THIRD

THE HARPER & ROW READER

Liberal Education Through
Reading and Writing

MARSHALL W. GREGORY
Butler University

WAYNE C. BOOTH
University of Chicago

EDITION

HarperCollins*Publishers*

Sponsoring Editor: Patricia Rossi
Development Editor: Sue Baugh
Project Editor: Melonie Parnes
Art Direction: Armen Kojoyian
Text Design: Maria Carella
Cover Design: Armen Kojoyian
Cover Illustration: Janie Paul
Production: Beth Maglione/Kathleen Donnelley
Compositor: ComCom Division of Haddon Craftsmen, Inc.
Printer and Binder: R. R. Donnelley & Sons, Company
Cover Printer: The Lehigh Press, Inc.

THE HARPER & ROW READER, Third Edition

Library of Congress Cataloging-in-Publication Data

The Harper & Row reader : liberal education through reading and
  writing / [compiled by] Marshall W. Gregory, Wayne C. Booth.—3rd
  ed.
      p.   cm.
  Includes indexes.
  ISBN 0-06-040840-5 (student ed.).—ISBN 0-06-040841-3 (teacher
ed.)
    1. College readers.   2. English language—Rhetoric.   I. Gregory,
  Marshall W., 1940–   . II. Booth, Wayne C.   III. Title: Harper and
  Row reader.
  PE1417.H276   1992
  808'.0427—dc20
                                                      91-16401 CIP

91 92 93 94   9 8 7 6 5 4 3 2 1

Brief Contents

Detailed Contents

✦

Preface

Through the first edition (1984), the second edition (1988), and the Brief Edition (1990), *The Harper & Row Reader* has met with such success as supports our belief that writing teachers want a reader to educate students' thinking while improving their writing. It is our conviction that the aims of both liberal education and writing are most successfully met when they are intertwined. That they *can* be intertwined is the foundation upon which this third edition of the *Reader* stands.

WHAT'S NEW IN THE THIRD EDITION?

What's mostly new is a large number of readings with increases in the percentage of women and minority authors. While the second edition included 24 percent new readings, the third edition includes 40 percent new readings. Women authors composed 16 percent of the total number in the second edition and 31 percent of the total in the third edition. In fact, women and minority authors play an even larger role in the third edition than the increase of percentages reveal. While the percentage of male authors is kept high by a large number of small pieces—the brief excerpts from Aquinas, Freud, and Nietzsche at the beginning of the chapter on feminism, for example, and the brief excerpts from Hobbes, Locke, Ogden and Richards, and Mark Johnson on metaphor—women and minority authors are represented with new essays of intellectual vitality and precision of prose.

One of the book's most successful features right from the beginning has been the inclusion of essays that "speak" to each other from opposite sides of a topic. Each chapter in this third edition continues to sign off with at least two essays cast in this role and we are very excited about the content of some of the new "contests." The quarrel over the value of and the values in a traditional liberal-arts education as conducted by Matthew Arnold, the high priest of humanism, and George Steiner, a post-modern critic of humanism, threatens to involve students in a meaningful debate about the values that should govern their own education. The quarrel about metaphor that concludes Chapter 3 is brand new and includes not only the traditional philosophers' attacks on metaphor, but a brilliant defense of metaphor by Cynthia Ozick. On the issue of censorship in the arts at the end of Chapter 4, Plato must now do battle not only with E. M. Forster, who was included in the second edition, but with André Brink, the South African novelist, and Margaret Atwood, the Canadian novelist. The hard-hitting clash at the end of Chapter 6 between Richard Dawkins' essay favoring sociobiology and Laurence Thomas' argument that evolution favors altruism, not selfishness, will nourish students' thinking for years. Rosemarie Tong opposing Andrea Dworkin on the law that would make pornography subject to civil rights suits creates a riveting ending to Chapter 8. Finally, C. S. Lewis at the end of Chapter 11 does battle no longer with Bertrand Russell who, over the years, simply seemed to rely more on sneer rather than argument. Lewis is now opposed by a new contestant, John Fowles, whose manifesto of appreciation for Christianity as a moral system is matched only by his hatred of the Christian church. The other chapters still include the Ideas in Debate section, complete with old friends. Throughout, all the voices in this book—those both in and out of the Ideas in Debate sections—exemplify the educated mind at work, inquiring with energy and moral responsibility into a diverse range of important issues. We firmly believe that both teachers and students will enjoy the education that attends the study of these controversies.

The third edition continues a change that was introduced in the second: the inclusion of a small number of literary pieces that possess a strong argumentative slant, such as Mary McCarthy's "Artists in Uniform," Shirley Jackson's "Flower Garden," and Stephen Spender's "In Railway Halls, on Pavements Near the Traffic." Such works allow students to see the rhetorical, argumentative, and polemical dimensions of such "literary" features as metaphor and narrative. This will not only enrich students' knowledge of how arguments actually get advanced in the world, but will also offer them and their teachers a welcome change of pace without throwing either them or the organization of the book into confusion.

A rhetorical index at the end of the text is especially designed for student use. It does not include references to all of the ideas, concepts, and people mentioned in the book, but it does index the references to, and most of the examples of, rhetorical devices and strategies. Thus if students are unclear, for example, about the meaning or use of analogy, a quick glance at the index will take them to a number of places where analogy is either discussed or exemplified. (As a further aid, a rhetorical table of contents is included in the Instructor's Manual.)

PURPOSE OF THE COURSE

We have assumed from the beginning that it is not only wasted effort in practice but indefensible in theory to attempt to train students to write without educating them. We assume, in other words, that writers must have something to say in order to have something to write, and that what they have to say will depend mainly on what they know, how they think, and who they are, not just on their mastery of isolated skills. We assume, further, that we write not just as thinkers but as moral agents attempting to do something in or to the world. Any attempt to teach writing as if it were something separate from character, or to reduce writing to the status of a "service skill," insults our students and shortchanges our culture.

Obviously, we cannot offer decisive proof for these assumptions—as opposed to views that we think are cynical, impoverished, or unjust—but we have not chosen them blindly. In what we know of empirical research and learning theory, we find no justification for believing that learning to write well can be divorced from the daily nourishment of trying to understand what other writers have said and then trying to respond with something worth saying.

The notion of "working" cannot be dodged. We were convinced from the beginning that the job we wanted to do would require a reader with a fair number of pieces both longer and harder than those in recent anthologies. Toughness for its own sake would no doubt be silly, but students cannot be stretched by what is already within easy reach. In each chapter we have thus included substantial essays, some of them once popular in readers but now abandoned, many of them never anthologized before.

The result, we believe, is a distinguished and engaging collection of essays. It is a controversial collection. In each chapter some essays confront others directly, while others address issues shared by other essays. Disagreement is found everywhere. The collection is also unusually wide-ranging. Even so, we obviously do not offer a complete list of topics important to liberal education, or a survey of the entire range of possible views about any one topic. Any critical reader will find that entire disciplines are either ignored or underrepresented; among the liberal arts, for example, we talk little about logic or grammar, but much about rhetoric. More particularly, many political, religious, and philosophical views go unmentioned. But we hope that our recommended approach to the readings will itself provide a way to compensate for our omissions and biases. In our introductions and questions, we have tried hard to avoid the suggestion, found in too many anthologies these days, that the authors and their editors are somehow privy to the one right way of looking at the world. And we assume that the kind of critical thinking we encourage throughout this book will in itself compensate, in the long run, for the inevitable gaps and distortions in our choice of selections.

METHODS

Thinking of the difficulties presented to beginners by many of our pieces, we have asked ourselves what kind of guidance we would have welcomed when we were beginning college students. The result is that we offer more extensive commentary than any other reader we have seen. Of course we have tried to modulate our editorial voice, according to the difficulty of the selections, by limiting our introductions to a paragraph for some simpler pieces, while demonstrating how to perform extensive analyses of some of the more difficult works. For those to whom our commentary seems excessive, the format makes it easy to skip our words and work exclusively on our selections.

The introductions to the readings provide only a minimum of biographical and bibliographical information; we concentrate instead on grappling with the issues. "Grappling" is the word, because we do not conceal our own inability to solve many of the issues raised. These works have stretched us as we have performed our editing, and they do so still. Too many anthologies have seemed to us to imply that their editors now have the whole of education taped and that the students' task is to discover what the editors claim to know already.

Similarly, we have not hesitated to raise questions for discussion that we ourselves cannot answer, though we hope to have raised none that would leave us tongue-tied. We have tried to strike a balance between relatively determinate questions about the authors' procedures and open-ended questions about the issues.

In our suggested essay topics we have, in contrast, suggested no topics that we could not happily write on ourselves. This has meant avoiding assignments that seem canned, arbitrary, abstract, or impossibly ambitious. Generally, our assignments place students in situations where they can aim for concrete objectives directed at specific audiences, choosing appropriate strategies and dealing with ideas raised or suggested by the piece they have just read. If they take our suggestions seriously, they will discover that learning to write well has become their own goal, not just the instructor's or the editors'.

ORGANIZATION

Our selections offer great flexibility to both students and teachers. Teachers and students can enter *The Harper & Row Reader,* Third Edition, at any of several levels of reading difficulty. For example, a class might well move through the whole text using mainly the shorter and less ambitious pieces, or a term could be built mainly on the longer and harder essays. Or a class of "middling" preparation might well choose to read all or most of the readings in a few chapters, beginning with the epigraphs that introduce a chapter and working right through to the toughest arguments at the end. Some classes might want entirely to ignore the sequence of our chapters and the order within them, though we hope—since our discussion material in general builds upon itself— that most classes will profit from following our organization.

We have, then, worked throughout in the conviction that reading, writing, and thinking are integrally related. No doubt every student will at some point need to pay special attention to isolated skills; some will profit from drill—in grammar, in reading techniques, in sentence combining. They will profit, that is, provided they have learned why the drill is important, and why learning to write well is something they should want for themselves, not something they do just for their teachers, their grades, or their parents.

To educate is always harder than to train, and the world will no doubt always find demonstrable uses for those who are trained without knowing what they have been trained *for.* But neither students nor their teachers should have to choose between a "useful" practical training and a "useless" liberal education. Anything truly liberating is also useful, and anything truly useful, when done well and with joy, is also liberating. The best versions of liberal and practical education are ultimately inseparable.

Regardless of any mistakes we have made in our own theory and practice, we feel quite sure about one thing: the required freshman composition course (whatever it is called and however it is staffed) can provide the most important experience of any student's college years and a continuing experience of self-education for the teacher. It can do so, that is, when it enables students and teachers together to repossess for themselves what others have learned in the past and then to engage each other pointedly and eagerly, sharing their thoughts about who they are and how they should try to live, here and now.

We would like to thank the following reviewers of this third edition for their helpful comments and suggestions: Bob Baker, Peru State College; Rudolph Bates, Furman University; John Bayer, St. Louis Community College; Suzanne Blaw, Southern Methodist University; Stanley Crowe, Furman University; Jennifer M. Ginn, North Carolina State University; Kristine Hansen, Brigham Young University; Francis A. Hubbard, Marquette University; George F. Kennedy, Washington State University; Mike Moran, University of Georgia; Nancy Posselt, Midlands Technical College; Brenda Schildgen; and Barbara Traister, Lehigh University.

Special thanks must go to Valiska Gregory and Phyllis Booth, whose support and criticism have been both constant and nourishing, and to those many students and teachers who have contacted us over the past ten years with suggestions and criticisms. They have helped sustain our energy and improve our work.

Marshall W. Gregory
Wayne C. Booth

THE COURSE, THE BOOK, AND SOME LEADING IDEAS

✦

SIX INTRODUCTORY ESSAYS

by
Marshall W. Gregory and Wayne C. Booth

WHY TAKE THIS COURSE?

Human beings deal constantly in words. We hardly ever stop talking, either audibly to each other or silently to ourselves. Life without language would be reduced to a thin circle of existence enclosing a blankness: the value of zero. To specialists who study brain structure or evolution, language may be a subject for inquiry, but to those who use it every day it is the one form of behavior that more than anything else makes human life possible. As fish are creatures of water and birds are creatures of air, human beings are creatures of words. Alfred North Whitehead sums up this point admirably: "The souls of men are the gift of language to mankind."

If Whitehead is right, language gives human beings abilities and pleasures available to no other species. It follows, then, that we become fully human when we most fully use and appreciate the gift of language. But unlike other creatures, which seem to realize their potential effortlessly so long as nothing inhibits their development, we language creatures can only reach our full potential with this mysterious, difficult, and wonderful gift through relentless exercise. Reading and writing courses aim to provide you with that exercise. Through steady practice, this course can promise you two benefits. First, you can strengthen your power to use language more effectively and you can learn to respond to it more sensitively. Second, this course promises you the uniquely human pleasure of the exercise itself; like good health, language skills need no justification beyond the satisfaction of possessing them for their own sake.

Just as exercise and discipline can improve our bodily health, they can also improve our "verbal health"—our power to use and respond to language. People often act as if being able to read a newspaper or ask for directions proves that they are fluent in their native tongue. But in fact most of us

3

perform even these basic language tasks less well than we could. People who think they "know how to read" often misread even the simplest news accounts, as all newspaper editors and reporters learn to their sorrow. And we all have had the experience of finding ourselves on the wrong side of town because we either asked for directions unclearly or received unclear directions from someone else. We can decrease the number of our confusions, misunderstandings, and misspeakings, but not without work, not without exercise, study, and discipline. The main objective of this course is to provide such systematic exercise in reading and writing. It may be the only course you will take, in fact, that is designed exclusively to provide such exercise.

If human beings are creatures of words in general, then their ability to use words *well* is made even more pressing by the modern conditions of work, politics, and leisure. The modern world depends increasingly on words as the primary tools for keeping itself in motion. A century ago, pioneers depended less on words than we do, but their survival skills have become our recreations. Tracking, hunting, canoeing, and riding are for us diversions, not a way of life. 4

In our world, we survive much more by our skill in handling words than by our skill in handling animals, rifles, or plows. In business, medicine, education, law enforcement, church work, psychiatry, social work, or selling—name the line of work and the general truth will hold: The modern world floats on a sea of memos, reports, forms, letters, speeches, minutes, manuals, and notes. Nurses and police officers spend as much time writing reports as they do handling cases. Accountants have to write complicated summaries to both their clients and their employers. People in business write an endless stream of memos to the executives above them and to the staffs below. Scientists in education and industry have to write accounts of their procedures and findings for both the agencies they serve and the general public. In all fields, jobs and promotions tend to go to those who read and write most effectively. 5

Contrary to what some people believe, the age of the computer is not diminishing our reliance on the old-fashioned use of words. Computers are in fact increasing our dependency. We authors are writing this essay, for example, on a computer loaded with a word-processing program. With the purchase of the computer we received four instruction manuals, each more than 150 pages long (in small type with thin margins). A fifth manual over 100 pages long tells us how to operate the word-processing program. On the advice of the dealer who sold us the machine, we wound up buying a sixth 400-page manual—just to clear up questions that the other manuals do not cover completely. The point is not only that somebody had to *write* those manuals, but that anyone who wants to know how to use computers well must know how to *read* them. Whether we are talking about reading or writing, computers are not going to let us off the hook about words. 6

The *utility* of reading and writing is not the most important justification, 7 however, for doing these activities well. It is true at one level that we must all practice the skills of literacy because the conditions of modern life force us to go into training. Since none of us plans to live under a rock or on a desert island, we have to acquire the skills necessary for competition and interaction in a complex world. But the metaphor of training and the reality of competition should not blind us to the fact that using language well and responding to it sensitively offer pleasures and rewards in and of themselves. Just as we all wish not merely to have health but to have *good* health, not merely to eat but to eat *well,* and not merely to be with people we know but with people we *love*—because these fulfillments enrich our lives—so we all wish that we could use language not only as a tool but as a pleasure. Watching a play, reading novels and poetry, playing word games with children, writing love letters, working crossword puzzles, and making puns all exhibit the joy we take in the presence of words shaped for uniquely human purposes. No one pays us for doing any of these things; we simply do them because a life in which they are present is better—richer, more interesting, more stimulating— than a life in which they are absent, regardless of practical conditions and circumstances. Because we are the only creatures who can use language at all, using it well always carries a rich array of rewards that go far beyond simple usefulness.

✦

Questions for Discussion

1. Discuss with your fellow students the reasons you were given in high school for taking a writing course, and relate the advantages, if any, that your counselors and teachers taught you to expect. Compare these views with the views that we give you in our short essay. Are there significant discrepancies? Which views seem most persuasive to you? Why?

2. Does our analogy in paragraph 1—As fish are creatures of water and birds are creatures of air, human beings are creatures of words—seem to over- state language's importance? If not, can you restate the point we are making in your own words? If it does, can you say where we are wrong?

3. If you are skeptical about the extent to which we all rely on language in non-practical ways, discuss with your classmates the way students use language to stimulate laughter (puns, jokes, satire, slang, double entendre, "in" words, innuendo, and so on), to express themselves (notes, letters, poems, diaries, letters to the editor, and so on), and to vent emotions (swear words, "psych up" talk, romantic talk, and so on). Or would you declare all these uses practical? If so, then what happens to the everyday definition of *practical* as "that which produces immediately useful or mea- surable results"? What *is* practical?

Suggested Essay Topics

1. Write a letter to one of your high school teachers or counselors arguing that the view of reading and writing you were given in high school was too narrow. Give your reasons and suggest how things might be improved for students still in high school.

2. Write a letter to us arguing that we exaggerate language's importance or that we underestimate the need to master practical uses of language— or objecting to some other part of our argument. Give your reasons for objecting and suggest how we should revise our case.

WHY USE A "READER" IN A WRITING COURSE?

The reason you have been asked to buy this book, called a "reader," 1 may not be immediately apparent. You may think that a writing class should deal mostly with writing, and that if you read even half of the material in this book you are going to spend a lot of time reading that you might better spend on writing. In addition, you may have been told that improving your writing is largely a matter of learning to avoid grammatical and spelling errors and that a "reader" will offer you no help in these areas. How can reading Plato's myth of the cave help you write an effective job application or a persuasive business letter?

The connections exist, but they are indirect. Seventeenth-century sail- 2 ors did not see at first what eating an orange a day had to do with sailing ships, and early nineteenth-century medical students did not see at first what antiseptics had to do with doctoring. But oranges prevented scurvy and antiseptics prevented infection, though for a long time nobody knew why. The connection between reading and writing is like these others. Though a full scientific explanation may never be found, experience shows that reading produces healthy effects on writing.

This book, then, is based on the assumption that good writing must 3 keep company with good reading. Obviously we cannot prove this claim about cause and effect because the relations are complex and irregular: Some people who read a lot do not write well. But we have never encountered a good writer who did not read a great deal. Every author who has earned a position in this book, for example, was a heavy reader, and so was every good writing student we have ever known. But we still call our claim an assumption, because we depend on it while waiting for the kind of scientific proof that in human affairs is seldom available.

Since the aim of a writing course is to help you write better prose, the 4 obvious questions to ask are, "How do people learn to write in the first place, and how do they then improve?" The same answer holds for both speaking and writing: We learn to speak and write by relying on instruction from others who already know how, and by then imitating their behavior.

As very young children, even as infants, our souls were stroked and 5 cradled into wakefulness by language. Rocked in the arms of language we early learned—although we could never have *said* that this was what we were learning—the rules of grammar in our native tongue. We learned at an astonishingly fast rate to say "She walks" rather than "Walks her" and "The water is boiling" rather than "Water boiling is the." We could not have told anyone that we were "using grammar," but knowing how to make these linguistic formations is what grammarians call knowing the "rules" of English.

There are many highly complicated and little understood processes that 6
occur during this period of language acquisition. At one level language learning occurs so deeply beneath consciousness that none of us can examine the process as it happens: We seem to have learned intuitively to say "went" instead of "goed" and to ask questions and give orders without referring to any conscious rules about interrogatives and direct objects. But an indispensable part of our learning is the conscious testing of what we have intuited. Children may act as if they are playing when they go through the steps of learning language, but it is very purposeful play. They *work* at acquiring language, and they work at it hard and persistently. They drill themselves and are drilled by their parents, making thousands of mistakes and receiving thousands of corrections, until they can finally say whole sentences and say them right: "The car went" instead of "The car goed."

The same process that taught us how to speak—constant exposure, 7
constant practice, and constant corrections—also teaches us how to write. We learn both intuitively and consciously, just as we learn to play tennis, play the piano, drive a car, or repair a radio both by the development of intuitive "feel" and by conscious practice. Once you are past the rock-bottom elementary stage of learning a skill (and in your use of English you are well past that point already), conscious imitation is going to work for you only if it is *intelligent* imitation: imitation that expresses independent thought, not mindless duplication.

Some people, for example, try to imitate classical paintings using the 8
paint-by-number technique. Anyone really interested in painting knows that this is both boring and useless. The pianist who wants to play as well as Vladimir Horowitz must do more than duplicate his execution of one piece. He must imitate Horowitz's *understanding;* he must play the music, not just the notes. No doubt there is a point, especially at the beginning, when simply trying to *sound like* Horowitz might teach the aspirant a good deal. But imitation-as-duplication can never be a sufficient means of developing independent skill. Writing, for reasons we discuss briefly in "What Is an Essay?" (pp. 10–14), seems to be the skill in which flat imitation is least instructive—but we must imitate, even so.

Acquiring the "feel" for any complicated skill requires, first, being in the 9
presence of models who already know the skills and, second, undertaking the discipline of sustained and thoughtful practice. Skimming over the assigned essays Monday through Thursday and then cramming the writing of the weekly essay into a 2- or 3-hour session mainly devoted to wishing you didn't have to do it does not even qualify as "hands-on experience"; any

tennis coach or violin teacher would laugh at such a lack of discipline and sustained practice. Getting the feel of good writing is even more complicated. The number of possible "moves," styles of play, and "partners" is much larger in the world of writing than in any of these other skills.

For any writer, master or beginner, reading well is part of the indispens- 10 able practice for writing well. Reading "well" means reading both accurately and sensitively, reading good writers, and reading a lot, not in spurts separated by periods of drought, but reading with regularity. When you were a child, talking was not something you listened to only occasionally, or only during the summer, or only for diversion, or only in fulfillment of an assignment. No, you swam in a sea of words until you became entirely adapted to your verbal environment, until you became in fact a "word creature." Learning to write requires the same immersion. Learning to write *well* means swimming in good company—the kind of company we have provided in this book.

But there is a further reason for reading your way into being a good 11 writer. When you were first learning how to talk, most of what you said centered around yourself. As you matured you learned to take into account other people and a larger slice of the world. Writing follows the same pattern of development. At first it probably seems more natural to write about yourself—your own feelings, desires, and views of things—than it does to write about events, issues, ideas, or problems in the "external" world. But just as maturing causes you to cease *talking* exclusively about yourself, so it also causes you to stop *writing* exclusively about yourself.

Some readers may protest here that a writer *must* write from personal 12 feelings and experiences. What else could one do? But the objection is based on a superficial notion of who we are and of how we "own" a "personal" feeling. Admitting that ideas and points of view are always in some sense personal does not erase the fundamental difference between self-absorption and fellow-feeling, between placing one's own ego at the center of the universe and having the capacity to embrace the feelings and ideas of others. Einstein once wrote that "the true value of a human being is determined primarily by the measure and the sense in which he has attained liberation from self." In this book we offer you a rich collection of "other selves" to listen to, to "talk to," and sometimes even to imitate.

If you work at these readings, if you engage fully with the problems 13 raised by the authors and grapple with their methods of arguing, you will intuit the shapes of good writing in the same way that you intuited the shapes of spoken English when you were a child. If you are also diligent in your practice, even if your first essays seem discouragingly inferior to these "professional" statements, you can progress rapidly.

Of course no one can promise how much progress you will make—there 14 are too many variables at work, your own commitment to learning being by far the most crucial. Do not be surprised if things fail to come easily or if your progress is uneven. You are not, after all, undertaking some trivial activity that anyone can easily master. You are trying to improve one of the skills that separates human beings most distinctively and most completely from all other creatures. Perhaps it could even be called a mystery, not just a skill. It is everyone's birthright, but it is possessed fully by none. Those few who are masters have penetrated the mystery, but they have also paid the dues of discipline and practice.

Questions for Discussion

1. Take an informal poll in your class. How many students estimate that they read 50 literary works a year beyond works assigned to them in school? How many read more, how many less? How many read hardly any? Then, using people's personal testimony as evidence, try to determine whether there is any correlation between success and ease of writing on the one hand and amount of reading on the other. Does your poll corroborate what we say about the connection between reading and writing?

2. Throughout our essay we make analogies between learning to write and learning other complicated skills such as playing some kinds of sports or playing a musical instrument. Can you develop this analogy further in discussion with your classmates? What do the training and discipline necessary to engage in sports or play music become when we think of the student writer? What changes, if any, does this analogy suggest that you should make in the way you approach writing or studying for this class?

3. Can you illustrate from your own experience our assertion that imitation is necessary in order to learn complicated skills but is never a sufficient means of learning such skills *well*? What skills have you learned (or may you be still learning) in which imitation has been a useful but limited tool? How do you know when to stop imitating and launch out on your own?

Suggested Essay Topics

1. You are the teacher of this class and a student has just come to you with a C essay and the request that you tell him how to make it "better." In addition to seeing that the student is weak in mechanical skills and logic, you also recognize that he simply has no intimacy with language. Write an extended note to your student (perhaps two typewritten pages) explaining what he needs to attend to if he is likely to make any real progress in learning to write better. Perhaps you could outline a course of "practice" or "training," as you might do for a weak athlete if you were a football or basketball coach.

2. At the beginning of paragraph 13 we say, "If you work at these readings, if you engage fully with the problems raised by the authors and grapple with their methods of arguing, you will intuit the shapes of good writing in the same way that you intuited the shapes of spoken English when you were a child." Write an essay directed to your fellow students in which

you explain what it means to "work at these readings" and to "engage fully with the problems raised by the authors." You might take our own essay and, by commenting on selections from it or on its overall structure or position, show how "working" and "engaging" with others' arguments is accomplished.

WHAT IS AN ESSAY?—
THE RANGE OF RHETORIC

Not long ago, the main meaning for the word *essay* was "an attempt," "a trial." In calling all of your "papers" *essays,* we want to underline that you should think of them as trial runs, attempts that you can always improve, no matter how good they are. Like all of our own "essays" throughout the book—this one for example—yours will always be in some sense unfinished, always asking for further improvement. We "try out" this or that solution, always hoping to make a better try later on. You will find that your best writing comes when you revise one attempt, after learning how other people view it, by "trying out" another one.   1

What is it that we try out? What do we attempt? We sometimes think that we are simply trying to solve a problem presented by a subject matter or a topic. But it is usually useful to add that we are also attempting to achieve some "rhetorical effect" on our potential readers. Each of your essays will attempt something never attempted before: your chosen rhetorical task. That task will always consist of three elements, each of them immensely variable: (1) the available reasons you can discover and turn into a line of argument to persuade the reader to see things your way (or, often enough, to discover for yourself what to believe); (2) your knowledge or hunches about the tastes, values, experiences, prejudices, or interests of your reader; and (3) your own resources of style and character.   2

If calling the effects of your essays "rhetorical" confuses you, it may be because many people take *rhetoric* to mean mere trickery or bombast or "cover-up"—the opposite of "substance" or "solid argument." But we use it here in a quite different, traditional sense. To us, rhetoric refers to the entire range of devices that writers and speakers use to communicate their ideas effectively. Thus whenever writers think about readers and about possible effects on them, they are thinking *rhetorically.* And even when writers do not themselves think about rhetorical effect, what they do can be "analyzed rhetorically" to discover whether in fact they have discovered the needed rhetorical resources for the task they have attempted.   3

In this sense of the word, no writer can avoid using rhetoric. The choice is only between good rhetoric and bad, and the judgment of good and bad will not depend only on whether or not the writer *intended* to "be rhetorical." Most writers find that they write best when they are clearest about their chosen rhetorical task. They think of what they write as designed to achieve some kind of communication—to produce in some specified audience this or   4 that rhetorical effect, such as persuading, informing, entertaining, or simply building a friendship.

Kinds of essays are as numerous as the kinds of possible effects we might aim for. Almost every effect that anybody could seek can be "essayed" in words; what's more, the same general task can be essayed in many different possible forms. For example, suppose I want to attack a political opponent or to prove that my friend should be president of the student body. The kinds of possible essays that I might use for my purposes vastly outnumber any one person's range: a solemn editorial; a mocking or ironic editorial; a letter campaign (and how many different forms might a letter take?); a long, fact-laden "report" on the conditions that call for new leadership; a biography of my enemy or my friend; and so on.

Because the choices among so many devices can seem threatening, some people have claimed that the best way to teach writing is to free students from having to think very hard about what is to be said: "Just tell students what to say, and let them practice how to say it. If they have to think hard—not only about a subject but about how to choose among rhetorical effects—they are sure to write badly." There is some truth to this claim. If you have to think about *too* much at once, if you are faced by overwhelming choices, you can sit in front of your desk helplessly frozen for hours. But something worse happens when you are forced to do "skill" assignments that are so specific and predetermined that you do not have to think about what *you* want to say or how you want to say it. Such assignments do not produce essays but mere mechanical exercises.

It is true that exercise, even if we do it according to someone else's drill, can be useful. Many human achievements depend on long hours of dull practice performed according to routines worked out by other people. If learning to play the cello or to be a fine swimmer requires endless hours of rote practice, why shouldn't writing?

The answer is that writing is more complicated, and thus harder to learn, than any other skill we can think of. It is in fact only superficially similar to developing athletic or musical skills. It *includes* routine but goes beyond it. The proof of this is quite simple: The success of any piece of writing depends to some degree on how it *departs* from standardization or routine repetitiveness, while most other skills *depend* on standardization and routine. A champion runner or swimmer, for example, tries to perfect a repeatable style that will produce a win in every race; nobody cares whether the swimmer's form exactly duplicates his or her previous form, so long as victory results. But if a writer hands in this week a duplicate of an essay that earned an A last week, it will receive an F—and possibly a conference about dishonesty.

Strange, isn't it? If you were able to "write well" last week, why shouldn't writing the same words this week also be judged favorably? The answer is that it would be no longer an essay, no longer an attempt to say something still worth saying. What is worth *your* saying is only something that *you* want to say to someone *now,* and since you are a constantly changing human being, you are unlikely to say exactly what you have said before to anyone. And what your readers (whether instructors or classmates) will want to read this week will not be a duplicate of what you have already said to them. In addition, repeating yourself robs you of learning. Writing is one of our most effective ways of learning, for it not only forces us to attend to other people's arguments and opinions, but also forces us to *think through* our own views. But in order to take advantage of writing-as-learning, we must constantly face the challenge of saying new things, facing new topics.

The most important part of each week's assignment will thus be *thinking* 10 *about your purpose* in writing. Of course in one sense the purpose will always be the same: to do the best essay you can do, or at least to show that you have made a genuine effort. But in every assignment you will be grappling with new ideas, and the clearer you are about the actual rhetorical task you are attempting, the better the results will be.

Spend some time, then, before you start writing (and from paragraph 11 to paragraph *as* you write), nagging yourself with the question: "What *am* I trying to do here, really?" Your answer may change as you write and rewrite, but if when working on each assignment you constantly relate your steps to an emerging notion of the job to be done, in a growing relation with some actual reader, you will find that notion guiding steps that otherwise would seem haphazard.

No one has ever made a complete list of the possible rhetorical effects, 12 that is, of all the possible goals you might "essay" to achieve, but there are several traditional classifications. One ancient tradition says that rhetoric will have one of three effects:

1. It will "move" us—that is, stir us to action, as when we change our vote or join a political movement.
2. It will teach us.
3. It will delight us, as when we read a beautiful poem or story.

Another interpretation says that rhetoric will do one of these three things:

1. Change our views about the *past* and about who was responsible for past events (*forensic rhetoric* of the kind studied by lawyers).
2. Change our decisions about how to act for a desired *future* (*deliberative rhetoric,* of the kind practiced by members of Congress or families deciding where to go for vacation).
3. Change our judgments about some person or institution in the *present* (*epideictic, display,* or *demonstrative rhetoric,* of the kind used for Fourth of July celebrations or college commencements).

Finally, some modern textbooks classify rhetorical tasks into four types:

1. Describing something (description).
2. Telling a story (narration).

3. Explaining something (exposition).
4. Making an argument (persuasion).

There's no need here at the beginning to worry about how these terms
and classifications relate to each other. We offer them now only as a checklist
to suggest questions that you can profitably ask yourself as you write. Instead
of merely "getting the paper done," make a habit of running through questions like these:

1. Am I trying to change the beliefs of my readers? If so, how?
   a. To persuade them to believe something about a subject they already
      care about?
   b. To consider seriously some question they have previously ignored?
   c. To open their minds to a possibility they had ruled out?
2. Am I trying to think something through for myself (and consequently
   for a reader who will be in a sense listening in)? If so, I should decide,
   as I must with question 1, whether it is in the nature of my topic to allow
   for some sort of decisive proof or only for probabilities.
3. Am I trying to provide thoughtful companionship for my readers, simply discussing issues and possibilities, with no effort to come to conclusions at all? (See the selection from Scott Sanders in Chapter 5, for
   example.)
4. Am I simply trying to entertain (by no means a contemptible task for
   an essayist)?
5. Am I perhaps trying to perform one of the following functions:
   · Explain a process, law, or rule?
   · Clarify a common confusion?
   · Console someone for a loss?
   · Warn someone?
   · Praise something or someone underrated?
   · Blame something or someone overpraised?
   · Lead someone to worship?
   · Shake someone's naive faith?
   · Complain about an injustice?
   · Show a relationship between things that people have commonly sepa-
     rated (that is, build a new synthesis)?
   · Separate things that people have previously mushed together (that is,
     perform a new analysis)?
   · Proclaim my love?
   · Get revenge?
   · Gain employment?
   · Correct an error?
   · Induce an attitude of peaceful meditation?
   · Incite to action?

Whatever your answers to these or other questions, your writing will 14
generally profit from asking them insistently. None of your specific choices
can be guided by the simple desire to "write a good essay." What you need,
in deciding what is good and what is bad, will always be some kind of answer
to questions like these.

STUDENT: What, then, is the intended rhetorical effect of your little essay on 15
      the essay?
  BOOTH: Well, it is to try to goad students into *thinking* about each essay,
      rather than simply going through the motions.
GREGORY: Do you think it will work?
  BOOTH: Why not? Hasn't it *sometimes* worked for us?

Questions for Discussion

1. Does "writing-as-learning" (¶9) make sense to you? Can you restate this
notion in your own words?

2. Discuss the limitations and strengths of the analogies that compare learning to write with learning sports and musical skills. In our two previous
essays we viewed these analogies as helpful; in this essay we suggest that
they are limited in their application. Discuss with your fellow students the
ways in which the analogies work and the points at which they (like all
analogies) eventually break down.

3. Contrast the popular view of rhetoric as a kind of verbal fakery or trickery
with the view we suggest here. Can you find references to rhetoric in
newspapers and magazines that take this derogatory, suspicious view? Do
you think that "mere rhetoric," as it is sometimes called, can be separated
from the substance of an argument or a position? Why or why not?

Suggested Essay Topics

1. Read Wendell Berry's essay "The Loss of the University" (p. 31) and write
an essay to your instructor arguing that the overall intent of Berry's essay
is to accomplish one of the rhetorical aims listed in paragraph 12: to stir
the audience to action, to teach, or to delight. Cite the particular passages
that seem to you to support your interpretation, and note the way that all
three aims may be exhibited to some extent in a single essay.

2. Write three different brief accounts of the same thing, the first one designed to move the audience, the second one designed to teach, and the
third one designed to delight. You might choose, perhaps, some campus
issue (required phys ed classes, dorm hours, tuition increases, inadequate
resources for commuters, inadequate resources for older students, and so
on) as the material to be worked up according to these three aims.

WHAT IS AN IDEA?

"I've got an idea; let's go get a hamburger." "All right, now, as sales representatives we must brainstorm for ideas to increase profits." "The way Ray flatters the boss gives you the idea he's bucking for a promotion, doesn't it?" "Hey, listen to this: I've just had an idea for attaching the boat to the top of the car without having to buy a carrier." "The idea of good defense is to keep pressure on the other team without committing errors ourselves." "What did you say that set of books was called? *The Great Ideas*? What does that mean?" 1

The word *idea,* as you can see, is used in a great many ways. In most of the examples just mentioned it means something like "intention," "opinion," or "mental image." The "idea" of going for a hamburger is really a mental picture of a possible action, just as the "idea" of a boat carrier is a mental image of a mechanical device. The "ideas" of good defense and Ray the flatterer are really opinions held by the speakers, while the appeal for "ideas" about how to increase profits is really an appeal for opinions (which may also involve mental images) from fellow workers. None of these examples, however, encompasses the meaning of *idea* as it has always been used by those who engage in serious discussions of politics, history, intellectual movements, and social affairs. Even the last example, an allusion to the famous set of books edited by Robert Maynard Hutchins and Mortimer Adler at the University of Chicago, does not yet express an idea; it only directs us toward a source where ideas may be encountered. 2

These uses of *idea* are entirely appropriate in their contexts. Words play different roles at different times. One can "fish" for either trout or compliments; and a scalp, an executive, and a toilet (in the Navy) are all "heads." Usually these different uses have overlapping, not opposed, meanings. For example, we wouldn't know what fishing for compliments meant unless we already knew what fishing for trout meant, and the "heads" we just referred to are all indications of position or place. In the same way, the different uses of the word *idea* overlap. Even the most enduring ideas may appear to some as "mere opinion." What, then, does *idea* mean in the context of serious talk, and what keeps some opinions and mental images from being ideas in our sense? 3

Three central features distinguish an idea from other kinds of mental constructs: 4

1. An idea is always connected to other ideas that lead to it, follow from it, or somehow support it. *Like a family member, an idea always exists amid a network of ancestors, parents, brothers, sisters, and cousins.* An idea could no more spring into existence by itself than a plant could grow without a seed, soil, and a suitable environment. For example, the idea that acts of racial discrimination are immoral grows out of and is surrounded by a complex of other, related ideas about the nature of human beings and the nature of moral conduct: Racial differences are irrelevant to human

nature, the sort of respect that is due to any human being *as* a human being is due equally to *all* human beings, it is immoral to deny to any human being the rights and privileges due to every human being, and so on. You can see that a great many other ideas surround, support, and follow from the leading idea.

2. An idea always has the capacity to generate other ideas. Ideas not only have ancestors and parents, but progeny. The idea that *racial* discrimination is immoral, for example, is the offspring of the idea that *any* sort of bigotry is wrong.

3. An idea is always capable of yielding more than one argument or position. An idea never has a fixed, once-and-for-all meaning, and it always requires interpretation and discussion. Whenever interpretation is required and discussion permitted, disagreements will exist. Ideas are always to some degree controversial, but the kind of controversy produced by the clash of ideas—unlike the kind of controversy produced by the clash of prejudices—is one in which *reasons* are offered and tested by both sides in the debate. As reasons are considered, positions that seemed fixed turn into ideas that move with argument. (See "What Is an Argument?" pp. 19–22, for further discussion.)

In recent years, for example, the idea that racial discrimination is immoral, combined with the idea that past discriminations should be compensated for, has led to the follow-up idea that minority groups should, in some cases, receive preferred treatment, such as being granted admission to medical school with lower scores than those of competing applicants from majority groups. Some people have charged that this is "reverse discrimination," while others advance arguments for such actions with great intellectual and moral vigor. Regardless of where you stand on this issue, you can see that interpretations of ideas yield a multiplicity of positions.   5

There are obviously many kinds of mental products that do not qualify as ideas according to these criteria. "Two plus two equals four," for example, is not an idea. Without reference to the ideas that lie behind it, it can neither be interpreted nor used. In and of itself, "two plus two equals four" is simply a brute fact, not an idea. However, as a statement it is clearly the product of ideas: the idea of quantity, the idea that the world can be understood and manipulated in terms of systems of numbers, and so on.   6

Many of our everyday notions, opinions, and pictures of things also fail to qualify as ideas. "I hate John" may be an intelligible utterance—it conveys the feelings of the speaker—but it is not an idea. The "parents" of this utterance lie in the psychology or biography of the speaker, not in other ideas, and it can neither yield its own offspring nor support an argument. "Catholics are sheep," "All communists are traitors," "Christianity is the only true religion," "Republicans stink," "Most people on welfare are cheaters," and "Premarital sex is OK if you know what you're doing" are all such non-ideas. With appropriate development or modification, some of these opinions could be turned into ideas, but what keeps them from qualifying as ideas in their   7 present form is that they are only minimally related (and in some instances totally unrelated) to other ideas. One sign that you are being offered mindless, bigoted, or fanatical opinions, not ideas, is the presence of emotion-charged generalizations, unsupported by evidence or argument. Catchwords, clichés, and code phrases ("welfare cheaters," "dumb jocks," "typical woman," "mad scientist") are a sure sign that emotions have shoved ideas out of the picture.

A liberal education is an education in ideas—not merely memorizing 8 them, but learning to move among them, balancing one against the other, negotiating relationships, accommodating new arguments, and returning for a closer look. Writing is one of the primary ways of learning how to perform this intricate dance *on one's own.* In American education, where the learning of facts and data is often confused with an education in ideas, thoughtful writing remains one of our best methods for learning how to turn opinions into ideas.

The attempt to write well forces us to clarify our thoughts. Because 9 every word in an essay (unlike those in a conversation) can be retrieved in the same form every time and then discussed, interpreted, challenged, and argued about, the act of putting words down on paper is more deliberate than speaking. It places more responsibility on us, and it threatens us with greater consequences for error. Our written words and ideas can be thrown back in our faces, either by our readers or simply by the page itself as we re-read. We are thus more aware when writing than when speaking that every word is a *choice,* one that commits us to a meaning in a way that another word would not.

One result is that writing forces us to develop ideas more systematically 10 and fully than speaking does. In conversation we can often get away with canyon-sized gaps in our arguments, and we can rely on facial expression, tone, gesture, and other "body language" to fill out our meanings when our words fail. But most of these devices are denied to us when we write. To make a piece of writing effective, every essential step must be filled in carefully, clearly, and emphatically. We cannot grab our listeners by the lapel or charm them with our ingratiating smile. The "grabbing" and the "charm" must somehow be put into words, and that always requires greater care than is needed in ordinary conversation.

Inexperienced writers often make the mistake of thinking that they 11 have a firmer grasp on their ideas than on their words. They frequently utter the complaint, "I know what I want to say; I just can't find the words for it." This claim is almost always untrue. It is easy to confuse an intuitive sense that you have something to say with the false sense that you already know precisely what that something is. When a writer is stuck for words, the problem is rarely a problem only of words. Inexperienced writers may think they need larger vocabularies when what they really need are clearer ideas and intentions. Being stuck for words indicates that the thought you want to convey is still vague, unformed, cloudy, and confused. Once you finally discover your concrete meaning, you will discover the proper words for expressing it at the same time. You may revise words later as meanings become *more* clear to you, but no writer ever stands in full possession of an idea without having enough words to express it.

Ideas are to writing as strength and agility are to athletic prowess: They 12 do not in themselves guarantee quality, but they are the muscle in all good writing prowess. Not all strong and agile athletes are champions, but all champion athletes are strong and agile. Not everyone who has powerful ideas is a great writer, but it is impossible for any writer even to be effective, much less achieve greatness, without them.

Questions for Discussion

1. Identify and discuss meanings of the word *idea* that we did not mention in our essay. Does an awareness of these different meanings allow you to pick your words with greater care?

2. We briefly indicated some of the family relationships among ideas based on the parent idea that discrimination against individuals is wrong. In discussion with your classmates, pick a few other ideas that interest you and map out some of the primary family relationships among them. You could discuss, for example, such ideas as the following: the universe is God's creation; the speed of light is an absolute; modern sexual mores are undermining the nuclear family (or are allowing more people more freedom and fulfillment than ever before); capitalism is the economic system most compatible with a democratic political system. The world is full of ideas (and non-ideas); the point is to see whether you can trace how one idea leads to other, related ideas. This exercise will also allow you to see that almost every idea is confronted eventually by its contrary, and is thus a source of controversy as well as enrichment.

3. Discuss our assertion in paragraph 8 that "a liberal education is an education in ideas." Contrast such an education with an education in skills. Is it possible to learn skills without learning ideas? Do you know people who know how to do certain activities by rote but who are poor at thinking through the rationale for doing them, or poor at criticizing what they do, or poor at looking for alternative ways of doing them? You might consider whether a technical education would ever be sufficient training by itself in how to deal with sophisticated or complex ideas.

Suggested Essay Topics

1. Look through some of the editorials or letters to the editor in the newspaper, and pick one that seems to you filled with either non-ideas or feeble ideas. Address a letter to the author showing him or her how weak the writing is in real ideas, and suggesting how the weak notions might have been turned into real ideas.

2. Take any field that interests you and show how it may be divided into techniques of performance on the one hand and the ideas that underlie technique on the other. Try to show the relationship. Football, ballet, architecture, and cooking are all suitable examples. In football, for example, some players only know how to run the plays they have memorized, but the coach (and other players, especially the quarterback) have to keep in mind the strategies that underlie the patterns, and they have to know how to adapt certain strategies for certain situations. You might consider whether the best performer is one who can both think *and* do. Does every great coach or choreographer have to also be a player or dancer? Make your essay an analysis of such questions.

WHAT IS AN ARGUMENT?

Everybody knows what an argument is. It is a dispute between two people. But the word has another meaning, a very old one that will be important in this book. When two people argue, they not only *have* an argument with each other; each of them *presents* an argument—a line of reasoning. Each arguer can present a case that is either strong or weak, regardless of what final position either one takes. Each one may hate "arguing" but still *argue* well.

What makes a good argument—a good case? We might think that it would be whatever convinces one party to accept the other's views. If George and Jeanne have an argument (in the first sense), and if Jeanne convinces George that she is right, doesn't that show that she presented the best argument—the best case? Not necessarily. Maybe George was a pushover. Maybe Jeanne was just very clever at concealing the flaws in her argument. A good argument, in the sense of a good *case,* must stand up under close *analysis* (see "What Is Analysis?" pp. 22–25). You may want to ask here questions that will come up again and again throughout your work in college: Stand up under *whose* analysis? Who are the experts who test our arguments, and how many of them are needed to decide that an argument is sound?

If there were simple answers to such questions, a college education would not require four years. If all the experts in the study of argument could agree on what makes a good or bad one, our lives would be simple. We could then just learn a set of neat tests, like using a circuit-tester to check for live wires, and then easily check out the relative strength of Jeanne's and George's arguments. But even the experts often disagree about which arguments justify changing our minds in a given case. Some people, including some of the authors in this volume, insist that an argument is not worth anything at all unless it consists of *hard proof*—evidence that usually involves numbers, statistics, laboratory reports, and calculations. But the curious fact is that even in the highly technical sciences like physics and chemistry, most disputes are not decisively settled with unarguable proof. Almost every argument includes steps that *some* people criticize as weak, leading to *further* disputes about whether those criticisms are right or not. Scientists do not consider such disputes unhealthy; continued disagreement about evidence and proof pumps life into the sciences. It should not distress us that such disputes mark most nonscientific matters as well.

The trouble comes when disagreement about which arguments should   4 carry real weight becomes so widespread and difficult that people get skeptical about finding any good arguments at all, especially when facing life's important and complex matters. In fact, one of the issues most disputed in our century is the degree to which genuinely good reasons are available for thinking together about such major decisions as whether or when to marry, how to vote, what causes to support, whether to believe in God, how to raise our children, how hard to work at getting an education, and a host of other problems that we cannot dodge but never have enough "scientific proof" to settle.

If even the experts do not agree, how can we, beginners all, hope to   5 improve our own arguments? Fortunately, we all have available two important resources. The first, possessed by everyone with or without a formal education, is commonsense experience. As the great American philosopher Charles Sanders Peirce said, "We generally reason correctly by nature: we are . . . in the main logical animals." But, he adds, "we are imperfectly so." Common sense, sometimes called "popular wisdom," although essential to life, can be highly unreliable. Still, if we learn how to make use of it, if we simply *pay attention* to one another's arguments, in class and out, and "use our heads" in a natural way, we can discover arguments that will save us from many a disaster, both intellectual and practical.

The truth is that simply to survive in our complex society—perhaps in   6 any society—everyone develops a fairly elaborate, though rough-and-ready, reasoning apparatus. We all have ways of asking whether a given conclusion "follows" from the reasons given—that is, whether an arguer has earned a given "therefore" or "thus" or "consequently." We Americans have a sturdy popular tradition of skeptical expressions that help us to avoid getting conned: "I'm from Missouri—you've got to show me," "Don't take any wooden nickels," "There's a sucker born every minute," "Tell me another good one," "I wasn't born yesterday, you know." Even when dealing with elaborate written arguments we can use popular wisdom of this kind, employing more deliberately our natural habit of making sense.

But fortunately we have a chance in college to master a second resource,   7 to go beyond common sense and learn a whole range of more formal, deliberate tests of *accuracy* about data, *cogency* of logical inference, and general *clarity* about the reasons for our beliefs. Some of you will later study formal logic and learn to apply elaborate and precise tests for judging whether two or more statements ("propositions") are logically tied together or not. In your rhetoric book you will find examples of fallacies—seemingly good arguments that are actually weak or not valid at all. (You may later find that in practice some arguments that are called fallacies in fact carry weight in some circumstances; things are never as simple as they seem.)

We cannot pretend in this book to take you through a complete and systematic introduction to every kind of good argument. But if you attend closely to our suggested questions for discussion and study the introductions and analyses that precede and follow the selections by Elaine Morgan and Karl R. Popper in Chapter 2, and then test the other authors and your own writing with the same kinds of questions, you will gradually develop confidence in deciding whether an argument carries real weight. But you will also learn, like your editors and teachers before you, that the task of analyzing and testing arguments is endless. As in so much else that you will study this year, college is just the beginning.

Questions for Discussion

1. Notice how closely connected are *argument* and *ideas.* Real arguments are fueled by real ideas. Sham arguments are made up of faked ideas or sheer prejudice. Divide up into groups of four or five students and examine the arguments in some editorials and letters to the editor. Consider whether the opinions advanced there constitute real arguments or not, and discuss together what the authors might do to strengthen their arguments.

2. Take some moral issue, such as students cheating on tests or husbands and wives cheating on their spouses or bank employees cheating on the books, and notice how difficult it is for people to agree about the *grounds* on which such behavior is to be condemned as wrong. Notice how much more confused things become when less stark matters requiring moral reasoning are introduced: whether pornography should be banned, whether the American Nazi party has the right to march in Jewish neighborhoods, whether taking drugs is wrong or merely a matter of personal choice, or whether it is morally wrong to cheat on one's income taxes. Try to determine why making arguments about these kinds of issues is so difficult. (If you get really interested in this topic, look at Alasdair MacIntyre's *After Virtue* and *Habits of the Heart* by Robert N. Bellah et al.) Ask yourself whether your education should aim at helping you reason better about moral issues, and how it might work toward achieving that aim.

Suggested Essay Topics

1. Write two versions of the same case, one which relies on mere assertion or emotional ploys, and a second which attempts to present a reasoned argument. Each essay should hold the same opinions and ask for the same response from the reader; the difference between them should be the way in which the case is advanced. Address the essays to someone you think needs convincing. At the end of the second essay, append a brief discussion about the relative merits of each case.

2. Read Anton Chekhov's short story "Gooseberries" (available in many different anthologies) and write an essay in which you make an argument either supporting or attacking Ivan Ivanych's criticism of his brother's notion of happiness. It is clear that Ivan Ivanych thinks there is something intrinsically wrong with his brother's definition of happiness and that his brother would be a better person if he would give up the idea of happiness he holds and replace it with another. Is it ever possible to criticize another person's notions of happiness, or are all such notions irretrievably private? In your essay, try to establish whether such criticisms can *ever* be validly made. If they may, on what grounds? If they may not, why not?

WHAT IS ANALYSIS?

We all practice two basic ways of thinking, whether we have names for them or not: We can delve inside something and try to separate its parts, or we can look at two or more things that seem separated and try to fit them together. Some theorists even claim that every new thought consists either of finding a new way of *analyzing* the parts or elements of the whole or a new way of *synthesizing* two or more elements into a single thing.   1

Analysis can be as complicated as trying to separate atomic particles or as simple as identifying the ingredients in a restaurant salad; synthesis can range from constructing an ambitious theory about the parts of the universe to a simple hunch that Deborah and Harry both vote Republican because their fathers are wealthy. Both analysis and synthesis can be performed either with highly deliberate methods, as in a scientific laboratory, or with quick intuitive leaps, as when we use metaphors or similes to describe people we know: "Percy is a pig," "Marie is a marshmallow," "My coach nags like a demon." Thus the most elaborate thought of the greatest genius is no different *in kind* from what everyone does a hundred times a day. The expert simply has (sometimes vastly) greater skill in discovering differences and similarities—in inventing possibilities and then testing them rigorously. Unfortunately, that skill cannot be learned or taught with formulas either simple or complex. If it could be, we would all be potential geniuses. But everyone can learn how to think better by *thinking about* these two fundamental ways of thinking.   2

Learning to analyze better as you read and prepare to write will be an essential part of that education in synthesis. Analysis usually looks easier than synthesis. Isn't it obvious that you can break something into parts more easily than you can put something together? To find out what something is made of—even if it is a complicated essay or a complex subject you plan to write about—all you have to do is tear at it for a while, like a vigorous child pulling a toy apart, until you finally have all the parts separated. But we all know that things don't work as simply as that. If, for example, you want to know how a clock or a toy works, pulling things apart at random will not give you knowledge, just a pile of meaningless fragments. A true analysis of any   3 machine seeks not only to separate its parts but also to discover the relation-ships that *make the parts work*—that is, to analyze each part's *function*. If we asked you to do a chemical analysis of a spoonful of some powder, and you came back saying, "I've counted all the grains, and there are 2456 parts," we'd know that you did not understand what *analysis* meant. If we asked you to analyze the workings of a watch, and you brought us five piles of parts labeled "metal parts," "plastic parts," "jewels," "numbers," and "dial," we'd know that you had been simply tearing it apart, not really analyzing. The popular complaint, "But you're comparing apples and oranges," reflects our common sense that *for some purposes* we need to distinguish differences rather than to dwell on similarities.

You will of course find yourself synthesizing every time you write an essay, because to make an essay *work* you must create a new synthesis—a new putting-together of words and ideas that nobody has ever put together in precisely this way before. That is one reason learning to write is so difficult. Even our sentences are almost all brand-new things in the world: They are combinations of words that, like these we are combining now, have never appeared in exactly this order before. Though our *ideas* are seldom entirely new, our ways of talking about them always require new syntheses. In this sense, all of your work this year—and not only in this course—will be an education in how to make better syntheses.

Among life's most difficult and important kinds of analyses are those we perform when we read an essay carefully. It is true that we cannot avoid performing some analysis, no matter how unconsciously we may go about it, for all reading goes from part to part, and the parts fit together in some way to make up a whole. We know that an author has put together sen-tences, paragraphs, sections, perhaps even chapters, to make something that he or she considers now to be a single thing—an essay or a book. But the joints in an essay's skeleton are often not obvious, and we sometimes do our carving at points that would surprise the author, especially if we are reading an argument about a topic new to us. We make up our minds too quickly that "this is a botched X, with the joints all wrong," when it is really a "fine Y, with every joint as it should be." In reading Mary McCarthy's account of her quarrel with the anti-Semitic Colonel in "Artists in Uniform" (Chapter 6) for example, it would be easy for a hasty reader to conclude that McCarthy is merely attacking the Colonel's bigotry. A closer reading, however, shows her attacking herself, not just the Colonel, for vi-olating all her own rules of fair argument in her eagerness to convert him into an egalitarian liberal.

Our best defense against mistaking what an essay says is thus a more careful analysis—a close and systematic look at how the parts form a whole. Most authors work hard to provide clues about the kind of creature they are creating; they build in "visible joints" that enable us to figure out the struc-ture of the skeleton. A full analysis of any work will take into account every such explicit aid—every *thus* and *therefore*, every *first* and *second*, every *we see, then,* and *on the other hand*. Throughout the book we illustrate how such analyses might be done, and our questions for discussion are often designed to help you see an essay's structure.

Fortunately, all of us naturally tend to take such clues into account, 7 provided that we are paying close attention. In conversation, whenever we are genuinely interested, we don't ignore such clues. If a friend says, "Now wait a minute, we're talking about two entirely different things here, and it's only the second one that matters to our discussion," we don't just ignore this analysis—not unless we are looking for a fight instead of a conversation. Paying the same close attention when we read will usually, though not always, uncover the clues that reveal the author's own analysis.

Discovering the author's own slicings in this way will often lead you 8 to your best thinking as you attempt further analysis, in effect saying to the author, "But you have not looked at this subject closely enough. You have divided it into two huge lumps, but there are really at least four distinct elements here, as follows: . . ." And such analytical thinking will automatically spill over into your own writing, as you organize your ideas, and then your words, according to the new analysis. Indeed, you will find that when you are stuck for something to say, a close *analytical* look at almost anything in the world will turn up interesting revisions of your own ideas—and when that happens, you will have something to say.

Can you now *analyze* the parts of this essay on analysis? What are the 9 joints that we authors see in the subject? What clues have we provided (that is, what transitions from part to part)? It is always a useful exercise to run through an essay, pencil in hand, underlining every word or phrase that flags a move to a new part. If your outlining is systematic in this way, rather than a random marking of whatever statements happen to catch your eye, you may be surprised at how much it helps both your understanding of an essay and your memory of how it works as an *argument*—or as some other kind of critter.

Questions for Discussion

1. Define *analysis* and *synthesis* as mental processes; give several examples of each.

2. Focus on three or four complex decisions that you have had to make, and try to determine whether you had to rely mainly on analysis or on synthesis or, as is more likely, on a movement back and forth between the two. In picking your college, for example, you undoubtedly lumped certain kinds of schools together in an act of synthesis (preppy, academically serious, beautiful campus, dull [or lively] social life, and so on), while at the same time you distinguished between them analytically ("Even though these two schools are both preppy, one has a much better chemistry department than the other"). The process of identifying the kinds of

mental processes you use in making decisions can be carried to great length. Work out two or more examples in some detail.

Suggested Essay Topics

1. Pick some *event* of interest to a particular audience and give an analytic account of it. That is, break the event down into its component parts, not just chronologically (which would be like merely separating the parts of a watch into respective piles, as in our example), but in such a way as to show how the parts make up the whole.

2. Pick some *literary work* and, in an essay directed to your instructor, provide a synthetic account of it. That is, show how it is like other works that are similar to it in important ways, and further, show how the similarities help explain the character of the work you have selected. (You may choose a musical work, a scientific theorem, or a sport if you do not want to write about a literary work.)

PART

TOWARD
A LIBERAL
EDUCATION

✦

TWO

♦ 1 ♦

EDUCATION

Images, Methods, and Aims

Ignorance is the night of the mind.
Efe Pygmies of Zaire

Never lose a holy curiosity.
Albert Einstein

Knowledge is capable of being its own end. Such is the
constitution of the human mind, that any kind of knowledge,
if it be really such, is its own reward.
John Henry Cardinal Newman

The pleasure of learning and knowing, though not the
keenest, is yet the least perishable of all pleasures.
A. E. Housman

Where there is much desire to learn, there of necessity
will be much arguing, much writing, many opinions; for opinion
in good men is but knowledge in the making.
John Milton

Whoso loveth instruction loveth knowledge: but he that
hateth reproof is brutish.
Proverbs 12:1

A little learning is a dangerous thing.
Alexander Pope

Human history becomes more and more a race between
education and catastrophe.
H. G. Wells

Wendell Berry

Is Wendell Berry's concern about special-ization among the disciplines in today's universities a concern of yours as well, or is it an issue you have thought little about? Whether specialization is considered good or bad depends, of course, on how one defines specialization and on how one defines the aims of a university. Nowhere does Berry give a very succinct definition of specialization, but he does build up his view of it gradually throughout the whole essay. On the purposes that should govern the aims of a university, however, Berry is both incisive and succinct. In paragraph 4 he says, "The thing being made in a university is humanity," and it is from this statement of ends that he infers the appropriate means of an education. You will have to determine as you read first, whether you agree with this statement of a university's ends and, second, whether Berry provides a compelling or convincing defense of his view.

Wendell Berry (b. 1934)—distinguished professor of English at the University of Kentucky, novelist, poet, and essayist—accuses academic and professional specializa-tions of employing vocabularies that reveal their abandonment of any ideal of general accessibility or social service. In paragraph 7 Berry warns that "[S]pecialized profes-sional language is thus not merely a contradiction in terms; it is a cheat and a hiding place; it may, indeed, be an ambush. At the very root of the idea of profession and professorship is the imperative to speak plainly in the common tongue." How can academic disciplines serve the public welfare if no one understands what they say?

As you think of your own college education, does Berry's accusation seem justified by the language employed in any of the courses you are taking right now? Can you use "the common tongue" to explain what you are learning in your classes to those who are not in them? Do the ideas or information you are learning have general accessibility, or are they more or less unintelligible to anyone outside the class? How easy would it be to "translate" the ideas or information in your classes into a generally accessible language? If such a translation would be difficult or impossible, do you view this as a problem? Why or why not?

All of these questions are issues of importance for Berry, who fears that the job of helping students develop "broadly informed human judgment" (¶22) is being obscured by the snowstorm of information now generated by specialized research within the academy's many and diverse disciplines. Like the issue of general accessibility, this issue of "broadly informed human judgment" is one that you can test from your own experience. Do you feel that your courses are helping you develop the abilities of thinking and evaluating that will help you play your role as informed citizen, or your potential roles as a mate and a parent, or your need to think clearly about ethical issues on the job and in everyday life, or your potential need to evaluate the effectiveness of your children's education better than if you had not taken the courses? If the answer is yes, can you say how the disciplinary orientation of the courses contributes to the acquisition of such broad skills on your part? If the answer is no, can you identify those points at which such skills might be developed in class even if they are now being ignored?

Regardless of how you answer these questions, you can count on Wendell Berry to help you face the relevant issues more thoughtfully and judiciously.

THE LOSS OF THE UNIVERSITY

From *Home Economics* (1987).

The predicament of literature within the university is not fundamentally different from the predicament of any other discipline, which is not fundamentally different from the predicament of language. That is, the various disciplines have ceased to speak to each other; they have become too specialized, and this overspecialization, this separation, of the disciplines has been enabled and enforced by the specialization of their languages. As a result, the modern university has grown, not according to any unifying principle, like an expanding universe, but according to the principle of miscellaneous accretion, like a furniture storage business.

I assume that there is a degree of specialization that is unavoidable because concentration involves a narrowing of attention; we can only do one thing at a time. I assume further that there is a degree of specialization that is desirable because good work depends upon sustained practice. If we want the best work to be done in teaching or writing or stone masonry or farming, then we must arrange for that work to be done by proven master workers, people who are prepared for the work by long and excellent practice.

But to assume that there is a degree of specialization that is proper is at the same time to assume that there is a degree that is improper. The impropriety begins, I think, when the various kinds of workers come to be divided and cease to speak to one another. In this division they become makers of *parts* of things. This is the impropriety of industrial organization, of which Eric Gill wrote, "Skill in making . . . degenerates into mere dexterity, i.e. skill in doing, when the workman . . . ceases to be concerned for the thing made or . . . has no longer any responsibility for the thing made and has therefore lost the knowledge of what it is that he is making. . . . The factory hand can only know what he is *doing*. What is being made is no concern of his."[1] Part of the problem in universities now (or part of the cause of the problem) is this loss of concern for the thing made and, back of that, I think, the loss of agreement on what the thing is that is being made.

The thing being made in a university is humanity. Given the current   4
influence of universities, this is merely inevitable. But what universities, at least the public-supported ones, are *mandated* to make or to help to make is human beings in the fullest sense of those words—not just trained workers or knowledgeable citizens but responsible heirs and members of human culture. If the proper work of the university is only to equip people to fulfill private ambitions, then how do we justify public support? If it is only to prepare citizens to fulfill public responsibilities, then how do we justify the teaching of arts and sciences? The common denominator has to be larger than either career preparation or preparation for citizenship. Underlying the idea of a university—the bringing together, the combining into one, of all the disciplines—is the idea that good work and good citizenship are the inevitable by-products of the making of a good—that is, a fully developed—human being. This, as I understand it, is the definition of the name *university*.

In order to be concerned for the thing made, in order even to know what   5
it is making, the university as a whole must speak the same language as all of its students and all of its graduates. There must, in other words, be a common tongue. Without a common tongue, a university not only loses concern for the thing made; it loses its own unity. Furthermore, when the departments of a university become so specialized that they can speak neither to each other nor to the students and graduates of other departments, then that university is displaced. As an institution, it no longer knows where it is, and therefore it cannot know either its responsibilities to its place or the effects of its irresponsibility. This too often is the practical meaning of "academic freedom": The teacher feels free to teach and learn, make and think, without concern for the thing made.

For example, it is still perfectly acceptable in land-grant universities for   6
agricultural researchers to apply themselves to the development of more productive dairy cows without considering at all the fact that this development necessarily involves the failure of many thousands of dairies and dairy farmers—that it has already done so and will inevitably continue to do so. The researcher feels at liberty to justify such work merely on the basis of the ratio between the "production unit" and the volume of production. And such work is permitted to continue, I suspect, because it is reported in language that is unreadable and probably unintelligible to nearly everybody in the university, to nearly everybody who milks cows, and to nearly everybody who drinks milk. That a modern university might provide a forum in which such researchers might be required to defend their work before colleagues in, say, philosophy or history or literature is, at present, not likely, nor is it likely, at present, that the departments of philosophy, history, or literature could produce many colleagues able or willing to be interested in the ethics of agricultural research.

Language is at the heart of the problem. To profess, after all, is "to 7
confess before"—to confess, I assume, before all who live within the neighborhood or under the influence of the confessor. But to confess before one's
neighbors and clients in a language that few of them can understand is not
to confess at all. The specialized professional language is thus not merely a
contradiction in terms; it is a cheat and a hiding place; it may, indeed, be an
ambush. At the very root of the idea of profession and professorship is the
imperative to speak plainly in the common tongue.

That the common tongue should become the exclusive specialty of a 8
department in a university is therefore a tragedy, and not just for the university and its worldly place; it is a tragedy for the common tongue. It means
that the common tongue, so far as the university is concerned, *ceases* to be the
common tongue; it becomes merely one tongue within a confusion of
tongues. Our language and literature cease to be seen as occurring in the
world, and begin to be seen as occurring within their university department
and within themselves. Literature ceases to be the meeting ground of all
readers of the common tongue and becomes only the occasion of a deafening
clatter *about* literature. Teachers and students read the great songs and stories
to learn *about* them, not to learn *from* them. The *texts* are tracked as by the
passing of an army of ants, but the power of songs and stories to affect life
is still little acknowledged, apparently because it is little felt.

The specialist approach, of course, is partly justifiable; in both speech 9
and literature, language does occur within itself. It echoes within itself, reverberating endlessly like a voice echoing within a cave, and speaking in answer
to its echo, and the answer again echoing. It must do this; its nature, in part,
is to do this.

But its nature also is to turn outward to the world, to strike its worldly 10
objects cleanly and cease to echo—to achieve a kind of rest and silence in
them. The professionalization of language and of language study makes the
cave inescapable; one strives without rest in the interior clamor.

The silence in which words return to their objects, touch them, and 11
come to rest is not the silence of the plugged ear. It is the world's silence, such
as occurs after the first hard freeze of autumn, when the weeks-long singing
of the crickets is suddenly stopped, and when, by a blessedly recurring
accident, all machine noises have stopped for the moment, too. It is a silence
that must be prepared for and waited for; it requires a silence of one's own.

The reverberations of language within itself are, finally, mere noise, no 12
better or worse than the noise of accumulated facts that grate aimlessly
against each other in think tanks and other hollow places. Facts, like words,
are not things but verbal tokens or signs of things that finally must be carried
back to the things they stand for to be verified. This carrying back is not
specialist work but an act generally human, though only properly humbled
and quieted humans can do it. It is an act that at once enlarges and shapes,
frees and limits us.

It is necessary, for example, that the word *tree* evoke memories that are 13
both personal and cultural. In order to understand fully what a tree is, we

must remember much of our experience with trees and much that we have heard and read about them. We destroy those memories by reducing trees to facts, by thinking of *tree* as a mere word, or by treating our memory of trees as "cultural history." When we call a tree a tree, we are not isolated among words and facts but are at once in the company of the tree itself and surrounded by ancestral voices calling out to us all that trees have been and meant. This is simply the condition of being human in this world, and there is nothing that art and science can do about it, except get used to it. But, of course, only specialized "professional" arts and sciences would propose or wish to do something about it.

This necessity for words and facts to return to their objects in the world 14 describes one of the boundaries of a university, one of the boundaries of book learning anywhere, and it describes the need for humility, restraint, exacting discipline, and high standards within that boundary.

Beside every effort of making, which is necessarily narrow, there must 15 be an effort of judgment, of criticism, which must be as broad as possible. That is, every made thing must be submitted to these questions: What is the quality of this thing as a human artifact, as an addition to the world of made and of created things? How suitable is it to the needs of human and natural neighborhoods?

It must, of course, sooner or later be submitted as well to the special 16 question: How good is this poem or this farm or this hospital as such? For it to have a human value, it obviously must be well made; it must meet the specialized, technical criteria; it must be *good* as such. But the question of its quality as such is not interesting—in the long run it is probably not even askable—unless we ask it under the rule of the more general questions. If we are disposed to judge apart from the larger questions, if we judge, as well as make, as specialists, then a good forger has as valid a claim to our respect as a good artist.

These two problems, how to make and how to judge, are the business 17 of education. But education has tended increasingly to ignore the doubleness of its obligation. It has concerned itself more and more exclusively with the problem of how to make, narrowing the issue of judgment virtually to the terms of the made thing itself. But the thing made by education now is not a fully developed human being; it is a specialist, a careerist, a graduate. In industrial education, the thing *finally* made is of no concern to the makers.

In some instances, this is because the specialized "fields" have grown 18 so complicated within themselves that the curriculum leaves no time for the broad and basic studies that would inform judgment. In other instances, one feels that there is a potentially embarrassing conflict between judgment broadly informed and the specialized career for which the student is being prepared; teachers of advertising techniques, for example, could ill afford for their students to realize that they are learning the arts of lying and seduction. In all instances, this narrowing is justified by the improbable assumption that young students, before they know anything else, know what they need to learn.

If the disintegration of the university begins in its specialist ideology, it is   19
enforced by a commercial compulsion to satisfy the customer. Since the student is now so much a free agent in determining his or her education, the department administrators and the faculty members must necessarily be preoccupied with the problem of how to keep enrollments up. Something obviously must be done to keep the classes filled; otherwise, the students will wander off to more attractive courses or to courses more directly useful to their proposed careers. Under such circumstances it is inevitable that requirements will be lightened, standards lowered, grades inflated, and instruction narrowed to the supposed requirements of some supposed career opportunity.

Dr. Johnson told Mrs. Thrale that his cousin, Cornelius Ford, "advised   20
him to study the Principles of every thing, that a general Acquaintance with Life might be the Consequence of his Enquiries—Learn said he the leading Precognita of all things . . . grasp the Trunk hard only, and you will shake all the Branches."[2] The soundness of this advice seems indisputable, and the metaphor entirely apt. From the trunk it is possible to "branch out." One can begin with a trunk and develop a single branch or any number of branches; although it may be possible to begin with a branch and develop a trunk, that is neither so probable nor so promising. The modern university, at any rate, more and more resembles a loose collection of lopped branches waving about randomly in the air. "Modern knowledge is departmentalized," H. J. Massingham wrote in 1943, "while the essence of culture is initiation into wholeness, so that all the divisions of knowledge are considered as the branches of one tree, the Tree of Life whose roots went deep into earth and whose top was in heaven."[3]

This Tree, for many hundreds of years, seems to have come almost   21
naturally to mind when we have sought to describe the form of knowledge. In Western tradition, it is at least as old as Genesis, and the form it gives us for all that we know is organic, unified, comprehensive, connective—and moral. The tree, at the beginning, was two trees: the tree of life and the tree of the knowledge of good and evil. Later, in our understanding of them, the two trees seem to have become one, or each seems to stand for the other—for in the world after the Fall, how can the two be separated? To know life is to know good and evil; to prepare young people for life is to prepare them to know the difference between good and evil. If we represent knowledge as a tree, we know that things that are divided are yet connected. We know that to observe the divisions and ignore the connections is to destroy the tree. The history of modern education may be the history of the loss of this image, and of its replacement by the pattern of the industrial machine, which subsists upon division—and by industrial economics ("publish or perish"), which is meaningless apart from division.

The need for broadly informed human judgment nevertheless remains,   22
and this need requires inescapably an education that is broad and basic. In

the face of this need, which is *both* private and public, "career preparation" is an improper use of public money, since "career preparation" serves merely private ends; it is also a waste of the student's time, since "career preparation" is best and most properly acquired in apprenticeships under the supervision of employers. The proper subject for a school, for example, is how to speak and write well, not how to be a "public speaker" or a "broadcaster" or a "creative writer" or a "technical writer" or a journalist or a practitioner of "business English." If one can speak and write well, then, given the need, one can make a speech or write an article or a story or a business letter. If one cannot speak or write well, then the tricks of a trade will be no help.

The work that should, and that can, unify a university is that of decid-   23
ing what a student should be required to learn—what studies, that is, consti-
tute the trunk of the tree of a person's education. "Career preparation," which has given so much practical support to academic specialization (and so many rewards to academic specialists) seems to have destroyed interest in this question. But the question exists and the failure to answer it (or even to ask it) imposes severe penalties on teachers, students, and the public alike. The penalties imposed on students and graduates by their failure to get a broad, basic education are, I think, obvious enough. The public penalties are also obvious if we consider, for instance, the number of certified expert speakers and writers who do not speak or write well, who do not know that they speak or write poorly, and who apparently do not care whether or not they speak or write honestly.

The penalties that this failure imposes on teachers are not so obvious,   24
mainly, I suppose, because so far the penalties have been obscured by re-
wards. The penalties for teachers are the same as those for students and the public, plus one more: The failure to decide what students should be required to learn keeps the teacher from functioning as, and perhaps from becoming, a responsible adult.

There is no one to teach young people but older people, and so the older   25
people must do it. That they do not know enough to do it, that they have never been smart enough or experienced enough or good enough to do it, does not matter. They must do it because there is no one else to do it. This is simply the elemental trial—some would say the elemental tragedy—of human life: the necessity to proceed on the basis merely of the knowledge that is available, the necessity to postpone until too late the question of the sufficiency and the truth of that knowledge.

There is, then, an inescapable component of trial and error in human   26
education; some things that are taught will be wrong because fallible humans are the teachers. But the reason for education, its constant effort and disci-
pline, is surely to reduce the young person's dependence on trial and error as far as possible. For it *can* be reduced. One should not have to learn everything, or the basic things, by trial and error. A child should not have to learn the danger of heat by falling into the fire. A student should not have to learn the penalties of illiteracy by being illiterate or the value of a good education by the "object lesson" of a poor one.

Teachers, moreover, are not providing "career preparation" so much as 27
they are "preparing young people for life." This statement is not the result
of educational doctrine; it is simply the fact of the matter. To prepare young
people for life, teachers must dispense knowledge and enlighten ignorance,
just as supposed. But ignorance is not only the affliction that teaching seeks
to cure; it is also the condition, the predicament, in which teaching is done,
for teachers do not know the life or the lives for which their students are
being prepared.

This condition gives the lie to the claims for "career preparation," since 28
students may not *have* the careers for which they have been prepared: The
"job market" may be overfilled; the requirements for this or that career may
change; the student may change, or the world may. The teacher, preparing
the student for a life necessarily unknown to them both, has no excusable
choice but to help the student to "grasp the Trunk."

Yet the arguments for "career preparation" continue to be made and to 29
grow in ambition. On August 23, 1983, for example, the Associated Press
announced that "the head of the Texas school board wants to require sixth-
graders to choose career 'tracks' that will point them toward jobs."[4] Thus,
twelve-year-old children would be "free to choose" the kind of life they wish
to live. They would even be free to change "career tracks," though, according
to the article, such a change would involve the penalty of a delayed graduation.

But these are free choices granted to children not prepared or ready to 30
make them. The idea, in reality, is to impose adult choices on children, and
these "choices" mask the most vicious sort of economic determinism. This
idea of education as "career track" diminishes everything it touches: education, teaching, childhood, the future. And such a thing could not be contemplated for sixth-graders, obviously, if it had not already been instituted in the
undergraduate programs of colleges and universities.

To require or expect or even allow young people to choose courses of 31
study and careers that they do not yet know anything about is not, as is
claimed, a grant of freedom. It is a severe limitation upon freedom. It means,
in practice, that when the student has finished school and is faced then,
appropriately, with the need to choose a career, he or she is prepared to
choose only one. At that point, the student stands in need of a freedom of
choice uselessly granted years before and forfeited in that grant.

The responsibility to decide what to teach the young is an adult respon- 32
sibility. When adults transfer this responsibility to the young, whether they
do it by indifference or as a grant of freedom, they trap themselves in a kind
of childishness. In that failure to accept responsibility, the teacher's own
learning and character are disemployed, and, in the contemporary industrialized education system, they are easily replaced by bureaucratic and methodological procedures, "job market" specifications, and tests graded by machines.

This question of what all young people should be expected to learn is 33
now little discussed. The reason, apparently, is the tacit belief that now, with

the demands of specialization so numerous and varied, such a question would be extremely hard, if not impossible, to answer. And yet this question appears to be as much within the reach of reason and common sense as any other. It cannot be denied, to begin with, that all the disciplines rest upon the knowledge of letters and the knowledge of numbers. Some rest more on letters than numbers, some more on numbers than letters, but it is surely true to say that people without knowledge of both letters and numbers are not prepared to learn much else. From there, one can proceed confidently to say that history, literature, philosophy, and foreign languages rest principally on the knowledge of letters and carry it forward, and that biology, chemistry, and physics rest on the knowledge of numbers and carry it forward. This provides us with a description of a probably adequate "core curriculum"—one that would prepare a student well both to choose a direction of further study and to go in that direction. An equally obvious need, then, is to eliminate from the curriculum all courses without content—that is, all courses in methodologies and technologies that could, and should, be learned in apprenticeships.

Besides the innate human imperfections already mentioned, other pain- 34 ful problems are involved in expecting and requiring students to choose the course of their own education. These problems have to do mainly with the diversity of gifts and abilities: that is, some people are not talented in some kinds of work or study; some, moreover, who are poor in one discipline may be excellent in another. Why should such people be forced into situations in which they must see themselves as poor workers or as failures?

The question is not a comfortable one, and I do not believe that it can 35 or should be comfortably answered. There is pain in the requirement to risk failure and pain in the failure that may result from that requirement. But failure is a possibility; in varying degrees for all of us, it is inescapable. The argument for removing the possibility of failure from schoolwork is therefore necessarily specious. The wrong is not in subjecting students to the possibility of failure or in calling their failures failures; the wrong is in the teacher's inability to see that failure in school is not necessarily synonymous with and does not necessarily lead to failure in the world. The wrong is in the failure to see or respect the boundaries between the school and the world. When those are not understood and respected, then the school, the school career, the diploma are all surrounded by such a spurious and modish dignity that failure in school *is* failure in the world. It is for this reason that it is so easy to give education a money value and to sell it to consumers in job lots.

It is a fact that some people with able minds do not fit well into schools 36 and are not properly valued by schoolish standards and tests. If such people fail in a school, their failure should be so called; a school's worth and integrity depend upon its willingness to call things by their right names. But, by the same token, a failure in school is no more than that; it does not necessarily imply or cause failure in the world, any more than it implies or causes stupidity. It is not rare for the judgment of the world to overturn the judgment of schools. There are other tests for human abilities than those given in schools, and there are some that cannot be given in schools. My own life has happened to acquaint me with several people who did not attend high school but who have been more knowledgeable in their "field" and who have had better things to say about matters of general importance than most of the doctors of philosophy I have known. This is not an "anti-intellectual" statement; it is a statement of what I take to be fact, and it means only that the uses of schools are limited—another fact, which schools prepare us to learn by surprise.

Another necessary consideration is that low expectations and standards 37 in universities encourage the lowering of expectations and standards in the high schools and elementary schools. If the universities raise their expectations and standards, the high schools and elementary schools will raise theirs; they will have to. On the other hand, if the universities teach high school courses because the students are not prepared for university courses, then they simply relieve the high schools of their duty and in the process make themselves unable to do their own duty. Once the school stoops to meet the student, the standards of judgment begin to topple at all levels. As standards are lowered—as they cease to be the measure of the students and come to be measured by them—it becomes manifestly less possible for students to fail. But for the same reason it becomes less possible for them to learn and for teachers to teach.

The question, then, is what is to determine the pattern of education. 38 Shall we shape a university education according to the previous schooling of the students, which we suppose has made them unfit to meet high expectations and standards, and to the supposed needs of students in some future still dark to us all? Or shall we shape it according to the nature and demands of the "leading Precognita of all things"—that is, according to the essential subjects of study? If we shape education to fit the students, then we clearly can maintain no standards; we will lose the subjects and eventually will lose the students as well. If we shape it to the subjects, then we will save both the subjects and the students. The inescapable purpose of education must be to preserve and pass on the essential human means—the thoughts and words and works and ways and standards and hopes without which we are not human. To preserve these things and to pass them on is to prepare students for life.

That such work cannot be done without high standards ought not to 39 have to be said. There are necessarily increasing degrees of complexity in the studies as students rise through the grades and the years, and yet the standards remain the same. The first-graders, that is, must read and write in simple sentences, but they read and write, even so, in the language of the King James Bible, of Shakespeare and Johnson, of Thoreau, Whitman, Dickinson, and Twain. The grade-schooler and the graduate student must study the same American history, and there is no excuse for falsifying it in order to make it elementary.

Moreover, if standards are to be upheld, they cannot be specialized, 40 professionalized, or departmented. Only common standards can be upheld—standards that are held and upheld in common by the whole community. When, in a university, for instance, English composition is made the responsibility exclusively of the English department, or of the subdepartment of freshman English, then the quality of the work in composition courses declines and the standards decline. This happens necessarily and for an obvious reason: If students' writing is graded according to form and quality in composition class but according only to "content" in, say, history class and if in other classes students are not required to write at all, then the message to the students is clear: namely, that the form and quality of their writing matters only in composition class, which is to say that it matters very little indeed. High standards of composition can be upheld only if they are upheld everywhere in the university.

Not only must the standards be held and upheld in common but they 41 must also be applied fairly—that is, there must be no conditions with respect to persons or groups. There must be no discrimination for or against any person for any reason. The quality of the individual performer is the issue, not the category of the performer. The aim is to recognize, reward, and promote good work. Special pleading for "disadvantaged" groups—whether disadvantaged by history, economics, or education—can only make it increasingly difficult for members of that group to do good work and have it recognized.

If the university faculties have failed to answer the question of the 42 internal placement of the knowledges of the arts and sciences with respect to each other and to the university as a whole, they have, it seems to me, also failed to ask the question of the external placement of these knowledges with respect to truth and to the world. This, of course, is a dangerous question, and I raise it with appropriate fear. The danger is that such questions should be *settled* by any institution whatever; these questions are the proper business of the people in the institutions, not of the institutions as such. I am arguing here against the specialist absorption in career and procedure that destroys what I take to be the indispensable interest in the question of the truth of what is taught and learned, as well as the equally indispensable interest in the fate and the use of knowledge in the world.

I would be frightened to hear that some university had suddenly taken 43 a lively interest in the question of what is true and was in the process of answering it, perhaps by a faculty vote. But I am equally frightened by the fashionable lack of interest in the question among university teachers individually. I am more frightened when this disinterest, under the alias of "objectivity," is given the status of a public virtue.

Objectivity, in practice, means that one studies or teaches one's subject 44 *as such,* without concern for its relation to other subjects or to the world—that is, without concern for its truth. If one is concerned, if one cares, about the truth or falsity of anything, one cannot be objective: one is glad if it is true and sorry if it is false; one believes it if it is judged to be true and disbelieves it if it is judged to be false. Moreover, the truth or falsity of some things cannot be objectively demonstrated, but must be determined by feeling and appearance, intuition and experience. And this work of judgment cannot take place at all with respect to one thing or one subject alone. The issue of truth rises out of the comparison of one thing with another, out of the study of the relations and influences between one thing and another and between one thing and many others.

Thus, if teachers aspire to the academic virtue of objectivity, they must 45 teach as if their subject has nothing to do with anything beyond itself. The teacher of literature, for example, must propose the study of poems as relics left by people who, unlike our highly favored modern selves, believed in things not subject to measurable proof; religious poetry, that is, may be taught as having to do with matters once believed but not believable. The poetry is to be learned *about;* to learn *from* it would be an embarrassing betrayal of objectivity.

That this is more than a matter of classroom technique is made suffi- 46 ciently evident in the current fracas over the teaching of the Bible in public schools. Judge Jackson Kiser of the federal district court in Bristol, Virginia, recently ruled that it would be constitutional to teach the Bible to public school students if the course is offered as an elective and "taught in an objective manner with no attempt made to indoctrinate the children as to either the truth or falsity of the biblical materials." James J. Kilpatrick, who discussed this ruling approvingly in one of his columns, suggested that the Bible might be taught "as Shakespeare is taught" and that this would be good because "the Bible is a rich lode of allusion, example and quotation." He warned that "The line that divides propaganda from instruction is a wavering line drawn on shifting sands," and he concluded by asserting that "Whatever else the Bible may be, the Bible is in fact literature. The trick is to teach it that way."[5]

The interesting question here is not whether young English-speakers 47 should know the Bible—they obviously should—but whether a book that so directly offers itself to our belief or disbelief can be taught "as literature." It clearly cannot be so taught except by ignoring "whatever else [it] may be," which is a very substantial part of it. The question, then, is whether it can be adequately or usefully taught as something less than it is. The fact is that the writers of the Bible did not think that they were writing what Judge Kiser and Mr. Kilpatrick call "literature." They thought they were writing the truth, which they expected to be believed by some and disbelieved by others. It is conceivable that the Bible could be well taught by a teacher who believes that it is true, by a teacher who believes that it is untrue, or by a teacher who believes that it is partly true. That it could be well taught by a teacher uninterested in the question of its truth is not conceivable. That a lively interest in the Bible could be maintained through several generations of teachers uninterested in the question of its truth is also not conceivable.

Obviously, this issue of the Bible in the public schools cannot be re- 48 solved by federal court decisions that prescribe teaching methods. It can only be settled in terms of the freedom of teachers to teach as they believe and in terms of the relation of teachers and schools to their local communities. It may be that in this controversy we are seeing the breakdown of the public school system, as an inevitable consequence of the breakdown of local communities. It is hard to believe that this can be remedied in courts of law.

My point, anyhow, is that we could not consider teaching the Bible "as 49 literature" if we were not already teaching literature "as literature"—as if we do not care, as if it does not matter, whether or not it is true. The causes of this are undoubtedly numerous, but prominent among them is a kind of shame among teachers of literature and other "humanities" that their truths are not objectively provable as are the truths of science. There is now an embarrassment about any statement that depends for confirmation upon experience or imagination or feeling or faith, and this embarrassment has produced an overwhelming impulse to treat such statements merely as artifacts, cultural relics, bits of historical evidence, or things of "aesthetic value." We will study, record, analyze, criticize, and appreciate. But we will not believe; we will not, in the full sense, know.

The result is a stance of "critical objectivity" that causes many teachers, 50 historians, and critics of literature to sound—not like mathematicians or chemists: their methodology does not permit that yet—but like ethologists, students of the behavior of a species to which they do not belong, in whose history and fate they have no part, their aim being, not to know anything for themselves, but to "advance knowledge." This may be said to work, as a textual mechanics, but it is not an approach by which one may know any great work of literature. That route is simply closed to people interested in what "they" thought "then"; it is closed to people who think that "Dante's world" or "Shakespeare's world" is far removed and completely alienated from "our world"; and it is closed to the viewers of poetic devices, emotional effects, and esthetic values.

The great distraction behind the modern fate of literature, I think, is 51 expressed in Coleridge's statement that his endeavor in *Lyrical Ballads* was "to transfer from our inward nature . . . a semblance of truth sufficient to procure for these shadows of imagination that willing suspension of disbelief for the moment, which constitutes poetic faith."[6] That is a sentence full of quakes and tremors. Is our inward nature true only by semblance? What is the difference, in a work of art, between truth and "semblance of truth"? What must be the result of separating "poetic faith" from faith of any other kind and then of making "poetic faith" dependent upon will?

The gist of the problem is in that adjective *willing,* which implies the 52 superiority of the believer to what is believed. This implication, I am convinced, is simply untrue. Belief precedes will. One either believes or one does not, and, if one believes, then one willingly believes. If one disbelieves, even unwillingly, all the will in the world cannot make one believe. Belief is involuntary, as is the Ancient Mariner's recognition of the beauty and sanctity of the water snakes:

A spring of love gushed from my heart,
And I blessed them unaware . . .

This involuntary belief is the only approach to the great writings. One may, assuredly, not believe, and we must, of course, grant unbelievers the right to read and comment as unbelievers, for disbelief is a legitimate response, because it is a possible one. We must be aware of the possibility that belief may be false, and of the need to awaken from false belief; "one need not step into belief as into an abyss."[7] But we must be aware also that to disbelieve is to remain, in an important sense, outside the work. When we are *in* the work, we are long past the possibility of any debate with ourselves about whether or not to be willing to believe. When we are *in* the work, we simply *know* that great Odysseus has come home, that Dante is in the presence of the celestial rose, that Cordelia, though her father carries her in his arms, is dead. If we know these things, we are apt to know too that Mary Magdalene mistook the risen Christ for the gardener—and are thus eligible to be taken lightly by objective scholars, and to be corrected by a federal judge.

We and these works meet in imagination; by imagination we know their truth. In imagination, there is no specifically or exclusively "poetic faith," just as there is no faith that is specifically or exclusively religious. Belief is the same wherever it happens, and its terms are invariably set by the imagination. One believes, that is, because one *sees,* not because one is informed. That is why, four hundred years after Copernicus, we still say, "The sun is rising."

When we read the ballad of Sir Patrick Spens we know that the knight and his men have drowned because "Thair hats they swam aboone,"* not because we have confirmed the event by the study of historical documents. And if our assent is forced also by the ballad of Thomas Rhymer,† far stranger than that of Sir Patrick, what are we to say? Must we go, believing, into the poem, and then return from it in disbelief because we find the story in no official record, have read of no such thing in the newspaper, and know nothing like it in our own experience? Or must we live with the poem, with our awareness of its power over us, as a piece of evidence that reality may be larger than we thought?

"Does that mean," I am asked, "that it's not possible for us to read Homer properly because we don't believe in the Greek gods?" I can only answer that I suspect that a proper reading of Homer will *result* in some manner of belief in his gods. How else explain their survival in the works of Christian writers into our own time? This survival has its apotheosis, it seems to me, in C. S. Lewis's novel, *That Hideous Strength,* at the end of which the Greek planetary deities reappear on earth as angels. Lewis wrote as a Christian who had read Homer, but he had read, obviously, as a man whose

---

*Above. In the medieval ballad of Sir Patrick Spens, Sir Patrick and his crew of Scottish nobles are drowned at sea, their cork-heeled shoes causing their bodies to float upside down, "aboon" their hats.

†Thomas the Rhymer is the earliest name in Scottish literature. He is supposed to have lived in the thirteenth century and to have written a romance, *Sir Tristrem.*

imagination was not encumbered with any such clinical apparatus as the willing suspension of disbelief. As such a reader, though he was a Christian, his reading had told him that the pagan gods retained a certain authority and commanded a certain assent. Like many of his forebears in English literary tradition, he yearned toward them. Their triumphant return, at the end of *That Hideous Strength,* as members of the heavenly hierarchy of Christianity, is not altogether a surprise. It is a profound resolution, not only in the novel itself, but in the history of English literature. One hears the ghosts of Spenser and Milton sighing with relief.

Questions of the authenticity of imaginings invite answers, and yet may 57 remain unanswered. For the imagination is not always subject to immediate proof or demonstration. It is often subject only to the slow and partial authentication of experience. It is subject, that is, to a practical, though not an exact, validation, and it is subject to correction. For a work of imagination to endure through time, it must prove valid, and it must survive correction. It is correctable by experience, by critical judgment, and by further works of imagination.

To say that a work of imagination is subject to correction is, of course, 58 to imply that there is no "world of imagination" as distinct from or opposed to the "real world." The imagination is *in* the world, is at work in it, is necessary to it, and is correctable by it. This correcting of imagination by experience is inescapable, necessary, and endless, as is the correcting of experience by imagination. This is the great general work of criticism to which we all are called. It is not literary criticism any more than it is historical or agricultural or biological criticism, but it must nevertheless be a fundamental part of the work of literary criticism, as it must be of criticisms of all other kinds. One of the most profound of human needs is for the truth of imagination to prove itself in every life and place in the world, and for the truth of the world's lives and places to be proved in imagination.

This need takes us as far as possible from the argument for works of 59 imagination, human artifacts, as special cases, privileged somehow to offer themselves to the world on their own terms. It is this argument and the consequent abandonment of the general criticism that have permitted the universities to organize themselves on the industrial principle, as if faculties and students and all that they might teach and learn are no more than parts of a machine, the purpose of which they have, in general, not bothered to define, much less to question. And largely through the agency of the universities, this principle and this metaphor now dominate our relation to nature and to one another.

If, for the sake of its own health, a university must be interested in 60 the question of the truth of what it teaches, then, for the sake of the world's health, it must be interested in the fate of that truth and the uses made of it in the world. It must want to know where its graduates live, where they work, and what they do. Do they return home with their knowledge to enhance and protect the life of their neighborhoods? Do they join the "upwardly mobile" professional force now exploiting and destroying local communities, both human and natural, all over the country? Has the work of the university, over the last generation, increased or decreased literacy and knowledge of the classics? Has it increased or decreased the general understanding of the sciences? Has it increased or decreased pollution and soil erosion? Has it increased or decreased the ability and the willingness of public servants to tell the truth? Such questions are not, of course, precisely answerable. Questions about influence never are. But they are askable, and the asking, should we choose to ask, would be a unifying and a shaping force.

NOTES

All notes are Berry's.

1. Eric Gill, *A Holy Tradition of Working,* ed. Brian Keeble (Ipswich: Golgonooza Press, 1983), p. 61.

2. W. Jackson Bate, *Samuel Johnson* (New York: Harcourt Brace Jovanovich, 1977), p. 51.

3. H. J. Massingham, *The Tree of Life* (London: Chapman & Hall, 1943).

4. "Texas School Board Chief Wants Sixth-Graders to Pick Job 'Tracks,' " *Courier-Journal* (Louisville, Ky.) Aug. 13, 1983.

5. "Plan to Teach the Bible as Literature May Wind up in the Supreme Court," *Courier-Journal* (Louisville, Ky.) Sept. 15, 1983.

6. Samuel Coleridge, *Biographia Literaria,* chapter 14.

7. Harry Mason, in a letter to the author.

Questions for Discussion

1. In paragraphs 9, 10, and 11, Berry's language becomes metaphorically charged. Are the metaphors and similes appropriate to his message? Do they work in the contexts where he uses them? Can you assess their strengths and weaknesses relative to Berry's objectives?

2. Whom do you identify as Berry's audience? What is your evidence for identifying one kind of audience rather than another?

3. How would you articulate in your own words Berry's statement in paragraph 12 that the "carrying back" of facts "to the things they stand for" can be done "only [by] properly humbled and quieted humans"? Why "humbled and quieted"? What does this phrase mean? Do you agree or disagree? Why?

4. In paragraphs 42–56, Berry constructs a fairly detailed critique of the academic ideal of "critical objectivity." For what reasons do you find this section convincing or not convincing? What does he mean by "critical objectivity"? Does he think it is or is not a proper ideal for education? For what reasons do you agree or disagree that ideas and issues should not be taught apart from considerations of their truth?

5. What does Berry mean in paragraph 54 by the statement that "Belief is the same wherever it happens, and its terms are invariably set by the imagination"? Can you challenge or corroborate this view with examples from your own beliefs?

Suggested Essay Topics

1. Construct a rebuttal directed to Berry himself of his critique of academic specialization. Provide, in other words, an argument for the other side of the case. A good way to begin might be to talk to three or four of your professors and have them give you the best reasons they can think of for defending and preserving disciplinary specialization. Ask them when, if ever, they think of specialization becoming excessive and see if their views agree with Berry's. Ask them what specialization has done *for* the disciplines and decide whether the *disadvantages* to education are as damaging as Berry thinks. Write your findings and reflections in an argument that makes the best case you can for disciplinary specialization.

2. In paragraphs 22–41 Berry constructs a detailed attack on education as "career preparation." If you agree with Berry's attack, then, for the sake of your own education, attempt to construct the best rebuttal you can. That is, make the best argument you can in favor of career training. Or, if you feel that even the best argument on this side is going to be feeble, write an essay to your classmates in which you discuss those points where Berry leaves himself most open to criticism from those who prefer career education. If you disagree with Berry's attack, then take three or four of his main points in this section and show *in detail,* by constructing criticism of his arguments and by providing alternative arguments of your own, why Berry's position is not convincing.

Malcolm X

Malcolm X (1925–1965) was a famous and powerful leader in the push for equal rights for blacks in the 1950s and 1960s. In The Autobiography of Malcolm X, *he describes the dramatic sequence of events that transformed him from Malcolm Little, street hustler and convicted thief, to political leader and outstanding evangelist for the Temple of Islam. In his devotion to Muslim teachings he journeyed to Mecca, and while there he became convinced that many of the teachings of the Temple of Islam were not true to the Muslim faith. On his return to America, he expressed his new convictions with characteristic forthrightness and power. He was assassinated in New York City in 1965 while preaching his new views. Some members of the Temple of Islam were convicted of the murder, but there is still controversy over who in fact killed him.*

The Autobiography *continues to be read as a passionate document expressing both private and public commitment to a cause. In the following selection, Malcolm X gives one of the most moving accounts we know of what it is like to engage in self-education. Of particular note is his growing realization of the value of language skill and his willingness to work at gaining it. Notice how the questions students often ask in school—Is this work going to be boring? Why is this so hard? Do I really have to do all of this work? Why is practice so important?—simply have no place in Malcolm X's mind. Because he has a clear picture of the goals he wants to achieve, he is willing to work hard at boring and routine matters the same way football players are willing to sweat and grunt in the heat of August practices because they want to look good in the cool of November games.*

If you are (or have been) unwilling to work hard at improving your reading and writing skills, perhaps it is because you have not internalized any of the goals your teachers have been telling you about. Perhaps you don't see them as your goals; you don't claim ownership of them. If this is the case, we ask you to read (or to reread) the essays in Part One of this book, especially the first two, conidering seriously our arguments about the advantages of improving one's language skills. Then turn back to this essay by Malcolm X who, it seems to us, gives a concrete illustration of the truth of our claims, an illustration that is moving and vivid because of the cost to Malcolm X himself. Ask yourself as you read whether you would ever be willing to pay as much in effort and dedication to acquire the rudiments of an education in reading and writing. And note how, as Malcolm X's reading moved from merely deciphering words to understanding ideas, he became aware of changes in his mind, in his feelings, and in his views of the world. Few essays better illustrate the transforming power of an education.

FREEDOM THROUGH LEARNING TO READ

From chapter 11, "Saved," of *The Autobiography of Malcolm X* (1964). The title is ours.

It was because of my letters that I happened to stumble upon starting   1
to acquire some kind of a homemade education.

I became increasingly frustrated at not being able to express what I   2
wanted to convey in letters that I wrote, especially those to Mr. Elijah
Muhammad.* In the street, I had been the most articulate hustler out there—I
had commanded attention when I said something. But now, trying to write
simple English, I not only wasn't articulate, I wasn't even functional. How
would I sound writing in slang, the way I would *say* it, something such as,
"Look, daddy, let me pull your coat about a cat, Elijah Muhammad—"

Many who today hear me somewhere in person, or on television, or   3
those who read something I've said, will think I went to school far beyond
the eighth grade. This impression is due entirely to my prison studies.

*Elijah Muhammad was a leader of the Black Muslims' Temple of Islam in the 1940s, 1950s, and
1960s.

It had really begun back in the Charlestown Prison, when Bimbi first   4
made me feel envy of his stock of knowledge. Bimbi had always taken charge
of any conversations he was in, and I had tried to emulate him. But every
book I picked up had few sentences which didn't contain anywhere from one
to nearly all of the words that might as well have been in Chinese. When I
just skipped those words, of course, I really ended up with little idea of what
the book said. So I had come to the Norfolk Prison Colony still going through
only book-reading motions. Pretty soon, I would have quit even these motions, unless I had received the motivation that I did.

I saw that the best thing I could do was get hold of a dictionary—to   5
study, to learn some words. I was lucky enough to reason also that I should
try to improve my penmanship. It was sad. I couldn't even write in a straight
line. It was both ideas together that moved me to request a dictionary along
with some tablets and pencils from the Norfolk Prison Colony school.

I spent two days just riffling uncertainly through the dictionary's pages.   6
I'd never realized so many words existed! I didn't know *which* words I needed
to learn. Finally, just to start some kind of action, I began copying.

In my slow, painstaking, ragged handwriting, I copied into my tablet   7
everything printed on that first page, down to the punctuation marks.

I believe it took me a day. Then, aloud, I read back, to myself, every-   8
thing I'd written on the tablet. Over and over, aloud, to myself, I read my own
handwriting.

I woke up the next morning, thinking about those words—immensely   9
proud to realize that not only had I written so much at one time, but I'd
written words that I never knew were in the world. Moreover, with a little
effort, I also could remember what many of these words meant. I reviewed
the words whose meanings I didn't remember. Funny thing, from the dictionary first page right now, that "aardvark" springs to my mind. The dictionary
had a picture of it, a long-tailed, long-eared, burrowing African mammal,
which lives off termites caught by sticking out its tongue as an anteater does
for ants.

I was so fascinated that I went on—I copied the dictionary's next page.   10
And the same experience came when I studied that. With every succeeding
page, I also learned of people and places and events from history. Actually
the dictionary is like a miniature encyclopedia. Finally the dictionary's A
section had filled a whole tablet—and I went on into the B's. That was the
way I started copying what eventually became the entire dictionary. It went
a lot faster after so much practice helped me to pick up handwriting speed.
Between what I wrote in my tablet, and writing letters, during the rest of my
time in prison I would guess I wrote a million words.

I suppose it was inevitable that as my word-base broadened, I could for   11
the first time pick up a book and read and now begin to understand what the
book was saying. Anyone who has read a great deal can imagine the new
world that opened. Let me tell you something: from then until I left that
prison, in every free moment I had, if I was not reading in the library, I was
reading on my bunk. You couldn't have gotten me out of books with a wedge.

Between Mr. Muhammad's teachings, my correspondence, my visitors—usually Ella and Reginald—and my reading of books, months passed without my even thinking about being imprisoned. In fact, up to then, I never had been so truly free in my life.

The Norfolk Prison Colony's library was in the school building. A 12 variety of classes was taught there by instructors who came from such places as Harvard and Boston universities. The weekly debates between inmate teams were also held in the school building. You would be astonished to know how worked up convict debaters and audiences would get over subjects like "Should Babies Be Fed Milk?"

Available on the prison library's shelves were books on just about 13 every general subject. Much of the big private collection that Parkhurst had willed to the prison was still in crates and boxes in the back of the library— thousands of old books. Some of them looked ancient: covers faded, old-time parchment-looking binding. Parkhurst, I've mentioned, seemed to have been principally interested in history and religion. He had the money and the special interest to have a lot of books that you wouldn't have in general circulation. Any college library would have been lucky to get that collection.

As you can imagine, especially in a prison where there was heavy 14 emphasis on rehabilitation, an inmate was smiled upon if he demonstrated an unusually intense interest in books. There was a sizable number of well-read inmates, especially the popular debaters. Some were said by many to be practically walking encyclopedias. They were almost celebrities. No university would ask any student to devour literature as I did when this new world opened to me, of being able to read and *understand.*

I read more in my room than in the library itself. An inmate who was 15 known to read a lot could check out more than the permitted maximum number of books. I preferred reading in the total isolation of my own room.

When I had progressed to really serious reading, every night at about 16 ten P.M. I would be outraged with the "lights out." It always seemed to catch me right in the middle of something engrossing.

Fortunately, right outside my door was a corridor light that cast a glow 17 into my room. The glow was enough to read by, once my eyes adjusted to it. So when "lights out" came, I would sit on the floor where I could continue reading in that glow.

At one-hour intervals the night guards paced past every room. Each 18 time I heard the approaching footsteps, I jumped into bed and feigned sleep. And as soon as the guard passed, I got back out of bed onto the floor area of that light-glow, where I would read for another fifty-eight minutes—until the guard approached again. That went on until three or four every morning. Three or four hours of sleep a night was enough for me. Often in the years in the streets I had slept less than that.

The teachings of Mr. Muhammad stressed how history had been "whit- 19 ened"—when white men had written history books, the black man simply had been left out. Mr. Muhammad couldn't have said anything that would have struck me much harder. I had never forgotten how when my class, me and all of those whites, had studied seventh-grade United States history back in Mason, the history of the Negro had been covered in one paragraph, and the teacher had gotten a big laugh with his joke, "Negroes' feet are so big that when they walk, they leave a hole in the ground."

This is one reason why Mr. Muhammad's teachings spread so swiftly all over the United States, among *all* Negroes, whether or not they became followers of Mr. Muhammad. The teachings ring true—to every Negro. You can hardly show me a black adult in America—or a white one, for that matter—who knows from the history books anything like the truth about the black man's role. In my own case, once I heard of the "glorious history of the black man," I took special pains to hunt in the library for books that would inform me on details about black history.

I can remember accurately the very first set of books that really impressed me. I have since bought that set of books and I have it at home for my children to read as they grow up. It's called *Wonders of the World.* It's full of pictures of archeological finds, statues that depict, usually, non-European people.

I found books like Will Durant's *Story of Civilization.* I read H. G. Wells' *Outline of History. Souls of Black Folk* by W. E. B. Du Bois gave me a glimpse into the black people's history before they came to this country. Carter G. Woodson's *Negro History* opened my eyes about black empires before the black slave was brought to the United States, and the early Negro struggles for freedom.

J. A. Rogers' three volumes of *Sex and Race* told about race-mixing before Christ's time; about Aesop being a black man who told fables; about Egypt's Pharaohs; about the great Coptic Christian Empires; about Ethiopia, the earth's oldest continuous black civilization, as China is the oldest continuous civilization.

Mr. Muhammad's teaching about how the white man had been created led me to *Findings in Genetics* by Gregor Mendel.* (The dictionary's G section was where I had learned what "genetics" meant.) I really studied this book by the Austrian monk. Reading it over and over, especially certain sections, helped me to understand that if you started with a black man, a white man could be produced; but starting with a white man, you never could produce a black man—because the white chromosome is recessive. And since no one disputes that there was but one Original Man, the conclusion is clear.

During the last year or so, in the *New York Times,* Arnold Toynbee used the word "bleached" in describing the white man. (His words were: "White [i.e. bleached] human beings of North European origin. . . .") Toynbee also referred to the European geographic area as only a peninsula of Asia. He said there is no such thing as Europe. And if you look at the globe, you will see for yourself that America is only an extension of Asia. (But at the same time Toynbee is among those who have helped to bleach history. He has written

---

*Gregor Mendel (1822–1884), Austrian Augustinian monk, father of genetic science.

that Africa was the only continent that produced no history. He won't write that again. Every day now, the truth is coming to light.)

I never will forget how shocked I was when I began reading about 26 slavery's total horror. It made such an impact upon me that it later became one of my favorite subjects when I became a minister of Mr. Muhammad's. The world's most monstrous crime, the sin and the blood on the white man's hands, are almost impossible to believe. Books like the one by Frederick Olmstead opened my eyes to the horrors suffered when the slave was landed in the United States. The European woman, Fannie Kimball, who had married a Southern white slaveowner, described how human beings were degraded. Of course I read *Uncle Tom's Cabin.* In fact, I believe that's the only novel I have ever read since I started serious reading.

Parkhurst's collection also contained some bound pamphlets of the 27 Abolitionist Anti-Slavery Society of New England. I read descriptions of atrocities, saw those illustrations of black slave women tied up and flogged with whips; of black mothers watching their babies being dragged off, never to be seen by their mothers again; of dogs after slaves, and of the fugitive slave catchers, evil white men with whips and clubs and chains and guns. I read about the slave preacher Nat Turner, who put the fear of God into the white slavemaster. Nat Turner wasn't going around preaching pie-in-the-sky and "non-violent" freedom for the black man. There in Virginia one night in 1831, Nat and seven other slaves started out at his master's home and through the night they went from one plantation "big house" to the next, killing, until by the next morning 57 white people were dead and Nat had about 70 slaves following him. White people, terrified for their lives, fled from their homes, locked themselves up in public buildings, hid in the woods, and some even left the state. A small army of soldiers took two months to catch and hang Nat Turner. Somewhere I have read where Nat Turner's example is said to have inspired John Brown to invade Virginia and attack Harper's Ferry nearly thirty years later, with thirteen white men and five Negroes.

I read Herodotus, "the father of History," or, rather, I read about him. 28 And I read the histories of various nations, which opened my eyes gradually, then wider and wider, to how the whole world's white men had indeed acted like devils, pillaging and raping and bleeding and draining the whole world's non-white people. I remember, for instance, books such as Will Durant's *The Story of Oriental Civilization,* and Mahatma Gandhi's accounts of the struggle to drive the British out of India.

Book after book showed me how the white man had brought upon the 29 world's black, brown, red, and yellow peoples every variety of the sufferings of exploitation. I saw how since the sixteenth century, the so-called "Christian trader" white man began to ply the seas in his lust for Asian and African empires, and plunder, and power. I read, I saw, how the white man never has gone among the non-white peoples bearing the Cross in the true manner and spirit of Christ's teachings—meek, humble, and Christlike.

I perceived, as I read, how the collective white man had been actually 30 nothing but a piratical opportunist who used Faustian machinations to make his own Christianity his initial wedge in criminal conquests. First, always "religiously," he branded "heathen" and "pagan" labels upon ancient non-white cultures and civilizations. The stage thus set, he then turned upon his non-white victims his weapons of war.

I read how, entering India—half a *billion* deeply religious brown people—the British white man, by 1759, through promises, trickery and manipulations, controlled much of India through Great Britain's East India Company. The parasitical British administration kept tentacling out to half of the subcontinent. In 1857, some of the desperate people of India finally mutinied—and, excepting the African slave trade, nowhere has history recorded any more unnecessary bestial and ruthless human carnage than the British suppression of the non-white Indian people.

Over 115 million African blacks—close to the 1930's population of the United States—were murdered or enslaved during the slave trade. And I read how when the slave market was glutted, the cannibalistic white powers of Europe next carved up, as their colonies, the richest areas of the black continent. And Europe's chancelleries for the next century played a chess game of naked exploitation and power from Cape Horn to Cairo.

Ten guards and the warden couldn't have torn me out of those books. Not even Elijah Muhammad could have been more eloquent than those books were in providing indisputable proof that the collective white man had acted like a devil in virtually every contact he had with the world's collective non-white man. I listen today to the radio, and watch television, and read the headlines about the collective white man's fear and tension concerning China. When the white man professes ignorance about why the Chinese hate him so, my mind can't help flashing back to what I read, there in prison, about how the blood forebears of this same white man raped China at a time when China was trusting and helpless. Those original white "Christian traders" sent into China millions of pounds of opium. By 1839, so many of the Chinese were addicts that China's desperate government destroyed twenty thousand chests of opium. The first Opium War was promptly declared by the white man. Imagine! Declaring *war* upon someone who objects to being narcotized! The Chinese were severely beaten, with Chinese-invented gunpowder.

The Treaty of Nanking made China pay the British white man for the destroyed opium: forced open China's major ports to British trade; forced China to abandon Hong Kong; fixed China's import tariffs so low that cheap British articles soon flooded in, maiming China's industrial development.

After a second Opium War, the Tientsin Treaties legalized the ravaging opium trade, legalized a British-French-American control of China's customs. China tried delaying that Treaty's ratification; Peking was looted and burned.

"Kill the foreign white devils!" was the 1901 Chinese war cry in the Boxer Rebellion. Losing again, this time the Chinese were driven from Peking's choicest areas. The vicious, arrogant white man put up the famous signs, "Chinese and dogs not allowed."

Red China after World War II closed its doors to the Western white world. Massive Chinese agricultural, scientific, and industrial efforts are described in a book that *Life* magazine recently published. Some observers inside Red China have reported that the world never has known such a hate-white campaign as is now going on in this non-white country where, present birth-rates continuing, in fifty more years Chinese will be half the earth's population. And it seems that some Chinese chickens will soon come home to roost, with China's recent successful nuclear tests.

Let us face reality. We can see in the United Nations a new world order 38 being shaped, along color lines—an alliance among the non-white nations. America's U.N. Ambassador Adlai Stevenson complained not long ago that in the United Nations "a skin game" was being played. He was right. He was facing reality. A "skin game" *is* being played. But Ambassador Stevenson sounded like Jesse James accusing the marshal of carrying a gun. Because who in the world's history ever has played a worse "skin game" than the white man?

Mr. Muhammad, to whom I was writing daily, had no idea of what a 39 new world had opened up to me through my efforts to document his teachings in books.

When I discovered philosophy, I tried to touch all the landmarks of 40 philosophical development. Gradually, I read most of the old philosophers, Occidental and Oriental. The Oriental philosophers were the ones I came to prefer; finally, my impression was that most Occidental philosophy had largely been borrowed from the Oriental thinkers. Socrates, for instance, traveled in Egypt. Some sources even say that Socrates was initiated into some of the Egyptian mysteries. Obviously Socrates got some of his wisdom among the East's wise men.

I have often reflected upon the new vistas that reading opened to me. 41 I knew right there in prison that reading had changed forever the course of my life. As I see it today, the ability to read awoke inside me some long dormant craving to be mentally alive. I certainly wasn't seeking any degree, the way a college confers a status symbol upon its students. My homemade education gave me, with every additional book that I read, a little bit more sensitivity to the deafness, dumbness, and blindness that was afflicting the black race in America. Not long ago, an English writer telephoned me from London, asking questions. One was, "What's your alma mater?" I told him, "Books." You will never catch me with a free fifteen minutes in which I'm not studying something I feel might be able to help the black man.

Yesterday I spoke in London, and both ways on the plane across the 42 Atlantic I was studying a document about how the United Nations proposes to insure the human rights of the oppressed minorities of the world. The American black man is the world's most shameful case of minority oppression. What makes the black man think of himself as only an internal United States issue is just a catch-phrase, two words, "civil rights." How is the black man going to get "civil rights" before first he wins his *human* rights? If the American black man will start thinking about his *human* rights, and then start thinking of himself as part of one of the world's great peoples, he will see he has a case for the United Nations.

I can't think of a better case! Four hundred years of black blood and 43
sweat invested here in America, and the white man still has the black man
begging for what every immigrant fresh off the ship can take for granted the
minute he walks down the gangplank.

But I'm digressing. I told the Englishman that my alma mater was books, 44
a good library. Every time I catch a plane, I have with me a book that I want
to read—and that's a lot of books these days. If I weren't out here every day
battling the white man, I could spend the rest of my life reading, just satisfying my curiosity—because you can hardly mention anything I'm not curious
about. I don't think anybody ever got more out of going to prison than I did.
In fact, prison enabled me to study far more intensively than I would have
if my life had gone differently and I had attended some college. I imagine that
one of the biggest troubles with colleges is there are too many distractions,
too much panty-raiding, fraternities, and boola-boola and all of that. Where
else but in a prison could I have attacked my ignorance by being able to study
intensely sometimes as much as fifteen hours a day?

Questions for Discussion

1. Does it seem to you that the following accusation is metaphorically true,
   literally true, or simply untrue: "The collective white man had acted like
   a devil in virtually every contact he had with the world's collective non-
   white man" (¶33)? What kinds of evidence would be required to prove or
   disprove such a claim? Can you think of examples that would seem to bear
   it out or to make it doubtful? Do you think Malcolm X uses his own
   examples fairly or unfairly?

2. Malcolm X expresses exhilaration at "being able to read and *understand*"
   (¶14). Is his delight entirely political and racial? Is there a part of him that
   thrills *as a person* to learning, not just as someone who wants to achieve
   political or religious goals? What evidence can you point to? Does the
   distinction between "reading politically" and "reading as a person" seem
   useful to you?

3. Is Malcolm X's distinction between "civil rights" and "human rights" (¶42)
   clear to you? How would you explain the difference to someone who had
   not read the *Autobiography*? Must one precede the other either in time or
   importance?

4. How would you describe Malcolm X's tone? (*Tone* is a word commonly
   used to suggest tone of voice, but we shall always use it to suggest the
   whole range of emotions that authors share with readers.) Does he sound
   angry, amused, hurt, outraged, friendly, aggressive, confiding, frank? Can
   you think of other adjectives that come closer to his implied relation with
   you? What sort of reader does he seem to address? (*Note:* Throughout this

text, you will find that asking about tone will be profitable, whether we remind you of it or not.)

5. In his account of Nat Turner (¶27), Malcolm X claims that Turner "put the fear of God into the white slavemaster" by killing 57 white people in one night. Is it clear whether the author approves or disapproves of this event? Would you respond differently, either to the event itself or to Malcolm X's account of it, if you knew whether the 57 murdered people were slaves or slavemasters? Field bosses? Children? Read about the life of Nat Turner in a good encyclopedia. What differences do you find between the account there and Malcolm X's? Are Malcolm X's claims about the biases of white historians relevant here?

6. In the light of what seems to be Malcolm X's purpose, does he make effective use of the Jesse James simile (¶38)? (A *simile* implies an analogy: A is to B as C is to D. For instance, winter relates to mittens as summer relates to swimsuits.) Can you work out the implied analogy of the Jesse James simile? Is it persuasive?

Suggested Essay Topics

1. Make a list of the possible motives that drove Malcolm X to be such a dedicated and persistent learner: for example, ambition, love of power, greed, desire to be known as a scholar, curiosity, boredom, hope of outsmarting other people, desire to improve the world. Then study the text again to see which ones seem most strongly suggested by what the author says. Write an essay designed to convince your classmates that your view of what drove him is the most likely one.

2. On the basis of Malcolm X's essay and your own experience, define the qualities and behavior of the good student. In an essay directed to fellow students (or, if you prefer, in a letter to your parents), evaluate your own persistence and eagerness in learning, and discuss whether you are a typical or exceptional student. In the course of your discussion, try to explain Malcolm X's assertion that while learning, "months passed without my even thinking about being imprisoned. In fact, up to then, I had never been so truly free in my life" (¶11).

Adrienne Rich

Since the 1960s, women have justified increased involvement in life outside of the home by constructing "gender critiques" of many segments of American life. They have pointed out the "gender gap" in hiring, in salaries, and in promotions; they have demanded maternity leaves and maternity benefits; and they have opened up one professional field after another to which the doors had been traditionally either closed or opened to only a few. In this terse and taut essay, Adrienne Rich (b. 1929)—noted poet, teacher, essayist, and feminist—examines the purpose of a college education from an unabashed gender perspective.

In asserting, however, that women must "claim" an education, not just receive one, Rich advances at least two notions that apply equally well to all students regardless of sex. The first notion says that students must assume personal responsibility for their education by taking themselves seriously as learners; the second says that learning must be active rather than passive. As you read, try to form a clear idea of what active versus passive learning means and what responsibilities both teachers and students must meet to ensure that active learning occurs. Consider the extent to which classes on your own campus stress active learning, and cite concrete examples of occasions or decisions that exemplify Rich's idea of taking personal responsibility for one's own education.

CLAIMING AN EDUCATION

From *On Lies, Secrets, and Silence* (1977).*

For this convocation, I planned to separate my remarks into two parts: 1
some thoughts about you, the women students here, and some thoughts about us who teach in a women's college. But ultimately, those two parts are indivisible. If university education means anything beyond the processing of human beings into expected roles, through credit hours, tests, and grades (and I believe that in a women's college especially it *might* mean much more), it implies an ethical and intellectual contract between teacher and student. This contract must remain intuitive, dynamic, unwritten; but we must turn to it again and again if learning is to be reclaimed from the depersonalizing and cheapening pressures of the present-day academic scene.

The first thing I want to say to you who are students, is that you cannot   2
afford to think of being here to *receive* an education; you will do much better to think of yourselves as being here to *claim* one. One of the dictionary definitions of the verb "to claim" is: *to take as the rightful owner; to assert in the face of possible contradiction.* "To receive" is *to come into possession of; to act as receptacle or container for; to accept as authoritative or true.* The difference is that between acting and being acted-upon, and for women it can literally mean the difference between life and death.

One of the devastating weaknesses of university learning, of the store   3
of knowledge and opinion that has been handed down through academic training, has been its almost total erasure of women's experience and thought from the curriculum, and its exclusion of women as members of the academic community. Today, with increasing numbers of women students in nearly every branch of higher learning, we still see very few women in the upper

*This talk was given at the Douglass College Convocation, September 6, 1977, and first printed in *The Common Woman,* a feminist literary magazine founded by Rutgers University women in New Brunswick, New Jersey.

levels of faculty and administration in most institutions. Douglass College itself is a women's college in a university administered overwhelmingly by men, who in turn are answerable to the state legislature, again composed predominantly of men. But the most significant fact for you is that what you learn here, the very texts you read, the lectures you hear, the way your studies are divided into categories and fragmented one from the other—all this reflects, to a very large degree, neither objective reality, nor an accurate picture of the past, nor a group of rigorously tested observations about human behavior. What you can learn here (and I mean not only at Douglass but any college in any university) is how *men* have perceived and organized their experience, their history, their ideas of social relationships, good and evil, sickness and health, etc. When you read or hear about "great issues," "major texts," "the mainstream of Western thought," you are hearing about what men, above all white men, in their male subjectivity, have decided is important.

Black and other minority peoples have for some time recognized that their racial and ethnic experience was not accounted for in the studies broadly labeled human; and that even the sciences can be racist. For many reasons, it has been more difficult for women to comprehend our exclusion, and to realize that even the sciences can be sexist. For one thing, it is only within the last hundred years that higher education has grudgingly been opened up to women at all, even to white, middle-class women. And many of us have found ourselves poring eagerly over books with titles like: *The Descent of Man; Man and His Symbols; Irrational Man; The Phenomenon of Man; The Future of Man; Man and the Machine; From Man to Man; May Man Prevail?; Man, Science and Society;* or *One-Dimensional Man*—books pretending to describe a "human" reality that does not include over one-half the human species.

Less than a decade ago, with the rebirth of a feminist movement in this country, women students and teachers in a number of universities began to demand and set up women's studies courses—to *claim* a woman-directed education. And, despite the inevitable accusations of "unscholarly," "group therapy," "faddism," etc., despite backlash and budget cuts, women's studies are still growing, offering to more and more women a new intellectual grasp on their lives, new understanding of our history, a fresh vision of the human experience, and also a critical basis for evaluating what they hear and read in other courses, and in the society at large.

But my talk is not really about women's studies, much as I believe in their scholarly, scientific, and human necessity. While I think that any Douglass student has everything to gain by investigating and enrolling in women's studies courses, I want to suggest that there is a more essential experience that you owe yourselves, one which courses in women's studies can greatly enrich, but which finally depends on you, in all your interactions with yourself and your world. This is the experience of *taking responsibility toward yourselves.* Our upbringing as women has so often told us that this should come second to our relationships and responsibilities to other people. We have been offered ethical models of the self-denying wife and mother; intellectual models of the brilliant but slapdash dilettante who never commits herself to anything the whole way, or the intelligent woman who denies her intelligence in order to seem more "feminine," or who sits in passive silence even when she disagrees inwardly with everything that is being said around her.

Responsibility to yourself means refusing to let others do your thinking, talking, and naming for you; it means learning to respect and use your own brains and instincts; hence, grappling with hard work. It means that you do not treat your body as a commodity with which to purchase superficial intimacy or economic security; for our bodies and minds are inseparable in this life, and when we allow our bodies to be treated as objects, our minds are in mortal danger. It means insisting that those to whom you give your friendship and love are able to respect your mind. It means being able to say, with Charlotte Brontë's *Jane Eyre*: "I have an inward treasure born with me, which can keep me alive if all the extraneous delights should be withheld or offered only at a price I cannot afford to give."

Responsibility to yourself means that you don't fall for shallow and easy solutions—predigested books and ideas, weekend encounters guaranteed to change your life, taking "gut" courses instead of ones you know will challenge you, bluffing at school and life instead of doing solid work, marrying early as an escape from real decisions, getting pregnant as an evasion of already existing problems. It means that you refuse to sell your talents and aspirations short, simply to avoid conflict and confrontation. And this, in turn, means resisting the forces in society which say that women should be nice, play safe, have low professional expectations, drown in love and forget about work, live through others, and stay in the places assigned to us. It means that we insist on a life of meaningful work, insist that work be as meaningful as love and friendship in our lives. It means, therefore, the courage to be "different"; not to be continuously available to others when we need time for ourselves and our work; to be able to demand of others—parents, friends, roommates, teachers, lovers, husbands, children—that they respect our sense of purpose and our integrity as persons. Women everywhere are finding the courage to do this, more and more, and we are finding that courage both in our study of women in the past who possessed it, and in each other as we look to other women for comradeship, community, and challenge. The difference between a life lived actively, and a life of passive drifting and dispersal of energies, is an immense difference. Once we begin to feel committed to our lives, responsible to ourselves, we can never again be satisfied with the old, passive way.

Now comes the second part of the contract. I believe that in a women's college you have the right to expect your faculty to take you seriously. The education of women has been a matter of debate for centuries, and old, negative attitudes about women's role, women's ability to think and take leadership, are still rife both in and outside the university. Many male professors (and I don't mean only at Douglass) still feel that teaching in a women's college is a second-rate career. Many tend to eroticize their women students—to treat them as sexual objects—instead of demanding the best of their minds. (At Yale a legal suit [*Alexander* v. *Yale*] has been brought against the university by a group of women students demanding a stated policy against sexual advances toward female students by male professors.) Many teachers, both men and women, trained in the male-centered tradition, are still handing the ideas and texts of that tradition on to students without teaching them to criticize its antiwoman attitudes, its omission of women as part of the species. Too often, all of us fail to teach the most important thing, which is that clear thinking, active discussion, and excellent writing are all necessary for intellectual freedom, and that these require *hard work.* Sometimes, perhaps in discouragement with a culture which is both antiintellectual and antiwoman, we may resign ourselves to low expectations for our students before we have given them half a chance to become more thoughtful, expressive human beings. We need to take to heart the words of Elizabeth Barrett Browning, a poet, a thinking woman, and a feminist, who wrote in 1845 of her impatience with studies which cultivate a "passive recipiency" in the mind, and asserted that "women want to be made to *think actively:* their apprehension is quicker than that of men, but their defect lies for the most part in the logical faculty and in the higher mental activities." Note that she implies a defect which can be remedied by intellectual training; *not* an inborn lack of ability.

I have said that the contract on the student's part involves that you demand to be taken seriously so that you can also go on taking yourself seriously. This means seeking out criticism, recognizing that the most affirming thing anyone can do for you is demand that you push yourself further, show you the range of what you *can* do. It means rejecting attitudes of "take-it-easy," "why-be-so-serious," "why-worry-you'll-probably-get-married-anyway." It means assuming your share of responsibility for what happens in the classroom, because that affects the quality of your daily life here. It means that the student sees herself engaged *with* her teachers in an active, ongoing struggle for a real education. But for her to do this, her teachers must be committed to the belief that women's minds and experience are intrinsically valuable and indispensable to any civilization worthy the name; that there is no more exhilarating and intellectually fertile place in the academic world today than a women's college—*if* both students and teachers in large enough numbers are trying to fulfill this contract. The contract is really a pledge of mutual seriousness about women, about language, ideas, methods, and values. It is our shared commitment toward a world in which the inborn potentialities of so many women's minds will no longer be wasted, raveled-away, paralyzed, or denied.

Questions for Discussion

1. Discuss with your classmates what Rich means by active and passive learning. Give examples of each from both high school and college. Can you make a list of advantages and disadvantages of each kind of learning, or do all the advantages fall on one side or the other? Are there different advantages and disadvantages for students as compared to teachers? Why or why not?

2. In paragraph 8 Rich lists many traits that she indirectly ascribes to women students in the past, traits that she advises present students to avoid. How many of these "traditional" traits do you and your class-mates see commonly exhibited by the women on your campus? Do the women in your class think that female students today are more willing to take responsibility for their own education than they were in 1977, when Rich wrote her essay? Do you see any differences between men and women on this score? What kind of evidence on either side of this question can you point to?

3. Rich says in paragraph 9 that students "have the right to expect your faculty to take you seriously." Do students in your class think they *are* generally taken seriously by the faculty at your college or university? Is there any feeling among students that women are taken less seriously than men?

4. Is there any feeling among students that women find it more difficult to take *themselves* seriously? If so, what reasons can be offered to explain this phenomenon? What are the clues that a teacher does or does not take students (or students of one sex) seriously?

5. What do students do or not do that *invites* teachers to view them seriously or dismissively? How much responsibility must students accept for setting the tone of their classes? What strategies are open to students who want to influence the tone of their classes?

Suggested Essay Topics

1. In a document addressed to the students and teachers of your college or university, write up a "Contract of Serious Education" in which you (1) define *serious education,* (2) state the teachers' responsibilities for making it happen, and (3) state the students' responsibilities for making it happen. Write the contract in plain, direct, forceful language, and focus on terms of such importance that you think every student and teacher in your institution should want to sign it.

2. Choose an idea, theory, concept, interpretation, or problem that you have recently encountered in one of your courses and put yourself in the position of a teacher required to teach it to a class of first-year college students. In your essay (directed to, say, your department head or someone responsible for overseeing your teaching), describe how you would go about teaching the idea or theory so that the students would engage in active rather

than passive learning. If this involves asking a series of questions, make the questions part of your essay (along with an explanation of what you hope to achieve by asking them). Finally, explain why the teaching techniques you have chosen will promote active learning.

— Oct 25
6:50 PM

Alfred North Whitehead

An English philosopher and mathematician, instructor of Bertrand Russell and later Russell's co-author on the Principia Mathematica, *and founder of a mode of thought called "process philosophy" (influential on scientists, philosophers, and theologians alike), Alfred North Whitehead (1861–1947) remains one of those figures in our day—like Plato, Aquinas, Kant, or Coleridge in earlier centuries—who seems to have become established as a permanent and almost official instructor of humankind. His technical writings, as in* Process and Reality, *are forbiddingly difficult, but his general writings, as in this piece, combine great depth of thought with a delightful clarity of style. Perhaps no one will ever find Whitehead easy to read; as he says in paragraph 11, "If it were easy, the book ought to be burned." But he has the kind of clarity we all seek, and his style is no more difficult than his ideas themselves require.*

As you work through his ideas about the aims of education, compare his description of a genuine education with an accurate description of your own education, both past and present, and with the aims of education as presented to you by your parents and high school counselors or teachers. You might use his essay as a source of new ideas about what is happening to you and your fellow students this year.

His main concerns seem to be (1) that whatever we learn should be truly useful (he takes pains to define what useful *means to us* now, *in a present that contains both the past and the future), (2) that all learning should constantly shift back and forth between general and specialized knowledge, and (3) that studying anything merely to pass a standardized exam kills all real learning.*

THE AIMS OF EDUCATION

From *"The Aims of Education" and Other Essays* (1929).

Culture is activity of thought, and receptiveness to beauty and humane feeling. Scraps of information have nothing to do with it. A merely well-informed man is the most useless bore on God's earth. What we should aim at producing is men who possess both culture and expert knowledge in some special direction. Their expert knowledge will give them the ground to start from, and their culture will lead them as deep as philosophy and as high as   1 art. We have to remember that the valuable intellectual development is self-development, and that it mostly takes place between the ages of sixteen and thirty. As to training, the most important part is given by mothers before the age of twelve. A saying due to Archbishop Temple illustrates my meaning. Surprise was expressed at the success in after-life of a man, who as a boy at Rugby had been somewhat undistinguished. He answered, "It is not what they are at eighteen, it is what they become afterwards that matters."

In training a child to activity of thought, above all things we must   2
beware of what I will call "inert ideas"—that is to say, ideas that are merely received into the mind without being utilized, or tested, or thrown into fresh combinations.

In the history of education, the most striking phenomenon is that   3
schools of learning, which at one epoch are alive with a ferment of genius, in a succeeding generation exhibit merely pedantry and routine. The reason is, that they are overladen with inert ideas. Education with inert ideas is not only useless: it is, above all things, harmful—*Corruptio optimi, pessima* [The corruption of the best is the worst]. Except at rare intervals of intellectual ferment, education in the past has been radically infected with inert ideas. That is the reason why uneducated clever women, who have seen much of the world, are in middle life so much the most cultured part of the community. They have been saved from this horrible burden of inert ideas. Every intellectual revolution which has ever stirred humanity into greatness has been a passionate protest against inert ideas. Then, alas, with pathetic ignorance of human psychology, it has proceeded by some educational scheme to bind humanity afresh with inert ideas of its own fashioning.

Let us now ask how in our system of education we are to guard against   4
this mental dryrot. We enunciate two educational commandments, "Do not teach too many subjects," and again, "What you teach, teach thoroughly."

The result of teaching small parts of a large number of subjects is the   5
passive reception of disconnected ideas, not illumined with any spark of vitality. Let the main ideas which are introduced into a child's education be few and important, and let them be thrown into every combination possible. The child should make them his own, and should understand their application here and now in the circumstances of his actual life. From the very beginning of his education, the child should experience the joy of discovery. The discovery which he has to make, is that general ideas give an understanding of that stream of events which pours through his life, which is his life. By understanding I mean more than a mere logical analysis, though that is included. I mean "understanding" in the sense in which it is used in the French proverb, "To understand all, is to forgive all." Pedants sneer at an education which is useful. But if education is not useful, what is it? Is it a talent, to be hidden away in a napkin? Of course, education should be useful, whatever your aim in life. It was useful to Saint Augustine and it was useful to Napoleon. It is useful, because understanding is useful.

I pass lightly over that understanding which should be given by the   6

literary side of education.* Nor do I wish to be supposed to pronounce on the
relative merits of a classical or a modern curriculum. I would only remark that
the understanding which we want is an understanding of an insistent present.
The only use of a knowledge of the past is to equip us for the present. No
more deadly harm can be done to young minds than by depreciation of the
present. The present contains all that there is. It is holy ground; for it is the
past, and it is the future.† At the same time it must be observed that an age
is no less past if it existed two hundred years ago than if it existed two
thousand years ago. Do not be deceived by the pedantry of dates. The ages
of Shakespeare and of Molière are no less past than are the ages of Sophocles
and of Virgil. The communion of saints is a great and inspiring assemblage,
but it has only one possible hall of meeting, and that is, the present; and the
mere lapse of time through which any particular group of saints must travel
to reach that meeting-place, makes very little difference.

Passing now to the scientific and logical side of education, we remember   7
that here also ideas which are not utilised are positively harmful. By utilising
an idea, I mean relating it to that stream, compounded of sense perceptions,
feelings, hopes, desires, and of mental activities adjusting thought to thought,
which forms our life. I can imagine a set of beings which might fortify their
souls by passively reviewing disconnected ideas. Humanity is not built that
way—except perhaps some editors of newspapers.

In scientific training, the first thing to do with an idea is to prove it. But   8
allow me for one moment to extend the meaning of "prove"; I mean—to
prove its worth. Now an idea is not worth much unless the propositions in
which it is embodied are true. Accordingly an essential part of the proof of
an idea is the proof, either by experiment or by logic, of the truth of the
propositions. But it is not essential that this proof of the truth should constitute the first introduction to the idea. After all, its assertion by the authority
of respectable teachers is sufficient evidence to begin with. In our first contact
with a set of propositions, we commence by appreciating their importance.
That is what we all do in after-life. We do not attempt, in the strict sense,
to prove or to disprove anything, unless its importance makes it worthy of
that honour. These two processes of proof, in the narrow sense, and of
appreciation, do not require a rigid separation in time. Both can be proceeded
with nearly concurrently. But in so far as either process must have the
priority, it should be that of appreciation by use.

Furthermore, we should not endeavour to use propositions in isolation.   9
Emphatically I do not mean, a neat little set of experiments to illustrate
Proposition I and then the proof of Proposition I, a neat little set of experiments to illustrate Proposition II and then the proof of Proposition II, and so
on to the end of the book. Nothing could be more boring. Interrelated truths

---

*By passing "lightly" over the "literary side of education," Whitehead is referring to what *we*
would call "the humanities," especially literature, philosophy, history, and languages. He largely
ignores these and discusses mainly scientific and mathematical examples because, first, he was
himself a mathematician and, second, his audience was the Mathematical Association.

†See Karl Popper's treatment of this same idea in "Utopia and Violence," p. 150, ¶34–37.

are utilised *en bloc,* and the various propositions are employed in any order, and with any reiteration. Choose some important applications of your theoretical subject; and study them concurrently with the systematic theoretical exposition. Keep the theoretical exposition short and simple, but let it be strict and rigid so far as it goes. It should not be too long for it to be easily known with thoroughness and accuracy. The consequences of a plethora of half-digested theoretical knowledge are deplorable.* Also the theory should not be muddled up with the practice. The child should have no doubt when it is proving and when it is utilising. My point is that what is proved should be utilised, and that what is utilised should—so far as is practicable—be proved. I am far from asserting that proof and utilisation are the same thing.

At this point of my discourse, I can most directly carry forward my   10
argument in the outward form of a digression. We are only just realising that the art and science of education require a genius and a study of their own; and that this genius and this science are more than a bare knowledge of some branch of science or of literature. This truth was partially perceived in the past generation; and headmasters, somewhat crudely, were apt to supersede learning in their colleagues by requiring left-hand bowling and a taste for football. But culture is more than cricket, and more than football, and more than extent of knowledge.

Education is the acquisition of the art of the utilisation of knowledge.   11
This is an art very difficult to impart. Whenever a textbook is written of real educational worth, you may be quite certain that some reviewer will say that it will be difficult to teach from it. Of course it will be difficult to teach from it. If it were easy, the book ought to be burned; for it cannot be educational. In education, as elsewhere, the broad primrose path leads to a nasty place. This evil path is represented by a book or a set of lectures which will practically enable the student to learn by heart all the questions likely to be asked at the next external examination.† And I may say in passing that no educational system is possible unless every question directly asked of a pupil at any examination is either framed or modified by the actual teacher of that pupil in that subject. The external assessor may report on the curriculum or on the performance of the pupils, but never should be allowed to ask the pupil a question which has not been strictly supervised by the actual teacher, or at least inspired by a long conference with him. There are a few exceptions to this rule, but they are exceptions, and could easily be allowed for under the general rule.

We now return to my previous point, that theoretical ideas should   12
always find important applications within the pupil's curriculum. This is not an easy doctrine to apply, but a very hard one. It contains within itself the problem of keeping knowledge alive, of preventing it from becoming inert, which is the central problem of all education.

---

*Recall the epigraph from Alexander Pope, "A little learning is a dangerous thing" (p. 29)
†External examinations are standardized tests administered by state employees, school inspectors, who are "external" to the school where they give the tests.

The best procedure will depend on several factors, none of which can be   13
neglected, namely, the genius of the teacher, the intellectual type of the pupils,
their prospects in life, the opportunities offered by the immediate surroundings of the school, and allied factors of this sort. It is for this reason that the
uniform external examination is so deadly. We do not denounce it because we
are cranks, and like denouncing established things. We are not so childish.
Also, of course, such examinations have their use in testing slackness. Our
reason of dislike is very definite and very practical. It kills the best part of
culture. When you analyse in the light of experience the central task of
education, you find that its successful accomplishment depends on a delicate
adjustment of many variable factors. The reason is that we are dealing with
human minds, and not with dead matter. The evocation of curiosity, of
judgment, of the power of mastering a complicated tangle of circumstances,
the use of theory in giving foresight in special cases—all these powers are not
to be imparted by a set rule embodied in one schedule of examination subjects.

I appeal to you, as practical teachers. With good discipline, it is always   14
possible to pump into the minds of a class a certain quantity of inert knowledge. You take a text-book and make them learn it. So far, so good. The child
then knows how to solve a quadratic equation. But what is the point of
teaching a child to solve a quadratic equation? There is a traditional answer
to this question. It runs thus: The mind is an instrument, you first sharpen
it, and then use it; the acquisition of the power of solving a quadratic equation
is part of the process of sharpening the mind. Now there is just enough truth
in this answer to have made it live through the ages. But for all its half-truth,
it embodies a radical error which bids fair to stifle the genius of the modern
world. I do not know who was first responsible for this analogy of the mind
to a dead instrument. For aught I know, it may have been one of the seven
wise men of Greece, or a committee of the whole lot of them. Whoever was
the originator, there can be no doubt of the authority which it has acquired
by the continuous approval bestowed upon it by eminent persons. But whatever its weight of authority, whatever the high approval which it can quote,
I have no hesitation in denouncing it as one of the most fatal, erroneous, and
dangerous conceptions ever introduced into the theory of education. The
mind is never passive; it is a perpetual activity, delicate, receptive, responsive
to stimulus. You cannot postpone its life until you have sharpened it. Whatever interest attaches to your subject-matter must be evoked here and now;
whatever powers you are strengthening in the pupil, must be exercised here
and now; whatever possibilities of mental life your teaching should impart,
must be exhibited here and now. That is the golden rule of education, and
a very difficult rule to follow.

The difficulty is just this: the apprehension of general ideas, intellectual   15
habits of mind, and pleasurable interest in mental achievement can be evoked
by no form of words, however accurately adjusted. All practical teachers
know that education is a patient process of the mastery of details, minute by
minute, hour by hour, day by day. There is no royal road to learning through
an airy path of brilliant generalisations. There is a proverb about the difficulty

of seeing the wood because of the trees. That difficulty is exactly the point which I am enforcing. The problem of education is to make the pupil see the wood by means of the trees.

The solution which I am urging, is to eradicate the fatal disconnection 16 of subjects which kills the vitality of our modern curriculum. There is only one subject-matter for education, and that is Life in all its manifestations. Instead of this single unity, we offer children—Algebra, from which nothing follows; Geometry, from which nothing follows; Science, from which nothing follows; History, from which nothing follows; a Couple of Languages, never mastered; and lastly, most dreary of all, Literature, represented by plays of Shakespeare, with philological notes and short analyses of plot and character to be in substance committed to memory. Can such a list be said to represent Life, as it is known in the midst of the living of it? The best that can be said of it is, that it is a rapid table of contents which a deity might run over in his mind while he was thinking of creating a world, and has not yet determined how to put it together.

Let us now return to quadratic equations. We still have on hand the 17 unanswered question. Why should children be taught their solution? Unless quadratic equations fit into a connected curriculum, of course there is no reason to teach anything about them. Furthermore, extensive as should be the place of mathematics in a complete culture, I am a little doubtful whether for many types of boys algebraic solutions of quadratic equations do not lie on the specialist side of mathematics. I may here remind you that as yet I have not said anything of the psychology or the content of the specialism, which is so necessary a part of an ideal education. But all that is an evasion of our real question, and I merely state it in order to avoid being misunderstood in my answer.

Quadratic equations are part of algebra, and algebra is the intellectual 18 instrument which has been created for rendering clear the quantitative aspects of the world. There is no getting out of it. Through and through the world is infected with quantity. To talk sense, is to talk in quantities. It is no use saying that the nation is large,—How large? It is no use saying that radium is scarce,—How scarce? You cannot evade quantity. You may fly to poetry and to music, and quantity and number will face you in your rhythms and your octaves. Elegant intellects which despise the theory of quantity, are but half developed. They are more to be pitied than blamed. The scraps of gibberish, which in their school-days were taught to them in the name of algebra, deserve some contempt.

This question of the degeneration of algebra into gibberish, both in 19 word and in fact, affords a pathetic instance of the uselessness of reforming educational schedules without a clear conception of the attributes which you wish to evoke in the living minds of the children. A few years ago there was an outcry that school algebra was in need of reform, but there was a general agreement that graphs would put everything right. So all sorts of things were extruded, and graphs were introduced. So far as I can see, with no sort of idea behind them, but just graphs. Now every examination paper has one or two questions on graphs. Personally I am an enthusiastic adherent of graphs. But I wonder whether as yet we have gained very much. You cannot put life into any schedule of general education unless you succeed in exhibiting its relation to some essential characteristic of all intelligent or emotional perception. It is a hard saying, but it is true; and I do not see how to make it any easier. In making these little formal alterations you are beaten by the very nature of things. You are pitted against too skilful an adversary, who will see to it that the pea is always under the other thimble.

Reformation must begin at the other end. First, you must make up your mind as to those quantitative aspects of the world which are simple enough to be introduced into general education; then a schedule of algebra should be framed which will about find its exemplification in these applications. We need not fear for our pet graphs, they will be there in plenty when we once begin to treat algebra as a serious means of studying the world. Some of the simplest applications will be found in the quantities which occur in the simplest study of society. The curves of history are more vivid and more informing than the dry catalogues of names and dates which comprise the greater part of that arid school study. What purpose is effected by a catalogue of undistinguished kings and queens? Tom, Dick, or Harry, they are all dead. General resurrections are failures, and are better postponed. The quantitative flux of the forces of modern society is capable of very simple exhibition. Meanwhile, the idea of the variable, of the function, of rate of change, of equations and their solution, of elimination, are being studied as an abstract science for their own sake. Not, of course, in the pompous phrases with which I am alluding to them here, but with that iteration of simple special cases proper to teaching. 20

If this course be followed, the route from Chaucer to the Black Death, from the Black Death to modern Labour troubles, will connect the tales of the mediēval pilgrims with the abstract science of algebra, both yielding diverse aspects of that single theme, Life. I know what most of you are thinking at this point. It is that the exact course which I have sketched out is not the particular one which you would have chosen, or even see how to work. I quite agree. I am not claiming that I could do it myself. But your objection is the precise reason why a common external examination system* is fatal to education. The process of exhibiting the applications of knowledge must, for its success, essentially depend on the character of the pupils and the genius of the teacher. Of course I have left out the easiest applications with which most of us are more at home. I mean the quantitative sides of sciences, such as mechanics and physics. 21

. . .

I must beg you to remember what I have been insisting on above. In the first place, one train of thought will not suit all groups of children. For example, I should expect that artisan children will want something more 22

*Common external exams are what Americans call "standardized exams"—tests made out by government employees or professional committees and administered to students on a mass scale ("in common").

concrete and, in a sense, swifter than I have set down here. Perhaps I am wrong, but that is what I should guess. In the second place, I am not contemplating one beautiful lecture stimulating, once and for all, an admiring class. That is not the way in which education proceeds. No; all the time the pupils are hard at work solving examples, drawing graphs, and making experiments, until they have a thorough hold on the whole subject. I am describing the interspersed explanations, the directions which should be given to their thoughts. The pupils have got to be made to feel that they are studying something, and are not merely executing intellectual minuets.

Finally, if you are teaching pupils for some general examination, the 23 problem of sound teaching is greatly complicated. Have you ever noticed the zig-zag moulding round a Norman arch? The ancient work is beautiful, the modern work is hideous. The reason is, that the modern work is done to exact measure, the ancient work is varied according to the idiosyncrasy of the workman. Here it is crowded, and there it is expanded. Now the essence of getting pupils through examinations is to give equal weight to all parts of the schedule. But mankind is naturally specialist. One man sees a whole subject, where another can find only a few detached examples. I know that it seems contradictory to allow for specialism in a curriculum especially designed for a broad culture. Without contradictions the world would be simpler, and perhaps duller. But I am certain that in education wherever you exclude specialism you destroy life.

. . .

Fortunately, the specialist side of education presents an easier problem 24 than does the provision of a general culture. For this there are many reasons. One is that many of the principles of procedure to be observed are the same in both cases, and it is unnecessary to recapitulate. Another reason is that specialist training takes place—or should take place—at a more advanced stage of the pupil's course, and thus there is easier material to work upon. But undoubtedly the chief reason is that the specialist study is normally a study of peculiar interest to the student. He is studying it because, for some reason, he wants to know it. This makes all the difference. The general culture is designed to foster an activity of mind; the specialist course utilises this activity. But it does not do to lay too much stress on these neat antitheses. As we have already seen, in the general course foci of special interest will arise; and similarly in the special study, the external connections of the subject drag thought outwards.

Again, there is not one course of study which merely gives general 25 culture, and another which gives special knowledge. The subjects pursued for the sake of a general education are special subjects specially studied; and, on the other hand, one of the ways of encouraging general mental activity is to foster a special devotion. You may not divide the seamless coat of learning. What education has to impart is an intimate sense for the power of ideas, for the beauty of ideas, and for the structure of ideas, together with a particular body of knowledge which has peculiar reference to the life of the being possessing it.

The appreciation of the structure of ideas is that side of a cultured mind   26
which can only grow under the influence of a special study. I mean that eye
for the whole chess-board, for the bearing of one set of ideas on another.
Nothing but a special study can give any appreciation for the exact formulation of general ideas, for their relations when formulated, for their service in
the comprehension of life. A mind so disciplined should be both more abstract and more concrete. It has been trained in the comprehension of abstract
thought and in the analysis of facts.

Finally, there should grow the most austere of all mental qualities; I   27
mean the sense for style. It is an æsthetic sense, based on admiration for the
direct attainment of a foreseen end, simply and without waste. Style in art,
style in literature, style in science, style in logic, style in practical execution
have fundamentally the same aesthetic qualities, namely, attainment and
restraint. The love of a subject in itself and for itself, where it is not the sleepy
pleasure of pacing a mental quarter-deck, is the love of style as manifested
in that study.

Here we are brought back to the position from which we started, the   28
utility of education. Style, in its finest sense, is the last acquirement of the
educated mind; it is also the most useful. It pervades the whole being. The
administrator with a sense for style hates waste; the engineer with a sense for
style economises his material; the artisan with a sense for style prefers good
work. Style is the ultimate morality of mind.

But above style, and above knowledge, there is something, a vague   29
shape like fate above the Greek gods. That something is Power. Style is the
fashioning of power, the restraining of power. But, after all, the power of
attainment of the desired end is fundamental. The first thing is to get there.
Do not bother about your style, but solve your problem, justify the ways of
God to man, administer your province, or do whatever else is set before you.

Where, then, does style help? In this, with style the end is attained   30
without side issues, without raising undesirable inflammations. With style
you attain your end and nothing but your end. With style the effect of your
activity is calculable, and foresight is the last gift of gods to men. With style
your power is increased, for your mind is not distracted with irrelevancies,
and you are more likely to attain your object. Now style is the exclusive
privilege of the expert. Whoever heard of the style of an amateur painter, of
the style of an amateur poet? Style is always the product of specialist study,
the peculiar contribution of specialism to culture.

English education in its present phase suffers from a lack of definite aim,   31
and from an external machinery which kills its vitality. Hitherto in this
address I have been considering the aims which should govern education. In
this respect England halts between two opinions. It has not decided whether
to produce amateurs or experts. The profound change in the world which the
nineteenth century has produced is that the growth of knowledge has given
foresight. The amateur is essentially a man with appreciation and with immense versatility in mastering a given routine. But he lacks the foresight
which comes from special knowledge. The object of this address is to suggest

how to produce the expert without loss of the essential virtues of the amateur. The machinery of our secondary education is rigid where it should be yielding, and lax where it should be rigid. Every school is bound on pain of extinction to train its boys for a small set of definite examinations. No headmaster has a free hand to develop his general education or his specialist studies in accordance with the opportunities of his school, which are created by its staff, its environment, its class of boys, and its endowments. I suggest that no system of external tests which aims primarily at examining individual scholars can result in anything but educational waste.

Primarily it is the schools and not the scholars which should be inspected. Each school should grant its own leaving certificates, based on its own curriculum. The standards of these schools should be sampled and corrected. But the first requisite for educational reform is the school as a unit, with its approved curriculum based on its own needs, and evolved by its own staff. If we fail to secure that, we simply fall from one formalism into another, from one dung-hill of inert ideas into another. 32

In stating that the school is the true educational unit in any national system for the safeguarding of efficiency, I have conceived the alternative system as being the external examination of the individual scholar. But every Scylla is faced by its Charybdis—or, in more homely language, there is a ditch on both sides of the road. It will be equally fatal to education if we fall into the hands of a supervising department which is under the impression that it can divide all schools into two or three rigid categories, each type being forced to adopt a rigid curriculum. When I say that the school is the educational unit, I mean exactly what I say, no larger unit, no smaller unit. Each school must have the claim to be considered in relation to its special circumstances. The classifying of schools for some purposes is necessary. But no absolutely rigid curriculum, not modified by its own staff, should be permissible. Exactly the same principles apply, with the proper modifications, to universities and to technical colleges. 33

When one considers in its length and in its breadth the importance of this question of the education of a nation's young, the broken lives, the defeated hopes, the national failures, which result from the frivolous inertia with which it is treated, it is difficult to restrain within oneself a savage rage. In the conditions of modern life the rule is absolute, the race which does not value trained intelligence is doomed. Not all your heroism, not all your social charm, not all your wit, not all your victories on land or at sea, can move back the finger of fate. To-day we maintain ourselves. To-morrow science will have moved forward yet one more step, and there will be no appeal from the judgment which will then be pronounced on the uneducated. 34

Questions for Discussion

1. What does Whitehead mean by "inert ideas"? What is bad about them? (You might read our essay on pp. 15–18, "What Is an Idea?") Why does a head full of inert ideas not contain real learning? Is the distinction between inert ideas and real learning one that you think most of your teachers have taken into account? Is your university or college different from high school in its commitment to genuine learning? *Should* there be a difference on this score between high school and college?

2. Do you agree with Whitehead's "two educational commandments" in paragraph 4? How do you decide how many subjects are "too many" (too many for what?), and what is the difference between thorough teaching and superficial teaching? Does the difference between *thorough* and *superficial* apply to students as well as teachers?

3. What does Whitehead mean by saying that "the understanding which we want is an understanding of an insistent present" (¶6)? When read out of context this comment may sound difficult or obscure, but do the examples in the remainder of the paragraph make it clear? How would you capture the meaning of paragraph 6 in your own words?

4. Whitehead insists that the metaphors teachers and students unconsciously work with largely determine what they do. Why does he object so strongly to the metaphor "the mind is an instrument" (¶14)? Can you think of other metaphors that teachers and students implicitly accept? For example, education as pouring knowledge into pitchers, education as training (as with animals), education as programming (as of computers)? Which of these metaphors do you like the best? Is your preferred metaphor fully adequate, or does it still fall short? What alternative metaphors can you create on your own—metaphors for either the mind or for learning—that accurately capture the most important aims of education?

5. Although Whitehead rejects the metaphor "the mind is an instrument," he uses many others (e.g., in ¶15, ¶29, and ¶30). Do these seem effective? Why? Why would an author choose a metaphor rather than saying something "straight out"?

6. By having "style" Whitehead seems to mean possessing the sophistication in any activity that comes from knowing it so intimately that one can move inside the activity by "feel," not thought. Dancers, scientists, athletes, and musicians may all exhibit style in this sense. Can you cite particular people who exhibit style in this way?

Suggested Essay Topics

1. Whitehead claims that all real learning involves going back and forth between general ideas and specialized knowledge. Write an essay directed to the narrowest teacher you have ever had (or to the dean or president of your university) explaining what Whitehead means by this notion and why it is crucial to all genuine education. Or, if you think Whitehead is

wrong, explain why students should be allowed to take only the specialized courses that they feel will be useful to their careers.

2. As a variation of topic 1, write a letter to the United States Secretary of Education arguing that our nation's specialists are too narrowly trained or that our generalists are too generally trained. Be sure to say what they are too general or specialized *for,* and give concrete examples from your personal experience as a student. In order to keep this essay from wandering off into abstractions, you might try contrasting the most widely trained (or knowledgeable) high school teacher you had with the one who seemed the most narrowly trained (or knowledgeable), and assessing their relative strengths and weaknesses as teachers.

Ideas in Debate

Matthew Arnold
George Steiner

Matthew Arnold

Matthew Arnold (1822–1888) first delivered "Literature and Science" as the Rede Lecture at Cambridge University. Following its delivery there, he revised it considerably, took out the references to Cambridge University, inserted references to the United States, and delivered it as a lecture during his American tour of 1883–1884.

During the period of nationwide campus turbulence of the 1960s, when the traditional liberal arts curriculum was attacked and in many places largely dismantled, Matthew Arnold's "Literature and Science" fell into neglect and, for some, into disrepute. His essay had for 90 years been considered a classic statement of the aims and advantages of a humanistic education, but when the traditional humanities came under attack, so did Arnold's defense of it. It may even be fair to say that Arnold's defense came under special attack. His formulation of the content of a liberal education—"to know the best which has been thought and said in the world" (¶8)—has been accused of being a shorthand disguise for privileging the writings and ideas of Western white males while excluding the writings and ideas of women, ethnic and racial minorities, and non-Western people.

In the 1980s, however, William Bennett, director of the National Endowment for the Humanities (NEH), and, later, Secretary of Education in the Reagan administration, fostered a national debate about the necessity of returning to a more classically oriented, traditional curriculum. This debate was further fired by the publication of E. D. Hirsch's Cultural Literacy: What Every American Needs to Know *(1987); of Lynne Cheney's* American Memory: A Report on the Humanities in the Nation's Public Schools *(1988) (as Bennett's successor at NEH, her voice has special significance for scholars looking to the NEH for funding); by Allan Bloom's* The Closing of the American Mind *(1988), a book that was, incredibly, on* The New York Times *best-seller list for many weeks; and by a host of other publications in popular magazines, in scholarly journals, and even in newspapers. Special conferences on the advantages and disadvantages of a revised curriculum—discussions often cast as debates about the "canon," those traditional texts of the kind Arnold recommends knowing in "Literature and Science"—have been vigorous and ongoing in academe for the past five or six years.*

Even though you are students, not college professors, this brief history is worth knowing because it bears directly and immediately on the curriculum made available to you in your own college or university. Because the passionate and intense debate about curricular issues continues, and because it directly affects both the kinds of courses you will take and the kinds of texts you will be assigned in those courses, it seems appropriate that you be given an opportunity, first, to read Arnold's classic statement for yourself and, second, to make up your own mind about its value as a definition of the education most worth having.

Arnold's formulation of the issues in 1884 is remarkably relevant to the curricular debate of the 1990s. In analyzing the value of a humanities education, Arnold tries to find the rock-bottom grounds on which an education composed largely of literature, languages, philosophy, history, and other texts (rather than one composed largely of scientific research or professional training) can be defended and promoted.

Arnold's fundamental claim seems to be that the only education any of us will ever find satisfying is one that includes with its content—its facts and knowledge— some view of not only the value of its contents but of the usefulness of its contents for deciding what kind of life to live. In paragraph 19, for example, Arnold says that we are all driven by the passion (which he calls a "power") to know which actions to choose (the power of "conduct"), to know how to learn (the power of "intellect and knowledge"), to know how to experience beauty (the power of "beauty"), and to know how to treat others (the power of "social life and manners"). Since these are the overriding concerns of everyone's life, it follows, at least for Arnold, that no education which fails to address these "powers"—no education which fails to cultivate them or take them into account—can satisfy us for long. And the only education which cultivates the basic human powers, connects learning and life, and Arnold claims, is a humanistic education: "Following our instinct for intellect and knowledge, we acquire pieces of knowledge; and presently, in the generality of men, there arises the desire to relate these pieces of knowledge to our sense for conduct, to our sense for beauty,—and there is weariness and dissatisfaction if the desire is baulked. Now in this desire lies, I think, the strength of that hold which letters [the humanities] have upon us" (¶19).

As you read, it will perhaps help you acquire a better focus on your own education if you consider the extent to which Arnold's claims may be true for you personally. How much of what you are learning (the power of intellect and knowledge) seems related to the actions you choose (the power of conduct), the forms of beauty you experience (the music you listen to, the prints or posters you buy, the styles you prefer, and so on), or the way you treat other people (the power of social life and manners). If the answer is "very little," can you contradict or corroborate Arnold's claim that such an education leads to "weariness and dissatisfaction"? If your answer is "a lot," is it true that the connections are created mainly in humanities courses rather than in science or professional courses? You should be able to decide much about the relevance of Arnold's position simply by testing it against your own experience as a student and learner.

LITERATURE AND SCIENCE

From *Discourses in America* (1885).

Practical people talk with a smile of Plato and of his absolute ideas;* and   1
it is impossible to deny that Plato's ideas do often seem unpractical and
impracticable, and especially when one views them in connexion with the life
of a great work-a-day world like the United States. The necessary staple of
the life of such a world Plato regards with disdain; handicraft and trade and
the working professions he regards with disdain; but what becomes of the life
of an industrial modern community if you take handicraft and trade and the
working professions out of it? The base mechanic arts and handicrafts, says
Plato, bring about a natural weakness in the principle of excellence in a man,
so that he cannot govern the ignoble growths in him, but nurses them, and
cannot understand fostering any other. Those who exercise such arts and
trades, as they have their bodies, he says, marred by their vulgar businesses,
so they have their souls, too, bowed and broken by them. And if one of these
uncomely people has a mind to seek self-culture and philosophy, Plato compares him to a bald little tinker, who has scraped together money, and has
got his release from service, and has had a bath, and bought a new coat, and
is rigged out like a bridegroom about to marry the daughter of his master who
has fallen into poor and helpless estate.†

Nor do the working professions fare any better than trade at the hands   2
of Plato. He draws for us an inimitable picture of the working lawyer, and
of his life of bondage; he shows how this bondage from his youth up has
stunted and warped him, and made him small and crooked of soul, encompassing him with difficulties which he is not man enough to rely on justice
and truth as means to encounter, but has recourse, for help out of them, to
falsehood and wrong. And so, says Plato, this poor creature is bent and
broken, and grows up from boy to man without a particle of soundness in
him, although exceedingly smart and clever in his own esteem.‡

One cannot refuse to admire the artist who draws these pictures. But   3
we say to ourselves that his ideas show the influence of a primitive and
obsolete order of things, when the warrior caste and the priestly caste were
alone in honour, and the humble work of the world was done by slaves. We
have now changed all that; the modern majesty consists in work, as Emerson
declares;§ and in work, we may add, principally of such plain and dusty kind
as the work of cultivators of the ground, handicraftsmen, men of trade and
business, men of the working professions. Above all is this true in a great
industrious community such as that of the United States.

Now education, many people go on to say, is still mainly governed by   4
the ideas of men like Plato, who lived when the warrior caste and the priestly

*Cf. Plato, *Republic*, X, 597B.
†Plato, *Republic*, vi, ix; also ix, xiii.
‡Plato, *Theaetetus*, 172–73.
§Ralph Waldo Emerson, "Literary Ethics," *Works*, Centenary Edition, vol. I, p. 179.

or philosophical class were alone in honour, and the really useful part of the community were slaves. It is an education fitted for persons of leisure in such a community. This education passed from Greece and Rome to the feudal communities of Europe, where also the warrior caste and the priestly caste were alone held in honour, and where the really useful and working part of the community, though not nominally slaves as in the pagan world, were practically not much better off than slaves, and not more seriously regarded. And how absurd it is, people end by saying, to inflict this education upon an industrious modern community, where very few indeed are persons of leisure, and the mass to be considered has not leisure, but is bound, for its own great good, and for the great good of the world at large, to plain labour and to industrial pursuits, and the education in question tends necessarily to make men dissatisfied with these pursuits and unfitted for them!

That is what is said. So far I must defend Plato, as to plead that his view   5
of education and studies is in the general, as it seems to me, sound enough, and fitted for all sorts and conditions of men, whatever their pursuits may be. "An intelligent man," says Plato, "will prize those studies which result in his soul getting soberness, righteousness, and wisdom, and will less value the others." I cannot consider *that* a bad description of the aim of education, and of the motives which should govern us in the choice of studies, whether we are preparing ourselves for a hereditary seat in the English House of Lords or for the pork trade in Chicago.

Still I admit that Plato's world was not ours, that his scorn of trade and   6
handicraft is fantastic, that he had no conception of a great industrial community such as that of the United States, and that such a community must and will shape its education to suit its own needs. If the usual education handed down to it from the past does not suit it, it will certainly before long drop this and try another. The usual education in the past has been mainly literary.* The question is whether the studies which were long supposed to be the best for all of us are practically the best now; whether others are not better. The tyranny of the past, many think, weighs on us injuriously in the predominance given to letters in education. The question is raised whether, to meet the needs of our modern life, the predominance ought not now to pass from letters to science; and naturally the question is nowhere raised with more energy than here in the United States. The design of abasing what is called "mere literary instruction and education," and of exalting what is called "sound, extensive, and practical scientific knowledge," is, in this intensely modern world of the United States, even more perhaps than in Europe, a very popular design, and makes great and rapid progress.

I am going to ask whether the present movement for ousting letters from   7
their old predominance in education, and for transferring the predominance in education to the natural sciences, whether this brisk and flourishing move-

*By "literary," Arnold does not mean imaginative literature exclusively. He means, rather (as with "letters" two sentences later), to refer to those studies that come to us as *texts in words* (distinguished from mathematics or an education in trade, business, nursing, or other professions).

ment ought to prevail, and whether it is likely that in the end it really will prevail. An objection may be raised which I will anticipate. My own studies have been almost wholly in letters, and my visits to the field of the natural sciences have been very slight and inadequate, although those sciences have always strongly moved my curiosity. A man of letters, it will perhaps be said, is not competent to discuss the comparative merits of letters and natural science as means of education. To this objection I reply, first of all, that his incompetence, if he attempts the discussion but is really incompetent for it, will be abundantly visible; nobody will be taken in; he will have plenty of sharp observers and critics to save mankind from that danger. But the line I am going to follow is, as you will soon discover, so extremely simple, that perhaps it may be followed without failure even by one who for a more ambitious line of discussion would be quite incompetent.

Some of you may possibly remember a phrase of mine which has been 8 the object of a good deal of comment; an observation to the effect that in our culture, the aim being *to know ourselves and the world,* we have, as the means to this end, *to know the best which has been thought and said in the world.* A man of science, who is also an excellent writer and the very prince of debaters, Professor Huxley, in a discourse at the opening of Sir Josiah Mason's college at Birmingham, laying hold of this phrase, expanded it by quoting some more words of mine, which are these: "The civilised world is to be regarded as now being, for intellectual and spiritual purposes, one great confederation, bound to a joint action and working to a common result; and whose members have for their proper outfit a knowledge of Greek, Roman, and Eastern antiquity, and of one another. Special local and temporary advantages being put out of account, that modern nation will in the intellectual and spiritual sphere make most progress, which most thoroughly carries out this programme."

Now on my phrase, thus enlarged, Professor Huxley remarks that when 9 I speak of the above-mentioned knowledge as enabling us to know ourselves and the world, I assert *literature* to contain the materials which suffice for thus making us know ourselves and the world. But it is not by any means clear, says he, that after having learnt all which ancient and modern literatures have to tell us, we have laid a sufficiently broad and deep foundation for that criticism of life, that knowledge of ourselves and the world, which constitutes culture. On the contrary, Professor Huxley declares that he finds himself "wholly unable to admit that either nations or individuals will really advance, if their outfit draws nothing from the stores of physical science. An army without weapons of precision, and with no particular base of operations, might more hopefully enter upon a campaign on the Rhine, than a man, devoid of a knowledge of what physical science has done in the last century, upon a criticism of life."

This shows how needful it is for those who are to discuss any matter 10 together, to have a common understanding as to the sense of the terms they employ,—how needful, and how difficult. What Professor Huxley says, implies just the reproach which is so often brought against the study of *belles lettres,* as they are called: that the study is an elegant one, but slight and ineffectual; a smattering of Greek and Latin and other ornamental things, of little use for any one whose object is to get at truth, and to be a practical man. So, too, Mr. Renan* talks of the "superficial humanism" of a school-course which treats us as if we were all going to be poets, writers, preachers, orators, and he opposes this humanism to positive science, or the critical search after truth. And there is always a tendency in those who are remonstrating against the predominance of letters in education, to understand by letters *belles lettres,* and by *belles lettres* a superficial humanism, the opposite of science or true knowledge.

But when we talk of knowing Greek and Roman antiquity, for instance, 11 which is the knowledge people have called the humanities, I for my part mean a knowledge which is something more than a superficial humanism, mainly decorative. "I call all teaching *scientific,"* says Wolf,† the critic of Homer, "which is systematically laid out and followed up to its original source. For example: a knowledge of classical antiquity is scientific when the remains of classical antiquity are connectedly studied in the original languages." There can be no doubt that Wolf is perfectly right; that all learning is scientific which is systematically laid out and followed up to its original sources, and that a genuine humanism is scientific.

When I speak of knowing Greek and Roman antiquity, therefore, as a 12 help to knowing ourselves and the world, I mean more than a knowledge of so much vocabulary, so much grammar, so many portions of authors in the Greek and Latin languages. I mean knowing the Greeks and Romans, and their life and genius, and what they were and did in the world; what we get from them, and what is its value. That, at least, is the ideal; and when we talk of endeavouring to know Greek and Roman antiquity, as a help to knowing ourselves and the world, we mean endeavouring so to know them as to satisfy this ideal, however much we may still fall short of it.

The same also as to knowing our own and other modern nations, with 13 the like aim of getting to understand ourselves and the world. To know the best that has been thought and said by the modern nations, is to know, says Professor Huxley, "only what modern *literatures* have to tell us; it is the criticism of life contained in modern literature." And yet "the distinctive character of our times," he urges, "lies in the vast and constantly increasing part which is played by natural knowledge." And how, therefore, can a man, devoid of knowledge of what physical science has done in the last century, enter hopefully upon a criticism of modern life?

Let us, I say, be agreed about the meaning of the terms we are using. 14 I talk of knowing the best which has been thought and uttered in the world; Professor Huxley says this means knowing *literature.* Literature is a large word; it may mean everything written with letters or printed in a book. Euclid's

---

*Joseph Ernest Renan (1823–1892), critic of French culture.

†Friedrich August Wolf (1759–1824), German critic and scholar, chiefly of Homer and ancient learning.

Elements and Newton's *Principia* are thus literature. All knowledge that reaches us through books is literature. But by literature Professor Huxley means *belles lettres.* He means to make me say, that knowing the best which has been thought and said by the modern nations is knowing their *belles lettres* and no more. And this is no sufficient equipment, he argues, for a criticism of modern life. But as I do not mean, by knowing ancient Rome, knowing merely more or less of Latin *belles lettres,* and taking no account of Rome's military, and political, and legal, and administrative work in the world; and as, by knowing ancient Greece, I understand knowing her as the giver of Greek art, and the guide to a free and right use of reason and to scientific method, and the founder of our mathematics and physics and astronomy and biology,—I understand knowing her as all this, and not merely knowing certain Greek poems, and histories, and treatises, and speeches,—so as to the knowledge of modern nations also. By knowing modern nations, I mean not merely know-ing their *belles lettres,* but knowing also what has been done by such men as Copernicus, Galileo, Newton, Darwin. "Our ancestors learned," says Profes-sor Huxley, "that the earth is the centre of the visible universe, and that man is the cynosure of things terrestrial; and more especially was it inculcated that the course of nature had no fixed order, but that it could be, and constantly was, altered." But for us now, continues Professor Huxley, "the notions of the beginning and the end of the world entertained by our forefathers are no longer credible. It is very certain that the earth is not the chief body in the material universe, and that the world is not subordinated to man's use. It is even more certain that nature is the expression of a definite order, with which nothing interferes." "And yet," he cries, "the purely classical education ad-vocated by the representatives of the humanists in our day gives no inkling of all this!"

In due place and time I will just touch upon that vexed question of 15 classical education; but at present the question is as to what is meant by knowing the best which modern nations have thought and said. It is not knowing their *belles lettres* merely which is meant. To know Italian *belles lettres* is not to know Italy, and to know English *belles lettres* is not to know England. Into knowing Italy and England there comes a great deal more, Galileo and Newton amongst it. The reproach of being a superficial humanism, a tincture of *belles lettres,* may attach rightly enough to some other disciplines; but to the particular discipline recommended when I proposed knowing the best that has been thought and said in the world, it does not apply. In that best I certainly include what in modern times has been thought and said by the great observers and knowers of nature.

There is, therefore, really no question between Professor Huxley and me 16 as to whether knowing the great results of the modern scientific study of nature is not required as a part of our culture, as well as knowing the products of literature and art. But to follow the processes by which those results are reached, ought, say the friends of physical science, to be made the staple of education for the bulk of mankind. And here there does arise a question

between those whom Professor Huxley calls with playful sarcasm "the Levites of culture," and those whom the poor humanist is sometimes apt to
regard as its Nebuchadnezzars.*

The great results of the scientific investigation of nature we are agreed   17
upon knowing, but how much of our study are we bound to give to the
processes by which those results are reached? The results have their visible
bearing on human life. But all the processes, too, all the items of fact, by
which those results are reached and established, are interesting. All knowledge is interesting to a wise man, and the knowledge of nature is interesting
to all men. It is very interesting to know, that, from the albuminous white
of the egg, the chick in the egg gets the materials for its flesh, bones, blood,
and feathers; while, from the fatty yolk of the egg, it gets the heat and energy
which enable it at length to break its shell and begin the world. It is less
interesting, perhaps, but still it is interesting, to know that when a taper
burns, the wax is converted into carbonic acid and water. Moreover, it is quite
true that the habit of dealing with facts, which is given by the study of nature,
is, as the friends of physical science praise it for being, an excellent discipline.
The appeal, in the study of nature, is constantly to observation and experiment; not only is it said that the thing is so, but we can be made to see that
it is so. Not only does a man tell us that when a taper burns the wax is
converted into carbonic acid and water, as a man may tell us, if he likes, that
Charon is punting his ferry-boat on the river Styx,† or that Victor Hugo is
a sublime poet, or Mr. Gladstone the most admirable of statesmen; but we
are made to see that the conversion into carbonic acid and water does actually
happen. This reality of natural knowledge it is, which makes the friends of
physical science contrast it, as a knowledge of things, with the humanist's
knowledge, which is, say they, a knowledge of words. And hence Professor
Huxley is moved to lay it down that, "for the purpose of attaining real
culture, an exclusively scientific education is at least as effectual as an exclusively literary education." And a certain President of the Section for Mechanical Science in the British Association is, in Scripture phrase, "very bold," and
declares that if a man, in his mental training, "has substituted literature and
history for natural science, he has chosen the less useful alternative." But
whether we go these lengths or not, we must all admit that in natural science
the habit gained of dealing with facts is a most valuable discipline, and that
every one should have some experience of it.

More than this, however, is demanded by the reformers. It is proposed   18
to make the training in natural science the main part of education, for the
great majority of mankind at any rate. And here, I confess, I part company

---

*Among the ancient Hebrews, the Levites supervised the ceremonies of traditional rites and
customs. Nebuchadnezzar was the king of Babylon who captured Jerusalem. Thus Huxley, the
scientist, is accusing the supporters of an exclusively classical education of being custom-bound,
while the classically oriented humanist is accusing the supporters of an exclusively scientific
education of being too materialistic and too practical.
†In Greek mythology, Charon is the immortal being who ferries souls across the river Styx into
Hades.

with the friends of physical science, with whom up to this point I have been agreeing. In differing from them, however, I wish to proceed with the utmost caution and diffidence. The smallness of my own acquaintance with the disciplines of natural science is ever before my mind, and I am fearful of doing these disciplines an injustice. The ability and pugnacity of the partisans of natural science make them formidable persons to contradict. The tone of tentative inquiry, which befits a being of dim faculties and bounded knowledge, is the tone I would wish to take and not to depart from. At present it seems to me, that those who are for giving to natural knowledge, as they call it, the chief place in the education of the majority of mankind, leave one important thing out of their account: the constitution of human nature. But I put this forward on the strength of some facts not at all recondite, very far from it; facts capable of being stated in the simplest possible fashion, and to which, if I so state them, the man of science will, I am sure, be willing to allow their due weight.

Deny the facts altogether, I think, he hardly can. He can hardly deny, 19 that when we set ourselves to enumerate the powers* which go to the building up of human life, and say that they are the power of conduct, the power of intellect and knowledge, the power of beauty, and the power of social life and manners,—he can hardly deny that this scheme, though drawn in rough and plain lines enough, and not pretending to scientific exactness, does yet give a fairly true representation of the matter. Human nature is built up by these powers; we have the need for them all. When we have rightly met and adjusted the claims of them all, we shall then be in a fair way for getting soberness and righteousness, with wisdom. This is evident enough, and the friends of physical science would admit it.

But perhaps they may not have sufficiently observed another thing: 20 namely, that the several powers just mentioned are not isolated, but there is, in the generality of mankind, a perpetual tendency to relate them one to another in divers ways. With one such way of relating them I am particularly concerned now. Following our instinct for intellect and knowledge, we acquire pieces of knowledge; and presently, in the generality of men, there arises the desire to relate these pieces of knowledge to our sense for conduct, to our sense for beauty,—and there is weariness and dissatisfaction if the desire is baulked. Now in this desire lies, I think, the strength of that hold which letters have upon us.

All knowledge is, as I said just now, interesting; and even items of 21 knowledge which from the nature of the case cannot well be related, but must stand isolated in our thoughts, have their interest. Even lists of exceptions have their interest. If we are studying Greek accents, it is interesting to know that *pais* and *pas,* and some other monosyllables of the same form of declension, do not take the circumflex upon the last syllable of the genitive plural, but vary, in this respect, from the common rule. If we are studying physiology, it is interesting to know that the pulmonary artery carries dark blood and

*By "powers" Arnold seems to mean "passions" or "desires and capacities."

the pulmonary vein carries bright blood, departing in this respect from the common rule for the division of labour between the veins and the arteries. But every one knows how we seek naturally to combine the pieces of our knowledge together, to bring them under general rules, to relate them to principles; and how unsatisfactory and tiresome it would be to go on for ever learning lists of exceptions, or accumulating items of fact which must stand isolated.

Well, that same need of relating our knowledge, which operates here   22
within the sphere of our knowledge itself, we shall find operating, also, outside that sphere. We experience, as we go on learning and knowing,—the vast majority of us experience,—the need of relating what we have learnt and known to the sense which we have in us for conduct, to the sense which we have in us for beauty.

A certain Greek prophetess of Mantineia in Arcadia, Diotima by   23
name, once explained to the philosopher Socrates that love, and impulse, and bent of all kinds, is, in fact, nothing else but the desire in men that good should for ever be present to them. This desire for good, Diotima assured Socrates, is our fundamental desire, of which fundamental desire every impulse in us is only some one particular form. And therefore this fundamental desire it is, I suppose,—this desire in men that good should be for ever present to them,—which acts in us when we feel the impulse for relating our knowledge to our sense for conduct and to our sense for beauty. At any rate, with men in general the instinct exists. Such is human nature. And the instinct, it will be admitted, is innocent, and human nature is preserved by our following the lead of its innocent instincts. Therefore, in seeking to gratify this instinct in question, we are following the instinct of self-preservation in humanity.

But, no doubt, some kinds of knowledge cannot be made to directly   24
serve the instinct in question, cannot be directly related to the sense for beauty, to the sense for conduct. These are instrument-knowledges; they lead on to other knowledges, which can. A man who passes his life in instrument-knowledges is a specialist. They may be invaluable as instruments to something beyond, for those who have the gift thus to employ them; and they may be disciplines in themselves wherein it is useful for every one to have some schooling. But it is inconceivable that the generality of men should pass all their mental life with Greek accents or with formal logic. My friend Professor Sylvester,* who is one of the first mathematicians in the world, holds transcendental doctrines as to the virtue of mathematics, but those doctrines are not for common men. In the very Senate House and heart of our English Cambridge I once ventured, though not without an apology for my profaneness, to hazard the opinion that for the majority of mankind a little of mathematics, even, goes a long way. Of course this is quite consistent with their being of immense importance as an instrument to something else; but

---

*James Joseph Sylvester (1814–1897); distinguished English mathematician at Johns Hopkins University and Oxford University.

it is the few who have the aptitude for thus using them, not the bulk of mankind.

The natural sciences do not, however, stand on the same footing with these instrument-knowledges. Experience shows us that the generality of men will find more interest in learning that, when a taper burns, the wax is converted into carbonic acid and water, or in learning the explanation of the phenomenon of dew, or in learning how the circulation of the blood is carried on, than they find in learning that the genitive plural of *pais* and *pas* does not take the circumflex on the termination. And one piece of natural knowledge is added to another, and others are added to that, and at last we come to propositions so interesting as Mr. Darwin's famous proposition that "our ancestor was a hairy quadruped furnished with a tail and pointed ears, probably arboreal in his habits."* Or we come to propositions of such reach and magnitude as those which Professor Huxley delivers, when he says that the notions of our forefathers about the beginning and the end of the world were all wrong, and that nature is the expression of a definite order with which nothing interferes. 25

Interesting, indeed, these results of science are, important they are, and we should all of us be acquainted with them. But what I now wish you to mark is, that we are still, when they are propounded to us and we receive them, we are still in the sphere of intellect and knowledge. And for the generality of men there will be found, I say, to arise, when they have duly taken in the proposition that their ancestor was "a hairy quadruped furnished with a tail and pointed ears, probably arboreal in his habits," there will be found to arise an invincible desire to relate this proposition to the sense in us for conduct, and to the sense in us for beauty. But this the men of science will not do for us, and will hardly even profess to do. They will give us other pieces of knowledge, other facts, about other animals and their ancestors, or about plants, or about stones, or about stars; and they may finally bring us to those great "general conceptions of the universe, which are forced upon us all," says Professor Huxley, "by the progress of physical science." But still it will be *knowledge* only which they give us; knowledge not put for us into relation with our sense for conduct, our sense for beauty, and touched with emotion by being so put; not thus put for us, and therefore, to the majority of mankind, after a certain while, unsatisfying, wearying. 26

Not to the born naturalist, I admit. But what do we mean by a born naturalist? We mean a man in whom the zeal for observing nature is so uncommonly strong and eminent, that it marks him off from the bulk of mankind. Such a man will pass his life happily in collecting natural knowledge and reasoning upon it, and will ask for nothing, or hardly anything, more. I have heard it said that the sagacious and admirable naturalist whom we lost not very long ago, Mr. Darwin, once owned to a friend that for his part he did not experience the necessity for two things which most men find so necessary to them,—religion and poetry; science and the domestic affec- 27

*One of the most controversial statements in Charles Darwin's *The Descent of Man* (1871).

tions, he thought, were enough. To a born naturalist, I can well understand
that this should seem so. So absorbing is his occupation with nature, so strong
his love for his occupation, that he goes on acquiring natural knowledge and
reasoning upon it, and has little time or inclination for thinking about getting
it related to the desire in man for conduct, the desire in man for beauty. He
relates it to them for himself as he goes along, so far as he feels the need; and
he draws from the domestic affections all the additional solace necessary. But
then Darwins are extremely rare. Another great and admirable master of
natural knowledge, Faraday,* was a Sandemanian. That is to say, he related
his knowledge to his instinct for conduct and to his instinct for beauty, by
the aid of that respectable Scottish sectary, Robert Sandeman.† And so
strong, in general, is the demand of religion and poetry to have their share
in a man, to associate themselves with his knowing, and to relieve and rejoice
it, that, probably, for one man amongst us with the disposition to do as
Darwin did in this respect, there are at least fifty with the disposition to do
as Faraday.

Education lays hold upon us, in fact, by satisfying this demand. Profes- 28
sor Huxley holds up to scorn mediæval education, with its neglect of the
knowledge of nature, its poverty even of literary studies, its formal logic
devoted to "showing how and why that which the Church said was true must
be true." But the great mediæval Universities were not brought into being,
we may be sure, by the zeal for giving a jejune and contemptible education.
Kings have been their nursing fathers, and queens have been their nursing
mothers, but not for this. The mediæval Universities came into being, because
the supposed knowledge, delivered by Scripture and the Church, so deeply
engaged men's hearts, by so simply, easily, and powerfully relating itself to
their desire for conduct, their desire for beauty. All other knowledge was
dominated by this supposed knowledge and was subordinated to it, because
of the surpassing strength of the hold which it gained upon the affections of
men, by allying itself profoundly with their sense for conduct, their sense for
beauty.

But now, says Professor Huxley, conceptions of the universe fatal to the 29
notions held by our forefathers have been forced upon us by physical science.
Grant to him that they are thus fatal, that the new conceptions must and will
soon become current everywhere, and that every one will finally perceive
them to be fatal to the beliefs of our forefathers. The need of humane letters,
as they are truly called, because they serve the paramount desire in men that
good should be for ever present to them,—the need of humane letters, to
establish a relation between the new conceptions, and our instinct for beauty,
our instinct for conduct, is only the more visible. The Middle Age could do
without humane letters, as it could do without the study of nature, because
its supposed knowledge was made to engage its emotions so powerfully.

*Michael Faraday (1791–1867), great physicist and chemist.
†Robert Sandeman (1718–1771), Scottish manufacturer, clergyman, and writer, who established
a Protestant-Christian sect.

Grant that the supposed knowledge disappears, its power of being made to engage the emotions will of course disappear along with it,—but the emotions themselves, and their claim to be engaged and satisfied, will remain. Now if we find by experience that humane letters have an undeniable power of engaging the emotions, the importance of humane letters in a man's training becomes not less, but greater, in proportion to the success of modern science in extirpating what it calls "mediæval thinking."

Have humane letters, then, have poetry and eloquence, the power here 30 attributed to them of engaging the emotions, and do they exercise it? And if they have it and exercise it, *how* do they exercise it, so as to exert an influence upon man's sense for conduct, his sense for beauty? Finally, even if they both can and do exert an influence upon the senses in question, how are they to relate to them the results,—the modern results,—of natural science? All these questions may be asked. First, have poetry and eloquence the power of calling out the emotions? The appeal is to experience. Experience shows that for the vast majority of men, for mankind in general, they have the power. Next, do they exercise it? They do. But then, *how* do they exercise it so as to affect man's sense for conduct, his sense for beauty? And this is perhaps a case for applying the Preacher's words: "Though a man labour to seek it out, yet he shall not find it; yea, farther, though a wise man think to know it, yet shall he not be able to find it."[1] Why should it be one thing, in its effect upon the emotions, to say, "Patience is a virtue," and quite another thing, in its effect upon the emotions, to say with Homer,

$$\tau\lambda\eta\tau\grave{o}\nu \ \gamma\grave{a}\rho \ \text{Μοῖραι} \ \theta\upsilon\mu\grave{o}\nu \ \theta\acute{\epsilon}\sigma\alpha\nu \ \grave{a}\nu\theta\rho\acute{\omega}\pi\omicron\iota\sigma\iota\nu—^2$$

"for an enduring heart have the destinies appointed to the children of men"? Why should it be one thing, in its effect upon the emotions, to say with the philosopher Spinoza, *Felicitas in eo consistit quod homo suum esse conservare potest*— "Man's happiness consists in his being able to preserve his own essence," and quite another thing, in its effect upon the emotions, to say with the Gospel, "What is a man advantaged, if he gain the whole world, and lose himself, forfeit himself?" How does this difference of effect arise? I cannot tell, and I am not much concerned to know; the important thing is that it does arise, and that we can profit by it. But how, finally, are poetry and eloquence to exercise the power of relating the modern results of natural science to man's instinct for conduct, his instinct for beauty? And here again I answer that I do not know *how* they will exercise it, but that they can and will exercise it I am sure. I do not mean that modern philosophical poets and modern philosophical moralists are to come and relate for us, in express terms, the results of modern scientific research to our instinct for conduct, our instinct for beauty. But I mean that we shall find, as a matter of experience, if we know the best that has been thought and uttered in the world, we shall find that the art and poetry and eloquence of men who lived, perhaps, long ago, who had the most limited natural knowledge, who had the most erroneous conceptions about many important matters, we shall find that this art, and poetry, and eloquence, have in fact not only the power of refreshing and delighting us, they have also the power,—such is the strength and worth, in essentials, of their authors' criticism of life,—they have a fortifying, and elevating, and quickening, and suggestive power, capable of wonderfully helping us to relate the results of modern science to our need for conduct, our need for beauty. Homer's conceptions of the physical universe were, I imagine, grotesque; but really, under the shock of hearing from modern science that "the world is not subordinated to man's use, and that man is not the cynosure of things terrestrial," I could, for my own part, desire no better comfort than Homer's line which I quoted just now,

$$\tau\lambda\eta\tau\grave{o}\nu\ \gamma\acute{a}\rho\ Mo\hat{\iota}\rho\alpha\iota\ \theta\upsilon\mu\grave{o}\nu\ \theta\varepsilon\sigma\alpha\nu\ \acute{a}\nu\theta\rho\acute{\omega}\pi o\iota\sigma\nu-$$

"for an enduring heart have the destinies appointed to the children of men"!

And the more that men's minds are cleared, the more that the results 31 of science are frankly accepted, the more that poetry and eloquence come to be received and studied as what in truth they really are,—the criticism of life by gifted men, alive and active with extraordinary power at an unusual number of points;—so much the more will the value of humane letters, and of art also, which is an utterance having a like kind of power with theirs, be felt and acknowledged, and their place in education be secured.

Let us therefore, all of us, avoid indeed as much as possible any invidi- 32 ous comparison between the merits of humane letters, as means of education, and the merits of the natural sciences. But when some President of a Section for Mechanical Science insists on making the comparison, and tells us that "he who in his training has substituted literature and history for natural science has chosen the less useful alternative," let us make answer to him that the student of humane letters only, will, at least, know also the great general conceptions brought in by modern physical science; for science, as Professor Huxley says, forces them upon us all. But the student of the natural sciences only, will, by our very hypothesis, know nothing of humane letters; not to mention that in setting himself to be perpetually accumulating natural knowledge, he sets himself to do what only specialists have in general the gift for doing genially. And so he will probably be unsatisfied, or at any rate incomplete, and even more incomplete than the student of humane letters only.

I once mentioned in a school-report, how a young man in one of our 33 English training colleges having to paraphrase the passage in *Macbeth* beginning,

"Can'st thou not minister to a mind diseased?"

turned this line into, "Can you not wait upon the lunatic?" And I remarked what a curious state of things it would be, if every pupil of our national schools knew, let us say, that the moon is two thousand one hundred and sixty miles in diameter, and thought at the same time that a good paraphrase for

"Can'st thou not minister to a mind diseased?"

was, "Can you not wait upon the lunatic?" If one is driven to choose, I think I would rather have a young person ignorant about the moon's diameter, but aware that "Can you not wait upon the lunatic?" is bad, than a young person whose education had been such as to manage things the other way.

Or to go higher than the pupils of our national schools. I have in my mind's eye a member of our British Parliament who comes to travel here in America, who afterwards relates his travels, and who shows a really masterly knowledge of the geology of this great country and of its mining capabilities, but who ends by gravely suggesting that the United States should borrow a prince from our Royal Family, and should make him their king, and should create a House of Lords of great landed proprietors after the pattern of ours; and then America, he thinks, would have her future happily and perfectly secured. Surely, in this case, the President of the Section for Mechanical Science would himself hardly say that our member of Parliament, by concentrating himself upon geology and mineralogy, and so on, and not attending to literature and history, had "chosen the more useful alternative."

If then there is to be separation and option between humane letters on the one hand, and the natural sciences on the other, the great majority of mankind, all who have not exceptional and overpowering aptitudes for the study of nature, would do well, I cannot but think, to choose to be educated in humane letters rather than in the natural sciences. Letters will call out their being at more points, will make them live more.

I said that before I ended I would just touch on the question of classical education, and I will keep my word. Even if literature is to retain a large place in our education, yet Latin and Greek, say the friends of progress, will certainly have to go. Greek is the grand offender in the eyes of these gentlemen. The attackers of the established course of study think that against Greek, at any rate, they have irresistible arguments. Literature may perhaps be needed in education, they say; but why on earth should it be Greek literature? Why not French or German? Nay, "has not an Englishman models in his own literature of every kind of excellence?" As before, it is not on any weak pleadings of my own that I rely for convincing the gainsayers; it is on the constitution of human nature itself, and on the instinct of self-preservation in humanity. The instinct for beauty is set in human nature, as surely as the instinct for knowledge is set there, or the instinct for conduct. If the instinct for beauty is served by Greek literature and art as it is served by no other literature and art, we may trust to the instinct of self-preservation in humanity for keeping Greek as part of our culture. We may trust to it for even making the study of Greek more prevalent than it is now. Greek will come, I hope, some day to be studied more rationally than at present; but it will be increasingly studied as men increasingly feel the need in them for beauty, and how powerfully Greek art and Greek literature can serve this need. Women will again study Greek, as Lady Jane Grey* did; I believe that in that chain of forts, with which the fair host of the Amazons are now engirdling our English universities, I find that here in America, in colleges like Smith College in Massachusetts, and Vassar College in the State of New York, and in the happy families of the mixed universities out West, they are studying it already.

Defuit una mihi symmetria prisca,—"The antique symmetry was the one 37 thing wanting to me," said Leonardo da Vinci; and he was an Italian. I will not presume to speak for the Americans, but I am sure that, in the English-man, the want of this admirable symmetry of the Greeks is a thousand times more great and crying than in any Italian. The results of the want show themselves most glaringly, perhaps, in our architecture, but they show them-selves, also, in all our art. *Fit details strictly combined, in view of a large general result nobly conceived;* that is just the beautiful *symmetria prisca* of the Greeks, and it is just where we English fail, where all our art fails. Striking ideas we have, and well-executed details we have; but that high symmetry which, with satisfy-ing and delightful effect, combines them, we seldom or never have. The glorious beauty of the Acropolis at Athens did not come from single fine things stuck about on that hill, a statue here, a gateway there;—no, it arose from all things being perfectly combined for a supreme total effect. What must not an Englishman feel about our deficiencies in this respect, as the sense for beauty, whereof this symmetry is an essential element, awakens and strengthens within him! what will not one day be his respect and desire for Greece and its *symmetria prisca,* when the scales drop from his eyes as he walks the London streets, and he sees such a lesson in meanness as the Strand, for instance, in its true deformity! But here we are coming to our friend Mr. Ruskin's province,† and I will not intrude upon it, for he is its very sufficient guardian.

And so we at last find, it seems, we find flowing in favour of the 38 humanities the natural and necessary stream of things, which seemed against them when we started. The "hairy quadruped furnished with a tail and pointed ears, probably arboreal in his habits," this good fellow carried hidden in his nature, apparently, something destined to develop into a necessity for humane letters. Nay, more; we seem finally to be even led to the further conclusion that our hairy ancestor carried in his nature, also, a necessity for Greek.

And therefore, to say the truth, I cannot really think that humane letters 39 are in much actual danger of being thrust out from their leading place in education, in spite of the array of authorities against them at this moment.

---

*A Greek scholar and humanist, (1537–1554), proclaimed queen in 1553, but executed in 1554.
†John Ruskin (1819–1900), art critic whose special concern was the correspondence between the character of a people and the architecture of that people. See especially Ruskin's "Traffic" in *The Crown of Wild Olive* (1866).

So long as human nature is what it is, their attractions will remain irresistible. As with Greek, so with letters generally: they will some day come, we may hope, to be studied more rationally, but they will not lose their place. What will happen will rather be that there will be crowded into education other matters besides, far too many; there will be, perhaps, a period of unsettlement and confusion and false tendency; but letters will not in the end lose their leading place. If they lose it for a time, they will get it back again. We shall be brought back to them by our wants and aspirations. And a poor humanist may possess his soul in patience, neither strive nor cry, admit the energy and brilliancy of the partisans of physical science, and their present favour with the public, to be far greater than his own, and still have a happy faith that the nature of things works silently on behalf of the studies which he loves, and that, while we shall all have to acquaint ourselves with the great results reached by modern science, and to give ourselves as much training in its disciplines as we can conveniently carry, yet the majority of men will always require humane letters; and so much the more, as they have the more and the greater results of science to relate to the need in man for conduct, and to the need in him for beauty.

NOTES

All notes are Arnold's.

1. *Ecclesiastes*, viii. 17
2. *Iliad*, xxiv. 49.

Questions for Discussion

1. How would you define in your own words the "instinct" Arnold refers to as "this desire in men that good should be for ever present to them" (¶23)?

2. In the contemporary curriculum at your college or university, which courses (or majors or programs or schools) fit Arnold's notion of "instrument-knowledges" (¶24)? What is the natural contrary of "instrument-knowledges"? What are the criteria by which "instrument-knowledges" are defined?

3. Why does Arnold say in paragraph 26 that science is unable to satisfy the "invincible desire to relate . . . [facts] to the sense in us for conduct, and to the sense in us for beauty"? If he is right, why? If he is wrong, why?

4. What does Arnold mean when he says that literature is "the criticism of life" (¶31)? What sense does *criticism* carry here? How do stories, poetry, and eloquence conduct such "criticism"?

Suggested Essay Topics

1. Arnold pictures a certain sequence that marks the educational process. First, we follow our passion for intellect and knowledge, which leads to the accumulation of "content," the knowledge of facts, figures, events, processes, definitions, dates, and so on. Second, we begin to feel a need—indeed, an internal demand—to know how our knowledge content bears on the actions we perform, on the forms of beauty we pursue, and on the standards we hold in our relations with other people. Third, this internal demand is either satisfied or not satisfied by the kind of education we receive. If it is satisfied, then we live a fuller, richer, and more controlled life. If it is not satisfied, then we feel "weariness and dissatisfaction" in carrying around loads of facts and other forms of knowledge we do not know the value of. In this essay, choose as your audience the one teacher who in your experience has been either the most or the least sensitive to the need for knowledge to "relate," to "connect," and explain to that teacher, in the first case, how you have been able to pursue "connectedness" as a consequence of his or her help. In the second case, explain to that teacher what was wrong with his or her instruction and make recommendations suggesting changes that will make his or her classroom a more vital, challenging, and truly educational site.

2. After you have read George Steiner's "In a Post-Culture" (the next essay), write a dialogue in which you picture Steiner and Arnold debating the value of a humanities education. Don't "give away" the argument to either man. Make each of them a strong representative of the best ideas in their respective positions. Then append a page in which you assess whether writing the dialogue has deepened your understanding or changed your mind about any of the important issues.

George Steiner

George Steiner was born in France in 1929 of Austrian-Jewish parents who had left Vienna for Paris in 1924. The whole family moved to the United States just before the German occupation of France in 1940 and became naturalized American citizens four years later. Despite his American and British connections, "Steiner identifies himself with the Central European Jewish intellectual tradition that produced Freud, Marx, and Einstein, a line cut brutally short by the holocaust. His sense of vocation is rooted in his obsession with 'the black mystery of what happened in Europe'—the rise of Nazism 'from the very core and locale of humanistic civilization'" (1983 Current Biography, p. 369). Perhaps second only to Elie Wiesel (see Chapter 11) in the incisiveness and voluminousness of his writings on the holocaust, Steiner has in book after book and essay after essay attempted to understand not only how the twentieth century slipped into hideous "political barbarism" (a frequent term of his), but especially how language could have been so employed as to make such horror seem inevitable or even to make it look like something noble. "Central to everything I am and believe and have written . . . [says Steiner] is my astonishment, naive as it seems to some people, that you can use human speech both to bless, to love, to build, to forgive and also to torture, to hate, to destroy, and to annihilate" (1983 Current Biography, *p. 369).*

The essay excerpted here attempts to analyze the problem of why the humanistic values and education of European culture proved so ineffective a barrier against the eruption of racial hatred and genocide during the 1930s and 1940s. In Steiner's view the tradition of humanistic education that goes back to the Greeks and Romans— traditionally called a liberal arts education—has been based on an assumption profoundly challenged by the holocaust: an assumption that humanistic education is in itself civilizing and humanizing. If a liberal arts education automatically humanizes one, asks Steiner, how does it happen that the butchers of Belsen and Buchenwald were in some cases the recipients of traditional humanistic educations obtained in the greatest universities of Europe? Many of the worst crimes of the holocaust, both of commission and omission—that is, both the commission of torture and the silent complicity of those who refused to object—were committed by people who had read the great classical works of Western civilization (Homer, Virgil, Dante, Goethe, and so on); who read poetry, went to the opera, and loved classical music; they were committed by people who had traveled abroad, spoke two or more languages, and to whom a cosmopolitan outlook and cultivated manners were second nature. Yet some of these people saw no inconsistency between their civilized education as connoisseurs of the arts and their barbaric practices as directors of the death camps at Auschwitz, Belsen, and Buchenwald. Or, if they did see an inconsistency, it seemed insufficiently important to provide a check against whatever other motives were driving them, especially the motive of racial hatred.

It won't do to say simply that the Nazis did the dirty work of Hitler's Third Reich all by themselves. It won't work to say that a small group of maniacal Aryan racists coerced millions of Europeans against their will to yield up the Jews for mass slaughter. The Nazis both depended upon and received the support—sometimes vocal, often silent, but always effective—of those millions of European citizens who would probably have revolted en masse *against the same crimes had the Nazis directed them against people of their own race and religion, but who closed their eyes in avoidance or even took a silent satisfaction in watching it happen to the Jews. Because the crimes of the Nazis and the crimes of those who were silently complicitous occurred on such a vast scale and involved every race and cultural group in Europe, the liberal-arts ideal of education to which they had all subscribed for centuries could not avoid being called into question.*

Steiner is not the first, although he is certainly among the most vocal, in trying to identify precisely how the long belief in education's humanizing effects was given its greatest challenge (some might say, given the lie) by events in Europe from the end of World War I to the end of World War II. In this essay he makes the clear argument, first, that the ancient tradition of humanistic education has much to answer for (incipient elitism and moral sterility, for example), and, second, that the ancient belief in the efficacy of humanistic education to form citizens of good character is at best naive and at worst a deliberate avoidance of the worst traits in our nature.

As you read, try to determine if Steiner is being fair to humanistic education as you have known and experienced it. Have teachers ever suggested to you that people are automatically improved in character by reading great works of literature or appreciating great works of art or music? If they have, have they produced arguments in support of their views? If they have not, on what grounds have they recommended that you learn to appreciate the liberal arts and the fine arts? Do you in fact feel that acquaintance with great works of literature, music, art, and philosophy either would have improved or has improved your character, made you more civilized? Do you feel that such acquaintance would or does make it more difficult for you to engage in acts of cruelty or hatred against others? These questions, difficult as they are to answer, have been given an urgency by events in the twentieth century that they never had in previous generations. You will of course not settle your mind about such complicated questions and issues on one sitting or as a consequence of one or two class discussions, but no matter how your thinking evolves, the vivid and compelling prose of George Steiner will probably accompany your reflections, enriching and challenging them.

IN A POST-CULTURE

From chapter 3 of *In Bluebeard's Castle: Some Notes Towards the Redefinition of Culture* (1971).

The third axiom* which we can no longer put forward without extreme   1
qualification is that which correlates humanism—as an educational program, as an ideal referent—to humane social conduct. The issue needs careful statement. The ideology of liberal education, of a classically based humanism in the nineteenth-century scheme of culture, is a working out of specific expectations of the Enlightment.† It takes place on many levels, among them university reform, revisions of the school syllabus, expansion of the educational base, adult instruction, the dissemination of excellence through low-cost books and periodicals. These expectations, Lockeian,‡ Jeffersonian if you will, had grown diffuse and self-evident, or self-evident because diffuse (universality entailing vagueness). But their central tenet was clear: that there was a natural progression from the cultivation of feeling and intellect in the individual to rational, beneficent behavior in and by the relevant society. The secular dogma of moral and political progress through education was pre-

---

*The other two "axioms" that Steiner has already discussed in this chapter—axioms which are as much under challenge today as the one he is now going to discuss—are (1) that the West is both racially and culturally superior to all other races and cultures and (2) that "the curve of Western history was ascendant" (p. 67), that progress forever was guaranteed.

†That period in Europe, roughly 1660–1900, that produced the main features of "liberal" thought: the theory of political equality, faith in reason, reliance on science, and a belief in the necessity of reforming the old feudal and aristocratically dominated social order.

‡John Locke (1632–1704), published liberal constitutional ideas on government in 1690 and liberal ideas on education in 1693.

cisely that: a transfer into the categories of schooling and public enlighten-ment—the lyceum, the public library, the workingmen's college—of those dynamics of illumination, of human growth towards ethical perfection that had once been theological and transcendentally elective. Thus the Jacobin slogan that the schoolroom was the temple and moral forum of a free people marks the secularization of a utopian, ultimately religious contract between the actuality and the potential of man.

Human folly and cruelty were directly expressive of ignorance, of that injustice whereby the great inheritance of philosophic, artistic, scientific achievements had been transmitted only to a privileged caste. For both Vol-taire* and Matthew Arnold†—and between them they may be said to date and define the generations of cultural promise—there is an obvious congru-ence between the cultivation of the individual mind through formal knowl-edge and a melioration in the commanding qualities of life. Though they argued in different idioms and brought different elements to their syllogism, Voltaire and Arnold regarded as established the crucial lemma that the humanities humanize. The root of the "humane" is explicit in both terms, and etymology knits them close. All this is familiar ground.

But the proposition needs to be refined. Although concepts of "nur-ture," of "culture," and of social melioration or perfectibility were intimately meshed and, often, interchangeable, the precise fabric of the relations be-tween them, of the instrumentalities that led from one to the other, continued to be examined. We do find a good deal of boisterous confidence in the immediate correlation of better schooling with an improved society—particu-larly in American progressive doctrines and Victorian socialism. But we find also, at a higher plane of debate, a continual awareness of the complexity of the equation. The *Essays on a Liberal Education,* edited by F. W. Farrar in 1867, two years before Arnold's *Culture and Anarchy* and three years before the Education Act, are a representative example of how the general axiom of improvement through humanism was revalued, as it were, from within. What concerned Farrar, Henry Sidgwick, and their colleagues was, precisely, the limitations of the classical canon.‡ They were engaged in reexamining the orthodox notion of a classical literacy, and they were testing its appropriate-ness to the needs of an increasingly technological and socially diversified community.

In the most incisive of these essays Sidgwick argues for the extension of the concept of necessary culture to include modern letters and some com-petence in the sciences. Greek and Latin literature can no longer be said to comprise all essential knowledge, even in an idealized, paradigmatic form: the claim of these literatures "to give the best teaching in mental, ethical, and political philosophy" is rapidly passing away. Physical science "is now so

---

*François-Marie Arouet Voltaire (1694–1778), a leading liberal philosopher of the Englighten-ment; author of *Cardide* (1759).

†English poet, critic, essayist, and school inspector (1822–1888), who proposed a program of liberal arts education that he thought would help keep society reasonable and humane.

‡Those classic works from the past most honored and most taught.

bound up with all the interests of mankind" that some familiarity with it is indispensable to an understanding of and participation in "the present phase of the progress of humanity." In short, the techniques and substantive content of cultural transmission were under vigorous debate even at the height of nineteenth-century optimism. What was *not* under debate was the compelling inference that such transmission, if and wherever rightly carried out, would lead necessarily to a more stable, humanely responsible condition of man. "A liberal education," wrote Sidgwick, with every implication of stating the obvious, "has for its object to impart the highest culture, to lead youths to the most full, vigorous, and harmonious exercise, according to the best ideal attainable, of their active, cognitive, and aesthetic faculties." Set in full play, extended, gradually and with due regard to differing degrees of native capacity, to an ever-widening compass of society and the globe, such education would ensure a steadily rising quality of life. Where culture flourished, barbarism was, by definition, a nightmare from the past.

We know now that this is not so. We know that the formal excellence   5
and numerical extension of education need not correlate with increased social stability and political rationality. The demonstrable virtues of the *Gymnasium**
or of the *lycée*† are no guarantor of how or whether the city will vote at the next plebiscite. We now realize that extremes of collective hysteria and savagery can coexist with a parallel conservation and, indeed, further development of the institutions, bureaucracies, and professional codes of high culture. In other words, the libraries, museums, theatres, universities, research centers, in and through which the transmission of the humanities and of the sciences mainly takes place, can prosper next to the concentration camps. The discriminations and freshness of their enterprise may well suffer under the surrounding impress of violence and regimentation. But they suffer surprisingly little. Sensibility (particularly that of the performing artist), intelligence, scruple in learning, carry forward as in a neutral zone. We know also—and here is knowledge thoroughly documented but in no way, as yet, incorporated in a rational psychology—that obvious qualities of literate response, of aesthetic feeling, can coexist with barbaric, politically sadistic behavior in the same individual. Men such as Hans Frank who administered the "final solution" in eastern Europe were avid connoisseurs and, in some instances, performers of Bach and Mozart. We know of personnel in the bureaucracy of the torturers and of the ovens who cultivated a knowledge of Goethe, a love of Rilke.‡ The facile evasion, "such men did not understand the poems they read or the music they knew and seemed to play so well," will not do. There simply is no evidence that they were more obtuse than anyone else to the

---

*A German word referring to a secondary school for students preparing to enter a university.
†The French counterpart of the German *gymnasium*.
‡In *Language and Silence* (1967), Steiner expresses this point even more bluntly: "We know now that a man can read Goethe or Rilke in the evening, and go to his day's work at Auschwitz in the morning. . . . In what way does this knowledge bear on literature and society, on the hope, grown almost axiomatic from the time of Plato to that of Matthew Arnold, that culture is a humanizing force, that the energies of spirit are transferable to those of conduct?"

humane genius, to the enacted moral energies of great literature and of art. One of the principal works that we have in the philosophy of language, in the total reading of Hölderlin's poetry, was composed almost within earshot of a death camp. Heidegger's* pen did not stop nor his mind go mute.

Whenever I cite this material, I am met with the objection: "Why are 6 you astonished? Why did you expect otherwise? One ought always to have known that culture and humane action, literacy and political impulse, are in no necessary or sufficient correlation." This objection sounds cogent, but it is in fact inadequate to the enormity of the case. The insights we now have into the negative or, at the least, dialectically paradoxical and parodistic relations between culture and society are something new, and morally bewildering. They would have impressed the Enlightenment and much of the nineteenth century as a morbid fantasy (it is precisely Kierkegaard's and Nietzsche's† premonitions on this issue that set them apart). Our present knowledge of a negative transfer from civilization to behavior, in the individual and the society, runs counter to the faith, to the operative assumptions, on which the progress of education, of general literacy, of scholarship and the dissemination of the arts were grounded. What we now know makes a mock of the vision of history penetrated, made malleable by, intelligence and educated feeling—a vision common to Jefferson and to Marx, as it was to Arnold and the reformers of 1867.‡ To say that one "ought" to have known is a facile use of language. *Had* the Enlightenment and the nineteenth century understood that there could be no presumption of a carry-over from civilization to civility, from humanism to the humane, the springs of hope would have been staunched and much of the immense liberation of the mind and of society achieved over four generations been rendered impossible. No doubt, confidence should have been less. Perhaps the trust in culture was itself hubristic and blind to the countercurrents and nostalgias for destruction it carried within. It may be that the incapacity of reason and of political will to impede the massacres of 1915–17 ought to have proved a final warning as to the fragility and mutually isolated condition of the fabric of culture.

But our insights here (and they are strangely absent from Eliot's§ own 7 *Notes* of 1948) come after the facts. They are themselves—this is the main point—a part of desolation. No less than our technical competence to build Hell on earth, so our knowledge of the failure of education, of literate tradition, to bring "sweetness and light"‖ to men, is a clear symptom of what is

---

*Martin Heidegger (1889–1976), German philosopher with definite ties to the Nazi party during World War II.

†Søren Kierkegaard (1813–1855), Danish philosopher, and Friedrich Nietzsche (1844–1900), German philosopher, both of whom rejected the Enlightenment's and the liberals' optimism about the perfectibility of human nature and society.

‡1867 was the year of the Second Reform Bill in England that enfranchised about one in three males.

§T. S. Eliot (1888–1965), British poet and critic; wrote *Notes Toward the Definition of Culture* in 1948.

‖"Sweetness and light" was Matthew Arnold's phrase, roughly translatable as "reasonableness and intelligence."

lost. We are forced now to return to an earlier, Pascalian* pessimism, to a model of history whose logic derives from a postulate of original sin. We can subscribe today, all too readily, to de Maistre's view that the barbarism of modern politics, the regress of educated, technologically inventive man into slaughter enact a necessary working out of the eschatology of the Fall. But there is in our reversion to these earlier, more "realistic" paradigms an element which is spurious and therefore psychologically corrosive. Unlike Pascal or de Maistre, very few of us in fact hold a dogmatic, explicitly religious view of man's personal and social disasters. For most of us the logic of original trespass and the image of history as purgatorial are, at best, a metaphor. Our pessimistic vision, unlike that of a true Jansenist,† has neither a rationale of causality nor a hope in transcendent remission. We are caught in the middle. We cannot echo Carducci's‡ famous salute to the future:

> *Salute, o genti umane affaticate!*
> *Tutto trapassa, e nullo può morir.*
> *Noi troppo odiammo e sofferimo. Amate:*
> *Il mondo è bello e santo è l'avvenir.§*

But we cannot respond either, with full, honest acquiescence, to the Pascalian diagnosis of the cruelties and absurdities of the historical condition as a natural consequence of a primal theological fault.

This instability of essential terrain and the psychological evasions   8 which it entails, characterize much of our current posture. At once realistic and psychologically hollow, our new stoic or ironic pessimism is a determinant of a post-culture. Not to have known about the inhuman potentialities of cultured man what we now know was a formidable privilege. In the generations from Voltaire to Arnold, absence of such knowledge was not innocence but rather an enabling program for civilization.

We may be able to group these "irreparables" under an inclusive head-   9 ing. The loss of a geographic-sociological centrality, the abandonment or extreme qualification of the axiom of historical progress, our sense of the failure or severe inadequacies of knowledge and humanism in regard to social action—all these signify the end of an agreed hierarchic value-structure. Those binary cuts which organized social perception and which represented the domination of the cultural over the natural code are now blurred or rejected outright. Cuts between Western civilization and the rest, between the learned and the untutored, between the upper and the lower strata of society, between the authority of age and the dependence of youth, between

---

*Blaise Pascal (1623–1662), French scientist and philosopher who held the conservative view that human beings are vain, weak, self-serving and incapable of finding truth with their own resources.

†Pascal was a Jansenist.

‡Bartolommeo Carducci (1560–c.1610)—Italian painter, sculptor, and architect.

§Hail to you, oh wearied races of men! / Everything passes, and nothing can die. / We have hated and borne too much. Love one another: / The world is beauteous and the future is holy.

the sexes. These cuts were not only diacritical—defining the identity of the two units in relation to themselves and to each other—they were expressly horizontal. The line of division separated the higher from the lower, the greater from the lesser: civilization from retarded primitivism, learning from ignorance, social privilege from subservience, seniority from immaturity, men from women. And each time, "from" stood also for "above." It is the collapse, more or less complete, more or less conscious, of these hierarchized, definitional value-gradients (and can there be value without hierarchy?) which is now the major fact of our intellectual and social circumstance.

The horizontal "cuts" of the classic order have been made vertical and often indistinct. 10

Never again, I imagine, will a white statesman write as did Palmerston* in 1863, at the occasion of a punitive action in far places, "I am inclined to think that our relations with Japan are going through the usual and unavoidable stages of the Intercourse of strong and Civilised nations with weaker and less civilised ones" (even the capitalization speaks loud). A ubiquitous anthropology, relativistic, non-evaluative in its study of differing races and cultures, now pervades our image of "self" and "others." "Countercultures" and aggregates of individualized, ad hoc reference are replacing set discriminations between learning and illiteracy. The line between education and ignorance is no longer self-evidently hierarchic. Much of the mental performance of society now transpires in a middle zone of personal eclecticism. The altering tone and substance of relations between age groups is a commonplace, and one that penetrates almost every aspect of social usage. So, more recently, is the fission of traditional sexual modes. The typologies of women's liberation, of the new politically, socially ostentatious homosexuality (notably in the United States) and of "unisex" point to a deep reordering or disordering of long-established frontiers. "So loosly disally'd," in Milton's telling phrase, men and women are not only maneuvering in a neutral terrain of indistinction, but exchanging roles—sartorially, psychologically, in regard to economic and erotic functions which were formerly set apart. 11

Again, a general rubric suggests itself. A common formlessness or search for new forms has all but undermined classic age-lines, sexual divisions, class structures, and hierarchic gradients of mind and power. We are caught in a Brownian movement† at every vital, molecular level of individuation and society. And if I may carry the analogy one step further, the membranes through which social energies are current are now permeable and nonselective. 12

It is widely asserted that the rate of social change we are experiencing is unprecedented, that metamorphoses and hybridizations across lines of time, of sexuality, of race, are now occurring more quickly than ever before. Does this rate and universality of change reflect verifiable organic transfor- 13

---

*Henry John Temple, 3rd Viscount Palmerston, (1784–1865), British Prime Minister, 1855–1865.
†A constant zigzag movement; after Robert Brown (1773–1858), who first demonstrated the constant zigzag movement of colloidal dispersions in a liquid medium.

mations? This is a very difficult question to pose accurately, let alone to answer. We "undergo" much of reality, sharply filtered and pre-sensed, through the instant diagnostic sociology of the mass media. No previous society has mirrored itself with such profuse fascination. At present, models and mythologies of fact, quite often astute and seemingly comprehensive, are offered at bewildering short intervals. This rapidity and "metadepth" of explanation may be obscuring the distinction between what is a matter of fashion, of surface coloration, and what occurs at the internal levels of a psychological or social system. What we know of the evolutionary time-scale makes it highly improbable that psychophysiological changes are happening in a dramatic, observable rhythm. To take an example: far-reaching correlations are being drawn between a revolution in sexual mores and the presumed lowering in the age of menstruation. It would appear that this phenomenology is susceptible of exact statistical inquiry. But, in fact, material and methodological doubts abound. What cultures or communities are affected, and how many cases within them would constitute a critical mass? Are we dealing with primary or secondary symptoms, with a physiological change or one in the context of awareness and social acceptance? Granted the fact, is the correlation legitimate, or are parallel but essentially dissociated mechanisms at work? Skepticism is in order.

Yet there ought also to be a certain largesse and vulnerability of imagi- 14
nation. It is conceivable, to put it modestly, that current changes in patterns of nutrition, of temperature control, of quick travel across climates and time zones, that the prolongation of the average life-span, and the ingestion of the therapeutic and narcotic substances, *are* bringing on genuine modification of personality, and marginally, perhaps, of physique. Such changes could be defined as "intermediary mutations," somewhere between the organic and the modish—in the strong sense of that term. We have no exact vocabulary in which to express second-order psychosocial or sociophysiological metamorphoses. Nevertheless, these seem to me to be the most important variant in the whole of post-culture.

Much of this is common ground. So, also, is the insight, first expressed 15
by Benda,* still the acutest of cultural critics, that the breakdown of classic hierarchies would occur from within. Wherever a decisive breach has been opened in the lines of order, the sappers have tunneled from inside the city. The conscience of privilege, of seniority, of mandarin rights has turned against itself.

Less widely asked is the question of whether certain core-elements in 16
the classic hierarchy of values are even worth reanimating? Is there a conceivable defense of the concept of culture against the two principal attacks now being pressed home? Particularly if we adhere to Eliot's central proposition "that culture is not merely the sum of several activities, but a *way of life.*"

It is on the fragility and cost of that "way of life" that the attack has 17
borne. Why labor to elaborate and transmit culture if it did so little to stem

*Julien Benda (1867–1956), French philosopher and writer.

the inhuman, if there were in it deep-set ambiguities which, at times, even solicited barbarism? Secondly: granted that culture was a medium of human excellence and intellectual vantage, was the price paid for it too high? In terms of social and spiritual inequality. In regard to the ontological imbalance—it ran deeper than economics—between the privileged locale of intellectual and artistic achievement, and the excluded world of poverty and underdevelopment. Can it have been accident that a large measure of ostentatious civilization—in Periclean Athens, in the Florence of the Medicis, in sixteenth-century England, in the Versailles of the *grand siècle* and the Vienna of Mozart—was closely correlate with political absolutism, a firm caste system, and the surrounding presence of a subject populace? Great art, music, and poetry, the science of Bacon and of Laplace,* flourish under more or less totalitarian modes of social governance. Can this be hazard? How vital are the affinities between power relations and classic literacy (relations initiated in the teaching process)? Is not the very notion of culture tautological with élitism? How many of its major energies feed on the violence which is disciplined, contained within, yet ceremonially visible, in a traditional or repressive society? Hence Pisarev's† critique, echoed later in Orwell, of art and letters as instrumentalities of caste and régime.

These are the challenges put contemptuously by the dropout and loud 18 in the four-letter graffiti of the "counter-culture." What good did high humanism do the oppressed mass of the community? What use was it when barbarism came? What immortal poem has ever stopped or mitigated political terror—though a number have celebrated it? And, more searchingly: Do those for whom a great poem, a philosophic design, a theorem, are, in the final reckoning, the supreme value, not help the throwers of napalm by looking away, by cultivating in themselves a stance of "objective sadness" or historical relativism?

I have tried to suggest, throughout this essay, that there is no adequate 19 answer to the question of the frailty of culture. We can construe all kinds of post facto insight into the lack of correlation between literacy and politics, between the inheritance of Weimar‡ and the reality of Buchenwald§ not many kilometers away. But diagnosis after the event is, at best, a shallow and partial comprehension. So far as I can see, much of the harrowing puzzle remains.

The question as to whether a high culture is not inevitably meshed with 20 social injustice can be answered. It is not difficult to formulate an apologia for civilization based firmly and without cant on a model of history as privi-

*Francis Bacon (1561–1626), British philosopher and author, and Pierre-Simon de Laplace (1749–1827), French astronomer and mathematician; each served under absolutist monarchs.

†Dimitry Ivanovich Pisarev (1840–1868), Russian critic; foremost representative of Russian nihilism.

‡The city in Germany where the constitutional assembly that created the German republic, 1919–1933, met.

§A Nazi concentration camp near Weimar.

lege, as hierarchic order. One can say simply that the accomplishments of art, of speculative imagining, of the mathematicaland empirical sciences have been, are, will be, to an overwhelming extent, the creation of the gifted few. In the perspective of the evolution of the species towards an even more complete enlistment of the potentialities of the cortex—and the sum of history may be precisely that—it is vital to preserve the kind of political system in which high gifts are recognized and afforded the pressures under which they flourish. The existence of a Plato, of a Karl Friedrich Gauss, of a Mozart may go a surprisingly long way towards redeeming that of man. The immense majority of human biographies are a gray transit between domestic spasm and oblivion. For a truly cultured sensibility to deny this, under pretexts of liberal piety, is not only mendacious but rank ingratitude. A culture "lived" is one that draws for continuous, indispensable sustenance on the great works of the past, on the truths and beauties achieved in the tradition. It does not reckon against them the social harshness, the personal suffering, which so often have generated or made possible the symphony, the fresco, the metaphysic. Where it is absolutely honest, the doctrine of a high culture will hold the burning of a great library, the destruction of Galois* at twenty-one, or the disappearance of an important score, to be losses paradoxically but none the less decidedly out of proportion with common deaths, even on a large scale.

This is a coherent position. It may accord with deep-seated biological 21 realities. For perfectly obvious reasons, however, it is a position which few today are ready to put forward publicly or with conviction. It flies too drastically in the face of doubts about culture which we have seen to be justified. It is too crassly out of tune with pervasive ideals of humane respect and social concern. There is something histrionic and psychologically suspect even in the bare exercise of stating an élitist canon.

But it is important to see just why this is so. Using the terms I have 22 indicated, and made with complete honesty, a contemporary defense of culture as "a way of life" will nevertheless have a void at its center. To argue for order and classic values on a purely immanent, secular basis is, finally, implausible. In stressing this point Eliot is justified, and the *Notes towards the Definition of Culture* remain valid. But if the core of a theory of culture is "religious," that term ought not to be taken, as it so largely was by Eliot, in a particular sectarian sense. If only because of its highly ambiguous implication in the holocaust, Christianity cannot serve as the focus of a redefinition of culture, and Eliot's nostalgia for Christian discipline is now the most vulnerable aspect of his argument. I mean "religious" in a particular and more ancient sense. What is central to a true culture is a certain view of the relations between time and individual death.

The thrust of will which engenders art and disinterested thought, the 23 engaged response which alone can ensure its transmission to other human beings, to the future, are rooted in a gamble on transcendence. The writer or

*Evariste Galois (1811–1832), French mathematician who made important contributions to group theory; killed in a duel.

thinker means the words of the poem, the sinews of the argument, the
personae of the drama, to outlast his own life, to take on the mystery of
autonomous presence and presentness. The sculptor commits to the stone the
vitalities against and across time which will soon drain from his own living
hand. Art and mind address those who are not yet, even at the risk, deliberately incurred, of being unnoticed by the living.

There is nothing natural, nothing self-evident in this wager against   24
mortality, against the common, unharried promises of life. In the overwhelming majority of cases—and the gambler on transcendence knows this in advance—the attempt will be a failure, nothing will survive. There may be a
cancerous mania in the mere notion of producing great art or philosophic
shapes—acts, by definition, free of utility and immediate reward. Flaubert
howled like a man racked at the thought that Emma Bovary—his creature,
his contrivance of arrayed syllables—would be alive and real, long after he
himself had gone to a painful death. There is a calm enormity, the more
incisive for its deliberate scriptural echo, in Pope's assertion that "to follow
Poetry as one ought, one must forget father and mother, and cleave to it
alone." For "Poetry" in that sentence, one can read mathematics, music,
painting, astrophysics, or whatever else consumes the spirit with total demand.

Each time, the equation is one of ambitious sacrifice, of the obsession   25
to outlast, to outmaneuver the banal democracy of death. To die at thirty-five
but to have composed *Don Giovanni,* to know, as did Galois during the last
night of his twenty-one-year existence, that the pages he was writing would
alter the future forms of algebra and of space. Perhaps an insane conceit,
using that term in its stylistic sense, but one that is the transcendent source
of a classic culture.

We hear it proclaimed at the close of Pindar's Third Pythian Ode (in   26
Lattimore's version):

> *I will work out the divinity that is busy within my mind*
> *and tend the means that are mine.*
> *Might God only give me luxury and its power,*
> *I hope I should find glory that would rise higher hereafter.*
> *Nestor and Sarpedon of Lykia we know,*
> *men's speech, from the sounding words that smiths of song in their wisdom*
> *built to beauty. In the glory of poetry achievement of men*
> *blossoms long; but of that the accomplishment is given to few.*

Note the modulation from poetic action to aristocratic truth —"but of that
the accomplishment is given to few." It is not accidental. The trope of immortality persists in Western culture, is central to it, from Pindar to the time of
Mallarmé's vision of *le Livre,* "tenté à son insu par quiconque a écrit," which
is the very aim of the universe. The obsession is crystallized once more,
memorably, in Eluard's phrase "le dur désir de durer." Without such "harsh
longing" there may be human love and justice, mercy and scruple. But can

there be a true culture? Can civilization as we know it be underwritten by an immanent view of personal and social reality? Can it be vital without a logic of relation between "the divinity that is busy within my mind" and the hunger for a "glory that would rise higher hereafter"? And it is precisely that logic, with its inference of active afterlife in and through artistic, intellectual creation, which is "religious."

This logic and its idiom are now eroded. The notion, axiomatic in classic 27 art and thought, of sacrificing present life, present humanity, to the marginal chance of future literary or intellectual renown, grates on modern nerves. To younger people today, the code of "glory" of intellect and creative act is highly suspect. Many would see in it no more than romantic bathos or a disguised perpetuation of élitist idols. There are currently, particularly in the the United States, some fashionable, silly theories about total revolutions of consciousness. Mutations of internal structure do not occur at such rate. But in this key matter of the equivocations between *poiesis*—the artist's, the thinker's creation—and death, deep shifts of perspective *are* discernible. Psychologically, there is a gap of light years between the sensibility of my own schooling, in the French formal vein, with its obvious stress on the prestige of genius and the compulsion of creative survival, and the posture of my students today. Do they still name city squares after algebraists?

The causes of this change are multiple. They may involve elements as 28 different as the standardization of death in two world wars and the "bomb culture," and the emergence of a new collectivism. An analysis of these currents lies outside the scope of this essay, but the symptoms are plain to see. They include the ideology of the "happening" and of autodestructive artifacts, with their emphasis on the immediacy, unrepeatability, and ephemeral medium of the work. Aleatory music is a striking case of the diminution of creative authority in favor of collaborative, spontaneous shadow-play (Werner Henze has declared that there is exploitation and the menace of arbitrary power in the very function of the composer). More and more literary texts and works of art now offer themselves as collective and/or anonymous. The poetics of ecstasy and of group feeling regard the imprint of a single "great name" on the process of creation as archaic vanity. The audience is no longer an informed echo to the artist's talent, a respondent to and transmitter of his singular enterprise; it is joint creator in a conglomerate of freewheeling, participatory impulse. Away with the presumptions of permanence in a classic *œuvre,* away with masters.

It would be absurd to try and pass judgment on the merits of this new 29 "leveling"—I use the word because there are obscure but substantive precedents in seventeenth-century Adamic and millenary dreams of all men as artists and equal singers of the moment. I am only saying that if this revaluation of the criteria of "lastingness," of individual mastery against time, is as radical and far-reaching as it now seems, the core of the very concept of culture will have been broken. If the gamble on transcendence no longer seems worth the odds and we are moving into a utopia of the immediate, the value-structure of our civilization will alter, after at least three millennia, in ways almost unforseeable.

Speaking with the serene malice of age and work done, Robert Graves 30 has recently asserted that "Nothing can stop the wide destruction of our ancient glories, amenities and pleasures." This may be too large a sweep, and in place of "destruction" it might be better to say "transmutation," "change." Nevertheless, it is almost certain that the old vocabulary is exhausted, that the forms of classic culture cannot be rebuilt on any general scale.

Questions for Discussion

1. In characterizing the views of nineteenth-century proponents of a traditional humanistic education, Steiner attributes a conviction to them that "where culture flourished, barbarism was, by definition, a nightmare from the past" (end of ¶ 4). Steiner seems to take it for granted that the inaccuracy of this view throws doubt on the truth of *any* claims positing a connection between one's character and one's education. Does it really seem reasonable to claim that education has *nothing* to do with your personal morality? Does the fact that some of the worst Nazi crimes were committed by people of "culture" with humanistic educations prove that education has no influence at all on character? Those in your class who tend to agree with Steiner and those who think he has overstated his case might consider debating the best reasons they can produce in support of each side.

2. George Steiner is clearly a product of the kind of education he questions the value of in this essay. Born of Austrian-Jewish parents in Paris, he has a cosmopolitan background. He took a baccalaureate in literature at the University of Paris in 1947. The following year he received a B.A. degree from the University of Chicago, and in 1950 he took an M.A. and won the Bell Prize in American literature at Harvard University. He is fluent in English, French, and German, and has a literary mastery of Greek, Latin, and most of the Romance languages. On a Rhodes scholarship, he went to Balliol College, Oxford University, where he won the Chancellor's Essay Prize for an essay titled "Malice" in 1952 and received his doctorate in philosophy in 1955. In addition to his writing, Steiner is an Extraordinary (that is, non-resident, although he is certainly extraordinary in the usual sense as well) Fellow of Churchill College, Cambridge University, and professor of English and comparative literature at the University of Geneva. His writing clearly shows the depth and breadth of his erudition. How easy would it be to separate George Steiner the moral (or immoral) person from his saturated education in the traditional Western values?

Where is the "real" Steiner if he is not both *in* and at the same time a *product* of that education? Do you think he could claim that he is whatever he would have been *without* this kind of education? If you think he would concede that his education has been instrumental in forming his character—or if, in any event, *you* feel that it has been instrumental—how does this view affect the argument about education that he raises in his essay?

3. In paragraph 17, Steiner asks a seemingly simple question: "Why labor to elaborate and transmit culture if it did so little to stem the inhuman, if there were in it deep-set ambiguities which, at times, even solicited barbarism?" Assuming for the moment that he is right, that culture is guilty of everything he accuses it of, does it therefore follow that culture should be abandoned, that it should never be taught? Can culture be defended only if it is perfectly innocent? Or can it be defended on some grounds and criticized on others?

4. In paragraphs 23–29, Steiner argues that one of the impulses that has always lain at the core of classical culture—the impulse for transcendence, the creation of works that will endure in time, transcending the life of their creator—has tended to produce "the master," the artist or the intellectual who, in his dedication to art, philosophy, mathematics, or some other discipline, achieves preeminent status. He further argues that reverence for the master is today being challenged by a more democratic and collaborative set of attitudes: "More and more literary texts and works of art now offer themselves as collective and/or anonymous. . . .

   Away with the presumptions of permanence in a classic *œuvre,* away with masters" (¶28). Do you find this attitude to be true in the classes you are taking at college? Do you find your teachers or other students expressing an attitude of irreverence or resentment toward the great masters of classical culture? If so, what feelings seem to justify this attitude? How were the masters and the classics of traditional culture treated in your high school education? What attitude do you think students *should* take toward them?

Suggested Essay Topics

1. One of the omissions in Steiner's essay is the concrete analysis of any particular work of classical culture. He does not show how the incipient elitism or barbarism that he accuses many classical works in the humanities of containing actually shows through in individual works. Decide whether you wish to support or attack Steiner's position and then do so by choosing a single work—one that you studied in high school or are studying now—and then analyzing its "message" or its qualities in order to show that it either does or does not contain incipient elitism or appeals to barbarism. Direct your essay to Steiner or to your fellow students.

2. Support or refute Steiner's position about traditional education by analyzing your own education and evaluating its influence on your basic values. Try to consider such issues as whether your education has made it more

or less likely, or whether it has had no influence at all, on the likelihood that you would ever commit any kind of wrong: thievery, violence, deceit, and so on; whether your education has increased, decreased, or had no influence on your ability to identify with the sorrows, sufferings, and joys of other people; whether your education plays a positive role, a negative role, or no role at all in the views you hold on such social issues as homelessness, poverty, public art, or public education.

+2+

REASON AND CRITICAL THINKING

Thinking Critically, Thinking Together

He who knows only his own side of the case, knows little of that.
His reasons may be good, and no one may have
been able to refute them. But if he is equally unable to refute
the reasons on the opposite side; if he does not
so much as know what they are, he has no ground
for preferring either opinion.
John Stuart Mill

If some great Power would agree to make me always think
what is true and do what is right, on condition of being turned into
a sort of clock and wound up every morning
before I got out of bed, I should instantly close with the offer.
Thomas Henry Huxley

Although it might belong to Socrates and other minds
of the like craft to acquire virtue by reason, the human race
would long since have ceased to be, had its preservation depended
only on the reasonings of the individuals composing it.
Rousseau

It is not the feeling sure of a doctrine (be it what it may)
which I call an assumption of infallibility. It is the undertaking
to decide that question *for others,* without allowing
them to hear what can be said on the contrary side.
John Stuart Mill

Stephen Jay Gould

Stephen Jay Gould (b. 1941) is a famous Harvard scientist who, in a series of books with such intriguing titles as The Flamingo's Smile, Hen's Teeth and Horse's Toes, *and* The Panda's Thumb, *has done much to interpret evolutionary theory for twentieth-century Americans. Like Thomas Huxley a century ago, he is a popularizer—but not a vulgar one. Instead of popularizing science by simplifying it or by patronizing his audience, Gould compliments his readers by assuming they are intelligent enough to follow a well-made argument about a complex subject. In addition, then, to being a respected scientist, Gould is also a forceful and clear writer, a noted lecturer, and a gifted teacher.*

In looking for concrete, dramatic examples of the possible advantages of critical thinking in everyday life, one could hardly do better than examine Gould's essay on how to think critically about statistics. Nothing less than Gould's life was at stake. It was crucial that he know how to interpret correctly the statistics relayed to him by his doctor. Having been diagnosed with one of the most serious forms of cancer, Gould read in the literature that the median life expectancy after the diagnosis of such cancer was eight months.

Did this statistic mean that Gould should expect to die in eight months? Most people would probably interpret the statistic in just this way. Gould, however, knows what statistics really mean in terms of predictability. He knows how much they "prove" and how much they do not. He arrived at a quite different interpretation than most of us would probably reach, and he is certain that his knowledge of how to interpret statistics has had much to do with keeping him alive.

One important issue Gould's essay raises is the relationship between critical thinking as a mode *of thinking and knowledge as the* content *we think about. "Critical thinking" has become something of a buzzword these days among teachers and administrators, as if teaching students to "think critically" were a panacea for*

*all educational ills. A significant number of educators are proposing special courses in
critical thinking that are supposed to teach a generic set of thinking skills useable in
any context.*

*But critical thinking is not that easy, not so transferable from one context to
another that a few easy tricks will make it possible. It is true that some features of
critical thinking will be common to different contexts, but it is also true that productive
critical thinking inside a context requires* knowledge of that context, *not just a
grasp of certain thinking* skills. *Gould had to be able to do more than ask the critical
questions "Why?", "What are the assumptions here?", and so on. He had to know
how statistics are generated, how they apply to a population, and how they are properly
interpreted. In other words, he shows that critical thinking occurs as a dynamic
relationship between content and method, between knowledge and the ways in which
we think about it.*

*Gould also shows that content and method even in a field that most people find
remote from their personal lives—statistics—can, in certain instances, have a deeply
human significance.*

THE MEDIAN ISN'T THE
MESSAGE

From Discover, June 1985.

My life has recently intersected, in a most personal way, two of Mark   1
Twain's famous quips. One I shall defer to the end of this essay. The other
(sometimes attributed to Disraeli), identifies three species of mendacity, each
worse than the one before—lies, damned lies, and statistics.

Consider the standard example of stretching truth with numbers—a   2
case quite relevant to my story. Statistics recognizes different measures of
an "average," or central tendency. The *mean* is our usual concept of an overall average—add up the items and divide them by the number of sharers
(100 candy bars collected for five kids next Halloween will yield 20 for each
in a just world). The *median,* a different measure of central tendency, is the
halfway point. If I line up five kids by height, the median child is shorter
than two and taller than the other two (who might have trouble getting
their mean share of the candy). A politician in power might say with pride,
"The mean income of our citizens is $15,000 per year." The leader of the
opposition might retort, "But half our citizens make less than $10,000 per
year." Both are right, but neither cites a statistic with impassive objectivity.
The first invokes a mean, the second a median. (Means are higher than
medians in such cases because one millionaire may outweigh hundreds of
poor people in setting a mean; but he can balance only one mendicant in
calculating a median).

The larger issue that creates a common distrust or contempt for statistics   3
is more troubling. Many people make an unfortunate and invalid separation
between heart and mind, or feeling and intellect. In some contemporary
traditions, abetted by attitudes stereotypically centered upon Southern California, feelings are exalted as more "real" and the only proper basis for
action—if it feels good, do it—while intellect gets short shrift as a hang-up
of outmoded elitism. Statistics, in this absurd dichotomy, often become the
symbol of the enemy. As Hilaire Belloc wrote, "Statistics are the triumph of
the quantitative method, and the quantitative method is the victory of sterility and death."

This is a personal story of statistics, properly interpreted, as profoundly   4
nurturant and life-giving. It declares holy war on the downgrading of intellect
by telling a small story about the utility of dry, academic knowledge about
science. Heart and head are focal points of one body, one personality.

In July 1982, I learned that I was suffering from abdominal mesothe-   5
lioma, a rare and serious cancer usually associated with exposure to asbestos.
When I revived after surgery, I asked my first question of my doctor and
chemotherapist: "What is the best technical literature about mesothelioma?"
She replied, with a touch of diplomacy (the only departure she has ever made
from direct frankness), that the medical literature contained nothing really
worth reading.

Of course, trying to keep an intellectual away from literature works   6
about as well as recommending chastity to *Homo sapiens,* the sexiest primate
of all. As soon as I could walk, I made a beeline for Harvard's Countway
medical library and punched mesothelioma into the computer's bibliographic
search program. An hour later, surrounded by the latest literature on abdominal mesothelioma, I realized with a gulp why my doctor had offered that
humane advice. The literature couldn't have been more brutally clear: mesothelioma is incurable, with a median mortality of only eight months after
discovery. I sat stunned for about fifteen minutes, then smiled and said to
myself: so that's why they didn't give me anything to read. Then my mind
started to work again, thank goodness.

If a little learning could ever be a dangerous thing, I had encountered   7
a classic example. Attitude clearly matters in fighting cancer. We don't know
why (from my old-style materialistic perspective, I suspect that mental states
feed back upon the immune system). But match people with the same cancer
for age, class, health, socioeconomic status, and, in general, those with positive attitudes, with a strong will and purpose for living, with commitment to
struggle, with an active response to aiding their own treatment and not just
a passive acceptance of anything doctors say, tend to live longer. A few
months later I asked Sir Peter Medawar, my personal scientific guru and a
Nobelist in immunology, what the best prescription for success against cancer
might be. "A sanguine personality," he replied. Fortunately (since one can't
reconstruct oneself at short notice and for a definite purpose), I am, if anything, even-tempered and confident in just this manner.

Hence the dilemma for humane doctors: since attitude matters so criti-   8
cally, should such a sombre conclusion be advertised, especially since few
people have sufficient understanding of statistics to evaluate what the statements really mean? From years of experience with the small-scale evolution
of Bahamian land snails treated quantitatively, I have developed this technical knowledge—and I am convinced that it played a major role in saving my
life. Knowledge is indeed power, in Bacon's proverb.

The problem may be briefly stated: What does "median mortality of   9
eight months" signify in our vernacular? I suspect that most people, without
training in statistics, would read such a statement as "I will probably be dead
in eight months"—the very conclusion that must be *avoided,* since it isn't so,
and since attitude matters so much.

I was not, of course, overjoyed, but I didn't read the statement in this   10
vernacular way either. My technical training enjoined a different perspective
on "eight months median mortality." The point is a subtle one, but profound—for it embodies the distinctive way of thinking in my own field of
evolutionary biology and natural history.

We still carry the historical baggage of a Platonic heritage that seeks   11
sharp essences and definite boundaries. (Thus we hope to find an unambiguous "beginning of life" or "definition of death," although nature often comes
to us as irreducible continua.) This Platonic heritage, with its emphasis on
clear distinctions and separated immutable entities, leads us to view statistical
measures of central tendency wrongly, indeed opposite to the appropriate
interpretation in our actual world of variation, shadings, and continua. In
short, we view means and medians as the hard "realities," and the variation
that permits their calculation as a set of transient and imperfect measurements of this hidden essence. If the median is the reality and variation around
the median just a device for its calculation, the "I will probably be dead in
eight months" may pass as a reasonable interpretation.

But all evolutionary biologists know that variation itself is nature's only   12
irreducible essence. Variation is the hard reality, not a set of imperfect measures for a central tendency. Means and medians are the abstractions. Therefore, I looked at the mesothelioma statistics quite differently—and not only
because I am an optimist who tends to see the doughnut instead of the hole,
but primarily because I know that variation itself is the reality. I had to place
myself amidst the variation.

When I learned about the eight-month median, my first intellectual   13
reaction was: fine, half the people will live longer; now what are my chances
of being in that half. I read for a furious and nervous hour and concluded,
with relief: damned good. I possessed every one of the characteristics conferring a probability of longer life: I was young; my disease had been recognized
in a relatively early stage; I would receive the nation's best medical treatment;
I had the world to live for; I knew how to read the data properly and not
despair.

5.10

Another technical point then added even more solace. I immediately 14
recognized that the distribution of variation about the eight-month median
would almost surely be what statisticians call "right skewed." (In a symmetrical distribution, the profile of variation to the left of the central tendency is
a mirror image of variation to the right. In skewed distributions, variation to
one side of the central tendency is more stretched out—left skewed if extended to the the left, right skewed if stretched out to the right) The distribution of variation had to be right skewed, I reasoned. After all, the left of the
distribution contains an irrevocable lower boundary of zero (since mesothelioma can only be identified at death or before). Thus there isn't much room
for the distribution's lower (or left) half—it must be scrunched up between
zero and eight months. But the upper (or right) half can extend out for years
and years, even if nobody ultimately survives. The distribution must be right
skewed, and I needed to know how long the extended tail ran—for I had
already concluded that my favorable profile made me a good candidate for
that part of the curve.

The distribution was, indeed, strongly right skewed, with a long tail 15
(however small) that extended for several years above the eight month median. I saw no reason why I shouldn't be in that small tail, and I breathed a
very long sigh of relief. My technical knowledge had helped. I had read the
graph correctly. I had asked the right question and found the answers. I had
obtained, in all probability, that most precious of all possible gifts in the
circumstances—substantial time. I didn't have to stop and immediately follow Isaiah's injunction to Hezekiah—set thine house in order: for thou shalt
die, and not live. I would have time to think, to plan, and to fight.

One final point about statistical distributions. They apply only to a 16
prescribed set of circumstances—in this case to survival with mesothelioma
under conventional modes of treatment. If circumstances change, the distribution may alter. I was placed on an experimental protocol of treatment
and, if fortune holds, will be in the first cohort of a new distribution with
high median and a right tail extending to death by natural causes at advanced old age.

It has become, in my view, a bit too trendy to regard the acceptance of 17
death as something tantamount to intrinsic dignity. Of course I agree with
the preacher of Ecclesiastes that there is a time to love and a time to die—and
when my skein runs out I hope to face the end calmly and in my own way.
For most situations, however, I prefer the more martial view that death is the
ultimate enemy—and I find nothing reproachable in those who rage mightily
against the dying of the light.

The swords of battle are numerous, and none more effective than 18
humor. My death was announced at a meeting of my colleagues in Scotland,
and I almost experienced the delicious pleasure of reading my obituary
penned by one of my best friends (the so-and-so got suspicious and checked;
he too is a statistician, and didn't expect to find me so far out on the [right]
tail). Still, the incident provided my first good laugh after the diagnosis. Just

think, I almost got to repeat Mark Twain's most famous line of all: the reports
of my death are greatly exaggerated.

Questions for Discussion

1. How many of you caught the pun in Gould's title, "The Median Isn't the
   Message"? Marshall McLuhan (1911–1980), the Canadian communications theorist, wrote a book (with Quentin Fiore), *The Medium Is the Message*
   (1967), the title of which became a thesis about modern culture so commonly used that, during the late sixties and early seventies, it had a
   meaning even for people who had never read or even heard of the book.
   Have you ever personally used or heard used "the medium is the message"? If so, did you know its origin? How does Gould's pun help him
   express his own thesis?

2. Does anyone in your class recognize the allusion to Theodore Roethke's
   poem in paragraph 17 ("I find nothing reproachable in those who rage
   mightily against the dying of the light")? Almost certainly someone will.
   If not, however, send a volunteer to look up the poem in the library and
   explain to the class both the allusion and Gould's use of it.

3. Does anyone in class recognize the classical allusion in Gould's statement
   that "when my skein runs out I hope to face the end calmly" (¶17)? Again,
   it is nearly certain that someone will, but, if not, find another volunteer
   to look up the "Fates" in a classical or mythological "companion" (a kind
   of dictionary or mini-encyclopedia on classical myths and literary topics)
   and report on the allusion and its use to the rest of the class.

4. Can you explain in your own words what Gould means by "variations is
   the hard reality, not a set of imperfect measures for a central tendency.
   Means and medians are the abstractions" (¶12)? How does this way of
   looking at means and medians differ from the way Gould thinks most
   people would look at them?

5. Why would a graph representing the mortality of mesothelioma sufferers
   be "skewed right"? What does this mean? Why would the left side of the
   graph be "scrunched up between zero and eight months" (¶14)?

Suggested Essay Topics

1. Conduct an informal (and not very scientific) survey in which you type
   two questions on a piece of paper, allowing three or four inches under each
   question for people's answers. Make question 1 the following: "Survival
   rates for mesothelioma, an asbestos-caused cancer, are described as 'a
   median mortality of eight months after discovery.' Explain what this description means." Make question 2: "Give appropriate reasons or definitions to support or explain the answer you gave to question 1." Make 10

or 15 copies of your questions and give them to people to answer. Then write an essay, directed at those who took the survey, in which you report on the various understandings of the sentences you asked them to interpret. Finally, evaluate the accuracy of the responses based on what Gould says about the proper interpretation of such statistics.

2. Choose from a newspaper, magazine, or other public source some statistic that interests you. Pick a statistic that is simply announced but not accompanied by the kinds of explanations that would explain its proper uses and interpretations. Take the statistic to some qualified expert on the faculty and try to get an explanation of how to interpret the statistic correctly, the kind of explanation that Gould provides for interpreting the statistic about survival rates for mesothelioma sufferers. (If the statistic you choose is about populations, for example, take it to a faculty member in sociology; if it is about mental health sufferers, take it to someone in clinical psychology; if it is about acid rain or some other environmental issue, take it to someone in environmental studies or chemistry; and so on.) Then write an essay directed to the author who used the statistic, either showing what the statistic really means, or at least showing what kinds of explanations and commentary needed to accompany the statistic to make it really meaningful to the reader.

Elaine Morgan

In this essay Elaine Morgan (b. 1920), Welsh author and teacher, criticizes male prejudices revealed in current evolutionary theory. Her criticism is not that all male biologists and anthropologists are malicious male chauvinists but that many of them are simply sloppy thinkers. Androcentric (male-centered) thinking has been around for so long, she argues (¶10), and has seemed so unquestionably true that few male scientists—despite their commitment, as scientists, to open-mindedness and neutral observation—can break through the crust of inherited prejudices and look clearly at evolutionary theory's supporting ideas and data.

She supports her own position by re-examining notions that have been long accepted as adequate accounts of human development. Without indulging in technical or abstract language, relying simply on careful reasoning and fresh vision, she shows that if scientists had thought as hard about women as they have about men, the inadequacy of their accounts would have been revealed long ago.

You have undoubtedly been told by your teachers over the years that having good reasons for your opinions is perhaps more important than having good opinions. And you may recall occasions on which being forced to support your opinions with good reasons made you see how few you had or how flimsy they were. The most useful part of your education is learning how to ask yourself the kind of penetrating questions that your best teachers have always asked you, learning how to criticize your own ideas by using the same hard tests they have employed. The purging of error, the straightening of twisted logic, the reformulation of ideas, and the search for new information in the light of new perspectives—these are the grounds of progress in all thinking.

By showing how to ask "Why?" and "How do you know that?" about "self-evident" opinions, Morgan exemplifies not only the healthy activity of critical thinking within a discipline but also the kind of critical thinking that education, at its best, teaches us to do on our own.

THE MAN-MADE MYTH

Chapter 1 of *The Descent of Woman* (1972).

According to the Book of Genesis, God first created man. Woman was not only an afterthought, but an amenity. For close on two thousand years this holy scripture was believed to justify her subordination and explain her inferiority; for even as a copy she was not a very good copy. There were differences. She was not one of His best efforts. 1

There is a line in an old folk song that runs: "I called my donkey a horse gone wonky." Throughout most of the literature dealing with the differences between the sexes there runs a subtle underlying assumption that woman is a man gone wonky; that woman is a distorted version of the original blueprint; that they are the norm, and we are the deviation. 2

It might have been expected that when Darwin came along and wrote an entirely different account of *The Descent of Man,* this assumption would have been eradicated, for Darwin didn't believe she was an afterthought: he believed her origin was at least contemporaneous with man's. It should have led to some kind of breakthrough in the relationship between the sexes. But it didn't. 3

Almost at once men set about the congenial and fascinating task of working out an entirely new set of reasons why woman was manifestly inferior and irreversibly subordinate, and they have been happily engaged in this ever since. Instead of theology they use biology, and ethology, and primatology, but they use them to reach the same conclusions. 4

They are now prepared to debate the most complex problems of economic reform not in terms of the will of God, but in terms of the sexual behavior patterns of the cichlid fish; so that if a woman claims equal pay or the right to promotion there is usually an authoritative male thinker around to deliver a brief homily on hormones, and point out that what she secretly intends by this, and what will inevitably result, is the "psychological castration" of the men in her life. 5

Now, that may look to us like a stock piece of emotional blackmail—like the woman who whimpers that if Sonny doesn't do as she wants him to do, then Mother's going to have one of her nasty turns. It is not really surprising 6 that most women who are concerned to win themselves a new and better status in society tend to sheer away from the whole subject of biology and origins, and hope that we can ignore all that and concentrate on ensuring that in the future things will be different.

I believe this is a mistake. The legend of the jungle heritage and the 7 evolution of man as a hunting carnivore has taken root in man's mind as firmly as Genesis ever did. He may even genuinely believe that equal pay will do something terrible to his gonads. He has built a beautiful theoretical construction, with himself on the top of it, buttressed with a formidable array of scientifically authenticated facts. We cannot dispute the facts. We should not attempt to ignore the facts. What I think we can do is to suggest that the currently accepted interpretation of the facts is not the only possible one.

I have considerable admiration for scientists in general, and evolution- 8 ists and ethologists in particular, and though I think they have sometimes gone astray, it has not been purely through prejudice. Partly it is due to sheer semantic accident—the fact that "man" is an ambiguous term. It means the species; it also means the male of the species. If you begin to write a book about man or conceive a theory about man you cannot avoid using this word. You cannot avoid using a pronoun as a substitute for the word, and you will use the pronoun "he" as a simple matter of linguistic convenience. But before you are halfway through the first chapter a mental image of this evolving creature begins to form in your mind. It will be a male image, and he will be the hero of the story: everything and everyone else in the story will relate to him.

All this may sound like a mere linguistic quibble or a piece of feminist 9 petulance. If you stay with me, I hope to convince you it's neither. I believe the deeply rooted semantic confusion between "man" as a male and "man" as a species has been fed back into and vitiated a great deal of the speculation that goes on about the origins, development, and nature of the human race.

A very high proportion of the thinking on these topics is androcentric 10 (male-centered) in the same way as pre-Copernican thinking was geocentric. It's just as hard for man to break the habit of thinking of himself as central to the species as it was to break the habit of thinking of himself as central to the universe. He sees himself quite unconsciously as the main line of evolution, with a female satellite revolving around him as the moon revolves around the earth. This not only causes him to overlook valuable clues to our ancestry, but sometimes leads him into making statements that are arrant and demonstrable nonsense.

The longer I went on reading his own books about himself, the more 11 I longed to find a volume that would begin: "When the first ancestor of the human race descended from the trees, she had not yet developed the mighty brain that was to distinguish her so sharply from all other species. . . ."

Of course, she was no more the first ancestor than he was—but she was 12 no *less* the first ancestor, either. She was there all along, contributing half the genes to each succeeding generation. Most of the books forget about her for most of the time. They drag her onstage rather suddenly for the obligatory chapter on Sex and Reproduction, and then say: "All right, love, you can go now," while they get on with the real meaty stuff about the Mighty Hunter with his lovely new weapons and his lovely new straight legs racing across the Pleistocene plains. Any modifications in her morphology are taken to be imitations of the Hunter's evolution, or else designed solely for his delectation.

Evolutionary thinking has been making great strides lately. Archeolo-   13
gists, ethologists, paleontologists, geologists, chemists, biologists, and physicists are closing in from all points of the compass on the central area of mystery that remains. For despite the frequent triumph dances of researchers coming up with another jawbone or another statistic, some part of the miracle is still unaccounted for. Most of their books include some such phrase as: ". . . the early stages of man's evolutionary progress remain a total mystery." "Man is an accident, the culmination of a series of highly improbable coincidences. . . ." "Man is a product of circumstances special to the point of disbelief." They feel there is still something missing, and they don't know what.

The trouble with specialists is that they tend to think in grooves. From   14
time to time something happens to shake them out of that groove. Robert Ardrey tells how such enlightenment came to Dr. Kenneth Oakley when the first Australopithecus remains had been unearthed in Africa: "The answer flashed without warning in his own large-domed head: 'Of course we believed that the big brain came first! We assumed that the first man was an Englishman!' " Neither he, nor Ardrey in relating the incident, noticed that he was still making an equally unconscious, equally unwarrantable assumption. One of these days an evolutionist is going to strike a palm against his large-domed head and cry: "Of course! We assumed the first human being was a man!"

First, let's have a swift recap of the story as currently related, for despite   15
all the new evidence recently brought to light, the generally accepted picture of human evolution has changed very little.

Smack in the center of it remains the Tarzanlike figure of the prehomi-   16
nid male who came down from the trees, saw a grassland teeming with game, picked up a weapon, and became a Mighty Hunter.

Almost everything about us is held to have derived from this. If we walk   17
erect it was because the Mighty Hunter had to stand tall to scan the distance for his prey. If we lived in caves it was because hunters need a base to come home to. If we learned to speak it was because hunters need to plan the next safari and boast about the last. Desmond Morris, pondering on the shape of a woman's breasts, instantly deduces that they evolved because her mate became a Mighty Hunter, and defends this preposterous proposition with the greatest ingenuity. There's something about the Tarzan figure which has them all mesmerized.

I find the whole yarn pretty incredible. It is riddled with mysteries, and   18
inconsistencies, and unanswered questions. Even more damning than the unanswered questions are the questions that are never even asked, because,

as Professor Peter Medawar has pointed out, "scientists tend not to ask themselves questions until they can see the rudiments of an answer in their minds." I shall devote this chapter to pointing out some of these problems before outlining a new version of the Naked Ape story [in following chapters not reprinted here] which will suggest at least possible answers to every one of them, and fifteen or twenty others besides.

The first mystery is, "What happened during the Pliocene?"   19

There is a wide acceptance now of the theory that the human story   20
began in Africa. Twenty million years ago in Kenya, there existed a flourishing population of apes of generalized body structure and of a profusion of types from the size of a small gibbon up to that of a large gorilla. Dr. L. S. B. Leakey has dug up their bones by the hundred in the region of Lake Victoria, and they were clearly doing very well there at the time. It was a period known as the Miocene. The weather was mild, the rainfall was heavier than today, and the forests were flourishing. So far, so good.

Then came the Pliocene drought. Robert Ardrey writes of it: "No man   21
can apprehend in terms of any possible human experience the duration of the Pliocene. Ten desiccated years were enough, a quarter of a century ago, to produce in the American Southwest that maelstrom of misery, the dust bowl. To the inhabitant of the region the ten years must have seemed endless. But the African Pliocene lasted twelve million."

On the entire African continent no Pliocene fossil bed has ever been   22
found. During this period many promising Miocene ape species were, not surprisingly, wiped out altogether. A few were trapped in dwindling pockets of forest and when the Pliocene ended they reappeared as brachiating apes—specialized for swinging by their arms.

Something astonishing also reappeared—the Australopithecines, first   23
discovered by Professor Raymond Dart in 1925 and since unearthed in considerable numbers by Dr. Leakey and others.

Australopithecus emerged from his horrifying twelve-million-year or-   24
deal much refreshed and improved. The occipital condyles of his skull suggest a bodily posture approaching that of modern man, and the orbital region, according to Sir Wilfred le Gros Clark, has "a remarkably human appearance." He was clever, too. His remains have been found in the Olduvai Gorge in association with crude pebble tools that have been hailed as the earliest beginning of human culture. Robert Ardrey says: "We entered the [Pliocene] crucible a generalized creature bearing only the human potential. We emerged a being lacking only a proper brain and a chin. What happened to us along the way?" The sixty-four-thousand-dollar question: "What happened to them? Where did they go?"

Second question: "Why did they stand upright?" The popular versions   25
skim very lightly over this patch of thin ice. Desmond Morris says simply: "With strong pressure on them to increase their prey-killing prowess, they became more upright—fast, better runners." Robert Ardrey says equally simply: "We learned to stand erect in the first place as a necessity of the hunting life."

But wait a minute. We were quadrupeds. These statements imply that 26
a quadruped suddenly discovered that he could move faster on two legs than
on four. Try to imagine any other quadruped discovering that—a cat? a dog?
a horse?—and you'll see that it's totally nonsensical. Other things being
equal, four legs are bound to run faster than two. The bipedal development
was violently unnatural.

Stoats, gophers, rabbits, chimpanzees, will sit or stand bipedally to gaze 27
into the distance, but when they want speed they have sense enough to use
all the legs they've got. The only quadrupeds I can think of that can move
faster on two legs than four are things like kangaroos—and a small lizard
called the Texas boomer, and he doesn't keep it up for long. The secret in
these cases is a long heavy counterbalancing tail which we certainly never
had. You may say it was a natural development for a primate because primates sit erect in trees—but *was* it natural? Baboons and macaques have been
largely terrestrial for millions of years without any sign of becoming bipedal.

George A. Bartholomew and Joseph B. Birdsell point out: ". . . the 28
extreme rarity of bipedalism among animals suggests that it is inefficient
except under very special circumstances. Even modern man's unique vertical
locomotion when compared to that of quadrupedal mammals, is relatively
ineffective. . . . A significant nonlocomotor advantage must have resulted."

What was this advantage? The Tarzanists suggest that bipedalism en- 29
abled this ape to race after game while carrying weapons—in the first instance, presumably pebbles. But a chimp running off with a banana (or a
pebble), if he can't put it in his mouth, will carry it in one hand and gallop
along on the others, because even *three* legs are faster than two. So what was
our ancestor supposed to be doing? Shambling along with a rock in each
hand? Throwing boulders that took two hands to lift?

No. There must have been a pretty powerful reason why we were 30
constrained over a long period of time to walk about on our hind legs *even
though it was slower.* We need to find that reason.

Third question: How did the ape come to be using these weapons, 31
anyway? Again Desmond Morris clears this one lightly, at a bound: "With
strong pressure on them to increase their prey-killing prowess . . . their hands
became strong efficient weapon-holders." Compared to Morris, Robert Ardrey is obsessed with weapons, which he calls "mankind's most significant
cultural endowment." Yet his explanation of how it all started is as cursory
as anyone else's: "In the first evolutionary hour of the human emergence we
became sufficiently skilled in the use of weapons to render redundant our
natural primate daggers" (i.e., the large prehominid canine teeth).

But wait a minute—how? and why? Why did one, and only one, species 32
of those Miocene apes start using weapons? A cornered baboon will fight a
leopard; a hungry baboon will kill and eat a chicken. He could theoretically
pick up a chunk of flint and forget about his "natural primate daggers," and
become a Mighty Hunter. He doesn't do it, though. Why did we? Sarel Eimerl
and Irven de Vore point out in their book *The Primates:*

"Actually, it takes quite a lot of explaining. For example, if an animal's 33 normal mode of defense is to flee from a predator, it flees. If its normal method of defense is to fight with its teeth, it fights with its teeth. It does not suddenly adopt a totally new course of action, such as picking up a stick or a rock and throwing it. The idea would simply not occur to it, and even if it did, the animal would have no reason to suppose that it would work."

Now primates do acquire useful tool-deploying habits. A chimpanzee 34 will use a stick to extract insects from their nests, and a crumpled leaf to sop up water. Wolfgang Köhler's apes used sticks to draw fruit toward the bars of their cage, and so on.

But this type of learning depends on three things. There must be leisure 35 for trial-and-error experiment. The tools must be either in unlimited supply (a forest is full of sticks and leaves) or else in *exactly the right place*. (Even Köhler's brilliant Sultan could be stumped if the fruit was in front of him and a new potential tool was behind him—he needed them both in view at the same time.) Thirdly, for the habit to stick, the same effect must result from the same action every time.

Now look at that ape. The timing is wrong—when he's faced with a 36 bristling rival or a charging cat or even an escaping prey, he won't fool around inventing fancy methods. A chimp sometimes brandishes a stick to convey menace to an adversary, but if his enemy keeps coming, he drops the stick and fights with hands and teeth. Even if we postulate a mutant ape cool enough to think, with the adrenalin surging through his veins, "There must be a better way than teeth," he still has to be lucky to notice that right in the middle of the primeval grassland there happens to be a stone of convenient size, precisely between him and his enemy. And when he throws it, he has to score a bull's-eye, first time and every time. Because if he failed to hit a leopard he wouldn't be there to tell his progeny that the trick only needed polishing up a bit; and if he failed to hit a springbok he'd think: "Ah well, that obviously doesn't work. Back to the old drawing board."

No. If it had taken all that much luck to turn man into a killer, we'd all 37 be still living on nut cutlets.

A lot of Tarzanists privately realize that their explanations of bipedal- 38 ism and weapon-wielding won't hold water. They have invented the doctrine of "feedback," which states that though these two theories are separately and individually nonsense, together they will just get by. It is alleged that the ape's bipedal gait, however unsteady, made him a better rock thrower (why?) and his rock throwing, however inaccurate, made him a better biped. (Why?) Eimerl and de Vore again put the awkward question: Since chimps can both walk erect and manipulate simple tools, "why was it only the hominids who benefited from the feed-back?" You may well ask.

Next question: Why did the naked ape become naked? 39

Desmond Morris claims that, unlike more specialized carnivores such as 40 lions and jackals, the ex-vegetarian ape was not physically equipped to "make lightning dashes after his prey." He would "experience considerable overheating during the hunt, and the loss of body hair would be of great value for the supreme moments of the chase."

This is a perfect example of androcentric thinking. There were two sexes   41
around at the time, and I don't believe it's ever been all that easy to part a
woman from a fur coat, just to save the old man from getting into a muck-
sweat during his supreme moments. What was supposed to be happening to
the female during this period of denudation?

Dr. Morris says: "This system would not work, of course, if the climate   42
was too intensely hot, because of damage to the exposed skin." So he is
obviously dating the loss of hair later than the Pliocene "inferno." But the
next period was the turbulent Pleistocene, punctuated by mammoth African
"pluvials," corresponding to the Ice Ages of the north. A pluvial was century
after century of torrential rainfall; so we have to picture our maternal ancestor
sitting naked in the middle of the plain while the heavens emptied, needing
both hands to keep her muddy grip on a slippery, squirming, equally naked
infant. This is ludicrous. It's no advantage to the species for the Mighty
Hunter to return home safe and cool if he finds his son's been dropped on
his head and his wife is dead of hypothermia.

This problem could have been solved by dimorphism—the loss of hair   43
could have gone further in one sex than the other. So it did, of course. But
unfortunately for the Tarzanists it was the stay-at-home female who became
nakedest, and the overheated hunter who kept the hair on his chest.

Next question: Why has our sex life become so involved and confusing?   44

The given answer, I need hardly say, is that it all began when man   45
became a hunter. He had to travel long distances after his prey and he began
worrying about what the little woman might be up to. He was also anxious
about other members of the hunting pack, because, Desmond Morris explains, "if the weaker males were going to be expected to cooperate on the
hunt, they had to be given more sexual rights. The females would have to
be more shared out."

Thus it became necessary, so the story goes, to establish a system of   46
"pair bonding" to ensure that couples remained faithful for life. I quote: "The
simplest and most direct method of doing this was to make the shared activities of the pair more complicated and more rewarding. In other words, to
make sex sexier."

To this end, the Naked Apes sprouted ear lobes, fleshy nostrils, and   47
everted lips, all allegedly designed to stimulate one another to a frenzy. Mrs.
A.'s nipples became highly erogenous, she invented and patented the female
orgasm, and she learned to be sexually responsive at all times, even during
pregnancy, "because with a one-male–one-female system, it would be dangerous to frustrate the male for too long a period. It might endanger the pair
bond." He might go off in a huff, or look for another woman. Or even refuse
to cooperate on the hunt.

In addition, they decided to change over to face-to-face sex, instead of   48
the male mounting from behind as previously, because this new method led
to "personalized sex." The frontal approach means that "the incoming sexual
signals and rewards are kept tightly linked with the identity signals from the
partner." In simpler words, you know who you're doing it with.

This landed Mrs. Naked Ape in something of a quandary. Up till then, 49
the fashionable thing to flaunt in sexual approaches had been "a pair of
fleshy, hemispherical buttocks." Now all of a sudden they were getting her
nowhere. She would come up to her mate making full-frontal identity signals
like mad with her nice new earlobes and nostrils, but somehow he just didn't
want to know. He missed the fleshy hemispheres, you see. The position was
parlous, Dr. Morris urges. "If the female of our species was going to successfully shift the interest of the male round to the front, evolution would have
to do something to make the frontal region more stimulating." Guess what?
Right the first time: she invested in a pair of fleshy hemispheres in the
thoracic region and we were once more saved by the skin of our teeth.

All this is good stirring stuff, but hard to take seriously. Wolf packs 50
manage to cooperate without all this erotic paraphernalia. Our near relatives
the gibbons remain faithful for life without "personalized" frontal sex, without elaborate erogenous zones, without perennial female availability. Why
couldn't we?

Above all, since when has increased sexiness been a guarantee of in- 51
creased fidelity? If the naked ape could see all this added sexual potential in
his own mate, how could he fail to see the same thing happening to all the
other females around him? What effect was that supposed to have on him,
especially in later life when he noticed Mrs. A.'s four hemispheres becoming
a little less fleshy than they used to be?

We haven't yet begun on the unasked questions. Before ending this 52
chapter I will mention just two out of many.

First: If female orgasm was evolved in our species for the first time to 53
provide the woman with a "behavioral reward" for increased sexual activity,
why in the name of Darwin has the job been so badly bungled that there have
been whole tribes and whole generations of women hardly aware of its
existence? Even in the sex-conscious U.S.A., according to Dr. Kinsey, it rarely
gets into proper working order before the age of about thirty. How could
natural selection ever have operated on such a rickety, unreliable, late-devel-
oping endowment when in the harsh conditions of prehistory a woman
would be lucky to survive more than twenty-nine years, anyway?

Second: Why in our species has sex become so closely linked with 54
aggression? In most of the higher primates sexual activity is the one thing in
life which is totally incompatible with hostility. A female primate can immediately deflect male wrath by presenting her backside and offering sex. Even
a male monkey can calm and appease a furious aggressor by imitating the
gesture. Nor is the mechanism confined to mammals. Lorenz tells of an irate
lizard charging down upon a female painted with male markings to deceive
him. When he got close enough to realize his mistake, the taboo was so
immediate and so absolute that his aggression went out like a light, and being
too late to stop himself he shot straight up into the air and turned a back
somersault.

Female primates admittedly are not among the species that can count 55
on this absolute chivalry at all times. A female monkey may be physically

chastised for obstreperous behavior; or a male may (on rare occasions) direct hostility against her when another male is copulating with her; but between the male and female engaged in it, sex is always the friendliest of interactions. There is no more hostility associated with it than with a session of mutual grooming.

How then have sex and aggression, the two irreconcilables of the animal kingdom, become in our species alone so closely interlinked that the words for sexual activity are spat out as insults and expletives? In what evolutionary terms are we to explain the Marquis de Sade, and the subterranean echoes that his name evokes in so many human minds? 56

Not, I think, in terms of Tarzan. It is time to approach the whole thing again right from the beginning: this time from the distaff side, and along a totally different route. 57

Questions for Discussion

1. Do you think that Morgan's sharpening of her feminist ax dulls her overall argument? Does she seem more intent on being a feminist thinker than a scientific thinker? Or do you think that her feminist examples are appropriate to her task?

2. Morgan's tone varies greatly from moment to moment. Often she sounds neutral, scientific: "We cannot dispute the facts. We should not attempt to ignore the facts. What I think we can do is to suggest that the currently accepted interpretation of the facts is not the only possible one" (¶7). But often enough she becomes ironic or even sarcastic: ". . . I don't believe it's ever been all that easy to part a woman from a fur coat, just to save the old man from getting into a muck-sweat during his supreme moments" (¶41); Mrs. A. "invented and patented the female orgasm" (¶47); "He may even genuinely believe that equal pay will do something terrible to his gonads" (¶7). Do you find these two styles compatible? Does she mix them effectively? What is the effect of mixing them? Do the passages with ironic zingers in them affect your view of her credibility? Why?

3. In paragraphs 25–30, Morgan discusses the emergence of bipedalism in human beings and argues that the conventional explanation—that walking upright made men faster and better hunters—simply does not hold water. Discuss in detail the objections she raises. Her questions are based on logic, not specialized knowledge. Do they make sense to you? Can you think of arguments that either support or undercut her criticisms?

4. The following "skeleton" outline is intended to reveal the connecting "joints" in Morgan's argument. Choose any essay you have read so far and try to bare the skeletal framework for it as we have done for Morgan's essay.

I. Paragraphs 1–14: *Introduction:* Morgan lays out the topic, thesis, and general form of her argument.

   A. Paragraphs 1–7: Exposition of *topic,* the relation between evolutionary theory in biology and the status of women in society. The *thesis* statement emerges in the last sentence of paragraph 7: "[T]he currently accepted interpretation of the facts is not the only possible one."

   B. Paragraphs 8–14: *General overview of argument* and beginning development. Even scientific thinkers do not think open-mindedly about evolution. She cites three reasons:

      1. Paragraphs 8–9: Language itself reinforces male prejudices.

      2. Paragraphs 10–13: Tradition reinforces male prejudices (brilliant metaphor from astronomy).

      3. Paragraphs 14: Narrowness of specialized thinking reinforces male prejudices; specialists tend to think "in grooves."

II. Paragraphs 15–56: *Detailed critique* of "grooved" views in evolutionary theory.

   A. Paragraphs 15–24: Summary of conventional views in current theory.

      1. Paragraphs 15–18: The development of human beings is largely built on the nature of early man as a "Mighty Hunter."

      2. Paragraphs 19–24: The standard problem that must be explained in anthropology.

   B. Paragraphs 25–30: The problem of how to explain the upright walk.

      1. Paragraph 25: The current explanation is based on the Mighty Hunter theory.

      2. Paragraphs 26–30: Critique that shows inadequacy of the current explanation.

   C. Paragraphs 31–38: The problem of how to explain emergence of weapons.

      1. Paragraph 31: The current explanation is based on the Mighty Hunter theory.

      2. Paragraphs 32–38: Critique—the necessities of hunting don't suffice as an explanation.

   D. Paragraphs 39–43: The problem of how to explain loss of hair.

      1. Paragraph 40: Again, the theory is based on the Mighty Hunter explanation.

      2. Paragraphs 41–43: Critique.

   E. Paragraphs 44–51: The problem of how to explain distinctive sexual practices of human beings.

      1. Paragraphs 45–49: Again we are given the conventional Mighty Hunter view.

      2. Paragraphs 50–56: Critique.

III. Paragraph 57: *Conclusion:* Reiteration of the thesis that current theory is inadequate to explain the data.

Suggested Essay Topics

1. In paragraph 10, Morgan compares androcentric thinking to pre-Copernican thinking and develops the comparison in a couple of sentences. In a short paper, begin by quoting the first three sentences of paragraph 10 and then continue by developing the comparison. You might go on to compare some early feminist (e.g., Margaret Sanger or Susan B. Anthony) to Copernicus, or compare male chauvinists to Copernicus's

contemporaries. The point of this essay is to give you practice in making an extended analogy work for you. Few devices are more powerful than extended analogies for packing meaning and effect into a compressed space. By contrast, nothing will seem less effective than an analogy that strikes a reader as far-fetched or inappropriate.

2. Pick an issue that is accompanied by widely accepted arguments that seem as objectionable to you as androcentric arguments seem to Morgan. Possible topics might include the arms race, space travel, a nuclear freeze, the "first-strike option," or abortion rights; or, if you wish to stick to issues you know firsthand, you might write on open dorm policies, tuition increases, the value of Greek-letter societies, or the money spent on athletics.

In an essay directed to your fellow students or in a memo or letter addressed to responsible officials, imitate Morgan's style of attack (¶25–30 or ¶31–38 provide a model). Begin with a short statement of the issue, proceed to give the conventional view you find objectionable, and then develop your objections, relying not on special information but on tight reasoning. Like Morgan, you do not have to replace the ideas you criticize with a whole new set; your objective is simply to point out as many flaws as possible in the arguments you are attacking. Try to go for the basic ideas, not trivialities.

William Golding

Everyone assumes they know how to think. But do people really know how to think as well as they assume? If they do, why is there so little clear thinking around? Why are most people's analyses and reactions to issues so full of clichés, prejudices, slogans, and rote formulas?

At one level it is clear that all human beings, even the dullest among us, are immensely intelligent and thoughtful. Even the slowest among ordinary folk can perform hundreds or thousands of complicated tasks such as driving cars, filling out loan applications, finding their way through complicated cities, and performing difficult occupational moves.

At another level, however, it is also clear that much of what people pass off as thinking is pretty feeble stuff. They either repeat what they hear other people say, or they simply retreat to their feelings and call them thinking. In part, the explanation for the scarcity of good thinking may not lie in the fact that most people are stupid, but in the fact that many issues are extremely complicated, open-ended, and subject to different interpretations. The explanation may also be that really good thinking is simply much harder than most of us suppose. Maybe most of us are capable of being good thinkers, but are not willing to work as hard at it as is necessary.

Perhaps most us tend to view thinking the way we view reading and writing.

That is, because all of us can perform each of these skills at some level, we give ourselves much more credit than we deserve for performing them well. Because we can read the newspaper we think we can read well. Because we can write a letter we assume we have mastered all the practical writing we need. And because we can think in some fashion or other about almost anything, we assume that we think powerfully when in fact we are mostly repeating what others have said or relying on stock notions.

In this essay the British novelist William Golding (b. 1911), author of The Lord of the Flies, *provides a humorous yet serious description of three levels of thinking. He draws his examples of each from his experience as a schoolboy, starting with grammar school and ending with his experience at the university. As you read, try to determine whether the three levels of schooling he talks about correspond to the three levels of thinking he describes. Consider whether you can verify his categories with examples from your own experience. Can you map Golding's progress from thinking as a "hobby" to thinking as a "professional"? Does the kind of thinking you are being taught in college fall within Golding's highest category?*

THINKING AS A HOBBY

From *Holiday,* August 1961.

While I was a boy, I came to the conclusion that there were three grades 1
of thinking; and since I was later to claim thinking as my hobby, I came to
an even stranger conclusion—namely, that I myself could not think at all.

I must have been an unsatisfactory child for grownups to deal with. I 2
remember how incomprehensible they appeared to me at first, but not, of
course, how I appeared to them. It was the headmaster of my grammar school
who first brought the subject of thinking before me—though neither in the
way, nor with the result he intended. He had some statuettes in his study.
They stood on a high cupboard behind his desk. One was a lady wearing
nothing but a bath towel. She seemed frozen in an eternal panic lest the bath
towel slip down any farther; and since she had no arms, she was in an
unfortunate position to pull the towel up again. Next to her, crouched the
statuette of a leopard, ready to spring down at the top drawer of a filing
cabinet labeled A–AH. My innocence interpreted this as the victim's last,
despairing cry. Beyond the leopard was a naked, muscular gentleman, who
sat, looking down, with his chin on his fist and his elbow on his knee. He
seemed utterly miserable.

Some time later, I learned about these statuettes. The headmaster had 3
placed them where they would face delinquent children, because they symbolized to him the whole of life. The naked lady was the Venus of Milo. She
was Love. She was not worried about the towel. She was just busy being
beautiful. The leopard was Nature, and he was being natural. The naked,
muscular gentleman was not miserable. He was Rodin's Thinker, an image of
pure thought. It is easy to buy small plaster models of what you think life
is like.

I had better explain that I was a frequent visitor to the headmaster's 4
study, because of the latest thing I had done or left undone. As we now say,
I was not integrated. I was, if anything, disintegrated; and I was puzzled.
Grownups never made sense. Whenever I found myself in a penal position
before the headmaster's desk, with the statuettes glimmering whitely above
him, I would sink my head, clasp my hands behind my back and writhe one
shoe over the other.

The headmaster would look opaquely at me, through flashing specta- 5
cles.

"What are we going to do with you?" 6

Well, what *were* they going to do with me? I would writhe my shoe some 7
more and stare down at the worn rug.

"Look up, boy! Can't you look up?" 8

Then I would look up at the cupboard, where the naked lady was frozen 9
in her panic and the muscular gentleman contemplated the hindquarters of
the leopard in endless gloom. I had nothing to say to the headmaster. His
spectacles caught the light so that you could see nothing human behind them.
There was no possibility of communication.

"Don't you ever think at all?" 10

No, I didn't think, wasn't thinking, couldn't think—I was simply wait- 11
ing in anguish for the interview to stop.

"Then you'd better learn—hadn't you?" 12

On one occasion the headmaster leaped to his feet, reached up and 13
plonked Rodin's masterpiece on the desk before me.

"That's what a man looks like when he's really thinking." 14

I surveyed the gentleman without interest or comprehension. 15

"Go back to your class." 16

Clearly there was something missing in me. Nature had endowed the 17
rest of the human race with a sixth sense and left me out. This must be so,
I mused, on my way back to the class, since whether I had broken a window,
or failed to remember Boyle's Law, or been late for school, my teachers
produced me one, adult answer: "Why can't you think?"

As I saw the case, I had broken the window because I had tried to hit 18
Jack Arney with a cricket ball and missed him; I could not remember Boyle's
Law because I had never bothered to learn it; and I was late for school because
I preferred looking over the bridge into the river. In fact, I was wicked. Were
my teachers, perhaps, so good that they could not understand the depths of
my depravity? Were they clear, untormented people who could direct their
every action by this mysterious business of thinking? The whole thing was
incomprehensible. In my earlier years, I found even the statuette of the
Thinker confusing. I did not believe any of my teachers were naked, ever.
Like someone born deaf, but bitterly determined to find out about sound, I
watched my teachers to find out about thought.

There was Mr. Houghton. He was always telling me to think. With a 19
modest satisfaction, he would tell me that he had thought a bit himself. Then
why did he spend so much time drinking? Or was there more sense in

drinking than there appeared to be? But if not, and if drinking were in fact ruinous to health—and Mr. Houghton was ruined, there was no doubt about that—why was he always talking about the clean life and the virtues of fresh air? He would spread his arms wide with the action of a man who habitually spent his time striding along mountain ridges.

"Open air does me good, boys—I know it!"   20

Sometimes, exalted by his own oratory, he would leap from his desk and   21
hustle us outside into a hideous wind.

"Now, boys! Deep breaths! Feel it right down inside you—huge   22
draughts of God's good air!"

He would stand before us, rejoicing in his perfect health, an open-air   23
man. He would put his hands on his waist and take a tremendous breath. You could hear the wind, trapped in the cavern of his chest and struggling with all the unnatural impediments. His body would reel with shock and his ruined face go white at the unaccustomed visitation. He would stagger back to his desk and collapse there, useless for the rest of the morning.

Mr. Houghton was given to high-minded monologues about the good   24
life, sexless and full of duty. Yet in the middle of one of these monologues, if a girl passed the window, tapping along on her neat little feet, he would interrupt his discourse, his neck would turn of itself and he would watch her out of sight. In this instance, he seemed to me ruled not by thought but by an invisible and irresistible spring in his nape.

His neck was an object of great interest to me. Normally it bulged a bit   25
over his collar. But Mr. Houghton had fought in the First World War along-side both Americans and French, and had come—by who knows what il-logic?—to a settled detestation of both countries. If either country happened to be prominent in current affairs, no argument could make Mr. Houghton think well of it. He would bang the desk, his neck would bulge still further and go red. "You can say what you like," he would cry, "but I've thought about this—and I know what I think!"

Mr. Houghton thought with his neck.   26

There was Miss Parsons. She assured us that her dearest wish was our   27
welfare, but I knew even then, with the mysterious clairvoyance of child-hood, that what she wanted most was the husband she never got. There was Mr. Hands—and so on.

I have dealt at length with my teachers because this was my introduc-   28
tion to the nature of what is commonly called thought. Through them I discovered that thought is often full of unconscious prejudice, ignorance and hypocrisy. It will lecture on disinterested purity while its neck is being re-morselessly twisted toward a skirt. Technically, it is about as proficient as most businessmen's golf, as honest as most politicians' intentions, or—to come near my own preoccupation—as coherent as most books that get writ-ten. It is what I came to call grade-three thinking, though more properly, it is feeling, rather than thought.

True, often there is a kind of innocence in prejudices, but in those days   29
I viewed grade-three thinking with an intolerant contempt and an incautious

mockery. I delighted to confront a pious lady who hated the Germans with the proposition that we should love our enemies. She taught me a great truth in dealing with grade-three thinkers; because of her, I no longer dismiss lightly a mental process which for nine-tenths of the population is the nearest they will ever get to thought. They have immense solidarity. We had better respect them, for we are outnumbered and surrounded. A crowd of grade-three thinkers, all shouting the same thing, all warming their hands at the fire of their own prejudices, will not thank you for pointing out the contradictions in their beliefs. Man is a gregarious animal, and enjoys agreement as cows will graze all the same way on the side of a hill.

Grade-two thinking is the detection of contradictions. I reached grade 30 two when I trapped the poor, pious lady. Grade-two thinkers do not stampede easily, though often they fall into the other fault and lag behind. Grade-two thinking is a withdrawal, with eyes and ears open. It became my hobby and brought satisfaction and loneliness in either hand. For grade-two thinking destroys without having the power to create. It set me watching the crowds cheering His Majesty the King and asking myself what all the fuss was about, without giving me anything positive to put in the place of that heady patriotism. But there were compensations. To hear people justify their habit of hunting foxes and tearing them to pieces by claiming that the foxes liked it. To hear our Prime Minister talk about the great benefit we conferred on India by jailing people like Pandit Nehru and Gandhi. To hear American politicians talk about peace in one sentence and refuse to join the League of Nations in the next. Yes, there were moments of delight.

But I was growing toward adolescence and had to admit that Mr. 31 Houghton was not the only one with an irresistible spring in his neck. I, too, felt the compulsive hand of nature and began to find that pointing out contradiction could be costly as well as fun. There was Ruth, for example, a serious and attractive girl. I was an atheist at the time. Grade-two thinking is a menace to religion and knocks down sects like skittles. I put myself in a position to be converted by her with an hypocrisy worthy of grade three. She was a Methodist—or at least, her parents were, and Ruth had to follow suit. But, alas, instead of relying on the Holy Spirit to convert me, Ruth was foolish enough to open her pretty mouth in argument. She claimed that the Bible (King James Version) was literally inspired. I countered by saying that the Catholics believed in the literal inspiration of Saint Jerome's *Vulgate,* and the two books were different. Argument flagged.

At last she remarked that there were an awful lot of Methodists, and 32 they couldn't be wrong, could they—not all those millions? That was too easy, said I restively (for the nearer you were to Ruth, the nicer she was to be near to) since there were more Roman Catholics than Methodists anyway; and they couldn't be wrong, could they—not all those hundreds of millions? An awful flicker of doubt appeared in her eyes. I slid my arm round her waist and murmured breathlessly that if we were counting heads, the Buddhists were the boys for my money. But Ruth had *really* wanted to do me good, because I was so nice. She fled. The combination of my arm and those countless Buddhists was too much for her.

That night her father visited my father and left, red-cheeked and indig- 33 nant. I was given the third degree to find out what had happened. It was lucky we were both of us only fourteen. I lost Ruth and gained an undeserved reputation as a potential libertine.

So grade-two thinking could be dangerous. It was in this knowledge, at 34 the age of fifteen, that I remember making a comment from the heights of grade two, on the limitations of grade three. One evening I found myself alone in the school hall, preparing it for a party. The door of the headmaster's study was open. I went in. The headmaster had ceased to thump Rodin's Thinker down on the desk as an example to the young. Perhaps he had not found any more candidates, but the statuettes were still there, glimmering and gathering dust on top of the cupboard. I stood on a chair and rearranged them. I stood Venus in her bath towel on the filing cabinet, so that now the top drawer caught its breath in a gasp of sexy excitement. "A-ah!" The portentous Thinker I placed on the edge of the cupboard so that he looked down at the bath towel and waited for it to slip.

Grade-two thinking, though it filled life with fun and excitement, did 35 not make for content. To find out the deficiencies of our elders bolsters the young ego but does not make for personal security. I found that grade two was not only the power to point out contradictions. It took the swimmer some distance from the shore and left him there, out of his depth. I decided that Pontius Pilate was a typical grade-two thinker. "What is truth?" he said, a very common grade-two thought, but one that is used always as the end of an argument instead of the beginning. There is a still higher grade of thought which says, "What is truth?" and sets out to find it.

But these grade-one thinkers were few and far between. They did not 36 visit my grammar school in the flesh though they were there in books. I aspired to them, partly because I was ambitious and partly because I now saw my hobby as an unsatisfactory thing if it went no further. If you set out to climb a mountain, however high you climb, you have failed if you cannot reach the top.

I *did* meet an undeniably grade-one thinker in my first year at Oxford. 37 I was looking over a small bridge in Magdalen Deer Park, and a tiny mustached and hatted figure came and stood by my side. He was a German who had just fled from the Nazis to Oxford as a temporary refuge. His name was Einstein.

But Professor Einstein knew no English at that time and I knew only 38 two words of German. I beamed at him, trying wordlessly to convey by my bearing all the affection and respect that the English felt for him. It is possible—and I have to make the admission—that I felt here were two grade-one thinkers standing side by side; yet I doubt if my face conveyed more than a formless awe. I would have given my Greek and Latin and French and a good slice of my English for enough German to communicate. But we were divided; he was as inscrutable as my headmaster. For perhaps five minutes we stood together on the bridge, undeniable grade-one thinker and breathless aspirant. With true greatness, Professor Einstein realized that any contact was better than none. He pointed to a trout wavering in midstream.

He spoke: *"Fisch."*   39

My brain reeled. Here I was, mingling with the great, and yet helpless   40
as the veriest grade-three thinker. Desperately I sought for some sign by which I might convey that I, too, revered pure reason. I nodded vehemently. In a brilliant flash I used up half my German vocabulary.

"Fisch. Ja. Ja."   41

For perhaps another five minutes we stood side by side. Then Professor   42
Einstein, his whole figure still conveying good will and amiability, drifted away out of sight.

I, too, would be a grade-one thinker. I was irreverent at the best of times.   43
Political and religious systems, social customs, loyalties and traditions, they all came tumbling down like so many rotten apples off a tree. This was a fine hobby and a sensible substitute for cricket, since you could play it all the year round. I came up in the end with what must always remain the justification for grade-one thinking, its sign, seal and charter. I devised a coherent system for living. It was a moral system, which was wholly logical. Of course, as I readily admitted, conversion of the world to my way of thinking might be difficult, since my system did away with a number of trifles, such as big business, centralized government, armies, marriage. . . .

It was Ruth all over again. I had some very good friends who stood by   44
me, and still do. But my acquaintances vanished, taking the girls with them. Young women seemed oddly contented with the world as it was. They valued the meaningless ceremony with a ring. Young men, while willing to concede the chaining sordidness of marriage, were hesitant about abandoning the organizations which they hoped would give them a career. A young man on the first rung of the Royal Navy, while perfectly agreeable to doing away with big business and marriage, got as red-necked as Mr. Houghton when I proposed a world without any battleships in it.

Had the game gone too far? Was it a game any longer? In those prewar   45
days, I stood to lose a great deal, for the sake of a hobby.

Now you are expecting me to describe how I saw the folly of my ways   46
and came back to the warm nest, where prejudices are so often called loyalties, where pointless actions are hallowed into custom by repetition, where we are content to say we think when all we do is feel.

But you would be wrong. I dropped my hobby and turned professional.   47

If I were to go back to the headmaster's study and find the dusty   48
statuettes still there, I would arrange them differently. I would dust Venus and put her aside, for I have come to love her and know her for the fair thing she is. But I would put the Thinker, sunk in his desperate thought, where

there were shadows before him—and at his back, I would put the leopard, crouched and ready to spring.

Questions for Discussion

1. What are the distinguishing features of each of Golding's levels of thinking? Do you know people who exemplify each kind? Are there persons in your college or university—administrators or professors, perhaps—whose wide recognizability make them good examples for the whole class to discuss? Are there times or occasions when even grade-three thinking is defensible? When? Why? If not, why not?

2. Can you point to details in paragraphs 4–16 that reveal Golding as a master storyteller? How do these narratives enhance his essay?

3. In what ways do the three statuettes seem to relate to Golding's three categories of thinking? Why does he rearrange the statuettes so that the leopard seems about to spring onto the back of the thinker? Does this rearrangement imply that Golding has reassessed the difficulty of thinking since he attended grammar school or since he gave it up as a hobby and turned professional?

4. Thinking as a hobby, as a game, seems to match which of Golding's levels of thinking? Does Golding reserve his highest praise for thinking as a hobby? If he offers criticism of this kind of thinking, what sort of criticism is it and in what paragraphs does he advance it?

5. Do you find that you can identify Golding's three levels of thinking with the kind of thinking that characterizes any particular group or organization in society? Is it possible to say that politicians, for example—or the clergy, business executives, or single-issue proponents—generally fall into one level of thinking rather than another? Can you point to exceptions within groups?

Suggested Essay Topics

1. In an essay directed to your classmates, draw a verbal portrait of the best "grade-one" thinker you have ever personally known. Provide at least one anecdote about this person's thinking habits. The point of your essay is to define your own version of first-rate thinking and to portray it as vividly as possible.

   As you write, think of the devices and strategies that Golding uses to achieve vividness: construction of little scenarios (¶4–16 and ¶37–42), use of images (Mr. Houghton's neck; people warming their hands at the fire of their own prejudices; the headmaster's opaque, flashing spectacles), and use of irony ("It is easy to buy small plaster models of what you think life is like"; "Were my teachers, perhaps, so good that they could not understand the depths of my depravity?"). Try to incorporate some of these devices into the writing of your own essay.

2. Go back through your memory's catalog of former teachers and, in imitation of Golding, pick out a few who exemplify his three levels of thinking. Write a feature article for a magazine or newspaper giving their traits, mannerisms, or examples that illustrate the category you placed them in. Make your descriptions of these teachers your main support in an essay designed to persuade your readers of the kind of thinking people should demand from teachers.

Ideas in Debate

Paul Tillich
Karl K. Popper
Kurt Vonnegut, Jr.

Paul Tillich

*P*aul Tillich (1886–1965) was a German
philosopher and theologian who attempted throughout his life and career to synthesize
modern culture and traditional Christianity. He came to the United States in 1933
when the Nazis barred him from teaching in German universities and became an
American citizen in 1940.

Are dreams of utopia destructive or creative? Does an interest in utopia, as some
claim, deflect our concern for the evils of the present because it rivets our attention on
impossible pictures of a perfect future? Or does an interest in utopia, as others claim,
stimulate fruitful criticism of the present, of the status quo, and thus provide us with
images of a perfect future which, once seen through the pictures of utopian dreamers,
we are then motivated to try to establish in our everyday world?

Tillich suggests that utopian dreams are capable of producing either one of these
consequences—and other consequences both better and worse. Tillich does not claim
that utopia is a neutral force that can be turned to either good or evil depending on
the character of the user, but he does claim that utopia's powerful energy calls for a
double response from human beings. In Tillich's view, utopianism must transcend itself
in order to be itself; that is, it must deal not only with the politics and time-order of
this world, the finite world we all live in physically, but it must also deal with the
infinite and timeless order of a perfect realm rooted in the divine, where we all have
our spiritual existence. The everyday world of politics and time Tillich calls the
"horizontal plane"; the transcendental world of divinely inspired visions he calls the
"vertical plane." Any version of utopia that limits itself to either of these planes
exclusively inevitably becomes destructive because such an exclusive focus will always
lead to disillusionment, bitterness, and the possibility of fanaticism.

Tillich's ideas are subtle, yet coherent. He finds in utopianism the same paradox
that most of us find in ourselves: that our strengths have a double edge and are often
the source of our weaknesses. Self-confident people frequently have a tendency to become
arrogant; beautiful people are frequently vain; smart people are often excessively
opinionated; people with well-developed ideas often react defensively and narrow-
mindedly when their ideas are criticized, and so on. As you read, identify the traits
in utopianism that Tillich identifies as both positive and negative, and try to assess

the usefulness or validity of his final recommendation that human beings always maintain a double stance toward utopianism as a guard against its negative power.

CRITIQUE AND JUSTIFICATION OF UTOPIA

From *Utopias and Utopian Thought,* ed. Frank E. Manuel (1965). [This article appeared originally as "Kritik and Rechtfertigung der Utopie," in *Politische Bedeutung der Utopie im Leben der Völker* (Berlin: Gebrüder Weiss, 1951).]

A thoroughgoing analysis of utopia would involve showing first that   1
it is rooted in the nature of man himself, for it is impossible to understand what it means for man "to have utopia" apart from this fundamental fact. Such an analysis would involve showing further that it is impossible to understand history without utopia for neither historical consciousness nor action can be meaningful unless utopia is envisaged both at the beginning and at the end of history. And, finally, such an analysis would show that all utopias strive to negate the negative itself in human existence; it is the negative in existence which makes the idea of utopia necessary. These are the three presuppositions for an evaluation of the meaning and characteristics of utopia, and they form the three bases on which this critique and justification will be undertaken. The evaluation itself will be developed in the following steps:

1. The positive characteristics of utopia
2. The negative characteristics of utopia
3. The transcendence of utopia

Any evaluation of utopia must begin with its *positive meaning,* and the   2
first positive characteristic to be pointed out is its *truth*—utopia is truth. Why is it truth? Because it expresses man's essence, the inner aim of his existence. Utopia shows what man is essentially and what he should have as *telos** of his existence. Every utopia is but one manifestation of what man has as inner aim and what he must have for fulfillment as a person. This definition stresses the social as much as the personal, for it is impossible to understand the one apart from the other. A socially defined utopia loses its truth if it does not at the same time fulfill the person, just as the individually defined utopia loses its truth if it does not at the same time bring fulfillment to society.

The art of healing serves as a useful illustration of this truth for, as   3
contemporary medical discussions concerning healing have shown, psychological disorders cannot be overcome in the individual and wholeness achieved in the fulfillment of his inner meaning if society at the same time

*Final purpose.

does not provide the surroundings in which health and fulfillment can be maintained. This is revealed in the despairing statement made to me once by a neurologist and analyst. "I have succeeded in healing men," he said, "but I have to send them back to the society from which they come, and I know they will return and beg for my help again." And it is equally true that healing of ills in society and social fulfillment cannot be achieved apart from wholeness in the person. This is the tragedy of the revolutionary movements of the past hundred years, all of which foundered inwardly, and many outwardly, because they expected to heal society without at the same time healing individuals who are the bearers of society. And so they failed. This is what it means to say that the personal and social aspects of utopia cannot be separated. Much of the tragedy of our own situation is rooted in the fact that we do not see it in its unity. If utopia expresses truth about human nature, it then follows that the rejection of utopia, whether cynically or philosophically, is a denial of this truth. Those who reject utopia are therefore lacking in that truth about man which utopia itself expresses. In evaluating utopia, the importance of this truth cannot be overstressed.

The second positive characteristic of utopia is its *fruitfulness,* which 4 stands in closest relationship to its truth. "Fruitfulness" means that utopia opens up possibilities which would have remained lost if not seen by utopian anticipation. Every utopia is an anticipation of human fulfillment, and many things anticipated in utopias have been shown to be real possibilities. Without this anticipatory inventiveness countless possibilities would have remained unrealized. Where no anticipating utopia opens up possibilities we find a stagnant, sterile present—we find a situation in which not only individual but also cultural realization of human possibilities is inhibited and cannot win through to fulfillment. The present, for men who have no utopia, is inevitably constricting; and, similarly, cultures which have no utopia remain imprisoned in the present and quickly fall back into the past, for the present can be fully alive only in tension between past and future. This is the fruitfulness of utopia—its ability to open up possibilities.

And the third positive characteristic of utopia is its *power:* utopia is 5 able to transform the given. Consideration of the great utopian movements of the past will make this immediately evident. Judaism is perhaps the most momentous utopian movement in history, for directly or indirectly it has elevated all mankind to another sphere of existence through its utopia based on the coming Kingdom of God. Bourgeois society with its utopia of the rational state—the "Third Age" of history—has revolutionized, directly or indirectly, the farthest corners of the earth and has thereby called into question and finally made altogether impossible all pre-bourgeois forms of existence. Similarly Marxism through its utopia of the classless society has revolutionized and transformed directly one half of the world and indirectly the other half. These are only three examples that show the power of utopia. In all three cases the question itself concerns something that has no present because it has no place—*ou topos,* "no-place"; but this utopia, which is nowhere, has proved itself the greatest of all powers over the given. The root of its power is the essential—the ontological—discontent* of man in every direction of his being. No utopia would have power if it were exclusively economic or exclusively intellectual or exclusively religious. Nor is it true, as a false analysis would have us believe, that it is those who are lowest in society in terms of power of being who are the real bearers of utopia because of their discontent. Rather, the bearers of utopia have been those who in the conflict between security and progress have chosen progress and then enlisted the help of the masses of discontented and used them for their victory, even though in the end the masses perhaps swallowed them up. It is a lesson of history that the bearers of utopia are never those who stand on the lowest rung of the economic ladder, whose discontent is basically economic and nothing more. On the contrary, the bearers of utopia are those who have sufficient power of being to achieve progress. One thinks of the French revolution where the proletariat contributed indispensable assistance but where it was the highly cultivated bourgeoisie who accomplished the revolution. One thinks of the Franciscan revolution where it was the most advanced figures of the order who revolted against the Church. Or one thinks of Marx's analysis of the avant-grade—those at once within the proletariat and yet in part outside who are the real bearers of utopia. This is to say that the power of utopia is *the power of man in his wholeness*—the power of man to push out of the ground of discontent, his ontological discontent, in all directions of being, where the economic plays no greater role than any other factor. The bearers of utopia are those who are able to transform reality, and it is in them that the power of utopia is anchored. So much for the positive meaning of utopia, the "Yes" which we must say to it.

But there is also a *negative meaning,* a "No" which we must say to it, and the first of utopia's negative characteristics is *untruth.* If we previously affirmed the truth of utopia, we must now show its untruth. Both are present together. The untruth of utopia is that it forgets the finitude and estrangement of man, it forgets that man as finite is a union of being and non-being, and it forgets that man under the conditions of existence is always estranged from his true or essential being and that it is therefore impossible to regard his essential being as attainable. One thinks, for example, of the idea of progress, an idea which, to be sure, takes account of man's finitude, at least for this life, yet often grants him development in an after-life. But it forgets that even in an "after-life" finitude would be expressed in every "moment," for the idea of progress belongs not to eternity but to the endless continuation of finitude.

While utopia does presuppose man's essential being, it fails to under- 7

Ontological discontent is discontent rooted in human nature itself, in the human power to be.

stand that man has fallen from that essence. "Fallenness" is meant here not in reference to a mythical event of the past but rather as a precise description of man's present condition. The untruth of utopia is its false view of man, and insofar as utopia builds on this untruth in its thought and action it can be dealt with only to the extent that it is shown that the "man" it presupposes is, in fact, *unestranged* man. Here utopia contradicts itself, for it is precisely the utopian contention that estranged man must be led out of his estrangement. But who will do this? Estranged man himself? The question is rather, how can estrangement itself be overcome? And if someone answers, of course not through men themselves but rather through inevitable economic or other processes, then the reply must be made that the understanding of these processes is itself a human act. And if the rejoinder comes, "But freedom is nothing but the knowledge of what is necessary," then we reply that even this knowing stands over against non-knowing, implying the possibility of a decision between them, and this *decision* itself is freedom. The statement "freedom is the knowledge of what is necessary" actually obscures rather than clarifies, for it misconstrues what is called "knowing," namely, the ability to participate in or contradict truth *beyond* necessity, and this ability we presuppose in every moment of our lives. Here is where the untruth of utopia lies. Its untruth is not that it imagines something fantastic in the future; that is unimportant here. What is important is that it actually puts forward a false view of man in contradiction of its own basic presupposition. For almost every utopia is a judgment of the extreme sinfulness of the present or of a social group or people or religion and an attempt to lead out of this situation, but it does not say how this is possible if there is radical estrangement. And this is the heart of utopia's untruth.

Once again we counter a positive characteristic of utopia with a corresponding negative in pointing, secondly, to the *unfruitfulness* of utopia—in addition to and over against its fruitfulness. The fruitfulness of utopia is its discovery of possibilities which can be realized only by pushing forward into the unlimitedness of possibility. The unfruitfulness of utopia is that it describes impossibilities as real possibilities—and fails to see them for what they are, impossibilities, or as oscillation between possibility and impossibility. In so doing, utopia succumbs to pure wishful thinking which, to be sure, has to do with the real (in that it is projected out of and onto real processes) but not with what is essentially human. It is the nature of "wish" to take impossibilities as realities, and this is true from the smallest wishes of children up to the most fantastic wishes of fairy tales. In utopia such wish-projection is self-defeating unrealism, and this is what we call its unfruitfulness. For this reason theologians and political philosophers such as Marx have rightly repudiated this tendency to unrealism in utopian imagination and have made utopia depend on real possibilities, which they show to be real possibilities without overstepping the limits of reality. They have taken care themselves to describe the wishful, unrealistic utopia as a fool's paradise, for those who regard action as something negative and those who have a very distorted view of man will of course visualize utopia in such wishful ways, but such utopias are indeed nothing but a fool's paradise. And this is the origin of the fantastic utopias—they conform not to essential possibilities but rather to a fantastically exaggerated wish for existence which itself has to be overcome. That is the unfruitfulness of utopia in contrast to its fruitfulness.

The third negative characteristic is the *impotence* of utopia in addition to and over against its power. The impotence of utopia is the fact that its negative content of untruth and unfruitfulness leads inevitably to disillusionment. This disillusionment must be discussed metaphysically, not psychologically. It is a disillusionment experienced again and again, and in such a profound way it disrupts man in the deepest levels of his being. Such disillusionment is an inevitable consequence of confusing the ambiguous preliminary with the unambiguous ultimate. However provisionally we live in the future, we actually live always in the preliminary and the ambiguous. But in the movement from present into future what utopia intended as final and therefore fixed as absolute proves contingent in the flux, and this contingency of something regarded as ultimate leads to bitter disillusionment. From this arise two consequences, both very destructive because of utopia's inability to surmount its transitoriness. The first is that those who suffer such disillusionment may become *fanatics against their own past.* This is especially true of those—the intelligentsia above all—who at some time in their life committed themselves to a utopia not as something preliminary but as something ultimate only to learn that not only was it *not* an ultimate, and thus merely preliminary and ambiguous, but in fact was something inherently demonic. This has happened to intelligentsia in America and is a sad and very puzzling fact of American existence—as it is of Western existence generally, and even beyond. This whole class of men represents today one of the most tragic groups in human society and, in a certain respect, one of the most dangerous, because their fanaticism, originally directed against themselves, infects all who have not shared it and whom they therefore take to be secret friends of everything they fanatically oppose. This is one side of the matter and one we must reckon with, though perhaps it is not possible to judge the extent to which this destructiveness characterizes the intellectual and political activity of such men. Yet it is one of the most serious consequences of utopia's impotence.

The other side is that the utopian activists, those who affirm the utopian goal and are able to hold to it despite its contingency and ambiguity, must guard against disillusionment in order to maintain themselves. To do so they resort to *terror.* Terror is an expression of corroding disillusionment in an actualized utopia; disillusionment is staved off through the political effects of terror. And this is the other side we must reckon with, which is just as understandable as the first.

In other words, through disillusionment and through reaction to possible disillusionment the impotence of utopia becomes a demonic force in society. It is just as in the physical realm and above all in the spiritual: "Nature abhors a vacuum." If a demon is driven out and the space remains empty, seven new demons appear to claim it; if a utopia, which is something preliminary, sets itself up as absolute, disillusionment follows. And to the empty place of disillusionment the demons flock; today, especially in Germany, we find ourselves struggling with them.

These are the negative characteristics of utopia, which are just as real 12 as its positive characteristics. But do not think that because the negative meaning is discussed after the positive that the negative is given the last word. The positive endures, but the negative makes its reality felt over against it, and the demand for a way beyond this negativity leads to *the transcendence of utopia.* Every living thing drives beyond itself, transcends itself. The moment in which it no longer does this, in which it remains bound within itself for the sake of internal or external security, the moment in which it no longer makes the experiment of life, in that moment it loses life. Only where life risks itself, stakes itself, and imperils itself in going beyond itself, only there can it be won. The fact that life transcends itself although at the same time it seeks to preserve itself is a universal description, a universal primal law or, as I call it, the ontological structure of being itself. And this structure of life, of wanting to remain within itself and to protect itself while it moves beyond itself, is valid also for utopia. As a consequence utopia is always and necessarily suspended between possibility and impossibility. The decision whether something is possible or impossible has as referent not present reality but something that is on the "other side" of reality, and it is because of this situation that *every utopia is a hovering, a suspension, between possibility and impossibility.* If one now considers what has been said concerning the negative characteristics of utopia, the question arises: Is it not possible to transcend this whole situation in which utopia finds itself? Is it not possible to overcome its negativity in this way not by transcending a little but by a complete and radical transcendence? To transcend a situation radically does not mean to move horizontally—in the sense of always going farther in a horizontal line—but to move vertically, to rise beyond the whole sphere of horizontal transcendence. This question concerns the possibility of transcending the structure of self-preservation and self-transcendence as such, of going beyond it radically in the vertical dimension—or perhaps more accurately, in that dimension where movement is both up and down, out of line and plane. This is a question that can be answered not merely theoretically but historically, from the development of culture itself, from which most utopias come.

If we consider the prophetic line of the Old Testament, we discover in 13 the great prophets a remarkable oscillation or dialectical movement between a partial transcendence, which we can call utopia in the political and social sense, and a radical transcendence that indicates the intrusion of something—

the divine—that breaks through the whole horizontal dimension. In the prophetic texts both occur ambiguously together. They are at once political, social, economic, and intellectual—all these elements are present and yet they at the same time go beyond and above everything which can be understood from history itself. They refer realistically to the world and yet they contain an apocalyptic element which transcends the world, and it is this duality, this doubleness, that is so charming in such descriptions, for example, as Isaiah's of the "peaceable kingdom" of animals and men in which the natural and visionary are intermingled and united. But, like all utopias of the vertical dimension, the prophetic utopias themselves were not able to prevent metaphysical disillusionment, a disillusionment as profound and destructive then as now.

In this situation the next stage of radical transcendence occurred, the 14 one we usually call "apocalyptic"—that is, the visionary unveiling (*apokalyptein,* to uncover) of something that is not within history but rather stands against history, "above" or "outside" history, and that makes itself known within history as a new creation. There occurs also a development of this stage in a transcendental way, where all socio-political contents were transcended without, however, negating them. In Christian eschatology,* as presented in the New Testament, we find still another stage has been reached: there all social and political contents have been transcended but only the heavenly kingdom itself is described, either in mystical colors or as loving union with the divine. And then there is a final stage, the mystical, where the term "utopia" itself becomes no longer applicable. This is not just the mystical form of Christianity alone but that more inclusive mysticism where fulfillment in the "beyond" completely extinguishes all finite contents. This mysticism, however, is hardly fulfillment at all but rather negation. Now if we view these developments in sequence, we see in the first an oscillation between the political and the transcendental-religious. In the second, the apocalyptic, we see the transcendence of the divine breaking into history but still as something which happens to this world, to transform it though "at the end of the age." In the third we see a transcendental conception in which the earth is "redeemed" or transformed in a more perfect way, yet where in the Christian form something still remains—the symbol "Kingdom of God." And "kingdom" to be sure is a socio-political symbol. Then we see the fourth stage, the mystical, where every political symbol disappears and where everything expressing utopia itself is transcended—not only personality and community but history and form as well.

If we look carefully at these four stages and ask what they have meant 15 for history, we find that the closer they were to the actual political situation the more they manifested both positive and negative characteristics of every utopia: their truth, their fruitfulness, and their power, but at the same time

---

*The Christian view of "final things" such as the end of time and the world, resurrection and judgment, and so on.

their untruth, their unfruitfulness, and their impotence. We find also that the closer they approached the mystical negation of every utopia, the less real were their socio-political contents and the less was said concerning the essential being of man, but the less threatening was the danger of metaphysical disillusionment, with its ruinous effects.

In response someone might say: Let us then give up every utopia, let us 16 reject not only the prophetic utopia with its secular consequences, and the eschatological, apocalyptic utopia which still maintains relevance to the world and its socio-political realities, and let us renounce even the Christian utopia—lest we miss the transcendent goal of utopia, the mystical union, the mystical fulfillment in the beyond. Perhaps there are people who choose this way as a result of great metaphysical disillusionment in their time, for it is a fact of history, as this discussion has indicated, that this way of escaping disillusionment has been taken.

But if we go this way, if we elevate utopia more and more into the 17 transcendent, out of the horizontal and into the vertical, then there arises the grave danger—and indeed the inevitable danger—that the truth, fruitfulness, and power of utopia will be sacrificed. This can happen in the form of reactionary religious conservatism which in utopian disillusionment not only misunderstands the truth of utopia but denies that truth and, far from affirming the present situation, preaches that denial together with the "fallenness" of the political realm. Such conservatism is a natural ally of a pure transcendental vision of human fulfillment. But those who hold such a view forfeit their influence over history. Even before World War I we found this to be true in Lutheranism where such a conservative transcendental form of utopia resisted every attempt to change reality. We found it also in certain forms of transcendental theology—that theology which in the name of a revelation given from "above" reality denies every realistic effort to better reality. We find it even in the half-religious, half-antireligious stance of certain existentialists who reject the idea of utopia in the name of an idea of absolute freedom of the individual without, however, concern for progress, individual or social. This is what happens if utopia is denied, if it is regarded as untrue, if its fruitfulness is disclaimed and its power thereby undermined. The consequences of this denial, as we know from history, have been extraordinary. A religious transcendentalism that denied utopia has condemned whole peoples to a passivity opposed to all actions which seek to change history and shape reality—and this has been partially the case in Germany. This is why revolutionary-utopian forces have set themselves against transcendentalism with such tremendous power so that now almost everywhere in the world they thrive on this opposition because religions at their center are either quite beyond any utopia, as the great mystical religions of the East, or have a transcendental utopia excluding political activity, as is the case in much of the West. Where this is true, the aggressive utopia is almost irresistible, and in a time of convulsive economic, political, and intellectual upheaval the passive strength of those who must resist such an onslaught has weakened to the extent that the aggressive utopia breaks through in all its revolu-

tionary power. This is a partial analysis of what has happened to a large part
of humanity in our own time.

Now, in conclusion, let me attempt briefly to formulate *how we should*   18
regard utopia on the basis of this analysis of its positive and negative meaning
and its transcendence. The problem for my generation in Germany came
alive when we returned from World War I and found ourselves in the midst
of a sharp conflict between a conservative Lutheranism with its transcendental utopia and a worldly utopian socialism with an exclusively immanent utopia.

Socialism had won the revolution because the strength of the conser-   19
vatives was destroyed or disorganized by the war. Yet the Lutherans, by
far the Protestant majority in Germany, rejected with distinct hostility the
horizontal utopia of the socialists and accused them of having a false view
of man—of being utopia in the sense of utopian untruth. At this time the
problem of the relation of politics and religion ceased to be abstract for us
and became highly concrete because of this postwar situation. From our
experience in the war and our own reflection we were certain of two
things: First, that a utopia of simple progress failed to take seriously the
finitude and estrangement of the human situation and thus would lead inevitably to metaphysical disillusionment; and, second, that a religion in
which utopia is exclusively transcendent cannot be an expression of the
New Being, of which the Christian message is witness. These were the two
firm convictions which impelled us to act, and in the power of these nega-
tions we then tried to understand what the truth, fruitfulness, and power
of utopia could mean if we did not fall prey to its untruth, unfruitfulness,
and impotence and the metaphysical disillusionment resulting from this
impotence. We answered that in the horizontal dimension something *can*
happen, something new, something realizable here and now, under present
circumstances and conditions, with their unique possibilities. We determined to press forward in order to become aware of our possibilities and
convert them into reality. We believed it to be an "hour of fulfillment" of
possibilities which earlier had been unable to come to fulfillment. Thus we
affirmed the idea of utopia. We felt that man's essential being cried out for
a new order and that this new order could be born at that historical moment for a definite historical period. That was one side, and that is why
we opposed the transcendental theology of Lutheranism.

On the other side, we fully understood the new order we sought was   20
a preliminary one and therefore ambiguous and not to be taken as absolute.
But then came those things of such horrible consequence—terror, and fanaticism turned against itself. Both show that every utopia, when actualized,
stands as a transitory reality and is therefore preliminary and ambiguous. We
were told that if we dared express such an idea—for which we often used the
Greek word *kairos* (the "right time," the hour of fulfillment which has come,
which previously had not been and which subsequently would no longer

be)—we would weaken the revolutionary forces of the socialist utopia by undermining the faith of those who fought for it. I have always maintained that the power of a movement, particularly a utopian movement, depends on its ability to demand an unconditional faith; and, if it is not granted such faith, then it is unable to actualize itself. The possibility that such faith will be undermined presents perhaps the most serious problem for the concept of *kairos,* one for which there is no adequate solution.

But there is a possible solution, if not a perfect one. Under certain 21 conditions every finite reality which is idolatrously regarded as absolute will inspire fanaticism. This is always a possibility because men will quickly commit themselves to any cause that promises certainty in their existence, and such total commitment produces an abundance of combative forces— the will to martyrdom, the readiness to surrender autonomy, and above all what one might call "ideocracy," total submission to the absolute authority of an idea endowed with divine sanction, even to the extent of becoming a substitute for God, no longer subject to doubt and therefore commanding unconditional adherence. This total commitment is always a possibility, and its power over men should never be underestimated. These are indeed powerful forces, but our question is this: Shall we let such forces, which inspire such fanatic, such idolatrous commitment, go unchallenged? Shall we let them have their way? If we do, they may for a time get the best of us, but then the moment comes in which the aggressive utopia shows it is nothing more than a finite form masquerading as an infinite, an absolute one; and at that moment it collides with other finite forms and is itself shattered in the collision.

This seems to me to be an unavoidable conclusion, and we must 22 choose whether to renounce the forces of fanaticism altogether or, despite the risk, to demand an unconditional commitment to them in the hour of need. In committing ourselves, however, we recognize that we are not committed to something absolute but to something preliminary and ambiguous. It is therefore not of divine inviolability but something we ourselves judge and, if need be, even reject; yet in the moment of action we are enabled to affirm it with an unqualified "Yes." This is true not only in the life of society but in our own lives, every moment, whenever we surrender ourselves to a thing or person—as in every love relationship. If we commit ourselves idolatrously, then metaphysical disillusionment is inevitable. Then the finite person or thing that has been made absolute collides with our own finite and is shattered in the collision. If, however, we say "Yes" to something whose finitude we admit, then the truth of utopia is on our side and this truth will ultimately triumph. I know how difficult it is; I know that from the heated debates in those years between the world wars in which we were repeatedly accused by the utopian side of undermining the forces of battle by appealing to this principle of final criticism. I believe history has proved us right.

This is one answer we gave then, and it is an answer I give today even   23
though the concrete situation itself has changed drastically. The second answer concerns the relation of the immanent and transcendental utopias—or
better, since these terms bear such misleading connotations, between the
horizontal and vertical utopias. This answer is *the idea of two orders,* one in the
horizontal plane, the order of finitude with its possibilities and impossibilities, its risks, its successes and failures; and another, a "vertical order" (the
term now used symbolically), an order which secular and religious utopias
have expressed in symbols such as "Kingdom of God," "Kingdom of
heaven," "Kingdom of justice," and "the consummation." We must always
bear in mind that in discussing such symbols we cannot in the least depict
literally what they may mean; we only know that no objective concept can
yield a meaningful statement about them. But we do have knowledge of these
two "orders" because both participate reciprocally in one another. The vertical order participates in the horizontal order—that is, the Kingdom of God
actualizes itself in historical events. It both actualizes itself and at the same
time is resisted, suppressed, vanquished. Yet it is this fighting Kingdom of
God in history that cannot disillusion because it does not confer utopian
finality to any place or time in history; rather it always makes itself known
again and again in ever new actualizations, so that the truth of utopia is
always borne out. This reciprocal participation of the two orders is the solution to the problem of utopia. A Kingdom of God that is not involved in
historical events, in utopian actualization in time, is not the Kingdom of God
at all but at best only a mystical annihilation of everything that can be
"kingdom"—namely, richness, fullness, manifoldness, individuality. And,
similarly, a Kingdom of God that is nothing but the historical process produces a utopia of endless progress or convulsive revolution whose catastrophic collapse eventuates in metaphysical disillusionment.

In the doctrine of the two orders we have both historical reality and   24
transhistorical fulfillment: We have the vertical, where alone fulfillment is
to be found, yet precisely where we are unable to see it but can only point
to it; and the horizontal, actualization in space and time but for that very
reason never full actualization but always partial, fragmentary, in this hour,
in that form. This is our double answer, and even in making it I would like
to say that every manifestation since the end of World War I, when these
ideas were conceived, has borne out this answer, and it seems to me today
to be still the solution. Whether one can speak at all today in the sense of
a *kairos,* as it was unquestionably possible to speak after World War I in
Germany—and in such a way as even to be heard beyond the borders of
Germany—no one indeed can judge, for we are already emerging from that
period into a new one. But my own deep feeling is that ours is a period in
which the *kairos,* the right time for utopian realization, lies far before us,
invisible, while only a void, an unfulfilled space, a vacuum, surrounds us.
But it should be taken as no more than a personal opinion if I have found
the situation after both world wars in Germany comparable with that in
America. That is not important. What is important are the principles to be

derived from the present situation as from that one, insofar always as we are able to describe our situation. What is important is the *idea* of utopia that overcomes utopia in its untruth and sustains it in its truth. Or, as I can perhaps say in summation of the whole discussion: *It is the spirit of utopia that conquers utopia.*

Questions for Discussion

1. What does Tillich seem to mean by the "fallenness" and "estrangement" of human beings in paragraph 7? From what have human beings fallen and become estranged, and what is their present condition?

2. Can you explain what Tillich seems to mean in paragraph 9 by the statement, "However provisionally we live in the future, we actually live always in the preliminary and the ambiguous"? What does the truth of this statement, in Tillich's view, have to do with how we should deal with utopian ideas?

3. Also in paragraph 9, Tillich talks about those people who become *"fanatics against their own past."* What does he seem to mean by this description? What danger does he see in such a fanaticism?

4. Tillich concedes that some people, in order to protect society from the potential destructiveness of utopianism, have recommended giving up utopian dreams altogether. What does Tillich feel to be the weakness of this recommendation (¶17)?

5. How would you express in your own words the meaning of Tillich's final sentence, *"It is the spirit of utopia that conquers utopia."*

Suggested Essay Topics

1. Using the *structure,* not the content, of Tillich's argument as a *model* for an argument of your own, choose a fairly complex idea or motive upon which people base their actions and, like Tillich, show that the object you are analyzing has strengths that are, in some forms, also its weaknesses. For example, you might show the negative and positive features of political activism, of working hard for grades, of taking others' feelings into consideration, or of wanting to be the best, and so on. Choose your audience based on the members' intrinsic interest in the particular topic you have chosen.

2. Write a dialogue in which Tillich and Popper (see the next essay) debate the value of utopianism in front of your class. Allow questions from the "audience" of you and your peers that the "speakers" try to answer. Make sure "your" Tillich and Popper talk productively; that is, they should use their terms the same way and really understand each others' points even when they disagree. Append a final page in which you assess whether the

writing of the dialogue helped you improve your understanding of Til-lich's and Popper's arguments.

Karl R. Popper

Philosopher Karl Popper (b. 1902) was born and educated in Vienna, but he taught and wrote at the University of London from 1945 until his retirement in 1969.

We are replacing our usual introduction with another demonstration of "How to Read an Argument." This demonstration is more extended than the one following Elaine Morgan's essay (Chapter 2). Here we offer first some suggestions about how to read an essay like Popper's. Then we follow the essay with an analysis that "walks through" the essay point by point.

How to Read an Argument:
Demonstration

By now you have seen that arguments re-veal a variety of purposes, tones, and shapes: sleek and streamlined, colloquial and chatty, complicated and interlocking, formal and lofty, and so on. The different varieties, moreover, require different kinds of reading skills.

Popper's essay, "Utopia and Violence," relies on (1) complex thought (the author troubles himself throughout to qualify, define, and explain with precision), (2) formal tone (he uses the vocabulary and sentence structure of someone engaged in a serious task directed at an educated audience), (3) analytical methodology (he elabo-rately separates his position into parts), and (4) intellectual intent (he primarily addresses his audience's capacity for thoughtful rather than emotional response).

To inexperienced readers such arguments often seem a tangle of briars in which they wander lost and frustrated, annoyed at the teacher for assigning such thorny stuff and becoming increasingly gloomy about the chances of escaping with any dignity or understanding. Unfortunately, there are no secret maps for keeping one's bearings inside such arguments—if there were, none of us would require either practice or intelligence. But there are some guideposts that can help to point us in the right direction. What follows here is a list of questions to ask as one reads essays like Popper's. Trying to fit the answers into a coherent reading of the text will move one toward a genuine "meeting" with a new and challenging author, even when, as is almost always the case, the text still refuses to yield itself up completely.

1. Topic.   What is the author's topic—the general area of interest and concern being dealt with?

2. Thesis.   *What is the author's thesis—that is, what specific proposition or hypothesis concerning the general* topic *is the author making? The* thesis *is a proposition that the author wants to persuade the reader to believe.*

3. Definitions of Terms.   *What words or phrases seem crucial to the author's argument, and what meanings, explicit or implied, does he or she focus on throughout the essay? It is only by thinking hard about definitions that we turn* words *into the* terms *that form the elements of an author's argument.*

4. Evidence: Facts, Examples, Statistics, Analogies, and the Like. *Good readers persistently ask authors, at every step in a given argument, "What's your evidence?" Authors often openly welcome the question, especially those who exhibit great care and formality in their reasoning. And most authors, if their tasks are at all serious, in some way anticipate our habit of questioning the evidence. But the answers will vary greatly from author to author and from subject to subject, both in kind and quality. For some subjects, some authors will ask us to take examples from "real life," or even invented examples, as hard proof. (Much of Einstein's evidence in his early papers consisted of "thought experiments" that could not possibly be carried out in reality.) Other authors will offer us extensive statistical analyses. Still others will depend on analogies; astronomers often have to do so. When used appropriately, examples and analogies count as evidence. They often constitute the only kinds of evidence we can lay our hands on. Thus they are not to be automatically despised or dismissed because they are not scientific or factual. One mark of a liberal education is to know what kinds of evidence are appropriate, or even possible, in a given subject. As Aristotle says, it is foolish to ask for greater precision of proof than a given subject allows.*

The only rule for the reader, then, is to check in every case to discover whether the required kind of evidence has in fact been offered. What an author says *supports a claim must really do so. Controversies in all areas of life often revolve around just this issue, because no one has ever been able to formulate a uniform "code of evidence" applicable to all cases of serious reasoning.*

The most frequently praised kind of evidence these days is probably "the facts." Even people who fiercely dispute their interpretation and significance generally agree that once "facts" are ascertained, they must *be taken into account. To many people, the "harder" or more solid a fact is, the more weight it carries: the height of Mt. Everest, the atomic weight of elements, the statistics about lung cancer, the life expectancy of American females, or the size of the gross national product. To others, a sensation, a feeling, a dream, an ambition, or a sense of awe can qualify as a fact.*

Obviously the whole realm of discourse would be a lot easier to manage if facts had an intrinsic, self-announcing quality that set them off into easily recognizable categories—but they do not. No datum simply is *a relevant fact; it* becomes *a fact in an argument as one decides how it can be used to support a conclusion. Nothing is more common than debaters denying the relevance, or even the solidity, of each other's facts. (See Edward Carr, "The Historian and His Facts," pp. 784–794, and the introduction to that essay.) Despite their elusiveness, however, they can be the strongest kind of evidence whenever both parties to a discussion can agree about what they are. To insert them successfully into an argument is like thumping a trump card on an opponent's ace.*

   5. Literary Devices. *Literary devices—such as personification, imagery, hyperbole, and irony—are sometimes powerfully persuasive. Metaphors are especially important. Sometimes their effect is local, limited to a particular sentence or paragraph, as when we said that reading some essays is like getting lost in a briar patch. But sometimes they exert a controlling influence over both the meaning and the structure of a whole argument. (For a discussion of metaphors, see the selection by Lakoff and Johnson beginning on p. 237, and for an example of an argument controlled throughout by a single dominant metaphor, see the selection by Plato beginning on p. 473.) If we had said, for example, that reading essays is like diving for pearls (you take a deep breath, plunge into alien waters, grab frantically at all of the oysters you can pry loose, and finally pop to the surface hoping you've snagged a pearl somewhere in your take), and if we had tried to make everything else we said about reading consistent with our pearl-diving metaphor,* then *we would have been operating under the influence of a controlling metaphor. Not every author relies on extended metaphors, and not all authors are even conscious of what metaphors they do use. But metaphors are usually present in an essay (some scholars, like Lakoff and Johnson, claim they are inescapable), and whenever metaphors occur, they, like all other literary devices, are crucially important.*

   6. Assumptions. *All arguments take some things for granted in order to get themselves launched. Even positions that rely, like Popper's, on close reasoning still rest on a foundation of (implied or stated) ideas, principles, or value judgments that the author simply* assumes *to be true; demonstrations of their truth are seldom offered, although they may be subject to rational criticism and defense elsewhere.*

   In order to make this argument about how to read certain kinds of essays, for example, we unavoidably rest our case on several assumptions. We assume, first, that the essays we read together have coherent meanings that are, on the whole, "public" and not just private. Otherwise we could not talk about ways of drawing out those meanings for general discussion. Second, we assume that it is better to get at an author's meaning by means of a systematic method, analyzing an argument for topic, thesis, definitions, assumptions, and so on. Third, we assume that this method can itself be discussed—it, too, is coherent and can be publicly assessed—and it can be duplicated and applied to any number of arguments. If we were operating on a contrary set of assumptions—that nonreplicable and unsystematic private intuitions were the foundation of all understanding—then we would have no business describing a method *for reading an essay.*

   Each of our assumptions, like those behind any argument, might be challenged and in turn defended. But whether we choose to accept or reject an author's assumptions, it is essential to our understanding to identify them.

7. Logical Coherence. *Once an author's assumptions have been uncovered, the reader is ready to ask questions about logical inference. We all feel that catching an author in an illogicality weighs heavily against a conclusion. Whenever authors contradict themselves, claim to have proved something that they have only asserted, cite inappropriate or inconclusive evidence, fail to cite evidence where it is necessary, ignore evidence that undercuts their case, call their opponents names instead of disproving their arguments, and jump over large areas of argumentative terrain that need to be surveyed, they have (at least partially) discredited their position. They may even have discredited themselves personally, giving the impression that they are "up to something" or that they are tackling a task beyond their abilities. In short, we all have a strong sense that the logical relationships within a position are among the most important determiners of its credibility.*

The logic of an argument can be assessed by readers in three ways: first, by analyzing the formal relationships between premises and conclusions, an activity that can be done in a highly technical way by logicians and philosophers but can also be done in a less technical way by the general reader (see the section on "logical fallacies" in your rhetoric book or handbook and "What Is an Argument?" in this book, pp. 19–21); second, by testing an author's claims against whatever knowledge, experience, and evidence of your own you happen to possess; and third, by testing an author's claims against your intuitions, sometimes even in the absence of hard evidence or reasons, about what makes "good sense."

None of these is an infallible test of an author's logic, but they are all that we have to work with. The places to look sharp for logical connections or illogical jumps are at points of transition, when terms of conclusion such as hence, therefore, and finally *appear, and at points where examples and metaphors are offered. These are the places where authors sometimes fail to link the parts of their arguments together tightly. The reader can test the "tightness" by going back to a concluding term and tracing the links that lead up to it or by asking critically whether the example or metaphor really applies in the way that the author claims.*

8. Overall Structure. *All the while you are asking our first seven questions about an essay, you are in fact working to discover the structure of the argument— progressing a long way toward discovering the steps, large and small, that the author is taking. A final way of checking your reconstruction is to look again at all of the "signals of transition" that provide clues about where the author* thinks *the argument has come from and where it is going: transitional paragraphs only one or two sentences long; words like* therefore, then, thus, so, hence, nevertheless, finally; *and designations of series, such as* first, second, what's more. *Though you may have attempted an outline of the essay at earlier points, it may sometimes be only at this final moment of synthesis that you can construct one that satisfies you fully.*

Now, keeping these eight guideposts in mind, read Popper's essay as critically as you can. Although we will offer our analysis of "Utopia and Violence" at the end of the essay, try to construct your own before you read ours. You will then be better able to assess whether we have followed our own guideposts well or badly.

UTOPIA AND VIOLENCE

From *Conjectures and Refutations: The Growth of Scientific Knowledge* (1963; 2d ed. 1965; 3d ed. 1969; we are reprinting from the 2d ed.).

There are many people who hate violence and are convinced that it is   1
one of their foremost and at the same time one of their most hopeful tasks
to work for its reduction and, if possible, for its elimination from human life.
I am among these hopeful enemies of violence. I not only hate violence, but
I firmly believe that the fight against it is not at all hopeless. I realize that the
task is difficult. I realize that, only too often in the course of history, it has
happened that what appeared at first to be a great success in the fight against
violence was followed by defeat. I do not overlook the fact that the new age
of violence which was opened by the two world wars is by no means at an
end. Nazism and Fascism are thoroughly beaten, but I must admit that their
defeat does not mean that barbarism and brutality have been defeated. On
the contrary, it is no use closing our eyes to the fact that these hateful ideas
achieved something like victory in defeat. I have to admit that Hitler succeeded in degrading the moral standards of our Western world, and that in
the world of today there is more violence and brutal force than would have
been tolerated even in the decade after the first world war. And we must face
the possibility that our civilization may ultimately be destroyed by those new
weapons which Hitlerism wished upon us, perhaps even within the first
decade* after the second world war; for no doubt the spirit of Hitlerism won
its greatest victory over us when, after its defeat, we used the weapons which
the threat of Nazism had induced us to develop. But in spite of all this I am
today no less hopeful than I have ever been that violence can be defeated.
It is our only hope; and long stretches in the history of Western as well as
of Eastern civilizations prove that it need not be a vain hope—that violence
can be reduced, and brought under the control of reason.

This is perhaps why I, like many others, believe in reason; why I call   2
myself a rationalist. I am a rationalist because I see in the attitude of reasonableness the only alternative to violence.

When two men disagree, they do so either because their opinions differ,   3
or because their interests differ, or both. There are many kinds of disagreement in social life which must be decided one way or another. The question
may be one which must be settled, because failure to settle it may create new
difficulties whose cumulative effects may cause an intolerable strain, such as
a state of continual and intense preparation for deciding the issue. (An arma-
ments race is an example.) To reach a decision may be a necessity.

*This was written in 1947. Today I should alter this passage merely by replacing "first" by
"second." [Popper's note.]

How can a decision be reached? There are, in the main, only two possi- 4
ble ways: argument (including arguments submitted to arbitration, for example to some international court of justice) and violence. Or, if it is interests
that clash, the two alternatives are a reasonable compromise or an attempt to
destroy the opposing interest.

A rationalist, as I use the word, is a man who attempts to reach decisions 5
by argument and perhaps, in certain cases, by compromise, rather than by
violence. He is a man who would rather be unsuccessful in convincing another man by argument than successful in crushing him by force, by intimi-
dation and threats, or even by persuasive propaganda.

We shall understand better what I mean by reasonableness if we con- 6
sider the difference between trying to convince a man by argument and trying
to persuade him by propaganda.

The difference does not lie so much in the use of argument. Propaganda 7
often uses argument too. Nor does the difference lie in our conviction that
our arguments are conclusive, and must be admitted to be conclusive by any
reasonable man. It lies rather in an attitude of give and take, in a readiness
not only to convince the other man but also possibly to be convinced by him.
What I call the attitude of reasonableness may be characterized by a remark
like this: "I think I am right, but I may be wrong and you may be right, and
in any case let us discuss it, for in this way we are likely to get nearer to a
true understanding than if we each merely insist that we are right."

It will be realized that what I call the attitude of reasonableness or the 8
rationalistic attitude presupposes a certain amount of intellectual humility.
Perhaps only those can take it up who are aware that they are sometimes
wrong, and who do not habitually forget their mistakes. It is born of the
realization that we are not omniscient, and that we owe most of our knowledge to others. It is an attitude which tries as far as possible to transfer to the
field of opinions in general the two rules of every legal proceeding: first, that
one should always hear both sides, and secondly, that one does not make a
good judge if one is a party to the case.

I believe that we can avoid violence only in so far as we practise this 9
attitude of reasonableness when dealing with one another in social life; and
that any other attitude is likely to produce violence—even a one-sided attempt to deal with others by gentle persuasion, and to convince them by
argument and example of those insights we are proud of possessing, and of
whose truth we are absolutely certain. We all remember how many religious
wars were fought for a religion of love and gentleness; how many bodies were
burned alive with the genuinely kind intention of saving souls from the
eternal fire of hell. Only if we give up our authoritarian attitude in the realm
of opinion, only if we establish the attitude of give and take, of readiness to
learn from other people, can we hope to control acts of violence inspired by
piety and duty.

There are many difficulties impeding the rapid spread of reasonableness. 10
One of the main difficulties is that it always takes two to make a discussion
reasonable. Each of the parties must be ready to learn from the other. You

cannot have a rational discussion with a man who prefers shooting you to being convinced by you. In other words, there are limits to the attitude of reasonableness. It is the same with tolerance. You must not, without qualification, accept the principle of tolerating all those who are intolerant; if you do, you will destroy not only yourself, but also the attitude of tolerance. (All this is indicated in the remark I made before—that reasonableness must be an attitude of *give and take.*)

An important consequence of all this is that we must not allow the 11 distinction between attack and defence to become blurred. We must insist upon this distinction, and support and develop social institutions (national as well as international) whose function it is to discriminate between aggression and resistance to aggression.

I think I have said enough to make clear what I intend to convey by 12 calling myself a rationalist. My rationalism is not dogmatic. I fully admit that I cannot rationally prove it. I frankly confess that I choose rationalism because I hate violence, and I do not deceive myself into believing that this hatred has any rational grounds. Or to put it another way, my rationalism is not self-contained, but rests on an irrational faith in the attitude of reasonableness. I do not see that we can go beyond this. One could say, perhaps, that my irrational faith in equal and reciprocal rights to convince others and be convinced by them is a faith in human reason; or simply, that I believe in man.

If I say that I believe in man, I mean in man as he is; and I should never 13 dream of saying that he is wholly rational. I do not think that a question such as whether man is more rational than emotional or *vice versa* should be asked: there are no ways of assessing or comparing such things. I admit that I feel inclined to protest against certain exaggerations (arising largely from a vulgarization of psycho-analysis) of the irrationality of man and of human society. But I am aware not only of the power of emotions in human life, but also of their value. I should never demand that the attainment of an attitude of reasonableness should become the one dominant aim of our lives. All I wish to assert is that this attitude can become one that is never wholly absent—not even in relationships which are dominated by great passions, such as love.*

My fundamental attitude towards the problem of reason and violence 14 will by now be understood; and I hope I share it with some of my readers and with many other people everywhere. It is on this basis that I now propose to discuss the problem of Utopianism.

I think we can describe Utopianism as a result of a form of rationalism, 15 and I shall try to show that this is a form of rationalism very different from the form in which I and many others believe. So I shall try to show that there exist at least two forms of rationalism, one of which I believe is right and the

---

*The existentialist Jaspers writes, "This is why love is cruel, ruthless; and why it is believed in, by the genuine lover, only if it is so." This attitude, to my mind, reveals weakness rather than the strength it wishes to show; it is not so much plain barbarism as an hysterical attempt to play the barbarian. (*Cf.* my *Open Society,* 4th edn., vol. II, p. 317.) [Popper's note.]

other wrong; and that the wrong kind of rationalism is the one which leads to Utopianism.

As far as I can see, Utopianism is the result of a way of reasoning which is accepted by many who would be astonished to hear that this apparently quite inescapable and self-evident way of reasoning leads to Utopian results. This specious reasoning can perhaps be presented in the following manner.

An action, it may be argued, is rational if it makes the best use of the available means in order to achieve a certain end. The end, admittedly, may be incapable of being determined rationally. However this may be, we can judge an action rationally, and describe it as rational or adequate, only relative to some given end. Only if we have an end in mind, and only relative to such an end, can we say that we are acting rationally.

Now let us apply this argument to politics. All politics consists of actions; and these actions will be rational only if they pursue some end. The end of a man's political actions may be the increase of his own power or wealth. Or it may perhaps be the improvement of the laws of the state, a change in the structure of the state.

In the latter case political action will be rational only if we first determine the final ends of the political changes which we intend to bring about. It will be rational only relative to certain ideas of what a state ought to be like. Thus it appears that as a preliminary to any rational political action we must first attempt to become as clear as possible about our ultimate political ends; for example the kind of state which we should consider the best; and only afterwards can we begin to determine the means which may best help us to realize this state, or to move slowly towards it, taking it as the aim of an historical process which we may to some extent influence and steer towards the goal selected.

Now it is precisely this view which I call Utopianism. Any rational and nonselfish political action, on this view, must be preceded by a determination of our ultimate ends, not merely of intermediate or partial aims which are only steps towards our ultimate end, and which therefore should be considered as means rather than as ends; therefore rational political action must be based upon a more or less clear and detailed description or blueprint of our ideal state, and also upon a plan or blueprint of the historical path that leads towards this goal.

I consider what I call Utopianism an attractive and, indeed, an all too attractive theory; for I also consider it dangerous and pernicious. It is, I believe, self-defeating, and it leads to violence.

That it is self-defeating is connected with the fact that it is impossible to determine ends scientifically. There is no scientific way of choosing between two ends. Some people, for example, love and venerate violence. For them a life without violence would be shallow and trivial. Many others, of whom I am one, hate violence. This is a quarrel about ends. It cannot be decided by science. This does not mean that the attempt to argue against violence is necessarily a waste of time. It only means that you may not be able to argue with the admirer of violence. He has a way of answering an argument with a bullet if he is not kept under control by the threat of counter-violence. If he is willing to listen to your arguments without shooting you, then he is at least infected by rationalism, and you may, perhaps, win him over. This is why arguing is no waste of time—as long as people listen to you. But you cannot, by means of argument, make people listen to argument; you cannot, by means of argument, convert those who suspect all argument, and who prefer violent decisions to rational decisions. You cannot prove to them that they are wrong. And this is only a particular case, which can be generalized. No decision about aims can be established by *purely* rational or scientific means. Nevertheless argument may prove extremely helpful in reaching a decision about aims.

Applying all this to the problem of Utopianism, we must first be quite   23
clear that the problem of constructing a Utopian blueprint cannot possibly be solved by science alone. Its aims, at least, must be given before the social scientist can begin to sketch his blueprint. We find the same situation in the natural sciences. No amount of physics will tell a scientist that it is the right thing for him to construct a plough, or an aeroplane, or an atomic bomb. Ends must be adopted by him, or given to him; and what he does *qua* [as] scientist is only to construct means by which these ends can be realized.

In emphasizing the difficulty of deciding, by way of rational argument,   24
between different Utopian ideals, I do not wish to create the impression that there is a realm—such as the realm of ends—which goes altogether beyond the power of rational criticism (even though I certainly wish to say that the realm of ends goes largely beyond the power of *scientific* argument). For I myself try to argue about this realm; and by pointing out the difficulty of deciding between competing Utopian blueprints, I try to argue rationally against choosing ideal ends of this kind. Similarly, my attempt to point out that this difficulty is likely to produce violence is meant as a rational argument, although it will appeal only to those who hate violence.

That the Utopian method, which chooses an ideal state of society as the   25
aim which all our political actions should serve, is likely to produce violence can be shown thus. Since we cannot determine the ultimate ends of political actions scientifically, or by purely rational methods, differences of opinion concerning what the ideal state should be like cannot always be smoothed out by the method of argument. They will at least partly have the character of religious differences. And there can be no tolerance between these different Utopian religions. Utopian aims are designed to serve as a basis for rational political action and discussion, and such action appears to be possible only if the aim is definitely decided upon. Thus the Utopianist must win over, or else crush, his Utopianist competitors who do not share his own Utopian aims and who do not profess his own Utopianist religion.

But he has to do more. He has to be very thorough in eliminating and   26
stamping out all heretical competing views. For the way to the Utopian goal is long. Thus the rationality of his political action demands constancy of aim for a long time ahead; and this can only be achieved if he not merely crushes

competing Utopian religions, but as far as possible stamps out all memory of them.

The use of violent methods for the suppression of competing aims 27 becomes even more urgent if we consider that the period of Utopian construction is liable to be one of social change. In such a time ideas are liable to change also. Thus what may have appeared to many as desirable at the time when the Utopian blueprint was decided upon may appear less desirable at a later date. If this is so, the whole approach is in danger of breaking down. For if we change our ultimate political aims while attempting to move towards them we may soon discover that we are moving in circles. The whole method of first establishing an ultimate political aim and then preparing to move towards it must be futile if the aim may be changed during the process of its realization. It may easily turn out that the steps so far taken lead in fact away from the new aim. And if we then change direction in accordance with our new aim we expose ourselves to the same risk. In spite of all the sacrifices which we may have made in order to make sure that we are acting rationally, we may get exactly nowhere—although not exactly to that "nowhere" which is meant by the word "Utopia."

Again, the only way to avoid such changes of our aims seems to be to 28 use violence, which includes propaganda, the suppression of criticism, and the annihilation of all opposition. With it goes the affirmation of the wisdom and foresight of the Utopian planners, of the Utopian engineers who design and execute the Utopian blueprint. The Utopian engineers must in this way become omniscient as well as omnipotent. They become gods. Thou shalt have no other Gods before them.

Utopian rationalism is a self-defeating rationalism. However benevo- 29 lent its ends, it does not bring happiness, but only the familiar misery of being condemned to live under a tyrannical government.

It is important to understand this criticism fully. I do not criticize politi- 30 cal ideals as such, nor do I assert that a political ideal can never be realized. This would not be a valid criticism. Many ideals have been realized which were once dogmatically declared to be unrealizable, for example, the establishment of workable and untyrannical institutions for securing civil peace, that is, for the suppression of crime within the state. Again, I see no reason why an international judicature and an international police force should be less successful in suppressing international crime, that is, national aggression and the ill-treatment of minorities or perhaps majorities. I do not object to the attempt to realize such ideals.

Wherein, then, lies the difference between those benevolent Utopian 31 plans to which I object because they lead to violence, and those other important and far-reaching political reforms which I am inclined to recommend?

If I were to give a simple formula or recipe for distinguishing between 32 what I consider to be admissible plans for social reform and inadmissible Utopian blueprints, I might say:

Work for the elimination of concrete evils rather than for the realization 33 of abstract goods. Do not aim at establishing happiness by political means.

Rather aim at the elimination of concrete miseries. Or, in more practical terms: fight for the elimination of poverty by direct means—for example, by making sure that everybody has a minimum income. Or fight against epidemics and disease by erecting hospitals and schools of medicine. Fight illiteracy as you fight criminality. But do all this by direct means. Choose what you consider the most urgent evil of the society in which you live, and try patiently to convince people that we can get rid of it.

But do not try to realize these aims indirectly by designing and working 34 for a distant ideal of a society which is wholly good. However deeply you may feel indebted to its inspiring vision, do not think that you are obliged to work for its realization, or that it is your mission to open the eyes of others to its beauty. Do not allow your dreams of a beautiful world to lure you away from the claims of men who suffer here and now. Our fellow men have a claim to our help; no generation must be sacrificed for the sake of future generations, for the sake of an ideal of happiness that may never be realized. In brief, it is my thesis that human misery is the most urgent problem of a rational public policy and that happiness is not such a problem. The attainment of happiness should be left to our private endeavours.

It is a fact, and not a very strange fact, that it is not so very difficult to 35 reach agreement by discussion on what are the most intolerable evils of our society, and on what are the most urgent social reforms. Such an agreement can be reached much more easily than an agreement concerning some ideal form of social life. For the evils are with us here and now. They can be experienced, and are being experienced every day, by many people who have been and are being made miserable by poverty, unemployment, national oppression, war and disease. Those of us who do not suffer from these miseries meet every day others who can describe them to us. This is what makes the evils concrete. This is why we can get somewhere in arguing about them; why we can profit here from the attitude of reasonableness. We can learn by listening to concrete claims, by patiently trying to assess them as impartially as we can, and by considering ways of meeting them without creating worse evils.

With ideal goods it is different. These we know only from our dreams 36 and from the dreams of our poets and prophets. They cannot be discussed, only proclaimed from the housetops. They do not call for the rational attitude of the impartial judge, but for the emotional attitude of the impassioned preacher.

The Utopianist attitude, therefore, is opposed to the attitude of reason- 37 ableness. Utopianism, even though it may often appear in a rationalist disguise, cannot be more than a pseudo-rationalism.

What, then, is wrong with the apparently rational argument which I 38 outlined when presenting the Utopianist case? I believe that it is quite true that we can judge the rationality of an action only in relation to some aims or ends. But this does not necessarily mean that the rationality of a political action can be judged only in relation to an *historical* end. And it surely does not mean that we must consider every social or political situation merely from the point of view of some preconceived historical ideal, from the point of view of an alleged ultimate aim of the development of history. On the contrary, if among our aims and ends there is anything conceived in terms of human happiness and misery, then we are bound to judge our actions in terms not only of possible contributions to the happiness of man in a distant future, but also of their more immediate effects. We must not argue that a certain social situation is a mere means to an end on the grounds that it is merely a transient historical situation. For all situations are transient. Similarly we must not argue that the misery of one generation may be considered as a mere means to the end of securing the lasting happiness of some later generation or generations; and this argument is improved neither by a high degree of promised happiness nor by a large number of generations profiting by it. All generations are transient. All have an equal right to be considered, but our immediate duties are undoubtedly to the present generation and to the next. Besides, we should never attempt to balance anybody's misery against somebody else's happiness.

With this the apparently rational arguments of Utopianism dissolve into 39 nothing. The fascination which the future exerts upon the Utopianist has nothing to do with rational foresight. Considered in this light the violence which Utopianism breeds looks very much like the running amok of an evolutionist metaphysics, of an hysterical philosophy of history, eager to sacrifice the present for the splendours of the future, and unaware that its principle would lead to sacrificing each particular future period for one which comes after it; and likewise unaware of the trivial truth that the ultimate future of man—whatever fate may have in store for him—can be nothing more splendid than his ultimate extinction.

The appeal of Utopianism arises from the failure to realize that we 40 cannot make heaven on earth. What I believe we can do instead is to make life a little less terrible and a little less unjust in each generation. A good deal can be achieved in this way. Much has been achieved in the last hundred years. More could be achieved by our own generation. There are many pressing problems which we might solve, at least partially, such as helping the weak and the sick, and those who suffer under oppression and injustice; stamping out unemployment; equalizing opportunities; and preventing international crime, such as blackmail and war instigated by men like gods, by omnipotent and omniscient leaders. All this we might achieve if only we could give up dreaming about distant ideals and fighting over our Utopian blueprints for a new world and a new man. Those of us who believe in man as he is, and who have therefore not given up the hope of defeating violence and unreason, must demand instead that every man should be given the right to arrange his life himself so far as this is compatible with the equal rights of others.

We can see here that the problem of the true and the false rationalisms 41 is part of a larger problem. Ultimately it is the problem of a sane attitude towards our own existence and its limitations—that very problem of which so much is made now by those who call themselves "Existentialists," the expounders of a new theology without God. There is, I believe, a neurotic and even an hysterical element in this exaggerated emphasis upon the fundamental loneliness of man in a godless world, and upon the resulting tension between the self and the world. I have little doubt that this hysteria is closely akin to Utopian romanticism, and also to the ethic of hero-worship, to an ethic that can comprehend life only in terms of "dominate or prostrate yourself." And I do not doubt that this hysteria is the secret of its strong appeal. That our problem is part of a larger one can be seen from the fact that we can find a clear parallel to the split between true and false rationalism even in a sphere apparently so far removed from rationalism as that of religion. Christian thinkers have interpreted the relationship between man and God in at least two very different ways. The sane one may be expressed by: "Never forget that men are not Gods; but remember that there is a divine spark in them." The other exaggerates the tension between man and God, and the baseness of man as well as the heights to which men may aspire. It introduces the ethic of "dominate or prostrate yourself" into the relationship of man and God. Whether there are always either conscious or unconscious dreams of godlikeness and of omnipotence at the roots of this attitude, I do not know. But I think it is hard to deny that the emphasis on this tension can arise only from an unbalanced attitude towards the problem of power.

This unbalanced (and immature) attitude is obsessed with the problem   42
of power, not only over other men, but also over our natural environment—over the world as a whole. What I might call, by analogy, the "false religion," is obsessed not only by God's power over men but also by His power to create a world; similarly, false rationalism is fascinated by the idea of creating huge machines and Utopian social worlds. Bacon's "knowledge is power" and Plato's "rule of the wise" are different expressions of this attitude which, at bottom, is one of claiming power on the basis of one's superior intellectual gifts. The true rationalist, by contrast, will always know how little he knows, and he will be aware of the simple fact that whatever critical faculty or reason he may possess he owes to intellectual intercourse with others. He will be inclined, therefore, to consider men as fundamentally equal, and human reason as a bond which unites them. Reason for him is the precise opposite of an instrument of power and violence: he sees it as a means whereby these may be tamed.

Analysis of "Utopia and Violence"

If we apply our method for reading an argument to Popper's essay, what does it yield? Let us look systematically at all eight guideposts.

1. Topic.   *Popper begins in paragraph 1 by making three claims: (1) that he along with many other persons hates violence, (2) that the world has become increasingly violent in the aftermath of the two world wars, and (3) that he remains nevertheless convinced that violence can be reduced and "brought under the control of reason." Doing so, he says, "is our only hope." Apparently, then, Popper's topic is the relationship between reason and violence. Notice, however, that this is only a general area of concern. Discovering that Popper is interested in the relationship between reason and violence does not reveal what direction his concern will take or what point about that relationship he wants to make. In other words, we know his topic but not his thesis.*

2. Thesis.   *Notice that paragraph 2 is very short, only two sentences long. Such paragraphs are often transitional. This one sums up the point of paragraph 1, but in doing so Popper manages to indicate clearly his thesis, the point he wants to make: "I see in the attitude of reasonableness the only alternative to violence."*

3. Definitions of Terms.   *We know from Popper's thesis statement that there are two crucial terms in his argument, reasonableness and violence. The second of these he does not define in any special way. He seems to take it for granted that we all know what violence is, and, indeed, his incidental allusions to violence are all conventional: people shooting each other, aggression between nations, certain kinds of oppression by political rulers, and so on.*

Reasonableness, however, has for him a very precise, special meaning, and he expends a considerable amount of effort and space clarifying this key term. He begins by saying what it is not. Reasonableness, he contends, is not merely knowing how to use reason in order to make arguments. Propagandists, tyrants, and oppressors of all sorts know how to use reason to make arguments. Rather, reasonableness "lies . . . in an attitude of give and take, in a readiness not only to convince the other man but also possibly to be convinced by him" (¶7).

But what does give-and-take mean? Primarily it means "humility," "the realization that we are not omniscient, and that we owe most of our knowledge to others" (¶8). (Notice, by the way, that Popper repeats this idea clearly at the end of his essay [¶42]: "The true rationalist . . . will always know . . . that whatever . . . reason he may possess he owes to intellectual intercourse with others." The more times an author repeats an idea in the course of an essay, especially if the repetitions come at key spots such as the beginning and the end, the more you are justified in assuming that the idea possesses central importance.)

In paragraph 9 we learn that humility is not only the admission that we have learned most of what we know from others, but that even our most precious values, even our certainties, are still susceptible to correction. Good intentions do not automatically produce good effects. In the Middle Ages torture was accepted as a device not only for discovering the truth, but also for making wrong-doers confess so that their souls might be saved even as their bodies perished. And in the modern period every violent revolution has produced mass killings by those whose sole professed aim was to create a better society. The number of victims maimed, tortured, and killed in any period would be much smaller if all certainties had been subject to give-and-take. Popper's point is that no belief, no matter how noble or true, allows us to assume our own infallibility; even if our opinions are true, we can never know them to be true in an absolute sense, and, in any event, inflicting pain, destruction, and violence, even in the interests of true opinions, involves us in an irreconcilable contradiction between the nobility of our aims and the ignobility of our methods.

Another term that Popper defines with precision (although it takes less effort because it is derived from his term reasonableness) is the word rationalist. A rationalist, as Popper uses the term, is simply a person committed to give-and-take, to tolerance, and to compromise (at least about conflicts of interest, if not about conflicts of opinion) when give-and-take is abandoned by those he is trying to talk to.

A fourth crucial term, utopianism, does not show up until paragraph 14. As with the term reasonableness, you can form a fairly clear notion of its importance in Popper's argument simply from the amount of discussion he devotes to its clarification. Reasonableness, it turns out, is the hero of his piece; utopianism is the villain. Notice here, by the way, how metaphors exert a controlling influence on one's understanding. The metaphor of "heroes versus villains," which comes from melodramas and westerns, is not used by Popper; we use it in trying to understand him. Notice further that if we were to base our analysis on this metaphor alone, we would trivialize his argument.

Yet our metaphor is appropriate if we apply it with caution, for Popper really intends not only to reveal the evil consequences of accepting utopianism, but to discredit it so thoroughly that no thinking person could retain faith in it after reading his argument. While avoiding melodramatic metaphors, he nevertheless suggests that this is a showdown, that he has viewed this evil phenomenon long enough to be convinced of its dangerousness, that he has thought out his arguments with care and precision, and that he is determined to leave no chink for utopianism to weasel through.

As he develops his views on utopianism at length (¶15–29), we see that he has two main charges to level against it: "It is, I believe, self-defeating, and it leads to violence" (¶21). If this were self-evident to everyone, merely to say it would be at once to express the argument and to prove it. But it is not self-evident, and that is what justifies drawing out the argument. Far from being obviously evil, utopianism, claims Popper, is "an all too attractive theory" (¶21) "which is accepted by many who would be astonished to hear" that it leads inescapably to violence (¶16). These claims place on Popper two burdens: first, to show how utopianism leads to violence and, second, to show why it is attractive (and, necessarily, why its attractiveness is illusory).

Utopianism is attractive because, by definition, it is a form of rationalism (although unlike reasonableness), and it may therefore seem a credible mode of thinking to anyone who values rationality (¶15). It looks rational because it engages in the process of constructing means to achieve already chosen ends (¶20). But, Popper claims, looks are in this case deceptive, for utopianism is "specious reasoning" (¶16), which is to say fair-looking but false.

The falseness of utopianism lies not so much in looking for means to achieve aims—this is rational enough—but in choosing aims that are so difficult to define and so impossible to achieve that they lead inevitably (or so he claims) to violence among those responsible for achieving them. "Utopianists" move "rationally" toward the ideal state, and that, says Popper, is where the trouble begins. Ideal ends, by definition, exist both so far removed from everyday experience and so far removed into the future that "differences of opinion concerning what the ideal state should be like cannot always be smoothed out by the method of argument. They will at least partly have the character of religious differences. And there can be no tolerance between these different Utopian religions" (¶25). Moreover, goals lying so far removed from experience and so far into the future cannot be kept in focus if competing views and shifts of goals are allowed. Thus, on its way toward the noble aim of creating a perfect society, utopianism always winds up employing means that not only create an imperfect society (presumably what we all begin with anyway) but the most imperfect form of society altogether: a totalitarianism that sacrifices everything in the present—the justice, comfort, security, and peace of the present generation—for the good of the ideal future state.

It should be clear by this point that a full understanding of crucial terms sometimes leads us to the very heart of an author's argument. This is not always true, but you should be alert to the possibility.

4. Evidence: Facts, Examples, Statistics, Analogies, and the Like. *Unlike many a serious thinker, Popper relies on few examples, no statistics, and practically no facts. The force of his essay rests almost wholly on the logical coherence of his arguments. Given his aim, one would expect that historical examples might have been useful, but he grounds the argument in logic alone, not on examples that others (presumably the utopianists) could explain away or quibble about. The only place where examples become telling is his catalog (¶33–35) of concrete ills that we should be trying to rid ourselves of: disease, poverty, crime, and so on. If we did not find these examples appropriate his argument would suffer, but because he sticks generally to the obvious ills that, as he says, everyone already recognizes, he runs little risk of discrediting himself with implausible examples. Insofar as the examples he does use are universally admitted to exist, they have the status of facts in his argument. He makes no appeal to other kinds of facts that are often thought useful, such as statistics, measurements, or polls.*

5. Literary Devices. *Popper relies no more on colorful literary devices and metaphors than he does on examples and collections of facts. Like almost all authors, he uses some metaphors, but these are strictly low-key and directly functional rather than "literary." He uses only the kind of metaphors we all use every day—as when he speaks of blueprints for society and moving in circles (¶27)—and their impact is restricted to small passages. None of them determines either his view of his topic or the structure of his essay. Perhaps the most potent metaphor in the whole essay is his allusion in paragraph 28 to "Utopian engineers" who think themselves "omniscient as well as omnipotent"—a metaphor that alludes to the view projected by George Orwell in* Nineteen Eighty-four *and used in a host of science fiction movies. But whether "engineers" is not more of a cliché than a vivid picture is an open question. It is certainly not the most chilling image for political oppressors that he might have* *picked. The restraint seems deliberate. Even in his final sentence, for example, where he speaks of taming the instruments of power and violence, at the terminal point where many authors would be tempted to pull out all the stops, Popper avoids any striving for a highly charged, triumphant, final chord. He seems vigorous but controlled from beginning to end. (Of course one might, as we suggested earlier, claim to see an unspoken master metaphor in the "showdown" or "war" Popper conducts between reason and violence. It is important to think about the implications of unspoken governing metaphors, but this sort of critique is better conducted at a stage following your first thorough analysis of the essay. See Lakoff and Johnson, pp. 237–247.)*

6. Assumptions.   *Perhaps because he is a philosopher, Popper is unusually clear about his assumptions. This is not the case with all writers; many authors seem guided by assumptions that they are only dimly aware of, and their conclusions and assumptions do not always seem consistent.*

The first assumption without which Popper's argument would be impossible, as he is well aware, is his "faith in human reason": "I believe in man," he says (¶12). Without this faith in the capacity of human beings not only to achieve understanding through reason but also to pattern behavior according to reason's light, writing this article would be a futile, self-contradictory undertaking.

Popper's second important assumption is about the limitations of reason. While he is advocating reasonableness with all the energy he can muster, he is only too aware that not everything can be decided on rational grounds alone, especially ultimate goals: "No decision about aims can be established by purely rational or scientific means" (¶22). For example, he says, "No amount of physics will tell a scientist that it is the right thing for him to construct a plough, or an aeroplane, or an atomic bomb" (¶23). This does not mean that all ends, as value judgments, are irrational impulse or whimsy, nor does it mean that they are incapable of reasoned defense. But it does mean that they are the product of vision, intuitions, and experience that go beyond logical argument.

This assumption plays a crucial role in Popper's argument, for if he assumed that final ends could be rationally determined, he would be undercutting his charge that utopianism's rational goals for the future lead to concrete evils in the present.

Popper's third crucial assumption is his belief that "no generation must be sacrificed for the sake of future generations, for the sake of an ideal of happiness that may never be realized" (¶34). He makes this same assertion another time or two in different words in the same paragraph, and utters it once again toward the end of paragraph 38: "We must not argue that a certain social situation is a mere means to an end on the grounds that it is merely a transient historical situation." The development of this assumption's meaning occupies the whole last section of the essay, from paragraphs 32–42.

At this point you may be wanting to say, "It is all very well to point out assumptions, and it is all very helpful when you do, but how do you recognize one in the first place? How did you know that these utterances contained assumptions?" It is a good question, but one to which there is no formulaic answer. The necessary skills are experience at reading arguments like this, experience at thinking about the kinds of ideas they contain, careful observation of the pattern of ideas and expression, and attention to logical connections. This may sound like a tall order for the inexperienced reader, but, as we said in "What Is an Argument?" (pp. 19–21), no one, not even the most inexperienced reader, comes to a piece of writing totally devoid of the powers of observation and logic. And every reader can detect the presence of important generalizations for which no extended argument is offered; they are what is assumed.

When readers who are paying close attention to what Popper is saying come, for example, to paragraph 32, they do not have to be college professors to observe that Popper's offer of "a simple formula or recipe" signals a shift of focus and tone. As the passage proceeds, Popper increasingly abandons neutrality of tone and addresses the reader in a more direct, personal, urgent way: "Do not try," he says, and "do not think," and "do not allow" (¶34). His increasing passion is one of the best clues that you are approaching a nodal point where assumptions lurk. Whenever an author's language becomes prescriptive and personal—"I feel," "I believe," "you must," "you must not"—chances are you are treading on the holy ground of fundamental assumptions.

7. Logical Coherence.

We saw earlier that Popper has two main charges to level against utopianism: that it is self-defeating and that it inevitably leads to violence. The first of these charges he supports convincingly, but the second seems less well supported. In paragraphs 22–28, for example, he launches into an extended argument about the procedure that turns utopian dreams into totalitarian states, but while he shows clearly that utopian ideals will always outpace achievement and are therefore self-defeating, he does not show that the inevitable consequence of this failure is violence. Even if he were able to show that that is what usually happens in fact, he would not have proved its inevitability in principle.

Why would Popper neglect to provide proof for such a crucial point, while elsewhere he demonstrates impressive logical rigor? We might be tempted to assign the status of "assumption" to this point, but Popper himself, as we have seen, is careful to separate his fundamental assumptions from assertions he means to support—and he does, it seems, intend to argue for the violent consequences of utopianism.

In a case like this, where logical coherence inexplicably breaks down, it is useful to search out any other failures or missing steps in the logic and to try to discern a motive behind the author's neglect. Another place where Popper has omitted steps in his argument is paragraph 38. Suddenly, without explanation, he introduces an element that seems totally unprepared for: "I believe that it is quite true that we can judge the rationality of an action only in relation to some aims or ends. But this does not necessarily mean that the rationality of a political action can be judged only in relation to an historical end." The abrupt insertion of a concern about historical ends right in the middle of his argument about ideal ends, without preparation or explanation, raises questions. There is a jump here in the logic that requires an explanation outside the boundaries of the argument itself.

Perhaps the explanation is that Popper, without ever naming Marxist philosophy in his article, is nevertheless constructing an argument against it. Other *writings of his show that he is an implacable foe of Marxist political philosophy, that he considers Marxist philosophers the most hopeless of all utopianists, and the Soviet Union the clearest example of how utopian dreams turn into totalitarian nightmares.*

Why, then, does he not mention that it is the Marxists' *historical ends that he objects to? The question is impossible to answer if the only answer lies in Popper's private motives. But the position itself suggests an answer. If he can demonstrate that all utopian thinking is equally invalid, then it* must *follow that Marxist thinking also stands condemned. But if he makes his quarrel with Marxism alone, he winds up with a weaker position even if he wins, for combating Marxism without combating utopianism means that he must attack Marxism on the basis of its policies, not its principles. He wants the stronger case that will discredit Marxism* and *its cousins once and for all, and the stronger case requires an attack on Marxism's underlying principles.*

Does this attack on Marxism undermine the logical coherence of Popper's essay? Probably not, since one can easily guess his motive for avoiding a direct attack. But it is surely a weakness of Popper's presentation that one cannot find a sufficient number of references within the essay to make this motive clear. And even putting his presentation aside, one illogicality clearly remains: He has not shown that Marxist utopianism must always *produce totalitarian states or, more generally, that utopianism must* always *lead to violence. It is difficult to say just how much this illogicality weakens his entire position. Here is where one must test the logic of a position with one's intuitions about what makes "good sense" and about the limits of our ability to prove generalizations concerning human possibilities.*

8. Overall Structure.   *The problem of how to discover a controlling structure in an argument is no different from the problem of how to discover a set of controlling assumptions. You have to pay close attention and then practice on essay after essay. From the beginning of Popper's essay it is apparent that he is concerned about violence and reasonableness, but it is not clear how the expression of that concern is going to be patterned until we come to paragraph 14. The careful reader will at this point observe that Popper explicitly defines what he has been up to for the first 13 paragraphs: "My fundamental attitude towards the problem of reason and violence will by now be understood." Building on this first clear indication of structure, let us see if we can discern the shape of the essay as a whole.*

I. Paragraphs 1–14: Introduction of topic, thesis, and definition of reasonableness.
   A. Paragraph 1, like most first paragraphs, is an introduction to the topic, the relationship between reason and violence.
   B. Paragraph 2 sums up paragraph 1 and states Popper's thesis.
   C. Paragraphs 3–9 refine the topic and thesis, mainly by providing a definition of *reasonableness* and by providing some appropriate concrete examples.
   D. Paragraphs 10–13 discuss the proper domain of reason, each paragraph adding a refinement to the idea.
   E. Paragraph 14 is transitional, introducing "the problem of Utopianism."

II. Paragraphs 15–29 express the main body of Popper's objections to utopianism.

    A. Paragraphs 15–21 argue that utopianism gives a rational appearance because it lays out goals and selects means for achieving them. This section ends with one of Popper's typical transitional paragraphs (¶21), just two sentences long, introducing a new direction to the discussion.

    B. Paragraphs 22–28 clarify the danger pointed to in the transitional paragraph.

        1. Paragraphs 22–24 begin to explain the danger.

        2. Paragraphs 25–28 become increasingly practical, culminating in a description of utopian planners as "engineers" who pretend to "become omniscient as well as omnipotent."

    C. Paragraph 29 is another two-sentence transition.

III. Paragraphs 30–40 make Popper's suggestions for how to avoid utopian thinking.

    A. Paragraphs 30–32 are a buildup to his catalog of non-utopian remedies.

        1. Paragraph 30 clarifies his critique: He wants the reader to be clear that he does not consider utopian thinking pernicious merely because it spins out ideals.

        2. Paragraph 31 seems to ask (not quite this bluntly), "Well, then, if ideal-oriented thinking isn't the problem, what is?"

        3. Paragraph 32 directly responds: "All right, I'll answer that question, but not by giving more criticisms, which I've already done. I will instead propose concrete remedies."

    B. Paragraphs 33–35 provide the concrete remedies. Popper here lists the ills that political planners should be trying to solve: the concrete evils of everyday life, the obvious ones that everybody already agrees about.

    C. Paragraphs 36–40 directly answer the question asked in paragraph 31, the answer made clearer now that we know what Popper's remedies are. The answer is that utopianism is not evil merely because it is idealistic; the problem is the *kinds* of ideals it commits itself to. Utopianism always assumes a dogmatic character, Popper claims, because it focuses on a future period of perfect happiness, and this seduces utopian-minded planners into thinking that they are justified in sacrificing the quality of present life for an anticipated, hoped-for, perfect, but always equally distant life in the future.

IV. Paragraphs 41–42 conclude Popper's case by positing the relationship between utopianism and general culture.

    A. Paragraph 41 argues that utopianism is one small current in a vast tide of anti-rational, hysterical, exaggerated, and immature responses to the problem of power afflicting Western culture in general. The essence of this attitude is that human beings in the modern world are given to thinking of themselves either as gods or worms, and both attitudes tend to give rulers a handy justification for walking over the people beneath them. If rulers are gods, they can do no wrong. If subjects are worms, they can be done no wrong. He sees this attitude also manifested in both religious and philosophical thinking, not just in political thinking.

    B. Paragraph 42 makes Popper's final point that this attitude, like the utopian thinking it spawns, always leads to violence. In response to that prospect, Popper ends where he began, by advocating reasonableness—intellectual humility and free give-and-take—as the only possible remedy.

Suggested Essay Topics

1. Write an essay addressed to Popper either supporting or attacking his claim that utopianism inevitably leads to violence. Unless you have fairly strong views about how his idea works in political movements, you will do better to relate his thesis to your personal experience of trying to reconcile ideal goals with practical necessities. You might, for example, make use of the popular expression "The perfect is the enemy of the good" and discuss how standards of perfection have sometimes prevented you from doing as well as you could. Or you might make use of opposing popular expressions ("Nothing ventured, nothing gained," "Difficult tasks take time; the impossible takes a little longer") by showing how striving for perfection has sometimes led to improved—though still imperfect—performance.

2. Read Plato's "Allegory of the Cave" (Chapter 6) and compare Plato's emphasis on the importance of the ideal with Popper's emphasis on the importance of the concrete. Discuss whether the ideal that Plato advocates is really the ideal that Popper fears and despises. If you think each author uses this term in the same way, discuss which of them makes the most persuasive case for his view. If you think that each of them uses the term in a different way, discuss the differences and explain why, despite their apparent contradictions of one another, they are not in disagreement because they are not talking about the same thing.

3. You may find it useful to vary topic 2 by turning it into a letter to Popper, arguing against his position using arguments derived from Plato, or vice versa.

Kurt Vonnegut, Jr.

Few statements carry as much meaning and significance for Americans as Jefferson's assertion that "all men are created equal." Despite the statement's ambiguity (equal in what sense?) and its inconsistent application (women and minorities have often been treated as if they were not equal), most Americans nevertheless feel that it expresses one of our nation's most distinctive and noble aspirations.

Yet it is clear that Kurt Vonnegut (b. 1922) thinks not only that this revered belief can become pernicious, but also that society is moving toward the evil conditions he portrays in his story. As a way of understanding this evil, you might ask yourself to what extent Vonnegut's depicted society is utopian. Equality is a good thing, right? All Americans believe in it, right? So what's wrong with a society in which equality is not only embraced in theory but enforced in practice—by impartial legislation? If people of superior ability will always take advantage of their inequality, doesn't handicapping them make sense as a way of evening out the chances of success for the rest of us? Isn't this exactly what Jefferson would have wanted, what his noble statement about equality leads to? Wouldn't getting rid of nasty competition and inequality make the world better, perhaps even perfect?

Maybe, and maybe not. Doesn't it finally depend on how we define "equal"? And on how we think "equal" ought to be protected or enforced? We have seen that Tillich considers utopian thinking inherently ambiguous, that Popper views it as an inevitable prelude to violence, and that Jefferson, if we can call his notions utopian, held the ideal of equality to be consistent with slavery for blacks and no votes for women. What does "equal" mean in these different contexts? Is it possible that Vonnegut's story concretely illustrates Popper's abstract thesis that utopian goals always lead to violence? Does Vonnegut oppose the ideal of equality on principle? If so, what principle? As you read "Harrison Bergeron," try to determine what kind of society Vonnegut would really prefer and what view of his fictional society Jefferson, Tillich, and Popper would take. Finally, try to determine your own views.

HARRISON BERGERON

From *Welcome to the Monkey House* (1961).

The year was 2081, and everybody was finally equal. They weren't only equal before God and the law. They were equal every which way. Nobody was smarter than anybody else. Nobody was better looking than anybody else. Nobody was stronger or quicker than anybody else. All this equality was due to the 211th, 212th, and 213th Amendments to the Constitution, and to the unceasing vigilance of agents of the United States Handicapper General.

Some things about living still weren't quite right, though. April, for instance, still drove people crazy by not being springtime. And it was in that clammy month that the H-G men took George and Hazel Bergeron's fourteen year-old son, Harrison, away.

It was tragic, all right, but George and Hazel couldn't think about it very hard. Hazel had a perfectly average intelligence, which meant she couldn't think about anything except in short bursts. And George, while his intelligence was way above normal, had a little mental handicap radio in his ear. He was required by law to wear it at all times. He was tuned to a government transmitter. Every twenty seconds or so, the transmitter would send out some sharp noise to keep people like George from taking unfair advantage of their brains.

George and Hazel were watching television. There were tears on Hazel's cheeks, but she'd forgotten for the moment what they were about.

On the television screen were ballerinas.

A buzzer sounded in George's head. His thoughts fled in panic, like bandits from a burglar alarm.

"That was a really pretty dance, that dance they just did," said Hazel.

"Huh?" said George.

"That dance—it was nice," said Hazel.   9

"Yup," said George. He tried to think a little about the ballerinas. They   10
weren't really very good—no better than anybody else would have been,
anyway. They were burdened with sash-weights and bags of birdshot, and
their faces were masked, so that no one, seeing a free and graceful gesture or
a pretty face, would feel like something the cat drug in. George was toying
with the vague notion that maybe dancers shouldn't be handicapped. But he
didn't get very far with it before another noise in his ear radio scattered his
thoughts.

George winced. So did two out of the eight ballerinas.   ·   11

Hazel saw him wince. Having no mental handicap herself, she had to   12
ask George what the latest sound had been.

"Sounded like somebody hitting a milk bottle with a ball peen ham-   13
mer," said George.

"I'd think it would be real interesting, hearing all the different sounds,"   14
said Hazel, a little envious. "All the things they think up."

"Um," said George.   15

"Only, if I was Handicapper General, you know what I would do?" said   16
Hazel. Hazel, as a matter of fact, bore a strong resemblance to the Handicapper General, a woman named Diana Moon Glampers. "If I was Diana Moon
Glampers," said Hazel, "I'd have chimes on Sunday—fast chimes. Kind of in
honor of religion."

"I could think, if it was just chimes," said George.   17

"Well—maybe make 'em real loud," said Hazel. "I think I'd make a good   18
Handicapper General."

"Good as anybody else," said George.   19

"Who knows better'n I do what normal is?" said Hazel.   20

"Right," said George. He began to think glimmeringly about his abnor-   21
mal son who was now in jail, about Harrison, but a twenty-one-gun salute
in his head stopped that.

"Boy!" said Hazel, "that was a doozy, wasn't it?"   22

It was such a doozy that George was white and trembling, and tears   23
stood on the rims of his red eyes. Two of the eight ballerinas had collapsed
to the studio floor, were holding their temples.

"All of a sudden you look so tired," said Hazel. "Why don't you stretch   24
out on the sofa, so's you can rest your handicap bag on the pillows, honey-
bunch." She was referring to the forty-seven pounds of birdshot in a canvas
bag, which was padlocked around George's neck. "Go on and rest the bag for
a little while," she said. "I don't care if you're not equal to me for a while."

George weighed the bag with his hands. "I don't mind it," he said. "I   25
don't notice it any more. It's just a part of me."

"You been so tired lately—kind of wore out," said Hazel. "If there was   26
just some way we could make a little hole in the bottom of the bag, and just
take out a few of them lead balls. Just a few."

"Two years in prison and two thousand dollars fine for every ball I took   27
out," said George. "I don't call that a bargain."

"If you could just take a few out when you came home from work," said   28
Hazel. "I mean—you don't compete with anybody around here. You just set
around."

"If I tried to get away with it," said George, "then other people'd get   29
away with it—and pretty soon we'd be right back to the dark ages again, with
everybody competing against everybody else. You wouldn't like that, would
you?"

"I'd hate it," said Hazel.   30

"There you are," said George. "The minute people start cheating on   31
laws, what do you think happens to society?"

If Hazel hadn't been able to come up with an answer to this question,   32
George couldn't have supplied one. A siren was going off in his head.

"Reckon it'd fall all apart," said Hazel.   33

"What would?" said George blankly.   34

"Society," said Hazel uncertainly. "Wasn't that what you just said?"   35

"Who knows?" said George.   36

The television program was suddenly interrupted for a news bulletin.   37
It wasn't clear at first as to what the bulletin was about, since the announcer,
like all announcers, had a serious speech impediment. For about half a minute, and in a state of high excitement, the announcer tried to say, "Ladies and
gentlemen—"

He finally gave up, handed the bulletin to a ballerina to read.   38

"That's all right—" Hazel said of the announcer, "he tried. That's the   39
big thing. He tried to do the best he could with what God gave him. He should
get a nice raise for trying so hard."

"Ladies and gentlemen—" said the ballerina, reading the bulletin. She   40
must have been extraordinarily beautiful, because the mask she wore was
hideous. And it was easy to see that she was the strongest and most graceful
of all the dancers, for her handicap bags were as big as those worn by
two-hundred-pound men.

And she had to apologize at once for her voice, which was a very unfair   41
voice for a woman to use. Her voice was a warm, luminous, timeless melody.
"Excuse me—" she said, and she began again, making her voice absolutely
uncompetitive.

"Harrison Bergeron, age fourteen," she said in a grackle squawk, "has   42
just escaped from jail, where he was held on suspicion of plotting to overthrow the government. He is a genius and an athlete, is under-handicapped,
and should be regarded as extremely dangerous."

A police photograph of Harrison Bergeron was flashed on the screen   43
upside down, then sideways, upside down again, then right side up. The
picture showed the full length of Harrison against a background calibrated
in feet and inches. He was exactly seven feet tall.

The rest of Harrison's appearance was Halloween and hardware. No-   44
body had ever borne heavier handicaps. He had outgrown hindrances faster
than the H-G men could think them up. Instead of a little ear radio for a
mental handicap, he wore a tremendous pair of earphones, and spectacles

with thick wavy lenses. The spectacles were intended to make him not only half blind, but to give him whanging headaches besides.

Scrap metal was hung all over him. Ordinarily, there was a certain symmetry, a military neatness to the handicaps issued to strong people, but Harrison looked like a walking junkyard. In the race of life, Harrison carried three hundred pounds. 45

And to offset his good looks, the H-G men required that he wear at all times a red rubber ball for a nose, keep his eyebrows shaved off, and cover his even white teeth with black caps at snaggle-tooth random. 46

"If you see this boy," said the ballerina, "do not—I repeat, do not—try to reason with him." 47

There was the shriek of a door being torn from its hinges. 48

Screams and barking cries of consternation came from the television set. The photograph of Harrison Bergeron on the screen jumped again and again, as though dancing to the tune of an earthquake. 49

George Bergeron correctly identified the earthquake, and well he might have—for many was the time his own home had danced to the same crashing tune. "My God—" said George, "that must be Harrison!" 50

The realization was blasted from his mind instantly by the sound of an automobile collision in his head. 51

When George could open his eyes again, the photograph of Harrison was gone. A living, breathing Harrison filled the screen. 52

Clanking, clownish, and huge, Harrison stood in the center of the studio. The knob of the uprooted studio door was still in his hand. Ballerinas, technicians, musicians, and announcers cowered on their knees before him, expecting to die. 53

"I am the Emperor!" cried Harrison. "Do you hear? I am the Emperor! Everybody must do what I say at once!" He stamped his foot and the studio shook. 54

"Even as I stand here—" he bellowed, "crippled, hobbled, sickened—I am a greater ruler than any man who ever lived! Now watch me become what I *can* become!" 55

Harrison tore the straps of his handicap harness like wet tissue paper, tore straps guaranteed to support five thousand pounds. 56

Harrison's scrap-iron handicaps crashed to the floor. 57

Harrison thrust his thumbs under the bar of the padlock that secured his head harness. The bar snapped like celery. Harrison smashed his headphones and spectacles against the wall. 58

He flung away his rubber-ball nose, revealed a man that would have awed Thor, the god of thunder. 59

"I shall now select my Empress!" he said, looking down on the cowering people. "Let the first woman who dares rise to her feet claim her mate and her throne!" 60

A moment passed, and then a ballerina arose, swaying like a willow. 61

Harrison plucked the mental handicap from her ear, snapped off her physical handicaps with marvelous delicacy. Last of all, he removed her mask. 62

She was blindingly beautiful.   63

"Now—" said Harrison, taking her hand, "shall we show the people the   64
meaning of the word dance? Music!" he commanded.

The musicians scrambled back into their chairs, and Harrison stripped 65
them of their handicaps, too. "Play your best," he told them, "and I'll make
you barons and dukes and earls."

The music began. It was normal at first—cheap, silly, false. But Harrison 66
snatched two musicians from their chairs, waved them like batons as he sang
the music as he wanted it played. He slammed them back into their chairs.

The music began again and was much improved.   67

Harrison and his Empress merely listened to the music for a while—   68
listened gravely, as though synchronizing their heartbeats with it.

They shifted their weights to their toes.   69

Harrison placed his big hands on the girl's tiny waist, letting her sense 70
the weightlessness that would soon be hers.

And then, in an explosion of joy and grace, into the air they sprang!   71

Not only were the laws of the land abandoned, but the law of gravity   72
and the laws of motion as well.

They reeled, whirled, swiveled, flounced, capered, gamboled, and spun. 73

They leaped like deer on the moon.   74

The studio ceiling was thirty feet high, but each leap brought the danc- 75
ers nearer to it.

It became their obvious intention to kiss the ceiling.   76

They kissed it.   77

And then, neutralizing gravity with love and pure will, they remained   78
suspended in air inches below the ceiling, and they kissed each other for a
long, long time.

It was then that Diana Moon Glampers, the Handicapper General, came   79
into the studio with a double-barreled ten-gauge shotgun. She fired twice,
and the Emperor and the Empress were dead before they hit the floor.

Diana Moon Glampers loaded the gun again. She aimed it at the musi-   80
cians and told them they had ten seconds to get their handicaps back on.

It was then that the Bergerons' television tube burned out.   81

Hazel turned to comment about the blackout to George. But George had   82
gone out into the kitchen for a can of beer.

George came back in with a beer, paused while a handicap signal shook   83
him up. And then he sat down again. "You been crying?" he said to Hazel.

"Yup," she said.   84

"What about?" he said.   85

"I forget," she said. "Something real sad on television."   86

"What was it?" he said.   87

"It's all kind of mixed up in my mind," said Hazel.   88

"Forget sad things," said George.   89

"I always do," said Hazel.   90

"That's my girl," said George. He winced. There was the sound of a   91
riveting gun in his head.

"Gee—I could tell that one was a doozy," said Hazel.   92
"You can say that again," said George.   93
"Gee—" said Hazel, "I could tell that one was a doozy."   94

Questions for Discussion

1. If "Harrison Bergeron" may be called a satire, what is the object, the butt, of the satire? Identify as specifically as you can who or what is being ridiculed.

2. Point out some of the specific devices of humor that Vonnegut uses. To what purpose does the humor seem directed?

3. The story relies heavily on dialogue. Try rewriting a section of dialogue (¶25–36, for example) as narrative commentary, using the same tone the narrator employs in the other, non-dialogue sections, and then discuss with the rest of the class what has been gained or lost by the revision.

Suggested Essay Topics

1. Write an essay directed to your classmates in which you compare the satire in Vonnegut's story with the satire from Elaine Morgan's "The Man-Made Myth" (Chapter 2) and in Swift's "Modest Proposal" (Chapter 7). Identify the satirical butt in each case, discuss the distinctive tone of each piece, and compare at least two satirical devices—ways of "sticking the needle" in the object being ridiculed.

2. Write a satire of your own, ridiculing some opinion, person, institution, custom, practice, or human trait. Satire is always *about* some detested object but seldom directed *to* that object. Usually the audience is composed of readers whom the satirist invites to stand *outside* the space occupied by the object, while reader and writer both laugh at the object *inside* the satirical space. You need to be clear, therefore, about the audience for whom you are writing and how the audience differs from the satirized object. Close to home, you could make fun of some ridiculous group or fashion on campus, or, farther afield, you could make fun of some public figure: an entertainer, perhaps, or a politician whose views you would like to hold up to scorn, or some national group whose beliefs you would like to scorn in writing.

+ 3 +

LANGUAGE

*Reading and Writing,
Words and Experience*

Reading is to the mind what exercise is to the body.
Richard Steele

Reading maketh a full man; conference a ready man and writing an exact man.
Sir Francis Bacon

For know you well, my dear Crito, that to
express oneself badly is not only faulty as far as the
language goes, but does some harm to the soul.
Socrates, in Plato's Phaedo

Without precision of meaning we damage not simply language,
but thought. The language we share is beautiful
and alarmingly complex. Try as we may, we are all likely to make
mistakes, and very few among us can claim to know the
English language to perfection. But we can try.
Robert Davies

Inspiration usually comes during work, rather than before it.
Madeline L'Engle

Style in its simplest definition, it seems to me, is sound—the sound
of self. It arises out of the whole concept of the work,
from the very pulsebeat of the writer and all that has gone
to make him, so that it is sometimes difficult to decide definitely where
technique and style have their firm boundary lines.
Eleanor Cameron

Rewriting isn't virtuous. It isn't something that ought to be done.
It is simply something that most writers find
they have to do to discover what they have to say
and how to say it.
Donald M. Murray

Marshall W. Gregory and Wayne C. Booth

CORRECTNESS AND ERRORS

For centuries people have claimed that the English language is in danger
of corruption and decay. Hundreds of books and articles have warned against
the "corruption" of English. In 1924, for example, R. W. Chapman, speaking
of "The Decay of Syntax," said that "the morbid state of modern English
prose is generally recognized by competent judges. . . . Any beauty in modern
English prose can be only the beauty of decay." As early as 1712 the great
satirist Jonathan Swift suggested that to combat the threat of change, which
he identified as decline, an "Academy" should be formed to establish and
preserve the correct forms. Some nations have established such bodies, and
to this day, in France and other nations, such official or semi-official "acade-
mies" issue formal decisions about which words or expressions will be given
a badge of approval.

Nobody has succeeded in establishing such an academy to oversee the
development of English. But many have tried, and many others have deplored
the seemingly chaotic way in which new and forbidden expressions make
their way from being outlawed—as "slang" or "foreign" or "vulgar" or "colloquial"—to being used by respected writers.

Many linguists have claimed that these purifying efforts are entirely
misguided. Since all languages are constantly changing, and since there is
never any clearly established authority to say which changes are good and
which are bad, our ideas about good English, claim these linguists, must
always shift according to the usage of whatever group we address. The
approved vocabulary, from this point of view, is not a matter of the intrinsic
superiority of some words over others. It is a matter of tradition, convention,
and political power. It is the vocabulary of the most powerful or traditionally
respected groups in society that gets honored, while the vocabulary of politically and socially marginalized groups becomes one of the marks by which

their inferior status is reinforced and perpetuated. To these linguists, there is no such thing as a "pure" vocabulary.

The "warfare" between the linguists and the purists has often been 4 bitter and confusing. It has been marked by much name-calling, and it reveals a good deal of puzzlement and anxiety on all sides. (See, for example, the controversy about *Webster's Third International Dictionary,* as recorded in *Dictionaries and That Dictionary,* edited in 1962 by Wilma Ebbitt and James Sledd.)

Few of us can hope to figure out the rights and wrongs of such an 5 elaborate and prolonged controversy. But we can profit from becoming aware of the issues and thinking about what our own practice will be. Our choices must always be dictated both by our effort to address different readers successfully and by our own knowledge, or lack of knowledge, about what expressions hinder our communication.

We soon learn that "correctness" is at best a mere beginning. Observing 6 correctness in writing is like observing the speed limit while driving: Following the "rules" may have the negative virtue of keeping you out of trouble, but, in and of itself, it cannot produce the positive virtue of good writing. Every beginner soon learns, moreover, that there is no end to the number of "mistakes" teachers can find in an essay; almost all of us have experienced a sense of hopelessness when we've seen our manuscripts marked again and again with corrections that seem endless.

Should teachers and students stop worrying, then, about correctness, 7 as "permissivists" have argued? We all know that if we do so, we will make a lot of trouble for ourselves. Some people will refuse to read what we write if they find it full of "errors," even when linguists point out that many of those very "errors" have been accepted by great authors from Shakespeare's time to the present. But deciding to concentrate on avoiding errors will not work either; we authors can attest to that. As we have worked on this book we have constantly discovered "errors," real or imaginary, in each other's writing, and we know from experience that, even after careful correction by editors at HarperCollins, our readers will discover faults we never dreamed of.

Thus our choices in this matter are complicated. If we wrote, "Neither 8 one of us don't know nothing about grammar," or if we commited many mispellings like these, and if you decided that we didn't know any better, you would probably stop using this book. But if we worried too much about catching every conceivable error, we would have to stop writing. So we all have a problem here—the problem of finding a livable "mean" between an overanxious care that makes writing either painful or impossible, on the one hand, and the carelessness that will leave readers confused or drive them away, on the other.

Like many problems in life, this one cannot be dodged. With every word 9 we utter, we either *meet* those we address or we *fail* to, and our success will depend in part on learning how, in any given situation, to be as "correct" as that situation requires. This in turn means that to learn to write well, we must learn to think hard about different situations and audiences. The kind of language accepted as correct English in a college essay may be fatal in a dormitory bull session, and vice versa. Different "discourse communities"— groups such as attorneys, doctors, historians, plumbers, police officers, and so on, who use a vocabulary peculiar to their "membership" and who expect different levels of formality or informality, logical rigor or logical looseness, personal formality of personal familiarity, and so on—exert demands on us which we must learn to meet in order to gain the serious attention of our audiences.

As you struggle to find appropriate language for your various writing 10 tasks, you may at times become almost immobilized for fear of committing errors you never dreamed of. When this happens, you should remind yourself of four points implicit in all of your work this year.

First, you are not alone. Every author in this book has depended on the 11 corrections of other people; most authors show their writing to friends before sending it to the printer, and all of them depend finally on copy editors whose professional task is to improve manuscripts. Our own discussions in this "reader," for example, have been re-written again and again, taking into account the corrections of so many readers, paid and unpaid, that we have lost count. That you need help with your writing is thus no disgrace.

Second, although possible errors in writing may seem infinite in num- 12 ber, the really crippling ones are relatively rare. If you think hard about the *kinds* of errors you find flagged in your papers, you can soon learn to avoid those that give you the most trouble. Seldom will a single error ever ruin an essay by itself.

Third, remember that you are learning correct ways of writing in part 13 by reading the essays here. Even when you are not thinking about errors at all, you are learning to avoid them simply by reading attentively to the texts you are assigned. If you had to memorize a full list of all the possible bad ways of writing, you would have reason to be discouraged. But by engaging with people who write well, you will automatically take in their ways—if you really pay attention.

Finally, don't forget that correctness is only a means to much more 14 important ends. You are learning to *say something worth saying;* and, if you face the challenges offered in this book, your writing will to a surprising degree "clean itself up." Most of the "errors" you now commit you would recognize yourself, if you really paid attention to your words as closely as the authors anthologized in this book have attended to theirs. And by following them in the close attention they practice, you will learn what it means to choose words that do their job.

One last hint: Nothing works quite so well for spotting errors as reading 15 your work aloud, slowly. Your worst errors will jump out at you when you hear yourself saying something that does not make good sense.

Helen Keller

The story of Helen Keller's life (1880–1968) is engrossing for the same reasons that all good memoirs are engrossing. They bring us into contact with an instructive, engaging mind, and they seem to offer us clues about how to face problems in our own lives. By presenting us with emotions that either parallel or differ from our own, memoirs confirm everyone's membership in the human community and simultaneously affirm everyone's individual uniqueness. Beyond this, however, Helen Keller's story offers us insight into a gripping topic larger than her life but on which her life and experience cast real illumination: the topic of how human beings acquire language and how, in acquiring it, they find, or perhaps create, their distinctively human nature.

Helen Keller was born a normal child, but at 19 months she was stricken with a severe disease that left her both blind and deaf. "Gradually," she says, "I got used to the silence and darkness that surrounded me, and forgot that it had ever been different." Despite the silence and darkness, the little girl came to understand a good deal of what was going on around her. She records that at age 5 she learned to fold and put away clean clothes, that she always knew when her mother and aunt were going out, and that she always wanted to accompany them. But without language she had no ideas, no means of living in a world of experience larger than immediate sensations and feelings, no way of holding on to memories or of formulating hopes and desires, no way of organizing the world conceptually, and, most important of all, no way of thinking her own thoughts and sharing them with others.

We are inclined to take language for granted. We live so much inside it that we no more think about it than we think about the beating of our own hearts or the air we breathe. But just as hearts may perform either well or poorly and air may be either pure or polluted, so our language may be used either more or less accurately, more or less sensitively, and more or less masterfully. Helen Keller was human, clearly, despite her immense handicap, but it is also clear that as she acquired language she came into an increasingly fuller ownership of her human birthright, an increasingly fuller experience of her own human nature.

This raises a question, doesn't it? If human nature and language are as intimately connected as Helen Keller's story suggests, and if language ownership is not an all-or-nothing thing but is instead mastered by degrees, does this not suggest that any enhancement or strengthening of our language will also enhance and strengthen our fundamental humanity? Is it possible, in other words, that being human (except in the most minimal biological sense) is not in itself an all-or-nothing thing? Is it possible that developing certain capacities within us may in fact bring us into fuller possession of what it means to be a human being? Helen Keller's story seems to suggest so.

If this suggestion is sound, implications for your own education follow. This view of language would clearly imply, for example, that courses that force you to deal with texts and thus increase your language power by constant exercise—humanities courses such as history, literature, languages, religion, and philosophy, to mention a few— may in fact be among the most useful courses you could take, useful if becoming more fully and powerfully human is useful. As you read, consider whether Helen Keller's story challenges any of your views or expectations about your own education, and whether her experience justifies your re-thinking or even re-tooling any of your educational ambitions.

THE KEY TO LANGUAGE

Our title for chapters 4 and 6 of *The Story of My Life* (1902).

The most important day I remember in all my life is the one on which my teacher, Anne Mansfield Sullivan, came to me. I am filled with wonder when I consider the immeasurable contrasts between the two lives which it connects. It was the third of March, 1887, three months before I was seven years old. 1

On the afternoon of that eventful day, I stood on the porch, dumb, expectant. I guessed vaguely from my mother's signs and from the hurrying to and fro in the house that something unusual was about to happen, so I went to the door and waited on the steps. The afternoon sun penetrated the mass of honeysuckle that covered the porch, and fell on my upturned face. My fingers lingered almost unconsciously on the familiar leaves and blossoms which had just come forth to greet the sweet southern spring. I did not know what the future held of marvel or surprise for me. Anger and bitterness had preyed upon me continually for weeks and a deep languor had succeeded this passionate struggle. 2

Have you ever been at sea in a dense fog, when it seemed as if a tangible white darkness shut you in, and the great ship, tense and anxious, groped her way toward the shore with plummet and sounding-line, and you waited with beating heart for something to happen? I was like that ship before my education began, only I was without compass or sounding-line, and had no way of knowing how near the harbour was. "Light! Give me light!" was the wordless cry of my soul, and the light of love shone on me in that very hour. 3

I felt approaching footsteps. I stretched out my hand as I supposed to my mother. Some one took it, and I was caught up and held close in the arms of her who had come to reveal all things to me, and, more than all things else, to love me. 4

The morning after my teacher came she led me into her room and gave me a doll. The little blind children at the Perkins Institution had sent it and Laura Bridgman had dressed it; but I did not know this until afterward. When I had played with it a little while, Miss Sullivan slowly spelled into my hand the word "d-o-l-l." I was at once interested in this finger play and tried to imitate it. When I finally succeeded in making the letters correctly I was flushed with childish pleasure and pride. Running downstairs to my mother I held up my hand and made the letters for doll. I did not know that I was spelling a word or even that words existed; I was simply making my fingers 5 go in monkey-like imitation. In the days that followed I learned to spell in this uncomprehending way a great many words, among them *pin, hat, cup* and a few verbs like *sit, stand* and *walk*. But my teacher had been with me several weeks before I understood that everything has a name.

One day, while I was playing with my new doll, Miss Sullivan put my big rag doll into my lap also, spelled "d-o-l-l" and tried to make me understand that "d-o-l-l" applied to both. Earlier in the day we had had a tussle over the words "m-u-g" and "w-a-t-e-r." Miss Sullivan had tried to impress it upon me that "m-u-g" is *mug* and that "w-a-t-e-r" is *water*, but I persisted in confounding the two. In despair she had dropped the subject for the time, only to renew it at the first opportunity. I became impatient at her repeated attempts and, seizing the new doll, I dashed it upon the floor. I was keenly delighted when I felt the fragments of the broken doll at my feet. Neither sorrow nor regret followed my passionate outburst. I had not loved the doll. In the still, dark world in which I lived there was no strong sentiment or tenderness. I felt my teacher sweep the fragments to one side of the hearth, and I had a sense of satisfaction that the cause of my discomfort was removed. She brought me my hat, and I knew I was going out into the warm sunshine. This thought, if a wordless sensation may be called a thought, made me hop and skip with pleasure.

We walked down the path to the well-house, attracted by the fragrance of the honeysuckle with which it was covered. Some one was drawing water and my teacher placed my hand under the spout. As the cool stream gushed over one hand she spelled into the other the word *water*, first slowly, then rapidly. I stood still, my whole attention fixed upon the motions of her fingers. Suddenly I felt a misty consciousness as of something forgotten—a thrill of returning thought; and somehow the mystery of language was revealed to me. I knew then that "w-a-t-e-r" meant the wonderful cool something that was flowing over my hand. That living word awakened my soul, gave it light, hope, joy, set it free! There were barriers still, it is true, but barriers that could in time be swept away.

I left the well-house eager to learn. Everything had a name, and each name gave birth to a new thought. As we returned to the house every object which I touched seemed to quiver with life. That was because I saw everything with the strange, new sight that had come to me. On entering the door I remembered the doll I had broken. I felt my way to the hearth and picked up the pieces. I tried vainly to put them together. Then my eyes filled with tears; for I realized what I had done, and for the first time I felt repentance and sorrow.

I learned a great many new words that day. I do not remember what they all were; but I do know that *mother, father, sister, teacher* were among them—words that were to make the world blossom for me, "like Aaron's rod, with flowers." It would have been difficult to find a happier child than I was as I lay in my crib at the close of that eventful day and lived over the joys it had brought me, and for the first time longed for a new day to come.

. . .

I had now the key to all language, and I was eager to learn to use it. 10
Children who hear acquire language without any particular effort; the words
that fall from others' lips they catch on the wing, as it were, delightedly, while
the little deaf child must trap them by a slow and often painful process. But
whatever the process, the result is wonderful. Gradually from naming an
object we advance step by step until we have traversed the vast distance
between our first stammered syllable and the sweep of thought in a line of
Shakespeare.

At first, when my teacher told me about a new thing I asked very few 11
questions. My ideas were vague, and my vocabulary was inadequate; but as
my knowledge of things grew, and I learned more and more words, my field
of inquiry broadened, and I would return again and again to the same subject,
eager for further information. Sometimes a new word revived an image that
some earlier experience had engraved on my brain.

I remember the morning that I first asked the meaning of the word, 12
"love." This was before I knew many words. I had found a few early violets
in the garden and brought them to my teacher. She tried to kiss me; but at
that time I did not like to have any one kiss me except my mother. Miss
Sullivan put her arm gently round me and spelled into my hand, "I love
Helen."

"What is love?" I asked.   13

She drew me closer to her and said, "It is here," pointing to my heart, 14
whose beats I was conscious of for the first time. Her words puzzled me very
much because I did not then understand anything unless I touched it.

I smelt the violets in her hand and asked, half in words, half in signs, 15
a question which meant, "Is love the sweetness of flowers?"

"No," said my teacher.   16

Again I thought. The warm sun was shining on us.   17

"Is this not love?" I asked, pointing in the direction from which the heat 18
came, "Is this not love?"

It seemed to me that there could be nothing more beautiful than the sun, 19
whose warmth makes all things grow. But Miss Sullivan shook her head, and
I was greatly puzzled and disappointed. I thought it strange that my teacher
could not show me love.

A day or two afterward I was stringing beads of different sizes in 20
symmetrical groups—two large beads, three small ones, and so on. I had made
many mistakes, and Miss Sullivna had pointed them out again and again with
gentle patience. Finally I noticed a very obvious error in the sequence and for
an instant I concentrated my attention on the lesson and tried to think how
I should have arranged the beads. Miss Sullivan touched my forehead and
spelled with decided emphasis, "Think."

In a flash I knew that the word was the name of the process that was 21
going on in my head. This was my first conscious perception of an abstract
idea.

For a long time I was still—I was not thinking of the beads in my lap, 22 but trying to find a meaning for "love" in the light of this new idea. The sun had been under a cloud all day, and there had been brief showers; but suddenly the sun broke forth in all its southern splendour.

Again I asked my teacher, "Is this not love?" 23

"Love is something like the clouds that were in the sky before the sun 24 came out," she replied. Then in simpler words than these, which at that time I could not have understood, she explained: "You cannot touch the clouds, you know; but you feel the rain and know how glad the flowers and the thirsty earth are to have it after a hot day. You cannot touch love either; but you feel the sweetness that it pours into everything. Without love you would not be happy or want to play."

The beautiful truth burst upon my mind—I felt that there were invisible 25 lines stretched between my spirit and the spirits of others.

From the beginning of my education Miss Sullivan made it a practice 26 to speak to me as she would speak to any hearing child; the only difference was that she spelled the sentences into my hand instead of speaking them. If I did not know the words and idioms necessary to express my thoughts she supplied them, even suggesting conversation when I was unable to keep up my end of the dialogue.

This process was continued for several years; for the deaf child does not 27 learn in a month, or even in two or three years, the numberless idioms and expressions used in the simplest daily intercourse. The little hearing child learns these from constant repetition and imitation. The conversation he hears in his home stimulates his mind and suggests topics and calls forth the spontaneous expression of his own thoughts. This natural exchange of ideas is denied to the deaf child. My teacher, realizing this, determined to supply the kinds of stimulus I lacked. This she did by repeating to me as far as possible, verbatim, what she heard, and by showing me how I could take part in the conversation. But it was a long time before I ventured to take the initiative, and still longer before I could find something appropriate to say at the right time.

The deaf and the blind find it very difficult to acquire the amenities of 28 conversation. How much more this difficulty must be augmented in the case of those who are both deaf and blind! They cannot distinguish the tone of the voice or, without assistance, go up and down the gamut of tones that give significance to words; nor can they watch the expression of the speaker's face, and a look is often the very soul of what one says.

[Attached here are two letters from Keller's revered teacher, Anne Mansfield Sullivan, which describe from the teacher's point of view the events that Keller has just narrated. What is interesting here are Sullivan's ideas about how language is learned by anyone, not just deaf children. Her description of young Helen turning more and more human as she acquires language is both moving and instructive.

Anne Sullivan was 14 years older than Helen Keller. Very early in her life she had been struck blind through illness and had entered the Perkins Institution for the blind the same year Helen was born. Later her sight was partially restored. The

*skills she learned at Perkins qualified her to be Keller's teacher. The letters here are
addressed to Mrs. Sophia C. Hopkins, a matron at the Perkins Institution who had
been like a mother to Sullivan. It is evident in these letters that Sullivan had a clear
idea of what she was doing and was critically analyzing the effectiveness of her means
of teaching Keller as she went along.]*

April 5, 1887.

1 I must write you a line this morning because something very important has happened. Helen has taken the second great step in her education. She has learned that *everything has a name, and that the manual alphabet is the key to everything she wants to know.*

2 In a previous letter I think I wrote you that "mug" and "milk" had given Helen more trouble than all the rest. She confused the nouns with the verb "drink." She didn't know the word for "drink," but went through the pantomime of drinking whenever she spelled "mug" or "milk." This morning, while she was washing, she wanted to know the name for "water." When she wants to know the name of anything, she points to it and pats my hand. I spelled "w-a-t-e-r" and thought no more about it until after breakfast. Then it occurred to me that with the help of this new word I might succeed in straightening out the "mug-milk" difficulty. We went out to the pump-house, and I made Helen hold her mug under the spout while I pumped. As the cold water gushed forth, filling the mug, I spelled "w-a-t-e-r" in Helen's free hand. The word coming so close upon the sensation of cold water rushing over her hand seemed to startle her. She dropped the mug and stood as one transfixed. A new light came into her face. She spelled "water" several times. Then she dropped on the ground and asked for its name and pointed to the pump and the trellis, and suddenly turning round she asked for my name. I spelled "Teacher." Just then the nurse brought Helen's little sister into the pump-house, and Helen spelled "baby" and pointed to the nurse. All the way back to the house she was highly excited, and learned the name of every object she touched, so that in a few hours she had added thirty new words to her vocabulary. Here are some of them: *Door, open, shut, give, go, come,* and a great many more.

3 P. S.—I didn't finish my letter in time to get it posted last night; so I shall add a line. Helen got up this morning like a radiant fairy. She had flitted from object to object, asking the name of everything and kissing me for very gladness. Last night when I got in bed, she stole into my arms of her own accord and kissed me for the first time, and I thought my heart would burst, so full was it of joy.

April 10, 1887.

4 I see an improvement in Helen from day to day, almost from hour to hour. Everything must have a name now. Wherever we go, she asks eagerly for the names of things she has not learned at home. She is anxious for her friends to spell, and eager to teach the letters to every one she meets. She drops the signs and pantomime she used before, as soon as she has words to supply their place, and the acquirement of a new word

affords her the liveliest pleasure. And we notice that her face grows more expressive each day.

I have decided not to try to have regular lessons for the present. I am going to treat Helen exactly like a two-year-old child. It occurred to me the other day that it is absurd to require a child to come to a certain place at a certain time and recite certain lessons, when he has not yet acquired a working vocabulary. I sent Helen away and sat down to think. I asked myself, *"How does a normal child learn language?"* The answer was simple, "By imitation." The child comes into the world with the ability to learn, and he learns of himself, provided he is supplied with sufficient outward stimulus. He sees people do things, and he tries to do them. He hears others speak, and he tries to speak. *But long before he utters his first word, he understands what is said to him.* I have been observing Helen's little cousin lately. She is about fifteen months old, and already understands a great deal. In response to questions she points out prettily her nose, mouth, eye, chin, cheek, ear. If I say, "Where is baby's other ear?" she points it out correctly. If I hand her a flower, and say, "Give it to mamma," she takes it to her mother. If I say, "Where is the little rogue?" she hides behind her mother's chair, or covers her face with her hands and peeps out at me with an expression of genuine roguishness. She obeys many commands like these: "Come," "Kiss," "Go to papa," "Shut the door," "Give me the biscuit." But I have not heard her try to say any of these words, although they have been repeated hundreds of times in her hearing, and it is perfectly evident that she understands them. These observations have given me a clue to the method to be followed in teaching Helen language. *I shall talk into her hand as we talk into the baby's ears.* I shall assume that she has the normal child's capacity of assimilation and imitation. *I shall use complete sentences in talking to her,* and fill out the meaning with gestures and her descriptive signs when necessity requires it; but I shall not try to keep her mind fixed on any one thing. I shall do all I can to interest and stimulate it, and wait for results.

Questions for Discussion

1. Keller's story makes clear that even in her pre-language existence she had a life of some feelings and emotions. She could experience anger, frustration, and pleasure. But the absence of language seems to have had a muting effect on even these; of other emotions she seems to have had little knowledge at all, especially emotions of companionship or tenderness. "In the still, dark world in which I lived," she says, "there was no strong sentiment of tenderness" (¶6). Does this surprise you? Would you have thought that language was essential to having a fully developed, mature emotional life? Does Keller's experience on this score corroborate the point we make in our comments about language's being intimately tied to the development of one's human capacities, one's basic human nature? If so, how? If not, why not?

2. According to the philosopher Alfred North Whitehead, "The souls of men are the gift from language to mankind." Helen Keller records her sudden discovery of the word *water* in similar terms: "I knew then that 'w-a-t-e-r' meant the wonderful cool something that was flowing over my hand. That living word awakened my soul, gave it light, hope, joy, set it free!" (¶7). What do you think these two writers mean by the assertion that language liberates or awakens the soul? Is this just gushy talk for an incommunicable emotional experience, or does it mean anything you can pin down in other words? If so, what other words?

3. "Everything had a name, and each name gave birth to a new thought," says Keller (¶8). Can you imagine our language devoid of the names of things? What would a language of all verbs, adverbs, and other parts of speech, but no nouns, be like? How would it alter human perception and experience? If this is too hard to imagine, picture a more limited case: a language with nouns but without proper names. Could we adapt to such a life, such a language? How? How would it alter our perception and experience?

4. In her pre-language stage, Keller reports that "I did not then understand anything unless I touched it" (¶14). We hear a lot of talk these days about re-discovering the kind of knowledge acquired through bodily sensations. The people who engage in this talk frequently assert the value of physical knowledge as an antidote to our tendency in modern society to distance everything with language that is too abstract, too conceptual, too removed from immediate experience. Use Helen Keller's story to help you construct a refutation of this view. Or, if you think this view is basically correct, show how Keller's acquisition of language is different from the kind of language being criticized by the "truth of the body" people.

5. Anne Sullivan reports that after Keller had begun to acquire language, "we notice that her face grows more expressive each day" (¶4). Why would this be the case? If you have ever had the opportunity to observe anyone with an extremely limited ownership of language, can you recall any notable features or absences of expressiveness that would throw light on Sullivan's meaning?

Suggested Essay Topics

1. Write an essay on discussion question 3 directed to your instructor. Or, if that kind of speculation seems too abstract, write a dialogue in which you picture two people—two students having lunch together in the cafeteria, for example—having a conversation in a version of English that includes nouns but no proper names. Address your writing to the kind of general reader who might see it in the creative writing section of a magazine or read it as a feature essay in a newspaper.

2. Go to the library and look up one of the numerous accounts of feral children—children raised in complete absence from human contact (usually by animals, as the accounts go)—and write an essay in which you compare the indoctrination of these children into human society to Helen Keller's

recovery of language. Conclude with appropriate observations about the nature and importance of language to human nature and experience. Direct the essay to your classmates. [One of the best-known accounts of a feral child is *The Wild Boy of Averyon* by Jean-Marc Gaspard Itard, translated by George and Muriel Humphrey (Prentice-Hall, 1962), which served as the inspiration for François Truffaut's film *L'Enfant sauvage (The Wild Child).*]

Bruno Bettelheim and Karen Zelan

*The psychologist Bruno Bettelheim (1903–1989) made important contributions in many fields: the study of mental disorders in children (*The Empty Fortress*), the nature of totalitarianism and the experience of the holocaust under the Nazis (*The Informed Heart*), the moral and social effects of different kinds of children's literature (*The Uses of Enchantment*). Karen Zelan (b. 1934) was a research colleague of Bettelheim's and is a child psychologist specializing in learning disorders. Together they conducted an extensive study of how children are taught to read and why the teaching so often fails.*

If you think back to when you were learning to read, you will remember that many children—you may even have been one of them—"hated school" and especially hated those moments when the teacher required each child to read a few words aloud. Bettelheim and Zelan argue that although learning to read must always be hard work, it can be work of the kind that leads to love, not hate—if the kind of reading that children do rewards them from the beginning with understanding and enjoyment. They find, however, that too many of today's reading texts cannot give such rewards because they are empty of human meaning. Most children, say Bettelheim and Zelan, will naturally rebel against such books and may, ultimately, learn to hate reading.

If Bettelheim and Zelan are right, they have discovered one main cause of many of America's educational problems. If you do not love to read, or if you have friends who say that they have never been "readers," the problem may well be traced to the kinds of stories, or non-stories, you were fed in the beginning years.

WHY CHILDREN DON'T LIKE TO READ

Originally published in *The Atlantic Monthly,* November 1981; reprinted as part of *On Learning to Read: The Child's Fascination with Meaning* (1981).

A child's attitude toward reading is of such importance that, more often   1
than not, it determines his scholastic fate. Moreover, his experiences in learning to read may decide how he will feel about learning in general, and even about himself as a person.

Family life has a good deal to do with the development of a child's   2
ability to understand, to use, and to enjoy language. It strongly influences his
impression of the value of reading, and his confidence in his intelligence and
academic abilities. But regardless of what the child brings from home to
school, the most important influence on his ability to read once he is in class
is how his teacher presents reading and literature. If the teacher can make
reading interesting and enjoyable, then the exertions required to learn how
will seem worthwhile.

A child takes great pleasure in becoming able to read some words. But   3
the excitement fades when the texts the child must read force him to reread
the same word endlessly. Word recognition—"decoding" is the term used by
educational theorists—deteriorates into empty rote learning when it does not
lead directly to the reading of meaningful content. The longer it takes the
child to advance from decoding to meaningful reading, the more likely it
becomes that his pleasure in books will evaporate. A child's ability to read
depends unquestionably on his learning pertinent skills. But he will not be
interested in learning basic reading skills if he thinks he is expected to master
them for their own sake. That is why so much depends on what the teacher,
the school, and the textbooks emphasize. From the very beginning, the child
must be convinced that skills are only a means to achieve a goal, and that the
only goal of importance is that he become literate—that is, come to enjoy
literature and benefit from what it has to offer.

A child who is made to read, "Nan had a pad. Nan had a tan pad. Dad   4
ran. Dad ran to the pad," and worse nonsense can have no idea that books
are worth the effort of learning to read. His frustration is increased by the fact
that such a repetitive exercise is passed off as a story to be enjoyed. The worst
effect of such drivel is the impression it makes on a child that sounding out
words on a page—decoding—is what reading is all about. If, on the contrary,
a child were taught new skills as they became necessary to understand a
worthwhile text, the empty achievement "Now I can decode some words"
would give way to the much more satisfying recognition "Now I am reading
something that adds to my life." From the start, reading lessons should
nourish the child's spontaneous desire to read books by himself.

Benjamin S. Bloom, professor of education at the University of Chicago,   5
has found that who will do well in school and who will do poorly is largely
determined by the end of the third grade. Thus, reading instruction during
the first three grades is crucial. Unfortunately, the primers used in most
American schools up to and sometimes through the third grade convey no
sense that there are rewards in store. And since poor readers continue to be
subjected to these primers well past the third grade, their reading can only
get worse as their interests and experience diverge further from the content
of the books.

· · ·

For many decades, textbooks have been used as the basis for reading   6
instruction by the vast majority of elementary school teachers, and they are
much worse today than [they were fifty years ago]. According to one study,

first readers published in the 1920s contained an average of 645 new words. By the late 1930s, this number had dropped to about 460 words. In the 1940s and 1950s, vocabulary declined further, to about 350 words. The vocabularies of primers in seven textbook series published between 1960 and 1963 ranged from 113 to 173 new words. More recent primers, compared with the 1920s editions, also have small vocabularies. For example, *Let's See the Animals,* published in 1970 by Bowmar/Noble, introduces 108 new words; *May I Come In?,* published in 1973, by Ginn & Company, introduces 219 new words; *Finding Places,* published by the American Book Company, in 1980, introduces 192 new words. Although in the 1920s few children went to kindergarten and little preschool reading instruction was given, by the 1970s, when many children were attending kindergarten and reading was consistently taught there, the first-grade primers contained only a quarter of the vocabulary presented to first-graders fifty years ago.

When they enter school, most children already know and use 4,000 or   7 more words. Nobody has to make a deliberate effort to teach them these words, with the exception of the first few learned in infancy. Children make words their own because they want to, because they find them pleasing and useful. Even the least verbal group of first-graders has mastered well over 2,000 words, thus invalidating the claim that children of culturally deprived families would be unfairly burdened by primers of larger vocabulary. This condescending assumption ignores the richness of daily life in even the poorest households. By encouraging the adoption of less challenging books, it has helped to deprive most children at school just as poverty deprives many children at home.

· · ·

Research in the teaching of reading, far from justifying the continuous   8 reduction in the number of words used in primers, fails to show any reason for it. It is therefore hard to understand why textbook publishers have pursued this course, and why educators have not rebelled. One possible explanation is that as primers become simpler, children, because they are bored, read them with less and less facility. The publishers, in response, make the books even simpler and, thus, even less effective.

Primers have no authors. Many people help to create the books, and the   9 financial investment required runs into the millions. (The sizable staff of one large publishing house worked for five years to produce a first-grade program alone.) Yet despite such prodigious effort and expense, all basic series are more or less alike. To recoup the large investment in a series, a publishing house must be able to sell it to schools all over the country. It cannot risk controversy.

We can cite two examples from our own experience. One publisher, in   10 an effort to improve a first-grade reader, came up with a story in which children bring a balloon home from a fair, whereupon a cat leaps on it and it bursts. The story would seem harmless enough to most people, but when the book was tested in an Illinois school system, cat-lovers were outraged: the story had maligned their pets, turned children against animals, and so on. The local school superintendent, who was coming up for re-election, decided to withdraw the book, and the publisher, fearing similar setbacks elsewhere, decided to drop the story.

Another publishing house was preparing a new edition of its widely 11 used series. One of us, asked to consult, objected in detail to the blandness of the stories proposed. The company's vice-president in charge of textbooks confessed that he, too, thought the stories would bore young readers, but he was obliged to keep in mind that neither children nor teachers buy textbooks: school boards and superintendents do. And their first concern is that no one mind their choices. Fairy tales, for example, would never do. Some people would complain that the stories insult stepmothers; others would find the punishment of evildoers too cruel.

The result of such constraints is a book full of endlessly repeated words 12 passed off as stories. Many teachers have told us that they don't like such a book, but assume that since a primer has been put together by experts, and approved by experts, it must be appropriate for children even if it is obnoxious to an adult. In the course of our research on the teaching of reading we have talked to children who were not so credulous. Many told us that their teachers must have faked an interest in the stories, or that they must think children are not very smart.

Fourth- and fifth-graders who had left the beginners' books behind 13 described their resentments to us quite clearly. One rather quiet boy, who preferred to read or work by himself and rarely participated in class, spoke up all on his own and with deep feeling. He had felt so ashamed to say the things written in primers that he could not bring himself to do it. And although he now liked reading a lot, he said, he still had a hard time reading aloud.

The first- and second-graders were as unhappy with their books as the 14 older children remembered being. They said they read only because they had to, and that on their own they would never choose such "junk." "It's all impossible," one of them said. When he was asked why, answers came from around the room: "The children aren't real!" "They aren't angry!" When one child exclaimed, "They aren't anything!" all agreed that there was nothing more to be said.

Textbook writers and publishers know that their books are dull, and 15 they have tried to make them more attractive by commissioning many colorful illustrations. For example, the number of pictures in primers of the Scott, Foresman series doubled between 1920 and 1962, from about one picture per one hundred words to nearly two per hundred words. The trouble with pictures is that the printed text becomes even less appealing in comparison. Words seem to be less vivid and to convey less information. Worse, being able to guess from the pictures what the text is about, a child who is reluctant to read has no incentive to learn.

The publishers' advice to teachers reinforces this syndrome. Typically, 16 the elaborate teachers' guides for each book in a series suggest that the class be asked questions about the pictures before reading the story. Yet there is evidence that pictures retard or interfere with learning to read. Consider the following report by a psychologist of reading, Eleanor J. Gibson: "Children in the second term of kindergarten were given practice with three-letter common words ('cat,' 'bed,' 'dog,' etc.) on flash cards. In one group, the word on the card was accompanied by the appropriate picture. In another, it appeared alone. Training trials, in which the experimenter pronounced the word as it was displayed to the child, alternated with test trials [in which] the child was shown the word alone and asked to say what it was. The picture group made significantly more errors and took longer . . . than the group without pictures. The pictorial redundancy appeared to be distracting rather than useful." Yet in most of the preprimers and primers in classrooms today, words are used primarily as labels and captions.

Learning to read is not an entertainment but hard work. Rather than face this directly, publishers seek to distract children with references to play. But allusions to strenuous physical activities make a child want to move, not think. Worse, a first-grader knows from his own experience just how complex a ball game can be. So a weak story about a ball game is most likely to convince the child that reading about a ball game is dull compared with playing in one.   17

In Harper & Row's "Janet and Mark" series (1966), school makes its first appearance in second grade in *All Through the Year.* The last section of the book is titled "Too Much Is Too Much of Anything," and the first story about the things that are too much, "A Feeling in the Air," is about school. "Everyone was waiting. . . . It was the last day of school. A little while, and it would be all over." The children are "daydreaming . . . of baseball and swimming and bicycle rides." In the last picture of the story, we see them streaming out of the school building, joyful to be released.   18

Psychoanalytic studies of the so-called "double bind" have shown that nothing is more confusing and disturbing to a child, or has more detrimental effects, than contradictory messages from an adult about important issues. Almost every preprimer and primer bears such contradictory messages. Tacitly, they say that the educational system, which requires the child to go to school and presents him with a book so that he may learn to read, holds that school and learning are serious business. But the explicit message of the text and pictures is that the child should think—that is, read—only about playing. The idea seems to be that a suggestion of what books are really for—to open new worlds of thought and imagination—would have the most undesirable consequences for the child's reading achievement.   19

From a psychoanalytic perspective, the primers' emphasis on play ensures that the books will be addressed solely to the child's pleasure-seeking ego—the earliest, most basic, but also most primitive motivating force in man. But as the child reaches school age, around age five, he should have learned to exchange (at least to some extent) living by the pleasure principle for making choices in accord with the reality principle. The primers, by presenting him almost exclusively with images of fun, throw the child back to the developmental phase he is trying, with difficulty, to outgrow. Such primers   20 insult the child's intelligence and his sense of worth, and the offense goes far to explain why children reject their reading books as empty. The books talk down to children; they do not take children's aspirations seriously.

In class, children read aloud. For some time to come, even if the child 21 does not voice what he is reading, he will form the words with his lips. Reading aloud feels to a child as if he were speaking to his teacher, or whoever might be listening to him. For that matter, it is not unusual for a child to think that his teacher wrote the book, and has planted messages for him in it. In a conversation, we wish to hold our listener's attention and impress him with what we have to say. But the teacher is oblivious of the child's impression that reading aloud is a sort of conversation; instead, the teacher listens carefully to make sure that the child reads the words as they are printed in the book, and corrects him when he fails. To do so is a teacher's duty, according to the teaching methods favored in this country; it may also be the only way a teacher can remain alert through the near-hypnotic effect of the words. In any case, the child experiences the teacher's interruptions as rejection, which certainly does not make reading more attractive to him.

Furthermore, a child may have good reason to make a mistake. Reading 22 for meaning is anything but passive, even when the content is absorbed exactly as presented. And the more intent a reader is on taking in the meaning, the more active he is in his reading. In order for a child to maintain the minimal interest necessary for reading a story, he may try to correct the story or improve it by misreading it. The barrenness of the text may tempt the child to project meaning where there is none.

The texts of preprimers and primers consist of words that can be readily 23 sounded out. But these words are often combined in sentences that no one would ever say. Such a text is actually harder for the beginner to read. For example, because the child usually learns early to recognize the words "store" and "man," one widely used basal text (*People Read,* one of the Bank Street readers) tells about a "store man" when referring to a salesman. Out of a wish to make learning to read easy, children who know the word that the text of, this story means to convey are asked to recognize and use in their reading a phrase that rarely comes up in writing or speech. To compound the irony, the phrase appears in a book whose title by implication promises to tell how everybody reads and what they read. The result is that children may be provoked to errors by the discrepancy between ordinary language and the uncommon language of the book.

We have spent a number of years observing school reading lessons, and 24 have learned that children make mistakes for many reasons, in addition to the obvious one of ignorance. For example, a first-grade boy was reading "Van's Cave," a story in the 1969 J. B. Lippincott series about a hunter and his dog, Spot. The story goes that the hunter shoots five ducks, which the dog retrieves. They then return to the cave, where they live. The man starts a fire on which he plans to roast the ducks. The text says: "Spot must not leave the ducks. He can see a wolf near the cave." This, inexplicably, is accompanied by a picture showing the dog asleep. The boy reversed the meaning of the sentence by reading, instead, "He can't see a wolf near the cave." It is possible that the boy did so because the picture shows the dog asleep. But it is more likely that the boy's knowledge of dog behavior made it seem unreasonable to him that a dog would sleep when it saw a wolf lurking nearby. A first-grader might also wish to believe that his dog would safeguard him. So the misreading of "can't" for "can," seemingly a simple error, reflects on one level the child's attempt to bring what the text says into accord with the picture. On another level, it may register the boy's protest against a dog that sleeps when its master needs protection. Finally, the misreading is a statement correctly describing normal dog behavior.

One first-grade girl complained about a story in McGraw-Hill's Sullivan Storybook series which told of a ball falling into a patch of tar. She thought it should have said that the ball fell into a puddle. The teacher, knowing that this phonics-based text used "patch of tar" in preference to "puddle" because these words are pronounced as printed, while "puddle" is pronounced "pud-del," said that perhaps the author of the story thought children would have difficulty in recognizing "puddle." By this she meant difficulty in decoding and reading the word. But the girl fastened on the exact words the teacher had used. She was indignant, and angrily exclaimed, "I know 'puddle' when I see it." We cannot say for sure that her remark did not simply reflect the fact that the word "puddle" was in her active vocabulary, while the words "patch of tar" were not, but the way she expressed herself suggests a more subtle reason for her sense of insult. She made it clear that she saw puddles in everyday life, not tar patches; and her reaction entailed the wish that teachers and those who write for children show respect for a child's experiences of the world.

Another smart first-grader puzzled his teacher because all year he had balked at reading, despite evidence that he knew how. On the day we observed him, the boy made numerous errors—for example, reading "stick" for "chick." This, the teacher told him, showed he had not mastered word beginnings and endings, and that he should therefore continue with his exercises. The boy refused.

The teacher then suggested that we read with him, upon which the boy strenuously protested that the workbook the teacher had assigned to him was boring. (The book, part of McGraw-Hill's Sullivan Programmed Reading series, is typical of most workbooks, in that the exercises require the student to fill in missing letters.) With our encouragement, the boy made one more attempt; again he read "stick" for "chick." But this time, before anyone had time to react, he corrected himself and angrily blurted out: "Fill in the blanks, that's all I get! Witch, witch, witch . . . ditch, ditch, ditch . . . stick, stick, stick. . . chick, chick, chick!" And that was it. He would not do any more reading with us that day. The boy had made error upon error, in this way giving vent to his negative feelings. But by pairing "witch" with "ditch," and "stick" with "chick," he showed that he understood well the different word beginnings and endings, and that his substitutions were not made in ignorance.

A couple of days later, we again asked the boy to read. He refused the 28
Sullivan series but was willing to try something more interesting. We settled
on *The Bear Detectives,* by Stan and Jan Berenstain. The story tells how Papa
Bear and his children hunt for a missing pumpkin, using a detective kit.
Although the small bears discover various clues to the pumpkin's whereabouts, they can't find it. After reading the story eagerly for some thirty
pages, the boy substituted the word "defective" for "detective": "He's in the
barn. This is it! Hand me that defective kit." Earlier he had read "detective"
correctly, demonstrating that he was well able to read the word—that he
knew what it designated and how it fit into the story. It seemed to us that
the boy, having read for so many pages that the detective kit was no help in
the search for the pumpkin, and carried away by the excited wish of the bears
to find it, was once more expressing his frustration with a text.

A few days later, this boy's workbook again required him to read a list 29
of words that, bereft of context, made no sense. He then read "dump" for
"jump." Responding to the feelings this misreading suggested, we asked,
"Who wants to dump this?" The boy immediately read the correct word,
"jump," and then nodded at us. When we asked him why he wanted to dump
the workbook, his unhesitating reply was, " 'Cause it's garbage."

Just as children are likely to change the words of a dull story in order 30
to make it more interesting, they are also likely to change the words of an
interesting story because they have a personal stake in the meaning. For
example, one competent first-grader read a story to us smoothly and with
interest and comprehension in her voice. The story was about tigers, and the
little girl made only one mistake: she consistently read "tigger" for "tiger."
It is easy to understand why this child would shy away from thinking about
dangerous tigers in favor of contemplating the harmless character of Tigger
in the Pooh books, which were favorites of hers. Her switch in thought
seemed to relieve her fear about what the ferocious beast would do next as
the story unfolded.

It requires considerable ingenuity on the part of first-graders to make 31
radical alterations in meanings by only the slightest change of letters. In the
examples of the boy reading about the dog and the wolf and the girl reading
about the tiger, the children retained all the letters of the printed word,
adding to them a single letter. By adding a "t," the boy substituted correct
animal behavior for an incorrect description of it, and by adding a "g," the
girl replaced an animal threatening danger and destruction with one symbol-
izing safety and pleasure. In the third example, by substituting one letter for
another in a nine-letter word, the child expressed his dissatisfaction with the
uselessness of an object that played a central role in the story he was reading.

When a child utters a word entirely different from the one printed in 32
the book, teachers are likely to assume, correctly, that the child's attention
has wandered, or that he may have given up on reading a word that is hard
for him. When what the child reads is only slightly different from what is
printed, teachers are also likely to conclude that the child has a problem—
faulty discrimination between letters—even though the error may change the

meaning of the sentence radically. They assume this despite the fact that the child has already read most letters as printed, suggesting that he was paying attention to the page and could recognize the letters correctly. But what if a child's substitution of one or a few letters makes good—though altered—sense within the context of a story? Perhaps he has perceived what the printed word signifies, decided that it is unacceptable, and found a solution that suits his purposes.

A teacher's reflex to catch and correct mistakes is but one example of 33 a situation that occurs over and over again in schools, and not only where beginners are taught to read: the educator's faith in abstract theories about how learning must proceed blinds him to the sophistication of the child's mind. The teacher's insistence on accuracy often barely hides the fact that what is involved is also a power play, in which the teacher uses her superior knowledge and her authority to gain her point. The child—consciously or, more often, subconsciously—reacts to being the victim of such a power play, and is antagonistic. Unfortunately, many children manage to defeat the teacher by refusing to learn; their victory robs them of their chance to be educated, and it deprives society of competent citizens.

It is not impossible to teach children to read while respecting their 34 intelligence and dignity. The primers used in Europe are generally far more difficult than those in use in this country. We believe their success is proved by the fact that at the end of the first grade, the average European child has a larger reading vocabulary than that of the average American child. More-over, reading retardation, the curse of so many young Americans, is much less common among European children and, when it occurs, is rarely as severe.

The most recent series of basic readers published in Switzerland stands 35 as a notable alternative to the American textbooks that we have complained about. The early reading program consists of three preprimers and one primer. The preprimers are loose-leaf booklets, each page (with a single exception) comprising a few short lines of text and an illustration. Since there are no pictures on the covers of the booklets, the child is encouraged to form his own opinion of what each booklet is about by reading.

The first preprimer is entitled *We are all here,* meaning "here to read 36 together." Its first page has only two words: "I am." And on this page there is no picture, no face to rival the child's own. The Swiss child's reading thus begins with the strongest statement of self-assertion imaginable. After six-teen more pages, each with a few words for the child to learn, there follow twenty-eight pages devoted either to snatches of well-known songs or to a few lines from popular fairy tales. In this way, the first preprimer leads easily to the next, *Once upon a time,* which is composed of five fairy tales from Grimm. Though quite simple, these versions are nonetheless faithful in all essentials to the originals.

The third Swiss preprimer, *Edi,* is about a little boy who might be the 37 peer of the children reading about him. The first page shows Edi with his school satchel on his back, standing between his father and mother. The story goes that Edi, who has eaten something that disagrees with him, gets sick and is sent to the country to stay with relatives and get well. We follow Edi's experiences on the farm until the end of the book, when he returns home, his health fully restored. There he finds that while he was away, his mother had a baby; Edi has a sister. Edi's story deals with two of the most critical events in a child's life: sickness and the birth of a sibling.

The primer of the Swiss series, *It's your turn,* meaning "it's your turn to 38 read," begins with counting rhymes and songs typically sung by children as accompaniment to their games. Since Swiss children know all these rhymes and songs, they know how the words they are decoding ought to sound, and so it is likely that at this more difficult level of reading, their attempts will be error-free. Thus the children's confidence in their ability to read this new, thicker, rather scary-looking book is supported, and they are ready for the remaining sections, which are longer and a little harder.

It's your turn has many colorful pictures that embellish the text without 39 giving away its meaning; the child *must* read in order to understand. For example, a poem by Christian Morgenstern, "Winternight," is illustrated by a picture of a town at night, covered with falling snow; the picture conveys the spirit of the poem but permits no conclusion about its substance. In addition to the Morgenstern poem, the book contains a number of other poems and short stories, many by famous German authors. The selection represents all periods of German literature: contemporary, Romantic, classical, and medieval, and legendary folktales, rhymes, and riddles.

This first Swiss reader, like its American counterparts, tries to introduce 40 children to reading by means of attractive and fairly easy material. The chief difference is that none of the pieces in the Swiss reader patronize the child; there is no deviation from ordinary language or ordinary usage. Children have been reciting the counting rhymes to each other for hundreds of years. No words are avoided because they might be difficult (as is done constantly in American primers)—and they prove not to be too hard, because the child who uses them in everyday conversation already knows what they mean, and is thus eager to master whatever technical obstacles they present on the page. In one way or another, all the stories appeal to children of primary age, but in none of them is there even the mention of active play. If anything, the pieces are on the contemplative side, though with a light touch. The most impressive difference between this book and American primers is the literary quality of many of its selections. The Swiss primer manages to introduce the child to literacy at the same time that it teaches him the rudiments of reading.

These primers, used in the German-speaking parts of Switzerland, have 41 a special lesson to teach American educators and publishers. It has been argued that our primers have to employ unnaturally simple words because many minority children speak a different language at home: Spanish, Chinese, "black English," and so on. But the language that *all* children growing up in the German parts of Switzerland speak—a dialect called *Schweizer Deutsch,* or Swiss German—is very different from the High German they must speak and read in school. Although during the first few months of school the children are allowed to speak to the teacher in their dialect, from the start they learn to read only the High German in which their primers are published. For some reason, Swiss children do not find this enforced bilingualism such a handicap that they fail to become able readers. We believe that their lack of difficulty is explained to a great extent by the fact that they like what they are given to read.

Questions for Discussion

1. Can you summarize the differences between the Swiss basic readers that the authors admire and the American texts they deplore? Is the difference to be found in the method of presentation, in the subject matter, or in both?

2. Compare your earliest memories of learning to read with those of your classmates. Are there strong differences among you about how pleasant or disagreeable it was? Can you remember the first book you really enjoyed? (Gregory remembers *Smoky the Crow,* Booth *The Wizard of Oz,* both from the second grade. Neither of us can remember a single reading from the first grade, except for the Dick and Jane books, which were dismal, dismal.)

3. What kind of persona do Bettelheim and Zelan project, judging from the way they write? Support your opinion by quoting their own words. (One result of getting an education should be an expansion of your vocabulary for describing people—their character, their ethos. When you ask, "What kind of person is he?" how many kinds do you have in mind?)

4. Bettelheim and Zelan suggest an analogy (¶7) between the child's learning to talk and learning to read: If children learn to talk "because they want to," obviously they will learn to read if they want to. (Compare our analogy of learning to talk with learning to write, pp. 6–7.) Do you think that the analogy is sound? In answering, remember that a fitting analogy does not require that *all* details in the comparison match perfectly, only that the directly pertinent elements do.

5. In what paragraphs do the authors provide evidence for their conclusions? Do different kinds of evidence carry different weight here? For example, is the account of Swiss schools and their success more or less persuasive than the quotations from the American primers?

6. In paragraph 21 the authors say that children experience reading aloud as conversation. Is silent reading also experienced as conversation? If you ask a book a question, can it ever be said to "reply"? Do some textbooks make us feel like holding a conversation, while some merely talk *at* us, and still others seem to address someone *behind* us, someone wearing an academic robe and mortarboard? (Most textbooks we authors remember from college had this last tone.) What makes the difference?

Suggested Essay Topics

1. In the children's literature section of the library, find a reading primer and do a careful book review from the point of view of Bettelheim and Zelan. Your basic question is, "Would it be a good book to learn to read from?" Be sure to do some thinking about the kind of reader you are addressing, whether librarians, elementary teachers, parents, or the children themselves.

2. This assignment is somewhat more ambitious. Read all or part of *The Uses of Enchantment* by Bettelheim. Then choose a short section from his defense of fairy tales and discuss whether it seems persuasive and why. Again you should think about whom you are trying to convince. For this assignment you might think of writing a letter to the editor of *The Atlantic Monthly* (where "Why Children Don't Like to Read" originally appeared) praising or condemning the authors for their argument. Or you might imagine yourself writing the authors directly, giving carefully considered reasons why you find their arguments strong or weak.

Saturday
11-20-93
4:43 PM

Peggy Rosenthal

Many linguists have argued that the categories and special features of any given language partly determine our perceptions of and our knowledge about reality. Peggy Rosenthal approaches this same set of issues in another way: by providing a detailed analysis of the full range of meanings of certain loaded words: those extended meanings that a careless, inattentive, unknowing, or superficial user can set reverberating without realizing it. Every historical age, she argues, uses particular words again and again, words that become packed with so many meanings from different sources that it becomes difficult to use them without heaving whole cartloads of connotations into our discussions—frequently without our seeing or thinking about them. The problem is that while these connotations may escape our notice, they may yet distort our meaning. The only cure, Rosenthal argues, is to become critically aware of words' varied layers. Doing so will allow us to choose words more carefully and use them more precisely.

Some of the words that crop up repeatedly in contemporary discourse—and treated by Rosenthal in Words and Values—*are* self, growth, development, relative, *and* relationship. *In the following excerpt from her book, Rosenthal invites you to consider contemporary notions of "self": a self that we, unlike former generations, are likely to think of as rooted in* private feelings *rather than in social function (the job, trade, craft, or profession we follow) or in divine purpose (the self as God-given and God-defined) or in social class (the self as defined by the duties and privileges of social standing). For many twentieth-century Americans, the self is defined by none of these external points of reference but almost by individual fiat, by what was called a few years ago "existential assertion." Even our absorption in and obsession with careers is not an external source of self-definition, for what we deem important is not so much what we do, but whether we feel good doing it. In today's world, few people would criticize others for leaving a career on the sole grounds that they felt "unhappy" or "unfulfilled" in it. In our culture few sources—including, perhaps, most churches— would challenge the primacy of everyone's "need" for "self-fulfillment."*

As you read, try to determine whether you think the modern notion of self is as satisfactory (or perhaps even as morally good) as the notions of self from these other sources just listed, sources that had the authority to define the self in former eras. Of course, you will also have to think about your criteria for "satisfactory" and "good." Do you hold happiness, for example, as a criterion for the "good" self? And do our self-derived notions of self make us happy? If we are not happy, does our unhappiness stem from the barrenness of our notions of self or from other sources? What other criteria might be useful? Fulfillment of social responsibilities (good citizenship)? Devotion to religious tenets (the righteous life)? Which criteria would you hold? Which notion of the self—your own self—do you prefer? Which notion, if any, do you find binding, or is each of us free to adopt any notion of self and self-fulfillment that pleases us most?

WORDS AND VALUES

From *Words and Values* (1984).

PREFACE

This book is a collection of biographical sketches of some of the leading figures of our time, though the figures aren't people but configurations of words. The purpose of tracing their lives is to find out how they got to be where they are today (how they got into their leading position) and what difference their being there makes in our own lives (what attitudes, beliefs, behavior we're led into by them).

The book therefore conceives of the leading words it examines as "leading" in two senses: as being currently "dominant" words, words in positions of power; and as "directing" us, from this dominant position, to think and act in certain ways. Each of the four parts of the book focuses on a group of very common leading words: words like *individual, feelings, develop, growth, alternative, opinion, relationship.* The words are examined to see where they get their popularity and their power, what meanings and values they carry as they move into different areas of our lives, and where they seem to be carrying us as they move along.

This view of our relation to the words we use perhaps appears a bit alarming. We aren't seen as leading our own language anywhere at all, but as being led by it. Our words, even our common everyday ones, are seen as an active force in our lives; our own position with respect to them is seen as passive. This is indeed a disturbing position to find ourselves in, but as the analysis proceeds we'll see that the normal operations of language do put us in this passive position: language works to give us much less control over "what we mean" than we generally assume we have. Even when we think we're choosing our words with care and giving them precise meanings, they can mean much more (or less) than we think; and when we use them carelessly, without thinking, they can still carry thoughts. These thoughts we're not aware of, these meanings we don't intend, can then carry us into certain beliefs and behavior—whether or not we notice where we're going.

But though the workings of language tend to put us in a passive position, this doesn't imply that our position must remain simply helpless. It will be helpless as long as we let ourselves remain blind to what our language is doing. But we have powers of critical detachment that we're always free to exercise with respect to any of our activities: so instead of letting ourselves be pulled along by the going terms of the day, we can always step back from them and look, from a position of critical detachment, at where they've come from and where they're going. Examining them from this distance, we'll be in a position to resist some of their pull if we want to; seeing more clearly where a certain set of words is going, we'll be able to decide how far we want to go along with it and where we'd perhaps rather switch to a different set of terms (and values and goals) instead. To encourage this critical distance, to enable us to make such choices, is the purpose of this book. 4

. . .

SELF

If the word *self* were a stone and the sentences we hear or read or say 5 were pathways, we'd probably be unable to get through an ordinary day without stumbling across all the stones in our way. The lines of best-sellers, popular magazines, and television talk shows are strewn with *self:* we're urged to fulfill ourselves, realize ourselves, know ourselves, be aware of (but not beware of) ourselves, love ourselves, create ourselves, feel good about ourselves, actualize ourselves, express ourselves, improve ourselves. Self-fulfillment therapy and self-improvement courses are booming businesses, run by alchemists who know how to turn the stones of *self* into gold. There is even in the city where I live an organization called The Self Center: a perfect title for our times, in which the self stands firmly in the center of our path, worshipped as our rock and our redeemer.

If we turn from the main roads of popular public discourse (and by 6 discourse I mean all uses of verbal language, both written and spoken) into the areas of special-interest groups, we still stumble upon *self* almost wherever we go. "Women's self-knowledge," "self-fulfillment," and "self-identification" are proclaimed as goals of the Women's Movement. "Energy self-sufficiency" is our nation's goal, and "Palestinian self-determination" a goal for many in the Middle East.

Even on the narrower roads of academic disciplines, the ground remains 7 familiar. We find *self* all over the place in the writings of philosophy: no surprise, since the self has been one of philosophy's prime subjects of study ever since the Renaissance. Recent philosophical books like *The Nature of the Self,* then, follow a time-honored tradition. But in the profession of literary criticism the hundreds of recent articles and books taking *self* as their subject ("Saul Bellow's Idea of Self," "The Divided Self in the Fiction of Henry James," "The Flexibility of the Self in Renaissance Literature," *Imagining a Self*) are a relatively new development, and an unexpected one unless we realize that literary criticism is much more in touch with popular concerns than is usually granted.

When we come to psychology, *self* is no longer just a stone that we trip   8
over, or pass by, or stoop to examine, on our way; it has swollen into a huge rock, even a cave, which we have to enter, explore, probe the depths of as we go through the discourse of the profession. And as we go through, we find ourselves coming full circle to where we began, since the cave of psychology opens onto the main road of popular discourse—even, we could say, spills onto it, considering the amount of best-seller material (*Games People Play; I'm OK, You're OK; Passages; Pulling Your Own Strings; Living, Loving, and Learning* is just some of it) that is the direct product of psychology.

Once we notice how often *self* turns up in our current public discourse,   9
both popular and specialized, we can easily see why *self* is a main term in our private discourse as well, and even in our private thoughts. The going terms of an age tend to be, naturally, the ones we think with, talk to our family and friends with, figure out things with. So it's no surprise that we often think these days in terms of *self,* seeing *myself* as the unquestioned justification for almost any action and as the goal toward which everything else must lead. Adolescents choosing a career are counseled, for example, to study themselves and know themselves fully in order to figure out which career will be best (meaning most self-fulfilling). We don't question whether, in laying our heavily weighted *self* on people who are already at the most self-absorbed stage of life, we might be burdening them unfairly, even preventing them from moving at all. Nor do we question our own or our friends' divorces when they're justified, as they often are, in terms of *self* (self-fulfillment, self-realization, etc.); there's no doubt that without the word *self,* and the values and concepts it currently brings with it, the divorce rate would be considerably lower than it is. . . .

Though I don't want to get bogged down here in methodology, I have   10
to make just one more distinction in order to be accurate about the way *self* pulls us: a distinction between the ways that a word's values, whether positive or negative, can be carried. Words lead complex lives and lead us along with them in complex ways; if we want to see how we're being led, rather than being led along blindly, we have to make an effort to follow our language with our eyes open to its subtle workings. What we see, then, when we look at how words carry their values, is that two different ways are possible. Some words carry their values inherently, in their very beings, so to speak: these are words whose referent* *is* a certain value, words like *good,*

*The object, concept, idea, or feeling a word names or to which it refers.

pleasure, comfortable, or, on the other side, *disgraceful, worthless, evil.* Many more words, though, carry their values not as inherent parts of themselves but *ad* herently, like labels stuck on their heads or behind their backs, or like little flags sticking up from them and bearing the imprint of a plus or a minus. These are words whose referent is not itself a value and which take on whatever attitude we have toward the referent at the time. Adherent values can therefore change over the years, as our attitudes do. For example, *sex* for the Victorians carried, at least on the surface of public discourse, a minus of untouchability, as if the word itself carried VD; whereas for us *sex* has become a bearer of all the good things of life, a word universally proclaimed from the rooftops by faces beaming with pleasure. Or *simple,* which once carried the positive sense of "guileless" or "sincere" when applied to a person, now tends to carry the negative scornful implication of "simple-minded" or "simple-ton." Adherent values can vary not only over time but for different speakers at the same time: *car* spoken by the president of General Motors carries a proud plus, but in the mouth and mind of an environmentalist fighting air pollution, or of an energy conservationist, it carries a menacing minus, the sign of the skull and crossbones.

Self's positive value today is of the adherent and almost universal kind, 11 like that of *sex.* Though critics of our self-concern have started speaking out in the past few years and so have begun to move *self* into the ambivalent category of *car, self* is still generally seen as an unquestionably good thing. But what's so good about it? What is there in *self* that we find so attractive? This is a question, really, about what *self* means to us. And it's a hard question to answer, not only because *self* has a variety of meanings, but also because *meaning* itself (and here another dual distinction is necessary) means at least two things. By *meaning* we mean the definition of a word: *jogging,* for example, means running at a slow, regular pace. But by *meaning* we also mean the concept or concepts carried by—or, as we usually say, "behind"—a word: *jogging* now carries the concept of good health, physical well-being, and even for some people mental well-being and peace of mind. Note that along with this concept of jogging as well-being (physical or mental) comes a positive value; the mere definition of jogging is neutral. Concepts often, as in this case, imply values: the attractiveness of jogging today seems to lie in the concepts behind it.

. . .

PSYCHOLOGY'S SLIPPERY SENSE OF
SELF

In 1956, a psychologist began his book with the statement: "Concern for 12 the self with all its contributing attributes and potentials is rapidly becoming a central focus of contemporary psychological inquiry." Today we might smile at the obviousness of such a statement, but our smile should be one not of scorn at its naiveté but of admiration at the astuteness of its prediction. *Self* and its compounds have indeed come to take up much of psychology's attention—so much that they fill, for example, fourteen columns of titles in the January–June 1982 *Psychological Abstracts* Subject Index (with *"Self Concept,"* *"Self Esteem,"* and *"Self Perception"* the longest entries) and seven inches of the Psychiatric Card Catalog at the University of Rochester Medical School (including titles like "On the Beginnings of a Cohesive Self," "The Finding and Becoming of Self," and "On the Development of the Experience of Mental Self, the Bodily Self, and Self Consciousness"). These statistics, though admittedly crude, confirm the sense of probably anyone who comes in contact with psychology (and is there anyone who doesn't?) that contemporary psychology is inseparable from *self.*

The "contemporary psychology" I refer to includes, as my reference to   13
the Psychiatric Card Catalog indicates, psychiatry and psychoanalysis and some of the psychotherapies as well. This inclusion is sure to rankle some members of these various disciplines who insist on the distinctness of their fields. But in the use they make of *self,* these fields are far from distinct. In fact, they seem to have developed their sense of *self* on common ground: ground initially laid by Freud (who, however, made no significant use of the term) and then sown and cultivated by workers with professional concerns and styles as varied as those of Jung, William James, Karen Horney, Carl Rogers, and Rollo May. The *self* produced by this crossbreeding has then spread into general public discourse from all the psychology-related fields except behaviorism, which has worked hard to hold back the spread. One field in particular, though, has been most strongly behind the push of *self* into popular discourse: the field known as "humanistic psychology" or "personal growth psychology" or "the human potential movement." Since my ultimate concern in this part of the book is with our popular sense of *self,* the psychology I have in mind when I talk about "psychology's *self"* is primarily this personal growth psychology. Primarily but not exclusively—because, as I've said, no *self* of any field of psychology is cut off from the *self* of the others.

What exactly *self* means for all these areas of psychology that make so   14
much of it is surprisingly difficult to discover. Soon after the above-quoted psychologist began his book by noting psychology's central "concern for the self," another psychologist began hers by noting that "in psychological discussions the word 'self' has been used in many different ways." And sixteen years later, those differences hadn't yet been resolved: a 1977 article in *Psychology in the Schools* complains that "currently scores of theories and definitions of 'self' are found in the literature." In trying to find out what *self* means for psychology, then, we can't hope simply to open a dictionary of psychology and find there a comprehensive definition. Nor, it turns out, can we go to the literature* itself to find clear statements of those scores of meanings: even though the self is one of psychology's central concerns, *the self* rarely gets directly defined by those concerned with it.

By "direct definition" I mean statements in the form "the self is. . . ."   15
Occasionally in the literature we find such a statement: for example, "The self is . . . the center from which one sees and is aware of . . . different 'sides' of

---

*The scholarly publications in a given field of research.

himself." More frequent, however, are indirect definitions of various kinds: definition by apposition ("it indicates that the person, the self, is generous"), by *or* ("the archetype of wholeness or of the self"), by *as* ("I speak now of the real self as that central inner force"), or by a combination of these ("conceiving ego or self as a constellation of interrelated attitudes"). Writers using grammatical forms such as these don't usually think of themselves as defining; yet these forms act as definitions, and in the absence of direct definitions we often have to rely on them to discover what writers mean by the words they use. Another, even more indirect, way of learning what is meant by psychology's *self* is by noticing the metaphors that *self* gets used in, or the terms that surround it. Even the terms that *self* gets opposed to will give us a clue about its definition: when we read, for example, that often a client "discovers that he exists only in response to the demands of others, that he seems to have no self of his own," we know that *self* is *not* exclusive responsiveness to others' demands and is some sort of opposition to those demands.

Reading through the writings of psychology, both technical and popu-   16
lar, with these various methods of definition as a guide, we can begin to sort out what psychologists have in mind by *self.* One thing they often seem to have in mind is that *self* is a goal of some kind. But the kind varies. It can be the goal of what sounds like a treasure hunt (the familiar "finding of one's self"), a trip ("the long journey to achieve selfhood"), a vegetable ("the maturation of the self"), or a vaguely Aristotelian process ("self-actualization is actualization of a self"). Sometimes, though, *self* seems not to be a goal but to have goals of its own: "the [mature] self now expresses . . . its intentions and goals." . . .

[In a section too technical to include here, Rosenthal continues to discuss notions of the self advanced by various psychologists. She alludes both to the founders of modern psychology, Sigmund Freud and Carl Jung, and to some of their modern heirs, the titles of whose writings reveal their relevance for Rosenthal's thesis: Rollo May, Man's Search for Himself *(1953); Willard Gaylin,* Feelings: Our Vital Signs *(1979); Karen Horney,* Neurosis and Human Growth *(1950); Carl Rogers,* On Becoming a Person *(1961); Abraham Maslow, "Self-Actualizing People: A Study of Psychological Health" (1958); and Erich Fromm, "Selfishness, Self-love, and Self-interest" (1958). Generalizing on the basis of their views, Rosenthal asserts that modern psychology has tended to link the concept of self more and more with other terms that possess positive value in the modern world, especially such terms as* feelings, individual, *and* unique. *The upshot of this tendency, she argues, has been to give us a notion of the self that is (1) always supposed to be unique (the authentic person) and (2) always supposed to feel good, especially about "itself." She concludes this discussion as follows.]*

What psychology did, we can now say in summary, was to link the   17
word *self* to these terms and to the concepts behind them; to give *self* and its associates scientific status by making them part of a technical vocabulary (without, however, developing for them clear or agreed-on definitions); and to link them all with teleologically weighted terms like *goal, growth,* and

health—thus offering us this extended network of terms, bright with the golden glow of scientific validity, as the ideal pattern for us to follow in our talk, our thinking, and our shaping of our lives.

OUR BEST-SELLING AND GOD-GIVEN
SELF

Have we accepted this *self* that psychology offers us? How much of our   18
sense of *self*, as we ordinarily use the word, comes from psychology? All, we might be tempted to say—especially when we notice how many of our best-sellers (those prime providers of terms for public, and private, discourse) either are written by psychologists or are, like *Passages,** popularizations of psychology. *Passages,* in fact, has itself become a passage: a conduit through which the terms of self-oriented psychology have poured into the main stream of general discourse.

While *self* is not a frequent term in *Passages,* the self as conceived by   19
psychology is the book's subject, and all the familiar *self* associations of psychology are there. The "inner realm" is for Sheehy where the action is; her study—like Freud's, Jung's, Maslow's, Gaylin's—is of our "internal life system." And her proudly positive *inner* is, in the best Rogersian fashion, set against an *outer* conceived as restrictive and artificial: when you move into midlife, "you are moving out of roles and into the self." This inner self—like May's, Maslow's, Rogers's—is the source (the only "authentic" source) of values: the move into the self is a move "away from external validations and accreditations, in search of an inner validation"; and "one of the great rewards of moving through the disassembling period to renewal [another positively loaded term] is coming to approve of oneself ethically and morally and quite independent of other people's standards and agenda."

"Coming to approve of oneself ethically and morally" turns out, in the   20
book—as in Gaylin and Rogers—to be inseparable from feeling good about oneself. Sheehy, as we would expect from our familiarity with *self*'s associates in psychology, makes much of *feeling,* both as a main subject and as a main term in her vocabulary. "How do we *feel* about our way of living in the world at any given time?" she asks as one of the book's central questions, letting her italics show where her emphasis lies.

But, of course, this emphasis on feelings is not only Sheehy's. It has   21
become—through *Passages* and all the other mass media productions through which psychology's terms come to us—the emphasis almost everywhere we go. When, for example, we go to meetings on the job, we find that once-objective business (a company's marketing changes, a college's curriculum

---

*Gail Sheehy's *Passages* (New York: Dutton, 1974) was a blockbuster best-seller that portrayed life as a series of passages and suggested that success in life is *not* finding yourself in middle age at the end of a passage leading to a future you don't want. The emphasis is on inner feelings as the final criteria: whether we "feel good" or "feel bad" about the choices we've made in life, whether those choices have been *authentic,* and whether they have been consistent with our *personal* values.

changes) has been sucked inside and comes out of speaker's mouths as "how I feel about these changes." If we go to church, we're likely to hear sermons on the importance of feeling good about ourselves and having a "positive self-image." And if we happen to go to medical school, we're likely to find the anatomy professor concentrating on how to "help the students deal with possible emotional tensions arising from the experience of the dissecting lab." The dissecting lab is no longer a classroom but an "experience"; an experience must be "felt"; and Sheehy's question "How do we *feel* about our way of living in the world at any given time?" seems to be asked now at every given time.

While we're asked constantly about our feelings, we're assured con-   22
stantly about our individual uniqueness. From Mister Rogers's assurance, to the four-year-old in each of us, that "you're a very special person" to Dr. Wayne Dyer's best-selling line that "you are unique in all the world" to Dr. Joyce Brothers's sales pitch that each of us should have "a unique and personal program" for success, psychology's line about the value of the individual seems to have spread everywhere. Or, more accurately (since the line isn't only psychology's), what has spread is psychology's version of a general humanist line: as *The Humanist* magazine reminds us, "the preciousness and dignity of the individual person is a central humanist value."

As pop psychology spreads the positive *unique–individual* line through our   23
culture, it necessarily spreads also the confusions and ambiguity that we saw running through psychology's use of the line. When, for example, Sheehy offers "each of us . . . the opportunity to emerge reborn, authentically unique, with an enlarged capacity to love ourselves and embrace others," she's offering us, along with that uniqueness, the ambiguity between given and goal that psychology leaves unresolved in *unique.* For if we have to "emerge" unique, we're presumably not unique already; yet our given uniqueness is one of the working assumptions that Sheehy takes over from developmental-personality psychology. To qualify the aimed-for uniqueness with *authentically* (and thus apparently to distinguish it from ordinary or inauthentic uniqueness) is to make no real qualification at all. *Authentic* is what we could call an "empty plus": it carries positive value but is void of content ("says nothing," as we often put it).

All my talk about the "spread" of psychology's *self,* via the popular   24
media into our common language, makes psychology sound like a creeping vine or like a virus spreading through the population or like a guerrilla force acting underground to take us over town by town (or term by term). These implications of my metaphor are, of course, inaccurate and unfair to psychology: psychology has no conspiracy against us, and it's not an alien force. It's part of us, part of our culture: the part, we could say, that studies for us what we want (even long) to know about our individual selves. If psychology gives us its *self,* this is because we ask for it.

So while we can truly say that we get psychology's *self* through the mass   25
media, we can't say that we get it against our will. Nor can we say, despite the dominant impression given by popular literature and by this analysis of it so far, that the *self* we get is entirely psychology's. Obviously, to a large

extent it is—so obviously, maybe, that this examination of how the mass media repeat psychology's lines has been, for many readers, simply repetitious. But if we now look more closely into these best-selling lines, we can see something more in them than what psychology alone has put there. In, for example, that promise of Sheehy's of "the opportunity to emerge reborn" there's a touch of evangelicalism that we can't say comes from psychology. Or, if it does—and there is, certainly, something of the promise of a new life in Maslow's and Rogers's goal of a new or renewed or higher self—it comes into both professional and pop psychology from elsewhere: from, originally, Christianity. There are other places, too, where Christianity enters into our sense of *self;* and we should look briefly at one of them in order to correct the impression that the *self* we get through the mass media, and hence our common sense of *self,* is entirely and simply psychology's.

In our common (both widespread and frequent) assertion of the value ²⁶ of each individual, we're indeed expressing what *The Humanist* called a "central humanist value." But before "the preciousness and dignity of the individual person" was a central humanist value, it was a central Christian value. By moving the locus of spiritual activity from external rites and laws into the individual, Christianity brought God's infinite value into each person. *Individual* and *internal* have thus always carried pluses for Christianity: the plus signs of God's presence in the individual. "Are you not aware that you are the temple of God, and that the Spirit of God dwells in you?" St. Paul asks rhetorically. One way of looking at what has happened to the positive term *individual* over the past two thousand years is to see the plus sign remaining over *individual* while the source of the world's plus, the Spirit of God, is gradually removed by the secular Renaissance–Romantic–psychology tradition. To St. Paul's question, psychology (speaking for secular humanism generally) answers no. And yet this answer doesn't decrease the value placed by us on the individual. In fact, it reinforces it.

This reinforcement works because we hear or see words but not the ²⁷ concepts behind them. Behind (or in) the Christian *individual* is the concept of God; behind (or in) the secular humanist *individual* is the concept of man alone. But while these concepts are far (infinitely far) apart, the words expressing them can be identical. Assertions of "our individual uniqueness" or "the preciousness of the individual" can sound exactly the same no matter who makes them. When Billy Graham asserts, for example, that "the central theme of the universe is the purpose and destiny of every individual," he sounds just like *The Humanist* (even though he means something different). And because Christian and secular voices can sound the same, each "sounds better" because we've heard the same line from the other; each, that is, lends its particular authority to the line. When Graham, then, tells us that each conversion process is "very personal" ("God looks at each of us differently, because each of us is different"), this sounds right because we've heard Mister Rogers telling us, since we were four, that each of us is special and different; and when Dr. Wayne Dyer assures each of us that "you are unique in all the world," we tend to believe it even more because we've heard it in church.

We've heard it even if we don't go to church—heard, that is, the Chris-   28
tian lines asserting the value of the individual. We tend to pride ourselves on
living in a secular culture; yet a culture in which a major television network
considers it profitable to broadcast Billy Graham during prime time, and in
which the *New York Times* regularly (religiously!) prints the Pope's addresses,
is hardly simply secular. Even those of us who grow up without opening the
Bible cannot have avoided contact with Christian lines. Where those lines
contradict the lines of a secular authority like psychology, of course we have
to choose which to follow. But where the lines overlap, as in assertions of the
worth of the individual, we can easily nod our approval to both. The fact that
Christianity places positive value on the individual just reinforces our sense
of that value, and thus adds to the positive sense of *self* that we get from
secular sources.

WHAT GOOD IS THE *SELF*?

If we return now to the original question of this chapter—the question   29
of how much of our sense of *self* comes from psychology—we find that the
answer has to be a bit complicated. In the area of *self* covered by *individual,*
our sense of positive value seems to come at least as much from Christianity
as from psychology, though the amount is hard to measure since in most
praise of the individual we can't tell where that praise is coming from. As for
the rest of the extensive area covered by *self* and its associated terms, we've
seen that while our common *self* is to a large extent psychology's, psychology's *self* is to a large extent not its own but that of four hundred years of
Western culture. The Renaissance's positive valuing of subjectivity, individuality, and creativity; seventeenth-century philosophy's positive valuing of
self-consciousness and identity; Romanticism's positive valuing of all these
along with internalness, freedom, and feelings—all this is carried on in psychology's *self.*

This is quite a lot of good (or goods) to be carried by a single word!   30
And yet there's still more. Because besides Christianity and psychology
(and through it the Renaissance–Romantic tradition), other powerful traditions and ideologies come into play in *self* and add their weight to the
word.

We've seen, for example, that *freedom* is one of the plus terms associated   31
with *self* in the Romantic tradition carried on by psychology; but *freedom,* along
with terms like *independence* and *self-determination,* has also been a plus word in
every expression of democratic political ideals since the French Revolution.
Furthermore, terms like *self-sufficiency* and *control,* which operate in close connection with the *freedom* set in both psychology and democratic political
discourse, are plus terms also in the ideology of modern technology. These
terms, of course, have different applications in each of these places. For
technology, *self-sufficiency* and *control* are terms applied primarily to machines
and ideal mechanical functioning; for democracy, these terms apply to governments and to people as political units; for psychology, they apply to

individual personality. Yet the application in each case is to something valued positively by the ideology or discipline concerned.

These terms then carry along with them, in all of their uses, the positive values of all the ideologies and disciplines and activities and traditions of thought in which they operate. I don't mean that they necessarily carry along the particular applications from these various places; nor do I mean that we're aware of all these sources adding their weight to a word we use. What I mean is that our sense of a word's positive value is increased, usually without our awareness, when that word carries positive value in ideologies and activities and so on other than the one we're consciously using it in—especially when those other sources of its value are themselves highly prized by our culture.

Take, for example, the call for independence in "Your Declaration of Independence," a 1977 *Harper's Bazaar* article: "Independence, simply, is the freedom to choose what is pertinent to your needs at any given time. It is a feeling of freedom that comes from within." Because of the neat overlap of political and psychological terms here, the positive political values of *independence* and *freedom* are brought to bear on the positive psychological values of *independence, needs, feeling,* and *within.* For the authors of this "Declaration," as well as for readers who respond positively to it, *independence* is attractive because it carries some of our most cherished political and psychological values; and it has this double attraction whether or not the authors and readers are aware of the sources of this attraction. Similarly, in the calls we've heard so often in recent years to "pull our own strings"—whether in ads like *Ms.* magazine's picture of a female marionette with text urging women to cut the strings that control them from outside, or in best-sellers like *Pulling Your Own Strings*—what is being appealed to is our generally and overwhelmingly positive sense of *self-sufficiency* and *control of our lives,* a sense which derives from the combined positive appeal of these terms in psychology, democracy, and technology. Because of the multiple strength of this appeal, then, we tend to go along unquestioningly with our sense that *self-sufficiency* is a good thing— pulled less by our own strings than by those of the powerful networks of meaning and value operating on the word from behind the scenes.

It's odd, maybe, to think of words working like this, apart from our awareness or our conscious intentions: we're so used to assuming our control of everything (we're so attracted by the idea of pulling our own strings) that we assume that, where our language is concerned, we can simply "say what we mean" as long as we just take a minute to choose our words carefully. That words can mean things apart from what we intend for them, that words say what *they* mean more than what *we* mean, is indeed disconcerting. Yet when we look at how our common language actually operates—when we look, for example, at why certain words attract us—we have to admit that it operates to a large extent outside of our conscious intentions. We can indeed increase the extent of our consciousness of its operations, as we're doing here, and thereby give ourselves more control over our language than we usually have. But unless we make this deliberate effort to watch how our words are working, we'll be worked on by them and manipulated by their meanings unawares.

One thing we've seen so far about the way words operate is that they 35
act as receptacles into which different disciplines and ideologies and traditions of thought pour their particular meanings, their favorite value-laden
concepts. The word *self,* we can now say, is the container of heavily weighted
meaning from some of our culture's most influential sources; it's a loaded
term. This is the case even though *self* has no precise definition, either in any
of the places where its value comes from or in our everyday use. If you ask
someone who speaks in terms of his self—who talks about fulfilling himself
or having a negative self-image or knowing his true self—what exactly he
means by his *self,* he's unlikely to be able to tell you. How could he have a
precise definition when the sources of his sense of *self* don't give him one?
What they give him instead of a definition is, as we've seen, a complex of
positively valued concepts—an overwhelmingly good (yes) feeling. And it
might be that if *self* had a tighter definition, it couldn't carry such a variety
of concepts. A definition is (by definition) a boundary, an assumption of
finiteness. A tightly defined word has definite boundaries and therefore limited room for concepts to fit into it. But a loosely defined word like *self* is
flexible, stretchy; its sides can move out easily to accommodate all the concepts that come into it from the various places where it operates. And the
more concepts it has room for, the more it then tends to draw in other terms
associated with these concepts—and thus the more likely it is to operate, by
itself or through its associates, in our everyday thought.

Our practically undefined *self,* then, brings with it an array of concepts: 36
mainly from the Renaissance, Romanticism, and psychology, but also from
Christianity, democracy, and technology (and from evolutionary theory
too . . . .). And these concepts carry almost unanimously positive value. No
wonder we're so filled with self: because *self* is filled with the prize concerns
of centuries of our culture.

Questions for Discussion

1. Can you think of other words that, like *self,* carry a lot of connotative
   baggage that many users may not be aware of? What about words like
   honor, duty, respect, responsibility, rights, liberty, and *patriotism*? Would they lend
   themselves to the kind of analysis that Rosenthal does of *self*? In class
   discussion can you begin to see some of the things that you would have
   to include in such an analysis of any one of these words (or another one
   of your own choice)?

2. In paragraph 3, Rosenthal says that "language works to give us much less
   control over 'what we mean' than we generally assume we have. Even
   when we think we're choosing our words with care and giving them
   precise meanings, they can mean much more (or less) than we think." Do

you agree with this as a general position about language, or does it sound to you as if she is overstating the case? Can you think of examples on either side of the question? Have you ever found yourself using a word or phrase that your listeners took in a much wider or narrower sense than you did? If so, give an account of that experience in class.

3. According to the Christian scheme of values that once held much wider sway than it does today, the role of the self was not to serve itself, not to achieve personal happiness above all things. Happiness was not in itself viewed as sinful, but the satisfaction or fulfillment of the self in a private sense was simply not taken to be the goal of existence. Human beings were created to do the will of God, not to serve the desires of the self. Human selfhood had been corrupt since the Fall (Adam and Eve's sin in the Garden of Eden) and was therefore not to be trusted as a guide to non-sinful behavior. Following God's will could lead the believer into many situations humiliating or stressful to the self—ridicule, poverty, persecution, or martyrdom, for example. In your view, how do modern Christians reconcile this traditional Christian view of the self with the modern view of the self based largely on twentieth-century psychology as described by Rosenthal? *Is* there any way to reconcile these views, to make them live together in peaceful co-existence? Or do most modern Christians simply fail to see that there is any divergence between these views of self? In class discussion, get as many Christians and non-Christians as possible to respond to these questions.

4. If any members of your class come from non-Western cultures or a non-Christian tradition, have them respond to Rosenthal's description of the twentieth-century American secular self from the perspective of their own cultural tradition. What important differences emerge? What kinds of insights might modern Americans learn about the self from non-Americans or non-Christians?

Suggested Essay Topics

1. In contemporary debates about moral issues it is clear that the perceived needs or feelings of the self are often given primacy over external moral standards. In the matter of cheating on exams, for example, you will often hear students arguing that "it's OK for you if you *feel* OK about it personally; I mean, everybody has to make up his own mind about these things." The same position is often taken about other kinds of behavior: premarital sex, drug use, abortion, cheating on income taxes, and so on. Choose an issue such as one of these, and write a dialogue in which one speaker gives support to the position that "X is right depending on how you feel about it," and the other supports some version of the position that "X can be viewed as wrong regardless of how you feel about it."

2. A variation on topic 1 is to choose one of these two positions about X and write an essay defending your views. If you choose this option, however, it will be important for you to find some way of bringing in the views of

the opposition. (You might try writing a dialogue.) At least show an awareness of what an intelligent opponent would say. Otherwise you will sound simplistic and naive. For example, you may really believe that abortion is not really a matter of personal feeling because the Bible says 'Thou shalt not kill' and abortion is a form of murder, but in this form it is an inadequate argument. Whether abortion is really a form of murder is exactly what the controversy is all about, and there are many sophisticated points on both sides that you need to be aware of before tackling this (or any other) complex issue. A better way to begin is to say something like, "I know what the proponents of abortion on demand have to say. Their position boils down to three basic arguments: . . ." and then give those arguments. Doing so will not only make you seem in control of your subject, which will enhance your rhetorical credibility, but will also give you concrete points to respond to as you develop your rebuttal.

George Orwell

George Orwell (1903–1950) was a British novelist, journalist, political commentator, and satirist. He is most famous as the author of two satiric fables warning of the dangers and exposing the operations of tyrannical governments, Animal Farm *(1945) and* Nineteen Eighty-four *(1949). These works have been translated into most major languages and are studied by scholars and schoolchildren alike.*

"Politics and the English Language" is almost as widely read as Orwell's fiction. Its title clearly indicates Orwell's central concern: "In our time," he says, "political speech and writing are largely the defence of the indefensible" (¶13). His thesis is that there is a direct and traceable relationship between political brutality and imprecise, vague, evasive, and cliché-ridden English. Immoral politics and bad writing reinforce each other, each one becoming in turn both a cause and an effect.

Three different groups contribute most directly to the deterioration of political language: (1) governments that want to find easier ways of masking their "indefensible" acts of brutality; (2) persons connected with brutal governments who have a vested interest in disguising their governments' acts; and (3) people who do not want to see political brutality for what it is because they do not want to take responsibility for stopping it.

In exposing this problem, Orwell is not completely pessimistic. Things are bad, he says, and getting worse all the time, but the state of neither politics nor language is hopeless. Political brutality and bad writing are not natural forces like the seasons; they are instead the product of choices. *Governments are not required to murder dissidents—they choose to. No one forces citizens to settle for language that disguises their government's murder of dissidents—they choose to. And what people choose at one time, they can reject at another time.*

Orwell's essay is an attempt to persuade us to reject perversions of politics and power by forcing us to attend to the language that supports them. The kind of world we live in, he says, is not just the world that happens to us; it is also the world we make. He insists that the effects of a hard-headed demand that world governments say clearly what they are doing and why they are doing it, combined with a hard-headed demand for clear and vigorous expression from ourselves, will improve both political conduct and the use of English.

After studying Orwell's essay, your class may want to subscribe to the **Quarterly Review of Doublespeak,** *published by the National Council of Teachers of English. The review annually announces the "Orwell Award" for the best book exposing abuse of language, and the "Doublespeak Award," a mock prize for "misuses of language with pernicious social or political consequences." In 1982 two of the Doublespeak Awards were given to Lawrence A. Kudlow, chief economist of the Office of Management and Budget, "for creating the phrase 'revenue enhancement,' which was used by the Reagan administration instead of the phrase 'tax increase,' " and to Secretary of the Interior James Watt, "who said, 'I never use the words Republicans and Democrats. It's liberals and Americans' " (see the January 1983 issue).*

POLITICS AND
THE ENGLISH LANGUAGE

From *"Shooting an Elephant" and Other Essays* (1950).

Most people who bother with the matter at all would admit that the English language is in a bad way, but it is generally assumed that we cannot by conscious action do anything about it. Our civilization is decadent and our language—so the argument runs—must inevitably share in the general collapse. It follows that any struggle against the abuse of language is a sentimental archaism, like preferring candles to electric light or hansom cabs to aeroplanes. Underneath this lies the half-conscious belief that language is a natural growth and not an instrument which we shape for our own purposes.

Now, it is clear that the decline of a language must ultimately have political and economic causes: it is not due simply to the bad influence of this or that individual writer. But an effect can become a cause, reinforcing the original cause and producing the same effect in an intensified form, and so on indefinitely. A man may take to drink because he feels himself to be a failure, and then fail all the more completely because he drinks. It is rather the same thing that is happening to the English language. It becomes ugly and inaccurate because our thoughts are foolish, but the slovenliness of our language makes it easier for us to have foolish thoughts. The point is that the process is reversible. Modern English, especially written English, is full of bad habits which spread by imitation and which can be avoided if one is willing to take the necessary trouble. If one gets rid of these habits one can think more clearly, and to think clearly is a necessary first step towards political regeneration: so that the fight against bad English is not frivolous and is not the exclusive concern of professional writers. I will come back to this presently, and I hope that by that time the meaning of what I have said here will have become clearer. Meanwhile, here are five specimens of the English language as it is now habitually written.

These five passages have not been picked out because they are especially bad—I could have quoted far worse if I had chosen—but because they illustrate various of the mental vices from which we now suffer. They are a little below the average, but are fairly representative samples. I number them so that I can refer back to them when necessary:

(1) I am not, indeed, sure whether it is not true to say that the Milton who once seemed not unlike a seventeenth-century Shelley had not become, out of an experience ever more bitter in each year, more alien [*sic*] to the founder of that Jesuit sect which nothing could induce him to tolerate.—Professor Harold Laski (Essay in *Freedom of Expression*)

(2) Above all, we cannot play ducks and drakes with a native battery of idioms which prescribes such egregious collocations of vocables as the Basic *put up with* for *tolerate* or *put at a loss* for *bewilder.*—Professor Lancelot Hogben (*Interglossa*)

(3) On the one side we have the free personality: by definition it is not neurotic, for it has neither conflict nor dream. Its desires, such as they are, are transparent, for they are just what institutional approval keeps in the forefront of consciousness; another institutional pattern would alter their number and intensity; there is little in them that is natural, irreducible, or culturally dangerous. But *on the other side,* the social bond itself is nothing but the mutual reflection of these self-secure integrities. Recall the definition of love. Is not this the very picture of a small academic? Where is there a place in this hall of mirrors for either personality or fraternity?—Essay on psychology in *Politics* (New York)

(4) All the "best people" from the gentlemen's clubs, and all the frantic fascist captains, united in common hatred of Socialism and bestial horror of the rising tide of the mass revolutionary movement, have turned to acts of provocation, to foul incendiarism, to medieval legends of poisoned wells, to legalize their own destruction of proletarian organizations, and rouse the agitated petty-bourgeoisie to chauvinistic fervor on behalf of the fight against the revolutionary way out of the crisis.—Communist pamphlet

(5) If a new spirit *is* to be infused into this old country, there is one thorny and contentious reform which must be tackled, and that is the humanization and galvanization of the B.B.C. Timidity here will bespeak canker and atrophy of the soul. The heart of Britain may be sound and of strong beat, for instance, but the British lion's roar at present is like that of Bottom in Shakespeare's *Midsummer Night's Dream*—as gentle as any sucking dove. A virile new Britain cannot continue indefinitely to be

traduced in the eyes or rather ears, of the world by the effete languors of Langham Place, brazenly masquerading as "standard English." When the Voice of Britain is heard at nine o'clock, better far and infinitely less ludicrous to hear aitches honestly dropped than the present priggish, inflated, inhibited, school-ma'amish arch braying of blameless bashful mewing maidens!—Letter in *Tribune*

Each of these passages has faults of its own, but, quite apart from avoidable ugliness, two qualities are common to all of them. The first is staleness of imagery; the other is lack of precision. The writer either has a meaning and cannot express it, or he inadvertently says something else, or he is almost indifferent as to whether his words mean anything or not. This mixture of vagueness and sheer incompetence is the most marked characteristic of modern English prose, and especially of any kind of political writing. As soon as certain topics are raised, the concrete melts into the abstract and no one seems able to think of turns of speech that are not hackneyed: prose consists less and less of *words* chosen for the sake of their meaning, and more and more of *phrases* tacked together like the sections of a prefabricated henhouse. I list below, with notes and examples, various of the tricks by means of which the work of prose-construction is habitually dodged:

Dying Metaphors. A newly invented metaphor assists thought by evoking a visual image, while on the other hand a metaphor which is technically "dead" (e.g. *iron resolution*) has in effect reverted to being an ordinary word and can generally be used without loss of vividness. But in between these two classes there is a huge dump of worn-out metaphors which have lost all evocative power and are merely used because they save people the trouble of inventing phrases for themselves. Examples are: *Ring the changes on, take up the cudgels for, toe the line, ride roughshod over, stand shoulder to shoulder with, play into the hands of, no axe to grind, grist to the mill, fishing in troubled waters, rift within the lute, on the order of the day, Achilles' heel, swan song, hotbed.* Many of these are used without knowledge of their meaning (what is a "rift," for instance?), and incompatible metaphors are frequently mixed, a sure sign that the writer is not interested in what he is saying. Some metaphors now current have been twisted out of their original meaning without those who use them even being aware of the fact. For example, *toe the line* is sometimes written *tow the line.* Another example is *the hammer and the anvil,* now always used with the implication that the anvil gets the worst of it. In real life it is always the anvil that breaks the hammer, never the other way about: a writer who stopped to think what he was saying would be aware of this, and would avoid perverting the original phrase.

Operators or *Verbal False Limbs.* These save the trouble of picking out appropriate verbs and nouns, and at the same time pad each sentence with extra syllables which give it an appearance of symmetry. Characteristic phrases are *render inoperative, militate against, make contact with, be subjected to, give rise to, give grounds for, have the effect of, play a leading part (role) in, make itself felt, take effect, exhibit a tendency to, serve the purpose of, etc., etc.* The keynote is the elimination of simple verbs. Instead of being a single word, such as *break, stop, spoil, mend, kill,* a verb becomes a *phrase,* made up of a noun or adjective tacked on to some general-purposes verb such as *prove, serve, form, play, render.* In addition, the passive voice is wherever possible used in preference to the active, and noun constructions are used instead of gerunds (*by examination of* instead of *by examin-ing*). The range of verbs is further cut down by means of the *-ize* and *de-*formations, and the banal statements are given an appearance of profundity by means of the *not un-* formation. Simple conjunctions and prepositions are replaced by such phrases as *with respect to, having regard to, the fact that, by dint of, in view of, in the interests of, on the hypothesis that;* and the ends of sentences are saved from anticlimax by such resounding common-places as *greatly to be desired, cannot be left out of account, a development to be expected in the near future, deserving of serious consideration, brought to a satisfactory conclusion,* and so on and so forth.

Pretentious Diction.   Words like *phenomenon, element, individual* (as noun), ⁷ *objective, categorical, effective, virtual, basic, primary, promote, constitute, exhibit, exploit, utilize, eliminate, liquidate,* are used to dress up simple statements and give an air of scientific impartiality to biased judgments. Adjectives like *epoch-making, epic, historic, unforgettable, triumphant, age-old, inevitable, inexorable, veritable,* are used to dignify the sordid processes of international politics, while writing that aims at glorifying war usually takes on an archaic color, its characteristic words being: *realm, throne, chariot, mailed fist, trident, sword, shield, buckler, banner, jackboot, clarion.* Foreign words and expressions such as *cul de sac, ancien régime, deus ex machina, mutatis mutandis, status quo, gleichschaltung, weltanschauung,* are used to give an air of culture and elegance. Except for the useful abbreviations *i.e., e.g.,* and *etc.,* there is no real need for any of the hundreds of foreign phrases now current in English. Bad writers, and especially scientific, political and socio-logical writers, are nearly always haunted by the notion that Latin or Greek words are grander than Saxon ones, and unnecessary words like *expedite, ameliorate, predict, extraneous, deracinated, clandestine, subaqueous* and hundreds of others constantly gain ground from their Anglo-Saxon opposite numbers.* The jargon peculiar to Marxist writing (*hyena, hangman, cannibal, petty bourgeois, these gentry, lacquey, flunkey, mad dog, White Guard,* etc.) consists largely of words and phrases translated from Russian, German or French; but the normal way of coining a new word is to use a Latin or Greek root with the appropriate affix and, where necessary, the *-ize* formation. It is often easier to make up words of this kind (*deregionalize, impermissible, extramarital, non-fragmentary* and so forth) than to think up the English words that will cover one's meaning. The result, in general, is an increase in slovenliness and vagueness.

*An interesting illustration of this is the way in which the English flower names which were in use till very recently are being ousted by Greek ones, *snapdragon* becoming *antirrhinum, forget-me-not* becoming *myosotis,* etc. It is hard to see any practical reason for this change of fashion: it is probably due to an instinctive turning-away from the more homely word and a vague feeling that the Greek word is scientific. [Orwell's note.]

Meaningless Words.   In certain kinds of writing, particularly in art crit-   8
icism and literary criticism, it is normal to come across long passages which
are almost completely lacking in meaning.* Words like *romantic, plastic, val-*
ues, human, dead, sentimental, natural, vitality, as used in art criticism, are strictly
meaningless, in the sense that they not only do not point to any discoverable object, but are hardly ever expected to do so by the reader. When one
critic writes, "The outstanding feature of Mr. X's work is its living quality," while another writes, "The immediately striking thing about Mr. X's
work is its peculiar deadness," the reader accepts this as a simple difference of opinion. If words like *black* and *white* were involved, instead of the
jargon words *dead* and *living,* he would see at once that language was being
used in an improper way. Many political words are similarly abused. The
word *Fascism* has now no meaning except in so far as it signifies "something not desirable." The words *democracy, socialism, freedom, patriotic, realistic,*
justice, have each of them several different meanings which cannot be
reconciled with one another. In the case of a word like *democracy,* not only
is there no agreed definition, but the attempt to make one is resisted from
all sides. It is almost universally felt that when we call a country democratic we are praising it: consequently the defenders of every kind of régime claim that it is a democracy, and fear that they might have to stop
using the word if it were tied down to any one meaning. Words of this
kind are often used in a consciously dishonest way. That is, the person
who uses them has his own private definition, but allows his hearer to
think he means something quite different. Statements like *Marshal Pétain*
was a true patriot, The Soviet Press is the freest in the world, The Catholic Church is
opposed to persecution, are almost always made with intent to deceive. Other
words used in variable meanings, in most cases more or less dishonestly,
are: *class, totalitarian, science, progressive, reactionary, bourgeois, equality.*

Now that I have made this catalogue of swindles and perversions, let   9
me give another example of the kind of writing that they lead to. This time
it must of its nature be an imaginary one. I am going to translate a passage
of good English into modern English of the worst sort. Here is a well-known
verse from *Ecclesiastes:*

"I returned and saw under the sun, that the race is not to the swift, nor
the battle to the strong, neither yet bread to the wise, nor yet riches to men
of understanding, nor yet favour to men of skill; but time and chance hap-
peneth to them all."

Here it is in modern English:

"Objective considerations of contemporary phenomena compels the
conclusion that success or failure in competitive activities exhibits no tend-

---

*Example: "Comfort's catholicity of perception and image, strangely Whitmanesque in range,
almost the exact opposite in aesthetic compulsion, continues to evoke that trembling atmospheric accumulative hinting at a cruel, an inexorably serene timelessness. . . . Wrey Gardiner
scores by aiming at simple bull's-eyes with precision. Only they are not so simple, and
through this contented sadness runs more than the surface bitter-sweet of resignation." (*Poetry
Quarterly* .) [Orwell's note.]

ency to be commensurate with innate capacity, but that a considerable element of the unpredictable must invariably be taken into account."

This is a parody, but not a very gross one. Exhibit (3), above, for 10
instance, contains several patches of the same kind of English. It will be seen
that I have not made a full translation. The beginning and ending of the
sentence follow the original meaning fairly closely, but in the middle the
concrete illustrations—race, battle, bread—dissolve into the vague phrase
"success or failure in competitive activities." This had to be so, because no
modern writer of the kind I am discussing—no one capable of using phrases
like "objective consideration of contemporary phenomena"—would ever
tabulate his thoughts in that precise and detailed way. The whole tendency
of modern prose is away from concreteness. Now analyse these two sentences
a little more closely. The first contains forty-nine words but only sixty syllables, and all its words are those of everyday life. The second contains thirty-
eight words of ninety syllables: eighteen of its words are from Latin roots,
and one from Greek. The first sentence contains six vivid images, and only
one phrase ("time and chance") that could be called vague. The second
contains not a single fresh, arresting phrase, and in spite of its ninety syllables
it gives only a shortened version of the meaning contained in the first. Yet
without a doubt it is the second kind of sentence that is gaining ground in
modern English. I do not want to exaggerate. This kind of writing is not yet
universal, and outcrops of simplicity will occur here and there in the worst-
written page. Still, if you or I were told to write a few lines on the uncertainty
of human fortunes, we should probably come much nearer to my imaginary
sentence than to the one from *Ecclesiastes.*

As I have tried to show, modern writing at its worst does not consist 11
in picking out words for the sake of their meaning and inventing images in
order to make the meaning clearer. It consists in gumming together long strips
of words which have already been set in order by someone else, and making
the results presentable by sheer humbug. The attraction of this way of writing
is that it is easy. It is easier—even quicker, once you have the habit—to say
In my opinion it is not an unjustifiable assumption that than to say *I think.* If you use
ready-made phrases, you not only don't have to hunt about for words; you
also don't have to bother with the rhythms of your sentences, since these
phrases are generally so arranged as to be more or less euphonious. When you
are composing in a hurry—when you are dictating to a stenographer, for
instance, or making a public speech—it is natural to fall into a pretentious,
Latinized style. Tags like *a consideration which we should do well to bear in mind* or
a conclusion to which all of us would readily assent will save many a sentence from
coming down with a bump. By using stale metaphors, similes and idioms, you
save much mental effort, at the cost of leaving your meaning vague, not only
for your reader but for yourself. This is the significance of mixed metaphors.
The sole aim of a metaphor is to call up a visual image. When these images
clash—as in *The Fascist octopus has sung its swan song, the jackboot is thrown into the
melting pot*—it can be taken as certain that the writer is not seeing a mental
image of the objects he is naming; in other words he is not really thinking.

Look again at the examples I gave at the beginning of this essay. Professor Laski (1) uses five negatives in fifty-three words. One of these is superfluous, making nonsense of the whole passage, and in addition there is the slip *alien* for akin, making further nonsense, and several avoidable pieces of clumsiness which increase the general vagueness. Professor Hogben (2) plays ducks and drakes with a battery which is able to write prescriptions, and, while disapproving of the everyday phrase *put up with,* is unwilling to look *egregious* up in the dictionary and see what it means; (3), if one takes an uncharitable attitude towards it, is simply meaningless: probably one could work out its intended meaning by reading the whole of the article in which it occurs. In (4), the writer knows more or less what he wants to say, but an accumulation of stale phrases chokes him like tea leaves blocking a sink. In (5), words and meaning have almost parted company. People who write in this manner usually have a general emotional meaning—they dislike one thing and want to express solidarity with another—but they are not interested in the detail of what they are saying. A scrupulous writer, in every sentence that he writes, will ask himself at least four questions, thus: What am I trying to say? What words will express it? What image or idiom will make it clearer? Is this image fresh enough to have an effect? And he will probably ask himself two more: Could I put it more shortly? Have I said anything that is avoidably ugly? But you are not obliged to go to all this trouble. You can shirk it by simply throwing your mind open and letting the ready-made phrases come crowding in. They will construct your sentences for you—even think your thoughts for you, to a certain extent—and at need they will perform the important service of partially concealing your meaning even from yourself. It is at this point that the special connection between politics and the debasement of language becomes clear.

In our time it is broadly true that political writing is bad writing. Where 12 it is not true, it will generally be found that the writer is some kind of rebel, expressing his private opinions and not a "party line." Orthodoxy, of whatever color, seems to demand a lifeless, imitative style. The political dialects to be found in pamphlets, leading articles, manifestos, White Papers and the speeches of under-secretaries do, of course, vary from party to party, but they are all alike in that one almost never finds in them a fresh, vivid, home-made turn of speech. When one watches some tired hack on the platform mechanically repeating the familiar phrases—*bestial atrocities, iron heel, bloodstained tyranny, free peoples of the world, stand shoulder to shoulder*—one often has a curious feeling that one is not watching a live human being but some kind of dummy: a feeling which suddenly becomes stronger at moments when the light catches the speaker's spectacles and turns them into blank discs which seem to have no eyes behind them. And this is not altogether fanciful. A speaker who uses that kind of phraseology has gone some distance towards turning himself into a machine. The appropriate noises are coming out of his larynx, but his brain is not involved as it would be if he were choosing his words for himself. If the speech he is making is one that he is accustomed to make over and over again, he may be almost unconscious of what he is saying, as one is when one utters the responses in church. And this reduced state of consciousness, if not indispensable, is at any rate favorable to political conformity.

In our time, political speech and writing are largely the defence of the 13 indefensible. Things like the continuance of British rule in India, the Russian purges and deportations, the dropping of the atom bombs on Japan, can indeed be defended, but only by arguments which are too brutal for most people to face, and which do not square with the professed aims of political parties. Thus political language has to consist largely of euphemism, question-begging and sheer cloudy vagueness. Defenceless villages are bombarded from the air, the inhabitants driven out into the countryside, the cattle machine-gunned, the huts set on fire with incendiary bullets: this is called *pacification.* Millions of peasants are robbed of their farms and sent trudging along the roads with no more than they can carry: this is called *transfer of population* or *rectification of frontiers.* People are imprisoned for years without trial, or shot in the back of the neck or sent to die of scurvy in Arctic lumber camps: this is called *elimination of unreliable elements.* Such phraseology is needed if one wants to name things without calling up mental pictures of them. Consider for instance some comfortable English professor defending Russian totalitarianism. He cannot say outright, "I believe in killing off your opponents when you can get good results by doing so." Probably, therefore, he will say something like this:

"While freely conceding that the Soviet régime exhibits certain features 14 which the humanitarian may be inclined to deplore, we must, I think, agree that a certain curtailment of the right to political opposition is an unavoidable concomitant of transitional periods, and that the rigors which the Russian people have been called upon to undergo have been amply justified in the sphere of concrete achievement."

The inflated style is itself a kind of euphemism. A mass of Latin words 15 falls upon the facts like soft snow, blurring the outlines and covering up all the details. The great enemy of clear language is insincerity. When there is a gap between one's real and one's declared aims, one turns as it were instinctively to long words and exhausted idioms, like a cuttlefish squirting out ink. In our age there is no such thing as "keeping out of politics." All issues are political issues, and politics itself is a mass of lies, evasions, folly, hatred and schizophrenia. When the general atmosphere is bad, language must suffer. I should expect to find—this is a guess which I have not sufficient knowledge to verify—that the German, Russian and Italian languages have all deteriorated in the last ten or fifteen years, as a result of dictatorship.

But if thought corrupts language, language can also corrupt thought. A 16 bad usage can spread by tradition and imitation, even among people who should and do know better. The debased language that I have been discussing is in some ways very convenient. Phrases like *a not unjustifiable assumption, leaves much to be desired, would serve no good purpose, a consideration which we should do well to bear in mind,* are a continuous temptation, a packet of aspirins always at one's elbow. Look back through this essay, and for certain you will find that I have again and again committed the very faults I am protesting against. By this morning's post I have received a pamphlet dealing with conditions in Germany. The author tells me that he "felt impelled" to write it. I open it at random, and here is almost the first sentence that I see: "[The Allies] have an opportunity not only of achieving a radical transformation of Germany's social and political structure in such a way as to avoid a nationalistic reaction in Germany itself, but at the same time of laying the foundations of a co-operative and unified Europe." You see, he "feels impelled" to write—feels, presumably, that he has something new to say—and yet his words, like cavalry horses answering the bugle, group themselves automatically into the familiar dreary pattern. This invasion of one's mind by ready-made phrases (*lay the foundations, achieve a radical transformation*) can only be prevented if one is constantly on guard against them, and every such phrase anaesthetizes a portion of one's brain.

I said earlier that the decadence of our language is probably curable. 17 Those who deny this would argue, if they produced an argument at all, that language merely reflects existing social conditions, and that we cannot influence its development by any direct tinkering with words and constructions. So far as the general tone or spirit of a language goes, this may be true, but it is not true in detail. Silly words and expressions have often disappeared, not through any evolutionary process but owing to the conscious action of a minority. Two recent examples were *explore every avenue* and *leave no stone unturned,* which were killed by the jeers of a few journalists. There is a long list of flyblown metaphors which could similarly be got rid of if enough people would interest themselves in the job; and it should also be possible to laugh the *not un-* formation out of existence,* to reduce the amount of Latin and Greek in the average sentence, to drive out foreign phrases and strayed scientific words, and, in general, to make pretentiousness unfashionable. But all these are minor points. The defence of the English language implies more than this, and perhaps it is best to start by saying what it does *not* imply.

To begin with it has nothing to do with archaism, with the salvaging 18 of obsolete words and turns of speech, or with the setting up of a "standard English" which must never be departed from. On the contrary, it is especially concerned with the scrapping of every word or idiom which has outworn its usefulness. It has nothing to do with correct grammar and syntax, which are of no importance so long as one makes one's meaning clear, or with the avoidance of Americanisms, or with having what is called a "good prose style." On the other hand it is not concerned with fake simplicity and the attempt to make written English colloquial. Nor does it even imply in every case preferring the Saxon word to the Latin one, though it does imply using the fewest and shortest words that will cover one's meaning. What is above all needed is to let the meaning choose the word, and not the other way about. In prose, the worst thing one can do with words is to surrender to them. When you think of a concrete object, you think wordlessly, and then, if you want

---

*One can cure oneself of the *not un-* formation by memorizing this sentence: *A not unblack dog was chasing a not unsmall rabbit across a not ungreen field.* [Orwell's note.]

to describe the thing you have been visualizing you probably hunt about till you find the exact words that seem to fit it. When you think of something abstract you are more inclined to use words from the start, and unless you make a conscious effort to prevent it, the existing dialect will come rushing in and do the job for you, at the expense of blurring or even changing your meaning. Probably it is better to put off using words as long as possible and get one's meaning as clear as one can through pictures or sensations. Afterwards one can choose—not simply *accept*—the phrases that will best cover the meaning, and then switch round and decide what impression one's words are likely to make on another person. This last effort of the mind cuts out all stale or mixed images, all prefabricated phrases, needless repetitions, and humbug and vagueness generally. But one can often be in doubt about the effect of a word or a phrase, and one needs rules that one can rely on when instinct fails. I think the following rules will cover most cases:

(i) Never use a metaphor, simile or other figure of speech which you are used to seeing in print.

(ii) Never use a long word where a short one will do.

(iii) If it is possible to cut a word out, always cut it out.

(iv) Never use the passive where you can use the active.

(v) Never use a foreign phrase, a scientific word or a jargon word if you can think of an everyday English equivalent.

(vi) Break any of these rules sooner than say anything outright barbarous.

These rules sound elementary, and so they are, but they demand a deep change of attitude in anyone who has grown used to writing in the style now fashionable. One could keep all of them and still write bad English, but one could not write the kind of stuff that I quoted in those five specimens at the beginning of this article.

I have not here been considering the literary use of language, but merely   19 language as an instrument for expressing and not for concealing or preventing thought. Stuart Chase and others have come near to claiming that all abstract words are meaningless, and have used this as a pretext for advocating a kind of political quietism. Since you don't know what Fascism is, how can you struggle against Fascism? One need not swallow such absurdities as this, but one ought to recognize that the present political chaos is connected with the decay of language, and that one can probably bring about some improvement by starting at the verbal end. If you simplify your English, you are freed from the worst follies of orthodoxy. You cannot speak any of the necessary dialects, and when you make a stupid remark its stupidity will be obvious, even to yourself. Political language—and with variations this is true of all political parties, from Conservatives to Anarchists—is designed to make lies sound truthful and murder respectable, and to give an appearance of solidity to pure wind. One cannot change this all in a moment, but one can at least change one's own habits, and from time to time one can even, if one jeers loudly enough, send some worn-out and useless phrase—some *jackboot, Achilles' heel, hotbed, melting pot, acid test, veritable inferno* or other lump of verbal refuse—into the dustbin where it belongs.

Questions for Discussion

1. Orwell begins by claiming that modern English is ugly, slovenly, and in decline. These charges must sound to many readers like highly subjective accusations, difficult if not impossible to document, and they are flatly denied by many scientific linguists. Does his claim seem to you convincing? (Remember that it is much easier to show that many people use language badly than to show that people in general speak and write worse now than they used to.) A second claim is that "the decline of a language must ultimately have political and economic causes" (¶2). How does Orwell argue for this position? Do you accept it? If not, would you say that he has a serious argument worth thinking about? If you are dubious, where do you think Orwell has gone wrong in his argument?

2. Orwell claims that one of the surest symptoms of a language's abuse is staleness of imagery (figurative language that no longer evokes mental pictures or concrete sensations). Consider the following images by Orwell himself. Are they stale or fresh? Do they evoke effective concrete pictures or feelings?

   a. Modern prose is "tacked together like the sections of a prefabricated hen-house" (¶4).
   b. "Now that I have made this catalogue of swindles and perversions . . ." (¶9).
   c. "[T]he writer knows more or less what he wants to say, but an accumulation of stale phrases chokes him like tea leaves blocking a sink" (¶11).
   d. The typical political speaker often seems "unconscious of what he is saying, as one is when one utters the responses in church" (¶12).
   e. "A mass of Latin words falls upon the facts like soft snow" (¶15).
   f. Insincerity in writing leads "instinctively to long words and exhausted idioms, like a cuttlefish squirting out ink" (¶15).
   g. Stock phrases "are a continuous temptation, a packet of aspirins always at one's elbow" (¶16).
   h. Any stock phrase is a "lump of verbal refuse" that should be sent "into the dustbin [garbage can] where it belongs" (¶19).

   Are all of these images equally effective? Are (f) and (g), for example, as good as (d) and (e)? (How do stock phrases resemble a packet of aspirins?) In general, does Orwell follow his own rule of using images that are fresh and effective?

3. Does the kind of argument Orwell constructs about the passage from Ecclesiastes (¶9–10)—counting the ratio of words to syllables—seem con-

vincing? That is, is it convincing to show that writing is flaccid by remarking on its unusually high number of syllables per word? Will the ratio he deplores *always* produce a flaccid effect? Can you rewrite the passage using many-syllabled words without being abstract and vague?

4. Do Orwell's "rules" for writing good English prose (¶18) sound like the rules you have read in English grammar texts? Do they sound easier or harder to follow? Does his argument convince you that following his rules will help you in your writing?

5. Do you think Orwell overstates his case when he says that writing good English "has nothing to do with correct grammar and syntax, which are of no importance so long as one makes one's meaning clear" (¶18)? Could you really write an effective business letter that was clear but ungrammatical? Do you find other points that seem to be overstated merely for strong effect?

Suggested Essay Topics

1. Select a document famous in American political history (such as the Declaration of Independence, Abraham Lincoln's Gettysburg Address or Second Inaugural Address, John F. Kennedy's Inaugural Address of 1960, or Hubert Humphrey's attack on "states' rights" at the Democratic National Convention in 1948). Read the whole speech and then evaluate one or two paragraphs according to Orwell's standards as summarized in paragraph 18 and defended throughout his essay. Direct your essay to your classmates, showing them why the speech you are examining is either a good or bad specimen of English prose, according to Orwell's standards.

2. Examine Orwell's own writing from the standpoint of his "rules" in paragraph 18, and write him a letter either commending or criticizing him for meeting (or not meeting) his own standards. Be sure to show concretely in particular passages how he either succeeds or fails. On the basis of Orwell's vocabulary, tone, and general stance, try to determine who he views as his audience, and assess whether, given that audience, Orwell meets its needs and expectations effectively.

Ideas in Debate

Marshall W. Gregory and Wayne C. Booth
Thomas Hobbes
John Locke
C.K. Ogden and I.A. Richards
Mark Johnson
George Lakoff and Mark Johnson
Cynthia Ozick

Marshall Gregory and Wayne C. Booth

CONTROVERSY OVER METAPHOR

Since at least the seventeen century in the Western world, many philos-   1
ophers and linguists, as well as everyday people whose professions and occupations never invite thought about language as such, have expressed a profound unease (sometimes intensely) about *metaphor* and its influence,
especially its alleged tendency to distort the objective truth of things.

In the history of metaphor's rejection as a means of expressing truth,   2
one of the notable features is that, until very recently, this rejection has been
so complete that it has not even been written about. In works on language
written by both linguists and philosophers, the insignificance or distorting
quality of metaphor is frequently alluded to, or there may be brief passages
that assert as much, but the main gauge of the profound dismissal of metaphor is that the dismissal is seldom alluded to. Neither linguists nor philosophers feel compelled to justify ignoring metaphor. Metaphor is simply a topic
that, traditionally, no serious analyst of language feels embarrassed to ignore.
When something is considered so insignificant that no one of note refers to
it, one does not have to defend skipping over it in one's own work. In what
is arguably the most influential book of the twentieth century in the philosophy of language—A. J. Ayer's *Language, Truth, and Logic* (1936)—*metaphor* does
not even appear in the index.

The grounds of metaphor's dismissal seems to be an assumption that the   3
world can be described in *literal* terms, and that descriptions of the world will
be more accurate if literal terms are used exclusively. Metaphorical language,
the refrain goes, is not literal but *emotive;* that is, it expresses states of feeling
and emotion, but does not describe objective reality. To use metaphorical
language in descriptions leads to confusion and chaos.

To see this assumption in operation, look at Irving M. Copi's brief   4
treatment of the issue in his *Introduction to Logic* (2nd edition, 1961), one of the
standard and most influential college texts for more than thirty years. A
portion of the text called "Emotive Words" sums up the modern view of
metaphor without ever treating it as a subject in its own right.

> We have already observed that one and the same sentence can serve
> both an informative and an expressive function. For the sentence to
> formulate a proposition, its words must have literal or cognitive meaning,
> referring to objects or events and their properties or relations. When it
> expresses an attitude or feeling, however, some of its words may also have
> an emotional suggestiveness or impact. . . .
>
> It might be thought that the emotive impact of a word or phrase is
> always connected with the properties possessed by the referent of that
> word or phrase. But consider the poet's phrase: "A rose by any other name
> would smell as sweet." It is true that the actual fragrance of the rose
> would remain the same through any change of name we might assign it.
> But it is doubtful if our attitude of approval would remain unchanged if
> we continually referred to roses as, say, "skunkweeds." The purveyors of
> canned horse mackerel sell much more of their product now that they call
> it "tuna fish". . . .
>
> The emotive meaning of a word may always be acquired by association,
> but these associations need not always be directly with the word's literal
> referent. . . .
>
> In this lively book entitled *How to Think Straight,* Robert Thouless made
> an experiment designed to show the importance of emotively colored
> words in poetry. There he examined two lines from Keats' "The Eve of
> St. Agnes":

> Full on this casement shone the wintry moon
> And threw warm gules on Madeline's fair breast.

> He proposed to show that their beauty arises primarily from the proper
> choice of emotionally colored words, by showing how that beauty is lost
> completely if those words are replaced by *neutral* ones. Selecting the words
> "casement," "gules," "Madeline," "fair," and "breast," Mr. Thouless
> wrote:

> *Casement* means simply a kind of window with emotional and romantic
> associations. *Gules* is the heraldic name for red, with the suggestion of

romance which accompanies all heraldry. *Madeline* is simply a girl's name, but one calling out favorable emotions absent from a relatively plain and straightforward name. *Fair* simply means, in objective fact, that her skin was white or uncolored—a necessary condition for the colors of the window to show—but also *fair* implies warm emotional preference for an uncolored skin rather than one which is yellow, purple, black, or any of the other colors which skin might be. *Breast* also has similar emotional meaning, and the aim of scientific description might have been equally well attained if it had been replaced by such a neutral word as *chest.*

Let us now try the experiment of keeping these two lines in a metrical form, but replacing all the emotionally colored words by neutral ones, while making as few other changes as possible. We may write:

"Full on this window shone the wintry moon,
Making red marks on Jane's uncolored chest."
No one will doubt that all of its poetic value has been knocked out of the passage by these changes. Yet the lines still mean the same in external fact; they still have the same objective meaning. It is only the emotional meaning which has been destroyed.

To the extent that humorous impact is to be included in emotive meaning, the revised lines of "poetry" have considerable emotive meaning, though very different from that possessed by the original verses. (pp. 37–40)

You can see how clear and unproblematic Copi assumes to be between "objective fact" on the one hand and "emotional impact" on the other. How easily Copi assumes that a "word's literal referent" is something just *there*, an obvious reality for anyone. Notice how he does not even pause to consider that emotion may in fact be an inseparable part of perception, or that "referents" may not only *not* be describable by a logical mind separated from its "feeling" component, but that the mind may not be divided into separable components to begin with. The assumption that there is an underlying "reality" on the one hand and "feelings" on the other completely dominates the analysis of the language of the Keats lines. Notice when "Madeline" is described as a girl's name that calls out "favorable emotions," the writer thinks it unnecessary even to question whether the "favor" is an attribute of anything but the name. (How can he be so sure that the "favorable emotions" don't correspond to something "real" in the referent?) And notice how, when it is conceded that the "poetic value" has been knocked out of Keats's line, the implication is clearly made that *nothing of any real value has been lost:* "It is *only* the emotional meaning which has been destroyed" (italics added).

In recent years the assumptions about language we have just been discussing have been called "positivist" or "objectivist." In the passages that follow, we have tried to develop the Ideas in Debate by giving some brief excerpts from the objectivist tradition, culminating with a brief summary of that tradition by Mark Johnson. In the last two essays, we present the other side of the case.

Because some of these pieces are very brief, we have suspended our usual practice of including Questions for Discussion and Suggested Essay Topics after every selection. Instead, we place them after Johnson's summary of the objectivist position, and then pick up our usual practice again with the essay by Cynthia Ozick and the subsequent ones.

Thomas Hobbes

Thomas Hobbes (1588–1679) was a British philosopher who contributed much to the tradition that culminated in positivism. As you can see in this brief excerpt, metaphor is clearly viewed as an aberrant use of language; metaphor is not what language was "ordained for" and leads, apparently, to inevitable deceit.

Whereas a very recent tradition of linguistic philosophy countering the positivist tradition claims that language is deeply and inextricably implicated with metaphor, and that metaphor is no more separable from language than sound is separable from hearing, Hobbes complacently assumes, as many after him have done, that metaphor not only can but should be avoided in the interests of clear speech. Assuming that human beings can place the "real names" of things in one pile and can then keep that pile completely separate from (and thus uncontaminated by) the other pile of "fake names" created by metaphor has been a constant feature of this tradition of thought.

ON SPEECH AND METAPHOR

Our title. From part 1, chapter 4 of *Leviathan, or the Matter, Forme, and Power of a Commonwealth Ecclesiasticall and Civil* (1651).

The use of speech. The general use of speech, is to transfer our mental discourse, into verbal; or the train of our thoughts, into a train of words; and that for two commodities, whereof one is the registering of the consequences of our thoughts; which being apt to slip out of our memory, and put us to a new labour, may again be recalled, by such words as they were marked by. So that the first use of names is to serve for *marks,* or *notes* of remembrance. Another is, when many use the same words, to signify, by their connexion and order, one to another, what they conceive, or think of each matter; and also what they desire, fear, or have any other passion for. And for this use they are called *signs.* Special uses of speech are these; first, to register, what by cogitation, we find to be the cause of any thing, present or past; and what we find things present or past may produce, or effect; which in sum, is acquiring of arts. Secondly, to show to others that knowledge which we have attained, which is, to counsel and teach one another. Thirdly, to make known to others our wills and purposes, that we may have the mutual help of one another. Fourthly, to please and delight ourselves and others, by playing with our words, for pleasure or ornament, innocently.

Abuses of speech. To these uses, there are also four correspondent abuses. First, when men register their thoughts wrong, by the inconstancy of the signification of their words; by which they register for their conception, that which they never conceived, and so deceive themselves. Secondly, when they use words metaphorically; that is, in other sense than that they are ordained for; and thereby deceive others. Thirdly, by words, when they declare that to be their will, which is not. Fourthly, when they use them to grieve one another; for seeing nature hath armed living creatures, some with teeth, some with horns, and some with hands, to grieve an enemy, it is but an abuse of speech, to grieve him with the tongue, unless it be one whom we are obliged to govern; and then it is not to grieve, but to correct and amend. . . .

Inconstant names. The names of such things as affect us, that is, which please and displease us, because all men be not alike affected with the same thing, nor the same man at all times, are in the common discourses of men of *inconstant* signification. For seeing all names are imposed to signify our conceptions, and all our affections are but conceptions, when we conceive the same things differently, we can hardly avoid different naming of them. For though the nature of that we conceive, be the same; yet the diversity of our reception of it, in respect of different constitutions of body, and prejudices of opinion, gives every thing a tincture of our different passions. And therefore in reasoning a man must take heed of words; which besides the signification of what we imagine of their nature, have a signification also of the nature, disposition, and interest of the speaker; such as are the names of virtues and vices; for one man calleth *wisdom,* what another calleth *fear;* and one *cruelty,* what another *justice;* one *prodigality,* what another *magnanimity;* and one *gravity,* what another *stupidity,* &c. And therefore such names can never be true grounds of any ratiocination. No more can metaphors, and tropes of speech: but these are less dangerous, because they profess their inconstancy; which the other do not.

John Locke

*Following in Hobbes' steps, John Locke
(1632–1704), the British philosopher known as the father of English empiricism, is
every bit as antagonistic toward metaphor and other figures of speech as his great
contemporary. By focusing on oratory and eloquence as the suspicious vehicles of
metaphor's deceptions, he implies that he is more concerned than Hobbes seems to be
about the public—that is, political—misuses of metaphorical language. His claim that
metaphor "move[s] the passions, and thereby mislead[s] the judgment" sounds like
Plato's argument against tragedy in Book X of the* Republic, *and, indeed, there is
a common strand connecting them. The strand is indignation against forms of language
that tend to obscure the description of things as they really are.*

*"If we would speak of things are they are," Locke says, we must avoid metaphor.
What neither Plato, Hobbes, nor Locke stop to consider is the possibility (1) that the
"areness" of "things as they are" cannot be comprehended except in language and (2)
that language cannot separate itself into uses that are strictly literal versus those that
are something else (figurative?, fanciful?, metaphorical?, poetic?, emotional?: the names
of "non-logical" uses of language are many, and most of them carry negative rather
than positive suggestions).*

ON FIGURATIVE LANGUAGE

Our title. From *An Essay Concerning Human Understanding* (1690).

34. . . . since wit and fancy find easier entertainment in the world than   1
dry truth and real knowledge, figurative speeches and allusion in language
will hardly be admitted as an imperfection or abuse of it. I confess, in discourses where we seek rather pleasure and delight than information and
improvement, such ornaments as are borrowed from them can scarce pass for
faults. But yet if we would speak of things as they are, we must allow that
all the art of rhetoric, besides order and clearness, all the artificial and figurative application of words eloquence hath invented, are for nothing else but
to insinuate wrong ideas, move the passions, and thereby mislead the judgment, and so indeed are perfect cheats, and, therefore, however laudable or
allowable oratory may render them in harangues and popular addresses, they
are certainly, in all discourses that pretend to inform or instruct, wholly to
be avoided; and where truth and knowledge are concerned, cannot but be
thought a great fault, either of the language or person that makes use of them.
What, and how various they are, will be superfluous here to take notice; the
books of rhetoric which abound in the world will instruct those who want
to be informed: only I cannot but observe how little the preservation and
improvement of truth and knowledge is the care and concern of mankind;
since the arts of fallacy are endowed and preferred. It is evident how much
men love to deceive and be deceived, since rhetoric, that powerful instrument
of error and deceit, has its established professors, is publicly taught, and has

always been had in great reputation: and, I doubt not, but it will be thought great boldness, if not brutality in me, to have said thus much against it. Eloquence, like the fair sex, has too prevailing beauties in it to suffer itself ever to be spoken against. And it is in vain to find fault with those arts of deceiving wherein men find pleasure to be deceived.

C. K. Ogden and I. A. Richards

Charles K. Ogden (1889–1957), British psychologist and linguist, and Ivor Armstrong Richards (1893–1979), English literary critic and professor at Cambridge and Harvard, were immensely influential within the tradition of objectivist views of language. The Meaning of Meaning, a study of language, thought, and symbolism, was first published in 1923 and went through eight editions, an immense number for a scholarly book. The last and eighth edition, moreover, survived into the sixties as a standard work on the philosophy of language. Between books like Copi's logic text, quoted in the Gregory and Booth introduction (pp. 223–226), and books like The Meaning of Meaning, several generations and thousands upon thousands of students and scholars were taught to think of metaphor as the positivists thought of it: as an emotive language function that expresses or calls up attitudes but that has nothing to do with truth or reality.

You can see in the brief excerpt from Ogden and Richards that this view completely dominates their analysis of language functions: "If we say 'The height of the Eiffel Tower is 900 feet' we are making a statement. . . . But if we say . . . 'Man is a worm' . . . we are most probably using words merely to evoke certain attitudes" (¶1). It is noteworthy that in all the thousands of times this same distinction crops up in works written from the objectivist tradition, it almost always appears in just this asserted rather than argued form. Ogden and Richards do not say why "Man is a worm" is not a statement. They just assume complacently and unproblematically, that because it is a metaphor it can't be a statement. Only verifiable statements like "The height of the Eiffel Tower is 900 feet" are statements.

The height of the Eiffel Tower is only verifiable, of course, if one knows what a foot is—that is, if one is acquainted with the English language and the conventions of measurement in the Western world (whether feet or meters)—and this knowledge is valued only if one has accepted certain assumptions, also mostly Western, about what kind of knowledge is most useful and honorable. But if this is what it means to "verify" the height of the Eiffel Tower—knowing the conventions of measurement and language used in a given culture and accepting the assumptions made by that culture about what forms of knowledge are most worth having—then what disqualifies "Man is a worm" from being a verifiable "statement"? As long as one knows the connotations and implications that the metaphor "worm" carries in our culture, and as long as one values the insight into the human condition that the metaphor conveys, is it not true, or at least arguable, that "Man is a worm" is as "verifiable" as "The height of the Eiffel Tower is 900 feet"? However, if metaphors are by definition ruled out of court, then they will not be seen as statements no matter how many criteria for "statements" they meet.

The point here is not to prove that Ogden and Richards are wrong. This analysis is too skimpy for that. The real point is that the views expressed by Ogden and Richards have been (1) extremely prevalent in Western culture, and (2) that they have been so prevalent that, until recently, they have received little critical analysis. They have largely been accepted as true without having to prove themselves against alternative views.

THE EMOTIVE USE OF WORDS

Our title. From *The Meaning of Meaning*, 8th ed. (1946).

In ordinary everyday speech each phrase has not one but a number of functions. We shall in our final chapter classify these under five headings; but here a twofold division is more convenient, the division between the *symbolic* use of words and the *emotive* use. The symbolic use of words is *statement;* the recording, the support, the organization and the communication of references. The emotive use of words is a more simple matter, it is the use of words to express or excite feelings and attitudes. It is probably more primitive. If we say "The height of the Eiffel Tower is 900 feet" we are making a statement, we are using symbols in order to record or communicate a reference, and our symbol is true or false in a strict sense and is theoretically verifiable. But if we say "Hurrah!" or "Poetry is a spirit" or "Man is a worm," we may not be making statements, not even false statements; we are most probably using words merely to evoke certain attitudes. 1

Each of these contrasted functions has, it will be seen, two sides, that of the speaker and that of the listener. Under the symbolic function are included both the symbolization of reference and its communication to the listener, *i.e.,* the causing in the listener of a similar reference. Under the emotive function are included both the expression of emotions, attitudes, moods, intentions, etc., in the speaker, and their communication, *i.e.,* their evocation in the listener. As there is no convenient verb to cover both expression and evocation, we shall in what follows often use the term 'evoke' to cover both sides of the emotive function, there being no risk of misunderstanding. In many cases, moreover, emotive language is used by the speaker not because he already has an emotion which he desires to express, but solely because he is seeking a word which will evoke an emotion which he desires to have; nor, of course, is it necessary for the speaker himself to experience the emotion which he attempts to evoke. 2

It is true that some element of reference probably enters, for all civilized 3 adults* at least, into almost all use of words, and it is always possible to import a reference, if it be only a reference to things in general. The two functions under consideration usually occur together but none the less they are in principle distinct. So far as words are used emotively no question as to their truth in the strict sense can directly arise. Indirectly, no doubt, truth in this strict sense is often involved. Very much poetry consist of statements, symbolic arrangements capable of truth or falsity, which are used not for the sake of their truth or falsity but for the sake of the attitudes which their acceptance will evoke. For this purpose it fortunately happens, or rather it is part of the poet's business to make it happen, that the truth or falsity matters not at all to the acceptance. Provided that the attitude or feeling is evoked the most important function of such language is fulfilled, and any symbolic function that the words may have is instrumental only and subsidiary to the evocative function.

This subtle interweaving of the two functions is the main reason why 4 recognition of their difference is not universal. The best test of whether our use of words is essentially symbolic or emotive is the question—"Is this true or false in the ordinary strict scientific sense?" If this question is relevant then the use is symbolic, if it is clearly irrelevant then we have an emotive utterance.

But in applying this test we must beware of two dangers. There is a 5 certain type of mind which although it uses evocative language itself cannot on reflection admit such a thing, and will regard the question as relevant upon all occasions. For a larger body of readers than is generally supposed poetry is unreadable for this reason. The other danger is more important. Corresponding in some degree to the strict sense of true and false for symbolic statements (True^S), there are senses which apply to emotive utterances (True^E). Critics often use True^E of works of art, where alternative symbols would be 'convincing' in some cases, 'sincere' in others, 'beautiful' in others, and so on. And this is commonly done without any awareness that True^E and True^S are different symbols. Further there is a purely evocative use of True— its use to excite attitudes of acceptance or admiration; and a purely evocative use of False—to excite attitudes of distrust or disapprobation. When so used these words, since they are evocative, cannot, except by accident, be replaced by others; a fact which explains the common reluctance to relinquish their employment even when the inconvenience of having symbols so alike superficially as True^S and True^E in use together is fully recognized. In general that affection for a word even when it is admitted to be ambiguous, which is such

---

*It is desirable to make the reservation, if only for educational purposes, for according to some authorities "ninety-nine per cent. of the words used in talking to a little child have no meaning for him, except that, as the expression of attention to him, they please him." Moreover, before the age of six or seven children "cannot hold a meaning before their minds without experiencing it in perceptual symbols, whether words or otherwise. . . . Hence the natural desire of the child to talk or be talked to, if he is asked even for a few minutes to sit still."—(W. E. Urwick, *The Child's Mind*, pp. 95, 102.) [Ogden and Richards' note.]

a common feature of discussion, is very often due to its emotive efficiency rather than to any real difficulty in finding alternative symbols which will support the same reference. It is, however, not always the sole reason, as we shall see when we come in our final chapter to consider the condition of word-dependence. . . .

We early begin to use language in order to learn language, but since it   6
is no mere matter of the acquisition of synonyms or alternative locutions, the same stressing of similarities between references and elimination of their differences through conflict is required. By these means we develop references of greater and greater abstractness, and metaphor, the primitive symbolization of abstraction, becomes possible. Metaphor, in the most general sense, is the use of one reference to a group of things between which a given relation holds, for the purpose of facilitating the discrimination of an analogous relation in another group. In the understanding of metaphorical language one reference borrows part of the context of another in an abstract form.

There are two ways in which one reference may appropriate part of the   7
context of another. Thus a reference to man may be joined with a reference to sea, the result being a reference to seamen. No metaphor is involved in this. When, on the other hand, we take arms against a sea of troubles, that part of the context of the reference to sea which is combined with the other references appears in an abstract form, *i.e.,* the relevant characters of the sea will not include attraction by the moon or being the resort of fishes. The poetic value of the metaphor depends in this case chiefly on the way in which the ceaseless recurrence of the waves accentuates the sense of hopelessness already present—as the Cuchulain legend well shows.

In fact the use of metaphor involves the same kind of contexts as   8
abstract thought, the important point being that the members shall only possess the relevant feature in common, and that irrelevant or accidental features shall cancel one another. All use of adjectives, prepositions, verbs, etc., depends on this principle. The prepositions are particularly interesting, the kinds of contexts upon which they depend being plainly different in extent and diversity of members. 'Inside' and 'outside,' it would appear, are the least complicated in context, and consequently, as might be expected, are easily retained in cases of disturbance of the speech functions. The metaphorical aspects of the greater part of language, and the ease with which any word may be used metaphorically, further indicate the degree to which, especially for educated persons, words have gained contexts through other words. Very simple folk with small and concrete vocabularies . . . on the other hand [use fewer metaphors] . . . since the majority of their words have naturally been acquired in direct connection with experience. Their language has throughout many of the characteristics of proper names. Hence in part their comparative freedom from confusions, but hence also the naïve or magical attitude to words. Such linguists may perhaps be said

to be beneath the level at which confusion, the penalty we pay for our power of abstraction, becomes possible.

NOTE

Ogden and Richard's note.

For other forms of Metaphor, see *Principles of Literary Criticism,* chapter XXXII.

Mark Johnson

Mark Johnson (b. 1949) provides here a succinct summary of the opinions about metaphor stated or implied in the views we have included from Copi, Hobbes, Locke, and Ogden and Richards. Johnson is the appropriate person to summarize the views of the objectivist tradition because, in his own philosophical work, he poses a direct challenge to it. You will see in Metaphors We Live By, *an excerpt from which comprises the next reading, that Johnson believes metaphors to be constitutive of thinking and perception, not just ornamental finery overlaid on the substance of "real" thinking.*

As Johnson makes clear, the grounds of controversy over metaphor have not only to do with views about language, but with views about the structure of reality. Metaphor has been rejected, or at best held in suspicion, by the positivist tradition because it tends, in Johnson's language, to "cut across experiential domains of different kinds" (¶4). By creating identity between unlike things—for example, "Man is a worm"—metaphor mingles domains that positivists believe are incapable of being mingled, at least not logically mingled. The "mingling" accomplished by metaphor violates the positivists' view that reality is formed of structures that are both discrete and that have definite categorical boundaries. If this is the truth about reality, then metaphor is naturally going to be viewed as a sloppy, confusing, and fundamentally fallacious way of describing the world. It may tickle our feelings, but it doesn't tell us the truth.

THE OBJECTIVIST VIEW OF METAPHOR

From *The Body in the Mind* (1987).

In the last two decades, metaphor has achieved a remarkable promi- 1 nence as an important problem in philosophy, psychology, linguistics, and other cognitive sciences. This trend stands in sharp contrast to an earlier view of metaphor as a derivative issue of only secondary importance. According to that extremely influential view, when all of the serious work of explaining meaning, truth, and speech-act structure was done, it was supposed that one could then employ the previously developed syntactic, semantic, and pragmatic apparatus to explain the workings of metaphor. Metaphor was thought to be either a deviant form of expression or a nonessential literary figure of speech. In either case, it was not regarded as cognitively fundamental.

This denial of any serious cognitive role for metaphor is principally the result of the long-standing popularity of the Objectivist assumptions about meaning that I listed in the Introduction. The relevant argument about metaphor runs as follows:

1. The most basic or fundamental level of description of reality is that of *literal* terms and propositions. The world consists of objects and events, with their properties and relations. Its basic categories are fixed, definite, and tied to the natures or essences of things in the world. "Literal concepts" or "literal terms" just are, by definition, those entities whose meanings specify truth conditions for the objects and events (with their properties and relations) that exist objectively in the world.

2. It follows that metaphorical statements cannot constitute a basic or fundamental level of description of objective reality for the following reason: metaphorical projections cross categorical boundaries—they cut across experiential domains of different kinds. So, metaphorical projections are not the sort of structures that could properly map onto a world that has discrete and definite categorical boundaries. A metaphorical utterance could only describe reality to the extent that it could be reduced to some set of literal propositions, which then fit or fail to fit the world.

3. Furthermore, if metaphors are not even fundamental, irreducible structures for *describing or reporting independently existing reality,* then they certainly cannot have a role in the *constitution of that reality.* That is, they cannot contribute to the creation of structure in our experience.

To sum up the Objectivist view of metaphor: the objective world has *its* structure, and our concepts and propositions, to be correct, must correspond to that structure. Only literal concepts and propositions can do that, since metaphors assert cross-categorical identities that do not exist objectively in reality. Metaphors may exist as cognitive processes of our understanding, but their meaning must be reducible to some set of literal concepts and propositions.

◆

Questions for Discussion

The Questions for Discussion and Sug-
gested Essay Topics refer back to the introduction to this Ideas in Debate section by
Gregory and Booth, and to the selections from Hobbes, Locke, Ogden and Richards,
and Johnson.

1. Without reading further than the essays in this reader on the issues raised by metaphor, and augmenting them with your personal experience, which view simply *feels,* intuitively, more true to you: the view that metaphor is constitutive of reality because it is a mode of perception and understanding, or the view that metaphor is an ornamental decoration overlaid on literal language? Whichever way you lean, give the best reasons you can to support your views.

2. Locke makes it clear that in his mind there exists an intimate connection between all the "figures" of language (as in "figure of speech"), such as metaphor and the potential deceits of rhetoric and eloquence. Is his suspicion verified by your own experience? Do dishonest people really rely more on metaphor and other figures of speech than honest people? Or is this just a prejudice held mainly by philosophers who value logic above everything else?

3. Do you agree with Ogden and Richards that "very simple folk" have "small and concrete vocabularies . . . since the majority of their words have naturally been acquired in direct connection with experience" (¶8)? It is probably true that "very simple folk," if by this designation Ogden and Richards are referring to those who are uneducated and untraveled, have *unlearned* vocabularies, but does it follow that they would have less *meta-phorical* vocabularies? Why or why not?

4. To us, Ogden and Richards' assertion that metaphor "borrows part of the context of another *in an abstract form"* (¶6, italics added) is not very clear. Since metaphors almost always tend to make things more concrete—one of their great uses, in fact, is to make concrete those abstract or invisible processes that are otherwise difficult to talk about, such as "I *grasp* your point" instead of "I am in a state of cognitive understanding of your point"—what can you propose as an explanation for Ogden and Richards' point?

5. When Ogden and Richards say "The best test of whether our use of words is essentially symbolic or emotive is the question—'Is this true or false in the ordinary strict scientific sense?' "(¶4), what do you understand by the phrase, "the ordinary strict scientific sense"? Ogden and Richards seem to think that "the ordinary strict scientific sense" is not only an easy thing to define, but an easy thing to arrive at. Do you agree? Why or why not?

6. Do you agree that in order for a metaphor to be credited with meaning,

the meaning "must be reducible to some set of literal concepts and propositions" (Johnson, ¶6), and that meanings which cannot be so reduced are just nonsense? Why or why not?

Suggested Essay Topics

1. Choose a brief but highly metaphorical passage of poetry and do to it what Thouless did to the two lines from Keats in the example cited by Copi in the Gregory and Booth introduction to this Ideas in Debate section. That is, "translate" it into "neutral" or "literal" language and then, in an essay addressed to Copi and Thouless, discuss how much *more* was lost from the passage than "merely" poetic beauty and "emotional impact." Show how the "meaning" that Copi and Thouless thinks is still intact (in the neutral language version) is not really the same meaning at all and is, in fact, not even close to the original meaning expressed in metaphorical language.

2. Carry a small notebook around with you for a few days and record in it a list of the metaphors and similes you hear people using in everyday conversation. Once you have collected 50 to 100 examples (this may sound like a lot, but, once you start listening for metaphors, you will realize how easy it is to collect 500 in a very brief span), devise two or three categories in which to arrange them. Make one category what Orwell calls "dead metaphors," the figures of speech we use so much that we are not aware of their metaphorical status ("I *see* your point," "You're *wasting* my time," "Please *retire* to the back of the line," and so on). Make another category something you might call "original metaphors," those figures of speech you are not aware of having heard before, ones that express a creative comparison by the speaker. If you have sufficient examples, you might have another category you call "literary metaphors," those that have not just originality but aesthetic beauty about them. You may think of other categories as well. Once you have made your categories, write an essay directed to your fellow students in which you report on your views about the frequency and the uses of metaphor in everyday language.

George Lakoff and Mark Johnson

*Is it true that all of us, not just poets, speak
in metaphors, whether we realize it or not? Is it perhaps even true that we live by
metaphors, that the way we experience the world is partly determined by the structure
of our metaphors? In* Metaphors We Live By, *George Lakoff (b. 1941), a linguist,
and Mark Johnson (b. 1949), a philosopher, suggest that metaphors not only make
our thoughts more vivid and interesting but that they actually structure our perceptions
and understanding. Thinking of marriage as a "contract agreement," for example,
leads to one set of expectations, while thinking of it as "team play," "a negotiated
settlement," "Russian roulette," "an indissoluble merger," or "a religious sacrament"
will carry different sets of expectations. When a government thinks of its enemies as
"turkeys" or "gooks" or "clowns," it does not take them as serious threats, but if they
are "pawns" in the hands of the communists, they are taken seriously indeed.*
Metaphors We Live By *has led many readers to a new recognition of how profoundly
metaphors not only shape our view of life in the present but set up the expectations
that determine what life will be for us in the future.*

METAPHORS WE LIVE BY

Our selection comprises chapters 1, 2, 3, and part of 4 of *Metaphors We Live By* (1980).

CONCEPTS WE LIVE BY

Metaphor is for most people a device of the poetic imagination and the
rhetorical flourish—a matter of extraordinary rather than ordinary language.
Moreover, metaphor is typically viewed as characteristic of language alone,
a matter of words rather than thought or action. For this reason, most people
think they can get along perfectly well without metaphor. We have found,
on the contrary, that metaphor is pervasive in everyday life, not just in
language but in thought and action. Our ordinary conceptual system, in terms
of which we both think and act, is fundamentally metaphorical in nature.

The concepts that govern our thought are not just matters of the intellect. They also govern our everyday functioning, down to the most mundane
details. Our concepts structure what we perceive, how we get around in the
world, and how we relate to other people. Our conceptual system thus plays
a central role in defining our everyday realities. If we are right in suggesting
that our conceptual system is largely metaphorical, then the way we think,
what we experience, and what we do every day is very much a matter of
metaphor.

But our conceptual system is not something we are normally aware of.
In most of the little things we do every day, we simply think and act more
or less automatically along certain lines. Just what these lines are is by no
means obvious. One way to find out is by looking at language. Since communication is based on the same conceptual system that we use in thinking and

acting, language is an important source of evidence for what that system is like.

Primarily on the basis of linguistic evidence, we have found that most   4
of our ordinary conceptual system is metaphorical in nature. And we have found a way to begin to identify in detail just what the metaphors are that structure how we perceive, how we think, and what we do.

To give some idea of what it could mean for a concept to be metaphori-   5
cal and for such a concept to structure an everyday activity, let us start with the concept ARGUMENT and the conceptual metaphor ARGUMENT IS WAR. This metaphor is reflected in our everyday language by a wide variety of expressions:

ARGUMENT IS WAR

Your claims are *indefensible.*

He *attacked every weak point* in my argument.

His criticisms were *right on target.*

I *demolished* his argument.

I've never *won* an argument with him.

You disagree? Okay, *shoot!*

If you use that *strategy,* he'll *wipe you out.*

He *shot down* all of my arguments.

It is important to see that we don't just *talk* about arguments in terms   6
of war. We can actually win or lose arguments. We see the person we are arguing with as an opponent. We attack his positions and we defend our own. We gain and lose ground. We plan and use strategies. If we find a position indefensible, we can abandon it and take a new line of attack. Many of the things we *do* in arguing are partially structured by the concept of war. Though there is no physical battle, there is a verbal battle, and the structure of an argument—attack, defense, counterattack, etc.—reflects this. It is in this sense that the ARGUMENT IS WAR metaphor is one that we live by in this culture; it structures the actions we perform in arguing.

Try to imagine a culture where arguments are not viewed in terms of   7
war, where no one wins or loses, where there is no sense of attacking or defending, gaining or losing ground. Imagine a culture where an argument is viewed as a dance, the participants are seen as performers, and the goal is to perform in a balanced and aesthetically pleasing way. In such a culture, people would view arguments differently, experience them differently, carry them out differently, and talk about them differently. But *we* would probably not view them as arguing at all: they would simply be doing something different. It would seem strange even to call what they were doing "arguing." Perhaps the most neutral way of describing this difference between their

culture and ours would be to say that we have a discourse form structured
in terms of battle and they have one structured in terms of dance.

This is an example of what it means for a metaphorical concept, namely,   8
ARGUMENT IS WAR, to structure (at least in part) what we do and how we
understand what we are doing when we argue. *The essence of metaphor is understanding and experiencing one kind of thing in terms of another.* It is not that arguments
are a subspecies of war. Arguments and wars are different kinds of things—
verbal discourse and armed conflict—and the actions performed are different
kinds of actions. But ARGUMENT is partially structured, understood, performed,
and talked about in terms of WAR. The concept is metaphorically structured,
the activity is metaphorically structured, and, consequently, the language is
metaphorically structured.

Moreover, this is the *ordinary* way of having an argument and talking   9
about one. The normal way for us to talk about attacking a position is to use
the words "attack a position." Our conventional ways of talking about arguments presuppose a metaphor we are hardly ever conscious of. The metaphor
is not merely in the words we use—it is in our very concept of an argument.
The language of argument is not poetic, fanciful, or rhetorical; it is literal. We
talk about arguments that way because we conceive of them that way—and
we act according to the way we conceive of things.

The most important claim we have made so far is that metaphor is not   10
just a matter of language, that is, of mere words. We shall argue that, on the
contrary, human *thought processes* are largely metaphorical. This is what we
mean when we say that the human conceptual system is metaphorically
structured and defined. Metaphors as linguistic expressions are possible precisely because there are metaphors in a person's conceptual system. Therefore, whenever in this book we speak of metaphors, such as ARGUMENT IS WAR,
it should be understood that *metaphor* means *metaphorical concept.*

THE SYSTEMATICITY OF
METAPHORICAL CONCEPTS

Arguments usually follow patterns; that is, there are certain things we   11
typically do and do not do in arguing. The fact that we in part conceptualize
arguments in terms of battle systematically influences the shape arguments
take and the way we talk about what we do in arguing. Because the metaphorical concept is systematic, the language we use to talk about that aspect
of the concept is systematic.

We saw in the ARGUMENT IS WAR metaphor that expressions from the   12
vocabulary of war, e.g., *attack a position, indefensible, strategy, new line of attack, win,
gain ground,* etc., form a systematic way of talking about the battling aspects
of arguing. It is no accident that these expressions mean what they mean
when we use them to talk about arguments. A portion of the conceptual
network of battle partially characterizes the concept of an argument, and the
language follows suit. Since metaphorical expressions in our language are tied

to metaphorical concepts in a systematic way, we can use metaphorical linguistic expressions to study the nature of metaphorical concepts and to gain
an understanding of the metaphorical nature of our activities.

To get an idea of how metaphorical expressions in everyday language   13
can give us insight into the metaphorical nature of the concepts that structure
our everyday activities, let us consider the metaphorical concept TIME IS MONEY
as it is reflected in contemporary English.

TIME IS MONEY
You're *wasting* my time.

This gadget will *save* you hours.

I don't *have* the time to *give* you.

How do you *spend* your time these days?

That flat tire *cost* me an hour.

I've *invested* a lot of time in her.

I don't *have enough* time to *spare* for that.

You're *running out* of time.

You need to *budget* your time.

Put aside some time for ping pong.

Is that *worth your while?*

Do you *have* much time *left?*

He's living on *borrowed* time.

You don't *use* your time *profitably.*

I *lost* a lot of time when I got sick.

Thank you for your time.

Time in our culture is a valuable commodity. It is a limited resource   14
that we use to accomplish our goals. Because of the way that the concept
of work has developed in modern Western culture, where work is typically
associated with the time it takes and time is precisely quantified, it has
become customary to pay people by the hour, week, or year. In our culture
TIME IS MONEY in many ways: telephone message units, hourly wages, hotel
room rates, yearly budgets, interest on loans, and paying your debt to society by "serving time." These practices are relatively new in the history of
the human race, and by no means do they exist in all cultures. They have
arisen in modern industrialized societies and structure our basic everyday
activities in a very profound way. Corresponding to the fact that we *act* as
if time is a valuable commodity—a limited resource, even money—we *conceive of* time that way. Thus we understand and experience time as the kind
of thing that can be spent, wasted, budgeted, invested wisely or poorly,
saved, or squandered.

TIME IS MONEY, TIME IS A LIMITED RESOURCE, and TIME IS A VALUABLE COMMODITY 15
are all metaphorical concepts. They are metaphorical since we are using our
everyday experiences with money, limited resources, and valuable commodities to conceptualize time. This isn't a necessary way for human beings to
conceptualize time; it is tied to our culture. There are cultures where time is
none of these things.

The metaphorical concepts TIME IS MONEY, TIME IS A RESOURCE, and TIME IS 16
A VALUABLE COMMODITY form a single system based on subcategorization, since
in our society money is a limited resource and limited resources are valuable
commodities. These subcategorization relationships characterize entailment
relationships between the metaphors. TIME IS MONEY entails that TIME IS A
LIMITED RESOURCE, which entails that TIME IS A VALUABLE COMMODITY.

We are adopting the practice of using the most specific metaphorical 17
concept, in this case TIME IS MONEY, to characterize the entire system. Of the
expressions listed under the TIME IS MONEY metaphor, some refer specifically
to money (*spend, invest, budget, profitably, cost*), others to limited resources (*use, use
up, have enough of, run out of*), and still others to valuable commodities (*have, give,
lose, thank you for*). This is an example of the way in which metaphorical
entailments can characterize a coherent system of metaphorical concepts and
a corresponding coherent system of metaphorical expressions for those concepts.

METAPHORICAL SYSTEMATICITY: HIGHLIGHTING AND HIDING

The very systematicity that allows us to comprehend one aspect of a 18
concept in terms of another (e.g., comprehending an aspect of arguing in
terms of battle) will necessarily hide other aspects of the concept. In allowing
us to focus on one aspect of a concept (e.g., the battling aspects of arguing),
a metaphorical concept can keep us from focusing on other aspects of the
concept that are inconsistent with that metaphor. For example, in the midst
of a heated argument, when we are intent on attacking our opponent's position and defending our own, we may lose sight of the cooperative aspects of
arguing. Someone who is arguing with you can be viewed as giving you his
time, a valuable commodity, in an effort at mutual understanding. But when
we are preoccupied with the battle aspects, we often lose sight of the cooperative aspects.

A far more subtle case of how a metaphorical concept can hide an aspect 19
of our experience can be seen in what Michael Reddy has called the "conduit
metaphor."[1] Reddy observes that our language about language is structured
roughly by the following complex metaphor:

IDEAS (or MEANINGS) ARE OBJECTS.

LINGUISTIC EXPRESSIONS ARE CONTAINERS.

COMMUNICATION IS SENDING.

The speaker puts ideas (objects) into words (containers) and sends them (along a conduit) to a hearer who takes the idea/objects out of the word/ containers. Reddy documents this with more than a hundred types of expressions in English, which he estimates account for at least 70 percent of the expressions we use for talking about language. Here are some examples:

THE CONDUIT METAPHOR

It's hard to *get* that idea *across to* him.

I *gave* you that idea.

Your reasons *came through* to us.

It's difficult to *put* my ideas *into* words.

When you *have* a good idea, try to *capture* it immediately *in* words.

Try to *pack* more thought *into* fewer words.

You can't simply *stuff* ideas *into* a sentence any old way.

The meaning is right there *in* the words.

Don't *force* your meanings *into* the wrong words.

His words *carry* little meaning.

The introduction *has* a great deal of thought *content*.

Your words seem *hollow*.

The sentence is *without* meaning.

The idea is *buried in* terribly dense paragraphs.

In examples like these it is far more difficult to see that there is anything hidden by the metaphor or even to see that there is a metaphor here at all. This is so much the conventional way of thinking about language that it is sometimes hard to imagine that it might not fit reality. But if we look at what the CONDUIT metaphor entails, we can see some of the ways in which it masks aspects of the communicative process.

First, the LINGUISTIC EXPRESSIONS ARE CONTAINERS FOR MEANINGS aspect of the CONDUIT metaphor entails that words and sentences have meanings in themselves, independent of any context or speaker. The MEANINGS ARE OBJECTS part of the metaphor, for example, entails that meanings have an existence independent of people and contexts. The part of the metaphor that says LINGUISTIC EXPRESSIONS ARE CONTAINERS FOR MEANING entails that words (and sentences) have meanings, again independent of contexts and speakers. These metaphors are appropriate in many situations—those where context differences don't matter and where all the participants in the conversation understand the sentences in the same way. These two entailments are exemplified by sentences like

The meaning is *right there in* the words,

which, according to the CONDUIT metaphor, can correctly be said of any sentence. But there are many cases where context does matter. Here is a celebrated one recorded in actual conversation by Pamela Downing:

Please sit in the apple-juice seat.

In isolation this sentence has no meaning at all, since the expression "apple-juice seat" is not a conventional way of referring to any kind of object. But the sentence makes perfect sense in the context in which it was uttered. An overnight guest came down to breakfast. There were four place settings, three with orange juice and one with apple juice. It was clear what the apple-juice seat was. And even the next morning, when there was no apple juice, it was still clear which seat was the apple-juice seat.

In addition to sentences that have no meaning without context, there 22
are cases where a single sentence will mean different things to different people. Consider:

We need new alternative sources of energy.

This means something very different to the president of Mobil Oil from what it means to the president of Friends of the Earth. The meaning is not right there in the sentence—it matters a lot who is saying or listening to the sentence and what his social and political attitudes are. The CONDUIT metaphor does not fit cases where context is required to determine whether the sentence has any meaning at all and, if so, what meaning it has.

These examples show that the metaphorical concepts we have looked 23
at provide us with a partial understanding of what communication, argument, and time are and that, in doing this, they hide other aspects of these concepts. It is important to see that the metaphorical structuring involved here is partial, not total. If it were total, one concept would actually *be* the other, not merely be understood in terms of it. For example, time isn't really money. If you *spend your time* trying to do something and it doesn't work, you can't get your time back. There are no time banks. I can *give you a lot of time,* but you can't give me back the same time, though you can *give me back the same amount of time.* And so on. Thus, part of a metaphorical concept does not and cannot fit.

On the other hand, metaphorical concepts can be extended beyond the 24
range of ordinary literal ways of thinking and talking into the range of what is called figurative, poetic, colorful, or fanciful thought and language. Thus, if ideas are objects, we can *dress them up in fancy clothes, juggle them, line them up nice and neat,* etc. So when we say that a concept is structured by a metaphor, we mean that it is partially structured and that it can be extended in some ways but not others.

ORIENTATIONAL METAPHORS

So far we have examined what we will call *structural metaphors,* cases 25
where one concept is metaphorically structured in terms of another. But there
is another kind of metaphorical concept, one that does not structure one
concept in terms of another but instead organizes a whole system of concepts
with respect to one another. We will call these *orientational metaphors,* since most
of them have to do with spatial orientation: up-down, in-out, front-back,
on-off, deep-shallow, central-peripheral. These spatial orientations arise
from the fact that we have bodies of the sort we have and that they function
as they do in our physical environment. Orientational metaphors give a
concept a spatial orientation; for example, HAPPY IS UP. The fact that the
concept HAPPY is oriented UP leads to English expressions like "I'm feeling *up*
today."

Such metaphorical orientations are not arbitrary. They have a basis in 26
our physical and cultural experience. Though the polar oppositions up-down,
in-out, etc., are physical in nature, the orientational metaphors based on them
can vary from culture to culture. For example, in some cultures the future is
in front of us, whereas in others it is in back. We will be looking at up-down
spatialization metaphors, which have been studied intensively by William
Nagy,[2] as an illustration. In each case, we will give a brief hint about how
each metaphorical concept might have arisen from our physical and cultural
experience. These accounts are meant to be suggestive and plausible, not
definitive.

HAPPY IS UP; SAD IS DOWN   27
I'm feeling *up.* That *boosted* my spirits. My spirits *rose.* You're in *high*
spirits. Thinking about her always gives me a *lift.* I'm feeling *down.* I'm
depressed. He's really *low* these days. I *fell* into a depression. My spirits
sank.

Physical basis: Drooping posture typically goes along with sadness and
depression, erect posture with a positive emotional state.

CONSCIOUS IS UP; UNCONSCIOUS IS DOWN   28
Get *up.* Wake *up.* I'm *up* already. He *rises* early in the morning. He *fell*
asleep. He *dropped* off to sleep. He's *under* hypnosis. He *sank* into a coma.

Physical basis: Humans and most other mammals sleep lying down and
stand up when they awaken.

HEALTH AND LIFE ARE UP;   29
SICKNESS AND DEATH ARE DOWN
He's at the *peak* of health. Lazarus *rose* from the dead. He's in *top* shape.
As to his health, he's way *up* there. He *fell* ill. He's *sinking* fast. He came
down with the flu. His health is *declining.* He *dropped* dead.

Physical basis: Serious illness forces us to lie down physically. When you're dead, you are physically down.

HAVING CONTROL OR FORCE IS UP;   30
BEING SUBJECT TO CONTROL OR
FORCE IS DOWN
I have control *over* her. I am *on top of* the situation. He's in a *superior* position. He's at the *height* of his power. He's in the *high* command. He's in the *upper* echelon. His power *rose.* He ranks *above* me in strength. He is *under* my control. He *fell* from power. His power is on the *decline.* He is my social *inferior.* He is *low man* on the totem pole.

Physical basis: Physical size typically correlates with physical strength, and the victor in a fight is typically on top.

MORE IS UP; LESS IS DOWN   31
The number of books printed each year keeps going *up.* His draft number is *high.* My income *rose* last year. The amount of artistic activity in this state has gone *down* in the past year. The number of errors he made is incredibly *low.* His income *fell* last year. He is *under*age. If you're too hot, turn the heat *down.*

Physical basis: If you add more of a substance or of physical objects to a container or pile, the level goes up.

FORESEEABLE FUTURE EVENTS ARE UP (AND AHEAD)   32
All *up*coming events are listed in the paper. What's coming *up* this week? I'm afraid of what's *up ahead* of us. What's *up?*

Physical basis: Normally our eyes look in the direction in which we typically move (ahead, forward). As an object approaches a person (or the person approaches the object), the object appears larger. Since the ground is perceived as being fixed, the top of the object appears to be moving upward in the person's field of vision.

HIGH STATUS IS UP; LOW STATUS IS DOWN   33
He has a *lofty* position. She'll *rise* to the *top.* He's at the *peak* of his career. He's *climbing* the ladder. He has little *upward* mobility. He's at the *bottom* of the social hierarchy. She *fell* in status.

Social and physical basis: Status is correlated with (social) power and (physical) power is UP.

GOOD IS UP; BAD IS DOWN   34
Things are looking *up.* We hit a *peak* last year, but it's been *downhill* ever since. Things are at an all-time *low.* He does *high-*quality work.

Physical basis for personal well-being: Happiness, health, life, and control—the things that principally characterize what is good for a person—are all UP.

VIRTUE IS UP; DEPRAVITY IS DOWN   35
He is *high*-minded. She has *high* standards. She is *upright.* She is an *upstanding* citizen. That was a *low* trick. Don't be *underhanded.* I wouldn't *stoop* to that. That would be *beneath* me. He *fell* into the *abyss* of depravity. That was a *low-down* thing to do.

Physical and social basis: GOOD IS UP for a person (physical basis), together with . . . SOCIETY IS A PERSON (in the version where you are *not* identifying with your society). To be virtuous is to act in accordance with the standards set by the society/person to maintain its well-being. VIRTUE IS UP because virtuous actions correlate with social well-being from the society/person's point of view. Since socially based metaphors are part of the culture, it's the society/person's point of view that counts.

RATIONAL IS UP; EMOTIONAL IS DOWN   36
The discussion *fell to the emotional* level, but I *raised* it back *up to the rational* plane. We put our *feelings* aside and had a *high-level intellectual* discussion of the matter. He couldn't *rise above* his *emotions.*

Physical and cultural basis: In our culture people view themselves as being in control over animals, plants, and their physical environment, and it is their unique ability to reason that places human beings above other animals and gives them this control. CONTROL IS UP thus provides a basis for MAN IS UP and therefore for RATIONAL IS UP.

NOTES

All notes are Lakoff's and Johnson's.

1. Michael Reddy, "The Conduit Metaphor," in A. Ortony, ed., *Metaphor and Thought* (Cambridge: Cambridge University Press, 1979).

2. William Nagy, "Figurative Patterns and Redundancy in the Lexicon" (Ph.D. diss., University of California at San Diego, 1974).

Questions for Discussion

1. Consider examples of metaphorical transfer in various activities—business, sex, politics, religion, education, sports, transportation, construction, and so on. Can you cite instances when persons in business, say, employ metaphors from sports or construction ("the sales *team*" or "the chairman of the board is the *architect* of our prosperity"), and vice versa? Do these

examples support Lakoff and Johnson's view that metaphors often structure our thinking? Can you think of categories of thought and perception where metaphors do not seem to play an important role?

2. In *The Educated Imagination,* Northrop Frye argues that the "motive for metaphor"—the reason that human beings devised metaphor in the first place—lies in the common human desire to live in a world that is a home, not just an environment. Metaphors create, through language, an identity between things. Consider, for example, the identity established between human beings and the animal world in comparisons such as "strong as an elephant," "sly as a fox," "dumb as an ox," and "playful as a kitten." This identity, Frye implies, allows us to feel at home in our world. Does Frye's theory ring true to you? Test it out by trying to come up with examples that both fit and don't fit. You might begin by discussing metaphors from patriotism and religion to see if they make us feel at home in our country ("America, *home* of the brave") and our cosmos ("God our *father*").

3. Can you think of examples of metaphors that contradict Lakoff and Johnson's assertion (¶34) that *up* is good and *down* is bad? When we say that a decision is "up in the air," meaning that it remains unsettled, do we mean something good or bad? Would one or two counterexamples really damage the authors' theory?

Suggested Essay Topics

1. Examine a group of metaphors clustered around a central concept (such as Lakoff and Johnson's in ¶13), and compare them to a group of metaphors clustered around a central concept in a good poem (such as Shakespeare's Sonnets 18 and 73). Even though we must grant that the two clusters are equally metaphorical, are there not startling differences between the *effects* of the metaphors in each group? Examine closely your two clusters of metaphors (if you don't like the Shakespeare sonnets, ask your instructor to recommend another good short poem), and write an essay explaining the differences in effect. (If Shakespeare had used metaphors as familiar as "You're *wasting* my time," would he have been more effective because more clear or less effective because too familiar?)

2. Listen carefully for a few nights to the metaphors used by athletes and sports broadcasters ("Iowa *trounced* Indiana," "quarterback *sneak,*" "a *shot* from the top of the *keyhole,*" "Michigan *up-ended* by UCLA," "Bears *dropped,*" etc.). Write a paper in which you (1) try to create categories that show where these metaphors come from (e.g., is "Princeton *pummels* Harvard" a metaphor from another sport, boxing?) and (2) try to argue whether a given sport would lose any significant interest or color if it had to give up its metaphors. Even if we did continue talking about our favorite sport, deprived of its typical metaphors, consider how much more abstract, dull, and time-consuming such colorless talk would be.

Cynthia Ozick

Cynthia Ozick (b. 1928)—essayist, author of two novels and three collections of short stories, 1982 Guggenheim Fellow, and recipient of a Mildred and Harold Strauss Living Award—poses in this essay a connection seldom made in today's society: a connection between moral behavior and imaginative capacity. She raises the question of whether human beings can create universal moral principles without the imaginative ability to put themselves in other people's shoes, to feel their life as though it were their own, to experience the world vicariously through other people's nerve endings, other people's eyes, and other people's ears. If Ozick is right in her suggestion that we can never raise our vision to the level of moral principle—moral codes that we hold to be universally true—without this ability for vicarious experience, then it follows that any mechanism which helps develop and express that ability would become an important object of study and attention.

In Ozick's view, metaphor is the mechanism by which we develop and express our imaginatively achieved insights and then raise them to the level of moral principles. To those who think of metaphor mainly as a kind of decoration used mainly by poets and other "creative" writers, Ozick's view must seem extravagant. Some might want to say that such a view places both an excessive burden and excessive importance on metaphor. Skeptics might reply to Ozick, "Oh, come on. You're exaggerating. As a creative writer you're simply inclined to overvalue metaphor. Most of us don't think about metaphor very much, and we certainly don't attach the kind of importance to it that you do. How can you say that metaphor is really one of the mechanisms necessary to moral life and to the establishment of moral principle?"

As you read, try to answer these questions as you believe Ozick might. In trying to think about metaphor as she does, you might consider the importance to her argument of the assertion she makes in paragraph 28 that metaphor "relies on what has been experienced before; it transforms the strange into the familiar." If one includes among "the strange," as Ozick seems to do, "the Other; the outsider; the alien; the slave; the oppressed; the sufferer; the outcast; the opponent; the barbarian who owns feelings and deserves rights" (¶20), then it may indeed follow, as she argues, that whatever mechanism helps transform the strange into the familiar would in fact operate as the basis for both moral conduct and the establishment of moral principle. Such a mechanism would allow us to see the outcast, the alien, and the Other as beings like ourselves. Metaphor—an act of language that asserts similarity or identity between things apparently dissimilar—would give us a basis for identifying with the pains, fear, and suffering of those different or alien to us, and in that identification may lie the only basis for moral conduct. Because the construction of identification between dissimilar agencies is the fundamental business of metaphor, it may follow that morality no less than poetry depends on it.

As in the case of all arguments, whether empirical or broadly speculative as this one is, you should try to test the assertions against not only logic but your own experience. Whether you wind up agreeing or disagreeing with Ozick, her speculations are both challenging and stimulating.

THE MORAL NECESSITY OF METAPHOR

From *Harper's Magazine,* May 1986.

1   Not long ago I was invited to read some tale of mine before an assembly of physicians who had, as it happened, a visionary captain. This man knew his Emerson: Emerson in "The American Scholar" had famously noted what he called the "amputation" of society, each trade and profession "ridden by the routine of . . . craft." "The priest becomes a form," Emerson wrote, "the attorney a statute-book; the mechanic a machine; the sailor a rope of the ship." And the doctor a CAT scan.

2   The doctors' visionary captain was out to ignite an Emersonian idea. He would set down among the doctors a fable-maker: a writer. What he had in mind was interpenetration, cutting through the dividing membrane of craft, peopling one cell with two temperaments. The purpose of the experiment would be to increase the doctors' capacity to imagine. The doctors, he explained, too often do not presume a connection of vulnerability between the catastrophe that besets the patient and the susceptibility of the doctors' own flesh; too often the doctors do not conceive of themselves as equally mortal, equally open to fortune's disasters. The writer, an imaginer by trade, will suggest a course of connecting, of entering into the tremulous spirit of the helpless, the fearful, the apart. The writer will demonstrate the contagion of passion and compassion that is known in medicine as empathy and in art as insight.

3   This, then, is the plan. The writer, though ignorant of every scientific punctilio, will command the leap into the Other. That is how tales are made.

4   And so, not suspecting what would come of it, I began to read out a narrative about a sexually active, intellectually sophisticated, faraway planet where the birth of children is no longer welcome, and finally, for prurient technological reasons, no longer possible. A number of children manage to get born anyhow, illicitly and improbably; and everything ends in barbarism and savagery. In short, a parable. Also a satire, outfitted in drollery and ribaldry. Drenched, above all, in metaphor. The tale of a lascivious planet too earnestly self-important to tolerate children could only have been directed against artifice and malice, sophistry and self-indulgence; it could only have pressed for fruitfulness and health, sanity and generosity, bloom and continuity. My story and its barren conclusion were, I thought, a contrivance that declared itself on the side of life; and therefore, presumably, on the side of the doctors themselves. In bringing metaphor to the doctors, surely I was obeying their captain, and opening the inmost valve of the imagining heart?

5   A rumbling. A stirring, a murmuring, a collective hiss. Here were the doctors, all at once ranked before me, a white-coated captious tribe, excited, resentful, bewildered, belligerent. They accused me of obscurantism. They wanted plain speech. They were appalled by metaphor (the shock of metaphor), by fable, image, echo, irony, satire, obliqueness, double meaning, the

call to interpret, the call to penetrate, the call to comment and diagnose. Before the use of metaphor they felt themselves stripped and defenseless; it was clear I had sickened them.

Now the argument may be urged that physicians are themselves abun- 6 dantly given over to metaphorical speech and thought; that they live every hour under the raucous wing of the Angel of Death and Crippling, whose devastating imagery they cannot deny, and whose symbols they read cell by cell, X-ray by X-ray; that ambiguity and interpretation are ineluctably in the grain of their tasks; that all medical literature, however hidden in obscure vocabularies in abstruse journals, is, case after case, a literature of redemption through parable: new cases remember past cases.

But dismiss all this. Say that the doctors have rejected metaphor as not 7 of their realm—as inimical to their gravity. They do it because they have one certainty: they know that, whatever else they may be, they are serious men and women. The struggle to heal, the will to repair the shattered, the will to redeem and make whole—this is what we mean when we speak of lives lived under the conscientious pressure of our moral nature. And metaphor, what is metaphor? Frivolity. Triviality. Lightness of mind. Baubles. To talk in metaphor to serious men and women, to talk *of* metaphor to serious men and women, is to disengage oneself from the great necessary bond of community. It is to cut oneself off from the heat of human pity—and all for the sake of a figure of speech.

If the doctors think this way—if numbers of other serious men and 8 women think this way—it may be, first, because they associate metaphor with writers and artists of every sort, and, secondly, because they associate writers and artists with what we always call inspiration. It isn't only that doctors like to keep away from inspiration on grounds of science and empiricism and predictability. Nor is it, for serious people, mainly a matter of valuing stability over spontaneity, or responsibility over elation. Something there is in inspiration that hints of wildness—a wildness even beyond the quick streak of possession, that brings resolution without warning. Serious people are used to feeling an at-homeness in their minds. Inspiration is an intruder, a kidnapper of reason, a burglar who shoots the watchdogs dead. Inspiration chases off sentries and censors and monitors. Inspiration instigates reckless cliff-walking; it sweeps its quarry to the edge of unfamiliar abysses. Inspiration is the secret sharer who flies out of pandemonium.*

All these characteristics do suggest that inspiration is allied to the stuff 9 of metaphor. Isn't metaphor the poetry-making faculty itself? And where does the poetry-making faculty derive from, if not from inspiration? It is in fact a truism to equate poetry and inspiration, metaphor and inspiration. Though truisms are sometimes at least partly true, my purpose is to tell something else about metaphor. I mean to persuade the doctors that metaphor belongs less to inspiration than it does to memory and pity. I want to argue

---

*The name of Satan's castle in Hell in Milton's *Paradise Lost.* Pandemonium was a wild and lawless place.

that metaphor is one of the chief agents of our moral nature, and that the more serious we are in life, the less we can do without it.

Begin, then, with the history of inspiration. Inspiration is one of those [10] ideas which can, without objection, claim a clear history; but never the history of poetry. Its genesis is in natural religion, or, rather, in the religion of nature. To come to Emerson again: in an essay rather unsuitably called "History"—it might more accurately have been named "Anti-History," since it annihilates the distinction between Then and Now—Emerson recounts a picturesque conversation with "a lady with whom I was riding in a forest [who] said to me that the woods always seemed to her *to wait,* as if the genii who inhabit them suspended their deeds until the wayfarer had passed on-ward; a thought which poetry has celebrated in the dance of the fairies, which breaks off on the approach of human feet." Now that is a very pretty story, but only because in Emerson's day the woods around Concord were safe, and the civilization of genii and fairies long finished. Inspiration may end in daydream or fancy, but it sets out in terror. For us Pan is all poetry, a charming faun with a flute; among the Greeks he caused panic. Fairies and all the other spirits of natural religion were once malevolent powers profoundly feared. Devout Anthenians on the third day of the important Anthesterion festival took the ceremony of frightening away the spirits as a somber religious duty. Emerson, reading history as benign nature, reads natural religion as a sublime illumination—"The idiot, the Indian, the child and the unschooled farmer's boy," he announces, "stand nearer to the light by which nature is to be read, than the dissector or the antiquary"—whereas for its historical adherents, its flesh-and-blood congregants, the religion of nature was mainly panic, dread, and desperate appeasement of the uncanny. Poetry, including Emersonian poetizing, seeps in only after two millennia have exhausted and silenced the fairies; only after the great god Pan is indisputably, unexaggeratedly, dead. In natural religion there are no metaphors; the genii are *there;* the poetry is not yet born.

The genii are there, potent and ubiquitous. They are in the birds and [11] in the beasts, in the brooks, in the muttering oaks—the majestic Zeus him-self got his start as a god who spoke out of the oak tree. Divinity lives even in a notched stick. In natural religion, there is nothing that is not an organ of omen, divination, enthusiasm. But when we reflect on this "enthusi-asm"—a Greek locution, *én theos,* the "god within"—there is one instance of it so celebrated that it comes to mind before all others. The syllables them-selves have turned into the full sweetness of poetry: the Oracle at Delphi; the sound of it is as beautiful as "nightingale." The cult of the Eleusinian mysteries remains a secret, a speculation, to this day; we know only that there was immersion in a river, that sacred cakes were eaten, a sacred potion drunk, and the birth of a holy infant proclaimed. The exalting ritual per-formed by the initiates, shrouded all through antiquity, had no public scribe or record-keeper. The events at Eleusis continue inscrutable. But about what went on at the shrine of Apollo at Delphi almost everything has

been disclosed. We can still follow its process, and there is nothing metaphoric in any of it.

Apollo was a latecomer to Delphi. Earthquake-prone, the place had once   12
belonged to Gaea, the earth goddess, and the shrine was built over a gorge,
or pit, a sort of saucer in the ground, within sight of the mountains of
Parnassus. Excavations have uncovered no crack or opening of any kind in
the floor of the saucer, but a certain gas was said to issue from a hole in the
earth: the narcotic stench of decomposition—below lay the carcass of the
terrible python Apollo slew. An underground stream flowed there, prophetic
waters called Kassotis; these too had narcotic properties. The agent of divination—the enthusiast, the sibyl possessed by the god—was at first, apparently,
a young virgin. Then the rules were changed, no one seems to know why, and
now the votary had to be a respectable, often married, woman of at least
fifty—she was, however, required to dress up as a maiden. This was the
Pythoness, or Pythia, Apollo's oracle, the incarnation of everything we mean,
in our own civilization and language, by inspiration.

Her method was to induce frenzy. She chewed the leaves of a narcotic   13
plant, drank from the narcotic spring, breathed in the narcotic vapor. A
number of attending priests, called the Holy Ones, members of important
local families, waited until she seemed on the brink of seizure and then led
her to a tripod, the seat of the god's speaking. These notables already had in
hand the question the god was to treat. The answer came, in the moment of
possession, from the mouth of the sibyl either as howls or murmurs—cas-
cades of gibberish flooded the shrine. When the Pythia's vatic fit was over,
the priests had to take up the task of interpretation, a role both intellectual
and political. It is conceivable that their interpretations were composed in
advance, since the questioner's predicament had been submitted in advance,
and often in writing. Being both human and bureaucratic, the priests now and
then accepted a bribe in exchange for a politically favorable interpretation.
Still, they were without doubt men of no small gifts: they were in fact
devoted to their ingenious versifying, and would sometimes set their interpretations in the meter of Homer or Hesiod, or else in succinctly ambiguous
prose that, no matter what the future brought, was always on the mark. The
replies of the oracle were famously broad, ranging from family court matters
to statecraft. The priests, like most priests everywhere, tended to think con-
servatively, though they were not unenlightened, and were capable of liberal
decisions: the occasional manumission of slaves, for instance. Delphi, the
fount of inspiration, was in essence the seat of pragmatism. Santayana,*
recalling that Plato too identifies madness with inspiration, and acknowledging that the "aboriginal madness" of the oracle could produce "faith, humility, courage, conformity," yet marvels that "the most intelligent and temper-
ate of nations submitted, in the most crucial matters, to the inspiration of
idiots."

*George Santayana (1863–1952), Spanish-American poet and philosopher.

All this does not mean to insinuate—it would be an untruth—that 14
because the oracle's infusion of the god-spirit at Delphi had nothing to do
with our idea of religion as conscience, Greece was a society that paid no
attention to the moral life. We know otherwise, from Socrates, Plato, and
Aristotle preeminently; we know otherwise from Greek drama, Greek poetry,
Greek history, Greek speculation. What else is the story of Antigone if not
a story of conscience? What else is tragedy if not moral seriousness? And
beyond these, the mind of science, the mind of art, are Greek. There is not
one Greece, but a hundred: heroes side by side with slaves, reason side by side
with magic, the self-restraint of Epictetus* side by side with sensuousness.
It is the Greeks, W. H. Auden† reminds us, "who have taught us, not to
think—that all human beings have always done—but to think about our
thinking." If one nation can be measured as more intelligent than all other
nations that ever were, or were to be, that is how we can measure the Greeks.
And the priestly interpretations at Delphi were themselves grounded in an
immensity of human understanding: ambiguity is psychology; ambiguity is
how we sort things out, how we decide. "Nothing in excess" is a Delphic
inscription.

Yet what was missing in the glory that was Greece was metaphor. 15
Perhaps this statement shocks you with its instant absurdity. You will want
to say, What? A nation of myth, and you claim it has no metaphor? Aren't
myths the greatest metaphors of all? And surely the most blatant? Or you will
want to listen again to the priestly interpretations at Delphi: aren't these, in
their fertility of implication, exactly what we mean by metaphoric language?

The answer in both instances, I think, is no. Remember that mythology 16
took on the inwardness of poetry only when the gods were no longer effica-
cious, only after they had ascended out of the reality of their belief system
into the misted charms of enchantment. And even now, when we read that
Apollo slew the python, what do we learn? We learn that snakes are dangerous and that the gods are brave and strong. For Apollo's constituents, the
aversion to snakes—and also their strange sacredness—was confirmed; so was
the reverence for Apollo. If there is a lesson, it is either that the bravery of
the gods ought to be emulated; or else that it is hubris to suppose the bravery
of the gods can be emulated. But why, you will say, why speak of "learning,"
of "lessons"? Do we go to the gods for schooling, or for self-revelation? Look,
you will say, how humanly resplendent: each god represents an aspect of
human passion. Here is beauty, here is lust, here is wisdom, here is chance,
here is courage, here is mendacity, here is war, and so on and so on. Isn't that
metaphoric enough for you?

Observe: there is no god or goddess who stands for the still, small voice 17
of conscience.

As for the Delphic riddles: they were recipes, not standards. They were 18

*Greek Stoic philosopher, (c. 55–c. 135 A.D.), originally a slave, who taught in Rome.
†Wystan Hugh Anden (1907–1973), American poet.

directions, not principles. Nor was there any consistent social compassion inherent in their readings. The oracle remembered nothing. The voice of conscience did not speak through the god at Delphi, or through any of the gods. Moral seriousness could be found again and again in Greece, especially among the geniuses; it could be found almost anywhere, except in religion, among the people. The reason is plain. Inspiration has no memory. Inspiration is spontaneity; its opposite is memory, which is history as judgment. When conscience flashed out of Greece, as it did again and again, it did so idiosyncratically, individually, without a base in a community model or a collective history. There was no heritage of a common historical experience to universalize ethical feeling. To put it otherwise: there was no will to create a universal moral parable; there was no will to enter and harness metaphor for the sake of a universal conscience.

By turning their religious life into poetry, we have long since universalized the Greeks. They are our psychology. We have ravished their cosmos and their beliefs to explain ourselves to ourselves. But that is our doing, not theirs. The Greeks, with all their astonishments, and in spite of the serenity of "Nothing in excess," were brutally parochial. This ravishingly civilized people kept slaves. Greeks enslaved foreigners and other Greeks. Anyone captured in war was dragged back as a slave, even if he was a Greek of a neighboring polis. In Athens slaves, especially women, were often domestic servants, but of 150,000 adult male slaves, 20,000 were set to work in the silver mines, in ten-hour shifts, in tunnels three feet high, shackled and lashed; the forehead of a retrieved runaway was branded with a hot iron. Aristotle called slaves "animate tools," forever indispensable, he thought, unless you were a utopian who believed in some future invention of automatic machinery. In Athens it was understood that the most efficient administrator of many slaves was someone who had himself been born into slavery and then freed; such a man would know, out of his own oppressive experience with severity, how to bear down hard. A foreigner who was not enslaved lived under prejudice and restriction. Demosthenes tells about the humiliation of a certain Euxitheus, a prosperous Athenian whose citizenship suddenly came under a cloud because his father happened to be overheard speaking with an un-Athenian accent. Euxitheus had to prove that his father had in fact been Athenian-born, or his own status would drop to that of resident alien, stripping him of his property and his rights, and endangering his freedom. That the Greeks called all foreigners "barbarians" is notorious enough; but it was not so much a category as a jeer. It imputed to all foreign languages the animal sound of a grunt or a bark: *bar-bar, bar-bar.*

So there is much irony in our having universalized Greece through poetizing it. The Greeks were not only not universalists; they scorned the idea. They were firm in despising the stranger. They had no pity for the stranger. As a society they never undertook to imagine what it was to be the Other; the outsider; the alien; the slave; the oppressed; the sufferer; the outcast; the opponent; the barbarian who owns feelings and deserves rights.

And that is because they did not, as a society, cultivate memory, or search out any historical metaphor to contain memory.

We come now to a jump. A short jump across the Mediterranean; a long 21 jump to the experience of another people, less lucky than the Greeks and— perhaps because less lucky—collectively obsessed with the imagination of pity; or call it the imagination of reciprocity. The Jews—they were named Hebrews then—were driven to a preoccupation with history and with memory almost at the start of their hard-pressed desert voyage into civilization. The distinguished Greeks had their complex polity, their stunning cities; in these great cities they nurtured unrivaled sophistications. The Jews began as primitives and nomads, naive shepherds as remote from scientific thinking as any other primitives; in their own culture, when at length they established their simple towns, they had no art or theater or athletics, and never would have. A good case can be made—though not a watertight one—that the Jews did not become students and scholars until they learned how from the Greeks; surely the classroom is a Greek innovation. And, finally, the Jews carried the memory of 400 years of torment. Unlike the citizen-Greeks, their history did not introduce civics; it introduced bricks without straw, and the Jews who escaped from Rameses' Egypt were a rough slave rabble, a mixed multitude; a rowdy, discontented, rebellious, ragtag mob. A nation of slaves is different from a nation of philosophers.

Out of that slavery a new thing was made. It should not be called a 22 philosophy, because philosophy was Greek, and this was an envisioning the Greeks had always avoided, or else had never wished to invent, or else had been unable to invent. I have all along been calling this new thing metaphor. It came about because thirty generations of slavery in Egypt were never forgotten—though not as a form of grudge-holding and memory; they are never the same. As for grudge-holding, it was forbidden to the ex-slave rabble. The helping hand, says Exodus, reaches out to your enemy. If you meet your enemy's donkey or ox going astray, you must bring it back to him. If you happen on your enemy's donkey collapsed under its burden, you may not pass by; you must help your enemy relieve the animal. The Egyptians were cruel enemies and crueler oppressors; the ex-slaves will not forget—not out of spite for the wrongdoers, but as a means to understand what it is to be an outcast, a foreigner, an alien of any kind. By turning the concrete memory of slavery into a universalizing metaphor of reciprocity, the ex-slaves discover a way to convert imagination into a serious moral instrument.

Now a fair representation of the Delphic Oracle is not the work of a 23 minute; this we have seen, and it is a paradox. Inspiration, which is as sudden and as transient as an electrical trajectory, takes a long time to delineate, possibly because latency (a hidden prior knowing) and unintelligibility are in its nature. It is in the nature of metaphor to be succinct. Four hundred years of bondage in Egypt, rendered as metaphoric memory, can be spoken in a moment; in a single sentence. What this sentence is, we know; we have built every idea of moral civilization on it. It is a sentence that conceivably sums up at the start every revelation that came afterward. It has given birth and tongue to saints and prophets, early and late. Its first dreamers are not its exclusive owners and operators; it belongs to everyone. That is the point of its having been dreamed into existence at all.

The sentence is easily identified. It follows sixteen verses behind "Love 24 thy neighbor as thyself," but, majestic as that is, it is not the most majestic, because its subject is not the most recalcitrant. Our neighbor is usually of our own tribe, and looks like us and talks like us. Our neighbor is usually familiar; our neighbor is usually not foreign, or of another race. "Love thy neighbor as thyself" is a glorious, civilizing, unifying sentence, an exhortation of consummate moral beauty, difficult of performance, difficult *in* performance. And it reveals at once the little seed of parable: the phrase "as thyself." "Thyself"—that universe of feeling—is the model. "As thyself" becomes the commanding metaphor. But we are still, with our neighbor, in Our Town. We are still, with the self, in psychology. We have not yet pentrated to history and memory. The more compelling sentence carries us there—Leviticus 19, verse 34—and you will hear in it history as metaphor, memory raised to parable:

> The stranger that sojourneth with you shall be unto you as the home-
> born among you, and you shall love him as yourself; because you were
> strangers in the land of Egypt.

Two chapters on, Leviticus 24, verse 22, insists further: "You shall have 25 one manner of law, the same for the stranger as for the home-born." A similar injunction appears in Exodus, and again in Deuteronomy, and again in Numbers. Altogether, this precept of loving the stranger, and treating the stranger as an equal both in emotion and under law, appears thirty-six times in the Pentateuch. It is there because a moral connection has been made with the memory of bondage. Leviticus 24, verse 22, demands memory, and then converts memory into metaphor: "Because you were strangers in the land of Egypt." Bondage becomes a metaphor of pity for the outsider; Egypt becomes the great metaphor of reciprocity. "And a stranger shall you not oppress," says Exodus 23, verse 8, "for you know the heart of a stranger, seeing you were strangers in the land of Egypt." There stands the parable; there stands the sacred metaphor of belonging, one heart to another. Without the metaphor of memory and history, we cannot imagine the life of the Other. We cannot imagine what it is to be someone else. Metaphor is the reciprocal agent, the universalizing force: it makes possible the power to envision the stranger's heart.

In the absence of this metaphoric capability, what are the consequences? 26 Nowhere beyond the reach of the Pentateuch did the alien and the home-born live under the same code. The Romans originally had a single word, *hostis,* to signify both enemy and stranger; in early Roman law, every alien was classed as an enemy, devoid of rights. In Germanic law the alien was *rechtsunfähig,* a pariah with no access to justice. The Greeks made slaves of the stranger and then taunted him with barks. There have been, and still are, religio-political systems that have incorporated the teaching of contempt, turning the closest neighbors into the most despised strangers—a loathing expressed in words like "untouchable," "dhimmi," "deicide." In our own country, slavery thrived under the wing of a freedom-proclaiming Constitution until the middle of the last century. And in 1945, a British camera on a single day in a single German deathcamp just liberated photographed a bulldozer sweeping into five pits 5,000 starved and abused human corpses at a time, a thousand to a pit, all of them having been judged unfit for the right to live.

By now you will have noticed that I have been quoting Scripture—a   27 temptation that is always perilous, not only because it is a famously devilish pastime but also because it induces the sermonizing tone, which for some reason always seems to settle in the nasal cavities. For this I apologize. My intended subject, after all, has not been national character or ethics or religion or history; it has not even, appearances to the contrary, been Matthew Arnold's fertile delta: Hebraism and Hellenism.* What I have been thinking of is *language*—explicitly the work of metaphor.

And it is time now to ask what metaphor *is*. One way to begin is to   28 recognize that metaphor is what inspiration is not. Inspiration is ad hoc and has no history. Metaphor relies on what has been experienced before; it transforms the strange into the familiar. This is the rule even of the simplest metaphor—Homer's wine-dark sea, for example. If you know wine, says the image, you will know the sea; the sea is for sailors, but wine is what we learn at home. Inspiration calls for possession and increases strangeness. Metaphor uses what we already possess and reduces strangeness. Inspiration belongs to riddle and oracle. Metaphor belongs to clarification and humane conduct. This is the meaning of the contrast between the Oracle at Delphi and the parable of servitude in Egypt. Inspiration attaches to the mysterious temples of anti-language. Metaphor overwhelmingly attaches to the house of language.

Should it, then, seem perplexing that both the oracle and the parable are   29 identically dedicated to interpretation? The chief business of the priests at Delphi is practical interpretation. The incessant allusion to Egyptian bondage is again for the purpose of usable interpretation. And still the differences are total. Because the Delphic priests must begin each time with a fresh-hatched inspiration, with the annihilation of experience, they cannot arrive at any universal principle or precept. Principles and precepts derive from an accumulation of old events. Delphi never has old events; every event in that place is singular; the cry from the tripod is blazingly individual, particular, peculiar unto itself. From the tripod rises the curse of nepenthe; amnesia;

---

*"Hebraism and Hellenism" was the title of a chapter in Matthew Arnold's analysis of Victorian society, *Culture and Anarchy* (1869). According to Arnold's famous formulation, "The governing idea of Hellenism is *spontaneity of consciousness;* that of Hebraism, *strictness of conscience.*

forgetting; nor is it the voice of the race of humanity and its continuities we hear. The tragedy of the Delphic priests is not that their interpretations are obliged to start from gibberish. After all, what goes in as raw gibberish comes out as subject to rational decision, and it is more than conceivable that social principles might be extracted from a body of such decisions. But the priests think consciously only of their own moment. Their system is not organized toward the universalizing formulation. The tragedy of the priests is that, cut off from the uses of history, experience, and memory, they are helpless to make the future. They may, in a manner of speaking, "prophesy," with whatever luck such prophets have, but they cannot construct a heritage. They have nothing to pass on. They cannot give birth to metaphor; one thing does not suggest another thing. In a place where each heart is meant to rave on in its uniqueness, there is no means for the grief of one heart to implicate the understanding of another heart. In the end, inspiration and its devices turn away from the hope of regeneration.

Nowadays much of American literature is included in this Delphic fix. 30 Certain novelists claim that fiction must express a pure autonomy—must become a self-sufficient language-machine—in order to be innovative; others strip language bare of any nuance. These aestheticians and minimalists, seeming opposites, both end inevitably in nihilism.* A certain style of poetry is so far committed to the exquisitely self-contained that it has long since given up on that incandescent dream we call criticism of life. Abandoning attachments, annihilating society, the airless verse of self-scrutiny ends, paradoxically, in loss of the self. A certain style of criticism becomes a series of overlapping solipsisms—consider those types of "deconstruction"† that end only in formulae. Insofar as these incommunicado literary movements are interested in interpretation at all, they have their ear at the Pythian tripod.

Metaphor, though never to be found at Delphi, is also a priest of 31 interpretation; but what it interprets is memory. Metaphor is compelled to press hard on language and storytelling; it inhabits language at its most concrete. As the shocking extension of the unknown into our most intimate, most feeling, most private selves, metaphor is the enemy of abstraction. Irony is of course implicit. Think how ironic it would be, declares the parable of Egypt, if you did *not* take the memory of slavery as your exemplar! Think how ironic your life would be if you passed through it without the power of connection! Novels, those vessels of irony and connection, are nothing if not metaphors. The great novels transform experience into idea because it is the way of metaphor to transform memory into a principle of continuity. By

---

*In philosophy, nihilism is the denial of the existence of any basis for knowledge or truth; in politics, the belief that all previous forms and institutions in society must be destroyed in order to make way for new ones.

†Deconstructionism is a movement in literary criticism which asserts that all texts ultimately "deconstruct" by contradicting themselves or "escaping" from the author's intentions; a view based on linguistic assumptions that language is too imprecise and too richly connotative to be contained or controlled entirely by authorial intentions or conventional definitions.

"continuity" I mean nothing less than literary seriousness, which is unquestionably a branch of life-seriousness.

Now, if all this has persisted in sounding more like a lecture in mor- 32 als than the meditation on language it professes to be, it may be worth turning to that astonishing comment in T. S. Eliot's* indispensable essay on what he terms "concentration" of experience. "Someone said," says Eliot in "Tradition and the Individual Talent," " 'The dead writers are remote from us because we *know* so much more than they did.' Precisely, and they are that which we know." He is speaking of the transforming effect of memory. The dead writers have turned metaphoric; they contain our experience, and they alter both our being and our becoming. Here we have an exact counterpart of biblical memory: *because you were strangers in Egypt.* Through metaphor, the past has the capacity to imagine us, and we it. Through metaphorical concentration, doctors can imagine what it is to be their patients. Those who have no pain can imagine those who suffer. Those at the center can imagine what it is to be outside. The strong can imagine what it is to be weak. Illuminated lives can imagine the dark. Poets in their twilight can imagine the borders of stellar fire. We strangers can imagine the familiar hearts of strangers.

Questions for Discussion

1. In what paragraph does Ozick state her *thesis?* What reasons can you find for her not stating it nearer to the beginning? Was her delay of the thesis effective for the overall success of her position?

2. State in your own words Ozick's distinction between *inspiration* and *metaphor.* Why does inspiration in her view have so little to do with moral principles? Why does metaphor have so much to do with moral principles?

3. What does Ozick mean when she says that we in modern times have universalized the Greeks, but that they in their own time did not universalize their own moral views?

4. In the Pentateuch, says Ozick, the "precept of loving the stranger, and treating the stranger as an equal both in emotion and under law . . . is there [thirty-six times] because a moral connection has been made with the memory of bondage. . . . Without the metaphor of memory and history, we cannot imagine the life of the Other" (¶25). Can you cite

---

*British poet and critic (1888–1965), immensely influential on aesthetic views during the modernist period (roughly 1914–1950). His single most influential essay was "Tradition and the Individual Talent" (1917), an attack on Romanticism's emphasis on originality and on art as an expression of the personality of the artist. Eliot was awarded the Nobel prize for literature in 1948.

examples of either successes or failures at identification with "the stranger" in literature, history, or your own experience illuminated by the ideas in this Ozick passage?

5. Our society generally tends to valorize ancient Greek culture as the birthplace of Western civilization and values. Were you shocked or dismayed by Ozick's uncomplimentary characterizations of the parochialism and brutality of Greek culture? Do you think she is being fair to the Greeks? What facts or reasons can you cite for either corroborating or cushioning Ozick's criticisms?

Suggested Essay Topics

1. This essay assignment involves some field research. Step 1: For three or four days carry a notebook with you wherever you go and record in it all the instances of other people's uses of metaphors and similes. (You may be amazed, when you really stop to listen, how many times metaphors and similes will be used in a single conversation.) Step 2: After you have collected your data—75 to 100 examples might do, depending on how varied the conversations were—develop categories into which different uses of metaphors and similes fit. In other words, make you categories refer to *kinds of uses* rather than linguistic construction or some other feature. Some metaphors and similes might be used to achieve humor, some to express sarcasm, some to make a point or description more vivid, some to explain an unfamiliar thing by comparing it to a familiar thing, and so on. Be especially attentive to any uses that establish *identity, similarity,* or *community* between persons or groups. Step 3: Write a report or an essay directed either to your fellow students or your instructor (or you might consider a general readership such as would read reports like yours in *Time* or *Newsweek*) based on your data and your analysis of it into categories. In your essay discuss the extent of reliance on metaphor and simile in everyday conversation, the kinds of uses to which they are put, and the effects on understanding and relationships you have observed.

2. If you find Ozick's view of metaphor exaggerated or unconvincing, write an essay directed to her in which you cite and analyze the passages that show the weaknesses of her argument. Try to do more than merely raise objections, or at least direct your objections to the main points of her essay rather than peripheral points, and suggest what corrections or modifications would be needed to make her position more convincing or accurate.

· 4 ·

IMAGINATION AND ART

The Nature and Value of Imagination

I am certain of nothing but the holiness of the heart's affections
and the truth of imagination—what the imagination seizes as
beauty must be truth—whether it existed before or not.
John Keats

States have been governed here and there, heaven knows how;
but not by poetry, it is certain. Literature is a seducer;
we had almost said a harlot. She may do to trifle with; but woe to the
state whose statesmen write verses, and whose lawyers
read more in Tom Moore [a poet] than in Brackton [a jurist].
This is a dangerous state of society. . . . The real happiness of man,
of the mass, not of the few, depends on the knowledge
of things, not on that of words.
Westminster Review

Then I asked: "Does a firm persuasion that a thing is so, make it so?"
He replied: "All Poets believe that it does, and in ages
of imagination this firm persuasion removed mountains;
but many are not capable of a firm persuasion of anything."
William Blake

We turn to stories and pictures and music because they show us
who and what and why we are, and what our relationship
is to life and death, what is essential, and what, despite the arbitrariness
of falling beams, will not burn.
Madeline L'Engle

Out of chaos the imagination frames a thing of beauty.
John Livingston Lowes

Jacob Bronowski

Jacob Bronowski (1908–1974), a famous mathematician and philosopher and creator of the highly acclaimed television series The Ascent of Man, *argues here that imagination—the ability "to make images and to move them about inside one's head in new arrangements"—is not only a uniquely human power but also the source of progress and invention in all human activities.*

By pointing out that every new line of inquiry or action in human affairs exists first in the mind as a model of something that might-be-but-is-not-yet, Bronowski is focusing on the importance of the human brain's twin powers to make pictures and to string out those pictures into connected sequences. This picture-making and picture-making-in-sequence ability seem to be the grounds of not only memory and forecasting, but also of invention and creativity as well. Memory and forecasting allow us to maintain connections with the past and the future, while invention and creativity allow us to construct alternatives to the status quo.

In addition, Bronowski's analysis of imagination reveals one important way that the arts and sciences overlap. Scientists and engineers no less than artists and poets rely on imagination as the seedbed of all flowering ideas. In claiming that the arts and the sciences are not enemies but allies, Bronowski attempts to apply a healing salve to one of the most unfortunate, unnecessary, and potentially disastrous wounds in modern culture: the split between the scientists and the humanists.

THE REACH OF IMAGINATION

From *Proceedings of the American Academy of Arts and Letters and the National Institute of Arts and Letters* 17 (1967) and *The American Scholar* 36 (1967).

For three thousand years, poets have been enchanted and moved and perplexed by the power of their own imagination. In a short and summary essay I can hope at most to lift one small corner of that mystery; and yet it is a critical corner. I shall ask, What goes on in the mind when we imagine? You will hear from me that one answer to this question is fairly specific: which is to say, that we can describe the working of the imagination. And when we describe it as I shall do, it becomes plain that imagination is a specifically *human* gift. To imagine is the characteristic act, not of the poet's mind, or the painter's, or the scientist's, but of the mind of man.

My stress here on the word *human* implies that there is a clear difference in this between the actions of men and those of other animals. Let me then start with a classical experiment with animals and children which Walter Hunter thought out in Chicago about 1910. That was the time when scientists were agog with the success of Ivan Pavlov in forming and changing the reflex actions of dogs, which Pavlov had first announced in 1903. Pavlov had been given a Nobel prize the next year, in 1904; although in fairness I should say that the award did not cite his work on the conditioned reflex, but on the digestive glands.

Hunter duly trained some dogs and other animals on Pavlov's lines. They were taught that when a light came on over one of three tunnels out of their cage, that tunnel would be open; they could escape down it, and were rewarded with food if they did. But once he had fixed that conditioned reflex, Hunter added to it a deeper idea: he gave the mechanical experiment a new dimension, literally—the dimension of time. Now he no longer let the dog go to the lighted tunnel at once; instead, he put out the light, and then kept the dog waiting a little while before he let him go. In this way Hunter timed how long an animal can remember where he has last seen the signal light to his escape route.

The results were and are staggering. A dog or a rat forgets which one of three tunnels has been lit up within a matter of seconds—in Hunter's experiment, ten seconds at most. If you want such an animal to do much better than this, you must make the task much simpler: you must face him with only two tunnels to choose from. Even so, the best that Hunter could do was to have a dog remember for five minutes which one of two tunnels had been lit up.

I am not quoting these times as if they were exact and universal: they surely are not. Hunter's experiment, more than fifty years old now, had many faults of detail. For example, there were too few animals, they were oddly picked, and they did not all behave consistently. It may be unfair to test a dog for what he *saw,* when he commonly follows his nose rather than his eyes. It may be unfair to test any animal in the unnatural setting of a laboratory cage. And there are higher animals, such as chimpanzees and other primates, which certainly have longer memories than the animals that Hunter tried.

Yet when all these provisos have been made (and met, by more modern experiments) the facts are still startling and characteristic. An animal cannot recall a signal from the past for even a short fraction of the time that a man can—for even a short fraction of the time that a child can. Hunter made comparable tests with six-year-old children, and found, of course, that they were incomparably better than the best of his animals. There is a striking and basic difference between a man's ability to imagine something that he saw or experienced, and an animal's failure.

Animals make up for this by other and extraordinary gifts. The salmon   7
and the carrier pigeon can find their way home as we cannot; they have, as it were, a practical memory that man cannot match. But their actions always depend on some form of habit: on instinct or on learning, which reproduce by rote a train of known responses. They do not depend, as human memory does, on calling to mind the recollection of absent things.

Where is it that the animal falls short? We get a clue to the answer, I   8
think, when Hunter tells us how the animals in his experiment tried to fix their recollection. They most often pointed themselves at the light before it went out, as some gun dogs point rigidly at the game they scent—and get the name *pointer* from the posture. The animal makes ready to act by building the signal into its action. There is a primitive imagery in its stance, it seems to me; it is as if the animal were trying to fix the light in its mind by fixing it in its body. And indeed, how else can a dog mark and (as it were) name one of three tunnels, when he has no such words as *left* and *right,* and no such numbers as *one, two, three?* The directed gesture of attention and readiness is perhaps the only symbolic device that the dog commands to hold on to the past, and thereby to guide himself into the future.

I used the verb *to imagine* a moment ago, and now I have some ground   9
for giving it a meaning. *To imagine* means to make images and to move them about inside one's head in new arrangements. When you and I recall the past, we imagine it in this direct and homely sense. The tool that puts the human mind ahead of the animal is imagery. For us, memory does not demand the preoccupation that it demands in animals, and it lasts immensely longer, because we fix it in images or other substitute symbols. With the same symbolic vocabulary we spell out the future—not one but many futures, which we weigh one against another.

I am using the word *image* in a wide meaning, which does not restrict   10
it to the mind's eye as a visual organ. An image in my usage is what Charles Peirce called a *sign,* without regard for its sensory quality. Peirce distinguished between different forms of signs, but there is no reason to make his distinction here, for the imagination works equally with them all, and that is why I call them all images.

Indeed, the most important images for human beings are simply words,   11
which are abstract symbols. Animals do not have words, in our sense: there is no specific center for language in the brain of any animal, as there is in the human brain. In this respect at least we know that the human imagination depends on a configuration in the brain that has only evolved in the last one or two million years. In the same period, evolution has greatly enlarged the front lobes in the human brain, which govern the sense of the past and the future; and it is a fair guess that they are probably the seat of our other images. (Part of the evidence for this guess is that damage to the front lobes in primates reduces them to the state of Hunter's animals.) If the guess turns out to be right, we shall know why man has come to look like a highbrow

or an egghead: because otherwise there would not be room in his head for his imagination.

The images play out for us events which are not present to our senses, 12 and thereby guard the past and create the future—a future that does not yet exist, and may never come to exist in that form. By contrast, the lack of symbolic ideas, or their rudimentary poverty, cuts off an animal from the past and the future alike, and imprisons him in the present. Of all the distinctions between man and animal, the characteristic gift which makes us human is the power to work with symbolic images: the gift of imagination.

This is really a remarkable finding. When Philip Sidney in 1580 de- 13 fended poets (and all unconventional thinkers) from the Puritan charge that they were liars, he said that a maker must imagine things that are not. Halfway between Sidney and us, William Blake said, "What is now proved was once only imagin'd." About the same time, in 1796, Samuel Taylor Coleridge for the first time distinguished between the passive fancy and the active imagination, "the living Power and prime Agent of all human Percep- tion." Now we see that they were right, and precisely right: the human gift is the gift of imagination—and that is not just a literary phrase.

Nor is it just a literary gift; it is, I repeat, characteristically human. 14 Almost everything that we do that is worth doing is done in the first place in the mind's eye. The richness of human life is that we have many lives; we live the events that do not happen (and some that cannot) as vividly as those that do; and if thereby we die a thousand deaths, that is the price we pay for living a thousand lives. (A cat, of course, has only nine.) Literature is alive to us because we live its images, but so is any play of the mind—so is chess: the lines of play that we foresee and try in our heads and dismiss are as much a part of the game as the moves that we make. John Keats said that the unheard melodies are sweeter, and all chess players sadly recall that the combinations that they planned and which never came to be played were the best.

I make this point to remind you, insistently, that imagination is the 15 manipulation of images in one's head; and that the rational manipulation belongs to that, as well as the literary and artistic manipulation. When a child begins to play games with things that stand for other things, with chairs or chessmen, he enters the gateway to reason and imagination together. For the human reason discovers new relations between things not by deduction, but by that unpredictable blend of speculation and insight that scientists call induction, which—like other forms of imagination—cannot be formalized. We see it at work when Walter Hunter inquires into a child's memory, as much as when Blake and Coleridge do. Only a restless and original mind would have asked Hunter's questions and could have conceived his experi- ments, in a science that was dominated by Pavlov's reflex arcs and was heading toward the behaviorism of John Watson.

Let me find a spectacular example for you from history. What is the 16 most famous experiment that you had described to you as a child? I will hazard that it is the experiment that Galileo is said to have made in Sidney's age, in Pisa about 1590, by dropping two unequal balls from the Leaning Tower. There, we say, is a man in the modern mold, a man after our own hearts: he insisted on questioning the authority of Aristotle and St. Thomas Aquinas, and seeing with his own eyes whether (as they said) the heavy ball would reach the ground before the light one. Seeing is believing.

Yet seeing is also imagining. Galileo did challenge the authority of   17
Aristotle, and he did look hard at his mechanics. But the eye that Galileo used was the mind's eye. He did not drop balls from the Leaning Tower of Pisa— and if he had, he would have got a very doubtful answer. Instead, Galileo made an imaginary experiment in his head, which I will describe as he did years later in the book he wrote after the Holy Office silenced him: the *Discorsi . . . intorno à due nuove scienze,* which was smuggled out to be printed in the Netherlands in 1638.

Suppose, said Galileo, that you drop two unequal balls from the tower   18
at the same time. And suppose that Aristotle is right—suppose that the heavy ball falls faster, so that it steadily gains on the light ball, and hits the ground first. Very well. Now imagine the same experiment done again, with only one difference: this time the two unequal balls are joined by a string between them. The heavy ball will again move ahead, but now the light ball holds it back and acts as a drag or brake. So the light ball will be speeded up and the heavy ball will be slowed down; they must reach the ground together because they are tied together, but they cannot reach the ground as quickly as the heavy ball alone. Yet the string between them has turned the two balls into a single mass which is heavier than either ball—and surely (according to Aristotle) this mass should therefore move faster than either ball? Galileo's imaginary experiment has uncovered a contradiction; he says trenchantly,

> You see how, from your assumption that a heavier body falls more rapidly than a lighter one, I infer that a (still) heavier body falls more slowly.

There is only one way out of the contradiction: the heavy ball and the light ball must fall at the same rate, so that they go on falling at the same rate when they are tied together.

This argument is not conclusive, for nature might be more subtle (when   19
the two balls are joined) than Galileo has allowed. And yet it is something more important: it is suggestive, it is stimulating, it opens a new view—in a word, it is imaginative. It cannot be settled without an actual experiment, because nothing that we imagine can become knowledge until we have trans- lated it into, and backed it by, real experience. The test of imagination is experience. But then, that is as true of literature and the arts as it is of science. In science, the imaginary experiment is tested by confronting it with physical experience; and in literature, the imaginative conception is tested by con- fronting it with human experience. The superficial speculation in science is dismissed because it is found to falsify nature; and the shallow work of art is discarded because it is found to be untrue to our own nature. So when Ella

Wheeler Wilcox died in 1919,* more people were reading her verses than Shakespeare's; yet in a few years her work was dead. It had been buried by its poverty of emotion and its trivialness of thought; which is to say that it had been proved to be as false to the nature of man as, say, Jean Baptiste Lamarck† and Trofim Lysenko‡ were false to the nature of inheritance. The strength of the imagination, its enriching power and excitement, lies in its interplay with reality—physical and emotional.

I doubt if there is much to choose here between science and the arts: the imagination is not much more free, and not much less free, in one than in the other. All great scientists have used their imagination freely, and let it ride them to outrageous conclusions without crying "Halt!" Albert Einstein fiddled with imaginary experiments from boyhood, and was wonderfully ignorant of the facts that they were supposed to bear on. When he wrote the first of his beautiful papers on the random movement of atoms, he did not know that the Brownian motion which it predicted could be seen in any laboratory. He was sixteen when he invented the paradox that he resolved ten years later, in 1905, in the theory of relativity, and it bulked much larger in his mind than the experiment of Albert Michelson and Edward Morley which had upset every other physicist since 1881. All his life Einstein loved to make up teasing puzzles like Galileo's, about falling lifts [elevators] and the detection of gravity; and they carry the nub of the problems of general relativity on which he was working.

Indeed, it could not be otherwise. The power that man has over nature and himself, and that a dog lacks, lies in his command of imaginary experience. He alone has the symbols which fix the past and play with the future, possible and impossible. In the Renaissance, the symbolism of memory was thought to be mystical, and devices that were invented as mnemonics (by Giordano Bruno, for example, and by Robert Fludd) were interpreted as magic signs. The symbol is the tool which gives man his power, and it is the same tool whether the symbols are images or words, mathematical signs or mesons. And the symbols have a reach and a roundness that goes beyond their literal and practical meaning. They are the rich concepts under which the mind gathers many particulars into one name, and many instances into one general induction. When a man says *left* and *right,* he is outdistancing the dog not only in looking for a light; he is setting in train all the shifts of meaning, the overtones and the ambiguities, between *gauche* and *adroit* and *dexterous,* between *sinister* and the sense of right. When a man counts *one, two, three,* he is not only doing mathematics; he is on the path to the mysticism

20

21

---

*American journalist and poet (1850–1919) who for many years published a daily poem for a syndicate of newspapers. She published over 20 volumes of verse but is now seldom read.

†French naturalist (1744–1829) who held that environmental adaptations could be genetically transmitted.

‡Soviet biologist (1898–1976) who developed a doctrine of genetics based partly on the ideas of Lamarck, which denied the existence of genes and plant hormones. His doctrine was eventually discredited, but not before greatly harming Soviet genetic research, agruicultural practices, and scientific education.

of numbers in Pythagoras and Vitruvius and Kepler, to the Trinity and the signs of the Zodiac.

I have described imagination as the ability to make images and to move 22
them about inside one's head in new arrangements. This is the faculty that is specifically human, and it is the common root from which science and literature both spring and grow and flourish together. For they do flourish (and languish) together; the great ages of science are the great ages of all the arts, because in them powerful minds have taken fire from one another, breathless and higgledy-piggledy, without asking too nicely whether they ought to tie their imagination to falling balls or a haunted island. Galileo and Shakespeare, who were born in the same year, grew into greatness in the same age; when Galileo was looking through his telescope at the moon, Shakespeare was writing *The Tempest;* and all Europe was in ferment, from Johannes Kepler to Peter Paul Rubens, and from the first table of logarithms by John Napier to the Authorised Version of the Bible.

Let me end with a last and spirited example of the common inspiration 23
of literature and science, because it is as much alive today as it was three hundred years ago. What I have in mind is man's ageless fantasy, to fly to the moon. I do not display this to you as a high scientific enterprise; on the contrary, I think we have more important discoveries to make here on earth than wait for us, beckoning, at the horned surface of the moon. Yet I cannot belittle the fascination which that ice-blue journey has had for the imagination of men, long before it drew us to our television screens to watch the tumbling of astronauts. Plutarch and Lucian, Ariosto and Ben Jonson wrote about it, before the days of Jules Verne and H. G. Wells and science fiction. The seventeenth century was heady with new dreams and fables about voyages to the moon. Kepler wrote one full of deep scientific ideas, which (alas) simply got his mother accused of witchcraft. In England, Francis Godwin wrote a wild and splendid work, *The Man in the Moone,* and the astronomer John Wilkins wrote a wild and learned one, *The Discovery of a New World.* They did not draw a line between science and fancy; for example, they all tried to guess just where in the journey the earth's gravity would stop. Only Kepler understood that gravity has no boundary, and put a law to it—which happened to be the wrong law.

All this was a few years before Isaac Newton was born, and it was all in 24
his head that day in 1666 when he sat in his mother's garden, a young man of twenty-three, and thought about the reach of gravity. This was how he came to conceive his brilliant image, that the moon is like a ball which has been thrown so hard that it falls exactly as fast as the horizon, all the way round the earth. The image will do for any satellite, and Newton modestly calculated how long therefore an astronaut would take to fall round the earth once. He made it ninety minutes, and we have all seen now that he was right; but Newton had no way to check that. Instead he went on to calculate how long in that case the distant moon would take to round the earth, if indeed it behaves like a thrown ball that falls in the earth's gravity, and if gravity obeyed a law of inverse squares. He found that the answer would be twenty-eight days.

In that telling figure, the imagination that day chimed with nature, and 25
made a harmony. We shall hear an echo of that harmony on the day when
we land on the moon, because it will be not a technical but an imaginative
triumph, that reaches back to the beginning of modern science and literature
both. All great acts of imagination are like this, in the arts and in science, and
convince us because they fill out reality with a deeper sense of rightness. We
start with the simplest vocabulary of images, with *left* and *right* and *one, two,
three,* and before we know how it happened the words and the numbers have
conspired to make a match with nature: we catch in them the pattern of mind
and matter as one.

Questions for Discussion

1. To test Bronowski's argument, picture yourself unable to forecast any
   event in your life beyond the completion of this assignment. Does the fact
   that you have to use your imagination to picture *not* having an imagination
   show the pervasiveness of imaginative activity?

2. As you look forward to the events of this coming weekend—a date, trip
   home, movie, or concert—does your foreknowledge exist in your head
   only as an abstraction, a string of words naming the events? Or does it
   consist of actual images—pictures—of yourself in the future?

3. Is imagination as Bronowski defines it coexistent with consciousness? As
   long as you are conscious, does the making of images in your mind ever
   totally cease? We sometimes talk about our minds being "blank," usually
   as an exaggerated way of saying we can't remember something, but is your
   mind ever *really* blank? How pervasive is your picture-making activity?

4. If one pole of imagination is the recollection of images from the past
   (memory), then the other pole is the creation of images about the future
   (forecasting). While our usual forecasts picture only what will or may
   happen, pictures of what is unlikely or impossible to happen can also come
   to mind (for example, imagining ourselves invisible, meeting a griffin at
   lunch, or going to class at the speed of light). Yet imagining impossible
   things, which is what fantasy and science fiction writers do all the time,
   can be made to seem plausible, even gripping. The movie *Frankenstein* was
   made in the 1930s and has become a classic; the television series *Star Trek*
   is nearly three decades old and still going strong. Does all this suggest the
   importance of imaginative activity for human beings? Does it suggest a
   distinction between imaginative and imaginary? Try putting this distinction into your own words.

5. What is the relationship between the quality of our lives and the quality
   of our imaginings? Does repeated exposure to images of brutality and
   violence on television actually make it easier to imagine doing brutal and

violent acts? If they become easier to imagine, do they become easier to do? Are children more susceptible to the implanting of images than older persons? If so, does this lend weight to Socrates' argument at the end of this chapter (in "Censorship") that the imaginative fare dished out to children ought to be censored?

Suggested Essay Topics

1. Paragraph 16 begins, "Let me find a spectacular example for you from history." For the next four paragraphs Bronowski not only gives us a spectacular example from history but also gives us a spectacular example of how to use an example. The four paragraphs could almost be lifted out as a miniature essay in themselves.

   Using these paragraphs as a model, develop some idea taken from Bronowski's essay. You might take as your thesis, for example, either of the two sentences at the beginning of paragraph 14: "Almost everything that we do that is worth doing is done in the first place in the mind's eye" or "The richness of human life is that we have many lives; we live the events that do not happen (and some that cannot) as vividly as those that do." Employing either of these sentences as a topic, think back to some experience that you anticipated keenly but that did *not* happen, and turn your account of the discrepancies between what you anticipated and what really happened into an extended example modeled on Bronowski's four paragraphs.

2. Write an account of one of your most vivid imaginative experiences, such as a dream, nightmare, daydream, fantasy, or ambition. After making the account as vivid as possible, describe the importance of this imagined experience to you or the role it plays in your life. Does it serve as motivation? As something you want to work toward? Something you want to avoid? Why do you remember it or keep coming back to it? Do imaginative constructions ever carry "lessons" in them more vividly or convincing than "lessons" learned from more direct forms of experience? If so, can your essay include an account of such "imaginative" forms of learning?

Ursula K. Le Guin

Whereas Bronowski inquires into the relationship between imagination and action, Le Guin (b. 1929) inquires into the relationship between imagination, truth, and maturity. In the course of her essay, which was originally delivered as a talk, Le Guin makes several controversial statements: that Americans disapprove of fantasy out of fear, that the disapproval of fantasy is merely a symptom of a more general disapproval of fiction, that the need for imaginative expression and development is fundamental to maturity, that the daily stock market report is a "masterpiece of total unreality," that the indulgence in formula fictions and pornography reflects a starved imagination looking for nourishment, and that mature adults are not those who have outgrown childhood but those who have carried their childhood with them as they have grown up, not out.

This is a great number of controversial statements, especially in so brief an essay, yet Le Guin does not seem to be merely thrashing about or lashing out at vaguely defined "enemies." Although she does not stop to provide a supportive argument for each of her controversial assertions (can you see reasons why she would not argue in more detail in this essay?), she nevertheless seems clearly in charge of her topic and unhesitatingly articulates the value and role of fantasy as she sees it.

Indeed, Le Guin's clarity of mind about the issues she raises—especially in combination with the firm certitude of her tone—challenges the reader to consider the supporting arguments that might be used to bolster her views. At the very least she invites her readers to reconsider the truth of a whole cluster of American commonplaces about "getting ahead," about "outgrowing" childhood, about the synonymity of truth and facts, and about the superior value of "realistic" fiction over fantasy.

WHY ARE AMERICANS AFRAID OF DRAGONS?

This essay originally appeared in *PNLA Quarterly* 38 (Winter 1974).

This was to be a talk about fantasy. But I have not been feeling very fanciful lately, and could not decide what to say; so I have been going about picking people's brains for ideas. "What about fantasy? Tell me something about fantasy." And one friend of mine said, "All right, I'll tell you something fantastic. Ten years ago, I went to the children's room of the library of such-and-such a city, and asked for *The Hobbit;** and the librarian told me, 'Oh, we keep that only in the adult collection; we don't feel that escapism is good for children.'" 1

My friend and I had a good laugh and shudder over that, and we agreed that things have changed a great deal in these past ten years. That kind of moralistic censorship of works of fantasy is very uncommon now, in the children's libraries. But the fact that the children's libraries have become oases in the desert doesn't mean that there isn't still a desert. The point of view from which that librarian spoke still exists. She was merely reflecting, in perfect good faith, something that goes very deep in the American character: a moral disapproval of fantasy, a disapproval so intense, and often so aggressive, that I cannot help but see it as arising, fundamentally, from fear. 2

So: Why are Americans afraid of dragons? 3

Before I try to answer my question, let me say that it isn't only Ameri- 4

*A fantasy novel by J. R. R. Tolkien (1892–1973), who also wrote the trilogy *The Lord of the Rings* and scholarly works on British medieval literature.

cans who are afraid of dragons. I suspect that almost all very highly technological peoples are more or less antifantasy. There are several national literatures which, like ours, have had no tradition of adult fantasy for the past
several hundred years: the French, for instance. But then you have the Germans, who have a good deal; and the English, who have it, and love it, and
do it better than anyone else. So this fear of dragons is not merely a Western,
or a technological, phenomenon. But I do not want to get into these vast
historical questions; I will speak of modern Americans, the only people I
know well enough to talk about.

In wondering why Americans are afraid of dragons, I began to realize   5
that a great many Americans are not only antifantasy, but altogether antifiction. We tend, as a people, to look upon all works of the imagination either
as suspect, or as contemptible.

"My wife reads novels. I haven't got the time."   6

"I used to read that science fiction stuff when I was a teenager, but of   7
course I don't now."

"Fairy stories are for kids. I live in the real world."   8

Who speaks so? Who is it that dismisses *War and Peace, The Time Machine,* 9
and *A Midsummer Night's Dream* with this perfect self-assurance? It is, I fear,
the man in the street—the hardworking, over-thirty American male—the
men who run this country.

Such a rejection of the entire art of fiction is related to several American 10
characteristics: our Puritanism, our work ethic, our profit-mindedness, and
even our sexual mores.

To read *War and Peace* or *The Lord of the Rings* plainly is not "work"—you   11
do it for pleasure. And if it cannot be justified as "educational" or as "self-
improvement," then, in the Puritan value system, it can only be self-indulgence or escapism. For pleasure is not a value, to the Puritan; on the contrary,
it is a sin.

Equally, in the businessman's value system, if an act does not bring in   12
an immediate, tangible profit, it has no justification at all. Thus the only
person who has an excuse to read Tolstoy or Tolkien is the English teacher,
because he gets paid for it. But our businessman might allow himself to read
a best-seller now and then: not because it is a good book, but because it is
a best-seller—it is a success, it has made money. To the strangely mystical
mind of the money-changer, this justifies its existence; and by reading it he
may participate, a little, in the power and mana of its success. If this is not
magic, by the way, I don't know what is.

The last element, the sexual one, is more complex. I hope I will not be   13
understood as being sexist if I say that, within our culture, I believe that this
antifiction attitude is basically a male one. The American boy and man is very
commonly forced to define his maleness by rejecting certain traits, certain
human gifts and potentialities, which our culture defines as "womanish" or
"childish." And one of these traits or potentialities is, in cold sober fact, the
absolutely essential human faculty of imagination.

Having got this far, I went quickly to the dictionary.   14

The *Shorter Oxford Dictionary* says: "Imagination. 1. The action of imagin- 15 ing, or forming a mental concept of what is not actually present to the senses; 2. The mental consideration of actions or events not yet in existence."

Very well; I certainly can let "absolutely essential human faculty" 16 stand. But I must narrow the definition to fit our present subject. By "imagination," then, I personally mean the free play of the mind, both intellectual and sensory. By "play" I mean recreation, re-creation, the recombination of what is known into what is new. By "free" I mean that the action is done without an immediate object of profit—spontaneously. That does not mean, however, that there may not be a purpose behind the free play of the mind, a goal; and the goal may be a very serious object indeed. Children's imaginative play is clearly a practicing at the acts and emotions of adulthood; a child who did not play would not become mature. As for the free play of an adult mind, its result may be *War and Peace,* or the theory of relativity.

To be free, after all, is not to be undisciplined. I should say that the 17 discipline of the imagination may in fact be the essential method or technique of both art and science. It is our Puritanism, insisting that discipline means repression or punishment, which confuses the subject. To discipline something, in the proper sense of the word, does not mean to repress it, but to train it—to encourage it to grow, and act, and be fruitful, whether it is a peach tree or a human mind.

I think that a great many American men have been taught just the 18 opposite. They have learned to repress their imagination, to reject it as something childish or effeminate, unprofitable, and probably sinful.

They have learned to fear it. But they have never learned to discipline 19 it at all.

Now, I doubt that the imagination can be suppressed. If you truly 20 eradicated it in a child, he would grow up to be an eggplant. Like all our evil propensities, the imagination will out. But if it is rejected and despised, it will grow into wild and weedy shapes; it will be deformed. At its best, it will be mere ego-centered daydreaming; at its worst, it will be wishful thinking, which is a very dangerous occupation when it is taken seriously. Where literature is concerned, in the old, truly Puritan days, the only permitted reading was the Bible. Nowadays, with our secular Puritanism, the man who refuses to read novels because it's unmanly to do so, or because they aren't true, will most likely end up watching bloody detective thrillers on the television, or reading hack Westerns or sports stories, or going in for pornography, from *Playboy* on down. It is his starved imagination, craving nourishment, that forces him to do so. But he can rationalize such entertainment by saying that it is realistic—after all, sex exists, and there are criminals, and there are baseball players, and there used to be cowboys— and also by saying that it is virile, by which he means that it doesn't interest most women.

That all these genres are sterile, hopelessly sterile, is a reassurance to 21 him, rather than a defect. If they were genuinely realistic, which is to say genuinely imagined and imaginative, he would be afraid of them. Fake real-

ism is the escapist literature of our time. And probably the ultimate escapist
reading is that masterpiece of total unreality, the daily stock market report.

Now what about our man's wife? She probably wasn't required to   22
squelch her private imagination in order to play her expected role in life, but
she hasn't been trained to discipline it, either. She is allowed to read novels,
and even fantasies. But, lacking training and encouragement, her fancy is
likely to glom on to very sickly fodder, such things as soap operas, and "true
romances," and nursy novels, and historico-sentimental novels, and all the
rest of the baloney ground out to replace genuine imaginative works by the
artistic sweatshops of a society that is profoundly distrustful of the uses of
the imagination.

What, then, are the uses of the imagination?   23

You see, I think we have a terrible thing here: a hardworking, upright,   24
responsible citizen, a full-grown, educated person, who is afraid of dragons,
and afraid of hobbits, and scared to death of fairies. It's funny, but it's also
terrible. Something has gone very wrong. I don't know what to do about it
but to try and give an honest answer to that person's question, even though
he often asks it in an aggressive and contemptuous tone of voice. "What's the
good of it all?" he says. "Dragons and hobbits and little green men—what's
the *use* of it?"

The truest answer, unfortunately, he won't even listen to. He won't hear   25
it. The truest answer is, "The use of it is to give you pleasure and delight."

"I haven't got the time," he snaps, swallowing a Maalox pill for his ulcer   26
and rushing off to the golf course.

So we try the next-to-truest answer. It probably won't go down much   27
better, but it must be said: "The use of imaginative fiction is to deepen your
understanding of your world, and your fellow men, and your own feelings,
and your destiny."

To which I fear he will retort, "Look, I got a raise last year, and I'm   28
giving my family the best of everything, we've got two cars and a color TV.
I understand enough of the world!"

And he is right, unanswerably right, if that is what he wants, and all   29
he wants.

The kind of thing you learn from reading about the problems of a hobbit   30
who is trying to drop a magic ring into an imaginary volcano has very little
to do with your social status, or material success, or income. Indeed, if there
is any relationship, it is a negative one. There is an inverse correlation between fantasy and money. That is a law, known to economists as Le Guin's
Law. If you want a striking example of Le Guin's Law, just give a lift to one
of those people along the roads who own nothing but a backpack, a guitar,
a fine head of hair, a smile, and a thumb. Time and again, you will find that
these waifs have read *The Lord of the Rings*—some of them can practically recite
it. But now take Aristotle Onassis, or J. Paul Getty: could you believe that
those men ever had anything to do, at any age, under any circumstances, with
a hobbit?

But, to carry my example a little further, and out of the realm of   31 economics, did you ever notice how very gloomy Mr. Onassis and Mr. Getty and all those billionaires look in their photographs? They have this strange, pinched look, as if they were hungry. As if they were hungry for something, as if they had lost something and were trying to think where it could be, or perhaps what it could be, what it was they've lost.

Could it be their childhood? 32

So I arrive at my personal defense of the uses of the imagination, 33 especially in fiction, and most especially in fairy tale, legend, fantasy, science fiction, and the rest of the lunatic fringe. I believe that maturity is not an outgrowing, but a growing up: that an adult is not a dead child, but a child who survived. I believe that all the best faculties of a mature human being exist in the child, and that if these faculties are encouraged in youth they will act well and wisely in the adult, but if they are repressed and denied in the child they will stunt and cripple the adult personality. And finally, I believe that one of the most deeply human, and humane, of these faculties is the power of imagination: so that it is our pleasant duty, as librarians, or teachers, or parents, or writers, or simply as grownups, to encourage that faculty of imagination in our children, to encourage it to grow freely, to flourish like the green bay tree, by giving it the best, absolutely the best and purest, nourishment that it can absorb. And never, under any circumstances, to squelch it, or sneer at it, or imply that it is childish, or unmanly, or untrue.

For fantasy is true, of course. It isn't factual, but it is true. Children 34 know that. Adults know it too, and that is precisely why many of them are afraid of fantasy. They know that its truth challenges, even threatens, all that is false, all that is phony, unnecessary, and trivial in the life they have let themselves be forced into living. They are afraid of dragons, because they are afraid of freedom.

So I believe that we should trust our children. Normal children do not 35 confuse reality and fantasy—they confuse them much less often than we adults do (as a certain great fantasist pointed out in a story called "The Emperor's New Clothes"). Children know perfectly well that unicorns aren't real, but they also know that books about unicorns, if they are good books, are true books. All too often, that's more than Mummy and Daddy know; for, in denying their childhood, the adults have denied half their knowledge, and are left with the sad, sterile little fact: "Unicorns aren't real." And that fact is one that never got anybody anywhere (except in the story "The Unicorn in the Garden," by another great fantasist, in which it is shown that a devotion to the unreality of unicorns may get you straight into the loony bin). It is by such statements as, "Once upon a time there was a dragon," or "In a hole in the ground there lived a hobbit"—it is by such beautiful non-facts that we fantastic human beings may arrive, in our peculiar fashion, at the truth.

Questions for Discussion

1. How would you explain in your own words Le Guin's implied distinction between escapism and fantasy? Why, in Le Guin's view, are they not the same? Which one is preferable? Why do many Americans confuse them?

2. In paragraphs 12 and 21, Le Guin makes two extremely unconventional references to institutionalized forms of moneymaking. In paragraph 12 she calls the mind of the moneychanger "strangely mystical" and refers to his tendency to be interested in stories of great monetary success as "magic." In paragraph 21 she calls the daily stock market report "that masterpiece of total unreality." In neither paragraph does she pause to provide a detailed explanation of what she means. On the basis of your reading of the whole essay, what do you think she means? If you were to fill out this part of her argument as you think she might have done, what would you say?

3. Once you have answered question 2, the obvious follow-up is, do you *agree* with Le Guin's view of the "unrealistic" character of moneymaking and stock investing? Since many people, perhaps most, think of moneymaking as extremely practical, what sense does Le Guin make by referring to it as "unrealistic"?

4. How would you explain in your own words Le Guin's assertion that "[f]ake realism is the escapist literature of our time" (paragraph 21)? What does she seem to mean? Give some appropriate examples to illustrate the kind of thing she is referring to.

5. Do you agree or disagree with Le Guin in paragraph 34 that "fantasy is true, of course. It isn't factual, but it is true"? How would you restate this assertion in your own words? What reasons can you offer for corroborating or contradicting it? Is the converse—that facts can be false—ever true?

Suggested Essay Topics

1. Jump ahead and read Plato's argument from book 2 of *The Republic* (which we have titled "Censorship"). Then write a dialogue in which you picture Plato and Le Guin arguing the relative advantages and disadvantages of allowing children to read "untrue" stories. Try to make sure, first, that you render each writer's position accurately and, second, that you make each writer truly meet the other's arguments.

2. Choose a particular work of fantasy that you like (you may use movies and TV programs as well as literature) and, in the kind of essay that you might send to a science fiction journal, analyze whether the work lives up to Le Guin's assertion in paragraph 27 that "[t]he use of imaginative fiction is to deepen your understanding of your world, and your fellow men, and your own feelings, and your destiny." If the essay is to be effective, the challenge you must meet is to be concrete and detailed and to focus on specific parts of the work in question (plot, language, characterizations, whatever) *and* on the way they are used to meet the goals set out by Le Guin.

Richard Wright

In their essay, "Why Children Don't Like to Read" (Chapter 3), Bruno Bettelheim and Karen Zelan assert that a child "will not be interested in learning basic reading skills if he thinks he is expected to master them for their own sake. . . . The child must be convinced that skills are only a means to achieve a goal." If "for their own sake" means that children are taught reading skills as a dead-end activity, leading to nothing more exciting or illuminating than good or bad grades on reading tests, surely Bettelheim and Zelan are right. But if children are given worthy goals that can be met by learning to read—goals that belong to them as well as to the teacher—then presumably they will be motivated to learn eagerly. At that point there is not much distance between learning reading skills "for their own sake" and learning them to achieve goals. No two poles could be farther apart than the reading goals in today's minimum-achievement classroom, where reading is often taught as a mechanical activity that goes nowhere, and the goals of Richard Wright's (1908–1960) passionate reader in "The Library Card."

"I hungered for books," he says, "[for] new ways of looking and seeing. It was not a matter of believing what I read, but of feeling something new, of being affected by something that made the look of the world different" (¶23). "It would have been impossible for me to have told anyone what I derived from these novels, for it was nothing less than a sense of life itself" (¶28). Clearly, books for this young narrator are doorways into a wider existence than he could ever have experienced on his own, and in his eagerness to reach that wider existence he opened one door after another. What does this experience suggest about the way reading should be taught to children in school? And what does it suggest about the kinds of reading they ought to do?

As you read, consider whether most of us share the narrator's hunger for a wider existence than our ordinary one. Is it possible to see people's interest in television, movies, plays, and song as different aspects of this hunger to be taken beyond our own lives, to learn how others see, feel, and think? If most of us do share this hunger (and if there are some who do not, why don't they?), why is the satisfying of this hunger not more frequently offered as the goal of learning to read? Six-year-old children may not be ready for a theoretical discussion of the issues, but isn't it true that they will certainly recognize the difference between reading as a narrow mechanical end and reading as a means of learning about the immense world around them? And at the high school and college levels, what is the proportion of reading that is done for sheer pleasure and general learning as compared to the reading that is done to acquire specific information? Does Richard Wright's account of how his world opened up make you wish you could take time to read more in your own life?

THE LIBRARY CARD

Chapter 13 of *Black Boy* (1937).

One morning I arrived early at work and went into the bank lobby   1
where the Negro porter was mopping. I stood at a counter and picked up the
Memphis *Commercial Appeal* and began my free reading of the press. I came
finally to the editorial page and saw an article dealing with one H. L.
Mencken.* I knew by hearsay that he was the editor of the *American Mercury,*
but aside from that I knew nothing about him. The article was a furious
denunciation of Mencken, concluding with one, hot, short sentence:
Mencken is a fool.

I wondered what on earth this Mencken had done to call down upon   2
him the scorn of the South. The only people I had ever heard denounced in
the South were Negroes, and this man was not a Negro. Then what ideas did
Mencken hold that made a newspaper like the *Commercial Appeal* castigate him
publicly? Undoubtedly he must be advocating ideas that the South did not
like. Were there, then, people other than Negroes who criticized the South?
I knew that during the Civil War the South had hated northern whites, but
I had not encountered such hate during my life. Knowing no more of
Mencken than I did at that moment, I felt a vague sympathy for him. Had
not the South, which had assigned me the role of a non-man, cast at him its
hardest words?

Now, how could I find out about this Mencken? There was a huge   3
library near the riverfront, but I knew that Negroes were not allowed to
patronize its shelves any more than they were the parks and playgrounds of
the city. I had gone into the library several times to get books for the white
men on the job. Which of them would now help me to get books? And how
could I read them without causing concern to the white men with whom I
worked? I had so far been successful in hiding my thoughts and feelings from
them, but I knew that I would create hostility if I went about the business
of reading in a clumsy way.

I weighed the personalities of the men on the job. There was Don, a Jew;   4
but I distrusted him. His position was not much better than mine and I knew
that he was uneasy and insecure; he had always treated me in an offhand,
bantering way that barely concealed his contempt. I was afraid to ask him to
help me get books; his frantic desire to demonstrate a racial solidarity with
the whites against Negroes might make him betray me.

Then how about the boss? No, he was a Baptist and I had the suspicion   5
that he would not be quite able to comprehend why a black boy would want
to read Mencken. There were other white men on the job whose attitudes
showed clearly that they were Kluxers or sympathizers, and they were out
of the question.

*Henry Louis Mencken (1880–1956)—American journalist and writer; founder, coeditor, and
editor of *American Mercury* from 1924–1933. Mencken was an extremely incisive and opinionated
writer and was embroiled in many controversies throughout his entire life.

There remained only one man whose attitude did not fit into an anti- 6
Negro category, for I had heard the white men refer to him as a "Pope lover."
He was an Irish Catholic and was hated by the white Southerners. I knew that
he read books, because I had got him volumes from the library several times.
Since he, too, was an object of hatred, I felt that he might refuse me but would
hardly betray me. I hesitated, weighing and balancing the imponderable
realities.

One morning I paused before the Catholic fellow's desk. 7

"I want to ask you a favor," I whispered to him.

"What is it?"

"I want to read. I can't get books from the library. I wonder if you'd let
me use your card?"

He looked at me suspiciously.

"My card is full most of the time," he said.

"I see," I said and waited, posing my question silently.

"You're not trying to get me into trouble, are you, boy?" he asked, 8
staring at me.

"Oh, no, sir."

"What book do you want?"

"A book by H. L. Mencken."

"Which one?"

"I don't know. Has he written more than one?"

"He has written several."

"I didn't know that."

"What makes you want to read Mencken?" 9

"Oh, I just saw his name in the newspaper," I said.

"It's good of you to want to read," he said. "But you ought to read the
right things."

I said nothing. Would he want to supervise my reading?

"Let me think," he said. "I'll figure out something."

I turned from him and he called me back. He stared at me quizzically.

"Richard, don't mention this to the other white men," he said.

"I understand," I said. "I won't say a word."

A few days later he called me to him.

"I've got a card in my wife's name," he said. "Here's mine." 10

"Thank you, sir."

"Do you think you can manage it?"

"I'll manage fine," I said.

"If they suspect you, you'll get in trouble," he said.

"I'll write the same kind of notes to the library that you wrote when
you sent me for books," I told him. "I'll sign your name."

He laughed.

"Go ahead. Let me see what you get," he said.

That afternoon I addressed myself to forging a note. Now, what were 11
the names of books written by H. L. Mencken? I did not know any of them.
I finally wrote what I thought would be a foolproof note: *Dear Madam: Will*

you please let this nigger boy—I used the word "nigger" to make the librarian feel that I could not possibly be the author of the note—*have some books by H. L. Mencken?* I forged the white man's name.

I entered the library as I had always done when on errands for whites, 12 but I felt that I would somehow slip up and betray myself. I doffed my hat, stood a respectful distance from the desk, looked as unbookish as possible, and waited for the white patrons to be taken care of. When the desk was clear of people, I still waited. The white librarian looked at me.

"What do you want, boy?"

As though I did not possess the power of speech, I stepped forward and 13 simply handed her the forged note, not parting my lips.

"What books by Mencken does he want?" she asked.

"I don't know, ma'am," I said, avoiding her eyes.

"Who gave you this card?"

"Mr. Falk," I said.

"Where is he?"

"He's at work, at the M——— Optical Company," I said. "I've been in 14 here for him before."

"I remember," the woman said. "But he never wrote notes like this."

Oh, God, she's suspicious. Perhaps she would not let me have the 15 books? If she had turned her back at that moment, I would have ducked out the door and never gone back. Then I thought of a bold idea.

"You can call him up, ma'am," I said, my heart pounding.   16

"You're not using these books, are you?" she asked pointedly.

"Oh, no, ma'am. I can't read."

"I don't know what he wants by Mencken," she said under her breath.

I knew now that I had won; she was thinking of other things and the 17 race question had gone out of her mind. She went to the shelves. Once or twice she looked over her shoulder at me, as though she was still doubtful. Finally she came forward with two books in her hands.

"I'm sending him two books," she said. "But tell Mr. Falk to come in 18 next time, or send me the names of the books he wants. I don't know what he wants to read."

I said nothing. She stamped the card and handed me the books. Not 19 daring to glance at them, I went out of the library, fearing that that woman would call me back for further questioning. A block away from the library I opened one of the books and read a title: *A Book of Prefaces.* I was nearing my nineteenth birthday and I did not know how to pronounce the word "preface." I thumbed the pages and saw strange words and strange names. I shook my head, disappointed, looked at the other book; it was called *Prejudices.* I knew what that word meant; I had heard it all my life. And right off I was on guard against Mencken's books. Why would a man want to call a book *Prejudices?* The word was so stained with all my memories of racial hate that I could not conceive of anybody using it for a title. Perhaps I had made a mistake about Mencken? A man who had prejudices must be wrong.

When I showed the books to Mr. Falk, he looked at me and frowned. 20

"That librarian might telephone you," I warned him.

"That's all right," he said. "But when you're through reading those books, I want you to tell me what you get out of them."

That night in my rented room, while letting the hot water run over my 21 can of pork and beans in the sink, I opened *A Book of Prefaces* and began to read. I was jarred and shocked by the style, the clear, clean, sweeping sentences. Why did he write like that? And how did one write like that? I pictured the man as a raging demon, slashing with his pen, consumed with hate, denouncing everything American, extolling everything European or German, laughing at the weaknesses of people, mocking God, authority. What was this? I stood up, trying to realize what reality lay behind the meaning of the words . . . Yes, this man was fighting, fighting with words. He was using words as a weapon, using them as one would use a club. Could words be weapons? Well, yes, for here they were. Then, maybe, perhaps, I could use them as a weapon? No. It frightened me. I read on and what amazed me was not what he said, but how on earth anybody had the courage to say it.

Occasionally I glanced up to reassure myself that I was alone in the 22 room. Who were these men about whom Mencken was talking so passionately? Who was Anatole France? Joseph Conrad? Sinclair Lewis, Sherwood Anderson, Dostoevski, George Moore, Gustave Flaubert, Maupassant, Tolstoy, Frank Harris, Mark Twain, Thomas Hardy, Arnold Bennett, Stephen Crane, Zola, Norris, Gorky, Bergson, Ibsen, Balzac, Bernard Shaw, Dumas, Poe, Thomas Mann, O. Henry, Dreiser, H. G. Wells, Gogol, T. S. Eliot, Gide, Baudelaire, Edgar Lee Masters, Stendhal, Turgenev, Huneker, Nietzsche, and scores of others? Were these men real? Did they exist or had they existed? And how did one pronounce their names?

I ran across many words whose meanings I did not know, and I either 23 looked them up in a dictionary or, before I had a chance to do that, encountered the word in a context that made its meaning clear. But what strange world was this? I concluded the book with the conviction that I had somehow overlooked something terribly important in life. I had once tried to write, had once reveled in feeling, had let my crude imagination roam, but the impulse to dream had been slowly beaten out of me by experience. Now it surged up again and I hungered for books, new ways of looking and seeing. It was not a matter of believing or disbelieving what I read, but of feeling something new, of being affected by something that made the look of the world different.

As dawn broke I ate my pork and beans, feeling dopey, sleepy. I went 24 to work, but the mood of the book would not die; it lingered, coloring everything I saw, heard, did. I now felt that I knew what the white men were feeling. Merely because I had read a book that had spoken of how they lived and thought, I identified myself with that book. I felt vaguely guilty. Would I, filled with bookish notions, act in a manner that would make the whites dislike me?

I forged more notes and my trips to the library became frequent. Reading grew into a passion. My first serious novel was Sinclair Lewis's *Main Street*. 25

It made me see my boss, Mr. Gerald, and identify him as an American type. I would smile when I saw him lugging his golf bags into the office. I had always felt a vast distance separating me from the boss, and now I felt closer to him, though still distant. I felt now that I knew him, that I could feel the very limits of his narrow life. And this had happened because I had read a novel about a mythical man called George F. Babbitt.

The plots and stories in the novels did not interest me so much as the 26 point of view revealed. I gave myself over to each novel without reserve, without trying to criticize it; it was enough for me to see and feel something different. And for me, everything was something different. Reading was like a drug, a dope. The novels created moods in which I lived for days. But I could not conquer my sense of guilt, my feeling that the white men around me knew that I was changing, that I had begun to regard them differently.

Whenever I brought a book to the job, I wrapped it in newspaper—a 27 habit that was to persist for years in other cities and under other circumstances. But some of the white men pried into my packages when I was absent and they questioned me.

"Boy, what are you reading those books for?"

"Oh, I don't know, sir."

"That's deep stuff you're reading, boy."

"I'm just killing time, sir."

"You'll addle your brains if you don't watch out."

I read Dreiser's* *Jennie Gerhardt* and *Sister Carrie* and they revived in me 28 a vivid sense of my mother's suffering; I was overwhelmed. I grew silent, wondering about the life around me. It would have been impossible for me to have told anyone what I derived from these novels, for it was nothing less than a sense of life itself. All my life had shaped me for the realism, the naturalism of the modern novel, and I could not read enough of them.

Steeped in new moods and ideas, I bought a ream of paper and tried to 29 write; but nothing would come, or what did come was flat beyond telling. I discovered that more than desire and feeling were necessary to write and I dropped the idea. Yet I still wondered how it was possible to know people sufficiently to write about them? Could I ever learn about life and people? To me, with my vast ignorance, my Jim Crow station in life, it seemed a task impossible of achievement. I now knew what being a Negro meant. I could endure the hunger. I had learned to live with hate. But to feel that there were feelings denied me, that the very breath of life itself was beyond my reach, that more than anything else hurt, wounded me. I had a new hunger.

In buoying me up, reading also cast me down, made me see what was 30 possible, what I had missed. My tension returned, new, terrible, bitter, surging, almost too great to be contained. I no longer *felt* that the world about me was hostile, killing; I *knew* it. A million times I asked myself what I could do

---

*Theodore Dreiser (1871–1945)—American writer of the "naturalist" school who, like other naturalist novelists, depicted human beings as the passive or determined products of their environment. The naturalists tended to pessimism and they chose subjects that stressed the sordid and ugly sides of life. *Jennie Gerhardt* was published in 1911; *Sister Carrie* in 1900.

to save myself, and there were no answers. I seemed forever condemned, ringed by walls.

I did not discuss my reading with Mr. Falk, who had lent me his library   31
card; it would have meant talking about myself and that would have been too painful. I smiled each day, fighting desperately to maintain my old behavior, to keep my disposition seemingly sunny. But some of the white men discerned that I had begun to brood.

"Wake up there, boy!" Mr. Olin said one day.   32

"Sir!" I answered for the lack of a better word.

"You act like you've stolen something," he said.

I laughed in the way I knew he expected me to laugh, but I resolved to   33
be more conscious of myself, to watch my every act, to guard and hide the new knowledge that was dawning within me.

If I went north, would it be possible for me to build a new life then?   34
But how could a man build a life upon vague, unformed yearnings? I wanted to write and I did not even know the English language. I bought English grammars and found them dull. I felt that I was getting a better sense of the language from novels than from grammars. I read hard, discarding a writer as soon as I felt that I had grasped his point of view. At night the printed page stood before my eyes in sleep.

Mrs. Moss, my landlady, asked me one Sunday morning: 35

"Son, what is this you keep on reading?"

"Oh, nothing. Just novels."

"What you get out of 'em?"

"I'm just killing time," I said.

"I hope you know your own mind," she said in a tone which implied that she doubted if I had a mind.

I knew of no Negroes who read the books I liked and I wondered if any   36
Negroes ever thought of them. I knew that there were Negro doctors, lawyers, newspapermen, but I never saw any of them. When I read a Negro newspaper I never caught the faintest echo of my preoccupation in its pages. I felt trapped and occasionally, for a few days, I would stop reading. But a vague hunger would come over me for books, books that opened up new avenues of feeling and seeing, and again I would forge another note to the white librarian. Again I would read and wonder as only the naïve and unlettered can read and wonder, feeling that I carried a secret, criminal burden about with me each day.

That winter my mother and brother came and we set up housekeeping,   37
buying furniture on the installment plan, being cheated and yet knowing no way to avoid it. I began to eat warm food and to my surprise found that regular meals enabled me to read faster. I may have lived through many illnesses and survived them, never suspecting that I was ill. My brother obtained a job and we began to save toward the trip north, plotting our time, setting tentative dates for departure. I told none of the white men on the job that I was planning to go north; I knew that the moment they felt I was thinking of the North they would change toward me. It would have made

them feel that I did not like the life I was living, and because my life was completely conditioned by what they said or did, it would have been tantamount to challenging them.

I could calculate my chances for life in the South as a Negro fairly clearly now. 38

I could fight the southern whites by organizing with other Negroes, as my grandfather had done. But I knew that I could never win that way; there were many whites and there were but few blacks. They were strong and we were weak. Outright black rebellion could never win. If I fought openly I would die and I did not want to die. News of lynchings were frequent. 39

I could submit and live the life of a genial slave, but that was impossible. All of my life had shaped me to live by my own feelings, and thoughts. I could make up to Bess and marry her and inherit the house. But that, too, would be the life of a slave; if I did that, I would crush to death something within me, and I would hate myself as much as I knew the whites already hated those who had submitted. Neither could I ever willingly present myself to be kicked, as Shorty had done. I would rather have died than do that. 40

I could drain off my restlessness by fighting with Shorty and Harrison. I had seen many Negroes solve the problem of being black by transferring their hatred of themselves to others with a black skin and fighting them. I would have to be cold to do that, and I was not cold and I could never be. 41

I could, of course, forget what I had read, thrust the whites out of my mind, forget them; and find release from anxiety and longing in sex and alcohol. But the memory of how my father had conducted himself made that course repugnant. If I did not want others to violate my life, how could I voluntarily violate it myself? 42

I had no hope whatever of being a professional man. Not only had I been so conditioned that I did not desire it, but the fulfillment of such an ambition was beyond my capabilities. Well-to-do Negroes lived in a world that was almost as alien to me as the world inhabited by whites. 43

What, then, was there? I held my life in my mind, in my consciousness each day, feeling at times that I would stumble and drop it, spill it forever. My reading had created a vast sense of distance between me and the world in which I lived and tried to make a living, and that sense of distance was increasing each day. My days and nights were one long, quiet, continuously contained dream of terror, tension, and anxiety. I wondered how long I could bear it. 44

Questions for Discussion

1. Having been deprived of learning, the young narrator views it as a great privilege. He does not view learning as a way of gaining power in the world or of increasing his income—those thoughts do not seem even to cross his

mind—but simply as a way of learning about lives, thoughts, and feelings other than his own. Discuss with your classmates the extent to which you think student apathy about learning derives from its being forced on children as a requirement rather than held out as a privilege. If you were to try to influence students in grade school and high school to become more enthusiastic readers and learners, what changes or tactics would you recommend? What new instructions would you give to teachers and administrators? What changes of behavior or attitude would you recommend to students themselves?

2. What is the social function of "boy" used as a form of address to blacks? Can you suggest why the whites in the story constantly repeat this term?

3. Why does the narrator in paragraphs 24 and 26 say that he felt guilty for the reading he was doing?

4. In trying to learn to write, the narrator says that he "bought English grammars" but "felt that I was getting a better sense of the language from novels than from grammars." Does this ring true to you? Do you think that increasing your reading will automatically improve your grammar? Would a steady reader ever have to study grammar formally in order to use it correctly? As you think about the answer to this question, consider the grammar of pre-school children who have never studied grammar. If they are surrounded by grammatically correct speakers, is their own grammar generally correct? If so, does this fact suggest an answer to the question of whether you can learn grammar from reading as well as by listening?

5. In discussion with your classmates, compare the various English and reading teachers you have had over the years. How many students think their teachers were successful at instilling a love of reading? How many think their teachers were poor? Are there similarities among the good teachers? Among the bad?

Suggested Essay Topics

1. In paragraph 24 the young narrator reports that after an all-night orgy of reading, "I went to work, but the mood of the book would not die; it lingered, coloring everything I saw, heard, did." If you have ever had this kind of experience yourself—the experience of a book's mood, characters, and events occupying your mind so vividly that they colored the world around you—give a specific account of the book's lingering effects. After reading Sinclair Lewis's *Main Street,* for example, the narrator achieves an entirely new understanding of his boss; he learns something about his boss's values and inner life that he could never have learned firsthand. Can you give an account of any similar experience, when a book gave you a fresher perspective or a deeper understanding of some (formerly inscrutable) person or event? Direct your essay to your classmates, with the aim of explaining how the book achieved its effect.

2. Re-read a book that was a favorite of yours when you were a child. Then write an essay explaining how you would present this book to children

today if you were a parent or a teacher using it to teach reading. Think back on your own experience with reading teachers, either in school or at home, and explain the strategies you would employ to lift children up to a love of reading. If it seems appropriate, pick a passage or two and discuss your selection in detail.

Zora Neale Hurston

In "Figure and Fancy" Zora Neale Hurston (b. 1901–1960), Afro-American novelist, recounts the main influence that stirred her artistic imagination and eventually turned her into a writer: stories. Stories that she heard as a child being told by the men and women sitting around the general store; stories that she made up, like a patchwork quilt, from scraps of memory, song, and folklore passed among the adults in her small community; stories that transformed the everyday world of tedium, dust, and work into a world of beauty and breathtaking possibilities.

Hurston does not here talk about imagination and writing. This is not an analytical essay written in a voice of academic detachment or clinical objectivity. This is, instead, a voice rich with remembering, a voice so steeped in memory that it seems warmed by the same sun that shone on Huston as a girl, a voice that loves the feel of recreating in words the reality of past time.

Clearly, for Hurston, stories were the soil in which her imagination grew, the nourishment on which it fed. But is this not equally true for us all? Even though few of us ever become professional writers of stories, all of us are raised on stories, and all of us are just as inclined to pass stories around as are the figures Hurston describes. She shows them swapping tales as they sit on the benches and boxes of the general store. As Hurston's deep emotional investment in stories reveals, stories are not just entertainment, they are a necessary ingredient in the acculturation of all human beings. We could not become human without stories, for stories constitute by far the overwhelming source of those contrasts and comparisons with others on which we depend for the gradual identification of our own nature, of our sameness and difference from other human beings. We know thousands more people from stories than we know in "real life" (think of the thousands of people you know from song lyrics alone—not to mention people that we have met in stories on television, in movies, and in plays, parables, sermons, fairy tales, commercials, religious writings, short stories, and novels!). Think of how impoverished your mental and emotional life would be if all of your acquaintances from stories were suddenly erased from your mind!

That there are no non-story-telling cultures, and apparently never have been, suggests that stories are in the fabric of human nature itself. Human beings may have begun by basing their stories on life, but, once a story is told, life can turn around and base itself on the fictional model. Whatever the truth of a story's origins, the fact is that by now our culture is so saturated with stories that the dynamic interchange between them and real life is both constant and undeniable. We live life by telling stories about it that make it intelligible, meaningful, and vivid. Story-telling is in fact a primary mode of living. Hurston's essay captures the primordial joy in stories that is perhaps the most fundamental birthright of all.

FIGURE AND FANCY

Chapter 5 of Hurston's autobiography, *Dust Tracks on a Road* (1942).

Nothing that God ever made is the same thing to more than one person. 1
That is natural. There is no single face in nature, because every eye that looks upon it, sees it from its own angle. So every man's spice-box seasons his own food.

Naturally, I picked up the reflections of life around me with my own 2
instruments, and absorbed what I gathered according to my inside juices.

There were the two churches, Methodist and Baptist, and the school. 3
Most people would say that such institutions are always the great influences in any town. They would say that because it sounds like the thing that ought to be said. But I know that Joe Clarke's store was the heart and spring of the town.

Men sat around the store on boxes and benches and passed this world 4
and the next one through their mouths. The right and the wrong, the who, when and why was passed on, and nobody doubted the conclusions. Women stood around there on Saturday nights and had it proven to the community that their husbands were good providers, put all of their money in their wives' hands and generally glorified them. Or right there before everybody it was revealed that one man was keeping some other woman by the things the other woman was allowed to buy on his account. No doubt a few men found that their wives had a brand new pair of shoes oftener than he could afford it, and wondered what she did with her time while he was off at work. Sometimes he didn't have to wonder. There were no discreet nuances of life on Joe Clarke's porch. There was open kindness, anger, hate, love, envy and its kinfolks, but all emotions were naked, and nakedly arrived at. It was a case of "make it and take it." You got what your strengths would bring you. This was not just true of Eatonville. This was the spirit of that whole new part of the state at the time, as it always is where men settle new lands.

For me, the store porch was the most interesting place that I could think 5
of. I was not allowed to sit around there, naturally. But, I could and did drag my feet going in and out, whenever I was sent there for something, to allow whatever was being said to hang in my ear. I would hear an occasional scrap of gossip in what to me was adult double talk, but which I understood at times. There would be, for instance, sly references to the physical condition of women, irregular love affairs, brags on male potency by the parties of the first part, and the like. It did not take me long to know what was meant when a girl was spoken of as "ruint" or "bigged."

For instance, somebody would remark, "Ada Dell is ruint, you know."   6
"Yep, somebody was telling me. A pitcher can go to the well a long time, but
its bound to get broke sooner or later." Or some woman or girl would come
switching past the store porch and some man would call to her, "Hey, Sugar!
What's on de rail for de lizard?" Then again I would hear some man say, "I
got to have my ground-rations. If one woman can't take care of it, I gits me
another one." One man told a woman to hold her ear close, because he had
a bug to put in her ear. He was sitting on a box. She stooped over to hear
whatever it was he had to whisper to her. Then she straightened up sharply
and pulled away from him. "Why, you!" she exclaimed. "The idea of such
a thing! Talking like dat to me, when you know I'm a good church-worker,
and you a deacon!" He didn't seem to be ashamed at all. "Dat's just de point
I'm coming out on, sister. Two clean sheets can't dirty one 'nother, you
know." There was general laughter, as the deacon moved his foot so that I
could get in the store door. I happened to hear a man talking to another in
a chiding manner and say, "To save my soul, I can't see what you fooled with
her for. I'd just as soon pick up an old tin can out of the trash pile."

But what I really loved to hear was the menfolks holding a "lying"   7
session. That is, straining against each other in telling folk tales. God, Devil,
Brer Rabbit, Brer Fox, Sis Cat, Brer Bear, Lion, Tiger, Buzzard, and all the
wood folk walked and talked like natural men. The wives of the story-tellers
might yell from backyards for them to come and tote some water, or chop
wood for the cook-stove and never get a move out of the men. The usual
rejoinder was, "Oh, she's got enough to go on. No matter how much wood
you chop, a woman will burn it all up to get a meal. If she got a couple of
pieces, she will make it do. If you chop up a whole boxful, she will burn every
stick of it. Pay her no mind." So the story-telling would go right on.

I often hung around and listened while Mama waited on me for the   8
sugar or coffee to finish off dinner, until she lifted her voice over the tree tops
in a way to let me know that her patience was gone: "You Zora-a-a! If you
don't come here, you better!" That had a promise of peach hickories in it, and
I would have to leave. But I would have found out from such story-tellers
as Elijah Moseley, better known as "Lige," how and why Sis Snail quit her
husband, for instance. You may or may not excuse my lagging feet, if you
know the circumstances of the case:

One morning soon, Lige met Sis Snail on the far side of the road. He   9
had passed there several times in the last few years and seen Sis Snail headed
towards the road. For the last three years he had stepped over her several
times as she crossed the road, always forging straight ahead. But this morning
he found her clean across, and she seemed mighty pleased with herself, so
he stopped and asked her where she was headed for.

"Going off to travel over the world," she told him. "I done left my   10
husband for good."

"How come, Sis Snail? He didn't ill-treat you in no ways, did he?"   11

"Can't exactly say he did, Brother Lige, but you take and take just so   12
much and then you can't take no more. Your craw gits full up to de neck.

De man gits around too slow to suit me, and look like I just can't break him of it. So I done left him for good. I'm out and gone. I gits around right fast, my ownself, and I just can't put up with nobody dat gits around as slow as he do."

"Oh, don't leave de man too sudden, Sis Snail. Maybe he might come 13 to move round fast like you do. Why don't you sort of reason wid de poor soul and let him know how you feel?"

"I done tried dat until my patience is all wore out. And this last thing 14 he done run my cup over. You know I took sick in de bed—had de misery in my side so bad till I couldn't rest in de bed. He heard me groaning and asked me what was de matter. I told him how sick I was. Told him, 'Lawd, I'm so sick!' So he said 'If you's sick like dat, I'll go git de doctor for you.' I says, 'I sho would be mighty much obliged if you would.' So he took and told me, 'I don't want you laying there and suffering like dat. I'll go git de doctor right away. Just lemme go git my hat.'

"So I laid there in de bed and waited for him to go git de doctor. Lawd! 15 I was so sick! I rolled from pillar to post. After seven I heard a noise at de door, and I said, 'Lawd, I'm so glad! I knows dats my husband done come back wid de doctor.' So I hollered out and asked, 'Honey, is dat you done come back wid de doctor?' And he come growling at me and giving me a short answer wid, 'Don't try to rush me. I ain't gone yet.' It had done took him seven years to git his hat and git to de door. So I just up and left him."

Then one late afternoon, a woman called Gold, who had come to town 16 from somewhere else, told the why and how of races that pleased me more than what I learned about race derivations later on in Ethnology. This was her explanation:

God did not make folks all at once. He made folks sort of in His spare 17 time. For instance one day He had a little time on his hands, so He got the clay, seasoned it the way He wanted it, then He laid it by and went on to do something more important. Another day He had some spare moments, so He rolled it all out, and cut out the human shapes, and stood them all up against His long gold fence to dry while He did some important creating. The human shapes all got dry, and when He found time, He blowed the breath of life in them. After that, from time to time, He would call everybody up, and give them spare parts. For instance, one day He called everybody and gave out feet and eyes. Another time He give out toe-nails that Old Maker figured they could use. Anyhow, they had all that they got up to now. So then one day He said, "Tomorrow morning, at seven o'clock *sharp,* I aim to give out color and git it over wid. Everybody be here on time. I got plenty of creating to do tomorrow, and I want to give out this color and get it over wid. *Everybody* be 'round de throne at seven o'clock tomorrow morning!"

So next morning at seven o'clock, God was sitting on His throne with 18 His big crown on His head and seven suns circling around His head. Great multitudes was standing around the throne waiting to get their color. God sat up there and looked, east, and He looked west, and He looked north and He looked Australia, and blazing worlds were falling off His teeth. So He looked over to His left and moved His hands over a crowd and said, "You's yellow people!" They all bowed low and said, "Thank you, God," and they went on off. He looked at another crowd, moved His hands over them and said, "You's red folks!" They made their manners and said, "Thank you, Old Maker," and they went on off. He looked towards the center and moved His hand over another crowd and said, "You's white folks!" They bowed low and said, "Much obliged, Jesus," and they went on off. Then God looked way over to the right and said, "Look here, Gabriel, I miss a lot of multitudes from around the throne this morning." Gabriel looked too, and said, "Yessir, there's a heap of multitudes missing from round de throne this morning." So God sat there an hour and a half and waited. Then He called Gabriel and said, "Looka here, Gabriel, I'm sick and tired of this waiting. I got plenty of creating to do this morning. You go find them folks and tell 'em they better hurry on up here and they expect to get any color. Fool with me, and I won't give out no more."

So Gabriel run on off and started to hunting around. Way after while, he found the missing multitudes lying around on the grass by the Sea of Life, fast asleep. So Gabriel woke them up and told them, "You better get up from there and come on up to the throne and get your color. Old Maker is might wore out from waiting. Fool with Him and He won't give out no more color."

So as the multitudes heard that, they all jumped up and went running towards the throne hollering, "Give us our color! We want our color! We got just as much right to color as anybody else." So when the first ones got to the throne, they tried to stop and be polite. But the ones coming up behind got to pushing and shoving so till the first ones got shoved all up against the throne so till the throne was careening all over to one side. So God said, "Here! Here! Git back! Git back!" But they was keeping up such a racket that they misunderstood Him, and thought He said, "Git black!" So they just got black, and kept the thing a-going.

In one way or another, I heard dozens more of these tales. My father and his preacher associates told the best stories on the church. Papa, being moderator of the South Florida Baptist Association, had numerous preacher visitors just before the Association met, to get the politics of the thing all cut and dried before the meetings came off. After it was decided who would put such and such a motion before the house, who would second it, and whom my father would recognize first and things like that, a big story-telling session would get under way on our front porch, and very funny stories at the expense of preachers and congregations would be told.

No doubt, these tales of God, the Devil, animals and natural elements seemed ordinary enough to most people in the village. But many of them stirred up fancies in me. It did not surprise me at all to hear that the animals talked. I had suspected it all along. Or let us say, that I wanted to suspect it. Life took on a bigger perimeter by expanding on these things. I picked up glints and gleams out of what I heard and stored it away to turn it to my own uses. The wind would sough through the tops of the tall, long-leaf pines and say things to me. I put in the words that the sounds put into me. Like "Woo woo, you wooo!" The tree was talking to me, even when I did not catch the words. It was talking and telling me things. I have mentioned the tree near our house that got so friendly I named it "the loving pine." Finally all of my playmates called it that too. I used to take a seat at the foot of that tree and play for hours without any toys. We talked about everything in the world. Sometimes we just took it out in singing songs. That tree had a mighty fine bass voice when it really took a notion to let it out.

There was another tree that used to creep up close to the house around 23 sundown and threaten me. It used to put on a skull-head with a crown on it every day at sundown and make motions at me when I had to go out on the back porch to wash my feet after supper before going to bed. It never bothered around during the day. It was just another pine tree about a hundred feet tall then, standing head and shoulders above a grove. But let the dusk begin to fall, and it would put that crown on its skull and creep in close. Nobody else ever seemed to notice what it was up to but me. I used to wish it would go off somewhere and get lost. But every evening I would have to look to see, and every time, it would be right there, sort of shaking and shivering and bowing its head at me. I used to wonder if sometime it was not going to come in the house.

When I began to make up stories I cannot say. Just from one fancy to 24 another, adding more and more detail until they seemed real. People seldom see themselves changing.

So I was making little stories to myself, and have no memory of how 25 I began. But I do remember some of the earliest ones.

I came in from play one day and told my mother how a bird had talked 26 to me with a tail so long that while he sat up in the top of the pine tree his tail was dragging the ground. It was a soft beautiful bird tail, all blue and pink and red and green. In fact I climbed up the bird's tail and sat up the tree and had a long talk with the bird. He knew my name, but I didn't know how he knew it. In fact, the bird had come a long way just to sit and talk with me.

Another time, I dashed into the kitchen and told Mama how the lake 27 had talked with me, and invited me to walk all over it. I told the lake I was afraid of getting drowned, but the lake assured me it wouldn't think of doing *me* like that. No, indeed! Come right on and have a walk. Well, I stepped out on the lake and walked all over it. It didn't even wet my feet. I could see all the fish and things swimming around under me, and they all said hello, but none of them bothered me. Wasn't that nice?

My mother said that it was. My grandmother glared at me like open- 28 faced hell and snorted.

"Luthee!" (She lisped.) "You hear dat young 'un stand up here and lie 29 like dat? And you ain't doing nothing to break her of it? Grab her! Wring her coat tails over her head and wear out a handful of peach hickories on her back-side! Stomp her guts out! Ruin her!"

"Oh, she's just playing," Mama said indulgently. 30

"Playing! Why dat lil' heifer is lying just as fast as a horse can trot. Stop 31 her! Wear her back-side out. I bet if I lay my hands on her she'll stop it. I vominates a lying tongue."

Mama never tried to break me. She'd listen sometimes, and sometimes   32
she wouldn't. But she never seemed displeased. But her mother used to foam
at the mouth. I was just as sure to be hung before I got grown as gun was
iron! The least thing Mama could do to straighten me out was to smack my
jaws for me. She outraged my grandmother scandalously by not doing it.
Mama was going to be responsible for my downfall when she stood up in
judgment. It was a sin before the living justice, that's what it was. God knows,
grandmother would break me or kill me, if she had her way. Killing me looked
like the best one, anyway. All I was good for was to lay up and wet the bed
half of the time and tell lies, besides being the spitting image of dat good-for-
nothing yaller bastard. I was the punishment God put on Mama for marrying
Papa. I ought to be thrown in the hogslops, that's what. She could beat me
as long as I last.

I knew that I did not have to pay too much attention to the old lady   33
and so I didn't. Furthermore, how was she going to tell me what I was doing
inside? I could keep my inventions to myself, which was what I did most of
the time.

One day, we were going to have roasting-ears for dinner and I was   34
around while Mama was shucking the corn. I picked up an inside chunk and
carried it off to look at it. It was such a delicate, blushy green. I crawled under
the side of the house to love it all by myself.

In a few minutes, it had become Miss Corn-Shuck, and of course needed   35
some hair. So I went back and picked up some cornsilk and tied it to the
pointed end. We had a lovely time together for a day or two, and then Miss
Corn-Shuck got lonesome for some company.

I do not think that her lonesomeness would have come down on her as   36
it did, if I had not found a cake of sweet soap in Mama's dresser drawer. It
was a cake of Pears' scented soap. It was clear like amber glass. I could see
straight through it. It delighted my senses just as much as the tender green
corn-shuck. So Miss Corn-Shuck fell in love with Mr. Sweet Smell then and
there. But she said she could not have a thing to do with him unless he went
and put on some clothes. I found a piece of red and white string that had come
around some groceries and made him a suit of clothes. Being bigger in the
middle than he was on either end, his pants kept falling off—sometimes over
his head and sometimes the other way. So I cut little notches in his sides
around the middle and tied his suit on. To other people it might have looked
like a cake of soap with a bit of twine tied around it, but Miss Corn-Shuck
and I knew he had on the finest clothes in the world. Every day it would be
different, because Mr. Sweet Smell was very particular about what he wore.
Besides he wanted Miss Corn-Shuck to admire him.

There was a great mystery about where Mr. Sweet Smell came from. I   37
suppose if Mama had been asked, she would have said that it was the
company soap, since the family used nothing but plain, yellow Octagon
laundry soap for bathing. But I had not known it was there until I happened
to find it. It might have been there for years. Whenever Miss Corn-Shuck
asked him where his home was, he always said it was a secret which he would

tell her about when they were married. It was not very important anyway. We knew he was some very high-class man from way off—the farther off the better.

But sad to say, Miss Corn-Shuck and Mr. Sweet Smell never got mar- 38 ried. They always meant to, but before very long, Miss Corn-Cob began to make trouble. We found her around the kitchen door one day, and she followed us back under the house and right away started her meanness. She was jealous of Miss Corn-Shuck because she was so pretty and green, with long silky hair, and so Miss Corn-Cob would make up all kinds of mean stories about her. One day there was going to be a big party and that was the first time the Spool People came to visit. They used to hop off of Mama's sewing machine one by one until they were a great congregation—at least fifteen or so. They didn't do anything much besides second the motion on what somebody else did and said, so they must have been the common people.

Reverend Door-Knob was there, too. He used to live on the inside of 39 the kitchen door, but one day he rolled off and came under the house to be with us. Unconsciously he behaved a lot like Mayor Joe Clarke. He was roundish and reddish brown, and used to laugh louder than anything when something funny happened. The spool people always laughed whenever he laughed. They used to cry too, whenever Mr. Sweet Smell or Miss Corn-Shuck cried. They were always doing whatever they saw other people do. That was the way the Spool People were.

When Mr. Sweet Smell left his fine house in the dresser drawer that day, 40 he came through the kitchen and brought a half can of condensed milk for the refreshments. Everybody liked condensed milk for refreshment. Well, Miss Corn-Cob sneaked around and ate up all the refreshments and then she told everybody that Miss Corn-Shuck ate it. That hurt Mr. Sweet Smell's feelings so bad till he went home and so he didn't marry Miss Corn-Shuck that day. Reverend Door-Knob was so mad with Miss Corn-Cob that he threw her clear over the house and she landed in the horse trough, which everybody said, served her just right.

But not getting married that day sort of threw Mr. Sweet Smell in a kind 41 of fever. He was sick in the bed for several days. Miss Corn-Shuck went to see him every day, and that was very nice. He rubbed off some of his smell on her because she was so nice to come to see him.

Some people might have thought that Miss Corn-Shuck's green dress 42 had faded and her silky hair all dried up. But that was because they didn't know any better. She just put on a brownish cloak over it, so it wouldn't get dirty. She would let me see it any time I wanted to. That was because she liked me better than anyone else except Mr. Sweet Smell. She lay under the mattress of my bed every night. Mr. Sweet Smell always went home to the dresser drawer. The Spool People slept on the sill under the house because Reverend Door-Knob used to sleep there. They couldn't do a thing unless they saw somebody else doing it. They wore a string around their waist, trying to dress up like Mr. Sweet Smell.

Miss Corn-Cob played a very mean trick once. Miss Corn-Shuck and 43
Mr. Sweet Smell were going to get married down by the lake. The lake had
kindly moved into the washbasin for the occasion. A piece of cold corn-
bread had turned into a magnificent cake. Plenty of egg-nogg had come out
of a cake of shaving soap. The bride and groom were standing side by side
and ready. When what did Miss Corn-Cob do? She shoved Reverend Door-
Knob into the lake, because she knew he couldn't swim. Here everybody
was waiting and nobody would have known where the preacher was if one
of the Spool People had not seen him kicking down at the bottom of the
lake and rescued him.

While he was getting dry and putting on a fresh suit of clothes, Miss 44
Corn-Cob sent out old dominecker rooster to steal the wedding cake. So the
wedding had to be put off until Christmas because then there would be plenty
of cake for everybody. The Spool People said they were glad of it, because
there ought to be enough cake to go around if you wanted a really nice
wedding. The lake told everybody good-bye, jumped out in the yard and
went on home. It could not stay off too long, because it would be missed and
people would not know what to think.

Miss Corn-Cob went and hid down a gopher hole for a whole week. 45
Every night she used to cry so loud that we could hear her at the house. You
see she was scared of the dark. Her mama gave her a good whipping when
she got back home and everybody stood around and said, "Goody! Goody!
Goody! Goody! Goody!" Because that makes everybody feel bad. That is, no
child likes to hear another one gloating "Goody!" when he is in trouble.

They all stayed around the house for years, holding funerals and al- 46
most weddings and taking trips with me to where the sky met the ground.
I do not know exactly when they left me. They kept me company for so
long. Then one day they were gone. Where? I do not know. But there is an
age when children are fit company for spirits. Before they have absorbed
too much of earthy things to be able to fly with the unseen things that soar.
There came a time when I could look back on the fields where we had
picked flowers together but they, my friends, were nowhere to be seen. The
sunlight where I had lost them was still of Midas gold, but that which
touched me where I stood had somehow turned to gilt. Nor could I return
to the shining meadow where they had vanished. I could not ask of others
if they had seen which way my company went. My friends had been too
shy to show themselves to others. Now and then when the sky is the right
shade of blue, the air soft, and the clouds are sculptured into heroic shapes,
I glimpse them for a moment, and believe again that the halcyon days have
been.

When inanimate things ceased to commune with me like natural men, 47
other dreams came to live with me. Animals took on lives and characteristics
which nobody knew anything about except myself. Little things that people
did or said grew into fantastic stories.

There was a man who turned into an alligator for my amusement. All 48 he did was live in a one-room house by himself down near Lake Belle. I did the rest myself. He came into the village one evening near dusk and stopped at the store. Somebody teased him about living out there by himself, and said that if he did not hurry up and get married, he was liable to go wild.

I saw him tending his little garden all day, and otherwise just being a natural man. But I made an image of him for after dark that was different. In my imagination, his work-a-day hands and feet became the reptilian claws of an alligator. A tough, knotty hide crept over him, and his mouth became a huge snout with prong-toothed, powerful jaws. In the dark of the night, when the alligators began their nightly mysteries behind the cloaking curtain of cypress trees that all but hid Lake Belle, I could see him crawling from his door, turning his ugly head from left to right to see who was looking, then gliding down into the dark waters to become a 'gator among 'gators. He would mingle his bellow with other bull 'gator bellows and be strong and terrible. He was the king of 'gators and the others minded him. When I heard the thunder of bull 'gator voices from the lake on dark nights, I used to whisper to myself, "That's Mr. Pendir! Just listen at him!"

I kept adding detail. For instance, late one afternoon, my mother had taken me for a walk down around Lake Belle. On our way home, the sun had set. It was good and dark when we came to the turning-off place that would take us straight home. At that spot, the trees stood apart, and the surface of the lake was plain. I saw the early moon laying a shiny track across the water. After that, I could picture the full moon laying a flaming red sword of light across the water. It was a road of yellow-red light made for Mr. Pendir to tread. I could see him crossing the lake down this flaming road wrapped in his awful majesty, with thousands on thousands of his subject-'gators moving silently along beside him and behind him in an awesome and mighty convoy.

I added another chapter to the Pendir story when a curious accident happened in the village. One old woman, Mrs. Bronson, went fishing in Blue Sink late one afternoon and did not return. The family, who had opposed the idea of a woman of Mrs. Bronson's age going off to Blue Sink to fish so late in the day, finally became worried and went out to hunt for her. They went around the edge of the lake with lanterns and torches and called and called, but they could not see her, and neither did she answer. Finally, they found her, though people were beginning to be doubtful about it. Blue Sink drops down abruptly from its shores, and is supposed to be bottomless. She was in the lake, at the very edge, still alive, but unable to crawl out. She did not even cry out when she heard herself being called and could discern the moving lanterns. When she was safely home in bed, she said that she had sat there till sundown because she knew the fish would begin to bite. She did catch a few. But just as black dark came on, a terrible fear came on her somehow, and something like a great wind struck her and hurled her into the water. She had fallen on the narrow inside rim of the lake, otherwise she would have sunk into the hidden deeps. She said that she screamed a few times for help, but something rushed across Blue Sink like a body-fied wind and commanded her to hush-up. If she so much as made another sound, she would never get out of that lake alive. That was why she had not answered when she was called, but she was praying inside to be found.

The doctor came and said that she had suffered a stroke. One whole side 52 of her body was paralyzed, so when she tumbled over into the lake, she could not get out. Her terror and fear had done the rest. She must have had two or three horrible hours lying there in the edge of the water, hard put to it to keep her face above water, and expecting the attack of an alligator, water moccasin, gar fish, and numerous other creatures which existed only in her terrified mind. It is a wonder that she did not die of fright.

Right away, I could see the mighty tail of Mr. Pendir slapping Old Lady 53 Bronson into the lake. Then he had stalked away across the lake like the Devil walking up and down in the earth. But when she had screamed, I pictured him re-crossing to her, treading the red-gold of his moon-carpet, with his mighty minions swimming along beside him, his feet walking the surface like a pavement. The soles of his feet never even being damp, he drew up his hosts around her and commanded her to hush.

The old woman was said to dabble in hoodoo, and some said that Pendir 54 did too. I had heard often enough that it was the pride of one hoodoo doctor to "throw it back on the one that done it." What could be more natural then than for my 'gator-man to get peeved because the old lady had tried to throw something he did back on him? Naturally, he slapped her in to the lake. No matter what the doctor said, I knew the real truth of the matter.

I told my playmates about it and they believed it right away. I got bold 55 and told them how I had seen Mr. Pendir turning into a 'gator at night and going down into the lake and walking the water. My chums even believed part of it in a way. That is, they liked the idea and joined in the game. They became timid in the presence of the harmless little man and on the sly would be looking for 'gator signs on him. We pretended a great fear of him. Lest we meet him in 'gator form some night and get carried off into the lake, and die on that terrible road of light.

I told them how he couldn't die anyway. That is, he couldn't die any- 56 more. He was not a living man. He had died a long time ago, and his soul had gone to the 'gators. He had told me that he had no fear of death because he had come back from where other folks were going.

The truth of the matter was, that poor Mr. Pendir was the one man in 57 the village who could not swim a lick. He died a very ordinary death. He worked too long in the hot sun one day, and some said on an empty stomach, and took down sick. Two days later he just died and was buried and stayed where he was put. His life had not agreed with my phantasy at any point. He had no female relatives around to mourn loud and make his funeral entertaining, even, and his name soon ceased to be called. The grown folks of the village never dreamed what an exciting man he had been to me. Even after he was dead and buried, I would go down to the edge of Lake Belle to see if I could run across some of his 'gator hides that he had sloughed off at daybreak when he became a man again. My phantasies were still fighting against the facts.

Questions for Discussion

1. If there is any truth to the analogy that stories nurture the imagination the way food nurtures the body, then it follows that different kinds of psychic food may be better, "healthier," for the imagination than other kinds, just as some kinds of digestible foods may nurture a healthier body than others. Is there "junk food" for the mind just as there is for the body? What are the criteria for deciding what stories are "junk," and, if you feel that this might justifiably describe some stories, what are some of the possible consequences of devouring narrative "junk"?

2. If you accept the analogy between food for the body and stories-as-food for the imagination, identify with your classmates the kinds of stories that are better for people than others. Say what *better* means. If you do not accept the analogy, discuss with your classmates the reasons why.

3. Compare examples of stories you were told and that you read (in your family) with stories read in the families of other people in your class. Are the *categories* the same? That is, do most of the families represented by the students in your class tell and read the same *kinds* of stories, even though the specific content may be different? If such commonality does indeed exist, does it raise any suggestions about a common culture and about how we learn to position ourselves in culture? (Did you all read, for example, children's stories? Which ones? Do people in your family read science fiction? romance novels? detective novels? biographies? essays? histories? war stories? or others? What others?)

4. Try to describe a person who has never read or been told any stories. What kinds of knowledge could such a person know of the world and of human nature? What kinds of knowledge could such a person not know? (If any of you know the *Autobiography* of John Stuart Mill or *Hard Times* by Charles Dickens, in which the character of Louisa Gradgrind is based on John Stuart Mill, you may find the depictions in these works useful as a starting point in trying to respond to these questions).

Suggested Essay Topics

1. In an essay directed to the general public—the people you picture reading essays in magazines such as *Harper's* or the *Atlantic Monthly*—recount, as Hurston does (she is your model for this essay), the kinds of occasions on which you absorbed stories in your childhood, the interest you had in the stories, and the content of a few of them. Perhaps your family occasion for stories was the children's bedtime; perhaps you got more stories from

your grandparents or other relatives or neighbors than from your parents; perhaps you were one of those childhood bookworms; or perhaps you got stories from some other source. In any event, give an account of the circumstances, your interests, and some description of content.

2. In an essay directed to your instructor, analyze how you were affected by some of the stories that you remember as being important during your childhood because you loved them so much and heard (or read) them so often. If you can, try to obtain copies of some of those stories and re-read them. Are they the same stories that you would like to pass on to your own or to others' children? Explain your answer in terms of the criteria you now think should be employed to guide children's reading. Assess whether or not your childhood reading was wisely directed. Explain what kinds of stories you would want your own children exposed to, and why you favor some over others.

Susan Sontag

Is modern art, like modern science, becoming too abstruse and technical to be understood by anyone except specialists? Has art changed its function from that of providing a commentary and criticism on life to that of providing new modes of sensory exploration and experience? Can modern art, by incorporating modern technology and becoming experimental in the same way that science is experimental, promote a more unified culture than the one that is currently said to be divided by loyalty to either science or literature?

These are the kinds of questions that vitally interest Susan Sontag (b. 1933). She is the most articulate propounder of such questions on the contemporary scene. Since 1965 she has, in article after article and book after book, tried to discover and explain the intersections between metaphor, art, and language on the one hand, and culture and sensibility on the other.

In examining these intersections, Sontag seems to have become convinced that the conditions of modern life, particularly changes resulting from technology, have prompted creative changes in art that are antagonistic to older, more traditional kinds of artistic programs. The speed of modern life, its crowdedness, its technical advances in cinematography and acoustic reproduction, its pluralism, its relatively higher interest in form rather than content—all these factors and more, she implies, have created a new sensibility in culture, one that most modern artists are eager both to explore and take advantage of. These conditions of modern life, for example, have led to an emphasis on technique, on form, on cool distance rather than passionate engagement, on intellectual playfulness rather than moral seriousness, and so on. The novel, claims Sontag, is the only art form lagging far behind the other arts in exploring ways of incorporating the modern sensibility into art.

Although Sontag emphasizes art's ability to modify consciousness and organize new modes of sensibility (¶7), you may want to question whether this aim really is, as she claims, a new function, or whether this is what art has always done. Wasn't it precisely art's power to modify consciousness and organize new modes of sensibility that caused Plato to be so suspicious of it in ancient Greece, Philip Sidney to be so laudatory of it in Renaissance England, and William Faulkner to claim for it, in his Nobel Prize acceptance speech of 1950, the power to help human beings not only survive but prevail in the face of the bomb and other stresses of twentieth century life? Or is Sontag talking about a different modification of consciousness and a different kind of sensibility? This may be a question you will want to answer for yourself as you read.

ONE CULTURE AND THE NEW SENSIBILITY

From *Against Interpretation and Other Essays* (1965).

In the last few years there has been a good deal of discussion of a purported chasm which opened up some two centuries ago, with the advent of the Industrial Revolution, between "two cultures," the literary-artistic and the scientific.* According to this diagnosis, any intelligent and articulate modern person is likely to inhabit one culture to the exclusion of the other. He will be concerned with different documents, different techniques, different problems; he will speak a different language. Most important, the type of effort required for the mastery of these two cultures will differ vastly. For the literary-artistic culture is understood as a general culture. It is addressed to man insofar as he is man; it is culture or, rather, it promotes culture, in the sense of culture defined by Ortega y Gasset: that which a man has in his possession when he has forgotten everything that he has read. The scientific culture, in contrast, is a culture for specialists; it is founded on remembering and is set down in ways that require complete dedication of the effort to comprehend. While the literary-artistic culture aims at internalization, ingestion—in other words, cultivation—the scientific culture aims at accumulation and externalization in complex instruments for problem-solving and specific techniques for mastery.

Though T. S. Eliot derived the chasm between the two cultures from a period more remote in modern history, speaking in a famous essay of a "dissociation of sensibility" which opened up in the 17th century, the connection of the problem with the Industrial Revolution seems well taken. There is a historic antipathy on the part of many literary intellectuals and artists to those changes which characterize modern society—above all, industrialization and those of its effects which everyone has experienced, such as the proliferation of huge impersonal cities and the predominance of the

*See C. P. Snow and Loren Eiseley essays in Chapter 10.

anonymous style of urban life. It has mattered little whether industrialization, the creature of modern "science," is seen on the 19th and early 20th
century model, as noisy smoky artificial processes which defile nature and
standardize culture, or on the newer model, the clean automated technology
that is coming into being in the second half of the 20th century. The judgment
has been mostly the same. Literary men, feeling that the status of humanity
itself was being challenged by the new science and the new technology,
abhorred and deplored the change. But the literary men, whether one thinks
of Emerson and Thoreau and Ruskin in the 19th century, or of 20th century
intellectuals who talk of modern society as being in some new way incomprehensible, "alienated," are inevitably on the defensive. They know that the
scientific culture, the coming of the machine, cannot be stopped.

The standard response to the problem of "the two cultures"—and the   3
issue long antedates by many decades the crude and philistine statement of
the problem by C. P. Snow in a famous lecture some years ago—has been a
facile defense of the function of the arts (in terms of an ever vaguer ideology
of "humanism") or a premature surrender of the function of the arts to
science. By the second response, I am not referring to the philistinism of
scientists (and those of their party among artists and philosophers) who
dismiss the arts as imprecise, untrue, at best mere boys. I am speaking of
serious doubts which have arisen among those who are passionately engaged
in the arts. The role of the individual artist, in the business of making unique
objects for the purpose of giving pleasure and educating conscience and
sensibility, has repeatedly been called into question. Some literary intellectuals and artists have gone so far as to prophesy the ultimate demise of the
art-making activity of man. Art, in an automated scientific society, would be
unfunctional, useless.

But this conclusion, I should argue, is plainly unwarranted. Indeed, the   4
whole issue seems to me crudely put. For the question of "the two cultures"
assumes that science and technology are changing, in motion, while the arts
are static, fulfilling some perennial generic human function (consolation?
edification? diversion?). Only on the basis of this false assumption would
anyone reason that the arts might be in danger of becoming obsolete.

Art does not progress, in the sense that science and technology do. But   5
the arts do develop and change. For instance, in our own time, art is becoming
increasingly the terrain of specialists. The most interesting and creative art of
our time is *not* open to the generally educated; it demands special effort; it
speaks a specialized language. The music of Milton Babbitt and Morton
Feldman, the painting of Mark Rothko and Frank Stella, the dance of Merce
Cunningham and James Waring demand an education of sensibility whose
difficulties and length of apprenticeship are at least comparable to the difficulties of mastering physics or engineering. (Only the novel, among the arts,
at least in America, fails to provide similar examples.) The parallel between
the abstruseness of contemporary art and that of modern science is too
obvious to be missed. Another likeness to the scientific culture is the history-
mindedness of contemporary art. The most interesting works of contempo-

rary art are full of references to the history of the medium; so far as they comment on past art, they demand a knowledge of at least the recent past. As Harold Rosenberg has pointed out, contemporary paintings are themselves acts of criticism as much as of creation. The point could be made as well of much recent work in the films, music, the dance, poetry, and (in Europe) literature. Again, a similarity with the style of science—this time, with the accumulative aspect of science—can be discerned.

The conflict between "the two cultures" is in fact an illusion, a temporary phenomenon born of a period of profound and bewildering historical change. What we are witnessing is not so much a conflict of cultures as the creation of a new (potentially unitary) kind of sensibility. This new sensibility is rooted, as it must be, in *our* experience, experiences which are new in the history of humanity—in extreme social and physical mobility; in the crowdedness of the human scene (both people and material commodities multiplying at a dizzying rate); in the availability of new sensations such as speed (physical speed, as in airplane travel; speed of images, as in the cinema); and in the pan-cultural perspective on the arts that is possible through the mass reproduction of art objects.

What we are getting is not the demise of art, but a transformation of the function of art. Art, which arose in human society as a magical-religious operation, and passed over into a technique for depicting and commenting on secular reality, has in our own time arrogated to itself a new function—neither religious, nor serving a secularized religious function, nor merely secular or profane (a notion which breaks down when its opposite, the "religious" or "sacred," becomes obsolescent). Art today is a new kind of instrument, an instrument for modifying consciousness and organizing new modes of sensibility. And the means for practicing art have been radically extended. Indeed, in response to this new function (more felt than clearly articulated), artists have had to become self-conscious aestheticians: continually challenging their means, their materials and methods. Often, the conquest and exploitation of new materials and methods drawn from the world of "non-art"—for example, from industrial technology, from commercial processes and imagery, from purely private and subjective fantasies and dreams—seems to be the principal effort of many artists. Painters no longer feel themselves confined to canvas and paint, but employ hair, photographs, wax, sand, bicycle tires, their own toothbrushes and socks. Musicians have reached beyond the sounds of the traditional instruments to use tampered instruments and (usually on tape) synthetic sounds and industrial noises.

All kinds of conventionally accepted boundaries have thereby been challenged: not just the one between the "scientific" and the "literary-artistic" cultures, or the one between "art" and "non-art"; but also many established distinctions within the world of culture itself—that between form and content, the frivolous and the serious, and (a favorite of literary intellectuals) "high" and "low" culture.

The distinction between "high" and "low" (or "mass" or "popular") culture is based partly on an evaluation of the difference between unique and mass-produced objects. In an era of mass technological reproduction, the work of the serious artist had a special value simply because it was unique, because it bore his personal, individual signature. The works of popular culture (and even films were for a long time included in this category) were seen as having little value because they were manufactured objects, bearing no individual stamp—group concoctions made for an undifferentiated audience. But in the light of contemporary practice in the arts, this distinction appears extremely shallow. Many of the serious works of art of recent decades have a decidedly impersonal character. The work of art is reasserting its existence as "object" (even as manufactured or mass-produced object, drawing on the popular arts) rather than as "individual personal expression."

The exploration of the impersonal (and trans-personal) in contemporary 10 art is the new classicism; at least, a reaction against what is understood as the romantic spirit dominates most of the interesting art of today. Today's art, with its insistence on coolness, its refusal of what it considers to be sentimentality, its spirit of exactness, its sense of "research" and "problems," is closer to the spirit of science than of art in the old-fashioned sense. Often, the artist's work is only his idea, his concept. This is a familiar practice in architecture, of course. And one remembers that painters in the Renaissance often left parts of their canvases to be worked out by students, and that in the flourishing period of the concerto the cadenza at the end of the first movement was left to the inventiveness and discretion of the performing soloist. But similar practices have a different, more polemical meaning today, in the present post-romantic era of the arts. When painters such as Joseph Albers, Ellsworth Kelly, and Andy Warhol assign portions of the work, say, the painting in of the colors themselves, to a friend or the local gardener; when musicians such as Stockhausen, John Cage, and Luigi Nono invite collaboration from performers by leaving opportunities for random effects, switching around the order of the score, and improvisations—they are changing the ground rules which most of us employ to recognize a work of art. They are saying what art need not be. At least, not necessarily.

The primary feature of the new sensibility is that its model product is 11 not the literary work, above all, the novel. A new non-literary culture exists today, of whose very existence, not to mention significance, most literary intellectuals are entirely unaware. This new establishment includes certain painters, sculptors, architects, social planners, film-makers, TV technicians, neurologists, musicians, electronics engineers, dancers, philosophers, and sociologists. (A few poets and prose writers can be included.) Some of the basic texts for this new cultural alignment are to be found in the writings of Nietzsche, Wittgenstein, Antonin Artaud, C. S. Sherrington, Buckminster Fuller, Marshall McLuhan, John Cage, André Breton, Roland Barthes, Claude Lévi-Strauss, Siegfried Gidieon, Norman O. Brown, and Gyorgy Kepes.

Those who worry about the gap between "the two cultures," and this 12 means virtually all literary intellectuals in England and America, take for granted a notion of culture which decidedly needs reexamining. It is the notion perhaps best expressed by Matthew Arnold (in which the central cultural act is the making of literature, which is itself understood as the criticism of culture). Simply ignorant of the vital and enthralling (so called "avant-garde") developments in the other arts, and blinded by their personal investment in the perpetuation of the older notion of culture, they continue to cling to literature as the model for creative statement.

What gives literature its preeminence is its heavy burden of "content," 13 both reportage and moral judgment. (This makes it possible for most English and American literary critics to use literary works mainly as texts, or even pretexts, for social and cultural diagnosis—rather than concentrating on the properties of, say, a given novel or a play, as an art work.) But the model arts of our time are actually those with much less content, and a much cooler mode of moral judgment—like music, films, dance, architecture, painting, sculpture. The practice of these arts—all of which draw profusely, naturally, and without embarrassment, upon science and technology—are the locus of the new sensibility.

The problem of "the two cultures," in short, rests upon an uneducated, 14 uncontemporary grasp of our present cultural situation. It arises from the ignorance of literary intellectuals (and of scientists with a shallow knowledge of the arts, like the scientist-novelist C. P. Snow himself) of a new culture, and its emerging sensibility. In fact, there can be no divorce between science and technology, on the one hand, and art, on the other, any more than there can be a divorce between art and the forms of social life. Works of art, psychological forms, and social forms all reflect each other, and change with each other. But, of course, most people are slow to come to terms with such changes—especially today, when the changes are occurring with an unprecedented rapidity. Marshall McLuhan has described human history as a succession of acts of technological extension of human capacity, each of which works a radical change upon our environment and our ways of thinking, feeling, and valuing. The tendency, he remarks, is to upgrade the old environment into art form (thus Nature became a vessel of aesthetic and spiritual values in the new industrial environment) "while the new conditions are regarded as corrupt and degrading." Typically, it is only certain artists in any given era who "have the resources and temerity to live in immediate contact with the environment of their age. . . . That is why they may seem to be 'ahead of their time'. . . . More timid people prefer to accept the . . . previous environment's values as the continuing reality of their time. Our natural bias is to accept the new gimmick (automation, say) as a thing that can be accommodated in the old ethical order." Only in the terms of what McLuhan calls the old ethical order does the problem of "the two cultures" appear to be a genuine problem. It is not a problem for most of the creative artists of our time (among whom one could include very few novelists) because most of these artists have broken, whether they know it or not, with the Matthew Arnold notion of culture, finding it historically and humanly obsolescent.

The Matthew Arnold notion of culture defines art as the criticism of 15 life—this being understood as the propounding of moral, social, and political ideas. The new sensibility understands art as the extension of life—this being understood as the representation of (new) modes of vivacity. There is no necessary denial of the role of moral evaluation here. Only the scale has changed; it has become less gross, and what it sacrifices in discursive explicitness it gains in accuracy and subliminal power. For we are what we are able to see (hear, taste, smell, feel) even more powerfully and profoundly than we are what furniture of ideas we have stocked in our heads. Of course, the proponents of "the two cultures" crisis continue to observe a desperate contrast between unintelligible, morally neutral science and technology, on the one hand, and morally committed, human-scale art on the other. But matters are not that simple, and never were. A great work of art is never simply (or even mainly) a vehicle of ideas or of moral sentiments. It is, first of all, an object modifying our consciousness and sensibility, changing the composition, however slightly, of the humus that nourishes all specific ideas and sentiments. Outraged humanists, please note. There is no need for alarm. A work of art does not cease being a moment in the conscience of mankind, when moral conscience is understood as only one of the functions of consciousness.

Sensations, feelings, the abstract forms and styles of sensibility count. 16 It is to these that contemporary art addresses itself. The basic unit for contemporary art is not the idea, but the analysis of an extension of sensations. (Or if it is an "idea," it is about the form of sensibility.) Rilke described the artist as someone who works "toward an extension of the regions of the individual senses"; McLuhan calls artists "experts in sensory awareness." And the most interesting works of contemporary art (one can begin at least as far back as French symbolist poetry) are adventures in sensation, new "sensory mixes." Such art is, in principle, experimental—not out of an elitist disdain for what is accessible to the majority, but precisely in the sense that science is experimental. Such an art is also notably apolitical and undidactic, or, rather, infradidactic.

When Ortega y Gasset wrote his famous essay "The Dehumanization 17 of Art" in the early 1920s, he ascribed the qualities of modern art (such as impersonality, the ban on pathos, hostility to the past, playfulness, willful stylization, absence of ethical and political commitment) to the spirit of youth which he thought dominated our age.[1] In retrospect, it seems this "dehumanization" did not signify the recovery of childlike innocence, but was rather a very adult, knowing response. What other response than anguish, followed by anesthesia and then by wit and the elevating of intelligence over sentiment, is possible as a response to the social disorder and mass atrocities of our time, and—equally important for our sensibilities, but less often remarked on—to the unprecedented change in what rules our environment from the intelligible and visible to that which is only with difficulty intelligible, and is invisible? Art, which I have characterized as an instrument for modifying and educating sensibility and consciousness, now operates in an environment which cannot be grasped by the senses.

Buckminster Fuller has written: 18

In World War I industry suddenly went from the visible to the invisible base, from the track to the trackless, from the wire to the wireless, from visible structuring to invisible structuring in alloys. The big thing about World War I is that *man went off the sensorial spectrum forever* as the prime criterion of accrediting innovations. . . . All major advances since World War I have been in the *infra* and the *ultra* sensorial frequencies of the electromagnetic spectrum. All the important technical affairs of men today are invisible. . . . The old masters who were sensorialists, have unleashed a Pandora's box of non-sensorially controllable phenomena, which they had avoided accrediting up to that time. . . . Suddenly they lost their true mastery, because from then on they didn't personally understand what was going on. If you don't understand you cannot master. . . . Since World War I have old masters been extinct. . . .

But, of course, art remains permanently tied to the senses. Just as one 19 cannot float colors in space (a painter needs some sort of surface, like a canvas, however neutral and textureless), one cannot have a work of art that does not impinge upon the human sensorium. But it is important to realize that human sensory awareness has not merely a biology but a specific history, each culture placing a premium on certain senses and inhibiting others. (The same is true for the range of primary human emotions.) Here is where art (among other things) enters, and why the interesting art of our time has such a feeling of anguish and crisis about it, however playful and abstract and ostensibly neutral morally it may appear. Western man may be said to have been undergoing a massive sensory anesthesia (a concomitant of the process that Max Weber calls "bureaucratic rationalization") at least since the Industrial Revolution, with modern art functioning as a kind of shock therapy for both confounding and unclosing our senses.

One important consequence of the new sensibility (with its abandon- 20 ment of the Matthew Arnold idea of culture) has already been alluded to— namely, that the distinction between "high" and "low" culture seems less and less meaningful. For such a distinction—inseparable from the Matthew Arnold apparatus—simply does not make sense for a creative community of artists and scientists engaged in programming sensations, uninterested in art as a species of moral journalism. Art has always been more than that, anyway.

Another way of characterizing the present cultural situation, in its most 21 creative aspects, would be to speak of a new attitude toward pleasure. In one sense, the new art and the new sensibility take a rather dim view of pleasure. (The great contemporary French composer, Pierre Boulez, entitled an important essay of his twelve years ago, "Against Hedonism in Music.") The seriousness of modern art precludes pleasure in the familiar sense—the pleasure of a melody that one can hum after leaving the concert hall, of characters in a novel or play whom one can recognize, identify with, and dissect in terms of realistic psychological motives, of a beautiful landscape or a dramatic moment represented on a canvas. If hedonism means sustaining the old ways in which we have found pleasure in art (the old sensory and psychic modalities), then the new art is anti-hedonistic. Having one's sensorium challenged or stretched hurts. The new serious music hurts one's ears, the new painting does not graciously reward one's sight, the new films and the few interesting new prose works do not go down easily. The commonest complaint about the films of Antonioni or the narratives of Beckett or Burroughs is that they are hard to look at or to read, that they are "boring." But the charge of boredom is really hypocritical. There is, in a sense, no such thing as boredom. Boredom is only another name for a certain species of frustration. And the new languages which the interesting art of our time speaks are frustrating to the sensibilities of most educated people.

But the purpose of art is always, ultimately, to give pleasure—though   22 our sensibilities may take time to catch up with the forms of pleasure that art in a given time may offer. And, one can also say that, balancing the ostensible anti-hedonism of serious contemporary art, the modern sensibility is more involved with pleasure in the familiar sense than ever. Because the new sensibility demands less "content" in art, and is more open to the pleasures of "form" and style, it is also less snobbish, less moralistic—in that it does not demand that pleasure in art necessarily be associated with edification. If art is understood as a form of discipline of the feelings and a programming of sensations, then the feeling (or sensation) given off by a Rauschenberg painting might be like that of a song by the Supremes. The brio and elegance of Budd Boetticher's *The Rise and Fall of Legs Diamond* or the singing style of Dionne Warwick can be appreciated as a complex and pleasurable event. They are experienced without condescension.

This last point seems to me worth underscoring. For it is important to   23 understand that the affection which many younger artists and intellectuals feel for the popular arts is not a new philistinism (as has so often been charged) or a species of anti-intellectualism or some kind of abdication from culture. The fact that many of the most serious American painters, for example, are also fans of "the new sound" in popular music is *not* the result of the search for mere diversion or relaxation; it is not, say, like [the composer] Schoenberg also playing tennis. It reflects a new, more open way of looking at the world and at things in the world, our world. It does not mean the renunciation of all standards: there is plenty of stupid popular music, as well as inferior and pretentious "avant-garde" paintings, films, and music. The point is that there *are* new standards, new standards of beauty and style and taste. The new sensibility is defiantly pluralistic; it is dedicated both to an excruciating seriousness and to fun and wit and nostalgia. It is also extremely history-conscious; and the voracity of its enthusiasms (and of the supercession of these enthusiasms) is very high-speed and hectic. From the vantage point of this new sensibility, the beauty of a machine or of the solution to a mathematical problem, of a painting by Jasper Johns, of a film by Jean-Luc Godard, and of the personalities and music of the Beatles is equally accessible.

NOTE

Reference is Sontag's.

Ortega remarks, in this essay: "Were art to redeem man, it could do so only by saving him from the seriousness of life and restoring him to an unexpected boyishness."

Questions for Discussion

1. Modern artists, says Sontag, have "repeatedly called into question" art's role of "making unique objects for the purpose of giving pleasure and educating conscience and sensibility" (¶3). She makes it clear that the role of art thus defined is a *traditional* role and that the *modern* role of art is to be a "new kind of instrument, an instrument for modifying consciousness and organizing new sensibility" (¶7). Do you agree or disagree? Why? Do you agree or disagree that the two functions are mutually exclusive, as Sontag implies? Why?

2. In paragraph 10 Sontag characterizes modern art as "closer to the spirit of science than of art in the old-fashioned sense." Only the novel, she maintains, sticks to traditional modes, techniques, and content in the face of the other arts' ready embrace of new, technology-based techniques and a new, distanced view of content in favor of form. If she is right, can you think of any reasons that would explain the novel's loyalty to traditional modes of story-telling? Is it to the novel's credit or discredit that it has proven more resistant to "innovation" than the other arts? (In order to speculate about the answer to this question, you will of course have to make some kind of assumption about what you take the "job" of the novel to be.)

3. "[T]he model arts of our time are actually those with much less content, and much cooler mode of moral judgment [than literary texts]," says Sontag (¶13). What does she mean by a "cooler" mode of moral judgment? Cooler than what? Can you tell whether she thinks this is a good or bad feature of modern art? If she thinks a "cooler" mode of moral judgment is preferable, *why* does she seem to think so?

4. "The new sensibility understands art as the extension of life—this being understood as the representation of (new) modes of vivacity" because modern art understands that "we are what we are able to see (hear, taste, smell, feel) even more powerfully and profoundly than we are what furniture of ideas we have stocked in our heads" (¶15). Do you agree with the second part of this assertion, that we are what we are in consequence of being *bodies* more than having *ideas?* What reasons on either side can you present? What implications follow from either view for morality, for feeling, and for art?

5. The new sensibility, says Sontag, is "uninterested in art as a species of moral journalism" (¶20). Do you take this comment to be a depreciation of traditional art? Why or why not? If this comment is in fact an expression of contempt for traditional art, do you agree or disagree with it? Why or why not? When she immediately follows up the comment quoted here with the statement that "[a]rt has always been more than that, anyway," how would she define "more" and can you tell whether she means to place all moral concerns in art in the "lesser" category of "moral journalism"?

Suggested Essay Topics

1. Select your favorite art form—cinema, music, painting, sculpture, literature, or whatever—and compare two works within that form, one that you would call "traditional" and another that you would call "avant-garde." In an essay directed to Sontag, support or rebut her views about the "new sensibility" based on your "reading" of the art works you have chosen to compare.

2. Although Sontag seems very dismissive of traditional art's focus on content and moral judgment, particularly in the literary arts (calling Matthew Arnold's view of literature as a "criticism of life" nothing but "moral journalism"), it could be argued that her own program of art as "an instrument for modifying consciousness and organizing new modes of sensibility" (¶7) is itself an ethical program calling for moral judgment. If Sontag really believes that "we are what we are able to see (hear, taste, smell, feel) even more powerfully than we are what furniture of ideas we have stocked in our heads" (¶15), then it follows that works of art that powerfully influence what Sontag calls our *sensorium* powerfully influence *what we are*. This is ethical influence by anyone's definition. For the purposes of this essay, then, choose any powerful work of art from any medium and, in an essay directed to your fellow students, analyze, first, the way the work educates or modifies the sensibilities of the auditor, and, second, analyze the possible or potential long-range *effects* of such modifications.

Ideas in Debate

Plato
E.M. Forster
André Brink
Margaret Atwood

Plato

In The Republic, Plato *(c. 427–347
B.C.) constructs a series of long conversations between Socrates and some of his fellow
citizens. The time is about 450 B.C.; the place is Athens, center of Greek culture; and
the topic they are discussing is "justice" and how they would go about constructing
the best sort of society to achieve it. They are discussing, in other words, what an ideal
society would look like—how it would educate its citizens to live just and beautiful
lives, keep itself solvent, protect itself, administer its laws, and worship its gods. They
try to consider everything, in short, that the creators of a state would have to make
decisions about if they were to build it from the ground up.*

*The state they talk about is "ideal" not in the sense that it is sheer fantasy
or so outlandish that it bears no resemblance to the society everyone already knows.
Instead, their state is ideal in the sense that its creators are imagining themselves free
to make it without having to solve all the practical problems that would hit them if
they were to cast off their old state and start over. They do not have to deal, for example,
with people's resistance to change, people's fears of the unknown, or the disruptions
that would occur if established ways of doing things were suddenly abandoned.*

*One of the most important questions they discuss is how they should educate
the state's rulers—"guardians"—in their youth. In addressing this problem Socrates
pictures a committee of older guardians, all philosophers—that is, lovers of truth, not
professionals—setting out a curriculum for the younger guardians who will actually
conduct the day-to-day business of the state when they grow up. Socrates bases his
educational ideas on the assumption that the kind of training a society gives its youth
determines the kind of adults that society gets. This was not a novel idea even then,
but few thinkers have pursued its implications as thoroughly and vigorously as
Socrates.*

*It seems obvious to him that if education feeds both the mind and the character
of a society's youth, then only first-rate fare should be proffered to them. In trying to
decide what is first-rate, Socrates picks a quarrel with literature. Stories, he claims,
feed youth with lies that teach them to disrespect the gods and imitate the immoral
behavior of heroes in myths, legends, and poems. He recommends protecting youth from*

corrupt literature by state censorship. Judges are to decide on the acceptability of stories and poems before they are given to children to read.

Our selection opens where Socrates is just beginning to bare the heart of his argument.

CENSORSHIP

Our title for this portion of *The Republic,* book 2.

Then he who is to be a really good and noble guardian of the State will   1
require to unite in himself philosophy and spirit and swiftness and strength?
Undoubtedly.
Then we have found the desired natures; and now that we have found them, how are they to be reared and educated? Is not this an inquiry which may be expected to throw light on the greater inquiry which is our final end—How do justice and injustice grow up in States? For we do not want either to omit what is to the point or to draw out the argument to an inconvenient length.
Adeimantus thought that the inquiry would be of great service to us.   2
Then, I said, my dear friend, the task must not be given up, even if somewhat long.
Certainly not.
Come then, and let us pass a leisure hour in story-telling, and our story shall be the education of our heroes.
By all means.
And what shall be their education? It would be hard, I think, to find a better than the traditional system, which has two divisions, gymnastic for the body, and music for the soul.
True.
Presumably we shall begin education with music, before gymnastic can   3
begin.
By all means.
And when you speak of music, do you include literature or not?
I do.
And literature may be either true or false?
Yes.
Both have a part to play in education, but we must begin with the false?
I do not understand your meaning, he said.
You know, I said, that we begin by telling children stories which, though not wholly destitute of truth, are in the main fictitious; and these stories are told them when they are not of an age for gymnastics.
Very true.
That was my meaning when I said that we must teach music before gymnastics.
Quite right, he said.

You know also that the beginning is the most important part of any   4
work, especially in the case of a young and tender thing; for that is the time
at which the character is being formed and the desired impression is more
readily taken.

Quite true.

And shall we just carelessly allow children to hear any casual tales
which may be devised by casual persons, and to receive into their minds ideas
for the most part the very opposite of those which we shall wish them to have
when they are grown up?

We cannot.

Then the first thing will be to establish a censorship of the writers of   5
fiction, and let the censors receive any tale of fiction which is good, and reject
the bad; and we will persuade mothers and nurses to tell their children the
authorized ones only. Let them fashion the mind with such tales, even more
fondly than they mould the body with their hands; but most of those which
are now in use must be discarded.

Of what tales are you speaking? he said.

You may find a model of the lesser in the greater, I said; for they must
both be of the same type, and the same spirit ought to be found in both of
them.

Very likely, he replied; but I do not as yet know what you would term   6
the greater.

Those, I said, which are narrated by Homer and Hesiod, and the rest of
the poets, who have ever been the great story-tellers of mankind.

But which stories do you mean, he said; and what fault do you find with
them?

A fault which is fundamental and most serious, I said; the fault of saying
what is false, and doing so for no good purpose.

But when is this fault committed?

Whenever an erroneous representation is made of the nature of gods
and heroes,—as when a painter paints a picture not having the shadow of a
likeness to his subject.

Yes, he said, that sort of thing is certainly very blameable; but what are
the stories which you mean?

First of all, I said, there was that greatest of all falsehoods on great   7
subjects, which the misguided poet told about Uranus,—I mean what Hesiod
says that Uranus did, and how Cronus retaliated on him.* The doings of
Cronus, and the sufferings which in turn his son inflicted upon him, even if
they were true, ought certainly not to be lightly told to young and thoughtless
persons; if possible, they had better be buried in silence. But if there is an
absolute necessity for their mention, a chosen few might hear them in a
mystery, and they should sacrifice not a common pig, but some huge and

*Uranus, the first lord of the universe, is depicted as having thrown his children into Tartarus,
a dark pit under the earth. He was eventually attacked and defeated by Cronus, his youngest
but strongest son, who drove Uranus away with a sickle made by Uranus's wife, Gaea. Cronus
was in turn eventually dethroned by his son, Zeus.

unprocurable victim, so that the number of the hearers may be very few indeed.

Why, yes, said he, those stories are extremely objectionable.

Yes, Adeimantus, they are stories not to be repeated in our State; the young man should not be told that in committing the worst of crimes he is far from doing anything outrageous; and that even if he chastises in savage fashion his father when he does wrong, he will only be following the example of the first and greatest among the gods.

I entirely agree with you, he said; in my opinion those stories are quite unfit to be repeated.

Neither, if we mean our future guardians to regard the habit of lightly 8 quarrelling among themselves as of all things the basest, should any word be said to them of the wars in heaven, and of the plots and fightings of the gods against one another, for they are not true. No, we shall never mention the battles of the giants, or let them be embroidered on garments; and we shall be silent about the innumerable other quarrels of gods and heroes with their friends and relatives. If we intend to persuade them that quarrelling is unholy, and that never up to this time has there been any hatred between citizens, then the stories which old men and old women tell them as children should be in this strain; and when they grow up, the poets also should be obliged to compose for them in a similar spirit. But the narrative of Hephaestus binding Hera his mother, or how on another occasion his father sent him flying for taking her part when she was being beaten, and all the battles of the gods in Homer—these tales must not be admitted into our State, whether they are supposed to have an allegorical meaning or not. For a young person cannot judge what is allegorical and what is literal; anything that he receives into his mind at that age is likely to become indelible and unalterable; and therefore it is most important that the tales which the young first hear should be models of virtuous thoughts.

There you are right, he replied; but if anyone asks where are such 9 models to be found and of what tales are you speaking—how shall we answer him?

I said to him, You and I, Adeimantus, at this moment are not poets, but founders of a State: now the founders of a State ought to know the general forms in which poets should cast their tales, and the limits which must be observed by them, but to make the tales is not their business.

Very true, he said; but what are these forms of theology which you 10 mean?

Something of this kind, I replied:—God* is always to be represented as he truly is, whatever be the sort of poetry, epic, lyric or tragic, in which the representation is given.

Right.

And is he not truly good? And must he not be represented as such?

Certainly.

*See discussion question 4 on p. 315.

And no good thing is hurtful?

No, indeed.

And that which is not hurtful hurts not?

Certainly not.

And that which hurts not does no evil?

No.

And can that which does no evil be a cause of evil?

Impossible.

And the good is advantageous?

Yes.

And therefore the cause of well-being?

Yes.

It follows therefore that the good is not the cause of all things, but of those which are as they should be; and it is not to be blamed for evil.

Assuredly.

Then God, if he be good, is not the author of all things, as the many 11 assert, but he is the cause of a few things only, and not of most things that occur to men. For few are the goods of human life, and many are the evils, and the good is to be attributed to God alone; of the evils the causes are to be sought elsewhere, and not in him.

That appears to me to be most true, he said.

Then we must not listen to Homer or to any other poet who is guilty of the folly of saying that

> Two casks lie at the threshold of Zeus, full of lots, one of good, the
> other of evil lots;

and that he to whom Zeus gives a mixture of the two

> Sometimes meets with evil fortune, at other times with good;

but that he to whom is given the cup of unmingled ill,

> Him wild hunger drives o'er the beauteous earth.

And again—

> Zeus, who is the dispenser of good and evil to us.

And if anyone asserts that the violation of oaths and treaties, which was really the work of Pandarus, was brought about by Athena and Zeus, or that the strife and competition between the gods was instigated by Themis and Zeus, he shall not have our approval; neither will we allow our young men to hear the words of Aeschylus, that

> God plants guilt among men when he desires utterly to destroy a house.

And if a poet writes of the sufferings of Niobe—the subject of the 12
tragedy in which these iambic verses occur—or of the house of Pelops, or of
the Trojan war or on any similar theme, either we must not permit him to
say that these are the works of God, or if they are of God, he must devise
some explanation of them such as we are seeking: he must say that God did
what was just and right, and they were the better for being punished. But that
those who are punished are miserable, and that God is the author of their
misery—the poet is not to be permitted to say; though he may say that the
wicked were miserable because they required to be punished, and were benefited by receiving punishment from God; but that God being good is the
author of evil to anyone is to be denied. We shall insist that it is not said or
sung or heard in verse or prose by anyone whether old or young in any
well-ordered commonwealth. Such a fiction would be impious, disastrous to
us, and inconsistent with itself.

I agree with you, he replied, and am ready to give my assent to the law.

Questions for Discussion

1. In the poems and legends Socrates refers to in paragraphs 6–8, Greek
   heroes and gods are often shown behaving out of greed, spite, envy,
   jealousy, disrespect, and pride—almost the whole range of human vices.
   Do you think Socrates is right in saying that young people will more likely
   commit vices themselves if they have "seen" them committed by gods and
   heroes in stories?

2. Socrates advances his argument about literature and character by means
   of an analogy with food and health. (For references to analogy, see the
   Rhetorical Index.) Can you state the analogy? Do you agree with it? Are
   feminists and minority representatives using this same analogy when they
   object to the moral effects of stories in which women, say, or blacks are
   depicted in demeaning ways? Do *you* object to such stories? On what
   grounds? Can you provide examples for class discussion?

3. If you accept Socrates' analogy and thus accept his definition of the problem, do you also accept his solution? Do you think that censorship is (1)
   a desirable solution or (2) a workable solution? In thinking about censorship, consider these questions:
   a. What is the possibility that the apparatus of censorship (committees,
      police, courts, suits, countersuits, and so on) might threaten the health
      of the state more than bad literature?
   b. Who is going to keep the censors pure? What happens if they need
      censoring? Who decides?
   c. How can a society be sure that its censors will never make a mistake?

   d. How does a society blend all the competing standards for purity into one workable set of guidelines?

   e. Does free discussion disappear in a censored society?

   f. What happens to artistic expression in a censored society? (What about art in Nazi Germany or the Soviet Union under Stalin, Khrushchev, and Brezhnev? If no one in your class knows anything about such art, you might elect a committee to look into it and prepare a report for the rest of the class.)

4. In Benjamin Jowett's translation of Plato, from which we have excerpted the selections by Plato in this book, you will notice that both the terms *God* and *the gods* are used. Such terms cause problems in all translations, not only because of their inherent ambiguities but because they carry so many different meanings for modern readers. We should therefore be alert to probe *possible* meanings rather than settling on one meaning that the words have had for us in other contexts. The warning may be especially important in reading Plato. Francis Cornford, in his preface to his translation of *The Republic,* says, "Some authors can be translated almost word for word. . . . This method cannot do justice to the matter and the manner of Plato's discourse. . . . Many key-words, such as 'music,' 'gymnastic,' 'virtue,' 'philosophy,' have shifted their meaning or acquired false associations for English ears." Cornford tells us that Plato "uses the singular 'god' and the plural 'the gods' with an indifference startling to the modern monotheist," and in his translation he avoids the form *God* entirely, in the belief that there is no notion in Plato quite like what is suggested to most modern readers by the term.

    If no one in your class knows ancient Greek to assist in discussing the possible meanings of *God* and *the gods* in this selection, some students might be given the special assignment of consulting two or three other standard translations—the Paul Shorey translation in the Loeb Classical Library series, for example, or the Cornford translation. They could then photocopy the passages about *God* and *the gods,* or other troublesome passages, and bring them to class.

    You may be shocked by the differences you find. Are they so great that they make reading the translations useless? What sorts of advice can you give yourself about reading other translations, on the basis of what you have found in comparing these translations?

Suggested Essay Topics

1. Clearly, Socrates is concerned about the moral influence of models that children meet in the stories they read. If children see Greek gods and heroes misbehaving, they will bend, like pliant plants, in those directions without realizing what is happening to them.

    Write an essay directed to a group of parents warning them that some of the models held out to children today are objectionable on the grounds given by Socrates. (You might watch some kids' programs, such as Saturday morning cartoons, in order to make your argument concrete and detailed.) Your purpose is to make a case, with illustrative examples, that the visual models children see on television are "bad" for them. You will, of course, have to say what you mean by *bad* and explain how important the problem is for society as a whole.

2. Read through a group of children's books in the library. Do you find material that you object to? Are there demeaning or stereotypical portrayals of minority groups, women, children, immigrants, or others? Try to find some old books from the late 1940s or early 1950s. Do you notice any difference between the depictions of stereotyped groups in older books as compared to more recent ones?

   If you find offensive material, choose an appropriate audience (your parents, the books' publishers, a grade-school teacher, etc.) and write an essay showing why the books you name are not good reading fare for young children. Be specific: Indicate why you find the material objectionable; indicate the ages you think make sensible cutoff points for parental or school supervision of youngsters' reading; say whether you think supervision ought to include actual censorship; and, if so, say why you accept censoring children's reading but not that of adults.

Plato

Many pages after Socrates has laid out his argument in The Republic *for censoring the reading of youngsters (his argument in the preceding selection), he again picks up his quarrel with literature. This time he attacks even more strongly, for he not only repeats his claims about the immoral influence of many kinds of literature but widens his argument to include most other kinds of representative art as well. For him the examples from literature, painting, and statuary are all interchangeable because they are all "imitations." The problem with imitations, we learn, is that they lead one away from truth by portraying shallow surfaces, not deep realities. Many readers have agreed with his earlier argument about the effects of literature on youngsters—witness the steady stream of criticism against the images that children are exposed to on television every day—but his later argument has proved harder to accept or even understand.*

His criticisms boil down to three main points. First, literature is inescapably entangled with falsehoods because it imitates appearances only, not underlying realities. Second, literature is not really useful in any significant way: poems and dramas, for example, do not make legislators more wise or generals more courageous. Third, literature constantly excites the weaker parts of human nature—the passions generally, but especially our fear of suffering—and thus undermines the strength of our nobler parts, reason and self-control. All three criticisms combine to make a serious charge about the immoral effects of most literature and to justify Socrates' claim that these bad effects should be prevented by state-enforced censorship.

Since all present-day concerns about the moral effects of literature (including television, movies, or dramas) ultimately echo Socrates' moral concerns, reading The Republic *carefully will provide insight into one of the most enduring debates in our history.*

THE SEDUCTIONS OF ART

Our title for this portion of *The Republic,* book 10.

Of the many excellences which I perceive in the order of our State, there   1
is none which upon reflection pleases me better than the rule about poetry.

To what do you refer?

To our refusal to admit the imitative kind of poetry, for it certainly ought not to be received; as I see far more clearly now that the parts of the soul have been distinguished.

What do you mean?

Speaking in confidence, for you will not denounce me to the tragedians and the rest of the imitative tribe, all poetical imitations are ruinous to the understanding of the hearers, unless as an antidote they possess the knowledge of the true nature of the originals.

Explain the purport of your remark.

Well, I will tell you, although I have always from my earliest youth had   2
an awe and love of Homer which even now makes the words falter on my lips, for he seems to be the great captain and teacher of the whole of that noble tragic company; but a man is not to be reverenced more than the truth, and therefore I will speak out.

Very good, he said.

Listen to me then, or rather, answer me.

Put your question.

Can you give me a general definition of imitation? For I really do not myself understand what it professes to be.

A likely thing, then, that I should know.

There would be nothing strange in that, for the duller eye may often see a thing sooner than the keener.

Very true, he said; but in your presence, even if I had any faint notion, I could not muster courage to utter it. Will you inquire yourself?

Well then, shall we begin the inquiry at this point, following our   3
usual method: Whenever a number of individuals have a common name, we assume that there is one corresponding idea or form:—do you understand me?

I do.

Let us take, for our present purpose, any instance of such a group; there are beds and tables in the world—many of each, are there not?

Yes.

But there are only two ideas or forms of such furniture—one the idea of a bed, the other of a table.

True.

And the maker of either of them makes a bed or he makes a table for our use, in accordance with the idea—that is our way of speaking in this and similar instances—but no artificer makes the idea itself: how could he?

Impossible.

And there is another artificer,—I should like to know what you would   4 say of him.

Who is he?

One who is the maker of all the works of all other workmen.

What an extraordinary man!

Wait a little, and there will be more reason for your saying so. For this is the craftsman who is able to make not only furniture of every kind, but all that grows out of the earth, and all living creatures, himself included; and besides these he can make earth and sky and the gods, and all the things which are in heaven or in the realm of Hades under the earth.

He must be a wizard and no mistake.

Oh! you are incredulous, are you? Do you mean that there is no such maker or creator, or that in one sense there might be a maker of all these things but in another not? Do you see that there is a way in which you could make them all yourself?

And what way is this? he asked.

An easy way enough; or rather, there are many ways in which the feat   5 might be quickly and easily accomplished, none quicker than that of turning a mirror round and round—you would soon enough make the sun and the heavens, and the earth and yourself, and other animals and plants, and furniture and all the other things of which we were just now speaking, in the mirror.

Yes, he said; but they would be appearances only.

Very good, I said, you are coming to the point now. And the painter too is, as I conceive, just such another—a creator of appearances, is he not?

Of course.

But then I suppose you will say that what he creates is untrue. And yet   6 there is a sense in which the painter also creates a bed? Is there not?

Yes, he said, but here again, an appearance only.

And what of the maker of the bed? Were you not saying that he too makes, not the idea which according to our view is the real object denoted by the word bed, but only a particular bed?

Yes, I did.

Then if he does not make a real object he cannot make what *is*, but only some semblance of existence; and if any one were to say that the work of the maker of the bed, or of any other workman, has real existence, he could hardly be supposed to be speaking the truth.

Not, at least, he replied, in the view of those who make a business of these discussions.

No wonder, then, that his work too is an indistinct expression of truth.

No wonder.

Suppose now that by the light of the examples just offered we inquire who this imitator is?

If you please.

Well then, here we find three beds: one existing in nature, which is made by God, as I think that we may say—for no one else can be the maker?   7

No one, I think.

There is another which is the work of the carpenter?

Yes.

And the work of the painter is a third?

Yes.

Beds, then, are of three kinds, and there are three artists who superintend them: God, the maker of the bed, and the painter?

Yes, there are three of them.

God, whether from choice or from necessity, made one bed in nature and one only; two or more such beds neither ever have been nor ever will be made by God.

Why is that?

Because even if He had made but two, a third would still appear behind them of which they again both possessed the form, and that would be the real bed and not the two others.

Very true, he said.

God knew this, I suppose, and He desired to be the real maker of a real   8 bed, not a kind of maker of a kind of bed, and therefore He created a bed which is essentially and by nature one only.

So it seems.

Shall we, then, speak of Him as the natural author or maker of the bed?

Yes, he replied; inasmuch as by the natural process of creation He is the author of this and of all other things.

And what shall we say of the carpenter—is not he also the maker of a bed?

Yes.

But would you call the painter an artificer and maker?

Certainly not.

Yet if he is not the maker, what is he in relation to the bed?

I think, he said, that we may fairly designate him as the imitator of that which the others make.

Good, I said; then you call him whose product is third in the descent from nature, an imitator?

Certainly, he said.

And so if the tragic poet is an imitator, he too is thrice removed from   9
the king and from the truth; and so are all other imitators.

That appears to be so.

Then about the imitator we are agreed. And what about the painter?—
Do you think he tries to imitate in each case that which originally exists in
nature, or only the creations of artificers?

The latter.

As they are or as they appear? You have still to determine this.

What do you mean?

I mean to ask whether a bed really becomes different when it is seen
from different points of view, obliquely or directly or from any other point
of view? Or does it simply appear different, without being really so? And the
same of all things.

Yes, he said, the difference is only apparent.

Now let me ask you another question: Which is the art of painting
designed to be—an imitation of things as they are, or as they appear—of
appearance or of reality?

Of appearance, he said.

Then the imitator is a long way off the truth, and can reproduce all   10
things because he lightly touches on a small part of them, and that part an
image. For example: A painter will paint a cobbler, carpenter, or any other
artisan, though he knows nothing of their arts; and, if he is a good painter,
he may deceive children or simple persons when he shows them his picture
of a carpenter from a distance, and they will fancy that they are looking at
a real carpenter.

Certainly.

And surely, my friend, this is how we should regard all such claims:
whenever any one informs us that he has found a man who knows all the
arts, and all things else that anybody knows, and every single thing with a
higher degree of accuracy than any other man—whoever tells us this, I think
that we can only retort that he is a simple creature who seems to have been
deceived by some wizard or imitator whom he met, and whom he thought
all-knowing, because he himself was unable to analyse the nature of knowledge and ignorance and imitation.

Most true.

And next, I said, we have to consider tragedy and its leader, Homer; for   11
we hear some persons saying that these poets know all the arts; and all things
human; where virtue and vice are concerned, and indeed all divine things too;
because the good poet cannot compose well unless he knows his subject, and
he who has not this knowledge can never be a poet. We ought to consider
whether here also there may not be a similar illusion. Perhaps they may have
come across imitators and been deceived by them; they may not have remembered when they saw their works that these were thrice removed from the
truth, and could easily be made without any knowledge of the truth, because

they are appearances only and not realities? Or, after all, they may be in the right, and good poets do really know the things about which they seem to the many to speak so well?

The question, he said, should by all means be considered.   12

Now do you suppose that if a person were able to make the original as well as the image, he would seriously devote himself to the image-making branch? Would he allow imitation to be the ruling principle of his life, as if he had nothing higher in him?

I should say not.

But the real artist, who had real knowledge of those things which he chose also to imitate, would be interested in realities and not in imitations; and would desire to leave as memorials of himself works many and fair; and, instead of being the author of encomiums, he would prefer to be the theme of them.

Yes, he said, that would be to him a source of much greater honour and profit.

Now let us refrain, I said, from calling Homer or any other poet to   13 account regarding those arts to which his poems incidentally refer: we will not ask them, in case any poet has been a doctor and not a mere imitator of medical parlance, to show what patients have been restored to health by a poet, ancient or modern, as they were by Asclepius; or what disciples in medicine a poet has left behind him, like the Asclepiads. Nor shall we press the same question upon them about the other arts. But we have a right to know respecting warfare, strategy, the administration of States and the education of man, which are the chiefest and noblest subjects of his poems, and we may fairly ask him about them. "Friend Homer," then we say to him, "if you are only in the second remove from truth in what you say of virtue, and not in the third—not an image maker, that is, by our definition, an imitator— and if you are able to discern what pursuits make men better or worse in private or public life, tell us what State was ever better governed by your help? The good order of Lacedaemon is due to Lycurgus, and many other cities great and small have been similarly benefited by others; but who says that you have been a good legislator to them and have done them any good? Italy and Sicily boast of Charondas, and there is Solon who is renowned among us; but what city has anything to say about you?" Is there any city which he might name?

I think not, said Glaucon; not even the Homerids themselves pretend that he was a legislator.

. . .

The poet with his words and phrases may be said to lay on the colours   14 of the several arts, himself understanding their nature only enough to imitate them; and other people, who are as ignorant as he is, and judge only from his words, imagine that if he speaks of cobbling, or of military tactics, or of anything else, in metre and harmony and rhythm, he speaks very well—such is the sweet influence which melody and rhythm by nature have. For I am

sure that you know what a poor appearance the works of poets make when
stripped of the colours which art puts upon them, and recited in simple prose.
You have seen some examples?

Yes, he said.   15

They are like faces which were never really beautiful, but only bloom-
ing, seen when the bloom of youth has passed away from them?

Exactly.

Come now, and observe this point: The imitator or maker of the image
knows nothing, we have said, of true existence; he knows appearances only.
Am I not right?

Yes.

Then let us have a clear understanding, and not be satisfied with half
an explanation.

Proceed.

Of the painter we say that he will paint reins, and he will paint a bit?
Yes.

And the worker in leather and brass will make them?
Certainly.

But does the painter know the right form of the bit and reins? Nay,   16
hardly even the workers in brass and leather who make them; only the
horseman who knows how to use them—he knows their right form.

Most true.

And may we not say the same of all things?
What?

That there are three arts which are concerned with all things: one which
uses, another which makes, a third which imitates them?

Yes.

And the excellence and beauty and rightness of every structure, animate
or inanimate, and of every action of man, is relative solely to the use for which
nature or the artist has intended them.

True.

Then beyond doubt it is the user who has the greatest experience of   17
them, and he must report to the maker the good or bad qualities which
develop themselves in use; for example, the flute-player will tell the flute-
maker which of his flutes is satisfactory to the performer; he will tell him how
he ought to make them, and the other will attend to his instructions?

Of course.

So the one pronounces with knowledge about the goodness and badness   18
of flutes, while the other, confiding in him, will make them accordingly?

True.

The instrument is the same, but about the excellence or badness of it
the maker will possess a correct belief, since he associates with one who
knows, and is compelled to hear what he has to say; whereas the user will
have knowledge?

True.

But will the imitator have either? Will he know from use whether or no that which he paints is correct or beautiful? or will he have right opinion from being compelled to associate with another who knows and gives him instructions about what he should paint?

Neither.

Then an imitator will no more have true opinion than he will have [19] knowledge about the goodness or badness of his models?

I suppose not.

The imitative poet will be in a brilliant state of intelligence about the theme of his poetry?

Nay, very much the reverse.

And still he will go on imitating without knowing what makes a thing good or bad, and may be expected therefore to imitate only that which appears to be good to the ignorant multitude?

Just so.

Thus far then we are pretty well agreed that the imitator has no knowledge worth mentioning of what he imitates.

. . .

But we have not yet brought forward the heaviest count in our accusa- [20] tion:—the power which poetry has of harming even the good (and there are very few who are not harmed), is surely an awful thing?

Yes, certainly, if the effect is what you say.

Hear and judge: The best of us, as I conceive, when we listen to a passage of Homer or one of the tragedians, in which he represents some hero who is drawling out his sorrows in a long oration, or singing, and smiting his breast— the best of us, you know, delight in giving way to sympathy, and are in raptures at the excellence of the poet who stirs our feelings most.

Yes, of course I know.

But when any sorrow of our own happens to us, then you may observe [21] that we pride ourselves on the opposite quality—we would fain be quiet and patient; this is considered the manly part, and the other which delighted us in the recitation is now deemed to be the part of a woman.

Very true, he said.

Now can we be right in praising and admiring another who is doing that which any one of us would abominate and be ashamed of in his own person?

No, he said, that is certainly not reasonable.

Nay, I said, quite reasonable from one point of view.

What point of view?

If you consider, I said, that when in misfortune we feel a natural hunger [22] and desire to relieve our sorrow by weeping and lamentation, and that this very feeling which is starved and suppressed in our own calamities is satisfied and delighted by the poets;—the better nature in each of us, not having been sufficiently trained by reason or habit, allows the sympathetic element to break loose because the sorrow is another's; and the spectator fancies that there can be no disgrace to himself in praising and pitying any one who while professing to be a brave man, gives way to untimely lamentation; he thinks that the pleasure is a gain, and is far from wishing to lose it by rejection of the whole poem. Few persons ever reflect, as I should imagine, that the contagion must pass from others to themselves. For the pity which has been nourished and strengthened in the misfortunes of others is with difficulty repressed in our own.

How very true!

And does not the same hold also of the ridiculous? There are jests which 23 you would be ashamed to make yourself, and yet on the comic stage, or indeed in private, when you hear them, you are greatly amused by them, and are not at all disgusted at their unseemliness;—the case of pity is repeated;— there is a principle in human nature which is disposed to raise a laugh, and this, which you once restrained by reason because you were afraid of being thought a buffoon, is now let out again; and having stimulated the risible faculty at the theatre, you are betrayed unconsciously to yourself into playing the comic poet at home.

Quite true, he said.

And the same may be said of lust and anger and all the other affections, 24 of desire and pain and pleasure, which are held to be inseparable from every action—in all of them poetry has a like effect; it feeds and waters the passions instead of drying them up; she lets them rule, although they ought to be controlled if mankind are ever to increase in happiness and virtue.

I cannot deny it.

Therefore, Glaucon, I said, whenever you meet with any of the eulogists 25 of Homer declaring that he has been the educator of Hellas, and that he is profitable for education and for the ordering of human things, and that you should take him up again and again and get to know him and regulate your whole life according to him, we may love and honour those who say these things—they are excellent people, as far as their lights extend; and we are ready to acknowledge that Homer is the greatest of poets and first of tragedy writers; but we must remain firm in our conviction that hymns to the gods and praises of famous men are the only poetry which ought to be admitted into our State.

Questions for Discussion

1. Is it true that artists, whether they paint imitations in colors or in words, are only dealing in appearances, not reality? Doesn't this depend on how one defines the artist's real object of imitation? Would you say that a writer of short stories or movie scripts, for example, imitates only the appearances of human conduct and feeling or imitates instead the eternal, "real" qualities in human nature? To argue the issue, pick an example of a short story or movie that almost everyone in class knows.

2. If most art deals only with superficial appearances, how can one account

for the facts (a) that art is found in all cultures, (b) that works of art are among the most treasured artifacts any culture possesses, and (c) that some works of art, such as those of Shakespeare and Homer, are found to be interesting to large numbers of readers, generation after generation, century after century, despite large shifts in language, society, and style?

3. Is it fair for Socrates to take it as an argument against literature that poems never helped a ruler govern a state (¶13)? Cannot the same thing be said of music, chess, football, fashions, fishing, senior proms, sky diving, and a thousand other activities that human beings devote invention, time, energy, and money to? Is art in some way more significant—and potentially more dangerous—than these other leisure-time activities? Would these things also have to be outlawed in an ideal state?

4. What would it be like to live in a world without art of any kind? (In thinking about such a condition, it is helpful to use a very broad definition of *art,* including all the "entertainment" that "imitates" life—even computer games and Lazer Tag.)

Suggested Essay Topics

1. In paragraph 24 Socrates says that poetry "feeds and waters the passions instead of drying them up; she lets them rule, although they ought to be controlled. . . ." Pick a literary work (or television program, movie, or play) that you think either supports or contradicts this assertion. Write an essay directed to the class explaining whether the work whips up the passions and whether you agree with Socrates that this is a bad thing.

2. A variation on topic 1: If you are familiar with any pornographic works, pick a vivid one and write an essay to your fellow students arguing either that Socrates' assertion about the passions provides a useful way of attacking the moral effects of pornography or that Socrates is wrong because pornography has the socially beneficial effect of releasing potentially destructive passions rather than whipping them up. If you take the latter option, explain why you think pornography decreases rather than increases the passions.

E. M. Forster

For the same reason that a flute is almost always less noticeable in a symphony than a trumpet, writers like E. M. Forster (1879–1970) almost always sound less interesting when placed in direct debate with writers like Plato. Plato stands out. He has brilliance, vividness, cleverness, and polish. E. M. Forster is quiet. His mind is subtle, and he shades his meanings delicately. When he says, for example, that the artist "legislates through creating. And he creates through his sensitiveness and his power to impose form" (¶13), he hasn't given us a quotable nugget, a philosophical analogy, or made us laugh. But he has made us think. Like

Plato, Forster has staying power because he deals intelligently with interesting ideas. The more closely a reader attends to Forster, the more rewards he yields.

The phrase "art for art's sake" emerged toward the end of the nineteenth century as a kind of slogan or battle cry. It was at first used primarily by avant-garde artists and critics who wanted to free art from all non-artistic standards and goals. They opposed the idea that art should ever try—or be asked to try—to teach moral truths, improve the world, or take positions about history, politics, or religion. Art, they insisted, exists only for itself. Its purpose is to achieve beauty, not to soil its aesthetic purity by embracing the world's coarseness or getting caught up in its controversies. The extremists in this group felt that art was the only goal worth pursuing in life, that art was the only dimension of life worth full respect and effect.

But not everyone who defended "art for art's sake" was an extremist. Forster's views about art fall somewhere between those hard heads who argue that works of imagination are valueless in a scientific and industrial world, and the self-conscious aesthetes of the late nineteenth century (such as Oscar Wilde and James Whistler) who liked to shock the middle classes by sometimes claiming that art is the only thing that matters in life. Precisely where he falls between these two positions you must decide for yourself, but it is clear that Forster thinks art serves a valuable function beyond mere aesthetic beauty. It may be that art can only serve larger ends through its beauty— rather than through direct argument, say—but if beauty is a totally self-reflexive quality, if it produces nothing beyond itself and has no consequences in the real world, then its elevation to a position of supreme importance is not likely to be taken seriously by many people. Artists themselves, in fact, are often eager for their works to be viewed as truthful or profound, not merely beautiful. Try to determine as precisely as you can Forster's views about the ends that art serves and its means of serving them. If art serves its own ends but in doing so also serves other ends, what are they? Are these other ends served directly or indirectly? And most important, are these other ends merely incidental, or are they essential? If the latter, why are they essential, and for whom?

ART FOR ART'S SAKE

An address delivered before the American Academy of Arts and Letters in New York, 1949, and published in *Two Cheers for Democracy* (1951).

I believe in art for art's sake. It is an unfashionable belief, and some of my   1
statements must be of the nature of an apology. Fifty years ago I should have
faced you with more confidence. A writer or a speaker who chose "Art for Art's
Sake" for his theme fifty years ago could be sure of being in the swim, and
could feel so confident of success that he sometimes dressed himself in esthetic
costumes suitable to the occasion—in an embroidered dressing gown, perhaps,
or a blue velvet suit with a Lord Fauntleroy collar; or a toga, or a kimono, and
carried a poppy or a lily or a long peacock's feather in his medieval hand.*

---

*The aesthetes, a group of mostly young men and women in the arts who captured a lot of public attention at the turn of the century, were noted (like the rebellious youth groups of the 1960s) for dressing extravagantly.

Times have changed. Not thus can I present either myself or my theme today. My aim rather is to ask you quietly to reconsider for a few minutes a phrase which has been much misused and much abused, but which has, I believe, great importance for us—has, indeed, eternal importance.

Now we can easily dismiss those peacock's feathers and other affecta-   2
tions—they are but trifles—but I want also to dismiss a more dangerous heresy, namely the silly idea that only art matters, an idea which has some-how got mixed up with the idea of art for art's sake, and has helped to discredit it. Many things, besides art, matter. It is merely one of the things that matter, and high though the claims are that I make for it, I want to keep them in proportion. No one can spend his or her life entirely in the creation or the appreciation of masterpieces. Man lives, and ought to live, in a complex world, full of conflicting claims, and if we simplified them down into the esthetic he would be sterilised. Art for art's sake does not mean that only art matters, and I would also like to rule out such phrases as "The Life of Art," "Living for Art," and "Art's High Mission." They confuse and mislead.

What does the phrase mean? Instead of generalising, let us take a spe-   3
cific instance—Shakespeare's *Macbeth,* for example, and pronounce the words, *"Macbeth* for *Macbeth's* sake." What does that mean? Well, the play has several aspects—it is educational, it teaches us something about legend-ary Scotland, something about Jacobean England, and a good deal about human nature and its perils. We can study its origins, and study and enjoy its dramatic technique and the music of its diction. All that is true. But *Macbeth* is furthermore a world of its own, created by Shakespeare and ex-isting in virtue of its own poetry. It is in this aspect *Macbeth* for *Macbeth's* sake, and that is what I intend by the phrase "art for art's sake." A work of art—whatever else it may be—is a self-contained entity, with a life of its own imposed on it by its creator. It has internal order. It may have external form. That is how we recognise it.

Take for another example that picture of Seurat's which I saw two years   4
ago in Chicago—*"La Grande Jatte."* Here again there is much to study and to enjoy: the pointillism, the charming face of the seated girl, the nineteenth-century Parisian Sunday sunlight, the sense of motion in immobility. But here again there is something more; *"La Grande Jatte"* forms a world of its own, created by Seurat and existing by virtue of its own poetry: *"La Grande Jatte" pour "La Grande Jatte": l'art pour l'art.* Like *Macbeth* it has internal order and internal life.

It is to the conception of order that I would now turn. This is important   5
to my argument, and I want to make a digression, and glance at order in daily life, before I come to order in art.

In the world of daily life, the world which we perforce inhabit, there   6
is much talk about order, particularly from statesmen and politicians. They tend, however, to confuse order with orders, just as they confuse creation with regulations. Order, I suggest, is something evolved from within, not something imposed from without; it is an internal stability, a vital harmony,

and in the social and political category, it has never existed except for the convenience of historians. Viewed realistically, the past is really a series of *dis*orders, succeeding one another by discoverable laws, no doubt, and certainly marked by an increasing growth of human interference, but disorders all the same. So that, speaking as a writer, what I hope for today is a disorder which will be more favourable to artists than is the present one, and which will provide them with fuller inspirations and better material conditions. It will not last—nothing lasts—but there have been some advantageous disorders in the past—for instance, in ancient Athens, in Renaissance Italy, eighteenth-century France, periods in China and Persia—and we may do something to accelerate the next one. But let us not again fix our hearts where true joys are not to be found. We were promised a new order after the first world war through the League of Nations. It did not come, nor have I faith in present promises, by whomsoever endorsed. The implacable offensive of Science forbids. We cannot reach social and political stability for the reason that we continue to make scientific discoveries and to apply them, and thus to destroy the arrangements which were based on more elementary discoveries. If Science would discover rather than apply—if, in other words, men were more interested in knowledge than in power—mankind would be in a far safer position, the stability statesmen talk about would be a possibility, there could be a new order based on vital harmony, and the earthly millennium might approach. But Science shows no signs of doing this: she gave us the internal combustion engine, and before we had digested and assimilated it with terrible pains into our social system, she harnessed the atom, and destroyed any new order that seemed to be evolving. How can man get into harmony with his surroundings when he is constantly altering them? The future of our race is, in this direction, more unpleasant than we care to admit, and it has sometimes seemed to me that its best chance lies through apathy, uninventiveness, and inertia. Universal exhaustion might promote that Change of Heart which is at present so briskly recommended from a thousand pulpits. Universal exhaustion would certainly be a new experience. The human race has never undergone it, and is still too perky to admit that it may be coming and might result in a sprouting of new growth through the decay.

I must not pursue these speculations any further—they lead me too far 7 from my terms of reference and maybe from yours. But I do want to emphasize that order in daily life and in history, order in the social and political category, is unattainable under our present psychology.

Where is it attainable? Not in the astronomical category, where it was 8 for many years enthroned. The heavens and the earth have become terribly alike since Einstein. No longer can we find a reassuring contrast to chaos in the night sky and look up with George Meredith to the stars, the army of unalterable law,* or listen for the music of the spheres. Order is not there. In the entire universe there seem to be only two possibilities for it. The first of them—which again lies outside my terms of reference—is the divine order,

*An allusion to George Meredith's poem "Lucifer by Starlight."

the mystic harmony, which according to all religions is available for those who can contemplate it. We must admit its possibility, on the evidence of the adepts, and we must believe them when they say that it is attained, if attainable, by prayer. "O thou who changest not, abide with me," said one of its poets. *"Ordina questo amor, o tu che m'ami,"* said another: "Set love in order, thou who lovest me." The existence of a divine order, though it cannot be tested, has never been disproved.

The second possibility for order lies in the esthetic category, which is   9
my subject here: the order which an artist can create in his own work, and to that we must now return. A work of art, we are all agreed, is a unique product. But why? It is unique not because it is clever or noble or beautiful or enlightened or original or sincere or idealistic or useful or educational—it may embody any of those qualities—but because it is the only material object in the universe which may possess internal harmony. All the others have been pressed into shape from outside, and when their mold is removed they collapse. The work of art stands up by itself, and nothing else does. It achieves something which has often been promised by society, but always delusively. Ancient Athens made a mess—but the *Antigone* stands up. Renaissance Rome made a mess—but the ceiling of the Sistine got painted. James I made a mess—but there was *Macbeth.* Louis XIV—but there was *Phèdre.* Art for art's sake? I should just think so, and more so than ever at the present time. It is the one orderly product which our muddling race has produced. It is the cry of a thousand sentinels, the echo from a thousand labyrinths; it is the lighthouse which cannot be hidden: *c'est le meilleur témoignage que nous puissions donner de notre dignité.* * *Antigone* for *Antigone's* sake, *Macbeth* for *Macbeth's,* "La Grande Jatte" pour "La Grande Jatte."

If this line of argument is correct, it follows that the artist will tend to   10
be an outsider in the society to which he has been born, and that the nineteenth-century conception of him as a Bohemian† was not inaccurate. The conception erred in three particulars: it postulated an economic system where art could be a full-time job, it introduced the fallacy that only art matters, and it overstressed idiosyncrasy and waywardness—the peacock-feather aspect—rather than order. But it is a truer conception than the one which prevails in official circles on my side of the Atlantic—I don't know about yours: the conception which treats the artist as if he were a particularly bright government advertiser and encourages him to be friendly and matey with his fellow citizens, and not to give himself airs.

Estimable is mateyness, and the man who achieves it gives many a   11
pleasant little drink to himself and to others. But it has no traceable connection with the creative impulse, and probably acts as an inhibition on it. The artist who is seduced by mateyness may stop himself from doing the one thing which he, and he alone, can do—the making of something out of words or sounds or paint or clay or marble or steel or film which has internal

*"It is the best testimony of our dignity that we can give." [Forster's translation.]
†Unconventional, anti-establishment.

harmony and presents order to a permanently disarranged planet. This seems worth doing, even at the risk of being called uppish by journalists. I have in mind an article which was published some years ago in the London *Times,* an article called "The Eclipse of the Highbrow," in which the "Average Man" was exalted, and all contemporary literature was censured if it did not toe the line, the precise position of the line being naturally known to the writer of the article. Sir Kenneth Clark, who was at that time director of our National Gallery, commented on this pernicious doctrine in a letter which cannot be too often quoted. "The poet and the artist," wrote Clark, "are important precisely because they are not average men; because in sensibility, intelligence, and power of invention they far exceed the average." These memorable words, and particularly the words "power of invention," are the Bohemian's passport. Furnished with it, he slinks about society, saluted now by a brickbat and now by a penny, and accepting either of them with equanimity. He does not consider too anxiously what his relations with society may be, for he is aware of something more important than that—namely the invitation to invent, to create order, and he believes he will be better placed for doing this if he attempts detachment. So round and round he slouches, with his hat pulled over his eyes, and maybe with a louse in his beard, and—if he really wants one—with a peacock's feather in his hand.

If our present society should disintegrate—and who dare prophesy that   12
it won't?—this old-fashioned and démodé figure will become clearer: the Bohemian, the outsider, the parasite, the rat—one of those figures which have at present no function either in a warring or a peaceful world. It may not be dignified to be a rat, but many of the ships are sinking, which is not dignified either—the officials did not build them properly. Myself, I would sooner be a swimming rat than a sinking ship—at all events I can look around me for a little longer—and I remember how one of us, a rat with particularly bright eyes called Shelley, squeaked out, "Poets are the unacknowledged legislators of the world," before he vanished into the waters of the Mediterranean.

What laws did Shelley propose to pass? None. The legislation of the   13
artist is never formulated at the time, though it is sometimes discerned by future generations. He legislates through creating. And he creates through his sensitiveness and his power to impose form. Without form the sensitiveness vanishes. And form is as important today, when the human race is trying to ride the whirlwind, as it ever was in those less agitating days of the past, when the earth seemed solid and the stars fixed, and the discoveries of science were made slowly, slowly. Form is not tradition. It alters from generation to generation. Artists always seek a new technique, and will continue to do so as long as their work excites them. But form of some kind is imperative. It is the surface crust of the internal harmony, it is the outward evidence of order.

My remarks about society may have seemed too pessimistic, but I   14
believe that society can only represent a fragment of the human spirit, and that another fragment can only get expressed through art. And I wanted to take this opportunity, this vantage ground, to assert not only the existence of art but its pertinacity. Looking back into the past, it seems to me that that

is all there has ever been: vantage grounds for discussion and creation, little vantage grounds in the changing chaos, where bubbles have been blown and webs spun, and the desire to create order has found temporary gratification, and the sentinels have managed to utter their challenges, and the huntsmen, though lost individually, have heard each other's calls through the impenetrable wood, and the lighthouses have never ceased sweeping the thankless seas. In this pertinacity there seems to me, as I grow older, something more and more profound, something which does in fact concern people who do not care about art at all.

15   In conclusion, let me summarize the various categories that have laid claim to the possession of Order.

16   (1) The social and political category. Claim disallowed on the evidence of history and of our own experience. If man altered psychologically, order here might be attainable; not otherwise.

17   (2) The astronomical category. Claim allowed up to the present century, but now disallowed on the evidence of the physicists.

18   (3) The religious category. Claim allowed on the evidence of the mystics.

19   (4) The esthetic category—the subject of this article. Claim allowed on the evidence of various works of art; and on the evidence of our own creative impulses, however weak these may be, or however imperfectly they may function. Works of art, in my opinion, are the only objects in the material universe to possess internal order, and that is why, though I don't believe that only art matters, I do believe in Art for Art's Sake.

Questions for Discussion

1. The long third sentence of paragraph 14 contains a series of images that suggest what the world is like and the function art serves in that world. Discuss with your classmates the qualities of the world suggested by these images and where art fits in as a human endeavor.

2. When the artist "presents order to a permanently disarranged planet" (¶11), does he or she, in Forster's view, do so in order "to do the world good"? Does Forster think this *should* be the artist's aim? Should the making of the work itself or the possible effects of the work be of most concern to the artist? If the former, then how are the wider effects of art achieved, beyond merely being beautiful?

3. In paragraph 9 Forster says that "a work of art . . . is the only material object in the universe which may possess internal harmony. All the others have been pressed into shape from outside, and when their mold is removed they collapse." How would you state the meaning of these two sentences in your own words? What would serve as good examples of two material objects that match his description?

Suggested Essay Topics

1. Consider for a moment some of the many ways available to a writer for establishing the internal order, or harmony, that Forster values so highly:

   a. Logical harmony: placing ideas in such an order that they "track" one another and thus develop coherently

   b. Thematic harmony: sticking to the same subject, or to appropriate subdivisions of the same subject, throughout an entire essay, story, or poem

   c. Tonal harmony: maintaining either the same tone throughout or modulating the variations in ways appropriate to the dominant tone

   d. Imagistic harmony: giving the reader pictures—through the use of metaphor, analogy, example, and comparisons of abstract qualities with physical senses ("I was so mad I could taste it in the back of my mouth")—that are appropriate to the subject and each other

   e. Formal harmony: designing a piece of writing so that its parts are of appropriate size and consistency

   f. Point-of-view harmony: maintaining the same perspective on a topic that is assumed at the beginning (if you were writing a personal essay assuming the point of view—for comic purposes, say—of someone who was dizzy, confused, naive, and bumbling, inserting sharply perceptive comments by other people would violate the initial point of view and, if done inadvertently, could ruin an essay)

   These modes of harmony (and others) are, of course, not mutually exclusive; a given essay may employ all of them. For this assignment, choose an essay, short story, or poem that you like, one that seems harmonious, and address an essay to your instructor in which you discuss three of four of the main kinds of harmony in your selection. Analyze how they work, and evaluate whether the author employed them effectively.

2. Write a dialogue between Forster and Plato in which you portray them as debating, in front of your class, one of the following topics: "The Relationship Between Art and Social Progress," "The Role of Literary Studies in High School and College Education," "The Effect on Civilization If All Works of Art Were Suddenly to Disappear," or "The Relationship between Art and Truth.'"

André Brink

*A*ndré Brink (b. 1935) is a South African novelist and essayist who, like Nadine Gordimer, Alan Paton, and others, has challenged the apartheid policies of the South African government, instituted in 1948 with the victory of the Dutch-based National Party over the previously long-standing,

English-based power structure. Having lived all his professional life at odds with and at risk from an oppressive political regime, Brink knows something of what it is like to be an outsider, and he has seen first-hand the degradations created by political oppression and institutional lies. In this essay he explores the role of the writer in such a situation, in such a society.

Should the artist stick to "art for art's sake" or, in the face of political oppression and social injustice, should the artist take a political stand and lend his or her voice to the struggle for political and social justice? Should artists use their art to expose and to oppose injustice? Is art a morally and politically neutral activity? These are questions that have been passionately debated among artists and thinkers over many centuries and in many different social and political contexts. Each time the debate arises, it is colored by the particular facts of the social and political context of the debaters' own society.

In Brink's view, the context of politics and social policy in his own country is dominated by two things: a laager *mentality and by apartheid, which is the major political expression of that mentality. In the history of the Dutch immigrants who "settled" the South African territory, the* laager—*an enclosed camp surrounded by a circle of wagons—occupies a special significance in the minds and imagination of South Africans. It is a physical expression of the belief on the part of those on the inside that everyone on the outside is a hostile alien. That mentality generates a great pressure for conformity, loyalty, and cohesiveness among the* laager *inhabitants who are feeling beleaguered by outside forces. The* laager *mentality, Brink contends, dominates the Afrikaners' views of the world and makes it immensely difficult for any one of them to oppose the actions of their fellow Afrikaners. Apartheid is the major tool for keeping the encampment intact and for keeping the outside forces—in this case, the political and social aspirations of the black majority—weak and subordinate.*

In such a context, Brink sees the task of the writer, difficult as the task may be, as that of pricking the conscience of the oppressors, of standing up for humane values in an inhumane context, of educating and challenging the minds and hearts of his audience: "What the writer does essentially implies that his work, if it is worthwhile, acts as a conscience in the world" (¶22). In a society of oppression and injustice, "art for art's sake" loses much of its appeal because it tends to remove art from commitment and engagement, from the arena where art may lend aid to the fight against injustice.

On the other hand, does the writer who focuses mainly on political and social aims lose the freedom to be concerned with such essential artistic issues as aesthetics, form, and technique? Does the artist who gets too involved in the noisy fracas of political debate lose the ability to hear the small, quiet voice of the internal muse? To what extent must the artist give up his or her attentiveness to private impulse and vision in order to support the collective impulses and public vision of his or her contemporaries, especially of those who are suffering from injustice? All these questions, and more, are explored and illuminated by the passion of Brink's concern and the clarity of his prose.

WRITERS AND WRITING IN
THE WORLD

"Writers and Writing in the World" is a collation of two lectures delivered at the University of
Natal, Pietermaritzburg and Durban, July 1969. Published in *Writing in a State of Siege* (1983).

Writers and their writing exist in the world: even the most private poem,   1
written for the poet's personal enjoyment and hidden in his bottom drawer,
presupposes a reader. Without functioning within a process of communication, it remains only partially realized.

But does this mean that the literary work is inevitably directed towards   2
the fulfillment of some social function? Can it be taken for granted that the
writer and his work can count on a form of social effect?

I

To explore this, one should of course be careful to distinguish between the   3
nature of a work and its possible effect: there is a wide difference between
what the work *is* and what it *does*—or what can be done with or to it.
Notre-Dame in Paris, has, among other things, been used as a stable, a
church, a court of law and a sanctuary for criminals and beggars: but it
remains, in the final analysis, a *building*. As with buildings, literature has
been used and abused in many ways—by authors and readers alike. Books
have been used to flatter tyrants or to contribute to their fall; to prove
theories or disprove them; to fight sinful lust or to stimulate the reader's
sexuality; to praise women or to hurl abuse at them; they have been used
to inspire men, to convey beauty, to kindle barbecue fires or to prop up
rickety shelves.

But the uses to which books have been put need not have anything to   4
do with the function implicit in literature. A specific example: so many critics
have attacked the Sestigers* on the grounds that their books might impair the
morals of youthful readers. None of these vociferous critics seems to blame
the Bible for the fact that many passages and chapters in it are constantly used
by adolescents for sexual titillation. Even a book written with the noblest of
intentions can be misused by malicious or idiotic or even well-meaning
readers.

But this should not lead us into another pitfall: that, namely, of the   5
"author's intention." Author's intentions are erratic and unpredictable and
most unreliable. T. S. Eliot once explained, perhaps with the wisdom of
hindsight, that he had intended *Murder in the Cathedral* as anti-Nazi propaganda: it is to be doubted whether any reader would have guessed this, had
Eliot not mentioned it himself. (Incidentally, this may be the case with several

---

*The Sestigers were a group of South African artists—filmmakers, poets, dramatists, and so
on—who in the 1960s engaged in criticism of the government for its racist policies. That they
were Afrikaan writers, not English, made them especially threatening to the government, who
saw their attempts to make a European perspective and liberal ideas current in South Africa as
undermining Afrikaan culture.

works in Afrikaans* as well: novels and poems express their social comment in cryptic symbols which, in a good work, become important in their own right but, in a bad work, degenerate into escapism.) Yet whether or not Eliot's play is anti-Nazi has nothing to do with the fact that it is an outstanding work of art.

And there are numerous other examples. *Don Quixote* was originally 6 written as a devastating comment on the tradition of picaresque novels and on the Spanish conquistadores but its lasting greatness has little to do with the impulses which prompted its writing in the first place.

The greatest novel in nineteenth-century Dutch literature, Multatuli's 7 *Max Havelaar,* was written to expose the intolerable conditions in the East Indies: the book ends with a personal, passionate plea to the Prince of Orange himself. The book was an enormous success: but everybody was so moved by the characters in their own right that no one paid any attention to the plight of the Javanese.

There are many modern examples, too: probably no other playwright 8 in our century has been more "committed" than Brecht: yet we have the word of a leading producer that when pure fantasy is required in Polish theatre, it is Brecht† who is performed. At the same time that "absurd" classic of the modern stage, *Waiting for Godot,* ‡ has been performed in Poland as the epitome of *théâtre engagé:* because there the waiting of Estragon and Vladimir§ could be interpreted politically as the waiting of the inmates of Auschwitz.

There is another example of the latter sort: when Pasternak‖ was first 9 confronted with official condemnation, he retired into silence. When he emerged, it was to publish the purest lyrical poetry. And yet these poems were interpreted as political provocation: because to write lyrical verse in a social context where political commitment or flattery of the system is not only expected but required, amounts to a challenge in itself. And so we are back where we started: i.e., the author's intentions may be almost universally regarded as irrelevant for the eventual quality of his work.

Even so, one cannot deny that much of the persuasive passion of *Don* 10 *Quixote* or the *Max Havelaar* derives precisely from the anger of a committed author, and that without that flame no mind would have been set alight by those works. Similarly, the agony and rage of James Baldwin or LeRoi Jones determine much of the compelling quality of their writing: it is as if the violence of their commitment is enhanced within the dimensions of their work.

---

*Afrikaans is the language (derived from Dutch) of the white minority in South Africa.

†Bertolt Brecht (1898–1956), German playwright and poet, famous for his plays of political and social criticism.

‡Written by Samuel Beckett (b. 1906) in 1954, *Waiting for Godot* portrays Estragon and Vladimir standing, futilely waiting for Godot, who never arrives.

§Estragon and Vladimir, two characters in *Waiting for Godot.*

‖Boris Pasternak (1890–1960), Russian poet and novelist; Nobel Prize winner, 1958; novels include *Doctor Zhivago* (1957); was censured by Soviet government for winning Nobel Prize.

This happens, too, in Nadine Gordimer's* *The Late Bourgeois World,* but   11
not in *An Occasion for Loving.* And it is interesting to note that *The Late Bourgeois World* is banned in South Africa whereas *An Occasion for Loving* is not, although the latter, with its theme of love-across-the-colour-bar, may seem much more "inflammable" in the South African context than the first. But its flame is short-lived, while that of *The Late Bourgeois World* transcends the original anger and becomes, in the process, more "dangerous"—which, in literature, often appears to be synonymous with "great."

II

What we have found so far, is that although a writer's personal intention may   12
have little to do with the success of his work, the *quality* of his anger may enlarge the scope of his work. And obviously the quality of his anger will be related, however tenuously, to the causes of that anger: the tantrum of a child who has been refused a sweet may be explosive in its own right but is much more restricted in its "human scope" than the rage of a person fighting for justice in the face of suffering. I shall in due course explore more fully the meanings I attach to this vague and over-exposed term "human scope." For the moment, what requires our attention is an acknowledgement of the fact that, in turning to the nature and sources of anger, we have shifted our focus from the *work* to the *writer.* And although both act as agents in the world, the range of their possible functions should not be confused.

I have referred to Pasternak and to the political weight attached even   13
to his utterly non-political poems. Of course he exerted an even greater influence on the world at large through *Doctor Zhivago.* And yet it remains true that thousands, perhaps millions of people in the West were moved by Pasternak's "stand," by what he represented, even though they may never have read his book. Just as millions have been inspired by those other Russian dissidents, Sinyavsky and Daniel, even though most know nothing whatsoever about their work.

We admire them because they exemplify resistance to oppression; be-   14
cause in them something courageous has survived, not for them alone, but for all people.

On a much, much smaller scale the same phenomenon has become   15
evident in South Africa with the advent of the Sestigers. Through their resistance to traditional pressures within their puritanical society and their revolt against obsolescence in letters and ethics, the impact of their renewal went far beyond the frontiers of literature. Their work became, first, a cultural, then a political phenomenon. Social attitudes within Afrikanerdom are assessed, even today, on the basis of whether a person is "for" or "against" the Sestigers.† And this applies as much to people who have read their work

*Nadine Gordimer (1923–), contemporary white South African novelist.

†Those "for" the Sestigers are liberals looking to change traditional Afrikaan culture. Those "against" them favor keeping South African society unchanged.

as to a multitude who haven't. The ripple effect has even gone beyond Afrikanerdom itself: to many English speakers in the country and, even more significantly, to a large number of coloureds and blacks (who have never read a word of the Sestigers) this work has come to signify a revolt against an entire oppressive system. In the process, the Sestigers have acquired an importance out of all proportion to what they have actually achieved in terms of literature.

I am not trying to denigrate what has been written by these writers. Some outstanding work has, in fact, been produced; and Afrikaans letters after Breytenbach and Etienne Leroux,* to name but two, can never be quite the same as before. But what concerns me most at the moment is that the peculiar social function fulfilled by (or forced on?) writers of the Sestiger generation also imposes an enormous social, moral and political responsibility on us all.

Whether we like it or not, in our particular situation, in *this* country, we have assumed, through what we have written, a responsibility not only to our métier but also, by implication, to every individual who reacts to our words.

III

Can the writer be described as a Pippa passing through the world, singing a song that alters something, and creates something, in each listener who hears it? Perhaps it would do greater justice to his function to see him as a Pied Piper: provided the image also conveys the essential fact that, in luring rats and children from their ordinary occupations, he also assumes responsibility for them.

But it is a responsibility different from that of the politician, the sociologist or the preacher. The writer remains a *writer:* the nature of his choice—to write rather than to go to Parliament or be a good Calvinist—implies a different relationship with the world.

We must face the simple fact that the actual effect of art as such is intimate and personal. The theatre critic Eric Bentley pointed out that Beethoven's Ninth Symphony has done less to create brotherhood among men than any performance by the Salvation Army. But he also insists that it would be ridiculous to reject Beethoven for that reason. What happens inside you when you see *Lear* or read *Crime and Punishment* or look at *Guernica* or listen to the *Well-tempered Clavichord* may be insignificant in comparison to the effects of a bomb, a speech by Mao Tse-Tung, a new law by Vorster† or a riot in Harlem . . .‡ but that it *has* an effect which, in its own right, can be tremendous, cannot be denied. And it should never be underestimated.

The work of art cannot—and need not—be justified on religious, political, moral or other grounds. But it satisfies a need in man which is as vital

*Breytenbach and Leroux were two writers prominent among the Sestigers.

†John Vorster (1915–1983), a former prime minister of the South African government and staunch upholder of its racist policies.

‡Ellipses are Brink's.

as hunger, even though it may not be recognized as readily. Like hunger, it is a personal need. But in its intimacy it is extremely significant. For it can expand an awareness of the human condition.

What the writer does essentially implies that his work, if it is worth- 22 while, acts as a conscience in the world.

IV

The operation of this conscience will, to a large extent, depend on the nature 23 of the world within which it functions. Or, to be more precise, on what the writer perceives to be the nature of his world, since it is only from a profound involvement in the problems of his world that the writer turns to writing.

Now our world has been defined in innumerable ways, and these need 24 not be mutually exclusive. But it seems to me that in *Art and Revolution* John Berger offered a diagnosis particularly relevant to the South Africa we live in today.

In Berger's view, shared by many others, most of the problems in the 25 world today are related to the exploitation and degradation of people all over the world, and to their struggle to liberate themselves from the most humiliating of these forms of exploitation and degradation. This involves primarily the struggle in the Third World to become free from the imperialism of Europe, the United States and Russia—freedom, above all, from exploitation: economic, but also mental, moral, spiritual: freedom from the attitude that other people are there to be used, not as people, but as commodities. In the way Africans, coloureds and Indians have been reduced to commodities in our country.

Let us be quite clear about this aspect of the situation in our world: 26 two-thirds of the people in the world are being exploited, deceived and humiliated by the remaining third. If this condition is accepted or, worse, institutionalized (as in South Africa), it can only be aggravated. For imperialism, whether economic or moral, is insatiable. We have reached a situation where no acceptance or justification of the status quo is permissible. Because the "wretched of the earth," the dispossessed, the disinherited, have their identity taken from them. And once a man's identity is denied, a struggle is initiated which cannot end before he has found his place and his name again. This suffering is not reserved for the already deprived: it exists in a peculiarly agonizing form in the minds of those who are *aware* of it: our torture, says Berger, is the existence of others as unequals. (Fanon:* "Leave this Europe where they are never done talking of Man, yet murder men everywhere they find them.")

One may ask: is there anything new in this condition? Has there not 27 always been suffering and injustice and oppression? Of course. But until recently the condition of the world was not wholly intolerable—because the

*Frantz Omar Fanon (1925–1961), French West Indian psychoanalyst who developed the theory that some neuroses are socially generated and authored anti-colonial writings.

full measure of the truth was not known. Earlier, Europeans could deceive themselves, John Berger points out, by believing that they represented humanity at its most civilized: so they were not forced to abandon a final belief in equality, as the issue could be deferred while they exploited inequality. And the exploited natives of the world were not aware of the scale of what was perpetrated against them. Today South Americans, Asians and Africans have discovered the whole extent of what is taking place. And this creates despair. And fury. (Baldwin:* We live in rage and pain, in rage and pain.") Mass communications have propagated these events around the world; and "no man can claim that he has not personally SEEN the intolerable condition of the world."

And the essence of this condition is, as Berger so eloquently points out, 28 the fact that a minority of people are exploiting the markets and the minds of the rest, and regard them as expendable. Which means, he says, that each individual who fights imperialism in our world is also fighting for human meaning.

This, it seems to me, indicates a function of writers in our terrifying and 29 sordid world: to keep the voice of humanity alive; to ensure the survival of human values.

V

Of course, "human values," like the "human scope" I referred to earlier, is 30 a notoriously vague term. Yet it is by no means impossible to attempt a clearer definition. For obvious reasons such a definition should start from a look at the individual human being, in order to find out which values in him can be so precious and at the same time so basic that the artist is willing to risk everything—time, the respect of others, peace of mind, love, even money—to fight for the preservation of their dignity.

We can start with the simplest characteristic of an individual: he is 31 animate. Though most people seem more dead than alive, the biological fact is that man is alive and not dead.

And, if this is the simplest characteristic of the human being—that he 32 is alive—it is part of his dignity that he should have the right to live, and that no one should force him to die. But is this really as simple as it seems? Is it simple in a country where more crimes are punishable by death than in any other country in the world?

We must proceed. A person lives, we have decided. But what does that 33 imply: *to live?* Again on the very basic level: it means to grow, to change, to move. On the other end of the scale lie decay and death.

And if the human condition begins with being alive, and if being alive 34 demands that a person should move, should grow, and, in the process, change, then these will be human values worth rebelling for: then people

*Roger Nash Baldwin (1884–1981), American reformer; founder (1920) and director (1920–1950) of the American Civil Liberties Union.

should have the *right* to move, to grow and to change. And they should not be subjected unnecessarily to that which hampers growth, movement, change and which precipitates decay and death.

These attributes of life are not mere physical processes. They have 35 metaphysical equivalents. For animals and plants, too, live. They, too, move and grow and change. But the human being is supposed to differ from them in his possession of reason, in his awareness of—or quest for, or even uncertainty about—"something more." People are the only creatures on earth not satisfied with being what they are. They want to be more, to become more, to become different.

Let us not argue about the soul. Let us accept what we more or less know 36 and what we can more or less prove:

The human being has intelligence. In other words, he does not only 37 experience, but he can interpret, associate, relate, anticipate experience. If he has this faculty, he also has the duty to use and develop it in the name of that movement, growth and change which we have identified on the biological level. And once again this implies that people should be respected in this dignity which lies in their *right* to think, to relate, to interpret. They should not be hampered in these processes: they should not be hindered in their task of relating today to yesterday and tomorrow.

Part of the means people have developed to express and embody these 38 processes is to be found in language. People can speak, and read, and write: they should have a *right* to speak, to read, to write.

These activities all touch upon the individual's urge to communicate, 39 which may be his most urgent physical and metaphysical need. And so he should have the right to communicate—or at least to *try* to communicate on all the levels of communication available to him, including the sexual, which is not only a biological function but the expression of a metaphysical enquiry. And so I should demand for him the right to choose his sexual partners and to interpret his sexual experience.

VI

But with communication we have crossed the border between the individual 40 as a lonely being and that same individual as a social being. This is the consequence of human consciousness—and perhaps one of the noblest attributes which distinguish people from other animals: they can relate their experience to that of others. They can compare. What the individual demands, he demands not only for himself, but for others as well. Philogenesis* is inextricably linked to ontogenesis.† Here, too, we must accept that the metaphysical is rooted in the physical: for if a person lives, he has the urge to perpetuate his existence and to safeguard it.

In an absolutely personal sense this might lead to the negation or even 41

*The origin and development of a species.
†The origin and development of an individual.

annihilation of others. But because of the social dimension the individual's urge to protect himself implies that he should not harm others—since that might invite retaliation. Consequently I can only feel truly safe if I also protect the safety of others. Whatever one does through one's freedom of choice, should never unduly impair the freedom of others. Which means that freedom must be measured with justice.

In an absolute sense, as Camus* insisted, these conditions are mutually   42
exclusive: absolute freedom includes the freedom of the strong to suppress the weak; absolute justice curtails all separate liberties. Consequently they can only co-exist in a relative sense. They force one to accept that the human domain is the relative; which, by the same token, implies that one's freedom and one's justice can always be improved and enlarged. And it means that the writer should constantly rebel against the set of circumstances which imperil or curtail the freedom and justice of the individuals in *his* society and *his* world.

In the light of all this one can now return to the view of the writer as   43
the rebel who fights in the name of the essentially human values—against everything which threatens the human, against everything which is essentially *inhuman*.

VII

Let us not underestimate this task, and most especially not when it concerns   44
the writer and his work in South Africa. For judging by its security legislation (aggravated by the recent introduction of a Bureau of State Security, so aptly abbreviated as BOSS), its past laws and influx control laws, its Group Areas Act and its Immorality Act . . .† this is not a "human" country. The entire system which determines every aspect of private and communal life in the country is a contradiction of all the basic attributes we have termed "human": movement; growth; change; communication; the right to think, to read, to speak, to write; the right to choose a sexual partner and relate one's experience to that of others; the right not to be killed; the small, precious, personal right to be—to be in awareness, in compassion, in humility, in defiance, in anger, in pain, and—if it must be so—in violence.

However, if I am pleading a literary cause, it is the cause of a literature   45
wholly committed to humanity, which requires a peculiar *awareness* in those who write in this country. Awareness not of one's subjective problems only, and not only of the situation of the small *laager*‡ of a few million whites . . .§ but awareness of the country as a whole and of its relation to the fierce world

---

*Albert Camus (1913–1960), French novelist, essayist, and playwright; Nobel Prize, 1957; leading exponent of post–World War II disillusionment; explored existentialist themes in his writings.
†Ellipses are Brink's.
‡In South Africa, a temporary camp within an encircling barricade of wagons. Brink uses the term metaphorically to stand for the Afrikaaner's attitude that the whole society exists as an enclosed camp surrounded by hostile forces.
§Ellipses are Brink's.

around us. Awareness, and courage, and humility. And a sense of loyalty to the truth, and to the imperative need to speak it fearlessly.

Will it have any "effect"? I have pointed out how *in*effectual writing can 46 be in practical terms. But also, I hope, of how wide its limits are. There are revolutions of many sorts in our world; Régis Debray, the young French revolutionary serving a thirty-year sentence in Bolivia, wrote "Poor gun without a word, poor word without a gun."

We are indeed living in the midst of a revolutionary situation which 47 manifests itself in many ways and on many levels.

The revolution I am involved in as a writer, is a revolution in the 48 conscience of my people. Perhaps it is not much I can accomplish—and I must demand of myself to be honest and to admit when an attitude becomes nothing more than rationalization. Indeed, it is a slow process. One can reach one person here, another there; after a long time we may still be only a handful. But I remember the words of Éluard:*

> They were but a handful—
> Suddenly they were a crowd.

And it is in the light of this that I should like to repeat the dictum of Debray, but now reversed: "Poor word without a gun: poor gun without a word."

Questions for Discussion

1. To what extent should artists worry about the social effects of their work? To what extent do they have a responsibility for trying to make sure that the effects of their work are socially positive?

2. If you feel that artists should not have to be "relevant" or have to "speak to" the political and social conditions of their society and times, how would you, if you were South African, evaluate the work of a white South African painter or novelist whose work ignored the political tensions and moral problems of apartheid? How would you evaluate the art of an Afro-American writer whose work showed no special consciousness of what it means to be black in a society that once fought a civil war over slavery?

3. Is Brink saying that a writer, in order to be politically relevant, has to deal explicitly with political themes in all of his or her work? Does he provide examples of writers whose work, while not explicitly political, nevertheless has a political dimension of significance? How can a nonpolitical work have a political impact?

*Paul Éluard (1895–1952), French poet; a founder of the Surrealist movement; turned from verse experimentation to poetry of political militance; active in the Resistance during World War II. Paul Éluard is the pseudonym for Eugène Grindel.

4. Can you point out any strengths and weaknesses in Brink's method of defining "human values" in section V, paragraphs 30–39? How does he arrive at his definition? What values does it allow him to stress? What issues does he pass over that you would like to see more fully developed?

Suggested Essay Topics

1. Choose a favorite story of yours that you think makes a political point or conveys a political point of view. [If you cannot think of any, you might choose from a couple of very brief ones by Kurt Vonnegut—"Harrison Bergeron" (in Chapter 2) or "Report on the Barnhouse Effect"—or James Thurber's "The Greatest Man in the World," or Albert Camus's "The Guest"; or Ralph Ellison's "Battle Royal" (in Chapter 7) and Joyce Carol Oates' "How I Contemplated the World from the Detroit House of Correction and Began My Life Over Again" (in Chapter 12). Or you could choose a story that is longer and more indirect, but intriguing, such as Thomas Mann's "Mario and the Magician."] In an essay directed to your instructor, analyze what you take to be the political message or political suggestiveness of the story. Include in your analysis an evaluation of whether the story *as a story* is harmed or helped by the political dimension of awareness.

2. This assignment involves more preparation than most, but, if you have a special interest in South African issues, you will find it rewarding. Read a novel by either André Brink or Nadine Gordimer (Brink's *A Dry White Season* or Gordimer's *July's People* would be excellent choices) and evaluate it from the point of view, using the criteria, that Brink develops in "Writers and Writing in the World." Direct your essay to other students interested in these issues.

Margaret Atwood

Canadian novelist Margaret Atwood (b. 1939) discusses with passion the question of whether artists (including writers) should be "political" or should stick to art. It is a vexing issue for artists, who are sometimes criticized for being too remote but who are also criticized, at least by some, when they speak out on political issues they are then accused of knowing nothing about. In some cases the "criticism" takes very serious forms, ranging from bans on the publication or exhibition of the works of those artists officially disapproved of to the imprisonment or execution of the artists themselves.

The question of what artists owe their society cannot be separated from the question of what all citizens owe. Artists, after all, are also citizens. If they are exempt from political involvement on the grounds that they must remain uncontaminated, that they must devote themselves to art alone, why are the rest of us not exempt on other grounds? We are all too busy, too harried, and too intent on the pursuit of personal goals to be political. It is never convenient or easy. Those who take politics seriously simply do it because they feel it is their duty, their way of making a contribution. Should artists feel the same way? Should our society expect artists to be as political as anyone else?

Since the time of the Romantic poets in the early nineteenth century, there has been a persistent notion in society that geniuses of all sorts have to be given special latitude, that they are not to be judged by the same moral, social, or political standards as the rest of humanity. While this view has been frequently criticized, it is still around. As you read Margaret Atwood, assess her views on this subject and determine the extent to which you agree.

A DISNEYLAND OF THE SOUL

From *The Writer and Human Rights* (1983).

The subject we have come together to address increases in importance   1
as the giants of this world move closer and closer to violent and fatal confrontation. Broadly put, it is: what is the writer's responsibility, if any, to the society in which he or she lives? The question is not a new one; it's been with us at least since the time of Plato; but more and more the answers of the world's governments have taken the form of amputation: of the tongue, of the soul, or of some other part of the body, such as the head.

We in Canada are ill-equipped to come to grips even with the problem,   2
let alone the solution. We live in a society in which the main consensus seems to be that the artist's duty is to entertain and divert, nothing more. Occasionally, our critics get a little heavy and start talking about the human condition. But on the whole, audiences prefer that art be not a mirror held up to life but a Disneyland of the soul, containing Romanceland, Spyland, Pornoland, and all the other Escapelands which are so much more agreeable than the complex truth. When we take an author seriously, we prefer to believe that her vision derives from her individual and subjective and neurotic, tortured soul—we like artists to have tortured souls—not from the world she is looking at. Sometimes our artists believe this version too, and the ego takes over. *I, me,* and *mine* are our favorite pronouns; *we, us,* and *ours* are low on the list. The artist is not seen as a lens for focusing the world but as a solipsism. We are good at analyzing an author's production in terms of her craft. We are not good at analyzing it in terms of her politics, and by and large we do not do so.

By "politics" I do not mean how you voted in the last election, although   3
that is included. I mean who is entitled to do what to whom, with impunity; who profits by it; and who therefore eats what. Such material enters a writer's work not because the writer is or is not consciously political but because a writer is an observer, a witness, and such observations are the air she breathes. They are the air all of us breathe; the only difference is that the

author looks, and then writes down what she sees. What she sees depends on how closely she looks and at what, but look she must.

In some countries, an author is censored not only for what he says but for how he says it. An unconventional style is therefore a declaration of artistic freedom. Here we are eclectic; we don't mind experimental styles; in fact, we devote learned journals to their analysis; but our critics sneer at anything they consider "heavy social commentary" or—a worse word— "message." Stylistic heavy guns are dandy, as long as they aren't pointed anywhere in particular. We like the human condition as long as it's seen as personal and individual. Placing politics and poetics in two watertight compartments is a luxury, just as specialization of any kind is a luxury, and it is possible only in a society where luxuries abound. Most countries cannot afford such luxuries; this North American way of thinking is alien to them. It was even alien in North America not long ago. We've already forgotten that in the 1950s many artists, both in the United States and here, were persecuted solely on the grounds of their presumed politics. Which leads us to another mistaken Canadian belief: the belief that it can't happen here.

It has happened here, many times. Although our country is one of the most peaceful and prosperous on earth, although we do not shoot artists here, although we do not execute political opponents, and although this is one of the few remaining countries in which we can have a gathering like this without expecting to be arrested or blown up, we should not overlook the fact that Canada's record on civil rights issues is less than pristine. Our treatment of our native peoples has been shameful. This is the country in which citizens of Japanese origin were interned during the Second World War and had their property stolen. (When a government steals property it is called "confiscation.") It is also the country in which thousands of our citizens were arrested, jailed, and held without warrant or explanation, during the War Measures Act, a scant eleven years ago. There was no general outcry in either case. Worse things have not happened not because we are genetically exempt but because we lead pampered lives.

Our methods, in Canada, of controlling artists are not violent, but they do exist. We control through the marketplace and through critical opinion. We are also controlled by the economics of culture, which in Canada still happen to be those of a colonial branch plant. In 1960 the number of Canadian books published here was minute, and the numbers sold pathetic. Things have changed very much in twenty years, but Canadian books still account for a mere 25 per cent of the overall book trade and paperback books for under 5 per cent. Talking about this situation is considered nationalist chauvinism. Nevertheless, I suppose we are lucky to have any per cent at all; they haven't yet sent in the marines, and if they do it won't be over books but over oil.

We in this country should use our privileged position not as a shelter from the world's realities but as a platform from which to speak. Many are denied their voices; we are not. A voice is a gift; it should be cherished and used, to utter fully human speech if possible. Powerlessness and silence go

together. One of the first efforts made in any totalitarian takeover is to
suppress the writers, the singers, the journalists, those who are the collective
voice. Get rid of the union leaders and pervert the legal system and what you
are left with is a reign of terror.

As we read the newspapers, we learn we are, right now, in a state of war.   8
The individual wars may not be large and they are being fought far from here,
but there is really only one war: the war between those who would like the
future to be, in the words of George Orwell, a boot grinding forever into a
human face, and those who would like it to be a state of something we still
dream of as freedom. The battle shifts according to the ground occupied by
the enemy. Greek myth tells of a man called Procrustes, who was a great
equalizer. He had a system for making all human beings the same size: if they
were too small, he stretched them; if they were too tall, he cut off their feet
or their heads. The Procrustes of today is the international operator, not
confined to any one ideology or religion. The world is full of perversions of
the notion of equality, just as it is full of perversions of the notion of freedom.
True freedom is not being able to do whatever you like to whomever you
want to do it to. Freedom that exists as a result of the servitude of others is
not true freedom.

The most lethal weapon in the world's arsenal is not the neutron bomb   9
or chemical warfare but the human mind that devises such things and puts
them to use. But it is the human mind that can also summon up the power
to resist, can imagine a better world than the one before it, can retain memory
and courage in the face of unspeakable suffering. Oppression involves a
failure of the imagination: the failure to imagine the full humanity of other
human beings. If the imagination were a negligible thing and the act of
writing a mere frill, as many in this society would like to believe, regimes all
over the world would not be at such pains to exterminate them. The ultimate
desire of a Procrustes is a population of lobotomized zombies. The writer,
unless he is a mere word processor, retains three attributes that power-mad
regimes cannot tolerate: a human imagination, in the many forms it may take;
the power to communicate; and hope. It may seem odd for me to speak of
hope in the midst of what many of my fellow Canadians will call a bleak
vision, but as the American writer Flannery O'Connor said, people without
hope do not write novels.

Questions for Discussion

1. What does Atwood mean by her metaphor, "a Disneyland of the soul"
   (¶2)? What connotations are conveyed by "Disneyland"? Is it an effective
   metaphor in relation to Atwood's purpose?
2. What is Atwood's definition of "politics"? Do you think her definition is
   appropriate or useful? Why or why not?

3. Can you tell whether Atwood is a political liberal or conservative? What opinions or comments support your view?

4. Can you support Atwood's claim that "[p]owerlessness and silence go together" (¶7) with examples from American social life (either past or present)? Do you agree that those who have a voice, and thus power, have a responsibility to use it on behalf of those who do not?

Suggested Essay Topics

1. Looking up entries under "Joseph McCarthy" in the *Readers' Guide to Periodical Literature* from 1950–1954, select a few accounts of his attacks on artists in literature and entertainment, and read them. Then, in an essay directed to your classmates, give an account of some of the hostile comments and attitudes that were directed by McCarthy and members of his Senate committee to writers and others who objected to his "investigations." Try to reveal some of the underlying assumptions about the role of artists in society by those both answering and asking the questions. Finally, try to use this material in formulating your own ideas about artistic responsibility.

2. If artists are given freedom to speak or create as they wish, they may offend people. There are many people in society today who are angry about sexually explicit and violent lyrics in rock songs; angry about the Mapplethorpe exhibit, which contains photographs that were sexually explicit and anti-religious; angry about pornography in film and theater; and so on. Such anger is not new. D. H. Lawrence's *Lady Chatterly's Lover,* Henry Miller's *Tropic of Cancer,* and Mark Twain's *Huckleberry Finn* are works that have been attacked and banned for different reasons in different places. For this essay, choose a work of art, literature, or music that is or has been controversial and either defend its right to be displayed or read freely, or attack its content and suggest what you feel is an appropriate response to it.

PART

THE
INDIVIDUAL
AND SOCIETY

✦

THREE

✦ 5 ✦

PERSONAL GOALS

What Should I Become?

Sow an act, and you reap a habit. Sow a habit, and you reap
a character. Sow a character, and you reap a destiny.
Charles Reade

Do not ask for success; success is for swine.
Anonymous

The only infallible criterion of wisdom to vulgar judgments—success.
Edmund Burke

To burn always with this hard, gemlike flame, to maintain
this ecstasy, is success in life.
Walter Pater

What is the chief end of man? To glorify God
and to enjoy him forever.
Shorter Catechism

He that can apprehend and consider vice with all her baits
and seeming pleasures, and yet abstain, and yet distinguish, and yet prefer
that which is truly better, he is the true wayfaring Christian.
I cannot praise a fugitive and cloistered virtue,
unexercised and unbreathed, that never sallies out and
sees her adversary, but slinks out of the race, where that immortal garland
is to be run for, not without dust and heat.
Assuredly we bring not innocence into the world, we bring
impurity much rather: that which purifies us is trial,
and trial is by what is contrary.
John Milton

That action is best, which procures the greatest happiness for
the greatest number.
Francis Hutcheson
(followed by many later utilitarians)

Phyllis Rose

This chapter focuses on personal goals: not simply on what we want out of life, *but on what we want to make out of* ourselves. *We are all prone to carry on internal conversations such as, "If I do X, which I already know is the* right *thing to do, how will others see me? Will they understand me, how will they judge me? If I don't do X because I fear being misunderstood or disliked, how will I live with myself? What kind of person will I have become then?"*

Asking such questions can underscore for us all just how vulnerable the self can sometimes feel. Don't we all share a certain shrinking when we anticipate criticism or rejection? Don't we all know that sweet flow of energy and jubilation when we have just received assurance that we, our precious selves, are indeed admired or loved? In an insightful essay, Phyllis Rose (b. 1942) takes note of these two poles and describes a typical human movement: the pendulum swing we all make between self-love and self-loathing or, in the jargon of the day, between being "up" about ourselves and being "down" about ourselves.

In the best tradition of the comic essay that makes a serious point while being funny, Rose shows that she knows us, that she knows how we all go up and down in our self-esteem. But of course she could know such a private thing about us only if in fact it is both private and universal. Rose knows us because in this respect she is us. She knows that we are all heirs to the human capacity for despair and hope, joy and sorrow.

So what do we make of our swings? Is this simply the way it is? Does self-consciousness doom us to eternal pendulum swings of feeling? Perhaps, but are we really helpless? Wouldn't things be better if we were more in control? Wouldn't life have been better even for the successful George Eliot referred to in Rose's essay if she hadn't had to spend so much emotion worrying about whether she was a noodle? Wouldn't Rose like to give up those days when she feels like an impostor? And wouldn't we all like to turn our paralyzing fears into liberating energies?

Rose's examples offer us suggestions—no recipes, but suggestions—for liberating ourselves. That the successful people of the world share our fears about achievement and self-worth suggests that we may be wrong to take it all so seriously, to take every

occasion of self-loathing as if it were The End. Can we infer from Rose's examples
that we take ourselves too seriously most of the time, whether we're feeling up or down?
If so, those life-or-death dramas when we feel like failures or frauds may be nothing
but our own emotional hype. Knowing this might lower some of our soaring highs,
but it might also take some of the depths out of our sagging lows. We might just discover
that life doesn't have to be a constant switch between Ferris wheel heights and roller
coaster plunges. In any event, Rose's fine essay invites us to take a hard look at the
various selves we create inside.

HEROIC FANTASIES, NERVOUS DOUBTS

From *The New York Times* "Hers" column (March 22, 1984).

Recently a young man presented a bouquet to the secretary of the   1
English department. She was astounded. "But I don't even know you!" she
said. He quickly explained that he was just the florist's messenger; the card
would tell her who had sent the flowers. They came, as it happened, from a
grateful professor. But what strikes me is that for a split second she thought
a complete stranger was offering her flowers, and although this surprised her
it was not inconceivable.

Why should it be? Don't we all harbor fantasies of a brass band's   2
arriving at our door one day to play in our honor? Of Warren Beatty's
standing on our front step with a red ribbon around his neck? I know I do.
Like gold coins in a garbage dump, sprinkled here and there in the midst of
our self-distrust are these glittering visions of our worth and importance. We
may suspect during many waking hours that we have no worth or importance
and at the same time hope that the world, perhaps in the form of a young
man bearing flowers, will one day pay them tribute.

Such fantasies seem to me entirely healthy, as bankable as my meta-   3
phorical gold coins. Sometimes they are linked to myths we hold about our
lives. Everyone, for example, has a story about his or her birth. I have always
been told and believed that I was born in Doctors Hospital with the fleet
massing in the East River beneath my mother's window for the invasion of
North Africa. Was the fleet really massing in the East River for the invasion
of North Africa? An easy question to answer for certain, but I never will, for
the facts in this case, as in many others, are less important to me than their
significance, the myth.

Some part of me thinks—has always thought—that the invasion of   4
North Africa was an elegant pretext, a cover story, an excuse. World War II
or no, the fleet would have been there festively "massing"—I imagine this to
consist of a lot of nuzzling between ships and blowing of horns—in honor
of my birth. The fleet massed for me the way the fairies gathered for the birth
of Sleeping Beauty. The fleet bestowed blessings on me and wished me well

in life. On successive birthdays I have waited for the fleet, in some form, to
return. It never does. Nevertheless, whatever is strong in my ego may be said
to be strong because I believe that the fleet massed below my mother's
window on the day of my birth.

The expectation that the world will congratulate us for living tends to   5
focus on birthdays, and usually what happens on birthdays is nothing. I'm
speaking of adults. Indeed, that's one way you can tell when you're grown
up: nothing happens on your birthday. I knew I was grown up when I turned
38 and even my mother forgot my birthday. I was so depressed after looking
through the mail that I went back to bed. My son, then 8, found me there,
the shades drawn on a bright Saturday afternoon. I disclosed the problem.
"Don't move," he said. "I'll be right back." Half an hour later he returned and
thrust something large at me in a brown paper bag. "You don't have to use
these," he said, "but I want you to have them." He had grabbed all his
capital—$2—had gone to the nearest store and had bought the biggest thing
he could get for his money: a five-pound bag of potatoes. Now I have a special
place in my heart for potatoes. Still, it's not the fleet or a brass band or Warren
Beatty.

The average person's mixture of arrogance and self-loathing, of daring   6
and fear, never ceases to amaze me. We want to bring down the house. We
want the house to stand, protecting us. We want to be invulnerable through
strength. We want to be invulnerable because there's nothing there to hurt.
We want to be everything and nothing. I sometimes believe I am the prize
package my kindly parents always told me I was. But just as often getting out
of bed in the morning seems a plucky thing to do. (At such moments of
existential panic,* I find enormously helpful the phrase "another day, another
dollar," which takes this risky business of getting out of bed away from
metaphysics and into the realm of the practical, where it belongs.)

Often I think I'm the only person for the job, whatever the job may be: 7
cooking pasta al pesto, planning a trip, writing a certain biography. But often
I feel like an impostor as writer, teacher, human being. I like attention but
I suffer from stage fright. If I had to say what it is I'm afraid of, I guess it's
that my self won't be there when I need it. I'm afraid people will see through
me and find there's nothing there.

I once appeared on a TV talk show with Joey Skaggs, the artist who   8
specializes in putting things over on people. For example, he will announce
that he intends to windsurf from Hawaii to California or that, as king of the
gypsies, he is calling for a work stoppage of gypsies to protest the term gypsy
moth. People believe him, and that constitutes the work of art. He is a media
artist, a public-relations artist. I like his work and envy his talent. Before the
TV show we chatted. He showed me his clippings, an enormous scrapbook

*The existential philosophers who were influential in the post–World War II period were given
to insisting that human beings had to *assert* their personal worth in the face of a meaningless
universe. Rose is joking on how panicky that act of self-assertion can make her.

full of them. Worried that I would be found invisible when I appeared on TV, I could not bring myself to look at this massive evidence of Joey Skaggs's reality. I guess he thought I was bored by it or contemptuous. "It's hard to take in all at once," he said. I told him that wasn't the problem. "It makes me feel like nothing by comparison," I said. Joey, a nice man, conned me into comfort. "Believe me," he said, waving his hand to take in the studio and his clipping book, "it's all this that's nothing."

I used to think these problems of self-esteem were peculiarly female. 9
Now I'm not sure. When I began teaching 14 years ago I was convinced that establishing authority in the classroom was more of a problem for me than for my male colleagues. Before the start of each semester I had terrible anxiety dreams: I would go to composition class prepared to teach Shakespeare or vice versa, I would suddenly be called upon to lecture on the history of Japanese theater or to announce the Harvard-Yale game, I would forget to show up for the first class or I would show up naked. That dream in particular seemed to me a woman's dream. Women are not bred to authority, I thought. If I set myself up as an authority, people will see I'm a fraud.

At this time, the early 70's, I found myself at a New Haven dinner party 10
seated next to a Yale geologist who was about to retire after a long and distinguished teaching career. Professor Flint told me that there were many things he would miss about teaching but one thing he would not miss: the nightmares he had at the start of every semester in which he presented himself at the podium for the first lecture and discovered he was naked.

Perhaps we should all have tapes of loved ones telling us the stories of 11
our lives in mythic form—how the fleet massed and so on—just as Olympic athletes have think-positive tapes prescribed by their sports psychologists. Few of us need tapes to remind us how insignificant we are. The anxieties speak for themselves. There was a Roman emperor who had a slave at his side all the time to remind him he was mortal. But probably more of us are like George Eliot,* who, according to her companion, needed a slave at her side constantly whispering, "You are not a noodle."

Questions for Discussion

1. Most people have both anxiety dreams and wish-fulfillment dreams. Without getting embarrassingly personal, can you and your classmates share some of these dreams? Is there a great deal of similarity among them? If not, does this suggest that we are more different in this respect than the

---

*George Eliot, the pseudonym of Mary Ann Evans (1819–1880), one of the most successful and critically acclaimed novelists of the nineteenth century. Her novels include *Adam Bede* (1859) and *Middlemarch* (1871–1872).

introduction and Rose's essay suggests? If they are similar, does this corroborate the suggestion than we are all pretty much alike in this respect regardless of past successes?

2. In how many places and in how many different forms do you find the swing from self-love to self-loathing recorded? Do the lyrics to some songs, for example, express the former, while the lyrics to others express inner doubts and fears? Can you give examples? What about characters on TV programs and in the movies? What about characters in drama? Hamlet, for example—if we take his soliloquies to express private thought—goes up and down in his own self-estimation much more than anyone else in the play knows. Do you find Hamlet's pattern repeated in other characters in other plays? At a quite different literary level, what about cartoons? Garfield the cat seems the epitome of arrogant self-confidence, but when he gets down on himself about his weight, he becomes another cat altogether. What other instances of our preoccupation with how we feel about ourselves can you cite from the culture around you?

3. How many people do you know who do not seem ever to need the slave whispering, "You are not a noodle," but who in fact could sometimes use another slave to whisper, "You are overbearing, egotistical, and obnoxious"? Do you think these people have their own moments of barren self-confidence, or are there a few of us who never lose our grip on who we want to be? If the latter, what we have said so far is wrong; self-doubt is only widespread but not really universal. What is your opinion? Can you support it with examples?

Suggested Essay Topics

1. St. Paul's definition of love (p. 388) suggests that the self finds its most complete fulfillment not in taking in assurance and affection but in passing these on to others. If you have ever been the recipient of a gift of love when you felt that you needed it most, when you were feeling like a barren thing, your own worst self, give an account of the experience—why you needed it, how the gift was given, the effects it worked—addressed to your classmates as an example of the kind of help we may be to one another in times of stress or trouble.

2. If you have ever given such a gift as described in topic 1, give an account of what motivated you, how you knew the gift was needed, what it cost you, and the effects it had—not to pat yourself on the back as a good person but to record what you learned or how you grew.

Margaret Sanger

*M*argaret *Sanger (1883–1966) was the earliest influential advocate for the spread of birth-control information in America. In 1921, working against intense opposition, she organized the first American birth-control conference, and she continued to write books and publish magazines on the subject over several decades. In this essay Sanger recounts the episodes that led up to the crucial moment when she made her lifelong commitment to the cause of birth-control education.*

As Sanger makes her way steadily toward the greatest decision of her life, she makes the reader aware of all that she will have to fight against in forging an unconventional path, especially difficult for a woman in her era. She will have to fight to reduce her own ignorance, fight the taboo against speaking out on sexual matters, fight against religious opposition, and, finally, fight against those who would dismiss her as an unfeminine radical at best, a meddling crackpot at worst.

Notice how the issue that was to dominate Sanger's life does not gain sharp focus until she becomes acquainted with the poor, who suffered most from excessive childbearing. Once she starts working among them, she learns to see them not as statistics or generalized "unfortunates" but as individuals (¶15). We can almost always endure reports of the catastrophes of anonymous masses with less discomfort than we can the minor troubles of people whom we know as individuals. Our sympathies are always more quickly awakened and brought into play by concrete images than by vague abstractions. Sanger is presumably aware of this tendency in her readers as she works to portray the suffering poor as vividly as possible without lapsing into lurid or implausible melodrama.

THE TURBID EBB AND FLOW OF MISERY

Chapter 7 of *An Autobiography* (1938). Sanger has taken her chapter title from a line in Matthew Arnold's poem "Dover Beach."

> Every night and every morn
> Some to misery are born.
> Every morn and every night
> Some are born to sweet delight.
> Some are born to sweet delight,
> Some are born to endless night.
> WILLIAM BLAKE

During these years [about 1912] in New York trained nurses were in great demand. Few people wanted to enter hospitals; they were afraid they might be "practiced" upon, and consented to go only in desperate emergencies. Sentiment was especially vehement in the matter of having babies. A woman's own bedroom, no matter how inconveniently arranged, was the usual place for her lying-in. I was not sufficiently free from domestic duties to be a general nurse, but I could ordinarily manage obstetrical cases because I was notified far enough ahead to plan my schedule. And after serving my two weeks I could get home again.

Sometimes I was summoned to small apartments occupied by young clerks, insurance salesmen, or lawyers, just starting out, most of them under thirty and whose wives were having their first or second baby. They were always eager to know the best and latest method in infant care and feeding. In particular, Jewish patients, whose lives centered around the family, welcomed advice and followed it implicitly.

But more and more my calls began to come from the Lower East Side, as though I were being magnetically drawn there by some force outside my control. I hated the wretchedness and hopelessness of the poor, and never experienced that satisfaction in working among them that so many noble women have found. My concern for my patients was now quite different from my earlier hospital attitude. I could see that much was wrong with them which did not appear in the physiological or medical diagnosis. A woman in childbirth was not merely a woman in childbirth. My expanded outlook included a view of her background, her potentialities as a human being, the kind of children she was bearing, and what was going to happen to them.

The wives of small shopkeepers were my most frequent cases, but I had carpenters, truck drivers, dishwashers, and pushcart vendors. I admired intensely the consideration most of these people had for their own. Money to pay doctor and nurse had been carefully saved months in advance—parents-in-law, grandfathers, grandmothers, all contributing.

As soon as the neighbors learned that a nurse was in the building they came in a friendly way to visit, often carrying fruit, jellies, or gefüllter fish made after a cherished recipe. It was infinitely pathetic to me that they, so poor themselves, should bring me food. Later they drifted in again with the excuse of getting the plate, and sat down for a nice talk; there was no hurry. Always back of the little gift was the question, "I am pregnant (or my daughter, or my sister is). Tell me something to keep from having another baby. We cannot afford another yet."

I tried to explain the only two methods I had ever heard of among the middle classes, both of which were invariably brushed aside as unacceptable. They were of no certain avail to the wife because they placed the burden of responsibility solely upon the husband—a burden which he seldom assumed. What she was seeking was self-protection she could herself use, and there was none.

Below this stratum of society was one in truly desperate circumstances. The men were sullen and unskilled, picking up odd jobs now and then, but more often unemployed, lounging in and out of the house at all hours of the day and night. The women seemed to slink on their way to market and were without neighborliness.

These submerged, untouched classes were beyond the scope of organized charity or religion. No labor union, no church, not even the Salvation

Army reached them. They were apprehensive of everyone and rejected help of any kind, ordering all intruders to keep out; both birth and death they considered their own business. Social agents, who were just beginning to appear, were profoundly mistrusted because they pried into homes and lives, asking questions about wages, how many were in the family, had any of them ever been in jail. Often two or three had been there or were now under suspicion of prostitution, shoplifting, purse snatching, petty thievery, and, in consequence, passed furtively by the big blue uniforms on the corner.

The utmost depression came over me as I approached this surreptitious   9 region. Below Fourteenth Street I seemed to be breathing a different air, to be in another world and country where the people had habits and customs alien to anything I had ever heard about.

There were then approximately ten thousand apartments in New York 10 into which no sun ray penetrated directly; such windows as they had opened only on a narrow court from which rose fetid odors. It was seldom cleaned, though garbage and refuse often went down into it. All these dwellings were pervaded by the foul breath of poverty, that moldy, indefinable, indescribable smell which cannot be fumigated out, sickening to me but apparently unnoticed by those who lived there. When I set to work with antiseptics, their pungent sting, at least temporarily, obscured the stench.

I remember one confinement case to which I was called by the doctor 11 of an insurance company. I climbed up the five flights and entered the airless rooms, but the baby had come with too great speed. A boy of ten had been the only assistant. Five flights was a long way; he had wrapped the placenta in a piece of newspaper and dropped it out the window into the court.

Many families took in "boarders," as they were termed, whose small 12 contributions paid the rent. These derelicts, wanderers, alternately working and drinking, were crowded in with the children; a single room sometimes held as many as six sleepers. Little girls were accustomed to dressing and undressing in front of the men, and were often violated, occasionally by their own fathers or brothers, before they reached the age of puberty.

Pregnancy was a chronic condition among the women of this class. 13 Suggestions as to what to do for a girl who was "in trouble" or a married woman who was "caught" passed from mouth to mouth—herb teas, turpentine, steaming, rolling downstairs, inserting slippery elm, knitting needles, shoe-hooks. When they had word of a new remedy they hurried to the drugstore, and if the clerk were inclined to be friendly he might say, "Oh, that won't help you, but here's something that may." The younger druggists usually refused to give advice because, if it were to be known, they would come under the law; midwives were even more fearful. The doomed women implored me to reveal the "secret" rich people had, offering to pay me extra to tell them; many really believed I was holding back information for money. They asked everybody and tried anything, but nothing did them any good. On Saturday nights I have seen groups of from fifty to one hundred with their shawls over their heads waiting outside the office of a five-dollar abortionist.

Each time I returned to this district, which was becoming a recurrent 14 nightmare, I used to hear that Mrs. Cohen "had been carried to a hospital, but had never come back," or that Mrs. Kelly "had sent the children to a neighbor and had put her head into the gas oven." Day after day such tales were poured into my ears—a baby born dead, great relief—the death of an older child, sorrow but again relief of a sort—the story told a thousand times of death from abortion and children going into institutions. I shuddered with horror as I listened to the details and studied the reasons back of them— destitution linked with excessive childbearing. The waste of life seemed utterly senseless. One by one worried, sad, pensive, and aging faces marshaled themselves before me in my dreams, sometimes appealingly, sometimes accusingly.

These were not merely "unfortunate conditions among the poor" such 15 as we read about. I knew the women personally. They were living, breathing, human beings, with hopes, fears, and aspirations like my own, yet their weary, misshapen bodies, "always ailing, never failing," were destined to be thrown on the scrap heap before they were thirty-five. I could not escape from the facts of their wretchedness; neither was I able to see any way out. My own cozy and comfortable family existence was becoming a reproach to me.

Then one stifling mid-July day of 1912 I was summoned to a Grand 16 Street tenement. My patient was a small, slight Russian Jewess, about twenty-eight years old, of the special cast of feature to which suffering lends a madonna-like expression. The cramped three-room apartment was in a sorry state of turmoil. Jake Sachs, a truck driver scarcely older than his wife, had come home to find the three children crying and her unconscious from the effects of a self-induced abortion. He had called the nearest doctor, who in turn had sent for me. Jake's earnings were trifling, and most of them had gone to keep the none-too-strong children clean and properly fed. But his wife's ingenuity had helped them to save a little, and this he was glad to spend on a nurse rather than have her go to a hospital.

The doctor and I settled ourselves to the task of fighting the septicemia. 17 Never had I worked so fast, never so concentratedly. The sultry days and nights were melted into a torpid inferno. It did not seem possible there could be such heat, and every bit of food, ice, and drugs had to be carried up three flights of stairs.

Jake was more kind and thoughtful than many of the husbands I had 18 encountered. He loved his children, and had always helped his wife wash and dress them. He had brought water up and carried garbage down before he left in the morning, and did as much as he could for me while he anxiously watched her progress.

After a fortnight Mrs. Sachs' recovery was in sight. Neighbors, ordinar- 19 ily fatalistic as to the results of abortion, were genuinely pleased that she had survived. She smiled wanly at all who came to see her and thanked them gently, but she could not respond to their hearty congratulations. She appeared to be more despondent and anxious than she should have been, and spent too much time in meditation.

At the end of three weeks, as I was preparing to leave the fragile patient 20
to take up her difficult life once more, she finally voiced her fears, "Another
baby will finish me, I suppose?"

"It's too early to talk about that," I temporized. 21

But when the doctor came to make his last call, I drew him aside. "Mrs. 22
Sachs is terribly worried about having another baby."

"She well may be," replied the doctor, and then he stood before her and 23
said, "Any more such capers, young woman, and there'll be no need to send
for me."

"I know, doctor," she replied timidly, "but," and she hesitated as 24
though it took all her courage to say it, "what can I do to prevent it?"

The doctor was a kindly man, and he had worked hard to save her, but 25
such incidents had become so familiar to him that he had long since lost
whatever delicacy he might once have had. He laughed good-naturedly. "You
want to have your cake and eat it too, do you? Well, it can't be done."

Then picking up his hat and bag to depart he said, "Tell Jake to sleep 26
on the roof."

I glanced quickly at Mrs. Sachs. Even through my sudden tears I could 27
see stamped on her face an expression of absolute despair. We simply looked
at each other, saying no word until the door had closed behind the doctor.
Then she lifted her thin, blue-veined hands and clasped them beseechingly.
"He can't understand. He's only a man. But you do, don't you? Please tell me
the secret, and I'll never breathe it to a soul. *Please!*"

What was I to do? I could not speak the conventionally comforting 28
phrases which would be of no comfort. Instead, I made her as physically easy
as I could and promised to come back in a few days to talk with her again.
A little later, when she slept, I tiptoed away.

Night after night the wistful image of Mrs. Sachs appeared before me. 29
I made all sorts of excuses to myself for not going back. I was busy on other
cases; I really did not know what to say to her or how to convince her of my
own ignorance; I was helpless to avert such monstrous atrocities. Time rolled
by and I did nothing.

The telephone rang one evening three months later, and Jake Sachs' 30
agitated voice begged me to come at once; his wife was sick again and from
the same cause. For a wild moment I thought of sending someone else, but
actually, of course, I hurried into my uniform, caught up my bag, and started
out. All the way I longed for a subway wreck, an explosion, anything to keep
me from having to enter that home again. But nothing happened, even to
delay me. I turned into the dingy doorway and climbed the familiar stairs
once more. The children were there, young little things.

Mrs. Sachs was in a coma and died within ten minutes. I folded her still 31
hands across her breast, remembering how they had pleaded with me, begging so humbly for the knowledge which was her right. I drew a sheet over
her pallid face. Jake was sobbing, running his hands through his hair and
pulling it out like an insane person. Over and over again he wailed, "My God!
My God! My God!"

I left him pacing desperately back and forth, and for hours I myself 32 walked and walked and walked through the hushed streets. When I finally arrived home and let myself quietly in, all the household was sleeping. I looked out my window and down upon the dimly lighted city. Its pains and griefs crowded in upon me, a moving picture rolled before my eyes with photographic clearness: women writhing in travail to bring forth little babies; the babies themselves naked and hungry, wrapped in newspapers to keep them from the cold; six-year-old children with pinched, pale, wrinkled faces, old in concentrated wretchedness, pushed into gray and fetid cellars, crouching on stone floors, their small scrawny hands scuttling through rags, making lamp shades, artificial flowers; white coffins, black coffins, coffins, coffins interminably passing in never-ending succession. The scenes piled one upon another on another. I could bear it no longer.

As I stood there the darkness faded. The sun came up and threw its 33 reflection over the house tops. It was the dawn of a new day in my life also. The doubt and questioning, the experimenting and trying, were now to be put behind me. I knew I could not go back merely to keeping people alive.

I went to bed, knowing that no matter what it might cost, I was finished 34 with palliatives and superficial cures; I was resolved to seek out the root of evil, to do something to change the destiny of mothers whose miseries were vast as the sky.

Questions for Discussion

1. In paragraphs 1–8, Sanger refers to three distinct social levels. What are they? What characterizes each one? How do they differ?

2. Compare Sanger's organization with the cinematographic device of the panorama. Paragraphs 1–15 begin as if from far above the city and the crowd; subsequent paragraphs begin to focus on things in more detail, and they continue to do so with increasing vividness until the Sachses' story begins in paragraph 16. Can you trace the progress of this organization in more detail? What are its effects?

3. In paragraph 25, Sanger gives the doctor on the Sachs case credit for being "a kindly man." Does his response to Mrs. Sachs's plea justify this credit? Can you defend his comments in paragraphs 25–26 in any way?

Suggested Essay Topics

1. Select a moment or an episode in your own life that you now see was decisive in giving you a sense of direction about something specific—for example, whether or not to go to college, to get engaged, to register for the draft, or to stand up for an unpopular cause. In an essay addressed to your fellow students, recount that moment or episode as Sanger does, giving

your readers a vivid picture of the buildup of feelings and ideas that led to your decision. (Naturally, you will have to pick a decision that was dramatic and trying for you, not one that you made casually or that someone else made for you.)

2. In an essay directed to the (real or imaginary) school board in your hometown, make an argument recommending or opposing classes on sex education that would include information on contraceptives. Like Sanger, you should use concrete illustrations to buttress your argument (you may make them up, if necessary, but write about them as if they were firsthand observations). You should also make clear, as she does, the principle you are defending or the goal you are pursuing.

Robert Stone

Robert Stone (b. 1937), a college pot smoker and former cocaine abuser, here draws a portrait both of users and causes. Neither are pretty. "I remember watching an elegant and beautiful woman who was trying cocaine for the first time. The lady, serving herself liberally, had a minor indelicate accident. For a long time she simply sat there contentedly with her nose running, licking her lips. The woman was a person of such imposing presence that watching her get high was like watching an angel turn into an ape; she hung there at a balancing point somewhere midway along the anthropoid spectrum" (¶14).

How do you feel about taking drugs? Do you distinguish among kinds, viewing some as less dangerous or culpable than others? Do you shun them all? Are you a free indulger? Do you think of drugs as mere entertainment, something to indulge in while you're young and in college, but something that you'll abandon later on? Do you think some drugs—all drugs—should be legalized? For what reasons?

Stone clearly sees drug use in this country as connected with the pressure for success and the anxiety about achieving or not achieving success that plagues many people's lives. In a society moving so fast that comparisons between one's own degree of success and that of others is made difficult—when everyone is moving so fast, how can you tell if you are really ahead and by how much?—and in a society that makes many feel that a life not materially successful is by definition a failure, the anxiety that drives people to seek help in feeling successful and looking successful by taking drugs is a powerful force.

Is it any wonder that even the least successful people—those whose status is so low in society that you might think they had given up on the rat race—are among the most eager users of drugs? Perhaps they need illusory supports even more desperately than the yuppies and baby-boomers Stone refers to in his essay: the high rollers and hardball players who take coke not only to get pumped up but simply to show that they can afford it, that they too can travel in the same circles as the fast and beautiful people. But if the drug is in demand even among the gutter trudgers and deadbeats of society, does this mean that the pressure for success is so great that no one, not even the person for whom conventional success is no longer an option, is exempt? If this is the case, is it any wonder that the young of both rich and poor get caught up in the web of illusion, that they fly high, crash low, then search frantically for more intense illusions and ultimately find themselves dependent, devoid of cash, dignity, or hope?

Regardless of your views on drug usage, Robert Stone's essay will provoke your thinking. He is not writing as a doctor, as a moralist, or as a political reactionary. He has been a player in the drug scene itself, and his witness is all the more frightening because of its personal authenticity.

A HIGHER HORROR OF THE WHITENESS: COCAINE'S COLORING OF THE AMERICAN PSYCHE

From *Harper's Magazine,* December 1986.

One day in New York last summer I had a vision near Saint Paul's   1
Chapel of Trinity Church. I had walked a lot of the length of Manhattan, and it seemed to me that a large part of my time had been spent stepping around men who stood in the gutter snapping imaginary whips. Strangers had approached me trying to sell Elavil, an antidepressant. As I stood on Broadway I reflected that although I had grown to middle age seeing strange sights, I had never thought to see people selling Elavil on the street. Street Elavil, I would have exclaimed, that must be a joke!

I looked across the street from Saint Paul's and the daylight seemed   2
strange. I had gotten used to thinking of the Wall Street area as a part of New York where people looked healthy and wholesome. But from where I stood half the men waiting for the light to change looked like Bartleby the Scrivener.* Everybody seemed to be listening in dread to his own heartbeat. They're all loaded, I thought. That was my vision. Everybody was loaded on cocaine.

In the morning, driving into Manhattan, the traffic had seemed particu-   3
larly demonic. I'd had a peculiar exchange with a bridge toll taker who seemed to have one half of a joke I was expected to have the other half of. I didn't. Walking on Fourteenth Street, I passed a man in an imitation leopard-skin hat who was crying as though his heart would break. At Fourth Avenue I was offered the Elavil. Elavil relieves the depression attendant on the deprivation of re-refined cocaine—"crack"—which is what the men cracking the imaginary whips were selling. Moreover, I'd been reading the papers. I began to think that I was seeing stoned cops, stoned grocery shop-

*See the short story "Bartleby" (1853) by Herman Melville (1819–1891).

pers, and stoned boomers.* So it went, and by the time I got to lower Broadway I was concerned. I felt as though I were about to confront the primary
process of hundreds of thousands of unsound minds. What I was seeing in
my vision of New York as super-stoned Super City was cocaine in its role
of success drug.

Not many years ago, people who didn't use cocaine didn't have to know   4
much about it. Now, however, it's intruding on the national perception rather
vigorously. The National Institute on Drug Abuse reported almost six million
current users in 1985, defining a current user as one who took cocaine at least
once in the course of the month preceding the survey. The same source in the
same year reckoned that more than twenty-two million people had tried
cocaine at least once during their lives.

So much is being heard about cocaine, principally through television,   5
that even people who live away from the urban centers are beginning to
experience it as a factor in their lives. Something of the same thing happened
during the sixties, when Americans in quiet parts of the country began to feel
they were being subjected to civil insurrection day in and day out.

One aspect that even people who don't want to know anything about   6
cocaine have been compelled to recognize is that people get unpleasantly
weird under its influence. The term "dope fiend" was coined for cocaine users.
You can actually seem unpleasantly weird to yourself on coke, which is one
of its greatest drawbacks.

In several ways the ubiquity of cocaine and its derivative crack have   7
helped the American city to carry on its iconographic function as Vision of
Hell. Over the past few years some of the street choreography of Manhattan
has changed slightly. There seems to be less marijuana in the air. At the
freight doors of garment factories and around construction sites people cluster smoking something odorless. At night in the ghettos and at the borders
of ghettos, near the tunnels and at downtown intersections, an enormous ugly
argument seems to be in progress. Small, contentious groups of people drift
across the avenues, sometimes squaring off at each other, moving from one
corner to the next, the conformation breaking up and re-forming. The purchase of illegal drugs was always a sordid process, but users and dealers
(pretty much interchangeable creatures) used to attempt adherence to an
idealized vision of the traffic in which smoothie dealt with smoothie in a
confraternity of the hip. Crack sales tend to start with a death threat and
deteriorate rapidly. The words "die" and "motherfucker" are among the most
often heard. Petty race riots between white suburban buyers and minority
urban sellers break out several times an hour. Every half block stand people
in various states of fury, mindless exhilaration, and utter despair—all of it
dreadfully authentic yet all of it essentially artificial.

On the day of my visionary walk through the city I felt beset by a drug   8

*Probably short for "baby-boomers."

I hadn't even been in the same room with for a year. New York always seems to tremble on the brink of entropy—that's why we love her even though she doesn't love us back. But that afternoon it felt as though white crystal had seeped through the plates and fouled the very frame of reference. There was an invisible whiteness deep down things, not just the glistening mounds in their little tricorn Pyramid papers tucked into compacts and under pocket handkerchiefs but, I thought, a metaphysical whiteness. It seemed a little out of place at first. I was not in California. I was among cathedrals of commerce in the midst of a city hard at work. I wondered why the sense of the drug should strike most vividly on Wall Street. It might be the shade of Bartleby,* I thought, and the proximity of the harbor. The whiteness was Melvillean, like the whiteness of the Whale.

In the celebrated chapter on whiteness in *Moby-Dick,* Melville frequently 9 mentions the Andes—not Bolivia, as it happens, but Lima, "the strangest saddest city thou canst see. . . . There is a higher horror in the whiteness of her woe." Higher horror seemed right. I had found a Lima of the mind.

"But not yet," Melville writes, "have we solved the incantation of this 10 whiteness and learned why it appeals with such power to the soul . . . and yet should be as it is, the intensifying agent in things the most appalling to mankind . . . a dumb blankness full of meaning in a wide landscape of snows—a colorless all-color of atheism from which we shrink."

I was in the city to do business with some people who tend toward 11 enthusiasms, toward ardor and mild obsession. Behind every enthusiasm, every outburst of ardor, every mildly obsessive response, I kept scouring the leprous white hand of narcosis. It's a mess when you think everybody's high. I liked it a lot better when the weirdest thing around was me.

We old-time pot smokers used to think we were cute with our instant 12 redefinitions and homespun minimalism. Our attention had been caught by a sensibility a lot of us associated with black people. We weren't as cute as we thought, but for a while we were able to indulge the notion that a small community of minds was being nurtured through marijuana. In a very limited way, in terms of art and music, we were right. In the early days we divided into two camps. Some of us were elitists who thought we had the right to get high because we were artists and musicians and consciousness was our profession and the rest of the world, the "squares," could go to hell. Others of us hoped the insights we got from using drugs like pot could somehow change the world for the better. To people in the latter camp, it was vaguely heartening when a walker in the city could smell marijuana everywhere. The present coke-deluded cityscape is another story.

Cocaine was never much to look at. All drugs have their coarse prac- 13 ticalities, so in the use of narcotics and their paraphernalia, dexterity and savoir-faire are prized. Coke, however, is difficult to handle gracefully. For

*In Melville's short story, a clerk employed by a Wall Street lawyer.

one thing, once-refined cocaine works only in solution with blood, mucus, or saliva, a handicap to éclat that speaks for itself.

I remember watching an elegant and beautiful woman who was trying 14
cocaine for the first time. The lady, serving herself liberally, had a minor indelicate accident. For a long time she simply sat there contentedly with her nose running, licking her lips. This woman was a person of such imposing presence that watching her get high was like watching an angel turn into an ape; she hung there at a balancing point somewhere midway along the anthropoid spectrum.

The first person I ever saw use cocaine was a poet I haven't seen for 15
twenty-five years. It was on the Lower East Side, one night during the fifties, in an age that's as dead now as Agamemnon. Coltrane's "My Favorite Things" was on the record player. The poet was tall and thin and pale and self-destructive, and we all thought that was a great way to be. After he'd done up, his nose started to bleed. The bathtub was in the kitchen, and he sat down on the kitchen floor and leaned his head back against it. You had to be there.

Let me tell you, I honor that man. I honor him for his lonely indepen- 16
dence and his hard outcast's road. I think he was one of the people who, in the fifties, helped to make this country a lot freer. Maybe that's the trouble. Ultimately, nothing is free, in the sense that you have to pay up somewhere along the line.

My friend the poet thought cocaine lived someplace around midnight 17
that he was trying to find. He would not have expected it to become a commonplace drug. He would not have expected over 17 percent of American high school students to have tried it, even thirty years later, any more than he would have expected that one quarter of America's high school students would use marijuana. He was the wild one. In hindsight, we should have known how many of the kids to come would want to be the wild ones too.

A few weeks after my difficult day in the city I was sitting in my car 18
in a New England coastal village leafing through my mail when for some reason I became aware of the car parked beside mine. In the front seat were two teenage girls whose tan summer faces seemed aglow with that combination of apparent innocence and apparent wantonness adolescence inflicts. I glanced across the space between our cars and saw that they were doing cocaine. The car windows were rolled up against the bay breeze. The drug itself was out of sight, on the car seat between them. By turns they descended to sniff. Then both of them sat upright, *bolt upright* might be the way to put it, staring straight ahead of them. They licked their fingers. The girl in the driver's seat ran her tongue over a pocket mirror. The girl beside her looked over at me, utterly untroubled by my presence; there was a six-inch length of peppermint-striped soda straw in her mouth. There are people I know who cannot remove a cigarette from its pack with someone standing behind them, who between opening the seal and lighting up perform the most elaborate pantomimes of guilty depravity. Neither of these children betrayed the

slightest cautious reflex, although we couldn't have been more than a few hundred yards from the village police station. The girl with the straw between her teeth and I looked at each other for an instant and I saw something in her eyes, but I don't know what it was. It wasn't guilty pleasure or defiance or flirtatiousness. Its intellectual aspect was crazy and its emotional valence was cold.

A moment later, the driver threw the car into reverse and straight into 19
the path of an oncoming postal truck, which fortunately braked in time. Then they were off down the road, headed wherever they thought their state of mind might make things better. One wondered where.

Watching their car disappear, I could still see the moment of their highs. 20
Surfacing, they had looked frosted, their faces streaked with a cotton-candied, snotty sugary excitement, a pair of little girls having their afternoon at the fair, their carnival goodies, and all the ride in a few seconds flat. Five minutes from the parking lot, the fairy lights would be burned out. Their parents would find them testy, sarcastic, and tantrum prone. Unless, of course, they had more.

The destructiveness of cocaine today is a cause for concern. What form 21
is our concern to take?

American politicians offer a not untypical American political response. 22
The Democrats say they want to hang the dealers. The Republicans say they want to hang them and throw their bones to the dogs. Several individuals suggest that the military be used in these endeavors. Maybe all the partisan competition for dramatic solutions will produce results. Surely some of our politically inspired plans must work some of the time.

I was talking with a friend of mine who's a lawyer recently. Like many 23
lawyers, she once used a lot of cocaine, although she doesn't anymore. She and I were discussing the satisfactions of cocaine abuse and the lack thereof, and she recounted the story of a stock-trading associate of hers who was sometimes guided in his decisions by stimulants. One day, all of his clients received telephone calls informing them that the world was coming to an end and that he was supervising their portfolios with that in mind. The world would end by water, said the financier, but the right people would turn into birds and escape. He and some of his clients were already growing feathers and wattles.

"Some gonna fly and some gonna die," the broker intoned darkly to his 24
startled customers.

We agreed that while this might be the kind of message you'd be glad 25
to get from your Yaqui soothsayer, it hardly qualified as sound investment strategy. (Although, God knows, the market can be that way!)

"But sometimes," she said, "you feel this illusion of lucidity. Of excel- 26
lence."

I think it's more that you feel like you're *about* to feel an illusion of 27
lucidity and excellence. But lucidity and excellence are pretty hot stuff, even

in a potential state, even as illusion. Those are very contemporary goals and quite different from the electric twilight that people were pursuing in the sixties.

"I thought of cocaine as a success drug," one addict is reported saying 28 in a recent newspaper story. Can you blame him? It certainly looks like a success drug, all white and shiny like an artificial Christmas morning. It glows and it shines just as success must. And success is back! The faint sound you hear at the edges of perception is the snap, crackle, and pop of winners winning and losers losing.

You can tell the losers by their downcast eyes bespeaking unseemly 29 scruple and self-doubt. You can tell the winners by their winning ways and natty strut; look at them stepping out there, all confidence and hard-edged realism. It's a new age of vim and vigor, piss and vinegar and cocaine. If we work hard enough and live long enough, we'll all be as young as the President.*

Meanwhile, behold restored as lord of creation, pinnacle of evolution 30 and progress, alpha and omega† of the rationalized universe, Mr. Success, together with his new partner and pal, Ms. Success. These two have what it takes; they've got heart, they've got drive, they've got aggression. It's a no-fault world of military options and no draft. Hey, they got it all.

Sometimes, though, it gets scary. Some days it's hard to know whether 31 you're winning or not. You're on the go but so's the next guy. You're moving fast but so is she. Sometimes you're afraid you'd think awful thoughts if you had time to think. That's why you're almost glad there isn't time. How can you be sure you're on the right track? You might be on the wrong one. Everybody can't be a winner or there wouldn't be a game. "Some gonna fly and some gonna die."

Predestinarian‡ religion generated a lot of useful energy in this republic. 32 It cast a long December shadow, a certain slant of light on winter afternoons. Things were grim with everybody wondering whether he was chosen, whether he was good enough, really, truly good enough and not just faking. Finally, it stopped being useful. We got rid of it.

It's funny how the old due bills come up for presentation. We had Faith 33 and not Works. Now we've got all kinds of works and no faith. And people still wonder if they've got what it takes.

When you're wondering if you've got what it takes, wondering whether 34 you're on the right track and whether you're going to fly, do you sometimes want a little pick-me-up? Something upbeat and cool with nice lines, something that shines like success and snaps you to, so you can step out there

*An ironic statement: At the time of the writing of this essay President Ronald Reagan was in his seventies.

†"Alpha and omega": beginning and end.

‡The theological belief that some people, the "elect," are predestined to go to heaven, while others are predestined to go to hell.

feeling aggressive, like a million-dollar Mr. or Ms.? And after that, would you like to be your very own poet and see fear—yes, I said fear—in a handful of dust? Have we got something for you! Something white.

On the New York morning of which I've spoken I beheld its whiteness. 35 How white it really is, and what it does, was further described about 130 years ago by America's God-bestowed prophet, who delineated the great American success story with the story of two great American losers, Bartleby and Ahab.* From *Moby-Dick*:

> And when we consider that . . . theory of the natural philosophers, that all other earthly hues—every stately or lovely emblazoning—the sweet tinges of sunset skies and woods; yea, and the gilded velvets of butterflies, and the butterfly cheeks of young girls; all these are but the subtile deceits, not actually inherent in substance, but only laid on from without; and when we proceed further, and consider that the mystical cosmetic which produces every one of her hues, the great principle of light, for ever remains white or colorless in itself, and if operating without medium upon matter, would touch all objects, even tulips and roses, with its own blank tinge—pondering all this, the palsied universe lies before us a leper; and like wilful travellers in Lapland, who refuse to wear colored and coloring glasses upon their eyes, so the wretched infidel gazes himself blind at the monumental white shroud that wraps all the prospect around him.

All over America at this moment pleasurable surges of self-esteem are 36 fading. People are discovering that the principal thing one does with cocaine is run out of it.

If cocaine is the great "success drug," is there a contradiction in that it 37 brings such ruin not only to the bankers and the lawyers but to so many of the youngest, poorest Americans? I think not. The poor and the children have always received American obsessions as shadow and parody. They too can be relied on to "go for it."

"Just say no!" we tell them and each other when we talk about crack 38 and cocaine. It is necessary that we say this because liberation starts from there.

But we live in a society based overwhelmingly on appetite and self- 39 regard. We train our young to be consumers and to think most highly of their own pleasure. In this we face a contradiction that no act of Congress can resolve.

In our debates on the subject of dealing with drug abuse, one of the 40 recurring phrases has been "the moral equivalent of war." Not many of those who use it, I suspect, know its origin.

In 1910, the philosopher William James wrote an essay discussing the 41 absence of values, the "moral weightlessness" that seemed to characterize modern times. James was a pacifist. Yet he conceded that the demands of

---

*Ahab was the ill-fated pursuer of the white whale, Moby-Dick, in Melville's novel, *Moby-Dick* (1851).

battle were capable of bringing forth virtues like courage, loyalty, community, and mutual concern that seemed in increasingly short supply as the new
century unfolded. As a pacifist and a moralist, James found himself in a
dilemma. How, he wondered, can we nourish those virtues without having
to pay the dreadful price that war demands? We must foster courage, loyalty,
and the rest, but we must not have war. Very well, he reasoned, we must find
the *moral equivalent of war.*

    Against these drugs can we ever, rhetoric aside, bring any kind of real 42
heroism to bear? When they've said no to crack, can we someday give them
something to say yes to?

Questions for Discussion

1. Do you feel as negative about drug use as Stone does? Are your opinions
   based on personal experience or the first-hand observation of others?
   Where in his account of users and causes do you find Stone weakest, and
   where do you find him most convincing? What is he trying to convince
   you *of?* What is Stone's thesis?

2. Who in class can explain the appropriateness of Stone's several allusions
   to Herman Melville and to Melville's many and complicated views of
   whiteness in *Moby-Dick?* If no one can explicate this allusion, perhaps it
   would be useful and interesting to request a specialist in nineteenth-
   century American fiction, most likely to be found in the English Department, to read Stone's essay and make an appearance in your class to discuss
   Stone's Melvillian references.

3. What is the point to Stone's account of the two New England girls he
   caught doing cocaine in the front seat of their car (¶¶18–20)? Stone seemed
   positively frightened by what he saw. Why?

4. What rhetorical or emotional effects does Stone achieve by slipping into
   a kind of huckster's lingo, a salesman's patter, in paragraphs 30 and 34?

5. After pointing out the ruinous consequences of cocaine use, Stone goes on
   to say, "But we live in a society based overwhelmingly on appetite and
   self-regard. We train our young to be consumers and to think most highly
   of their own pleasure. In this we face a contradiction that no act of Congress can resolve" (¶39). Does this claim about the nature of the attraction
   of cocaine for young people seem to you insightful or off the point? What
   reasons can you give for your answer?

Suggested Essay Topics

1. In the last paragraph of his essay, Stone suggests, without elaborating the
   point, that part of the reason for extensive drug use among the young in
   this country is the lack of anything for them to believe in beyond material

pursuits and physical pleasures. If you think he is right, develop his point for him. In an essay directed to Stone's own audience—that is, a general audience of fairly well-educated readers—take his final point as the thesis of your own essay and develop appropriate supporting arguments to make your case convincing.

2. If you have ever had experience with drug dependency (including alcohol, the most commonly used and abused drug in the world) either in your own person or by living with another person who was (is) dependent, write an essay addressed to someone who has not had such experience, detailing what you take to be the worst aspects of drug dependency and explaining how you dealt with the problem.

Susan Neville

Do you expect to know the same people all your life, to have friends who will not just be called *"life-long," but who will really have such a place in your life? Do you expect to maintain intimacy all your days (or theirs) with family members—cousins, aunts, uncles, grandparents—that you were close to as a child? Or do you already have the intuition that estrangements will occur, that your going away to college or moving from your hometown or traveling abroad will create a gulf that in some ways will never be re-crossed? And if you do know that, does the anticipation of that loss seem a sad diminishment, or do you feel that such changes are just the inevitable accompaniments of growing up, that everyone has to face separation from family and friends, and that the future is sufficiently full of promise to make up for such losses?*

One consideration, potentially unpleasant and perhaps a little frightening, that necessarily enters into the question of "What Should I Become?" (the subtitle of this chapter) is that choosing who to become is not always a matter of simply choosing what you want and then getting it. We may become some things over which we have little or no control, such as becoming distant and separated from people we once lived closely with. In "Cousins," Susan Neville (b. 1951) explores the complex arrangements of connectedness, estrangement, and loss that are inevitable accompaniments to ordinary living.

The connectedness comes naturally, a spontaneous consequence of children being raised together, sharing the same experiences, knowing each others' parents and houses, going to the same schools, and having the same expectations of life. Children do not see estrangement and separation coming, and when it does come it is not brought by anyone's failure or shallowness or treachery. It comes, rather, just because people change, grow, or move away to get an education and make their own lives. Then, at a funeral or during a Christmas holiday, or on a summer visit, they find unexpectedly that it has happened, that they are no longer what they once were to each other, that they no longer know how to share the same intimacy they once did. It is no one's fault, but it is a loss, this disappearance of connections that once supported one like a net.

Neville's sensitive and nostalgic, yet hardheaded and realistic, probing of this issue invites us all to think about the connections we most value and the ones we might work hardest to maintain as we try to answer the question, "What should I become?"

COUSINS

From *The Invention of Flight* (1984). Winner of the Flannery O'Connor Prize for short fiction, 1984.

We share some of the same relatives and, if diagrammed, they would hold us together like hinges or bonds drawn in geometric shapes between hydrogen, say, and oxygen in water, or any other elements that fuse. But it's a tenuous fusion; there are many other relatives that we don't share, and if one of these other relatives draws a family tree I am not included, unfastened and set to drift because I am related only in that my mother is sister to their father and my blood does not flow directly to the treasure we all hope to find, hidden in our genes and only waiting to be recognized, some man or woman centuries before whose life was important enough to justify the secret knowledge that we deserve more, much more, recognition from the world than we have ever received.

There is one grandmother between us. They have another, a millionaire's wife with orange pink hair who has been lying in bed for three years from a hip that healed months after it was broken. I had another grandmother who had cancer hidden for ten years behind the denim overalls she wore all summer while she nurtured zucchini, cherries, corn. She died one week after the doctor made her lie down, finally, for some rest. It would be interesting if something could be, but nothing can be, inferred from that. It says nothing about my character or about my cousins'. I am not related by blood to their mother, but we have the same thighs. My oldest cousin is not related by blood to my father, but they share a nose. My own brother does not look at all like me; he looks like a man I saw once, for a brief instant, in a shopping mall, buying a pearl-handled umbrella.

When we were children we could say that we were good friends, close friends. At Christmas, the oldest girl cousin and I got matching dolls from our shared grandmother. There is a photograph at the bottom of a glass paperweight in my mother's bedroom where the three cousins and my brother and I are falling out of an overstuffed chair. We look like we know each other well. At age eleven I got very fat and had a permanent that was too tight; then I got tall and thin. Five years later, when she was eleven, my oldest cousin did the same thing. For a while she was like a spring following me. When we were children I knew them so well that I could have summed up each one of them in a sentence if I had been asked to, looking past those things that were contradictory until I found what was continuous. I could say that the oldest one cried tears without making a sound, the middle one cried with more sound than tears, and no one had ever seen the youngest one cry. If you knew these things about them, then you knew everything you needed to know.

But there seems to come a time when the relationship between in- 4 dividuals becomes set, a concrete wall, when past that point if one of the individuals changes it demands change in all of the others, a recognition of the change, a breathing. And if the others refuse, the wall breaks down into separate blocks and that is all. In the case of my cousins and me, the break- down is my fault, although it's possible that I am making myself too central, that actually, because I am five years older than the oldest of them, I am only on the periphery, an observer, unimportant. I admit that possibly each one of them and my brother and I would all rush to assign the guilt to ourselves, that it does underline our importance, but in this case I can't help feeling that it is truly I who have caused it because they are the ones who have stayed in the same place, the same houses, and done nothing more than grow older and I am the one who moved away and have tried to come back, but never for good.

The summer before I left for college was when our relationship was set 5 for me. I was the only teenager; my brother and our oldest cousin were twelve. At dinner they performed for me and for each other. When it was my turn to perform, I gave them secrets: names of rock groups, clothing stores, high school teachers that would serve as passwords, keys to the exciting life they supposed I led. I grew used to being the sage, used to the openness of them, the transparency of children. Then I left for college, came back for brief visits, graduated, began to work in another state, and—returning for visits at Christmas and Thanksgiving—found that I was becoming obsolete, that the secrets no longer resided in me. I was no longer needed. I am ashamed to admit that I was hurt by this, found it difficult to speak with them. It was difficult for me to change. I suppose that I am selfish or too easily intimidated. Perhaps I am shy. They were different people, aware of themselves, able to think about their actions secretly at the same time that they performed them—a definition, I suppose, of adulthood. It seems so much more alienating when you watch it grow, when there is suddenly something that needs to be broken down between people who were, at one time, close. I suppose that parents feel this, I'm not sure. I know that it is profoundly sad. With strangers it is more easily broken down. There is no false assumption that you know each other, that it is not necessary to begin at the beginning.

And worse, there is the feeling, unthinkable, that we are the seeds 6 scattered by a single tree, in the hopes that one will take. William and Henry James are a rarity. There is only one Joyce, one Shakespeare, one Pasteur, one Michelangelo. Raised as we were, similarly, we cannot occupy the same space. As teenagers, all of our ambitions ran deep. Only mine are becoming tempered by the demands of practical things. I am slowly beginning to realize that teaching is not something that I make my living at temporarily until I become a famous actress, a playwright. It is what I do, what I am. My cousins do not want to hear this, that it might happen to them. I had been sent out to test the waters, and am no longer trustworthy. Perhaps I am exaggerating. Perhaps I am feeling, right now, the price of my restlessness.

Early this year their father died, my uncle, my aunt's husband, my mother's brother, my grandmother's son. It is important that he is understood in this way, how he was connected to all of us, because he had been the central bond. He had had a heart condition for years. Still, his death was unexpected. He was in his middle forties, slender, handsome like one of the singers my mother loved, Perry Como—a slimmer Frank Sinatra. He had given up salt and Cokes and this was supposed to have protected him. My aunt found him slumped over a stove that he was moving into his appliance store.   7

At one time he had wanted to be a pharmacist. Every man I knew who was his age, my father's age, had wanted to be a doctor or a pharmacist. But they had all gone into business. My own father, who started his studies in pre-medicine, spends his life writing reports on the viscosity of nail polish, the solidity of brushes. The only ones who remembered these ambitions, who spoke of them often as if they were still alive, as if they formed part of the characters of the sons, were the grandmothers.   8

I thought of pharmacy when my mother called to tell me of my uncle's death and I thought of my cousins as they had been when we were small children. This one's an actress, my mother would say, this one a doctor. This one's a poet, this one a composer, this one a politician, my Aunt Mary would counter. I asked how everyone was taking it and my mother told me that my aunt and my grandmother had both collapsed, but that they were doing better now. There are so many "I's" in this that it will be difficult to believe that the real action is going on elsewhere, where I am not. I can imagine the slumping, the collapsing, the initial grief, but I cannot convey it clearly. I am afraid of flying, of the loss of control, it is possibly the thing that keeps me in one place for any period of time, but I flew home that afternoon. By the time I arrived, people had begun to pull themselves together, to behave as though they were calm. No one knew how to act as, here too, the real drama took place in the places where we are separate.   9

The funeral seems important in the history of my cousins and me. The funeral home was huge—subdued lighting, gleaming parquet floors. I had never seen such furniture, such carpeting and drapes. There were boxes with tissues sticking out like sails or pale limp hands, lying discreetly on marble-topped tables; hidden in odd corners, small private rooms for crying.   10

I can see my grandmother sitting on a pink velvet antique chair. She has chosen the lowest chair in the room and still her feet don't touch the floor. There are no longer any stores in town that carry her shoe size, and she is wearing a larger size with cloth stuffed into the toes and her white legs are swinging, ever so slightly. The last time I saw my uncle, a year and a half ago, she was buttoning the top button of his winter coat, turning up his collar. She and my mother are both wearing navy blue. It is proper, my mother says, but not as dreary as black. She is a few inches taller than my grandmother. Some day her shoe size also will be extinct. They are both sitting there holding   11 white gloves, with their hands folded over their purses. Before we left the house they had come into my room again and again, asking whether this necklace was too gaudy or these earrings were becoming. For lunch we had cantaloupe and cottage cheese, carefully garnished with parsley. My grandmother leans over to my mother and asks if she thinks the cantaloupe will set well on their stomachs. My mother says she's sure it will and my grandmother sits back up, comforted. My aunt and my oldest cousin wear slacks, simple blouses, and when they first arrive the rest of us look overdressed, showy. Mary doesn't own a dress, my grandmother whispers to me, a little too loudly.

We walk into the room where my uncle is lying in a mahogany casket. 12 It is obvious from the way one cousin touches another's arm or the arm of my aunt that they have bonded together, that when they turn they put on their calm looks, the looks reserved for strangers. I feel like an outsider. We begin to look at each other, briefly, then at the flowers, and we move to the back of the room, away from the body. We circle the walls, looking at the cards as if we are at a museum. How lovely, I say to my oldest cousin, these roses. And these, she says, these apricot glads. I look at her shoes, half a size larger than my mother's, the same size as my own, and I wonder if the world will outgrow us also, as if everything contains some magical yeast, some incredible fermentation, and the women in my family are being left behind, and I almost say something like this to my cousin while looking at a brass goblet, some roses, some cut glass. The boy cousin leaves us, moves to sit in a chair near his father. He straightens his tie, is careful with the jacket of his suit. He will have nothing to do with our talk of flowers.

I see the room filling with people. Each of the family members is sur- 13 rounded by satellites, friends, distant relatives. When friends come, we are animated. It is wearing, this talk, but we find ourselves interested; we are amazed at how some people are so young still, how some are so old. For long periods of time I forget that my uncle is there, my eyes never moving to the front of the room. I hear Aunt Mary laughing and watch her Indian wrestle with her daughter's boyfriend. My words begin to come easily; I walk up, excited, to where the boy cousin is sitting, watching his father, but when I get there all I ask is the name of a flower, the waxy looking red bloom that is shaped like an ear. He shrugs, will keep his vigil, and I wonder why I did not say more.

Our grandmother, suddenly afraid that there might be something to 14 religion and wanting him to be comfortable, her son, asks my aunt if we shouldn't have a proper funeral. My aunt says no, a small gathering at the gravesite, maybe a psalm, and after that no dinner, no gathering. I overhear the middle cousin whispering to a friend. What is this called, what we're doing? Is this a wake we are having? We have no names for tradition.

I see my middle cousin, her hair the color, the cut of Jean Harlow's.* 15 I show her where there are Cokes downstairs. We sit on a sofa and I ask her

*Famous American movie actress (1911–1937) of the 1930s; her trademark was shoulder-length, platinum blonde hair.

where she's going to go to college when she is through with high school, what she'll do after that. She shakes her hair, stretches her long legs in front of her, says that she plans to go into music, that she hopes to write a Broadway musical, an opera, a symphony. She says that she will keep her father's name, that she will never change it for any other man. She tells me that she changed the spelling of her first name two years ago, from a "y" on the end to an "e." She says she noticed that I spelled it the wrong way on all the Christmas cards I sent the family, but that I can keep spelling it that way because she is changing it back to "y." I feel absurdly angry at this. I want to tell her, of course, that I should have known, that it was the same thing her older sister had done at her age, the same thing I had done, that it was not, as she felt, original. I want to tell her that she may not have the strength for that, that her talent may not be as great as she suspects. And because I hesitate before I wish her success and because I find, when I do say it, that I do not at that moment mean it, I suddenly am convinced—even though for me the idea of sin has little substance—that what I am feeling is somehow, inexorably, sinful. My cousin leaves and I wonder if everyone becomes this confused at funerals, and I remember a cousin of my mother's who, at the death of their grandmother, seemingly bothered less by the presence of death than by the realization that she was, herself, fully alive, left her husband and children and became legendarily promiscuous for a time.

Later, six or seven of my grandmother's friends come in a group. They 16 have been at a birthday party of the oldest one of their friends. They are all my grandmother's height. They had walked together on the first day of grade school. They tell me these stories. The phone wires flame between them, every day, in different patterns. Each day they make a connection. Here I am surrounded by people who know each other well. Most of the people I have known keep friends for three or four years and then someone moves, or everyone moves. At first we write letters and then we stop. And if we run into each other a few years later, we are different people. I can't imagine what it would be like to have a friend for over sixty years, if I would begin to know what is the same about me from decade to decade, if I would have the depth that is necessary when you're not always starting over. Two of my grandmother's cousins are in the group. They have grown up together, gone the same ways, belong to the same clubs and women's groups. One would not join without the others.

The time for visitation ends and two men in black suits clear the room 17 of people and we are forced once again to stand by the casket. My aunt stands by her husband, looking like a girl, face flushed from the talk, excited. The muscles melt as one of the men from the funeral home puts a crank into the casket, waiting for us to take a last look at his handiwork before he lowers the lid, as nonchalant as if he's offering us, please, one last chocolate. I remember that my uncle's blood has been drained from him, that he has been denied even the comfort of his own blood, and I think of that same blood in all of us, bits of tubing cut and fastened, then unfastened.

He looks so pretty, my grandmother says, still holding onto my mother, 18 he looks so peaceful. He's dead, my aunt says, just dead and that's all. Her shoulders slump forward. The man in the black suit begins to lower the lid slowly and we all huddle together, touch arms, bits of glass coming together finally in a pattern. On my arm I can feel the texture of skin through the soft blouses of my oldest and middle cousin and it feels like my skin. I feel my face and it is a cousin's face; my mother's voice is in my throat. And I think that there is no one I love more than this. *Please God, let them be as great as they can be. Keep the old ones strong and the young ones strong, and when one goes, as this one, please God, let him live within us so that we are greater, not smaller, from his passing.* Then cousins break forward, a last look. And then we all break apart, head for separate cars.

In the morning we watch two young boys in paint-splattered jeans and   19
khaki jackets try to crank the casket into the vault. They have difficulty getting all four sides level and I think that if we weren't there they might let it fall and be done with it. They get it down finally, with much banging and chipping of mahogany, and there is silence, a green wind, and I think that I can hear my cousins' voices but am afraid that I am only hearing my own. And then my cousins and my aunt get into their car. My brother gets into his, Aunt Mary's father into another. My mother and grandmother take me to the airport and they return to their homes.

At Christmas we all get together, but it's built up again and we've lost   20
the stimulus to break it down. We rush through dinner, gifts are sparse, several of us have the beginnings of a cold. We are dressed carelessly. Later we will all wash our hair to go out with friends. When it's time to leave we feel relief. It is a scene we will repeat many times.

Questions for Discussion

1. If you have ever been to the funeral of a relative, as Neville depicts her narrator doing in "Cousins," what feelings and thoughts about family and connectedness did the experience arouse in you? Were your feelings like the narrator's or were they different? Why?

2. Have you ever had the experience of moving so far away from close family members or friends that former intimacy was made impossible? How keenly did you feel the loss? What was it like the first time you returned for a visit? Could you pick up where you had left off as if nothing had changed? If not, did you experience that separateness as a sadness? Why or why not?

3. Do you expect or desire to return to your hometown to make a living after college? Why or why not? Do you anticipate having some of the same friends for life? Why or why not?

4. What is your personal reaction to the prayer in paragraph 18? Do you find it moving? Why or why not? What is your reaction to the prayer as a critical reader of stories? What function does the prayer serve in advancing the story or helping to develop the character of the narrator? Would the story be damaged or improved if the prayer were omitted? Why or why not?

Suggested Essay Topics

1. This essay suggestion is an extension of discussion question 2. If you have ever had the experience of moving away from close family members or friends (or had them move away from you), write an essay directed to your classmates in which you analyze the feelings that the move aroused in you. Did you feel diminished by the loss? Frightened? Lonely? Angry? Whatever your feelings were, this is an opportunity to identify them and to try to understand what gave rise to them. After describing your feelings, go on in your essay to analyze what those feelings reveal about your need for certain forms of connectedness; suggest what role such connections play in your life. Finally, say whether you think there is any point in working at maintaining certain connections in your life and, if you do think there is a point to it, discuss what that point is and suggest what you are going to *do* in your life to maintain them.

2. In an essay directed to your family, perhaps in the form of a letter, undertake to evaluate your family's success or failure in maintaining nourishing relationships with other family members or friends. The point here is not necessarily to press blame, but to analyze what opportunities for such relationships have been lost or prized by your family, and what the consequences have been for its members. Indicate to your audience the hopes you have for your own future family relationships.

Patricia Hampl

Patricia Hampl (b. 1946), American writer of Czech descent, explores in this essay the theme of the chapter—"What Should I Become?"—by trying to see how she fits as an individual within the context of two larger social domains: on the one hand, the Czech past to which her family, but not she (because born in America), still has direct links and ties, and on the other hand, the American present of the 1960s which provided the turbulent context for her adolescent and young-adult years.

The old saying—"How can I know what I mean 'til I see what I say?"— captures Hampl's sense of what it was like trying to determine what she should "become" as a young girl and woman. Its as if she was saying "How can I know what I want to become until I know who I've been?" Who she has been, of course, is whatever her family has been. They are her inescapable context, and in this essay she expresses the frustration she felt with them as a young woman for believing that they had not been anything. The members of her family, without "the ghost of a pretension" (¶14) "have always been polite enough to feel that nothing has ever happened to them" (¶24). "In fact, is it a heritage," she asks, to belong to a family that has "discarded" its past "because it was not only useless but simply without interest" (¶14)?

But the larger context affecting her perplexity about who to "become" is the context of an American society divided against itself over the Vietnam War. Speaking of her own generation, Hampl says, "We had lost the national connection and were heartsick in a cultural way" (¶18), a statement that raises the interesting question of the extent to which all of us rely on a "national connection" as an essential component of our personal development. If it is true that Hampl needed a "national connection" which the confusion, polarization, and anger of the time prevented her from enjoying, is it true that everyone needs such a connection? Many would say yes. They would argue that both the context and the boundaries of who we may become are set not by us but by our culture, our "national connection." They could go on to add the argument that even the concepts, the ideas, and the language with which we think about the possible kinds of selves we might become are all social inheritances, not individual accomplishments.

If this is true, then it may follow that trying to grow up in an excessively turbulent era may present young people at a certain stage of their development with definite problems. Adding anger and polarization to the already bewildering uncertainty of adolescence, and then to the already bewildering pluralism of American society as well, may simply make a "national connection" seem terminally impossible.

Does the lack of a "national connection" make anyone feel incomplete? Hampl's experience suggests that it may: "[A]t home I didn't talk psychology, I talked politics, arguing with a kind of angry misery whose depths confused me" (¶18), as if the problem were not an internal neurosis but a public pathology. Without putting it in these words, Hampl raises the question of whether young people might not need the affirmation of and connection with a broad stream of public consensus which, precisely because it is so generally accepted, they can set aside for the time being (while they are trying to find themselves) in order to concentrate on their personal development.

In the absence of such a broad current of public consensus, however, young people may be thrust too early into public discourse where, if Hampl's experience is typical, they carry their immaturity with them—making them miserable—and contributing little of substance to public policy. But, they have no other choice because they need a public consensus as the base of their own personal development.

Whatever your views on these issues, Patricia Hampl writes of the intersections among memory, family, and nation in a memorable and vivid way.

A ROMANTIC EDUCATION

From *A Romantic Education* (1981).*

I was five and was sitting on the floor of the vestibule hallway of my 1
grandmother's house where the one bookcase had been pushed. The bookcase
wasn't in the house itself—ours wasn't a reading family. I was holding in my
lap a book of sepia photographs bound in a soft brown cover, stamped in
flaking gold with the title *Zlatá Praha.* Golden Prague, views of the nineteenth
century.

The album felt good, soft. First, the Hradčany Castle and its gardens, 2
then a close-up of the astronomical clock, a view of the baroque jumble of
Malá Stream. Then a whole series of photographs of the Vltava River, each
showing a different bridge, photograph after pale photograph like a wild rose
that opens petal by petal, exposing itself effortlessly, as if there were no such
thing as regret. All the buildings in the pictures were hazy, making it seem
that the air, not the stone, held the contour of the baroque villas intact.

I didn't know how to read yet, and the Czech captions under the pic- 3
tures were no more incomprehensible to me than English would have been.
I liked the soft, fleshlike pliancy of the book. I knew the pictures were of
Europe, and that Europe was far away, unreachable. Still, it had something
to do with me, with my family. I sat in the cold vestibule, turning the pages
of the Prague album. I was flying; I was somewhere else. I was not in St. Paul,
Minnesota, and I was happy.

My grandmother appeared at the doorway. Her hands were on her stout 4
hips, and she wanted me to come out of the unheated hallway. She wanted
me to eat coffee cake in the kitchen with everybody else, and I had been hard
to find. She said, "Come eat," as if this were the family motto.

As she turned to go, she noticed the album. In a second she was down 5
on the floor with me, taking the album carefully in her hands, turning the
soft, felt pages. "Oh," she said, "Praha." She looked a long time at one
picture, I don't remember which one, and then she took a white handkerchief
out of her pinafore apron pocket, and dabbed at the tears under her glasses.
She took off the wire-rim glasses and made a full swipe.

Her glasses had made deep hollows on either side of her nose, two small 6
caves. They looked as if, with a poke, the skin would give way like a ripe
peach, and an entrance would be exposed into her head, into the skull, a
passageway to the core of her brain. I didn't want her head to have such
wounds. Yet I liked them, these unexpected dips in a familiar landscape.

"So beautiful," she was crying melodramatically over the album. "So 7
beautiful." I had never seen an adult cry before. I was relieved, in some odd
way, that there was crying in adulthood, that crying would not be taken
away.

My grandmother hunched down next to me in the hallway; she held the 8 album, reciting the gold-stamped captions as she turned the pages and dabbed at her eyes. She was having a good cry. I wanted to put my small finger into the two little caves of puckered skin, the eyeless sockets on either side of her large, drooping nose. Strange wounds, I wanted to touch them. I wanted to touch her, my father's mother. She was so *foreign.*

Looking repeatedly into the past, you do not necessarily become fascinated with your own life, but rather with the phenomenon of memory. The act of remembering becomes less autobiographical; it begins to feel tentative, aloof. It becomes blessedly impersonal. 9

The self-absorption that seems to be the impetus and embarrassment of autobiography turns into (or perhaps always was) a hunger for the world. Actually, it begins as hunger for *a* world, one gone or lost, effaced by time or a more sudden brutality. But in the act of remembering, the personal environment expands, resonates beyond itself, beyond its "subject," into the endless and tragic recollection that is history. 10

We look at old family photographs in which we stand next to black, boxy Fords and are wearing period costumes, and we do not gaze fascinated because there we are young again, or there we are standing, as we never will again in life, next to our mother. We stare and drift because there we are . . .* historical. It is the dress, the black car that dazzle us now and draw us beyond our mother's bright arms which once caught us. We reach into the attractive impersonality of something more significant than ourselves. 11

We embrace the deathliness and yet we are not dead. We are impersonal and yet ourselves. The astonishing power and authority of memory derive from this paradox. Here, in memory, we live *and* die. We do "live again" in memory, but differently: in history as well as in biography. And when these two come together, forming a narrative, they approach fiction. The imprecision of memory causes us to create, to extend remembrance into narrative. It sometimes seems, therefore, that what we remember is not—could not be—true. And yet it is *accurate.* The imagination, triggered by memory, is satisfied that this is so. 12

We trust memory against all the evidence: it is selective, subjective, cannily defensive, unreliable as fact. But a single red detail remembered—a hat worn in 1952, the nail polish applied one summer day by an aunt to her toes, separated by balls of cotton, as we watched—has more real blood than the creatures around us on a bus as, for some reason, we think of that day, that hat, those bright feet. That world. This power of memory probably comes from its kinship with the imagination. In memory each of us is an artist: each of us creates. The Kingdom of God, the nuns used to tell us in school, is within you. We may not have made a religion of memory, but it is our passion, and along with (sometimes in opposition to) science, our authority. It is a kingdom of its own. 13

*Ellipses are Hampl's.

Psychology, which is somehow *our* science, the claustrophobic disci- 14
pline of the century, has made us acknowledge the value of remembering—
even at the peril of shame.* But it is especially difficult to reach back into the
merely insignificant, into a family life where, it seemed, nothing happened,
where there wasn't the ghost of a pretension. That is a steelier resistance
because to break through what is unimportant and as anonymous as dirt a
greater sense of worthlessness must be overcome. At least shame is interesting; at least it is hidden, the sign of anything valuable. But for a past to be
overlooked, discarded because it was not only useless but simply without
interest—that is a harsher heritage. In fact, is it a heritage?

It seems as if I spent most of my twenties holding a lukewarm cup of 15
coffee, hunched over a table, talking. Innumerable cups of coffee, countless
tables: the booths of the Gopher Grill at the University of Minnesota where,
probably around 1965, I first heard myself use the word *relationship;* a little
later, the orange formica table of a federal prison where "the man I live with"
(there still is no other term) was serving a sentence for draft resistance; and
the second-hand tables of a dozen apartments, the wooden farmhouse table
of a short-lived commune—table after table, friend after friend, rehashing
our hardly ended (or not ended) childhoods. I may have the tables wrong;
maybe the formica one was in the farmhouse, the oak one in the prison,
maybe the chairs in the prison were orange and the table gray. But they are
fixtures, nailed down, not to be moved: memories.

This generation has written its memoirs early; we squeezed every child- 16
hood lemon for all it was worth: my mother this, my father that. Our self-
absorption was appalling. But I won't go back—not yet—on that decade. It
was also the time when my generation, as "a generation," was most political,
most involved. The people I sat with, picking at our individual pasts, wearing
nightgowns till noon as we analyzed within a millimeter our dreams and their
meanings (that is, how they proved this or that about our parents), finally put
on our clothes, went outside and, in various ways that are too easily forgotten, tried to end a war which we were the first, as a group, to recognize was
disastrous. In fact, our protest against the war is what made us a generation,
even to ourselves.

Perhaps no American generation—certainly not our parents who were 17
young during the Depression—had a childhood as long as ours. The war kept
us young. We stayed in school, endlessly, it seemed, and our protest kept us
in the child's position: we alternately "rebelled" against and pestered the
grownups for what we wanted—an end to the war. Those who fought the
war had no such long, self-reflective youths. Childhood belonged to us, who
stayed at home. And we became the "sixties generation."

Our certainty that the war was wrong became entangled with our 18

---

*An indirect reference to Freudian psychoanalysis which, in its treatment of neuroses, takes the
patient back in memory to the confrontation with a hitherto repressed event about which the
patient feels traumatized or ashamed.

analysis of our families and our psyches not only because we were given to self-reflection and had a lot of time on our hands. We combed through our dreams and our childhoods with Jung's *Man and His Symbols* at the ready, and were looking for something, I now think, that was neither personal nor familial and perhaps not even psychological. We had lost the national connection and were heartsick in a cultural way. I don't think we knew that; I didn't, anyway. But at home I didn't talk psychology, I talked politics, arguing with a kind of angry misery whose depths confused me and made my family frightened for me, and probably of me. But there was no real argument—I did all the talking; my family, gathered for Sunday dinner, looked glumly at the gravy on their plates as if at liquid Rorschach blots that might suggest why I, the adored child, had come to this strange pass. They weren't "for the war," but the belligerent way I was against it dismayed them and caused them to fall silent, waiting for me to stop. I had opinions, I spoke of my "position" on things.

One night my uncle, trying to meet me halfway, said, "Well, when I was   19
in Italy during the War . . ."

"How do you defend that analogy?" I snapped at him, perhaps partly   20
because for them "the War" was still the Second World War. My family couldn't seem, for a long time, to *focus* on Vietnam. But my uncle retreated in the face of the big guns of my new English-major lingo.

On Thanksgiving one year I left the table to find *I. F. Stone's Weekly** and   21
read parts of it to the assembled family in a ringing, triumphantly angry voice. "But," my father said when I finished, as if I. F. Stone had been compiling evidence about me and not the Johnson† administration, "you used to be so *happy*—the happiest person I ever met."

"What does that have to do with anything?" I said.   22

Yet he was right. My unhappiness (but I didn't think of myself as   23
unhappy) was a confusion of personal and public matters, and it was made more intense by the fact that I had been happy ("the happiest person!") and now I couldn't remember what that happiness had been—just childhood? But many childhoods are miserable. And I couldn't remember exactly how the happiness stopped. I carry from that time the feeling that private memory is not just private and not just memory. Yet the resistances not against memory but against the significance of memory remain strong.

I come from people who have always been polite enough to feel that   24
nothing has ever happened to them. They have worked, raised families, played cards, gone on fishing trips together, risen to grief and admirable bitterness and, then, taken patiently the early death that robbed them of a brother, a son. They have not dwelt on things. To dwell, that appropriate word, as if the past were a residence, faintly morbid and barbaric: the dwell-

---

*I. F. Stone (1907–1989), an American journalist and political commentator whose *I. F. Stone Weekly* was for decades an important source of ideas and views for anti-establishment critics of American culture and politics.

†Lyndon Johnson (1908–1973), U.S. president, 1963–1969, responsible for enlarging the Vietnam War and exciting violent protest.

ings of prehistoric men. Or, the language of the Bible: "The Word was made flesh, and dwelt amongst us."

I have dwelt, though. To make a metaphor is to make a fuss, and I am 25 a poet, though it seems that is something one cannot claim for oneself; anyway, I write poetry. I am enough of them, my kind family, to be repelled by the significance of things, to find poetry, with its tendency to make connections and to break the barriers between past and present, slightly embarrassing.

It would be impossible to look into the past, even a happy one (espe- 26 cially a happy one), were it not for the impersonality that dwells in the most intimate fragments, the integuments that bind even obscure lives to history and, eventually, history to fiction, to myth.

I will hold up negative after family negative to the light. I will dwell. 27 Dwell in the house of the dead and in the living house of my relatives. I'm after junk. I want to make something out of what my family says is nothing. I suppose that is what I was up to when my grandmother called me out of the vestibule, away from the bookcase and the views of Prague, to eat my dinner with everybody else.

Questions for Discussion

1. Do you share Hampl's need for a "national connection"? To what extent do you feel the need to belong not just to your group of friends or to your family, but to your country? Is the pride you take in your country an important component of your personal life? If you find it hard to be proud of your country, do you feel the absence of this connection as a hurt or a wound? Why or why not?

2. Explain in your own words what Hampl means when she says in paragraph 25, "To make a metaphor is to make a fuss." Does this comment reveal anything about her literary method throughout the essay?

3. What do you make of the contrast between her family's tendency "to be repelled by the significance of things" (¶25) and her own tendency "to make a fuss" (¶25)? And what of the added wrinkle in that picture of her, in the last sentence, leaving the vestibule where she had been having a private and happy time "to eat my dinner with everybody else" (¶27)? Is Hampl merely confused, or does she capture the reality of the complexity of one's relations with family? Or is it something else altogether she is after?

4. Do you agree with her characterization of memory (in ¶13) as so compelling that we trust it "against all the evidence. . . . In memory each of us is an artist: each of us creates." What does she mean by this statement? Do you think it is true? Why or why not?

Suggested Essay Topics

1. If you have ever been, or if you now are, in rebellion against your family for one reason or another, write an essay about you and them which, like Hampl's, attempts to characterize each party with sensitivity and accuracy. Direct your essay not to your family, but to a friend or to the members of your class, and describe the dynamic between you and your family. Try not to be self-serving, but don't avoid making judgments. What is it, really, that you are in rebellion against? Can you be very precise about it? Can you get far enough outside of your feelings to describe things as they are? (When you are done, you may want to consider showing your essay to your family after all.)

2. Try taking the title of this chapter as the title of your next essay: "What Should I Become?" This is a dangerous assignment. It is very easy to write drippy, vacuous stuff in response to such an assignment. How do you do it without becoming drippy and vacuous? You might try the following. *First,* imagine yourself facing some concrete and complex problem or dilemma. Define it: My girl friend is pregnant, my husband objects to my going back to college, I don't know which job offer to take, I don't know how to tell my friend that what he or she is doing is wrong, or some other such problem. *Second,* make a decision. Describe in your essay the response you have chosen. *Third,* connect the decision you have made with the kind of person you want to be. "I decided upon Course A rather than Course B because I want to be *this* kind of person rather than *that* kind of person." Develop your description of what you want to become at sufficient length so that someone who does not know you firsthand would have the feeling of knowing you from reading your essay.

IDEAS IN DEBATE

St. Paul
Robert Coles
Shirley Jackson
Ayn Rand

St. Paul

*O*f all the parts of the New Testament,
the thirteenth chapter of First Corinthians is probably better known than any except
the stories about Christ's birth. It is quoted so often that readers may rush through
the familiar words with the impression that they are easy to understand. But everyone who studies them carefully will find that the chapter can yield more than one
meaning. Part of our difficulty is that translators do not agree on the best English
equivalent for the Greek word agape, here translated as love. The translators who
wrote the King James Version of the Bible, nearly four centuries ago, chose charity.
Both of these English terms are deeply ambiguous, even more ambiguous, scholars
tell us, than agape, which was distinguished by the Greeks from the term for
sexual love (eros) and the term for loving friendship (philia).

Obviously, some of the meanings that we associate with either English term
cannot possibly fit what Paul claims to be the most important of all human spiritual
qualities: Agape has nothing to do with such phrases as "to love sport" or "to give
generously to a charity." But the difficulties we find here in determining meaning run
far deeper than simply explaining the Greek words that lie behind the English. Paul
is attempting to describe a condition of the soul that is essentially beyond literal
definition; no words for that condition could ever be freed of all vagueness. Whatever
Paul means by love or charity, it is not something that could be pinned down once
and for all. In talking of such matters, he cannot avoid a tone that is oblique,
suggestive, oracular, or even a bit gnomic. It is as if he had just come down from a
mountaintop with a message from God himself. (See discussion questions 4–8 for "I
Owe Nothing to My Brothers" by Ayn Rand, in this chapter.)

We suggest that you read the passage several times, aloud and silently, first
in the modern translation that we reprint from the New English Bible and then in
a copy of the King James Version. You will probably find, like many another student
of the chapter, that even after studying it for an hour or so you are still puzzled about
many words and phrases. You may also find, like many readers before you, that the
puzzlement is part of the power the words contain. Though all guides to good writing

*tell us to be "as clear as possible," some of the world's greatest writing is about matters
that can never be reduced to clear and simple propositions.*

*Of course some statements that offer multiple suggestions and meanings may
appear to be rich when they are not; they may be merely confused or even badly
written. Unfortunately, there is no infallible test in reading prose for separating real
gold from fool's gold. Readers are forced to rely on the same powers of judgment and
discrimination in reading prose as they use when "reading" people. We meet phonies
both in person and in prose, but by keeping a sharp eye for details and a sharp ear
for tone we can separate truly rich writing from the merely muddled.*

*What we can certainly become clear about is the source of our problems. As
you prepare for class discussion, try to determine the sources both of what hostile critics
would call vagueness and what friendly readers might call spiritual richness. Can you
see why such a passage would have become one of the most frequently quoted religious
pronouncements of all time?*

*Note that we print the traditional verse numbers as well as our usual paragraph
numbers.*

I CORINTHIANS 13

And now I will show you the best way of all.   1

[1]I may speak in tongues of men or of angels, but if I am without love,   2
I am a sounding gong or a clanging cymbal. [2]I may have the gift of prophecy,
and know every hidden truth; I may have faith strong enough to move
mountains; but if I have no love, I am nothing. [3]I may dole out all I possess,
or even give my body to be burnt, but if I have no love, I am none the better.

[4]Love is patient; love is kind and envies no one. Love is never boastful,
[5]nor conceited, nor rude; never selfish, not quick to take offence. Love keeps   3
no score of wrongs; [6]does not gloat over other men's sins, but delights in the
truth. [7]There is nothing love cannot face; there is no limit to its faith, its hope,
and its endurance.

[8]Love will never come to an end. Are there prophets? their work will   4
be over. Are there tongues of ecstasy? they will cease. Is there knowledge?
it will vanish away; [9]for our knowledge and our prophecy alike are partial,
[10]and the partial vanishes when wholeness comes. [11]When I was a child, my
speech, my outlook, and my thoughts were all childish. When I grew up, I
had finished with childish things. [12]Now we see only puzzling reflections in
a mirror, but then we shall see face to face. My knowledge now is partial; then
it will be whole, like God's knowledge of me. [13]In a word, there are three
things that last for ever: faith, hope, and love; but the greatest of them all is
love.

◆

Questions for Discussion

1. As we have suggested, guides to good writing often tell us that if a passage is written well, the reader should be able to summarize its meaning in one sentence. Can you summarize Paul's meaning in a sentence? In a paragraph? If so, can you get all other members of the class to accept your summary? If your class cannot agree on a summary, does this show the passage to be bad writing?

2. How would you state the purpose of the passage? Does it seem to be different from the meaning? Can you see anything in the purpose you have described that would force an author to be vague in meaning? Can you see any way in which an author could write with simple clarity about such matters?

3. How is the chapter organized? Do all of the sentences in each paragraph contribute to the same general point, as your own sentences are often expected to do? (Note that the paragraphing has been provided by modern translators; only the verse divisions appear in earlier printings.) What is the effect of the passage's organization?

4. We could describe verses 4–7 as Paul's effort to define an indefinable word by giving examples of what love *is,* while verses 1–3 give examples of what love *is not.* Do you see anything in either set of examples that would explain why modern translators would find the word *love* to be clearer than the word *charity*?

Suggested Essay Topics

1. Make a short list of words that might carry some of the meaning that Paul gives to *agape;* for example, *generosity, fellow feeling, compassion, sympathy,* or *large-mindedness.* Then write a brief paper (no more than one page) defending or rejecting the one that seems most nearly adequate or most inadequate for its job in Paul's chapter.

2. Choose some general quality or trait that you admire in other people; if possible, find one that you admire more than any other. Don't worry about whether it is one that everyone else would value to the same degree; after all, Paul must have known that many of his readers would disagree with his praise of love/charity/*agape,* or he would not have troubled to write his "praise poem." Write a passage praising the quality you have chosen; "imitate" Paul as much as you like, but try to find language that you think will appeal not only to your classmates but to all the world.

Robert Coles

*Robert Coles (b. 1929) is one of a small
number of social scientists who can write effectively both to specialists and to the general
reading public. His best-known works are the three volumes of* Children of Crisis
*(see his reference notes 7 and 8), based on his experiences observing and thinking about
how Americans deal with racial prejudice, and his book* The Moral Life of Children
*(1986). If you read the selection carefully, you will find more direct clues about the
author's biography than most of our selections have revealed. You will also find that
he gives innumerable hints about himself while he* seems *to be talking about other
matters. In reading an essay on character, attention to such hints about the author's
own character is especially important.*

*As Coles says, his present interest in what makes a good or bad character and
in how to talk about character began about 1950 when he was in college. That interest
has grown as he has observed how some people of limited education reveal in their
actions a kind of tough inner quality that is not covered by terms like* personality
or reputation *or* psychological makeup. *As you read the essay reporting his visits
to three highly contrasting schools, notice how he is able to show a mastery of fairly
complicated psychological terms while at the same time admitting their final inadequacy for talking about character.*

*As you follow him, try to develop your own picture of the people whose opinions
he reports, and think about how they compare with the students, teachers, and
administrators in your school.*

*In reading this piece, especially the first time through, it is important not to
worry too much about any words that you may not be able to define precisely. Some
of them will be understood fully only by professionals (for example,* counterphobic
and borderline personality *in ¶5), some of them are made clear by the context, and
some do not matter to Coles's argument except as examples of terms that do not do justice
to the topic of character. You might simply underline or circle words that you don't
quite "get" so that on a second reading you can reduce your difficulties by looking up
the essential words before you tackle each new paragraph.*

ON THE NATURE OF
CHARACTER
Some Preliminary Field Notes

From *Daedalus: Proceedings of the American Academy of Arts and Sciences,* Fall 1981.

In the Harvard College of the decade after the Second World War,   1
Gordon Allport was a significant figure indeed—interested always in connecting the newly influential social sciences to the ethical and religious concerns
of earlier social and psychological scholars: William James, of course, and
William McDougall, and farther back, J. S. Mill or John Locke. I still remember a lecture of Allport's in 1950 in which he stressed the distinction between

character and personality. He was forever anxious to acknowledge Freud's perceptive, trenchant thrusts into the outer precincts of consciousness, while at the same time remind us what Freud could afford to ignore about himself and certain others: a moral center that was, quite simply, *there.* No amount of psychoanalysis, even an interminable stretch of it, Allport cautioned us— drawing on Freud's givens with respect to human development—can provide a strong conscience to a person who has grown up in such a fashion as to become chronically dishonest, mean-spirited, a liar. "Psychoanalysis can provide insight, can help us overcome inhibitions," we were told, "but it was not meant to be an instrument of 'character building.' " I found recently my old college notes, found that sentence. I had put a big question mark above the phrase "character building," as if to say: What is it, really? I had heard the expression often enough in the Boy Scouts, in Sunday School, and, not least, from my somewhat Puritanical parents. They set great store by virtues they referred to as self-discipline, responsibility, honesty (often described as "the best policy"), and not least, the one my mother most commonly mentioned, "good conduct." Could it be that a social *scientist,* in the middle of the twentieth century, was mentioning such qualities in a college lecture—was, in fact, asking us to consider how they might be evaluated in people, with some accuracy and consistency?[1]

At that time such efforts were still being made, notably by Robert [2] Havighurst and Hilda Taba and their colleagues at the University of Chicago.[2] But as I got nearer and nearer to becoming a doctor, then a pediatrician, then a child psychiatrist, I heard less and less about "character" and more and more about "character disorders"—certain elements of psychopathology that many psychoanalysts today connect with the vicissitudes of what is called "psychosexual development."[3] In his early productive years, before he turned fanciful—if not deranged—Wilhelm Reich placed great emphasis on what he called "character reactions," the particular way each person works out his or her psychodynamic fate. "In the main," he once said, "character proves to be a narcissistic defense mechanism."[4] No doubt such a generalization can be helpful; we are brought closer to the subliminal workings of the mind, and to its historic necessities of symbolic expression and self-protection, in the face of turmoil generated from within, never mind the stresses that "life" manages to bring. But at some point, even the most factual-minded or dispassionately "rational" of psychoanalytic observers, anxious to maintain a "value-free" posture, would be tempted to observe that there is more to the assessment of human beings than an analysis (even one "in-depth") of narcissistic defense mechanisms can provide.

Hitler's mechanisms, Stalin's, those of any number of murderers or [3] thieves, surely offered what Reich called a "character armor"—as do, right now, the mechanisms employed by Mother Theresa's unconscious, and that belonging to Dom Helder of Brazil's Recife, or to such among us in America as Robert Penn Warren or Eudora Welty or, until her death recently, Dorothy Day. At some point the issue becomes decidedly moral—or, in today's flat, impoverished language, a "normative matter." If I may call upon Gordon

Allport again, "character is personality evaluated," a descriptive notion that may make up, in its everyday usefulness, for whatever is lost so far as "psychodynamic relevance" goes.

How we go about doing that evaluation is a matter of great import. In recent years character has been of little concern for many of us whose interest is mental life, or the social and cultural life of human beings. The very word may suggest a prescientific age; may remind us of pietistic avowals or moralistic banalities many of us have tried to put behind us; may bring up the spectre of a word being used to protect the privileges of the well-born, the powerful—as if what is at issue is etiquette, polish, a certain appearance or manner of talking and carrying oneself. How much fairer, some say, to judge people through their academic performance, or through standardized tests: no risk of subjectivity, not to mention self-serving partiality. Still, it is not only Emerson, in another age, who suggested that "character is higher than intellect," and who observed that "a great soul will be strong to live, as well as strong to think."[5] Walker Percy today reminds us of those "who get all A's and flunk life."[6] And surely, a century that has witnessed learned individuals like Jung and Heidegger embrace Nazism, not to mention any number of intellectuals preach uncritically the virtues of Stalinist totalitarianism, is not going to be completely uninterested in such distinctions as the age-old polarity of knowledge as against wisdom.

In my own working life the question of "character" came up in the early 1960s when my wife and I were getting to know the black children who initiated school desegregation in the South, often against high odds—mob violence, even—and the young men and women who made up the nonviolent sit-in movement. I remember the clinical appraisals, psychological histories, and socioeconomic comments I wrote then. I remember my continuing effort to *characterize* those children, those youths—as if one weighty, academically acceptable adjective after another would, in sum, do the job. Ruby was from a "culturally deprived," a "culturally disadvantaged," family. Tessie's grandmother was illiterate. Lawrence was counterphobic, suffering "deep down" from a mix of anxiety and depression. Martha "projected" a lot. George was prone to "reaction-formations." Jim seemed to have a "character disorder," even a "borderline personality." Fred might well become psychotic later on. Meanwhile, these youthful American citizens were walking past grown men and women who were calling them the foulest of names, who were even threatening to kill them—and such hecklers were escaping sociological and psychological scrutiny in the bargain, while any number of judges were ordering "evaluations" by my kind to be done on sit-in students who were violating the (segregationist) laws, and who were thought to be (and eventually declared by doctors to be) "sick" or "delinquent" or "troubled" or "sociopathic" or "psychopathic." A historic crisis had confronted a region politically, and in so doing, had ripped open the political, economic, racial aspects of our manner of judging others—the direct connection between what the Bible calls "principalities and powers," and what in our everyday life is "normal" or "proper" behavior. One day, as I mumbled some statements suffused with the words of psychiatric theory to "explain" a given child's behavior, my wife said, "You are making her sound as if she ought to be on her way to a child guidance clinic, but she is walking into a school building—and no matter the threats, she is holding her head up high, even smiling at her obscene hecklers. Last night she even prayed for them!"

It was my wife's judgment that Ruby Bridges, aged six, was demonstrating to all the world *character*. Even if cognitive psychologists were to declare such a child not old enough to make certain recognitions or distinctions; even if other theorists were to find Ruby unable to do very much moral reasoning or analysis; even if still other social scientists or clinicians were to emphasize her severe "problems"—her imitative habits, her fearful responses, her Oedipal tensions, her moments of blind obedience or terror-struck submission; even if she were to demonstrate to any number of curious observers—armed with questions, tests, stories to be analyzed, crayons to be used on drawing paper—certain handicaps, developmental difficulties, emotional impasses or disorders, cognitive blocks, age-related blind spots; nevertheless, she was managing to face those mobs with a quiet, stoic dignity that impressed her teachers, newspaper reporters, and federal marshals (who escorted her each day to and from school). One of her teachers, as a matter of fact, said that she herself could never submit to such a daily scene—suggesting that moral *behavior* is not necessarily the same thing as a capacity for moral *thinking;* that character may not be something one ascertains through questionnaires or through experiments done on a university campus.

Against such vexing theoretical difficulties (which had become for me a matter of continuing astonishment, if not haunting confusion), a chance to talk again with young people in a variety of school situations was most welcome. My wife and I had spent years visiting a number of Atlanta's high schools, though not George Washington Carver School.[7] We had spent a season visiting a high school north of Chicago, though not Highland Park High School.[8] And we have children in the private schools of New England, though not St. Paul's School. I decided to keep trying to gain some sense of the variations in the moral life of the young by emphasizing that subject in my planned visits to these three schools, in the hope that more and more of what Anna Freud calls "direct observation" (as opposed to eagerly speculative and all too inclusive and unqualified generalizations) will help us to understand where "personality" ends and "character" begins in the mind's life.

The "methodology" is thoroughly simple—a mere beginning in exploration, but perhaps not an altogether futile way to learn something about certain young people. I asked the principals of the two public high schools and the headmaster of the private school to "select two teachers qualified to judge character"; those teachers would, in turn, select four or so students who, they believe, possess "character" or "high character." When the principals of Highland Park and Carver asked what I meant by such a word, such an expression, I replied simply that I was trying to find out precisely *that*. I told each principal that I wanted to speak with all the students chosen together, rather than separately, and that I wanted to meet also with the two teachers together.

I went to St. Paul's School first. The headmaster had arranged for two   9
teachers to select four students, and we met in a classroom a good distance from the headmaster's office. We were, in a sense, free—no classes, no one to interrupt or keep an eye on what was to be a full morning's discussion. I told the students, two young men and two young women, that I wanted to explore the meaning to them of "character," and we were, with no hesitation, off to a sustained inquiry.

The word was not a strange one for these students; they had heard it   10
used repeatedly, they said, though none had ever really stopped to think about its meaning. Early on one of the young women said, "We talk about 'human nature' or 'personality' or 'identity'; I suppose in the past they talked about 'character.' " Yet these students were quite articulate as they sifted and sorted among themselves and their classmates in search of a definition, a way of looking at a particular subject. In no time a whole school was being morally scrutinized: the "jocks," the "beautiful people," the "social butterflies," the "freaks," the "party people," the "grinds," various teachers, and the "goodly heritage," a phrase many who have gone to St. Paul's have heard again and again.

Much time was spent struggling with the question of arrogance, with   11
the temptation of self-importance and self-centeredness—a personal hazard these four were not loath to acknowledge. They were in a school known as one of the best in America. They were, in different ways, doing well there— one academically; one as a scholar-athlete; one for showing concern and compassion for others, near and afar; one as a person trusted and liked by a wide assortment of classmates. Yet they worried that their success was a temptation to "become stuck-up," as one put it. Self-righteousness and self-consciousness were additional hazards—elements likely to shut a person off, making that person less responsive to other people. Gradually, how one responds to others took on high importance. One of the young men put it this way: "I tend to be a private person. I like to take long walks by myself. At times I don't want company. I want to hold onto my individuality. But I like to be with others, too. I like to be a *friend*. I'd like to think that if someone were in trouble, he'd turn to me, and I'd be there, and I'd put that person's trouble above my needs, including taking a solitary walk!"

Other topics came up frequently: the tension between adjustment to the   12
demands of various cliques and the private values a given individual feels to be important—or put differently, the tension between loyalty to one's friends and loyalty to one's own memories, habits, yearnings; the tension between one's competitive side and one's regard for others; and more crudely, the tension between one's wish to win and one's willingness to help others. The word "honesty" was mentioned over and over—an Augustinian examina-

tion,* done with today's psychological panache: who is "really" honest, and for what "underlying" reasons? Moreover, does it "pay" in this society to be honest all the time? When do honesty and self-effacement turn into "masochism"? When does pride in one's convictions turn into a bullying egotism? If you really do have "a sense of yourself," are you not in danger of being smug, self-serving, all too sure of your own significance? When does popularity reduce one's individuality to the point that one belongs to a herd, has lost a mind of one's own?

Such questions were asked quite earnestly, and always with regard to the matter at hand: the characteristics of character. When pressed by one another (I ended up being, most of the time, a listener), the students offered lists: a person who sticks to a set of principles; a person who can risk unpopularity, yet is commanding enough to gain the respect of others; a person who has the courage to be himself, herself; a person who is open-minded, who plays fair with others, who doesn't lie and cheat and, interestingly enough, deceive himself, herself. These were students who believed such qualities to be only partially present. These were students, in fact, who had a decidedly dialectical turn of mind: "You can try to be a better person, but it's a struggle. You can be humble, and that way, intimidate people. You can use humility. It's hard to know what's genuine in people. Sometimes people pretend to be something, but they're really just the opposite. They flip and they flop. I don't like people who are sanctimonious. They lecture others, and people take it, but it's out of fear, or there is guilt, and it's being exploited. Every once in a while, I prefer someone who puts his cards on the table and shows he's a real pain in the neck to these holier-than-thou types. Character doesn't mean being a goody-goody person! If you're that kind of person, there's a lot of meanness, probably, inside you, or competitiveness that you're not letting on about to others. Maybe you don't know about it yourself!"

These were, obviously, what we would now call a psychologically sophisticated breed of youth. Yet, they were (thank God!) not anxious to have all human behavior a matter of psychology or psychopathology—or sociology, either: "There are reasons we end up being one kind of person or another kind of person, but when you actually become that person (when you're nice to others most of the time), then that's a true achievement. A lot of people don't become nice, and it's no excuse to say you had a bad childhood or you never had the right luck. I think you have to take your troubles and overcome them!" The Puritan spirit lives still in the woods of southern New Hampshire, no matter the references—and they were many—to "adolescence," "identity," Sigmund Freud's ideas, the latest notions of what "motivates" people, what makes us "anxious" or "strung out" or "ambivalent."

More than anything else, these four youths grappled with what used to be commonly called "the meaning of life" in philosophy lectures (before the advent of logical positivism, computers, the libido theory, and a strictly

13

14

15

*In his *Confessions,* St. Augustine (354–430) examines his moral and spiritual qualities in great detail, always in Christian terms.

materialist view of life, liberty, the pursuit of happiness). One of the young men said this toward the end of our meeting time: "What matters—don't you think?—is what you *do* with your life. I've tried to be independent, to have my own thoughts, but to listen to others. I hope to live comfortably, but I hope I won't be greedy and selfish. I don't know what our responsibilities are—to ourselves and our friends and family and neighbors, and to others in places abroad I'll never even see. Even today, this is a big world. What are we supposed to do? We're lucky to be here at St. Paul's. We have such a good life. What do we owe others? Isn't that 'character'—what you decide to do for others, not just yourself?"

The "great suck of self," Walker Percy calls it in *The Second Coming*—the inevitable pull toward our own thoughts, our own wishes, our navels. Adolescence is not the only period of self-absorption, these youths seemed already to know. For them, one is likely to be neither bad nor good. For them, character was no categorical trait. For them, character is not a possession, but something one searches for: a quality of mind and heart one struggles for, sometimes with a bit more success than at other times. Not one of these four wanted to spell out a definition, set down a compulsory series of attributes, offer a list of candidates. One heard from their mouths expressions of confusion, annoyance, vanity, self-satisfaction, self-criticism, self-doubt, self-assurance. One heard, maybe most of all, tentativeness—a reluctance to speak definitively about an aspect of human behavior one student kept describing as "hard to pin down," but also as "important to consider when you're thinking about someone." 16

The two teachers I met at St. Paul's School, a middle-aged man who taught math, a young woman who taught English, had met, discussed the subject of "character," and added to one another's notions, so that, in the end, there was a final written statement available: 17

- The aggregate of distinctive qualities belonging to an individual
- Moral vigor or firmness, especially as acquired through self-discipline
- The ability to respond to a setback
- The ability to form an attachment to ideals of a larger community or organization than oneself, and to exert one's influence for the good of the greater body
- The possession of a sense of humor that allows one to see that there is more to life than living
- The ability to be an *individual* in a crowd of *different* people
- A sense of self that has been found through experience
- The ability to allow others to be individuals, even though they may be different
- The ability to disagree with others without condemning (or losing respect for) the individual one disagrees with
- A sensitivity toward the feelings of others
- An understanding of the wholeness of other people's personalities or character (even when it is different from one's own)

These were two individuals who had thought long and hard about a 18
vexing subject—whom to choose, and why? A very bright person, involved
in many activities, able to speak coherently and easily, headed straight for
Harvard, as against a quiet person who defers to the ideas of others in a
classroom, does well, but "not all that well," yet in numerous moments seems
to reach out for others, not to save them, or turn them into psychiatric cases,
but simply "to do a good turn"? A marvelous athlete who also is a leader in
many ways during the course of a school year, as against a hardworking
youth who is most often self-effacing, yet managed to stand up once or twice
on a matter of ethical principle, no matter the risks and the penalties? And
surely a host of alternatives, because, as one teacher put it, "when you judge
'character,' you judge the overall person and compare him, or her, to others,
and you do so over time, the school year."

In Highland Park, north of Chicago, a somewhat different arrangement 19
had been made. The principal of this suburban high school had selected two
teachers, as I requested, but they had picked four students each—seven girls
and one boy, interestingly enough. We met in a room across the hall from the
principal's office. Twice he asked how we were doing, offered water, tea,
coffee—in general, showed a distinct, active interest in our discussions. He
himself had thought about the word "character," and as with so many of us,
found it a bit puzzling and elusive. So did the students I spent a winter
morning with. Several of them said that character had a lot to do with
personality; in fact, declared "a good personality" or a "well-rounded person"
to be equivalent descriptions to "good character" or "high character." Two
young women dissented, however: "Character has to do with honesty. You
can be popular, and have a shrink's seal of approval, but not have character!"

We fairly quickly got into a discussion of ethnic and racial tensions—in 20
the school, in our society as a whole. At St. Paul's the cliques were enumerated, as if they threatened individuality, hence character, through the requirements of social cohesion; at Highland Park High School the dominant
social divisions, at least for these students, had to do with class and race:
Italians and Jews, "working people" and "wealthier people," blacks and
whites.

I was given some outspoken lessons in how one's family life affects 21
one's situation in school, and not least, one's character: "It all depends on who
you are! Some kids want to go to an Ivy League school; that's all that's on
their minds. They put up a good front, to show they have 'character'; they
join clubs, and have all these hobbies and interests, so as to impress the
teachers and the people who read college applications. Some kids have to
work while going to school. They try to get a good deal, a job that pays well.
They're making contacts even now for later on. It's built into their 'character'
that the world is tough, and you have to know people to get ahead. A lot of
the black kids are here because there's a military base in the school district.
They come and then they go. It's hard to figure them out. It's in their 'character' to stay away from us whites. There's a lot of tension among us whites.

Go into the johns, and you'll see a lot of writing! [I went, and I saw the ethnic slurs.] But a lot of the time we get along pretty well. We've got brainy ones here, headed for college since they were born, and don't get in their way, or else! We've got kids who will work in a store or a factory, and not be ashamed. They see the world different. They take different courses. They have their own code."

The speaker is a wry, outspoken, somewhat detached young woman,   22 bound for college, but "not a fancy one." She is neither Italian nor Jewish, but Anglo-Irish. She had made a certain virtue out of marginality, and the others in the room seemed a bit deferential: "She isn't pushed around by anyone. She's her own person. She can mingle with anyone. She doesn't put on airs with anyone." The associations moved relentlessly from social situation to moral conduct—not the first time, or the last, such a progression would be made for me in the course of this study. "You have to know where the person is coming from," I was told several times. Explain! "Well, if you've got a lot going for you, then you can be more relaxed. True, you can be a tightwad and be rich; but it's easier to be generous if you've got a lot behind you!" On the other hand, one student insisted, "there's still room for being poor and good in this world!" She persisted: "I know some kids, right in this school, and they're not here now, they weren't chosen to be here, and they're from pretty poor families, compared to others; their fathers just get by, make a living. And they would give you the shirt off their backs, those kids: that's character. And they wouldn't go talking about what they've done, bragging, and showing off—*that's* character! Some people, they know how to play up to the teachers, and they get a big reputation, but what's the *truth* about them? What are they like when no one is looking, and what are they like when no one is listening?"

We touched many bases. Class and character. Egotism and character.   23 Psychology and character. Smartness and character. Motivation and character. Caring and character. Manners and character. To be stuck-up. To be considerate. To be a help when a person needs help—a flat tire, a car ride, a pencil or piece of paper, a loan of money, a sympathetic ear. To take risks, extend oneself to others, brave social pressures. Grade-mongers. Leaders and followers. Hypocrites. People who have one or another veneer. The "way-down-deep truth" of a person. A final test of character: sickness, financial straits, a disaster. Character and mental health.

Part of [the movie] *Ordinary People* had been made in Highland Park. The   24 students had watched the filming, and they wondered: If one is hurt, bewildered, "seeing a shrink," can one have the "mental peace" to demonstrate character? Consumerism, selfishness—can one defy them, develop "an ability not to be absorbed with objects"? And at some interesting and suggestive length: literature as a means of understanding character, as in *To Kill a Mockingbird* (Atticus had character, he was open-minded, stood up for what he believed, no matter the risks and costs, and so was a "moral man"); or as in *Macbeth* (Lady Macbeth was a "bad person," a "bad character"). And politics: Lincoln and Eisenhower and Truman had character; Johnson lacked it, as do

Nixon and Carter. "All politicians probably lie," one student observed, "and maybe all people do, but some just keep on lying, and you can't trust them, and you don't like them, and they're just no damn good, and you can tell, after awhile, even if they tell you they pray every other minute! The truth about a person's character eventually comes out, *eventually.*"

Such faith was not universally shared. There was much talk of appear- 25 ance as against reality: the way people present themselves to others, as opposed to some inner truth about each of us. In contrast to the students at St. Paul's School, these students were distinctly more interested in the relationship between a person's social, economic, ethnic, or racial background—a person's circumstances—and that person's behavior, hence character. And it did come down to that, they all agreed at the end: "You are the way you act—in the long run." What did that qualification mean? Well, it goes like this: "Some people can put on an act. But if you keep your wits, and keep an eye on them, you find out the truth about them. If they're good people, kind to others, not just wrapped up in themselves, you'll find it out. If they're putting on a production, you'll find that out." No one, in that regard, seemed to have any doubts about his or her ultimate psychological acuity—or about the long-run dramatic capacities of one or another individual.

There was, as we were ending, a spirited, occasionally tense discussion 26 of tests, grades, the criteria used by colleges and graduate schools to evaluate people. "I know kids who get all A's, and would murder their parents, their brothers and sisters, if they stood in their way," one youth offered. Yes, but there's plenty of nastiness to go around, others said, even among those who do poorly in school. What *should* various committees of admission do? How *does* one make a fairly accurate moral judgment about a person? Numbers may not tell enough. Multiple choice questions may not do justice to life's strangeness—the ironies and ambiguities, the complexities and inconsistencies and contradictions we all struggle with, though some with more decency and integrity and generosity of spirit than others. But how do we arrive at an estimate of a person's essential kindness with respect to others—in the face of thousands of importunate applicants, each putting on the very best face possible? Don't interviews have *their* hazards, the unpredictable variations of mood and temperament, the nuances of subjectivity which can, alas, of a sudden, amount to outright prejudice? We ended on an eclectic note—the desirability of taking a lot into consideration when accepting people for a job, a place in a college, and yes, when judging that elusive concept "character." The last person to leave the room, the young woman who spoke least, said that she thought "character meant being kind and good, even when there was no one to reward you for being kind and good."

These were students acutely aware of the divisions in this society—as 27 Tillie Olsen put it in her story *O Yes,* the ways we "sort." The two Highland Park High School teachers were similarly sensitive to issues of "class and caste," as the splits among us have sometimes been described. Actually, the teachers were themselves a bit split. The assistant principal, a man, is quite in touch with the more academic students of the school; whereas the woman teacher is very much involved with those students who are working at jobs while trying to get through Highland Park—and who are headed, mostly, for what many social scientists would call "service jobs," or membership in the "working class," or the "lower-middle to middle-middle-class," and on and on. The two did not argue, however; in fact, they largely echoed the sentiments of their chosen students: "Grades aren't the whole story, by any means"; and very emphatically, "Character has something to do with moral life."

Both teachers worried about class—expressed concern, for instance, that 28 "mere etiquette" can deceive, or insisted that human scoundrels, like wolves, find sheepskins ("social veneer") aplenty to wear. I heard practically nothing about class-connected deceit at St. Paul's, a lot about it at Highland Park—and character seemed to require, everyone agreed, an impressive absence of such a tendency. Moreover, psychiatry and psychoanalysis were even more prominently mentioned than at St. Paul's—a way of getting to the "deeper truth" about people, hence to a judgment of their character. (Fallout from *Ordinary People*?) As already mentioned, disturbed people were described as less likely to show high character. When I mentioned Gandhi's personal eccentricities, if not moments of cruelty, vanity, thoughtlessness, the students were ready, all too ready, to take the clue, the hint, and write him off as sick. When I reminded them that he was, yet, a rather impressive moral leader, the students worried about the burdens placed on his family, and about his own psychiatric ones.

If I had a little trouble persuading this group of students and their 29 teachers that, neurosis or no neurosis, a person's moral motives can affect his or her character, they had no trouble letting me know that a neighborhood, a level of income, the possession of a given nationality, can all affect a person's character. The teachers especially emphasized the distinction between the quietly considerate person, as against the demonstrative, if not flamboyant, doer of public good deeds, a performer of sorts. "Some students want to get A in character, too," one teacher said, as we broke off, a reminder that not only can life be unfair, as one American president took pains to remind us, but virtue can be unfairly perceived—when, in truth, sins are being shrewdly masked. As Flannery O'Connor observed, through the comic irony of a title to one of her stories, a good man is hard to find—and maybe, when the pressures are high, almost impossible to take for granted.

At George Washington Carver High School, in Atlanta, Georgia, I had 30 quite another discussion, with the principal ready to point out the extreme hazards to what he called "character formation" well before I saw (in a room that belonged, really, to his office suite) the four children (two boys and two girls) and two teachers (both women, one who teaches math, the other, biology). "There is a problem with drugs," he explained. "There is a problem with poverty, with terrible poverty, with welfare homes, with absent fathers, with unemployment all over the place." He gave me a lively lecture on the school's history—once a "dumping ground for school failures," now a "place of hope," much connected to businesses that offer promising black youths a great variety of jobs, a chance "to enter the mainstream," in the principal's words. In time I was able to begin talking with the four selected youths, though not before being told emphatically: "Character is something you have to build, right here in this school, every day. You have to lay down the law, and see that it's enforced. Character means discipline and hard work and looking to the future and getting there!" Of the three school leaders, Carver's principal was the only one to volunteer (or hazard) such an explication.

The students were not averse to this line of reasoning. These were 31 young people who were determined to find jobs, determined to be hard workers, strong parents—and not reluctant to explain why such a commitment was connected to a definition, in their minds, of the word "character": "A lot of us, even here, with the principal and the teachers bearing down every minute on us, have trouble reading and writing. We're not going to college, most of us. We're going to try to get a job and hold onto it! It takes character, I think, to do that—not take the easy way out and drink or use drugs or say the white man is on our backs, so what the devil can we do! To me, character is being stubborn. It's staying in there, it's getting out of a hole, and breathing the fresh air, and not falling down anymore."

My wife and I spent three years in Atlanta, talking with youths such 32 as these—young black men and women trying, in the face of adversity, to forge a better life for themselves. These were more outspoken and self-assured individuals than the ones we got to know in the early 1960s. They were quick to describe themselves as "job-hungry" and as full of determination, willfulness, hopeful anticipation. They were not, though, uninterested in some of the refinements of psychology I had heard discussed in Illinois and New Hampshire: "There's success and success. It's not only getting there, it's how you get there. If you have character, that means you keep trying, no matter how hard it is, and you don't lose your soul while you're doing that. You have to say to yourself, 'I'll go so far and no farther.' You have to draw the line, and if you do, and you can hold to it, you've got character." Nods all around, followed by smiles of recognition as the temptations get mentioned: white devils and black devils who offer serious distractions in the form of drugs and booze, bribes and payoffs, an assortment of "tricks." These are street-smart kids, and they have lots of savvy about Atlanta politics, Atlanta vice, Atlanta hypocrisy, black and white alike. Their moralism and self-conscious, urgently stated rectitude is hard earned, if (they seem to know) not entirely invulnerable.

One pushes the word "character," gets responses connected to hardship, 33 ambition, the requirements of people living on the edge, hence with little interest in metaphysical or metapsychological speculation. Character? Why, J. R. in *Dallas* lacks it, utterly; Dr. King had it, that's for sure. Character? A lot of big shots may seem to have it, but too bad more people don't know who is scratching whose back. On the other hand, there's a woman who works in a Howard Johnson's motel, and she lost her husband from cancer, and she has five kids, and she has two of them out of high school and in good jobs, and the other three are headed that way, and she doesn't stand for any foolishness, *none,* and she takes those kids to church every Sunday, and they pray hard and long, and she has character, in case anyone wants to know! The church—at long last it comes up in a talk about character! Not in a school that bears the name of St. Paul, no less; and not in a school where Catholics and Jews seem ready to square off at each other all day, every day; but in Carver, you bet. Each of these four high-school-age Americans (no fools about getting high or about the demands of the flesh or about the various shortcuts people take) goes to church on Sundays, and if there is reluctance sometimes (the joy of a late sleep), there is, after all, no real choice: "We have to go. Our mother says we have to go, and once we're there, I don't half mind! I like it there. I'll make my kids go, too."

Much talk of "uplift." Much reference to "building" oneself into "a   34
stronger person," getting "on the map." How? There are auto repair shops. There are radio and TV repair shops. There are cosmetology shops. There are dry-cleaning places. There are tailoring and sewing and shoe repair places. There is a big airport, and people work there—on engines if they are on top, otherwise as cleaning people or doing errands, or driving buses and taxis, "lots of things." (No angst about capitalism at Carver!) If you get one of those jobs, and you hold onto it; if you get yourself a girlfriend or a boyfriend, and they become a wife or a husband, and you become a father or a mother, and you "stay with it," and be good to your family, earn them a living, take care of them; if you remain loyal to your church, and pray to God when you're weak; if you don't forget your people, and try to lend a hand to the ones who didn't make it, who stumbled and fell and are hurt and sad and wondering what the point of it all is, and maybe have done wrong, done it too many times—if all that is "inscribed on your soul," then, by God, you have character, and it's important to say "by God," because it's "His grace that does things."

"I'm not as small after church as I am before church," one of these four   35
told me—a lifeline that rescues at least one American, temporarily, from "the culture of narcissism." As for "good manners," they aren't superficial at all; they tell of something very deep down, no matter what so-called depth psychologists have to say, not to mention those who make of them religious figures: "You can tell a person by how he speaks to you. If he's respectful, then he's good; if he gives you the shoulder, then he's bad. I don't care if someone has a lot of bad in him. If he keeps it a secret from the whole world, then he's way out front. If he shows his bad self to everyone, he's putting it on us, man, and it's hard enough without that—another hassle to deal with. My grandmother tells us: 'Keep your mouth shut if there's no good to come out of it. Keep your mischief to yourself. We've all got it—but some of us don't show it off.' She's right; she has character."

Some other virtues that bespeak character: punctuality; how you carry   36
yourself; an ability to laugh, when there's a good excuse for crying or shouting or shaking your fists; how you speak—with clear enunciation of words, so that others may hear you; self-respect, as measured by neatness and choice

of clothes, as well as respect for others, as measured by a smile, a please, a thank you; obedience—to your elders, to the law, to your own self-evident ideas of what is right and wrong. "We all stray," said one of the young women, "but if we try hard not to keep repeating ourselves, and if we're not afraid to learn from our mistakes, and if we're willing to work hard, and sacrifice, then we have character." Pieties, all those remarks, the skeptical, psychoanalyzed liberal Yankee muses—fighting off embarrassment, wonder, a touch of awe, and emotional memories of other youths in other Atlanta spots, youths similarly hard-pressed, who managed to "overcome," and youths similarly unwilling to be self-pitying in the face of the severe inequities of this life.

The two teachers—my wife got to know so many very much like these 37 two: tough-minded, outspoken, a touch contemptuous of anyone who wants to offer sympathy, never mind condolences. They are demanding, insistent, forceful women: "Let these kids work hard, and better themselves, and be good members of their families, and they'll show character; that's how, the only way!" And candidly, bluntly, unapologetically: "We chose the best we have to talk with you. We chose the smart ones, the ones who could talk with you and get themselves across. We have others here who would tax your patience and understanding. Maybe they have 'character,' too. I don't think character is the property of the lucky and the smart and the successful, no sir. But to me, character means an active person, who is ready to face the world, and make a mark on it. That's why I chose these kids. They're ready, they're ready to turn their backs on all their troubles, our troubles, and be good—be full of action. 'Never be lazy,' I tell my kids at home, and here in school. There's that expression: going to meet 'the man.' Well, I say we can become 'the man' ourselves. We can take control of our own lives, be our own masters. It may be preachy of me to talk like this, but we've got to pep-talk ourselves, and then *get on with it!* I pray to God—we need His help badly—that more and more of these kids at Carver *will* get on with it."

On the way home, back North again, I took out my books and papers: 38 notes to write, ideas to savor, comparisons to make. There it was, the wonderful message that Kierkegaard gave us over a century ago, the message I often wish a few of us theorists of moral development would keep in constant mind: "Morality is character, character is that which is engraved (χαράσσοω); but the sand and the sea have no character and neither has abstract intelligence, for character is really inwardness. Immorality, as energy, is also character; but to be neither moral nor immoral is merely ambiguous, and ambiguity enters into life when the qualitative distinctions are weakened by a gnawing reflection."[9]

He was a great one for leaps, that nineteenth century version of the 39 melancholy (if spiritedly so) Dane. I wondered on my flight home whether he might somewhere in this universe be smiling, be assenting to the message, the slightly hectoring statement delivered by that mathematics teacher, and later by her tough, occasionally *very* tough, principal, who told me that he had "a lot of bad characters" to deal with, but damned if he couldn't "take them

on," "turn them around," "convert their wasted energy into useful energy."
It all sounded slightly like the noise of strained braggadocio: I'll talk big, and
hope for the best. It all sounded exaggerated, romantic—like Kierkegaard. It
all sounded pretty good, though, to those four young people and two of their
teachers.

REFERENCES

All references are Coles's.

1. A good summary of Allport's sensitive moral and psychological writing is found in *Personality: A Psychological Interpretation* (New York: Holt, 1937).

2. See R. J. Havighurst and H. Taba, *Adolescent Character and Personality* (New York: Wiley, 1949). Also, more recently, R. Havighurst and R. Peck, *The Psychology of Character Development* (New York: Wiley, 1960).

3. See *Disorders of Character,* by Joseph Michaels (Springfield, Illinois: Thomas, 1955), for a sugges-tive discussion, with a first-rate bibliography.

4. Wilhelm Reich, *Character Analysis,* 3d ed. (New York: Farrar, Straus & Giroux, 1972), p. 169.

5. In his well-known oration, "The American Scholar," delivered before Harvard's Phi Beta Kappa Society on August 31, 1837.

6. Walker Percy, *The Second Coming* (New York: Farrar, Straus & Giroux, 1980). See also his wonderful collection of essays, which take up the same theme again and again, *The Message in the Bottle* (New York: Farrar, Straus & Giroux, 1975).

7. See my *Children of Crisis: A Study of Courage and Fear,* vol. 1 (Boston: Atlantic-Little, Brown, 1967).

8. See the section "Schools" in volume 3 of *Children of Crisis: The South Goes North* (Boston: Atlantic-Little, Brown, 1967).

9. Søren Kierkegaard, *The Present Age,* translated by Alexander Dru (New York: Harper & Row, 1962), p. 43.

Questions for Discussion

1. If a stranger had conducted interviews in your high school, would the
   principal have provided the interviewer with a quiet classroom "a good
   distance from the headmaster's office" (¶9)? Or would the principal have
   kept things closely under control, "in a room that belonged, really, to his
   office suite" (¶30)? What meanings or effects does Coles add to his piece
   with these details?

2. Can you construct a simple, clear summary of Coles's main point? Can you
   say whether he flatly admires or condemns any of the three schools?

3. Often an author will provide a careful summary in a final paragraph or
   two. Does Coles summarize, in paragraphs 38 and 39, what he thinks *we*
   should think? If not, why not? If so, what is the message?

4. Much of Coles's presentation consists of short accounts of what *other*
   people said and did, instead of statements about what *he* thinks. Which

of the accounts seems to you most memorable or most forceful for his purposes?

5. Do you or your acquaintances ever talk about character? If so, do you use the term *character,* or do you use other terms to refer to the same thing?

6. Make two lists, in separate columns, of all the qualities you most admire and dislike in any person (yourself included). Don't worry about whether your terms are used in polite company or formal writing. And don't worry about whether your opinions will be "correct." Just consider yourself as going into a strange environment, as Coles did, to discover what people think, but this time *you* are the *subject* under study.

7. What kind of person does Coles seem to be? Does he lead you to infer that he has character? How would it alter your picture of him if he had omitted references to his wife, especially his admission that she always seems to discern character ahead of him? (See, for example, ¶5 and ¶6.)

Suggested Essay Topics

1. From the definitions of *good character* reported by Coles, choose the one that satisfies you best. Then write a portrait of a person who seems to be a good example of that kind of character. Try to include as much lively detail about actions or statements as you can remember (or invent). Some of Coles's devices for portraying Ruby Bridges (¶6) may suggest ways of doing your portrait.

2. Think over the people you know or have seen portrayed in movies or on TV. Choose three whose characters seem to be sharply defined or uncommon. Then write one paragraph about each person, *in the language of that person.* For example, "I doan take any a that kinda crap from anybody, see? You step on me, I'm gonna step right back. See what I mean?" Or "I'm just the sort of person who finds it extremely difficult to talk about myself. I cannot explain precisely what I mean, but I seem to want to keep in my own corner and watch the world go by. It's really unusual for me to be talking to you like this, but there was just something about you that made me open up." Write an essay directed to your classmates in which you discuss the character of each of your "speakers."

Shirley Jackson

The subtitle of this chapter—"What Should I Become?"—asks a question about character. It does not ask who we want to be, as if all we had to do were to choose and then have the matter forever settled. It asks instead who we want to become, *implying that character is not a static thing, that it is in constant formation as a consequence of the choices we make in everyday living. Earlier in this chapter, St. Paul provided us with one of our culture's most influential and long-lasting definitions of the goals of character. St. Paul states clearly that the goal of character is love: "In a word, there are three things that last forever: faith, hope, and love; but the greatest of them all is love" (p. 388).*

Over the centuries this brief statement has seemed to many people to express a fundamental criterion of good character. Viewed as St. Paul seems to view it, the power to give and to receive love is the greatest source of good within and among individuals. With it one may be open to change and generous to others, for love unstops the ears and stirs the heart to charity. Those who can love may sometimes be weak and sometimes make mistakes, but they do not fall willingly into malice. Accepting love creates self-respect, and giving love creates fellow-feeling. Both are the enemy of malice. People who lack this power, however, may be led to malice through their own emptiness. They will be victims of whatever social forces get to them first. They will have no motives for generosity beyond their training in good manners or the promptings of self-interest and nothing to prop up their self-esteem but the goodwill of their neighbors, which must be purchased at the price of conforming to community conventions and accepted truths. People who cannot love can seldom afford to point out their neighbors' inadequacies, for they have no internal strength to fall back on if their neighbors reject them. They must thus pay the price of conformity even if the community's accepted truths are really cruel falsehoods.

In Shirley Jackson's (1919–1965) "Flower Garden" we see this principle illustrated and dramatized. A woman is jarred out of her ordinary habits and faced with a crisis: whether to challenge or to accept her community's racism. She is called upon to love another person, not romantically but charitably. She is called upon to be fair, decent, and just. Both her fundamental sympathies and her conscience stir her to answer this call with courage and justice. But to do so she must face the real possibility of losing her place in a small community where place is almost everything. She even faces the possibility, more remote but still real, of losing her home and family. In the midst of this dilemma her character hangs in the balance. Will she have enough courage? Does she love justice more than social position? She cannot dodge these issues. She must choose, and the choice she makes will constitute a decision about character, about who she is to become.

The narrator allows us to see that up to the present, Mrs. Winning has lived in a state of silent, resentful, incipient rebellion against the cold self-importance of her husband's family. She has longed for a life of independence symbolized by the cottage, and of passion and warmth symbolized by the flower garden. But when the opportunity of allying herself with another person who shares her longing for independence and warmth, and who is thus a natural friend and companion, brings her into conflict with her family's and community's disapproval, she cannot face her potential losses. We see her at the story's end turning away from new possibilities—new possibilities for herself, literally her "self," and her community—and turning toward conformity, toward sameness, and toward a falsehood that wounds both victim and victimizer.

As you read, compare Mrs. Winning's shaping of her character with that of Margaret Sanger (Chapter 5) and Richard Wright (Chapter 4), who also faced crises of character. Does St. Paul's formulation about love give you a way of explaining the differences among these three people? Would it be helpful to augment the religious and mythical perspectives with theories of personality from psychology or sociology? Finally, regardless of what theories we appeal to, one fundamental question remains: What would each of us have done in Mrs. Winning's place? Surely we can see that to have chosen other than she did would have been costly. Who among us would have had the necessary strength to give and receive the needed love? There are no easy answers.

FLOWER GARDEN

From *The Lottery* (1948).

After living in an old Vermont manor house together for almost eleven years, the two Mrs. Winnings, mother and daughter-in-law, had grown to look a good deal alike, as women will who live intimately together, and work in the same kitchen and get things done around the house in the same manner. Although young Mrs. Winning had been a Talbot, and had dark hair which she wore cut short, she was now officially a Winning, a member of the oldest family in town and her hair was beginning to grey where her mother-in-law's hair had greyed first, at the temples; they both had thin sharp-featured faces and eloquent hands, and sometimes when they were washing dishes or shelling peas or polishing silverware together, their hands, moving so quickly and similarly, communicated more easily and sympathetically than their minds ever could. Young Mrs. Winning thought sometimes, when she sat at the breakfast table next to her mother-in-law, with her baby girl in the high-chair close by, that they must resemble some stylized block print for a New England wallpaper; mother, daughter, and granddaughter, with perhaps Plymouth Rock or Concord Bridge in the background. 1

On this, as on other cold mornings, they lingered over their coffee, unwilling to leave the big kitchen with the coal stove and the pleasant atmosphere of food and cleanliness, and they sat together silently sometimes until the baby had long finished her breakfast and was playing quietly in the special baby corner, where uncounted Winning children had played with almost identical toys from the same heavy wooden box. 2

"It seems as though spring would never come," young Mrs. Winning said. "I get so tired of the cold." 3

"Got to be cold some of the time," her mother-in-law said. She began to move suddenly and quickly, stacking plates, indicating that the time for sitting was over and the time for working had begun. Young Mrs. Winning, rising immediately to help, thought for the thousandth time that her mother-in-law would never relinquish the position of authority in her own house until she was too old to move before anyone else. 4

"And I wish someone would move into the old cottage," young Mrs. Winning added. She stopped halfway to the pantry with the table napkins and said longingly, "If only *someone* would move in before spring." Young Mrs. Winning had wanted, long ago, to buy the cottage herself, for her 5 husband to make with his own hands into a home where they could live with their children, but now, accustomed as she was to the big old house at the top of the hill where her husband's family had lived for generations, she had only a great kindness left toward the little cottage, and a wistful anxiety to see some happy young people living there. When she heard it was sold, as all the old houses were being sold in these days when no one could seem to find a newer place to live, she had allowed herself to watch daily for a sign that someone new was coming; every morning she glanced down from the back porch to see if there was smoke coming out of the cottage chimney, and every day going down the hill on her way to the store she hesitated past the cottage, watching carefully for the least movement within. The cottage had been sold in January and now, nearly two months later, even though it seemed prettier and less worn with the snow gently covering the overgrown garden and icicles in front of the blank windows, it was still forlorn and empty, despised since the day long ago when Mrs. Winning had given up all hope of ever living there.

Mrs. Winning deposited the napkins in the pantry and turned to tear   6
the leaf off the kitchen calendar before selecting a dish towel and joining her mother-in-law at the sink. "March already," she said despondently.

"They *did* tell me down at the store yesterday," her mother-in-law said,   7
"that they were going to start painting the cottage this week."

"Then that *must* mean someone's coming!"   8

"Can't take more than a couple of weeks to paint inside that little   9
house," old Mrs. Winning said.

It was almost April, however, before the new people moved in. The   10
snow had almost melted and was running down the street in icy, half-solid rivers. The ground was slushy and miserable to walk on, the skies grey and dull. In another month the first amazing green would start in the trees and on the ground, but for the better part of April there would be cold rain and perhaps more snow. The cottage had been painted inside, and new paper put on the walls. The front steps had been repaired and new glass put into the broken windows. In spite of the grey sky and the patches of dirty snow the cottage looked neater and firmer, and the painters were coming back to do the outside when the weather cleared. Mrs. Winning, standing at the foot of the cottage walk, tried to picture the cottage as it stood now, against the picture of the cottage she had made years ago, when she had hoped to live there herself. She had wanted roses by the porch; that could be done, and the neat colorful garden she had planned. She would have painted the outside white, and that too might still be done. Since the cottage had been sold she had not gone inside, but she remembered the little rooms, with the windows over the garden that could be so bright with gay curtains and window boxes, the small kitchen she would have painted yellow, the two bedrooms upstairs with slanting ceilings under the eaves. Mrs. Winning looked at the cottage for a long time, standing on the wet walk, and then went slowly on down to the store.

The first news she had of the new people came, at last, from the grocer 11 a few days later. As he was tying the string around the three pounds of hamburger the large Winning family would consume in one meal, he asked cheerfully, "Seen your new neighbors yet?"

"Have they moved in?" Mrs. Winning asked. "The people in the cot- 12 tage?"

"Lady in here this morning," the grocer said. "Lady and a little boy, 13 seem like nice people. They say her husband's dead. Nice-looking lady."

Mrs. Winning had been born in the town and the grocer's father had 14 given her jawbreakers and licorice in the grocery store while the present grocer was still in high school. For a while, when she was twelve and the grocer's son was twenty, Mrs. Winning had hoped secretly that he would want to marry her. He was fleshy now, and middle-aged, and although he still called her Helen and she still called him Tom, she belonged now to the Winning family and had to speak critically to him, no matter how unwillingly, if the meat were tough or the butter price too high. She knew that when he spoke of the new neighbor as a "lady" he meant something different than if he had spoken of her as a "woman" or a "person." Mrs. Winning knew that he spoke of the two Mrs. Winnings to his other customers as "ladies." She hesitated and then asked, "Have they really moved in to stay?"

"She'll have to stay for a while," the grocer said drily. "Bought a week's 15 worth of groceries."

Going back up the hill with her package Mrs. Winning watched all the 16 way to detect some sign of the new people in the cottage. When she reached the cottage walk she slowed down and tried to watch not too obviously. There was no smoke coming from the chimney, and no sign of furniture near the house, as there might have been if people were still moving in, but there was a middle-aged car parked in the street before the cottage and Mrs. Winning thought she could see figures moving past the windows. On a sudden irresistible impulse she turned and went up the walk to the front porch, and then, after debating for a moment, on up the steps to the door. She knocked, holding her bag of groceries in one arm, and then the door opened and she looked down on a little boy, about the same age, she thought happily, as her own son.

"Hello," Mrs. Winning said. 17

"Hello," the boy said. He regarded her soberly. 18

"Is your mother here?" Mrs. Winning asked. "I came to see if I could 19 help her move in."

"We're all moved in," the boy said. He was about to close the door, but 20 a woman's voice said from somewhere in the house, "Davey? Are you talking to someone?"

"That's my mommy," the little boy said. The woman came up behind 21 him and opened the door a little wider. "Yes?" she said.

Mrs. Winning said, "I'm Helen Winning. I live about three houses up 22 the street, and I thought perhaps I might be able to help you."

"Thank you," the woman said doubtfully. She's younger than I am, 23

Mrs. Winning thought, she's about thirty. And pretty. For a clear minute Mrs. Winning saw why the grocer had called her a lady.

"It's so nice to have someone living in this house," Mrs. Winning said 24 shyly. Past the other woman's head she could see the small hallway, with the larger living-room beyond and the door on the left going into the kitchen, the stairs on the right, with the delicate stair-rail newly painted; they had done the hall in light green, and Mrs. Winning smiled with friendship at the woman in the doorway, thinking, She *has* done it right; this is the way it should look after all, she knows about pretty houses.

After a minute the other woman smiled back, and said, "Will you come 25 in?"

As she stepped back to let Mrs. Winning in, Mrs. Winning wondered 26 with a suddenly stricken conscience if perhaps she had not been too forward, almost pushing herself in. . . . "I hope I'm not making a nuisance of myself," she said unexpectedly, turning to the other woman. "It's just that I've been wanting to live here myself for so long." Why did I say that, she wondered; it had been a very long time since young Mrs. Winning had said the first thing that came into her head.

"Come see *my* room," the little boy said urgently, and Mrs. Winning 27 smiled down at him.

"I have a little boy just about your age," she said. "What's your name?" 28

"Davey," the little boy said, moving closer to his mother. "Davey Wil- 29 liam MacLane."

"My little boy," Mrs. Winning said soberly, "is named Howard Talbot 30 Winning."

The little boy looked up at his mother uncertainly, and Mrs. Winning, 31 who felt ill at ease and awkward in this little house she so longed for, said, "How old are you? My little boy is five."

"I'm five," the little boy said, as though realizing it for the first time. 32 He looked again at his mother and she said graciously, "Will you come in and see what we've done to the house?"

Mrs. Winning put her bag of groceries down on the slim-legged table 33 in the green hall, and followed Mrs. MacLane into the living-room, which was L-shaped and had the windows Mrs. Winning would have fitted with gay curtains and flower-boxes. As she stepped into the room, Mrs. Winning realized, with a quick wonderful relief, that it was really going to be all right, after all. Everything, from the andirons in the fireplace to the books on the table, was exactly as Mrs. Winning might have done if she were eleven years younger; a little more informal, perhaps, nothing of quite such good quality as young Mrs. Winning might have chosen, but still richly, undeniably right. There was a picture of Davey on the mantel, flanked by a picture which Mrs. Winning supposed was Davey's father; there was a glorious blue bowl on the low coffee table, and around the corner of the L stood a row of orange plates on a shelf, and a polished maple table and chairs.

"It's lovely," Mrs. Winning said. This could have been mine, she was 34 thinking, and she stood in the doorway and said again, "It's perfectly lovely."

Mrs. MacLane crossed over to the low armchair by the fireplace and   35
picked up the soft blue material that lay across the arm. "I'm making curtains," she said, and touched the blue bowl with the tip of one finger. "Somehow I always make my blue bowl the center of the room," she said. "I'm
having the curtains the same blue, and my rug—when it comes!—will have
the same blue in the design."

"It matches Davey's eyes," Mrs. Winning said, and when Mrs. MacLane   36
smiled again she saw that it matched Mrs. MacLane's eyes too. Helpless
before so much that was magic to her, Mrs. Winning said *'Have* you painted
the kitchen yellow?"

"Yes," Mrs. MacLane said, surprised. "Come and see." She led the way   37
through the L, around past the orange plates to the kitchen, which caught the
late morning sun and shone with clean paint and bright aluminum; Mrs.
Winning noticed the electric coffeepot, the waffle iron, the toaster, and
thought, *She* couldn't have much trouble cooking, not with just the two of
them.

"When I have a garden," Mrs. MacLane said, "we'll be able to see it   38
from almost all the windows." She gestured to the broad kitchen windows,
and added, "I love gardens. I imagine I'll spend most of my time working in
this one, as soon as the weather is nice."

"It's a good house for a garden," Mrs. Winning said. "I've heard that   39
it used to be one of the prettiest gardens on the block."

"I thought so too," Mrs. MacLane said. "I'm going to have flowers on   40
all four sides of the house. With a cottage like this you can, you know."

Oh, I know, I know, Mrs. Winning thought wistfully, remembering the   41
neat charming garden she could have had, instead of the row of nasturtiums
along the side of the Winning house, which she tended so carefully; no
flowers would grow well around the Winning house, because of the heavy
old maple trees which shaded all the yard and which had been tall when the
house was built.

Mrs. MacLane had had the bathroom upstairs done in yellow, too, and   42
the two small bedrooms with overhanging eaves were painted green and rose.
"All garden colors," she told Mrs. Winning gaily, and Mrs. Winning, thinking
of the oddly matched, austere bedrooms in the big Winning house, sighed and
admitted that it would be wonderful to have window seats under the eaved
windows. Davey's bedroom was the green one, and his small bed was close
to the window. "This morning," he told Mrs. Winning solemnly, "I looked
out and there were four icicles hanging by my bed."

Mrs. Winning stayed in the cottage longer than she should have; she felt   43
certain, although Mrs. MacLane was pleasant and cordial, that her visit was
extended past courtesy and into curiosity. Even so, it was only her sudden
guilt about the three pounds of hamburger and dinner for the Winning men
that drove her away. When she left, waving good-bye to Mrs. MacLane and
Davey as they stood in the cottage doorway, she had invited Davey up to play
with Howard, Mrs. MacLane up for tea, both of them to come for lunch some
day, and all without the permission of her mother-in-law.

Reluctantly she came to the big house and turned past the bolted front 44
door to go up the walk to the back door, which all the family used in the
winter. Her mother-in-law looked up as she came into the kitchen and said
irritably, "I called the store and Tom said you left an hour ago."

"I stopped off at the old cottage," Mrs. Winning said. She put the 45
package of groceries down on the table and began to take things out quickly,
to get the doughnuts on to a plate and the hamburger into the pan before too
much time was lost. With her coat still on and her scarf over her head she
moved as fast as she could while her mother-in-law, slicing bread at the
kitchen table, watched her silently.

"Take your coat off," her mother-in-law said finally. "Your husband 46
will be home in a minute."

By twelve o'clock the house was noisy and full of mud tracked across 47
the kitchen floor. The oldest Howard, Mrs. Winning's father-in-law, came in
from the farm and went silently to hang his hat and coat in the dark hall
before speaking to his wife and daughter-in-law; the younger Howard, Mrs.
Winning's husband, came in from the barn after putting the truck away and
nodded to his wife and kissed his mother; and the youngest Howard, Mrs.
Winning's son, crashed into the kitchen, home from kindergarten, shouting,
"Where's dinner?"

The baby, anticipating food, banged on her high-chair with the silver 48
cup which had first been used by the oldest Howard Winning's mother. Mrs.
Winning and her mother-in-law put plates down on the table swiftly, knowing after many years the exact pause between the latest arrival and the serving
of food, and with a minimum of time three generations of the Winning family
were eating silently and efficiently, all anxious to be back about their work:
the farm, the mill, the electric train; the dishes, the sewing, the nap. Mrs.
Winning, feeding the baby, trying to anticipate her mother-in-law's gestures
of serving, thought, today more poignantly than ever before, that she had at
least given them another Howard, with the Winning eyes and mouth, in
exchange for her food and her bed.

After dinner, after the men had gone back to work and the children were 49
in bed, the baby for her nap and Howard resting with crayons and coloring
book, Mrs. Winning sat down with her mother-in-law over their sewing and
tried to describe the cottage.

"It's just perfect," she said helplessly. "Everything is so pretty. She 50
invited us to come down some day and see it when it's all finished, the
curtains and everything."

"I was talking to Mrs. Blake," the elder Mrs. Winning said, as though 51
in agreement. "She says the husband was killed in an automobile accident.
She had some money in her own name and I guess she decided to settle down
in the country for the boy's health. Mrs. Blake said he looked peakish."

"She loves gardens," Mrs. Winning said, her needle still in her hand for 52
a moment. "She's going to have a big garden all around the house."

"She'll need help," the elder woman said humorlessly, "that's a mighty 53
big garden she'll have."

"She has the *most* beautiful blue bowl, Mother Winning. You'd love it, 54 it's almost like silver."

"Probably," the elder Mrs. Winning said after a pause, "probably her 55 people came from around here a ways back, and *that's* why she's settled in these parts."

The next day Mrs. Winning walked slowly past the cottage, and slowly 56 the next, and the day after, and the day after that. On the second day she saw Mrs. MacLane at the window, and waved, and on the third day she met Davey on the sidewalk. "When are you coming to visit my little boy?" she asked him, and he stared at her solemnly and said, "Tomorrow."

Mrs. Burton, next-door to the MacLanes, ran over on the third day they 57 were there with a fresh apple pie, and then told all the neighbors about the yellow kitchen and the bright electric utensils. Another neighbor, whose husband had helped Mrs. MacLane start her furnace, explained that Mrs. MacLane was only very recently widowed. One or another of the townspeople called on the MacLanes almost daily, and frequently, as young Mrs. Winning passed, she saw familiar faces at the windows, measuring the blue curtains with Mrs. MacLane, or she waved to acquaintances who stood chatting with Mrs. MacLane on the now firm front steps. After the MacLanes had been in the cottage for about a week Mrs. Winning met them one day in the grocery and they walked up the hill together, and talked about putting Davey into the kindergarten. Mrs. MacLane wanted to keep him home as long as possible, and Mrs. Winning asked her, "Don't you feel terribly tied down, having him with you all the time?"

"I like it," Mrs. MacLane said cheerfully, "we keep each other com- 58 pany," and Mrs. Winning felt clumsy and ill-mannered, remembering Mrs. MacLane's widowhood.

As the weather grew warmer and the first signs of green showed on the 59 trees and on the wet ground, Mrs. Winning and Mrs. MacLane became better friends. They met almost daily at the grocery and walked up the hill together, and twice Davey came up to play with Howard's electric train, and once Mrs. MacLane came up to get him and stayed for a cup of coffee in the great kitchen while the boys raced round and round the table and Mrs. Winning's mother-in-law was visiting a neighbor.

"It's such an old house," Mrs. MacLane said, looking up at the dark 60 ceiling. "I love old houses; they feel so secure and warm, as though lots of people had been perfectly satisfied with them and they *knew* how useful they were. You don't get that feeling with a new house."

"This dreary old place," Mrs. Winning said. Mrs. MacLane, with a 61 rose-colored sweater and her bright soft hair, was a spot of color in the kitchen that Mrs. Winning knew she could never duplicate. "I'd give anything in the world to live in your house," Mrs. Winning said.

"I love it," Mrs. MacLane said. "I don't think I've ever been so happy. 62 Everyone around here is so nice, and the house is so pretty, and I planted a lot of bulbs yesterday." She laughed. "I used to sit in that apartment in New York and dream about planting bulbs again."

Mrs. Winning looked at the boys, thinking how Howard was half-a- 63 head taller, and stronger, and how Davey was small and weak and loved his mother adoringly. "It's been good for Davey already," she said. "There's color in his cheeks."

"Davey loves it," Mrs. MacLane agreed. Hearing his name Davey came 64 over and put his head in her lap and she touched his hair, bright like her own. "We'd better be getting home, Davey boy," she said.

"Maybe our flowers have grown some since yesterday," said Davey. 65

Gradually the days became miraculously long and warm, and Mrs. 66 MacLane's garden began to show colors and became an ordered thing, still very young and unsure, but promising rich brilliance for the end of the summer, and the next summer, and summers ten years from now.

"It's even better than I hoped," Mrs. MacLane said to Mrs. Winning, 67 standing at the garden gate. "Things grow so much better here than almost anywhere else."

Davey and Howard played daily after the school was out for the sum- 68 mer, and Howard was free all day. Sometimes Howard stayed at Davey's house for lunch, and they planted a vegetable patch together in the MacLane back yard. Mrs. Winning stopped for Mrs. MacLane on her way to the store in the mornings and Davey and Howard frolicked ahead of them down the street. They picked up their mail together and read it walking back up the hill, and Mrs. Winning went more cheerfully back to the big Winning house after walking most of the way home with Mrs. MacLane.

One afternoon Mrs. Winning put the baby in Howard's wagon and with 69 the two boys they went for a long walk in the country. Mrs. MacLane picked Queen Anne's lace and put it into the wagon with the baby; and the boys found a garter snake and tried to bring it home. On the way up the hill Mrs. MacLane helped pull the wagon with the baby and the Queen Anne's lace, and they stopped halfway to rest and Mrs. MacLane said, "Look, I believe you can see my garden all the way from here."

It was a spot of color almost at the top of the hill and they stood looking 70 at it while the baby threw the Queen Anne's lace out of the wagon. Mrs. MacLane said, "I always want to stop here to look at it," and then, "Who is that *beautiful* child?"

Mrs. Winning looked, and then laughed. "He *is* attractive, isn't he," she 71 said. "It's Billy Jones." She looked at him herself, carefully, trying to see him as Mrs. MacLane would. He was a boy about twelve, sitting quietly on a wall across the street, with his chin in his hands, silently watching Davey and Howard.

"He's like a young statue," Mrs. MacLane said. "So brown, and will you 72 look at that face?" She started to walk again to see him more clearly, and Mrs. Winning followed her. "Do I know his mother and fath—?"

"The Jones children are half-Negro," Mrs. Winning said hastily. "But 73
they're all beautiful children; you should see the girl. They live just outside
town."

Howard's voice reached them clearly across the summer air. "Nigger," 74
he was saying, "nigger, nigger boy."

"Nigger," Davey repeated, giggling. 75

Mrs. MacLane gasped, and then said, *"Davey,"* in a voice that made 76
Davey turn his head apprehensively. Mrs. Winning had never heard her
friend use such a voice, and she too watched Mrs. MacLane.

"Davey," Mrs. MacLane said again, and Davey approached slowly. 77
"What did I hear you say?"

"Howard," Mrs. Winning said, "leave Billy alone." 78

"Go tell that boy you're sorry," Mrs. MacLane said. "Go at once and 79
tell him you're sorry."

Davey blinked tearfully at his mother and then went to the curb and 80
called across the street, "I'm sorry."

Howard and Mrs. Winning waited uneasily, and Billy Jones across the 81
street raised his head from his hands and looked at Davey and then, for a long
time, at Mrs. MacLane. Then he put his chin on his hands again.

Suddenly Mrs. MacLane called, "Young man—Will you come here a 82
minute, please?"

Mrs. Winning was surprised, and stared at Mrs. MacLane, but when the 83
boy across the street did not move, Mrs. Winning said sharply, "Billy! Billy
Jones! Come here at once!"

The boy raised his head and looked at them, and then slid slowly down 84
from the wall and started across the street. When he was across the street and
about five feet from them he stopped, waiting.

"Hello," Mrs. MacLane said gently, "what's your name?" 85

The boy looked at her for a minute and then at Mrs. Winning, and Mrs. 86
Winning said, "He's Billy Jones. Answer when you're spoken to, Billy."

"Billy," Mrs. MacLane said. "I'm sorry my little boy called you a name, 87
but he's very little and he doesn't always know what he's saying. But he's
sorry, too."

"Okay," Billy said, still watching Mrs. Winning. He was wearing an old 88
pair of blue jeans and a torn white shirt, and he was barefoot. His skin and
hair were the same color, the golden shade of a very heavy tan, and his hair
curled lightly; he had the look of a garden statue.

"Billy," Mrs. MacLane said, "how would you like to come and work for 89
me? Earn some money?"

"Sure," Billy said. 90

"Do you like gardening?" Mrs. MacLane asked. Billy nodded soberly. 91
"Because," Mrs. MacLane went on enthusiastically, "I've been needing some-
one to help me with my garden, and it would be just the thing for you to do."
She waited a minute and then said, "Do you know where I live?"

"Sure," Billy said. He turned his eyes away from Mrs. Winning and for 92 a minute looked at Mrs. MacLane, his brown eyes expressionless. Then he looked back at Mrs. Winning, who was watching Howard up the street.

"Fine," Mrs. MacLane said. "Will you come tomorrow?"   93

"Sure," Billy said. He waited for a minute, looking from Mrs. MacLane   94
to Mrs. Winning, and then ran back across the street and vaulted over the wall where he had been sitting. Mrs. MacLane watched him admiringly. Then she smiled at Mrs. Winning and gave the wagon a tug to start it up the hill again. They were nearly at the MacLane cottage before Mrs. MacLane finally spoke. "I just can't stand that," she said, "to hear children attacking people for things they can't help."

"They're strange people, the Joneses," Mrs. Winning said readily. "The   95
father works around as a handyman; maybe you've seen him. You see—" she dropped her voice—"the mother was white, a girl from around here. A local girl," she said again, to make it more clear to a foreigner. "She left the whole litter of them when Billy was about two, and went off with a white man."

"Poor children," Mrs. MacLane said.   96

"They're all right," Mrs. Winning said. "The church takes care of them, 97
of course, and people are always giving them things. The girl's old enough to work now, too. She's sixteen, but. . . ."

"But what?" Mrs. MacLane said, when Mrs. Winning hesitated.   98

"Well, people talk about her a lot, you know," Mrs. Winning said.   99
"Think of her mother, after all. And there's another boy, couple of years older than Billy."

They stopped in front of the MacLane cottage and Mrs. MacLane   100
touched Davey's hair. "Poor unfortunate child," she said.

"Children *will* call names," Mrs. Winning said. "There's not much you   101
can do."

"Well . . ." Mrs. MacLane said. "Poor child."   102

The next day, after the dinner dishes were washed, and while Mrs.   103
Winning and her mother-in-law were putting them away, the elder Mrs. Winning said casually, "Mrs. Blake tells me your friend Mrs. MacLane was asking around the neighbors how to get hold of the Jones boy."

"She wants someone to help in the garden, I think," Mrs. Winning said   104
weakly. "She needs help in that big garden."

"Not *that* kind of help," the elder Mrs. Winning said. "You tell her   105
about them?"

"She seemed to feel sorry for them," Mrs. Winning said, from the   106
depths of the pantry. She took a long time settling the plates in even stacks in order to neaten her mind. She *shouldn't* have done it, she was thinking, but her mind refused to tell her why. She should have asked me first, though, she thought finally.

The next day Mrs. Winning stopped off at the cottage with Mrs. Ma-   107
cLane after coming up the hill from the store. They sat in the yellow kitchen and drank coffee, while the boys played in the back yard. While they were discussing the possibilities of hammocks between the apple trees there was

a knock at the kitchen door and when Mrs. MacLane opened it she found a man standing there, so that she said, "Yes?" politely, and waited.

"Good morning," the man said. He took off his hat and nodded his head   108
at Mrs. MacLane. "Billy told me you was looking for someone to work your garden," he said.

"Why . . ." Mrs. MacLane began, glancing sideways uneasily at Mrs.   109
Winning.

"I'm Billy's father," the man said. He nodded his head toward the back   110
yard and Mrs. MacLane saw Billy Jones sitting under one of the apple trees, his arms folded in front of him, his eyes on the grass at his feet.

"How do you do," Mrs. MacLane said inadequately.   111

"Billy told me you said for him to come work your garden," the man   112
said. "Well, now, I think maybe a summer job's too much for a boy his age, he ought to be out playing in the good weather. And that's the kind of work I do anyway, so's I thought I'd just come over and see if you found anyone yet."

He was a big man, very much like Billy, except that where Billy's hair   113
curled only a little, his father's hair curled tightly, with a line around his head where his hat stayed constantly and where Billy's skin was a golden tan, his father's skin was darker, almost bronze. When he moved, it was gracefully, like Billy, and his eyes were the same fathomless brown. "Like to work this garden," Mr. Jones said, looking around. "Could be a mighty nice place."

"You were very nice to come," Mrs. MacLane said. "I certainly do need   114
help."

Mrs. Winning sat silently, not wanting to speak in front of Mr. Jones.   115
She was thinking, I wish she'd ask me first, this is impossible . . . and Mr. Jones stood silently, listening courteously, with his dark eyes on Mrs. MacLane while she spoke. "I guess a lot of the work would be too much for a boy like Billy," she said. "There are a lot of things I can't even do myself, and I was sort of hoping I could get someone to give me a hand."

"That's fine, then," Mr. Jones said. "Guess I can manage most of it," he   116
said, and smiled.

"Well," Mrs. MacLane said, "I guess that's all settled, then. When do   117
you want to start?"

"How about right now?" he said.   118

"Grand," Mrs. MacLane said enthusiastically, and then, "Excuse me for   119
a minute," to Mrs. Winning over her shoulder. She took down her gardening gloves and wide straw hat from the shelf by the door. "Isn't it a lovely day?" she asked Mr. Jones as she stepped out into the garden while he stood back to let her pass.

"You go along home now, Bill," Mr. Jones called as they went toward   120
the side of the house.

"Oh, why not let him stay?" Mrs. MacLane said. Mrs. Winning heard   121
her voice going on as they went out of sight. "He can play around the garden, and he'd probably enjoy . . ."

For a minute Mrs. Winning sat looking at the garden, at the corner   122

around which Mr. Jones had followed Mrs. MacLane, and then Howard's face
appeared around the side of the door and he said, "Hi, is it nearly time to eat?"

"Howard," Mrs. Winning said quietly, and he came in through the door   123
and came over to her. "It's time for you to run along home," Mrs. Winning
said. "I'll be along in a minute."

Howard started to protest, but she added, "I want you to go right away.   124
Take my bag of groceries if you think you can carry it."

Howard was impressed by her conception of his strength, and he lifted   125
down the bag of groceries; his shoulders, already broad out of proportion, like
his father's and his grandfather's, strained under the weight, and then he
steadied on his feet. "Aren't I strong?" he asked exultantly.

"*Very* strong," Mrs. Winning said. "Tell Grandma I'll be right up. I'll just   126
say good-bye to Mrs. MacLane."

Howard disappeared through the house; Mrs. Winning heard him walk-   127
ing heavily under the groceries, out through the open front door and down
the steps. Mrs. Winning rose and was standing by the kitchen door when
Mrs. MacLane came back.

"You're not ready to go?" Mrs. MacLane exclaimed when she saw Mrs.   128
Winning with her jacket on. "Without finishing your coffee?"

"I'd better catch Howard," Mrs. Winning said. "He ran along ahead."   129

"I'm sorry I left you like that," Mrs. MacLane said. She stood in the   130
doorway beside Mrs. Winning, looking out into the garden. "How *wonderful*
it all is," she said, and laughed happily.

They walked together through the house; the blue curtains were up by   131
now, and the rug with the touch of blue in the design was on the floor.

"Good-bye," Mrs. Winning said on the front steps.   132

Mrs. MacLane was smiling, and following her look Mrs. Winning   133
turned and saw Mr. Jones, his shirt off and his strong back shining in the sun
as he bent with a scythe over the long grass at the side of the house. Billy
lay nearby, under the shade of the bushes; he was playing with a grey kitten.
"I'm going to have the finest garden in town," Mrs. MacLane said proudly.

"You won't have him working here past today, will you?" Mrs. Win-   134
ning asked. "Of course you won't have him any longer than just today?"

"But surely—" Mrs. MacLane began, with a tolerant smile, and Mrs.   135
Winning, after looking at her for an incredulous minute, turned and started,
indignant and embarrassed, up the hill.

Howard had brought the groceries safely home and her mother-in-law   136
was already setting the table.

"Howard says you sent him home from MacLane's," her mother-in-law   137
said, and Mrs. Winning answered briefly, "I thought it was getting late."

The next morning when Mrs. Winning reached the cottage on her way   138
down to the store she saw Mr. Jones swinging the scythe expertly against the
side of the house, and Billy Jones and Davey sitting on the front steps
watching him. "Good morning, Davey," Mrs. Winning called, "is your
mother ready to go downstreet?"

"Where's Howard?" Davey asked, not moving.   139

"He stayed home with his grandma today," Mrs. Winning said brightly.   140
"Is your mother ready?"

"She's making lemonade for Billy and me," Davey said. "We're going   141
to have it in the garden."

"Then tell her," Mrs. Winning said quickly, "tell her that I said I was   142
in a hurry and that I had to go on ahead. I'll see her later." She hurried on
down the hill.

In the store she met Mrs. Harris, a lady whose mother had worked for   143
the elder Mrs. Winning nearly forty years before. "Helen," Mrs. Harris said,
"you get greyer every year. You ought to stop all this running around."

Mrs. Winning, in the store without Mrs. MacLane for the first time in   144
weeks, smiled shyly and said that she guessed she needed a vacation.

"Vacation!" Mrs. Harris said. "Let that husband of yours do the house-   145
work for a change. He doesn't have nuthin' else to do."

She laughed richly, and shook her head. "Nuthin' else to do," she said.   146
"The Winnings!"

Before Mrs. Winning could step away Mrs. Harris added, her laughter   147
penetrated by a sudden sharp curiosity: "Where's that dressed-up friend of
yours get to? Usually downstreet together, ain't you?"

Mrs. Winning smiled courteously, and Mrs. Harris said, laughing again,   148
"Just couldn't believe those shoes of hers, first time I seen them. Them shoes!"

While she was laughing again Mrs. Winning escaped to the meat   149
counter and began to discuss the potentialities of pork shoulder earnestly
with the grocer. Mrs. Harris only says what everyone else says, she was
thinking, are they talking like that about Mrs. MacLane? Are they laughing
at her? When she thought of Mrs. MacLane she thought of the quiet house,
the soft colors, the mother and son in the garden; Mrs. MacLane's shoes were
green and yellow platform sandals, odd-looking certainly next to Mrs. Winning's solid white oxfords, but so inevitably right for Mrs. MacLane's house,
and her garden. . . . Mrs. Harris came up behind her and said, laughing again,
"What's she got, that Jones fellow working for her now?"

When Mrs. Winning reached home, after hurrying up the hill past the   150
cottage, where she saw no one, her mother-in-law was waiting for her in front
of the house, watching her come the last few yards. "Early enough today,"
her mother-in-law said. "MacLane out of town?"

Resentful, Mrs. Winning said only, "Mrs. Harris nearly drove me out   151
of the store, with her jokes."

"Nothing wrong with Lucy Harris getting away from that man of hers   152
wouldn't cure," the elder Mrs. Winning said. Together, they began to walk
around the house to the back door. Mrs. Winning, as they walked, noticed
that the grass under the trees had greened up nicely, and that the nasturtiums
beside the house were bright.

"I've got something to say to you, Helen," the elder Mrs. Winning said   153
finally.

"Yes?" her daughter-in-law said.   154

"It's the MacLane girl, about her, I mean. You know her so well, you   155
ought to talk to her about that colored man working there."

"I suppose so," Mrs. Winning said.   156

"You *sure* you told her? You told her about those people?"   157

"I told her," Mrs. Winning said.   158

"He's there every blessed day," her mother-in-law said. "And working   159
out there without his shirt on. He goes in the house."

And that evening Mr. Burton, next-door neighbor to Mrs. MacLane,   160
dropped in to see the Howard Winnings about getting a new lot of shingles
at the mill; he turned, suddenly, to Mrs. Winning, who was sitting sewing
next to her mother-in-law at the table in the front room, and raised his voice
a little when he said, "Helen, I wish you'd tell your friend Mrs. MacLane to
keep that kid of hers out of my vegetables."

"Davey?" Mrs. Winning said involuntarily.   161

"No," Mr. Burton said, while all the Winnings looked at the younger   162
Mrs. Winning, "no, the other one, the colored boy. He's been running loose
through our back yard. Makes me sort of mad, that kid coming in spoiling
other people's property. You know," he added, turning to the Howard Winnings, "you know, that does make a person mad." There was a silence, and
then Mr. Burton added, rising heavily, "Guess I'll say good-night to you
people."

They all attended him to the door and came back to their work in   163
silence. I've got to do something, Mrs. Winning was thinking, pretty soon
they'll stop coming to me first, they'll tell someone else to speak to *me*. She
looked up, found her mother-in-law looking at her, and they both looked
down quickly.

Consequently Mrs. Winning went to the store the next morning earlier 164
than usual, and she and Howard crossed the street just above the MacLane
house, and went down the hill on the other side.

"Aren't we going to see Davey?" Howard asked once, and Mrs. Win-   165
ning said carelessly, "Not today, Howard. Maybe your father will take you
out to the mill this afternoon."

She avoided looking across the street at the MacLane house, and hurried 166
to keep up with Howard.

Mrs. Winning met Mrs. MacLane occasionally after that at the store or 167
the post office, and they spoke pleasantly. When Mrs. Winning passed the
cottage after the first week or so, she was no longer embarrassed about going
by, and even looked at it frankly once or twice. The garden was going
beautifully; Mr. Jones's broad back was usually visible through the bushes,
and Billy Jones sat on the steps or lay on the grass with Davey.

One morning on her way down the hill Mrs. Winning heard a conversa-   168
tion between Davey MacLane and Billy Jones; they were in the bushes
together and she heard Davey's high familiar voice saying, "Billy, you want
to build a house with me today?"

"Okay," Billy said. Mrs. Winning slowed her steps a little to hear.   169

"We'll build a big house out of branches," Davey said excitedly, "and 170 when it's finished we'll ask my mommy if we can have lunch out there."

"You can't build a house just out of branches," Billy said. "You ought 171 to have wood, and boards."

"And chairs and tables and dishes," Davey agreed. "And walls." 172

"Ask your mommy can we have two chairs out here," Billy said. "Then 173 we can pretend the whole garden is our house."

"And I'll get us some cookies, too," Davey said. "And we'll ask my 174 mommy and your daddy to come in our house." Mrs. Winning heard them shouting as she went down along the sidewalk.

You have to admit, she told herself as though she were being strictly 175 just, you have to admit that he's doing a lot with that garden; it's the prettiest garden on the street. And Billy acts as though he had as much right there as Davey.

As the summer wore on into long hot days undistinguishable one from 176 another, so that it was impossible to tell with any real accuracy whether the light shower had been yesterday or the day before, the Winnings moved out into their yard to sit after supper, and in the warm darkness. Mrs. Winning sometimes found an opportunity of sitting next to her husband so that she could touch his arm; she was never able to teach Howard to run to her and put his head in her lap, or inspire him with other than the perfunctory Winning affection, but she consoled herself with the thought that at least they were a family, a solid respectable thing.

The hot weather kept up, and Mrs. Winning began to spend more time 177 in the store, postponing the long aching walk up the hill in the sun. She stopped and chatted with the grocer, with other young mothers in the town, with older friends of her mother-in-law's, talking about the weather, the reluctance of the town to put in a decent swimming pool, the work that had to be done before school started in the fall, chickenpox, the P.T.A. One morning she met Mrs. Burton in the store, and they spoke of their husbands, the heat, and the hot-weather occupations of their children before Mrs. Burton said: "By the way, Johnny will be six on Saturday and he's having a birthday party; can Howard come?"

"Wonderful," Mrs. Winning said, thinking. His good white shorts, the 178 dark blue shirt, a carefully wrapped present.

"Just about eight children," Mrs. Burton said, with the loving careless- 179 ness mothers use in planning the birthday parties of their children. "They'll stay for supper, of course—send Howard down about three-thirty."

"That sounds so nice," Mrs. Winning said. "He'll be delighted when I 180 tell him."

"I thought I'd have them all play outdoors most of the time," Mrs. 181 Burton said. "In this weather. And then perhaps a few games indoors, and supper. Keep it simple—*you* know." She hesitated, running her finger around and around the top rim of a can of coffee. "Look," she said, "I hope you won't mind me asking, but would it be all right with you if I didn't invite the MacLane boy?"

Mrs. Winning felt sick for a minute, and had to wait for her voice to 182
even out before she said lightly, "It's all right with me if it's all right with
you; why do you have to ask *me?"*

Mrs. Burton laughed. "I just thought you might mind if he didn't 183
come."

Mrs. Winning was thinking, Something bad has happened, somehow 184
people think they know something about me that they won't say, they all
pretend it's nothing, but this never happened to me before; I live with the
Winnings, don't I? "Really," she said, putting the weight of the old Winning
house into her voice, "why in the *world* would it bother me?" Did I take it too
seriously, she was wondering, did I seem too anxious, should I have let it go?

Mrs. Burton was embarrassed, and she set the can of coffee down on 185
the shelf and began to examine the other shelves studiously. "I'm sorry I
mentioned it at all," she said.

Mrs. Winning felt that she had to say something further, something to 186
state her position with finality, so that no longer would Mrs. Burton, at least,
dare to use such a tone to a Winning, presume to preface a question with "I
hope you don't mind me asking." "After all," Mrs. Winning said carefully,
weighing the words, "she's like a second mother to Billy."

Mrs. Burton, turning to look at Mrs. Winning for confirmation, 187
grimaced and said, "Good Lord, Helen!"

Mrs. Winning shrugged and then smiled and Mrs. Burton smiled and 188
then Mrs. Winning said, "I do feel so sorry for the little boy, though."

Mrs. Burton said, "Such a sweet little thing, too." 189

Mrs. Winning had just said, "He and Billy are together *all* the time 190
now," when she looked up and saw Mrs. MacLane regarding her from the end
of the aisle of shelves; it was impossible to tell whether she had heard them
or not. For a minute Mrs. Winning looked steadily back at Mrs. MacLane, and
then she said, with just the right note of cordiality. "Good morning, Mrs.
MacLane. Where is your little boy this morning?"

"Good morning, Mrs. Winning," Mrs. MacLane said, and moved on 191
past the aisle of shelves, and Mrs. Burton caught Mrs. Winning's arm and
made a desperate gesture of hiding her face and, unable to help themselves,
both she and Mrs. Winning began to laugh.

Soon after that, although the grass in the Winning yard under the maple 192
trees stayed smooth and green, Mrs. Winning began to notice in her daily
trips past the cottage that Mrs. MacLane's garden was suffering from the heat.
The flowers wilted under the morning sun, and no longer stood up fresh and
bright; the grass was browning slightly and the rose bushes Mrs. MacLane
had put in so optimistically were noticeably dying. Mr. Jones seemed always
cool, working steadily; sometimes bent down with his hands in the earth,
sometimes tall against the side of the house, setting up a trellis or pruning
a tree, but the blue curtains hung lifelessly at the windows. Mrs. MacLane
still smiled at Mrs. Winning in the store, and then one day they met at the
gate of Mrs. MacLane's garden and, after hesitating for a minute, Mrs. Mac-

Lane said, "Can you come in for a few minutes? I'd like to have a talk, if you have time."

"Surely," Mrs. Winning said courteously, and followed Mrs. MacLane up 193 the walk, still luxuriously bordered with flowering bushes, but somehow disenchanted, as though the summer heat had baked away the vivacity from the ground. In the familiar living-room Mrs. Winning sat down on a straight chair, holding herself politely stiff, while Mrs. MacLane sat as usual in her armchair.

"How is Davey?" Mrs. Winning asked finally, since Mrs. MacLane did 194 not seem disposed to start any conversation.

"He's very well," Mrs. MacLane said, and smiled as she always did 195 when speaking of Davey. "He's out back with Billy."

There was a quiet minute, and then Mrs. MacLane said, staring at the 196 blue bowl on the coffee table, "What I wanted to ask you is, what on earth is gone wrong?"

Mrs. Winning had been holding herself stiff in readiness for some such 197 question, and when she said, "I don't know what you mean," she thought, I sound exactly like Mother Winning, and realized, I'm enjoying this, just as *she* would; and no matter what she thought of herself she was unable to keep from adding, "*Is* something wrong?"

"Of course," Mrs. MacLane said. She stared at the blue bowl, and said 198 slowly, "When I first came, everyone was so nice, and they seemed to like Davey and me and want to help us."

That's wrong, Mrs. Winning was thinking, you mustn't ever talk about 199 whether people like you, that's bad taste.

"And the garden was going so well," Mrs. MacLane said helplessly. 200 "And now, no one ever does more than just speak to us—I used to say 'Good morning' over the fence to Mrs. Burton, and she'd come to the fence and we'd talk about the garden, and now she just says 'Morning' and goes in the house—and no one ever smiles, or anything."

This is dreadful, Mrs. Winning thought, this is childish, this is com- 201 plaining. People treat you as you treat them, she thought; she wanted desperately to go over and take Mrs. MacLane's hand and ask her to come back and be one of the nice people again; but she only sat straighter in the chair and said, "I'm sure you must be mistaken. I've never heard anyone speak of it."

"*Are* you sure?" Mrs. MacLane turned and looked at her. "Are you sure 202 it isn't because of Mr. Jones working here?"

Mrs. Winning lifted her chin a little higher and said, "Why on earth 203 would anyone around here be rude to you because of Jones?"

Mrs. MacLane came with her to the door, both of them planning vigor- 204 ously for the days some time next week when they would all go swimming, when they would have a picnic, and Mrs. Winning went down the hill thinking, The nerve of her, trying to blame the colored folks.

Toward the end of the summer there was a bad thunderstorm, breaking 205 up the prolonged hot spell. It raged with heavy wind and rain over the town all night, sweeping without pity through the trees, pulling up young bushes and flowers ruthlessly; a barn was struck on one side of town, the wires pulled down on another. In the morning Mrs. Winning opened the back door to find the Winning yard littered with small branches from the maples, the grass bent almost flat to the ground.

Her mother-in-law came to the door behind her. "Quite a storm," she said, "did it wake you?" 206

"I woke up once and went to look at the children," Mrs. Winning said. "It must have been about three o'clock." 207

"I was up later," her mother-in-law said. "I looked at the children too; they were both asleep." 208

They turned together and went in to start breakfast. 209

Later in the day Mrs. Winning started down to the store; she had almost reached the MacLane cottage when she saw Mrs. MacLane standing in the front garden with Mr. Jones standing beside her and Billy Jones with Davey in the shadows of the front porch. They were all looking silently at a great branch from one of the Burtons' trees that lay across the center of the garden, crushing most of the flowering bushes and pinning down what was to have been a glorious tulip bed. As Mrs. Winning stopped, watching, Mrs. Burton came out on to her front porch to survey the storm damage, and Mrs. Mac-Lane called to her, "Good morning, Mrs. Burton, it looks like we have part of your tree over here." 210

"Looks so," Mrs. Burton said, and she went back into her house and closed the door flatly. 211

Mrs. Winning watched while Mrs. MacLane stood quietly for a minute. Then she looked up at Mr. Jones almost hopefully and she and Mr. Jones looked at one another for a long time. Then Mrs. MacLane said, her clear voice carrying lightly across the air washed clean by the storm: "Do you think I ought to give it up, Mr. Jones? Go back to the city where I'll never have to see another garden?" 212

Mr. Jones shook his head despondently, and Mrs. MacLane, her shoulders tired, went slowly over and sat on her front steps and Davey came and sat next to her. Mr. Jones took hold of the great branch angrily and tried to move it, shaking it and pulling until his shoulders tensed with the strength he was bringing to bear, but the branch only gave slightly and stayed, clinging to the garden. 213

"Leave it alone, Mr. Jones," Mrs. MacLane said finally. "Leave it for the next people to move!" 214

But still Mr. Jones pulled against the branch, and then suddenly Davey stood up and cried out, "There's Mrs. Winning! Hi, Mrs. Winning!" 215

Mrs. MacLane and Mr. Jones both turned, and Mrs. MacLane waved and called out, "Hello!" 216

Mrs. Winning swung around without speaking and started, with great dignity, back up the hill toward the old Winning house. 217

✦

Questions for Discussion

1. In paragraph 10 Mrs. Winning thinks back on her earlier dreams of living in the cottage. What do her specific dreams of decorating and colors suggest about her inner life? About her distance from the other Winnings? About how happy she is?

2. What does the fact that the same people see each other every day—at the grocery store, at the post office, and on the single main street—suggest about the closeness of community standards? How is the size of a town a force for conformity?

3. How do the names of the Winnings, especially the men's names, suggest the view that the Winnings take of their own importance? How does the location of the Winning house reinforce this view?

4. What is the significance for Mrs. Winning's inner life that "no flowers would grow well around the Winning house, because of the heavy old maple trees which shaded all the yard and which had been tall when the house was built" (¶41)?

5. What is the significance for Mrs. Winning's inner life that when her husband comes in from the farm for the noon meal, he "nodded to his wife and kissed his mother" (¶47)?

6. What does Mrs. Winning's explanation of the name-calling episode (¶101) suggest about her character? What can we "read" in her joining Mrs. Burton's laughter in paragraph 191? Above all, what is suggested by her realization in paragraph 197 that she *enjoys* sounding just like Mother Winning?

7. What features in the Winning family make you sympathize with Mrs. Winning's position? What is suggested about the function and status of women in the Winning family by Mrs. Winning's silent thought that "she had at least given them another Howard, with the Winning eyes and mouth, in exchange for her food and bed" (¶48)?

Suggested Essay Topics

1. Write an essay to your class in which, speaking as Mrs. Winning, you explain your actions as they must have appeared to you. Allow Mrs. Winning to make the best case in her own defense that you can imagine, allowing her, perhaps, to predict the consequences if she had taken a different tack; in short, allow her to construct her own standards. After you have given her her say, conclude with a page of response in which you determine which parts of her justification are valid and which are not.

2. Write a dialogue or conversation in which you picture Mrs. MacLane and Mrs. Winning meeting years later and discussing the events recorded in Jackson's story. The conversation could go in many different directions; you will have to choose one direction and stick with it. There could be recriminations and counteraccusations. You could invent any number of evil consequences for either or both women. Or you could have them

arrive at an understanding of each other, seeing each other's limitations but also the pressure they were under at the time, and being willing to forgive. Or you could imagine a host of other kinds of confrontations. Try to keep in mind, however, that the story is fundamentally about possibilities of character and that your conversation should both express and illuminate the character of the women involved.

Ayn Rand

Ayn Rand (1905–1982) was born and educated in Russia, where as a young woman she experienced the Bolshevik Revolution and the extreme restrictions of individual freedom that Soviet collectivization imposed. A naturalized American citizen, she published a series of novels and essays urging the pursuit of freedom through a total individualism. The Fountainhead *(1943), probably her best-known novel, portrays a version of the great architect, Frank Lloyd Wright, as a model of the achievements possible for a creative and uninhibited individual. Her credo is perhaps best summarized in the oath sworn by the citizens of an imaginary community described in* Atlas Shrugged *(1957): "I will never live for the sake of another man, nor ask any other man to live for mine."*

The following excerpt is from Anthem, *a novelette portraying the fate of a courageous dissenter in a totalitarian state. The excerpt is a hymn of praise sung by the hero to his god—himself. As you read, you might think of similar attitudes expressed in your time—though in a different style (for example, in the 1970s best-seller* Looking Out for No. 1 *by Robert J. Ringer).*

I OWE NOTHING
TO MY BROTHERS

Our title for chapter 11 of *Anthem* (1938).

I AM. I THINK. I WILL. 1

My hands . . . My spirit . . . My sky . . . My forest . . . This earth of 2
mine. . . .

What must I say besides? These are the words. This is the answer. 3

I stand here on the summit of the mountain. I lift my head and I spread 4
my arms. This, my body and spirit, this is the end of the quest. I wished to know the meaning of things. I am the meaning. I wished to find a warrant

for being. I need no warrant for being, and no word of sanction upon my being. I am the warrant and the sanction.

It is my eyes which see, and the sight of my eyes grants beauty to the   5
earth. It is my ears which hear, and the hearing of my ears gives its song to the world. It is my mind which thinks, and the judgment of my mind is the only searchlight that can find the truth. It is my will which chooses, and the choice of my will is the only edict I must respect.

Many words have been granted me, and some are wise, and some are   6
false, but only three are holy: "I will it!"

Whatever road I take, the guiding star is within me; the guiding star and   7
the loadstone which point the way. They point in but one direction. They point to me.

I know not if this earth on which I stand is the core of the universe or   8
if it is but a speck of dust lost in eternity. I know not and I care not. For I know what happiness is possible to me on earth. And my happiness needs no higher aim to vindicate it. My happiness is not the means to any end. It is the end. It is its own goal. It is its own purpose.

Neither am I the means to any end others may wish to accomplish. I am   9
not a tool for their use. I am not a servant of their needs. I am not a bandage for their wounds. I am not a sacrifice on their altars.

I am a man. This miracle of me is mine to own and keep, and mine to   10
guard, and mine to use, and mine to kneel before!

I do not surrender my treasures, nor do I share them. The fortune of my   11
spirit is not to be blown into coins of brass and flung to the winds as alms for the poor of the spirit. I guard my treasures: my thought, my will, my freedom. And the greatest of these is freedom.

I owe nothing to my brothers, nor do I gather debts from them. I ask   12
none to live for me, nor do I live for any others. I covet no man's soul, nor is my soul theirs to covet.

I am neither foe nor friend to my brothers, but such as each of them shall   13
deserve of me. And to earn my love, my brothers must do more than to have been born. I do not grant my love without reason, nor to any chance passer-by who may wish to claim it. I honor men with my love. But honor is a thing to be earned.

I shall choose friends among men, but neither slaves nor masters. And   14
I shall choose only such as please me, and them I shall love and respect, but

neither command nor obey. And we shall join our hands when we wish, or walk alone when we so desire. For in the temple of his spirit, each man is alone. Let each man keep his temple untouched and undefiled. Then let him join hands with others if he wishes, but only beyond his holy threshold.

For the word "We" must never be spoken, save by one's choice and as   15
a second thought. This word must never be placed first within man's soul, else it becomes a monster, the root of all the evils on earth, the root of man's torture by men, and of an unspeakable lie.

The word "We" is as lime poured over men, which sets and hardens to   16
stone, and crushes all beneath it, and that which is white and that which is black are lost equally in the grey of it. It is the word by which the depraved steal the virtue of the good, by which the weak steal the might of the strong, by which the fools steal the wisdom of the sages.

What is my joy if all hands, even the unclean, can reach into it? What   17
is my wisdom, if even the fools can dictate to me? What is my freedom, if all creatures, even the botched and the impotent, are my masters? What is my life, if I am but to bow, to agree and to obey?

But I am done with this creed of corruption.   18

I am done with the monster of "We," the word of serfdom, of plunder, 19
of misery, falsehood and shame.

And now I see the face of god, and I raise this god over the earth, this 20
god whom men have sought since men came into being, this god who will grant them joy and peace and pride.

This god, this one word: 21

"I."   22

✦

Questions for Discussion

1. People who like to think in slogans called the 1970s and 1980s "the me decades." *Anthem* was written in the 1930s, sometimes called "the decade of social responsibility." Does the position expressed in "I Owe Nothing to My Brothers" seem to resemble or to contrast with the basic beliefs that have been fashionable since you became aware of "beliefs" at all?

2. The doctrine proclaimed in this excerpt from *Anthem* is in one sense deliberately "anti-social." Does it seem to you finally dangerous to society? Give your reasons. What do you think Rand would reply to anyone who claimed that she cared only about the welfare of the selfish and powerful?

3. Phrases like "the me decade," "the decade of social responsibility," "the apathetic decade" (the 1950s), and "the decade of protest" (the 1960s) at best cover only a limited number of the trends and topics of a given period. People pick them up as a way of talking easily about the past, but when we press our memories or do research we usually find more exceptions than illustrations. Ayn Rand might say that our tendency to use these catchphrases in our thinking is just one more example of our being too dependent on other people. Yet she inevitably depends, as we all do, on earlier thinkers (Nietzsche, perhaps, for the glorification of the independent "I"; Thomas Jefferson, for the inalienable right to the pursuit of happiness; Aristotle, for the relentless pursuit of rationality). Thus her ideas, like those of every other thinker, can almost all be traced to predecessors. Does this unavoidable kinship with earlier thinkers seriously undermine Rand's notion that each individual should attempt to worship and serve only the "I"? How does her "I" relate to the "we" who have thought similar thoughts?

4. Although Ayn Rand often advocates reliance on reason as the ultimate test of truth, the tone of this chapter from *Anthem* is "oracular"; it resembles what we might call the "prophetic" tone of I Corinthians 13 (pp. 387–389). Compare, for example, Rand's paragraph 18 with St. Paul's verse 11. The voice in "I Owe Nothing to My Brothers" is that of an "oracle," one who speaks to us from the "summit of the mountain" (like Moses at Mt. Sinai), uttering truths that seem to have come from a higher source than is available to ordinary mortals. Conclusions are pronounced without the usual kinds of supporting evidence, and each assertion is loaded with an unusually strong emotional commitment. Indeed, the whole utterance is couched in the language of scripture ("guiding star," ¶7; "miracle," ¶10; "fortune of my spirit," ¶11; "covet," ¶12; "temple" and "holy," ¶14; and so on). Go through the passage slowly and list all of the other "scriptural" devices used by the speaker—not just those that explicitly echo the Bible but any device or turn of phrase suggesting that "these utterances are not to be tested by the usual tests. Do not question my word; it comes from on high."

5. When two oracles seem to contradict each other, as do St. Paul and Rand, how are we to deal with them? One simple way would be to dismiss *all* such writing and speaking as absurd because it cannot be tested with rational tests. Another way would be to listen to one of the two voices uncritically: *My* prophet is simply right and yours self-evidently wrong. Can you think of other possibilities?

6. One possible answer to question 5 would be this: When oracles conflict, there may be *some* truth in each, and the way to find out how much is to

slow down and think about the *consequences,* both intellectual and practical, of taking the oracles seriously. Oracles do not, in themselves, usually talk about consequences; their tone suggests that life would be simple if we would only give up every reservation and follow the true doctrine. But as readers who want to learn from them, provided that they really have anything worthwhile to teach, we can step back a bit and ask what their message would mean to our effort to build livable worlds for ourselves. First what do you think would be the consequences, for you, if you decided to put into practice the values expressed by Rand? Second, what would be the consequences for *you* if everyone you know decided to live by these values?

7. Another way to test an oracle is to ask whether the utterance is consistent within itself. Do you detect any internal inconsistencies in Rand's message? In St. Paul's?

8. The 1980s saw a remarkable growth in the popularity and influence of TV evangelists, claiming to offer us a saving truth. One good question to ask of these oracles, a question surprisingly often neglected by people who jump and join, is this: "What is there in it for *you*—the prophet?" Does the question yield different results when asked of St. Paul and when asked of Rand or of the TV evangelists?

Note: The executor of Miss Ayn Rand's estate, Mr. Leonard Peikoff, responding to our request to reprint this selection from *Anthem,* suggested that some of our discussion questions seriously misrepresent her thought.

> Miss Rand repudiates all forms of mysticism and religion; she advocates exclusive reliance on reason as a means of cognition, and she has written an entire book defining her conception of "reason" (*Introduction to Objectivist Epistemology*). To liken her method or approach, therefore, to that of St. Paul, and to describe her viewpoint as "oracular," is unacceptable in point of accuracy and scholarship. *Anthem* is, of course, a novelette, not a philosophical treatise; as such each sentence does not come equipped with lengthy exegesis or geometric demonstration. But this does not mean that the viewpoint is "oracular." Within its own context, the reasons *are* advanced: the events of the preceding story give the rationale for the summarizing conclusion which you wish to quote. For a full proof of Ayn Rand's ethical viewpoint, including a discussion of the meta-ethical problems of validation involved, I would refer you to her book *The Virtue of Selfishness*.

Suggested Essay Topics

1. "I owe nothing to my brothers, nor do I gather debts from them" (¶12). Imagine a friend of yours who, after reading Rand's chapter from *Anthem*, has decided that her celebration of "I" as against "We" is sound guidance for life. Write *one* of the following letters:
   a. A letter arguing against the decision, concentrating on why this one statement seems factually doubtful

b. A letter arguing in support of her views, concentrating on wl statement seems sound to you

c. A letter debating the pros and cons of the position, describing as many reasons as you can for and against saying that you "owe" something to your brothers (and sisters)

2. Most of your essays will attempt to give more supporting evidence for your claims than is appropriate in "prophetic" writing. But this topic is your chance to climb onto your own mountaintop and shout whatever truths you would like the whole world to believe. Choose your favorite cause—some behavior or set of beliefs you'd like the whole world to adopt—and let yourself go. (One possibility: a hymn to the god "We," in answer to Rand's celebration of the great god "I.")

✦ 6 ✦

THE INDIVIDUAL
AND SOCIETY

The Duties of the Citizen,
the Beliefs of the Individual

Power tends to corrupt; absolute power corrupts absolutely.
Lord Acton

Liberty means responsibility. That is why most men dread it.
George Bernard Shaw

Authority and power are two different things: *Power* is the force
by means of which you can oblige others to obey you.
Authority is the *right* to direct and comment, to be listened to or obeyed
by others. Authority requests power. Power without authority
is tyranny.
Jacques Maritain

If all mankind minus one were of one opinion,
and only one person were of the contrary opinion,
mankind would be no more justified in
silencing that one person, than he, if he had the power,
would be justified in silencing mankind.
John Stuart Mill

For discipline is the channel in which our acts run strong
and deep; where there is no direction, the deeds of men run shallow
and wander and are wasted.
Ursula K. Le Guin

The tree of liberty must be refreshed from time to time with
the blood of patriots and tyrants. It is its natural manure.
Thomas Jefferson

Strange it is, that men should admit the validity of the arguments
for free discussion, but object to their being "pushed to an extreme";
not seeing that unless the reasons are good
for an extreme case, they are not good for any case.
John Stuart Mill

start
12-7-93

Scott Russell Sanders

Although society *in the theme of this chapter, "The Individual and Society," is often taken to refer to the larger society made up of everyone in it,* society *also refers to those smaller communities that we are all members of, including the societies comprised of our families, friends, and neighborhoods. In many cases these smaller societies influence us more than the larger society, for we carry on a more intimate commerce with them. We look more often for approval to the members of our small and intimate societies than to members of the larger society; we also flinch more readily at the disapproval of these same persons.*

For all of us, the society of our families extends backwards in time, bridging the past and the present. Some of us are unfortunate enough not to know much about the individuals in our own family's past. Grandparents were left in Europe, perhaps, or other foreign countries; families got scattered, somehow, never to be reunited; or family generations failed to live long enough to establish extended relations with their children and grandchildren. But many others are fortunate enough to have continuity with their family's past, and it is almost always true that such ties are viewed as a precious entitlement by those who have them. Intimacy and continuity with the past seem to help one, as in Scott Sanders' (b. 1945) case, achieve a sense of present identity. It helps you know who you are if you know who your forbearers have been: where they came from, how they lived, what they valued, and how they spent their days.

The fullness of all these associations is richly conveyed in Sanders' essay about his father, stimulated by the news of his father's death on a cold February morning. The carpenter's tools Sanders is using when the news of his father's death arrives are a legacy from that same man, who inherited them in his turn from his father, Sanders' grandfather. Sanders reflects on the tools—their shape, the uses to which they have been put, the family stories associated with them, the memories of using them in childhood, his long apprenticeship of learning how to use them properly, and, finally, the comparisons between the tools and their former owners suggested by the occasion.

All of these reflections allow Sanders to speak at more than one level: as an essayist, as a grieving son, and as a remembering grandson. As he speaks from these various levels, he finds the continuity that makes the present death in his family not less grievous, but somehow less terminal, less final. Already Sanders' own son is beginning to use the inherited family tools in the same clumsy but eager way that Sanders did when he was his own son's age. The inheritance continues.

THE INHERITANCE OF TOOLS

From *North American Review,* 1986; reprinted in Sanders' collection of essays, *The Paradise of Bombs* (1987).

At just about the hour when my father died, soon after dawn one   1
February morning when ice coated the windows like cataracts, I banged my thumb with a hammer. Naturally I swore at the hammer, the reckless thing, and in the moment of swearing I thought of what my father would say: "If you'd try hitting the nail it would go in a whole lot faster. Don't you know your thumb's not as hard as that hammer?" We both were doing carpentry that day, but far apart. He was building cupboards at my brother's place in Oklahoma; I was at home in Indiana, putting up a wall in the basement to make a bedroom for my daughter. By the time my mother called with news of his death—the long distance wires whittling her voice until it seemed too thin to bear the weight of what she had to say—my thumb was swollen. A week or so later a white scar in the shape of a crescent moon began to show above the cuticle, and month by month it rose across the pink sky of my thumbnail. It took the better part of a year for the scar to disappear, and every time I noticed it I thought of my father.

The hammer had belonged to him, and to his father before him. The   2
three of us have used it to build houses and barns and chicken coops, to upholster chairs and crack walnuts, to make doll furniture and bookshelves and jewelry boxes. The head is scratched and pockmarked, like an old plowshare that has been working rocky fields, and it gives off the sort of dull sheen you see on fast creek water in the shade. It is a finishing hammer, about the weight of a bread loaf, too light, really, for framing walls, too heavy for cabinet work, with a curved claw for pulling nails, a rounded head for pounding, a fluted neck for looks, and a hickory handle for strength.

The present handle is my third one, bought from a lumberyard in   3
Tennessee, down the road from where by brother and I were helping my father build his retirement house. I broke the previous one by trying to pull sixteen-penny nails out of floor joists—a foolish thing to do with a finishing hammer, as my father pointed out. "You ever hear of a crowbar?" he said. No telling how many handles he and my grandfather had gone through before me. My grandfather used to cut down hickory trees on his farm, saw them into slabs, cure the planks in his hayloft, and carve handles with a drawknife. The grain in hickory is crooked and knotty, and therefore

tough, hard to split, like the grain in the two men who owned this hammer before me.

After proposing marriage to a neighbor girl, my grandfather used this hammer to build a house for his bride on a stretch of river bottom in northern Mississippi. The lumber for the place, like the hickory for the handle, was cut on his own land. By the day of the wedding he had not quite finished the house, and so right after the ceremony he took his wife home and put her to work. My grandmother had worn her Sunday dress for the wedding, with a fringe of lace tacked on around the hem in honor of the occasion. She removed this lace and folded it away before going out to help my grandfather nail siding on the house. "There she was in her good dress," he told me some fifty-odd years after that wedding day, "holding up them long pieces of clapboard while I hammered, and together we got the place covered up before dark." As the family grew to four, six, eight, and eventually thirteen, my grandfather used this hammer to enlarge his house room by room, like a chambered nautilus expanding its shell.

By and by the hammer was passed along to my father. One day he was up on the roof of our pony barn nailing shingles with it, when I stepped out the kitchen door to call him for supper. Before I could yell, something about the sight of him straddling the spine of that roof and swinging the hammer caught my eye and made me hold my tongue. I was five or six years old, and the world's commonplaces were still news to me. He would pull a nail from the pouch at his waist, bring the hammer down, and a moment later the *thunk* of the blow would reach my ears. And that is what had stopped me in my tracks and stilled my tongue, that momentary gap between seeing and hearing the blow. Instead of yelling from the kitchen door, I ran to the barn and climbed two rungs up the ladder—as far as I was allowed to go—and spoke quietly to my father. On our walk to the house he explained that sound takes time to make its way through air. Suddenly the world seemed larger, the air more dense, if sound could be held back like any ordinary traveler.

By the time I started using this hammer, at about the age when I discovered the speed of sound, it already contained houses and mysteries for me. The smooth handle was one my grandfather had made. In those days I needed both hands to swing it. My father would start a nail in a scrap of wood, and I would pound away until I bent it over.

"Looks like you got ahold of some of those rubber nails," he would tell me. "Here, let me see if I can find you some stiff ones." And he would rummage in a drawer until he came up with a fistful of more cooperative nails. "Look at the head," he would tell me. "Don't look at your hands, don't look at the hammer. Just look at the head of that nail and pretty soon you'll learn to hit it square."

Pretty soon I did learn. While he worked in the garage cutting dovetail joints for a drawer or skinning a deer or tuning an engine, I would hammer nails. I made innocent blocks of wood look like porcupines. He did not talk much in the midst of his tools, but he kept up a nearly ceaseless humming, slipping in and out of a dozen tunes in an afternoon, often running back over the same stretch of melody again and again, as if searching for a way out. When the humming did cease, I knew he was faced with a task requiring great delicacy or concentration, and I took care not to distract him.

He kept scraps of wood in a cardboard box—the ends of two-by-fours, 9 slabs of shelving and plywood, odd pieces of molding—and everything in it was fair game. I nailed scraps together to fashion what I called boats or houses, but the results usually bore only faint resemblance to the visions I carried in my head. I would hold up these constructions to show my father, and he would turn them over in his hands admiringly, speculating about what they might be. My cobbled-together guitars might have been alien space-ships, my barns might have been models of Aztec temples, each wooden contraption might have been anything but what I had set out to make.

Now and again I would feel the need to have a chunk of wood shaped 10 or shortened before I riddled it with nails, and I would clamp it in a vise and scrape at it with a handsaw. My father would let me lacerate the board until my arm gave out, and then he would wrap his hand around mine and help me finish the cut, showing me how to use my thumb to guide the blade, how to pull back on the saw to keep it from binding, how to let my shoulder do the work.

"Don't force it," he would say, "just drag it easy and give the teeth a 11 chance to bite."

As the saw teeth bit down, the wood released its smell, each kind with 12 its own fragrance, oak or walnut or cherry or pine—usually pine because it was the softest, easiest for a child to work. No matter how weathered and gray the board, no matter how warped and cracked, inside there was this smell waiting, as of something freshly baked. I gathered every smidgen of sawdust and stored it away in coffee cans, which I kept in a drawer of the workbench. When I did not feel like hammering nails, I would dump my sawdust on the concrete floor of the garage and landscape it into highways and farms and towns, running miniature cars and trucks along miniature roads. Looming as huge as a colossus, my father worked over and around me, now and again bending down to inspect my work, careful not to trample my creations. It was a landscape that smelled dizzyingly of wood. Even after a bath my skin would carry the smell, and so would my father's hair, when he lifted me for a bedtime hug.

I tell these things not only from memory but also from recent observa- 13 tion, because my own son now turns blocks of wood into nailed porcupines, dumps cans full of sawdust at my feet and sculpts highways on the floor. He learns how to swing a hammer from the elbow instead of the wrist, how to lay his thumb beside the blade to guide a saw, how to tap a chisel with a wooden mallet, how to mark a hole with an awl before starting a drill bit. My daughter did the same before him, and even now, on the brink of teenage aloofness, she will occasionally drag out my box of wood scraps and carpenter something. So I have seen my apprenticeship to wood and tools re-enacted in each of my children, as my father saw his own apprenticeship renewed in me.

The saw I use belonged to him, as did my level and both of my squares, 14 and all four tools had belonged to his father. The blade of the saw is the bluish color of gun barrels, and the maple handle, dark from the sweat of hands, is inscribed with curving leaf designs. The level is a shaft of walnut two feet long, edged with brass and pierced by three round windows in which air bubbles float in oil-filled tubes of glass. The middle window serves for testing if a surface is horizontal, the others for testing if a surface is plumb or vertical. My grandfather used to carry this level on the gun rack behind the seat in his pickup, and when I rode with him I would turn around to watch the bubbles dance. The larger of the two squares is called a framing square, a flat steel elbow, so beat up and tarnished you can barely make out the rows of numbers that show how to figure the cuts on rafters. The smaller one is called a try square, for marking right angles, with a blued steel blade for the shank and a brass-faced block of cherry for the head.

I was taught early on that a saw is not to be used apart from a square: 15 "If you're going to cut a piece of wood," my father insisted, "you owe it to the tree to cut it straight."

Long before studying geometry, I learned there is a mystical virtue in 16 right angles. There is an unspoken morality in seeking the level and the plumb. A house will stand, a table will bear weight, the sides of a box will hold together, only if the joints are square and the members upright. When the bubble is lined up between two marks etched in the glass tube of a level, you have aligned yourself with the forces that hold the universe together. When you miter the corners of a picture frame, each angle must be exactly forty-five degrees, as they are in the perfect triangles of Pythagoras, not a degree more or less. Otherwise the frame will hang crookedly, as if ashamed of itself and of its maker. No matter if the joints you are cutting do not show. Even if you are butting two pieces of wood together inside a cabinet, where no one except a wrecking crew will ever see them, you must take pains to ensure that the ends are square and the studs are plumb.

I took pains over the wall I was building on the day my father died. Not 17 long after that wall was finished—paneled with tongue-and-groove boards of yellow pine, the nail holes filled with putty and the wood all stained and sealed—I came close to wrecking it one afternoon when my daughter ran howling up the stairs to announce that her gerbils had escaped from their cage and were hiding in my brand new wall. She could hear them scratching and squeaking behind her bed. Impossible! I said. How on earth could they get inside my drum-tight wall? Through the heating vent, she answered. I went downstairs, pressed my ear to the honey-colored wood, and heard the *scritch scritch* of tiny feet.

"What can we do?" my daughter wailed. "They'll starve to death, 18 they'll die of thirst, they'll suffocate."

"Hold on," I soothed. "I'll think of something." 19

While I thought and she fretted, the radio on her bedside table delivered 20 us the headlines: Several thousand people had died in a city in India from a poisonous cloud that had leaked overnight from a chemical plant. A nuclear-powered submarine had been launched. Rioting continued in South Africa. An airplane had been hijacked in the Mediterranean. Authorities calculated that several thousand homeless people slept on the streets within sight of the Washington Monument. I felt my usual helplessness in the face of all these calamities. But here was my daughter, weeping because her gerbils were holed up in a wall. This calamity I could handle.

"Don't worry," I told her. "We'll set food and water by the heating vent   21
and lure them out. And if that doesn't do the trick, I'll tear the wall apart until we find them."

She stopped crying and gazed at me. "You'd really tear it apart? Just for   22
my gerbils? The *wall?*" Astonishment slowed her down only for a second, however, before she ran to the workbench and began tugging at drawers, saying, "Let's see, what'll we need? Crowbar. Hammer. Chisels. I hope we don't have to use them—but just in case."

We didn't need the wrecking tools. I never had to assault my handsome   23
wall, because the gerbils eventually came out to nibble at a dish of popcorn. But for several hours I studied the tongue-and-groove skin I had nailed up on the day of my father's death, considering where to begin prying. There were no gaps in that wall, no crooked joints.

I had botched a great many pieces of wood before I mastered the right   24
angle with a saw, botched even more before I learned to miter a joint. The knowledge of these things resides in my hands and eyes and the webwork of muscles, not in the tools. There are machines for sale—powered miter boxes and radial-arm saws, for instance—that will enable any casual soul to cut proper angles in boards. The skill is invested in the gadget instead of the person who uses it, and this is what distinguishes a machine from a tool. If I had to earn my keep by making furniture or building houses, I suppose I would buy powered saw and pneumatic nailers; the need for speed would drive me to it. But since I carpenter only for my own pleasure or to help neighbors or to remake the house around the ears of my family, I stick with hand tools. Most of the ones I own were given to me by my father, who also taught me how to wield them. The tools in my workbench are a double inheritance, for each hammer and level and saw is wrapped in a cloud of knowing.

All of these tools are a pleasure to look at and to hold. Merchants would   25
never paste NEW NEW NEW! signs on them in stores. Their designs are old because they work, because they serve their purpose well. Like folk songs and aphorisms and the grainy bits of language, these tools have been pared down to essentials. I look at my claw hammer, the distillation of a hundred generations of carpenters, and consider that it holds up well beside those other classics—Greek vases, Gregorian chants, *Don Quixote,* barbed fish hooks, candles, spoons. Knowledge of hammering stretches back to the earliest humans who squatted beside fires, chipping flints. Anthropologists have a lovely name for those unworked rocks that served as the earliest hammers. "Dawn stones," they are called. Their only qualification for the work, aside from

hardness, is that they fit the hand. Our ancestors used them for grinding corn, tapping awls, smashing bones. From dawn stones to this claw hammer is a great leap in time, but no great distance in design or imagination.

On that iced-over February morning when I smashed my thumb with 26 the hammer, I was down in the basement framing the wall that my daughter's gerbils would later hide in. I was thinking of my father, as I always did whenever I built anything, thinking how he would have gone about the work, hearing in memory what he would have said about the wisdom of hitting the nail instead of my thumb. I had the studs and plates nailed together all square and trim, and was lifting the wall into place when the phone rang upstairs. My wife answered, and in a moment she came to the basement door and called down softly to me. The stillness in her voice made me drop the framed wall and hurry upstairs. She told me my father was dead. Then I heard the details over the phone from my mother. Building a set of cupboards for my brother in Oklahoma, he had knocked off work early the previous afternoon because of cramps in his stomach. Early this morning, on his way into the kitchen of my brother's trailer, maybe going for a glass of water, so early that no one else was awake, he slumped down on the linoleum and his heart quit.

For several hours I paced around inside my house, upstairs and down, 27 in and out of every room, looking for the right door to open and knowing there was no such door. My wife and children followed me and wrapped me in arms and backed away again, circling and staring as if I were on fire. Where was the door, the door, the door? I kept wondering. My smashed thumb turned purple and throbbed, making me furious. I wanted to cut it off and rush outside and scrape away the snow and hack a hole in the frozen earth and bury the shameful thing.

I went down into the basement, opened a drawer in my workbench, 28 and stared at the ranks of chisels and knives. Oiled and sharp, as my father would have kept them, they gleamed at me like teeth. I took up a clasp knife, pried out the longest blade, and tested the edge on the hair of my forearm. A tuft came away cleanly, and I saw my father testing the sharpness of tools on his own skin, the blades of axes and knives and gouges and hoes, saw the red hair shaved off in patches from his arms and the backs of his hands. "That will cut bear," he would say. He never cut a bear with his blades, now my blades, but he cut deer, dirt, wood. I closed the knife and put it away. Then I took up the hammer and went back to work on my daughter's wall, snugging the bottom plate against a chalk line on the floor, shimming the top plate against the joists overhead, plumbing the studs with my level, making sure before I drove the first nail that every line was square and true.

◆

Questions for Discussion

1. Sanders begins an account of the day of his father's death in the first sentence of the essay but breaks off and does not return to this account until paragraph 26. What is going on rhetorically and emotionally in the essay in the intervening 24 paragraphs? Is Sanders' return to this account more effective in paragraph 26 than if he had finished it in the first two or three paragraphs and then gone on to talk about the things he includes in the "inserted" 24 paragraphs? Why or why not?

2. Can you or others in the class give an account of material items—tools, jewelry, china, furniture, and so on—handed down through the generations in your families? Does the value of these items resonate with the same emotional connotations as Sanders' carpentry tools? How do you explain the symbolic significance of these kinds of material objects? What might be the point of talking or writing about such symbolic significance?

3. After reading Sanders' essay, do you think you know his father well? What qualities do you attribute to him? Could you write a paragraph or two about him, confident that you knew the man's character and not just some of his actions or his appearance? If so, how does Sanders succeed in conveying character? What descriptive or analytical strategies help him as a writer realize his purposes?

4. What does Sanders accomplish by such contrasts as that in paragraphs 14 and 16, where he packs paragraph 14 with objective information about tools and packs paragraph 16 with subjective and subtle suggestions about the values that lie behind the proper use of the tools: the "unspoken morality in seeking the level and the plumb"? What are the rhetorical effects of such contrasts?

Suggested Essay Topics

1. A parent does not have to be dead for Sanders' kind of essay to be an appropriate tribute, nor is the person who plays an important role in one's life always a parent. Using Sanders' essay as a model, write an essay of your own about someone who has been powerfully influential in your life, and, like Sanders, try to use the essay to express not only your own feelings about this person, but to capture that person's objective reality, the wholeness or heft of the person's character. Imagine your audience to be the same as Sanders': the kind of person who might read *Harper's Magazine* or *The New Yorker* or *Atlantic Monthly* or *The New York Times Magazine*.

2. Write an essay to your fellow students or to any other group of people you imagine to have read Sanders' essay and take as your task the job of explaining the manner and effectiveness of Sander's use of metaphor and simile. Almost every paragraph has at least one striking image made up of a metaphor or a simile: "a white scar in the shape of a crescent moon began to show above the cuticle, and month by month it rose across the pink sky of my thumbnail" (¶1), "my grandfather used this hammer to enlarge his

house room by room, like a chambered nautilus expanding its shell" (¶4), "I made innocent blocks of wood look like porcupines" (¶8), "I studied the tongue-and-groove skin I had nailed up" (¶23), and so on. There are many others. If you imagine these and other such passages as either missing or rewritten in "neutral" language, what happens to the emotional suggestiveness of the essay? Make your own essay an attempt to explain the kinds and content of suggestions that Sanders achieves by his use of metaphorical language.

Martin Luther King, Jr.

Martin Luther King, Jr. (1929–1968), a leader of the American civil rights movement, first achieved national prominence during the late 1950s and early 1960s. The scope of his social vision, the moral integrity of his commitment to nonviolence, the authority of his voice, and the generous, incandescent passion of his love for an America not yet realized marked King early as a force larger than any local or particular movement pushing for social change. In 1964 he was awarded the Nobel Peace Prize. In 1968 he was assassinated while on a visit to Memphis, Tennessee, lending support to a strike for higher wages by the garbage workers of that city.

Like Socrates, who persistently reminded his fellow Athenians that they cared more for custom, comfort, and security than for the pursuit of truth or the cultivation of their souls, King reminded his fellow Americans that they cared more for the color of their fellow citizens' skins than for compassion, dignity, or justice. Also like Socrates, who chose to accept execution as a subversive rather than live in exile from his beloved Athens, King always made it clear that he attacked the practices of his country out of love, not hatred. Socrates could be unmerciful in flogging his friends' inconsistencies, hypocrisies, and deceptions and still show that he preferred their company to all others—that he needled them only because he loved them. In the same way, King could express annoyance, disappointment, frustration, and anger at his fellow Americans' foot-dragging on the issue of social justice (especially the foot-dragging of the self-styled "moderate liberal") and still show that what he wanted was for this country to live up to the dream of its best self.

The title of the piece reprinted here is factual; King wrote this letter while he was indeed in prison. The immediate circumstances and local history of the conflict are partially explained in the letter itself. But of course the significance of such matters shifts for us depending on our perspective. For Booth, who was 42 years old when the letter was written, to re-read it now is to experience again the excitement and admiration he felt at the time. For Gregory, who in 1963 was freshly graduated from an isolated, predominantly white college in central Indiana and who had never before faced seriously the problem of racial injustice, the movement King championed produced what he now considers a major awakening, a transformation of conscience and consciousness.

But for most of you who read this book, the events took place before you were born and probably seem to you part of the distant past.

For all of us the meaning of those events shifts as we learn more and more about what they led to. What does not shift, as our memories dim and we become more and more dependent on historical accounts, is our picture of the grandeur of King's achievement. King's letter, addressing the conscience of a nation and testing its moral resolve, embraces far more than Birmingham, Alabama, 1963, as it speaks to people of any time and any place who care about justice.

LETTER FROM BIRMINGHAM JAIL*

From *Why We Can't Wait* (1964).

April 16, 1963

MY DEAR FELLOW CLERGYMEN:

While confined here in the Birmingham city jail, I came across your   1
recent statement calling my present activities "unwise and untimely." Seldom do I pause to answer criticism of my work and ideas. If I sought to answer all the criticisms that cross my desk, my secretaries would have little time for anything other than such correspondence in the course of the day, and I would have no time for constructive work. But since I feel that you are men of genuine good will and that your criticisms are sincerely set forth, I want to try to answer your statement in what I hope will be patient and reasonable terms.

I think I should indicate why I am here in Birmingham, since you have   2
been influenced by the view which argues against "outsiders coming in." I have the honor of serving as president of the Southern Christian Leadership Conference, an organization operating in every southern state, with head-quarters in Atlanta, Georgia. We have some eighty-five affiliated organizations across the South, and one of them is the Alabama Christian Movement for Human Rights. Frequently we share staff, educational and financial resources with our affiliates. Several months ago the affiliate here in Birmingham asked us to be on call to engage in a nonviolent direct-action program if such were deemed necessary. We readily consented, and when the hour came we lived up to our promise. So I, along with several members of my staff, am here because I was invited here. I am here because I have organizational ties here.

---

*This response to a published statement by eight fellow clergymen from Alabama (Bishop C. C. J. Carpenter, Bishop Joseph A. Durick, Rabbi Hilton L. Grafman, Bishop Paul Hardin, Bishop Holan B. Harmon, the Reverend George M. Murray, the Reverend Edward V. Ramage and the Reverend Earl Stallings) was composed under somewhat constricting circumstances. Begun on the margins of the newspaper in which the statement appeared while I was in jail, the letter was continued on scraps of writing paper supplied by a friendly Negro trusty, and concluded on a pad my attorneys were eventually permitted to leave me. Although the text remains in substance unaltered, I have indulged in the author's prerogative of polishing it for publication. [King's note.]

But more basically, I am in Birmingham because injustice is here. Just 3
as the prophets of the eighth century B.C. left their villages and carried their
"thus saith the Lord" far beyond the boundaries of their home towns, and
just as the Apostle Paul left his village of Tarsus and carried the gospel of
Jesus Christ to the far corners of the Greco-Roman world, so am I compelled
to carry the gospel of freedom beyond my own home town. Like Paul, I must
constantly respond to the Macedonian call for aid.

Moreover, I am cognizant of the interrelatedness of all communities and 4
states. I cannot sit idly by in Atlanta and not be concerned about what
happens in Birmingham. Injustice anywhere is a threat to justice everywhere.
We are caught in an inescapable network of mutuality, tied in a single garment of destiny. Whatever affects one directly, affects all indirectly. Never
again can we afford to live with the narrow, provincial "outside agitator"
idea. Anyone who lives inside the United States can never be considered an
outsider anywhere within its bounds.

You deplore the demonstrations taking place in Birmingham. But your 5
statement, I am sorry to say, fails to express a similar concern for the conditions that brought about the demonstrations. I am sure that none of you
would want to rest content with the superficial kind of social analysis that
deals merely with effects and does not grapple with underlying causes. It is
unfortunate that demonstrations are taking place in Birmingham, but it is
even more unfortunate that the city's white power structure left the Negro
community with no alternative.

In any nonviolent campaign there are four basic steps: collection of the 6
facts to determine whether injustices exist; negotiation; self-purification; and
direct action. We have gone through all these steps in Birmingham. There can
be no gainsaying the fact that racial injustice engulfs this community. Birmingham is probably the most thoroughly segregated city in the United
States. Its ugly record of brutality is widely known. Negroes have experienced
grossly unjust treatment in the courts. There have been more unsolved bombings of Negro homes and churches in Birmingham than in any other city in
the nation. These are the hard, brutal facts of the case. On the basis of these
conditions, Negro leaders sought to negotiate with the city fathers. But the
latter consistently refused to engage in good-faith negotiation.

Then, last September, came the opportunity to talk with leaders of 7
Birmingham's economic community. In the course of the negotiations, certain
promises were made by the merchants—for example, to remove the stores'
humiliating racial signs. On the basis of these promises, the Reverend Fred
Shuttlesworth and the leaders of the Alabama Christian Movement for
Human Rights agreed to a moratorium on all demonstrations. As the weeks
and months went by, we realized that we were the victims of a broken
promise. A few signs, briefly removed, returned; the others remained.

As in so many past experiences, our hopes had been blasted, and the 8
shadow of deep disappointment settled upon us. We had no alternative
except to prepare for direct action, whereby we would present our very bodies
as a means of laying our case before the conscience of the local and the

national community. Mindful of the difficulties involved, we decided to undertake a process of self-purification. We began a series of workshops on nonviolence, and we repeatedly asked ourselves: "Are you able to accept blows without retaliating?" "Are you able to endure the ordeal of jail?" We decided to schedule our direct-action program for the Easter season, realizing that except for Christmas, this is the main shopping period of the year. Knowing that a strong economic-withdrawal program would be the by-product of direct action, we felt that this would be the best time to bring pressure to bear on the merchants for the needed change.

Then it occurred to us that Birmingham's mayoral election was coming   9 up in March, and we speedily decided to postpone action until after election day. When we discovered that the Commissioner of Public Safety, Eugene "Bull" Connor, had piled up enough votes to be in the run-off, we decided again to postpone action until the day after the run-off so that the demonstrations could not be used to cloud the issues. Like many others, we waited to see Mr. Connor defeated, and to this end we endured postponement after postponement. Having aided in this community need, we felt that our direct-action program could be delayed no longer.

You may well ask: "Why direct action? Why sit-ins, marches and so   10 forth? Isn't negotiation a better path?" You are quite right in calling for negotiation. Indeed, this is the very purpose of direct action. Nonviolent direct action seeks to create such a crisis and foster such a tension that a community which has constantly refused to negotiate is forced to confront the issue. It seeks so to dramatize the issue that it can no longer be ignored. My citing the creation of tension as part of the work of the nonviolent-resister may sound rather shocking. But I must confess that I am not afraid of the word "tension." I have earnestly opposed violent tension, but there is a type of constructive, nonviolent tension which is necessary for growth. Just as Socrates felt that it was necessary to create a tension in the mind so that individuals could rise from the bondage of myths and half-truths to the unfettered realm of creative analysis and objective appraisal, so must we see the need for nonviolent gadflies to create the kind of tension in society that will help men rise from the dark depths of prejudice and racism to the majestic heights of understanding and brotherhood.

The purpose of our direct-action program is to create a situation so   11 crisis-packed that it will inevitably open the door to negotiation. I therefore concur with you in your call for negotiation. Too long has our beloved Southland been bogged down in a tragic effort to live in monologue rather than dialogue.

One of the basic points in your statement is that the action that I and   12 my associates have taken in Birmingham is untimely. Some have asked: "Why didn't you give the new city administration time to act?" The only answer that I can give to this query is that the new Birmingham administration must be prodded about as much as the outgoing one, before it will act. We are sadly mistaken if we feel that the election of Albert Boutwell as mayor will bring the millennium to Birmingham. While Mr. Boutwell is a much more gentle person than Mr. Connor, they are both segregationists, dedicated to maintenance of the status quo. I have hope that Mr. Boutwell will be reasonable enough to see the futility of massive resistance to desegregation. But he will not see this without pressure from devotees of civil rights. My friends, I must say to you that we have not made a single gain in civil rights without determined legal and nonviolent pressure. Lamentably, it is an historical fact that privileged groups seldom give up their privileges voluntarily. Individuals may see the moral light and voluntarily give up their unjust posture; but, as Reinhold Niebuhr* has reminded us, groups tend to be more immoral than individuals.

We know through painful experience that freedom is never voluntarily 13 given by the oppressor; it must be demanded by the oppressed. Frankly, I have yet to engage in a direct-action campaign that was "well timed" in the view of those who have not suffered unduly from the disease of segregation. For years now I have heard the word "Wait!" It rings in the ear of every Negro with piercing familiarity. This "Wait" has almost always meant "Never." We must come to see, with one of our distinguished jurists, that "justice too long delayed is justice denied."

We have waited for more than 340 years for our constitutional and 14 God-given rights. The nations of Asia and Africa are moving with jetlike speed toward gaining political independence, but we still creep at horse-and-buggy pace toward gaining a cup of coffee at a lunch counter. Perhaps it is easy for those who have never felt the stinging darts of segregation to say, "Wait." But when you have seen vicious mobs lynch your mothers and fathers at will and drown your sisters and brothers at whim; when you have seen hate-filled policemen curse, kick and even kill your black brothers and sisters; when you see the vast majority of your twenty million Negro brothers smothering in an airtight cage of poverty in the midst of an affluent society; when you suddenly find your tongue twisted and your speech stammering as you seek to explain to your six-year-old daughter why she can't go to the public amusement park that has just been advertised on television, and see tears welling up in her eyes when she is told that Funtown is closed to colored children, and see ominous clouds of inferiority beginning to form in her little mental sky, and see her beginning to distort her personality by developing an unconscious bitterness toward white people; when you have to concoct an answer for a five-year-old son who is asking: "Daddy, why do white people treat colored people so mean?"; when you take a cross-country drive and find it necessary to sleep night after night in the uncomfortable corners of your automobile because no motel will accept you; when you are humiliated day in and day out by nagging signs reading "white" and "colored"; when your first name becomes "nigger," your middle name becomes "boy" (however old you are) and your last name becomes "John," and your wife and mother are never given the respected title "Mrs."; when you are harried by day and

---

*American clergyman and theologian (1892–1971). The book King refers to is *Moral Man and Immoral Society* (1932).

haunted by night by the fact that you are a Negro, living constantly at tiptoe stance, never quite knowing what to expect next, and are plagued with inner fears and outer resentments; when you are forever fighting a degenerating sense of "nobodiness"—then you will understand why we find it difficult to wait. There comes a time when the cup of endurance runs over, and men are no longer willing to be plunged into the abyss of despair. I hope, sirs, you can understand our legitimate and unavoidable impatience.

You express a great deal of anxiety over our willingness to break laws. 15 This is certainly a legitimate concern. Since we so diligently urge people to obey the Supreme Court's decision of 1954 outlawing segregation in the public schools, at first glance it may seem rather paradoxical for us consciously to break laws. One may well ask: "How can you advocate breaking some laws and obeying others?" The answer lies in the fact that there are two types of laws: just and unjust. I would be the first to advocate obeying just laws. One has not only a legal but a moral responsibility to obey just laws. Conversely, one has a moral responsibility to disobey unjust laws. I would agree with St. Augustine that "an unjust law is no law at all."

Now, what is the difference between the two? How does one determine 16 whether a law is just or unjust? A just law is a man-made code that squares with the moral law or the law of God. An unjust law is a code that is out of harmony with the moral law. To put it in the terms of St. Thomas Aquinas: An unjust law is a human law that is not rooted in eternal law and natural law. Any law that uplifts human personality is just. Any law that degrades human personality is unjust. All segregation statutes are unjust because segregation distorts the soul and damages the personality. It gives the segregator a false sense of superiority and the segregated a false sense of inferiority. Segregation, to use the terminology of the Jewish philosopher Martin Buber, substitutes an "I–it" relationship for an "I–thou" relationship and ends up relegating persons to the status of things. Hence segregation is not only politically, economically and sociologically unsound, it is morally wrong and sinful. Paul Tillich has said that sin is separation. Is not segregation an existential expression of man's tragic separation, his awful estrangement, his terrible sinfulness? Thus it is that I can urge men to obey the 1954 decision of the Supreme Court, for it is morally right; and I can urge them to disobey segregation ordinances, for they are morally wrong.

Let us consider a more concrete example of just and unjust laws. An 17 unjust law is a code that a numerical or power majority group compels a minority group to obey but does not make binding on itself. This is *difference* made legal. By the same token, a just law is a code that a majority compels a minority to follow and that it is willing to follow itself. This is *sameness* made legal.

Let me give another explanation. A law is unjust if it is inflicted on a 18 minority that, as a result of being denied the right to vote, had no part in enacting or devising the law. Who can say that the legislature of Alabama which set up that state's segregation laws was democratically elected? Throughout Alabama all sorts of devious methods are used to prevent

Negroes from becoming registered voters, and there are some counties in which, even though Negroes constitute a majority of the population, not a single Negro is registered. Can any law enacted under such circumstances be considered democratically structured?

Sometimes a law is just on its face and unjust in its application. For instance, I have been arrested on a charge of parading without a permit. Now, there is nothing wrong in having an ordinance which requires a permit for a parade. But such an ordinance becomes unjust when it is used to maintain segregation and to deny citizens the First-Amendment privilege of peaceful assembly and protest. 19

I hope you are able to see the distinction I am trying to point out. In no sense do I advocate evading or defying the law, as would the rabid segregationist. That would lead to anarchy. One who breaks an unjust law must do so openly, lovingly, and with a willingness to accept the penalty. I submit that an individual who breaks a law that conscience tells him is unjust, and who willingly accepts the penalty of imprisonment in order to arouse the conscience of the community over its injustice, is in reality expressing the highest respect for law. 20

Of course, there is nothing new about this kind of civil disobedience. It was evidenced sublimely in the refusal of Shadrach, Meshach and Abednego to obey the laws of Nebuchadnezzar, on the ground that a higher moral law was at stake. It was practiced superbly by the early Christians, who were willing to face hungry lions and the excruciating pain of chopping blocks rather than submit to certain unjust laws of the Roman Empire. To a degree, academic freedom is a reality today because Socrates practiced civil disobedience. In our own nation, the Boston Tea Party represented a massive act of civil disobedience. 21

We should never forget that everything Adolf Hitler did in Germany was "legal" and everything the Hungarian freedom fighters did in Hungary was "illegal." It was "illegal" to aid and comfort a Jew in Hitler's Germany. Even so, I am sure that, had I lived in Germany at the time, I would have aided and comforted my Jewish brothers. If today I lived in a Communist country where certain principles dear to the Christian faith are suppressed, I would openly advocate disobeying that country's antireligious laws. 22

I must make two honest confessions to you, my Christian and Jewish brothers. First, I must confess that over the past few years I have been gravely disappointed with the white moderate. I have almost reached the regrettable conclusion that the Negro's great stumbling block in his stride toward freedom is not the White Citizen's Counciler or the Ku Klux Klanner, but the white moderate, who is more devoted to "order" than to justice; who prefers a negative peace which is the absence of tension to a positive peace which is the presence of justice; who constantly says: "I agree with you in the goal you seek, but I cannot agree with your methods of direct action"; who paternalistically believes he can set the timetable for another man's freedom; who lives by a mythical concept of time and who constantly advises the Negro to wait for a "more convenient season." Shallow understanding from 23 people of good will is more frustrating than absolute misunderstanding from people of ill will. Lukewarm acceptance is much more bewildering than outright rejection.

I had hoped that the white moderate would understand that law and 24
order exist for the purpose of establishing justice and that when they fail in this purpose they become the dangerously structured dams that block the flow of social progress. I had hoped that the white moderate would understand that the present tension in the South is a necessary phase of the transition from an obnoxious negative peace, in which the Negro passively accepted his unjust plight, to a substantive and positive peace, in which all men will respect the dignity and worth of human personality. Actually, we who engage in nonviolent direct action are not the creators of tension. We merely bring to the surface the hidden tension that is already alive. We bring it out in the open, where it can be seen and dealt with. Like a boil that can never be cured so long as it is covered up but must be opened with all its ugliness to the natural medicines of air and light, injustice must be exposed, with all the tension its exposure creates, to the light of human conscience and the air of national opinion before it can be cured.

In your statement you assert that our actions, even though peaceful, 25
must be condemned because they precipitate violence. But is this a logical assertion? Isn't this like condemning a robbed man because his possession of money precipitated the evil act of robbery? Isn't this like condemning Socrates because his unswerving commitment to truth and his philosophical inquiries precipitated the act by the misguided populace in which they made him drink hemlock? Isn't this like condemning Jesus because his unique God-consciousness and never-ceasing devotion to God's will precipitated the evil act of crucifixion? We must come to see that, as the federal courts have consistently affirmed, it is wrong to urge an individual to cease his efforts to gain his basic constitutional rights because the quest may precipitate violence. Society must protect the robbed and punish the robber.

I had also hoped that the white moderate would reject the myth con- 26
cerning time in relation to the struggle for freedom. I have just received a letter from a white brother in Texas. He writes: "All Christians know that the colored people will receive equal rights eventually, but it is possible that you are in too great a religious hurry. It has taken Christianity almost two thousand years to accomplish what it has. The teachings of Christ take time to come to earth." Such an attitude stems from a tragic misconception of time, from the strangely irrational notion that there is something in the very flow of time that will inevitably cure all ills. Actually, time itself is neutral; it can be used either destructively or constructively. More and more I feel that the people of ill will have used time much more effectively than have the people of good will. We will have to repent in this generation not merely for the hateful words and actions of the bad people but for the appalling silence of the good people. Human progress never rolls in on wheels of inevitability; it comes through the tireless efforts of men willing to be co-workers with God, and without this hard work, time itself becomes an ally of the forces of social

stagnation. We must use time creatively, in the knowledge that the time is always ripe to do right. Now is the time to make real the promise of democracy and transform our pending national elegy into a creative psalm of brotherhood. Now is the time to lift our national policy from the quicksand of racial injustice to the solid rock of human dignity.

You speak of our activity in Birmingham as extreme. At first I was rather 27 disappointed that fellow clergymen would see my nonviolent efforts as those of an extremist. I began thinking about the fact that I stand in the middle of two opposing forces in the Negro community. One is a force of complacency, made up in part of Negroes who, as a result of long years of oppression, are so drained of self-respect and a sense of "somebodiness" that they have adjusted to segregation; and in part of a few middle-class Negroes who, because of a degree of academic and economic security and because in some ways they profit by segregation, have become insensitive to the problems of the masses. The other force is one of bitterness and hatred, and it comes perilously close to advocating violence. It is expressed in the various black nationalist groups that are springing up across the nation, the largest and best-known being Elijah Muhammad's Muslim movement. Nourished by the Negro's frustration over the continued existence of racial discrimination, this movement is made up of people who have lost faith in America, who have absolutely repudiated Christianity, and who have concluded that the white man is an incorrigible "devil."

I have tried to stand between these two forces, saying that we need 28 emulate neither the "do-nothingism" of the complacent nor the hatred and despair of the black nationalist. For there is the more excellent way of love and nonviolent protest. I am grateful to God that, through the influence of the Negro church, the way of nonviolence became an integral part of our struggle.

If this philosophy had not emerged, by now many streets of the South 29 would, I am convinced, be flowing with blood. And I am further convinced that if our white brothers dismiss as "rabble-rousers" and "outside agitators" those of us who employ nonviolent direct action, and if they refuse to support our nonviolent efforts, millions of Negroes will, out of frustration and despair, seek solace and security in black-nationalist ideologies—a development that would inevitably lead to a frightening racial nightmare.

Oppressed people cannot remain oppressed forever. The yearning for 30 freedom eventually manifests itself, and that is what has happened to the American Negro. Something within has reminded him of his birthright of freedom, and something without has reminded him that it can be gained. Consciously or unconsciously, he has been caught up by the *Zeitgeist,* and with his black brothers of Africa and his brown and yellow brothers of Asia, South America and the Caribbean, the United States Negro is moving with a sense of great urgency toward the promised land of racial justice. If one recognizes this vital urge that has engulfed the Negro community, one should readily understand why public demonstrations are taking place. The Negro has many pent-up resentments and latent frustrations, and he must release them. So let him march; let him make prayer pilgrimages to the city hall; let him go on freedom rides—and try to understand why he must do so. If his repressed emotions are not released in nonviolent ways, they will seek expression through violence; this is not a threat but a fact of history. So I have not said to my people: "Get rid of your discontent." Rather, I have tried to say that this normal and healthy discontent can be channeled into the creative outlet of nonviolent direct action. And now this approach is being termed extremist.

But though I was initially disappointed at being categorized as an ex- 31 tremist, as I continued to think about the matter I gradually gained a measure of satisfaction from the label. Was not Jesus an extremist for love: "Love your enemies, bless them that curse you, do good to them that hate you, and pray for them which despitefully use you, and persecute you." Was not Amos an extremist for justice: "Let justice roll down like waters and righteousness like an ever-flowing stream." Was not Paul an extremist for the Christian gospel: "I bear in my body the marks of the Lord Jesus." Was not Martin Luther an extremist: "Here I stand; I cannot do otherwise, so help me God." And John Bunyan: "I will stay in jail to the end of my days before I make a butchery of my conscience." And Abraham Lincoln: "This nation cannot survive half slave and half free." And Thomas Jefferson: "We hold these truths to be self-evident, that all men are created equal . . ." So the question is not whether we will be extremists, but what kind of extremists we will be. Will we be extremists for hate or for love? Will we be extremists for the preservation of injustice or for the extension of justice? In that dramatic scene on Calvary's hill three men were crucified. We must never forget that all three were crucified for the same crime—the crime of extremism. Two were extremists for immorality, and thus fell below their environment. The other, Jesus Christ, was an extremist for love, truth and goodness, and thereby rose above his environment. Perhaps the South, the nation and the world are in dire need of creative extremists.

I had hoped that the white moderate would see this need. Perhaps I was 32 too optimistic; perhaps I expected too much. I suppose I should have realized that few members of the oppressor race can understand the deep groans and passionate yearnings of the oppressed race, and still fewer have the vision to see that injustice must be rooted out by strong, persistent and determined action. I am thankful, however, that some of our white brothers in the South have grasped the meaning of this social revolution and committed themselves to it. They are still all too few in quantity, but they are big in quality. Some—such as Ralph McGill, Lillian Smith, Harry Golden, James McBride Dabbs, Ann Braden and Sarah Patton Boyle—have written about our struggle in eloquent and prophetic terms. Others have marched with us down name-less streets of the South. They have languished in filthy, roach-infested jails, suffering the abuse and brutality of policemen who view them as "dirty nigger-lovers." Unlike so many of their moderate brothers and sisters, they have recognized the urgency of the moment and sensed the need for powerful "action" antidotes to combat the disease of segregation.

Let me take note of my other major disappointment. I have been so 33 greatly disappointed with the white church and its leadership. Of course, there are some notable exceptions. I am not unmindful of the fact that each of you has taken some significant stands on this issue. I commend you, Reverend Stallings, for your Christian stand on this past Sunday, in welcoming Negroes to your worship service on a nonsegregated basis. I commend the Catholic leaders of this state for integrating Spring Hill College several years ago.

But despite these notable exceptions, I must honestly reiterate that I have been disappointed with the church. I do not say this as one of those negative critics who can always find something wrong with the church. I say this as a minister of the gospel, who loves the church; who was nurtured in its bosom; who has been sustained by its spiritual blessings and who will remain true to it as long as the cord of life shall lengthen. 34

When I was suddenly catapulted into the leadership of the bus protest in Montgomery, Alabama, a few years ago, I felt we would be supported by the white church. I felt that the white ministers, priests and rabbis of the South would be among our strongest allies. Instead, some have been outright opponents, refusing to understand the freedom movement and misrepresenting its leaders; all too many others have been more cautious than courageous and have remained silent behind the anesthetizing security of stained-glass windows. 35

In spite of my shattered dreams, I came to Birmingham with the hope that the white religious leadership of this community would see the justice of our cause and, with deep moral concern, would serve as the channel through which our just grievances could reach the power structure. I had hoped that each of you would understand. But again I have been disappointed. 36

I have heard numerous southern religious leaders admonish their worshipers to comply with a desegregation decision because it is the law, but I have longed to hear white ministers declare: "Follow this decree because integration is morally right and because the Negro is your brother." In the midst of blatant injustices inflicted upon the Negro, I have watched white churchmen stand on the sideline and mouth pious irrelevancies and sanctimonious trivialities. In the midst of a mighty struggle to rid our nation of racial and economic injustice, I have heard many ministers say: "Those are social issues, with which the gospel has no real concern." And I have watched many churches commit themselves to a completely otherworldly religion which makes a strange, un-Biblical distinction between body and soul, between the sacred and the secular. 37

I have traveled the length and breadth of Alabama, Mississippi and all the other southern states. On sweltering summer days and crisp autumn mornings I have looked at the South's beautiful churches with their lofty spires pointing heavenward. I have beheld the impressive outlines of her massive religious-education buildings. Over and over I have found myself asking: "What kind of people worship here? Who is their God? Where were their voices when the lips of Governor Barnett dripped with words of inter- 38 position and nullification? Where were they when Governor Wallace gave a clarion call for defiance and hatred? Where were their voices of support when bruised and weary Negro men and women decided to rise from the dark dungeons of complacency to the bright hills of creative protest?"

Yes, these questions are still in my mind. In deep disappointment I have 39 wept over the laxity of the church. But be assured that my tears have been tears of love. There can be no deep disappointment where there is not deep love. Yes, I love the church. How could I do otherwise? I am in the rather unique position of being the son, the grandson and the great-grandson of preachers. Yes, I see the church as the body of Christ. But, oh! How we have blemished and scarred that body through social neglect and through fear of being nonconformists.

There was a time when the church was very powerful—in the time 40 when the early Christians rejoiced at being deemed worthy to suffer for what they believed. In those days the church was not merely a thermometer that recorded the ideas and principles of popular opinion; it was a thermostat that transformed the mores of society. Whenever the early Christians entered a town, the people in power became disturbed and immediately sought to convict the Christians for being "disturbers of the peace" and "outside agitators." But the Christians pressed on, in the conviction that they were "a colony of heaven," called to obey God rather than man. Small in number, they were big in commitment. They were too God-intoxicated to be "astronomically intimidated." By their effort and example they brought an end to such ancient evils as infanticide and gladiatorial contests.

Things are different now. So often the contemporary church is a weak, 41 ineffectual voice with an uncertain sound. So often it is an archdefender of the status quo. Far from being disturbed by the presence of the church, the power structure of the average community is consoled by the church's silent—and often even vocal—sanction of things as they are.

But the judgment of God is upon the church as never before. If today's 42 church does not recapture the sacrificial spirit of the early church, it will lose its authenticity, forfeit the loyalty of millions, and be dismissed as an irrelevant social club with no meaning for the twentieth century. Every day I meet young people whose disappointment with the church has turned into outright disgust.

Perhaps I have once again been too optimistic. Is organized religion too 43 inextricably bound to the status quo to save our nation and the world? Perhaps I must turn my faith to the inner spiritual church, the church within the church, as the true *ekklesia* and the hope of the world. But again I am thankful to God that some noble souls from the ranks of organized religion have broken loose from the paralyzing chains of conformity and joined us as active partners in the struggle for freedom. They have left their secure congregations and walked the streets of Albany, Georgia, with us. They have gone down the highways of the South on tortuous rides for freedom. Yes, they have gone to jail with us. Some have been dismissed from their churches, have lost the support of their bishops and fellow ministers. But they have acted in the faith that right defeated is stronger than evil triumphant. Their witness has been the spiritual salt that has preserved the true meaning of the gospel in these troubled times. They have carved a tunnel of hope through the dark mountain of disappointment.

I hope the church as a whole will meet the challenge of this decisive 44 hour. But even if the church does not come to the aid of justice, I have no despair about the future. I have no fear about the outcome of our struggle in Birmingham, even if our motives are at present misunderstood. We will reach the goal of freedom in Birmingham and all over the nation, because the goal of America is freedom. Abused and scorned though we may be, our destiny is tied up with America's destiny. Before the pilgrims landed at Plymouth, we were here. Before the pen of Jefferson etched the majestic words of the Declaration of Independence across the pages of history, we were here. For more than two centuries our forebears labored in this country without wages; they made cotton king; they built the homes of their masters while suffering gross injustice and shameful humiliation—and yet out of a bottomless vitality they continued to thrive and develop. If the inexpressible cruelties of slavery could not stop us, the opposition we now face will surely fail. We will win our freedom because the sacred heritage of our nation and the eternal will of God are embodied in our echoing demands.

Before closing I feel impelled to mention one other point in your state- 45 ment that has troubled me profoundly. You warmly commended the Bir-mingham police force for keeping "order" and "preventing violence." I doubt that you would have so warmly commended the police force if you had seen its dogs sinking their teeth into unarmed, nonviolent Negroes. I doubt that you would so quickly commend the policemen if you were to observe their ugly and inhumane treatment of Negroes here in the city jail; if you were to watch them push and curse old Negro women and young Negro girls; if you were to see them slap and kick old Negro men and young boys; if you were to observe them, as they did on two occasions, refuse to give us food because we wanted to sing our grace together. I cannot join you in your praise of the Birmingham police department.

It is true that the police have exercised a degree of discipline in handling 46 the demonstrators. In this sense they have conducted themselves rather "non-violently" in public. But for what purpose? To preserve the evil system of segregation. Over the past few years I have consistently preached that nonvi-olence demands that the means we use must be as pure as the ends we seek. I have tried to make clear that it is wrong to use immoral means to attain moral ends. But now I must affirm that it is just as wrong, or perhaps even more so, to use moral means to preserve immoral ends. Perhaps Mr. Connor and his policemen have been rather nonviolent in public, as was Chief Pritch-ett in Albany, Georgia, but they have used the moral means of nonviolence to maintain the immoral end of racial injustice. As T. S. Eliot has said: "The last temptation is the greatest treason: To do the right deed for the wrong reason."

I wish you had commended the Negro sit-inners and demonstrators of 47

Birmingham for their sublime courage, their willingness to suffer and their amazing discipline in the midst of great provocation. One day the South will recognize its real heroes. They will be the James Merediths, with the noble sense of purpose that enables them to face jeering and hostile mobs, and with the agonizing loneliness that characterizes the life of the pioneer. They will be old, oppressed, battered Negro women, symbolized in a seventy-two-year-old woman in Montgomery, Alabama, who rose up with a sense of dignity and with her people decided not to ride segregated buses, and who responded with ungrammatical profundity to one who inquired about her weariness: "My feets is tired, but my soul is at rest." They will be the young high school and college students, the young ministers of the gospel and a host of their elders, courageously and nonviolently sitting in at lunch counters and willingly going to jail for conscience' sake. One day the South will know that when these disinherited children of God sat down at lunch counters, they were in reality standing up for what is best in the American dream and for the most sacred values in our Judaeo-Christian heritage, thereby bringing our nation back to those great wells of democracy which were dug deep by the founding fathers in their formulation of the Constitution and the Declaration of Independence.

Never before have I written so long a letter. I'm afraid it is much too   48
long to take your precious time. I can assure you that it would have been much shorter if I had been writing from a comfortable desk, but what else can one do when he is alone in a narrow jail cell, other than write long letters, think long thoughts and pray long prayers?

If I have said anything in this letter that overstates the truth and indicates   49
an unreasonable impatience, I beg you to forgive me. If I have said anything that understates the truth and indicates my having a patience that allows me to settle for anything less than brotherhood, I beg God to forgive me.

I hope this letter finds you strong in the faith. I also hope that circum-   50
stances will soon make it possible for me to meet each of you, not as an integrationist or a civil-rights leader but as a fellow clergyman and a Christian brother. Let us all hope that the dark clouds of racial prejudice will soon pass away and the deep fog of misunderstanding will be lifted from our fear-drenched communities, and in some not too distant tomorrow the radiant stars of love and brotherhood will shine over our great nation with all their scintillating beauty.

Yours for the cause of Peace and Brotherhood,
MARTIN LUTHER KING, JR.

Questions for Discussion

1. What reasons does King give for taking time to answer the critics whose letter provoked this reply when he ignores most of his other critics?

2. Do you agree that "[a]nyone who lives inside the United States can never be considered an outsider anywhere within its bounds" (¶4)? Have you heard arguments to the contrary? Do you find King convincing on this question?

3. Can you give an explanation and a justification for the four steps in any nonviolent campaign that King lays out in paragraph 6? Can you explain and justify the order of the steps?

4. How does "direct action" differ from violence (¶¶8, 10, and 11)?

5. Stylistically, King is master of certain devices that are particularly effective in oral delivery. Identify the device used in paragraph 14, and comment on its effectiveness. What happens to the rhetorical power of the paragraph if you alter the wording to destroy the device—even if you retain the meaning?

6. Can you explain in your own words King's distinction between a "just" and an "unjust" law? Does he support the distinction with convincing argument? Why is it important for him to spend so much space (¶¶15–22) supporting the validity of this distinction?

7. Why does King find the "white moderate" more objectionable (in some ways) than the outspoken segregationist? Do you think he is justified in his feeling?

8. What is King's criticism of the church with respect to social justice? Do you think the church in America has become less silent and evasive since King criticized it in 1963?

Suggested Essay Topics

1. Powerful metaphors abound in King's letter in almost every paragraph. Pick several that strike you as most impressive and analyze the power they impart to King's prose. One clear way of doing this is to replace each metaphor with a literal statement—the best you can write—and see what happens to the power of the statement. (It may strengthen your analysis if you consider which of the five senses each metaphor appeals to.) Address your paper either to your instructor or to someone you know whose writing seems to suffer from a poverty of metaphor. Remember that your own tone should vary somewhat, depending on which kind of reader you are trying to convince.

2. Choose some injustice that you have experienced firsthand or know something about, and write two contrasting arguments about it. Address the first one to a sympathetic judge who has asked for a *factual* or *skeletal* account of your argument. Make it as lean, as undoctored, as unliterary as you can. Then write a second account of the same issue, but this time use as much of the kind of stylistic heightening that King uses as you possibly can. Don't worry about being too flowery; treat the assignment as an experiment in packing in rather than cutting out—a chance to try out all kinds of appeals that can reinforce the skeleton of an argument.

Mary McCarthy

Mary McCarthy's (b. 1912) "Artists in Uniform," first published in 1953, raises several important issues about the individual in relationship to the community. Part of the drama inside the story derives from the drama that was occurring outside of the story. In the early 1950s the cold war—the period of Soviet-American antagonism and military feinting that began at the end of World War II and led to the Cuban missile crisis of 1963—was in full swing and America was in the throes of a "red scare." Grade-school children were regularly drilled on how to climb dutifully under their desks in the event of a nuclear attack, people dug bomb shelters in their back yards, the signing of "loyalty oaths" was proposed as a prerequisite to some kinds of employment, and a series of books, articles, movies, and TV programs all fed the fear that communists were infiltrating every level of American society. Senator Joseph McCarthy (no relation to Mary McCarthy) was reinforcing that fear with his notorious Senate "hearings," in which artists, intellectuals, academics, and other political liberals were harassed, bullied, humiliated, and defamed in front of the whole country. Television, in its infancy as a mass commodity, seized on the hearings as one of its early "media events."

McCarthy's "hearings" did not succeed in unearthing any proven communists or conspiracies during the entire period of its operations. But they did succeed in scaring into silence most politicians who wanted to speak up in favor of civil liberties, and they fostered a climate of fear and suspicion in which political liberals might at any time or place—even in a passenger train winding its way across Indiana in a heat wave—find themselves the targets of insinuations or accusations that their patriotism was weak, that their loyalty was suspect, or that they were "soft on communism."

In a police state, such social pressures can be an effective mechanism for strangling dissent, criticism, or innovative thinking before the words ever get uttered. In a democracy, such pressure threatens to cut off democratic processes at the root. Conformity becomes enforced not by the secret police at the door but by the fear of majority opinion. In "Bedfellows," an essay by E. B. White, says that "democracy, if I understand it at all, is a society in which the unbeliever feels undisturbed and at home. If there were only half a dozen unbelievers in America, their well-being would be a test of our democracy, their tranquillity would be its proof. . . . The concern of a democracy is that no honest man shall feel uncomfortable, I don't care who he is, or how nutty he is" (from Essays of E. B. White, 1956).

But the narrator in "Artists in Uniform" does not feel comfortable. Discovering with shock that her sophisticated clothing has revealed her to the men in the club car as not just an artist but an artist of an intellectual, "liberal" stamp—as if she were in uniform—she immediately feels vulnerable to potential attacks on her political beliefs. Yet her contempt for the cliché-ridden, knee-jerk mentality of her car companions spurs her to go on the attack herself, to attempt to overturn their vague accusations about communism among academics and Jews. The trouble is, she does not really possess any more facts about communism among these groups than do her opponents, and in the attempt to speak for pure reason and a liberal, unprejudiced mentality, she finds herself committing every intellectual sin she detests in the others.

Although McCarthy records elsewhere that the primary events of this story really happened to her, we should be leery of assuming that every detail of speech, thought, and action is a biographical fact. Regardless of how much the biography and the fiction overlap (or fail to), McCarthy portrays a character caught up in issues of importance for us all. As you read, consider the possibility that McCarthy writes this story not as an exposé of the Colonel—his prejudice is of the garden variety: common, rank, easily recognizable—but as an exposé of herself (or of people generally like her): the intellectual who sets up her own fall through excessive pride. Notice her smugness as she says, "[I]t seemed to me that the writer or intellectual had a certain missionary usefulness in just such accidental gatherings as this, if he spoke not as an intellectual but as a normal member of the public" (¶3)—as if the "normal public" were too stupid to form sound opinions without guidance from intellectuals such as she, who will of course avoid condescending to their inferiors by pretending to be normal themselves. Here is condescension with a vengeance, not merely committing the sin of pride but pretending to be noble.

Consider, however, whether the story may contain a larger object of attack than either of the main characters. Is it possible that the story's larger target is a society that fosters extremist positions, that permits conformity to be a cover for non-thinkers like the Colonel while forcing intellectuals like McCarthy's narrator into defensive positions that short-circuit clear thinking? McCarthy invites us to consider seriously the uniforms we ourselves may wear and how we react to the perceived uniforms of others.

ARTISTS IN UNIFORM

From *On the Contrary* (1953).

> The Colonel went out sailing,
> He spoke with Turk and Jew . . .

"Pour it on Colonel," cried the young man in the Dacron suit excitedly, making his first sortie into the club-car conversation. His face was white as Roquefort and of a glistening, cheese-like texture; he had a shock of tow-colored hair, badly cut and greasy, and a snub nose with large gray pores. Under his darting eyes were two black craters. He appeared to be under some intense nervous strain and had sat the night before in the club car drinking bourbon with beer chasers and leafing magazines which he frowningly tossed aside, like cards into a discard heap. This morning he had come in late, with a hangdog, hangover look, and had been sitting tensely forward on a settee, smoking cigarettes and following the conversation with little twitches of the nose and quivers of the body, as a dog follows a human conversation, veering its mistrustful eyeballs from one speaker to another and raising its head eagerly at its master's voice. The Colonel's voice, rich and light and plausible, had in fact abruptly risen and swollen, as he pronounced his last sentence.

"I can tell you one thing," he said harshly. "They weren't named Ryan or Murphy!"

A sort of sigh, as of consummation, ran through the club car. "Pour it 2 on, Colonel, give it to them, Colonel, that's right, Colonel," urged the young man in a transport of admiration. The Colonel fingered his collar and modestly smiled. He was a thin, hawklike, black-haired handsome man with a bright blue bloodshot eye and a well-pressed, well-tailored uniform that did not show the effects of the heat—the train, westbound for St. Louis, was passing through Indiana, and, as usual in a heat-wave, the air-conditioning had not met the test. He wore the Air Force insignia, and there was something in his light-boned, spruce figure and keen, knifelike profile that suggested a classic image of the aviator, ready to cut, piercing, into space. In base fact, however, the Colonel was in procurement,* as we heard him tell the mining engineer who had just bought him a drink. From several silken hints that parachuted into the talk, it was patent to us that the Colonel was a man who knew how to enjoy this earth and its pleasures: he led, he gave us to think, a bachelor's life of abstemious dissipation and well-rounded sensuality. He had accepted the engineer's drink with a mere nod of the glass in acknowledgment, like a genial Mars quaffing a libation; there was clearly no prospect of his buying a second in return, not if the train were to travel from here to the Mojave Desert. In the same way, an understanding had arisen that I, the only woman in the club car, had become the Colonel's perquisite; it was taken for granted, without an invitation's being issued, that I was to lunch with him in St. Louis, where we each had a wait between trains—my plans for seeing the city in a taxicab were dished.

From the beginning, as we eyed each other over my volume of Dickens 3 ("*The Christmas Carol?*" suggested the Colonel, opening relations), I had guessed that the Colonel was of Irish stock, and this, I felt, gave me an advantage, for he did not suspect the same of me; strangely so, for I am supposed to have the map of Ireland written on my features. In fact, he had just wagered, with a jaunty, sidelong grin at the mining engineer, that my people "came from Boston from way back," and that I—narrowed glance, running, like steel measuring-tape, up and down my form—was a professional sculptress. I might have laughed this off, as a crudely bad guess like his *Christmas Carol,* if I had not seen the engineer nodding gravely, like an idol, and the peculiar young man bobbing his head up and down in mute applause and agreement. I was wearing a bright apple-green raw silk blouse and a dark-green rather full raw silk skirt, plus a pair of pink glass earrings; my hair was done up in a bun. It came to me, for the first time, with a sort of dawning horror, that I had begun, in the course of years, without ever guessing it, to look irrevocably Bohemian.† Refracted from the three men's eyes was a

---

*Procurement is a clerking, not a combat, function. The procurement clerk edits purchase requests, invites bids from suppliers, and makes out orders for procurement of materials—in this case for the Air Force.

†Unconventional, anti-establishment, scornful of middle-class values.

strange vision of myself as an artist, through and through, stained with my occupation like the dyer's hand. All I lacked, apparently, was a pair of sandals. My sick heart sank to my Ferragamo shoes; I had always particularly preened myself on being an artist in disguise. And it was not only a question of personal vanity—it seemed to me that the writer or intellectual had a certain missionary usefulness in just such accidental gatherings as this, if he spoke not as an intellectual but as a normal member of the public. Now, thanks to the Colonel, I slowly became aware that my contributions to the club-car conversation were being watched and assessed as coming from *a certain quarter.* My costume, it seemed, carefully assembled as it had been at an expensive shop, was to these observers simply a uniform that blazoned a caste and allegiance just as plainly as the Colonel's khaki and eagles. *"Gardez,"* [take care] I said to myself. But, as the conversation grew tenser and I endeavored to keep cool, I began to writhe within myself, and every time I looked down, my contrasting greens seemed to be growing more and more lurid and taking on an almost menacing light, like leaves just before a storm that lift their bright undersides as the air becomes darker. We had been speaking, of course, of Russia,* and I had mentioned a study that had been made at Harvard of political attitudes among Iron Curtain refugees. Suddenly, the Colonel had smiled. "They're pretty Red at Harvard, I'm given to understand," he observed in a comfortable tone, while the young man twitched and quivered urgently. The eyes of all the men settled on me and waited. I flushed as I saw myself reflected. The woodland greens of my dress were turning to their complementary red, like a color-experiment in psychology or a traffic light changing. Down at the other end of the club car, a man looked up from his paper. I pulled myself together. "Set your mind at rest, Colonel," I remarked dryly. "I know Harvard very well and they're conservative to the point of dullness. The only thing crimson is the football team." This disparagement had its effect. "So . . . ?" queried the Colonel. "I thought there was some professor. . . ." I shook my head. "Absolutely not. There used to be a few fellow-travelers, but they're very quiet these days, when they haven't absolutely recanted. The general atmosphere is more anti-Communist than the Vatican." The Colonel and the mining engineer exchanged a thoughtful stare and seemed to agree that the Delphic oracle that had just pronounced knew whereof it spoke. "Glad to hear it," said the Colonel. The engineer frowned and shook his fat wattles; he was a stately, gray-haired, plump man with small hands and feet and the pampered, finical tidiness of a small-town widow. "There's so much hearsay these days," he exclaimed vexedly. "You don't know *what* to believe."

I reopened my book with an air of having closed the subject and read a paragraph three times over. I exulted to think that I had made a modest contribution to sanity in our times, and I imagined my words pyramiding like a chain letter—the Colonel telling a fellow-officer on the veranda of a club

*In the early 1950s, at the height of the cold war, talk of Soviet-American antagonisms was common enough to be referred to by an "of course."

in Texas, the engineer halting a works-superintendent in a Colorado mine shaft: "I met a woman on the train who claims . . . Yes, absolutely. . . ." Of course, I did not know Harvard as thoroughly as I pretended, but I forgave myself by thinking it was the convention of such club-car symposia in our positivistic country to speak from the horse's mouth.

Meanwhile, across the aisle, the engineer and the Colonel continued their talk in slightly lowered voices. From time to time, the Colonel's polished index-fingernail scratched his burnished black head and his knowing blue eye forayed occasionally toward me. I saw that still I was a doubtful quantity to them, a movement in the bushes, a noise, a flicker, that was figuring in their crenelated thought as "she." The subject of Reds in our colleges had not, alas, been finished; they were speaking now of another university and a woman faculty-member who had been issuing Communist statements. This story somehow, I thought angrily, had managed to appear in the newspapers without my knowledge, while these men were conversant with it; I recognized a big chink in the armor of my authority. Looking up from my book, I began to question them sharply, as though they were reporting some unheard-of natural phenomenon. "When?" I demanded. "Where did you see it? What was her name?" This request for the professor's name was a headlong attempt on my part to buttress my position, the implication being that the identities of all university professors were known to me and that if I were but given the name I could promptly clarify the matter. To admit that there was a single Communist in our academic system whose activities were hidden from me imperiled, I instinctively felt, all the small good I had done here. Moreover, in the back of my mind, I had a supreme confidence that these men were wrong: the story, I supposed, was some tattered piece of misinformation they had picked up from a gossip column. Pride, as usual, preceded my fall. To the Colonel, the demand for the name was not specific but generic: what *kind* of name was the question he presumed me to be asking. "Oh," he said slowly with a luxurious yawn, "Finkelstein or Fishbein or Feinstein."* He lolled back in his seat with a side glance at the engineer, who deeply nodded. There was a voluptuary pause, as the implication sank in. I bit my lip, regarding this as a mere diversionary tactic. "Please!" I said impatiently. "Can't you remember exactly?" The Colonel shook his head and then his spare cheekbones suddenly reddened and he looked directly at me. "I can tell you one thing," he exclaimed irefully. "They weren't named Ryan or Murphy."

The Colonel went no further; it was quite unnecessary. In an instant, the young man was at his side, yapping excitedly and actually picking at the military sleeve. The poor thing was transformed, like some creature in a fairy tale whom a magic word releases from silence. "That's right, Colonel," he happily repeated. "I know them. *I* was at Harvard in the business school, studying accountancy. I left. I couldn't take it." He threw a poisonous glance at me, and the Colonel, who had been regarding him somewhat doubtfully, now put on an alert expression and inclined an ear for his confidences. The

*Jewish-sounding names—which makes the Colonel's comment an anti-Semitic slur.

man at the other end of the car folded his newspaper solemnly and took a seat by the young man's side. "They're all Reds, Colonel," said the young man. "They teach it in the classroom. I came back here to Missouri. It made me sick to listen to the stuff they handed out. If you didn't hand it back, they flunked you. Don't let anybody tell you different." "You are wrong," I said coldly and closed my book and rose. The young man was still talking eagerly, and the three men were leaning forward to catch his every gasping word, like three astute detectives over a dying informer, when I reached the door and cast a last look over my shoulder at them. For an instant, the Colonel's eye met mine, and I felt his scrutiny processing my green back as I tugged open the door and met a blast of hot air, blowing my full skirt wide. Behind me, in my fancy, I saw four sets of shrugging brows.

In my own car, I sat down, opposite two fat nuns, and tried to assemble my thoughts. I ought to have spoken, I felt, and yet what could I have said? It occurred to me that the four men had perhaps not realized why I had left the club car with such abruptness: was it possible that they thought I was a Communist, who feared to be unmasked? I spurned this possibility, and yet it made me uneasy. For some reason, it troubled my *amour-propre** to think of my anti-Communist self living on, so to speak, green in their collective memory as a Communist or fellow-traveler. In fact, though I did not give a fig for the men, I hated the idea, while a few years ago I should have counted it a great joke. This, it seemed to me, was a measure of the change in the social climate. I had always scoffed at the notion of liberals "living in fear" of political demagoguery in America, but now I had to admit that if I was not fearful, I was at least uncomfortable in the supposition that anybody, anybody whatever, could think of me, precious me, as a Communist.† A remoter possibility was, of course, that back there my departure was being ascribed to Jewishness, and this too annoyed me. I am in fact a quarter Jewish, and though I did not "hate" the idea of being taken for a Jew, I did not precisely like it, particularly under these circumstances. I wished it to be clear that I had left the club car for intellectual and principled reasons; I wanted those men to know that it was not I, but my principles, that had been offended. To let them conjecture that I had left because I was Jewish would imply that only a Jew could be affronted by an anti-Semitic outburst: a terrible idea. Aside from anything else, it voided the whole concept of transcendence, which was very close to my heart, the concept that man is more than his circumstances, more even than himself.

However you looked at the episode, I said to myself nervously, I had not acquitted myself well. I ought to have done or said something concrete and unmistakable. From this, I slid glassily to the thought that those men ought to be punished, the Colonel, in particular, who occupied a responsible

7

8

---

*Self-pride.

†This was the period in which Senator Joseph McCarthy was holding his notorious "hearings," in which he frequently accused artists and intellectuals of being communists. Such accusations, which could not be rebutted in a Senate hearing as they could have been in a court of law, ruined several careers and cost others both heavy loss of income and great personal anguish.

position. In a minute, I was framing a businesslike letter to the Chief of Staff, deploring the Colonel's conduct as unbecoming to an officer and identifying him by rank and post, since unfortunately I did not know his name. Earlier in the conversation, he had passed some comments on "Harry"* that bordered positively on treason, I said to myself triumphantly. A vivid image of the proceedings against him presented itself to my imagination: the long military tribunal with a row of stern soldierly faces glaring down at the Colonel. I myself occupied only an inconspicuous corner of this tableau, for, to tell the truth, I did not relish the role of the witness. Perhaps it would be wiser to let the matter drop . . . ? We were nearing St. Louis now; the Colonel had come back into my car, and the young accountant had followed him, still talking feverishly. I pretended not to see them and turned to the two nuns, as if for sanctuary from this world and its hatreds and revenges. Out of the corner of my eye, I watched the Colonel, who now looked wry and restless; he shrank against the window as the young man made a place for himself amid the Colonel's smart luggage and continued to express his views in a pale breathless voice. I smiled to think that the Colonel was paying the piper. For the Colonel, anti-Semitism was simply an aspect of urbanity, like a knowledge of hotels or women. This frantic psychopath of an accountant was serving him as a nemesis, just as the German people had been served by their psychopath, Hitler. Colonel, I adjured him, you have chosen, between him and me; measure the depth of your error and make the best of it! No intervention on my part was now necessary; justice had been meted out. Nevertheless, my heart was still throbbing violently, as if I were on the verge of some dangerous action. What was I to do, I kept asking myself, as I chatted with the nuns, if the Colonel were to hold me to that lunch? And I slowly and apprehensively revolved this question, just as though it were a matter of the most serious import. It seemed to me that if I did not lunch with him—and I had no intention of doing so—I had the dreadful obligation of telling him why.

He was waiting for me as I descended the car steps. "Aren't you coming to lunch with me?" he called out and moved up to take my elbow. I began to tremble with audacity. "No," I said firmly, picking up my suitcase and draping an olive-green linen duster over my arm. "I can't lunch with you." He quirked a wiry black eyebrow. "Why not?" he said. "I understood it was all arranged." He reached for my suitcase. "No," I said, holding on to the suitcase. "I can't." I took a deep breath. "I have to tell you. I think you should be *ashamed* of yourself, Colonel, for what you said in the club car." The Colonel stared; I mechanically waved for a red-cap, who took my bag and coat and went off. The Colonel and I stood facing each other on the emptying platform. "What do you mean?" he inquired in a low, almost clandestine tone. "Those anti-Semitic remarks," I muttered, resolutely. "You ought to be *ashamed.*" The Colonel gave a quick, relieved laugh. "Oh, come now," he protested. "I'm sorry," I said. "I can't have lunch with anybody who feels that

9

*Harry Truman, president of the United States from 1946 to 1952.

way about the Jews." The Colonel put down his attaché case and scratched
the back of his lean neck. "Oh, come now," he repeated, with a look of
amusement. "You're not Jewish, are you?" "No," I said quickly. "Well,
then . . ." said the Colonel, spreading his hands in a gesture of bafflement.
I saw that he was truly surprised and slightly hurt by my criticism, and this
made me feel wretchedly embarrassed and even apologetic, on my side, as
though I had called attention to some physical defect in him, of which he
himself was unconscious. "But I might have been," I stammered. "You had
no way of knowing. You oughtn't to talk like that." I recognized, too late, that
I was strangely reducing the whole matter to a question of etiquette: "Don't
start anti-Semitic talk before making sure there are no Jews present." "Oh,
hell," said the Colonel, easily. "I can tell a Jew." "No, you can't," I retorted,
thinking of my Jewish grandmother, for by Nazi criteria I was Jewish. "Of
course I can," he insisted. "So can you." We had begun to walk down the
platform side by side, disputing with a restrained passion that isolated us like
a pair of lovers. All at once, the Colonel halted, as though struck with a
thought. "What *are* you, anyway?" he said meditatively, regarding my dark
hair, green blouse, and pink earrings. Inside myself, I began to laugh. "Oh,"
I said gaily, playing out the trump I had been saving, "I'm Irish, like you,
Colonel." "How did you know?" he said amazedly. I laughed aloud. "I can
tell an Irishman," I taunted. The Colonel frowned. "What's your family
name?" he said brusquely. "McCarthy." He lifted an eyebrow, in defeat, and
then quickly took note of my wedding ring. "That your maiden name?" I
nodded. Under this peremptory questioning, I had the peculiar sensation that
I get when I am lying; I began to feel that "McCarthy" was a nom de plume,*
a coinage of my artistic personality. But the Colonel appeared to be satisfied.
"Hell," he said, "come on to lunch, then. With a fine name like that, you and
I should be friends." I still shook my head, though by this time we were
pacing outside the station restaurant; my baggage had been checked in a
locker; sweat was running down my face and I felt exhausted and hungry.
I knew that I was weakening and I wanted only an excuse to yield and go
inside with him. The Colonel seemed to sense this. "Hell," he conceded.
"You've got me wrong. I've got nothing against the Jews. Back there in the
club car, I was just stating a simple fact: you won't find an Irishman sounding
off for the Commies. You can't deny that, can you?"

His voice rose persuasively; he took my arm. In the heat, I wilted and   10
we went into the air-conditioned cocktail lounge. The Colonel ordered two
old-fashioneds. The room was dark as a cave and produced, in the midst of
the hot midday, a hallucinated feeling, as though time had ceased, with the
weather, and we were in eternity together. As the Colonel prepared to relax,
I made a tremendous effort to guide the conversation along rational, purposive lines; my only justification for being here would be to convert the Colonel.
"There *have* been Irishmen associated with the Communist party," I said
suddenly, when the drinks came. "I can think of two." "Oh, hell," said the

*Assumed name, pen name.

Colonel, "every race and nation has its traitors. What I mean is, you won't find them in numbers. You've got to admit that the Communists in this country are 90 per cent Jewish." "But the Jews in this country aren't 90 per cent Communist," I retorted.

As he stirred his drink, restively, I began to try to show him the reasons 11 why the Communist movement in America had attracted such a large number, relatively, of Jews: how the Communists had been anti-Nazi when nobody else seemed to care what happened to the Jews in Germany; how the Communists still capitalized on a Jewish fear of fascism; how many Jews had become, after Buchenwald,* traumatized by this fear. . . .

But the Colonel was scarcely listening. An impatient frown rested on 12 his jaunty features. "I don't get it," he said slowly. "Why should you be for them, with a name like yours?" "I'm *not* for the Communists," I cried. "I'm just trying to explain to you—" "For the Jews," the Colonel interrupted, irritable now himself. "I've heard of such people but I never met one before." "I'm not 'for' them," I protested. "You don't understand. I'm not for *any* race or nation. I'm against those who are against them." This word, *them,* with a sort of slurring circle drawn round it, was beginning to sound ugly to me. Automatically, in arguing with him, I seemed to have slipped into the Colonel's style of thought. It occurred to me that defense of the Jews could be a subtle and safe form of anti-Semitism, an exercise of patronage: as a rational Gentile, one could feel superior both to the Jews and the anti-Semites. There could be no doubt that the Jewish question evoked a curious stealthy lust or concupiscence. I could feel it now vibrating between us over the dark table. If I had been a good person, I should unquestionably have got up and left.

"I don't get it," repeated the Colonel. "How were you brought up? Were 13 your people this way too?" It was manifest that an odd reversal had taken place; each of us regarded the other as "abnormal" and was attempting to understand the etiology of a disease. "Many of my people think just as you do," I said, smiling coldly. "It seems to be a sickness to which the Irish are prone. Perhaps it's due to the potato diet," I said sweetly, having divined that the Colonel came from a social stratum somewhat lower than my own.

But the Colonel's hide was tough. "You've got me wrong," he reiterated, 14 with an almost plaintive laugh. "I don't dislike the Jews. I've got a lot of Jewish friends. Among themselves, they think just as I do, mark my words. I tell you what it is," he added ruminatively, with a thoughtful prod of his muddler, "I draw a distinction between a kike and a Jew." I groaned. "Colonel, I've never heard an anti-Semite who didn't draw that distinction. You know what Otto Kahn† said? 'A kike is a Jewish gentleman who has just left the room.'" The Colonel did not laugh. "I don't hold it against some of them," he persisted, in a tone of pensive justice. "It's not their fault if they

---

*A Nazi extermination camp.

†American banker and philanthropist (1867–1934), born in Germany (naturalized in 1917), president of the Metropolitan Opera Company (1918–1931); perhaps the greatest patron of the arts in U.S. history.

were born that way. That's what I tell them, and they respect me for my honesty. I've had a lot of discussions; in procurement, you have to do business with them, and the Jews are the first to admit that you'll find more chiselers among their race than among the rest of mankind." "It's not a race," I interjected wearily, but the Colonel pressed on. "If I deal with a Jewish manufacturer, I can't bank on his word. I've seen it again and again, every damned time. When I deal with a Gentile, I can trust him to make delivery as promised. That's the difference between the two races. They're just a different breed. They don't have standards of honesty, even among each other." I sighed, feeling unequal to arguing the Colonel's personal experience.

"Look," I said, "you may be dealing with an industry where the Jewish 15 manufacturers are the most recent comers and feel they have to cut corners to compete with the established firms. I've heard that said about Jewish cattle-dealers, who are supposed to be extra sharp. But what I think, really, is that you notice it when a Jewish firm fails to meet an agreement and don't notice it when it's a Yankee." "Hah," said the Colonel. "They'll tell you what I'm telling you themselves, if you get to know them and go into their homes. You won't believe it, but some of my best friends are Jews," he said, simply and thoughtfully, with an air of originality. "They may be *your* best friends, Colonel," I retorted, "but you are not theirs. I defy you to tell me that you talk to them as you're talking now." "Sure," said the Colonel, easily. "More or less." "They must be very queer Jews you know," I observed tartly, and I began to wonder whether there indeed existed a peculiar class of Jews whose function in life was to be "friends" with such people as the Colonel. It was difficult to think that all the anti-Semites who made the Colonel's assertion were the victims of a cruel self-deception.

A dispirited silence followed. I was not one of those liberals who be- 16 lieved that the Jews, alone among peoples, possessed no characteristics whatever of a distinguishing nature—this would mean they had no history and no culture, a charge which should be leveled against them only by an anti-Semite. Certainly, types of Jews could be noted and patterns of Jewish thought and feeling: Jewish humor, Jewish rationality, and so on, not that every Jew reflected every attribute of Jewish life or history. But somehow, with the Colonel, I dared not concede that there was such a thing as a Jew: I saw the sad meaning of the assertion that a Jew was a person whom other people thought was Jewish.

Hopeless, however, to convey this to the Colonel. The desolate truth 17 was that the Colonel was extremely stupid, and it came to me, as we sat there, glumly ordering lunch, that for extremely stupid people anti-Semitism was a form of intellectuality, the sole form of intellectuality of which they were capable. It represented, in a rudimentary way, the ability to make categories, to generalize. Hence a thing I had noted before but never understood: the fact that anti-Semitic statements were generally delivered in an atmosphere of profundity. Furrowed brows attended these speculative distinctions between a kike and a Jew, these little empirical laws that you can't know one without knowing them all. To arrive, indeed, at the idea of a Jew was, for these

grouping minds, an exercise in Platonic thought, a discovery of essence,* and
to be able to add the great corollary, "Some of my best friends are Jews," was
to find the philosopher's cleft between essence and existence. From this, it
would seem, followed the querulous obstinacy with which the anti-Semite
clung to his concept; to be deprived of this intellectual tool by missionaries
of tolerance would be, for persons like the Colonel, the equivalent of Western
man's losing the syllogism: a lapse into animal darkness. In the club car, we
had just witnessed an example: the Colonel with his anti-Semitic observation
had come to the mute young man like the paraclete, bearing the gift of
tongues.

Here in the bar, it grew plainer and plainer that the Colonel did not 18
regard himself as an anti-Semite but merely as a heavy thinker. The idea
that I considered him anti-Semitic sincerely outraged his feelings. "Prejudice" was the last trait he could have imputed to himself. He looked on me,
almost respectfully, as a "Jew lover," a kind of being he had heard of but
never actually encountered, like a centaur or a Siamese twin, and the interest of relating this prodigy to the natural state of mankind overrode any
personal distaste. There I sat, the exception which was "proving" or testing
the rule, and he kept pressing me for details of my history that might explain my deviation in terms of the norm. On my side, of course, I had
become fiercely resolved that he would learn nothing from me that would
make it possible for him to dismiss my anti-anti-Semitism as the product of
special circumstances: I was stubbornly sitting on the fact of my Jewish
grandmother like a hen on a golden egg. I was bent on making *him* see
himself as a monster, a deviation, a heretic from Church and State. Unfortunately, the Colonel, owing perhaps to his military training, had not the
glimmering of an idea of what democracy meant; to him, it was simply a
slogan that was sometimes useful in war. The notion of an ordained inequality was to him "scientific."

"Honestly," he was saying in lowered tones, as our drinks were taken 19
away and the waitress set down my sandwich and his corned-beef hash,
"don't you, brought up the way you were, feel about them the way I do? Just
between ourselves, isn't there a sort of inborn feeling of horror that the very
word, Jew, suggests?" I shook my head, roundly. The idea of an *innate* anti-
Semitism was in keeping with the rest of the Colonel's thought, yet it shocked
me more than anything he had yet said. "No," I sharply replied. "It doesn't
evoke any feeling one way or the other." "Honest Injun?" said the Colonel.
"Think back; when you were a kid, didn't the word, Jew, make you feel
sick?"† There was a dreadful sincerity about this that made me answer in an
almost kindly tone. "No, truthfully, I assure you. When we were children,
we learned to call the old-clothes man a sheeny, but that was just a dirty word

---

*For Plato, every object in *this* world—the world perceivable by the physical senses—is merely
a shadow of its *essential* identity, a non-material version of itself existing on a spiritual plane. Thus
to discover the "essence" of a thing is to discover the ultimate truth about it.

†Compare the similarity of the Colonel's views with the views of Hitler in *Mein Kampf,* pp.
596–604).

to us, like 'Hun' that we used to call after workmen we thought were Germans."

"I don't get it," pondered the Colonel, eating a pickle. "There must be 20 something wrong with you. Everybody is born with that feeling. It's natural; it's part of nature." "On the contrary," I said. "It's something very unnatural that you must have been taught as a child." "It's not something you're *taught,* " he protested. "You must have been," I said. "You simply don't remember it. In any case, you're a man now; you must rid yourself of that feeling. It's psychopathic, like that horrible young man on the train." "You thought he was crazy?" mused the Colonel, in an idle, dreamy tone. I shrugged my shoulders. "Of course. Think of his color. He was probably just out of a mental institution. People don't get that tattletale gray except in prison or mental hospitals." The Colonel suddenly grinned. "You might be right," he said. "He was quite a case." He chuckled.

I leaned forward. "You know, Colonel," I said quickly, "anti-Semitism 21 is contrary to the Church's teaching. God will make you do penance for hating the Jews. Ask your priest; he'll tell you I'm right. You'll have a long spell in Purgatory, if you don't rid yourself of this sin. It's a deliberate violation of Christ's commandment, 'Love thy neighbor.' The Church holds that the Jews have a sacred place in God's design. Mary was a Jew and Christ was a Jew. The Jews are under God's special protection. The Church teaches that the millennium can't come until the conversion of the Jews; therefore, the Jews must be preserved that the Divine Will may be accomplished. Woe to them that harm them, for they controvert God's Will!" In the course of speaking, I had swept myself away with the solemnity of the doctrine. The Great Reconciliation between God and His chosen people, as envisioned by the Evangelist, had for me at that moment a piercing, majestic beauty, like some awesome Tintoretto. I saw a noble spectacle of blue sky, thronged with gray clouds, and a vast white desert, across which God and Israel advanced to meet each other, while below in hell the demons of disunion shrieked and gnashed their teeth.

"Hell," said the Colonel, jovially. "I don't believe in all that. I lost my 22 faith when I was a kid. I saw that all this God stuff was a lot of bushwa." I gazed at him in stupefaction. His confidence had completely returned. The blue eyes glittered debonairly; the eagles glittered; the narrow polished head cocked and listened to itself like a trilling bird. I was up against an air man with a bird's-eye view, a man who believed in nothing but the law of kind: the epitome of godless materialism. "You still don't hold with that bunk?" the Colonel inquired in an undertone, with an expression of stealthy curiosity. "No," I confessed, sad to admit to a meeting of minds. "You know what got me?" exclaimed the Colonel. "That birth-control stuff. Didn't it kill you?" I made a neutral sound. "I was beginning to play around," said the Colonel, with a significant beam of the eye, "and I just couldn't take that guff. When I saw through the birth-control talk, I saw through the whole thing. They claimed it was against nature, but I claim, if that's so, an operation's against nature. I told my old man that when he was having his kidney stones out.

You ought to have heard him yell!" A rich, reminiscent satisfaction dwelt in the Colonel's face.

This period of his life, in which he had thrown off the claims of the spiritual and adopted a practical approach, was evidently one of those "turning points" to which a man looks back with pride. He lingered over the story of his break with church and parents with a curious sort of heat, as though the flames of old sexual conquests stirred within his body at the memory of those old quarrels. The looks he rested on me, as a sharer of that experience, grew more and more lickerish and assaying. "What got *you* down?" he finally inquired, settling back in his chair and pushing his coffee cup aside. "Oh," I said wearily, "it's a long story. You can read it when it's published." "You're an author?" cried the Colonel, who was really very slow-witted. I nodded, and the Colonel regarded me afresh. "What do you write? Love stories?" He gave a half-wink. "No," I said. "Various things. Articles. Books. Highbrowish stories." A suspicion darkened in the Colonel's sharp face. "That McCarthy," he said. "Is that your pen name?" "Yes," I said, "but it's my real name too. It's the name I write under *and* my maiden name." The Colonel digested this thought. "Oh," he concluded.

A new idea seemed to visit him. Quite cruelly, I watched it take possession. He was thinking of the power of the press and the indiscretions of other military figures, who had been rewarded with demotion. The consciousness of the uniform he wore appeared to seep uneasily into his body. He straightened his shoulders and called thoughtfully for the check. We paid in silence, the Colonel making no effort to forestall my dive into my pocketbook. I should not have let him pay in any case, but it startled me that he did not try to do so, if only for reasons of vanity. The whole business of paying, apparently, was painful to him; I watched his facial muscles contract as he pocketed the change and slipped two dimes for the waitress onto the table, not daring quite to hide them under the coffee cup—he had short-changed me on the bill and the tip, and we both knew it. We walked out into the steaming station and I took my baggage out of the checking locker. The Colonel carried my suitcase and we strolled along without speaking. Again, I felt horribly embarrassed for him. He was meditative, and I supposed that he too was mortified by his meanness about the tip.

"Don't get me wrong," he said suddenly, setting the suitcase down and turning squarely to face me, as though he had taken a big decision. "I may have said a few things back there about the Jews getting what they deserved in Germany." I looked at him in surprise; actually, he had not said that to me. Perhaps he had let it drop in the club car. "But that doesn't mean I approve of Hitler." "I should hope not," I said. "What I mean is," said the Colonel, "that they probably gave the Germans a lot of provocation, but that doesn't excuse what Hitler did." "No," I said, somewhat ironically, but the Colonel was unaware of anything satiric in the air. His face was grave and determined; he was sorting out his philosophy for the record. "I mean, I don't approve of his methods," he finally stated. "No," I agreed. "You mean, you don't approve of the gas chamber." The Colonel shook his head very severely. "Absolutely not! That was terrible." He shuddered and drew out a handkerchief and slowly wiped his brow. "For God's sake," he said, "don't get me wrong. I think they're human beings." "Yes," I assented, and we walked along to my track. The Colonel's spirits lifted, as though, having stated his credo, he had both got himself in line with public policy and achieved an autonomous thought. "I mean," he resumed, "you may not care for them, but that's not the same as killing them, in cold blood, like that." "No, Colonel," I said.

He swung my bag onto the car's platform and I climbed up behind it. 26 He stood below, smiling, with upturned face. "I'll look for your article," he cried, as the train whistle blew. I nodded, and the Colonel waved, and I could not stop myself from waving back at him and even giving him the corner of a smile. After all, I said to myself, looking down at him, the Colonel was "a human being." There followed one of those inane intervals in which one prays for the train to leave. We both glanced at our watches. "See you some time," he called. "What's your married name?" "Broadwater," I called back. The whistle blew again. "Brodwater?" shouted the Colonel, with a dazed look of unbelief and growing enlightenment; he was not the first person to hear it as a Jewish name, on the model of Goldwater. "B-r-o-a-d," I began, automatically, but then I stopped. I disdained to spell it out for him; the victory was his. "One of the chosen, eh?" his brief grimace commiserated. For the last time, and in the final fullness of understanding, the hawk eye patrolled the green dress, the duster, and the earrings; the narrow flue of his nostril contracted as he curtly turned away. The train commenced to move.

Questions for Discussion

1. Why is McCarthy's narrator so upset in paragraph 3 to realize that she has been discovered as an artist: "I had always particularly preened myself on being an artist in disguise"? What criticism or support can you offer for her desire to stay unknown as an artist among strangers?

2. What quality in the central figure's character is revealed when she says, "I exulted to think that I had made a modest contribution to sanity in our times, and I imagined my words pyramiding like a chain letter" (¶4)?

3. The reader gradually realizes that the narrator, in conversing with the Colonel, is not only deceiving herself about her own motives but is also being dishonest in her mode of arguing (attacking the Colonel, for example, with Church doctrines that she herself does not believe). Later, however, in writing it all down as a story, she seems completely honest and judgmental about her faults. To what degree does her subsequent honesty redeem her character in the reader's eyes? Are there any who dislike her as a person at the end of the story? For what reasons?

4. What does the narrator mean at the end of paragragh 12 when she says, "If I had been a good person, I should unquestionably have got up and left"? Why does she make this judgment? Do you agree with it? What do you think you would have done in her place?

5. Why does the narrator say at the end, "I disdained to spell it out for him; the victory was his"? What victory? Why does she not tell him that Broadwater is not a Jewish name? She has argued so hard and spent so much energy trying to convert the Colonel, why does she let him walk away thinking that he now knows why she objected to his anti-Semitism?

Suggested Essay Topics

1. If you have ever felt unfair pressure to conform to majority opinion, write an essay in which you give an account of the experience, explaining how you felt and analyzing, as McCarthy does, the source of the pressure. Finally, evaluate your behavior in the face of it. Address your essay to a sympathetic friend to whom you want to give as complete an account of the experience as possible.

2. The quotation from E. B. White included in the introduction could be countered with the old aphorism "The majority should rule," an aphorism with which most of us probably agree. But where is the line that, when crossed, turns "majority rule" into "suppression of dissent"? And where is the line that, when crossed, turns the individual rights of the few into tyranny of the underdog? Choose some particular case that interests you and analyze it, attempting to uphold the rights of the individual (or the minority) against the will of the majority or, if the case warrants it, the rights of the majority against the will of the individual (or the minority). You might consider, for example, the justice of upholding minority quotas for job openings or for admission into schools, especially when the quotas seem to force the hiring or admission of minority candidates less qualified than others. Or you might discuss the right of men's and women's private clubs to ban members of the opposite sex, the prohibition of girls from Little League baseball, or some similar matter.

Plato

Plato's Republic, *a much longer work from which "The Allegory of the Cave" is taken, covers many topics as its characters discourse on the question, "What is justice and how can it be made the reigning principle of the state?" (For more on* The Republic, *see the introductions to "Censorship," pp. 309–310, "The Seductions of Art," p. 317, and "The Education of Women," p. 625.) Some of the topics discussed include education (the goals as well as the curriculum), the role of women, the rearing of children, the censorship of literature, and, in this portion, the criteria for choosing the highest rulers in the state.*

Plato (c. 427–347 B.C.) assumes that a state wants its most talented, most virtuous, and wisest persons as rulers, but he realizes that unless it is self-evident who these persons are, simply saying that they are the ones most wanted doesn't automatically put them in power. Obviously, one must have some criterion for deciding who they are. The criterion that Plato invariably holds for determining wisdom and virtue is knowledge, not so much the amount of knowledge as the kind of knowledge. Specifically, he judges wisdom and virtue to be products of the knowledge of truth.

But this raises another problem: He cannot determine his criterion of knowledge until he constructs a criterion for truth, especially the highest kind of truth. To do that is the purpose of "The Allegory of the Cave." He constructs his allegory—really an extended analogy—to express his theory of what the world is like and to define the highest kind of truth that it contains (¶¶1–16). Once he has accomplished that purpose, he is ready to apply the definition yielded by the analogy to the practical business of deciding who shall rule the state (¶¶17–26).

Plato's view of the world is what philosophers call dualistic, which simply means that he believes in two realms of reality. Dualism assumes that there is, on the one hand, the tangible realm of matter—the entire realm of physical entities, including all forms of nature and our own bodies—and, on the other, the intangible realm of spiritual entities, which Plato called "Ideas." It is important to understand that Plato does not suppose that Ideas are created by any activity or force in the world of matter. Ideas are not in themselves created in people's brains or by nature; they have their own independent (what some philosophers call objective) existence. (Since dualism is a common view in most of the world's religions, this idea should not sound totally strange or unfamiliar. Any belief in an eternal, non-material, unchanging God is an example of a dualistic view, unless the belief treats our ordinary world as sheer illusion.)

What is distinctive about Plato's dualism is the relationship he posits between Ideas and matter. Specialists quarrel about just how Plato sees this relationship, but we can clarify it, within limits, by contrasting it with Christian views. Christianity posits that the ultimate non-material force in the universe, God, is related to the world of matter by having initially created it, having invested it with a purpose and a destiny, and having sustained an interest in its goings on. To Christians the world of physical forms is both real and important because God created it.

However, even though some versions of Christianity have borrowed heavily from his thought, no mainstream Christian view is identical to Plato's. Contrary to Christianity's appreciation of the world as a creation of God, Plato devalues the world of physical reality altogether. From his point of view, the physical forms perceived by the physical senses are merely inferior shadows of Ideas. Because any truth about physical forms can therefore only be a secondary shadow version of primary truth, Plato devotes much discussion to the ways that human beings can escape the constant pull of their physical nature, which dulls and blocks their intellectual perceptions. His remedy is self-discipline acquired by a lifelong, life-governing commitment to rational inquiry: the self-discipline of the true philosopher. The philosopher systematically hardens himself against the appetites and entanglements of worldly attractions: physical pleasure, the exercise of power, the accumulation of money, or the achievement of social status.

The reason Plato assumes that non-material Ideas are superior to (simply more real and therefore more true than) material entities is that Ideas, unlike material objects, are perfect, eternal, and unchanging. The physical world may appear to be solid and enduring, but a moment's reflection reminds us that even granite mountains eventually turn into hillocks, that whole oceans have dried into deserts, that the continents were once a solid landmass, and that most of the species of animals that ever lived on the earth are now extinct. Particle physics tells us that the atoms making up solid-seeming matter are mostly composed of empty space and that their particles are dancing a miniature cosmic dance, the steps of which are eternally unpredictable. All matter, in other words, is in a constant state of flux, flow, alteration, deterioration, change, death, and rebirth. Plato's Ideas, however, having no physical substance, are not subject to the laws that govern physical emergence and change. They are the unchanging counterpart of what we express only fleetingly and glimpse only obscurely in the course of our physical existence.

"The Allegory of the Cave" is Plato's way of expressing all of this (and much more) in a compact, vivid way. The figures chained in the dark cave, looking at the shadows of things and mistaking them for realities, represent ordinary human beings chained to the appetites and allurements of physical existence. Their resistance to being unchained and disciplined for the arduous ascent into the true light of original forms, the Ideas, represents most people's resistance to new thought. It especially represents the fuss that some people make when they are asked to abandon the clichés, maxims, customs, and inherited bits of wisdom that they have been using to organize their lives—when they are asked to start thinking critically rather than slipping into secondhand beliefs without checking to see if they really fit.

Plato's allegory thus extends beyond representing kinds of truth and knowledge to suggest how the quality of knowledge we seek determines the quality of life we embrace. He claims that true freedom and happiness cannot be found in doing or acquiring the things that most people usually associate with freedom: having power, money, and prestige. He never tires of pointing out that these possessions only tighten the chains that keep most people's backs to the light and their eyes focused on shadows. The Platonic point of view says that freedom and happiness are found not by focusing on oneself but by focusing on something both larger than and external to oneself, something that compels and lifts one's vision above the mundane preoccupations that most people mistake as significant. The road to such unconventional and lofty concerns is steep and arduous, but Plato argues that it is worth the discipline and energy it requires, for the glimpse thus obtained of higher truths satisfies the soul as none of our ordinary pursuits ever can.

THE ALLEGORY OF THE CAVE

Our title for this portion of *The Republic*, book 7.

And now, I said, let me show in a figure how far our nature is enlight- 1
ened or unenlightened:—Behold! human beings housed in an underground
cave, which has a long entrance open towards the light and as wide as the
interior of the cave; here they have been from their childhood, and have their
legs and necks chained, so that they cannot move and can only see before
them, being prevented by the chains from turning round their heads. Above
and behind them a fire is blazing at a distance, and between the fire and the
prisoners there is a raised way; and you will see, if you look, a low wall built
along the way, like the screen which marionette players have in front of them,
over which they show the puppets.

I see.

And do you see, I said, men passing along the wall carrying all sorts of 2
vessels, and statues and figures of animals made of wood and stone and
various materials, which appear over the wall? While carrying their burdens,
some of them, as you would expect, are talking, others silent.

You have shown me a strange image, and they are strange prisoners.

Like ourselves, I replied; for in the first place do you think they have 3
seen anything of themselves, and of one another, except the shadows which
the fire throws on the opposite wall of the cave?

How could they do so, he asked, if throughout their lives they were
never allowed to move their heads?

And of the objects which are being carried in like manner they would
only see the shadows?

Yes, he said.

And if they were able to converse with one another, would they not
suppose that the things they saw were the real things?

Very true.

And suppose further that the prison had an echo which came from the 4
other side, would they not be sure to fancy when one of the passers-by spoke
that the voice which they heard came from the passing shadow?

No question, he replied.

To them, I said, the truth would be literally nothing but the shadows
of the images.

That is certain.

And now look again, and see in what manner they would be re- 5
leased from their bonds, and cured of their error, whether the process
would naturally be as follows. At first, when any of them is liberated and
compelled suddenly to stand up and turn his neck round and walk and
look towards the light, he will suffer sharp pains; the glare will distress
him, and he will be unable to see the realities of which in his former
state he had seen the shadows; and then conceive someone saying to him
that what he saw before was an illusion, but that now, when he is

approaching nearer to being and his eye is turned towards more real existence, he has a clearer vision,—what will be his reply? And you may further imagine that his instructor is pointing to the objects as they pass and
requiring him to name them,—will he not be perplexed? Will he not
fancy that the shadows which he formerly saw are truer than the objects
which are now shown to him?

Far truer.

And if he is compelled to look straight at the light, will he not have a 6
pain in his eyes which will make him turn away to take refuge in the objects
of vision which he can see, and which he will conceive to be in reality clearer
than the things which are now being shown to him?

True, he said.

And suppose once more, that he is reluctantly dragged up that steep and 7
rugged ascent, and held fast until he is forced into the presence of the sun
himself, is he not likely to be pained and irritated? When he approaches the
light his eyes will be dazzled, and he will not be able to see anything at all
of what are now called realities.

Not all in a moment, he said.

He will require to grow accustomed to the sight of the upper world. And 8
first he will see the shadows best, next the reflections of men and other objects
in the water, and then the objects themselves; and, when he turned to the
heavenly bodies and the heaven itself, he would find it easier to gaze upon
the light of the moon and the stars at night than to see the sun or the light
of the sun by day?

Certainly.

Last of all he will be able to see the sun, not turning aside to the illusory 9
reflections of him in the water, but gazing directly at him in his own proper
place, and contemplating him as he is.

Certainly.

He will then proceed to argue that this is he who gives the seasons and 10
the years, and is the guardian of all that is in the visible world, and in a certain
way the cause of all things which he and his fellows have been accustomed
to behold?

Clearly, he said, he would arrive at this conclusion after what he had
seen.

And when he remembered his old habitation, and the wisdom of the 11
cave and his fellow-prisoners, do you not suppose that he would felicitate
himself on the change, and pity them?

Certainly, he would.

And if they were in the habit of conferring honours among themselves 12
on those who were quickest to observe the passing shadows and to remark
which of them went before and which followed after and which were together, and who were best able from these observations to divine the future,
do you think that he would be eager for such honours and glories, or envy
those who attained honour and sovereignty among those men? Would he not
say with Homer,

"Better to be a serf, labouring for a landless master,"

and to endure anything, rather than think as they do and live after their manner?

Yes, he said, I think that he would consent to suffer anything rather than live in this miserable manner.

Imagine once more, I said, such a one coming down suddenly out of the   13
sunlight, and being replaced in his old seat; would he not be certain to have his eyes full of darkness?

To be sure, he said.

And if there were a contest, and he had to compete in measuring the   14
shadows with the prisoners who had never moved out of the cave, while his sight was still weak, and before his eyes had become steady (and the time which would be needed to acquire this new habit of sight might be very considerable), would he not make himself ridiculous? Men would say of him that he had returned from the place above with his eyes ruined; and that it was better not even to think of ascending; and if anyone tried to loose another and lead him up to the light, let them only catch the offender, and they would put him to death.

No question, he said.

This entire allegory, I said, you may now append, dear Glaucon, to the   15
previous argument; the prison-house is the world of sight, the light of the fire is the power of the sun, and you will not misapprehend me if you interpret the journey upwards to be the ascent of the soul into the intellectual world according to my surmise, which, at your desire, I have expressed—whether rightly or wrongly God knows. But, whether true or false, my opinion is that in the world of knowledge the Idea of good appears last of all, and is seen only with an effort; although, when seen, it is inferred to be the universal author of all things beautiful and right, parent of light and of the lord of light in the visible world, and the immediate and supreme source of reason and truth in the intellectual; and that this is the power upon which he who would act rationally either in public or private life must have his eye fixed.

I agree, he said, as far as I am able to understand you.

Moreover, I said, you must agree once more, and not wonder that those   16
who attain to this vision are unwilling to take any part in human affairs; for their souls are ever hastening into the upper world where they desire to dwell; which desire of theirs is very natural, if our allegory may be trusted.

Yes, very natural.

. . .

Then, I said, the business of us who are the founders of the State will   17
be to compel the best minds to attain that knowledge which we have already shown to be the greatest of all, namely, the vision of the good; they must make the ascent which we have described; but when they have ascended and seen enough we must not allow them to do as they do now.

What do you mean?

They are permitted to remain in the upper world, refusing to descend   18 again among the prisoners in the cave, and partake of their labours and honours, whether they are worth having or not.

But is not this unjust? he said; ought we to give them a worse life, when they might have a better?

You have again forgotten, my friend, I said, the intention of our law, 19 which does not aim at making any one class in the State happy above the rest; it seeks rather to spread happiness over the whole State, and to hold the citizens together by persuasion and necessity, making each share with others any benefit which he can confer upon the State; and the law aims at producing such citizens, not that they may be left to please themselves, but that they may serve in binding the State together.

True, he said, I had forgotten.

Observe, Glaucon, that we shall do no wrong to our philosophers but 20 rather make a just demand, when we oblige them to have a care and providence of others; we shall explain to them that in other States, men of their class are not obliged to share in the toils of politics; and this is reasonable, for they grow up spontaneously, against the will of the governments in their several States; and things which grow up of themselves, and are indebted to no one for their nurture, cannot fairly be expected to pay dues for a culture which they have never received. But we have brought you into the world to be rulers of the hive, kings of yourselves and of the other citizens, and have educated you far better and more perfectly than they have been educated, and you are better able to share in the double duty. Wherefore each of you, when his turn comes, must go down to rejoin his companions, and acquire with them the habit of seeing things in the dark. As you acquire that habit, you will see ten thousand times better than the inhabitants of the cave, and you will know what the several images are and what they represent, because you have seen the beautiful and just and good in their truth. And thus our State, which is also yours, will be a reality and not a dream only, and will be administered in a spirit unlike that of other States, in which men fight with one another about shadows only and are distracted in the struggle for power, which in their eyes is a great good. Whereas the truth is that the State in which those who are to govern have least ambition to do so is always the best and most quietly governed, and the State in which they are most eager, the worst.

Quite true, he replied.

And will our pupils, when they hear this, refuse to take their turn at the 21 toils of State, when they are allowed to spend the greater part of their time with one another in the heavenly light?

Impossible, he answered; for they are just men, and the commands 22 which we impose upon them are just. But there can be no doubt that every one of them will take office as a stern necessity, contrary to the spirit of our present rulers of State.

Yes, my friend, I said; and there lies the point. You must contrive for 23 your future rulers another and a better life than that of a ruler, and then you may have a well-ordered State; for only in the State which offers this, will they rule who are truly rich, not in gold, but in virtue and wisdom, which are the true blessings of life. Whereas if men who are destitute and starved of such personal goods go to the administration of public affairs, thinking to enrich themselves at the public expense, order there can never be; for they will be fighting about office, and the civil and domestic broils which thus arise will be the ruin of the rulers themselves and of the whole State.

Most true, he replied.

And the only life which looks down upon the life of political ambition 24 is that of true philosophy. Do you know of any other?

Indeed, I do not, he said.

And those who govern should not "make love to their employment?" 25 For, if they do there will be rival lovers, and they will fight.

No question.

Whom, then, will you compel to become guardians of the State? Surely 26 those who excel in judgement of the means by which a State is administered, and who at the same time have other honours and another and a better life than that of politics?

None but these, he replied.

Questions for Discussion

1. To make sure that you understand Plato's allegory, draw a line down a sheet of paper, dividing it into two vertical halves. On the left side make a column (a numbered list) of all the specific items Plato refers to in his allegory. Leave none of them out: chains, fire, cave, and so on. On the right side make a list of items, with corresponding numbers, that identify what those on the left side might represent in our "real" life. In other words, anatomize the allegory.

2. Do you believe, like Plato, that reality includes a realm of intangible entities that have their own objective existence? What arguments can you make in support of such a position? What arguments can you make against it? (Remember that whatever you assert now will be only a start on immensely complex problems.)

3. If you do believe in an objective realm of intangible entities, what is its relationship to the realm of tangible entities? Is one realm superior or more real than the other, as Plato believes? Is one realm truer than the other? What arguments can you make to support your position one way or another?

4. Do you agree with Plato that the highest rulers in a state ought to be those who care least for the power and prestige of the job? Do you agree that the more people care about these material things, the more their vision of just leadership is obscured and distorted? Can you provide examples that reinforce or discredit this argument?

Suggested Essay Topics

1. Plato says that earthly life is like living in a dark cave where we can see only the dusky shadows of things. Create and develop an extended analogy of your own—one that allows for allegorical development. You might try "Social life is like playing different roles in different dramas," "Dating is like playing chess (or organizing a military campaign or establishing a dictatorship)," "Getting educated is like eating in a cafeteria." Address your allegory to your fellow students. Your objective, like Plato's, is to make an otherwise abstract concept vividly, concretely clear to your reader.

2. Write a letter to one of the governing bodies of your college or university (the president's administrative council or the faculty senate, for example), arguing that the officers of the student government should *not* be elected from among the candidates who *want* the job (argue in fact that their wanting it is sufficient to disqualify them from getting it), but that students should be persuaded to serve by those already in power on the basis of their intelligence, honesty, and clearheadedness. They should be urged to accept office as a matter of public duty, not private ambition. Support your position with inferences drawn from Plato's allegory. Your purpose is to show how the present process of selecting leaders only leads to petty bickering, political infighting, and shortsighted policies.

Sissela Bok

Sissela Bok (b. 1934) here challenges the excuses that politicians and government leaders most frequently give for lying to the public. Lying, officials say, is sometimes necessary "to protect national security"; or to prevent a public crisis and is therefore "for the public's own good"; or "to prevent error and confusion" on the grounds that some issues are too complicated for the general public to understand.

There have been many reports in recent years that the American public has grown extremely cynical about the honesty of politicians in general. This cynicism seems to have intensified especially since the Vietnam War (from 1965–1972, during Lyndon Johnson's and Richard Nixon's administrations), and the Watergate scandal (in 1972–1973, during Richard Nixon's administration), and since the Iran-Contra scandal (in 1989, during Ronald Reagan's administration). These three events shocked Americans with the knowledge that lying as official policy has at times— more frequently than anyone 30 years ago would have ever had predicted—penetrated to the very core of national leadership. Regardless of whether all politicians and government leaders are guilty of lying to the public, the repeated spectacle of lying on the part of the highest leaders leads many people to generalize that most, if not all, politicians are liars most, if not all, of the time.

Although it is not fully answered, a very important question implied here is whether there really is any genuine, substantive difference between the so-called noble lie told for the public good and the other kind of lie—the "ignoble lie"?—told in order to advance or protect one's selfish interests. Is there really such a thing as the "noble lie," or is this term of honor merely a cover-up for the one-and-only kind of lie, the lie told to manipulate others and protect oneself? Bok's essay forces one to think about this issue in concrete terms.

Another issue raised, but not fully answered here is the role the public may play in agreeing to its own deception. Bok contends that if people are going to be deceived by government leaders, they ought to debate and to agree openly and beforehand on the *kinds* of lies they will allow officials to tell and the kinds they will not. This *position obviously raises thorny questions about how those categories should be or might be defined and whether it is even possible—much less desirable—to do so. But it is at least a start on a* possible *solution.*

Once an electorate allows its officials to lie to the public, how does it then establish lines across which further lies will be obviously unjustified or indefensible? What happens to a community or a society in which trust among individuals and classes and between the governed and the governors has been eroded away by a social atmosphere in which no one can believe anything anyone else says? Is it possible to separate personal honesty from public dishonesty? That is, if the public discourse in a society is corrupted with distrust because no one can believe the stated pronouncements and opinions of officials, then does this state of things at the public level make it more difficult for people to have a clear view of what honesty entails at the private level?

Some of these important views are discussed and all of these important views are implied by Bok's clear and challenging essay.

LIES FOR THE PUBLIC GOOD

From *Lying: Moral Choice in Public and Private Life* (1978).

> "How then," said I, "might we contrive one of those opportune false-hoods of which we were just now speaking, so as by one noble lie to persuade if possible the rulers themselves, but failing that the rest of the city?"
>
> [. . .] "While all of you are brothers," we will say, "yet God in fashioning those of you who are fitted to hold rule mingled gold in their generation, for which reason they are most precious—but in their helpers silver and iron and brass in the farmers and other craftsmen."
>
> [. . .] "Do you see any way of getting them to believe this tale?" "No, not these themselves," he said, "but I do, their sons and successors and the rest of mankind who come after." "Well," said I, "even that would have a good effect in making them more inclined to care for the state and one another."
>
> Plato, *The Republic*

HUGO   And do you think the living will agree to your schemes?
HOEDERER We'll get them to swallow them little by little.
HUGO   By lying to them?
HOEDERER By lying to them sometimes.
HOEDERER I'll lie when I must, and I have contempt for no one. I
                wasn't the one who invented lying. It grew out of a
                society divided into classes, and each one of us has in-
                herited it from birth. We shall not abolish lying by
                refusing to tell lies, but by using every means at hand
                to abolish classes.

                                                      Jean-Paul Sartre, *Dirty Hands*

THE NOBLE LIE

In earlier chapters three circumstances have seemed to liars to provide   1
the strongest excuse for their behavior—a crisis where overwhelming harm
can be averted only through deceit; complete harmlessness and triviality to
the point where it seems absurd to quibble about whether a lie has been
told; and the duty to particular individuals to protect their secrets. I have
shown how lies in times of crisis can expand into vast practices where the
harm to be averted is less obvious and the crisis less and less immediate;
how white lies can shade into equally vast practices no longer so harmless,
with immense cumulative costs; and how lies to protect individuals and to
cover up their secrets can be told for increasingly dubious purposes to the
detriment of all.

When these three expanding streams flow together and mingle with yet   2
another—a desire to advance the public good—they form the most dangerous
body of deceit of all. These lies may not be justified by an immediate crisis
nor by complete triviality nor by duty to any one person; rather, liars tend
to consider them as right and unavoidable because of the altruism that motivates them. I want . . . to turn to this far-flung category.

Naturally, there will be large areas of overlap between these lies and   3
those considered earlier. But the most characteristic defense for these lies is
a separate one, based on the benefits they may confer and the long-range
harm they can avoid. The intention may be broadly paternalistic, as when
citizens are deceived "for their own good," or only a few may be lied to for
the benefit of the community at large. Error and self-deception mingle with
these altruistic purposes and blur them; the filters through which we must try
to peer at lying are thicker and more distorting than ever in these practices.
But I shall try to single out, among these lies, the elements that are consciously and purposely intended to benefit society.

A long tradition in political philosophy endorses some lies for the sake   4
of the public. Plato, in the passage quoted at the head of this chapter first used
the expression "noble lie" for the fanciful story that might be told to people
in order to persuade them to accept class distinctions and thereby safeguard
social harmony. According to this story, God Himself mingled gold, silver,

iron, and brass in fashioning rulers, auxiliaries, farmers, and craftsmen, intending these groups for separate tasks in a harmonious hierarchy.

The Greek adjective which Plato used to characterize this falsehood expresses a most important fact about lies by those in power: this adjective is *"gennaion,"* which means "noble" in the sense of both "high-minded" and "well-bred." The same assumption of nobility, good breeding, and superiority to those deceived is also present in Disraeli's statement that a gentleman is one who knows when to tell the truth and when not to. In other words, lying is excusable when undertaken for "noble" ends by those trained to discern these purposes.

Rulers, both temporal and spiritual, have seen their deceits in the benign light of such social purposes. They have propagated and maintained myths, played on the gullibility of the ignorant, and sought stability in shared beliefs. They have seen themselves as high-minded and well-bred—whether by birth or by training—and as superior to those they deceive. Some have gone so far as to claim that those who govern have a *right* to lie. The powerful tell lies believing that they have greater than ordinary understanding of what is at stake; very often, they regard their dupes as having inadequate judgment, or as likely to respond in the wrong way to truthful information.

At times, those who govern also regard particular circumstances as too uncomfortable, too painful, for most people to be able to cope with rationally. They may believe, for instance, that their country must prepare for long-term challenges of great importance, such as a war, an epidemic, or a belt-tightening in the face of future shortages. Yet they may fear that citizens will be able to respond only to short-range dangers. Deception at such times may seem to the government leaders as the only means of attaining the necessary results.

The perspective of the liar is paramount in all such decisions to tell "noble" lies. If the liar considers the responses of the deceived at all, he assumes that they will, once the deceit comes to light and its benefits are understood, be uncomplaining if not positively grateful. The lies are often seen as necessary merely at one *stage* in the education of the public. Thus Erasmus, in commenting on Plato's views, wrote:

> [. . .][H]e sets forth deceitful fictions for the rabble, so that the people might not set fire to the magistracy, and similar falsifications by which the crass multitude is deceived in its own interest, in the same way that parents deceive children and doctors the sick.
> [. . .]Thus for the crass multitude there is need of temporary promises, figures, allegories, parables [. . .] so that little by little they might advance to loftier things.

Some experienced public officials are impatient with any effort to question the ethics of such deceptive practices (except actions obviously taken for private ends). They argue that vital objectives in the national interest require a measure of deception to succeed in the face of powerful obstacles. Negotiations must be carried on that are best left hidden from public view; bargains must be struck that simply cannot be comprehended by a politically unsophisticated electorate. A certain amount of illusion is needed in order for public servants to be effective. Every government, therefore, has to deceive people to some extent in order to lead them.

These officials view the public's concern for ethics as understandable   10
but hardly realistic. Such "moralistic" concerns, put forth without any understanding of practical exigencies, may lead to the setting of impossible standards; these could seriously hamper work without actually changing the underlying practices. Government officials could then feel so beleaguered that some of them might quit their jobs; inefficiency and incompetence would then increasingly afflict the work of the rest.

If we assume the perspective of the deceived—those who experience the   11
consequences of government deception—such arguments are not persuasive. We cannot take for granted either the altruism or the good judgment of those who lie to us, no matter how much they intend to benefit us. We have learned that much deceit for private gain masquerades as being in the public interest. We know how deception, even for the most unselfish motive, corrupts and spreads. And we have lived through the consequences of lies told for what were believed to be noble purposes.

Equally unpersuasive is the argument that there always has been gov-   12
ernment deception, and always will be, and that efforts to draw lines and set standards are therefore useless annoyances. It is certainly true that deception can never be completely absent from most human practices. But there are great differences among societies in the kinds of deceit that exist and the extent to which they are practiced, differences also among individuals in the same government and among successive governments within the same society. This strongly suggests that it is worthwhile trying to discover why such differences exist and to seek ways of raising the standards of truthfulness that can have an effect.

The argument that those who raise moral concerns are ignorant of   13
political realities, finally, ought to lead, not to a dismissal of such inquiries, but to a more articulate description of what these realities are, so that a more careful and informed debate could begin. We have every reason to regard government as more profoundly injured by a dismissal of criticism and a failure to consider standards than by efforts to discuss them openly. If duplicity is to be allowed in exceptional cases, the criteria for these exceptions should themselves be openly debated and publicly chosen. Otherwise government leaders will have free rein to manipulate and distort the facts and thus escape accountability to the public.

The effort to question political deception cannot be ruled out so sum-   14
marily. The disparagement of inquiries into such practices has to be seen as the defense of unwarranted power—power bypassing the consent of the governed. In the pages to come I shall take up just a few cases to illustrate both the clear breaches of trust that no group of citizens could desire, and circumstances where it is more difficult to render a judgment.

EXAMPLES OF POLITICAL DECEPTION

In September 1964, a State Department official, reflecting a growing   15
administration consensus, wrote a memorandum advocating a momentous
deceit of the American public. He outlined possible courses of action to cope
with the deteriorating military situation in South Vietnam. These included a
stepping up of American participation in the "pacification" in South Vietnam
and a "crescendo" of military action against North Vietnam, involving heavy
bombing by the United States. But an election campaign was going on; the
President's Republican opponent, Senator Goldwater, was suspected by the
electorate of favoring escalation of the war in Vietnam and of brandishing
nuclear threats to the communist world. In keeping with President Johnson's
efforts to portray Senator Goldwater as an irresponsible war hawk, the memorandum ended with a paragraph entitled "Special considerations during the
next two months," holding that:

> During the next two months, because of the lack of "rebuttal time"
> before election to justify particular actions which may be distorted to the
> U.S. public, we must act with special care—signaling to . . . [the South
> Vietnamese] that we are behaving energetically despite the restraints of
> our political season, and to the U.S. public that we are behaving with good
> purpose and restraint.

As the campaign wore on, President Johnson increasingly professed to   16
be the candidate of peace. He gave no indication of the growing pressure for
escalation from high administrative officials who would remain in office
should he win; no hint of the hard choice he knew he would face if reelected.
Rather he repeated over and over again that:

> [T]he first responsibility, the only real issue in this campaign, the only
> thing you ought to be concerned about at all, is: Who can best keep the
> peace?

The stratagem succeeded; the election was won; the war escalated.   17
Under the name of Operation Rolling Thunder, the United States launched
massive bombing raids over North Vietnam early in 1965. In suppressing
genuine debate about these plans during the election campaign and masquerading as the party of peace, government members privy to the maneuver
believed that they knew what was best for the country and that history
would vindicate them. They meant to benefit the nation and the world by
keeping the danger of a communist victory at bay. If a sense of *crisis* was
needed for added justification, the Domino Theory strained for it: one regime
after another was seen as toppling should the first domino be pushed over.

But why the deceit, if the purposes were so altruistic? Why not espouse   18
these purposes openly before the election? The reason must have been that
the government could not count on popular support for the scheme. In the
first place, the sense of crisis and threat from North Vietnam would have been

far from universally shared. To be forthright about the likelihood of escalation might lose many votes; it certainly could not fit with the campaign to
portray President Johnson as the candidate most likely to keep the peace.
Second, the government feared that its explanations might be "distorted" in
the election campaign, so that the voters would not have the correct information before them. Third, time was lacking for the government to make an
effort at educating the people about all that was at issue. Finally, the plans
were not definitive; changes were possible, and the Vietnamese situation
itself very unstable. For all these reasons, it seemed best to campaign for
negotiation and restraint and let the Republican opponent be the target for
the fear of United States belligerence.

President Johnson thus denied the electorate any chance to give or to   19
refuse consent to the escalation of the war in Vietnam. Believing they had
voted for the candidate of peace, American citizens were, within months,
deeply embroiled in one of the cruelest wars in their history. Deception of
this kind strikes at the very essence of democratic government. It allows those
in power to override or nullify the right vested in the people to cast an
informed vote in critical elections. Deceiving the people for the sake of the
people is a self-contradictory notion in a democracy, unless it can be shown
that there has been genuine consent to deceit. The actions of President Johnson were therefore inconsistent with the most basic principle of our political
system.

What if all governments felt similarly free to deceive provided they   20
believed the deception genuinely necessary to achieve some important public
end? The trouble is that those who make such calculations are always susceptible to bias. They overestimate the likelihood that the benefit will occur and
that the harm will be averted; they underestimate the chances that the deceit
will be discovered and ignore the effects of such a discovery on trust; they
underrate the comprehension of the deceived citizens, as well as their ability
and their right to make a reasoned choice. And, most important, such a
benevolent self-righteousness disguises the many motives for political lying
which could *not* serve as moral excuses: the need to cover up past mistakes;
the vindictiveness; the desire to stay in power. These self-serving ends provide the impetus for countless lies that are rationalized as "necessary" for the
public good.

As political leaders become accustomed to making such excuses, they   21
grow insensitive to fairness and to veracity. Some come to believe that any
lie can be told so long as they can convince themselves that people will be
better off in the long run. From there, it is a short step to the conclusion that,
even if people will not be better off from a particular lie, they will benefit by
all maneuvers to keep the right people in office. Once public servants lose
their bearings in this way, all the shabby deceits of Watergate—the fake
telegrams, the erased tapes, the elaborate cover-ups, the bribing of witnesses
to make them lie, the televised pleas for trust—become possible.

While Watergate may be unusual in its scope, most observers would   22
agree that deception is part and parcel of many everyday decisions in govern-

ment. Statistics may be presented in such a way as to diminish the gravity of embarrassing problems. Civil servants may lie to members of Congress in order to protect programs they judge important, or to guard secrets they have been ordered not to divulge. If asked, members of Congress who make deals with one another to vote for measures they would otherwise oppose deny having made such deals. False rumors may be leaked by subordinates who believe that unwise executive action is about to be taken. Or the leak may be correct, but falsely attributed in order to protect the source.

Consider the following situation and imagine all the variations on this 23 theme being played in campaigns all over the United States, at the local, state, or federal level:

A big-city mayor is running for reelection. He has read a report recom- 24 mending that he remove rent controls after his reelection. He intends to do so, but believes he will lose the election if his intention is known. When asked, at a news conference two days before his election, about the existence of such a report, he denies knowledge of it and reaffirms his strong support of rent control.

In the mayor's view, his reelection is very much in the public interest, 25 and the lie concerns questions which he believes the voters are unable to evaluate properly, especially on such short notice. In all similar situations, the sizable bias resulting from the self-serving element (the desire to be elected, to stay in office, to exercise power) is often clearer to onlookers than to the liars themselves. This bias inflates the alleged justifications for the lie—the worthiness, superiority, altruism of the liar, the rightness of his cause, and the inability of those deceived to respond "appropriately" to hearing the truth.

These common lies are now so widely suspected that voters are at a loss 26 to know when they can and cannot believe what a candidate says in campaigning. The damage to trust has been immense. I have already referred to the poll which found 69 percent of Americans agreeing, both in 1975 and 1976, that the country's leaders had consistently lied to the American people over the past ten years. Over 40 percent of the respondents also agreed that:

> Most politicians are so similar that it doesn't really make much differ-
> ence who gets elected.

Many refuse to vote under such circumstances. Others look to appear- 27 ance or to personality factors for clues as to which candidate might be more honest than the others. Voters and candidates alike are the losers when a political system has reached such a low level of trust. Once elected, officials find that their warnings and their calls to common sacrifice meet with disbelief and apathy, even when cooperation is most urgently needed. Law suits and investigations multiply. And the fact that candidates, should they win, are not expected to have meant what they said while campaigning, nor held accountable for discrepancies, only reinforces the incentives for them to bend the truth the next time, thus adding further to the distrust of the voters.

Political lies, so often assumed to be trivial by those who tell them,   28
rarely are. They cannot be trivial when they affect so many people and when
they are so peculiarly likely to be imitated, used to retaliate, and spread from
a few to many. When political representatives or entire governments arrogate
to themselves the right to lie, they take power from the public that would
not have been given up voluntarily.

DECEPTION AND CONSENT

Can there be exceptions to the well-founded distrust of deception in   29
public life? Are there times when the public itself might truly not care about
possible lies, or might even prefer to be deceived? Are some white lies so
trivial or so transparent that they can be ignored? And can we envisage public
discussion of more seriously misleading government statements such that
reasonable persons could consent to them in advance?

White lies, first of all, are as common to political and diplomatic affairs   30
as they are to the private lives of most people. Feigning enjoyment of an
embassy gathering or a political rally, toasting the longevity of a dubious
regime or an unimpressive candidate for office—these are forms of politeness
that mislead few. It is difficult to regard them as threats to either individuals
or communities. As with all white lies, however, the problem is that they
spread so easily, and that lines are very hard to draw. Is it still a white lie for
a secretary of state to announce that he is going to one country when in reality
he travels to another? Or for a president to issue a "cover story" to the effect
that a cold is forcing him to return to the White House, when in reality an
international crisis made him cancel the rest of his campaign trip? Is it a white
lie to issue a letter of praise for a public servant one has just fired? Given the
vulnerability of public trust, it is never more important than in public life to
keep the deceptive element of white lies to an absolute minimum, and to hold
down the danger of their turning into more widespread deceitful practices.

A great deal of deception believed not only innocent but highly justified   31
by public figures concerns their private lives. Information about their marriages, their children, their opinions about others—information about their
personal plans and about their motives for personal decisions—all are theirs
to keep private if they wish to do so. Refusing to give information under these
circumstances is justifiable—but the right to withhold information is not the
right to lie about it. Lying under such circumstances bodes ill for conduct in
other matters.*

Certain additional forms of deception may be debated and authorized   32
in advance by elected representatives of the public. The use of unmarked
police cars to discourage speeding by drivers is an example of such a practice.
Various forms of unannounced, sometimes covert, auditing of business and

*A lie by an experienced adult in a position of authority about private matters that can be
protected by a refusal to speak is therefore much less excusable than a lie by the school child
described by Bonhoeffer in Chapter XI: too frightened by the bullying teacher to be able to stand
up to him or think of a non-deceptive "way out" on the spur of the moment. [Bok's note.]

government operations are others. Whenever these practices are publicly regulated, they can be limited so that abuses are avoided. But they must be *openly* debated and agreed to in advance, with every precaution against abuses of privacy and the rights of individuals, and against the spread of such covert activities. It is not enough that a public official assumes that consent would be given to such practices.

Another type of deceit has no such consent in advance: the temporizing 33 or the lie when truthful information at a particular *time* might do great damage. Say that a government is making careful plans for announcing the devaluation of its currency. If the news leaks out to some before it can be announced to all, unfair profits for speculators might result. Or take the decision to make sharp increases in taxes on imported goods in order to rescue a tottering economy. To announce the decision beforehand would lead to hoarding and to exactly the results that the taxes are meant to combat. Thus, government officials will typically seek to avoid any premature announcement and will refuse to comment if asked whether devaluation or higher taxes are imminent. At times, however, official spokesment will go further and falsely deny that the actions in question will in fact take place.

Such lies may well be uttered in good faith in an effort to avoid harmful 34 speculation and hoarding. Nevertheless, if false statements are made to the public only to be exposed as soon as the devaluation or the new tax is announced, great damage to trust will result. It is like telling a patient that an operation will be painless—the swifter the disproof, the more likely the loss of trust. In addition, these lies are subject to all the dangers of spread and mistake and deterioration of standards that accompany all deception.

For these reasons, it is far better to refuse comment than to lie in such 35 situations. The objection may be made, however, that a refusal to comment will be interpreted by the press as tantamount to an admission that devaluation or higher taxes are very near. Such an objection has force only if a government has not already established credibility by letting it be known earlier that it would never comment on such matters, and by strictly adhering to this policy at all times. Since lies in these cases are so egregious, it is worth taking care to establish such credibility in advance, so that a refusal to comment is not taken as an invitation to monetary speculation.

Another form of deception takes place when the government regards 36 the public as frightened, or hostile, and highly volatile. In order not to create a panic, information about early signs of an epidemic may be suppressed or distorted. And the lie to a mob seeking its victim is like lying to the murderer asking where the person he is pursuing has gone. It can be acknowledged and defended as soon as the threat is over. In such cases, one may at times be justified in withholding information; perhaps, on rare occasions, even in lying. But such cases are so rare that they hardly exist for practical purposes.

The fact that rare circumstances exist where the justification for govern- 37 ment lying seems powerful creates a difficulty—these same excuses will often be made to serve a great many more purposes. For some governments or public officials, the information they wish to conceal is almost never of the

requisite certainty, the time never the right one, and the public never sufficiently dispassionate. For these reasons, it is hard to see how a practice of
lying to the public about devaluation or changes in taxation or epidemics
could be consented to in advance, and therefore justified.

Are there any exceptionally dangerous circumstances where the state of   38
crisis is such as to justify lies to the public for its own protection? We have
already discussed lying to enemies in an acute crisis. Sometimes the domestic
public is then also deceived, at least temporarily, as in the case of the U-2
incident. Wherever there is a threat—from a future enemy, as before World
War II, or from a shortage of energy—the temptation to draw upon the
excuses for deceiving citizens is very strong. The government may sincerely
doubt that the electorate is capable of making the immediate sacrifices needed
to confront the growing danger. (Or one branch of the government may lack
confidence in another, for similar reasons, as when the administration mis-
trusts Congress.) The public may seem too emotional, the time not yet ripe
for disclosure. Are there crises so exceptional that deceptive strategies are
justifiable?

Compare, for instance, what was said and left unsaid by two United   39
States Presidents confronted by a popular unwillingness to enter a war: President Lyndon Johnson, in escalating the war in Vietnam, and President Franklin D. Roosevelt, in moving the country closer to participating in World War
II, while making statements such as the following in his 1940 campaign to be
reelected:

> I have said this before, but I shall say it again and again and again: Your
> boys are not going to be sent into any foreign wars.

By the standards set forth in this chapter, President Johnson's covert   40
escalation and his failure to consult the electorate concerning the undeclared
war in Vietnam was clearly unjustifiable. Consent was bypassed; there was
no immediate danger to the nation which could even begin to excuse deceiving the public in a national election on grounds of an acute crisis.

The crisis looming before World War II, on the other hand, was doubt-   41
less much greater. Certainly this case is a difficult one, and one on which
reasonable persons might not be able to agree. The threat was unprecedented;
the need for preparations and for support of allies great; yet the difficulties
of alerting the American public seemed insuperable. Would this crisis, then,
justify proceeding through deceit?

To consent even to such deception would, I believe, be to take a fright-   42
ening step. Do we want to live in a society where public officials can resort
to deceit and manipulation whenever they decide that an exceptional crisis
has arisen? Would we not, on balance, prefer to run the risk of failing to rise
to a crisis honestly explained to us, from which the government might have
saved us through manipulation? And what protection from abuse do we
foresee should we surrender this choice?

In considering answers to these questions, we must take into account   43

more than the short-run effects of government manipulation. President
Roosevelt's manner of bringing the American people to accept first the possibility, then the likelihood, of war was used as an example by those who
wanted to justify President Johnson's acts of dissimulation. And these acts
in turn were pointed to by those who resorted to so many forms of duplicity
in the Nixon administration. Secrecy and deceit grew at least in part because
of existing precedents.

The consequences of spreading deception, alienation, and lack of trust   44
could not have been documented for us more concretely than they have in
the past decades. We have had a very vivid illustration of how lies undermine
our political system. While deception under the circumstances confronting
President Roosevelt may in hindsight be more excusable than much that
followed, we could no more consent to it in advance than to all that came
later.

Wherever lies to the public have become routine, then, very special   45
safeguards should be required. The test of public justification of deceptive
practices is more needed than ever. It will be a hard test to satisfy, the more
so the more trust is invested in those who lie and the more power they wield.
Those in government and other positions of trust should be held to the
highest standards. Their lies are not ennobled by their positions; quite the
contrary. Some lies—notably minor white lies and emergency lies rapidly
acknowledged—may be more *excusable* than others, but only those deceptive
practices which can be openly debated and consented to in advance are
justifiable in a democracy.

Questions for Discussion

1. What are some of the views held by people in your class about the media
   "spots" and "bites" that are employed in American elections for public
   office? Take a poll. Do most people in the class believe the content of
   television and radio advertisements purporting to "tell it like it is" about
   the different candidates? If not, what *do* they base their decisions on when
   they vote? What recommendations can be made about how to improve
   things?
2. Do any students in your class have the kind of international experience
   that would allow them to contrast what happens in American elections
   with what happens in those of other countries? If so, are the contrasts
   suggestive of reforms that might be made in American election campaigns?
   If not, you might explore the possibility of inviting a guest to the class who
   can provide this contrast.
3. When you know about a lie, but do not expose it, do you become complicitous in it? For example, if you see someone cheating on a test and do not

report it, are you as guilty as the cheater? Would you be as guilty as the cheater if the instructor had explicitly said that all students should report any instance of cheating?

4. How culpable are "white lies": "I love that dress" when you really hate it, or "Yes, I'd be happy to have lunch with you" when what you really want is to eat a solitary lunch and read the final chapter of an exciting mystery, but you do not want to hurt your acquaintance's feelings?

5. Are you seriously offended when public officials are exposed as liars, or is it so commonplace that you have come to accept it? Do you feel that there really is such a thing as the "noble lie," the justifiable lie told for "the public's own good"? If so, what is an example of such a lie? If not, what reasons can you offer for disallowing the noble lie?

Suggested Essay Topics

1. Imagine yourself in this situation. You are the president of a Greek fraternity or sorority house on your campus. Some unknown group of students has perpetrated a prank that got out of control and has caused several thousand dollars worth of damage. You are the only person who knows that the guilty persons are members of your house. You would personally like to see them punished or at least held responsible. However, you know that if their identity is exposed, your house, whose well-being is partly in your hands as president, may be seriously censured by the university—it may even lose its existence on this campus—and you feel responsible for protecting the public good, the happiness of those innocent members of your house who will be hurt if the house is severely punished or thrown off campus. Write an essay directed to your instructor explaining whether you would turn your house members in or not. Give your reasons, making clear in your essay that you have considered the arguments on the other side of whatever position you take.

2. Imagine yourself in this situation. You are the new president of the United States and you are writing a memo to your internal staff and the members of your cabinet. Your purpose is not just to order your staff and cabinet members to maintain honesty with the public, but to make an argument, saying why you think such honesty is essential to good government. You are taking special care to answer those of your audience who may feel about "national security" the way Sissela Bok (¶9) says some "experienced" public officials feel.

Mary Ellen Goodman

To what degree are human beings social creatures? To what degree are we determined by our environment? How much freedom do we have to negotiate a personal independence between the desires that are "really our own" and the desires that society has programmed in us? What does really our own mean? Is everything put in us from the outside or do we have internal ways of seeing, feeling, and valuing that are our own in some unique or exclusive way? Or can even desires of internal origin be really ours if they are hard-wired into us as part of the basic human equipment we are born with?

The issues raised by these questions and implied by the title to this chapter, "The Individual and Society," are nowhere better displayed than in Mary Ellen Goodman's research on the development of racial awareness in four-year-olds. Goodman's observations convey the discouraging suggestion that racist attitudes and racist ways of valuing are picked up so early in the home, that is, in homes where racist attitudes are held by adults, that nonracist attitudes taught at school or elsewhere will have to fight for space on ground that has already been coopted by racist views absorbed from families. Racist attitudes seem firmly established even in four-year-old children who come from families where adults hold racist attitudes.

Because children are not born with racist attitudes, it is clear that they learn them. What Goodman's research suggests is that they learn them much earlier and in more detail than anyone might think. One view suggested by this fact is that socialization of all sorts begins earlier than one might think. Looking at children's attitudes about race suggests that their attitudes about everything, not just race, begin to be formed by the influence of attitudes in the social milieu from an extremely early age, perhaps from the moment they are born.

Thus five-year-olds do not arrive at school in pristine innocence. Even by age four they have learned much about their world: how to value certain attributes, including lightness or darkness of skin; how to classify not just things, but people; and how to employ the language of exclusivity. School may be an influence on them, but it will certainly not be the first influence, nor the only influence, and probably not the dominant influence. More often than not, schools are in the position of having to fight attitudes rather than form them. They especially have to fight those attitudes that are antisocial, discriminatory, and racist.

As you think to your future (perhaps your present) as (potential) parents and to your role as citizens who have a stake in living with other citizens who are enlightened rather than negatively programmed about race, Goodman's essay offers to help clarify your ideas and to give a realistic sense of what kinds of psychic and social forces you may have to deal with.

RACE AWARENESS IN YOUNG CHILDREN

From *Race Awareness in Young Children* (1952).

"WHAT AM I?"

It was Helen who asked one day, "What am I?" Helen's father has a sense of humor, and it did not fail him at a rather crucial moment. "You are," he said, "a tantalizin' brown! So's your mother, and so am I." 1

Helen was satisfied, and happy—for the moment. She was four and a half then, but she had asked the question before. Her mother thinks she wasn't more than three the first time, and 2

> "She got a different answer. I said, 'You're an American, and so am I, and so's your father.' At nursery school the other day, she asked the teacher, 'What are you?' Mrs. X. said, 'I'm an American,' and Helen drew herself up very proud and said, 'I'm an American too.' . . . And then a little while back Mary said she'd rather play with David than Helen. Mary said, 'He's white and you're colored.' But Helen wasn't takin' that. She came right back with, 'Oh no I'm not. I'm a tantalizin' brown!' " 3

THE PROCESS OF BECOMING A PERSON

Helen's case is both like and unlike those of others of our four-year-olds. She is forthright and relatively shockproof, like her father and mother. She asks and has been lucky enough to get answers that contributed to her comfort at the moment and provided her with an answer to give to others when she needed one. She has been given reason, both at home and at school, to feel that almost anything can be asked and a satisfying answer will be forthcoming. In this way she is unlike most of our children. There are those who ask and get evasive answers or none at all. After a while they stop asking and make up their own answers. 4

Whatever the process of getting them, answers they must have, at four and five and even three. By three the consciousness of self is coming into focus, and inseparable from it is the consciousness of others. By the time the child can put into words the question *"Who* am I," he already has some sense of himself as a person, and a sense of mother and father, sisters and brothers and playmates, as outside the boundaries of "me." The baby had no real sense of himself, and the idea of the "me" has been a gradual growth, a result of living with people (as such), of living with people who observe a certain "style" of life, and of living with unique and individualized people. The growth of the *ego* has meant developing a sense of separateness, and this is both rewarding and painful. It is rewarding to feel separate and hence autonomous, but it is painful at times to find oneself outside others and alone. 5

THE FOUR-YEAR-OLD PERSON

The four-year-old has a strong sense of self. He has learned to enjoy his 6
autonomy, if his growth is healthy, and,

> "... having found a firm solution of his problem of autonomy, the child
> of four and five is faced with the next step—and with the next crisis.
> Being firmly convinced that he *is* a person, the child must now find out
> *what kind* of a person he is going to be... He begins to make comparisons
> and is apt to develop untiring curiosity about differences... He tries to
> comprehend possible future roles."

Our four-year-old has also a sense of others. It grows, as does the 7
self-awareness, through making comparisons, finding likenesses and differences.

> "He is beginning to sense himself as only one among many, ... he has
> a definite consciousness of kind, of his own kind, (and) a fundamental
> noetic attitude... (He has) a dim intent to generalize and to order ...
> experience."

He has social interest and

> "... an awareness of the attitudes and opinions of others, ... a
> consciousness of social milieu and ... maturing social insight."

Such being the case, the interest our children show in identifying, 8
describing, classifying, evaluating, and comparing themselves and others is
quite in line with reasonable expectations. Their interest in characteristics or
behavior having to do with what adults call race, nationality, or religion is
a part of these general interests and inclinations. From this point of view,
Tony's flat "I'm not no girl—I'm a boy" has something in common with
Elaine's "I got curly yellow hair" and with Gerry's "I had my birthday. I'm
five." All of these are simple and accurate descriptions of the self. "My
mother has a coat like yours"—"my baby sister wears diapers"—"my daddy
goes to work at night"—"my brother got a bike too"—these are bits of what
the child sees in his mind's eye when he thinks of some of the others. Again
they are simple and accurate pictures, reflecting awareness of sex, age, personal attributes, family roles, clothes, time, and personal possessions. They
are natural enough and unremarkable.

Considering the adult world, it is also natural enough that certain judg- 9
ments of right and wrong, good and bad, pretty and ugly, etc., etc., should
begin to be made. Our children are not merely exercising their eyes and ears
and minds in recording the objective features of people, things, and behavior.
They are at the same time learning to see, hear, and think along the lines
followed by their models. Jimmie is learning the *culture* of mid-century Amer-

ica in the somewhat distinctive forms it takes in New Dublin, the Harding-Dover area, Morton Street, the Walker's flat, Coleman House Nursery School, and possibly a few other places. He did not arrive in the world equipped with an ego, but has had to grow his own, with the help of other people. Neither did he come equipped with a culture—with a yearning for ice-cream cones rather than toasted worms, a bike rather than a birchbark canoe, or the idea that living in a frame tenement, using the bathroom, or going to nursery school are among the "of course" things of life.

By four Jimmie has already learned a quite staggering number of the 10 ways of his world—an amazing number in view of the fact that he came into it quite naked, culturally as well as physically. He had only a body—a body stocked with possibilities, a large number of which would appear in due course. Some of them appear almost inevitably—like the color and size and curiosity of our four-year-old. Others probably do or do not appear to a degree depending upon the nature and force of the pressures brought to bear. Some of the pressures themselves operate quite automatically and almost inevitably. If he lives in Harding or Dover, he will learn to speak English. Other pressures may operate as automatically though they are less inevitable—being denied meat on Friday or pork every day, for example. And some may be quite as effective though not at all inevitable, like having a father who breaks up furniture when he comes home drunk. Whatever the particular combination may have been, our four-year-old has already done a good deal of more or less subtly directed unfolding. In the process he has learned many of the ways *and* many of the *values* current in his world.

The learning of values, and of attitudes, means learning to want, to 11 desire, to prefer certain kinds of things, activities, people, and personal traits or attributes. Conversely, it means learning to not want, not desire, and not prefer other things, activities, etc., or to have some "in-between" feelings.

The child's feelings, whether for, against, or in-between, are not neces- 12 sarily always the same, nor do they necessarily seem to add up to a neatly logical total. Yet it is possible to see, when we know a good deal about the whole child and his life situation, that he is growing into a fitting shape. That particular combination and intensity of pressures under which he grows does not wholly determine his shaping. The pressures meet resistances of different sorts and degrees. The human material is plastic, but neither completely nor uniformly so. Still, if we knew enough about the complex properties of the material, about the intricate angles described by the mold, about the effects of degrees of pressure and the significance of timing, *if* we knew enough about all this, we should almost surely be able to see that the shape does fit. The "if" looms very large. Here we can offer only outline drawings and estimates.

Look at William, for example. Yesterday William valued the company 13 of girls. His attitude toward them was admiring, very friendly, and actively seeking. "I want to walk with a girl," he said firmly as Mrs. D. lined up the nursery school four-year-olds to go on a little excursion. Today William can hardly wait for John to get to school—he wants to continue a game they started on the slide just before closing time yesterday. He refuses to let Irma play with him, but he accepts Ned, at least until John arrives. This is a boy's game. Right now he values the company of boys and his attitudes toward girls are not what they were. But counting the number of times William seeks out girls as against the number recorded for Billy makes it plain that Billy's values and attitudes are different. Billy says, "I don't play with girls—I don't like girls," and generally his actions are in accord.

William's attitude toward girls has background in his experience and support from other of his attitudes. The pieces seem to fit together. Or, more accurately perhaps, we can see enough of the pieces to draw an outline and estimate dynamics.   14

William has a gentle father who is affectionate and kind toward his mother. She is gentle and affectionate with William, and he is devoted to her almost to the point of overdependence. For perhaps half his lifetime, his special playmate has been the only child of his age on the block, and that child happens to be a girl. William has a little sister who is "just crazy about him" and who "thinks everything he does is just right." In view of this somewhat unusual *combination* of circumstances, it is perhaps not surprising that William's orientation toward the opposite sex is favorable, and somewhat more favorable than is common among his fellows. It is relevant, too, that William is a "positive" child—he is more likely to make strong statements about the things he is "for" than about the things he is "against," and he probably has more positive than negative feelings.   15

Billy, on the other hand, leans toward negative attitudes and toward expressions of not-liking, not-wanting, etc. His low valuation of girls may be both an expression of his personal negativism and of an attitude common among boys his age or a little older. The background pressures are less clear in his case than in William's, though his little life has been turbulent enough to account for some negativism in him. Hence the negatives current in the culture of his world press in on soft spots. Growing up with three older children in a two-room shack on an alley, living with a careless, tired mother and with a father who is perennially out of work, drunk, or "away" (in jail) could account for some negativism. Billy, however, does not look like a young delinquent. He occasionally "blows up" at school, but he is generally quite happy, friendly, and cooperative. One might expect more than an occasional spell of temper or "moodiness," silence about home when he is at school, a sullen refusal to go to school now and then, an occasional rejection of girls— and of other "kinds of people."   16

Helen and William and Billy and the rest of our four-year-olds are making progress toward finding out *what* they are. In order to know what they are, they must at the same time know more about what other people are. They now know themselves to be one person—one girl or boy—among many small or large boys and girls, sons and daughters, who live with fathers and mothers, brothers and sisters. They have developed a sense of self and a sense of others, and they see more and more of the details about themselves and others. They are learning that these details have meanings, and they are   17 learning to interpret the details "correctly," i.e., to value them as some others around them do.

Our 103 children, chattering with one another, with their parents or 18
teachers or with Observers (the writer or an assistant), give us evidence that they are doing these kinds of things:

1. They are perceiving (registering) the objective features of people, things, and behavior, and making classifications on the basis of these perceptions;
2. They are becoming used to a great number of doings and ways of doing, and are increasingly practicing these ways themselves;
3. They are learning to like the things that other people like, and to dislike the things other people dislike.

SEEING AND PIGEONHOLING PEOPLE

The first process, perceiving and classifying, inevitably extends to fea 19
tures and groups which the adult world calls "racial." When we speak here of "race" we are not following the anthropologist's definitions (and the plural is advisedly used). We are following the "common-sense" definition, which in fact makes rather little logical "sense" but is certainly "common" enough. It is weird logic indeed which puts into one pigeonhole labeled "Negro" people who may in *fact* have little but their humanness in common. It happens because they are *believed* to have much else in common and because those elements are *believed* to be important. The beliefs make all the difference. Cultural definitions like this common definition of race are based on *beliefs* which often bear little or no resemblance to the *facts.* But in the "real" world outside classrooms, libraries, and laboratories, it is the beliefs that count.

Young children first see the more conspicuous features of people, and 20
the more conspicuous differences between them. They base their classifications on these. Vivien says: "this girl (white doll) belongs to this boy (white doll); this girl (brown doll) belongs to this boy (brown doll)." She is spontaneously classifying on the simple basis of the rather marked color differences between the dolls.

Most of our children made such classifications, either in respect to dolls, 21
pictured people, or real people. The tendency to see the classificatory features is stronger, however, when the child is looking at representations than when he is looking at real people. The view is less obstructed by personality. But he does see the racial attributes of real people, including himself. Herman observes correctly: "My mother's brown-skinned." Stefan offers: "My mother's *that* white." Carol M. says: "See how colored my hands are." When Vivien informs us: "I got a white brother," she may be offering a simple description, but she is more likely making a classification. She knows that he is not literally white—like a piece of chalk, for example.

Classification was undoubtedly being made when Thomas looked 22
thoughtfully at the children in his room at school and said: "There are two

white children here and all the rest are colored." An adult would have said the same, and the "colored" ranged from very light to medium dark. Thomas called Rose "Blackie," and Rose is fair enough to make some grown-ups wonder "what is she?" So we know that Thomas classifies, and does so in a more grown-up way than most of his fellows.

Norman and Sam were sharp at color perception and classification, too. [23] Norman started something in his group at school when he asked his teacher (teasingly she felt), "What color are you?" Sam picked up the question and answered it for her—"She's brown." Norman agreed: "She's brown and I'm brown." This was more than simple description, because Mrs. D. is very considerably browner than Norman. Sam added: "Yes, and I'm brown too," and he proceeded to name a number of children and teachers, not all of whom were present, labeling each "white," "brown," or "colored."

Hair form as well as skin color is a feature of interest, but it is a [24] secondary basis for classification. Donald, Sam, and Norman discussed the hair of the children around them. They said some (the Negro children) had "curly" hair, and some (the white children) had "straight" hair or "curly-at-the-bottom" hair. Comments about hair—its form, color, length, and the style in which it is worn—are very common. The children stroke or finger one another's hair occasionally, when heads and hands happen to be in proximity. Deep interest is sometimes expressed by the way they do it. But when they say that so-and-so is "white" and go on to explain "why," they rarely mention hair. When they do it is hair color rather than form that is noted. "Because he has that kind of face—hands—legs—eyes" is usual. It is the unusual child who adds "and he has white hair" (i.e., the kind whites have).

Our children are seeing physical traits and grouping people in terms of [25] them. They do not always label the resulting groups just as their parents might, nor do they know that they are talking about what their parents would call "race." But what they are doing is otherwise very much like the "noticing" and labeling that the grown-ups do.

LEARNING THE "OF COURSE" WAYS
OF LIFE

We have said that there is a second important process going on in our [26] children—the process of accepting an ever greater number of the ways of their world. The racial—and interracial—ways are no exceptions. The race-ways are, however, less obvious and more complex than a good many other kinds of ways. Hence Eddie H. has learned to eat with a fork and spoon rather than his fingers (most of the time), to put on and take off his clothes, to say "thank you" and "please" (sometimes), to ride a tricycle and use crayons and paints, and to do a thousand other things that American four-year-olds do.

So far, however, Eddie H. has not learned to do the things that older [27] white children often do when they encounter colored children. He has not learned to say "no—I don't want to play with you—you're colored," as his six-year-old sister has. Nor has he learned, like seven-year-old John, to stop uncertainly beside the wading pool at the "Center" when he sees the colored children in it, and then go home and tell his mother he's not going there any more, "because there are too many colored." He has not learned to "gang up" with other white boys on the way home from school to "get" that colored kid who had him down in the school yard when the teacher pulled them apart. Four-year-old Eddie hasn't even learned to yell "nigger," but four-year-old Nathan and a few others have.

Our white Eddies and brown Irmas play together on the street or in 28 nursery school with few "racial incidents." But if we were to conclude from this that they "pay no attention at all to race," we would be quite wrong. The casual visitor in the "mixed" nursery school, or the passer-by on the street, concludes just that, and goes away happily reassured that this is an age of racial innocence. Even parents and teachers are inclined to overlook the significance of the few clues they do get. They may be too busy to notice. They may also be ignoring or selectively forgetting matters which are distasteful because Americans like to believe in the "purity" of childhood. Precocious sexuality shocks them and so does precocious raciality. But the crux of the matter is that the public behavior of our Eddies and Irmas does not tell the whole story.

The whole story comes out only when these children are given repeated 29 chances to "think out loud" just as freely as they can be encouraged to do. In the making of this study, we gave them the chances and the encouragement. We gave them time—weeks or even months—to get acquainted with us before we invited them, one by one, to "come and play with our puzzles" (or doll house, or pictures, or dolls). They accepted happily and went with us to the testing room where we had quiet and privacy. They played, and we watched, listened, recorded, and asked some carefully calculated questions. For eight months most of these children were under our eyes at least two days a week, and during that period each of them "visited" our room at least four times to play with the four different sets of materials. During those visits we learned that four-year-olds see and hear and sense much more about race than one would suppose after watching them at school or even at home.

Sarah (w) is an excellent example. At her nursery school there were a 30 few Negro children, and one Negro teacher. But week after week her behavior at school gave no indication that she either noticed or cared about color. Yet the Observer's final report on her behavior during the play interviews reads as follows:

> "Awareness of race differences is accurate and verbalized. She is clearly 31
> aware of what she calls 'black people' and has rather strong feelings about
> them. She shows a rather consistent rejection of Negroes. She is clearly
> aware that 'blacks' are very different people from 'whites.'"

The case of Joan G. (N) points up the discrepancy between what her 32 mother knew of her awareness and what we came to know. Mothers do not necessarily tell all, of course, even to someone they have come to know fairly well and even though that someone is an eager listener with a genuine interest in mother's pride and joy. But after allowing for this factor, and for plain lapses of memory or observation, a large discrepancy appears between what Mrs. G. told us and what we knew. At home Joan had once referred to a nursery school child as "white," and she had once asked whether a certain other friend were "white." That was all of the evidence for awareness, and Mrs. G. was sure that "Joan makes no difference in her judgment (of people) on a basis of color." Alone with the Observer, Joan repeatedly described and labeled dolls or pictured people as "white," "brown," or "colored." She volunteered comments about real people too: "My daddy's colored. My mommy's colored." Most notable of all, this child of less than four and a half offered what strikes the adult ear as an acute commentary on American society. Joan told us:

> *"The people that are white, they can go up. The people that are brown, they have to* 33
> *go down."*

The evidence is overwhelming that many of our children have devel- 34 oped awareness and feelings far in excess of their habits of expressing them in behavior. Those ways of expressing racialism which are common among older children and their parents are rarely a part of our four-year-old's accumulation of learned ways of doing. But much that is relevant to his later doings has already taken its place in that complex system we call his personality.

LEARNING THE WANT-AND-LIKE
WAYS OF LIFE

This is the third of the important types of development which we have 35 noted as characteristic of our children. It is a matter of the learning of values about people and attitudes toward them. We have seen that some personal details strike the senses of our children early and forcefully—skin, hair, and eye color among them. As they become aware of such items and begin to sort people into color kinds, they also begin to value differently both the items and the kinds.

Some of this differential valuing would develop even if it were not 36 among the life-ways of our children's people. There are uniquely personal reasons for preferring blue eyes to brown, creamy skin to coffee-colored, or straight hair to tightly curled. *Having* any of these attributes can be a reason for liking them—or for not liking them—depending upon how much you like yourself. And *not having* any of them can be a reason for liking or not liking them—depending upon how much you like the people who do have them. But it is hard to draw a line between the uniquely personal reasons and the reasons which reside in the social world and filter into the personal system after a time. How much you like yourself and certain other people is not wholly a matter of your independent and objective judgment based on your objective experience. It feels very much as though it were, but this proves only how deep culture goes. Our experience with ourselves and with others is always seen and felt in ways which are partly determined by culture.

So Joan M. (N) is not expressing a purely original point of view, based 37 on the cold, hard facts of her experience, when she says "black people—I hate 'em." Nor has Stefan (w) been uninfluenced by culturally patterned points of view. He says he'd rather play with the white than with the brown boy (in the picture) *"because* he's white." And later: "All I like is the white one (girl in picture). *Not* the black one—the white one." Norman says of a pictured Negro boy: "He's a freshie! Look at his face—I don't like that kind of face." The face in question is hardly to be seen, and what does show looks to the casual observer quite an unremarkable medium brown. Vivien (w) says that the white lady "is better than the colored lady" in the same picture. The opinion is not that of a neutral judge. Billy (w) is not neutral either when he looks at two pictured men, both ordinary and unremarkable, and says: *"A good man—and a black one."*

Here are expressions of positive or negative *valuing,* and in no uncertain 38 terms. To "hate" black people, and to not like the "kind" of face a brown boy is assumed to have; to choose the white over the brown boy to play with "because" he's white, and to like only the white boy; to see the white woman as "better" than the brown; to set "black" against "good"—these are expressions of strong feelings. Nor are they the only evaluations made by these particular children. If we had nothing more in the way of evidence concerning their individual feeling tones, we might question the significance of the single statement. But there is much else on the record for Joan M., Stefan, Norman, Vivien, Billy, and a good many others. The value-laden comments from each of them add up to an unmistakable total. Not all our children feel so strongly, or perhaps they are not so much given to putting their feelings into words. But a fourth of them said enough to make it clear that, among our four-year-olds, their systems of race-related values are strongly entrenched.

The process of learning how other people place Negroes and whites on 39 various scales of value is well under way. But *attitudes,* we have said, are involved in our four-year-old's learning too. Having an attitude means being "ready" and "set" to act in a particular way, when and if you meet a certain kind of situation. Acquiring an attitude is like cocking a gun—the person and the gun are thereafter poised for action. Triggering comes for the person when the appropriate situation is met. There will be no shooting until and unless all of the necessary elements have accumulated: the person, his values, his attitudes—and a situation. Values are an indispensable part of the ensemble. They supply the push—the feeling power which carries the individual into action. Some recurrent actions become so automatic that little or no emotional steam goes into them. The more common daily habits of a people are of this sort. Life-ways of a less recurrent and less unanimously accepted sort involve more feeling, and race-ways are among them.

Our children are "building up steam" about race. Simultaneously they 40 are getting "ready" and "set" to go into action one day. They seldom go into action now (beyond the talking-about-it kind of action) for one or both of two reasons: (1) the steam is not yet up, i.e., they don't yet feel strongly enough, however vehement their statements, to do anything about it; (2) they have not yet learned to go through certain motions, like yelling "nigger" when the other kids do it, simply as one of the relatively automatic gestures copied from others around them. In either case the necessary attitude (or attitudes) is missing.

The necessary attitudes may be missing, in spite of firmly held and 41 strongly felt values about colored and white. They may be missing in spite of opportunities for copying. This can happen when some other values, like fair play, politeness, kindness, etc., are strong enough to block the development of antagonistic race attitudes, or to block the copying of actions which depend upon antagonistic attitudes. The child may have built up strong feelings—out of his personal experience as he has learned to see it, out of what he sees and hears of other people's feelings, and in response to his particular needs. Yet these may be kept in check by countercurrents pouring from the same wells—from his perceptions of personal experience, from his sample of culturally patterned attitudes and values, and from his own psychic imperatives.

WE AND THEY

Our four-year-olds have come a long way. The possibilities packed in 42 each of these erstwhile blobs of protoplasm have unfolded, as the blobs themselves expanded. Both processes have meanwhile been affected by the push and pull of a great variety of forces outside them. So each child has come to feel himself a separate person, but close to other persons, as an "I" within the "We." He has also come to sense the existence of persons a greater distance away, the existence of "They." "They" may be the people in the next flat or on the next block, the children next door or in another school, or any one of a hundred other kinds, with their reciprocal "we'." But here our interest is focused upon racial "we's" and "they's." We have already seen a little of the making of "we-they" thinking and feeling. Now we will look to the nature of that thinking and feeling in Negro children and in white.

. . .

Questions for Discussion

1. Paragraph 18 conveys a powerful picture of the dynamic between development of the individual as an individual and development of the individual as a product of social influences. Items 1 and 2 seem to exhibit the former; item 3 seems to exhibit the latter. Which of these two plays the

greater role in one's development as a person? Why do you answer as you do? What experience or knowledge can you use to support your views?

2. In paragraph 36, Goodman observes that "How much you like yourself and certain other people is not wholly a matter of your independent and objective judgment based on your objective experience. It feels very much as though it were, but this proves only how deep culture goes." Do you agree or disagree with this statement? Why or why not? What reasons or evidence can you muster to support your opinions?

3. Does the fact that children learn racial attitudes so early suggest why some attitudes linger so long in society and why they take so long to change? Is it fair to say that some of these attitudes are set "for life" at a very young age? Is it easier to change attitudes established early or ones established later? Why?

4. How do attitudes and "facts" learned later interact with attitudes and "facts" learned earlier when the later ones contradict the earlier ones? Does later learning erase earlier learning? Does later learning not take root because the hard-set attitudes from early learning do not allow it to? Do the two kinds of learning simply get piled on top of one another, providing two bases for reacting to things in life? In what circumstances does later learning displace earlier learning?

Suggested Essay Topics

1. Write a letter directed to your parents or extended family members recalling the kinds of attitudes that were expressed in your family, however indirectly, about race and racial issues (whether you really send it or not will be up to you). Analyze the influence of these attitudes on you and evaluate whether those attitudes have been "good" or "bad" for your own socialization. If you have criticisms to offer or suggestions to make about the rearing of younger children still in the family, make clear the criteria you are using in your judgments. If you are still in basic agreement with the attitudes of your family, make clear the grounds of your approval.

2. Tolerance is very easy to subscribe to at an abstract level and sometimes very difficult to perform at a concrete, personal level. Imagine that someone in your family—a sibling, a favorite aunt or uncle, or a single parent—has just announced that he or she is preparing to marry someone of a different race, religion, or ethnic background than the one you share with this person. In an essay addressed basically to yourself, but in language that you would not mind sharing with a general audience who will become participants in your internal meditations, analyze as honestly as you can how you would feel about this turn of events. Try to imagine the event as vividly as you can, in all of its details and potential consequences, and then imagine how you would react. Try to trace your reactions to their roots and include an account of whether you have learned anything new about yourself and your attitudes.

Ideas in Debate

Richard Dawkins
Laurence Thomas

Richard Dawkins

*P*artly *through the influence of Richard Dawkins's (b. 1941)* **The Selfish Gene** *(1976),* sociobiology *has become an arena of hotly contested views about human nature, human purposiveness, and human survival. As the two obvious word stems in* sociobiology *suggest (social + biology), sociobiology is the attempt to develop a body of social theory based on a biological interpretation of human nature and behavior. In Dawkins' case, the biological interpretation to which he attaches most importance is the theory of natural selection first advanced by Charles Darwin in* **On the Origin of Species by Means of Natural Selection** *(1859).*

While Darwin purports to explain how animals survive in their environments, eventually producing in themselves genetic adaptations that explain the differences among species, Dawkins purports to explain the underlying mechanism that governs adaptive behavior. Darwin focuses on animals and their behavior; Dawkins focuses on the underlying causes that drive *their behavior. He locates these causes in the genes, in whose DNA, "instructions for survival," he finds a biological explanation for many different kinds of social behavior that have traditionally been explained as acts of will, purposiveness, and intellect. To Dawkins, animal bodies, including human ones, are "survival machines" driven by the "desire" of genes to perpetuate themselves, to remain alive and to prosper in the gene pool.*

Dawkins concedes the controversial nature of his views in the very title of his book, The Selfish Gene, *which implies the human beings are selfish in a fundamental, deep-structure way: in their biological makeup itself. If his claims are true, then human beings' views about most forms of altruistic behavior will have to be relabeled as* so-called *altruistic behavior. Dawkins, in short, strongly challenges the view that human beings really have the capacity to behave disinterestedly. He challenges even more strongly the view that they can ever behave in ways that* genuinely *threaten the survival of their genes.*

Dawkins' arguments rely heavily on metaphor and analogy, which are present not merely to adorn or to clarify; they are also constitutive components of the argument itself. You are likely to view his arguments as strong or weak, therefore, insofar as you view his metaphors and analogies as sound or farfetched. As you read, assess carefully the soundness or weakness of the metaphors and analogies. Do they seem appropriate and on target? Or do they fudge the issues? Do they mask important

503

weaknesses in Dawkins' position itself? One way to begin to answer these questions is to try to come up with metaphors or analogies other than Dawkins' that either corroborate or challenge his own.

THE GENE MACHINE

(From *The Selfish Gene* (1976).

THIS book should be read almost as though it were science fiction. It is   1
designed to appeal to the imagination. But it is not science fiction: it is science.
Cliché or not, "stranger than fiction" expresses exactly how I feel about the
truth. We are survival machines—robot vehicles blindly programmed to preserve the selfish molecules known as genes. This is a truth which still fills me
with astonishment. Though I have known it for years, I never seem to get
fully used to it. One of my hopes is that I may have some success in astonishing others.

· · ·

INTELLIGENT life on a planet comes of age when it first works out the   2
reason for its own existence. If superior creatures from space ever visit earth,
the first question they will ask, in order to assess the level of our civilization,
is: "Have they discovered evolution yet?" Living organisms had existed on
earth, without ever knowing why, for over three thousand million years
before the truth finally dawned on one of them. His name was Charles
Darwin. To be fair, others had had inklings of the truth, but it was Darwin
who first put together a coherent and tenable account of why we exist.
Darwin made it possible for us to give a sensible answer to the curious child
whose question heads this chapter [Why are People?]. We no longer have to
resort to superstition when faced with the deep problems: Is there a meaning
to life? What are we for? What is man? After posing the last of these questions, the eminent zoologist G. G. Simpson put it thus: "The point I want to
make now is that all attempts to answer that question before 1859 are worthless and that we will be better off if we ignore them completely."

Today the theory of evolution is about as much open to doubt as the   3
theory that the earth goes round the sun, but the full implications of Darwin's
revolution have yet to be widely realized. Zoology is still a minority subject
in universities, and even those who choose to study it often make their
decision without appreciating its profound philosophical significance. Philosophy and the subjects known as 'humanities' are still taught almost as if
Darwin had never lived. No doubt this will change in time. In any case, this
book is not intended as a general advocacy of Darwinism. Instead, it will
explore the consequences of the evolution theory for a particular issue. My
purpose is to examine the biology of selfishness and altruism.

· · ·

Before beginning on my argument itself, I want to explain briefly what   4
sort of an argument it is, and what sort of an argument it is not. If we were

told that a man had lived a long and prosperous life in the world of Chicago gangsters, we would be entitled to make some guesses as to the sort of man he was. We might expect that he would have qualities such as toughness, a quick trigger finger, and the ability to attract loyal friends. These would not be infallible deductions, but you can make some inferences about a man's character if you know something about the conditions in which he has survived and prospered. The argument of this book is that we, and all other animals, are machines created by our genes. Like successful Chicago gangsters, our genes have survived, in some cases for millions of years, in a highly competitive world. This entitles us to expect certain qualities in our genes. I shall argue that a predominant quality to be expected in a successful gene is ruthless selfishness. This gene selfishness will usually give rise to selfishness in individual behavior. However, as we shall see, there are special circumstances in which a gene can achieve its own selfish goals best by fostering a limited form of altruism at the level of individual animals. "Special" and "limited" are important words in the last sentence. Much as we might wish to believe otherwise, universal love and the welfare of the species as a whole are concepts which simply do not make evolutionary sense.

This brings me to the first point I want to make about what this book 5 is *not*. I am not advocating a morality based on evolution. I am saying how things have evolved. I am not saying how we humans morally ought to behave. I stress this, because I know I am in danger of being misunderstood by those people, all too numerous, who cannot distinguish a statement of belief in what is the case from an advocacy of what ought to be the case. My own feeling is that a human society based simply on the gene's law of universal ruthless selfishness would be a very nasty society in which to live. But unfortunately, however much we may deplore something, it does not stop it being true. This book is mainly intended to be interesting, but if you would extract a moral from it, read it as a warning. Be warned that if you wish, as I do, to build a society in which individuals cooperate generously and unselfishly towards a common good, you can expect little help from biological nature. Let us try to *teach* generosity and altruism, because we are born selfish. Let us understand what our own selfish genes are up to, because we may then at least have the chance to upset their designs, something which no other species has ever aspired to.

. . .

Some people object to what they see as an excessively gene-centred 6 view of evolution. After all, they argue, it is whole individuals with all their genes who actually live or die. I hope I have said enough in this chapter to show that there is really no disagreement here. Just as whole boats win or lose races, it is indeed individuals who live or die, and the *immediate* manifestation of natural selection is nearly always at the individual level. But the long-term consequences of non-random individual death and reproductive success are manifested in the form of changing gene frequencies in the gene pool. With reservations, the gene pool plays the same role for the modern replicators as the primeval soup did for the original ones. Sex and chromosomal crossing-over have the effect of preserving the liquidity of the modern equivalent of the soup. Because of sex and crossing-over the gene pool is kept well stirred, and the genes partially shuffled. Evolution is the process by which some genes become more numerous and others less numerous in the gene pool. It is good to get into the habit, whenever we are trying to explain the evolution of some characteristic, such as altruistic behaviour, of asking ourselves simply: "what effect will this characteristic have on frequencies of genes in the gene pool?" At times, gene language gets a bit tedious, and for brevity and vividness we shall lapse into metaphor. But we shall always keep a sceptical eye on our metaphors, to make sure they can be translated back into gene language if necessary.

As far as the gene is concerned, the gene pool is just the new sort of soup   7
where it makes its living. All that has changed is that nowadays it makes its living by cooperating with successive groups of companions drawn from the gene pool in building one mortal survival machine after another. It is to survival machines themselves, and the sense in which genes may be said to control their behaviour, that we turn in the next chapter.

Survival machines began as passive receptacles for the genes, providing   8
little more than walls to protect them from the chemical warfare of their rivals and the ravages of accidental molecular bombardment. In the early days they 'fed' on organic molecules freely available in the soup.* This easy life came to an end when the organic food in the soup, which had been slowly built up under the energetic influence of centuries of sunlight, was all used up. A major branch of survival machines, now called plants, started to use sunlight directly themselves to build up complex molecules from simple ones, re-enacting at much higher speed the synthetic processes of the original soup. Another branch, now known as animals, "discovered" how to exploit the chemical labours of the plants, either by eating them, or by eating other animals. Both main branches of survival machines evolved more and more ingenious tricks to increase their efficiency in their various ways of life, and new ways of life were continually being opened up. Sub-branches and sub-sub-branches evolved, each one excelling in a particular specialized way of making a living: in the sea, on the ground, in the air, underground, up trees, inside other living bodies. This sub-branching has given rise to the immense diversity of animals and plants which so impresses us today.

Both animals and plants evolved into many-celled bodies, complete   9
copies of all the genes being distributed to every cell. We do not know when, why, or how many times independently, this happened. Some people use the metaphor of a colony, describing a body as a colony of cells. I prefer to think of the body as a colony of *genes,* and of the cell as a convenient working unit for the chemical industries of the genes.

Colonies of genes they may be but, in their behaviour, bodies have   10
undeniably acquired an individuality of their own. An animal moves as a coordinated whole, as a unit. Subjectively I feel like a unit, not a colony. This

*The primeval ocean in which life began.

is to be expected. Selection has favoured genes which cooperate with others. In the fierce competition for scarce resources, in the relentless struggle to eat other survival machines, and to avoid being eaten, there must have been a premium on central coordination rather than anarchy within the communal body. Nowadays the intricate mutual coevolution of genes has proceeded to such an extent that the communal nature of an individual survival machine is virtually unrecognizable. Indeed many biologists do not recognize it, and will disagree with me.

Fortunately for what journalists would call the 'credibility' of the rest 11 of this book, the disagreement is largely academic. Just as it is not convenient to talk about quanta and fundamental particles when we discuss the workings of a car, so it is often tedious and unnecessary to keep dragging genes in when we discuss the behaviour of survival machines. In practice it is usually convenient, as an approximation, to regard the individual body as an agent 'trying' to increase the numbers of all its genes in future generations. I shall use the language of convenience. Unless otherwise stated, "altruistic behaviour" and "selfish behaviour" will mean behaviour directed by one animal body toward another.

This chapter is about *behaviour*—the trick of rapid movement which has 12 been largely exploited by the animal branch of survival machines. Animals became active go-getting gene vehicles: gene machines. The characteristic of behaviour, as biologists use the term, is that it is fast. Plants move, but very slowly. When seen in highly speeded-up film, climbing plants look like active animals. But most plant movement is really irreversible growth. Animals, on the other hand, have evolved ways of moving hundreds of thousands of times faster. Moreover, the movements they make are reversible, and repeatable an indefinite number of times.

The gadget which animals evolved to achieve rapid movement was the 13 muscle. Muscles are engines which, like the steam engine and the internal combustion engine, use energy stored in chemical fuel to generate mechanical movement. The difference is that the immediate mechanical force of a muscle is generated in the form of tension, rather than gas pressure as in the case of the steam and internal combustion engines. But muscles are like engines in that they often exert their force on cords, and levers with hinges. In us the levers are known as bones, the cords as tendons, and the hinges as joints. Quite a lot is known about the exact molecular ways in which muscles work, but I find more interesting the question of how muscle contractions are *timed*.

Have you ever watched an artificial machine of some complexity, a 14 knitting or sewing machine, a loom, an automatic bottling factory, or a hay baler? Motive power comes from somewhere, an electric motor say, or a tractor. But much more baffling is the intricate timing of the operations. Valves open and shut in the right order, steel fingers deftly tie a knot round a hay bale, and then at just the right moment a knife shoots out and cuts the string. In many artificial machines timing is achieved by that brilliant invention the cam. This translates simple rotary motion into a complex rhythmic pattern of operations by means of an eccentric or specially shaped wheel. The principle of the musical box is similar. Other machines such as the steam organ and the pianola use paper rolls or cards with holes punched in a pattern. Recently there has been a trend towards replacing such simple mechanical timers with electronic ones. Digital computers are examples of large and versatile electronic devices which can be used for generating complex timed patterns of movements. The basic component of a modern electronic machine like a computer is the semiconductor, of which a familiar form is the transistor.

Survival machines seem to have bypassed the cam and the punched card 15 altogether. The apparatus they use for timing their movements has more in common with an electronic computer, although it is strictly different in fundamental operation. The basic unit of biological computers, the nerve cell or neurone, is really nothing like a transistor in its internal workings. Certainly the code in which neurones communicate with each other seems to be a little bit like the pulse codes of digital computers, but the individual neurone is a much more sophisticated data-processing unit than the transistor. Instead of just three connections with other components, a single neurone may have tens of thousands. The neurone is slower than the transistor, but it has gone much further in the direction of miniaturization, a trend which has dominated the electronics industry over the past two decades. This is brought home by the fact that there are some ten thousand million neurones in the human brain: you could pack only a few hundred transistors into a skull.

Plants have no need of the neurone, because they get their living with- 16 out moving around, but it is found in the great majority of animal groups. It may have been "discovered" early in animal evolution, and inherited by all groups, or it may have been rediscovered several times independently.

Neurones are basically just cells, with a nucleus and chromosomes like 17 other cells. But their cell walls are drawn out in long, thin, wire-like projections. Often a neurone has one particularly long "wire" called the axon. Although the width of an axon is microscopic, its length may be many feet: there are single axons which run the whole length of a giraffe's neck. The axons are usually bundled together in thick multi-stranded cables called nerves. These lead from one part of the body to another carrying messages, rather like trunk telephone cables. Other neurones have short axons, and are confined to dense concentrations of nervous tissue called ganglia, or, when they are very large, brains. Brains may be regarded as analogous in function to computers. They are analogous in that both types of machine generate complex patterns of output, after analysis of complex patterns of input, and after reference to stored information.

The main way in which brains actually contribute to the success of 18 survival machines is by controlling and coordinating the contractions of muscles. To do this they need cables leading to the muscles, and these are called motor nerves. But this leads to efficient preservation of genes only if the timing of muscle contractions bears some relation to the timing of events in the outside world. It is important to contract the jaw muscles only when the jaws contain something worth biting, and to contract the leg muscles in running patterns only when there is something worth running towards or away from. For this reason, natural selection favoured animals which became equipped with sense organs, devices which translate patterns of physical events in the outside world into the pulse code of the neurones. The brain is connected to the sense organs—eyes, ears, taste-buds etc.—by means of cables called sensory nerves. The workings of the sensory systems are particularly baffling, because they can achieve far more sophisticated feats of pattern-recognition than the best and most expensive man-made machines; if this were not so, all typists would be redundant, superseded by speech-recognizing machines, or machines for reading handwriting. Human typists will be needed for many decades yet.

There may have been a time when sense organs communicated more or less directly with muscles; indeed, sea anemones are not far from this state today, since for their way of life it is efficient. But to achieve more complex and indirect relationships between the timing of events in the outside world and the timing of muscular contractions, some kind of brain was needed as an intermediary. A notable advance was the evolutionary 'invention' of memory. By this device, the timing of muscle contractions could be influenced not only by events in the immediate past, but by events in the distant past as well. The memory, or store, is an essential part of a digital computer too. Computer memories are more reliable than human ones, but they are less capacious, and enormously less sophisticated in their techniques of information-retrieval.   19

One of the most striking properties of survival-machine behaviour is its apparent purposiveness. By this I do not just mean that it seems to be well calculated to help the animal's genes to survive, although of course it is. I am talking about a closer analogy to human purposeful behaviour. When we watch an animal "searching" for food, or for a mate, or for a lost child, we can hardly help imputing to it some of the subjective feelings we ourselves experience when we search. These may include "desire" for some object, a "mental picture" of the desired object, an "aim" or "end in view." Each one of us knows, from the evidence of his own introspection, that, at least in one modern survival machine, this purposiveness has evolved the property we call "consciousness." I am not philosopher enough to discuss what this means, but fortunately it does not matter for our present purposes because it is easy to talk about machines which behave *as if* motivated by a purpose, and to leave open the question whether they actually are conscious. These machines are basically very simple, and the principles of unconscious purposive behaviour are among the commonplaces of engineering science. The classic example is the Watt steam governor.   20

The fundamental principle involved is called negative feedback, of which there are various different forms. In general what happens is this. The "purpose machine," the machine or thing that behaves as if it had a conscious purpose, is equipped with some kind of measuring device which measures the discrepancy between the current state of things, and the "desired" state. It is built in such a way that the larger this discrepancy is, the harder the machine works. In this way the machine will automatically tend to reduce the   21 discrepancy—this is why it is called *negative* feedback—and it may actually come to rest if the 'desired' state is reached. The Watt governor consists of a pair of balls which are whirled round by a steam engine. Each ball is on the end of a hinged arm. The faster the balls fly round, the more does centrifugal force push the arms towards a horizontal position, this tendency being resisted by gravity. The arms are connected to the steam valve feeding the engine, in such a way that the steam tends to be shut off when the arms approach the horizontal position. So, if the engine goes too fast, some of its steam will be shut off, and it will tend to slow down. If it slows down too much, more steam will automatically be fed to it by the valve, and it will speed up again. Such purpose machines often oscillate due to over-shooting and time-lags, and it is part of the engineer's art to build in supplementary devices to reduce the oscillations.

The "desired" state of the Watt governor is a particular speed of rota-   22
tion. Obviously it does not consciously desire it. The "goal" of a machine is simply defined as that state to which it tends to return. Modern purpose machines use extensions of basic principles like negative feedback to achieve much more complex "life-like" behaviour. Guided missiles, for example, appear to search actively for their target, and when they have it in range they seem to pursue it, taking account of its evasive twists and turns, and sometimes even "predicting" or "anticipating" them. The details of how this is done are not worth going into. They involve negative feedback of various kinds, "feed-forward", and other principles well understood by engineers and now known to be extensively involved in the working of living bodies. Nothing remotely approaching consciousness needs to be postulated, even though a layman, watching its apparently deliberate and purposeful behaviour, finds it hard to believe that the missile is not under the direct control of a human pilot.

It is a common misconception that because a machine such as a guided   23
missile was originally designed and built by conscious man, then it must be truly under the immediate control of conscious man. Another variant of this fallacy is "computers do not really play chess, because they can only do what a human operator tells them." It is important that we understand why this is fallacious, because it affects our understanding of the sense in which genes can be said to "control" behaviour. Computer chess is quite a good example for making the point, so I will discuss it briefly.

Computers do not yet play chess as well as human grand masters, but   24
they have reached the standard of a good amateur. More strictly, one should say *programs* have reached the standard of a good amateur, for a chess-playing program is not fussy which physical computer it uses to act out its skills. Now, what is the role of the human programmer? First, he is definitely not manipulating the computer from moment to moment, like a puppeteer pulling strings. That would be just cheating. He writes the program, puts it in the computer, and then the computer is on its own: there is no further human intervention, except for the opponent typing in his moves. Does the programmer perhaps anticipate all possible chess positions, and provide the computer

with a long list of good moves, one for each possible contingency? Most certainly not, because the number of possible positions in chess is so great that the world would come to an end before the list had been completed. For the same reason, the computer cannot possibly be programmed to try out "in its head" all possible moves, and all possible follow-ups, until it finds a winning strategy. There are more possible games of chess than there are atoms in the galaxy. So much for the trivial non-solutions to the problem of programming a computer to play chess. It is in fact an exceedingly difficult problem, and it is hardly surprising that the best programs have still not achieved grand master status.

The programmer's actual role is rather more like that of a father teaching his son to play chess. He tells the computer the basic moves of the game, not separately for every possible starting position, but in terms of more economically expressed rules. He does not literally say in plain English "bishops move in a diagonal," but he does say something mathematically equivalent, such as, though more briefly: "New coordinates of bishop are obtained from old coordinates, by adding the same constant, though not necessarily with the same sign, to both old x coordinate and old y coordinate." Then he might program in some "advice," written in the same sort of mathematical or logical language, but amounting in human terms to hints such as "don't leave your king unguarded," or useful tricks such as "forking" with the knight. The details are intriguing, but they would take us too far afield. The important point is this. When it is actually playing, the computer is on its own, and can expect no help from its master. All the programmer can do is to set the computer up *beforehand* in the best way possible, with a proper balance between lists of specific knowledge, and hints about strategies and techniques. 25

The genes too control the behaviour of their survival machines, not directly with their fingers on puppet strings, but indirectly like the computer programmer. All they can do is to set it up beforehand; then the survival machine is on its own, and the genes can only sit passively inside. Why are they so passive? Why don't they grab the reins and take charge from moment to moment? The answer is that they cannot because of time-lag problems. This is best shown by another analogy, taken from science fiction. *A for Andromeda* by Fred Hoyle and John Elliot is an exciting story, and, like all good science fiction, it has some interesting scientific points lying behind it. Strangely, the book seems to lack explicit mention of the most important of these underlying points. It is left to the reader's imagination. I hope the authors will not mind if I spell it out here. 26

There is a civilization 200 light years away, in the constellation of Andromeda. They want to spread their culture to distant worlds. How best to do it? Direct travel is out of the question. The speed of light imposes a theoretical upper limit to the rate at which you can get from one place to another in the universe, and mechanical considerations impose a much lower limit in practice. Besides, there may not be all that many worlds worth going to, and how do you know which direction to go in? Radio is a better way of communicating with the rest of the universe, since, if you have enough power 27 to broadcast your signals in all directions rather than beam them in one direction, you can reach a very large number of worlds (the number increasing as the square of the distance the signal travels). Radio waves travel at the speed of light, which means the signal takes 200 years to reach earth from Andromeda. The trouble with this sort of distance is that you can never hold a conversation. Even if you discount the fact that each successive message from earth would be transmitted by people separated from each other by twelve generations, it would be just plain wasteful to attempt to converse over such distances.

This problem will soon arise in earnest for us: it takes about four 28 minutes for radio waves to travel between earth and Mars. There can be no doubt that spacemen will have to get out of the habit of conversing in short alternating sentences, and will have to use long soliloquies or monologues, more like letters than conversations. As another example, Roger Payne has pointed out that the acoustics of the sea have certain peculiar properties, which mean that the exceedingly loud "song" of the humpback whale could theoretically be heard all the way round the world, provided the whales swim at a certain depth. It is not known whether they actually do communicate with each other over very great distances, but if they do they must be in much the same predicament as an astronaut on Mars. The speed of sound in water is such that it would take nearly two hours for the song to travel across the Atlantic Ocean and for a reply to return. I suggest this as an explanation for the fact that the whales deliver a continuous soliloquy, without repeating themselves, for a full eight minutes. They then go back to the beginning of the song and repeat it all over again, many times over, each complete cycle lasting about eight minutes.

The Andromedans of the story did the same thing. Since there was no 29 point in waiting for a reply, they assembled everything they wanted to say into one huge unbroken message, and then they broadcast it out into space, over and over again, with a cycle time of several months. Their message was very different from that of the whales, however. It consisted of coded instructions for the building and programming of a giant computer. Of course the instructions were in no human language, but almost any code can be broken by a skilled cryptographer, especially if the designers of the code intended it to be easily broken. Picked up by the Jodrell Bank radio telescope, the message was eventually decoded, the computer built, and the program run. The results were nearly disastrous for mankind, for the intentions of the Andromedans were not universally altruistic, and the computer was well on the way to dictatorship over the world before the hero eventually finished it off with an axe.

From our point of view, the interesting question is in what sense the 30 Andromedans could be said to be manipulating events on Earth. They had no direct control over what the computer did from moment to moment; indeed they had no possible way of even knowing the computer had been built, since the information would have taken 200 years to get back to them. The decisions and actions of the computer were entirely its own. It could not even refer back to its masters for general policy instructions. All its instructions had to be built-in in advance, because of the inviolable 200 year barrier. In principle, it must have been programmed very much like a chess-playing computer, but with greater flexibility and capacity for absorbing local information. This was because the program had to be designed to work not just on earth, but on any world possessing an advanced technology, any of a set of worlds whose detailed conditions the Andromedans had no way of knowing.

Just as the Andromedans had to have a computer on earth to take day-to-day decisions for them, our genes have to build a brain. But the genes are not only the Andromedans who sent the coded instructions; they are also the instructions themselves. The reason why they cannot manipulate our puppet strings directly is the same: time-lags. Genes work by controlling protein synthesis. This is a powerful way of manipulating the world, but it is slow. It takes months of patiently pulling protein strings to build an embryo. The whole point about behaviour, on the other hand, is that it is fast. It works on a time-scale not of months but of seconds and fractions of seconds. Something happens in the world, an owl flashes overhead, a rustle in the long grass betrays prey, and in milliseconds nervous systems crackle into action, muscles leap, and someone's life is saved—or lost. Genes don't have reaction-times like that. Like the Andromedans, the genes can only do their best *in advance* by building a fast executive computer for themselves, and programming it in advance with rules and "advice" to cope with as many eventualities as they can "anticipate." But life, like the game of chess, offers too many different possible eventualities for all of them to be anticipated. Like the chess programmer, the genes have to "instruct" their survival machines not in specifics, but in the general strategies and tricks of the living trade.

As J. Z. Young has pointed out, the genes have to perform a task analogous to prediction. When an embryo survival machine is being built, the dangers and problems of its life lie in the future. Who can say what carnivores crouch waiting for it behind what bushes, or what fleet-footed prey will dart and zig-zag across its path? No human prophet, nor any gene. But some general predictions can be made. Polar bear genes can safely predict that the future of their unborn survival machine is going to be a cold one. They do not think of it as a prophecy, they do not think at all: they just build in a thick coat of hair, because that is what they have always done before in previous bodies, and that is why they still exist in the gene pool. They also predict that the ground is going to be snowy, and their prediction takes the form of making the coat of hair white and therefore camouflaged. If the climate of the Arctic changed so rapidly that the baby bear found itself born into a tropical desert, the predictions of the genes would be wrong, and they would pay the penalty. The young bear would die, and they inside it.

Prediction in a complex world is a chancy business. Every decision that a survival machine takes is a gamble, and it is the business of genes to program brains in advance so that on average they take decisions which pay

31

32

33

off. The currency used in the casino of evolution is survival, strictly gene survival, but for many purposes individual survival is a reasonable approximation. If you go down to the water-hole to drink, you increase your risk of being eaten by predators who make their living lurking for prey by water-holes. If you do not go down to the water-hole you will eventually die of thirst. There are risks whichever way you turn, and you must take the decision which maximizes the long-term survival chances of your genes. Perhaps the best policy is to postpone drinking until you are very thirsty, then go and have one good long drink to last you a long time. That way you reduce the number of separate visits to the water-hole, but you have to spend a long time with your head down when you finally do drink. Alternatively the best gamble might be to drink little and often, snatching quick gulps of water while running past the water-hole. Which is the best gambling strategy depends on all sorts of complex things, not least the hunting habit of the predators, which itself is evolved to be maximally efficient from their point of view. Some form of weighing up of the odds has to be done. But of course we do not have to think of the animals as making the calculations consciously. All we have to believe is that those individuals whose genes build brains in such a way that they tend to gamble correctly are as a direct result more likely to survive, and therefore to propagate those same genes.

We can carry the metaphor of gambling a little further. A gambler must 34 think of three main quantities, stake, odds, and prize. If the prize is very large, a gambler is prepared to risk a big stake. A gambler who risks his all on a single throw stands to gain a great deal. He also stands to lose a great deal, but on average high-stake gamblers are no better and no worse off than other players who play for low winnings with low stakes. An analogous comparison is that between speculative and safe investors on the stock market. In some ways the stock market is a better analogy than a casino, because casinos are deliberately rigged in the bank's favour (which means, strictly, that high-stake players will on average end up poorer than low-stake players; and low-stake players poorer than those who do not gamble at all. But this is for a reason not germane to our discussion). Ignoring this, both high-stake play and low-stake play seem reasonable. Are there animal gamblers who play for high stakes, and others with a more conservative game? In Chapter 9 we shall see that it is often possible to picture males as high-stake high-risk gamblers, and females as safe investors, especially in polygamous species in which males compete for females. Naturalists who read this book may be able to think of species which can be described as high-stake high-risk players, and other species which play a more conservative game. I now return to the more general theme of how genes make "predictions" about the future.

One way for genes to solve the problem of making predictions in rather 35 unpredictable environments is to build in a capacity for learning. Here the program may take the form of the following instructions to the survival machine: "Here is a list of things defined as rewarding: sweet taste in the mouth, orgasm, mild temperature, smiling child. And here is a list of nasty things: various sorts of pain, nausea, empty stomach, screaming child. If you should happen to do something which is followed by one of the nasty things, don't do it again, but on the other hand repeat anything which is followed by one of the nice things." The advantage of this sort of programming is that it greatly cuts down the number of detailed rules which have to be built into the original program; and it is also capable of coping with changes in the environment which could not have been predicted in detail. On the other hand, certain predictions have to be made still. In our example the genes are predicting that sweet taste in the mouth, and orgasm, are going to be "good" in the sense that eating sugar and copulating are likely to be beneficial to gene survival. The possibilities of saccharine and masturbation are not anticipated according to this example; nor are the dangers of over-eating sugar in our environment where it exists in unnatural plenty.

Learning-strategies have been used in some chess-playing computer [36] programs. These programs actually get better as they play against human opponents or against other computers. Although they are equipped with a repertoire of rules and tactics, they also have a small random tendency built into their decision procedure. They record past decisions, and whenever they win a game they slightly increase the weighting given to the tactics which preceded the victory, so that next time they are a little bit more likely to choose those same tactics again.

One of the most interesting methods of predicting the future is simula- [37] tion. If a general wishes to know whether a particular military plan will be better than alternatives, he has a problem in prediction. There are unknown quantities in the weather, in the morale of his own troops, and in the possible countermeasures of the enemy. One way of discovering whether it is a good plan is to try it and see, but it is undesirable to use this test for all the tentative plans dreamed up, if only because the supply of young men prepared to die 'for their country' is exhaustible, and the supply of possible plans is very large. It is better to try the various plans out in dummy runs rather than in deadly earnest. This may take the form of full-scale exercises with "North-land" fighting "Southland" using blank ammunition, but even this is expensive in time and materials. Less wastefully, war games may be played, with tin soldiers and little toy tanks being shuffled around a large map.

Recently, computers have taken over large parts of the simulation func- [38] tion, not only in military strategy, but in all fields where prediction of the future is necessary, fields like economics, ecology, sociology, and many others. The technique works like this. A model of some aspect of the world is set up in the computer. This does not mean that if you unscrewed the lid you would see a little miniature dummy inside with the same shape as the object simulated. In the chess-playing computer there is no 'mental picture' inside the memory banks recognizable as a chess board with knights and pawns sitting on it. The chess board and its current position would be represented by lists of electronically coded numbers. To us a map is a miniature scale model of a part of the world, compressed into two dimensions. In a computer, a map would more probably be represented as a list of towns and other spots, each with two numbers—its latitude and longitude. But it does not matter how the computer actually holds its model of the world in its head, provided that it holds it in a form in which it can operate on it, manipulate it, do experiments with it, and report back to the human operators in terms which they can understand. Through the technique of simulation, model battles can be won or lost, simulated airliners fly or crash, economic policies lead to prosperity or to ruin. In each case the whole process goes on inside the computer in a tiny fraction of the time it would take in real life. Of course there are good models of the world and bad ones, and even the good ones are only approximations. No amount of simulation can predict exactly what will happen in reality, but a good simulation is enormously preferable to blind trial and error. Simulation could be called vicarious trial and error, a term unfortunately pre-empted long ago by rat psychologists.

If simulation is such a good idea, we might expect that survival ma- 39
chines would have discovered it first. After all, they invented many of the other techniques of human engineering long before we came on the scene: the focusing lens and the parabolic reflector, frequency analysis of sound waves, servo-control, sonar, buffer storage of incoming information, and countless others with long names, whose details don't matter. What about simulation? Well, when you yourself have a difficult decision to make involving unknown quantities in the future, you do go in for a form of simulation. You *imagine* what would happen if you did each of the alternatives open to you. You set up a model in your head, not of everything in the world, but of the restricted set of entities which you think may be relevant. You may see them vividly in your mind's eye, or you may see and manipulate stylized abstractions of them. In either case it is unlikely that somewhere laid out in your brain is an actual spatial model of the events you are imagining. But, just as in the computer, the details of how your brain represents its model of the world are less important than the fact that it is able to use it to predict possible events. Survival machines which can simulate the future are one jump ahead of survival machines who can only learn on the basis of overt trial and error. The trouble with overt trial is that it takes time and energy. The trouble with overt error is that it is often fatal. Simulation is both safer and faster.

The evolution of the capacity to simulate seems to have culminated in 40
subjective consciousness. Why this should have happened is, to me, the most profound mystery facing modern biology. There is no reason to suppose that electronic computers are conscious when they simulate, although we have to admit that in the future they may become so. Perhaps consciousness arises when the brain's simulation of the world becomes so complete that it must include a model of itself. Obviously the limbs and body of a survival machine must constitute an important part of its simulated world; presumably for the same kind of reason, the simulation itself could be regarded as part of the world to be simulated. Another word for this might indeed be "self-awareness," but I don't find this a fully satisfying explanation of the evolution of consciousness, and this is only partly because it involves an infinite regress—if there is a model of the model, why not a model of the model of the model . . . ?

Whatever the philosophical problems raised by consciousness, for the 41
purpose of this story it can be thought of as the culmination of an evolutionary trend towards the emancipation of survival machines as executive deci-
sion-takers from their ultimate masters, the genes. Not only are brains in
charge of the day-to-day running of survival-machine affairs, they have also
acquired the ability to predict the future and act accordingly. They even have
the power to rebel against the dictates of the genes, for instance in refusing
to have as many children as they are able to. But in this respect man is a very
special case, as we shall see.

What has all this to do with altruism and selfishness? I am trying to 42
build up the idea that animal behaviour, altruistic or selfish, is under the
control of genes in only an indirect, but still very powerful, sense. By dictating the way survival machines and their nervous systems are built, genes
exert ultimate power over behaviour. But the moment-to-moment decisions
about what to do next are taken by the nervous system. Genes are the primary
policy-makers; brains are the executives. But as brains became more highly
developed, they took over more and more of the actual policy decisions, using
tricks like learning and simulation in doing so. The logical conclusion to this
trend, not yet reached in any species, would be for the genes to give the
survival machine a single overall policy instruction: do whatever you think
best to keep us alive.

Analogies with computers and with human decision-taking are all very 43
well. But now we must come down to earth and remember that evolution in
fact occurs step-by-step, through the differential survival of genes in the gene
pool. Therefore, in order for a behaviour pattern—altruistic or selfish—to
evolve, it is necessary that a gene "for" that behaviour should survive in the
gene pool more successfully than a rival gene or allele 'for' some different
behaviour. A gene for altruistic behaviour means any gene which influences
the development of nervous systems in such a way as to make them likely
to behave altruistically. Is there any experimental evidence for the genetic
inheritance of altruistic behaviour? No, but that is hardly surprising, since
little work has been done on the genetics of any behaviour. Instead, let me
tell you about one study of a behaviour pattern which does not happen to
be obviously altruistic, but which is complex enough to be interesting. It
serves as a model for how altruistic behaviour might be inherited.

Honey bees suffer from an infectious disease called foul brood. This 44
attacks the grubs in their cells. Of the domestic breeds used by beekeepers,
some are more at risk from foul brood than others, and it turns out that the
difference between strains is, at least in some cases, a behavioural one. There
are so-called hygienic strains which quickly stamp out epidemics by locating
infected grubs, pulling them from their cells and throwing them out of the
hive. The susceptible strains are susceptible because they do not practise this
hygienic infanticide. The behaviour actually involved in hygiene is quite
complicated. The workers have to locate the cell of each diseased grub,
remove the wax cap from the cell, pull out the larva, drag it through the door
of the hive, and throw it on the rubbish tip.

Doing genetic experiments with bees is quite a complicated business for   45
various reasons. Worker bees themselves do not ordinarily reproduce, and so
you have to cross a queen of one strain with a drone (= male) of the other,
and then look at the behaviour of the daughter workers. This is what W. C.
Rothenbuhler did. He found that all first-generation hybrid daughter hives
were non-hygienic: the behaviour of their hygienic parent seemed to have
been lost, although as things turned out the hygienic genes were still there
but were recessive, like human genes for blue eyes. When Rothenbuhler
'back-crossed' first-generation hybrids with a pure hygienic strain (again of
course using queens and drones), he obtained a most beautiful result. The
daughter hives fell into three groups. One group showed perfect hygienic
behaviour, a second showed no hygienic behaviour at all, and the third went
half way. This last group uncapped the wax cells of diseased grubs, but they
did not follow through and throw out the larvae. Rothenbuhler surmised that
there might be two separate genes, one gene for uncapping, and one gene for
throwing-out. Normal hygienic strains possess both genes, susceptible strains
possess the alleles—rivals—of both genes instead. The hybrids who only
went half way presumably possessed the uncapping gene (in double dose) but
not the throwing-out gene. Rothenbuhler guessed that his experimental
group of apparently totally non-hygienic bees might conceal a subgroup
possessing the throwing-out gene, but unable to show it because they lacked
the uncapping gene. He confirmed this most elegantly by removing caps
himself. Sure enough, half of the apparently non-hygienic bees thereupon
showed perfectly normal throwing-out behaviour.

This story illustrates a number of important points which came up in   46
the previous chapter. It shows that it can be perfectly proper to speak of "a
gene for behaviour so-and-so" even if we haven't the faintest idea of the
chemical chain of embryonic causes leading from gene to behaviour. The
chain of causes could even turn out to involve learning. For example, it could
be that the uncapping gene exerts its effect by giving bees a taste for infected
wax. This means they will find the eating of the wax caps covering disease-
victims rewarding, and will therefore tend to repeat it. Even if this is how the
gene works, it is still truly a gene "for uncapping" provided that, other things
being equal, bees possessing the gene end up by uncapping, and bees not
possessing the gene do not uncap.

Secondly it illustrates the fact that genes "cooperate" in their effects on   47
the behaviour of the communal survival machine. The throwing-out gene is
useless unless it is accompanied by the uncapping gene and vice versa. Yet
the genetic experiments show equally clearly that the two genes are in principle quite separable in their journey through the generations. As far as their
useful work is concerned you can think of them as a single cooperating unit,
but as replicating genes they are two free and independent agents.

For purposes of argument it will be necessary to speculate about genes   48
"for" doing all sorts of improbable things. If I speak, for example, of a
hypothetical gene "for saving companions from drowning," and you find
such a concept incredible, remember the story of the hygienic bees. Recall

that we are not talking about the gene as the sole antecedent cause of all the complex muscular contractions, sensory integrations, and even conscious decisions, which are involved in saving somebody from drowning. We are saying nothing about the question of whether learning, experience, or environmental influences enter into the development of the behaviour. All you have to concede is that it is possible for a single gene, other things being equal and lots of other essential genes and environmental factors being present, to make a body more likely to save somebody from drowning than its allele would. The difference between the two genes may turn out at bottom to be a slight difference in some simple quantitative variable. The details of the embryonic developmental process, interesting as they may be, are irrelevant to evolutionary considerations. Konrad Lorenz has put this point well.

The genes are master programmers, and they are programming for their 49 lives. They are judged according to the success of their programs in coping with all the hazards which life throws at their survival machines, and the judge is the ruthless judge of the court of survival. We shall come later to ways in which gene survival can be fostered by what appears to be altruistic behaviour. But the obvious first priorities of a survival machine, and of the brain that takes the decisions for it, are individual survival and reproduction. All the genes in the "colony" would agree about these priorities. Animals therefore go to elaborate lengths to find and catch food; to avoid being caught and eaten themselves; to avoid disease and accident; to protect themselves from unfavourable climatic conditions; to find members of the opposite sex and persuade them to mate; and to confer on their children advantages similar to those they enjoy themselves. I shall not give examples—if you want one just look carefully at the next wild animal that you see. But I do want to mention one particular kind of behaviour because we shall need to refer to it again when we come to speak of altruism and selfishness. This is the behaviour that can be broadly labelled *communication*.

A survival machine may be said to have communicated with another 50 one when it influences its behaviour or the state of its nervous system. This is not a definition I would like to have to defend for very long, but it is good enough for present purposes. By influence I mean direct causal influence. Examples of communication are numerous: song in birds, frogs, and crickets; tailwagging and hackle-raising in dogs; "grinning" in chimpanzees; human gestures and language. A great number of survival-machine actions promote their genes' welfare indirectly by influencing the behavior of other survival machines. Animals go to great lengths to make this communication effective. The songs of birds enchant and mystify successive generations of men. I have already referred to the even more elaborate and mysterious song of the humpback whale, with its prodigious range, its frequencies spanning the whole of human hearing from subsonic rumblings to ultrasonic squeaks. Mole-crickets amplify their song to stentorian loudness by singing down in a burrow which they carefully dig in the shape of a double exponential horn, or megaphone. Bees dance in the dark to give other bees accurate information about the direction and distance of food, a feat of communication rivalled only by human language itself.

The traditional story of ethologists is that communication signals evolve 51 for the mutual benefit of both sender and recipient. For instance, baby chicks influence their mother's behaviour by giving high piercing cheeps when they are lost or cold. This usually has the immediate effect of summoning the mother, who leads the chick back to the main clutch. This behaviour could be said to have evolved for mutual benefit, in the sense that natural selection has favoured babies who cheep when they are lost, and also mothers who respond appropriately to the cheeping.

If we wish to (it is not really necessary), we can regard signals such as 52 the cheep call as having a meaning, or as carrying information: in this case "I am lost." The alarm call given by small birds, which I mentioned in Chapter I, could be said to convey the information "There is a hawk." Animals who receive this information and act on it are benefited. Therefore the information can be said to be true. But do animals ever communicate false information; do they ever tell lies?

The notion of an animal telling a lie is open to misunderstanding, so I 53 must try to forestall this. I remember attending a lecture given by Beatrice and Allen Gardner about their famous 'talking' chimpanzee Washoe (she uses American Sign Language, and her achievement is of great potential interest to students of language). There were some philosophers in the audience, and in the discussion after the lecture they were much exercised by the question of whether Washoe could tell a lie. I suspected that the Gardners thought there were more interesting things to talk about, and I agreed with them. In this book I am using words like "deceive" and "lie" in a much more straight-forward sense than those philosophers. They were interested in conscious intention to deceive. I am talking simply about having an effect functionally equivalent to deception. If a bird used the "There is a hawk" signal when there was no hawk, thereby frightening his colleagues away, leaving him to eat all their food, we might say he had told a lie. We would not mean he had deliberately intended consciously to deceive. All that is implied is that the liar gained food at the other birds' expense, and the reason the other birds flew away was that they reacted to the liar's cry in a way appropriate to the presence of a hawk.

Many edible insects, like the butterflies of the previous chapter, derive 54 protection by mimicking the external appearance of other distasteful or sting-ing insects. We ourselves are often fooled into thinking that yellow and black striped hover-flies are wasps. Some bee-mimicking flies are even more perfect in their deception. Predators too tell lies. Angler fish wait patiently on the bottom of the sea, blending in with the background. The only conspicuous part is a wriggling worm-like piece of flesh on the end of a long "fishing rod," projecting from the top of the head. When a small prey fish comes near, the angler will dance its worm-like bait in front of the little fish, and lure it down to the region of the angler's own concealed mouth. Suddenly it opens its jaws, and the little fish is sucked in and eaten. The angler is telling a lie, exploiting the little fish's tendency to approach wriggling worm-like objects. He is saying "Here is a worm," and any little fish who "believes" the lie is quickly eaten.

Some survival machines exploit the sexual desires of others. Bee orchids 55 induce bees to copulate with their flowers, because of their strong resemblance to female bees. What the orchid has to gain from this deception is pollination, for a bee who is fooled by two orchids will incidentally carry pollen from one to the other. Fireflies (which are really beetles) attract their mates by flashing lights at them. Each species has its own particular dot-dash flashing pattern, which prevents confusion between species, and consequent harmful hybridization. Just as sailors look out for the flash patterns of particular lighthouses, so fireflies seek the coded flash patterns of their own species. Females of the genus *Photuris* have "discovered" that they can lure males of the genus *Photinus* if they imitate the flashing code of a *Photinus* female. This they do, and when a *Photinus* male is fooled by the lie into approaching, he is summarily eaten by the *Photuris* female. Sirens and Lorelei spring to mind as analogies, but Cornishmen will prefer to think of the wreckers of the old days, who used lanterns to lure ships on to the rocks, and then plundered the cargoes which spilled out of the wrecks.

Whenever a system of communication evolves, there is always the 56 danger that some will exploit the system for their own ends. Brought up as we have been on the "good of the species" view of evolution, we naturally think first of liars and deceivers as belonging to different species: predators, prey, parasites, and so on. However, we must expect lies and deceit, and selfish exploitation of communication to arise whenever the interests of the genes of different individuals diverge. This will include individuals of the same species. As we shall see, we must even expect that children will deceive their parents, that husbands will cheat on wives, and that brother will lie to brother.

Even the belief that animal communication signals originally evolve to 57 foster mutual benefit, and then afterwards become exploited by malevolent parties, is too simple. It may well be that all animal communication contains an element of deception right from the start, because all animal interactions involve at least some conflict of interest. The next chapter introduces a powerful way of thinking about conflicts of interest from an evolutionary point of view.

Questions for Discussion

1. Write a paragraph or two (to be shared in class discussion) assessing some of Dawkins's important metaphors and analogies ("survival machine," "gene machine," "biological computers," "the casino of evolution," "the living trade," and so on). How effective are his metaphors? Do they do what Dawkins wants them to do? What *does* he want them to do? Apart from effectiveness, however, are his metaphors appropriate? That is, are

they accurate, fair, and illuminating? Or are they strained, farfetched, and confusing?

2. Does Dawkins adequately support his view (in ¶26) that genes "control the behaviour of their survival machines, not directly with their fingers on puppet strings, but indirectly like the computer programmer"? What support does he provide? What kind of support is *available* for supporting such a claim? Is this claim convincing? Why or why not?

3. Can Dawkins's claim in paragraphs 34 to 38 that genes "make predictions" be translated into scientific language? Is there anyone in class who can explain in scientific terms what he means by this claim? When the claim is translated into the scientific language of natural selection, does it mean exactly the same thing as it means in Dawkins's metaphorical language?

4. The emergence of "subjective consciousness," claims Dawkins in paragraph 40, is "the most profound mystery facing modern biology." Ask your instructor to help you divide your class into two groups. One group is to jump ahead in the *Reader* and read Joseph Wood Krutch's essay, "The Meaning of Awareness," in Chapter 10. Krutch attempts to provide an answer to Dawkins's "profound mystery," and he attempts to do it in the scientific "language" of natural selection. Have the students who agree to read Krutch report on his position to the other half of the class. Then have the listening half of the class construct a collective response either supporting or attacking Krutch's solution to the mystery. Peer discussion groups will be necessary for the completion of this activity.

Suggested Essay Assignments

1. In the preface, Dawkins identifies three distinct audiences who he imagined were looking over his shoulder as he wrote his book.

> Three imaginary readers looked over my shoulder while I was writing, and I now dedicate the book to them. First the general reader, the layman. For him I have avoided technical jargon almost totally, and where I have had to use specialized words I have defined them. I now wonder why we don't censor most of our jargon from learned journals too. I have assumed that the layman has no special knowledge, but I have not assumed that he is stupid. Anyone can popularize science if he oversimplifies. I have worked hard to try to popularize some subtle and complicated ideas in non-mathematical language, without losing their essence. I do not know how far I have succeeded in this, nor how far I have succeeded in another of my ambitions: to try to make the book as entertaining and gripping as its subject matter deserves. I have long felt that biology ought to seem as exciting as a mystery story, for a mystery story is exactly what biology is. I do not dare to hope that I have conveyed more than a tiny fraction of the excitement which the subject has to offer.
>
> My second imaginary reader was the expert. He has been a harsh critic, sharply drawing in his breath at some of my analogies and figures of speech. His favourite phrases are 'with the exception of'; 'but on the other hand'; and 'ugh'. I listened to him attentively, and even completely re-

wrote one chapter entirely for his benefit, but in the end I have had to tell the story my way. The expert will still not be totally happy with the way I put things. Yet my greatest hope is that even he will find something new here; a new way of looking at familiar ideas perhaps; even stimulation of new ideas of his own. If this is too high an aspiration, may I at least hope that the book will entertain him on a train?

The third reader I had in mind was the student, making the transition from layman to expert. If he still has not made up his mind what field he wants to be an expert in, I hope to encourage him to give my own field of zoology a second glance. There is a better reason for studying zoology than its possible 'usefulness', and the general likeableness of animals. This reason is that we animals are the most complicated and perfectly-designed pieces of machinery in the known universe. Put it like that, and it is hard to see why anybody studies anything else! For the student who has already committed himself to zoology, I hope my book may have some educational value. He is having to work through the original papers and technical books on which my treatment is based. If he finds the original sources hard to digest, perhaps my nonmathematical interpretation may help, as an introduction and adjunct.

There are obvious dangers in trying to appeal to three different kinds of reader. I can only say that I have been very conscious of these dangers, but that they seemed to be outweighed by the advantages of the attempt.

Write an essay directed to a general audience of your peers, for example, your fellow classmates, in which you assess Dawkins' success or failure in meeting the needs of his three audiences. Assess also the appropriateness of his disclaimers to each of his audiences about what he *cannot* do in his book. Suggest in your essay what he might have done or what he should not have done to meet his audiences more effectively. If you think he has met the needs of his different audiences admirably, identify the particular strategies of tone, diction, example, argument, and so on that help Dawkins's writing to succeed.

2. In paragraph 5, Dawkins claims that he is "not advocating a morality based on evolution. I am saying how things have evolved. I am not saying how we humans morally ought to behave." By claiming that he is merely describing the way things *are,* not how they *should be,* Dawkins has taken himself off the hook for seeming to advocate any particular social policies or general attitudes based on the alleged, ingrained selfishness of human nature. He also seems to have taken selfish behavior itself off the hook: It is, after all, just an inevitable part of our nature. Write an essay directed to Dawkins himself in which, first, you critique his claim that he is merely *describing* things objectively—"as they are." Is his account really just a description, or is it in fact an interpretation? Second, critique his effort to separate his "description" from the advocacy of any particular kind of moral stance or general attitude about others. Can Dawkins really say in all fairness that his description recommends no particular response to the way people behave? Test his view by asking yourself, and perhaps other people as well, whether his position makes it easier, harder, or has no

influence on your ability to censure selfish or antisocial behavior. You may also want to assess how Dawkins' position influences your tendency to censure your own "selfish" behavior.

Laurence Thomas

Is altruistic behavior—doing things for the sake of others rather than ourselves, sometimes at the sacrifice of our own self-interest—merely an illusion because human beings are biologically "determined" to be selfish, as Dawkins claims in the preceding essay? Or is altruism a reality supported by our biological nature, as Laurence Thomas (b. 1949) argues in the present essay? In the eyes of its detractors, biological determinism—the "selfish gene" view of human nature—is objectionable because it undermines human will (by teaching that it is merely illusory) and because it denies the reality of such virtues as compassion, generosity, self-sacrifice, and self-control (by teaching that they are merely disguised forms of selfishness).

Those who argue against the selfish gene view seldom argue on the same grounds as those who advance it. That is, the opponents of the selfish gene view typically argue the case for human freedom and virtue on ethical or religious grounds, not scientific grounds. They justify their belief in the reality of freedom and virtue on ethical principles, on teachings found in the Bible (or other religious texts), and on teachings advanced by different religions. Laurence Thomas's position, however, is noteworthy precisely because he opposes biological determinism by appealing to the same scientific views that are usually employed to support it, especially the Darwinian principle of natural selection.

The "exchange" between Dawkins and Thomas illustrates an important feature about the relationship between data *and* facts *on the one hand and* interpretation *on the other: The meaning and significance of data and facts are never self-announcing. They become meaningful only when they are interpreted. Equally important all data and facts will support a variety of interpretations. Sometimes, as in the case of Dawkins and Thomas, different interpretations will be so far apart that they really oppose each other on every important point, yet the facts each arguer appeals to are the "same." Dawkins and Thomas both appeal to the principle of natural selection, yet they come to nearly contrary conclusions.*

This does not mean that all arguments are equally meaningless or unproductive because none of them ever yields unquestionable or unchallengeable truth. However, it does mean that all arguments are probably more tentative, conditional, and hypothetical—less conclusive and less certain—than most arguers would like to admit. There are not many issues for which a good case on the "other side" cannot be made. Awareness of this should not necessarily soften our commitments, but it should make our arguments more flexible. We do not have to give up our loves and hatreds simply because we know that people can make good arguments on the "other side" of our own views. But it should at least make us listen *more sensitively to our opponents' counterarguments. Their being on the other side does not automatically make them wrong and us right. When we know this, we begin to turn ourselves into better arguers for our favored positions.*

THE BIOLOGICAL BASIS OF ALTRUISM

From *Living Morally: A Psychology of Moral Character* (1989).

Love is surely a form of altruism. Morality can be grafted upon the   1
natural affection of parental love. The capacity to love is essential not just to the survival but to the very flourishing of the human species. Parental love, in particular, is indisputably important to the flourishing of the child; and this love, I argue, has been selected for.* With an eye toward showing its relevance to morality, an account of the nature of parental love is offered. This kind of love is characterized as transparent, which I contrast with opaque love. On the view being presented, then, morality has biological foundations. Understandably, there is a reluctance to view morality in this way. This reluctance stems from two sources. One is the threat of biological determinism. The other is the fear that if morality is given biological underpinnings, then the altruism is taken out of morality, and altruism thus becomes a mere illusion rather than a reality. For the idea of genes maximizing their own numbers in the gene pool is at the heart of sociobiological explanations; and, prima facie, it would not seem that altruism can be squared with a maximizing notion of this sort. While I shall address the first concern briefly, my primary aim in this chapter will be to show that biology is not incompatible with an altruistic morality. I begin, though, with a few remarks concerning the former. Needless to say, I cannot hope to settle the issue of biological determinism here. However, I hope to dispel a few worries.

MORALITY AND SOCIOBIOLOGY

Crudely put, biological determinism is the view that most, if not all,   2
aspects of human behavior are controlled or, at any rate, strongly influenced by our genetic make-up. We may think of this as thorough-going biological determinism. That some aspects of human behavior are so influenced is too obvious for words. What should be noted, though, is this: From the fact that some aspects of a given kind of human activity may be biologically determined, it is a mistake to infer that all aspects of that activity are biologically determined; hence, it is a mistake to invoke thoroughgoing biological determinism with respect to that activity. For example, consider the sex drive, the presence of which everyone regards as purely a matter of biological determi-

*That is, biologically, according to the Darwinian principle of natural selection.

nation. This drive is known for manifesting itself, upon occasion, quite independently of our wishes. Still, by no stretch of the imagination does it follow that people have no choice as to when or why or whether they engage in sexual activity. When people do so clearly depends upon, inter alia,* tastes, preferences, and opportunity. Reasons abound for why people engage in or refrain from sexual activity: personal ones (for example, to get even or to prove themselves), religious ones, political ones, and so on. Finally, a person may opt for celibacy and thus avoid sexual activity with others entirely.

Obviously enough, none of this entails that thoroughgoing biological 3 determinism does not obtain. But on the strength of the foregoing considerations, what can be said with complete confidence is this: We have no reason to suppose that just because some aspects of a given human activity are biologically determined, then thoroughgoing biological determinism obtains with respect to that activity. For in view of what we now know, it is clear that a person would be maintaining a false view if he held that since the sex drive is biologically determined, all sexual activity is.

Now, I have not addressed, and shall not address, the general problem 4 of determinism—namely, whether human action is free or determined. And, of course, to diffuse the threat of biological determinism is not in any way to resolve the general problem of determinism. But given our concerns, that should not be necessary. The issue for us is whether we straightaway have an objection to morality's having biological foundations on the grounds that thoroughgoing biological determinism holds, as I have developed this notion. It suffices for our purposes, then, if it can be shown that we do not. To put the matter another way, it might be thought that taking a biological approach to morality thereby makes one especially susceptible to the difficulties of thoroughgoing determinism. As we have seen, however, this surmise is mistaken.

I turn now to the second reason why people are reluctant to allow that 5 morality can have biological foundation, namely, that the altruism is taken out of morality, so that seemingly altruistic acts are, in the final analysis, really selfish ones. It is not difficult to see how one might come to think this. On a typical reading of a sociobiological account of human behavior, the ultimate motivating force behind each human being's behavior is the drive to maximize her or his gene pool.[1] All manifestations of altruism are to be thus explained, even parental altruism in human beings, since the sociobiological argument is that parents best maximize their gene pool by caring for their children until the latter are in turn able to have progeny (grandchildren). Yet on the face of it, not only does this explanation for parental altruism seem manifestly false, but it would also seem that altruism toward non-kin does not neatly admit of a sociobiological explanation.

Consider a typical instance of parental love. Two parents hear their 6 five-year-old child screaming desperately. It turns out that the child is being attacked by several vicious dogs. We suppose that if the parents genuinely

---

*Among other things.

love the child, then without any regard for their own well-being they will attempt to rescue her. In particular, we suppose that the parents will be motivated to rescue their child simply out of their love for her, and that in no way will a desire to maximize their gene pool figure into an explanation of their attempt. Most parents would surely regard it as the cruelest of statements if someone were to claim that in the last analysis what motivated them to rescue their child was the desire and hope that she would give them grandchildren, thereby contributing to the survival of their (the parents') genes. The problem is that a sociobiological account of human behavior would seem to commit us to saying just that—or so it is objected.

As for altruism toward non-kin, Mother Teresa* would seem to be a 7 tremendous embarrassment to the theory. Whatever else is true, her altruistic behavior does not serve her gene pool in any way at all. To be sure, Mother Teresa represents an extreme display of altruism. Still, it would not seem that less extreme displays of altruism admit neatly of a sociobiological explanation. Consider helping a stranger who has just been robbed, or making a substantial and anonymous donation to charity. Is there any reason whatsoever to suppose that such acts serve the gene pool of the agents who perform them, let alone that people perform such acts with that thought in mind? Surely not.

I believe that with regard to human altruism, a sociobiological explanation of human behavior does not present the sort of difficulties that many have attributed to it. True enough, sociobiologists have not helped matters by describing genes in metaphorical ways, as having intentions, purposes, and the like.[2] But I hope to show that notwithstanding this abuse of language, sociobiology does not take the altruism out of altruism. That is, I hope to show that it allows for genuine altruism.

Let us begin by distinguishing between motive altruism and unwitting 9 altruism, on the one hand, and motive selfishness and unwitting selfishness, on the other. With motive altruism, a benefit is intentionally bestowed upon someone at some cost or risk to oneself without regard to future gain (keeping in mind that simply foregoing a benefit can count as incurring a cost [see Trivers 1971], and that from the standpoint of sociobiological theory, to do something at a risk to oneself is to do something at a cost to oneself). With unwitting altruism, while it is true that someone has benefited from one's behavior (which was at some cost to oneself), the benefit was in no way intended; indeed, unwitting altruism does not make reference to intentions or motives of any sort. Motive altruism is what is generally regarded as genuine altruism. It is the kind of altruism required by altruism moral theories. Motive selfishness and unwitting selfishness are to be understood in analogous ways with respect to the term selfishness. Thus, motive selfishness is what is generally regarded as genuine selfishness.

---

*Mother Teresa (Agnes Gonxha Bojaxhui), born in Yugoslavia in 1910, founded the Missionaries of Charity in India in 1950 and was awarded the Pope John XXIII Peace Prize in 1971 and the Nobel Peace Prize in 1979.

Of significance is that while unwitting altruism entails neither motive   10
nor unwitting selfishness, unwitting altruism is compatible with unwitting
selfishness. That is, individual X may gain from having unwittingly benefited
individual Y, since benefiting someone at a risk to oneself does not entail a
loss to oneself; indeed, it is compatible with a gain. An illustration of this will
be given below. The charge that sociobiology takes the altruism out of altruism holds only if what is presented as motive altruism in fact turns out to be
motive selfishness. Unwitting selfishness does not take the altruism out of
altruism.

Sociobiologists frequently talk about animals (such as calling birds) and   11
insects (such as ants and bees) benefiting others. And the theories of kin
selection and reciprocal altruism are currently two of the most basic ways of
explaining altruism in species. Roughly speaking, kin selection tells us how
natural selection tends to operate upon social groups who interact with a fair
degree of frequency; reciprocal altruism tells us how natural selection operates upon individuals with a degree of dependence upon one another, of
whom longevity is characteristic, who tend to interact over a reasonably long
period of time.[3] The latter is meant to explain altruism between different
species and non-kin. With neither, however, does motive altruism turn out
to be motive selfishness. Each explains how unwitting altruism might come
about as a result of natural selection, and how this unwitting altruism results
in unwitting selfishness in that the individual's gene pool is benefited. If so,
then the claim that sociobiology takes the altruism out of altruism turns out
to be false. A brief discussion of the two theories will render these points
more perspicuous.

A most important consequence of the theory of kin selection is that it   12
makes possible a very satisfactory evolutionary account of parental altruism.
But even here it is important to realize that the altruism that the theory of
kin selection is intended to capture is primarily unwitting altruism rather than
motive altruism. The intuitive idea behind the theory of kin selection is this:
The degree to which an individual is disposed to help another is directly a
function of the degree of genetic relatedness between the two individuals. So,
other things equal, we are more disposed to help our siblings than our first
cousins, our first cousins than our second cousins, our second than our third,
and so on. Full brothers and sisters, on the one hand, and parents and children, on the other, have the same degree of genetic relatedness, the members
of each pair having half of their genes in common. Only identical twins have
a greater degree of genetic relatedness, since both have exactly the same set
of genes. Other things equal, then, the theory of kin selection tells us that
parents should be just as disposed to help their baby siblings as they are to
help their own offspring. We rarely have siblings who are completely in our
charge and who are the same age as our own offspring, so we rarely feel a
conflict between the two.

It is easy to see why the theory of kin selection makes possible a very   13
satisfactory evolutionary account of parental altruism. Given a choice between helping any two creatures, an individual does more to ensure the

continuation of his gene pool by helping the one whose gene pool is more in common with his own. The greater the degree of genetic relatedness, the more disposed the individual to ensure the continuation of his own gene pool. In terms of genetic relatedness, the score is tied between an individual's siblings, his own offspring, and his parents. But in terms of who is most likely to need help and where providing help is most likely to promote the continuation of his gene pool, an individual does the best by helping his own offspring. For an individual's gene pool will continue only if there are individuals in the next generation who have genes in common with that pool. Even if the individual's siblings have children, he will still do better to help his own children, since the degree of genetic relatedness between him and his own offspring (which is one-half) will be greater than that between him and his siblings' offspring (which is one-quarter). The exception is when the sibling is an identical twin, in which case the degree of genetic relatedness between him and his twin's children will be the same as that between him and his own children.

Supposing, for the sake of argument, that the theory of kin selection is 14 certainly applicable to human beings, observe that it was not introduced simply to explain altruism, especially parental altruism, in humans.[4] On the contrary, it was intended to explain altruism among species generally (cf. Bertram 1978). Put another way, the theory was in no way designed to explain the altruistic behavior of only those creatures who can engage in sophisticated computations, as well as have beliefs, about the degree of genetic relatedness of those whom they help. The importance of this observation is that it makes clear that the altruism explained by the theory is unwitting altruism and not motive altruism, and that the selfishness we get is unwitting selfishness and not motive selfishness. The theory in no way implies that parents (kin) are intentionally motivated to sacrifice for their offspring (kin) by the desire to ensure the continuation of their gene pool.

The foregoing remarks hold, mutatis mutandis,* for the theory of recip- 15 rocal altruism, which (as I said) is meant to explain altruism between different species and non-kin. We are not to suppose, for instance, that in issuing a warning call, which jeopardizes its life by making its whereabouts more easily determined by a predator, a calling bird reasons to itself that it is better that it, a single calling bird, should put its life in jeopardy than that the life of its neighboring calling birds should be endangered. We are not to impute intentions of the appropriate sort to a calling bird that gives a warning call. The benefit it bestows by giving a warning call is purely an instance of unwitting altruism, which has come about as a result of natural selection. Fish that clean the gills of an entirely different species of fish constitute an example of reciprocal altruism between species (Trivers 1971). The host fish has its gills cleaned, the cleaning fish obtains a meal. At no point are we to think that the two species—through arbitration or some such thing—have worked out a mutually satisfactory arrangement for finding food and having gills cleaned.

*That is, the necessary changes having been made.

In no way is motive altruism supposed. Rather, we have unwitting altruism and unwitting selfishness operating together.

My aim thus far has been to show that when sociobiologists talk about altruism, they generally mean unwitting altruism and unwitting selfishness as opposed to motive altruism and motive selfishness. While to show this is not, I realize, to show that sociobiology underwrites motive altruism, it is very much a step in that direction. For, since neither makes reference to motives or intentions of any sort—in particular, motive selfishness—it then follows that achieving motive altruism is not a matter of going against the biological grain of motive selfishness. But, as I shall now try to show in what follows, a very persuasive case can be made for the strong claim that sociobiology underwrites motive altruism.   16

To begin with, let us distinguish between what a person desires to do and what as a matter of biological constitution a person is disposed to do. Suppose, for example, that as a matter of biological constitution, the crying of an infant—any infant—automatically invokes altruistic feelings within us. We are spontaneously moved to attend to the child's needs in an affectionate way. And suppose, further, that this is of tremendous evolutionary advantage, since it ensures that we will be moved to care affectionately for our offspring in spite of the physical and emotional costs of doing so. Now, none of this would seem to be an obstacle to adults' displaying motive altruism toward infants. If anything, it is possible that the biological constitution of adults enables them to better carry through with their altruistic intentions toward infants. For adults could desire to behave in a caring and affectionate way toward infants and thus be delighted that they are so constituted biologically. We can want to be, and can take delight in being, constituted in the way that we are.[5] And an act is no less altruistic simply because, given our biological constitution, we are better able to execute our altruistic intentions.   17

If my presentation of sociobiology and unwitting altruism is sound, then the way in which we are biologically constituted, far from being at odds with motive altruism, better enables us to realize altruistic intentions. This is quite apparent with altruism among kin and with the theory of kin selection. In general, parents care deeply for their children and delight in the fact that they do. (The example that I sketched above with regard to our reactions to crying infants obviously has a foothold in reality.) From the standpoint of evolutionary theory, the theory of kin selection tells us that it pays for us to be biologically constituted so as to be especially concerned about the well-being of our children. Again, we are in general more favorably disposed toward our kin than toward others; and the theory of kin selection tells us that it pays for us to be biologically constituted so as to favor our kin over others.   18

Let us now look at motive altruism outside of kin relationships, for it is such manifestations of altruism that are especially the concern of the moral point of view. As I have already observed, the theory of reciprocal altruism was introduced to account for various manifestations of altruism outside of kin relationships. With its obvious affinity to contract theory, the idea behind the   19 theory of reciprocal altruism is a familiar one: when individuals frequently interact with one another they are better off cooperating to some extent than not doing so; in particular, everyone is better off with certain altruistic norms than not. For example, given how fragile infants are and how easy it is for them to get in harm's way, society is better off on balance if nearly everyone is moved to attend to the immediate needs of a crying infant, regardless of who the parents of the child are. So, the theory suggests a way of accounting for various altruistic norms among human beings. It is not supposed that individuals actually reason in this way, but only that from the standpoint of natural selection individuals are better off with respect to their gene pool's being maintained if they are disposed to comply with altruistic norms.

Now, the theory posits feelings of guilt and fear of expulsion from group membership as psychological mechanisms that have been selected for because they operate to ensure compliance with the altruistic norms of the group (Trivers 1971). It might be tempting to infer from this that the theory is therefore at odds with motive altruism as the explanation for why individuals comply with the altruistic norms of the group. However, this temptation should be resisted. Of course, if either feelings of guilt or fear of expulsion from the group is the only explanation for why a person follows an altruistic norm, then the person's compliance with the norm can hardly be said to stem from motive altruism. But the theory does not make this claim. To suppose that it does is to confuse an explanation for the way in which certain feelings may operate in our lives with how a person may be motivated to behave.

The thesis that feelings of guilt or fear of expulsion from the group operates to enhance compliance with the altruistic norms of the group does not entail that either of these psychological mechanisms is the only motive a person can have for complying with those norms. This can be easily seen by recalling a previous discussion in this section. It is obvious that the sex drive has been selected for precisely because of the importance of leaving behind progeny. Yet it hardly follows from this that it is only for the sake of leaving behind progeny that individuals are moved to satisfy this drive. Indeed, one need not give any thought at all to the idea.

Surprisingly, perhaps, support for the view that natural selection favors the compliance of human beings with altruistic norms comes from the theory of kin selection itself. The natural parent-offspring relationship among *Homo sapiens* is the longest and most complex among any species. This means that raising offspring to the point where they are able to leave behind progeny is a matter of considerable parental investment for human beings, requiring a great deal of time and energy.[6] In fact, the amount of care and attention that human offspring require is so great that humans would hardly be able to provide these things if the possibility for social cooperation among human beings did not exist. It is not just a morally good thing that human beings can live in harmony and, hence, engage in social cooperation with one another. The amount of care and attention that human offspring require necessitates that humans live this way at least to some extent.

I want to conclude this section with a very different sort of argument   23
for the view that biology allows for genuine altruism among human beings.

It is obvious that human beings do not procreate in the most efficient   24
of ways; enormous energy and time are spent engaging in activities that do
not constitute the procreative act but only lead up to it.[7] However pleasurable
the rituals (let us say) of sexual activity may be,[8] the fact is that from a strictly
procreative perspective, things proceed rather inefficiently. Indeed, in a very
straightforward sense, people would have a lot more time and energy (not to
mention money) left to attend to other things were sexual intercourse confined strictly to the procreative act. Hence, one might very well ask: How is
it that human beings have evolved so that things are not thus confined? That
is, what evolutionary advantage accrues to human beings in virtue of the
rituals of sexual intercourse?

One answer that immediately recommends itself is that such rituals   25
have an enormous bonding effect upon the involved parties, which in turn
contributes to their being cooperative in the venture of child rearing (cf.
Wilson 1978, p. 137 ff.). And this has an evolutionary advantage, given the
length and complexities of child rearing among human beings. But with this
truth, assuming it is that, we have not reached the end of the story.

The rituals of sexual intercourse primarily take place between non-kin.   26
But if such rituals have an enormous bonding effect upon the parties involved, then what follows rather interestingly is that the capacity for altruism
is more a part of our biological make-up than is often supposed. This follows
from the fact that altruism (or something very much like it) flows in the wake
of the formation of bonds between individuals. For the type of bond formed
is one of affection, which is surely one of the fountainheads of altruistic
behavior. If non-kin have the capacity for affectional bonding, for whatever
reason, then altruism can be no stranger to human beings. That this capacity
is evolutionarily advantageous because it increases cooperation in child rearing in no way militates against the truth of the point being made. Nor does
the fact that this capacity is supervenient upon sexual behavior. For it does
not follow from this that only sexual behavior can trigger this capacity.

My aim in this section has been to argue in a very general way for the   27
view that the biological make-up of human beings is compatible with their
being disposed to act in altruistic ways. To accomplish this task is not to show
that all human beings will act altruistically, but only that the claims of an
altruistic morality do not go entirely against the grain of our biological make-
up. In the sections that follow, I hope to render this conclusion more secure
by looking at a particular form of altruism, namely, love itself. I believe that
a certain form of love clearly has a biological basis. That conception of love
is characterized and defended in the section below.

LOVE: TRANSPARENT AND OPAQUE

There are various kinds of love: love between friends, romantic love,   28
familial love, and a special species of familial love, namely, parental love. Of

these various types of love, parental love is perhaps the most unique. In what follows, I shall attempt to characterize the uniqueness of this love and explain what distinguishes it from other types of love. I shall do this generally by contrasting parental love with romantic love.

Romantic love is a paradigmatic instance of what I shall call opaque love.[9] It is love for a person under a certain description of that person, where the description makes reference to various attributes of the individual: the person's character, personality, style, physical features, skills, or what have you. It is love grounded in the attributes of the person. One can be married to a person about whom one knows nothing, as with prearranged marriages,[10] but not romantically in love with a person about whom one knows nothing.

With romantic love, then, the description under which the person is loved is of considerable importance. Literally, a person may be loved under one description and not another. For example, suppose that unbeknownst to John, Susan leads two rather disparate lives. By day she is a major corporate executive; by night she is a drug dealer. Not only can we easily imagine John being quite in love with Susan the corporate executive, but not Susan the drug dealer, we can easily imagine him falling out of love with Susan upon discovering that she is a drug dealer.

Of course, I do not mean to suggest that romantic love is so description-sensitive that it cannot tolerate any departures from the description under which the person is loved. That would be untenable, clearly. It is radical departures that present a problem for romantic love; and depending upon the attributes that primarily serve to ground the love, some romantic loves are more vulnerable than others to departures from the description under which the person is loved. Presumably, love grounded in physical attractiveness is more vulnerable than love grounded in intellectual talent, since intellect tends to weather the circumstances of life better than physical attraction. Obesity, which tends to make one less attractive, rarely curtails one's intellectual powers. And if personality and traits of character are more durable than physical attributes, then love grounded in the former is less vulnerable than love grounded in the latter.

As I have characterized it, opaque love seems to be at odds with the romantic ideal that receives its fullest expression in the traditional marriage vows. The ideal is that regardless of how each changes, the parties involved shall love one another until death separates them. As I hope to show momentarily, it is a mistake to think that opaque love is completely at odds with this ideal or, at any rate, the spirit of it. But first it will help to introduce the notion of transparent love in connection with parental love.

(It is obvious that people have children for a myriad of reasons—to make up, to prove themselves, and so on. The account of transparent love offered is not meant to address all cases of having children, but only those in which the child is desired by the parents because of the joy they hope to experience in contributing to the flourishing of a new human being.)

I regard parental love, at least at the outset, as the paradigmatic instance of transparent love. Parents display considerable love for their children from the very moment the children are born. In fact, it can be plausibly argued that such love manifests itself even sooner than that; but the issue need not concern us here. (I conclude this section with some remarks about parental love and the severely retarded and deformed.) This makes it incontrovertible that such love cannot be grounded in the usual attributes: the child's character, personality, style, physical features, skills, and so on. Whether the just-born, as I shall say, by which I mean a child no more than a few weeks old, has anything like a developed character and personality is not clear. What is clear, though, is that a just-born's character and personality are not pronounced enough at the moment of birth to make a difference in the reaction of her or his parents. These fragile creatures are not sexy-looking or coy, they do not possess a sense of presence, they are without poise, they cannot flirt, and so on. They display none of the nonverbal behavior that so often serves to explain at least the beginnings of romantic love. Any given just-born may become an intellectual giant or a symbol of physical attractiveness, but this is not known at the moment of birth. Thus, to love a just-born infant is not merely to love a bundle of unrealized potential; rather, it is to love a being the nature of whose potential is unknown to one. A just-born infant may even be without a name for awhile.

I call parental love transparent because it is grounded simply in the fact [35] that the children in question are one's offspring. In due course, I shall slightly modify my description of the basis for transparent parental love.

Now, it may be argued that the fact that the child is one's own is surely [36] an attribute of the child—indeed, the attribute that grounds the love that the parents have for the child; hence, the distinction between opaque and transparent love collapses, since in both cases the love is grounded by the attributes of the object of the love. This objection, I think, misses the point of the distinction.

The attribute "my child" is not a quality-denoting attribute. It does not [37] pick out qualities that the child currently possesses or shall come to possess. The attribute indicates, and functions purely as an indicator of, the source of the child's origins, and not what the child is or shall be like. It applies equally to any child who has the same origins. Hold the origins fixed and one just-born is as good as another. It is in precisely this sense that the transparency of parental love mirrors the transparency of reference. Substitutions yield the same results.

By contrast, opaque love does not function purely as an indicator of [38] origins. To be sure, X may very well love Y because Y is a member of the so-and-so family. By one can ask X why a person's being a member of the so-and-so family is important. And something is very much amiss if X does not have a response other than Y is a member of the family. Thus, even here romantic love turns out not to function as a pure indicator of origins. By contrast, observe that no response other than X is my child is needed to explain why a person loves X.

Parenthetically, it should be noted that as the notion of transparency is [39] used in the theory of reference, it need not be held that no description whatsoever obtains in the case of transparent reference. If an object is being picked out at all, there has to be some description under which it is being picked out. So it is a mistake to think of transparent reference as involving no descriptions at all. Rather, the idea is that a fixed description has to suffice to pick out the object in question in all cases. Accordingly, then, the idea of transparent love is not to be understood as involving no descriptions whatsoever. Thus, without doing harm to the argument, it can be conceded that "my child" functions as a description. For the issue is whether that description suffices to ground parental love whatever else might be true. And the claim is that it does.

I have been arguing that parental love for the just-born is transparent. Children grow very rapidly. Ideally, parental love should remain transparent as the child grows. However, I have not argued that this is the case. I have not argued that once an object of someone's parental love, then always an object of that person's parental love. I want now to return to the apparent disparity between opaque love and the romantic ideal.

The traditional marriage vows suggest that romantic love that results in marriage should in effect become something rather like transparent love, in that the parties involved are supposed to love one another regardless of the changes that either might undergo. Thus, marital love is supposed to transcend, that is, not be grounded in, the attributes of the person. Instead, such love is supposed to be grounded in a deep and quintessential feature of the person. Indeed, it may be argued that unless this is the case we are quite easily replaceable by someone who just so happens to possess the very same attributes that we possess. And that, so it is argued, should not be.[11] Succinctly put, then, the claim is this: Unless marital love is grounded in some deep and quintessential feature of the person and, therefore, is not an instance of opaque love, the threat of attribute replaceability looms large. Ideally, marital love ought not to be, and is not, open to this threat. Hence, such marital love cannot be properly regarded as opaque love.

Clearly, the argument speaks to something important. There is something unsettling, if not altogether repugnant, about the idea that one's marital partner could just as easily love someone else if that person's set of attributes were identical to one's own. On the other hand, equally unsettling is the idea that marital love is as it ought to be only if one continues to love one's partner regardless of the changes that she or he undergoes. Surely, the kind of changes the person undergoes ought to make a difference. To speak in extremes, it is one thing if the person puts on a little weight; it is quite another if the person becomes an exceedingly wicked individual. Life being what it is, a change of the former type is to be expected. However, no one who gets married can be thought to have bargained for the latter. The objection (under consideration) to characterizing marital love as opaque love misses the mark because it loses sight of the developmental aspects of a marital relationship or it implicitly takes physical attributes to be the ground for the love throughout the marriage. People do not just get married. They get married and share their lives together.

There are the joyful and painful learning experiences, the hurdles that each has gotten the other over, and the like. If all goes well, each contributes significantly to the other's flourishing. And this fact suffices to defuse the threat of attribute replaceability as an ever-present problem.

Consider the following. Suppose John and Susan get married. Five years 43 pass and it is a good marriage. Each has contributed significantly to the other's flourishing. Having grown, they respectively now have the set alpha and beta of attributes. As it happens, there is a John* and a Susan* each having the set of attributes that, after five years of marriage, their counterparts John and Susan came to have. (Whether John* and Susan* know each other is irrelevant.) Needless to say, there could not be a more pertinent fact than that John and Susan developed with each other and not with their counterparts. It is to each other's flourishing that they contributed, with all that that involved, and not the flourishing of the counterparts. And it is to one another that each will be grateful and not someone who just so happens to have the identical set of properties. The distance they have travelled together qualitatively affects how they view and feel about each other. None of this is changed by the fact that John* and Susan* have the same attributes as their counterparts John and Susan. For Susan did not contribute to John*'s having his attributes, nor John to Susan*'s having hers.

If physical attributes are the ground of marital love, then it is much 44 easier to see how the threat of attribute replaceability could arise, though even here it is possible to tell a story in which the threat is minimized. Something that we have an emotional investment in is not easily replaced, even by something that is indistinguishable from it, as objects of sentimental value make clear. Although a father could get his daughter, who is now a professional potter, to make him a cup just like the one she made for him twenty years ago when she was six, and which he accidentally but irreparably broke, the replacement cup cannot really take the place of the original. For the significance that the father attached to that cup was inextricably tied to the fact that it was made by his daughter when she was six. Tears of joy came to his eyes when he unwrapped the cup, which was her birthday gift to him. Another cup that looked just like it simply would not invoke the same memories, at least not in the same way. For the original cup was a token of his daughter's love as expressed at the age of six. No other cup be a token of that! These considerations shore up the points made in the preceding paragraph.

If, as a result of having flourished together, John and Susan have traits 45 alpha and beta respectively, then the fact that there is a John* and a Susan* who have the exact same traits does not, on that account alone, pose any threat either to John or Susan. For both will have helped and been helped by each other. The depth of their sentiments will have been engaged by each other. Neither John* nor Susan* will have been anywhere in the picture. So, with romantic love it seems that the threat of replaceability would loom large in the lives of a couple only if it is allowed that a romantic relationship can be based entirely upon physical attraction and that the individuals' living and interacting together add nothing whatsoever to the relationship. But to call such a relationship an instance of romantic love is surely a misnomer.

Marital love is at its best when the involved individuals grow and flourish together. However, marital love is not always at its best, and the involved parties may part company. This is a very different phenomenon from simply being replaced by someone whose attributes are identical to one's own. After all, a couple can part company although neither party has another romantic interest on the horizon. With no difficulty, then, we can maintain that marital love is an instance of opaque love and yet do justice to the idea that the threat of attribute replaceability should not loom large in the background. [46]

Of course, if one understands the spirit of the traditional marriage vows to be that one should remain committed to one's partner, however she or he might change, then I have hardly shed any light on the matter. On the other hand, if the spirit of these vows is that, among other things, neither party to the marriage should feel threatened by the mere fact that there are others who have similar attributes, then I believe that our understanding of these vows has been enhanced. It is undoubtedly a wonderful thing when two people love one another until death separates them. But it is unquestionably a mistake to suppose that we have genuine love only when this is the case. In particular, we need not suppose that we have genuine love only when the object of our love is irreplaceable. From the fact that it is possible that someone could replace us in a love relationship, it in no way follows that the threat of being replaced hangs over us. After all, in a similar sense of the word *possible,* it is just as possible that the one who loves us could kill us; yet we rarely see that possibility as amounting to anything like a threat of death. [47]

Now, there is an independent reason for wanting romantic love, even in the ideal form of marital love, to be an instance of opaque love. The kind of love that is closest in character to romantic love is love between deep friends or companion friends, as I shall say. In fact, it is notoriously difficult to distinguish the love of companion friendships from romantic love, apart from maintaining that the latter, and not the former, has a sexual component, and the expression of affection is different. Perhaps these differences are just enough to yield a difference in kind. But what must be shown is not simply that a difference in kind exists as a result of these things, but that the love of complete friendship naturally stops short of these things. In due course, I shall question this line of reasoning. [48]

At any rate, with both kinds of love, the love in question is an expression of choice for a person of a certain kind. Second, in both instances the ideal is that the parties involved contribute significantly to each other's flourishing. Both types of relationship give deep expression to the idea that individuals can be mirrors to the souls of each other.[12] Yet no one would maintain that two people should remain deep friends regardless of the changes that either undergoes. In particular, no one would urge the continuation of a friendship with a person who has become irredeemably wicked.[13] [49]

The love that is characteristic of friendship is manifestly an instance of [50] opaque love. If Aristotle is right, the relevant attributes have to do with character (*Nicomachean Ethics,* Bk. 9). The threat of attribute replaceability does not loom large on the horizon of friendships thus grounded, and this provides us with an independent reason for thinking that no such threat need be present in the marital case simply because romantic love is grounded in the attributes of the person. This holds a fortiori* if the differences between the love of romance and the love of companion friendship are all but indistinguishable.

I have claimed that of the various types of love, parental love is perhaps   51
the most unique. As one might surmise, I want to say that that has to do with its being transparent, at least at the outset. Other familial loves may also tend toward transparency; however, it is reasonable to hold that, in general, transparent love receives its fullest expression in parental love. This is because among familial relationships, sustained altruism (which is not of the heroic or saintly sort) generally receives its greatest expression in parenthood. To be sure, when their parents are along in years, children often do things for them, if not support them outright; but such behavior is often motivated to some extent by the feeling on the children's part that they have acquired a debt of gratitude to their parents. Obviously enough, the altruism that parents display toward their just-born children simply cannot be so explained.

. . .

TRANSPARENT LOVE AND NATURAL SELECTION

Among the basic needs of a human infant the need for continuous love   52
from its parents (or parental surrogate) is said to be one of the most important, if not the most important.[14] If, as we shall see, this is indeed the case, then the fact that the human species continues to survive gives us reason enough to believe that not only do human beings have the capacity to meet this need, but that this capacity has been selected for.

. . .

There is a species of love—I have called it transparent love—that con-   53
sists of a concern for a person's well-being and is not tied to the person's performances. This is unconditional love not because one may never cease to have such love for an individual, but because there is no belief about that individual's behavior, performances, or what have you, that constitutes a conceptual bar to so loving that person. There is nothing a person can do, nothing a person can become, that would cause one, on conceptual grounds, to cease loving him.

These remarks show the importance of distinguishing between having   54
the psychological wherewithal to continue loving a person and having conditions that a person must meet if one is to continue loving her or him. It is possible not to be able to continue loving a person even though one wishes that one could, just as one may wish that one were more patient.

*All the more.

Suppose one's spouse is on a secret military assignment that will keep her away from home for three years. One may very well have no desire whatsoever not to go on loving her throughout the three years; yet it could turn out—much to one's own surprise even—that one lacks the psychological wherewithal to do so.

What I have called transparent love, or something very much like it, is thought to be one of the defining features of Christianity. And observe that while the Christian commandment to love one's enemies is regarded as exceedingly difficult,[15] doing so is not ruled out on conceptual grounds. It is not on a par with being commanded to square a circle (the logically impossible) or to leap tall buildings in a single bound (the physically impossible). Since transparent love is not tied to performances, it is compatible with disapproval. It is this distinctive feature that accounts for the significance and importance of parental love in the life of the child.

. . .

In view of these considerations, we may say that parental love engenders and sustains in the child basic psychological security, which we understand simply as a sense of worth that is in no way tied to performances. As a result of their displays of love, the child believes that his parents' acceptance of him and their desire to support him is not tied to his performances. Accordingly, the child believes that in the eyes of his parents he has worth regardless of whether his performances meet their approval.

Naturally, I do not mean to suggest that there is nothing at all to be said for parental approval and disapproval. I shall say something about that momentarily.

Now, basic psychological security is surely one of the keys that unlocks the door to a child's flourishing. Here is why. It is through exploratory behavior that a child learns how to master her environment and so to acquire a sense of competence.[16]

. . .

To sum up, then, I have tried to show the significance of parental love as an instance of transparent love. I have argued that the significance lies in the fact that such parental love engenders basic psychological security on the part of the child, and that this security, in addition to allaying or altogether precluding the fear of parental rejection, is one of the keys to the child's flourishing.

If the argument is sound, then from the standpoint of evolutionary theory we have reason to believe that the capacity for transparent love as manifested through parental love has been selected for. It will be recalled that a necessary condition for the survival of any species is that enough among each generation of adults succeed in leaving behind progeny who, in turn, succeed in doing the same. Far from playing a peripheral role in the survival of the human species, basic psychological security on the part of the child proves to be indispensable if the child is to have a chance of flourishing.

. . .

I have argued that the capacity for transparent parental love has been   59
selected for. What I have meant by the argument is that in general we have
the capacity for such love in virtue of being human—not in virtue of having
children. The psychological attitude of adults toward the children of others
and, especially, toward the prospect of having their own children would be
quite inexplicable if the capacity for parental love were triggered only by
actually having (or conceiving) children. Under such a view, we could make
little sense of the great joy that the very thought of having children gives to
people presently without them. Further, it seems that any view that gives
such weight to actually having (or conceiving) children puts males at an
enormous disadvantage with regard to the capacity for transparent love, since
it is females, and not men, who conceive and bear children. But there is
absolutely no reason to believe that, in comparison to women, men have a
diminished capacity for transparent parental love.

Now, perhaps the best and most compelling evidence that can be prof-   60
fered in support of the view that the capacity for transparent parental love
derives from being human is that some adults adopt children; and the love
these adults have for their (adopted) children is indistinguishable from the
richness and depth of love parents have for their natural children. Taken as
a class, the parents of adopted children are indistinguishable from the parents
of natural children when it comes to displaying love toward their children.
If the capacity for transparent parental love came only in the wake of having
natural offspring, or if it reached a particularly heightened form as a result
of natural offspring, then there should be a discernable difference between
the capacity of parents of adopted children to love their children vis-à-vis
that of parents of natural children to love theirs. (This would be true even
if the difference could be overcome.) None, however, is to be found.

LOVE, MORALITY, AND
SELF-INTEREST

If there is a biological basis for transparent love, then it follows that   61
there is a biological basis for what I called motive altruism, since love is an
altruistic concept. And if there is a biological basis for motive altruism, then
it follows that there is a measure of congruence between our biological make-
up and altruistic morality. In fact, an even stronger claim can be made,
namely, that our biological make-up is an ally of morality. This is so, at any
rate, if one regards love as a natural, and thus nonmoral, sentiment. For I have
argued that transparent love has a very straightforward evolutionary underpinning or, at any rate, that it is not implausible to suppose that this is so.
And if any sentiment embodies motive altruism, surely love does. Together,
these considerations entail that motive altruism itself has a basis in our
biological make-up. If so, then it follows that the altruism that morality calls
for has a biological underpinning.

. . .

NOTES

All notes are Thomas's.

1. Cf. Dawkins (1976), Trivers (1985), and Wilson (1975).

2. As the very title of his book, *The Selfish Gene*, might indicate, Dawkins (1976) is quite guilty of this. He writes: "I shall make use of the metaphor of the architect's plans, freely mixing the language of metaphor with the language of the real thing" (p.23). In his *Ever Since Darwin* (1977), Stephen J. Gould alerts the reader as follows: "I do not mean to attribute conscious will to creatures with such rudimentary brains [ants]. I use such prases as 'he would rather' only as a convenient shortcut for 'in the course of evolution, males [male ants] who did not behave this way have been placed at a selective disadvantage and gradually eliminated" (pp. 264–65). [For Gould, see *Reader*, Chapter 2.]

3. The theory was introduced by W.D. Hamilton (1964): the theory of reciprocal altruism was introduced by Robert L. Trivers (1971). My understanding of the former owes much to Maynard-Smith (1976, 1982).

4. See Wilson (1975), pp. 117–20. Gould (1977) writes: "Hamilton's theory of kin selection has had stunning success in explaining some persistent biological puzzles in the evolution of social behavior in the Hymenoptera—ants, bees, and wasps. Why has true sociality evolved independently at least eleven times in the Hymenoptera and only once among other insects (the termites)? Why are sterile worker castes always female in the Hymenoptera, but both male and female in termites? The answer seems to lie in the workings of kin selection within the unusual genetic system of the Hymenoptera" (p. 263). With great caution, Gould allows that the theory may be able to explain unwitting altruism among humans (p. 265).

5. This way of putting the point owes its inspiration to Frankfurt (1971).

6. On the topic of parental investment outside of the human context, see Trivers (1978).

7. Here and in what follows, I am much indebted to Wilson (1978), ch. 6. I have also profited from discussions with Andrew Manitsky.

8. Sexual foreplay and involved preparations that are done explicitly or implicitly with sexual intercourse in mind, for example, the intimate dinner or the purchasing of garments.

9. As the term *opaque* and its counterpart *transparent* suggest, the account of opaque and transparent love developed owes some of its inspiration to work in the philosophy of language, the theory of reference in particular, between transparent and opaque reference. See, for example, Kripke (1980). In borrowing terminology, one invariably runs the risk of being misunderstood. I hope to have kept misunderstandings to a minimum.

10. Cf. "And he [Hagar] dwelt in the wilderness of Paran: and his mother took him a wife out of the land of Egypt" (Genesis 21:21).

11. This argument is presented with great force in Kraut (1983) and Nozick (1974).

12. See Ch. 1, n. 1.

13. No one, including Aristotle, who no doubt made this very point first. See his *Nicomachean Ethics* (Bk. 9, Sec. 3).

14. Cf. Bowlby (1953). He writes" "What is believed to be essential for mental health is that an infant and young child should experience a warm, intimate, and continuous relationship with his mother (or permanent mother-substitute—one person who steadily 'mothers' him) in which both find satisfaction and enjoyment" (p.13). Bowlby develops this line of thought in *Attachment* (1969). Bowlby's general conclusions concerning the importance of parental love are now regarded as established. See Hinde (1978) and Rutter (1978). Gregory Vlastos (1962) writes that "constancy of affection in the face of variations of merit is one of the surest tests of whether a mother loves a child."

15. "But I say unto you, Love your enemies, bless them that curse you, do good to them that hate you" (Matthew 5:44). This form of Christian love is generally referred to as agape love. See Meilaender (1981) for an excellent discussion of the character and scope of agape love.

16. Here I follow Rutter (1978) and, especially, White (1963), ch. 3. See also Gruen (1988). It is worth mentioning that one of the central aims of White's work is to show that Freud's theory of the personality is inadequate—in particular, Freud's account of human motivation.

Questions for Discussion

1. What does Laurence mean by the distinction between "motive altruism" and "unwitting altruism" in paragraph 9?

2. Explain what Laurence means in paragraph 10 by his statement that "unwitting altruism is compatible with unwitting selfishness."

3. Explain Laurence's distinction between "opaque love" and "transparent love" (¶24–35). Can you create examples of each kind of love different from Laurence's own?

4. How important is the theory of evolution for Laurence's position? Where does he appeal to this theory and what use does he make of it?

5. What does Laurence's use of Latin phrases—inter alia (¶2), mutatis mutandis (¶15), and a fortiori (¶50)—imply about the identity of his audience as he sees it? Is his use of language appropriate to the audience he has selected?

Suggested Essay Topics

1. Construct an attack on either Dawkins's or Laurence's position and direct it to the author himself, showing where the argument fails to be convincing and providing counterarguments or counterexamples that show the inadequacy of either author's views.

2. If you favor Dawkins's position, create for him a rebuttal to Laurence's arguments about parental love and be sure to include an account of Laurence's argument about the love of parents for adopted children. If you favor Laurence's position, create for him a rebuttal of Dawkins's argument that genes control behavior the way the author of a software computer program controls the computer running the software. (You will have to consider whether this metaphor constitutes an appropriate analogy.) In writing either essay you may want to consider what it reveals, if anything, about the nature of either man's position that Dawkins, the scientist, relies more on metaphors in support of his position that does Laurence, the philosopher, who relies on examples, but not much on metaphors.

♦ 7 ♦

SOCIAL JUSTICE

Minorities and Majorities

To me, anti-Semitism is now the most shocking of all things.
It is destroying much more than the Jews; it is assailing the human mind
at its source, and inviting it to create false categories
before exercising judgment. I am sure we shall win through.
But it will take a long time. . . . For the moment
all we can do is to dig in our heels, and prevent silliness
from sliding into insanity.
E. M. Forster

The Negro wanted to feel pride in his race? With tokenism,
the solution was simple. If all twenty million Negroes would keep looking
at Ralph Bunche [former ambassador to the United Nations],
the one man in so exalted a post would
generate such a volume of pride that it could be cut into
portions and served to everyone.
Martin Luther King, Jr.

In giving freedom to the slave, we assure freedom
to the free—honorable alike in what we give and what we preserve.
Abraham Lincoln

There is no subject on earth so easily understood as that of
the American Indian. Each summer, work camps
disgorge teen-agers on various reservations.
Within one month's time the youngsters acquire a knowledge
of Indians that would astound a college professor.
Vine Deloria, Jr.

None can love freedom heartily, but good men; the rest love
not freedom, but licence.
John Milton

Chief Red Jacket and the Missionary

The story of injustices inflicted upon racial and ethnic minorities in American society, past and present, has been widely documented with case histories and statistics and explained with countless theories. These are useful and informative, but the whole issue has perhaps never been summed up with such simple and powerful eloquence as in the rejection by the Indians (in this episode) of the white man's religion, patronizingly pushed at them by a missionary whose every word reveals his intolerance toward everything Indian. The Indians say that they will accept the white man's religion when they see that it makes whites treat Indians more fairly. By this simple test they at once summarize and condemn the whole tradition of white hypocrisy and greed.

Why should the Indians accept a religion that has allowed the white man to justify the theft of Indian lands and the murder of Indian people? They have learned that listening to the white man always leads to being cheated. Their "smiling" acceptance of the missionary's refusal to shake their hands after they have rejected his religion shows that they clearly see through his professed intention to do them good and perceive his real intention, which is to add the robbery of their religion to the robbery of their lands and way of life.

The narrative that introduces and comments on the speeches is by the anonymous editor of the 1809 edition.

A NATIVE AMERICAN EPISODE

Speeches by Chief Red Jacket and
the Reverend Mr. Cram

From *Indian Speeches; Delivered by Farmer's Brother and Red Jacket, Two Seneca Chiefs* (1809). The title is ours.

[In the summer of 1805, a number of the principal Chiefs and Warriors 1
of the Six Nations, principally Senecas, assembled at Buffalo Creek, in the
state of New York, at the particular request of Rev. Mr. Cram, a Missionary
from the state of Massachusetts. The Missionary being furnished with an
Interpreter, and accompanied by the Agent of the United States for Indian
affairs, met the Indians in Council, when the following talk took place.]

FIRST, BY THE AGENT. "*Brothers of the Six Nations;* I rejoice to meet you at this 2
time, and thank the Great Spirit, that he has preserved you in health, and
given me another opportunity of taking you by the hand.

"*Brothers;* The person who sits by me, is a friend who has come a great 3
distance to hold a talk with you. He will inform you what his business is, and
it is my request that you would listen with attention to his words."

MISSIONARY. "*My Friends;* I am thankful for the opportunity afforded us 4
of uniting together at this time. I had a great desire to see you, and inquire
into your state and welfare; for this purpose I have travelled a great distance,
being sent by your old friends, the Boston Missionary Society. You will
recollect they formerly sent missionaries among you, to instruct you in religion, and labor for your good. Although they have not heard from you for
a long time, yet they have not forgotten their brothers the Six Nations, and
are still anxious to do you good.

"*Brothers;* I have not come to get your lands or your money, but to 5
enlighten your minds, and to instruct you how to worship the Great Spirit
agreeably to his mind and will, and to preach to you the gospel of his son
Jesus Christ. There is but one religion, and but one way to serve God, and
if you do not embrace the right way, you cannot be happy hereafter. You
have never worshipped the Great Spirit in a manner acceptable to him; but
have, all your lives, been in great errors and darkness. To endeavor to remove
these errors, and open your eyes, so that you might see clearly, is my business
with you.

"*Brothers;* I wish to talk with you as one friend talks with another; and, 6
if you have any objections to receive the religion which I preach, I wish you
to state them; and I will endeavor to satisfy your minds, and remove the
objections.

"*Brothers;* I want you to speak your minds freely; for I wish to reason 7
with you on the subject, and, if possible, remove all doubts, if there be any
on your minds. The subject is an important one, and it is of consequence that
you give it an early attention while the offer is made you. Your friends, the
Boston Missionary Society, will continue to send you good and faithful

ministers, to instruct and strengthen you in religion, if, on your part, you are willing to receive them.

"*Brothers;* Since I have been in this part of the country, I have visited 8 some of your small villages, and talked with your people. They appear willing to receive instruction, but, as they look up to you as their older brothers in council, they want first to know your opinion on the subject.

"You have now heard what I have to propose at present. I hope you will 9 take it into consideration, and give me an answer before we part."

[After about two hours consultation among themselves, the Chief, com- 10 monly called by the white people, Red Jacket (whose Indian name is Sagu-yu-what-hah, which interpreted is *Keeper awake*) rose and spoke as follows:]

"*Friend and Brother;* It was the will of the Great Spirit that we should meet 11 together this day. HE orders all things, and has given us a fine day for our Council. HE has taken his garment from before the sun, and caused it to shine with brightness upon us. Our eyes are opened, that we see clearly; our ears are unstopped, that we have been able to hear distinctly the words you have spoken. For all these favors we thank the Great Spirit; and HIM *only.*

"*Brother;* This council fire was kindled by you. It was at your request that 12 we came together at this time. We have listened with attention to what you have said. You requested us to speak our minds freely. This gives us great joy; for we now consider that we stand upright before you, and can speak what we think. All have heard your voice, and all speak to you now as one man. Our minds are agreed.

"*Brother;* You say you want an answer to your talk before you leave this 13 place. It is right you should have one, as you are a great distance from home, and we do not wish to detain you. But we will first look back a little, and tell you what our fathers have told us, and what we have heard from the white people.

"*Brother;* Listen to what we say. 14

"There was a time when our forefathers owned this great island. Their seats extended from the rising to the setting sun. The Great Spirit had made it for the use of Indians. HE had created the buffalo, the deer, and other animals for food. HE had made the bear and the beaver. Their skins served us for clothing. HE had scattered them over the country, and taught us how to take them. HE had caused the earth to produce corn for bread. All this HE had done for his red children, because HE loved them. If we had some disputes about our hunting ground, they were generally settled without the shedding of much blood. But an evil day came upon us. Your forefathers crossed the great water, and landed on this island. Their numbers were small. They found friends and not enemies. They told us they had fled from their country for fear of wicked men, and had come here to enjoy their religion. They asked for a small seat. We took pity on them, granted their request; and they sat down amongst us. We gave them corn and meat, they gave us poison [alluding, it is supposed, to ardent spirits] in return.

"The white people had now found our country. Tidings were carried 15 back, and more came amongst us. Yet we did not fear them. We took them to be friends. They called us brothers. We believed them, and gave them a larger seat. At length their numbers had greatly increased. They wanted more land; they wanted our country. Our eyes were opened, and our minds became uneasy. Wars took place. Indians were hired to fight against Indians, and many of our people were destroyed. They also brought strong liquor amongst us. It was strong and powerful, and has slain thousands.

"*Brother;* Our seats were once large and yours were small. You have now 16 become a great people, and we have scarcely a place left to spread our blankets. You have got our country, but are not satisfied; you want to force your religion upon us.

"*Brother;* Continue to listen. 17

"You say that you are sent to instruct us how to worship the Great Spirit agreeably to his mind, and, if we do not take hold of the religion which you white people teach, we shall be unhappy hereafter. You say that you are right and we are lost. How do we know this to be true? We understand that your religion is written in a book. If it was intended for us as well as you, why has not the Great Spirit given to us, and not only to us, but why did he not give to our forefathers, the knowledge of that book, with the means of understanding it rightly? We only know what you tell us about it. How shall we know when to believe, being so often deceived by the white people?

"*Brother;* You say there is but one way to worship and serve the Great 18 Spirit. If there is but one religion; why do you white people differ so much about it? Why not all agreed, as you can all read the book?

"*Brother;* We do not understand these things. 19

"We are told that your religion was given to your forefathers, and has been handed down from father to son. We also have a religion, which was given to our forefathers, and has been handed down to us their children. We worship in that way. It teaches us to be thankful for all the favors we receive; to love each other, and to be united. We never quarrel about religion.

"*Brother;* The Great Spirit has made us all, but he has made a great 20 difference between his white and red children. He has given us different complexions and different customs. To you He has given the arts. To these He has not opened our eyes. We know these things to be true. Since He has made so great a difference between us in other things; why may we not conclude that He has given us a different religion according to our understanding? The Great Spirit does right. He knows what is best for his children; we are satisfied.

"*Brother;* We do not wish to destroy your religion, or take it from you. 21 We only want to enjoy our own.

"*Brother;* We are told that you have been preaching to the white people 22 in this place. These people are our neighbors. We are acquainted with them. We will wait a little while, and see what effect your preaching has upon them. If we find it does them good, makes them honest and less disposed to cheat Indians; we will then consider again of what you have said.

"*Brother;* You have now heard our answer to your talk, and this is all we 23 have to say at present.

"As we are going to part, we will come and take you by the hand, and 24 hope the Great Spirit will protect you on your journey, and return you safe to your friends."

[As the Indians began to approach the missionary, he rose hastily from 25 his seat and replied, that he could not take them by the hand; that there was no fellowship between the religion of God and the works of the devil.

This being interpreted to the Indians, they smiled, and retired in a 26 peaceable manner.

It being afterwards suggested to the missionary that his reply to the 27 Indians was rather indiscreet; he observed, that he supposed the ceremony of shaking hands would be received by them as a token that he assented to what they had said. Being otherwise informed, he said he was sorry for the expressions.]

Questions for Discussion

1. What words and actions can you point to that reveal the unconscious bigotry of the missionary?

2. In light of the patronizing tone adopted by the missionary, how do you account for the mildness and friendliness of the Indians' reply? Clearly, this picture squares badly with the image of the "savage redskin" in novels and movies. What reasons can you offer for the persistence of this popular but degrading image? Which of those reasons is connected to the attitudes exhibited by the missionary?

3. What kind of research, and what kind of thinking about evidence, would be required to get a clear picture of what the Senecas were like at the time this speech was given? Do you think that any one account, whether from the perspective of Indians, of white Americans, or of some "neutral" historian from another nation, could capture the full story that lies behind Red Jacket's speech?

4. Do you think that the account of Indian history *from the Indians' point of view* (¶14–16) is generally accepted today by most white people? If it is, why do you think that more has not been done to right the obvious wrongs exposed in this history? If you think most white people reject the Indians' view, what other views do you think they hold?

Suggested Essay Topics

1. Write another answer to the missionary for the Indians, taking a tone of indignation, outrage, or bitterness. You may use the same content or add to it from your own store of information; the point is to alter the tone so that you change the effect of the message.

2. Write a speech that might serve as a reply to Red Jacket, made by someone who has *really listened* to his arguments. In planning your speech, you should think through the possible lines of argument and the possible tones you might take: humbly apologetic (moving toward explanation); firmly indignant about having been misunderstood and maligned; rational and unemotional, mustering anecdotes and other evidence to show that Indians after all *have* committed cruel acts; and so on. Then choose the tone (implying a character for yourself) that you think will be most likely to be taken as sympathetic, so that the Indians will be most likely to hear your side of the story.

Frederick Douglass

Many of you are familiar with the stirring rhythms, profound vision, and moral passion in the prose of Martin Luther King, who is probably the greatest of twentieth-century orators to write and speak in defense of a "liberty and justice" for all that really does cover all, *including African-Americans. Some of you will be less familiar, perhaps totally unfamiliar, with King's predecessor and nineteenth-century counterpart, Frederick Douglass (1817–1895). Slightly more than 100 years before King's "Letter from Birmingham Jail" (in Chapter 6) and "I Have a Dream," Frederick Douglass, born in slavery and bravely speaking to a society that still condoned slavery as a national institution, spoke with an outraged plainness, an authority based on personal experience, a sad and profound sense of common humanity, and a moral passion that, in its incandescence, matches King's own.*

Some of Douglass's readers today may recognize him as a stirring figure, but may consider him relevant only in a historical sense. After all, slavery has been long abolished, so what reason is there to read Douglass other than to see and hear the kinds of arguments and language that eventually helped overturn slavery? Others, however, may resist the idea that someone like Douglass is interesting or relevant merely as an historical figure.

Understood as an argument that not merely opposes slavery in its technical sense, but that oppose all forms of oppression in the broadest sense, the speech reprinted here remains a passionate manifesto in defense of equal opportunity, equal treatment under the law, and equal respect for the basic rights of all human beings. As an utterance that gives voice not only to the pain, the humiliation, and the outrage of those who are oppressed, but that resoundingly articulates the grounds upon which oppression is to be opposed, his speech remains as current today as it was when he delivered it in Rochester, New York, in 1852.

Many Americans today are perplexed and ashamed that so many of their fellow citizens—millions of them, in fact, and among them a preponderance of children—are so impoverished and neglected that they are forced to live without homes or other shelter, without the means of securing the most basic necessities of food and medical help, and without hope. Both those who are well off and those who are impoverished angrily wonder why "someone doesn't do something." Why are these circumstances allowed to persist, and, indeed, allowed to grow?

Reading Douglass will not answer this question directly, but reading him does invite us all to examine, much more vividly than we would be inclined to do without his powerful rhetoric, the grounds on which answers to this question may be based. When all of us feel in our bones the shame of certain circumstances as keenly as the people who suffer those circumstances, as keenly as Douglass feels the shame of those bound in slavery, then we will insist on answers instead of dwelling on plaintive questions. When others' pain is felt as our own, we will no longer look for someone else to "do something"; we will feel it necessary to do something ourselves. Surely one of the social functions of an eloquence as powerful as Douglass's is to make the realities he describes more vivid to us than we are able to do on our own, to awaken our imagination and sympathies, and, finally, to stir us to action.

Consider as you read how difficult Douglass's rhetorical position was in 1852. Denouncing slavery, even in the North, in a time when slavery was still a legal institution protected and aided by the law, custom, and religion was not only difficult in the rhetorical sense of persuading others to see things as Douglass saw them, but was dangerous to his person. Notice how carefully he builds credibility by showing his full understanding, in the first 30 paragraphs, of all that Americans deserve to be proud of. He lets his audience know that he understands and shares an American's pride and patriotism in the country that, in its Revolutionary War, withstood the tyranny of the (then) strongest country in the world.

However, notice also how, once he has clearly shown his familiarity with the grounds of American pride and superiority, he is then in a much more credible position than he might otherwise have been to show that the hypocrisy and degradation of slavery stain and undermine those very principles that Americans are used to viewing as the special marks of their virtue and superiority. Finally, once he has established his point about national hypocrisy, notice how he drives the point home to the hilt. He hammers away at it, showing its presence in every light possible, especially its presence in American churches, which mostly stood silently to the side on the slavery question or actively preached compliance with such enactments as the Fugitive Slave Law because slavery was, after all, "legal."

THE MEANING OF JULY FOURTH FOR THE NEGRO

From *The Life and Writings of Frederick Douglass, Pre-Civil War Decade, 1850–1860,* Volume II, edited by Philip S. Foner (1950).

THE MEANING OF JULY FOURTH FOR THE NEGRO, SPEECH AT ROCHESTER, NEW YORK, JULY 5, 1852

Mr. President, Friends and Fellow Citizens:

He who could address this audience without a quailing sensation, has 1 stronger nerves than I have. I do not remember ever to have appeared as a speaker before any assembly more shrinkingly, nor with greater distrust of my ability, than I do this day. A feeling has crept over me quite unfavorable to the exercise of my limited powers of speech. The task before me is one which requires much previous thought and study for its proper performance. I know that apologies of this sort are generally considered flat and unmeaning. I trust, however, that mine will not be so considered. Should I seem at ease, my appearance would much misrepresent me. The little experience I have had in addressing public meetings, in country school houses, avails me nothing on the present occasion.

The papers and placards say that I am to deliver a Fourth of July 2 Oration. This certainly sounds large, and out of the common way, for me. It is true that I have often had the privilege to speak in this beautiful Hall, and to address many who now honor me with their presence. But neither their familiar faces, nor the perfect gage I think I have of Corinthian Hall seems to free me from embarrassment.

The fact is, ladies and gentlemen, the distance between this platform 3 and the slave plantation, from which I escaped, is considerable—and the difficulties to be overcome in getting from the latter to the former are by no means slight. That I am here to-day is, to me, a matter of astonishment as well as of gratitude. You will not, therefore, be surprised, if in what I have to say I evince no elaborate preparation, nor grace my speech with any high sounding exordium. With little experience and with less learning, I have been able to throw my thoughts hastily and imperfectly together; and trusting to your patient and generous indulgence, I will proceed to lay them before you.

This, for the purpose of this celebration, is the Fourth of July. It is the 4 birthday of your National Independence, and of your political freedom. This, to you, is what the Passover was to the emancipated people of God. It carries your minds back to the day, and to the act of your great deliverance; and to the signs, and to the wonders, associated with that act, and that day. This celebration also marks the beginning of another year of your national life; and reminds you that the Republic of America is now 76 years old. I am glad, fellow-citizens, that your nation is so young. Seventy-six years, though a good old age for a man, is but a mere speck in the life of a nation. Three score years and ten is the allotted time for individual men; but nations number their years by thousands. According to this fact, you are, even now, only in the beginning of your national career, still lingering in the period of childhood. I repeat, I am glad this is so. There is hope in the thought, and hope is much needed, under the dark clouds which lower above the horizon. The eye of the reformer is met with angry flashes, portending disastrous times; but his heart may well beat lighter at the thought that America is young, and that she is still in the impressible stage of her existence. May he not hope that high lessons of wisdom, of justice and of truth, will yet give direction to her destiny? Were the nation older, the patriot's heart might be sadder, and the reformer's brow heavier. Its future might be shrouded in gloom, and the hope of its prophets go out in sorrow. There is consolation in the thought that America is young.—Great streams are not easily turned from channels, worn deep in the course of ages. They may sometimes rise in quiet and stately majesty, and inundate the land, refreshing and fertilizing the earth with their mysterious properties. They may also rise in wrath and fury, and bear away, on their angry waves, the accumulated wealth of years of toil and hardship. They, however, gradually flow back to the same old channel, and flow on as serenely as ever. But, while the river may not be turned aside, it may dry up, and leave nothing behind but the withered branch, and the unsightly rock, to howl in the abyss-sweeping wind, the sad tale of departed glory. As with rivers so with nations.

Fellow-citizens, I shall not presume to dwell at length on the associa-   5
tions that cluster about this day. The simple story of it is, that, 76 years ago, the people of this country were British subjects. The style and title of your "sovereign people" (in which you now glory) was not then born. You were under the British Crown. Your fathers esteemed the English Government as the home government; and England as the fatherland. This home government, you know, although a considerable distance from your home, did, in the exercise of its parental prerogatives, impose upon its colonial children, such restraints, burdens and limitations, as, in its mature judgment, it deemed wise, right and proper.

But your fathers, who had not adopted the fashionable idea of this day,   6
of the infallibility of government, and the absolute character of its acts, presumed to differ from the home government in respect to the wisdom and the justice of some of those burdens and restraints. They went so far in their excitement as to pronounce the measures of government unjust, unreasonable, and oppressive, and altogether such as ought not to be quietly submitted to. I scarcely need say, fellow-citizens, that my opinion of those measures fully accords with that of your fathers. Such a declaration of agreement on my part would not be worth much to anybody. It would certainly prove nothing as to what part I might have taken had I lived during the great controversy of 1776. To say now that America was right, and England wrong, is exceedingly easy. Everybody can say it; the dastard, not less than the noble brave, can flippantly discant on the tyranny of England towards the American

Colonies. It is fashionable to do so; but there was a time when, to pronounce against England, and in favor of the cause of the colonies, tried men's souls. They who did so were accounted in their day plotters of mischief, agitators and rebels, dangerous men. To side with the right against the wrong, with the weak against the strong, and with the oppressed against the oppressor! here lies the merit, and the one which, of all others, seems unfashionable in our day. The cause of liberty may be stabbed by the men who glory in the deeds of your fathers. But, to proceed.

Feeling themselves harshly and unjustly treated, by the home govern- 7 ment, your fathers, like men of honesty, and men of spirit, earnestly sought redress. They petitioned and remonstrated; they did so in a decorous, respect- ful, and loyal manner. Their conduct was wholly unexceptionable. This, however, did not answer the purpose. They saw themselves treated with sovereign indifference, coldness and scorn. Yet they persevered. They were not the men to look back.

As the sheet anchor takes a firmer hold, when the ship is tossed by the 8 storm, so did the cause of your fathers grow stronger as it breasted the chilling blasts of kingly displeasure. The greatest and best of British statesmen admit- ted its justice, and the loftiest eloquence of the British Senate came to its support. But, with that blindness which seems to be the unvarying character- istic of tyrants, since Pharaoh and his hosts were drowned in the Red Sea, the British Government persisted in the exactions complained of.

The madness of this course, we believe, is admitted now, even by 9 England; but we fear the lesson is wholly lost on our present rulers.

Oppression makes a wise man mad. Your fathers were wise men, and 10 if they did not go mad, they became restive under this treatment. They felt themselves the victims of grievous wrongs, wholly incurable in their colonial capacity. With brave men there is always a remedy for oppression. Just here, the idea of a total separation of the colonies from the crown was born! It was a startling idea, much more so than we, at this distance of time, regard it. The timid and the prudent (as has been intimated) of that day were, of course, shocked and alarmed by it.

Such people lived then, had lived before, and will, probably, ever have 11 a place on this planet; and their course, in respect to any great change (no matter how great the good to be attained, or the wrong to be redressed by it), may be calculated with as much precision as can be the course of the stars. They hate all changes, but silver, gold and copper change! Of this sort of change they are always strongly in favor.

These people were called Tories in the days of your fathers; and the 12 appellation, probably, conveyed the same idea that is meant by a more mod- ern, though a somewhat less euphonious term, which we often find in our papers, applied to some of our old politicians.

Their opposition to the then dangerous thought was earnest and power- 13 ful; but, amid all their terror and affrighted vociferations against it, the alarming and revolutionary idea moved on, and the country with it.

On the 2d of July, 1776, the old Continental Congress, to the dismay 14 of the lovers of ease, and the worshipers of property, clothed that dreadful idea with all the authority of national sanction. They did so in the form of a resolution; and as we seldom hit upon resolutions, drawn up in our day, whose transparency is at all equal to this, it may refresh your minds and help my story if I read it.

> "Resolved, That these united colonies are, and of right, ought to be free   15
> and Independent States; that they are absolved from all allegiance to the
> British Crown; and that all political connection between them and the
> State of Great Britain is, and ought to be, dissolved."

Citizens, your fathers made good that resolution. They succeeded; and   16
to-day you reap the fruits of their success. The freedom gained is yours; and you, therefore, may properly celebrate this anniversary. The 4th of July is the first great fact in your nation's history—the very ringbolt in the chain of your yet undeveloped destiny.

Pride and patriotism, not less than gratitude, prompt you to celebrate   17
and to hold it in perpetual remembrance. I have said that the Declaration of Independence is the ringbolt to the chain of your nation's destiny; so, indeed, I regard it. The principles contained in that instrument are saving principles. Stand by those principles, be true to them on all occasions, in all places, against all foes, and at whatever cost.

From the round top of your ship of state, dark and threatening clouds   18
may be seen. Heavy billows, like mountains in the distance, disclose to the leeward huge forms of flinty rocks! That bolt drawn, that chain broken, and all is lost. Cling to this day—cling to it, and to its principles, with the grasp of a storm-tossed mariner to a spar at midnight.

The coming into being of a nation, in any circumstances, is an interest-   19
ing event. But, besides general considerations, there were peculiar circumstances which make the advent of this republic an event of special attractiveness.

The whole scene, as I look back to it, was simple, dignified and sublime.   20
The population of the country, at the time, stood at the insignificant number of three millions. The country was poor in the munitions of war. The population was weak and scattered, and the country a wilderness unsubdued. There were then no means of concert and combination, such as exist now. Neither steam nor lightning had then been reduced to order and discipline. From the Potomac to the Delaware was a journey of many days. Under these, and innumerable other disadvantages, your fathers declared for liberty and independence and triumphed.

Fellow-citizens, I am not wanting in respect for the fathers of this   21
republic. The signers of the Declaration of Independence were brave men. They were great men, too—great enough to give frame to a great age. It does not often happen to a nation to raise, at one time, such a number of truly great men. The point from which I am compelled to view them is not, certainly, the most favorable; and yet I cannot contemplate their great deeds with less

than admiration. They were statesmen, patriots and heroes, and for the good they did, and the principles they contended for, I will unite with you to honor their memory.

They loved their country better than their own private interests; and, 22 though this is not the highest form of human excellence, all will concede that it is a rare virtue, and that when it is exhibited it ought to command respect. He who will, intelligently, lay down his life for his country is a man whom it is not in human nature to despise. Your fathers staked their lives, their fortunes, and their sacred honor, on the cause of their country. In their admiration of liberty, they lost sight of all other interests.

They were peace men; but they preferred revolution to peaceful submis- 23 sion to bondage. They were quiet men; but they did not shrink from agitating against oppression. They showed forbearance; but that they knew its limits. They believed in order; but not in the order of tyranny. With them, nothing was "settled" that was not right. With them, justice, liberty and humanity were "final"; not slavery and oppression. You may well cherish the memory of such men. They were great in their day and generation. Their solid manhood stands out the more as we contrast it with these degenerate times.

How circumspect, exact and proportionate were all their movements! 24 How unlike the politicians of an hour! Their statesmanship looked beyond the passing moment, and stretched away in strength into the distant future. They seized upon eternal principles, and set a glorious example in their defence. Mark them!

Fully appreciating the hardships to be encountered, firmly believing in 25 the right of their cause, honorably inviting the scrutiny of an on-looking world, reverently appealing to heaven to attest their sincerity, soundly comprehending the solemn responsibility they were about to assume, wisely measuring the terrible odds against them, your fathers, the fathers of this republic, did, most deliberately, under the inspiration of a glorious patriotism, and with a sublime faith in the great principles of justice and freedom, lay deep, the corner-stone of the national super-structure, which has risen and still rises in grandeur around you.

Of this fundamental work, this day is the anniversary. Our eyes are met 26 with demonstrations of joyous enthusiasm. Banners and pennants wave exultingly on the breeze. The din of business, too, is hushed. Even mammon seems to have quitted his grasp on this day. The ear-piercing fife and the stirring drum unite their accents with the ascending peal of a thousand church bells. Prayers are made, hymns are sung, and sermons are preached in honor of this day; while the quick martial tramp of a great and multitudinous nation, echoed back by all the hills, valleys and mountains of a vast continent, bespeak the occasion one of thrilling and universal interest—a nation's jubilee.

Friends and citizens, I need not enter further into the causes which led 27 to this anniversary. Many of you understand them better than I do. You could instruct me in regard to them. That is a branch of knowledge in which you feel, perhaps, a much deeper interest than your speaker. The causes which led to the separation of the colonies from the British Crown have never lacked for a tongue. They have all been taught in your common schools, narrated at your firesides, unfolded from your pulpits, and thundered from your legislative halls, and are as familiar to you as household words. They form the staple of your national poetry and eloquence.

I remember, also, that, as a people, Americans are remarkably familiar 28 with all facts which make in their own favor. This is esteemed by some as a national trait—perhaps a national weakness. It is a fact, that whatever makes for the wealth or for the reputation of Americans and can be had cheap! will be found by Americans. I shall not be charged with slandering Americans if I say I think the American side of any question may be safely left in American hands.

I leave, therefore, the great deeds of your fathers to other gentlemen 29 whose claim to have been regularly descended will be less likely to be disputed than mine!

My business, if I have any here to-day, is with the present. The accepted 30 time with God and His cause is the ever-living now.

> Trust no future, however pleasant,
>   Let the dead past bury its dead;
> Act, act in the living present,
>   Heart within, and God overhead.

We have to do with the past only as we can make it useful to the present and to the future. To all inspiring motives, to noble deeds which can be gained from the past, we are welcome. But now is the time, the important time. Your fathers have lived, died, and have done their work, and have done much of it well. You live and must die, and you must do your work. You have no right to enjoy a child's share in the labor of your fathers, unless your children are to be blest by your labors. You have no right to wear out and waste the hard-earned fame of your fathers to cover your indolence. Sydney Smith tells us that men seldom eulogize the wisdom and virtues of their fathers, but to excuse some folly or wickedness of their own. This truth is not a doubtful one. There are illustrations of it near and remote, ancient and modern. It was fashionable, hundreds of years ago, for the children of Jacob to boast, we have "Abraham to our father," when they had long lost Abraham's faith and spirit. That people contented themselves under the shadow of Abraham's great name, while they repudiated the deeds which made his name great. Need I remind you that a similar thing is being done all over this country to-day? Need I tell you that the Jews are not the only people who built the tombs of the prophets, and garnished the sepulchers of the righteous? Washington could not die till he had broken the chains of his slaves. Yet his monument is built up by the price of human blood, and the traders in the bodies and souls of men shout—"We have Washington to *our father.* "—Alas! that it should be so; yet so it is.

> *The evil that men do, lives after them,*
> *The good is oft interred with their bones.*

Fellow-citizens, pardon me, allow me to ask, why am I called upon to 31 speak here to-day? What have I, or those I represent, to do with your national independence? Are the great principles of political freedom and of natural justice, embodied in that Declaration of Independence, extended to us? and am I, therefore, called upon to bring our humble offering to the national altar, and to confess the benefits and express devout gratitude for the blessings resulting from your independence to us?

Would to God, both for your sakes and ours, that an affirmative answer 32 could be truthfully returned to these questions! Then would my task be light, and my burden easy and delightful. For *who* is there so cold, that a nation's sympathy could not warm him? Who so obdurate and dead to the claims of gratitude, that would not thankfully acknowledge such priceless benefits? Who so stolid and selfish, that would not give his voice to swell the hallelujahs of a nation's jubilee, when the chains of servitude had been torn from his limbs? I am not that man. In a case like that, the dumb might eloquently speak, and the "lame man leap as an hart."

But such is not the state of the case. I say it with a sad sense of the 33 disparity between us. I am not included within the pale of this glorious anniversary! Your high independence only reveals the immeasurable distance between us. The blessings in which you, this day, rejoice, are not enjoyed in common.—The rich inheritance of justice, liberty, prosperity and independence, bequeathed by your fathers, is shared by you, not by me. The sunlight that brought light and healing to you, has brought stripes and death to me. This Fourth of July is *yours,* not *mine. You* may rejoice, *I* must mourn. To drag a man in fetters into the grand illuminated temple of liberty, and call upon him to join you in joyous anthems, were inhuman mockery and sacrilegious irony. Do you mean, citizens, to mock me, by asking me to speak to-day? If so, there is a parallel to your conduct. And let me warn you that it is dangerous to copy the example of a nation whose crimes, towering up to heaven, were thrown down by the breath of the Almighty, burying that nation in irrevocable ruin! I can to-day take up the plaintive lament of a peeled and woe-smitten people!

"By the rivers of Babylon, there we sat down. Yea! we wept when we 34 remembered Zion. We hanged our harps upon the willows in the midst thereof. For there, they that carried us away captive, required of us a song; and they who wasted us required of us mirth, saying, Sing us one of the songs of Zion. How can we sing the Lord's song in a strange land? If I forget thee, O Jerusalem, let my right hand forget her cunning. If I do not remember thee, let my tongue cleave to the roof of my mouth."

Fellow-citizens, above your national, tumultuous joy, I hear the mourn- 35 ful wail of millions! whose chains, heavy and grievous yesterday, are, to-day, rendered more intolerable by the jubilee shouts that reach them. If I do forget, if I do not faithfully remember those bleeding children of sorrow this day, "may my right hand forget her cunning, and may my tongue cleave to the roof of my mouth!" To forget them, to pass lightly over their wrongs, and to chime in with the popular theme, would be treason most scandalous and shocking, and would make me a reproach before God and the world. My subject, then, fellow-citizens, is American slavery. I shall see this day and its popular characteristics from the slave's point of view. Standing there identified with the American bondman, making his wrongs mine, I do not hesitate to declare, with all my soul, that the character and conduct of this nation never looked blacker to me than on this 4th of July! Whether we turn to the declarations of the past, or to the professions of the present, the conduct of the nation seems equally hideous and revolting. America is false to the past, false to the present, and solemnly binds herself to be false to the future. Standing with God and the crushed and bleeding slave on this occasion, I will, in the name of humanity which is outraged, in the name of liberty which is fettered, in the name of the constitution and the Bible which are disregarded and trampled upon, dare to call in question and to denounce, with all the emphasis I can command, everything that serves to perpetuate slavery—the great sin and shame of America! "I will not equivocate; I will not excuse"; I will use the severest language I can command; and yet not one word shall escape me that any man, whose judgment is not blinded by prejudice, or who is not at heart a slaveholder, shall not confess to be right and just.

But I fancy I hear some one of my audience say, "It is just in this 36 circumstance that you and your brother abolitionists fail to make a favorable impression on the public mind. Would you argue more, and denounce less; would you persuade more, and rebuke less; your cause would be much more likely to succeed." But, I submit, where all is plain there is nothing to be argued. What point in the anti-slavery creed would you have me argue? On what branch of the subject do the people of this country need light? Must I undertake to prove that the slave is a man? That point is conceded already. Nobody doubts it. The slaveholders themselves acknowledge it in the enactment of laws for their government. They acknowledge it when they punish disobedience on the part of the slave. There are seventy-two crimes in the State of Virginia which, if committed by a black man (no matter how ignorant he be), subject him to the punishment of death; while only two of the same crimes will subject a white man to the like punishment. What is this but the acknowledgment that the slave is a moral, intellectual, and responsible being? The manhood of the slave is conceded. It is admitted in the fact that Southern statute books are covered with enactments forbidding, under severe fines and penalties, the teaching of the slave to read or to write. When you can point to any such laws in reference to the beasts of the field, then I may consent to argue the manhood of the slave. When the dogs in your streets, when the fowls of the air, when the cattle on your hills, when the fish of the sea, and the reptiles that crawl, shall be unable to distinguish the slave from a brute, *then* will I argue with you that the slave is a man!

For the present, it is enough to affirm the equal manhood of the Negro 37 race. Is it not astonishing that, while we are ploughing, planting, and reaping, using all kinds of mechanical tools, erecting houses, constructing bridges, building ships, working in metals of brass, iron, copper, silver and gold; that, while we are reading, writing and ciphering, acting as clerks, merchants and secretaries, having among us lawyers, doctors, ministers, poets, authors, editors, orators and teachers; that, while we are engaged in all manner of enterprises common to other men, digging gold in California, capturing the whale in the Pacific, feeding sheep and cattle on the hill-side, living, moving, acting, thinking, planning, living in families as husbands, wives and children, and, above all, confessing and worshipping the Christian's God, and looking hopefully for life and immortality beyond the grave, we are called upon to prove that we are men!

Would you have me argue that man is entitled to liberty? that he is the 38
rightful owner of his own body? You have already declared it. Must I argue the wrongfulness of slavery? Is that a question for Republicans? Is it to be settled by the rules of logic and argumentation, as a matter beset with great difficulty, involving a doubtful application of the principle of justice, hard to be understood? How should I look to-day, in the presence of Americans, dividing, and subdividing a discourse, to show that men have a natural right to freedom? speaking of it relatively and positively, negatively and affirmatively. To do so, would be to make myself ridiculous, and to offer an insult to your understanding.—There is not a man beneath the canopy of heaven that does not know that slavery is wrong *for him.*

What, am I to argue that it is wrong to make men brutes, to rob them 39
of their liberty, to work them without wages, to keep them ignorant of their relations to their fellow men, to beat them with sticks, to flay their flesh with the lash, to load their limbs with irons, to hunt them with dogs, to sell them at auction, to sunder their families, to knock out their teeth, to burn their flesh, to starve them into obedience and submission to their masters? Must I argue that a system thus marked with blood, and stained with pollution, is *wrong?* No! I will not. I have better employment for my time and strength than such arguments would imply.

What, then, remains to be argued? Is it that slavery is not divine; that 40
God did not establish it; that our doctors of divinity are mistaken? There is blasphemy in the thought. That which is inhuman, cannot be divine! *Who* can reason on such a proposition? They that can, may; I cannot. The time for such argument is passed.

At a time like this, scorching irony, not convincing argument, is needed. 41
O! had I the ability, and could reach the nation's ear, I would, to-day, pour out a fiery stream of biting ridicule, blasting reproach, withering sarcasm, and stern rebuke. For it is not light that is needed, but fire; it is not the gentle shower, but thunder. We need the storm, the whirlwind, and the earthquake. The feeling of the nation must be quickened; the conscience of the nation must be roused; the propriety of the nation must be startled; the hypocrisy of the nation must be exposed; and its crimes against God and man must be proclaimed and denounced.

What, to the American slave, is your 4th of July? I answer; a day that 42 reveals to him, more than all other days in the year, the gross injustice and cruelty to which he is the constant victim. To him, your celebration is a sham; your boasted liberty, an unholy license; your national greatness, swelling vanity; your sounds of rejoicing are empty and heartless; your denunciation of tyrants, brass-fronted impudence; your shouts of liberty and equality, hollow mockery; your prayers and hymns, your sermons and thanksgivings, with all your religious parade and solemnity, are, to Him, mere bombast, fraud, deception, impiety, and hypocrisy—a thin veil to cover up crimes which would disgrace a nation of savages. There is not a nation on the earth guilty of practices more shocking and bloody than are the people of the United States, at this very hour.

Go where you may, search where you will, roam through all the monar- 43
chies and despotisms of the Old World, travel through South America, search out every abuse, and when you have found the last, lay your facts by the side of the everyday practices of this nation, and you will say with me, that, for revolting barbarity and shameless hypocrisy, American reigns without a rival.

Take the American slave-trade, which we are told by the papers, is 44
especially prosperous just now. Ex-Senator Benton tells us that the price of men was never higher than now. He mentions the fact to show that slavery is in no danger. This trade is one of the peculiarities of American institutions. It is carried on in all the large towns and cities in one-half of this confederacy; and millions are pocketed every year by dealers in this horrid traffic. In several states this trade is a chief source of wealth. It is called (in contradistinction to the foreign slave-trade) *"the internal slave-trade."* It is, probably, called so, too, in order to divert from it the horror with which the foreign slave-trade is contemplated. That trade has long since been denounced by this government as piracy. It has been denounced with burning words from the high places of the nation as an execrable traffic. To arrest it, to put an end to it, this nation keeps a squadron, at immense cost, on the coast of Africa. Everywhere, in this country, it is safe to speak of this foreign slave-trade as a most inhuman traffic, opposed alike to the laws of God and of man. The duty to extirpate and destroy it, is admitted even by our doctors of divinity. In order to put an end to it, some of these last have consented that their colored brethren (nominally free) should leave this country, and establish themselves on the western coast of Africa! It is, however, a notable fact that, while so much execration is poured out by Americans upon all those engaged in the foreign slave-trade, the men engaged in the slave-trade between the states pass without condemnation, and their business is deemed honorable.

Behold the practical operation of this internal slave-trade, the American 45
slave-trade, sustained by American politics and American religion. Here you will see men and women reared like swine for the market. You know what is a swine-drover? I will show you a man-drover. They inhabit all our Southern States. They perambulate the country, and crowd the highways of the nation, with droves of human stock. You will see one of these human flesh jobbers, armed with pistol, whip, and bowie-knife, driving a company of a hundred men, women, and children, from the Potomac to the slave market

at New Orleans. These wretched people are to be sold singly, or in lots, to suit purchasers. They are food for the cotton-field and the deadly sugar-mill. Mark the sad procession, as it moves wearily along, and the inhuman wretch who drives them. Hear his savage yells and his blood-curdling oaths, as he hurries on his affrighted captives! There, see the old man with locks thinned and gray. Cast one glance, if you please, upon that young mother, whose shoulders are bare to the scorching sun, her briny tears falling on the brow of the babe in her arms. See, too, that girl of thirteen, weeping, *yes!* weeping, as she thinks of the mother from whom she has been torn! The drove moves tardily. Heat and sorrow have nearly consumed their strength; suddenly you hear a quick snap, like the discharge of a rifle; the fetters clank, and the chain rattles simultaneously; your ears are saluted with a scream, that seems to have torn its way to the centre of your soul! The crack you heard was the sound of the slave-whip; the scream you heard was from the woman you saw with the babe. Her speed had faltered under the weight of her child and her chains! that gash on her shoulder tells her to move on. Follow this drive to New Orleans. Attend the auction; see men examined like horses; see the forms of women rudely and brutally exposed to the shocking gaze of American slave-buyers. See this drove sold and separated forever; and never forget the deep, sad sobs that arose from that scattered multitude. Tell me, citizens, where, under the sun, you can witness a spectacle more fiendish and shocking. Yet this is but a glance at the American slave-trade, as it exists, at this moment, in the ruling part of the United States.

I was born amid such sights and scenes. To me the American slave-trade is a terrible reality. When a child, my soul was often pierced with a sense of its horrors. I lived on Philpot Street, Fell's Point, Baltimore, and have watched from the wharves the slave ships in the Basin, anchored from the shore, with their cargoes of human flesh, waiting for favorable winds to waft them down the Chesapeake. There was, at that time, a grand slave mart kept at the head of Pratt Street, by Austin Woldfolk. His agents were sent into every town and county in Maryland, announcing their arrival, through the papers, and on flaming *"hand-bills,"* headed cash for Negroes. These men were generally well dressed men, and very captivating in their manners; ever ready to drink, to treat, and to gamble. The fate of many a slave has depended upon the turn of a single card; and many a child has been snatched from the arms of its mother by bargains arranged in a state of brutal drunkenness. [46]

The flesh-mongers gather up their victims by dozens, and drive them, chained, to the general depot at Baltimore. When a sufficient number has been collected here, a ship is chartered for the purpose of conveying the forlorn crew to Mobile, or to New Orleans. From the slave prison to the ship, they are usually driven in the darkness of night; for since the anti-slavery agitation, a certain caution is observed. [47]

In the deep, still darkness of midnight, I have been often aroused by the dead, heavy footsteps, and the piteous cries of the chained gangs that passed our door. The anguish of my boyish heart was intense; and I was often [48] consoled, when speaking to my mistress in the morning, to hear her say that the custom was very wicked; that she hated to hear the rattle of the chains and the heart-rending cries. I was glad to find one who sympathized with me in my horror.

Fellow-citizens, this murderous traffic is, to-day, in active operation in this boasted republic. In the solitude of my spirit I see clouds of dust raised on the highways of the South; I see the bleeding footsteps; I hear the doleful wail of fettered humanity on the way to the slave-markets, where the victims are to be sold like *horses, sheep,* and *swine,* knocked off to the highest bidder. There I see the tenderest ties ruthlessly broken, to gratify the lust, caprice and rapacity of the buyers and sellers of men. My soul sickens at the sight. 49

> *Is this the land your Fathers loved,*
> *The freedom which they toiled to win?*
> *Is this the earth whereon they moved?*
> *Are these the graves they slumber in?*

But a still more inhuman, disgraceful, and scandalous state of things remains to be presented. By an act of the American Congress, not yet two years old, slavery has been nationalized in its most horrible and revolting form. By that act, Mason and Dixon's line has been obliterated; New York has become as Virginia; and the power to hold, hunt, and sell men, women and children, as slaves, remains no longer a mere state institution, but is now an institution of the whole United States. The power is co-extensive with the star-spangled banner, and American Christianity. Where these go, may also go the merciless slave-hunter. Where these are, man is not sacred. He is a bird for the sportsman's gun. By that most foul and fiendish of all human decrees, the liberty and person of every man are put in peril. Your broad republican domain is hunting ground for *men. Not* for thieves and robbers, enemies of society, merely, but for men guilty of no crime. Your law-makers have commanded all good citizens to engage in this hellish sport. Your President, your Secretary of State, your *lords, nobles,* and ecclesiastics enforce, as a duty you owe to your free and glorious country, and to your God, that you do this accursed thing. Not fewer than forty Americans have, with in the past two years, been hunted down and, without a moment's warning, hurried away in chains, and consigned to slavery and excruciating torture. Some of these have had wives and children, dependent on them for bread; but of this, no account was made. The right of the hunter to his prey stands superior to the right of marriage, and to *all* rights in this republic, the rights of God included! For black men there is neither law nor justice, humanity nor religion. The Fugitive Slave *Law* makes mercy to them a crime; and bribes the judge who tries them. An American judge gets ten dollars for every victim he consigns to slavery, and five, when he fails to do so. The oath of any two villains is sufficient, under this hell-black enactment, to send the most pious and exemplary black man into the remorseless jaws of slavery! His own testimony is nothing. He 50 can bring no witnesses for himself. The minister of American justice is bound by the law to hear but *one* side; and *that* side is the side of the oppressor. Let this damning fact be perpetually told. Let it be thundered around the world that in tyrant-killing, king-hating, people-loving, democratic, Christian America the seats of justice are filled with judges who hold their offices under an open and palpable *bribe,* and are bound, in deciding the case of a man's liberty, *to hear only his accusers!*

In glaring violation of justice, in shameless disregard of the forms of 51 administering law, in cunning arrangement to entrap the defenceless, and in diabolical intent this Fugitive Slave Law stands alone in the annals of tyrannical legislation. I doubt if there be another nation on the globe having the brass and the baseness to put such a law on the statute-book. If any man in this assembly thinks differently from me in this matter, and feels able to disprove my statements, I will gladly confront him at any suitable time and place he may select.

I take this law to be one of the grossest infringements of Christian 52 Liberty, and, if the churches and ministers of our country were not stupidly blind, or most wickedly indifferent, they, too, would so regard it.

At the very moment that they are thanking God for the enjoyment of 53 civil and religious liberty, and for the right to worship God according to the dictates of their own consciences, they are utterly silent in respect to a law which robs religion of its chief significance and makes it utterly worthless to a world lying in wickedness. Did this law concern the *"mint, anise, and cummin"*—abridge the right to sing psalms, to partake of the sacrament, or to engage in any of the ceremonies of religion, it would be smitten by the thunder of a thousand pulpits. A general shout would go up from the church demanding *repeal, repeal, instant repeal!*—And it would go hard with that politician who presumed to solicit the votes of the people without inscribing this motto on his banner. Further, if this demand were not complied with, another Scotland would be added to the history of religious liberty, and the stern old covenanters would be thrown into the shade. A John Knox* would be seen at every church door and heard from every pulpit, and Fillmore† would have no more quarter than was shown by Knox to the beautiful, but treacherous, Queen Mary of Scotland.‡ The fact that the church of our country (with

*John Knox (1513–1572) was leader of the reformation (the separation of the Protestant church from the Catholic church) in Scotland. He set the austere moral tone of the Church of Scotland and shaped its democratic form of government. Thus Douglass's reference to "another Scotland" in the previous sentence is a reference to national movements in favor of freedom and opposed to tyranny.

†Millard Fillmore (1800–1874) was president of the United States at the time of Douglass's address. Fillmore was vice president under Zachary Taylor and completed Taylor's term when Taylor died in 1850. He was defeated for the presidency in his own right in 1852. Fillmore signed the new Fugitive Slave Law of 1850, thus alienating abolitionists.

‡Mary Stuart (1542–1587) was the Catholic queen of Scotland who wished to return Scotland to Catholicism, but was forced by the nation's Protestant partisans to abdicate the throne in favor of her Protestant son, who later became both king of Scotland as James VI and of England as James I. Knox was one of Mary's principal opponents.

fractional exceptions) does not esteem "the Fugitive Slave Law"* as a declaration of war against religious liberty, implies that that church regards religion simply as a form of worship, an empty ceremony, and *not* a vital principle, requiring active benevolence, justice, love, and good will towards man. It esteems sacrifice above mercy; psalm-singing above right doing; solemn meetings above practical righteousness. A worship that can be conducted by persons who refuse to give shelter to the houseless, to give bread to the hungry, clothing to the naked, and who enjoin obedience to a law forbidding these acts of mercy is a curse, not a blessing to mankind. The Bible addresses all such persons as "scribes, pharisees, hypocrites, who pay tithe of *mint, anise,* and *cummin,* and have omitted the weightier matters of the law, judgment, mercy, and faith."

But the church of this country is not only indifferent to the wrongs of the slave, it actually takes sides with the oppressors. It has made itself the bulwark of American slavery, and the shield of American slave-hunters. Many of its most eloquent Divines, who stand as the very lights of the church, have shamelessly given the sanction of religion and the Bible to the whole slave system. They have taught that man may, properly, be a slave; that the relation of master and slave is ordained of God; that to send back an escaped bondman to his master is clearly the duty of all the followers of the Lord Jesus Christ; and this horrible blasphemy is palmed off upon the world for Christianity.

For my part, I would say, welcome infidelity! welcome atheism! welcome anything! in preference to the gospel, *as preached by those Divines!* They convert the very name of religion into an engine of tyranny and barbarous cruelty, and serve to confirm more infidels, in this age, than all the infidel writings of Thomas Paine, Voltaire, and Bolingbroke† put together have done! These ministers make religion a cold and flinty-hearted thing, having neither principles of right action nor bowels of compassion. They strip the love of God of its beauty and leave the throne of religion a huge, horrible, repulsive form. It is a religion for oppressors, tyrants, man-stealers, and *thugs.* It is not that *"pure and undefiled religion"* which is from above, and which is *"first pure, then peaceable, easy to be entreated,* full of mercy and good fruits, *without partiality, and without hypocrisy."* But a religion which favors the rich against the poor; which exalts the proud above the humble; which divides mankind into two classes, tyrants and slaves; which says to the man in chains, *stay there;* and to the oppressor, *oppress on;* it is a religion which may be professed and enjoyed

*The Fugitive Slave Law was first enacted by Congress in 1793 and mandated the right of a slaveowner to recover a runaway slave. This law made it illegal for those who opposed slavery, even in nonslavery states, to interfere with a slaveowner's attempts to remove runaway slaves from northern refuges and return them to southern slavery. A new Fugitive Slave Act passed by Congress and signed by President Fillmore in 1850 strengthened the act of 1793 and was bitterly opposed by abolitionists.

†Thomas Paine (1737–1809), American political philosopher; Francois-Marie Arouet, "Voltaire" (1694–1778), French philopher and athiest; and Henry St. John, 1st Viscount Bolingbroke (1678–1751), English politician and writer, were eighteenth-century figures all noted for their religious skepticism and hostility toward churches.

by all the robbers and enslavers of mankind; it makes God a respecter of persons, denies his fatherhood of the race, and tramples in the dust the great truth of the brotherhood of man. All this we affirm to be true of the popular church, and the popular worship of our land and nation—a religion, a church, and a worship which, on the authority of inspired wisdom, we pronounce to be an abomination in the sight of God. In the language of Isaiah, the American church might be well addressed, "Bring no more vain oblations; incense is an abomination unto me: the new moons and Sabbaths, the calling of assemblies, I cannot away with; it is iniquity, even the solemn meeting. Your new moons, and your appointed feasts my soul hateth. They are a trouble to me; I am weary to bear them; and when ye spread forth your hands I will hide mine eyes from you. Yea! when ye make many prayers, I will not hear. Your hands are full of blood; cease to do evil, learn to do well; seek judgment; relieve the oppressed; judge for the fatherless; plead for the widow."

The American church is guilty, when viewed in connection with what 56 it is doing to uphold slavery; but it is superlatively guilty when viewed in its connection with its ability to abolish slavery.

The sin of which it is guilty is one of omission as well as of commission. 57 Albert Barnes but uttered what the common sense of every man at all observant of the actual state of the case will receive as truth, when he declared that "There is no power out of the church that could sustain slavery an hour, if it were not sustained in it."

Let the religious press, the pulpit, the Sunday School, the conference 58 meeting, the great ecclesiastical, missionary, Bible and tract associations of the land array their immense powers against slavery, and slave-holding; and the whole system of crime and blood would be scattered to the winds, and that they do not do this involves them in the most awful responsibility of which the mind can conceive.

In prosecuting the anti-slavery enterprise, we have been asked to spare 59 the church, to spare the ministry; but *how*, we ask, could such a thing be done? We are met on the threshold of our efforts for the redemption of the slave, by the church and ministry of the country, in battle arrayed against us; and we are compelled to fight or flee. From *what* quarter, I beg to know, has proceeded a fire so deadly upon our ranks, during the last two years, as from the Northern pulpit? As the champions of oppressors, the chosen men of American theology have appeared—men honored for their so-called piety, and their real learning. The Lords of Buffalo, the Springs of New York, the Lathrops of Auburn, the Coxes and Spencers of Brooklyn, the Gannets and Sharps of Boston, the Deweys of Washington, and other great religious lights of the land have, in utter denial of the authority of *Him* by whom they professed to be called to the ministry, deliberately taught us, against the example of the Hebrews, and against the remonstrance of the Apostles, *that we ought to obey man's law before the law of God.*

My spirit wearies of such blasphemy; and how such men can be sup- 60 ported, as the "standing types and representatives of Jesus Christ," is a mystery which I leave others to penetrate. In speaking of the American church, however, let it be distinctly understood that I mean the *great mass* of the religious organizations of our land. There are exceptions, and I thank God that there are. Noble men may be found, scattered all over these Northern States, of whom Henry Ward Beecher, of Brooklyn; Samuel J. May, of Syracuse; and my esteemed friend (Rev. R. R. Raymond) on the platform, are shining examples; and let me say further, that, upon these men lies the duty to inspire our ranks with high religious faith and zeal, and to cheer us on in the great mission of the slave's redemption from his chains.

One is struck with the difference between the attitude of the American church towards the anti-slavery movement, and that occupied by the churches in England towards a similar movement in that country. There, the church, true to its mission of ameliorating, elevating and improving the condition of mankind, came forward promptly, bound up the wounds of the West Indian slave, and restored him to his liberty. There, the question of emancipation was a high religious question. It was demanded in the name of humanity, and according to the law of the living God. The Sharps, the Clarksons, the Wilberforces, the Buxtons, the Burchells, and the Knibbs were alike famous for their piety and for their philanthropy. The anti-slavery movement *there* was not an anti-church movement, for the reason that the church took its full share in prosecuting that movement: and the anti-slavery movement in this country will cease to be an anti-church movement, when the church of this country shall assume a favorable instead of a hostile position towards that movement.

Americans! your republican politics, not less than your republican religion, are flagrantly inconsistent. You boast of your love of liberty, your superior civilization, and your pure Christianity, while the whole political power of the nation (as embodied in the two great political parties) is solemnly pledged to support and perpetuate the enslavement of three millions of your countrymen. You hurl your anathemas at the crowned headed tyrants of Russia and Austria and pride yourselves on your Democratic institutions, while you yourselves consent to be the mere *tools* and *body-guards* of the tyrants of Virginia and Carolina. You invite to your shores fugitives of oppression from abroad, honor them with banquets, greet them with ovations, cheer them, toast them, salute them, protect them, and pour out your money to them like water; but the fugitives from your own land you advertise, hunt, arrest, shoot, and kill. You glory in your refinement and your universal education; yet you maintain a system as barbarous and dreadful as ever stained the character of a nation—a system begun in avarice, supported in pride, and perpetuated in cruelty. You shed tears over fallen Hungary, and make the sad story of her wrongs the theme of your poets, statesmen, and orators, till your gallant sons are ready to fly to arms to vindicate her cause against the oppressor; but, in regard to the ten thousand wrongs of the American slave, you would enforce the strictest silence, and would hail him as an enemy of the nation who dares to make those wrongs the subject of public discourse! You are all on fire at the mention of liberty for France or for Ireland; but are as cold as an iceberg at the thought of liberty for the

enslaved of America. You discourse eloquently on the dignity of labor; yet
you sustain a system which, in its very essence, casts a stigma upon labor.
You can bare your bosom to the storm of British artillery to throw off a
three-penny tax on tea; and yet wring the last hard earned farthing from the
grasp of the black laborers of your country. You profess to believe "that, of
one blood, God made all nations of men to dwell on the face of all the earth,"
and hath commanded all men, everywhere, to love one another; yet you
notoriously hate (and glory in your hatred) all men whose skins are not
colored like your own. You declare before the world, and are understood by
the world to declare that you *"hold these truths to be self-evident, that all men are
created equal; and are endowed by their Creator with certain inalienable rights; and that among
these are, life, liberty, and the pursuit of happiness;* and yet, you hold securely, in a
bondage which, according to your own Thomas Jefferson, *"is worse than ages
of that which your fathers rose in rebellion to oppose,"* a seventh part* of the inhabitants
of your country.

Fellow-citizens, I will not enlarge further on your national inconsisten-   63
cies. The existence of slavery in this country brands your republicanism as
a sham, your humanity as a base pretense, and your Christianity as a lie. It
destroys your moral power abroad: it corrupts your politicians at home. It
saps the foundation of religion; it makes your name a hissing and a bye-word
to a mocking earth. It is the antagonistic force in your government, the only
thing that seriously disturbs and endangers your *Union.* It fetters your progress; it is the enemy of improvement; the deadly foe of education; it fosters
pride; it breeds insolence; it promotes vice; it shelters crime; it is a curse to
the earth that supports it; and yet you cling to it as if it were the sheet anchor
of all your hopes. Oh! be warned! be warned! a horrible reptile is coiled up
in your nation's bosom; the venomous creature is nursing at the tender breast
of your youthful republic; *for the love of God, tear away,* and fling from you the
hideous monster, and *let the weight of twenty millions crush and destroy it forever!*

But it is answered in reply to all this, that precisely what I have now   64
denounced is, in fact, guaranteed and sanctioned by the Constitution of the
United States; that, the right to hold, and to hunt slaves is a part of that
Constitution framed by the illustrious Fathers of this Republic.

Then, I dare to affirm, notwithstanding all I have said before, your   65
fathers stooped, basely stooped

> *To palter with us in a double sense:*
> *And keep the word of promise to the dear,*
> *But break it to the heart.*

And instead of being the honest men I have before declared them to be,   66
they were the veriest impostors that ever practised on mankind. This is the
inevitable conclusion, and from it there is no escape; but I differ from those
who charge this baseness on the framers of the Constitution of the United
States. It is a slander upon their memory, at least, so I believe. There is not

time now to argue the constitutional question at length; nor have I the ability to discuss it as it ought to be discussed. The subject has been handled with masterly power by Lysander Spooner, Esq., by William Goodell, by Samuel E. Sewall, Esq., and last, though not least, by Gerrit Smith, Esq. These gentlemen have, as I think, fully and clearly vindicated the Constitution from any design to support slavery for an hour.

Fellow-citizens! there is no matter in respect to which the people of the 67 North have allowed themselves to be so ruinously imposed upon as that of the pro-slavery character of the Constitution. In that instrument I hold there is neither warrant, license, nor sanction of the hateful thing; but interpreted, as it ought to be interpreted, the Constitution is a glorious liberty document. Read its preamble, consider its purposes. Is slavery among them? Is it at the gateway? or is it in the temple? it is neither. While I do not intend to argue this question on the present occasion, let me ask, if it be not somewhat singular that, if the Constitution were intended to be, by its framers and adopters, a slaveholding instrument, why neither slavery, slaveholding, nor slave can anywhere be found in it. What would be thought of an instrument, drawn up, legally drawn up, for the purpose of entitling the city of Rochester to a tract of land, in which no mention of land was made? Now, there are certain rules of interpretation for the proper understanding of all legal instruments. These rules are well established. They are plain, common-sense rules, such as you and I, and all of us, can understand and apply, without having passed years in the study of law. I scout the idea that the question of the constitutionality, or unconstitutionality of slavery, is not a question for the people. I hold that every American citizen has a right to form an opinion of the constitution, and to propagate that opinion, and to use all honorable means to make his opinion the prevailing one. Without this right, the liberty of an American citizen would be as insecure as that of a Frenchman. Ex-Vice-President Dallas tells us that the constitution is an object to which no American mind can be too attentive, and no American heart too devoted. He further says, the Constitution, in its words, is plain and intelligible, and is meant for the home-bred, unsophisticated understandings of our fellow-citizens. Senator Berrien tells us that the Constitution is the fundamental law, that which controls all others. The charter of our liberties, which every citizen has a personal interest in understanding thoroughly. The testimony of Senator Breese, Lewis Cass, and many others that might be named, who are everywhere esteemed as sound lawyers, so regard the constitution. I take it, therefore, that it is not presumption in a private citizen to form an opinion of that instrument.

Now, take the Constitution according to its plain reading, and I defy the 68 presentation of a single pro-slavery clause in it. On the other hand, it will be found to contain principles and purposes, entirely hostile to the existence of slavery.

I have detained my audience entirely too long already. At some future 69 period I will gladly avail myself of an opportunity to give this subject a full and fair discussion.

Allow me to say, in conclusion, notwithstanding the dark picture I   70
have this day presented, of the state of the nation, I do not despair of this
country. There are forces in operation which must inevitably work the
downfall of slavery. "The arm of the Lord is not shortened," and the doom
of slavery is certain. I, therefore, leave off where I began, with hope. While
drawing encouragement from "the Declaration of Independence," the great
principles it contains, and the genius of American Institutions, my spirit is
also cheered by the obvious tendencies of the age. Nations do not now
stand in the same relation to each other that they did ages ago. No nation
can now shut itself up from the surrounding world and trot round in the
same old path of its fathers without interference. The time was when such
could be done. Long established customs of hurtful character could formerly fence themselves in, and do their evil work with social impunity.
Knowledge was then confined and enjoyed by the privileged few, and the
multitude walked on in mental darkness. But a change has now come over
the affairs of mankind. Walled cities and empires have become unfashionable. The arm of commerce has borne away the gates of the strong city.
Intelligence is penetrating the darkest corners of the globe. It makes its
pathway over and under the sea, as well as on the earth. Wind, steam, and
lightning are its chartered agents. Oceans no longer divide, but link nations
together. From Boston to London is now a holiday excursion. Space is comparatively annihilated.—Thoughts expressed on one side of the Atlantic are
distinctly heard on the other.

The far off and almost fabulous Pacific rolls in grandeur at our feet. The   71
Celestial Empire, the mystery of ages, is being solved. The fiat of the Almighty, "Let there be Light," has not yet spent its force. No abuse, no outrage
whether in taste, sport or avarice, can now hide itself from the all-pervading
light. The iron shoe, and crippled foot of China must be seen in contrast with
nature. Africa must rise and put on her yet unwoven garment. "Ethiopia shall
stretch out her hand unto God."* In the fervent aspirations of William Lloyd
Garrison, I say, and let every heart join in saying it:

> God speed the year of jubilee
> The wide world o'er!
> When from their galling chains set free,
> Th' oppress'd shall vilely bend the knee,
> And wear the yoke of tyranny   5
> Like brutes no more.
> That year will come, and freedom's reign,
> To man his plundered rights again
> Restore.

*Douglass's general point about light is that oppressive abuses, in a day of international travel,
cannot be hidden as before and will cry for redress. The "crippled foot of China" is a reference
to foot binding and "Ethiopia" is here used as a term for all African people.

God speed the day when human blood   10
Shall cease to flow!
In every clime be understood,
The claims of human brotherhood,
And each return for evil, good,
Not blow for blow;   15
That day will come all feuds to end,
And change into a faithful friend
Each foe.

God speed the hour, the glorious hour,
When none on earth   20
Shall exercise a lordly power,
Nor in a tyrant's presence cower;
But to all manhood's stature tower,
By equal birth!
That hour will come, to each, to all,   25
And from his prison-house, to thrall
Go forth.

Until that year, day, hour, arrive,
With head, and heart, and hand I'll strive,
To break the rod, and rend the gyve,   30
The spoiler of his prey deprive—
So witness Heaven!
And never from my chosen post,
Whate'er the peril or the cost,
Be driven.   35

Questions for Discussion

1. What is the function of "your," the sixth word in the second sentence of paragraph 4? How does this word prepare you for the change of tone and content that is to come later, beginning with paragraph 30?

2. How would you describe, first, the function of the parallel clauses that Douglass uses in paragraph 25 and, second, their rhetorical effect? If you rewrite the paragraph not making it intentionally ugly, but getting rid of the parallel constructions, what changes for the better or worse result?

3. Why does Douglass spend so much time—a full 29 paragraphs—speaking sympathetically, understandingly, and admiringly of American political and social principles? Is he sincere or insincere? What is the effect on his audience?

4. Another instance of Douglass's use of parallelism occurs in paragraph 35, where he says,

> I will, in the name of humanity which is outraged, in the name of liberty which is fettered, in the name of the constitution and the Bible which are disregarded and trampled upon . . . ! "I will not equivocate; I will not excuse"; . . . .

Is parallelism a device more appropriate and useful for oral delivery than for written expression? Why or why not? Or does such parallelism work differently in spoken as opposed to written prose? Is Douglass's use of it effective? Why or why not?

5. How is it possible for Douglass to include the two following utterances in the same speech without appearing to (or in fact) contradicting himself? "Fellow-citizens . . . the signers of the Declaration of Independence were brave men. They were great men, too . . . and for the good they did, and the principles they contended for, I will unite with you to honor their memory" (¶21). Yet in paragraphs 42 and 43 he says, "There is not a nation on the earth guilty of practices more shocking and bloody than are the people of the United States, at this very hour. . . . [F]or revolting barbarity and shameless hypocrisy, America reigns without a rival." Do both of these judgments come off as reasoned and sound? If so, how much does the projection of a particular *ethos,* or character, on Douglass's part affect the reader's assessment of the writer's judgments? What *is* Douglass's ethos? Is it appropriate to his task? Does he maintain the same ethos throughout his talk?

Suggested Essay Topics

1. Try your hand at writing a stirring, uplifting manifesto full of passion and moral authority. This is not an easy task to do well. What *is* easy is to sound pompous, empty, windy, and unduly certain about everything under the sun. However, all rhetorical stances have their special dangers and the reality of things is that when this stance is convincingly assumed, few types of utterances can be more effective. So give it a try. Choose some group of persons, some individual, or some issue about which you feel you can develop a full-blown rhetorical treatment, choose an audience appropriate to your choice of topic, and then mount your soap box. If you slip on your own soap, you will at least have learned more fully how to admire those who can speak successfully in this vein. (If you really do not feel up to this task, you might try the reverse of it: writing a parody or a satire of someone who attempts such a rhetorical undertaking, but simply comes off as a fatuous ass.)

2. In an essay directed to your instructor, analyze Douglass's essay by answering the following questions.
   a. What is Douglass's purpose and who is his audience? How does his awareness of audience help shape his purpose and how does he use his purpose to help shape his audience?

b. What devices of invention does Douglass employ? That is, to what sources does he go to find examples arguments? The standard sources of invention are the audience (what you know about them and what you think they expect), memory, conversation with others, observation, history, and the known facts about the subject itself.

c. What kinds of arguments, evidence, or facts does Douglass use in support of his claims?

d. What is the shape or design of Douglass's position? Where do the major organizational shifts in the development of his essay appear? How are they signaled?

e. How effectively does he employ devices of cohesion, those connections such as *however, therefore, although, but,* and so on that keep the reader on track sentence by sentence?

f. What image of his character, or *ethos,* does Douglas project of himself as a person? How does that character add to or detract from the effectiveness of Douglass's argument?

(If this is too large an undertaking for a single essay, leave out questions b, d, and e for now, with the understanding that a full analysis of Douglass's effects would in another essay have to take them into account.)

Ralph Ellison

Ralph Ellison (b. 1914) became famous almost overnight with the publication in 1952 of his novel Invisible Man, *the story of a young black man's trek toward self-identity. In a society that tells him he has no right to an identity except that given to him by whites, almost all of whom treat him with contempt, a trek toward identity meets almost impossible conditions. Most of us feel that we have a right not only to our own sense of selfhood but also to be surrounded by people who give us affection, encouragement, guidance, and hope.*

Through the use of symbol and metaphor, "Battle Royal" implies an argument about the position of blacks in a white-dominated power structure. Simply put, blacks must do battle in order to survive, but they must lose their naïveté if they are to battle successfully. As long as they allow whites to set the terms and conditions of battle, as long as they allow whites to set blacks battling against other blacks, and as long as they allow whites to reward them with cheap and phony payoffs that only underscore their inferior status, they will be duped into thinking they are winning a skirmish here and there (a scholarship to an all-black college, for example), but they will lose the royal battle, the battle for dignity, freedom, and self-esteem.

One of the most evocative symbols in the story is the naked dancer. As you read, try to determine how Ellison uses this symbol. Does "the small American flag tattooed upon her belly" (¶7) make her a symbol? If so, of what? Of all the false seductions that whites have held out to blacks who are eager to embrace America's noble slogans about freedom and equality but who are never allowed to join in the dance? The message to blacks has historically been one of "desire but don't possess," "admire but don't touch." And the callous way the white men toss the dancer in the air, defiling her out of sheer lust or greed, seems to highlight their profound ignorance of the grounds of their own freedom and to provide a sad commentary on their profound corruption.

The realization "that I am nobody but myself" (¶1) sounds simple, but to realize what this means in the only way that counts—to be in possession of one's own conscience, one's own sense of worth, and one's own sense of dignity, and to be able to hold to these in spite of social pressure, failure, or disappointment—this is not so simple. When family or society gives us double messages or lies, the realization can be made even harder. As you read, consider in what ways your own experience, whether you are a member of a minority or not, parallels and diverges from the central character's. Perhaps each of us has to fight a battle royal of some kind on the road to self-knowledge. The young man in the story has to identify the real enemy before he can begin to fight effectively, before he can even choose the right battle. How does he do this? What, or who, is his real enemy? His story invites us all to identify the battles that are most necessary or meaningful for us personally.

BATTLE ROYAL

From *Invisible Man* (1952).

It goes a long way back, some twenty years. All my life I had been looking for something, and everywhere I turned someone tried to tell me what it was. I accepted their answers too, though they were often in contradiction and even self-contradictory. I was naïve. I was looking for myself and asking everyone except myself questions which I, and only I, could answer. It took me a long time and much painful boomeranging of my expectations to achieve a realization everyone else appears to have been born with: That I am nobody but myself. But first I had to discover that I am an invisible man!

And yet I am no freak of nature, nor of history. I was in the cards, other things having been equal (or unequal) eighty-five years ago. I am not ashamed of my grandparents for having been slaves. I am only ashamed of myself for having at one time been ashamed. About eighty-five years ago they were told that they were free, united with others of our country in everything pertaining to the common good, and, in everything social, separate like the fingers of the hand. And they believed it. They exulted in it. They stayed in their place, worked hard, and brought up my father to do the same. But my grandfather is the one. He was an odd old guy, my grandfather, and I am told I take after him. It was he who caused the trouble. On his deathbed he called my father to him and said, "Son, after I'm gone I want you to keep up the fight. I never told you, but our life is a war and I have been a traitor all my born days, a spy in the enemy's country ever since I give up my gun back in the Reconstruction. Live with your head in the lion's mouth. I want you to overcome 'em with yeses, undermine 'em with grins, agree 'em to

death and destruction, let 'em swoller you till they vomit or bust wide open."
They thought the old man had gone out of his mind. He had been the meekest
of men. The younger children were rushed from the room, the shades drawn
and the flame of the lamp turned so low that it sputtered on the wick like
the old man's breathing. "Learn it to the younguns," he whispered fiercely;
then he died.

But my folks were more alarmed over his last words than over his dying.   3
It was as though he had not died at all, his words caused so much anxiety.
I was warned emphatically to forget what he had said and, indeed, this is the
first time it has been mentioned outside the family circle. It had a tremendous
effect upon me, however. I could never be sure of what he meant. Grandfather
had been a quiet old man who never made any trouble, yet on his deathbed
he had called himself a traitor and a spy, and he had spoken of his meekness
as a dangerous activity. It became a constant puzzle which lay unanswered
in the back of my mind. And whenever things went well for me I remembered
my grandfather and felt guilty and uncomfortable. It was as though I was
carrying out his advice in spite of myself. And to make it worse, everyone
loved me for it. I was praised by the most lily-white men of the town. I was
considered an example of desirable conduct—just as my grandfather had
been. And what puzzled me was that the old man had defined it as *treachery.*
When I was praised for my conduct I felt a guilt that in some way I was doing
something that was really against the wishes of the white folks, that if they
had understood they would have desired me to act just the opposite, that I
should have been sulky and mean, and that that really would have been what
they wanted, even though they were fooled and thought they wanted me to
act as I did. It made me afraid that some day they would look upon me as
a traitor and I would be lost. Still I was more afraid to act any other way
because they didn't like that at all. The old man's words were like a curse.
On my graduation day I delivered an oration in which I showed that humility
was the secret, indeed, the very essence of progress. (Not that I believed
this—how could I, remembering my grandfather?—I only believed that it
worked.) It was a great success. Everyone praised me and I was invited to give
the speech at a gathering of the town's leading white citizens. It was a triumph
for our whole community.

It was in the main ballroom of the leading hotel. When I got there I   4
discovered that it was on the occasion of a smoker, and I was told that since
I was to be there anyway I might as well take part in the battle royal to be
fought by some of my schoolmates as part of the entertainment. The battle
royal came first.

All of the town's big shots were there in their tuxedos, wolfing down   5
the buffet foods, drinking beer and whiskey and smoking black cigars. It was
a large room with a high ceiling. Chairs were arranged in neat rows around
three sides of a portable boxing ring. The fourth side was clear, revealing a
gleaming space of polished floor. I had some misgivings over the battle royal,
by the way. Not from a distaste for fighting, but because I didn't care too
much for the other fellows who were to take part. They were tough guys who

seemed to have no grandfather's curse worrying their minds. No one could mistake their toughness. And besides, I suspected that fighting a battle royal might detract from the dignity of my speech. In those pre-invisible days I visualized myself as a potential Booker T. Washington.* But the other fellows didn't care too much for me either, and there were nine of them. I felt superior to them in my way, and I didn't like the manner in which we were all crowded together into the servants' elevator. Nor did they like my being there. In fact, as the warmly lighted floors flashed past the elevator we had words over the fact that I, by taking part in the fight, had knocked one of their friends out of a night's work.

We were led out of the elevator through a rococo hall into an anteroom and told to get into our fighting togs. Each of us was issued a pair of boxing gloves and ushered out into the big mirrored hall, which we entered looking cautiously about us and whispering, lest we might accidentally be heard above the noise of the room. It was foggy with cigar smoke. And already the whiskey was taking effect. I was shocked to see some of the most important men of the town quite tipsy. They were all there—bankers, lawyers, judges, doctors, fire chiefs, teachers, merchants. Even one of the more fashionable pastors. Something we could not see was going on up front. A clarinet was vibrating sensuously and the men were standing up and moving eagerly forward. We were a small tight group, clustered together, our bare upper bodies touching and shining with anticipatory sweat; while up front the big shots were becoming increasingly excited over something we still could not see. Suddenly I heard the school superintendent, who had told me to come, yell, "Bring up the shines, gentlemen! Bring up the little shines!"

We were rushed up to the front of the ballroom, where it smelled even more strongly of tobacco and whiskey. Then we were pushed into place. I almost wet my pants. A sea of faces, some hostile, some amused, ringed around us, and in the center, facing us, stood a magnificent blonde—stark naked. There was a dead silence. I felt a blast of cold air chill me. I tried to back away, but they were behind me and around me. Some of the boys stood with lowered heads, trembling. I felt a wave of irrational guilt and fear. My teeth chattered, my skin turned to goose flesh, my knees knocked. Yet I was strongly attracted and looked in spite of myself. Had the price of looking been blindness, I would have looked. The hair was yellow like that of a circus kewpie doll, the face heavily powdered and rouged, as though to form an abstract mask, the eyes hollow and smeared a cool blue, the color of a baboon's butt. I felt a desire to spit upon her as my eyes brushed slowly over her body. Her breasts were firm and round as the domes of East Indian temples, and I stood so close as to see the fine skin texture and beads of pearly perspiration glistening like dew around the pink and erected buds of her nipples. I wanted at one and the same time to run from the room, to sink through the floor, or go to her and cover her from my eyes and the eyes of the others with my body; to feel the soft thighs, to caress her and destroy her,

6

7

*Black American teacher and leader (1856–1915).

to love her and murder her, to hide from her, and yet to stroke where below the small American flag tattooed upon her belly her thighs formed a capital V. I had a notion that of all in the room she saw only me with her impersonal eyes.

And then she began to dance, a slow sensuous movement; the smoke   8 of a hundred cigars clinging to her like the thinnest of veils. She seemed like a fair bird-girl girdled in veils calling to me from the angry surface of some gray and threatening sea. I was transported. Then I became aware of the clarinet playing and the big shots yelling at us. Some threatened us if we looked and others if we did not. On my right I saw one boy faint. And now a man grabbed a silver pitcher from a table and stepped close as he dashed ice water upon him and stood him up and forced two of us to support him as his head hung and moans issued from his thick bluish lips. Another boy began to plead to go home. He was the largest of the group, wearing dark red fighting trunks much too small to conceal the erection which projected from him as though in answer to the insinuating low-registered moaning of the clarinet. He tried to hide himself with his boxing gloves.

And all the while the blonde continued dancing, smiling faintly at the   9 big shots who watched her with fascination, and faintly smiling at our fear. I noticed a certain merchant who followed her hungrily, his lips loose and drooling. He was a large man who wore diamond studs in a shirtfront which swelled with the ample paunch underneath, and each time the blonde swayed her undulating hips he ran his hand through the thin hair of his bald head and, with his arms upheld, his posture clumsy like that of an intoxicated panda, wound his belly in a slow and obscene grind. This creature was completely hypnotized. The music had quickened. As the dancer flung herself about with a detached expression on her face, the men began reaching out to touch her. I could see their beefy fingers sink into the soft flesh. Some of the others tried to stop them and she began to move around the floor in graceful circles, as they gave chase, slipping and sliding over the polished floor. It was mad. Chairs went crashing, drinks were spilt, as they ran laughing and howling after her. They caught her just as she reached a door, raised her from the floor, and tossed her as college boys are tossed at a hazing, and above her red, fixed-smiling lips I saw the terror and disgust in her eyes, almost like my own terror and that which I saw in some of the other boys. As I watched, they tossed her twice and her soft breasts seemed to flatten against the air and her legs flung wildly as she spun. Some of the more sober ones helped her to escape. And I started off the floor, heading for the anteroom with the rest of the boys.

Some were still crying and in hysteria. But as we tried to leave we were   10 stopped and ordered to get into the ring. There was nothing to do but what we were told. All ten of us climbed under the ropes and allowed ourselves to be blindfolded with broad bands of white cloth. One of the men seemed to feel a bit sympathetic and tried to cheer us up as we stood with our backs against the ropes. Some of us tried to grin. "See that boy over there?" one of the men said. "I want you to run across at the bell and give it to him right

in the belly. If you don't get him, I'm going to get you. I don't like his looks."
Each of us was told the same. The blindfolds were put on. Yet even then I
had been going over my speech. In my mind each word was as bright as flame.
I felt the cloth pressed into place, and frowned so that it would be loosened
when I relaxed.

But now I felt a sudden fit of blind terror. I was unused to darkness. It 11
was as though I had suddenly found myself in a dark room filled with
poisonous cottonmouths. I could hear the bleary voices yelling insistently for
the battle royal to begin.

"Get going in there!"   12

"Let me at the big nigger!"   13

I strained to pick up the school superintendent's voice, as though to   14
squeeze some security out of that slightly more familiar sound.

"Let me at those black sonsabitches!" someone yelled.   15

"No, Jackson, no!" another voice yelled. "Here, somebody, help me hold   16
Jack."

"I want to get at that ginger-colored nigger. Tear him limb from limb,"   17
the first voice yelled.

I stood against the ropes trembling. For in those days I was what they   18
called ginger-colored, and he sounded as though he might crunch me between
his teeth like a crisp ginger cookie.

Quite a struggle was going on. Chairs were being kicked about and I   19
could hear voices grunting as with a terrific effort. I wanted to see, to see more
desperately than ever before. But the blindfold was as tight as a thick skin-
puckering scab and when I raised my gloved hands to push the layers of white
aside a voice yelled, "Oh, no you don't, black bastard! Leave that alone!"

"Ring the bell before Jackson kills him a coon!" someone boomed in the   20
sudden silence. And I heard the bell clang and the sound of feet scuffling
forward.

A glove smacked against my head. I pivoted, striking out stiffly as   21
someone went past, and felt the jar ripple along the length of my arm to my
shoulder. Then it seemed as though all nine of the boys had turned upon me
at once. Blows pounded me from all sides while I struck out as best I could.
So many blows landed upon me that I wondered if I were not the only
blindfolded fighter in the ring, or if the man called Jackson hadn't succeeded
in getting me after all.

Blindfolded, I could no longer control my motions. I had no dignity. I   22
stumbled about like a baby or a drunken man. The smoke had become thicker
and with each new blow it seemed to sear and further restrict my lungs. My
saliva became like hot bitter glue. A glove connected with my head, filling
my mouth with warm blood. It was everywhere. I could not tell if the
moisture I felt upon my body was sweat or blood. A blow landed hard against
the nape of my neck. I felt myself going over, my head hitting the floor.
Streaks of blue light filled the black world behind the blindfold. I lay prone,
pretending that I was knocked out, but felt myself seized by hands and
yanked to my feet. "Get going, black boy! Mix it up!" My arms were like lead,

my head smarting from blows. I managed to feel my way to the ropes and held on, trying to catch my breath. A glove landed in my midsection and I went over again, feeling as though the smoke had become a knife jabbed into my guts. Pushed this way and that by the legs milling around me, I finally pulled erect and discovered that I could see the black, sweat-washed forms weaving in the smoky-blue atmosphere like drunken dancers weaving to the rapid drumlike thuds of blows.

Everyone fought hysterically. It was complete anarchy. Everybody 23 fought everybody else. No group fought together for long. Two, three, four, fought one, then turned to fight each other, were themselves attacked. Blows landed below the belt and in the kidney, with the gloves open as well as closed, and with my eye partly opened now there was not so much terror. I moved carefully, avoiding blows, although not too many to attract attention, fighting from group to group. The boys groped about like blind, cautious crabs crouching to protect their mid-sections, their heads pulled in short against their shoulders, their arms stretched nervously before them, with their fists testing the smoke-filled air like the knobbed feelers of hypersensitive snails. In the corner I glimpsed a boy violently punching the air and heard him scream in pain as he smashed his hand against a ring post. For a second I saw him bent over holding his hand, then going down as a blow caught his unprotected head. I played one group against the other, slipping in and throwing a punch then stepping out of range while pushing the others into the melee to take the blows blindly aimed at me. The smoke was agonizing and there were no rounds, no bells at three minute intervals to relieve our exhaustion. The room spun around me, a swirl of lights, smoke, sweating bodies surrounded by tense white faces. I bled from both nose and mouth, the blood spattering upon my chest.

The men kept yelling, "Slug him, black boy! Knock his guts out!"   24
"Uppercut him! Kill him! Kill that big boy!"   25
Taking a fake fall, I saw a boy going down heavily beside me as though 26 we were felled by a single blow, saw a sneaker-clad foot shoot into his groin as the two who had knocked him down stumbled upon him. I rolled out of range, feeling a twinge of nausea.

The harder we fought the more threatening the men became. And yet, 27 I had begun to worry about my speech again. How would it go? Would they recognize my ability? What would they give me?

I was fighting automatically when suddenly I noticed that one after 28 another of the boys was leaving the ring. I was surprised, filled with panic, as though I had been left alone with an unknown danger. Then I understood. The boys had arranged it among themselves. It was custom for the two men left in the ring to slug it out for the winner's prize. I discovered this too late. When the bell sounded two men in tuxedos leaped into the ring and removed the blindfold. I found myself facing Tatlock, the biggest of the gang. I felt sick at my stomach. Hardly had the bell stopped ringing in my ears than it clanged again and I saw him moving swiftly toward me. Thinking of nothing else to do I hit him smash on the nose. He kept coming, bringing the rank sharp violence of stale sweat. His face was a black blank of a face, only his eyes alive—with hate of me and aglow with a feverish terror from what had happened to us all. I became anxious. I wanted to deliver my speech and he came at me as though he meant to beat it out of me. I smashed him again and again, taking his blows as they came. Then on a sudden impulse I struck him lightly and as we clinched, I whispered, "Fake like I knocked you out, you can have the prize."

"I'll break your behind," he whispered hoarsely.   29

"For *them*?"   30

"For *me*, sonofabitch."   31

They were yelling for us to break it up and Tatlock spun me half around   32 with a blow, and as a joggled camera sweeps in a reeling scene, I saw the howling red faces crouching tense beneath the cloud of blue-gray smoke. For a moment the world wavered, unraveled, flowed, then my head cleared and Tatlock bounced before me. The fluttering shadow before my eyes was his jabbing left hand. Then falling forward, my head against his damp shoulder, I whispered.

"I'll make it five dollars more."   33

"Go to hell!"   34

But his muscles relaxed a trifle beneath my pressure and I breathed,   35 "Seven?"

"Give it to your ma," he said, ripping me beneath the heart.   36

And while I still held him I butted him and moved away. I felt myself   37 bombarded with punches. I fought back with hopeless desperation. I wanted to deliver my speech more than anything else in the world, because I felt only these men could judge truly my ability, and now this stupid clown was ruining my chances. I began fighting carefully now, moving in to punch him and out again with my greater speed. A lucky blow to his chin and I had him going too—until I heard a loud voice yell, "I got my money on the big boy."

Hearing this, I almost dropped my guard. I was confused: Should I try   38 to win against the voice out there? Would not this go against my speech, and was not this a moment for humility, for nonresistance? A blow to my head as I danced about sent my right eye popping like a jack-in-the-box and settled my dilemma. The room went red as I fell. It was a dream fall, my body languid and fastidious as to where to land, until the floor became impatient and smashed up to meet me. A moment later I came to. An hypnotic voice said FIVE emphatically. And I lay there, hazily watching a dark red spot of my own blood shaping itself into a butterfly, glistening and soaking into the soiled gray world of the canvas.

When the voice drawled TEN I was lifted up and dragged to a chair. I   39 sat dazed. My eye pained and swelled with each throb of my pounding heart and I wondered if now I would be allowed to speak. I was wringing wet, my mouth still bleeding. We were grouped along the wall now. The other boys ignored me as they congratulated Tatlock and speculated as to how much they would be paid. One boy whimpered over his smashed hand. Looking up front, I saw attendants in white jackets rolling the portable ring away and placing a small square rug in the vacant space surrounded by chairs. Perhaps, I thought, I will stand on the rug to deliver my speech.

Then the M.C. called to us, "Come on up here boys and get your money." 40

We ran forward to where the men laughed and talked in their chairs, 41 waiting. Everyone seemed friendly now.

"There it is on the rug," the man said. I saw the rug covered with coins 42 of all dimensions and a few crumpled bills. But what excited me, scattered here and there, were the gold pieces.

"Boys, it's all yours," the man said. "You get all you grab." 43

"That's right, Sambo," a blond man said, winking at me confidentially. 44

I trembled with excitement, forgetting my pain. I would get the gold and 45 the bills, I thought. I would use both hands. I would throw my body against the boys nearest me to block them from the gold.

"Get down around the rug now," the man commanded, "and don't 46 anyone touch it until I give the signal."

"This ought to be good," I heard. 47

As told, we got around the square rug on our knees. Slowly the man 48 raised his freckled hand as we followed it upward with our eyes.

I heard, "These niggers look like they're about to pray!" 49

Then, "Ready," the man said. "Go!" 50

I lunged for a yellow coin lying on the blue design on the carpet, 51 touching it and sending a surprised shriek to join those rising around me. I tried frantically to remove my hand but could not let go. A hot, violent force tore through my body, shaking me like a wet rat. The rug was electrified. The hair bristled up on my head as I shook myself free. My muscles jumped, my nerves jangled, writhed. But I saw that this was not stopping the other boys. Laughing in fear and embarrassment, some were holding back and scooping up the coins knocked off by the painful contortions of the others. The men roared above us as we struggled.

"Pick it up, goddamnit, pick it up!" someone called like a bass-voiced 52 parrot. "Go on, get it!"

I crawled rapidly around the floor, picking up the coins, trying to avoid 53 the coppers and to get greenbacks and the gold. Ignoring the shock by laughing, as I brushed the coins off quickly, I discovered that I could contain the electricity—a contradiction, but it works. Then the men began to push us onto the rug. Laughing embarrassedly, we struggled out of their hands and kept after the coins. We were all wet and slippery and hard to hold. Suddenly I saw a boy lifted into the air, glistening with sweat like a circus seal, and dropped, his wet back landing flush upon the charged rug, heard him yell and saw him literally dance upon his back, his elbows beating a frenzied tattoo upon the floor, his muscles twitching like the flesh of a horse stung by many flies. When he finally rolled off, his face was gray and no one stopped him when he ran from the floor amid booming laughter.

"Get the money," the M.C. called. "That's good hard American cash!" 54

And we snatched and grabbed, snatched and grabbed. I was careful not 55 to come too close to the rug now, and when I felt the hot whiskey breath descend upon me like a cloud of foul air I reached out and grabbed the leg of a chair. It was occupied and I held on desperately.

"Leggo nigger! Leggo!"   56

The huge face wavered down to mine as he tried to push me free. But   57
my body was slippery and he was too drunk. It was Mr. Colcord, who owned a chain of movie houses and "entertainment palaces." Each time he grabbed me I slipped out of his hands. It became a real struggle. I feared the rug more than I did the drunk, so I held on, surprising myself for a moment by trying to topple *him* upon the rug. It was such an enormous idea that I found myself actually carrying it out. I tried not to be obvious, yet when I grabbed his leg, trying to tumble him out of the chair, he raised up roaring with laughter, and, looking at me with soberness dead in the eye, kicked me viciously in the chest. The chair leg flew out of my hand and I felt myself going and rolled. It was as though I had rolled through a bed of hot coals. It seemed a whole century would pass before I would roll free, a century in which I was seared through the deepest levels of my body to the fearful breath within me and the breath seared and heated to the point of explosion. It'll all be over in a flash, I thought as I rolled clear. It'll all be over in a flash.

But not yet, the men on the other side were waiting, red faces swollen   58
as though from apoplexy as they bent forward in their chairs. Seeing their fingers coming toward me I rolled away as a fumbled football rolls off the receiver's fingertips, back into the coals. That time I luckily sent the rug sliding out of place and heard the coins ringing against the floor and the boys scuffling to pick them up and the M.C. calling, "All right, boys, that's all. Go get dressed and get your money."

I was limp as a dish rag. My back felt as though it had been beaten with   59
wires.

When we had dressed the M.C. came in and gave us each five dollars,   60
except Tatlock, who got ten for being last in the ring. Then he told us to leave. I was not to get a chance to deliver my speech, I thought. I was going out into the dim alley in despair when I was stopped and told to go back. I returned to the ballroom, where the men were pushing back their chairs and gathering in groups to talk.

The M.C. knocked on a table for quiet. "Gentlemen," he said, "we   61
almost forgot an important part of the program. A most serious part, gentlemen. This boy was brought here to deliver a speech which he made at his graduation yesterday . . ."

"Bravo!"   62

"I'm told that he is the smartest boy we've got out there in Greenwood.   63
I'm told that he knows more big words than a pocket-sized dictionary."

Much applause and laughter.   64

"So now, gentlemen, I want you to give him your attention."   65

There was still laughter as I faced them, my mouth dry, my eye throb-   66
bing. I began slowly, but evidently my throat was tense, because they began shouting, "Louder! Louder!"

"We of the younger generation extol the wisdom of that great leader   67
and educator," I shouted, "who first spoke these flaming words of wisdom.
'A ship lost at sea for many days suddenly sighted a friendly vessel. From the
mast of the unfortunate vessel was seen a signal: "Water, water; we die of
thirst!" The answer from the friendly vessel came back: "Cast down your
bucket where you are." The captain of the distressed vessel, at last heeding
the injunction, cast down his bucket, and it came up full of fresh sparkling
water from the mouth of the Amazon River.' And like him I say, and in his
words, 'To those of my race who depend upon bettering their condition in
a foreign land, or who underestimate the importance of cultivating friendly
relations with the Southern white man, who is his next-door neighbor, I
would say: "Cast down your bucket where you are"—cast it down in making
friends in every manly way of the people of all races by whom we are
surrounded. . . .' "

I spoke automatically and with such fervor that I did not realize that the   68
men were still talking and laughing until my dry mouth, filling up with blood
from the cut, almost strangled me. I coughed, wanting to stop and go to one
of the tall brass, sand-filled spittoons to relieve myself, but a few of the men,
especially the superintendent, were listening and I was afraid. So I gulped it
down, blood, saliva, and all, and continued. (What powers of endurance I had
during those days! What enthusiasm! What a belief in the rightness of
things!) I spoke even louder in spite of the pain. But still they talked and still
they laughed, as though deaf with cotton in dirty ears. So I spoke with greater
emotional emphasis. I closed my ears and swallowed blood until I was nau-
seated. The speech seemed a hundred times as long as before, but I could not
leave out a single word. All had to be said, each memorized nuance considered, rendered. Nor was that all. Whenever I uttered a word of three or more
syllables a group of voices would yell for me to repeat it. I used the phrase
"social responsibility" and they yelled:

"What's that word you say, boy?"   69
"Social responsibility," I said.   70
"What?"   71
"Social . . ."   72
"Louder."   73
". . . responsibility."   74
"More!"   75
"Respon—"   76
"Repeat!"   77
"—sibility."   78

The room filled with the uproar of laughter until, no doubt, distracted   79
by having to gulp down my blood, I made a mistake and yelled a phrase I
had often seen denounced with newspaper editorials, heard debated in private.

"Social . . ."   80
"What?" they yelled.   81
". . . equality—"   82

The laughter hung smokelike in the sudden stillness. I opened my eyes, 83
puzzled. Sounds of displeasure filled the room. The M.C. rushed forward.
They shouted hostile phrases at me. But I did not understand.

A small dry mustached man in the front row blared out, "Say that 84
slowly, son!"

"What sir?" 85

"Social responsibility, sir," I said. 86

"You weren't being smart, were you, boy?" he said, not unkindly. 87

"No, sir!" 88

"You sure that about 'equality' was a mistake?" 89

"Oh, yes, sir," I said. "I was swallowing blood." 90

"Well, you had better speak more slowly so we can understand. We 91
mean to do right by you, but you've got to know your place at all times. All
right, now, go on with your speech."

I was afraid. I wanted to leave but I wanted also to speak and I was afraid 92
they'd snatch me down.

"Thank you, sir," I said, beginning where I had left off, and having them 93
ignore me as before.

Yet when I finished there was a thunderous applause. I was surprised 94
to see the superintendent come forth with a package wrapped in white tissue
paper, and, gesturing for quiet, address the men.

"Gentlemen, you see that I did not overpraise this boy. He makes a good 95
speech and some day he'll lead his people in the proper paths. And I don't
have to tell you that that is important in these days and times. This is a good,
smart boy, and so to encourage him in the right direction, in the name of the
Board of Education I wish to present him a prize in the form of this . . ."

He paused, removing the tissue paper and revealing a gleaming calfskin 96
brief case.

". . . in the form of this first-class article from Shad Whitmore's shop." 97

"Boy," he said, addressing me, "take this prize and keep it well. Con- 98
sider it a badge of office. Prize it. Keep developing as you are and some day
it will be filled with important papers that will help shape the destiny of your
people."

I was so moved that I could hardly express my thanks. A rope of bloody 99
saliva forming a shape like an undiscovered continent drooled upon the
leather and I wiped it quickly away. I felt an importance that I had never
dreamed.

"Open it and see what's inside," I was told. 100

My fingers a-tremble, I complied, smelling the fresh leather and finding 101
an official-looking document inside. It was a scholarship to the state college
for Negroes. My eyes filled with tears and I ran awkwardly off the floor.

I was so overjoyed; I did not even mind when I discovered that the gold 102
pieces I had scrambled for were brass pocket tokens advertising a certain
make of automobile.

When I reached home everyone was excited. Next day the neighbors 103 came to congratulate me. I even felt safe from grandfather, whose deathbed curse usually spoiled my triumphs. I stood beneath his photograph with my brief case in hand and smiled triumphantly into his stolid black peasant's face. It was a face that fascinated me. The eyes seemed to follow everywhere I went.

That night I dreamed I was at a circus with him and that he refused to   104
laugh at the clowns no matter what they did. Then later he told me to open my brief case and read what was inside and I did, finding an official envelope stamped with the state seal; and inside the envelope I found another and another, endlessly, and I thought I would fall of weariness. "Them's years," he said. "Now open that one." And I did and in it I found an engraved document containing a short message in letters of gold. "Read it," my grandfather said. "Out loud."

"To Whom It May Concern," I intoned. "Keep This Nigger-Boy Run-   105
ning."

I awoke with the old man's laughter ringing in my ears.   106

(It was a dream I was to remember and dream again for many years after.   107
But at that time I had no insight into its meaning. First I had to attend college.)

Questions for Discussion

1. What is your own interpretation of the grandfather's message in paragraph 2? What does he mean when he says "our life is a war and I have been a traitor all my born days"?

2. What is meant (in the young man's dream) by the official document inscribed, "To Whom It May Concern, Keep This Nigger-Boy Running" (¶105)? What is the significance of this document's being contained in "an official envelope stamped with the state seal"? How does "running" tie in with the young man's willingness to fight and his gratitude over the scholarship to college?

3. Why is it significant that the smoker is attended by "the most important men of the town . . . bankers, lawyers, judges, doctors, fire chiefs, teachers, merchants. Even one of the more fashionable pastors" (¶6)? What do these men represent in the story?

4. In what sense might it be true to say that the young man, who thinks he sees how the game of progress and social advancement must be played, begins to see more clearly the *real* truth of his situation when he is placed in the blindfold (¶11)?

5. Why is it ironic that the young man "attempts to squeeze some security" out of the school superintendent's voice as the fight begins (¶14)? What does this say about his naïveté?

6. A corrupt system corrupts not just the victimizers but the victims as well. How is the truth of this statement corroborated by the young man's question, "What would they give me?" in paragraph 27?

7. What does the young man mean when he says that "I had to [experience] much painful boomeranging of my expectations" before he could discover "that I am nobody but myself . . ." (¶1)?

Suggested Essay Topics

1. Have you ever felt invisible in Ellison's narrator's sense of the term—felt that some persons, no matter what you do or say to them, will always fail to see you for what you are, will always insist on seeing instead some image of you or of "your kind" that they have already formed in their own heads? If you have ever experienced this feeling, give an account of it in an essay directed to your fellow students. Use Ellison's analysis to help you explain what it feels like to be treated this way and how you dealt (or are dealing) with it. Your purpose is to try to define the condition of invisibility as *you* have experienced it (with appropriate examples) so that your readers will know not only what the condition has been like, but what it has meant (or means) in your life.

2. After thinking about topic 1, write an editorial or a letter to the editor of your campus newspaper, arguing that everyone should wake up and *look* at the *individuals* on campus instead of making them invisible by lumping them into groups and types. Identify the group stereotypes that make individuals invisible (dumb jocks, dizzy blonds, stupid administrators, and so on), and make your editorial or letter a ringing assertion of these people's right to be viewed and judged as individuals, not as predictable representatives of groups.

Jonathan Swift

Jonathan Swift (1667–1745) was born and educated in Dublin, Ireland, was ordained as an Anglican priest, and from 1713 on held the post of dean of St. Patrick's in Dublin. He wrote on church doctrine, social matters, and politics (especially on the relations between Ireland and England). The latter two topics gave him great scope for his immense gifts as a satirist. He wielded his pen like a scalpel and dissected the objects of his ridicule with deadly accuracy, energy, and finesse. What sets Swift above many other brilliant satirists is the scope and depth of his moral vision. He does not just satirize absurdities like comedians on late-night television, jabbing the needle quickly and then running to the next topic. His ridicule goes far beyond merely accurate observation and enters the realm of informed vision. He shows us not simply that human stupidity, greed, or self-deception exists but also how things might be better. It is important to remember that Swift is a satirist, not a cynic: While he thinks many people bad, he does not think all people hopeless. Even as he flays his targets, hanging up the pelts of their hypocrisies and absurdities to swing in the wind of public scrutiny, he points out possible remedies for the evils he attacks.

The main satiric device in "A Modest Proposal" is irony: saying one thing and meaning the opposite. (Irony is a much more sophisticated device than this rough definition implies, but we have insufficient space here for a thorough discussion.) Even this simple definition, however, makes one thing clear: The reader somehow has to know that a meaning beyond the surface meaning must be decoded. Any reader who does not recognize a piece as satire will simply take the surface meaning at face value—and, in the case of "A Modest Proposal," will make a horrible mistake.

As you read, try to spot places where Swift lets you know that a deep decoding is necessary. What are the clues? He cannot use any of the visual or auditory signals that satirists often rely on, such as inflection, body language, gesture, or facial expression. Yet by the second sentence of paragraph 4, far in advance of the outrageous proposal in paragraph 9, you know you are in the presence of a satiric voice. How is the satiric intent conveyed? Are there any sections in which the satire is dropped in favor of straightforward recommendations? If so, where? If not, how do you decide whether his essay includes any positive proposals and where they are stated? Try to decipher not only the satire but the means by which the satire is accomplished.

A MODEST PROPOSAL

First published as "A Modest Proposal for Preventing the Children of Poor People from Being a Burden to Their Parents or the Country" (1729).

It is a melancholy object to those who walk through this great town* or travel in the country, when they see the streets, the roads, and cabin doors, crowded with beggars of the female sex, followed by three, four, or six children, all in rags and importuning every passenger for an alms. These mothers, instead of being able to work for their honest livelihood, are forced to employ all their time in strolling to beg sustenance for their helpless infants, who, as they grow up, either turn thieves for want of work, or leave their dear native country to fight for the Pretender in Spain, or sell themselves to the Barbadoes.†

I think it is agreed by all parties that this prodigious number of children in the arms, or on the backs, or at the heels of their mothers, and frequently of their fathers, is in the present deplorable state of the kingdom a very great additional grievance; and therefore whoever could find out a fair, cheap, and easy method of making these children sound, useful members of the com-

---

*Dublin, capital city of Ireland.

†The pretender to the throne of England was James Stuart (1688–1766), son of the deposed James II. Barbados is an island in the West Indies.

monwealth would deserve so well of the public as to have his statue set up for a preserver of the nation.

But my intention is very far from being confined to provide only for the children of professed beggars; it is of a much greater extent, and shall take in the whole number of infants at a certain age who are born of parents in effect as little able to support them as those who demand our charity in the streets.

As to my own part, having turned my thoughts for many years upon this important subject, and maturely weighed the several schemes of other projectors, I have always found them grossly mistaken in their computation. It is true, a child just dropped from its dam may be supported by her milk for a solar year, with little other nourishment; at most not above the value of two shillings,* which the mother may certainly get, or the value in scraps, by her lawful occupation of begging; and it is exactly at one year old that I propose to provide for them in such a manner as instead of being a charge upon their parents or the parish, or wanting food and raiment for the rest of their lives, they shall on the contrary contribute to the feeding, and partly to the clothing, of many thousands.

There is likewise another great advantage in my scheme, that it will prevent those voluntary abortions, and that horrid practice of women murdering their bastard children, alas, too frequent among us, sacrificing the poor innocent babes, I doubt, more to avoid the expense than the shame, which would move tears and pity in the most savage and inhuman breast.

The number of souls in this kingdom being usually reckoned one million and a half, of these I calculate there may be about two hundred thousand couple whose wives are breeders; from which number I subtract thirty thousand couples who are able to maintain their own children, although I apprehend there cannot be so many under the present distress of the kingdom; but this being granted, there will remain an hundred and seventy thousand breeders. I again subtract fifty thousand for those women who miscarry, or whose children die by accident or disease within the year. There only remain an hundred and twenty thousand children of poor parents annually born. The question therefore is, how this number shall be reared and provided for, which, as I have already said, under the present situation of affairs, is utterly impossible by all the methods hitherto proposed. For we can neither employ them in handicraft or agriculture; we neither build houses (I mean in the country) nor cultivate land. They can very seldom pick up a livelihood by stealing till they arrive at six years old, except where they are of towardly parts;† although I confess they learn the rudiments much earlier, during which time they can however be looked upon only as probationers, as I have been informed by a principal gentleman in the county of Cavan, who protested to me that he never knew above one or two instances under the age

*The British pound sterling was made up of twenty shillings; five shillings made a crown.
†*Towardly* means "advanced"; *parts* refers to abilities or talents.

of six, even in a part of the kingdom so renowned for the quickest proficiency in that art.

I am assured by our merchants that a boy or a girl before twelve years   7
old is no salable commodity; and even when they come to this age they will not yield above three pounds, or three pounds and half a crown at most on the Exchange; which cannot turn to account either to the parents or the kingdom, the charge of nutriment and rags having been at least four times that value.

I shall now therefore humbly propose my own thoughts, which I hope   8
will not be liable to the least objection.

I have been assured by a very knowing American of my acquaintance   9
in London, that a young healthy child well nursed is at a year old a most delicious, nourishing, and wholesome food, whether stewed, roasted, baked, or boiled; and I make no doubt that it will equally serve in a fricassee or a ragout.

I do therefore humbly offer it to public consideration that of the hun-   10
dred and twenty thousand children, already computed, twenty thousand may be reserved for breed, whereof only one fourth part to be males, which is more than we allow to sheep, black cattle, or swine; and my reason is that these children are seldom the fruits of marriage, a circumstance not much regarded by our savages, therefore one male will be sufficient to serve four females. That the remaining hundred thousand may at a year old be offered in sale to the persons of quality and fortune through the kingdom, always advising the mother to let them suck plentifully in the last month, so as to render them plump and fat for a good table. A child will make two dishes at an entertainment for friends; and when the family dines alone, the fore or hind quarter will make a reasonable dish, and seasoned with a little pepper or salt will be very good boiled on the fourth day, especially in winter.

I have reckoned upon a medium that a child just born will weigh twelve   11
pounds, and in a solar year if tolerably nursed increaseth to twenty-eight pounds.

I grant this food will be somewhat dear, and therefore very proper for   12
landlords, who, as they have already devoured most of the parents, seem to have the best title to the children.

Infant's flesh will be in season throughout the year, but more plentiful   13
in March, and a little before and after. For we are told by a grave author, an eminent French physician,* that fish being a prolific diet, there are more children born in Roman Catholic countries about nine months after Lent than at any other season; therefore, reckoning a year after Lent, the markets will be more glutted than usual, because the number of popish infants is at least three to one in this kingdom; and therefore it will have one other collateral advantage, by lessening the number of Papists among us.

I have already computed the charge of nursing a beggar's child (in which   14
list I reckon all cottagers, laborers, and four fifths of the farmers) to be about

*François Rabelais (1494?–1553), French satirist, author of *Pantagruel* (1532) and *Gargantua* (1534).

two shillings per annum, rags included; and I believe no gentleman would repine to give ten shillings for the carcass of a good fat child, which, as I have said, will make four dishes of excellent nutritive meat, when he hath only some particular friend or his own family to dine with him. Thus the squire will learn to be a good landlord, and grow popular among the tenants; the mother will have eight shillings net profit, and be fit for work till she produces another child.

Those who are more thrifty (as I must confess the times require) may 15 flay the carcass; the skin of which artificially* dressed will make admirable gloves for ladies, and summer boots for fine gentlemen.

As to our city of Dublin, shambles† may be appointed for this purpose 16 in the most convenient parts of it, and butchers we may be assured will not be wanting; although I rather recommend buying the children alive, and dressing them hot from the knife as we do roasting pigs.

A very worthy person, a true lover of his country, and whose virtues 17 I highly esteem, was lately pleased in discoursing on this matter to offer a refinement upon my scheme. He said that many gentlemen of this kingdom, having of late destroyed their deer, he conceived that the want of venison might be well supplied by the bodies of young lads and maidens, not exceeding fourteen years of age nor under twelve, so great a number of both sexes in every country being now ready to starve for want of work and service; and these to be disposed of by their parents, if alive, or otherwise by their nearest relations. But with due deference to so excellent a friend and so deserving a patriot, I cannot be altogether in his sentiments; for as to the males, my American acquaintance assured me from frequent experience that their flesh was generally tough and lean, like that of our schoolboys, by continual exercise, and their taste disagreeable; and to fatten them would not answer the charge. Then as to the females, it would, I think with humble submission, be a loss to the public, because they soon would become breeders themselves: and besides, it is not improbable that some scrupulous people might be apt to censure such a practice (although indeed very unjustly) as a little bordering upon cruelty; which, I confess, hath always been with me the strongest objection against any project, how well soever intended.

But in order to justify my friend, he confessed that this expedient was 18 put into his head by the famous Psalmanazar, a native of the island Formosa, who came from thence to London above twenty years ago, and in conversation told my friend that in his country when any young person happened to be put to death, the executioner sold the carcass to persons of quality as a prime dainty; and that in his time the body of a plump girl of fifteen, who was crucified for an attempt to poison the emperor, was sold to his Imperial Majesty's prime minister of state, and other great mandarins of the court, in joints from the gibbet, at four hundred crowns. Neither indeed can I deny that if the same use were made of several plump young girls in this town, who

*Skillfully, artistically.
†Slaughterhouses.

without one single groat to their fortunes cannot stir abroad without a chair,*
and appear at the playhouse and assemblies in foreign fineries which they
never will pay for, the kingdom would not be the worse.

Some persons of a desponding spirit are in great concern about that vast 19
number of poor people who are aged, diseased, or maimed, and I have been
desired to employ my thoughts what course may be taken to ease the nation
of so grievous an encumbrance. But I am not in the least pain upon that
matter, because it is very well known that they are every day dying and
rotting by cold and famine, and filth and vermin, as fast as can be reasonably
expected. And as to the younger laborers, they are now in almost as hopeful
a condition. They cannot get work, and consequently pine away for want of
nourishment to a degree that if at any time they are accidentally hired to
common labor, they have not strength to perform it; and thus the country and
themselves are happily delivered from the evils to come.

I have too long digressed, and therefore shall return to my subject. I 20
think the advantages by the proposal which I have made are obvious and
many, as well as of the highest importance.

For first, as I have already observed, it would greatly lessen the number 21
of Papists, with whom we are yearly overrun, being the principal breeders of
the nation as well as our most dangerous enemies; and who stay at home on
purpose to deliver the kingdom to the Pretender, hoping to take their advantage by the absence of so many good Protestants, who have chosen rather to
leave their country than stay at home and pay tithes against their conscience
to an Episcopal curate.† ⨯

Secondly, the poorer tenants will have something valuable of their own, 22
which by law may be made liable to distress, and help to pay their landlord's
rent, their corn and cattle being already seized and money a thing unknown.

Thirdly, whereas the maintenance of an hundred thousand children, 23
from two years old and upward, cannot be computed at less than ten shillings
a piece per annum, the nation's stock will be thereby increased fifty thousand
pounds per annum, besides the profit of a new dish introduced to the tables
of all gentlemen of fortune in the kingdom who have any refinement in taste.
And the money will circulate among ourselves,‡ the goods being entirely of
our own growth and manufacture.

Fourthly, the constant breeders, besides the gain of eight shillings ster- 24
ling per annum by the sale of their children, will be rid of the charge of
maintaining them after the first year.

Fifthly, this food would likewise bring great custom to taverns, where 25
the vintners will certainly be so prudent as to procure the best receipts for
dressing it to perfection, and consequently have their houses frequented by

*Sedan chair, an enclosed chair set on horizontal poles, in which the occupant could be conveyed
from place to place by two carriers, one in front and one in back.

†Swift blamed much of Ireland's poverty on large Protestant landowners who, not wanting to
pay Anglican (Episcopal) Church tithes (taxes), lived abroad and thus spent their Irish-made
money abroad, depriving the Irish economy of their income.

‡That is, among the Irish themselves.

all the fine gentlemen, who justly value themselves upon their knowledge in good eating; and a skillful cook, who understands how to oblige his guests, will contrive to make it as expensive as they please.

Sixthly, this would be a great inducement to marriage, which all wise 26 nations have either encouraged by rewards or enforced by laws and penalties. It would increase the care and tenderness of mothers toward their children, when they were sure of a settlement for life to the poor babes, provided in some sort by the public, to their annual profit instead of expense. We should see an honest emulation among the married women, which of them could bring the fattest child to the market. Men would become as fond of their wifes during the time of their pregnancy as they are now of their mares in foal, their cows in calf, or sows when they are ready to farrow; nor offer to beat or kick them (as is too frequent a practice) for fear of a miscarriage.

Many other advantages might be enumerated. For instance, the addition 27 of some thousand carcasses in our exportation of barreled beef, the propagation of swine's flesh, and improvement in the art of making good bacon, so much wanted among us by the great destruction of pigs, too frequent at our tables, which are no way comparable in taste or magnificence to a well-grown, fat, yearling child, which roasted whole will make a considerable figure at a lord mayor's feast or any other public entertainment. But this and many others I omit, being studious of brevity.

Supposing that one thousand families in this city would be constant 28 customers for infants' flesh, besides others who might have it at merry meetings, particularly weddings and christenings, I compute that Dublin would take off annually about twenty thousand carcasses, and the rest of the kingdom (where probably they will be sold somewhat cheaper) the remaining eighty thousand.

I can think of no one objection that will possibly be raised against this 29 proposal, unless it should be urged that the number of people will be thereby much lessened in the kingdom. This I freely own, and it was indeed one principal design in offering it to the world. I desire the reader will observe, that I calculate my remedy for this one individual kingdom of Ireland and for no other that ever was, is, or I think ever can be upon earth. Therefore let no man talk to me of other expedients: of taxing our absentees at five shillings a pound: of using neither clothes nor household furniture except what is of our own growth and manufacture: of utterly rejecting the materials and instruments that promote foreign luxury: of curing the expensiveness of pride, vanity, idleness, and gaming* in our women: of introducing a vein of parsimony, prudence, and temperance: of learning to love our country, in the want of which we differ even from Laplanders and the inhabitants of Topinamboo: of quitting our animosities and factions, nor acting any longer like the Jews, who were murdering one another at the very moment their city† was taken: of being a little cautious not to sell our

---

*Gambling.
†Jerusalem, sacked by the Romans in A.D. 70.

country and conscience for nothing: of teaching landlords to have at least one degree of mercy toward their tenants: lastly, of putting a spirit of honesty, industry, and skill into our shopkeepers; who, if a resolution could now be taken to buy only our native goods, would immediately unite to cheat and exact upon us in the price, the measure, and the goodness, nor could ever yet be brought to make one fair proposal of just dealing, though often and earnestly invited to it.

Therefore I repeat, let no man talk to me of these and the like expedi- 30 ents, till he hath at least some glimpse of hope that there will ever be some hearty and sincere attempt to put them in practice.

But as to myself, having been wearied out for many years with offer- 31 ing vain, idle, visionary thoughts, and at length utterly despairing of success, I fortunately fell upon this proposal, which, as it is wholly new, so it hath something solid and real, of no expense and little trouble, full in our own power, and whereby we can incur no danger in disobliging England. For this kind of commodity will not bear exportation, the flesh being of too tender a consistence to admit a long continuance in salt, although perhaps I could name a country* which would be glad to eat up our whole nation without it.

After all, I am not so violently bent upon my own opinion as to reject 32 any offer proposed by wise men, which shall be found equally innocent, cheap, easy, and effectual. But before something of that kind shall be advanced in contradiction to my scheme, and offering a better, I desire the author or authors will be pleased maturely to consider two points. First, as things now stand, how they will be able to find food and raiment for an hundred thousand useless mouths and backs. And secondly, there being a round million of creatures in human figure throughout this kingdom, whose sole subsistence put into a common stock would leave them in debt two millions of pounds sterling, adding those who are beggars by profession to the bulk of farmers, cottagers, and laborers, with their wives and children who are beggars in effect; I desire those politicians who dislike my overture, and may perhaps be so bold to attempt an answer, that they will first ask the parents of these mortals whether they would not at this day think it a great happiness to have been sold for food at a year old in the manner I prescribe, and thereby have avoided such a perpetual scene of misfortunes as they have since gone through by the oppression of landlords, the impossibility of paying rent without money or trade, the want of common sustenance, with neither house nor clothes to cover them from the inclemencies of the weather, and the most inevitable prospect of entailing the like or greater miseries upon their breed forever.

I profess, in the sincerity of my heart, that I have not the least personal 33 interest in endeavoring to promote this necessary work, having no other motive than the public good of my country, by advancing our trade, providing for infants, relieving the poor, and giving some pleasure to the rich. I have

---

*England, of course, against whose occupation of Ireland many Irish are still resentful.

no children by which I can propose to get a single penny; the youngest being nine years old, and my wife past childbearing.

Questions for Discussion

1. If the satirist Swift is delivering a message that has to be decoded, not the message that is stated, who is delivering the surface message? What does Swift achieve by not speaking "straight," in his own voice? How can you determine the amount of distance between the persona and Swift himself?

2. In the original edition of Swift's essay, most of paragrapph 29 is italicized. Can you think of any rhetorical reasons—purpose, tone, arguments, style, and so on—that would justify Swift's use of italics as a visual sign here? What is the purpose of paragraph 29? Does the purpose differ from that of of Swift's other paragraphs? How does paragraph 29 fit into the rest of the essay?

3. Does it matter for Swift's satire whether his persona's statistics are accurate or not? Do you think they are bogus or real? Regardless of the answer to this question, what *rhetorical* effect do they serve? What kind of *character* do they help establish for the persona? How do they fit into Swift's overall satire?

4. Who receives the strongest attack from Swift: the British landlords, the Irish leaders, or the Irish people in general? How do you know?

5. What would the "proposal" gain or lose if the final paragraph were dropped? Does it provide a fitting conclusion for the satire? If so, how? If not, why not?

6. How does the animal imagery—dam, breeder, carcass, and so on—contribute to the satire? Can you think of any other terms that would serve Swift's purpose as well? If not, what does this suggest about the craftedness of the satire?

Suggested Essay Topics

1. Write your own satire making fun of some group, person, institution, or human trait. Address it not to your target but to people that you would like to join you in contempt or ridicule of the target.

2. Write two different versions of the same attack, one in a satirical voice, the other as a straightforward denunciation. In a satire you can say you "love" something, and, if the satire is working, the reader will know that you hate it. In a straightforward denunciation you simply say that you hate what you hate. But satire's greater relative complexity does not mean that it is always better for all purposes. After you have done your two versions, write a final paragraph or two evaluating which version works better.

Stephen Spender

Most of the readings in this chapter deal
with different versions of racial or ethnic discrimination, but there is one form of
discrimination in modern life that embraces all races, ages, and sexes: the discrimination against the urban poor—not those who are struggling to stay economically afloat,
and not those whose lives are scrimped and scraped by insufficient income, but those
who have no income, those who have gone under: the bag ladies, the hobos, and the
winos who beg on the streets, live in the alleys, and sleep on the warm-air gratings
of every large American city. They are the unemployed and, in many cases, the
unemployable; they are homeless, hopeless, and habituated to neglect. Many of us stop
noticing these degraded and unaided folk after a while; we don't wish to see what we
cannot understand or help.

Fortunately, however, others not only look but see and in the intensity of their
gaze make us look again. They invite us to see what we were too embarrassed or hurried
to notice the first time. Spender's (b. 1909) poem captures a moment of intense seeing
of these urban poor. He looks at them without sentimentality and insists that we do
the same. He admonishes us to "paint here no draped despairs" (l. 12), but to look
on wounds that are raw, ugly, and personal, not statistical.

IN RAILWAY HALLS,
ON PAVEMENTS
NEAR THE TRAFFIC

From *Collected Poems* (1934).

In railway halls, on pavements near the traffic,
They beg, their eyes made big by empty staring
And only measuring Time, like the blank clock.

No, I shall wave no tracery of pen-ornament
To make them birds upon my singing-tree: 5
Time merely drives these lives which do not live
As tides push rotten stuff along the shore.

—There is no consolation, no, none,
In the curving beauty of that line
Traced on our graphs through History, where the oppressor   10
    Starves and deprives the poor.

Paint here no draped despairs, no saddening clouds
Where the soul rests, proclaims eternity.

But let the wrong cry out as raw as wounds
This time forgets and never heals, far less transcends.   15

1933

Questions for Discussion

1. Why is the clock in line 3 described as "blank"? In what sense is Spender using *blank*?
2. To what do "tracery of pen-ornament" (l. 4) and "singing-tree" (l. 5) refer? Are these appropriate metaphors? How do they aid the poem's effectiveness?
3. Graph lines may have a "curving beauty" (l. 9), but why does Spender find them so sinister? Why is he angry?
4. What is his final judgment about "this time" (l. 15) and its treatment of the poor he is describing?

Suggested Essay Topics

1. Choose some group that is discriminated against that is generally as invisible to most of us as the urban poor, and write an indignant letter to the editor of the city newspaper in which you attempt to make this group really visible and awaken the conscience of your fellow citizens about the plight of the real people in the group.
2. Try writing a "social protest" poem of your own, focusing on any groups and taking any tone you choose. Direct the poem toward the kind of general reader who might see it as a published piece in your campus literary magazine.

IDEAS IN DEBATE

Adolf Hitler
Malcolm Hay

Adolf Hitler

Into Mein Kampf *(My Struggle), Adolf Hitler (1889–1945) poured all of the weird fantasies, twisted logic, and racial hatred of a person who seems never to have loved or to have been loved by anyone. (The idolatry he received as Führer was another kind of thing.) His father was a shoemaker, and his mother, who was his father's third wife, had been a maid in the first wife's home. The father died when Hitler was 13; the mother died two years later.*

At age 15, then, Hitler found himself alone in the world and made his way to Vienna, Austria, where he hoped to study art. He lived in Vienna for about nine years, until 1912, existing in miserable poverty, failing his entrance exam into the art academy, and finding himself unable to take up architecture, a second ambition, because he had never completed his secondary education. He squeezed out a barren existence as a building construction worker and also tried painting postcards and selling pictures. But these efforts brought in only pennies. In 1912 Hitler moved to Munich, where he continued to make a scanty living as a commercial artist. He served as a soldier in the German army, 1914–1918, and was wounded in 1916. After the war he became more and more absorbed in political activity, joining the German Workers' party in 1919 and discovering that he was a speaker. He began to gather around him a group of misfits and thugs who with him participated in the "Beer Hall Putsch" of November 8–9, 1923, when Hitler was 34. With the failure of the putsch, he was sentenced to prison on the charge of treason, and while there he began writing Mein Kampf *at the suggestion of Rudolf Hess. He was pardoned the next year by a government that was habitually lenient toward right-wing agitators.*

In Hitler's account of his Vienna years in Mein Kampf *we get a clear picture of his emerging hatred of Jews. At them he directs all the pent-up rage and the psychopathological fury of a man who, small in every sense, had lived a life unloved, unexciting, unrewarded, unsuccessful, and unpromising. This rage was later to transform itself into the calculated murder of more than 6 million Jews.*

However, as Malcolm Hay makes clear in the next selection, "The Persecution of Jews" (pp. 604–621), Hitler's choice of the Jews as a scapegoat for his frustrations was not random, idiosyncratic, or accidental. Hatred of Jews was an ancient tradition in Europe, both within the Christian church and outside of it. Anti-Semitism was thus a "safe" outlet for the expression of hatreds that Hitler during his Vienna years had neither the imagination nor the influence to vent on other, more powerful groups. The Jews were traditional targets.

We pick up Hitler's story at the point where he tells of coming under the influence of the mayor of Vienna, Karl Lueger, whose newspaper, Volksblatt, *was rabidly anti-Semitic. He begins by saying that when he first came to Vienna he disliked both Lueger and his anti-Semitic bias. As the account progresses he records how he gradually came to see anti-Semitism as, for him, an inevitable position.*

IS THIS A JEW?

From *Mein Kampf.* We are reprinting from the translation by Ralph Manheim. *Mein Kampf* was originally published in 1925. The title is ours.

These occasions slowly made me acquainted with the man and the movement, which in those days guided Vienna's destinies: Dr. Karl Lueger* and the Christian Social Party.   1

When I arrived in Vienna, I was hostile to both of them.   2

The man and the movement seemed 'reactionary' in my eyes.   3

My common sense of justice, however, forced me to change this judg-   4
ment in proportion as I had occasion to become acquainted with the man and his work; and slowly my fair judgment turned to unconcealed admiration. Today, more than ever, I regard this man as the greatest German mayor of all times.

How many of my basic principles were upset by this change in my   5
attitude toward the Christian Social movement!

My views with regard to anti-Semitism thus succumbed to the passage   6
of time, and this was my greatest transformation of all.

It cost me the greatest inner soul struggles, and only after months of   7
battle between my reason and my sentiments did my reason begin to emerge victorious. Two years later, my sentiment had followed my reason, and from then on became its most loyal guardian and sentinel.

At the time of this bitter struggle between spiritual education and cold   8
reason, the visual instruction of the Vienna streets had performed invaluable services. There came a time when I no longer, as in the first days, wandered blindly through the mighty city; now with open eyes I saw not only the buildings but also the people.

Once, as I was strolling through the Inner City, I suddenly encountered   9
an apparition in a black caftan† and black hair locks. Is this a Jew? was my first thought.

*In 1897, Karl Lueger (1844–1910), as a member of the anti-Semitic Christian Social Party, became mayor of Vienna and kept the post until his death. He also edited the violently anti-Semitic newspaper *Volksblatt,* which influenced Hitler's views about race, nation, and patriotism. At first opposed by the Court for his radical nationalism and anti-Semitism, toward the end of Lueger's career he became more moderate and was reconciled with the emperor.

†An ankle-length, coat-like garment, often striped, with very long sleeves and a sash.

For, to be sure, they had not looked like that in Linz. I observed the man   10
furtively and cautiously, but the longer I stared at this foreign face, scrutiniz-
ing feature for feature, the more my first question assumed a new form:

Is this a German?   11

As always in such cases, I now began to try to relieve my doubts by   12
books. For a few hellers I bought the first anti-Semitic pamphlets of my life.
Unfortunately, they all proceeded from the supposition that in principle the
reader knew or even understood the Jewish question to a certain degree.
Besides, the tone for the most part was such that doubts again arose in me,
due in part to the dull and amazingly unscientific arguments favoring the
thesis.

I relapsed for weeks at a time, once even for months.   13

The whole thing seemed to me so monstrous, the accusations so bound-   14
less, that, tormented by the fear of doing injustice, I again became anxious
and uncertain.

Yet I could no longer very well doubt that the objects of my study were   15
not Germans of a special religion, but a people in themselves; for since I had
begun to concern myself with this question and to take cognizance of the
Jews, Vienna appeared to me in a different light than before. Wherever I went,
I began to see Jews, and the more I saw, the more sharply they became
distinguished in my eyes from the rest of humanity. Particularly the Inner
City and the districts north of the Danube Canal swarmed with a people
which even outwardly had lost all resemblance to Germans.

And whatever doubts I may still have nourished were finally dispelled   16
by the attitude of a portion of the Jews themselves.

Among them there was a great movement, quite extensive in Vienna,   17
which came out sharply in confirmation of the national character of the Jews:
this was the *Zionists.* *

It looked, to be sure, as though only a part of the Jews approved this   18
viewpoint, while the great majority condemned and inwardly rejected such
a formulation. But when examined more closely, this appearance dissolved
itself into an unsavory vapor of pretexts advanced for mere reasons of expedi-
ence, not to say lies. For the so-called liberal Jews did not reject the Zionists
as non-Jews, but only as Jews with an impractical, perhaps even dangerous,
way of publicly avowing their Jewishness.

Intrinsically they remained unalterably of one piece.   19

In a short time this apparent struggle between Zionistic and liberal Jews   20
disgusted me; for it was false through and through, founded on lies and
scarcely in keeping with the moral elevation and purity always claimed by
this people.

The cleanliness of this people, moral and otherwise, I must say, is a   21
point in itself. By their very exterior you could tell that these were no lovers

---

*Those Jews who believed that Judaism was not only a religion but conferred a *national* status
as well. Zionists thus believe in a Jewish state, not just a Jewish faith.

of water, and, to your distress, you often knew it with your eyes closed. Later I often grew sick to my stomach from the smell of these caftan-wearers. Added to this, there was their unclean dress and their generally unheroic appearance.

All this could scarcely be called very attractive; but it became positively 22 repulsive when, in addition to their physical uncleanliness, you discovered the moral stains on this 'chosen people.'

In a short time I was made more thoughtful than ever by my slowly 23 rising insight into the type of activity carried on by the Jews in certain fields.

Was there any form of filth or profligacy, particularly in cultural life, 24 without at least one Jew involved in it?

If you cut even cautiously into such an abscess, you found, like a maggot 25 in a rotting body, often dazzled by the sudden light—a kike!

What had to be reckoned heavily against the Jews in my eyes was when 26 I became acquainted with their activity in the press, art, literature, and the theater.* All the unctuous reassurances helped little or nothing. It sufficed to look at a billboard, to study the names of the men behind the horrible trash they advertised, to make you hard for a long time to come. This was pestilence, spiritual pestilence, worse than the Black Death of olden times, and the people was being infected with it! It goes without saying that the lower the intellectual level of one of these art manufacturers, the more unlimited his fertility will be, and the scoundrel ends up like a garbage separator, splashing his filth in the face of humanity. And bear in mind that there is no limit to their number; bear in mind that for one Goethe Nature easily can foist on the world ten thousand of these scribblers who poison men's souls like germ-carriers of the worse sort, on their fellow men.

It was terrible, but not to be overlooked, that precisely the Jew, in 27 tremendous numbers, seemed chosen by Nature for this shameful calling.

Is this why the Jews are called the 'chosen people'? 28

I now began to examine carefully the names of all the creators of 29 unclean products in public artistic life. The result was less and less favorable for my previous attitude toward the Jews. Regardless how my sentiment might resist, my reason was forced to draw its conclusions.

The fact that nine tenths of all literary filth, artistic trash, and theatrical 30 idiocy can be set to the account of a people, constituting hardly one hundredth of all the country's inhabitants, could simply not be talked away; it was the plain truth.

And I now began to examine my beloved 'world press' from this point 31 of view.

And the deeper I probed, the more the object of my former admiration 32 shriveled. The style became more and more unbearable; I could not help

*There is not much evidence that Hitler really knew the art, literature, and theatre of his day. These criticisms seem to be parrotings of *Volksblatt* editorials. It was attitudes such as these that eventually led to the Nazi burning of books and the denunciation of writings by "racially inferior" authors.

rejecting the content as inwardly shallow and banal; the objectivity of exposition now seemed to me more akin to lies than honest truth; and the writers were—Jews.

A thousand things which I had hardly seen before now struck my 33 notice, and others, which had previously given me food for thought, I now learned to grasp and understand.

I now saw the liberal attitude of this press in a different light; the lofty 34 tone in which it answered attacks and its method of killing them with silence now revealed itself to me as a trick as clever as it was treacherous; the transfigured raptures of their theatrical critics were always directed at Jewish writers, and their disapproval never struck anyone but Germans. The gentle pinpricks against William II revealed its methods by their persistency, and so did its commendation of French culture and civilization. The trashy content of the short story now appeared to me as outright indecency, and in the language I detected the accents of a foreign people; the sense of the whole thing was so obviously hostile to Germanism that this could only have been intentional.

But who had an interest in this? 35

Was all this a mere accident? 36

Gradually I became uncertain. 37

The development was accelerated by insights which I gained into a 38 number of other matters. I am referring to the general view of ethics and morals which was quite openly exhibited by a large part of the Jews, and the practical application of which could be seen.

Here again the streets provided an object lesson of a sort which was 39 sometimes positively evil.

The relation of the Jews to prostitution and, even more, to the white- 40 slave traffic, could be studied in Vienna as perhaps in no other city of Western Europe, with the possible exception of the southern French ports. If you walked at night through the streets and alleys of Leopoldstadt,* at every step you witnessed proceedings which remained concealed from the majority of the German people until the War gave the soldiers on the eastern front occasion to see similar things, or, better expressed, forced them to see them.

When thus for the first time I recognized the Jew as the cold-hearted, 41 shameless, and calculating director of this revolting vice traffic in the scum of the big city, a cold shudder ran down my back.

But then a flame flared up within me. I no longer avoided discussion of 42 the Jewish question; no, now I sought it. And when I learned to look for the Jew in all branches of cultural and artistic life and its various manifestations, I suddenly encountered him in a place where I would least have expected to find him.

---

*Second District of Vienna, separated from the main part of the city by the Danube Canal. Formerly the ghetto, it still has a predominantly Jewish population. [Original editor's note]

When I recognized the Jew as the leader of the Social Democracy,* 43 the scales dropped from my eyes. A long soul struggle had reached its conclusion.

Even in my daily relations with my fellow workers, I observed the 44 amazing adaptability with which they adopted different positions on the same question, sometimes within an interval of a few days, sometimes in only a few hours. It was hard for me to understand how people who, when spoken to alone, possessed some sensible opinions, suddenly lost them as soon as they came under the influence of the masses. It was often enough to make one despair. When, after hours of argument, I was convinced that now at last I had broken the ice or cleared up some absurdity, and was beginning to rejoice at my success, on the next day to my disgust I had to begin all over again; it had all been in vain. Like an eternal pendulum their opinions seemed to swing back again and again to the old madness.

All this I could understand: that they were dissatisfied with their lot and 45 cursed the Fate which often struck them so harshly; that they hated the employers who seemed to them the heartless bailiffs of Fate; that they cursed the authorities who in their eyes were without feeling for their situation; that they demonstrated against food prices and carried their demands into the streets: this much could be understood without recourse to reason. But what inevitably remained incomprehensible was the boundless hatred they heaped upon their own nationality, despising its greatness, besmirching its history, and dragging its great men into the gutter.

This struggle against their own species, their own clan, their own home- 46 land, was as senseless as it was incomprehensible. It was unnatural.

It was possible to cure them temporarily of this vice, but only for days 47 or at most weeks. If later you met the man you thought you had converted, he was just the same as before.

His old unnatural state had regained full possession of him. 48

. . .

I gradually became aware that the Social Democratic press was directed 49 predominantly by Jews; yet I did not attribute any special significance to this circumstance, since conditions were exactly the same in the other papers. Yet one fact seemed conspicuous: there was not one paper with Jews working on it which could have been regarded as truly national, according to my education and way of thinking.

I swallowed my disgust and tried to read this type of Marxist press 50 production, but my revulsion became so unlimited in so doing that I endeavored to become more closely acquainted with the men who manufactured these compendiums of knavery.

From the publisher down, they were all Jews. 51

I took all the Social Democratic pamphlets I could lay hands on and 52

*Socialism, the political theory at the opposite end of the political spectrum from the fascism which Hitler later brought to Germany.

sought the names of their authors: Jews.* I noted the names of the leaders; by far the greatest part were likewise members of the 'chosen people,' whether they were representatives in the Reichsrat or trade-union secretaries, the heads of organizations or street agitators. It was always the same gruesome picture. The names of the Austerlitzes, Davids, Adlers, Ellenbogens, etc., will remain forever graven in my memory. One thing had grown clear to me: the party with whose petty representatives I had been carrying on the most violent struggle for months was, as to leadership, almost exclusively in the hands of a foreign people; for, to my deep and joyful satisfaction, I had at last come to the conclusion that the Jew was no German.

Only now did I become thoroughly acquainted with the seducer of our people.   53

A single year of my sojourn in Vienna had sufficed to imbue me with the conviction that no worker could be so stubborn that he would not in the end succumb to better knowledge and better explanations. Slowly I had become an expert in their own doctrine and used it as a weapon in the struggle for my own profound conviction.   54

Success almost always favored my side.   55

The great masses could be saved, if only with the gravest sacrifice in time and patience.   56

But a Jew could never be parted from his opinions.   57

At that time I was still childish enough to try to make the madness of their doctrine clear to them; in my little circle I talked my tongue sore and my throat hoarse, thinking I would inevitably succeed in convincing them how ruinous their Marxist madness was; but what I accomplished was often the opposite. It seemed as though their increased understanding of the destructive effects of Social Democratic theories and their results only reinforced their determination.   58

The more I argued with them, the better I came to know their dialectic. First they counted on the stupidity of their adversary, and then, when there was no other way out, they themselves simply played stupid. If all this didn't help, they pretended not to understand, or, if challenged, they changed the subject in a hurry, quoted platitudes which, if you accepted them, they immediately related to entirely different matters, and then, if again attacked, gave ground and pretended not to know exactly what you were talking about. Whenever you tried to attack one of these apostles, your hand closed on a jelly-like slime which divided up and poured through your fingers, but in the next moment collected again. But if you really struck one of these fellows so telling a blow that, observed by the audience, he couldn't help but agree, and if you believed that this had taken you at least one step forward, your amazement was great the next day. The Jew had not the slightest recollection of the day before, he rattled off his same old nonsense as though nothing at all had happened, and, if indignantly challenged, affected amazement; he   59

*The facts do not support this assertion that the leadership of Austrian Social Democracy was primarily Jewish.

couldn't remember a thing, except that he had proved the correctness of his assertions the previous day.

Sometimes I stood there thunderstruck.   60

I didn't know what to be more amazed at: the agility of their tongues 61 or their virtuosity at lying.

Gradually I began to hate them.   62

All this had but one good side: that in proportion as the real leaders or 63 at least the disseminators of Social Democracy came within my vision, my love for my people inevitably grew. For who, in view of the diabolical craftiness of these seducers, could damn the luckless victims? How hard it was, even for me, to get the better of this race of dialectical liars! And how futile was such success in dealing with people who twist the truth in your mouth, who without so much as a blush disavow the word they have just spoken, and in the very next minute take credit for it after all.

No. The better acquainted I became with the Jew, the more forgiving 64 I inevitably became toward the worker.

Questions for Discussion

1. If you have ever talked to a fanatical bigot of any kind, compare the "reasoning" you encountered then with that in *Mein Kampf.* What seems to be the real root of the hatred that emerges in this kind of bigotry? Is it a common root, or does it vary unpredictably from person to person? This is too big a question to answer factually, of course. But it may be useful to share impressions and speculations with your classmates.

2. Notice the self-conscious abandonment of reason in favor of feeling in paragraph 7. What would have been the effect of this move on Hitler's emerging racial hatred?

3. What is the intended rhetorical effect of the imagery that Hitler employs in paragraphs 25, 26, 53, and 59?

4. Discuss the similarities of opinion about Jews in *Mein Kampf,* paragraphs 21–25, with the opinions of the Colonel in "Artists in Uniform" (p. 466 ¶19).

5. It is sometimes said that everyone views the members of *some* groups more favorably than others, which is to say that everyone is prejudiced to some degree, if by prejudice we mean the expectation that individual members of certain groups will behave less admirably than the members of our own group. Do you think that this is so? Is it true of you? If it is, are you "bigoted"? If you think that you are not but still admit that you allow preconceptions about *groups* to affect your judgment of *individuals,* how would you define *bigotry* and *prejudice* as distinct from your behavior?

6. It is sometimes said that America is experiencing a new increase in acts of bigotry: attacks on individuals merely because they belong to this or that group; mailing of anonymous hate-mail to members of minority groups; publication of journals that include incitement to bigotry. Have you noted any such behavior on your own campus? If so, what do you think might be an effective way to combat it?

Suggested Essay Topics

1. In "Artists in Uniform" (pp. 457–469), Mary McCarthy's narrator, talking with the anti-Semitic Colonel, says,

> It came to me . . . that for extremely stupid people anti-Semitism was a form of intellectuality, the sole form of intellectuality of which they were capable. It represented, in a rudimentary way, the ability to make categories, to generalize. Hence a thing I had noted before but never understood: the fact that anti-Semetic statements were generally delivered in an atmosphere of profundity. . . . To arrive, indeed, at the idea of a Jew was, for these grouping minds, an exercise in Platonic thought, a discovery of essence. . . . From this, it would seem, followed the querulous obstinacy with which the anti-Semite clung to his concept; to be deprived of this intellectual tool by missionaries of tolerance would be, for persons like the Colonel, the equivalent of Western man's losing the syllogism: a lapse into animal darkness. (¶17)

If you agree that this analysis accurately lays bare the cause of much bigotry in general and is not limited to anti-Semitism, write an essay that analyzes some example of bigotry that you know firsthand, and base your analysis on the perspective provided by McCarthy in the quoted passage.

2. A variation of topic 1: Use McCarthy's perspective as the basis of your analysis of some example of bigotry found in a work of fiction.

Malcolm Hay

In the book from which this excerpt is taken, Europe and the Jews: The Pressure of Christendom on the People of Israel for 1900 Years, *Malcolm Hay (1881–1962) addresses one of the most troublesome of all human questions: Why do the members of one human group hate other groups so much that they are eager to exterminate them? His form of the question—Who is to blame for a given historical crime?—presents one of the most difficult of all writing tasks. To support any conclusions about such broad and elusive questions requires an immense amount of careful research, and to grapple with such emotion-charged matters requires great courage and tact. The author is sure to offend many readers, especially those groups that he blames for crimes they have accused others of committing.*

Through more than 300 pages packed with carefully chosen quotations, Hay argues three main points. First, it is a mistake to blame only Hitler and the Germans for the killing of millions of Jews during World War II; if we in the nations that opposed Hitler had responded with concrete aid as reports of extermination camps filtered into the Allied countries, hundreds of thousands, perhaps millions, of Jews might have been saved. Second, the reason for our indifference to the fate of innocent millions was that we had been taught, by one major "Christian" tradition, that Jews deserved to die because they had killed Christ. Third, the Jews did not kill Christ; Christ was killed, as three of the four Gospels make clear, by Roman soldiers. The Jews who connived in Christ's death were a small group who had to plot secretly with the Romans for fear of resistance from the main body of Jews.

As a Christian himself, Hay is in a better position for making these points than if he were Jewish. Some people would be more tempted to question his objectivity if he clearly had a personal stake in making his case. But in arguing about such complex matters, it is never enough to have a good, seemingly "objective" platform to stand on; final success depends on the quality of our reasoning and the evidence we offer.

As you read this selection (less than one-tenth of Hay's argument), it is important to avoid making up your mind with final assurance. After all, it would take months, perhaps years, of study to check out the reliability of his hundreds of quotations (we have omitted his references to save space) and to reach a point of confident personal understanding of the issues he raises. What we all can do, however, is enlarge our grasp of the issues and our sense of the possible ways of thinking about them. As you read, you may want to question yourself about your own prejudices and your justified beliefs and about possible ways of removing the prejudices and deepening and refining the convictions.

THE PERSECUTION OF JEWS

A Christian Scandal

Our title for chapter 1, "The Golden Mouth," of *Europe and the Jews: The Pressure of Christendom on the People of Israel for 1900 Years* (1950).

Suffer no man and no cause to escape the undying penalty which history has the power to inflict on wrong.—Lord Acton

So I considered again all the oppressions that are done under the sun;
And beheld the tears of such as were oppressed, and they had no com-
    forter;
And on the side of the oppressors there was power,
But they had no comforter.

Wherefore I praised the dead that are already dead
More than the living that are yet alive;
But better than they both is he that hath not yet been,
Who hath not seen the evil that is done under the sun.
Ecclesiastes IV: 1–3

Men are not born with hatred in their blood. The infection is usually 1
acquired by contact; it may be injected deliberately or even unconsciously,
by parents, or by teachers. Adults, unless protected by the vigor of their
intelligence, or by a rare quality of goodness, seldom escape contagion. The
disease may spread throughout the land like the plague, so that a class, a
religion, a nation, will become the victim of popular hatred without anyone
knowing exactly how it all began; and people will disagree, and even quarrel
among themselves, about the real reason for its existence; and no one foresees
the inevitable consequences.

For hatred dealeth perversely, as St. Paul might have said were he 2
writing to the Corinthians at the present time, and is puffed up with pride;
rejoiceth in iniquity; regardeth not the truth. These three things, therefore,
corrupt the world: disbelief, despair, and hatred—and of these, the most
dangerous of all is hatred.

In the spring of 1945, three trucks loaded with eight to nine tons of 3
human ashes, from the Sachsenhausen concentration camp, were dumped
into a canal in order to conceal the high rate of Jewish executions. When a
German general was asked at Nuremberg how such things could happen, he
replied: "I am of the opinion that when for years, for decades, the doctrine
is preached that Jews are not even human, such an outcome is inevitable."
This explanation, which gets to the root of the matter, is, however, incomplete. The doctrine which made such deeds inevitable had been preached, not
merely for years or for decades, but for many centuries; more than once
during the Middle Ages it threatened to destroy the Jewish people. "The
Jews," wrote Léon Bloy, "are the most faithful witnesses, the most authentic
remainders, of the candid Middle Ages which hated them for the love of God,
and so often wanted to exterminate them." In those days the excuse given
for killing them was often that they were "not human," and that, in the
modern German sense, they were "nonadaptable"; they did not fit into the
mediaeval conception of a World State.

The German crime of genocide—the murder of a race—has its logical 4
roots in the mediaeval theory that the Jews were outcasts, condemned by God
to a life of perpetual servitude, and it is not, therefore, a phenomenon completely disconnected from previous history. Moreover, responsibility for the
nearly achieved success of the German plan to destroy a whole group of
human beings ought not to be restricted to Hitler and his gangsters, or to the
German people. The plan nearly succeeded because it was allowed to develop
without interference.

"It was an excellent saying of Solon's," wrote Richard Bentley, "who 5
when he was asked what would rid the world of injuries, replied: 'If the

bystanders would have the same resentment with those that suffer wrong.' "
The responsibility of bystanders who remained inactive while the German
plan proceeded was recognized by one European statesman, by the least
guilty of them all, Jan Masaryk, who had helped to rescue many thousands
from the German chambers of death. Masaryk said:

> I am not an expert on the Near East and know practically nothing about
> pipe-lines. But one pipe-line I have watched with horror all my life; it is
> the pipe-line through which, for centuries, Jewish blood has flowed
> sporadically, and with horrible, incessant streams from 1933 to 1945. I will
> not, I cannot, forget this unbelievable fact, and I bow my head in shame
> as one of those who permitted this greatest of wholesale murders to
> happen, instead of standing up with courage and decision against its
> perpetrators before it was too late.

Even after the Nuremberg Laws of 1935, every frontier remained closed [6]
against Jews fleeing from German terror, although a few were sometimes
allowed in by a back door. Bystanders from thirty-two countries attended a
conference at Evian, in 1938, to discuss the refugee problem; they formed a
Permanent Intergovernmental Department in London to make arrangements
for the admission of Jewish immigrants from Germany. The question of
saving Jewish children by sending them to Palestine was not on the agenda
of the Committee for assistance to refugees. "Up to August, 1939, the Committee had not succeeded in discovering new opportunities of immigration,
though negotiations were proceeding with San Domingo, Northern Rhodesia,
the Philippines and British Guiana."
An American writer asked in 1938: [7]

> What is to be done with these people, with the millions who are
> clawing like frantic beasts at the dark walls of the suffocating chambers
> where they are imprisoned? The Christian world has practically aban-
> doned them, and sits by with hardly an observable twinge of conscience
> in the midst of this terrible catastrophe. The Western Jews, still potent
> and powerful, rotate in their smug self-satisfied orbits, and confine them-
> selves to genteel charity.

Until Germany obtained control of the greater part of Western Europe [8]
her policy had been directed mainly to compulsory Jewish emigration. But
victories in 1940 had opened up new possibilities; and the Jews were therefore
driven into ghettos in Poland and neighboring areas, where arrangements
were being made for the "final solution," which was proclaimed in 1942, and
put into action throughout all Germany and German-occupied territories.
"What should be done with them," asked Hans Frank, governor general of
occupied Poland, on December 16th, 1941. The German answer was no longer
a secret. "I must ask you, gentlemen," said the governor, "to arm yourselves
against all feelings of pity. We must annihilate the Jews wherever we find
them."

Hitler, in 1941, was still waiting to see what the Christian world was   9
going to do. Had the Allies opened their doors wide, even then, at least a
million people, including hundreds of thousands of children, could have been
saved. But no doors anywhere were widely opened. Few hearts anywhere
were deeply moved. In Palestine, in the corner secured to Jews by the decision
of the League of Nations, the entries by land and by sea were guarded by
British soldiers and British sailors. Great numbers, especially in Poland,
would have fled from the impending terror: *"If only they could,"* wrote Jacques
Maritain in 1938, "if only other countries would open their frontiers." The
German government at that time, and even after, was not always unwilling,
and in 1939 and 1940, was still prepared to let them go on certain conditions.
"The Allies were told that if the Jews of Germany were to receive certificates
to Palestine, or visas for any other country, they could be saved. Although
for Jews to remain in Germany meant certain death, the pieces of paper
needed to save human lives were not granted."

These pieces of paper were not provided, even to save the lives of   10
children. In April, 1943, the Swedish government agreed to ask the German
government to permit twenty thousand children to leave Germany for Sweden, provided that Sweden should be relieved of responsibility for them after
the war. These children would have been saved had the British government
given them certificates for Palestine. But even to save twenty thousand children from being slaughtered by the Germans, "it was not possible," said a
British minister in the House of Commons, "for His Majesty's Government
to go beyond the terms of policy approved by Parliament."

About the same time, in 1943, the Germans were considering an offer   11
by the Red Cross and the British to evacuate seventy thousand children from
Rumania to Palestine. Negotiations dragged on with the usual lack of vigor.
And the Germans were persuaded by the Mufti of Jerusalem and Raschid Ali
Gailani, prime minister of Iraq, who at the time were living, at German
expense, in Berlin, to reject the plan. So the seventy thousand children were
sent to the gas chambers.

More than a million children, including uncounted thousands of new-   12
born infants, were killed by the Germans; most of them could have been
saved had the countries of the world been determined to save them. But the
doors remained closed. The children were taken away from their parents and
sent, crowded in the death trains, and alone, to the crematoria of Auschwitz
and Treblinka, or to the mass graves of Poland and Western Russia.

The German method of burying people in communal pits was a great   13
improvement on the old system, once considered to be inhuman, of making
each condemned man dig his own grave. The shooting of about two million
people, whose bodies could not be left lying about, presented a difficult
problem owing to the shortage of labor. Jewish women and children, weakened by torture and by long internment in concentration camps, were physically incapable of digging; and the men, when put on the list for "special
treatment," were, as a rule, reduced to such a condition by hard labor on
meager rations that they could hardly walk. The mass grave was an obvious

necessity; but the German stroke of genius was the idea of making their victims get into the grave before they were shot, thus saving the labor of lifting two million dead bodies and throwing them in. Many hundreds of these death pits were dug in Central Europe until the Germans began to apply to extermination their well-known scientific efficiency. One of the largest pits, at Kerch, was examined in 1942 by officials of the Russian army:

> It was discovered that this trench, one kilometer in length, four meters wide, and two meters deep, was filled to overflowing with bodies of women, children, old men, and boys and girls in their teens. Near the trench were frozen pools of blood. Children's caps, toys, ribbons, torn off buttons, gloves, milkbottles, and rubber comforters, small shoes, galoshes, together with torn off hands and feet, and other parts of human bodies, were lying nearby. Everything was spattered with blood and brains.

What happened at Dulmo, in the Ukraine, reported by a German witness, Hermann Graebe, is one of the grimmest short stories that has ever been told in the bloody record of inhuman history. Graebe was manager of a building contractor's business at Dulmo. On October 5, 1942, he went as usual to his office and there was told by his foreman of terrible doings in the neighborhood. All the Jews in the district, about five thousand of them, were being liquidated. About fifteen hundred were shot every day, out in the open air, at a place nearby where three large pits had been dug, thirty meters long and three meters deep. Graebe and his foreman, who was intensely agitated, got into a car and drove off to the place. They saw a great mound of earth, twice the length of a cricket pitch and more than six feet high—a good shooting range. Near the mound were several trucks packed with people. Guards with whips drove the people off the trucks. The victims all had yellow patches sewn onto their garments, back and front—the Jewish badge. From behind the earth mound came the sound of rifle shots in quick succession. The people from the lorries, men, women and children of all ages, were herded together near the mound by an SS man armed with a dog whip. They were ordered to strip. They were told to put down their clothes in tidy order, boots and shoes, top clothing and underclothing.

Already there were great piles of this clothing, and a heap of eight hundred to a thousand pairs of boots and shoes. The people undressed. The mothers undressed the little children, "without screaming or weeping," reported Graebe, five years after. They had reached the point of human suffering where tears no longer flow and all hope has long been abandoned. "They stood around in family groups, kissed each other, said farewells, and waited." They were waiting for a signal from the SS man with a whip, who was standing by the pit. They stood there waiting for a quarter of an hour, waiting for their turn to come, while on the other side of the earth mound, now that the shots were no longer heard, the dead and dying were being packed into the pit. Graebe said:

I heard no complaints, no appeal for mercy. I watched a family of about eight persons, a man and a woman both about fifty, with their grown up children, about twenty to twenty-four. An old woman with snow-white hair was holding a little baby in her arms, singing to it and tickling it. The baby was cooing with delight. The couple were looking at each other with tears in their eyes. The father was holding the hand of a boy about ten years old and speaking to him softly; the boy was fighting his tears . . .

Then suddenly came a shout from the SS man at the pit. They were ready to deal with the next batch. Twenty people were counted off, including the family of eight. They were marched away behind the earth mound. Graebe and his foreman followed them. They walked round the mound and saw the tremendous grave, nearly a hundred feet long and nine feet deep. "People were closely wedged together and lying on top of each other so that only their heads were visible. Nearly all had blood running over their shoulders from their heads." They had been shot, in the usual German way, in the back of the neck. "Some of the shot people were still moving. Some were lifting their arms and turning their heads to show that they were still alive." 16

The pit was already nearly full; it contained about a thousand bodies. The SS man who did the shooting was sitting on the edge of the pit, smoking a cigarette, with a tommy gun on his knee. The new batch of twenty people, the family of eight and the baby carried in the arms of the woman with snow-white hair, all completely naked, were directed down steps cut in the clay wall of the pit, and clambered over the heads of the dead and the dying. They lay down among them. "Some caressed those who were still alive and spoke to them in a low voice." Then came the shots from the SS man, who had thrown away his cigarette. Graebe looked into the pit "and saw the bodies were twitching, and some heads lying already motionless on top of the dead bodies that lay under them." 17

The Jews who died in this manner at Dulmo were the most fortunate ones. They were spared torture in laboratory tests carried out by German doctors in order to find out how much agony the human body can endure before it dies; they were spared the choking terror of death in the gas chamber where hundreds of people at a time, squeezed together as tightly as the room could hold them, waited for the stream of poison to be turned on, while members of the German prison staff stood listening for ten or fifteen minutes until the screaming ceased, until all sounds had ceased, and they could safely open the door to the dead. And when the door was opened, the torture was not yet over. Four young Jews, whose turn would come perhaps with the next batch, dressed in a special sanitary uniform, with high rubber boots and long leather gauntlets, and provided with grappling irons, were compelled to drag out the pale dead bodies; and another group of young men was waiting to load the bodies onto a cart and drive them to the crematorium; and they knew that their turn, too, would soon come. 18

Responsibility for these deeds which have dishonored humanity does 19 not rest solely with Hitler and the men who sat in the dock at Nuremberg. Another tribunal will judge the bystanders, some of them in England, who watched the murderous beginnings, and then looked away and in their hearts secretly approved. "The Jewish blood shed by the Nazis," writes J.-P. Sartre, "is upon the heads of all of us."

As Maxim Gorky said more than thirty years ago, one of the greatest crimes of which men are guilty, is indifference to the fate of their fellow men. This responsibility of the indifferent was recognized by Jacques Maritain a few years before the final act of the tragedy. "There seems to be a spirit," he said in 1938, "which, without endorsing excesses committed against Jews . . . and without professing anti-Semitism, regards the Jewish drama with the indifference of the rational man who goes coldly along his way." It was this spirit of indifference, this cold aloofness of the bystanders, which made it possible for Hitler to turn Europe into a Jewish cemetery. Christian responsibility has, however, been recognized by one English bystander who for many years had never failed "to have the same resentment with those that suffer wrong": "In our own day, and within our own civilization," writes Dr. James Parkes, "more than six million deliberate murders are the consequence of the teachings about Jews for which the Christian Church is ultimately responsible, and of an attitude to Judaism which is not only maintained by all the Christian Churches, but has its ultimate resting place in the teaching of the New Testament itself."

Repressing the instinct to make excuses, read the following words written by a survivor of Auschwitz:

> German responsibility for these crimes, however overwhelming it may be, is only a secondary responsibility, which has grafted itself, like a hideous parasite, upon a secular tradition, which is a Christian tradition. How can one forget that Christianity, chiefly from the eleventh century, has employed against Jews a policy of degradation and of pogroms, which has been extended—among certain Christian people—into contemporary history, which can be observed still alive to-day in most Catholic Poland, and of which the Hitlerian system has been only a copy, atrociously perfected.

Even in countries where pogroms are unknown, it was the coldness, the indifference of the average man which made the Jewish drama in Europe possible. "I am convinced," wrote Pierre van Paassen, "that Hitler neither could nor would have done to the Jewish people what he has done . . . if we had not actively prepared the way for him by our own unfriendly attitude to the Jews, by our selfishness and by the anti-Semitic teaching in our churches and schools."

The way was prepared by a hatred which has a long history. The inoculation of the poison began long ago in the nurseries of Christendom. Millions of children heard about Jews for the first time when they were told the story of how Christ was killed by wicked men; killed by the Jews;

crucified by the Jews. And the next thing they learned was that God had punished these wicked men and had cursed the whole of their nation for all time, so that they had become outcasts and were unfit to associate with Christians. When these children grew up, some of them quarreled among themselves about the meaning of the word of Christ and about the story of his life, death and resurrection; and others were Christians only in name; but most of them retained enough Christianity to continue hating the perfidious people, the Christ-killers, the deicide [i.e., god-murdering] race.

Although the popular tradition that "the Jews" crucified Christ goes   24
back to the beginnings of the Christian Church, no justification for it can be found in the New Testament. St. Matthew, St. Mark and St. Luke all took special care to impress upon their readers the fact that the Jewish people, their own people, were not responsible for, and were for the most part ignorant of, the events which led up to the apprehension, the trial and the condemnation of Christ. St. Matthew's account of what happened does not provide any opportunity for people to differ about his meaning. He states quite clearly in his twenty-sixth chapter that "the Jews" had nothing to do with the plot against Christ. He explains who the conspirators were, and why they had to do their work in secret. "Then were gathered together the Chief Priests and the Ancients of the people into the court of the High Priest who is called Caiphas. And they consulted together that by subtlety they might apprehend Jesus and put him to death." Secrecy was essential to the plans of the plotters because they "feared the multitude" (Matthew XXI:46). They were afraid that "the Jews" might find out what was brewing and start a riot.

The plot which ended on Calvary began to take shape for the first time   25
at that gathering in the court of Caiphas. These men were engaged upon an enterprise which they knew would not meet with public approval. They had no mandate from the Jewish people for what they were about to do. They did not represent the two or three million Jews who at that time lived in Palestine, or another million who lived in Egypt, or the millions more who were scattered all over the Roman Empire. At least three-quarters of all these people lived and died without ever hearing the name of Christ.

The conspirators did not even represent the wishes of the Jewish popu-   26
lation in and around Jerusalem. They were afraid, explained Matthew, of arresting Jesus "on the festival day, lest there should be a tumult among the people."

They had to act promptly; they had to avoid publicity. They employed   27
the crowd of idlers and ruffians which can be always collected for an evil purpose, to provide a democratic covering for what they proposed to do. This crowd formed a majority of the people present at the trial; these were the men who, when Pilate, the pioneer of appeasement, tried to save Christ from their fury, replied with the fateful words which Matthew recorded in the twenty-seventh chapter of his Gospel: "And the whole people answering said: 'His blood be upon us and upon our children.'" Although "the whole people," as Matthew explained, meant only the people present "who had been persuaded by the High Priest and the Ancients" (XXVII:20), his text has been used for

centuries by countless Christian preachers as a stimulant to hate and an excuse for anti-Jewish pogroms. "O cursed race!" thundered Bossuet from his pulpit, "your prayer will be answered only too effectively; that blood will pursue you even unto your remotest descendants, until the Lord, weary at last of vengeance, will be mindful, at the end of time, of your miserable remnant."

St. Mark, also, records that the Jewish people had nothing to do with the plot and that if they had known about it they would have expressed violent disapproval. "The Chief Priests and the Pharisees sought how they might destroy him. For they feared him because the whole multitude was in admiration of his doctrine" (XI:18). "They sought to lay hands upon him, but they feared the people" (XII:12). They sought to lay hold on him and kill him, but they said, "not on the festival day, lest there should be a tumult among the people" (XIV:2). ²⁸

St. Luke tells the same story with the same emphasis. "And the Chief Priests and the Scribes, and the rulers of the people, sought to destroy him. And they found not what to do to him; for all the people were very attentive to hear him" (XIX:47, 48). "The Chief Priests and the Scribes sought to lay hands on him . . . but they feared the people" (XX:19). "And the Chief Priests and the Scribes sought how they might put Jesus to death; but they feared the people" (XXII:2). ²⁹

This Christian tradition, which made "the Jews" responsible for the death of Christ, first took shape in the Fourth Gospel. St. John deals with the historical beginnings of the Christian Church even more fully than with the ending of the era which preceded the foundation of Christianity. Unlike the other evangelists, he wrote as one outside the Jewish world, as one hostile to it. He was already disassimilated. His Gospel contains the first hint of hostility, the first suggestion of a religious Judaeophobia. He almost invariably employs the phrase "the Jews" when the context shows, and the other evangelists confirm, that he is referring to the action or to the opinions of the High Priests and the Ancients. ³⁰

Whereas Matthew, Mark and Luke all wrote as if they had foreseen, and were trying to refute in advance, the accusation which would be brought against their fellow-countrymen, John, by his repeated use of the phrase "the Jews," puts into the mind of his readers the idea that they were all guilty. Although Matthew, for instance, says that when Jesus healed the man with a withered hand on the Sabbath, "the Pharisees made a consultation how they might destroy him," John, reporting a similar incident, indicts, not the Pharisees, but "the Jews": "*The Jews* therefore said to him that was healed: it is not lawful for thee to take up thy bed . . . therefore did *the Jews* persecute Jesus because he did these things on the Sabbath" (V:10, 16). ³¹

When John tells the story of the blind man, he begins by relating what the Pharisees said, but after the man received his sight his parents are reported to have "feared *the Jews,*" although it is obvious from the context that they feared the Pharisees. In the same chapter, John wrote that "*the Jews* had agreed among themselves that if any man should confess him to be the Christ, he should be put out of the synagogue." This agreement had been reached, not ³²

by the Jews, but by the Chief Priests and the Ancients. In the tenth chapter which deals with the action and behavior of this political group, we read that

> a dissension rose again among *the Jews* . . . and many of them said: He hath a devil and is mad . . . In Solomon's Porch *the Jews* therefore came to him and said to him . . . If thou be the Christ tell us plainly . . . *The Jews* then took up stones to stone him . . . *The Jews* answered him—For a good work we stone thee not, but for blasphemy.

John was more careful in his choice of words when he described the details of the crucifixion. He laid special emphasis on the fact that Christ was crucified, not by the Jews, but by Roman soldiers. "The soldiers therefore, when they had crucified him took his garments . . . and also his coat . . . they said to one another: Let us not cut it, but let us cast lots for it . . . and the soldiers indeed did these things" (XIX:23, 24). Nevertheless, in John's story of the apprehension, trial and death of Christ, responsibility is laid, as much as inference can lay it, on the whole Jewish people; a prominence is given to the action of "the Jews" which the events as recorded by the other evangelists do not justify. 33

Père Lagrange suggested that John made use of the phrase "the Jews," as a literary device to save constant repetition of the words "High Priests and Pharisees." It is a pity that this interpretation of John's meaning did not occur to any of the early Fathers. When Origen wrote at the beginning of the fourth century that "the Jews . . . nailed Christ to the cross," he also may have meant something different from what he said—but for many centuries his words were taken as literally true by all Christendom. And consequently, as an English historian in our own time has admitted, "The crime of a handful of priests and elders in Jerusalem was visited by the Christian Churches upon the whole Jewish race." 34

This tradition has been handed on without much respect for the actual facts as related in the Gospels. Thus, in the thirteenth century, a pious monk, Jacques de Vitry, went to the Holy Land, visited the site of Calvary and sat in meditation, as he recorded in his Chronicle, "on the very spot where *the Jews* divided the garments of Christ, and for his tunic cast lots." 35

. . .

Margery Kempe, a slightly later visionary . . . , in her description of the Passion [i.e., the suffering and crucifixion], which she imagined she had actually witnessed, followed the common conviction that Jews had nailed Christ to the cross. "Sche beheld how the cruel Jewys leydyn his precyows body to the Crosse and sithyn tokyn a long nayle . . . and wyth gret vilnes and cruelnes thei dreuyn it thorw hys hande" [She beheld how the cruel Jews laid his precious body to the Cross and then took a long nail . . . and with great villainy and cruelty they drove it through his hand]. Pictures of Jews hammering in the nails helped to encourage both hatred and piety. A writer at the beginning of the sixteenth century mentions "a Church where there was placed a Jew, of wood, before the Saviour, grasping a hammer." 36

Pious ingenuity reached a new peak in Spain where, in the first quarter   37
of the eighteenth century, two hundred years after all the Jews had been
expelled, hatred continued to flourish alongside Christian faith and Christian
superstition. A collection of the fables popular in the Middle Ages, printed
in 1728, entitled *Centinela Contra Judios,* revived the belief that certain Jews, who
were "born with worms in their mouth . . . were descended from a Jewess who
ordered the locksmith who made the nails to crucify Christ to make the points
blunt so that the pain of crucifixion would be greater." In the seventeenth
century a zealous Catholic who was trying to convert Spinoza asked him to
remember "the terrible and unspeakably severe punishments by which the
Jews were reduced to the last stages of misery and calamity because they were
the authors of Christ's crucifixion."

In order to fortify these traditions, Christian commentators tended in-   38
creasingly to ignore the obvious meaning of the Gospel texts and sometimes
substituted the phrase "the Jews" where John himself had written "the High
Priests and the Pharisees."

. . .

In Russia popular Christianity produced a pattern of hate similar to that   39
of Western Europe. When the Czarina Elizabeth (1741–1761) was asked to
admit Jews into the country for economic reasons, she replied: "I do not wish
to obtain any benefits from the enemies of Christ." More than a hundred
years later, in 1890, when Alexander III was shown the draft of an official
report recommending some relaxation of the oppression from which the Jews
of his empire were suffering, he noted in the margin: "But we must not forget
that the Jews crucified Christ."

. . .

From the earliest times to the present day, readers of the Fourth Gospel,   40
with rare exceptions, have taken the phrase "the Jews" in its literal sense
without any shading of meaning. Consequently the whole literature of Christendom has contributed throughout the centuries to consolidate a tradition
not sanctioned by the text of the Synoptic Gospels—one that has brought
immeasurable suffering upon countless numbers of innocent human beings:
the tradition that "the Jewish nation condemned Christ to be crucified."
Joseph Klausner writes:

> The Jews, *as a nation,* were far less guilty of the death of Jesus than the
> Greeks, as a nation, were guilty of the death of Socrates; but who now
> would think of avenging the blood of Socrates the Greek upon his coun-
> trymen, the present Greek race? Yet these nineteen hundred years past,
> the world has gone on avenging the blood of Jesus the Jew upon his
> countrymen, the Jews, who have already paid the penalty, and still go on
> paying the penalty, in rivers and torrents of blood.

The extent of Jewish responsibility for the apprehension, trial and death   41
of Christ was defined by the highest authority of the Christian Church, St.
Peter, whose judgment corrects the bias shown, a generation later, in the

Fourth Gospel. The first papal pronouncement on this question was addressed by St. Peter to "Ye men of Israel," a gathering which had assembled in "the Porch which is called Solomon's"; it was addressed to those men only, in that place, and at that time. St. Peter did not acquit these men of guilt; he knew that they had taken some active part in the plot and at the trial; they were, he told them, accessories to the crime. But the final words he used have often been ignored: "And now, brethren, I know you did it through ignorance; as did also your rulers."

Ignorance, defined by Maimonides as "the want of knowledge respect- 42 ing things the knowledge of which can be obtained," is acceptable as an excuse only when it is not culpable. Abelard, in the twelfth century, may have extended too widely the proposition that where there is ignorance there can be no sin, when he said that the rulers of Israel acted "out of zeal for their law," and should therefore be absolved from all guilt. Christian tradition, especially in the early centuries, practically ignored St. Peter's statement that the "rulers" acted through ignorance. St. John Chrysostom, indeed, flatly contradicted St. Peter when he wrote that "the Jews . . . erred not ignorantly but with full knowledge." Whatever degree of guilt the "rulers" may have incurred, there is surely no justification for excluding them from the benefit of the petition and the judgment of Christ—"Father, forgive them for they know not what they do" (Luke XXIII:34). In the Gospel text these words refer quite clearly to the Roman soldiers, and not to the Jews.

The belief current in the Middle Ages which Abelard attacked and St. 43 Bernard defended was that "the Jews" were all guilty; that they had acted with deliberate malice; that their guilt was shared by the whole Jewish people, for all time, and that they, and their children's children to the last generation, were condemned to live in slavery as the servants of Christian princes. That was not the doctrine of St. Peter. If Christians had always remembered his words, the history of the Jews in their long exile would perhaps have been very different, and the civilization of the West might not have witnessed the degradation of humanity which was achieved by the Germans in their death camps and gas chambers.

In spite of St. Peter's judgment the popular Christian doctrine has al- 44 ways been that anyone, whether pagan or Christian, who has at any time persecuted, tortured or massacred Jews has acted as an instrument of Divine wrath. A chronicler, writing in the early years of the thirteenth century, admired the patience of God, who "after the Jews had crucified Our Lord, waited for forty-eight years before chastising them." According to Fleury, who wrote, in the first quarter of the eighteenth century, an enormous and still useful ecclesiastical history, God began to take reprisals against the Jews in the year 38 of the Christian era. In that year, anti-Jewish riots broke out in Alexandria. The rioters were secretly encouraged by Flaccus, the Roman commissioner in Egypt, who took no effective measures to prevent the mob from burning down synagogues, breaking into Jewish shops, and scattering the merchandise into the streets of the city. Flaccus showed his "neutrality" by attempting to disarm, not the rioters, but their victims. "He had searches made in the houses of the Jews on the pretext of disarming the nation, and several women were taken away and tormented when they refused to eat swine's flesh." A great number of Jews were murdered, and their bodies dragged through the streets. "In this manner," wrote Fleury in 1732, "divine vengeance began to be manifested against the Jews."

The sacking of Jerusalem and the destruction of the Temple, in the year 45 70, when more than a million people were massacred with a brutality to which the world has once again become accustomed, were regarded by many pious Christians as part of God's plan of revenge. "The Jews," wrote Sulpicius Severus, "were thus punished and exiled throughout the whole world, for no other account than for the impious hands they laid upon Christ." This interpretation of the event has been repeated for centuries.

. . .

There are therefore still some people who believe that the Jews were 46 cursed out of Palestine because they had behaved in a manner displeasing to God. If nations were liable to be dispossessed for such a reason, very few of them would enjoy security of tenure. "The Curse," as J.-P. Sartre has recently pointed out, was "geographical."

. . .

To justify the persecution of Jews, two excuses . . . were available to 47 Christians: either the Christians were acting in self-defense, or they were carrying out the will of God. The teaching of the early Fathers made the second excuse plausible. There was no direct incitement to violence. Athanasius did not tell the people to go out and beat up Jews. But he told them that "the Jews were no longer the people of God, but rulers of Sodom and Gomorrah"; and he asked the ominous question: "What is left unfulfilled, that they should now be allowed to disbelieve with impunity?"

When St. Ambrose told his congregations that the Jewish synagogue 48 was "a house of impiety, a receptacle of folly, which God himself has condemned," no one was surprised when the people went off and set fire to one. St. Ambrose accepted responsibility for the outrage. "I declare that I set fire to the synagogue, or at least that I ordered those who did it, that there might not be a place where Christ was denied. If it be objected to me that I did not set the synagogue on fire here, I answer it began to be burnt by the judgment of God." He told the Emperor that people who burnt a synagogue ought not to be punished, such action being a just reprisal because Jews, in the reign of the Emperor Julian, had burnt down Christian churches. In any case, he added, since the synagogues contained nothing of any value, "what could the Jews lose by the fire?" When they complained to the Emperor, he was indignant at their impertinence. They had no place in a court of law, he declared, because nothing they said could ever be believed. "Into what calumnies will they not break out, who, by false witness, calumniated even Christ!"

The Emperor, however, who did not approve of fire-raising propaganda, 49 endeavored to protect the synagogues from the fury of the mob. He received a letter, from an unexpected quarter, asking him to revoke the orders he had given for punishing the offenders, a letter dispatched from the top of a pillar by St. Simeon Stylites. This ascetic, who achieved distinction by living for thirty-six years on top of a pillar fifty feet high, had given up, as G. F. Abbott remarked, "all worldly luxuries except Jew-hatred." He is not the only saint who was unable to renounce the consolations of anti-Semitism.

In the fourth century the natural goodness of men, and even saintliness, 50 did not always operate for the benefit of Jews. St. Gregory of Nyssa, with the eloquence for which he was famous, composed against them a comprehensive indictment:

> Slayers of the Lord, murderers of the prophets, adversaries of God, haters of God, men who show contempt for the law, foes of grace, enemies of their father's faith, advocates of the devil, brood of vipers, slanderers, scoffers, men whose minds are in darkness, leaven of the Pharisees, assembly of demons, sinners, wicked men, stoners, and haters of righteousness.

Such exaggeration may have been an offense against charity, but it is 51 not so harmful to the soul as the modern hypocrisy which pretends that the early Christian Fathers were invariably models of proper Christian behavior. "Our duty," wrote Basnage in the seventeenth century, "is to excuse the Fathers in their Extravagance, instead of justifying them, lest such forcible Examples should authorize Modern Divines, and confirm the Hatred and Revenge of writers."

St. John Chrysostom, the Golden-Mouthed, one of the greatest of the 52 Church Fathers, spent his life, in and out of the pulpit, trying to reform the world. Christian writers, of varying shades of belief, have agreed in admiring his fervent love for all mankind, in spite of the fact that he was undoubtedly a socialist. "Chrysostom," said a Protestant divine, "was one of the most eloquent of the preachers who, ever since apostolic times, have brought to men the Divine tidings of truth and love." "A bright cheerful gentle soul," wrote Cardinal Newman, "a sensitive heart, a temperament open to emotion and impulse; and all this elevated, refined, transformed by the touch of heaven,—such was St. John Chrysostom."

Yet in this kindly gentle soul of the preacher who brought to men the 53 tidings of truth and love, was hidden a hard core of hatred. "It must be admitted," wrote an honest French hagiographer, "that, in his homilies against the Jews, he allowed himself to be unduly carried away by an occasional access of passion."

A great deal more than this must be admitted.

The violence of the language used by St. John Chrysostom in his 54 homilies against the Jews has never been exceeded by any preacher whose sermons have been recorded. Allowances must, no doubt, be made for the custom of the times, for passionate zeal, and for the fear that some tender shoots of Christian faith might be chilled by too much contact with Jews. But no amount of allowance can alter the fact that these homilies filled the minds of Christian congregations with a hatred which was transmitted to their children, and to their children's children, for many generations. These homilies, moreover, were used for centuries, in schools and in seminaries where priests were taught to preach, with St. John Chrysostom as their model—where priests were taught to hate, with St. John Chrysostom as their model.

There was no "touch of heaven" in the language used by St. John 55 Chrysostom when he was preaching about Jewish synagogues. "The synagogue," he said, "is worse than a brothel . . . it is the den of scoundrels and the repair of wild beasts . . . the temple of demons devoted to idolatrous cults . . . the refuge of brigands and debauchees, and the cavern of devils."

The synagogue, he told his congregations in another sermon, was 56 "a criminal assembly of Jews . . . a place of meeting for the assassins of Christ . . . a house worse than a drinking shop . . . a den of thieves; a house of ill fame, a dwelling of iniquity, the refuge of devils, a gulf and abyss of perdition." And he concluded, exhausted at length by his eloquence: "Whatever name even more horrible could be found, will never be worse than the synagogue deserves."

These sermons have not been forgotten; nor has contempt for Judaism 57 diminished among the Christian congregations since they were first preached more than fifteen hundred years ago.

. . .

In reply to some Christians who had maintained that Jewish synagogues 58 might be entitled to respect because in them were kept the writings of Moses and the prophets, St. John Chrysostom answered: Not at all! This was a reason for hating them more, because they use these books, but willfully misunderstand their meaning. "As for me, I hate the synagogue. . . . I hate the Jews for the same reason."

It is not difficult to imagine the effect such sermons must have had upon 59 congregations of excitable Orientals. Not only every synagogue, Chrysostom told them, but every Jew, was a temple of the devil. "I would say the same things about their souls." And he said a great deal more. It was unfit, he proclaimed, for Christians to associate with a people who had fallen into a condition lower than the vilest animals. "Debauchery and drunkenness had brought them to the level of the lusty goat and the pig. They know only one thing, to satisfy their stomachs, to get drunk, to kill and beat each other up like stage villains and coachmen."

. . .

When the usual allowances have been made for the manners of the time, 60 pious zeal, oriental imagery, and for any context, setting, or background which might be urged in mitigation, these are words difficult to justify. This condemnation of the people of Israel, in the name of God, was not forgotten. It helped to strengthen the tradition of hate handed on through the Dark Ages and welcomed by mediaeval Christendom, a tradition which has disfigured the whole history of Western Europe.

For many centuries the Jews listened to the echo of those three words 61
of St. John Chrysostom, the Golden-Mouthed: "God hates you."

Questions for Discussion

1. There are some passages in the chapter that might be misunderstood
   because Hay speaks with "tongue in cheek," using irony: for example,
   "The German method of burying people in communal pits was a great
   improvement on the old system" (¶13) or "most of them retained enough
   Christianity to continue hating the perfidious people, the Christ-killers"
   (¶23). What is Hay really saying with these words? What does he gain by
   seeming to say something else? How many other ironic passages can you
   find?

2. Occasionally Hay addresses his reader in direct form (for example, the
   opening phrase of ¶21). Who *is* this reader? Why do you think Hay breaks
   the conventions of most scholarly writing to become personal in this way?

3. People are sure to respond to this kind of writing in diverse ways, depending on their prior beliefs. Christians are challenged directly to reappraise
   their traditions. In a sense all other readers are bystanders or eavesdrop-
   pers, watching Christians debate about a great wrong that Hay accuses
   them of having committed. Jewish readers, in contrast, may find the piece
   too painful to read because of the gruesome details about the Holocaust.
   Those who are neither Jewish nor Christian may initially feel less concerned—until they examine their own prejudices and reconsider the history of other atrocities that have been committed by groups they are
   affiliated with. It is important in discussing matters of this kind to recognize that we are *all* implicated in human prejudice, past and present. A
   college classroom is a rare place where we can discuss such matters without
   fearing reprisal from authorities or rival gangs, and we should be willing
   to risk talking frankly with each other.

   With these difficulties and opportunities in mind, see now whether
   you and your classmates can discuss your deepest prejudices about groups
   without falling into a pointless or angry shouting match. Do you assume,
   with or without what you consider to be good evidence, that people of any
   one group are going to be on "the level of the lusty goat and the pig," that
   they will "know only one thing, to satisfy their stomachs, to get drunk,
   to kill and beat each other up like stage villains" (¶59)?

4. If in discussing question 3 you have found strong hostility between two
   or more groups represented in the class, organize a discussion by assigning
   contrary roles—for example, have a Christian defend the case for Jews, a
   Jew speak for American blacks or Indians, a person of French descent
   defend the English, and so on. Your task, if you take one of these roles,

is to show why the prejudice against "your" group is absurd or cruel or mistaken. Try to make your argument as free of name-calling as possible, depending instead on whatever evidence and reasons seem compelling.

5. Some classes have tried the experiment of "practicing" discrimination against a given group for a day or two—a prejudicial treatment invented for the occasion: "No one with blue eyes will be allowed to speak until Friday," "Everyone taller than 5 feet 10 inches must arrive 10 minutes early," and so on. If you are by now fairly easy with each other in class discussion, try inventing such a group (for example, people not from a given part of the country or state, people from a certain kind of school, or people who intend to be science or English majors). Then "give them the treatment." Make the kinds of jokes about them (or about you, if you're one of the victims) that people make about minority groups. Seat them at the back of the room or in specially created "ghettos," "reservations," or "barrios." Require them to address the rest of the class as "ma'am" and "sir." Do this as long as the victims can stand it and then discuss how it felt, to both the oppressors and the oppressed.

Suggested Essay Topics

1. If you have ever been the victim of injustice based on someone's seeing you as a member of a condemned group, write an account of how it happened and how it felt. (Decide in advance whether you are addressing readers who are already sympathetic to your cause or readers who may share the feelings of your persecutors.) You will have noticed that Hay achieves some of his most powerful effects by using vivid stories. Don't hesitate to be just as vivid in your use of the details of your story.

2. If you have ever committed what you now consider to be an injustice against someone as a result of seeing that person as a member of a given group rather than as an individual, write an account of the event describing how it felt both at the time and when you later decided that you had been unjust. Before you write, study topic 1.

✦ 8 ✦

WOMEN AND MEN

From Sexism to Feminism

EPIGRAPHS FROM
THE SEXIST TRADITION

There is a good principle which created order, light and man,
and an evil principle which created chaos, darkness and woman.
Pythagoras

Women, then, are only children of a larger growth:
they have an entertaining tattle, and sometimes wit;
but for solid reasoning good-sense, I never knew
in my life one that had it, or who reasoned or acted consequentially
for four and twenty hours together.
Lord Chesterfield

Man is the only male animal who beats his female.
He is therefore the most brutal of all males—unless woman is the most
unbearable of all females, which, after all, is quite plausible.
Georges Courteline

Beat thy wife every morning; if thou know not why, she doth.
Arab saying

Frailty, thy name is woman!
Shakespeare (spoken by Hamlet, about his mother)

The world is full of care, much like unto a bubble;
Women and care, and care and women, and women and care
and trouble.
Reverend Nathaniel Ward
(attributed to a lady at the Court of the Queen of Bohemia)

Ever hear of a woman loving a poor man?
Pagnol

EPIGRAPHS FROM
THE FEMINIST TRADITION

All that has been written by men about women must be suspect,
for they are both judge and interested party.
Poulain La Barre

So the image of woman [in advertising] appears plastered on every surface
imaginable, smiling interminably. An apple pie evokes
a glance of tender beatitude, a washing machine causes hilarity,
a cheap box of chocolates brings forth meltingly
joyous gratitude, a Coke is the cause of a rictus of
unutterable brilliance, even a new stick-on bandage
is saluted by a smirk of satisfaction.
Germaine Greer

Total masculinity is an ideal of the frustrated, not a fact of biology.
Harold Rosenberg

It is impossible for a sex or a class to have economic freedom
until everybody has it, and until economic freedom is attained
for everybody, there can be no real freedom for anybody.
Suzanne LaFollette

I long to hear that you have declared an independancy
[for the thirteen colonies]—and by the way in the new Code of
Laws which I suppose it will be necessary for you
to make I desire you would Remember the Ladies, and be more
generous and favorable to them than your ancestors. Do not put
such unlimited power into the hands of the Husbands.
Remember all Men would be tyrants if they could. If
perticuliar care and attention is not paid to the Ladies we are determined
to foment a Rebelion, and will not hold ourselves bound by
any Laws in which we have no voice, or Representation.
Letter from Abigail Adams to John Adams

Yes, ye lordly, ye haughty sex, our souls are by nature *equal* to
yours; the same breath of God animates, enlivens, and invigorates us.
Judith Sargent Murray

I believe that our future salvation lies in a movement
away from sexual polarization and the prison of gender
toward a world in which individual roles
and the modes of personal behavior can be freely chosen.
Carolyn Heilbrun

Marshall W. Gregory and Wayne C. Booth

THE TRADITIONAL ABASEMENT OF WOMEN

Until fairly recently, almost all discussions of men and women were by men, and almost all assumed the inferiority, if not the downright viciousness, of women. Occasionally a philosopher like Plato might speculate about what would happen if women were ever given education and rights genuinely equal to those of men (see pp. 625–633), and a few wrote about women as ideal, angelic creatures, far above their wicked menfolk. But whole libraries have been written "proving" that women's intrinsic inferiority justifies social servitude.

One of the most frequently quoted documents in this tradition was Aristotle's argument, in *On the Generation of Animals,* that a woman is a "misbegotten male." In the conception of a child, the "male principle" provides, he said, a form or shape, while the "female principle" provides the matter on which the shape is imposed by the semen. If the imposition of form is successful, a male child is born. If it is a partial failure, a female child—a botched male—results. The male thus provides the "active" role, the female the "passive." According to this view, a highly convenient one for males, nature invites and justifies whatever subordination a given culture chooses to impose on women.

Aristotle was quoted by almost all theorists for about 2000 years. Jewish, Christian, and Islamic theologians borrowed and extended his arguments to buttress their teachings about how a male God founded the universe and how females, from the beginning, were either responsible for or at least symbolic of its instabilities and limitations. His influence can be seen clearly in the brief passage we quote here from Thomas Aquinas (c. 1225–1274), which itself achieved wide influence as a standard Christian way of explaining the story of Adam and Eve. The passages by Nietzsche (1844–1900) and Freud (1856–1939) show that the downgrading of women has hardly been confined to religious theorists; many a secular author has heaped abuse on women, some of it (like that of Schopenhauer, the philosopher, and Strindberg, the playwright) even more aggressively woman-hating (or *misogynistic*) than the passages we quote.

In one respect we are clearly being unjust to such wide-ranging thinkers and prolific writers as Nietzsche and Freud by quoting only snippets from them. All writers can be made to look silly, thoughtless, or incoherent by editing that disembowels their positions. Knowing this, our readers need to understand that we are not trying to take cheap shots at the writers included here. The more creative sides of their thinking are passed over. Our point is not primarily about these specific thinkers at all. We quote from Aquinas, Nietzsche, and Freud not to pillory them but to illustrate some of the content of a centuries-long tradition that precedes them, includes them, and extends far beyond them. They did not create this tradition, but they are symptomatic of it. Thus, while it may be unfair to the wider range and substance of their thought to reprint them so briefly, they help us to make a valid point about hostility to women in Western culture. When feminists argue in favor of fairness and equality for women, their opponent is not one writer or a few male chauvinists but rather a whole set of misogynistic attitudes that thinkers like those reprinted here have helped energize and perpetuate.

Feminist writers of recent times, both male and female, have had to write under the immense pressure of this tradition of contempt, and they have often shown a sense of frustration in trying to deal with it. How does one find arguments to combat opinions that seem so wrongheaded yet deep-seated? How does one argue with dogmas uttered by authors who otherwise seem fair-minded and sane? It is no wonder that some writers find it impossible to remain cool and dispassionate in the face of past and present abuses.

The truth may be that there are no decisive arguments that could prove either natural inferiority or natural equality. Like arguments about religious belief, discussion of such matters depends on our deepest assumptions about life and on our experience. Such arguments are never settled once and for all; experience is too rich and diverse for that. But we need no resolution of debate to tell us how important is the quest in modern times for a new way of thinking and talking that will no longer debase or ignore one half of humanity.

Plato

Plato's Republic *is a long series of discussions between Socrates and some of his fellow Athenians concerning the ideally just society and the nature of justice itself. (See the introductions to other selections from* The Republic *in Chapter 4.) In the parts of* The Republic *where Socrates argues*

*for censorship of the arts and for what characterizes kinds of knowledge (Chapter 4),
the discussions are aimed at one central concern: how the education of society's future
"guardians" determines the goodness or badness of their future leadership. Here we
have selected a passage that focuses not on the content of education but on those who
are educated—not on what but on whom.*

*Socrates argues that in an ideally just society women should have equal oppor-
tunities for equal rule with men. He makes two proposals that hypothetically turn
Athenian social conventions upside down. He argues, first, that women should hold
all public offices equally with men and, second, that women should receive the same
education as men. It is an index of the rigor of Plato's mind that he is able to construct
a coherent argument even when his thinking violates every social convention of his
time. And it is an index of how deeply ingrained sexist conventions still are today
that women are left fighting an uphill battle for the fair and equal treatment that Plato
imagined for them 2300 years ago.*

*As is his way, Socrates begins his argument without pausing to take into
account the prejudices of his time. He never stops to wonder whether his listeners will
think him daft or dangerous; he simply plunges into hard thinking, attacking every
subject in its most direct form. Either women are equal to men with respect to all the
capacities that make a good ruler, or they are not. He quickly establishes that they
are equal in this sense and immediately pursues the implications of this position: no
quibbling, no hedging, no appeals to authority, and no loopholes for the male chauvinists whom he might offend.*

*When Socrates says in paragraph 1 that "the drama of the men has been
played out," he means that he has already discussed the role of men in the ideal
republic. Having gone on in his discussion to other things, Socrates has just been
asked by one of his companions to backtrack and take up the question of the role of
women in his hypothetical new state. He begins to do this with the comment, "I
must retrace my steps." The argument for female equality is complete from this point
to the end of the selection. The questions come from Socrates, the answers from his
companions.*

THE EDUCATION OF WOMEN

Our title for this portion of *The Republic,* book 5.

Well, I replied, I suppose that I must retrace my steps and say what I   1
perhaps ought to have said before in the proper place. The drama of the men
has been played out, and now properly enough comes the turn of the women,
especially in view of your challenge.

For men born and educated like our citizens there can, in my opinion,   2
be no right possession and use of women and children unless they follow the
path on which we sent them forth. We proposed, as you know, to treat them
as watchdogs of the herd.

True.

Let us abide by that comparison in our account of their birth and   3
breeding, and let us see whether the result accords with our design.

What do you mean?

What I mean may be put into the form of a question, I said: Are female   4
sheepdogs expected to keep watch together with the males, and to go hunting
with them and share in their other activities? or do we entrust to the males
the entire and exclusive care of the flocks, while we leave the females at home,
because we think that the bearing and suckling their puppies is labour enough
for them?

No, he said, they share alike; the only difference between them is that   5
the males are regarded as stronger and the females as weaker.

But can you use different animals for the same purpose, unless they are   6
bred and fed in the same way?

You cannot.   7

Then if women are to have the same duties as men, they must have the   8
same education?

Yes.   9

The education which was assigned to the men was music and gymnastic.   10

Yes.   11

Then women also must be taught music and gymnastic and military   12
exercises, and they must be treated like the men?

This is the inference, I suppose.   13

I fully expect, I said, that our proposals, if they are carried out, being   14
unusual, may in many respects appear ridiculous.

No doubt of it.   15

Yes, and the most ridiculous thing of all will be the sight of women   16
naked in the palaestra, exercising with the men, even when they are no longer
young; they certainly will not be a vision of beauty, any more than the
enthusiastic old men who in spite of wrinkles and ugliness continue to frequent the gymnasia.

Yes, indeed, he said: according to present notions the proposal would   17
be thought ridiculous.

But then, I said, as we have determined to speak our minds, we must   18
not fear the jests of the wits which will be directed against this sort of
innovation; how they will talk of women's attainments both in music and
gymnastic, and above all about their wearing armour and riding upon horse-
back.

Very true, he replied.   19

Yet having begun we must go forward to the rough places of the law;   20
at the same time begging of these gentlemen for once in their life to be serious.
Not long ago, as we shall remind them, the Hellenes were of the opinion,
which is still generally received among the barbarians, that the sight of a
naked man was ridiculous and improper; and when first the Cretans and then
the Lacedaemonians introduced the custom of stripping for exercise, the wits
of that day might equally have ridiculed the innovation.

No doubt.   21

But no doubt when experience showed that to let all things be uncov- 22
ered was far better than to cover them up, the ludicrous effect to the outward
eye vanished before what reason had proved to be best, and the man was
perceived to be a fool who directs the shafts of his ridicule at any other sight
but that of folly and vice, or seriously inclines to weigh the beautiful by any
other standard but that of the good.

Very true, he replied.   23

First, then, let us come to an understanding whether the course we 24
propose is possible or not: let us admit any arguments put forward by comedians or persons more seriously inclined, and tending to show whether in the
human race the female is able to take part in all the occupations of the male,
or in some of them only, or in none; and to which class the art of war belongs.
That will be the best way of commencing the inquiry, and will probably lead
to the soundest conclusion.

That will be much the best way.   25

Shall we take the other side first and begin by arguing against ourselves; 26
in this manner the adversary's position will not be undefended.

Why not? he said.   27

Then let us put a speech into the mouths of our opponents. They will 28
say: 'Socrates and Glaucon, no adversary is needed to convict you, for you
yourselves, at the first foundation of the State, admitted the principle that
everybody was to do the one work suited to his own nature.' And certainly,
if I am not mistaken, such an admission was made by us. 'And do not the
natures of men and women differ very much indeed?' And we shall reply: Of
course they do. Then we shall be asked, 'Whether the tasks assigned to men
and to women should not be different, and such as are agreeable to their
different natures?' Certainly they should. 'But if so, have you not fallen into
a serious inconsistency in saying that men and women, whose natures are so
entirely different, ought to perform the same actions?'—What defence will
you make for us, my good sir, against these objections?

That is not an easy question to answer when asked suddenly; and I shall 29
and I do beg of you to draw out the case on our side.

These are the objections, Glaucon, and there are many others of a like 30
kind, which I foresaw long ago; they made me afraid and reluctant to take
in hand any law about the possession and nurture of women and children.

By Zeus, he said, the problem to be solved is anything but easy.   31

Why yes, I said, but the fact is that when a man is out of his depth, 32
whether he has fallen into a little swimming-bath or into mid ocean, he has
to swim all the same.

Very true.   33

And must not we swim and try to reach the shore, while hoping that 34
Arion's dolphin or some other miraculous help may save us?

I suppose so, he said.   35

Well then, let us see if any way of escape can be found. We acknowl- 36
edged—did we not?—that different natures ought to have different pursuits,
and that men's and women's natures are different. And now what are we

saying? that different natures ought to have the same pursuits,—this is the inconsistency which is charged upon us.

Precisely. 37

Verily, Glaucon, I said, glorious is the power of the art of disputation! 38

Why do you say so? 39

Because I think that many a man falls into the practice against his will. 40 When he thinks that he is reasoning he is really disputing, just because he does not know how to inquire into a subject by distinguishing its various aspects, but pursues some verbal opposition in the statement which has been made. That is the difference between the spirit of contention and that of fair discussion.

Yes, he replied, that is a fairly common failing, but does it apply at 41 present to us?

Yes, indeed; for there is a danger of our getting unintentionally into 42 verbal contradiction.

In what way? 43

Why, we valiantly and pugnaciously insist upon the verbal truth that 44 different natures ought to have different pursuits, but we never considered at all what was the meaning of sameness or difference of nature, or with what intention we distinguished them when we assigned different pursuits to different natures and the same to the same natures.

Why, no, he said, that was never considered by us. 45

I said: Yet it seems that we should be entitled to ask ourselves whether 46 there is not an opposition in nature between bald men and hairy men; and if this is admitted by us, then, if bald men are cobblers, we should forbid the hairy men to be cobblers, and conversely?

That would be a jest, he said. 47

Yes, I said, a jest; and why? because we were not previously speaking 48 of sameness or difference in *any* sense; we were concerned with one *form* of difference or similarity, namely that which would affect the pursuit in which a man is engaged; we should have argued, for example, that a physician and one who is in mind a physician may be said to have the same nature.

True. 49

Whereas the physician and the carpenter have different natures? 50

Certainly. 51

And if, I said, the male and female sex appear to differ in their fitness 52 for any art or pursuit, we should say that such pursuit or art ought to be assigned to one or the other of them; but if the difference consists only in women bearing and men begetting children, this does not amount to a proof that a woman differs from a man in respect of the sort of education she should receive; and we shall therefore continue to maintain that our guardians and their wives ought to have the same pursuits.

Quite rightly, he said. 53

Only then shall we ask our opponent to inform us with reference to 54 which of the pursuits or arts of civic life the nature of a woman differs from that of a man?

That will be quite fair.   55

And perhaps he, like yourself a moment ago, will reply that to give a   56
sufficient answer on the instant is not easy; but that given time for reflection
there is no difficulty.

Yes, perhaps.   57

Suppose then that we invite such an objector to accompany us in the   58
argument, in the hope of showing him that there is no occupation peculiar
to women which need be considered in the administration of the State.

By all means.   59

Let us say to him: Come now, and we will ask you a question:—when   60
you spoke of a nature gifted or not gifted in any respect, did you mean to
say that one man will acquire a thing easily, another with difficulty? the first,
after brief instruction, is able to discover a great deal more for himself,
whereas the other, after much teaching and application, cannot even preserve
what he has learnt; or again, did you mean that the one has a body which
is a good servant to his mind, while the body of the other is a hindrance to
him? Would not these be the sort of differences which distinguish the man
gifted by nature from the one who is ungifted?

No one will deny that.   61

And can you mention any pursuit of mankind in which the male sex   62
has not all these gifts and qualities in a higher degree than the female? Need
I waste time in speaking of the art of weaving, and the preparation of pan-
cakes and preserves in which womankind is generally thought to have some
skill, and in which for her to be beaten by a man is of all things the most
absurd?

You are quite right, he replied, in maintaining that one sex greatly excels   63
the other in almost every field. Although many women are in many things
superior to many men, yet on the whole what you say is true.

And if so, my friend, I said, there is no special faculty of administration   64
in a state which a woman has because she is a woman, or which a man has
by virtue of his sex, but the gifts of nature are alike diffused in both; all the
pursuits of men can naturally be assigned to women also, but in all of them
a woman is weaker than a man.

Very true.   65

Then are we to impose all our enactments on men and none of them on   66
women?

That will never do.   67

Because we shall say that a woman too may, or may not, have the gift   68
of healing; and that one is a musician, and another has no music in her nature?

Very true.   69

And it can hardly be denied that one woman has a turn for gymnastic   70
and military exercises, and another is unwarlike and hates gymnastics?

I think not.   71

And one woman is a philosopher, and another is an enemy of philoso-   72
phy; one has spirit, and another is without spirit?

That is also true. 73

Then one woman will have the temper of a guardian, and another not. 74
For these, as you remember, were the natural gifts for which we looked in
the selection of the male guardians.

Yes. 75

Men and women alike possess the qualities which make a guardian; 76
they differ only in their comparative strength or weakness.

Obviously. 77

Therefore those women who have such qualities are to be selected as 78
the companions and colleagues of men who also have them and whom they
resemble in capacity and in character?

Very true. 79

But ought not the same natures to be trained in the same pursuits? 80

They ought. 81

Then we have come round to the previous point that there is nothing 82
unnatural in assigning music and gymnastic to the guardian women.

Certainly not. 83

The law which we then enacted was agreeable to nature, and therefore 84
not an impossibility or mere aspiration; it is rather the contrary practice,
which prevails at present, that is a violation of nature.

That appears to be true. 85

We had to consider, first, whether our proposals were possible, and 86
secondly whether they were the most beneficial?

Yes. 87

And the possibility has been acknowledged? 88

Yes. 89

The very great benefit has next to be established? 90

Quite so. 91

You will admit that the same education which makes a man a good 92
guardian will make a woman a good guardian; especially if the original nature
of both is the same?

Yes. 93

I should like to ask you a question. 94

What is it? 95

Is it your opinion that one man is better than another? Or do you think 96
them all equal?

Not at all. 97

And in the commonwealth which we were founding do you conceive 98
the guardians who have been brought up on our model system to be more
perfect men, or the cobblers whose education has been cobbling?

What a ridiculous question! 99

You have answered me, I replied: in fact, our guardians are the best of 100
all our citizens?

By far the best. 101

And will not the guardian women be the best women? 102

Yes, by far the best.   103

And can there be anything better for the interests of the State than that   104
the men and women of a State should be as good as possible?

There can be nothing better.   105

And this is what the arts of music and gymnastic, when present in such   106
manner as we have described, will accomplish?

Certainly.   107

Then we have made an enactment not only possible but in the highest   108
degree beneficial to the State?

True.   109

Then let the guardian women strip, for their virtue will be their robe,   110
and let them share in the toils of war and the defence of their country; only
in the distribution of labours the lighter are to be assigned to the women, who
are the weaker natures, but in other respects their duties are to be the same.
And as for the man who laughs at naked women exercising their bodies from
the best of motives, in his laughter he is plucking

A fruit of unripe wisdom,

and he himself is ignorant of what he is laughing at, or what he is about;—for
that is, and ever will be, the best of sayings, *That the useful is noble and the hurtful
is base.*

Questions for Discussion

1. Do you accept Socrates' analogy between human beings and dogs (¶2–5)?
   He makes it clear that sexual differences between dogs are merely incidental to the activities they perform as dogs and that sexual differences between human beings are similarly incidental. They have no significant
   bearing on what men and women are capable of doing *as human beings* and
   thus cannot be used as argument for limiting the roles that members of
   either sex are invited to play in society. Regardless of what you decide
   about the analogy, what do you think of his general argument? Can you
   imagine how it would strike you if you were of the opposite sex?

2. Would you vote for a woman for president? How many students in your
   class would do so? How many would vote for a woman senator or member
   of Congress, but *not* for a woman president? How many would vote for
   a woman president of your student government? As you take these straw
   votes, be sure to look as closely as possible at the arguments that can be
   offered for various positions. Be sure to think back on what Socrates would
   be likely to say about your arguments. You might also want to look at the
   facts in your situation: How many of the top positions in various student

activities are held by women? If there is a discrepancy between your expressed views and the facts of campus life, how do you explain it?

3. One could argue that Socrates' position is clearly not feminist in the modern sense of supporting a political and social movement. He gives no indication that he is motivated by the desire to correct actual injustices to women. He is instead drawing a rational picture of what the ideal society would look like. He is thus not speaking for a "special-interest group" with an ax to grind but for society as a whole. By concentrating on what is rational as against what is irrational, Socrates keeps the issue of sexual justice from getting bogged down in debates about private and petty interests or decisions about what to do *now*. A critic of Plato might argue:

> If we want to get something *done* in the world of practical politics, Socrates' tone of dispassionate inquiry is not much help. To be effective in the world, we must be passionate, committed, and rhetorically flamboyant. While thinkers like Socrates pursue dispassionate inquiry, with their "on the one hand" and "on the other hand," the issues are actually settled by people of action, not of thought. After all, no matter how cogent Plato's presentation of Socrates' case may be, Plato seems to have produced no discernible improvement for women in Greece.

After discussing this criticism, what do you conclude about the value of Socrates' tone? Would you recommend it to present-day feminists, male and female?

Suggested Essay Topics

1. After thinking about discussion question 3, write an essay directed to a committed feminist in which you attempt to argue that feminist issues should be couched in terms of human liberation, not just women's liberation. Take the Socratic position that the ultimate goal should be the perfection of society as a whole and that women, although having no less stake in this goal than men, certainly have no more stake in it than anyone else, including men. Try to make your reader see that if successful, programs to benefit special-interest groups only turn present inequalities upside down rather than erasing them and that if such programs are unsuccessful, they simply discredit those who have supported them.

2. This is a reversal of topic 1: Address an essay to Socrates (or to anyone who chooses to write on topic 1) arguing that human liberation and the perfection of society are too large and too vague to serve as political objectives. Argue that it is all very well to have these as ultimate aims, but that political and social changes are created only by special pressure groups who know how to coerce or intimidate established seats of power.

St. Thomas Aquinas

THE PRODUCTION OF WOMAN

Whether Woman Should Have Been Made in the First Production of Things

"Question 92" from the *Summa Theologica* (1265–1272). There are four "articles" in the Question, of which we reprint part of the first.

We proceed thus to the First Article:—

Objection 1. It would seem that woman should not have been made in the first production of things. For the Philosopher [Aristotle] says that the *female is a misbegotten male.* But nothing misbegotten or defective should have been in the first production of things. Therefore woman should not have been made at that first production.

Obj. 2. Further, subjection and limitation were a result of sin, for to the woman was it said after sin (Genesis iii. 16): *Thou shalt be under the man's power;* and Gregory says that, *Where there is no sin, there is no inequality.* But woman is naturally of less strength and dignity than man, *for the agent is always more honorable than the patient,* as Augustine says. Therefore woman should not have been made in the first production of things before sin.

Obj. 3. Further, occasions of sin should be cut off. But God foresaw that woman would be an occasion of sin to man. Therefore He should not have made woman.

On the contrary, It is written (Genesis ii. 18): *It is not good for man to be alone; let us make him a helper like to himself.*

I answer that, It was necessary for woman to be made, as the Scripture says, as *a helper* to man; not, indeed, as a helpmate in other works, as some say, since man can be more efficiently helped by another man in other works; but as a helper in the work of generation. This can be made clear if we observe the mode of generation carried out in various living things. Some living things do not possess in themselves the power of generation, but are generated by an agent of another species; and such are those plants and animals which are generated, without seed, from suitable matter through the active power of the heavenly bodies. Others possess the active and passive generative power together, as we see in plants which are generated from seed. For the noblest vital function in plants is generation, and so we observe that in these the active power of generation invariably accompanies the passive power. Among perfect animals, the active power of generation belongs to the male sex, and the passive power to the female. And as among animals there is a vital operation nobler than generation, to which their life is principally directed, so it happens that the male sex is not found in continual union with the female in perfect animals, but only at the time of coition; so that we may consider that by coition the male and female are one, as in plants they are always united, even though in some cases one of them preponderates, and in some the other. But man is further ordered to a still nobler work of life, and that is intellectual operation. Therefore there was greater reason for the distinction of these two powers in man; so that the female should be produced separately from the male, and yet that they should be carnally united for generation. Therefore directly after the formation of woman, it was said: *And they shall be two in one flesh* (Genesis ii. 24).

Reply Obj. 1. As regards the individual nature, woman is defective and misbegotten, for the active power in the male seed tends to the production of a perfect likeness according to the masculine sex; while the production of woman comes from defect in the active power, or from some material indisposition, or even from some external influence, such as that of a south wind, which is moist, as the Philosopher observes. On the other hand, as regards universal human nature, woman is not misbegotten, but is included in nature's intention as directed to the work of generation. Now the universal intention of nature depends on God, Who is the universal Author of nature. Therefore, in producing nature, God formed not only the male but also the female.

Reply Obj. 2. Subjection is twofold. One is servile, by virtue of which a superior makes use of a subject for his own benefit; and this kind of subjection began after sin. There is another kind of subjection, which is called economic or civil, whereby the superior makes use of his subjects for their own benefit and good; and this kind of subjection existed even before sin. For the good of order would have been wanting in the human family if some were not governed by others wiser than themselves. So by such a kind of subjection woman is naturally subject to man, because in man the discernment of reason predominates.

Friedrich Nietzsche

THE UGLINESS OF WOMAN

Our title for part 7, "Our Virtues," aphorism 232, of *Beyond Good and Evil* (1886).

Woman wants to become self-reliant—and for that reason she is beginning to enlighten men about "woman as such": *this* is one of the worst developments of the general *uglification* of Europe. For what must these clumsy attempts of women at scientific self-exposure bring to light! Woman has much reason for shame; so much pedantry, superficiality, schoolmarmishness, petty presumption, petty licentiousness and immodesty lies concealed in woman—one only needs to study her behavior with children!—and so far all this was at bottom best repressed and kept under control by *fear* of man. Woe when "the eternally boring in woman"*—she is rich in that!—is permit-

*Allusion to "the Eternal-Feminine" in the penultimate line of Goethe's *Faust.*

ted to venture forth! When she begins to unlearn thoroughly and on principle her prudence and art—of grace, of play, of chasing away worries, of lightening burdens and taking things lightly—and her subtle aptitude for agreeable desires!

Even now female voices are heard which—holy Aristophanes!—are 2 frightening: they threaten with medical explicitness what woman *wants* from man, first and last. Is it not in the worst taste when woman sets about becoming scientific that way? So far enlightenment of this sort was fortunately man's affair, man's lot—we remained "among ourselves" in this; and whatever women write about "woman," we may in the end reserve a healthy suspicion whether woman really *wants* enlightenment about herself—whether she *can* will it—

Unless a woman seeks a new adornment for herself that way—I do 3 think adorning herself is part of the Eternal-Feminine?—she surely wants to inspire fear of herself—perhaps she seeks mastery. But she does not *want* truth: what is truth to woman? From the beginning, nothing has been more alien, repugnant, and hostile to woman than truth—her great art is the lie, her highest concern is mere appearance and beauty. Let us men confess it: we honor and love precisely *this* art and *this* instinct in woman—we who have a hard time and for our relief like to associate with beings under whose hands, eyes, and tender follies our seriousness, our gravity and profundity almost appear to us like folly.

Finally I pose the question: has ever a woman conceded profundity to 4 a woman's head, or justice to a woman's heart? And is it not true that on the whole "woman" has so far been despised most by woman herself—and by no means by us?

We men wish that woman should not go on compromising herself 5 through enlightenment—just as it was man's thoughtfulness and consideration for woman that found expression in the church decree: *mulier taceat in ecclesia* [woman should be silent in church]! It was for woman's good when Napoleon gave the all too eloquent Madame de Staël to understand: *mulier taceat in politicis* [woman should be silent in politics]! And I think it is a real friend of women that counsels them today: *mulier taceat de muliere* [woman should be silent about woman]!

Sigmund Freud

FEMININITY

From lecture 33 of *New Introductory Lectures on Psycho-analysis* (1933).

As you hear, then, we ascribe a castration complex to women as well. 1
And for good reasons, though its content cannot be the same as with boys.
In the latter the castration complex arises after they have learnt from the sight
of the female genitals that the organ which they value so highly need not
necessarily accompany the body. At this the boy recalls to mind the threats
he brought on himself by his doings with that organ, he begins to give
credence to them and falls under the influence of fear of castration, which will
be the most powerful motive force in his subsequent development. The
castration complex of girls is also started by the sight of the genitals of the
other sex. They at once notice the difference and, it must be admitted, its
significance too. They feel seriously wronged, often declare that they want
to "have something like it too," and fall a victim to "envy for the penis,"
which will leave ineradicable traces on their development and the formation
of their character and which will not be surmounted in even the most favourable cases without a severe expenditure of psychical energy. The girl's recognition of the fact of her being without a penis does not by any means imply
that she submits to the fact easily. On the contrary, she continues to hold on
for a long time to the wish to get something like it herself and she believes
in that possibility for improbably long years; and analysis can show that, at
a period when knowledge of reality has long since rejected the fulfilment of
the wish as unattainable, it persists in the unconscious and retains a considerable cathexis of energy. The wish to get the longed-for penis eventually in
spite of everything may contribute to the motives that drive a mature woman
to analysis, and what she may reasonably expect from analysis—a capacity,
for instance, to carry on an intellectual profession—may often be recognized
as a sublimated modification of this repressed wish.

One cannot very well doubt the importance of envy for the penis. You 2
may take it as an instance of male injustice if I assert that envy and jealousy
play an even greater part in the mental life of women than of men. It is not
that I think these characteristics are absent in men or that I think they have
no other roots in women than envy for the penis; but I am inclined to attribute
their greater amount in women to this latter influence.

. . .

The discovery that she is castrated is a turning-point in a girl's growth. 3
Three possible lines of development start from it: one leads to sexual inhibition or to neurosis, the second to change of character in the sense of a
masculinity complex, the third, finally, to normal femininity. We have learnt
a fair amount, though not everything, about all three.

The essential content of the first is as follows: the little girl has hith- 4
erto lived in a masculine way, has been able to get pleasure by the excita-

tion of her clitoris and has brought this activity into relation with her sexual wishes directed towards her mother, which are often active ones; now, owing to the influence of her penis-envy, she loses her enjoyment in her phallic sexuality. Her self-love is mortified by the comparison with the boy's far superior equipment and in consequence she renounces her masturbatory satisfaction from her clitoris, repudiates her love for her mother and at the same time not infrequently represses a good part of her sexual trends in general. No doubt her turning away from her mother does not occur all at once, for to begin with the girl regards her castration as an individual misfortune, and only gradually extends it to other females and finally to her mother as well. Her love was directed to her *phallic* mother; with the discovery that her mother is castrated it becomes possible to drop her as an object, so that the motives for hostility, which have long been accumulating, gain the upper hand. This means, therefore, that as a result of the discovery of women's lack of a penis they are debased in value for girls just as they are for boys and later perhaps for men.

Questions for Discussion

1. Restate Aristotle's position about the biological inferiority of women in your own words. Do you know people who take the view that men are "naturally" superior in some ways to women? What traits or abilities do these people ascribe to men and women? Do any of the assumptions about innate masculine and feminine traits match your own experience and observation? If so, which ones? If not, how do you react when you find yourself placed within categories that don't fit?

2. Is Nietzsche's denigration of women foreign to you, or is it the same denigration you hear nowadays, only less antagonistically and abrasively stated? In paragraph 4, for example, Nietzsche claims that " 'woman' has so far been despised most by woman herself." While this is strong language, is its content any different from that of the commonly bandied cliché that women are catty about other women? Can Nietzsche's other insults be restated in contemporary terms? If so, what does this say about contemporary views of women?

3. Ask the teacher to appoint three or four members of the class to ask various members of the psychology department whether they think Freud's notion of "penis envy" is taken seriously today by psychoanalysts and what they themselves think of the notion. Report back to the class.

4. Have two or three members of the class examine the wording of the Catholic marriage ceremony (or different versions of it) to see whether any traces of Aquinas's views about the relationship between men and women are reflected in it. Compare the Catholic ceremony to a few Protestant

versions. Are there any interesing differences with respect to the roles of men and women?

Suggested Essay Topics

1. Read chapters 3 and 4 ("Biological Facts and Social Consequences" and "Who Said 'The Inferior Sex'?") of *The Natural Superiority of Women* by Ashley Montagu (Macmillan, 1952). Using Montagu as a starting point, but not limiting yourself to him if you have other scholars or scientists to cite (Montagu offers an annotated bibliography at the end of his book), construct your own rebuttal to Aristotle's views of the natural inferiority of women.

2. In a small notebook that you should carry around with you until this assignment is completed, record for a two-week period all the instances in which you hear people expressing belief in "natural" differences between men and women. Whether the remarks you overhear are insulting or not, comment on the extent to which you think they are inaccurate, misleading, or limiting for either sex, and address your essay to people whose (perhaps unseen) prejudices you would like to make visible.

Margaret Mead

Margaret Mead (1901–1978) first became famous in the 1930s as an anthropologist. Her book Growing Up in New Guinea *remains a classic in its field, despite recent controversy about her method. Over the years she acquired an international reputation not only as an anthropologist but also as a commentator on human affairs in general, especially on issues like environmental pollution, women's rights, and the threat of nuclear war. A good example of her work of this kind is* A Rap on Race, *which she wrote with James Baldwin in the 1960s.*

In the following selection from her autobiography, Blackberry Winter, *Mead discusses how her mother's and grandmother's examples taught her early in life that "the mind is not sex-typed." According to Mead's account, her grandmother's stories were of crucial importance in forming her character and shaping her general view of the world. As you read, compare her account of the importance of stories with what Plato (in Chapter 4) has to say about the roles that stories and imitation play in the formation of character.*

THE MIND IS NOT SEX-TYPED

From chapter 5, "On Being a Granddaughter," of *Blackberry Winter: My Earlier Years* (1972). The title is ours.

Grandma had no sense at all of ever having been handicapped by being   1
a woman. I think she played as strong a role among her brothers and sisters as her elder brother, who was a famous Methodist preacher. Between them they kept up an active relationship with their parents in Winchester and, returning often for visits, they supervised, stimulated, and advised the less adventurous members of the family. This has now become my role among some of the descendants of my grandmother's sisters, who still live in various small towns and large cities in Ohio.

Grandma was a wonderful storyteller, and she had a set of priceless,   2
individually tailored anecdotes with which American grandparents of her day brought up children. There was the story of the little boys who had been taught absolute, quick obedience. One day when they were out on the prairie, their father shouted, "Fall down on your faces!" They did, and the terrible prairie fire swept over them *and they weren't hurt.* There was also the story of three boys at school, each of whom received a cake sent from home. One hoarded his, and the mice ate it; one ate all of his, and he got sick; and who do you think had the best time?—why, of course, the one who shared his cake with his friends. Then there was the little boy who ran away from home and stayed away all day. When he came home after supper, he found the family sitting around the fire and nobody said a word. Not a word. Finally, he couldn't stand it anymore and said, "Well, I see you have the same old cat!" And there was one about a man who was so lazy he would rather starve than work. Finally, his neighbors decided to bury him alive. On the way to the cemetery they met a man with a wagon-load of unshelled corn. He asked where they were going. When they told him that they were going to bury that no-good man alive, the owner of the corn took pity on him and said, "I tell you what. I will give you this load of corn. All you will have to do is shell it." But the lazy man said, "Drive on, boys!"

Because Grandma did so many things with her hands, a little girl could   3
always tag after her, talking and asking questions and listening. Side by side with Grandma, I learned to peel apples, to take the skin off tomatoes by plunging them into scalding water, to do simple embroidery stitches, and to knit. Later, during World War I, when I had to cook for the whole household, she taught me a lot about cooking, for example, just when to add a lump of butter, something that always had to be concealed from Mother, who thought that cooking with butter was extravagant.

While I followed her about as she carried out the endless little house-   4
hold tasks that she took on, supplementing the work of the maids or doing more in between maids—and we were often in between—she told me endless tales about Winchester. She told me about her school days and about the poor children who used to beg the cores of apples from the rich children who had

whole apples for lunch. She told me about Em Eiler, who pushed Aunt Lou off a rail fence into a flooded pasture lot; about Great-aunt Louisian, who could read people's minds and tell them everything they had said about her and who had been a triplet and so small when she was born that she would fit into a quart cup; about Grace, who died from riding a trotting horse too hard, which wasn't good for girls; and about the time Lida cut off Anna Louise's curls and said, "Now they won't say 'pretty little girl' anymore." My great-grandfather used to say such a long grace, she told me, that one of her most vivid memories was of standing, holding a log she had started to put on the fire, for what seemed to be hours for fear of interrupting him. All this was as real to me as if I had lived it myself. I think that if anyone had tried to repeat the Bridie Murphy case,* I could easily have impersonated, in trance, the child and girl my grandmother had been.

One of the stories I loved most was about the time the Confederate 5 soldiers came through the village and shot down the flag. In the face of the danger, my grandmother's younger sister ran out and held the flag aloft. It was only another Barbara Frietchie episode and the story gained a great deal from the fact that we had learned to recite, " 'Shoot, if you must, this old gray head,/But spare your country's flag,' she said." But this particular Barbara Frietchie had been young and was my great-aunt. Later, I tried to immortalize her in a story called "A Strip of Old Glory," which was published in the Doylestown High School magazine, of which I was the editor.

I never saw Winchester until recently, when the town was holding its 6 sesquicentennial celebration. I took my daughter with me, and as we walked through the streets, I looked at houses that were completely familiar. I saw the house in which my great-grandparents had lived and in which my father's cousin Cally had heard the sound of a ghostly coffin bumping on the stairs until her mother made her get down on her knees and promise never again to indulge in that strange, outlandish Aunt-Louisian kind of behavior. I saw the house in which the Bradfords had lived and where they had been such warm hosts to the next generation. And I recognized the sites of the fires. For part of the history of Winchester, a little town that never grew, is written in fire.

I was treated as an honored guest in a handsome house with peacocks 7 on the lawn that had been bought by a successful man who had returned from a large city to buy the house where he had once been the stableboy. The husband of one of my cousins also was being honored for his success, and people told me how pleased they were; as a boy he had been so poor, they explained, that he had had to ride a horse bareback to school. One of the peculiarities of the little town, which was never reflected in my grandmother's stories because she saw life ethically and not in class terms, was its incredible snobbishness. This came home to me as I watched how people with

*A celebrated case in which an American woman was alleged to have provided accounts, under hypnosis, of having lived various lives in previous states of existence, one of them as an Irish girl named Bridie Murphy.

strange ticks and deformities seldom seen in a city entered the house humbly in order to shake the hands of the guests of a leading citizen who now owned the garage, as once her father had owned the livery stable.

My grandmother was indifferent to social class, but in her stories she told me about poor people, unfortunate people, people who were better off, and no-count people who drank or gambled or deserted their wives and children. Her own family, for all their pride and their handsome noses, had a fair number of charming, no-count men in each generation and, appropriately, a fair number of women who married the same kind of men. There were a number of stern, impressive women and an occasional impressive man, but a lot of weak ones, too—that is the family picture. My cousins suspect that our great-grandfather was not a very strong character, but that he was kept in hand by our great-grandmother.

This indifference to social class irritated my mother, who used to complain that Grandma could get interested in the most ordinary people. Sometimes she went on a holiday to the seaside. When she came home she told us endless narratives about the lives of the ordinary people with whom she sat on the steps of the seaside hotel. This used to make Mother mutter. Grandma and Mother looked a good deal alike. They were of the same height and weight, and had similar enough features so that people often mistook them for mother and daughter. This, too, did not please Mother.

Mother never ceased to resent the fact that Grandma lived with us, but she gave her her due. Grandma never "interfered"—never tried to teach the children anything religious that had not previously been introduced by my mother, and in disagreements between my mother and father she always took my mother's side. When my father threatened to leave my mother, Grandma told him firmly that she would stay with her and the children.

. . .

I think it was my grandmother who gave me my ease in being a woman. She was unquestionably feminine—small and dainty and pretty and wholly without masculine protest or feminist aggrievement. She had gone to college when this was a very unusual thing for a girl to do, she had a firm grasp of anything she paid attention to, she had married and had a child, and she had a career of her own. All this was true of my mother, as well. But my mother was filled with passionate resentment about the condition of women, as perhaps my grandmother might have been had my grandfather lived and had she borne five children and had little opportunity to use her special gifts and training. As it was, the two women I knew best were mothers and had professional training. So I had no reason to doubt that brains were suitable for a woman. And as I had my father's kind of mind—which was also his mother's—I learned that the mind is not sex-typed.

♦

Questions for Discussion

1. How did Mead's mother and grandmother differ in their attitudes about a woman's place in society (¶11)? Is it clear which woman Mead admires more? Is it clear which woman she prefers to use as a role model?

2. Can you tell whether Mead sympathizes more with her mother's or her grandmother's attitudes about social class (¶8–9)? Where do your own sympathies lie on this issue?

3. Does Mead sound defensive about being a woman? Does she sound masculine? Feminine? Or is this distinction simply irrelevant when talking about the workings of the intellect? From what you have read, would you predict that Mead ever gave much time to helping the feminist movement? Or would you expect her simply to have gone around it? (You can find out for sure by reading Part 3 of *Blackberry Winter*.)

Suggested Essay Topics

1. In an essay directed to the other students in your class, compare the importance of stories in Margaret Mead's childhood with the importance of such stories in your own childhood. Give an account of the kinds of stories that taught you, as the stories in Mead's background taught her, how to view issues and events in the world: the role of women, poor people, your own family history, and so on.

2. Using Mead's description of her grandmother as a model, create a corresponding portrait of someone in your own family who played a crucial role in the formation of your character. Try to be as specific as Mead is about *how* your family member exerted influence. (You might choose to address your account to the model directly or to the other members of your family.)

Lorraine Hansberry

Although she only lived to age 34, Lorraine Hansberry (1930–1965) wrote at least one classic play. A Raisin in the Sun, *four other plays that she did not live to see produced, and many occasional pieces, some of which are only now being collected and published. When she was 29,* Raisin *won the Best Play of the Year award from the New York Drama Critics. Hansberry was the first black playwright to receive this honor.*

Hansberry's argument, while undeniably about the relationship between the sexes, focuses more on personal goals than on sex-specific roles. Hansberry is concerned with the difficulty facing anyone who wants to become a whole person in a society that imposes stereotypes on both men and women. Thus Hansberry's topic focuses less on how men and women treat each other than on how society tells them they should *treat each other and on the resulting strains, indignities, and impoverishments that afflict both sexes when they try to meet society's demands.*

Hansberry suggests that neither men nor women can be free to discover, or create, the best version of themselves when they are reared in traditions that impose on men the necessity of always pretending to be superior and strong and impose on women the necessity of always propping up men and massaging their egos as if they were children too weak to face the truth about their own defects. Such impositions, Hansberry asserts, not only insult both men and women but also retard all progress in society.

In response to worriers who fear that women's liberation will produce unsexed or masculine women, Hansberry asserts that what will emerge instead is more interesting women and more completely developed men. She further assumes that most men and women will welcome such changes and that those who do fear change and thus attempt to block it are not preserving a golden past but preventing the emergence of a more lustrous future.

The somewhat breezy colloquial style of this piece is a function of its having been written (and published) originally not as a scholarly essay but as a feature article intended for a popular magazine. As a professional writer, Hansberry was master of a variety of styles for a variety of occasions.

IN DEFENSE OF THE EQUALITY OF *MEN*

This essay, probably written in 1961, was intended for publication in a popular magazine to be called *The Fair Sex.* The magazine never appeared.

1   There is currently mushrooming in the land, a voluminous body of opinion in which scores of magazine writers, television panelists, and conference speakers with weighted eyebrows and ominous sentences allude to a peril in the Republic such as might herald a second coming of the British. Book, speech, and dissertation titles make the matter explicit: "Modern Woman—The Lost Sex";* "Trousered Mothers and Dishwashing Dads"; "American Man in a Woman's World"; etc.

2   Women, it is said, have ceased being, of all things, *women.* The conclusion has now been drawn in many circles that womanhood's historical insistance on ever-increasing measures of equality has resulted in women becoming "the imitations of men"—and, it is sometimes added, with something of a Calvinist shout: "Very bad imitations!"

3   The total theme of the alarm is that the "roles of the sexes are disappearing," and according to one analyst: "We are drifting toward a social structure made up of he-women and she-men." Which, all will admit, if it is true, is pretty scary business!

4   To aid in the terror, some contemporary schools of psychoanalytical

*Title of an influential book (1947) by Marynia Farnham and Ferdinand Lundberg.

thought have been right in there giving leadership, guiding the worried along paths of "explanation" which have to do with their own preoccupations with "phallus envy," "castration complexes," and the rest of it: the inevitable result being that large numbers of people are now inclined to speak of the hardly new quest for universal equality as a neurotic disorder! "A disorder," we are informed, which seems to be sweeping other modern civilizations as well. For what else could be at the root, for example, of the "trouble in Australia," where a study reveals that sixty percent of the husbands in Melbourne reported that they help their wives with the dishes and yet another twenty-two percent get breakfast for the family in the mornings?

It appears that the horrified commentators have taken note of some very real disorders in modern life and deduced, rather automatically, that the causes must lie in the disintegration of our most entrenched traditions. Yet few of these seers, remarkably enough, seem to have seriously considered the alternative: that the problems might in fact lie in the lingering *life* of certain of our traditions.

There are, to be sure, other observers—a counter force holding their own—who suggest that, at best, the alarm is rooted in archaic concepts and, at worst, is in itself presumptious as the dickens! Striking a note of rationality, they argue that what we are dealing with is the oldest phenomena of the planet: *change.* The implication being that, contrary to negative legends, the human race possesses an incredible capacity to adapt itself, physically and psychologically, to its own ever-improving technological condition. Thus, modern man—modern urban man in particular—has begun to lose his *reasons* for the retention of formerly rigid notions of occupational, avocational, or even psychic categorizations which were apparently essential to his forebears in their more primitive social systems.

Affairs behind executive or professorial desks have tended to make "brute strength" irrelevant; World War II showed that virtually the same thing was true for the assembly line. And even if there were wild boars and such things still to be hunted for survival, the force required on the trigger of an automatic weapon is hardly the same once needed to pummel something with a stone axe. Increasingly, it is a human being's thinking capacity, not his bulk, which most equips him for modern life; whatever there once was of a realistic reason for physique determining labor is rapidly disappearing. In that light it is not extraordinary to behold the human attitude also changing. If modern trade unionism, white-collar labor, and the eight-hour day have contrived to diminish the laboring hours of the husband, it is to his credit that he has begun of his own volition to apply his new and hard-won leisure to sharing some part of his wife's still often twelve-to-fourteen-hour workday. It suggests that more than being a question for concern, it is one for celebration inasmuch as for the first time in history the family may now be growing toward a circumstantial reality which will allow it to become the truly harmonized, cooperative unit the human dream has always longed for it to be.

The current aspiration for the retention of ancient polarized concepts of strict divisions of labor reflects a social order which has effectively kept womanhood in her well known second-class situation, but which is less often criticised for imposing *upon males* the most unreasonable and unnecessary burdens of "superiority" and "authority," which, in fact, work only to insult their humanness and *deny the reality of their civilized state.*

Most apologists for a male supremacist culture do not dream that they   9
savagely downgrade *men* in their efforts to provide them with a socially guaranteed place of privilege on the human scale. Yet, it was not romanticism alone, but also shimmering human practicality, which led the great humanist thinkers and artists of history to postulate, in poetry and prose, the ideas that, for instance, the rich must be inevitably degraded, in *human* terms, in a world where so many starve; that the educated remain, in large measure, untested for their wisdom when so few can read or write. And, certainly, in our own time, in the United States, it has become increasingly clear that white Americans are among the most compromised people on the face of the earth, because of their steady demonstration of their fear of running a non-handicapped race with their black countrymen.

If modern males are suffering from high percentages of ulcer, heart   10
ailment, and a thousand-and-one nervous disorders, this might well be the burden imposed on their nervous systems from subjecting the reality of present-day life to the totems and taboos* of the primeval, medieval, and Victorian past. As in all questions where nonconformity carries heavy penalties, great numbers of males are naturally reticent to articulate their dissent from the "favors" heaped upon them. But, occasionally, usually in the more acceptable guise of "explaining" to women how to give artificially contrived sustenance to the male ego, the plea can be discerned. John Kord Lagemann provides an excellent example in an article in *Redbook* entitled "The Male Sex": "The average male would be happy to drop the he-man pose if he didn't feel it would mean losing face as a man. It isn't because of his male instinct that he shies away from washing dishes, changing diapers, working under a woman boss or enjoying string quartets and modern art. It's because he suspects that other people, including his wife—despite their protestations to the contrary—still look on these chores and pastimes as 'unnatural' for a man."

We have all become so preoccupied with the "usurpation of the male's   11
authority by the female" that we have neglected to analyse the vestigial presumption of that self-awarded authority; in so doing, we have also neglected to be outraged and shocked by the equally widespread assumption that men are in reality inferior human beings who have to be "propped up." The institutional acceptance of woman as a second-class human being carries its own dynamic which inadvertantly must, of necessity, present men as flagrantly unintelligent and somewhat dehumanized creatures. In "Making Marriage Work," featured in a widely read woman's magazine, the professor-analyst author tackled what might seem, to the excessively civilized, a re-

*An allusion to Sigmund Freud's (1856–1939) *Totem and Taboo* (1913).

solved question: *"Should a Husband Strike His Wife?"* Bending to enlightenment, the writer opined, "It is impossible to condone such behavior." He then went on, however, to modify that bit of radical abandon by advising his readers that the "provocation" by wives was undoubtedly far greater than they realized. He offered the following directions to wives as to how best avoid their partially deserved beatings: "Gauge his mood; avoid arguments; indulge his whims; help him relax; share his burdens; keep love alive."

Now it must be clear that any group of human beings who *could* impose 12 such saintly behavior on themselves at will, presumably after their own fairly exhausting and temper-rousing workdays, would be a superior lot indeed. But rather more outrageous is the assumption that men must be placated, outwitted, humored, and patronized like the family pet of whom we do not expect rationality and emotional control. One wonders how the writer supposes the criminal charge of "assault" ever found its way to the law books (evolved as it was by *male* representatives of social authority who could not apparently find within *themselves* justification for such behavior regardless of the sex of the victim).

Many men have cast wary eyes at the false crutches handed their sex: 13 Shakespeare toyed freely with pompous assumptions of masculine superiority in several of his works; Mark Twain in his witticisms; Zola in his novels; Frederick Douglass from the antislavery podium; August Bebel in his great studies; John Stuart Mill in his essays; Whitman in his poetry; William Godwin in the stuff of his life and his writings; Karl Marx in the development of his economic theories; and, of course, in our own time, George Bernard Shaw in almost every wise and irreverent word he wrote. None of these figures found themselves diminished by an impending "threat" of the equality of women; most of them took the position that its accomplishment bode but another aspect of the liberation of *men,* in all senses of that might word.

It required, in fact, the industrial revolution and the winds of *égalité* from 14 the American and French revolutions before history could thrust forward a woman to set down the case for the "Rights of Woman" in 1792. That the brilliant Jacobin Englishwoman Mary Wollstonecraft did so raised all the stormy outrage that the conservative thinkers of her time, male and female, could muster.* That the outrage has lingered and all but obscured her name and her book is a revealing indicator of the unfinished character of what is sometimes called, improperly, the "sexual revolution."

It is worth the digression to remark that whole generations have come 15 to maturity believing that "feminists," upper- or lowercase, were strident, ludicrous creatures in incongruous costumes of feathered hats and oversized bloomers, who marched about, mainly through the saloons of the land, conking poor, peaceful, beer-guzzling males over the head. The image successfully erases a truer and more cogent picture. In deed and oratory, in their recognition of direct political action as opposed to parlor and bedroom wheedling of

---

*A reference to Mary Wollstonecraft's (1759–1797) *Vindication of the Rights of Woman* (1792), a powerful attack on sexist conventions and assumptions.

husbands and fathers as the true key to social transformation, American Feminist leaders, in particular, set a path that a grateful society will undoubtedly, in time, celebrate. The scope of their understanding of the evils of their times is summed up magnificently in a portion of a speech by Susan B. Anthony as she addressed the court where she was being sentenced to jail for voting in the state of New York in 1879: "Your denial of my right to vote is the denial of my right of consent as one of the governed, the denial of my right of representation as one of the taxed, the denial of my right to a trial by a jury of my peers. . . . But, yesterday, the same man-made forms of law declared it a crime punishable with a $1,000 fine and six months' imprisonment, for you, or me, or any of us, to give a cup of cold water, a crust of bread, or a night's shelter to a panting fugitive as he was tracking his way to Canada. And every man or woman in whose veins coursed a drop of human sympathy violated that wicked law, reckless of consequences, and was justified in doing so. As then, the slaves who got their freedom must yet take it over, or under, or through the unjust forms of law, precisely so now must women, to get their right to a voice in this Government, take it; I have taken mine, and mean to take it at every possible opportunity."

This thrilling American patriot, not less than the Franklin radicals or the 16 Jeffersonian democrats—and like scores of other Feminists—put her comfort, and in some brutal instances her very life, upon the line in order to do no more and certainly no less than enlarge the Constitutional promises of the American Republic to include the largest numbers of its people of both sexes. As is apparent from the text of her speech she and the other leaders of the Feminist movement (Lucretia Mott, Elizabeth Cady Stanton, Sojourner Truth, and Harriet Tubman, among many*) gave equally of their energies to the greatest issue of their time, the antislavery struggle, as their spiritual descendants were to give theirs, in another period, to prison reform, the eradication of illiteracy, conservation, and the crowning achievement of the abolition of child labor. We might well long for the day when the knowledge of the debt all society owes to organized womanhood in bringing the human race closer together, not pushing it farther apart, will still the laughter in the throats of the now uninformed.

Nonetheless, the lingering infamy in which "feminism" is generally 17 held helps to explain the mystery of the widespread notion that the emancipation of the modern American woman is an accomplished fact, despite all evidence that she does not universally get "equal pay for equal work," that she is discouraged flatly in many occupations and government posts, and that her advance into executive positions is held stringently in check. It also helps to explain the eager mythology of the "tyranny of women" who allegedly rule over the home and even the wealth of the nation. In his book *America as a Civilization,* Max Lerner replies to the myth thusly: "The catch is

*Lucretia Mott (1793–1880), feminist and reformer; Elizabeth Cady Stanton (1815–1902), feminist and co-worker with Anthony (see above); Sojourner Truth (c.1797–1883), former slave and feminist (see above); Harriet Tubman (1820?–1913), fugitive slave and rescuer of slaves.

that women hold their purchasing power largely as wives and have acquired their wealth mainly as widows; economically they are disbursing agents, not principals. . . . The real control of the wealth is in the hands of male trustees, lawyers and bankers. Few women are directors of big corporations, just as there are few who form government policies. . . . The minority of women who are powerful in their ownership of wealth are functionless with respect to their wealth, because they lack strategic control of it."

As for the "tyranny of Mom," Mom has been effectively toppled from 18 her pedestal without society taking a second look to discover, if all those dreadful things are really true about her, *how* she got that way. Our culture has been slow to assume responsibility for ordinary women who have been told, starting with the cradle, that home and husband and children will be the sources of all reward in life, the foundations of all true happiness; it has had almost nothing to say about what she should do with herself when the children are grown and her husband is exhausted and bored with excessive attention, preoccupied as he is with other aspects of the world. Mah-jong and matinees in the city seem to her to lack purpose, and, whether we like it or not, that is the thing that human beings tend to crave: purpose.

The glaring fact is that Mom's life needs liberation as much as everyone 19 else's. To say so is to be thought of as attacking the "bedrock of our way of life" and all of that, but it must be said. Mom must be allowed to think of herself, as Simone de Beauvoir has insisted brilliantly,* as a human being first and a mother second. Housewives insist on identifying themselves, to the frustration of the experts, as *"only* housewives" because, apparently, they perceive that housework and care of the family is but humankind's necessity of function: things requisite to existence; essentials which should permit us to . . . something else. We do not live to wash our faces and eat our meals, we wash our faces and eat our meals in order to participate in the world: in the classroom, in the factory, in the office, in the shop, in the national and international halls of government, in the scientific laboratory and in the studios where the arts are created. *The Feminists did not create the housewife's dissatisfaction with her lot—the Feminists came from out of the only place they could have come—the housewives of the world!* Satisfaction for the housewife, then, lies not in a new program of propaganda to exalt what remains, and always will remain, drudgery; but in the continued effort to reduce it to a hardly perceptible (if ever necessary) interruption in the pursuit of productive labors and creative expression. Satisfaction lies in allowing and encouraging men to freely assume more and more equal relationship with their children and their wives. The argument against this is difficult to understand since the more interesting the lives of the parents (both parents), the more interesting we have every right to expect future generations to be.

One area of the national life where the estate of woman is certainly 20 never debated, and may be passed over quickly, is in the newest crop of "for Men Only" magazines where the whole thing has been resolved by reducing

*In *The Second Sex* (1949).

the entire relationship between men and women to a long and rather boring (not to add mechanical) tableaux of simple-minded and degrading animal essences. There, Woman the Child, Woman the Animal, Woman Upside-down-and-naked, Woman the Harem Fantasy—is replete with no conflict and no aspiration, the sex-object of men who cannot fathom the nature of their own delusions. The symptomatic fumes of Romanesque decay which exude from the same pages, where some of the world's most established writers are obliged, like musicians in a whorehouse, to appear between "play-mates," is stultifying. To say so, however, is not to long for a new wave of "banning": that unfortunate practice always ends up by lynching the brave new thoughts in the world and merely covering up our social filth. It is to long for a deeper appraisal of what we really want for ourselves and our children; to long for a cultural climate where Mrs. Roosevelt's* image will be projected to our young men and women with more regularity than the current courte-sans.

It is, finally, a longing that another generation of girls will not have to 21 grow up under a certain pragmatism which insists that men do not like "brainy" women. That notion is a terrible cheat to all, and one of the most belittling indictments of men. Girls are better taught to "reach for the stars" even in the matter of seeking or accepting a mate. The grim possibility is that she who "hides her brains" will, more than likely, end up with a mate who is only equal to a woman with "hidden brains" or none at all. That hardly gives the children of such a union a robust start in life. To hide one's mental capacity is a personality disfigurement which is even more grotesque than to flaunt it—which, at least, boasts *pride.*

There *are* men who find love affairs of stature enough. Men who neither 22 desire nor tolerate affected vacuity: who wish mutuality and stimulation. In this writer's experience *those* are the exciting men; they exist. A woman who is willing to be herself and pursue her own potentials—it is time it was said—runs not so much the risk of loneliness as the challenge of exposure to more interesting men—and people in general.

There are, it is true, perhaps larger numbers of men who have mistaken 23 WOMAN herself for the antagonism between the sexes. And, heaven knows, women passionately, often hysterically, feed the delusion. But is *is* a delusion: it is the codified barriers *between* the sexes that cause the trouble. Accordingly, some men are overwhelmed by the pressures upon their "masculinity" as they understand it, and move through life in perpetual states of agitation because, they are certain, of their persecution by women. Some of them, a few, become pathological woman-haters and proceed to hate all women: those in their "place" at home; and those "out of it." They have hatred of the women who will not sleep with them and hatred for those who will. Their hostility should not be met with hostility: they are frightened and pathetic

*Eleanor Roosevelt (1884–1962), widow of President Franklin D. Roosevelt, was the first U.S. delegate to the United Nations (1945) and one of the authors of the Universal Declaration of Human Rights (1948).

human beings, as much caught in a social trap as their feminine counterparts who, it is true, get more and uglier attention in popular conversation and literature. These people are the most extreme victims of the *inequality* between the sexes; the rest of us are victims in other ways. In their situation, a member of the opposite sex does not have to open his or her mouth, they just have to *be* and they have offended. The weight is put upon our shoulders when we are hardly out of the womb, *all* of us, and it is more than a little tragic, this exaggerated sense of alienation from one another that we are taught. Having paid such terrible prices for it, need we despair for its passing?

With the barriers should go many of the arbitrary definitions structured 24 into our very language from out of the past: the classification of occupations, activities, roles by gender; the built-in assumption of maleness in certain words; the adjectives which still confuse and confine us in our thinking and make it possible for serious sociologists and psychologists to draw conclusions from "masculine-feminine" charts which are based on nothing other than conditioned concepts of what is "natural" (for whom?). Within that scale, male journalists, firemen and policemen have scored "less masculine" than other men, such as laborers, because of their occupational interest in "womanish" concerns like the human condition and saving lives! Among women, domestic servants score the highest "femininity" ratings of all— because of their demonstrated "interest" in cleaning house!

At the heart of this incredible mish-mosh of nonsense is the time- 25 honored but perfectly silly habit of attributing to a given set of universally human capacities, a qualification which implies that they are unique to one sex, race, or culture. (It is by that outrage that the people of Europe and their descendants in North America innocently go on speaking of objective adjectives such as "modern" or even "progressive" as if they were virtually synonymous with the geographical noun "the West"—to the wonder (and fury) of at least two-thirds of the world. Modern ideas, one notes, function elsewhere and, in some instances, these days especially, with greater acceleration. It was not "the West," after all, that first punctured space* and it is the women of Ghana who vote and the women of Switzerland who do not.) Thus, women who seek objective fulfillment as people are not trying to be "men" (or good or bad "imitations" of them)—they are trying to be successful human beings.

Finally, it is not to be doubted that our clinging to the habits of the past 26 gives all of us some comfort in this thus-far-unexplained universe: it is always reassuring to think that our ancestors "did it" the same way. But in medicine the price of dogged superstition has too often been death, and in all human affairs there comes a time—to let go. With regard to the sexual connotations of words, can we all not think of what a dream will be realized for the race when the noun "soldier," for example, ceases to conjure up romantic notions of masculinity, but will instead have been unsexed and (at long last) put in its true place in history by the more accurate associations it recalls: "tragedy . . . the organized waste of human life and potential"?

*The Russians launched *Sputnik,* the first rocket-fueled satellite, in 1957.

None of this, we can rest easy, will dissipate the *true* distinction between 27
the sexes: that will not happen because nobody *desires* for it to happen. The
French have remarked on that matter for all time*—to which one need only
add another *"Vive!"*

Questions for Discussion

1. Although a feminist essay, "In Defense of the Equality of *Men"* perhaps
   discusses men more than it discusses women. Is the title merely ironic? Is
   it ironic at all? If so, what is ironic about it? If it is ironic, who or what
   is being attacked? If Hansberry seriously desires the equality of men, what
   reasons does she offer and what social or psychological forces does she
   think oppose it?

2. As a dramatist, Hansberry captures the rhythms of spoken speech so
   masterfully that she manages to make even a prose essay sound like an
   extended monologue delivered by a lively, intelligent, and passionate
   speaker. This essay does not sound like an academically sanitized meditation. Demonstrate Hansberry's grasp of vernacular by reading paragraphs
   aloud in class, noting that Hansberry frequently uses sentence fragments
   where they would be used in spoken speech and even relies on a few
   slangy colloqualisms. Does this colloquial tone work throughout the essay,
   or does the author at times diminish the seriousness of her argument by
   lapsing too far into an unserious tone?

3. When Hansberry wrote this essay in 1961, she thought it accurate to refer
   to "the lingering infamy in which 'feminism' is generally held" (¶17). Do
   you think this description is still accurate, or do you think that society has
   come to accept feminism as socially and intellectually respectable? How
   many men and women in your class would not object to being identified
   in the campus newspaper—during an interview, say—as a "feminist"?
   How many men would object (or would not object) to dating a woman
   who called herself a feminist? Do the tallies produced by these questions
   surprise you? If so, can you identify the source of your mistaken predictions?

4. Ask each person in your class to write a one-word definition of "feminism," and then have each person read the definition aloud. If there is little
   agreement, are there at least any *patterns* of meaning, and can the class agree
   on an operational definition to use for the remainder of the discussion?

5. In paragraph 21 Hansberry refers to the often-repeated belief that "men
   do not like 'brainy' women." What is the response to this assertion among

*A reference to the French adage *Vive la différence*—"Long live the difference" (between men and
women).

the men and women in your class? Can any of the women recount the personal experience of feeling social pressure to disguise their intelligence or to remain silent about their superior grasp of information so as not to perform better than boys in school? Can any of the men contradict or corroborate the assertion on the basis of their personal experience? If some men in class admit to not liking "brainy women," what reasons do they offer?

Suggested Essay Topics

1. By using such reference works as the *Social Sciences and Humanities Index* and the *Readers' Guide to Periodical Literature,* find some anti-feminist essays from roughly the same period as Hansberry's essay and compare one of the best written of them with Hansberry's, pointing out to your audience (your own classmates) the opposing theses and the quality of the supporting arguments that each author uses.

2. Referring back to the subtitle of Chapter 5—"What Should I Become?"—, direct an essay to your classmates in which you discuss how the messages about sexuality and sex roles that you have heard all your life from family, relatives, and community (school, church, friends, and so on) have affected your sense of the possibilities of what you may or may not become. Note the strengths or anxieties that have been programmed into you by these messages, and give a concrete picture of the person you hope to become, focusing specifically on the role you expect to play as a man or woman relating to members of the opposite sex as mates, co-workers, and friends.

Francine Frank and Frank Ashen

The struggle to rid society of various kinds of oppression requires analysis on many fronts: political, historical, theological, ethical, and so on. The analysis given to us here by Francine Frank and Frank Ashen is linguistic. The oppression they object to is the unfair and destructive denigration of women as a group; the mechanism of oppression they are attempting to expose is buried so deep within our consciousness that it takes a deliberate and energetic effort at self-examination to see how it operates. It is the mechanism of language itself. Because language lies so deep within us, some of us may be more hostile and defensive when asked to change our linguistic habits than we would be if we were asked to change anything else. The common words by which we refer to everyday objects and experience are more than just useful tools to us; they seem a natural extension of reality itself. Words thus carry an emotional charge, an aura, a mystique that native speakers decode in sophisticated ways without having to think consciously about how they do it.

So it is with words that deprecate, condescend, or depreciate: words that put people down, rob them of their dignity, or diminish their worth as human beings. "Boy"—a generic term of address—could at one time be used by any white person to refer to any black male, regardless of the black man's age, merits, or social standing. The subtle difference between "I know the woman who lives in that house" and "I know the lady who lives in that house" will be picked up by any reasonably educated speaker of English. Frank and Ashen give us many examples of the way English may be used to keep women in an inferior social position, to keep them feeling inferior, useless, incompetent, or powerless. No native speaker has to take a course to learn the use of such language; rather, one almost has to take a course in order to unlearn it, to become aware enough to avoid it. The sexist bias runs deeper than most of us ever recognize until we are challenged to see it by the research and criticism of those who, like Frank and Ashen, spend much more time thinking about these issues than most people.

As you read, try to think of examples from your own experience or reading that support or even extend the authors' arguments. You might also consider to what extent the authors' linguistic examples of sexist language are mirrored in nonverbal aspects of life. Clearly, we have a great many verbal ways of expressing bias against people of despised religions, ethnic origins, and skin color. We have all heard the ugly terms. What about other ways of identifying who is "in" and who is "out" in certain social groups—at school, in the dorm, in the fraternity or sorority house, on the job, in the neighborhood, and in other areas? Can Frank and Ashen's argument help explain such nonverbal modes of differentiation? But when we are talking about language, Frank and Ashen invite us to think more critically about (and listen more carefully to) the uses of language that help create our social and emotional environment.

OF GIRLS AND CHICKS

Chapter 4 of *Language and the Sexes* (1983).

English is a sexist language! Angry women have often been driven to make such a statement. But is it accurate? Can we really label some languages as more sexist than others? In a recent movie, a rather obnoxious adolescent described his favorite pastime as "cruising chicks." If the adolescent had been female, she would not have had a parallel term to refer to finding boys. This asymmetry in vocabulary is a linguistic reflection of sexism in our society.

One of the more intriguing and controversial hypotheses of modern linguistics is the idea that the grammatical structure of a language may influence the thought processes of speakers of that language. Regardless of the truth of that idea, known among linguists as the Sapir-Whorf hypothesis, it seems clear that we can gain insights into the culture and attitudes of a group by examining the language of that group. Eskimos live in an environment in which the condition of snow is vital to survival, and they therefore have a large number of distinct words for different kinds of snow. Most Hindi speakers live in areas of India where it does not snow and, as a result, Hindi has only a single word equivalent to the two English words *snow* and *ice*. In

Modern English, the plethora of words such as *road, avenue, freeway, highway, boulevard, street, turnpike, expressway, parkway, lane,* and *interstate* might lead one to conclude that automobiles are very important to Americans, while the relative scarcity of words for various types of kinfolk would suggest that extended familial relationships are not very important to Americans. (We do not, for example, have separate words for our mother's brother and our father's brother.) In this chapter, we will look at the linguistic treatment of women in English for clues to the attitudes towards women held by speakers of English.

First let us consider what the last members of the following groups have in common: Jack and Jill, Romeo and Juliet, Adam and Eve, Peter, Paul and Mary, Hansel and Gretel, Roy Rogers and Dale Evans, Tristan and Isolde, Guys and Dolls, Abelard and Heloise, man and wife, Dick and Jane, Burns and Allen, Anthony and Cleopatra, Sonny and Cher, Fibber Magee and Molly,* Ferdinand and Isabella, Samson and Delilah, and Stiller and Meara. That's right, it is a group of women who have been put in their place. Not that women must always come last: Snow White gets to precede all seven of the dwarfs, Fran may follow Kukla, but she comes before Ollie,† Anna preceded the King of Siam, although it must be noted that, as colonialism waned, she was thrust to the rear of the billing in "The King and I."‡ Women with guns are also able to command top billing, as in Frankie and Johnny, and Bonnie and Clyde. The moral is clear: a woman who wants precedence in our society should either hang around with dwarfs or dragons, or shoot somebody. "Women and children first" may apply on sinking ships, but it clearly doesn't apply in the English language.

Not only are women put off, they are also put down, numerically and otherwise. In the real world, women slightly outnumber men. But the world created for American schoolchildren presents a different picture. In an article describing the preparation of a dictionary for schoolchildren, Alma Graham recounts the imbalance discovered in schoolbooks in all subjects in use in the early 1970s. A computer analysis of five million words in context revealed many subtle and not-so-subtle clues to the status of women in American society. The numbers alone tell us a lot: men outnumber women seven to one, boys outnumber girls two to one; girls are even in the minority in home economics books, where masculine pronouns outnumber feminine ones two to one. In general, the pronouns *he, him,* and *his* outnumber *she, her,* and *hers* by a ratio of four to one.

When the linguistic context of the above pronouns was analyzed to see if they were generics, referring to people regardless of sex it was found that of 940 examples, almost eighty percent clearly referred to male human beings; next came references to male animals, to persons such as sailors and farmers,

3
4
5

---

*Popular radio entertainers in the 1930s and 1940s.

†*Kukla, Fran, and Ollie* was a popular TV show in the 1950s. Fran was a human who interacted with the puppets Kukla and Ollie.

‡The 1950s Broadway musical *The King and I* was based on a book titled *Anna and the King of Siam.*

who were assumed to be male, and only thirty-two pronouns were true generics. In another set of words, we do find more women: mothers outnumber fathers, and wives appear three times as often as husbands. However, children are usually labelled by referring to a male parent (Jim's son rather than Betty's son), most mothers have sons rather than daughters, and so do most fathers. There are twice as many uncles as aunts and every first born child is a son. It is not altogether clear from all this how the race reproduces itself without dying out in a few generations. Notice further that, although the word *wife* is more frequent, expressions like *the farmer's wife, pioneers and their wives,* etc., indicate that the main characters are male.

Consider now another area of our language. English has a large number   6
of nouns which appear to be neutral with regard to sex, but actually are covertly masculine. Although the dictionary may define *poet* as one who writes poetry, a woman who writes poetry appears so anomalous or threatening to some, that they use the special term *poetess* to refer to her. There is no corresponding term to call attention to the sex of a man who writes poetry, but then we find nothing remarkable in the fact that poetry is written by men. Of course, if a woman is sufficiently meritorious, we may forgive her her sex and refer to her as a poet after all, or, wishing to keep the important fact of her sex in our consciousness, we may call her a *woman poet.* However, to balance the possible reward of having her sex overlooked, there remains the possibility of more extreme punishment; we may judge her work so harshly that she will be labelled a *lady poet.* Once again, the moral is clear: people who write poetry are assumed to be men until proven otherwise, and people identified as women who write poetry are assumed to be less competent than sexually unidentified (i.e., presumably male) people who write poetry.

If the phenomenon we have been discussing were limited to poetry, we   7
might not regard it as very significant; after all, our society tends to regard poets as somewhat odd anyway. But, in fact, it is widespread in the language. There is a general tendency to label the exception, which in most cases turns out to be women. Many words with feminine suffixes, such as *farmerette, authoress,* and *aviatrix,* have such a clear trivializing effect, that there has been a trend away from their use and a preference for *woman author* and the like. The feminines of many ethnic terms, such as *Negress* and *Jewess,* are considered particularly objectionable. Other words, such as *actress* and *waitress,* seem to have escaped the negative connotations and remain in use. However, we note that waiters often work in more expensive establishments than do waitresses, that actresses belong to "Actor's Equity," and that women participants in theatrical groups have begun to refer to themselves as "actors." On rare occasions, this presumption of maleness in terms which should be sexually neutral, works to women's advantage. If someone is called a *bastard,* either as a general term of abuse, or as a statement of the lack of legal marital ties between that person's parents, we assume that person is a male. While an illegitimate child may be of either sex, only men are bastards in common usage. Although the dictionary seems to regard this as a sex-neutral term, a recent dictionary of slang gives the term *bastarda* as a "female bastard/law, Black."[1]

Sometimes the feminine member of a pair of words has a meaning   8
which is not only inferior to the masculine one, but also different from it.
Compare, for instance, a *governor* with a *governess* or a *major* with a *majorette.* Ella
Grasso was the governor of Connecticut, and a high ranking woman in the
U.S. Army would certainly not be a majorette. In a large number of cases, the
supposed feminine form does not even exist to refer to a woman occupying
a "male" position. Women, for example, may be United States Senators, but
there is no such thing as a *Senatress.* Often, where the feminine noun does
exist, it will acquire sexual overtones not found in the original: compare a
mistress with a *master.*

The last effect even spills over to adjectives applied to the two sexes.   9
A *virtuous* man may be patriotic or charitable or exhibit any one of a number
of other admirable traits; a *virtuous* woman is chaste. (The word *virtue* is, itself,
derived from the Latin word for *man.*) Similarly, consider Robin Lakoff's
example[2] of the different implications involved in saying *He is a professional*
versus *She is a professional.** Although adjectives also may come in seemingly
equivalent pairs like *handsome* and *pretty,* they prove not to be equivalent in
practice; it is a compliment to call a woman *handsome* and an insult to call a
man *pretty.* In other cases, where pairs of adjectives exist, one term covers both
sexes and the other one tends to refer only to one sex, usually females. So,
members of both sexes may be *small,* but only women seem to be *petite;* both
boys and girls may have a *lively* personality, but when did you last meet a
vivacious boy?

In addition to this use of certain adjectives almost exclusively to refer   10
to women, descriptions of women typically include more adjectives and
expressions referring to physical appearance than do descriptions of men. The
media clearly reflect this tendency; a report on an interview with a well-
known woman rarely fails to mention that she is *attractive* or *stylish,* or to say
something about her clothes or the color of her hair or eyes, even if the
context is a serious one like politics or economics, where such details have
no importance. Readers are also likely to be informed of the number and ages
of her children. Men are not treated in a parallel fashion.

Verbs turn out to be sex-differentiated also. Prominent among such   11
verbs are those which refer to women's linguistic behavior and reflect some
of the stereotypes discussed in an earlier chapter. Women, for example, may
shriek and *scream,* while men may *bellow.* Women and children (girls?) hold a
virtual monopoly on *giggling,* and it seems that men rarely *gossip* or *scold.* There
are also a large number of sex-marked verbs which refer to sexual intercourse.
In their article, "Sex-marked Predicates in English," Julia P. Stanley and
Susan W. Robbins note the abundance of terms which describe the male role
in sexual intercourse, and the lack of parallel terms for women's role.[3]
Women are thus assigned a passive role in sex by our language.

Another set of words which are presumably sex-neutral are the ones   12

*Traditionally, the word *professional,* applied to a woman, has been used as a euphemism for
prostitute.

that end in -*man*. This suffix, which is pronounced with a different vowel from the one in the word *man*, supposedly indicates a person of either sex. It is commonly found in words designating professions—*salesman, postman, congressman*, for example—and in some other expressions such as *chairman* and *freshman*. However, the very fact that there exist female counterparts for many of these words, such as *chairwoman* and *congresswoman*, indicates that they are thought of as typically male and, as in the case of poets, when a woman is referred to, her sex must be clearly indicated. In the case of *salesman*, there are a variety of feminine forms: *saleswoman, saleslady*, and *salesgirl*. Although they appear to be synonymous, they convey significant social distinctions; someone referred to as a *saleslady* or a *salesgirl* probably works in a retail establishment such as a department store or a variety store. A woman who sells mainframe computers to large corporations would be called a *saleswoman*, or even a *salesman*. The more important the position, the less likely it is to be held by a -*girl* or a -*lady*, and the more likely it is to be the responsibility of a -*man*.

If speakers of English often have a choice of using separate words for men and women, of pretending that a single word with a male marker like *chairman* refers to both sexes, or of using a truly sex-neutral term like *chairperson* or *chair*, speakers of some other languages do not enjoy such freedom. They are constrained by the grammar of their languages to classify the nouns they use according to something called gender. Grammatical gender is a feature of most European languages and of many others as well. Depending on the language, nouns may be classified according to whether they are animate or inanimate, human or non-human, male or female, or, in the case of inanimate objects, the class may depend on shape or some other characteristic. In some languages, meaning plays little part in determining noun class or gender; it may be predictable from the phonetic shape of the words, or it may be completely arbitrary. In the European tradition, genders are labelled *masculine* and *feminine* and, if there is a third noun class, *neuter*. This is in spite of the fact that most words included in all three of these classes represent inanimate objects like *tables* and *doors*, abstract concepts like *freedom*, or body parts like *head, toe, nose*, etc. Some of us English speakers may begin to wonder about the strange world view of speakers of languages which classify books as masculine and tables as feminine, especially when we notice that the word for nose is feminine in Spanish, but masculine in French and Italian. It turns out, however, that they are not following some animistic practice whereby inanimate objects are thought of as having sexual attributes; in the modern European languages at least, grammatical gender is, for most nouns, a purely arbitrary classification, often the result of linguistic tradition and of a number of historical accidents. The labels come from the fact that most nouns referring to males belong to one class and most nouns referring to females belong to another class and, following the human practice of classifying everything in terms of ourselves, we extend the distinguishing labels to all nouns. There are, not surprisingly, exceptions to this prevalent mode of classification, which lead to the oddity of such words as the French *sentinelle*, 'guard', being grammatically feminine,

13

although most guards are men, while two German words for 'young woman,' *Fräulein* and *Mädchen,* are grammatically neuter.

Are speakers of languages with grammatical gender completely strait- 14 jacketed by their grammar and forced to be sexist? We will return to this question in the final chapter. For now, we note that in these languages, the masculine forms usually serve as generics and are considered the general forms, in much the same way as the *-man* words are in English. Just as there are often alternatives to these masculine words in English, other languages also have many words that are potentially neutral and can belong to either gender, depending on the sex of the person referred to—French *poète* and Spanish *poeta* are examples, despite the dictionaries' classification of them as masculine. Yet speakers often insist on signalling the sex of women poets by adding suffixes parallel to the English *-ess, poétesse* and *poetisa* being the French and Spanish equivalents, or by tacking on the word for woman, as in *femme médecin,* one term for a 'woman doctor' in French.

Although it is true that the masculine forms serve as the unmarked or 15 neutral terms in many languages, this does not seem to be a universal feature of human languages, as some have claimed. Iroquoian languages use feminine nouns as unmarked or generic terms; however, in the case of Iroquoian occupational terms, which are composed of a pronoun and a verb (literally translated as 'she cooks' or 'he cooks'), the sex-typing of the job determines whether the masculine or feminine pronoun is used. In Modern Standard Arabic many nouns switch to the feminine gender when they are pluralized. In many European languages, abstract nouns are predominantly in the femi-nine gender.

English nouns no longer exhibit grammatical gender, but the language 16 does have a large number of words that refer to members of one sex only. In addition, when we do not know the sex of the person referred to by a noun such as *writer* or *student,* the choice of the pronoun will, as in Iroquois, often depend on culturally defined sex roles. *Teacher,* therefore, is usually *she,* while *professor, doctor,* and *priest* usually go with *he.* This brings us to the question of the "generic" use of *he* and the word *man.*

In the case of the word *man,* as in *Man is a primate,* it has been argued 17 that this usage is independent of sex, that it refers to all members of the species, and that it is just an etymological coincidence that the form for the species is the same as that for the male members of the species. Certainly, using the same form for the entire species and for half the species creates the possibility of confusion, as those colonial women discovered who rashly thought that the word *man* in the sentence "All men are created equal" included them. More confusion may come about when we use phrases like *early man.* Although this presumably refers to the species, notice how easy it is to use expressions like *early man and his wife* and how hard it is to say things like *man is the only animal that menstruates* or even *early woman and her husband.* As with the poetical examples discussed earlier, the common theme running through these last examples is that the male is taken as the normal, that masculine forms refer both to the sex and the species, while women are the exception, usually absorbed by the masculine, but needing special terms when they become noticeable.

If the above examples have not convinced you that *man* as a generic is   18
at best ambiguous, consider the following quote from Alma Graham:

> If a woman is swept off a ship into the water, the cry is "Man over-board!" If she is killed by a hit-and-run driver, the charge is "manslaugh-ter." If she is injured on the job, the coverage is "workmen's compensa-tion." But if she arrives at a threshold marked "Men Only," she knows the admonition is not intended to bar animals or plants or inanimate objects. It is meant for her.[4]

Historically, *man* did start out as a general term for human beings, but   19
Old English also had separate sex-specific terms: *wif* for women and *wer* or *carl* for men. The compound term *wifman* (female person) is the source for today's *woman,* but the terms for males were lost as *man* came to take on its sex-specific meaning, thus creating the confusion we have been discussing. For an authoritative opinion on the modern meaning of this word, we could turn to the *Oxford English Dictionary,* which notes that the generic use of *man* is obsolete: "in modern apprehension *man* as thus used primarily denotes the male sex, though by implication referring also to women." We note that the "modern apprehension" referred to was the late nineteenth century. If any-thing, the situation is even clearer today.

An even shorter word which is supposed to include women but often   20
excludes them is the pronoun *he.* Observers have long pointed out the incon-venience of the ambiguity of this form and the advantages of having a true generic singular pronoun, which would be sex-neutral. In the absence of such a sex-neutral pronoun, speakers of English have been expected to utter sen-tences such as *Everybody should bring his book tomorrow,* where the *everybody* referred to includes forty women and just one man. For centuries, speakers and writers of English have been happily getting around this obstacle by using *they* in such situations, yielding sentences such as *Everybody should bring their book tomor-row.* Unfortunately, since the middle of the eighteenth century, prescriptive grammarians have been prescribing the use of *he* in these situations and attacking the use of *they,* by arguing that the use of *they* is a violation of the rule for pronoun agreement, i.e., a singular noun such as *everybody* should not take a plural pronoun such as *they.*

Although the prescriptive grammarians have not explained why it is all   21
right for a female person such as *Mary* to be referred to by a masculine pronoun such as *he,* they have managed to make many people feel guilty about breaking the law when they use *they* in such sentences. As a result, many of us consciously avoid the use of *they* in these contexts, and some of us avoid the use of such sentences at all. Ann Bodine quotes a writer of a grammatical handbook advocating the latter course when faced with the need to formulate the sentence, "Everyone in the class worried about the midyear history exam, but he all passed."[5] In 1850, an actual law was passed on the

subject when the British Parliament, in an attempt to shorten the language in its legislation, declared: "in all acts words importing the masculine gender shall be deemed and taken to include females. . ."[6] The importance of shortening the language of legislation can clearly be seen by Parliament's use of "deemed and taken." Statements similar to Parliament's are found in leases and other legal contracts today, but, as Casey Miller and Kate Swift point out in *The Handbook of Nonsexist Writing for Writers, Editors and Speakers*, "it was often conveniently ignored. In 1879, for example, a move to admit female physicians to the all-male Massachusetts Medical Society was effectively blocked on the grounds that the society's by-laws describing membership used the pronoun *he.*"[7] Julia Stanley is one of a number of writers who have discredited the "myth of generics" in English. Her essay contains many examples of ambiguous and "pseudo-generic" usages.[8]

Rather than rely on authority or opinion, some scholars have conducted experiments to determine whether or not today's speakers of English perceive the forms *man* and *he* as generic. In one study, Joseph Schneider and Sally Hacker asked some students to find appropriate illustrations for an anthropology book with chapter headings like "Man and His Environment," and "Man and His Family;" another group of students was given titles like "Family Life" and "Urban Life." The students who were assigned titles with the word *man* chose more illustrations of men only, while the second group chose more pictures showing men, women, and children. Other studies have confirmed our tendency to interpret *he* and *man* as masculine unless the context clearly indicates they are meant generically, the contrary of what is usually claimed. One experiment, conducted by Wendy Martyna, that tested the usage and meaning of these words among young people, found that women and men may be using the terms quite differently. The men's usage appears to be based on sex-specific (male) imagery, while the women's usage is based instead on the prescription that *he* should be used when the sex of the person is not specified. Things can now run smoothly with women believing that they are included while men know otherwise. 22

Being treated as a trivial exception, being made to go to the rear linguistically, or even being made to disappear, are not the worst things that happen to women in the English language. Our lopsided lexicon is well supplied with unpleasant labels for women. Many, although by no means all of these, are slang words. The editor of the 1960 edition of the *Dictionary of American Slang* writes that "most American slang is created and used by males." This observation may be prejudiced by the fact that most collectors of American slang are males, but in any case, the words referring to women should give us an idea of the attitudes of American men towards women. The dictionaries reveal an unpleasant picture indeed. 23

Disregarding the obscene terms, and that is quite a task, since the list of obscene words for women is long, if monotonous, we still find term after term referring to women in a sexually derogatory way. Consider the following small sample: *chick, hussy, tart, broad, dame,* and *bimbo.* In one study, "The Semantic Derogation of Women," Muriel Schulz found over one thousand 24 words and phrases which put women in their place in this way.[9] She analyzes a long series of words which started out as harmless terms or had a positive meaning, and gradually acquired negative connotations. It would seem that men find it difficult to talk about women without insulting them. The opposite is not true—few of the words have masculine counterparts. After going through the lists compiled by Schulz and other writers, one may begin to wonder about the popular belief that men talk about more serious topics than do women. Unless, of course, sexual jokes and insults constitute a serious topic, men should scarcely need so many derogatory terms. An interesting, if depressing, party game is to try to think of positive labels which are used for women.

Let's examine a few examples of words for women, their meanings and their histories. The woman of the house, or *housewife,* became a *hussy* with the passage of time, and eventually the word had to be reinvented with its original meaning. So much for the dignity of housewives. *Madam* and *mistress* did not change in form, but they took on new sex related meanings, while *Sir* and *master* participate in no double entendres. Many of the most insulting words began life as terms of endearment and evolved into sexual slurs. *Tart,* originally a term of endearment like *sweetie-pie,* came to mean a sexually desirable woman and then a prostitute, while *broad* originally meant a young woman. *Girl* started out meaning a child of either sex, then took on the following meanings at various stages: a female child, a servant, a prostitute, and a mistress. The process then seemed to reverse itself and *girl* has gone back to meaning a female child most of the time, although some of the other meanings remain. *Whore,* which has the same root as Latin *carus* 'dear', referred at first to a lover of either sex, then only to females, and finally came to mean prostitute. Almost all the words for female relatives—*mother, aunt, daughter,* and the like—have at one time or another been euphemisms for prostitute. Stanley analyzes 220 terms used to describe sexually promiscuous women.[10] This is just a sample of a much larger group, although there are relatively few words to describe sexually promiscuous men. Even though most of the derogatory terms for women originated as positive words, some of them did not: *shrew,* for example, never had a favorable connotation.

There are many animal metaphors used to insult both men and women, *dog* being an example. However, here too, there seem to be more terms of abuse for women: *chick* is one example, another is *cow,* which has been "a rude term for a woman" since the mid 1600s according to one recent dictionary of slang. Side by side with *dog,* which can be used for both sexes, we find *bitch,* limited to women. We know of no animal terms of abuse which are limited to men. In another semantic area, there is the large group of terms used both to label and to address women as objects to be consumed: *tomato, honey, cookie, sweetie-pie,* and *peach* are but a few examples. These are not necessarily derogatory and some of them, like *honey,* can be used by women to address men, but most refer largely or exclusively to women, and there is no parallel set used to refer to men. The food terms have not escaped the process of pejoration which commonly afflicts words for women, as is shown by the example of *tart,* which was included in our discussion of derogatory words.

In an earlier chapter we discussed some of the similarities between   27 stereotypes about the way women speak and beliefs about the speech of other powerless groups. Not surprisingly, there are also many derogatory labels for such groups in the form of ethnic and racial slurs and, like women, they are the butt of many jokes. Once again we find that Black women are doubly insulted. In the words of Patricia Bell Scott, "the English language has dealt a 'low-blow' to the self-esteem of developing Black womanhood."[11] After consulting the 1960 *American Thesaurus of Slang,* Scott states: "From a glance at the synonyms used to describe a Black person, especially a Black woman, one readily senses that there is something inherently negative about 'being Black' and specifically about being a Black woman. The words listed under the heading 'Negress,' in itself an offensive term, have largely negative and sexual connotations."[12] Some of the milder terms listed include *Black doll, femmoke,* and *nigger gal.* Black women do not seem to be treated much better by Black English. Scott also examined handbooks of Black language and found "a preoccupation with physical attractiveness, sex appeal, and skin color, with the light-skinned Black women receiving connotations of positiveness." She concludes that "much of Black English has also dealt Black Womanhood a 'low-blow.' "[13]

At the beginning of this chapter we asserted that one can determine a   28 great deal about the attitudes of a group of speakers by examining their linguistic usage. At the end of this chapter we must conclude that the attitudes towards women reflected in the usage of English speakers are depressing indeed. They have sometimes been belittled and treated as *girls;* at other times, they have been excluded or ignored by the pretense of "generic" terms; they have frequently been defined as sex objects or insulted as prostitutes, or, on the contrary, placed on a pedestal, desexed, and treated with deference, as *ladies.* It is no wonder that many women have rebelled against being the object of such language and have become creators and advocates of new usages designed to bring equity to the English language.

REFERENCES

All references are Frank and Ashen's.

1. Richard A. Spears, *Slang and Euphemism* (Middle Village, New York: Jonathan David, 1981), p. 21.

2. Robin Lakoff, *Language and Woman's Place* (New York: Harper & Row, 1975), p. 30.

3. Julia P. Stanley and Susan W. Robbins, "Sex-marked Predicates in English," *Papers in Linguistics* 11 (1978): 494.

4. Alma Graham, "The Making of a Nonsexist Dictionary," in *Language and Sex,* ed. Barrie Thorn and Nancy Henley (New York: Newbury House, 1975), p. 62.

5. Ann Bodine, "Androcentrism in Prescriptive Grammar: Singular 'They,' Sex-indefinite 'He' and 'He and She,' " *Language in Society* 4 (1975): 140.

6. Ibid., 136.

7. Casey Miller and Kate Swift, *The Handbook of Nonsexist Writing for Writers, Editors and Speakers* (New York: Lippincott & Crowell, 1980), p. 37.

8. Julia P. Stanley, "Gender-Marking in American English: Usage and Reference," in *Sexism and Language,* ed. Alleen Pace Nilsen, Haig Bosmajian, H. Lee Gershuny, and Julia P. Stanley (Urbana, Ill.: National Council of Teachers of English, 1977), pp. 43–74.

9. Muriel Schulz, "The Semantic Derogation of Women," in *Language and Sex,* ed. Barrie Thorn and Nancy Henley (Cambridge, Mass.: Newbury House, 1975), pp. 64–75.

10. Julia P. Stanley, "Paradigmatic Woman: The Prostitute," in *Papers in Language Variation,* ed. David L. Shores and Carol P. Hines (University, Ala.: University of Alabama Press, 1977).

11. Patricia Bell Scott, "The English Language and Black Womanhood: A Low Blow at Self-esteem," *Journal of Afro-American Issues* 2 (1974): 220.

12. Ibid.

13. Ibid., 220–221.

Questions for Discussion

1. Here are some words that refer to women or to activities attributed mainly to women. Following each word is one or more earlier meanings. Comment on political, social, linguistic, and sexual implications. Do you see a sexist pattern in the way the meanings of these words have changed over the years? What are some possible ways of accounting for the pattern?
   a. *shrew:* a malicious, evil, cunning man
   b. *termagant:* a male Saracen idol
   c. *harlot:* a young, base fellow
   d. *scold:* from Old Norse, a poet or lampooner
   e. *baggage:* a worthless fellow
   f. *frump:* a derisive snort > a jeer > ill humor > a cross, dowdy man or woman
   g. *witch:* originally either male or female
   h. *gossip: godsib,* "god-relative" > a familiar acquaintance
   i. *mistress:* feminine of *master*
   j. *madam:* "my lady"

2. Here are some other insulting terms for women: *broad, chippy, drab, floozy, slattern, slut, strumpet, trollop, troll, trot, doxy, hag, harridan, crone, biddy, harpy, vamp, nag, whore, bitch, piece, lay, tail, hen, old maid, wallflower, unladylike, unfeminine, snit, chit, tart, hussy.* What aspects of female reference do most of these words focus on? How many masculine counterparts to these words can you come up with? If there are many fewer insulting terms for men, what does this suggest about the relative differences between men and women, historically, in education, political clout, and social dominance?

3. Consider the way animal terms and animal imagery are employed to make value judgments, to praise, or to insult. Here is a list of animal images, many of them similes, that we use in everyday conversation. Discuss which of them refer mainly to women, which refer mainly to men, and

which may refer to either sex. Note which are insulting. Is there a higher percentage of insulting images among the terms that refer mainly to women? If so, why?

a. eats like a bird, pecks at food
b. acts like a minx
c. a real fox, real foxy
d. talks catty
e. leads a dog's life, works like a dog
f. stubborn as a mule
g. works like a horse
h. looks fishy
i. fishing for compliments
j. gullible as a fish
k. bull-headed
l. to cry crocodile tears
m. dumb as an ox
n. act like a goose
o. old bat
p. feel sheepish
q. quarrelsome as a shrew
r. busy as a beaver
s. mild as a lamb
t. filthy as a pig, eat like a pig
u. feel squirrely
v. graceful as a swan
w. playful as a kitten
x. act like a jackass
y. timid as a mouse, quiet as a mouse
z. bull in a china shop

Suggested Essay Topics

1. For 3 weeks conduct an experiment of your own. Buy yourself a small notebook, such as a 3-by-5-inch spiral pad, and carry it with you at all times. In it jot down all the terms of insult that you hear used in reference to men and women. After you have recorded a phrase or term once, make a mark after it for every repeated use that you hear. Also for each term jot down the social context in which it was used (formal, informal, in class, etc.), and record the sex of the speaker. Finally, record whether the sex of the audience was single or mixed. After 3 weeks of keeping records, organize your material and present it in an essay directed to your classmates, drawing whatever implications and conclusions you think are warranted about the way men and women talk about one another on your campus. You might consider making this a feature article or letter to the editor in the campus newspaper. Finally, although this is not part of the essay assignment as such, discuss in class any strong differences that show up in the records of men and women. See if you can determine, for

example, whether women talking together without men use more, less, or about the same number of insulting terms for men as men use when they are talking together without women.

2. Referring to the reference notes after the Frank and Ashen essay, select three of the following five sources to read more fully: Robin Lakoff, *Language and Woman's Place;* Alma Graham, "The Making of a Nonsexist Dictionary"; Muriel Schulz, "The Semantic Derogation of Women"; Julia P. Stanley, "Paradigmatic Woman: The Prostitute"; Patricia Bell Scott, "The English Language and Black Womanhood: A Low Blow at Self-esteem." After reading three of these sources, write an article for the campus newspaper in which you make the best arguments you can against sexist language usage, providing appropriate examples of its occurrence in the language and analyzing the pernicious social, political, and psychological effects it has on both users and referents.

Betty Roszak

Betty Roszak (b. 1933) is a writer, feminist, and co-editor with her husband, Theodore Roszak, of Masculine/Feminine, *the anthology in which the following essay first appeared.*

The temptation to misread is always strongest when we read essays that include, or seem to include, opinions that we find powerfully appealing or powerfully repulsive. We are more likely to notice statements with a high emotional charge, and more likely to remember them later on, forgetting the original supporting arguments. No doubt you have noticed how newspapers often emphasize a startling event or stirring statement so strongly that they sacrifice accuracy. Even when extracted sentences are quoted accurately, and they often are not, extraction itself always produces some *distortion. By quoting out of context, reporters even directly reverse an author's meaning because they fail, for example, to recognize or acknowledge that a passage was written ironically or that it in fact describes a position that the author was attempting to refute.*

The danger seems especially strong in an essay like this one. No matter where we stand on the issues Roszak raises, they are charged with emotion, and we are thus even more tempted than usual to notice only the charged moments and overlook how they work within the whole piece.

Any speedy reader can quickly discover here, for example, that Roszak is a feminist and that, like all feminists, she seeks to change things. She "favors abortion" and is convinced that men have on the whole been unjust to women. Whether we like these opinions or not, we are likely to let them overshadow her main points unless we discipline ourselves to the kind of reading that cares more about understanding others than feeding our prejudices or pet ideas. In short, to label the essay or the author with loose, general terms like pro-abortionist *or* radical *is to commit the fault that many*

*good thinkers, including Roszak, warn us about: the fault of polarizing opinions on
every issue into two, and often* only *two, positions and thus artificially simplifying
what is actually rich and many-sided.*

*As you read, then, resist deciding what the author's main point is until you
have not only read through the whole piece once or twice but thought about how it
is all put together—and why. Can you prepare a summary that would lead the author
to say, "Yes, that was my main point; you have understood"?*

*By now you've learned not to expect any simple rules for grasping an author's
true intention before deciding whether you agree or not. But there are two obvious
questions by which you can test your command of an author's intention, both of them
useful in reading Roszak. Ask yourself, "If I were writing this piece, trying to say
what I think she is saying, would I begin or end it the way she does?" Then ask,
"If this essay were my own, would I introduce what I take to be her thesis with the
title she uses?" Whenever the answer is "no" to one or both of these questions, either
the author has chosen badly or you should try out another possible view of the author's
intention.*

THE HUMAN CONTINUUM

From *Masculine/Feminine: Readings in Sexual Mythology and the Liberation of Women,* edited by Betty
Roszak and Theodore Roszak (1969).

Recent years have seen a resurgence of feminism that has taken main-   1
stream America by surprise. It began with the discontent of lonely middle-
class suburban housewives, whose malady was given a name by Betty Friedan
in her immensely influential book, *The Feminine Mystique.* But it didn't become
what we know as a "women's liberation movement" until the growth of the
New Left from the civil rights and peace movements of the early 1960's. It
wasn't until then that hundreds of young women, many of whom were
seasoned veterans of antiwar and antisegregationist activities, began to realize
the anomaly of their situation. Here they were, radical women involved in
a struggle for human equality and an end to oppression, willing to dedicate
years of effort to effecting political change, and what were they being allowed
to do? Typing, mimeographing, addressing envelopes, sweeping, providing
coffee and sexual diversion for the vigorous young men who were making all
the decisions. Far from going forward together to change the world, men and
women were once more stuck (and this time with a vengeance) with their
time-honored roles: the men to think and act; the women to serve and drudge.
The last equality—that between women and men—was never even mentioned. In fact, movement women found that they were even worse off than
apolitical women, because they were aware of and extremely sensitive to the
hypocrisies of their male colleagues who talked idealistically of equality, but
who acted scornful of women in their everyday lives. The rhetoric of equality
was directed at black, brown, and Third World *men* only. The New Left of
the late sixties had begun to take on a tough, aggressively male tone, born

of the idolization of Ché Guevara, guerrilla warfare, and admiration for the exaggerated, overcompensating manliness of the Black Panthers. As nonviolence, exemplified by Martin Luther King, Jr., became discredited by revolutionary and black militancy, so the tough style became a political requirement. In deference to this new brutalism men found it easy to take the necessary traditional he-man attitude toward women, the attitude of dominance and power. This left women in a bewildering dilemma. Were they to remain in a movement which allowed them to exist only as lackeys and silently submissive bedmates, or would they refuse to accept a subordinate status?

As this dilemma is being resolved today, there sounds in the background the laughter of contemptuous radical men: "Crazy feminist bitches!" The words merely echo a shared male ridicule that knows no class lines. Women find themselves of necessity beginning to re-examine the traditions of misogyny that even radical men have unknowingly inherited. 2

In our cultural past "Woman" was the symbol of sex; and sex, though necessary, was at the same time known to be an abhorrent evil, a degrading passion. In the Middle Ages, the masculine world view of the church dared not make light of women. Church authorities of the fifteenth century, ever on the alert for the malevolence of the devil, used a popular handbook on the identification and treatment of witches, the *Malleus Maleficarum,* in searching out evil in the form of women. "What else is woman," says this medieval antisubversive activities manual, "but a foe to friendship, an unescapable punishment, a necessary evil, a natural temptation, a desirable calamity, a domestic danger, a delectable detriment, an evil of nature painted with fair colors?" By the eighteenth century, Rousseau, one of France's most prolific proponents of democratic equality, could write with impunity, "Women have in general no love of any art; they have no proper knowledge of any; and they have no genius," thus curtly dismissing half of humanity to a status of hopeless inferiority. By mid-nineteenth century, the "evil of nature" had turned into an object of scorn, and Schopenhauer's indictment of women as "that undersized, narrow-shouldered, broad-hipped, and short-legged race," denied women even their beauty, their "fair colors," along with their intellectual capacity. 3

Today's predominantly male society no longer sees women as evil, at least on the surface. The ambivalent fear and attraction of the Middle Ages has changed along with the prevailing attitude toward sex. Now that sexuality has lost its mystery, the once dangerous and seductive female can be safely ignored and denied her power. The fear has turned to ridicule. One cannot ignore evil, but one can pretend that the ridiculous does not exist. Men irritably ask the rhetorical question (echoing Freud), "What do women want?" meaning, of course, that anything women want is absurd. The question is asked not of individual women but of the world, and in an exasperated tone, as if women were dumb and couldn't answer. The false barrier continues to be built: "We" cannot understand "Them." Why are "They" so res- 4 tive? Further communication between the sexes seems useless. Always it is men talking to men about women.

The fact of ridicule is constantly with us. When it was proposed in 1969 5 in the British House of Commons that attention be paid to developing a contraceptive pill for men, "the idea provoked hearty laughter," according to Paul Vaughan in the London *Observer.* Moreover, he tells us, the British government has rejected outright any allocation of funds for research on a pill for men. When the question was under discussion in the House of Lords, one Labour peer advised the government to ignore " 'these do-gooders who take all the fun out of life' (laughter)." Researchers explain their reluctance to tamper with the male germ cells. Yet the same researchers have not hesitated to tamper with the female germ cells in developing the pill for women. Nor have unpleasant side effects or hazards to women's health deterred them, while they quickly stopped research on a substance being tested on men because it was noted that when men drank alcohol while taking it, their eyes became reddened! Doctors have been known to laugh at the mention of labor pains during childbirth and in the not too distant past have been willing to stand by, calmly withholding anesthetics while women underwent great agonies in labor. So, too, male legislators have laughed at the idea of the legalization of abortion, hinting at unprecedented promiscuity (on the part of women, not men) if such a thing were allowed. Meanwhile, thousands of desperate women die each year as the direct result of male laws making abortion illegal.

Women are learning the meaning of this male laughter and indiffer- 6 ence in the face of the most hazardous and serious biological enterprise women undertake, willingly or not. And in cultural enterprises, whenever women attempt to enter any of the male-dominated professions (who ever heard of a woman chairman of the board, a woman orchestra conductor, a woman Chief Justice, a woman President or a woman getting equal pay for equal work?), we again hear the familiar laughter of male ridicule. If we look at the image of woman men present to us in novels, drama, or advertising, we see a scatterbrained, helpless flunky, or a comical sex-pot, or a dumb beast of burden. Is this what they mean when they exhort us in popular song to "enjoy being a girl"? But women are beginning to relearn the old lesson: in this male-dominated world, it is a misfortune to be born female.

From the very moment of birth a higher value is placed by his society 7 on the male infant, a value which accumulates and accelerates into his adult life. By the time the female infant has grown into adulthood, however, if she has learned society's lessons well, she will have come to acquiesce in her second-class status—to accept unconsciously the burden of her inferiority. No matter what honors she wins, what her exploits, what her achievements or talents, she will always be considered a woman first, and thus inferior to the least honored, talented and worthy male of that society—foremost a sexual being, still fair game for his aggressive sexual fantasies. As Albert

Memmi puts it, ". . . every man, no matter how low he may be, holds women in contempt and judges masculinity to be an inestimable good."

Male society's disparagement of women has all the force of an uncon-   8 scious conspiracy. It is even more subtle than the racist and colonial oppressions to which it is so closely allied, because it is softened and hidden by the silken padding of eroticism. We women grow to think that because we are wanted as lovers, wives, and mothers, it might be because we are wanted as human beings. But if by chance or natural inclination we attempt to move outside these male-defined and male-dependent roles, we find that they are, in reality, barriers.

For many women this is the first inkling of the fact of oppression.   9 Pressed from birth into the mold of an exclusively sexual being, the growing girl soon develops what Sartre calls the "phantom personality"; she comes to feel that she is what "they" tell her she is. This other self envelops her like a second skin. When she begins to experience a natural sense of constriction (which is growth), her real feelings clash with what "they" say she should feel. The more forceful and vital she is, the more she will have to repress her real feelings, because girls are to be passive and manipulatable. She becomes frightened, suspicious, anxious about herself. A sense of malaise overcomes her. She must obey the social prohibitions which force her back into the mold of the sexual being. She is not to desire or act, but to *be* desired and acted upon. Many women give up the struggle right there and dully force themselves to remain stunted human beings. The butterfly must not be allowed to come forth from its chrysalis: her vitality is only allowed guilty expression in certain private moments or is turned into sullen resentment which smolders during all her unfulfilled life.

Family and home, which look like a refuge and a sanctuary, turn out to   10 be the same kind of trap. Beyond the marriage ghetto there is outright rejection and exclusion. In the work world there are lower wages, union and employer discrimination, the prohibitive cost of child care. In the professions mere tokenism takes the place of acceptance and equality. The same is true in government and political activity. The single woman knows only too well the psychological exclusionism practiced by male society. She is suspect, or comic, if over a certain age. All men assume she would be married if she could—there must be something psychologically wrong with her if she isn't. And single women have the added burden of not being socially acceptable without an "escort"—a man, any man.

Further, women are the nonexistent people in the very life of the nation   11 itself—now more so even than the blacks who have at last forced themselves into the nation's consciousness. The invisible man has become the invisible *woman.* William James called it a "fiendish punishment" that "one should be turned loose on society and remain absolutely unnoticed by all the members thereof." Yet that is the treatment male society metes out to those women who wish to escape from the male-defined erotic roles. Left out of the history books, not credited with a past worth mentioning in the masculine chronicles of state, women of today remain ignorant of women's movements of the past and the important role individual women have played in the history of the human race. Male historical scholarship sees the suffragists and feminists of the nineteenth century as figures of fun, worthy of only a paragraph here and there, as footnotes on the by-ways of social customs, far from the main roads of masculine endeavor: the wars, political intrigues, and diplomatic maneuverings which make up the history of power.

With the blacks and other oppressed minorities, women can say, "How 12 can we hope to shape the future without some knowledge of our past?" If the historic heroines of feminism are ignored or treated trivially, today's women are hindered from dealing with their own repression. This undermining of self-confidence is common to all oppressed peoples, along with the doubts of the reality of one's own perceptions. Women's self-rejection as worthwhile human beings thus becomes an inevitable extension of the cycle of oppression.

But radical women have begun to rebel against the false, exclusively 13 sexual image men have created for them. And in rebelling, many women are seeing the need for bypassing the marriage ghetto altogether. They are recognizing the true nature of the institution of marriage as an economic bargain glossed over by misty sentimentalizing. Wash off the romantic love ideal, and underneath we see the true face of the marriage contract. It is grimly epitomized by the immortal slogan found chalked on innumerable honeymoon getaway cars: "She got him today; he'll get her tonight." Or, as put more sophisticatedly by Robert Briffault, "Whether she aims at freedom or a home a woman is thrown back on the defense of her own interests; she must defend herself against man's attempt to bind her, or sell herself to advantage. Woman is to man a sexual prey; man is to woman an economic prey." And this kind of oppression cuts across all economic class lines, even though there may be social differences between streetwalker Jane X, housewife Joan Y, and debutante Jacqueline Z. One may sell her body for a few dollars to the likeliest passerby; one for a four-bedroomed house in the suburbs; and one for rubies and yachts. But all must sell their bodies in order to participate in the bargain. Yet if women were to refuse to enter into the sexual bargain, they not only would refute the masculine idea of women as property, but they also would make it possible to free men from the equally self-destructive role of sole breadwinner. Thus there would be a chance to break the predatory cycle.

Beyond marriage and the old, outmoded roles, radical women are seek- 14 ing new ways of dealing with the oppressive institutions of society. No longer will they acquiesce in the pattern of dominance and submission. They are beginning to take control of their own lives, building new relationships, developing new modes of work, political activity, child rearing and education. Rejection of male exploitation must start with psychic as well as economic independence. The new female consciousness is going to develop cooperative forms of child care; women's centers as sanctuaries for talk, planning, and action; all-female communes where women can escape for a while from the all-pervading male influence; the sharing of domestic drudgery with men in cooperative living arrangements; the building up of competence and self-confidence in such previously male-dependent endeavors as general mechanical repair work, carpentry, and construction.

By rejecting the false self for so long imposed upon us and in which we   15
have participated unwittingly, we women can forge the self-respect necessary in order to discover our own true values. Only when we refuse to be made use of by those who despise and ridicule us, can we throw off our heavy burden of resentment. We must take our lives in our own hands. This is what liberation means. Out of a common oppression women can break the stereotypes of masculine-feminine and enter once more into the freedom of the human continuum.

Women's liberation will thus inevitably bring with it, as a concomitant,   16
men's liberation. Men, no less than women, are imprisoned by the heavy carapace of their sexual stereotype. The fact that they gain more advantages and privileges from women's oppression has blinded them to their own bondage which is the bondage of an artificial duality. This is the male problem: the positing of a difference, the establishment of a dichotomy emphasizing oppositeness. Men are to behave in this way; women in that; women do this; men do the other. And it just so happens that the way men behave and act is important and valuable, while what women do is unimportant and trivial. Instead of identifying both the sexes as part of humanity, there is a false separation which is to the advantage of men. Masculine society has insisted on seeing in sexuality that same sense of conflict and competition that it has imposed upon its relation to the planet as a whole. From the bedroom to the board room to the international conference table, separateness, differentiation, opposition, exclusion, antithesis have been the cause and goal of the male politics of power. Human characteristics belonging to the entire species have been crystallized out of the living flow of human experience and made into either/or categories. This male habit of setting up boundary lines between imagined polarities has been the impetus for untold hatred and destruction. Masculine/feminine is just one of such polarities among many, including body/mind, organism/environment, plant/animal, good/evil, black/white, feeling/intellect, passive/active, sane/insane, living/dead. Such language hardens what is in reality a continuum and a unity into separate mental images always in opposition to one another.

If we think of ourselves as "a woman" or "a man," we are already   17
participating in a fantasy of language. People become preoccupied with images of one another—surely the deepest and most desperate alienation there is. The very process of conceptualization warps our primary, unitary feelings of what we are. Mental images take the place of the primary stimuli of sex which involve the entire organism. Instead of a sense of identification, we have pornographic sex with its restrictive emphasis on genital stimulation. This "short circuiting between genitals and cortex" as William E. Galt calls it (in a brilliant article, "The Male-Female Dichotomy," in *Psychiatry,* 1943) is a peculiarly modern distortion of the original, instinctual nature of sex. We are suffering from D. H. Lawrence's "sex in the head." In childhood we know

sexuality as a generalized body response; the body is an erotic organ of sensation. To this Freud gave the nasty name of polymorphous perversity. But it is actually the restriction to localized genitality of the so-called "normal" adult that is perverted, in the sense of a twisting away from the original and primary body eroticism. Biological evidence indicates that the sex response is a primitive, gross sensory stimulation—diffused and nonlocalizable. Phallic man, however, wishes to assert the primacy of his aggressive organ. The ego of phallic man divides him off from the rest of the world, and in this symbolic division he maintains the deep-seated tradition of man *against* woman, wresting his sexual pleasure *from* her, like the spoils of war. The total body response must be repressed in order to satisfy the sharpness of his genital cravings.

But in the primary sexual response of the body, there is no differentiation between man or woman; there is no "man," there is no "woman" (mental images), just a shared organism responding to touch, smell, taste, sound. The sexual response can then be seen as one part of the species' total response to and participation in, the environment. We sense the world with our sensitive bodies as an ever-changing flow of relationships in which we move and partake. Phallic man sees the world as a collection of things from which he is sharply differentiated. If we consider the phenomenon of the orgasm in this light, we can see that its basic qualities are the same for male and female. There can be no real distinction between the feminine and masculine *self-abandonment* in a sexual climax. The self, or controlling power, simply vanishes. All talk of masculine or feminine orgasm misses this point entirely, because this is a surrender which goes beyond masculine or feminine. Yet how many men are there who are willing to see their own sexual vitality as exactly this self-surrender? 18

When men want desperately to preserve that which they deem masculine—the controlling power—then they insist on the necessity of the feminine as that which must be controlled and mastered. Men force themselves into the role of phallic man and seek always to be hard, to be tough, to be competitive, to assert their "manhood." Alan Watts wisely sees this masculine striving for rigidity as "nothing more than an emotional paralysis" which causes men to misunderstand the bisexuality of their own nature, to force a necessarily unsatisfactory sexual response, and to be exploitative in their relations with women and the world. 19

According to Plato's myth, the ancients thought of men and women as originally a single being cut asunder into male and female by an angry god.* There is a good biological basis to this myth; although the sexes are externally differentiated, they are still structurally homologous. Psychologically, too, the speculations of George Groddeck are apt: 20

Personal sex cuts right across the fundamental qualities of human nature; the very word suggests the violent splitting asunder of humanity

*The reference here is to Aristophanes' speech in the *Symposium*.

into male and female. *Sexus* is derived from *secare,* to cut, from which we also get *segmentum,* a part cut from a circle. It conveys the idea that man and woman once formed a unity, that together they make a complete whole, the perfect circle of the individuum and that both sections share the properties of this individuum. These suggestions are of course in harmony with the ancient Hebrew legend, which told how God first created a human being who was both male and female, Adam-Lilith, and later sawed this asunder.[1]

The dichotomizing of human qualities can thus be seen as a basic error in men's understanding of nature. Biologically, both sexes are always present in each. Perhaps with the overcoming of women's oppression, the woman in man will be allowed to emerge. If, as Coleridge said, great minds are androgynous, there can be no feminine or masculine ideal, but only as the poet realizes,

> . . . what is true is human,
> homosexuality, heterosexuality
> There is something more important:
>
> to be human
> in which kind
> is kind.[2]

REFERENCES

All references are Roszak's.

1. *The World of Man* (New York: Vision Press, 1951).
2. Clayton Eshleman, "Holding Duncan's Hand."

Questions for Discussion

1. What is the *main* thesis of Roszak's essay? Does your answer fit her choice of a title and a conclusion? (See again our questions at the end of the introduction, p. 666.)

2. Did any part of this essay make you feel angry or uncomfortable? Elated or supported? If not, what emotions did you feel? Can you explain the basis of your reaction?

3. Discuss with your classmates whether men and women respond differently to Roszak's essay. Do the men find in it a different thesis than the women do? Do the men react to it with different emotions?

4. Conduct a poll of your classmates on the question "Does Roszak argue her case persuasively, providing adequate evidence at each step for the beliefs

she wants us to accept?" Those who answer "no" should be asked to find unsupported assertions, and those who answer "yes" should be asked to explain why no further evidence is needed. After discussion, conduct the poll again. Are there any changes of vote? How do you account for the results of your experiment?

5. In paragraph 6, we find a parenthetical question that might be answered as follows: "Well, actually, we *have* heard by now of women who head boards, conduct symphony orchestras, and get equal pay for equal work. We now have a woman justice of the Supreme Court—not quite the same as chief justice or president, perhaps, but we're moving fast." Do you think that such a reply weakens Roszak's case? Why or why not?

6. When you hear terms like *radical, pro-abortionist, feminist,* and *militant* thrown about, do you think that the people who use these terms recognize that there may be different *kinds* of each one of them? Or does the use of such general terms almost automatically erase differences of kind? Through open discussion try to determine whether the class members who use any of these labels to describe themselves really belong to homogeneous groups or whether they retain individual differences despite the labels they accept.

Suggested Essay Topics

1. Roszak generalizes freely about the typical experience of males and females in our society. Your own experience, presumably, either matches or fails to match her generalizations. Write an autobiographical essay (or, if you prefer, a personal letter to Roszak) in which you describe as precisely as you can how you developed your picture of what it means to be male or female in our society. Don't try to describe any present inhibitions or anxieties. Your task is to dramatize how you first learned that "what a *man* does (or is like) is so-and-so, while what a *woman* does (or is like) is such-and-such." Then write a concluding paragraph or so appraising whether Roszak's picture fits your experience. (*Note:* Do not try to develop a general thesis about sex or sexual relations in American society or try to refute or support Roszak's whole position. Limit yourself to comparing your memories with her claims about what men and women are taught about themselves "from the very moment of birth" [¶7].)

2. In paragraph 18 Roszak talks about the necessity for men to learn "self-surrender" as an enlargement of sexual response. She also argues that the false distinction between male orgasm and female orgasm intensifies alienation between men and women. Write an essay directed to Roszak describing the earliest encounters you can remember with sexual images in fiction (novels, plays, movies, TV)—images that formed your first expectations about sex in general and about your role as a male or female partner. Looking at these images from Roszak's point of view, assess whether they were "good" for you or not. Be as clear as possible about the reasons for your judgment.

Ideas in Debate

Andrea Dworkin
Rosemarie Tong

Andrea Dworkin

How do you feel about pornography? Would you call it obscene, immoral, and sadistic or do these terms seem too heavy-handed and judgmental? Would you prefer terms such as juvenile, naughty, or dirty? Do you feel that pornography is criminal and that producers and consumers of it should be legally prosecuted? If so, for breaking what law? Are you ever a consumer of pornography yourself? Do you go to X-rated movies; rent videotapes from the "no-one-under-18-admitted" room at your local video store; buy magazines in which women (or, in some cases, men) are objectified, depicted as taking pleasure in being beaten, raped, or humiliated; or tell jokes in which the listener is expected to take pleasure in the "comic" antics of men possessing women sexually against their will or taking delight in sexually inflicted pain? Or, if you perform any of these acts, have you not considered them as the consumption of pornography but as mere entertainment or fun?

Whatever your views on this topic have been up to this point, Andrea Dworkin (b. 1946) will probably succeed in making you think more concretely and vividly about the production, consumption, and consequences of pornography than you ever have before. She is relentless in exposing the harm of pornography, relentless in refusing to let pornography be covered up or waved away with the usual sniggers, evasions, or clichés: She was probably asking for it, some women like that sort of thing, boys will be boys, women get what they advertise for, and so on.

Dworkin's denunciation are not simply exhortative or moralistic, however; she has been instrumental in pushing for the passage of laws in various cities that will allow women or other victims of pornography to sue the makers and sellers of pornography on the grounds that such acts constitute a violation of their civil rights. Even though such a law has been passed three times—twice in Minneapolis in 1983 and 1984 and once in Indianapolis in 1984—and has been discussed, but not passed in other cities as well. So far, it has been overturned as unconstitutional by the second federal appeals court. Thus there are no such laws on the books at present, but the agitation for them continues on the part of some, for whose interests Dworkin is the most vocal and compelling advocate.

Because Dworkin's examples of women who have been victimized by pornography are so vivid and her rhetoric of outraged protest is so strong, one cannot remain neutral about the issue in the presence of her prose. She forces us to think both in legal and moral terms about what it means, first, to depict women as enjoying rape and other forms of sexual brutality, and, second, what it means to enjoy such depictions. How do we view the women shown in pornography, the women who are depicted as enjoying being raped, beaten, and humiliated? Regardless of our own sex, do we think these women are somehow a breed apart, somehow fundamentally different from the women we know as wives, mothers, and sisters? Do we think because they are obviously "asking for it" that it is okay for them to "get it"? Is this just one aspect of what any normal woman might want, or are the women in pornography somehow pathological, crazy, or sick? If they are, what does it say about the men who believe this and still enjoy seeing pathological, crazy, sick women being tortured and raped?

Whether or not you agree with her legal remedy for pornography, Dworkin is a serious woman writing about a serious issue that she tackles with lucidity, determination, and, above all, an incandescent passion.

PORNOGRAPHY MUST BE STOPPED: "BEAVER'S ENDURED TOO MUCH TO TURN BACK NOW"

Our title. From chapter 6 and the introduction to *Pornography: Men Possessing Women* (1979). The introduction was written in 1989 when the book was reissued.

PORNOGRAPHY, A DEFINITION

Consider also our spirits that break a little each time we see ourselves in chains or full labial display for the conquering male viewer, bruised or on our knees, screaming a real or pretended pain to delight the sadist, pretending to enjoy what we don't enjoy, to be blind to the images of our sisters that really haunt us—humiliated often enough ourselves by the truly obscene idea that sex and the domination of women must be combined.

Gloria Steinem, "Erotica and Pornography"

Somehow every indignity the female suffers ultimately comes to be symbolized in a sexuality that is held to be her responsibility, her shame. Even the self-denigration required of the prostitute is an emotion urged upon all women, but rarely with as much success: not as frankly, not as openly, not as efficiently. It can be summarized in one four-letter word. And the word is not *fuck,* it's *cunt.* Our self-contempt originates in this: in knowing we are cunt. This is what we are supposed to be about—our essence, our offense.

Kate Millett, *The Prostitution Papers*

I can never have my fill of killing whores.

Euripides' Orestes, in *Orestes*

The word *pornography,* derived from the ancient Greek *porne* and *graphos,* 1
means "writing about whores." *Porne* means "whore," specifically and exclusively the lowest class of whore, which in ancient Greece was the brothel slut
available to all male citizens. The *porne* was the cheapest (in the literal sense),
least regarded, least protected of all women, including slaves. She was, simply
and clearly and absolutely, a sexual slave. *Graphos* means "writing, etching,
or drawing."

The word *pornography* does not mean "writing about sex" or "depictions 2
of the erotic" or "depictions of sexual acts" or "depictions of nude bodies"
or "sexual representations" or any other such euphemism. It means the
graphic depiction of women as vile whores. In ancient Greece, not all prostitutes were considered vile: only the *porneia.*

Contemporary pornography strictly and literally conforms to the 3
word's root meaning: the graphic depiction of vile whores, or, in our language, sluts, cows (as in: sexual cattle, sexual chattel), cunts. The word has
not changed its meaning and the genre is not misnamed. The only change
in the meaning of the word is with respect to its second part, *graphos:* now
there are cameras—there is still photography, film, video. The methods of
graphic depiction have increased in number and in kind: the content is the
same; the meaning is the same; the purpose is the same; the status of the
women depicted is the same; the sexuality of the women depicted is the
same; the value of the women depicted is the same. With the technologically advanced methods of graphic depiction, real women are required for
the depiction as such to exist.

The word *pornography* does not have any other meaning than the one 4
cited here, the graphic depiction of the lowest whores. Whores exist to
serve men sexually. Whores exist only within a framework of male sexual
domination. Indeed, outside that framework the notion of whores would be
absurd and the usage of women as whores would be impossible. The word
whore is incomprehensible unless one is immersed in the lexicon of male
domination. Men have created the group, the type, the concept, the epithet,
the insult, the industry, the trade, the commodity, the reality of woman as
whore. Woman as whore exists within the objective and real system of
male sexual domination. The pornography itself is objective and real and
central to the male sexual system. The valuation of women's sexuality in
pornography is objective and real because women are so regarded and so
valued. The force depicted in pornography is objective and real because
force is so used against women. The debasing of women depicted in pornography and intrinsic to it is objective and real in that women are so
debased. The uses of women depicted in pornography are objective and real
because women are so used. The women used in pornography are used in
pornography. The definition of women articulated systematically and consistently in pornography is objective and real in that real women exist
within and must live with constant reference to the boundaries of this def-

inition. The fact that pornography is widely believed to be "sexual representations" or "depictions of sex" emphasizes only that the valuation of women as low whores is widespread and that the sexuality of women is perceived as low and whorish in and of itself. The fact that pornography is widely believed to be "depictions of the erotic" means only that the debasing of women is held to be the real pleasure of sex. As Kate Millett wrote, women's sexuality is reduced to the one essential: "cunt . . . our essence, our offense."[1] The idea that pornography is "dirty" originates in the conviction that the sexuality of women is dirty and is actually portrayed in pornography; that women's bodies (especially women's genitals) are dirty and lewd in themselves. Pornography does not, as some claim, refute the idea that female sexuality is dirty: instead, pornography embodies and exploits this idea; pornography sells and promotes it.

In the United States, the pornography industry is larger than the re-   5
cord and film industries combined. In a time of widespread economic impoverishment, it is growing: more and more male consumers are eager to spend more and more money on pornography—on depictions of women as vile whores. Pornography is now carried by cable television; it is now being marketed for home use in video machines. The technology itself demands the creation of more and more *porneia* to meet the market opened up by the technology. Real women are tied up, stretched, hanged, fucked, gang-banged, whipped, beaten, and begging for more. In the photographs and films, real women are used as *porneia* and real women are depicted as *porneia.* To profit, the pimps must supply the *porneia* as the technology widens the market for the visual consumption of women being brutalized and loving it. One picture is worth a thousand words. The number of pictures required to meet the demands of the marketplace determines the number of *porneia* required to meet the demands of graphic depiction. The numbers grow as the technology and its accessibility grow. The technology by its very nature encourages more and more passive acquiescence to the graphic depictions. Passivity makes the already credulous consumer more credulous. He comes to the pornography a believer; he goes away from it a missionary. The technology itself legitimizes the uses of women conveyed by it.

In the male system, women are sex; sex is the whore. The whore is *porne*,   6
the lowest whore, the whore who belongs to *all* male citizens: the slut, the cunt. Buying her is buying pornography. Having her is having pornography. Seeing her is seeing pornography. Seeing her sex, especially her genitals, is seeing pornography. Seeing her in sex is seeing the whore in sex. Using her is using pornography. Wanting her means wanting pornography. Being her means being pornography.

. . .

[1]Kate Millett, *The Prostitution Papers* (New York: Avon Books, 1973), p. 95.

ANTI-PORNOGRAPHY, A MANIFESTO

1

> I did not hesitate to let it be known of me, that the white man who
> expected to succeed in whipping, must also succeed in killing me.
>
> Frederick Douglass, *Narrative*
> *of the Life of Frederick Douglass*
> *An American Slave Written by*
> *Himself*

In 1838, at the age of 21, Frederick Douglass* became a runaway slave,   7
a hunted fugitive. Though later renowned as a powerful political orator, he
spoke his first public words with trepidation at an abolitionist meeting—a
meeting of white people—in Massachusetts in 1841. Abolitionist leader William Lloyd Garrison recalled the event:

> He came forward to the platform with a hesitancy and embarrassment,
> necessarily the attendants of a sensitive mind in such a novel position.
> After apologizing for his ignorance, and reminding the audience that
> slavery was a poor school for the human intellect and heart, he proceeded
> to narrate some of the facts in his own history as a slave. . . . As soon
> as he had taken his seat, filled with hope and admiration, I rose . . .
> [and] . . . reminded the audience of the peril which surrounded this
> self-emancipated young man at the North,—even in Massachusetts, on
> the soil of the Pilgrim Fathers, among the descendants of revolutionary
> sires; and I appealed to them, whether they would ever allow him to be
> carried back into slavery—law or no law, constitution or no constitution.[1]

Always in danger as a fugitive, Douglass became an organizer for the abolitionists; the editor of his own newspaper, which advocated both abolition and
women's rights; a station chief for the underground railroad; a close comrade
of John Brown's; and the only person willing, at the Seneca Falls Convention
in 1848, to second Elizabeth Cady Stanton's resolution demanding the vote
for women. To me, he has been a political hero: someone whose passion for
human rights was both visionary and rooted in action; whose risk was real,
not rhetorical; whose endurance in pursuing equality set a standard for political honor. In his writings, which were as eloquent as his orations, his repudia-
tion of subjugation was uncompromising. His political intelligence, which
was both analytical and strategic, was suffused with emotion: indignation at
human pain, grief at degradation, anguish over suffering, fury at apathy and
collusion. He hated oppression. He had an empathy for those hurt by inequality that crossed lines of race, gender, and class because it was an empathy
animated by his own experience—his own experience of humiliation and his
own experience of dignity.

*For an essay by Frederick Douglass, see Chapter 7.

To put it simply, Frederick Douglass was a serious man—a man serious 8
in the pursuit of freedom. Well, you see the problem. Surely it is self-evident.
What can any such thing have to do with us—with women in our time?
Imagine—in present time—a woman saying, and meaning, that a man who
expected to succeed in whipping, must also succeed in killing her. Suppose
there were a politics of liberation premised on that assertion—an assertion not
of ideology but of deep and stubborn outrage at being misused, a resolute
assertion, a serious assertion by serious women. What are serious women; are
there any; isn't seriousness about freedom by women for women grotesquely
comic; we don't want to be laughed at, do we? What would this politics of
liberation be like? Where would we find it? What would we have to do?
Would we have to do something other than dress for success? Would we have
to stop the people who are hurting us from hurting us? Not debate them; stop
them. Would we have to stop slavery? Not discuss it; stop it. Would we have
to stop pretending that our rights are protected in this society? Would we
have to be so grandiose, so arrogant, so unfeminine, as to believe that the
streets we walk on, the homes we live in, the beds we sleep in, are *ours*—
belong to us—really belong to us: we decide what is right and what is wrong
and if something hurts us, it stops. It is, of course, gauche to be too sincere
about these things, and it is downright ridiculous to be serious. Intelligent
people are well mannered and moderate, even in pursuing freedom. Smart
women whisper and say please.

Now imagine Cherry Tart or Bunny or Pet or Beaver saying, and mean- 9
ing, that a man who expected to succeed in whipping must also succeed in
killing her. She says it; she means it. It is not a pornographic scenario in which
she is the dummy forced by the pimp-ventriloquist to say the ubiquitous
No-That-Means-Yes. It is not the usual sexual provocation created by pornographers using a woman's body, the subtext of which is: I refuse to be
whipped so whip me harder, whip me more; I refuse to be whipped, what I
really want is for you to kill me; whip me, then kill me; kill me, then whip
me; whatever you want, however you want it—was it good for you? Instead,
the piece on the page or in the film steps down and steps out: I'm real, she
says. Like Frederick Douglass, she will be hesitant and embarrassed. She will
feel ignorant. She will tell a first-person story about her own experience in
prostitution, in pornography, as a victim of incest, as a victim of rape, as
someone who has been beaten or tortured, as someone who has been bought
and sold. She may not remind her audience that sexual servitude is a poor
school for the human intellect and heart—sexually violated, often since childhood, she may not know the value of her human intellect or her human
heart—and the audience cannot be counted on to know that she deserved
better than she got. Will there be someone there to implore the audience to
help her escape the pornography—law or no law, constitution or no constitution; will the audience understand that as long as the pornography of her
exists she is a captive of it, a fugitive from it? Will the audience be willing
to fight for her freedom by fighting against the pornography of her, because,
as Linda Marchiano said of *Deep Throat*, "every time someone watches that

film, they are watching me being raped"?[2] Will the audience understand that she is standing in for those who didn't get away; will the audience understand that those who didn't get away were *someone*—each one was someone? Will the audience understand what stepping down from the page or out of the film cost her—what it took for her to survive, for her to escape, for her to dare to speak now about what happened to her then?

"I'm an incest survivor, ex-pornography model, and ex-prostitute," the woman says. "My incest story begins before preschool and ends many years later—this was with my father. I was also molested by an uncle and a minister . . . my father forced me to perform sexual acts with men at a stag party when I was a teenager. . . . My father was my pimp in pornography. There were three occasions from ages nine to sixteen when he forced me to be a pornography model . . . in Nebraska, so, yes, it does happen here."[3]

I was thirteen when I was forced into prostitution and pornography, the woman says. I was drugged, raped, gang-raped, imprisoned, beaten, sold from one pimp to another, photographed by pimps, photographed by tricks;* I was used in pornography and they used pornography on me; "[t]hey knew a child's face when they looked into it. It was clear that I was not acting of my own free will. I was always covered with welts and bruises. . . . It was even clearer that I was sexually inexperienced. I literally didn't know what to do. So they showed me pornography to teach me about sex and then they would ignore my tears as they positioned my body like the women in the pictures and used me."[4]

"As I speak about pornography, here, today," the woman says, "I am talking about my life." I was raped by my uncle when I was ten, by my stepbrother and stepfather by the time I was twelve. My stepbrother was making pornography of me by the time I was fourteen. "I was not even sixteen years old and my life reality consisted of sucking cocks, posing nude, performing sexual acts and actively being repeatedly raped."[5]

These are the women in the pictures; they have stepped out, though the pictures may still exist. They have become very serious women; serious in the pursuit of freedom. There are many thousands of them in the United States, not all first put in pornography as children though most were sexually molested as children, raped or otherwise abused again later, eventually becoming homeless and poor. They are feminists in the antipornography movement, and they don't want to debate "free speech." Like Frederick Douglass, they are fugitives from the men who made a profit off of them. They live in jeopardy, always more or less in hiding. They organize to help others escape. They write—in blood, their own. They publish sometimes, including their own newsletters. They demonstrate; they resist; they disappear when the danger gets too close. The Constitution has nothing for them—no help, no protection, no dignity, no solace, no justice. The law has nothing for them—

10

11

12

13

*Prostitutes' term for men who purchase sexual favors.

no recognition of the injuries done them by pornography, no reparations for what has been taken from them. They are real, and even though this society will do nothing for them, they are women who have resolved that the man who expects to succeed in whipping must also succeed in killing them. This changes the nature of the women's movement. It must stop slavery. The runaway slave is now part of it.

2

One new indulgence was to go out evenings alone. This I worked out carefully in my mind, as not only a right but a duty. Why should a woman be deprived of her only free time, the time allotted to recreation? Why must she be dependent on some man, and thus forced to please him if she wished to go anywhere at night?

A stalwart man once sharply contested my claim to this freedom to go alone. "Any true man," he said with fervor, "is always ready to go with a woman at night. He is her natural protector." "Against what?" I inquired. As a matter of fact, the thing a woman is most afraid to meet on a dark street is her natural protector. Singular.

Charlotte Perkins Gilman,
*The Living of Charlotte
Perkins Gilman: An Autobiography*

She was thirteen. She was at a Girl Scout camp in northern Wisconsin.   14
She went for a long walk in the woods alone during the day. She had long blond hair. She saw three hunters reading magazines, talking, joking. One looked up and said: "There's a live one." She thought they meant a deer. She ducked and started to run away. They meant her. They chased her, caught her, dragged her back to where they were camped. The magazines were pornography of women she physically resembled: blond, childlike. They called her names from the pornography: Little Godiva, Golden Girl, also bitch and slut. They threatened to kill her. They made her undress. It was November and cold. One held a rifle to her head; another beat her breasts with his rifle. All three raped her—penile penetration into the vagina. The third one couldn't get hard at first so he demanded a blow job. She didn't know what that was. The third man forced his penis into her mouth; one of the others cocked the trigger on his rifle. She was told she had better do it right. She tried. When they were done with her they kicked her: they kicked her naked body and they kicked leaves and pine needles on her. "[T]hey told me that if I wanted more, that I could come back the next day."[6]

She was sexually abused when she was three by a boy who was four-   15
teen—it was a "game" he had learned from pornography. "[I]t seems really bizarre to me to use the word 'boy' because the only memory I have of this person is as a three year old. And as a three year old he seemed like a really big man." When she was a young adult she was drugged by men who made and sold pornography. She remembers flashing lights, being forced onto a

stage, being undressed by two men and sexually touched by a third. Men were waving money at her: "one of them shoved it in my stomach and essentially punched me. I kept wondering how it was possible that they couldn't see that I didn't want to be there, that I wasn't there willingly."[7]

She had a boyfriend. She was twenty-one. One night he went to a stag 16 party and watched pornography films. He called her up to ask if he could have sex with her. She felt obligated to make him happy. "I also felt that the refusal would be indicative of sexual quote unquote hang-ups on my part and that I was not quote unquote liberal enough. When he arrived, he informed me that the other men at the party were envious that he had a girlfriend to fuck. They wanted to fuck too after watching the pornography. He informed me of this as he was taking his coat off." He had her perform oral sex on him: "I did not do this of my own volition. He put his genitals in my face and he said 'Take it all.'" He fucked her. The whole encounter took about five minutes. Then he dressed and went back to the party. "I felt ashamed and numb and I also felt very used."[8]

She was seventeen, he was nineteen. He was an art student. He used her 17 body for photography assignments by putting her body in contorted positions and telling her rape stories to get the expression he wanted on her face: fear. About a year later he had an assignment to do body casts in plaster. He couldn't get models because the plaster was heavy and caused fainting. She was a premed student. She tried to explain to him how deleterious the effects of the plaster were. "When you plut plaster on your body, it sets up, it draws the blood to the skin and the more area it covers on your body, the more blood is drawn to your skin. You become dizzy and nauseous and sick to your stomach and finally faint." He needed his work to be exhibited, so he needed her to model. She tried. She couldn't stand the heat and the weight of the plaster. "He wanted me to be in poses where I had to hold my hands up over my head, and they would be numb and they would fall. He eventually tied my hands over my head." They got married. During the course of their marriage he began to consume more and more pornography. He would read excerpts to her from the magazines about group sex, wife swapping, anal intercourse, and bondage. They would go to pornography films and wet T-shirt contests with friends. "I felt devastated and disgusted watching it. I was told by those men that if I wasn't as smart as I was and if I would be more sexually liberated and more sexy that I would get along a lot better in the world and that they and a lot of other men would like me more. About this time I started feeling very terrified. I realized that this wasn't a joke anymore." She asked her mother for help but was told that divorce was a disgrace and it was her responsibility to make the marriage work. He brought his friends home to act out the scenarios from the pornography. She found the group sex humiliating and disgusting, and to prevent it she agreed to act out the pornography in private with her husband. She began feeling suicidal. He was transferred to an Asian country in connection with his job. The pornography in the country where they now lived was more violent. He took her to live sex shows where women had sex with animals, especially snakes.

Increasingly, when she was asleep he would force intercourse on her. Then he started traveling a lot, and she used his absence to learn karate. "One night when I was in one of those pornographic institutions, I was sitting with a couple of people that I had known, watching the women on stage and watching the different transactions and the sales of the women and the different acts going on, and I realized that my life wasn't any different than these women except that it was done in the name of marriage. I could see how I was being seasoned to the use of pornography and I could see what was coming next. I could see more violence and I could see more humiliation and I knew at that point I was either going to die from it, I was going to kill myself, or I was going to leave. And I was feeling strong enough that I left. . . . Pornography is not a fantasy, it was my life, reality."[9]

At the time she made this statement, she couldn't have been older than 18 twenty-two. She was terrified that the people would be identifiable, and so she spoke in only the most general terms, never specifying their relationship to her. She said she had lived in a house with a divorced woman, that woman's children, and the ex-husband, who refused to leave. She had lived there for eighteen years. During that time, "the woman was regularly raped by this man. He would bring pornographic magazines, books, and paraphernalia into the bedroom with him and tell her that if she did not perform the sexual acts that were being done in the 'dirty' books and magazines he would beat and kill her. I know about this because my bedroom was right next to hers. I could hear everything they said. I could hear her screams and cries. In addition, since I did most of the cleaning in the house, I would often come across the books, magazines, and paraphernalia that were in the bedroom and other rooms of the house. . . . Not only did I suffer through the torture of listening to the rapes and tortures of a woman, but I could see what grotesque acts this man was performing on her from the pictures in the pornographic materials. I was also able to see the systematic destruction of a human being taking place before my eyes. At the time I lived with the woman, I was completely helpless, powerless in regard to helping this woman and her children in getting away from this man." As a child, she was told by the man that if she ever told or tried to run away he would break her arms and legs and cut up her face. He whipped her with belts and electrical cords. He made her pull her pants down to beat her. "I was touched and grabbed where I did not want him to touch me." She was also locked in dark closets and in the basement for long periods of time.[10]

She was raped by two men. They were acting out the pornographic 19 video game "Custer's Revenge." She was American Indian; they were white. "They held me down and as one was running the tip of his knife across my face and throat he said, 'Do you want to play Custer's Last Stand? It's great. You lose but you don't care, do you? You like a little pain, don't you, squaw.' They both laughed and then he said, 'There is a lot of cock in Custer's Last Stand. You should be grateful, squaw, that all-American boys like us want you. Maybe we will tie you to a tree and start a fire around you.' "[11]

Her name is Jayne Stamen. She is currently in jail. In 1986, she hired 20 three men to beat up her husband. She wanted him to know what a beating felt like. He died. She was charged with second-degree murder; convicted of first-degree manslaughter; sentenced to eight-and-a-half to twenty-five years. She was also convicted of criminal solicitation: in 1984 she asked some men to kill her husband for her, then reneged; she was sentenced on the criminal solicitation charge to two-and-a-third to seven years. The sentences are to run consecutively. She was tortured in her marriage by a man consumed by acting out pornography. He tied her up when he raped her; he broke bones; he forced anal intercourse; he beat her mercilessly; he penetrated her vagina with objects, "his rifle, or a long-necked wine decanter, or twelve-inch artificial rubber penises." He shaved the hair off her pubic area because he wanted, in his words, to "screw a baby's cunt." He slept with a rifle and kept a knife by the bed; he would threaten to cut her face with the knife if she didn't act out the pornography, and he would use the knife again if she wasn't showing pleasure. He called her all the names: whore, slut, cunt, bitch. "He used to jerk himself off on my chest while I was sleeping, or I would get woke up with him coming in my face and then he'd urinate on me." She tried to escape several times. He came after her armed with his rifle. She became addicted to alcohol and pills. "The papers stated that I didn't report [the violence] to the police. I did have the police at my home on several occasions. Twice on Long Island was for the gun threats, and once in Starrett City was also for the gun. The rest of the times were for the beatings and throwing me out of the house. A few times the police helped me get away from him with my clothes and the boys. I went home to my mom's. [He came after her with a rifle.] I went to the doctor's and hospitals on several occasions, too, but I could not tell the truth on how I 'hurt myself.' I always covered up for him, as I knew my life depended on that." The judge wouldn't admit testimony on the torture because he said the husband wasn't on trial. The defense lawyer said in private that he thought she probably enjoyed the abusive sex. Jayne's case will be appealed, but she may well have to stay in jail at Bedford Hills, a New York State prison for women, for the duration of the appeal because Women Against Pornography, a group that established the Defense Fund for Jayne Stamen, has not been able to raise bail money for her. Neither have I or others who care. It isn't chic to help such women; they aren't the Black Panthers.* Ironically, there are many women—and recently a teenage girl, a victim of incest—who have hired others to kill the men—husbands, fathers—who were torturing them because they could not bear to do it themselves. Or the woman pours gasoline on the bed when he sleeps and lights the fire. Jayne didn't hire the men to kill her husband; the real question may be, why not? why didn't she? Women don't understand self-defense the way men do—perhaps because sexual abuse destroys the self. We don't feel we have a right to kill just because we are being beaten, raped, tortured,

---

*A black militant protest group active during the 1960s.

and terrorized. We are hurt for a long time before we fight back. Then, usually, we are punished: "I have lived in a prison for ten years, meaning my marriage," says Jayne Stamen, ". . . and now they have me in a real prison."[12]

I've quoted from statements, all made in public forums, by women I 21 know well (except for Jayne Stamen; I've talked with her but I haven't met her). I can vouch for them; I know the stories are true. The women who made these particular statements are only a few of the thousands of women I have met, talked with, questioned: women who have been hurt by pornography. The women are real to me. I know what they look like standing tall; I've seen the fear; I've watched them remember; I've talked with them about other things, all sorts of things: intellectual issues, the weather, politics, school, children, cooking. I have some idea of their aspirations as individuals, the ones they lost during the course of sexual abuse, the ones they cherish now. I know them. Each one, for me, has a face, a voice, a whole life behind her face and her voice. Each is more eloquent and more hurt than I know how to convey. Since 1974, when my book *Woman Hating* was first published, women have been seeking me out to tell me that they have been hurt by pornography; they have told me how they have been hurt in detail, how much, how long, by how many. They thought I might believe them, initially, I think, because I took pornography seriously in *Woman Hating.* I said it was cruel, violent, basic to the way our culture sees and treats women—and I said the hate in it was real. Well, they knew that the hate in it was real because they had been sexually assaulted by that hate. One does not make the first tentative efforts to communicate about this abuse to those who will almost certainly ridicule one. Some women took a chance on me; and it was a chance, because I often did not want to listen. I had my limits and my reasons, like everyone else. For many years, I heard the same stories I have tried to encapsulate here: the same stories, sometimes more complicated, sometimes more savage, from thousands of women, most of whom hadn't dared to tell anyone. No part of the country was exempt; no age group; no racial or ethnic group; no "life-style" however "normal" or "alternative." The statements I have paraphrased here are not special: not more sadistic, not chosen by me because they are particularly sickening or offensive. In fact, they are not particularly sickening or offensive. They simply are what happens to women who are brutalized by the use of pornography on them.

Such first-person stories from women are dismissed by defenders of 22 pornography as "anecdotal"; they misuse the word to make it denote a story, probably fictive, that is small, trivial, inconsequential, proof only of some defect in the woman herself—the story tells us nothing about pornography but it tells us all we need to know about the woman. She's probably lying; maybe she really liked it; and if it did happen, how could anyone (sometimes referred to as "a smart girl like you") be stupid enough, simple-minded enough, to think that pornography had anything to do with it? Wasn't there, as one grinning adversary always asks, also coffee in the house? The coffee, he suggests, is more likely to be a factor in the abuse than the pornography—after all, the bad effects of coffee have been proven in the laboratory. What does one do when women's lives are worth so little—worth arrogant, self-satisfied ridicule and nothing else, not even the appearance, however false, of charity or concern? Alas, one answers: the man (the husband, the boy-friend, the rapist, the torturer—you or your colleague or your best friend or your buddy) wasn't reading the coffee label when he tied the knots; the directions he followed are found in pornography, and, frankly, they are not found anywhere else. The first-person stories are human experience, raw and true, not mediated by dogma or ideology *or* social convention; "human" is the trick word in the sentence. If one values women as human beings, one cannot turn away or refuse to hear so that one can refuse to care without bearing responsibility for the refusal. One cannot turn one's back on the women or on the burden of memory they carry. If one values women as human beings, one will not turn one's back on the women who are being hurt today and the women who will be hurt tomorrow.

Most of what we know about the experience of punishment, the experi- 23
ence of torture, the experience of socially sanctioned sadism, comes from the first-person testimony of individuals—"anecdotal" material. We have the first-person stories of Frederick Douglass and Sojourner Truth, of Primo Levy and Elie Wiesel, of Nadezhda Mandelstam and Aleksandr Solzhenitsyn. Others in the same or different circumstances of torture and terror have spoken out to bear witness. Often, they were not believed. They were shamed, not honored. We smelled the humiliation, the degradation, on them; we turned away. At the same time, their stories were too horrible, too impossible, too unpleasant; their stories indicted those who stood by and did nothing—most of us, most of the time. Respectfully, I suggest that the women who have experienced the sadism of pornography on their bodies—the women in the pornography and the women on whom the pornography is used—are also survivors; they bear witness, now, for themselves, on behalf of others. "Survivors," wrote Terrence Des Pres, "are not individuals in the bourgeois sense. They are living remnants of the general struggle, and certainly they know it."[13] Of these women hurt by pornography, we must say that they know it now. Before, each was alone, unspeakably alone, isolated in terror and humil-iated even by the will to live—it was the will to live, after all, that carried each woman from rape to rape, from beating to beating. Each had never heard another's voice saying the words of what had happened, telling the same story; because it is the same story, over and over—and none of those who escaped, survived, endured, are individuals in the bourgeois sense. These women will not abandon the meaning of their own experience. That meaning is: pornography is the orchestrated destruction of women's bodies and souls; rape, battery, incest, and prostitution animate it; dehumanization and sadism characterize it; it is war on women, serial assaults on dignity, identity, and human worth; it is tyranny. Each woman who has survived knows from the experience of her own life that pornography is captivity—the woman trapped in the picture used on the woman trapped wherever he's got her.

3

The burden of proof will be on those of us who have been victimized. If I [any woman] am able to prove that the picture you are holding, the one where the knife is stuffed up my vagina, was taken when my pimp forced me at gunpoint and photographed it without my consent, if my existence is proved real, I am coming to take what is mine. If I can prove that the movie you are looking at called *Black Bondage,* the one where my black skin is synonymous with filth and my bondage and my slavery is encouraged, caused me harm and discrimination, if my existence is proved real, I am coming to take what is mine. Whether you like it or not, the time is coming when you will have to get your fantasy *off my ass.*

> Therese Stanton, "Fighting for
> Our Existence" in *Changing Men*
> #15, Fall 1985

In the fall of 1983, something changed. The speech of women hurt by 24
pornography became public and real. It, they, began to exist in the sphere of
public reality. Constitutional lawyer Catharine A. MacKinnon and I were
hired by the City of Minneapolis to draft an amendment to the city's civil
rights law: an amendment that would recognize pornography as a violation
of the civil rights of women, as a form of sex discrimination, an abuse of
human rights. We were also asked to organize hearings that would provide
a legislative record showing the need for such a law. Essentially, the legislators needed to know that these violations were systematic and pervasive in
the population they represented, not rare, peculiar anomalies.

The years of listening to the private stories had been years of despair 25
for me. It was hopeless. I could not help. There was no help. I listened; I went
on my way; nothing changed. Now, all the years of listening were knowledge,
real knowledge that could be minded: a resource, not a burden and a curse.
I knew how women were hurt by pornography. My knowledge was concrete,
not abstract: I knew the ways it was used; I knew how it was made; I knew
the scenes of exploitation and abuse in real life—the lives of prostitutes,
daughters, girlfriends, wives; I knew the words the women said when they
dared to whisper what had happened to them; I could hear their voices in my
mind, in my heart. I didn't know that there were such women all around me,
everywhere, in Minneapolis that fall. I was heartbroken as women I knew
came forward to testify: though I listened with an outer detachment to the
stories of rape, incest, prostitution, battery, and torture, each in the service
of pornography, inside I wanted to die.

The women who came forward to testify at the hearings held by the 26
Minneapolis City Council on December 12 and 13, 1983, gave their names
and specified the area of the city in which they lived. They spoke on the
record before a governmental body in the city where they lived; there they
were, for family, neighbors, friends, employers, teachers, and strangers to see,
to remember. They described in detail sexual abuse through pornography as

it had happened to them. They were questioned on their testimony by Catharine MacKinnon and myself and also by members of the city council and sometimes the city attorney. There were photographers and television cameras. There were a couple of hundred people in the room. There was no safety, no privacy, no retreat, no protection; only a net of validation provided by the testimony of experts—clinical psychologists, prosecutors, experimental psychologists, social scientists, experts in sexual abuse from rape crisis centers and battered women's shelters, and those who worked with sex offenders. The testimony of these experts was not abstract or theoretical; it brought the lives of more women, more children, into the room: more rape, more violation through pornography. They too were talking about real people who had been hurt, sometimes killed; they had seen, known, treated, interviewed, numbers of them. A new social truth emerged, one that had been buried in fear, shame, and the silence of the socially powerless: no woman hurt by pornography was alone—she never had been; no woman hurt by pornography would ever be alone again because each was—truly—a "living remnant of the general struggle." What the survivors said was speech; the pornography had been, throughout their lives, a means of actively suppressing their speech. They had been turned into pornography in life and made mute; terrorized by it and made mute. Now, the mute spoke; the socially invisible were seen; the women were real; they mattered. This speech—their speech—was new in the world of public discourse, and it was made possible by the development of a law that some called censorship. The women came forward because they thought that the new civil rights law recognized what had happened to them, gave them recourse and redress, enhanced their civil dignity and human worth. The law itself gave them *existence:* I am real; they believed me; I count; social policy at last will take my life into account, validate my worth—me, the woman who was forced to fuck a dog; me, the woman he urinated on; me, the women he tied up for his friends to use; me, the woman he masturbated in; me, the woman he branded or maimed; me, the woman he prostituted; me, the woman they gang-raped.

The law was passed twice in Minneapolis in 1983 and 1984 by two 27 different city councils; it was vetoed each time by the same mayor, a man active in Amnesty International, opposing torture outside of Minneapolis. The law was passed in 1984 in Indianapolis with a redrafted definition that targeted violent pornography—the kind "everyone" opposes. The city was sued for passing it; the courts found it unconstitutional. The appeals judge said that pornography did all the harm we claimed—it promoted insult and injury, rape and assault, even caused women to have lower wages—and that these effects proved its power as speech; therefore, it had to be protected. In 1985, the law was put on the ballot by popular petition in Cambridge, Massachusetts. The city council refused to allow it on the ballot; we had to sue for ballot access; the civil liberties people opposed our having that access; we won the court case and the city was ordered to put the law on the ballot. We got 42 percent of the vote, a higher percentage than feminists got on the first women's suffrage referendum. In 1988, the law was on the ballot in Bellingham, Washington, in the presidential election; we got 62 percent of the vote. The city had tried to keep us off the ballot; again we had to get a court order to gain ballot access. The City of Bellingham was sued by the ACLU in federal court for having the law, however unwillingly; a federal district judge found the law unconstitutional, simply reiterating the previous appeals court decision in the Indianapolis case—indeed, there was a statement that the harms of pornography were recognized and not in dispute.

We have not been able to get the courts to confront a real woman 28 plaintiff suing a real pornographer for depriving her of real rights through sexual exploitation or sexual abuse. This is because the challenges to the civil rights law have been abstract arguments about speech, as if women's lives are abstract, as if the harms are abstract, conceded but not real. The women trapped in the pictures continue to be perceived as the free speech of the pimps who exploit them. No judge seems willing to look such a woman, three-dimensional and breathing, in the face and tell her that the pimp's use of her is his constitutionally protected right of speech; that he has a right to express himself by violating her. The women on whom the pornography is used in assault remain invisible and speechless in these court cases. No judge has had to try to sleep at night having heard a real woman's voice describing what happened to her, the incest, the rape, the gang rape, the battery, the forced prostitution. Keeping these women silent in courts of law is the main strategy of the free speech lawyers who defend the pornography industry. Hey, they love literature; they deplore sexism. If some women get hurt, that's the price we pay for freedom. Who are the "we"? What is the "freedom"? These speech-loving lawyers keep the women from speaking in court so that no judge will actually be able to listen to them.

Women continue speaking out in public forums, even though we are 29 formally and purposefully silenced in actual courts of law. Hearings were held by a subcommittee of the Senate Judiciary Committee on the effects of pornography on women and children; the Attorney General's Commission on Pornography listened to the testimony of women hurt by pornography; women are demanding to speak at conferences, debates, on television, radio. This civil rights law is taught in law schools all over the country; it is written about in law journals, often favorably; increasingly, it has academic support; and its passage has been cited as precedent in at least one judicial decision finding that pornography in the workplace can be legally recognized as sexual harassment. The time of silence—at least the time of absolute silence—is over. And the civil rights law developed in Minneapolis has had an impact around the world. It is on the agenda of legislators in England, Ireland, West Germany, New Zealand, Tasmania, and Canada; it is on the agenda of political activists all over the world.

The law itself is civil, not criminal. It allows people who have been hurt 30 by pornography to sue for sex discrimination. Under this law, it is sex discrimination to coerce, intimidate, or fraudulently induce anyone into pornography; it is sex discrimination to force pornography on a person in any place of employment, education, home, or any public place; it is sex discrimination to assault, physically attack, or injure any person in a way that is directly caused by a specific piece of pornography—the pornographers share responsibility for the assault; in the Bellingham version, it is also sex discrimination to defame any person through the unauthorized use in pornography of their name, image, and/or recognizable personal likeness; and it is sex discrimination to produce, sell, exhibit, or distribute pornography—to traffic in the exploitation of women, to traffic in material that probably causes aggression against and lower civil status for women in society.

The law's definition of pornography is concrete, not abstract. Pornography is defined as the graphic, sexually explicit subordination of women in pictures and/or words that also includes women presented dehumanized as sexual objects, things, or commodities; or women presented as sexual objects who enjoy pain or humiliation; or women presented as sexual objects who experience sexual pleasure in being raped; or women presented as sexual objects tied up or cut up or mutilated or bruised or physically hurt; or women presented in postures or positions of sexual submission, servility, or display; or women's body parts—including but not limited to vaginas, breasts, buttocks—exhibited such that women are reduced to those parts; or women presented as whores by nature; or women presented being penetrated by objects or animals; or women presented in scenarios of degradation, injury, torture, shown as filthy or inferior, bleeding, bruised, or hurt in a context that makes these conditions sexual. If men, children, or transsexuals are used in any of the same ways, the material also meets the definition of pornography. 31

For women hurt by pornography, this law simply describes reality; it is a map of a real world. Because the law allows them to sue those who have imposed this reality on them—especially the makers, sellers, exhibitors, and distributors of pornography—they have a way of redrawing the map. The courts now protect the pornography; they recognize the harm to women in judicial decisions—or they use words that say they recognize the harm—and then tell women that the Constitution protects the harm; profit is real to them and they make sure the pimps stay rich, even as women and their children are this country's poor. The civil rights law is designed to confront both the courts and the pornographers with a demand for substantive, not theoretical, equality. This law says: we have the right to stop them from doing this to us because we are human beings. "If my existence is proved real, I am coming to take what is mine," Therese Stanton wrote for every woman who wants to use this law. How terrifying that thought must be to those who have been using women with impunity. 32

Initially an amendment to a city ordinance, this law has had a global impact because: (1) it tells the truth about what pornography is and does; (2) it tells the truth about how women are exploited and hurt by the use of pornography; (3) it seeks to expand the speech of women by taking the pornographers' gags out of our mouths; (4) it seeks to expand the speech and enhance the civil status of women by giving us the courts as a forum in which we will have standing and authority; (5) it is a mechanism for redistributing power, taking it from pimps, giving it to those they have been exploiting for profit, 33 injuring for pleasure; (6) it says that women matter, including the women in the pornography. This law and the political vision and experience that inform it are not going to go away. We are going to stop the pornographers. We are going to claim our human dignity under law. One ex-prostitute, who is an organizer for the passage of this civil rights law, wrote: "Confronting how I've been hurt is the hardest thing that I've ever had to do in my life. A hard life, if I may say so."[14] She is right. Confronting the pornographers is easier—their threats, their violence, their power. Confronting the courts is easier—their indifference, their contempt for women, their plain stupidity. Confronting the status quo is easier. Patience is easier and so is every form of political activism, however dangerous. Beaver is real, all right. A serious woman—formidable even—she is coming to take what is hers.

. . .

[Section 4 of Dworkin's introduction to her book (five paragraphs long, here omitted) develops a comparison and a contrast between pornography that exploits women and Nazi films of the torture of Jews. This section also recounts the publishing history of her book.]

5

When I first wrote this book, I was going to use these lines from Eliza-   34
beth Barrett Browning's letters as an epigraph: "If a woman ignores these wrongs, then may women as a sex continue to suffer them; there is no help for any of us—let us be dumb and die."[18] I changed my mind, because I decided that no woman deserved what pornography does to women: no woman, however stupid or evil, treacherous or cowardly, venal or corrupt; no woman. I also decided that even if some women did, I didn't. I also remembered the brave women, the women who had survived, escaped; in the late 1970s, they were still silent, but I had heard them. I don't want them, ever, to be dumb and die; and certainly not because some other woman somewhere is a coward or a fool or a cynic or a Kapo. There are women who will defend pornography, who don't give a damn. There are women who will use pornography, including on other women. There are women who will work for pornographers—not as so-called models but as managers, lawyers, publicists, and paid writers of "opinion" and "journalism." There are women of every kind, all the time; there are always women who will ignore egregious wrongs. My aspirations for dignity and equality do not hinge on perfection in myself or in any other woman; only on the humanity we share, fragile as that appears to be. I understand Elizabeth Barrett Browning's desperation and the rage behind it, but I'm removing her curse. No woman's betrayal will make us dumb and dead—no more and never again. Beaver's endured too much to turn back now.

—Andrea Dworkin
New York City
March 1989

NOTES

All notes are Dworkin's.

1. William Lloyd Garrison, Preface, *Narrative of the Life of Frederick Douglass An American Slave Written by Himself,* Frederick Douglass, ed. Benjamin Quarles (Cambridge, Mass.: The Belknap Press of Harvard University Press, 1960), p. 5.

2. Public Hearings on Ordinances to Add Pornography as Discrimination Against Women, Minneapolis City Council, Government Operations Committee, December 12, and 13, 1983, in transcript available from Organizing Against Pornography, 734 East Lake Street, Minneapolis, Mn. 55407, p.16.

3. Name withheld, manuscript.

4. Sarah Wynter, pseudonym, manuscript, June 19, 1985.

5. Name withheld, manuscript; also testimony before the Subcommittee on Juvenile Justice of the Committee on the Judiciary, United States Senate, September 12, 1984.

6. See Public Hearings, Minneapolis, pp. 38–39.

7. See Public Hearings, Minneapolis, pp. 39–41.

8. See Public Hearings, Minneapolis, p. 41.

9. See Public Hearings, Minneapolis, pp. 42–46.

10. See Public Hearings, Minneapolis, pp. 65–66.

11. See Public Hearings, Minneapolis, pp. 66–67.

12. Direct quotations are from the Statement of Jayne Stamen, issued by Woman Against Pornography, February 14, 1988.

13. Terrence Des Pres, *The Survivor; An Anatomy of Life in the Death Camps* (New York: Pocket Books, 1977), p. 39.

14. Toby Summer, pseudonym, "Women, Lesbians and Prostitution: A Workingclass Dyke Speaks Out Against Buying Women for Sex," *Lesbian Ethics,* vol. 2 no. 3, Summer 1987, p. 37.

15. Elizabeth Barrett Browning, *Letters of Elizabeth Barrett Browning* in Mary Daly, *Gyn/Ecology: The Metaethics of Radical Feminism* (Boston: Beacon Press, 1978), p. 153.

Questions for Discussion

1. Do you accept Dworkin's definition of pornography presented in paragraph 31? Why or why not?

2. Do *Playboy, Hustler,* and *Playgirl* qualify as pornography? Why or why not? Do you think the reading of these magazines has any real effect on men and women—in men's views about the nature of women or what they enjoy, in women's views about themselves, or in society's views about what kind of protections, legal or otherwise, women should be granted from sexual abuse?

3. Do you think Dworkin is justified in asserting that pornography actually incites desire in men to abuse women sexually and in addition teaches them the mechanisms of abuse? Why or why not?

4. Do you agree or disagree that pornography ought to be punishable as a violation of the civil rights of women? Why or why not?

5. If you are a male, would it embarrass you, or would you feel uncomfortably self-conscious, watching a pornographic videotape with your girlfriend or wife? If so, why? Where would your embarrassment come from?

6. If you are a female, have you ever watched pornography in which women were depicted as enjoying being raped, beaten, or humiliated? How did it make you feel? Aroused? Indignant? Afraid? Ashamed? What emotions accompanied your viewing? Do you enjoy pornography in which men are the central figures? If so, on what grounds? If not, on what grounds?

Suggested Essay Topics

1. After reading Rosemarie Tong in the next essay, "Women, Sex, and the Law," write an essay to your classmates attacking or defending Dworkin's desire for a civil law allowing women to sue pornographers for violating their civil rights. Try to persuade them that Dworkin is either right or wrong and thus deserves either their full support or strong criticism. (If the former, suggest what might constitute appropriate forms of support.) In either case, take it as part of your writing task to show that you have really heard and considered the voice of the opposition and that you know what can be said against as well as for the position you favor.

2. Again directing your essay to your classmates, write an account of your reaction to specific instances of pornography. Rent a videotape or two; look at a few magazines; enter a "museum of adult pleasure" and take stock of the devices, films, magazines, and books offered for sale. Then write an account of your reaction to the pornography you have actually seen, perhaps using your reactions as the basis of support for or criticism of Dworkin, but mostly as a means of developing your own view of the character and consequences of pornography. (After reviewing this assignment, Dworkin advises us that women entering an "adult book shop" or "museum of adult pleasure" could be placing themselves in physical jeopardy. Perhaps only men should undertake this part of this assignment.)

Rosemarie Tong

On what grounds, if any, may pornography be legally repressed? When, if ever, may the sale of pornography be forbidden in shops, denied transport through the U.S. Post Office, prohibited in movie theaters, made illegal on commercial videotape, and so on?

While all feminists support freedom of the press, thought, and speech in a pluralistic society, the dissemination of pornography presents a vexing legal and moral problem that leads different people (not exclusively militant feminists) to argue that pornography ought to be treated as an exception, that pornography ought not *to be protected under the principle of free speech, free thought, or free press.*

Before the complexities of this issue can be productively engaged, pornography must be defined. Before one can decide whether a given act comes under the protection of the Bill of Rights or the Constitution, one has to know how to define that act. What is pornography? Is it the same thing as obscenity? Are there different kinds of pornography? Does the frequently employed distinction between soft-core and hard-core porn make sense? Is Playboy *a destructive magazine? How about* Hustler *and* Playgirl? *How about the videotapes available in the "18-or-older" room of your local video store? Are some forms of pornography more objectionable than others? If so, why? What are the features of the different kinds? Rosemarie Tong's careful, well-defined distinctions in the present essay help answer these questions.*

Tong is also helpful in determining what arguments can be made about pornography's effects. Does pornography, disgusting as it may be to some people, serve the socially useful function of providing a nonphysical outlet for aggressive and hostile energies that, in pornography's absence, may be acted out in real life rather than in the realm of phantasy? Does pornography, like a lightning rod, harmlessly carry off destructive energy, thus protecting society from damage? Or, to ask the opposite question, does pornography act as an incitement to contemptuous, destructive, and hostile acts directed toward women? Does pornography teach *men forms of women hating? Tong's essay is also helpful for supplying the arguments that can be used to answer these two questions.*

Even if you decide that pornography does indeed constitute an education in forms of women hating, the question remains whether that function justifies pornography's legal repression. Some would say that the Constitution is neutral about whom you hate and only takes notice of whom you harm. Others would say, "Yes, that's right, but pornography is *harmful to women, to all women." In a society where the sale of pornography in different forms reaches into the millions, every American needs to spend some time thinking about not only its effects, but its moral and legal status.*

WOMEN, SEX, AND THE LAW

From *Women, Sex, and the Law* (1984).

In 1979 Women Against Pornography (WAP) organized a march of 7,000 people through Times Square and held a conference with about 800 attendees. After the conference, an editor of *Playboy* called a woman participant he knew, angered that she had addressed the meeting. "How could you do that?" he demanded. "Don't you know that if the forces of censorship win, they will get you too?"[1] Like many others, this woman admitted that the editor had a point. Increasingly, feminists are concerned that a stance against pornography may be used to justify censorship. Their concern is not without warrant. For example, in parts of the country where regional censorship ordinances have been enforced, officials have classified feminists' works such as *Our Bodies, Ourselves, Fear of Flying,* and *The Joy of Sex* together with "Jane Birkin in Bondage," "Chester the Molester," and "The Joy of Pain." As a result of instances where fundamental differences between works on female sexuality have gone unrecognized, more and more feminist writers have been arguing that the antipornography campaign is a "hot and dangerous" issue for feminists,[2] not only because it is perilously in alliance with the New Right, but because it may be mistakenly viewed as "antisex." At a recent feminist conference, Alice Echols argued that the antiporn movement (as practice) and cultural feminism[3] (as ideology) may detrimentally "re-inforce and validate women's traditional sexual conservatism and manipulate their sense of themselves as culture's victims as well as its moral guardians."[4]

Echols and others have not dissuaded some feminist theorists from writing antipornography treatises or some feminist activists from organizing marches, boycotts, and teach-ins against pornography, but they have caused them to try to clarify their precise motives and exact aims. First, this chapter will schematize the position of feminist antipornographers, contrasting it with more traditional antipornography positions. Second, it will ask whether it is possible to shape legal remedies for women-degrading pornography that fit the contours of a pluralist democracy. Finally, it will be suggested that before any woman condemns all pornography, she should decide to what extent sexually explicit material plays a salutory as well as deleterious role in women's lives.

THE TRADITIONAL CONCEPT OF PORNOGRAPHY IN ANGLO-AMERICAN LAW

Groups such as Women Against Pornography, Take Back the Night (TBTN), and Women Against Violence in Pornography and the Media (WAVPM) insist that their concept of pornography is not to be confused with more traditional concepts of pornography, especially those embedded in Anglo-American law, which conflate the notion of pornography with obscenity. As David A. J. Richards notes, the term "pornography" (from the Greek *pornographos*) initially meant "writing of harlots." In this sense, pornography is indeed sexually explicit material consisting in graphic depictions of sexual organs and various modes of coitus. It is important that pornography not be equated with obscenity. The notion of sexually explicit depictions (pornography) is not the same idea as that of the abuse of a bodily/personal function (obscenity) that causes one to react with disgust (such as coprohagy*).[5]

Significantly, and not without serious consequences, pornography and the obscene were equated in Christian culture because theologians defined proper sexual functions in a particularly limited way: All sexual acts are improper except those in which the aim is procreation. Not only are extramarital and male homosexual or lesbian intercourse prohibited, but all "unnatural" forms of intercourse within conventional marriage as well as oral

*Eating excrement.

or anal sex. Furthermore, all depictions and descriptions that will lead to "illicit genital commotion" (masturbation) are prohibited. Thus, pornography is obscene not only in itself, but because it leads to extramarital sex, to non-vaginal intercourse within marriage, or to masturbation, which, according to the traditional Christian view, are "independently obscene acts" because they supposedly violate "minimum standards" of appropriate sexual functions, thereby causing "disgust."[6]

Richards points out that fear of "unnatural" sexuality probably accounts for the rash of obscenity legislation in England and the United States in the mid-nineteenth century. This legislation reflected a curious Victorian view that linked sexual indulgence, in general, and masturbation, in particular, to insanity and even to death. Since it was thought to aid and abet human sexual fantasy and subsequent sexual activity, pornography was condemned for medical as well as theological reasons. For example, Anthony Comstock, leader of the Committee for the Suppression of Vice, argued that those who read pornography invariably engaged in masturbation, and that those who masturbated either went crazy or died at a tender age. He never tired of noting pathological cases such as the one in which a thirteen-year-old girl supposedly wasted away to the shell of her former self after reading too many dirty books.[7]

Although our courts are no longer preoccupied with the evils of autoeroticism, they do continue to identify the pornographic with the obscene. However, unlike their nineteenth-century predecessors, today's courts do not automatically classify sexually explicit material as obscene/pornographic. As a result of several controversial cases involving massive public support for works of literature such as *Ulysses, Lady Chatterley's Lover,* and the *Memoirs of Fanny Hill,* the courts have had to distinguish between sexually explicit material that is obscene/pornographic and sexually explicit material that is not. In order to make these distinctions, the courts have proposed more or less unsuccessful definitions of obscenity, and therefore, in their terms, of pornography. The test currently employed is the one that was articulated in *Miller* v. *California* (1973). In deciding whether or not, an instance of sexually explicit material is obscene/pornographic, the trier of-fact (judge or juror) must ask himself or herself:

(a) Whether "the average person, applying contemporary community standards," would find that the work, taken as a whole, appeals to the prurient interest
(b) Whether the work depicts or describes, in a patently offensive way, sexual conduct specifically defined by the applicable state law
(c) Whether the work, taken as a whole, lacks serious literary, artistic, political or scientific value[8]

If a work appeals to the "prurient interest," is "patently offensive," and "lacks serious . . . value," it is obscene/pornographic.

According to many critics, including some feminists, the *Miller* test is seriously flawed not only because it is difficult to operationalize phrases such as "prurient interest," "patently offensive," and "lacks serious . . . value," but also because it is not certain which, if any, of these criteria suggest a legitimate reason for legal restriction of sexually explicit material. That something appeals to prurience, which the dictionary defines as a lustful, itching desire, is not necessarily a reason to control it legally. Unless it can be empirically established, for example, that occasionally giving into one's prurient interests is more enervating than rejuvenating, more socially destructive than socially creative, then the law has no good reason to restrict this form of self-expression. Likewise, that something "lacks serious . . . value" is not necessarily a reason to control it legally. To ban sexually explicit material simply because it has no serious value is not only to make an arrogant, global judgment about its worth, but also to forget that even if such material is not of serious value it may still serve a social function. Finally, that something is "patently offensive" is not necessarily a reason to control it legally. Since the sensitivities of persons vary enormously, what one person finds patently offensive, another will find manifestly unoffensive. Therefore, unless a sexually explicit depiction is likely to offend persons whose sensitivities are neither under- nor overdeveloped, and unless those who take offense at the depiction are unable to avoid it without disrupting their own lives, the law has no good reason to restrict its discreet production, procurement, and enjoyment.

If the *Miller* test is as flawed as its critics insist, then what, if anything,   8 does make or would make sexually explicit material somehow morally objectionable and/or legally restrictable? Feminists have found it difficult not only to distinguish between those modes of pornography they think are objectionable (women-degrading) and those modes of pornography they think are unobjectionable, but also to suggest appropriate legal remedies for the former.

TOWARD A DEFINITION OF WOMEN-DEGRADING PORNOGRAPHY

In a searing critique, Deirdre English takes to task Women Against   9 Violence in Pornography and the Media's attempt to distinguish between pornographic modes that supposedly degrade women (hard-core porn and soft-core porn) and pornographic modes that supposedly do not degrade women (erotica). According to WAVPM, erotica is not women-degrading because it is "personal, emotional; has 'lightness'; is refreshing; has an element of trust or caring or love; is natural, circular."[9] In contrast, hard-core porn and, to a lesser extent, soft-core porn[10] is women-degrading because it "is defined by penis, men, is for the titillation of men; shows a power imbalance; suggests violence; is heavy; [depicts] bodies contorted; [shows] no reciprocity between people, gratification at someone's expense; is voyeuristic, linear, something you can buy and sell."[11]

Deirdre English comments: "Can't you buy and sell erotica? Is looking   10 at sexual representations voyeuristic? The penis is pornographic; the 'circle' is erotic? Hmm."[12] As a result of this and related criticisms, the general public as well as some feminists have come to believe that degradation is in the subjective eye of the beholder, and that attempts to provide criteria for objectionable (women-degrading) pornography are doomed. Such pessimism, however, may be premature. Feminists have advanced at least two plausible tests for identifying women-degrading pornography: It depicts disrespect for women's wishes as sexual beings and it falsely portrays women's wishes as sexual beings.[13] A close examination of these tests will reveal why feminists have regarded women-degrading pornography as a real and serious problem rather than a manufactured and trivial issue.

The type of pornography to which feminists are most opposed is best 11 termed gyno-thanatica (from the Greek words for "woman" and "death or a destructive principle").[14] Unlike gyno-erotic pornography (from the Greek words for "woman" and "love or a creative principle"), which depicts women being integrated, constituted, or focused by creative sexual forces, gyno-thanatic pornography depicts women being disintegrated, dismembered, or disoriented by destructive sexual forces. When gyno-thanatic pornography first appeared, feminists called attention to the way in which it displayed men disrespecting women's ends as sexual beings. The standard way to indicate disrespect for another person's ends (such as happiness and perfection) is deliberately to ignore that person's wants and needs in one's transactions with him or her; and the usual means of calling attention to this fact is to point out that person x has not secured person y's consent to action z. Along this line of reasoning, depictions of sexual exchanges in which men do whatever they please to women without taking into account their interests, needs, and wants as sexual beings are portrayals of men failing to respect women properly. Comments Gloria Steinem:

> Look at any depiction of sex in which there is clear force, or an unequal power that spells coercion. It may be very blatant, with weapons of torture or bondage, wounds and bruises, some clear humiliation, or an adult's sexual power being used over a child. It may be much more subtle: a physical attitude of conqueror and victim, the use of race or class to imply the same thing, perhaps a very unequal nudity, with one person exposed and vulnerable while the other is clothed. In either case, there is no sense of equal choice or equal power.[15]

Therefore, any time a man is portrayed as foisting himself sexually upon a woman as proof of his superiority, he is depicted as degrading her.

Interestingly, feminists have recently deepened their critique of gyno- 12 thanatic pornography. Although they continue to object to its coercive—especially violent—features, they are also objecting to its tendency to depict women as creatures who welcome or seek out male sexual abuse. Whereas the feminists anthologized in Laura Lederer's *Take Back the Night*[16] concentrate on magazines like *Bondage*, which feature depictions of men torturing women (businessmen systematically applying hot irons, scissors, torches, and knives to the breasts and vaginas of their secretaries), in *Pornography and Silence: Cul-*

ture's Revenge Against Nature, [17] Susan Griffin concentrates on the connections among pornography, anti-Semitism, and sadism, arguing that in the same way that Jews did not volunteer to be gassed, women do not volunteer to be sexually abused. Whatever their focus, however, feminists agree that gyno-thanatic pornography is women-degrading not only because it typically suggests that "sexuality and violence are congruent"[18] and that what women *want* as sexual beings is irrelevant, but also because it often relays pernicious lies about *what* women want as sexual beings, suggesting that "for women sex is essentially masochistic, humiliation pleasurable, physical abuse erotic."[19]

Significantly, critics chastize feminists for focusing on gyno-thanatic 13 pornography. In general, these critics are of two sorts: the type who thinks that feminists should not object to any kind of pornography, including gyno-thanatica, and the type who thinks that they should object to every kind of pornography, no matter how slightly it degrades, objectifies, or trivializes women.

The first type of critic is epitomized by Jean Bethke Elshtain, who argues 14 that members of Women Against Violence in Pornography and the Media have frightened women, plunging them ever deeper into the psychic terrors of female victimization. By setting up men as brutal enemies, as "implacable foes", feminists have increased women's incipient fears that they, too, will be victims of male violence or already are.[20] However, as Elshtain sees it, the *rise* of violence against women is a largely trumped-up issue. She notes, for example, that FBI statistics, as well as those available from the U.S. Justice Department's Bureau of Justice, show little overall change in the rate of reported forcible rapes from 1973 to 1978. This rate holds at two-tenths of 1 percent of households (an estimated 75,989 reported rapes in 1979 and an estimated 82,088 reported rapes in 1980).[21] Nevertheless, Elshtain observes that women have become increasingly preoccupied with and unnecessarily worried about their personal safety. Therefore, she concludes, to the extent that it contributes to women's perceptions of themselves as victims and to the degree that it causes women to limit their sexual contacts with men, the feminist antipornography movement must ask itself whether it is serving to lengthen rather than to shorten women's sexual oppression.

The second type of critic is epitomized by disillusioned members of 15 WAP, TBTN, and WAVPM who regret that the feminist antipornography movement has shriveled from an all-inclusive campaign against soft-core as well as hard-core porn to a narrowly focused attack on the most violent and most women-degrading modes of pornography. As these critics see it, everyone knows that women do not want to be tortured and killed, even if it is in the name of sexual expression. What everyone does not know, however, is that women are not by nature sexually voracious and indiscriminate creatures, always yielding gladly and responding orgasmically to the most perfunctory male advances. So what is needed is not so much a campaign against gyno-thanatica as a campaign against soft porn (sentimental soap operas, gushy romantic novels, "macho" spy films).

Although most feminist antipornographers admit that their critics' ob- 16 jections are not without merit, they do not think that they are unassailable. First, feminist antipornographers are not at all convinced that violence against women is a largely manufactured issue. They note, for example, that arguments such as Elshtain's reply on statistics of reported instances of rape. Such *reported* instances of rape must be balanced against *unreported* instances of rape, woman-battering, and sexual harassment. Despite certain improvements in the criminal justice system, most women still think twice or three times before they report a sex-related crime. These same women, however, may not be reluctant to communicate their woes through informal women's networks. As in the past, women today have their own lines of communication—the coffee-break chat, the casual conversation at the laundromat, the extended phone talk—and if the reports of those who work in battered-women's shelters and rape crisis centers are any index, violence against women is definitely on the rise. Second, although feminist antipornographers were originally convinced that soft porn was telling as many lies about women as hard porn, they have come to doubt the truth of their initial claim. Given women's continuing penchant for soft porn, some feminists are wondering whether the first antiporn movement was launched before women had had an opportunity to ascertain the "truth" about female sexuality and to decide how many, if any, lies about female sexuality were being told in soft-porn favorites like *Charlie's Angels* (a television series in which three female detectives, dressed for the most part in bikinis, pursue law, order, and attractive men); Harlequin or Silhouette romances (pulpy novels in which it takes about 50 pages for a reluctant first kiss and another 150 or so to get married); and *James Bond* thrillers (movies in which a "macho" spy alternates his time between pursuing heinous criminals and chasing curvacious women).

Of these two responses, the second is by far the most controversial. 17 Only a few years ago, feminists would have chided any woman who dared to read, for example, a Silhouette romance, and not without some cause. The typical plot of a Silhouette romance features a "poor, orphaned young woman of beauty and integrity who meets and falls for a powerful, wealthy, and slightly older man."[22] Although this man dominates the heroine throughout the book, "mocking her emotions" as he arouses her seething passions, in the final pages she learns what the reader has known all along, namely, that he has always loved her.[23] In short, the classic formula of a Silhouette romance is one of female sexual submission and male sexual dominance—scarcely a feminist theme. Although feminists are still inclined to agree with Ann Douglas that "it is a frightening measure of the still patriarchal quality of our culture that many women of all ages cosponsor male fantasies about themselves and enjoy peep shows into masculine myths about their sexuality as the surest means of self-induced excitation,"[24] they are increasingly willing to confront the possibility that Silhouette romances and other types of soft porn may not be presenting an entirely false view of female sexuality. Indeed, they observe that the relative place of responsiveness and initiative in women's sex lives is likely to remain an open question until women define themselves not only sexually but also ontologically. Comments Catherine MacKinnon:

> If women are socially defined such that female sexuality cannot be lived or spoken or felt or even somatically sensed apart from its enforced definition, so that it is its own lack, then there is no such thing as a woman as such, there are only walking embodiments of men's projected needs. For feminism, asking whether there is, socially, a female sexuality is the same as asking whether women exist.[25]

But even if women do not have all the answers to the questions "what is a woman" and "what is female sexuality," they do have some of the answers. It may make sense for women to discuss whether an issue of *Playboy* displaying a Great White Hunter disrobing a quivering "bunny" down to her itsy-bitsy cottontail is women-degrading, but feminist antipornographers are confident that it does not make sense for women to discuss whether an issue of *Hustler* displaying a woman being ground into meat is women-degrading. This is perhaps the reason why most feminists have decided to concentrate on blatant examples of women-degrading pornography (gyno-thanatica) rather than on more ambiguous instances of it. A woman may dream of her lover stripping her bare, but a vision of him reducing her to a bloody pulp can only strike her as a nightmare.

THE SEARCH FOR AN APPROPRIATE LEGAL RESPONSE TO GYNO-THANATICA

Hard as it is to convince people that at least gyno-thanatic pornography [18] is women-degrading, it is even harder to convince people that anything should be done about it. Feminist antipornographers have been severely criticized because of their search for appropriate legal as well as extralegal remedies (consciousness-raising conferences, seminars, and teach-ins) for gyno-thanatic pornography. According to the critics, there are sound legal grounds for restricting, say, gyno-thanatic *behavior*, but these grounds cannot be invoked to restrict mere *depictions* and *descriptions* of such behavior. A person's liberty to do as he or she pleases or sees fit—in this instance his or her liberty to engage in gyno-thanatic fantasies—may be limited only if it constitutes a violation of at least one of the four principles that this society generally accepts as legitimate reasons to restrict a man's or a woman's liberty.

In order of decreasing social acceptance, these principles are:

1. The harm principle—A person's liberty may be restricted to prevent physical or psychic injury to other specific individuals; likewise, a person's liberty may be restricted to prevent impairment or destruction of institutional practices and regulatory systems that are in the public interest.

2. The offense principle—A person's liberty may be restricted to prevent offense to other specific individuals, where "offense" is interpreted as behavior that causes feelings of embarrassment, shame, outrage, or disgust in those against whom it is directed.

3. The principle of legal paternalism—A person's liberty may be restricted to protect himself or herself from self-inflicted harm, or, in its extreme version, to guide that person, whether he or she likes it or not, toward his or her own good.

4. The principle of legal moralism—A person's liberty may be restricted to protect other specific individuals, but especially society as a whole from immoral behavior, where the word "immoral" means neither "harmful" nor "offensive," but something like "against the rule of a higher authority" (God) or "against a societal taboo."[26]

According to most liberals, acts such as sexual harassment, rape, and women-battering are clear violations of the harm principle, if not also of the offense, legal paternalism, and legal moralism principles. In contrast, mere depictions or mere descriptions of such acts do not constitute any violation of the harm principle; and if they do constitute some sort of offense to others, harm to self, or social "immorality," it is so slight as not to warrant the restriction of any individual's liberty to see, read, or hear what he or she pleases.

Like their liberal critics, feminists are not eager to restrict the liberty of any person. However, unlike their liberal critics, they think that two liberty-limiting principles—the harm principle and the offense principle—apply at least in the case of gyno-thanatica.[27] As they see it, these two principles can be invoked successfully when it comes to constructing a case not for the outright censorship of all forms of women-degrading pornography, but for the imposition of certain legal restrictions on the public display and public dissemination of the worst of this material (gyno-thanatica). Indeed, censorship has never been the *essential* goal of feminist antipornographers. Says Susan Brownmiller, one of women-degrading pornography's most vehement foes: "We are not saying 'Smash the presses' or 'Ban the bad ones,' but simply 'Get the stuff out of our sight.' "[28] What has been and remains one of the *peripheral* aims of feminists however, is the exploration of legal remedies aimed at putting a damper on the celebration of gyno-thanatica not in the *privacy* of a man's or a woman's castle, but in the *publicity* of an open marketplace. Although members of organizations such as WAP, TBTN, and WAVPM have not, to date, advanced an entirely acceptable legal remedy for gyno-thanatica, their arguments are illuminating and worth the measured consideration of those who oppose any legal restrictions on pornography whatsoever, as well as those who advocate limited legal restrictions of the worst and most conspicuous forms of it.

Arguments Invoking the Harm Principle

According to some feminists, gyno-thanatic pornography is harmful in one or both of two senses: (1) Although gyno-thanatic pornography may not be harmful per se, it causes men to engage in harmful behavior toward women; or (2) gyno-thanatic pornography is harmful per se since it consists in the defamation of women. Related as these two arguments are, they make substantially different points and should be considered separately.

1. *Argument One:* The first argument—that there is a causal connection   21 between viewing gyno-thanatic pornography and engaging in corresponding forms of behavior—is based on the commonsense belief that there is an intimate relationship between thought and action. In 1970 the Commission on Obscenity and Pornography denied the truth of this relationship inso- far as pornography/obscenity is concerned, concluding that there is "no evi- dence . . . that exposure to explicit sexual material plays a significant role in the causation of delinquent or criminal behavior among youth or adults."[29] That the commission came to such a conclusion is not surprising. Tradition- ally, two working models have guided researchers in their study of pornogra- phy and aggressive behavior: the catharsis model and the imitation model. When applied to any kind of pornography, including gyno-thanatic pornog- raphy, the catharsis model assumes that pornography is a harmless outlet for sexual aggressions. The imitation model assumes that pornography is a propadeutic* for sexually unacceptable behavior, especially sexual violence.

Most of the research done for the Commission on Obscenity and Por-   22 nography was guided by the catharsis model. Derived from psychoanalytic theory, the catharsis model predicts that women-degrading pornography serves society by allowing men to release, in a nonviolent manner, their instinctual sexual aggressions against women. Using this model, Donald L. Mosher found that "sex-calloused" attitudes, manifested in *verbal* approba- tion of the sexual exploitation of women, decreased among men who were exposed to pornographic films. That is, the men who saw these films were less likely—at least for twenty-four hours—to fill in the blank in "When a woman gets uppity, it's time to —her" with words such as "rape" or "smack." Mosher attributed this phenomenon to the fact that seeing pornography in the com- pany of only men satisfies the need for "macho" behavior—that is, it satisfies the need for endorsing "sex-calloused" attitudes on paper and for boasting about one's sexual prowess.[30]

On the basis of Mosher's study and other similar studies, the commis-   23 sion drew the conclusion that men who view any kind of sexually explicit material, be it gyno-erotic or gyno-thanatic, are less inclined to sexually abuse women after seeing such material than before seeing it. This conclusion was unwarranted for several reasons. In very few, if any instances, had Mosher exposed his audience to gyno-thanatic pornography. In fact, Mosher himself admitted that he usually used as test material a "better-than-aver- age" pornographic film (that is, a gyno-erotic film) because it showed "more affection and fewer genital close-ups" and because it appealed more to "sexu- ally uninhibited, experienced adults of both sexes" than "kinky," exclusively male-oriented films.[31] This suggests that if Mosher proved anything it was

*Introductory instruction.

that men who are exposed to erotic pornography—to sexually explicit descriptions and displays that show the involved parties caring about each other's desires and experiences as sexual beings—are less inclined to make women-degrading statements after seeing such material than before seeing it. But even if Mosher did prove this, he did not also prove, as the commission thought he had, that men who are disinclined to make women-degrading *statements* are also disinclined to engage in women-degrading *behavior*. There are always significant gaps between a subject's guarded statements in a scientist's laboratory and a subject's spontaneous behavior at home or on the street. And even if, contrary to fact, Mosher had proved everything the commission had hoped he would prove, it should have checked Mosher's hypotheses, data, and conclusions against those put forward by the competing, imitation model.

Unlike the catharsis model, the imitation model suggests that people   24
learn patterns of violence from role models. Aggression and anger are behaviors that are learned from the environment like any other social behavior. A child, for example, is not naturally militant. He learns warlike behavior from the games he plays, from the stories he reads, from the television programs he sees, and especially from the heroes he emulates. Using this model, recent researchers of gyno-thanatic pornography have suggested that the rapist, a pervasive figure in contemporary gyno-thanatica, functions as a role model for porn devotees. For example, in a paper entitled "Pornography Commission Revisited: Aggressive-Erotica and Violence Against Women," Professor Ed Donnerstein reported that angered males who had watched "aggressive erotica" (gyno-thanatica) displayed aggression to females but not to males. Donnerstein explained this phenomenon of "selective aggression" toward females by noting that in the typical gyno-thanatic film, the female plays the role of victim. Because she is observed to be the object of male violence in the fantasy world of depictions and descriptions, the female takes on what is called "aggressive cue value" in the real world. That is, she becomes an aggressive stimulus that, given certain conditions such as work-related anger on the part of the male spectator, can elicit aggressive responses in him. In short, once a woman is seen as a scapegoat, she will be the target for male aggression when that aggression seeks release.[32]

Should studies such as Donnerstein's be confirmed, the causal link   25
between viewing gyno-thanatica and perpetrating sexually abusive acts against women would be more firmly established. More credence could be given to Susan Brownmiller's view that the anti-female propaganda that permeates our nation's cultural output "promotes a climate in which acts of sexual hostility directed against women are not only tolerated but ideologically encouraged."[33] But even if empirical evidence of Donnerstein's sort were to increase, it would have to increase dramatically to support the claim that some early feminist antipornographers made: that gyno-thanatica constitutes a "clear and present danger" to women, that it causes men to rape, beat, and even murder women.

According to Wendy Kaminer, a feminist lawyer, not only would it be   26 difficult to support such a claim, but the clear-and-present-danger standard would in fact give greater legal protection to gyno-thanatica than contemporary obscenity law.[34] Under contemporary obscenity law, sexually explicit material that is judged obscene is classified as nonspeech on the grounds that there is no speech without thought, and that thought is not behind mere depictions and descriptions, especially those that appeal only to the prurient interest.[35] As many feminists see it, however, thought is reflected in the images of filmmakers, photographers, painters, dancers, and musicians no less than it is reflected in the words of journalists, essayists, novelists, and speechmakers. Therefore, if sexually explicit depictions and descriptions, including instances of gyno-thanatic pornography, communicate thought, then they constitute speech. But if gyno-thanatica constitutes speech, it has the prima facie protection of the First Amendment; and if it has this protection, it will be very difficult to establish that any instance of it presents a clear and present danger to society in general and to women in particular. In order to prove, for example, that *Snuff,* a film in which a sexually aroused man gives a "bitch" what "[she] wants" (supposedly, a death worse than being drawn and quartered),[36] the prosecution would have to show that as a result of viewing this horror, some male viewers would, as soon as the opportunity presented itself, sexually assault or even brutally murder women. But it is not at all certain whether viewing *Snuff* has the same sort of behavioral effect on an audience as yelling "Fire" in a crowded theater does. It may, however, have some sort of suggestive effect on viewers.

The fact that three schoolgirls raped a nine-year-old girl with a beer bottle only four days after *Born Innocent,* a film in which several schoolgirls used a "plumber's helper" to rape a girl, was aired on television does not seem to have been pure coincidence.[37] Nonetheless, courts are loathe to admit that there is a direct causal relation between adult persons seeing something and their acting out what they have seen. Even in the case of adolescents, courts are reluctant to recognize such causal connections. When 15-year-old Ronald Zamora argued that he had killed an aged neighborhood woman as a result of "prolonged, intense, involuntary, subliminal television intoxication,"[38] his defense fell on deaf ears. The jury convicted him of murder, not at all convinced that viewing *Kojak* and other violent television programs could have caused Zamora to act violently in real life. No one is quite sure how, or even if, fantasy may influence action; and even those who are convinced there is some causal relationship between the two tend to think that it is usually within a person's power to separate his real life from his fantasy life. This being the case, it is difficult to convince jury members that heinous sights and sounds can immediately propel persons to perpetrate heinous deeds.

2. *Argument Two:* Given, then, that there is so much confusion about whether or not seeing *x* is causally related to doing *x*, feminists have advanced a second argument against gyno-thanatic pornography. Like the causation argument, this one is based on the harm principle. Unlike the causation argument, this one claims that in and of themselves certain sexually explicit depictions and descriptions (such as gyno-thanatica) constitute a harm to

women akin to defamation. Defamatory communications are those that damage a person's reputation by expressing thoughts to third parties that either
diminish the esteem in which the defamed party is held or excite adverse
feelings or opinions against him/her.

The law of defamation covers not only verbal statements (written or   29
oral) but also nonverbal representations (cartoons, sketches, drawings, photographs, gestures), as well as modes of communication that combine verbal
statements with nonverbal representations (most films, television programs,
magazine articles). Defamatory communications belong to that class of
speech acts that do not have the protection of the First Amendment. Included
in this category are, as Helen Longino points out, "the incitement to violence
in volatile circumstances, the solicitation of crimes, perjury and misrepresen-
tation, slander, libel, and false advertising."[39] According to Longino and other
feminist antipornographers,

> that there are forms of proscribed speech shows that we accept limita-
> tions on the right to freedom of speech. The manufacture and distribution
> of material which defames and threatens all members of a class by its
> recommendation of abusive and degrading behavior toward some mem-
> bers of that class simply in virtue of their membership in it seems a clear
> candidate for inclusion on the list [of proscribed speech acts].[40]

In short, if it can be shown that gyno-thanatic pornography defames women,
then it will be possible for women as a group to bring, for example, civil suit
against pornographers for damages to their reputations.[41]

a. *Objection One:* There are several problems with this novel, legal ap-   30
proach to gyno-thanatic pornography. First, it is not at all clear that pornographers flash images of sexually abused women across the screen in order to
make statements, defamatory or otherwise, about women. According to many
students of film, the typical pornographer does not mean to *state* anything in
particular when he creates images of women who plead to be tortured or
killed during sexual exchanges with men. That is, he does not intend the
depiction of these gross images to produce specific effects in his audience (the
excitation of adverse feelings or opinions against women, for example) *by
means* of their recognition of his intention to make them have these specific,
negative feelings or opinions about women.[42] Supposedly, he does not intend
this because he realizes that people who patronize porn films come not to be
educated, but to release or relieve their sexual tensions. Says Deirdre English:
"Pornography is not understood to 'teach' anything, but to provide mechanisms that carry off the effluvia of socially banned sexual expressions."[43]

Cogent as this objection is, some feminist antipornographers note that   31
there could exist, for example, a Bertolt Brecht of pornography.[44] Such a
pornographer would refuse to entertain his audience, insisting instead on
educating them. By means of flashing images of sexually abused women
across the screen, he would intend to excite women-degrading feelings in his
audience, and he would, as Brecht did, try to force his audience to recognize

his intentions. In such a case, a group-defamation suit would be possible, and a Brechtian pornographer would have but two defenses: (1) that what he said about women is in fact true, or (2) that his audience misunderstood what he said.

Truth of course is a defense in standard defamation cases, whether the defamation is libelous (written or depicted) or slanderous (oral). If I publicly charge Smith with buggery and he sues me, I can defeat the suit by showing that he is indeed a buggerer. If the same rules prevail in group-defamation suits, then a Brechtian pornographer would be allowed to defend himself by establishing the truth of some proposition such as "all women are masochists and they like being masochists." This means that judges and jurors would be called upon to determine the truth of what amounts to an ideological claim.[45] They would be asked to decide whether it is Theodor Reik who is correct when he exclaims, "Feminine masochism of the woman? Sounds like a pleonasm. It is comparable to an expression like, 'the Negro has dark skin.' But the color of the skin is defined simply by the term Negro; a white Negro is no Negro,"[46] or whether it is instead Andrea Dworkin who is correct when she insists that women are not willing masochists but persons whose bodies have been "sexually colonized" and who are routinely forced to "volunteer," against their best interest, for male sexual abuse.[47] (Note that the term "masochist" is used here to denote not a woman who freely chooses to engage in sadomasochistic practices because they fulfill *her* sexual wants and needs as well as those of her sadist partner, but a woman who has been socially encouraged or conditioned to submit to sexual abuse, and even to risk her own physical and psychic destruction, if by so doing she is able to satisfy a *man's* gyno-thanatic impulses.)

Assuming that it is wise to let judges and jurors arbitrate the truth of general philosophies, a Brechtian pornographer would have difficulty proving that "all women are masochists and they like being masochists." But prove this he would have to. In a defamation suit the burden of proof would fall upon his shoulders, since "out of a tender regard for reputations the law presumes in the first instance that all defamation is false, and the defendant has the burden of pleading and proving its truth."[48] In short, women would not have to disprove that they are willing masochists; rather, the pornographer would have to prove that women are willing masochists.

Since this would be no easy task, a Brechtian pornographer might prefer to argue in his defense that his audience misinterpreted his message. He might claim that although his audience took him to say that "It's great that all women are masochists—nothing must be done to alter this wonderful state of affairs," what he intended to say through his film was that "It's a shame that all women are masochists—something must be done to alter this lamentable state of affairs." If this were the case, it would be unfair to accuse him of defamation. Why not instead accuse his audience of defamation?

Along these lines, B. Ruby Rich relates a story. One of her friends worked as an artist's model. Usually she refused to model for photographers because, with photographers, models have little control over who sees their bodies. Once, however, she violated her rule and modeled for a photographer friend who did a series of nude photographs of her that she thought were beautiful. Unfortunately, one of these photos was stolen from the photographer. The model went into a depression, tormented by the image of an unknown man masturbating to her photo. Ruby Rich asks: "Was that photograph erotic or pornographic?"[49] On the one hand, if the viewer's perceptions determine whether a depiction is "erotic" or "pornographic," then the photo of the woman was "pornographic." On the other hand, if the intentions of the photographer determine whether a depiction is "erotic" or "pornographic," then the photo of the woman was "erotic." But if, as suggests Rich, there is no way to decide whether a photographer's intentions or a viewer's perceptions determine the message of a photo, then there is no way to decide whether a photo is essentially "erotic" or essentially "pornographic." Indeed, continues Rich, there is no reason to think that any photograph has an essential meaning. Rather, there are as many interpretations and/or uses of a photograph as there are interpreters and users. The photographer's viewpoint is but one among many; and he should not be held responsible for viewpoints that diverge from his.[50]

Although this is probably the most accurate way to articulate complex   36
issues of perception and intention, if we are talking about standard defamation law, then the pornographer's intended statements—and not a specific audience's interpretations of them—determine whether defamation has been perpetrated or not. This being the case, our Brechtian pornographer will have to be given an opportunity to establish that his message was misunderstood, for example, by an exceptionally "hypersensitive" or "prudish" audience. If the largest majority of his audience takes him to be communicating a gynothanatic message, this will of course count against his defense. Nonetheless, our Brechtian pornographer will escape liability, if he can show that a "reasonable man,"[51] that is, a person of ordinary sensibilities, would not have interpreted his film as conveying gyno-thanatic ideas.[52]

b. *Objection Two:* Even if it could be established that most pornographers   37
intend to communicate women-degrading messages to their audiences—that they mean to activate the brains as well as the penises of their audience against women—the objection will be made that Anglo American law simply has no way to handle cases of group defamation.

Traditionally, the law of defamation is concerned with the protection   38
of an individual's reputation and not with the protection of a group's reputation, especially an unwieldy and huge group like women. John Salmond, the sage of torts, for example, dismissed as ridiculous any notion of a suit against someone for saying that all clergymen are hypocrites or all lawyers dishonest. According to Salmond, as the number of a defamed group swells, the extravagance of the defamer's assertions will discredit him or her. It is one thing to convince a person that some clergymen are hypocrites, that some lawyers are dishonest, and that some women are masochists. It is quite another matter to persuade a person that *all* clergymen are hypocrites, that *all* lawyers are dishonest, and that *all* women are masochists. And even if a few people were

convinced by such global generalizations, would this fact actually hurt any or all clergymen, lawyers, and women; and could this fact support anything but the most "speculative claim" for damages, either material or psychic?[53]

Once again this is a forceful set of objections to which feminists have responded more or less convincingly. Although there are no precise precedents for *civil* group-defamation suits in the United States, feminists note that the Supreme Court has upheld *criminal* statutes that protect groups from harms akin to defamation; such as from contempt, derision, or obloquy. For example, in a 1952 case, *Beuharnis* v. *Illinois,* the Supreme Court sustained the constitutionality of a state statute that made it unlawful to disseminate or display publicly any "lithography, moving picture, play, drama or sketch" portraying "depravity, criminality, unchastity, or lack of virtue of a class of citizens, of any race, color, creed or religion" thereby either exposing these citizens to "contempt, derision or obloquy" or producing a "breach of the peace or riots."[54] Given that the criminal law is a more onerous legal sanction than the civil law (it is, for example, more disgraceful to stand criminal trial than to be sued in a civil court), feminists point to *Beuharnis* not because they want to send pornographers to prison for publicly displaying and disseminating gyno-thanatica, but simply because the *Beuharnis* case sought to remedy the harms that *groups* sustain. Therefore, the case is a precedent for a civil group-defamation suit only in the weak sense that it encourages legal theorists to think in terms of collective harms—the type of harms that an entire race or an entire gender is likely to sustain.

If feminists have found only weak precedent for the concept of group defamation, they have found strong legal support for their claim that statements like "all women are masochists" cause harm to women as a group as well as to women as individuals. In a lengthy article on group defamation, David Reisman argues that statements like "all lawyers are dishonest" have had a negative effect on the legal community:

> The legal profession has suffered in esteem and influence from such reiterated remarks (it is noteworthy that Hollywood usually portrays lawyers as obfuscators or crooks . . .), and its members have directly suffered in pocket, for many persons are deterred, as we all know, from resorting to lawyers out of fear of excessive fees and other sharp practices.[55]

Reisman concludes by observing that no member of a racial or cultural minority—blacks, Jews, American Indians, Poles—escapes "some psychic or material hurt as a consequence of the attacks upon the group with which he is voluntarily or involuntarily identified."[56]

Taking their cue from Reisman, some members of WAP, TBTN, and WAVPM have argued that statements like "all women are willing masochists who both want and need sexual abuse" do indeed cause harm to women as a group and to women as individuals. When pressed to specify the harm done to women by gyno-thanatic statements, however, feminists hesitate. Either an act of defamation causes material damage (loss of business, opportunity, income, physical security) or it causes psychic distress. A claim that gyno-thanatic pornography does the first sort of harm to women requires some form of the causal argument—that is, some appeal to the notion that if men see gyno-thanatic visions and hear gyno-thanatic statements they will engage in gyno-thanatic acts (sexual harassment, rape, woman battering). But as noted in Argument One, this causal relationship is tenuous and unlikely to support a claim for material damages.

The second possible avenue, that pornography is harmful because it 42 causes psychic distress (insomnia, agitation, fear and trembling, hysteria) seems more promising. For example, feminist antipornographers claim that gyno-thanatic images have a profoundly upsetting effect on them. Neverthe-less, a significant number of women insist that the "pornophobia" of feminist antipornographers is a largely manufactured syndrome, an overreaction to sexually explicit fantasies that should not bother real women in the least. Interestingly, Reisman accounts for such divergent reactions by observing that adults who claim that nasty generalizations about their group (race, class, religion) are "mere idle blathering" remind him of children who chant "Sticks and stones can break my bones, but names can never hurt me" precisely because they are hurting.[57] Sometimes this may be so, but it is also possible for women not to be physically distressed by gyno-thanatica. Indeed, this is why at least some women have joined the anti-pornography movement. If this is the case, the persuasiveness of a civil suit on behalf of *all* women seems questionable.

c. *Objection Three:* Even if it could be established that women as a group 43 and women as individuals were materially damaged and/or psychically dis-tressed by gyno-thanatica, a third objection to the group defamation ap-proach remains: That it opens the flood gates to all manner of lawsuits. If women can sue the creators and purveyors of gyno-thanatic pornography for depicting and describing women as sexually warped masochists, then they can sue the producers of television commercials that portray women as rather unintelligent housewives who spend their days agonizing over what laundry detergent to use. That is, if women can sue pornographers for spreading deep and vicious lies about females as *sex* objects, then they can sue commercial artists for manufacturing falsehoods or half-truths about women's *gender* roles. And if women can initiate such suits, then industrialists can sue leftists who claim "all capitalists are bloodsuckers," and Italian-Americans can sue the producers of "The Untouchables" for conveying the impression that most Italians belong to the Mafia and spend Saturday nights machine-gunning whole neighborhoods.

In response to this objection, feminists admit that a society such as ours 44 cannot survive if not only individuals but also groups sue each other at a drop of a hat. If a constitutional democracy is to remain stable, both the virtue of democratic tolerance and that of mutual respect have to be practiced. The one cannot be sacrificed for the other. Therefore, potential litigants need tests to which they can appeal as they decide whether or not to bring suit against their defamers.

One such test may be the following: Defamatory statements are more 45 or less harmful to the extent that they attack the core of a person. As Carolyn M. Shafer and Marilyn Frye point out:

> In dealing with persons, one is dealing with behaving bodies, and it is these that have domains. . . . Since biological life and health are prerequisites for the pursuit of any other interests and goals whatever, everything necessary for their maintenance and sustenance evidently will fall very close to the center of the domain. Whatever has a relatively permanent effect on the person, whatever affects its relatively constant surroundings, whatever causes it discomfort or distress—in short, whatever a person has to live with—is likely to fall squarely within its domain.[58]

If Shafer's and Frye's analysis is correct, then defamatory depictions and descriptions directed against one's race or sexuality violate the center of a person's domain more grievously than those directed against one's national origin or gender role. One's race is not escapable in the same way that one's national origin is. Blacks stand out in a white population in a manner that Italian-Americans do not stand out in an American population. Similarly, a woman cannot transcend her biological sex as easily as she can belie gender stereotypes. Therefore, to defame persons on account of their race or sexuality, to suggest that those characteristics which constitute their essential persons are precisely those characteristics which make them less than fully human, is to do something more harmful to persons than to attack them on account of their national origin or gender role. If this is so, when courts are faced with the problem of balancing democratic tolerance against mutual respect, they may decide to tip the scales in favor of the former when it comes to civil suits involving ethnic group, gender role, religion, or profession and in favor of the latter when it comes to civil suits involving race or sex.

But even though this test is available, feminists realize that the group 46 defamation approach is not likely to work unless Objection Two above can be answered; and this is precisely the objection that cannot be met unless women *as a group* come to share the same negative reactions to gyno-thanatic pornography. If recent arguments between feminist antipornographers and feminist anti-antipornographers are any indication, however, a consensus will not be achieved tomorrow, if ever.

Arguments Invoking the Offense Principle

Realizing that it is difficult to convince society as a whole, women in 47 general, and every feminist in particular that gyno-thanatica is harmful either in the sense of causing men to engage in harmful behavior toward women or in the sense of constituting a group defamation to women, some feminist antipornographers have argued that gyno-thanatica is legally restrictable on other grounds; namely, on the grounds that it constitutes an offense to many onlookers. That is, the state may restrict the public display and dissemination of gyno-thanatic pornography not because such exhibitions harm all women, but simply because they give offense—cause responses of shame, disgust, embarrassment, or "boiling blood"—to many onlookers, especially women.

The main problem with this approach is that the offense principle is one of the weaker liberty-limiting principles. Ever since John Stuart Mill's time, there has been considerable debate as to whether any principle other than the harm principle can constitute a sufficient reason for limiting the liberty of a citizen. In general, the overwhelming sentiment has been that each citizen may do as he or she pleases, provided that he or she causes no other person harm. This being the case, the law may not restrict a person's liberty merely because he or she harms himself or herself, gives offense to others, or engages in "harmless" immoralities.

Significantly, it is not clear that Mill, who is usually regarded as the 48 main advocate of the preceding point of view, really espoused it in every detail. He seems, for example, to have conferred some validity upon the offense principle. At times, Mill relates harm to the violation of personal or property rights and offense to the violation of something less stringent than rights, such as aesthetic sensibilities. Whereas harms violate the law, offenses violate good manners, propriety, or custom. Nonetheless, offenses do not always fall entirely outside the scope of the law. Says Mill:

> There are many acts which, being directly injurious only to the agents themselves, ought not to be legally interdicted, but which, if done publicly, are a violation of good manners, and coming thus within the category of offenses against others, may rightfully be prohibited. Of this kind are offenses against public decency.[49]

But why may a "harmless" offense such as public nudity, be validly restricted? Is it not an instance of symbolic speech, a nonverbal or primarily nonverbal expression of opinion about the artificiality of clothing, entitled to the same protection that safeguards theological, philosophical, and political arguments that are verbal or primarily verbal?

Those who are not impressed by the merits of *offensive* symbolic speech 49 argue that, to the extent that it is really a commentary on obsolete social taboos, it is a mere *form* (and a second-rate one at that) of saying something that can be equally well said without using that form. In other words, nudists do not have to resort to self-exposure to get their message across; supposedly, they can get their message across better by giving a speech when fully clothed or by writing a book in the privacy of their own nudist colony. Mill suggests as much when he says that public indecencies that aim to communicate opinions in nonverbal modes are not as valuable as assertions, criticisms, advocacies, and debates.[60]

But this is not always true, especially in an age when nonverbal modes 50 of communication are intermingled with verbal modes of communication and when some entirely nonverbal modes of communication are understood to convey ideas and attitudes in a powerful manner not to be rivaled by verbal modes of communication. Indeed, the general direction of the Supreme Court has been to recognize these developments and to lend increasing First Amendment protection to modes of art, such as films, whose meaning cannot be conveyed through words at all or through words alone. This concession suggests that unjustified prohibitions on art forms such as punk music, modern dance, and mime would be unconstitutional.[61] In short, the First Amendment protects all *communications,* nonverbal as well as verbal; and it does not assign primacy of value to any specific mode of communication.

But if verbal modes of communication are not necessarily more valuable 51 than nonverbal modes of communication, then the main justification formerly given for legally restricting certain public indecencies evaporates. However, there may be another, better reason to restrict legally some offensive behavior; namely, that a pluralistic society can withstand only so much in the way of denigrating and degrading speakings, writings, soundings, and depictings before its viability is threatened. There are certain moral virtues or character traits, such as democratic tolerance and mutual respect, that citizens must exhibit if the democracy is to remain stable over time.[62]

This is probably the intuition behind Joel Feinberg's attempt to add 52 credence to the offense principles as a liberty-limiting principle. He argues that offensive expression may be restricted provided that it is universally offensive, publicly flaunted, and imposed on the beholders. An offense is of the universal sort when it can be expected to evoke reactions such as shame, embarrassment, repugnance, repulsion, or disgust in almost any person simply because he or she is a person, and not because he or she belongs to the Moral Majority, the Black Panthers, or the Society for Prevention of Cruelty to Animals.[63] Almost anyone would be disgusted by the sight of a man who defecated in public and then ate his feces in front of passersby. An offense is publicly flaunted when individuals can avoid it only by unreasonably inconveniencing themselves.[64] For example, someone would be unreasonably inconvenienced if the only way he could avoid blatantly offensive sights would be by foregoing his forays into the public marketplace except between the hours of 2:00 A.M. and 3:00 A.M. Finally, an offense is imposed on beholders when they have not voluntarily assumed risk of offense upon themselves. For example, a person would be so imposed upon if she were misled to think that a movie theater was featuring Walt Disney's *Bambi,* a sentimental tale about a fawn, when in fact it was featuring some pornographer's version of *Bambi,* where Bambi is a woman upon whom sexual abuse is heaped.

If Feinberg is correct, the implications are these. Considering almost any 53 account of women-degrading pornography, at least gyno-thanatica is universally offensive. Most women and perhaps most men are offended by depictions of men treating women as pieces of meat ready to be branded or butchered on the altar of male sexual entertainment. And even if the population as a whole is not offended by such depictions, some feminists note that Feinberg's standard of universality can be supplemented with the doctrine of retaliatory violence, a doctrine meant to offset such insensitivity. According to this doctrine, expressions like public cross-burnings, displays of swastikas, and "Polish jokes" may be curtailed if they are bound to upset, alarm, anger, or irritate those whom they insult in ways that will cause them to vent their anger in retaliatory aggression.[65]

An example will clarify the import of this doctrine. In a 1939 prosecution   54
for using disorderly, threatening, or insulting language/behavior in a public place, a strict orator named Ninfo was convicted for shouting from a soapbox, "If I had my way, I would hang all the Jews in this country. I wish I had $100,000 from Hitler. I would show those damn Jews what I would do, you mockies, you damn Jews, you scum."[66] Significantly, Ninfo was convicted on the grounds that a reasonable Jew could not be expected to listen to his words passively. If a reasonable Jew in Ninfo's audience were to lose his temper, then Ninfo and not the Jew would be responsible for the Jew's aggressive behavior. Therefore, to prevent such justified but nonetheless violent outbursts, the law demands that Ninfo either tone down his rhetoric or speak in a more private location where Jews are not likely to be in attendance. Analogously, whether or not gyno-thanatic pornography offends the entire population, provided that it is upsetting enough to prompt reasonable women to militant action, as it has in some cases where women have "trashed" gyno-thanatic displays, there may be cause for legal intervention. In such a case, it is not the women who should be prosecuted for the damage they cause, but the displayers of gyno-thanatic pornography for prompting such retaliatory violence.

Still, if those who take offense at gyno-thanatica can easily and effec-   55
tively avoid them, then such depictions and descriptions may not be legitimately restricted. In other words, no matter how universally offensive a gyno-thanatic film is and no matter how conducive to retaliatory violence it is, provided that it is not publicly flaunted or foisted upon unwilling spectators, it may be viewed in private no matter how many nonviewers are repulsed, embarrassed, shamed, or angered at the mere thought that others are viewing it. This seems to have been behind the Supreme Court's thinking in *Stanley* v. *Georgia,* the decision that held that Georgia could not convict Mr. Stanley merely for possessing in his home an obscene film for his own viewing.[67] After citing the First Amendment right of Mr. Stanley to receive information and ideas, the Court appealed to the constitutional right of privacy: "For also fundamental is the right to be free, except in very limited circumstances, from unwanted government intrusion into one's privacy."[68] Therefore, if gyno-thanatic pornography violates neither women's interests nor rights, if it simply wounds women's sensibilities, then, provided that it is not publicly displayed and disseminated, feminists must live with the knowledge that it is being viewed in the recesses of the so-called private realm.

CONCLUSION

Apparently, there is no ideal legal remedy for gyno-thanatic pornogra-   56
phy in particular or for women-degrading pornography in general. To date, all of the legal remedies advanced by feminist antipornographers have proved

to be somehow flawed or limited. Still it is possible to rank them in order of increasing cogency. The clear-and-present-danger approach is the most problematic. If gyno-thanatic pornography presents a threat of this magnitude to society, then it is not enough to restrict it when it appears in the *public* domain. It must also be restricted when it emerges in the *private* realm. If those who view gyno-thanatic material are caused to sexually abuse women, then as far as the law is concerned, it matters not whether they view it in public or in private. In either case, it is extremely dangerous and must be extirpated. But there is little consensus on just how dangerous gyno-thanatic pornography is. Although feminists are confident that gyno-thanatic images shape the way people think and act, they do not know how they do this or to what extent. And until they know the how and why of gyno-thanatica, the clear-and-present-danger approach should be resisted. After all, to invoke a test that ensnared antidraft protestors in both world wars and alleged "Communists" during the Cold War is to risk depriving citizens of their liberty unnecessarily; and it is extremely doubtful that feminists wish to add to such injustices if they can avoid it.[69]

Better than the clear-and-present-danger approach is the group defamation approach; but it, too, is fatally flawed. What seems to be central in the group-defamation approach is the "lie" that gyno-thanatica tells about women and their sexuality: That women love to be sexually abused by men. But lies about female sexuality are not confined to *Snuff, The Devil in Miss Jones,* and *Deep Throat.* Silhouette romances may be telling lies about female sexuality that encourage women to accept as natural their inferior status in the social structure. Moreover, all sorts of religious, psychological, and philosophical works tell "lies" about female sexuality. What is incoherent about the group-defamation approach is that it comes close to losing the connection between its principle of regulation (prevention of "lies" about female sexuality) and its object of regulation (control of sexually explicit material).[70] If feminist antipornographers want to prevent *lies* about women, then they must take on Freud as well as Hugh Hefner and the producers of *Snuff.* After all, the lies that stimulate the brain are more powerful than those that stimulate the penis—unless, of course, I am hopelessly misguided to think that men of Freud's stature have had a deeper effect on the way we think than men of Hefner's talents.

More adequate than either of the preceding legal approaches is the offense-principle approach. Assuming that a gyno-thanatic depiction or description is either universally offensive or sufficiently gross to make the blood of at least feminists boil, and provided that it is publicly flaunted or foisted upon unwilling spectators who have no reasonable way to avoid it, then the state may drive this material out of the public domain. Unfortunately, it is not that clear either where the public domain ends, or how blatant, brazen, and/or blaring a gyno-thanatic display must be before it constitutes an unavoidable assault upon an unwilling spectator's sense.

In this connection, the so-called Skokie crisis is instructive. In 1979 the National Socialist Party won the court's permission not only to march in the predominantly Jewish community of Skokie, but also to wear their swastikas, and this despite the fact that their message of anti-Semitism was all too familiar, their action was offensive to Gentiles as well as to Jews, and their mode of presentation deliberately unavoidable.[71] Although the court did not deny "that the proposed demonstration would seriously disturb, emotionally and mentally, at least some, and probably many, of the village's residents,"[72] it nonetheless proclaimed:

> It is better to allow those who preach racial hate to expend their venom in rhetoric rather than [for us to] be panicked into embarking on the dangerous course of permitting the government to decide what its citizens may see and hear. . . . The ability of American Society to tolerate the advocacy even of the hateful doctrines espoused by the plaintiffs without abandoning its commitment to freedom of speech and assembly is perhaps the best protection we have against the establishment of any Nazi-type regime in this country.[73]

As it so happened, the Nazis did not march in Skokie. Fearing retaliatory violence on the part of the Jews, they marched around Chicago's Grant Park instead. But what if the Nazis had marched that day in Skokie? Or what if they wanted to march every week in Skokie or to schedule systematically a march in a different Jewish community every weekend? Or what if, as Susan Brownmiller speculates, "the bookstores and movie theaters lining Forty-Second Street in New York City were devoted . . . to a systematized, commercially successful propaganda machine depicting the sadistic pleasures of gassing Jews or lynching blacks?"[74] Faced with such incidents, would not the courts reconsider their stance on democratic tolerance, stressing instead this nation's need to strike a better balance between the freedom to speak and the freedom not to listen? If so, feminists ask, should not the courts also attend to the fact that many bookstores and movie theaters are currently devoted "to the humiliation of women by rape and torture?"[75] In any event, even if the courts did do something about gyno-thanatic pornography, if only to restrict its *public* celebration to the Forty Second Streets of this nation, little would be gained. Pornography is a four-billion dollar a year enterprise; and as the years pass, it is becoming an increasingly slick business. Less of it is being publicly disseminated and displayed as more of it finds entrance into the home via video cassettes, cable television, and 16 mm. home films. Were laws against gyno-thanatica's *public* appearances passed and enforced, the process of its "privatization" would be accelerated. More and more video cassettes, for example, would be produced; and far from withering away, gyno-thanatica would thrive as men discovered the pleasures of watching it at home rather than in some shabby center-city theater.

Indeed, it is this last point which has persuaded many feminists largely to abandon the search for legal remedies. More of them are agreeing with Wendy Kaminer that "it makes little sense for feminists to focus on a legal 'war' against pornography or to direct much energy to reformulating obscenity prohibitions."[76] Not only does the effort seem disproportional to the outcome, but the outcome is one frought with danger, since, as Kaminer also points out, legislative or judicial control of pornography may not be possible without jeopardizing the legal principles and procedures that are essential to feminists' right to speak and, ultimately, feminists' freedom to control their sexual destinies.[77]

Realizing that Anglo-American law is such that it cannot provide remedies for every blight that poisons the human community in general and male-female sexual relations in particular, feminists are relying on extralegal means of persuasion—book writing, filmmaking, and consciousness-raising. Although feminists have been criticized for even these efforts, the criticisms seem excessive. To call a feminist "a moral prude," "a sexually repressed woman," or "an enemy of freedom" simply because she is not prepared to praise any and all sexually explicit material is to castigate someone because of her desire to make reasoned distinctions. [62]

Admittedly, a few feminist antipornographers have on occasion bombarded their captive audiences with the horrors of gyno-thanatica, appealing more to their "guts" than to their minds and forcing them to hasty conclusions. Amber Hollibaugh, for example, complains about the manner in which WAVPM has constructed its antiporn slide show: [63]

> There will be an image from a porn magazine of a woman tied up, beaten, right? And they'll say, *Hustler* magazine, 1976, and you're struck dumb by it, horrified! The next slide will be a picture of a woman with a police file, badly beaten by her husband. And the rap that connects these two is that the image of the woman tied and bruised in the pornographic magazine *caused* the beating that she suffered. The talk implies that her husband went and saw that picture, then came home and tried to re-create it in their bedroom. That is the guilt by association theory of pornography and violence. And I remember sitting and watching this slide show and being freaked out about both of those images. And having nowhere to react to the analysis and say, what the hell is going on? I found it incredibly manipulative.[78]

For similar reasons, Gayle Rubin condemns a WAVPM tour of New York's porn strip: [64]

> When I went on the WAVPM tour, everybody went and stood in front of the bondage material. It was like they had on blinders. And I said, look, there's oral sex over there! Why don't you look at that? And they were glued to the bondage rack. I started pulling out female dominance magazines, and saying, look, here's a woman dominating a man. What about that? It was like I wasn't there. People said, look at this picture of a woman being tied up![79]

But even though Hollibaugh and Rubin have a point—that the presentations they describe left no room for discussion—most feminist antipornographers are not as dogmatic as the ones they encountered. On the contrary, like those feminists who currently support pornography, those feminists who currently oppose it wish to explore its liberating as well as its enslaving features.

Of course, it is difficult to decide when sexually explicit material is a   65 source of sexual liberation and general freedom for humans and when it is a source of sexual oppression and general unfreedom. Although many feminists who endorse pornography admit that it can be a "bastion of sexism," they hasten to add that ordinarily it is a "vehicle of rebellion" against repressive, oppressive, and depressive sexual and moral norms. Indeed, these women claim that society has the pornographic imagination to thank for the "new openness about, say, nudity, lesbianism, oral-genital sex or even nonmarital sex";[80] and they insist that anyone who is for sexual liberation must also be for pornography. Therefore, to be a liberated woman is to enjoy sex is to enjoy pornography.

But *must* a liberated woman enjoy all sexual experiences and *must* she   66 enjoy all types of sexually explicit material? Susan Sontag is one woman who answers this question with a definite 'no.' As she sees it, the question to ask women is: What kind of sex are women being liberated to enjoy?

> Merely to remove the onus placed upon the sexual expressiveness of women is a hollow victory if the sexuality they become freer to enjoy remains the old one that converts women into objects. . . . This already "freer" sexuality mostly reflects a spurious idea of freedom: the right of each person, briefly, to exploit and dehumanize someone else. Without a change in the very norms of sexuality, the liberation of women is a meaningless goal. Sex as such is not liberating for women. Neither is more sex.[81]

As usual, Sontag has made a profound observation. The path to freedom is not through *Playgirl* or through male striptease joints; that is, women will not come into touch with their own sexuality by exploiting and dehumanizing men, or by trading the role of masochist for that of sadist, or by creating men-degrading pornography. Rather, if women are to understand what female sexuality means apart from men as well as in relation to men, then they must shatter the old sex roles and drown out this society's dominant, if not exclusive, discourse on sexuality; namely, sex = violence = death. But if women are to succeed, they must say something more than sex = nonviolence = life; for to say this is only to negate what men have said in the past.

It is difficult to say something new about sexuality and about its vehicle,   67 the body. It will take time for women to free their imagination from the definitions and concepts men have, because of certain social conditions, constructed for it. But free it they can. And when women achieve this feat, they will drown out gyno-thanatic discourse not with andro-thanatic discourse, but with multiple voices celebrating the incarnation of woman as woman. In this connection, Deirdre English describes one of the more "erotic sights" she ever saw:

> It was a hot summer day in Pennsylvania, and during a break in the weekend-long conference we gathered at an outdoor swimming pool. There were no men around, so we all stripped and swam naked—dozens of women, most of them perfect strangers. I had never really been struck before by how *different* women's bodies are from how they're "supposed to be," and how woman's body is unique.[82]

The more women learn to love their bodies, the less power men will have over women. Once women revere their bodies, and once they rejoice, revel, and relax in them, they will refuse to hand them over to anyone who would treat them cruelly and contemptuously. And once men as well as women realize that woman's sexuality is not "for-man," a real sexual liberation will be effected. At last, men and women will be able to relate to each other as sexed beings whose sexuality is an expression of personal uniqueness, rather than the reflection of any unilateral vision or universal prescription of how one sex should relate to the other.

NOTES

All notes are Tong's.

1. Deirdre English, "The Politics of Porn: Can Feminists Walk the Line?" *Mother Jones*, April 1980, p. 20.

2. Judith R. Walkowitz, "The Politics of Prostitution," *Signs: Journal of Women in Culture and Society* 6, no. 1 (Autumn 1980):123–35.

3. Cultural feminism is a school of thought that equates women's liberation with the development and preservation of a female counterculture. It advocates separatism from male values rather than men.

4. Deborah Sherman and Harriet Hirshorn, "Feminists and Sexuality: Background to a Debate," *WIN* 18 (October 15, 1982):9.

5. David A. J. Richards, *The Moral Criticism of the Law* (Encino, Calif.: Dickenson Publishing Co., 1977), p. 64.

6. Ibid., p. 64.

7. Ibid.

8. *Miller* v. *California*, 413 U.S. 15, 24 (1973).

9. English, "The Politics of Porn," p. 23.

10. I take the distinction between hard- and soft-core pornography to be this: Although both of these pornographic modes suggest male sexual domination and female sexual submission, only the former is tinged with violence.

11. English, "The Politics of Porn," p. 23.

12. Ibid.

13. I owe this distinction to Robert Fullinwider, Center for Philosophy and Public Policy, University of Maryland.

14. Rosemarie Tong, "Feminism, Pornography, and Censorship," *Social Theory and Practice* 8, no. 1 (Spring 1982):1–17.

15. Gloria Steinem, "What is Pornography?" *Take Back the Night,* Laura Lederer, ed. (New York: William Morrow, 1980), p. 39.

16. Lederer, ed., *Take Back the Night.*

17. Susan Griffin, *Pornography and Silence: Culture's Revenge Against Nature* (New York: Harper & Row, 1981).

18. Adrienne Rich, "Compulsory Heterosexuality and Lesbian Existence," *Signs: Journal of Women in Culture and Society* 5, no. 4 (1980):641.

19. Ibid.

20. Jean Bethke Elshtain, "The Victim Syndrome: A Troubling Turn in Feminism," *The Progressive* 46 (June 1982):43.

21. Ibid., pp. 42–43.

22. Martha Nelson, "The Sex Life of the Romance Novel," *Ms.,* February 1983, p. 97.

23. Ibid.

24. Ibid., p. 99.

25. Catherine A. MacKinnon, "Feminism, Marxism, Method, and the State: An Agenda for Theory," *Signs: Journal of Women in Culture and Society* 7, no. 3 (Spring 1982):534.

26. For a complete explanation of these four liberty-limiting principles, see Joel Feinberg, *Social Philosophy* (Englewood Cliffs, N. J.: Jersey: Prentice-Hall, 1973), pp. 36–55.

27. Feminists have eschewed the principle of legal paternalism, except to suggest that some women who view gyno-thanatica may harm themselves to the extent that they think less of themselves as persons or let themselves be treated as less than persons. Feminists have not, however, gone on to argue that women should be denied access to gyno-thanatica. There is little, if any, empirical evidence to establish the hypothesis that women who view women-degrading pornography in general or gyno-thanatica in particular lose their sense of self-respect. Indeed, the opposite may be true. Most women who willingly view such pornography may, after awhile, become so outraged by the sight of brutalized female flesh that their sense of self-respect is either retrieved or comes alive for the first time. Insofar as women are concerned, "Enough is enough" is a more probable response to *Snuff* than "Wow! What a turn-on." Likewise, regarding other issues, feminists have shunned the principle of legal moralism. Of all the purported liberty-limiting principles, the principle of legal moralism is the most problematic. It aims to restrict legally actions, descriptions, and depictions that are immoral, where "immoral" means something other than either "harmful" or "offensive." But because it is difficult to conceive what the term "immoral" can mean other than "harmful" or "offensive," feminists have not, like the Moral Majority, argued that women-degrading pornography in general and gyno-thanatic pornography in particular should be legally restricted simply because it is immoral—where "immoral" means "against the rule of a higher authority" (God) or "against a societal taboo."

28. Susan Brownmiller, "Let's Put Pornography Back in the Closet," in Lederer, ed., *Take Back the Night,* p. 255.

29. United States Commission on Obscenity and Pornography, *Report of the Commission on Obscenity and Pornography* (Washington, D.C.: U.S. Government Printing Office, 1970), p. 27.

30. Donald Mosher, "Sex Differences, Sex Guilt, and Explicitly Sexual Films," *The Journal of Social Issues* 29, no. 3 (March 1973):95–112.

31. Pauline B. Bart and Margaret Jozsa, "Dirty Books, Dirty Films, and Dirty Data," in Lederer, ed., *Take Back the Night,* p. 209.

32. Sarah J. McCarthy, "Pornography, Rape, and the Cult of Macho," *The Humanist* 40, no. 5 (September/October 1980):19.

33. Irene Diamond, "Pornography and Repression: A Reconsideration of 'Who' and 'What,'" in Lederer, ed., *Take Back the Night,* p. 191.

34. Wendy Kaminer, "Pornography and the First Amendment: Prior Restraints and Private Action," in Lederer, ed., *Take Back the Night,* p. 245.

35. Speaking for the majority in a decision that vindicated states' rights to ban publicly disseminated and/or publicly displayed obscenity, Justice Berger said: "We have directed our holdings, not at thoughts or speech, but at depiction and description of specifically defined sexual conduct

that states may regulate within limits designed to prevent infringement of First Amendment rights." *Paris Adult Theater I* v. *Slaton,* 413 U.S. 49 (1973).

36. For a full description of *Snuff's* plot, see Beverly LaBelle, "Snuff—*The Ultimate in Women-Hating*" in Lederer, ed., *Take Back the Night,* pp. 272–74.

37. Diana E. H. Russell with Laura Lederer, "Questions We Get Asked Most Often," in Lederer, ed., *Take Back the Night,* pp. 25–26.

38. Hugo A. Bedau, "Rough Justice: The Limits of Novel Defenses," *Hastings Center Report* 8 (December 1978):8.

39. Helen Longino, "Pornography, Oppression and Freedom: A Closer Look," in Lederer, ed., *Take Back the Night,* p. 50.

40. Ibid., p. 51.

41. Criminal statutes against *threatening* defamation are another possibility.

42. H. P. Grice, "Meaning," *Philosophical Review* 66 (1957):385.

43. English, "The Politics of Porn," p. 44.

44. Bertolt Brecht was an innovative German playwright who transcended the parameters of Greek theater. He did not believe that the primary function of tragic theater was cathartic; rather, he believed that it was didactic.

45. For a thorough discussion of the impact that sexist and racist language use has on women and minorities, see Part IV of Mary Vetterling-Braggin, ed., *Sexist Language: A Modern Philosophical Analysis* (Totowa, N.J.: Rowman and Littlefield, 1981), pp. 249–318.

46. Andrea Dworkin, "Pornography's Exquisite Volunteers, *Ms.,* March 1981, p. 96.

47. Ibid.

48. William C. Prosser, *Handbook of the Law of Torts,* 2d ed. (St. Paul, Minn.: West Publishing Co., 1955), p. 631.

49. B. Ruby Rich, "Anti-Porn: Soft Issue, Hard World," *The Village Voice* 20 (July 1982):17.

50. Ibid.

51. The "reasonable man" test is a standard test for liability applied to Anglo-American tort law. It is meant to serve as an objective check on the individual subjectivities of men and women who are not perfectly reasonable.

52. But all this is quite beside the point. Most pornographers are neither as artistically skilled nor as politically aware as Bertolt Brecht, and most consumers of porn would balk at attempts to intellectualize gyno-thanatic films. Does this mean that pornographers cannot be sued for defamation because they usually do not intend to say anything slanderous/libelous about women when they flash across the screen images of bruised and bloodied women, or because porn devotees do not usually link their feelings about women during a gyno-thanatic film with any didactic intentions they think the film's writers, producers, distributors, or displayers had? Does the magic of catharsis relieve the porn establishment of any causal responsibility for the exacerbation of women-despising attitudes in real life? I think not. If images reach into the lives of an audience, a point we stress when we discuss the impact of media violence on children's psyches, then they probably reach into the lives of any audience, young or old.

The law of defamation could be adopted in ways that would ascribe liability to members of the porn industry for publicly displaying gyno-thanatic material that is known, as the result of empirical tests on substantially similar material to lessen the esteem in which women are held or known to excite adverse feelings and opinions against women; and this, even though most porn consumers go to gyno-thanatic films, say, to be entertained and not to be educated, and even though most pornographers make gyno-thanatic films to entertain their audiences and not to educate them. In other words, there is no reason to insist that all defamations have to be intentional anymore than that all homicides have to be intentional. Just as the harmful effect counts more in cases of manslaughter than the lack of intent to kill, so, too, the harmful effect may count more in "negligent defamation" than the lack of explicit intent to damage the reputation of women.

53. David Reisman, "Democracy and Defamation: Control of Group Libel," *Columbia Law Review* 42 (May 1942): 770.

54. *Beuharnis* v. *Illinois,* 343 U.S. 250, 725 S. Ct. 725, 96 L. Ed. 918 (1952).

55. Reisman, "Democracy and Defamation," p. 770.

56. Ibid., p. 771.

57. Ibid.

58. Marilyn Frye and Carolyn M. Shafer, "Rape and Respect," in *Feminism and Philosophy,* Mary Vetterling-Braggin, ed., (Totowa, N.J.: Rowman and Littlefield, 1977), p. 337.

59. John Stuart Mill, *On Liberty,* David Spitz, ed., (New York: W. W. Norton, 1975), chap. 5, par. 7.

60. Joel Feinberg, *Rights, Justice and the Bounds of Liberty: Essays in Social Philosophy* (Princeton, N.J.: Princeton University Press, 1980), p. 71.

61. Richards, *The Moral Criticism of the Law,* p. 69.

62. Ibid., p. 25.

63. Feinberg, *Rights, Justice and the Bounds of Liberty,* p. 88.

64. Ibid., p. 89.

65. Ibid., p. 88.

66. Reisman, "Democracy and Defamation," p. 751.

67. *Stanley* v. *Georgia,* 405 U.S. 113 (1973).

68. Ibid.

69. Wendy Kaminer points out that "the standard was first enunciated by the Supreme Court in 1919 after the First World War, to allow for prosecutions for anti-draft pamphleteering under the Espionage Act; it was used in the early 1950's to uphold convictions for allegedly 'subversive' speech under the Smith Act; it has recently been invoked unsuccessfully by the government in an attempt to restrain the publication of the Pentagon Papers." Kaminer, "Pornography and the First Amendment," Lederer, ed., *Take Back the Night,* p. 245.

70. I owe this distinction to Robert Fullinwider.

71. Nat Hentoff, *The First Freedom* (New York: Delacorte, 1980), p. 312.

72. Ibid., p. 322.

73. Ibid.

74. Brownmiller, *Against Our Will: Men, Women and Rape,* p. 395.

75. Ibid.

76. Kaminer, "Pornography and the First Amendment," Lederer, ed., *Take Back the Night,* p. 246.

77. Ibid., p. 247.

78. Deirdre English, Amber Hollibaugh, and Gayle Rubin, "Talking Sex: A Conversation on Sexuality and Feminism," *Socialist Review* 11, no. 4 (July–August 1981):58.

79. Ibid.

80. English, "The Politics of Porn," p. 44.

81. Susan Sontag, "The Third World of Women," *Partisan Review* 40, no. 2 (1973):180–206, esp. 188.

82. English, "The Politics of Porn," p. 50.

Questions for Discussion

1. If you are a woman, would it bother you to know that a significant man in your life—your father, a close uncle, your grandfather, your husband, your fiance, your steady date—was a consumer of pornography? If so, why would it bother you? What would be the grounds of your discomfort?

Would you draw a line between the acceptability of some forms of pornography and others? Would *Playboy* be OK, but *Hustler* not? Do you think the significant man in your life would want you to know of his fondness for pornography? If not, why not?

2. If you are a man, are there forms of pornography that you feel can be harmlessly indulged? Do you think that the consistent reading of *Playboy* and *Hustler* or the frequent watching of pornographic movies and videos implies a contempt for women on your part? Are there some forms of pornography that turn you on and others that disgust you? Where do you draw your own lines (and why) for what is acceptable and not acceptable?

3. Does defining pornography seem a hopelessly subjective task? Is pornography all "in the eye of the beholder," or can some actions and depictions be defined as pornographic regardless of defenses from some people? What are the criteria you would use in answering this question?

4. State in your own words Tong's distinction between gyno-erotic and gyno-thanatic pornography? Do you agree that this is a valid distinction? Do you think this distinction is helpful or not in establishing the criteria for judging different kinds of pornography? Would the distinction be helpful or not in deciding which kinds of pornography ought to be legally censored? Is the validity of the distinction borne out by differences that you are personally aware of in different works of pornography?

Suggested Essay Topics

1. Write an essay directed to your classmates in which you analyze the underlying view of women in some particular work of pornography you know, and give the best reasons you can for having the work banned or otherwise repressed. Then attach a final page in which you summarize the best arguments for not repressing the work.

2. Write an essay directed to your classmates in which you define pornography in such a way that suggestive commercials and network television programs either do or do not fall within your definition, and then defend your inclusion or elimination of these works from your definition, attempting to answer the responses of the most intelligent critic of your position that you can imagine.

PART

PERSPECTIVES ON THE WORLD

✦

FOUR

✦ 9 ✦

HISTORICAL
PERSPECTIVES

Understanding the Present by Learning About the Past

Of the three dimensions of time, only the past is "real" in the absolute sense
that it has occurred, the future is only a concept,
and the present is that fateful split second in which all action takes place.
One of the most disturbing habits of the human mind
is its willful and destructive forgetting of what in its past
does not flatter or confirm its present point of view.
Katherine Anne Porter

Those who do not learn from history are doomed to repeat it.
Karl Marx

If men could learn from history, what lessons it might teach us!
But passion and party blind our eyes, and the light which experience gives
is a lantern on the stern, which shines only on the waves behind us!
Samuel Taylor Coleridge

History is bunk.
Henry Ford

History is philosophy teaching by examples.
Dionysius of Halicarnassus

History is the pack of tricks that the living play on the dead.
Voltaire

What is history but a fable agreed on?
Napoleon

No great man lives in vain. The history of the world is but
the biography of great men.
Thomas Carlyle

Genesis 1–2:3

Obviously history must somehow have begun "in the beginning," "when God began to create the heaven and the earth." Yet no one has ever observed our beginnings, and the anthropologists and cosmologists who try to account today for what happened "then" usually hedge their statements with apologies about guesswork. Ancient authors were less cautious. Most cultures have stories that begin as confidently as the following account from Genesis, the opening story of what Christians call the Old Testament and Jews call the Torah. (Both Jews and Christians use the term Pentateuch *to refer to the first five books of the Bible, the books that Moses is said to have received from God.) The authors of the world's many creation stories always* know *what happened "in the beginning," and the accounts usually explain, as only a story can, how and why things started and how and why they led to the way things are now.*

The creation story in the Bible does not even bow in the direction of trying to explain where God himself came from. Other traditions, such as that of the ancient Greeks, developed much more elaborate accounts of how the *beginning could be found* behind *other beginnings and of how mysterious and amorphous early gods begat later gods who in turn created this or that part of the world. But Genesis begins with a supreme creator unchallenged in his orders and finding it "all," at the end of the creative week, unambiguously "good."*

We reprint two translations of Genesis 1–2:3, the first from the King James or "Authorized" Version of the Bible (1611) and the second from a modern translation of the Torah by the Jewish Publication Society of America (1962). The words you will now read constitute perhaps the most-discussed text in Western history. Innumerable books have been written about them, and scholars often disagree over their interpretation. Perhaps you have read or heard them so often that you see no reason to study them further. Or you may have come to accept a history about beginnings that you think makes this one obsolete—something like "In the beginning was a Big

Bang, an explosion of an incredibly dense blob of mass or energy that expanded into the still-expanding universe we know today." Or you may believe that the words in Genesis recount a literal history that was written by Moses as one of five books given him by the Lord.

Whatever your view of when and where we began, you can recreate the wonder of this text, with its confident assertions, by asking simply, "What could lead anyone to tell this kind of history in this way to account for our beginnings?"

Note that we print the traditional verse numbers instead of our usual paragraph numbers. The verses in the King James Version correspond to those in the Torah.

GENESIS 1–2:3

From the King James Version

1.

[1]In the beginning God created the heaven and the earth. [2]And the earth was without form, and void; and darkness was upon the face of the deep. And the Spirit of God moved upon the face of the waters. [3]And God said, Let there be light: and there was light. [4]And God saw the light, that it was good: and God divided the light from the darkness. [5]And God called the light Day, and the darkness he called Night. And the evening and the morning were the first day.

[6]And God said, Let there be a firmament in the midst of the waters, and let it divide the waters from the waters. [7]And God made the firmament, and divided the waters which were under the firmament from the waters which were above the firmament: and it was so. [8]And God called the firmament Heaven. And the evening and the morning were the second day.

[9]And God said, Let the waters under the heaven be gathered together unto one place, and let the dry land appear: and it was so. [10]And God called the dry land Earth; and the gathering together of the waters called he Seas: and God saw that it was good. [11]And God said, Let the earth bring forth grass, the herb yielding seed, and the fruit tree yielding fruit after his kind, whose seed is in itself, upon the earth: and it was so. [12]And the earth brought forth grass, and herb yielding seed after his kind, and the tree yielding fruit, whose seed was in itself, after his kind: and God saw that it was good. [13]And the evening and the morning were the third day.

[14]And God said, Let there be lights in the firmament of the heaven to divide the day from the night; and let them be for signs, and for seasons, and for days, and years: [15]And let them be for lights in the firmament of the heaven to give light upon the earth: and it was so. [16]And God made two great lights; the greater light to rule the day, and the lesser light to rule the night: he made the stars also. [17]And God set them in the firmament of the heaven to give light upon the earth, [18]and to rule over the day and over the night, and to divide the light from the darkness: and God saw that it was good.

[19]And the evening and the morning were the fourth day. [20]And God said, Let the waters bring forth abundantly the moving creature that hath life, and fowl that may fly above the earth in the open firmament of heaven. [21]And God created great whales, and every living creature that moveth, which the waters brought forth abundantly, after their kind, and every winged fowl after his kind: and God saw that it was good. [22]And God blessed them, saying, Be fruitful, and multiply, and fill the waters in the seas, and let fowl multiply in the earth. [23]And the evening and the morning were the fifth day.

[24]And God said, Let the earth bring forth the living creature after his kind, cattle, and creeping thing, and beast of the earth after his kind: and it was so. [25]And God made the beast of the earth after his kind, and cattle after their kind, and every thing that creepeth upon the earth after his kind: and God saw that it was good.

[26]And God said, Let us make man in our image, after our likeness: and let them have dominion over the fish of the sea, and over the fowl of the air, and over the cattle, and over all the earth, and over every creeping thing that creepeth upon the earth. [27]So God created man in his own image, in the image of God created he him; male and female created he them. [28]And God blessed them, and God said unto them, Be fruitful, and multiply, and replenish the earth, and subdue it: and have dominion over the fish of the sea, and over the fowl of the air, and over every living thing that moveth upon the earth.

[29]And God said, Behold, I have given you every herb bearing seed, which is upon the face of all the earth, and every tree, in the which is the fruit of a tree yielding seed; to you it shall be for meat. [30]And to every beast of the earth, and to every fowl of the air, and to every thing that creepeth upon the earth, wherein there is life, I have given every green herb for meat: and it was so. [31]And God saw every thing that he had made, and, behold, it was very good. And the evening and the morning were the sixth day.

2.

[1]Thus the heavens and the earth were finished, and all the host of them. [2]And on the seventh day God ended his work which he had made; and he rested on the seventh day from all his work which he had made. [3]And God blessed the seventh day, and sanctified it: because that in it he had rested from all his work which God created and made.

GENESIS 1–2:3

From the Torah

1.

¹When God began to create the heaven and the earth—²the earth being unformed and void, with darkness over the surface of the deep and a wind from God sweeping over the water—³God said, "Let there be light"; and there was light. ⁴God saw that the light was good, and God separated the light from the darkness. ⁵God called the light Day, and the darkness He called Night. And there was evening and there was morning, a first day.

⁶God said, "Let there be an expanse in the midst of the water, that it may separate water from water." ⁷God made the expanse, and it separated the water which was below the expanse from the water which was above the expanse. And it was so. ⁸God called the expanse Sky. And there was evening and there was morning, a second day.

⁹God said, "Let the water below the sky be gathered into one area, that the dry land may appear." And it was so. ¹⁰God called the dry land Earth, and the gathering of waters He called Seas. And God saw that this was good. ¹¹And God said, "Let the earth sprout vegetation: seed-bearing plants, fruit trees of every kind on earth that bear fruit with the seed in it." And it was so. ¹²The earth brought forth vegetation: seed-bearing plants of every kind, and trees of every kind bearing fruit with the seed in it. And God saw that this was good. ¹³And there was evening and there was morning, a third day.

¹⁴God said, "Let there be lights in the expanse of the sky to separate day from night; they shall serve as signs for the set times—the days and the years; ¹⁵and they shall serve as lights in the expanse of the sky to shine upon the earth." And it was so. ¹⁶God made the two great lights, the greater light to dominate the day and the lesser light to dominate the night, and the stars. ¹⁷And God set them in the expanse of the sky to shine upon the earth, ¹⁸to dominate the day and the night, and to separate light from darkness. And God saw that this was good. ¹⁹And there was evening and there was morning, a fourth day.

²⁰God said, "Let the waters bring forth swarms of living creatures, and birds that fly above the earth across the expanse of the sky." ²¹God created the great sea monsters, and all the living creatures of every kind that creep, which the waters brought forth in swarms; and all the winged birds of every kind. And God saw that this was good. ²²God blessed them, saying, "Be fertile and increase, fill the waters in the seas, and let the birds increase on the earth." ²³And there was evening and there was morning, a fifth day.

²⁴God said, "Let the earth bring forth every kind of living creature: cattle, creeping things, and wild beasts of every kind." And it was so. ²⁵God made wild beasts of every kind and cattle of every kind, and all kinds of creeping things of the earth. And God saw that this was good. ²⁶And God said, "Let us make man in our image, after our likeness. They shall rule the fish of the sea, the birds of the sky, the cattle, the whole earth, and all the

creeping things that creep on earth." ²⁷And God created man in His image, in the image of God He created him; male and female He created them. ²⁸God blessed them and God said to them, "Be fertile and increase, fill the earth and master it; and rule the fish of the sea, the birds of the sky, and all the living things that creep on earth."

²⁹God said, "See, I give you every seed-bearing plant that is upon all the earth, and every tree that has seed-bearing fruit; they shall be yours for food. ³⁰And to all the animals on land, to all the birds of the sky, and to everything that creeps on earth, in which there is the breath of life, [I give] all the green plants for food." And it was so. ³¹And God saw all that He had made, and found it very good. And there was evening and there was morning, the sixth day.

2.

¹The heaven and the earth were finished, and all their array. ²On the seventh day God finished the work which He had been doing, and He ceased on the seventh day from all the work which He had done. ³And God blessed the seventh day and declared it holy, because on it God ceased from all the work of creation which He had done.

Questions for Discussion

1. If anyone in the class knows Hebrew well enough to read the original, ask him or her to bring the Torah and talk about other possible translations of passages that seem puzzling.

2. Do you see any logical order in the sequence of what God creates? How would that sequence compare with what you have been told in your biology classes?

3. If you believe that Genesis is completely "mythical," discuss what might be meant by that belief. Is the account fictional in the sense that a novel is? If so, why should so many people have treated it as sacred?

4. Read the next three chapters in either the Old Testament or the Torah. If you were to imagine that they were written in our own time, by a single author who was trying to account for "how things began," what problem or problems about the nature of our world would you say he or she was trying to solve?

5. In many regions of America today there are heated battles between "creationists" and "evolutionists." Usually such battles, whether in courtrooms, popular magazines, or scholarly journals, reveal that neither side fully appreciates the case made by the opponents. What is considered evidence by one side is dismissed as irrelevant or false by the other. If there are

proponents and opponents of these views in your class, discuss the kinds of reasons that might be counted as evidence by *both* groups.

Suggested Essay Topics

1. Read in an encyclopedia about the history of translations of the Bible. Then compare our two translations in detail, remembering that ultimately they come from the same Hebrew original. If you discern any patterns of difference in emphasis or meaning, write an essay attempting to account for them. Don't think that you must speak as a biblical scholar. Your task is not to provide a comparative linguistic or historical account but a rhetorical account. (See "What Is an Essay? The Range of Rhetoric" in Part One.) That is, analyze what seem to be different *effects* that different wordings in each translation aim at, and try to reconstruct a picture of the kind of audience that the translators must have had in mind.

2. Write an essay directed to anyone you are fairly sure will initially disagree with you, defending your view of the creation story in Genesis. Whether you view it as literal truth, as poetic myth, as allegory, or as primitive intuition, explain why you think your view is credible, and try to make it as convincing as possible to someone with an opposing view.

Gertrude Himmelfarb

A brief etymological summary suggests that human beings have always viewed history, stories, and knowledge as intimately connected, as if they were more like different facets of the same gem or different tones of the same voice rather than fundamentally different kinds of activities. The word History *came into the English language during the medieval period from the French* histoire, *meaning "story." (During the 250 years following the 1066 conquest of the Saxons by the Normans, who spoke French, some 40,000 French words were imported into the English language.) The French word, in its turn, had come from the Greek* historia, *meaning "a learning by inquiry," or "knowledge," and* historia *was built on the Greek base* eidenai, *meaning "to know." This quick sketch suggests that for human beings, telling stories is both a fundamental way of saying what we know (perhaps even of identifying what we know) and summarizing what we have known (telling history, the story of the past).*

In this chapter we attempt to give you an overview of a few different kinds of historical perspectives and reporting. If what we just said in the previous paragraph is right, these different ways of telling the story of the past are, in effect, different ways human beings have both of identifying what they know and of taking charge of it. In Genesis, for example, you can see history as myth, that fundamentally important, primordial way of telling a story that both identifies the origins of human existence and suggests the distinctive nature of human beings. In Edith Hamilton's "The Ever-Present Past" you can see how the story of the past is often turned into a story of usefulness for the present, in this case as a kind of lesson about how our society should educate its young. In Kai Erikson's "Of Accidental Judgments and Casual Slaughters" you can see how the story of the past is turned into a kind of warning for the future: "let us not repeat certain kinds of past mistakes; see the past and be better prepared for the future." In Peter Geyl and Arnold Toynbee's debate, you see an attempt to read the story of history on the grandest scale possible, to understand the rise and fall of different civilizations according to a story of maturation and decline. In Edward Hallett Carr's "The Historian and His Facts," you see an attempt to define the status of a historical fact.

In Gertrude Himmelfarb (b. 1922) we find a kind of history and story making different in intent from the kinds I have just discussed. The excerpt from Himmelfarb shows how a professional historian uses records from a bygone period, a period the details of which may be known to very few in the present, in order to reconstruct the story of a slice of that period and thus bring its feel, its movement, and its life, apparently remote, into freshness and motion once again. Without historians who retrieve the feel and the life of the past for us, we are likely to lose our contact with it and thus lose contact with a part of ourselves, that part most directly derivative rather than immediately constructed.

Note as you read the variety of sources that Himmelfarb uses as she attempts to recreate the feel of a slice of Victorian London (a quick look at the end notes will give you a summary). She makes use of the works of at least two poets, an etymology study, scholarly journals, many other works of history dealing with other aspects of the period (cities, railroads, industry, crime, and so on), a scholarly sociological study, a novel, letters, analyses written during the period itself, newspaper articles, biographies, and travelogues. To a historian, it is clear that very little from the past could ever be considered irrelevant. Thus to be a historian is to be a student of human nature, of human development, of ideas, of change, and of the connection between what we were and what we are becoming.

Himmelfarb's re-creation of the "culture of poverty" in Victorian London, especially the "discovery" of that culture by the Victorians themselves, provides a fascinating glimpse of connections that sound at once foreign and familiar. Do the problems of public waste and industrial pollution sound contemporary? Welcome to Victorian London. Do the problems of crime and homelessness sound contemporary? Welcome to Victorian London. Do the problems of overcrowding in urban areas and a vast gulf between the rich and poor sound contemporary? Welcome to Victorian London. Yet the differences are as striking as the similarities. In Himmelfarb's fine history, you can see how the professional historian helps us to live in both the past and the present at once, thus clarifying the former and enriching the latter.

THE "CULTURE OF POVERTY IN EARLY INDUSTRIAL ENGLAND"

From *The Idea of Poverty: England in the Early Industrial Age* (1983).

LONDON: A SPECIAL CASE

"Hell is a city much like London—a populous and a smoky city." Thus [1]
Shelley in 1819, voicing the familiar pastoral lament.[1] By the middle of the
century Shelley would have had more reason to complain, for the population
of London continued to grow at twice the national rate. During the first half
of the century, while the population of the country as a whole doubled, that
of London tripled; of the 18,000,000 people in England and Wales in 1851,
London had over 2,350,000, more than one-eighth of the whole. (Paris, the
next largest city in the world, doubled in the same period, bringing its population up to 1,000,000 by mid-century—but that was only one-thirty-fifth of
the total population of France.) This unprecedented increase in population
coincided with the building of the railroads and the laying out of new streets,
which put even greater strains on the most densely populated and poorest
areas—the slums, or "rookeries," as they were commonly known.*

"A populous and a smoky city." The most populous but not the smoki- [2]
est, the mining and mill towns of the midlands and north competing for that
distinction. Smoky enough, however, partly because of its populousness.
Millions of open fires spewed out their fumes (and much of their heat)
through as many chimney pots, producing that yellow fog which seems
romantic in retrospect but was in fact a noxious form of pollution. A good
measure of that smoke was also contributed by the railroads, gasworks, and
manufacturing establishments of the city. The industrial character of Victorian London tends to be overshadowed by the other qualities of the metropolis and by the more striking industrial development in other parts of the
country. But even in this respect London retained its primacy. In the middle
of the century it was still the major manufacturing center of England, more
diversified than Manchester or Birmingham and in this sense less dramatic,
but that very diversity provided its own drama.[3]

London was an invitation to superlatives. It was the largest center of [3]

---

*"Rookery" was the more common word through much of the century. It derived from the
"rookery," or rook's nest, that was the breeding place for that unattractive, harsh-voiced bird.
The unsavory connotation of the word was reinforced by the verb "to rook," meaning to cheat
or swindle, and by the noun "rook," a thief or swindler, or the crowbar used in housebreaking.
("Rook" in this sense went back to Elizabethan times.) More recent was "slum" which first
appeared in Vaux's *Flash Dictionary* in 1812 ("flash" also meaning "thief"). "Slum" had at first a
somewhat more innocuous meaning than "rookery"; supposedly derived from "slumber," it
designated a "sleepy, unknown back alley." In 1850, Cardinal Wiseman complained of the
"congealed labyrinths of lanes and courts, and alleys and slums" near Westminster Abbey.[2]
[Himmelfarb's note.]

industry, the largest port, the largest provider of services, the largest concentration of consumers, the largest source of all those needs, demands, and fancies that kept busy the "dark satanic mills" of the midlands and the "sweated workshops" of the East End.* It was also the political, cultural, and social center of the country, creating and disseminating the ideas and values that were reflected in the literature, legislation, and institutions of the age. The "provinces" had their distinctive cultures, but they were distinctively, consciously, sometimes aggressively provincial. London had a "moral density" (in Emile Durkheim's† expressive phrase) commensurate with its "material density," a critical mass of intellectual and social consciousness that gave it a unique position and power.[4]

London was unique, for good and ill. If Shelley saw it as an unmitigated "hell" and Cobbett as a "great wen," a malignant excrescence on the body politic, there were those for whom it was an unfailing source of pride and delight, even its offenses being so outsized as to evoke perverse admiration. It was common to speak of London as a microcosm of England, of the world, indeed of civilization, exhibiting in heightened form all the virtues and vices of modernity. One writer managed to find cause for celebration even in its smoke, "the sublime canopy that shrouds the City of the World."[5] Others adduced the familiar metaphor of the heart and the body. "It is the centre, to which and from which the lines are radiating, which connect it with every point in the circumference: it is the heart to which and from which the life-blood circulates through every artery and vein of the entire body."[6]‡

In the 1830s and 1840s, when both the material and the moral "dynamic" (again, Durkheim's term) were at their height, London seemed more than ever to be at the heart of things. This was true even of those matters that were not peculiar to London. The impact of Chartism,§ for example, was

*Blake's "dark Satanic Mills" is generally taken to be a condemnation of the cotton factories. In the preface to *Milton,* where the phrase appears, it refers to the universities and intellectual establishments which worshipped the false gods of Homer and Ovid, Plato and Cicero, instead of the Bible, Shakespeare, and Milton. The image of the mill, here and in his other poems, derives not from the cotton mill but from the iron and steel mills producing the weapons of war. It was militarism more than industrialism that exercised Blake. [Himmelfarb's note.]

†Emile Durkheim (1858–1917), French sociologist. [Our note.]

‡In one sense, London was less a center of England than Paris was of France. The English had proudly and successfully resisted the kind of centralization that France had always been prone to and that had been much intensified under Napoleon. The difference between the two countries might be symbolized by the location of their major universities—Oxford and Cambridge, the Sorbonne and the Ecole Polytechnique. Yet it was, paradoxically, the Englishman's much vaunted attachment to land and locality, his resistance to centralization and suspicion of the metropolis, that made the physical growth of London and its magnetic attraction all the more striking. The University of London was never a threat to the intellectual hegemony of Oxford and Cambridge, but its founding in 1828 had a symbolic significance that far outweighed its institutional importance. Blake, Carlyle, and Cobbett all ranted about the "infernal wen" while comfortably ensconced there (just as Rousseau praised Geneva while yearning for Paris). [Himmelfarb's note.]

§A movement among working-class people in the 1840s to extend the vote to them, have elections with secret ballots, pay legislators (thus freeing them from domination by the rich), and other liberal proposals. Chartism produced big rallies and much attention, but no results. [Our note.]

far greater in the provinces than in London. Yet it was London that gave birth to the movement and was the scene of its demise. Similarly the condition-of-England question was more urgent for the industrial north than for London. But it was London that brought that problem to the attention of the rest of the country, dramatized and publicized it, and proposed to alleviate it. The seat of Parliament, the location of the major newspapers and journals, the home of social critics, social reformers, and social commentators, London was the center of the newest "growth industry," one that was not listed in the official census returns but that was well known to contemporaries—the reform industry.

As London was the political, the financial, the commercial, the social,   6
and the cultural capital of England, so it was also the "capital of poverty." It was the poorest city, if only because it was the richest. "Real poverty," André Gide once said, "is that of cities, because it is there such a close neighbor to the excesses." This too was London's distinction: it was the city of excesses par excellence. An American visitor in 1849, eulogizing London as the "heart of the great world," was overwhelmed by both its grandeur and its poverty. "In the midst of the most extraordinary abundance, here are men, women, and children dying of starvation; and running alongside of the splendid chariot, with its gilded equipages, its silken linings, and its liveried footmen, are poor, forlorn, friendless, almost naked wretches, looking like the mere fragments of humanity."[7] In London the "two nations"* lived in the closest proximity—and were separated by the most impassable gulf.

The coexistence of poverty and riches was the least of the paradoxes for   7
which London was famous. Another was the anomaly familiar to the ancients: *Magna civitas, magna solitudo.* † The vision of a city so crowded that its very atmosphere was fetid—Rousseau meant it literally when he said that in the city "man's breath is deadly to his kind"[8]—was superimposed upon another image which had each man totally isolated from the neighbor who pressed so hard upon him, completely immersed in his own interests, absorbed by an *amour propre* ‡ that left no room for human compassion or social affections. Here, where each had most need of all, the "war of each against all" was being waged most ruthlessly.

The rookery was the symbol of that war, of a state of anarchy in which   8
the only law was the law of the jungle. The metaphors were familiar: the rookeries were "breeding grounds" for vice and disease, "schools" of crime and immorality. Inculcating no moral or religious habits, imposing no check on natural passions and inclinations, they gave the residents, as one contemporary critic put it, "a licence to do evil." Yet that critic also pointed out that there were in fact far fewer criminals in London than was commonly thought, less than one percent of the population. "It is the exception," he noted,

---

*The "nations" of the rich and the poor and the sub-title of Benjamin Disraeli's novel on the division between rich and poor: *Sybil, or, The Two Nations* (1845). [Our note.]

†A great city (is) a great solitude. [Our note.]

‡Self-esteem, vanity. [Our note.]

"rather than the mass, which is thus putrid."[9] But the exception was enough to putrefy the whole, to create the impression of a massive rookery in which crime and disease were as rampant as poverty. For Robert Southey the image conjured up by London was of a wilderness swarming with every kind of physical and moral pestilence, of misery and vice.

> London is the heart of your commercial system but it is also the hot-bed of corruption. It is at once the centre of wealth and the sink* of misery; the seat of intellect and empire, . . . and yet a wilderness wherein they, who live like wild beasts upon their fellow creatures, find prey and cover. . . . Ignorance and misery and vice are allowed to grow, and blossom and seed, not on the waste alone, but in the very garden and pleasure ground of society and civilization.[10]

There were counter-images, to be sure. In contrast to the spectacle of a swarming mass of people without community, there was the vision of a city composed of many small communities, the poorest of which, precisely because they were so crowded, were the most neighborly; even the rookery evoked the fantasy of a fraternity happily united in crime. Where some saw the coexistence of wealth and poverty as the dramatic evidence of social injustice, a standing invitation to envy, discontent, and dissension, others saw it as a means of social amelioration, the luxuries of the rich providing employment and sustenance for the poor and thus the opportunity to "better themselves." The *amour propre* which Rousseau took to be the great vice of mankind, a vice that flourished especially in the modern city, was transmuted by Smith† into the benign "self-interest" which, properly understood, became the most reliable (if unexalted) of social virtues and the most effective (if invisible) of social bonds. In "socializing" political economy, Smith also "socialized" the city.

One of Smith's disciples, Frederick Eden, defended the city against Rousseau. "Why is it," he quoted Rousseau, "that in a thriving city, the Poor are so miserable, while such extreme distress is hardly ever experienced in those countries where there are no instances of immense wealth?"[11] To which Eden gave the un-Rousseauean answer that the poor were poorer in the city because they were freer there. Unlike the agricultural laborer who was assured against want but only at the cost of his liberty (his freedom to move to another parish) and of his independence (his self-sufficiency), the town worker was free and independent—and, by the same token, more vulnerable and less secure in times of want. The poor themselves, Eden was convinced, preferred freedom even at the price of security. "A prisoner under the custody of his keeper, may perhaps be confident of receiving his bread and his water daily; yet, I believe, there are few who would not, even with the contingent possibility of starving, prefer a precarious chance of subsistence, from their

*Sewer. [Our note.]

†Adam Smith (1723–1790), Scottish economist whose *Inquiry Into the Nature and Causes of the Wealth of Nations* (1776) is commonly said to have laid the grounds for a capitalist economy. [Our note.]

own industry, to the certainty of regular meals in a gaol."[12] This defense of the city—the freedom to starve rather than the servitude of being fed—was not, to be sure, much of a recommendation; and it was hardly what Smith had in mind when he extolled freedom.

At a time when the condition of man was a subject of much agonizing, the condition of urban man, and of the Londoner particularly, began to be seen as the condition of modern man *in extremis:* spiritually and morally impoverished, anonymous, isolated, "alienated." So, too, the London poor seemed to be afflicted with a kind of poverty *in extremis,* a poverty that made them not so much a class apart, or even a "nation" apart (as in the "two nations" image), as a "race" apart. In fact the London poor were no poorer than the poor elsewhere and may even have been, on the average, less poor (although the poorest of them, the Spitalfields silk weavers, were in as depressed a state as any laborers in the country). Nor was the "anomie"* of London life as severe or pervasive as has been made out; neighborhoods, streets, workshops, even public houses, generated distinctive loyalties, sentiments, and associations. Still, there was unquestionably an acute sense of uprootedness experienced by large numbers of immigrants from the countryside and Ireland, by workers displaced from their old crafts and having to seek new occupations (silk weavers, for example, driven to the docks), and by families disoriented in unfamiliar surroundings.

Thus London, the least typical of places with the least typical kinds of poverty, somehow became archetypical. Not that any kind of poverty was "typical." Contemporaries were well aware that the kinds of poverty were as various as the degrees, that rural poverty was significantly different from urban, the poverty in a textile mill from that of a mining village, the poverty of a declining trade from that of a stable one, the poverty of old age from that of youth. Yet by the middle of the century the problem of poverty was more and more identified with the city, and, paradoxically, with that most uncommon city, the city beyond compare, the metropolis.

London became the "capital of poverty" in part by default, at a time when poverty ceased to be an urgent problem in the rest of the country. By the middle of the century, the general improvement in the economy and a series of melioratory measures had removed the condition-of-England question from the center of public attention. If the 1840s were never quite the "Bleak Age," nor the 1850s the "Golden Age," some historians have made them out to be, there was nevertheless a conspicuous improvement in the condition and morale of the poor.[13] Yet just at this time, when social tensions were abating, when there were no sensational Royal Commission reports and no dramatic demonstrations of popular discontent, attention turned to London, where an attentive observer might find, in the midst of unparalleled riches and unmistakable progress, new social problems and new forms of poverty. If Manchester was the "shock city" of the forties, London was the

*Rootlessness, disorganization, normlessness. It is a term first applied to communities and societies by Emile Durkheim. [Our note.]

"shock city" of the fifties, a new challenge to the social imagination and conscience.

In part London attained that dubious distinction because of the assidu- 14 ous efforts of one of the most remarkable chroniclers of the time, Henry Mayhew. Mayhew was a one-man Royal Commission. His methods of inquiry were somewhat unorthodox (but so were those of some of the Royal Commissioners), and his work was profoundly ambiguous in its intentions and implications. Yet he succeeded in popularizing a new idea and image of poverty, a poverty that was not so much an economic phenomenon as a cultural one—a "culture of poverty," as we have since learned to call it.

HENRY MAYHEW: DISCOVERER OF THE "POOR"

It was in the autumn of 1849 that Henry Mayhew launched the series 15 of articles that did more to focus attention upon poverty in London than any other single work. Until December 1850 the articles appeared in the *Morning Chronicle,* and then until February 1852 as weekly pamphlets (some of which were bound and issued as two volumes in 1851–52); a pamphlet series was briefly resumed in 1856; and the four-volume *London Labour and the London Poor* was published in 1861–62 and reprinted in 1864–65.[14]

Mayhew was a journalist, novelist, playwright, editor, humorist, satirist, 16 moralist, commentator, advertiser, children's writer, travel writer, amateur scientist, and entrepreneur of sorts—of a rather unconventional sort, specializing in such schemes as the production of artificial diamonds. His father was a prosperous London solicitor who thoroughly disapproved of him (to the point, eventually, of disinheriting him) and who was heartily disliked in turn. But some of his brothers (there were seventeen children in all) were more congenial: the oldest, Thomas, was the editor of Hetherington's *Penny Papers* and *The Poor Man's Guardian* until he committed suicide in 1834; Horace was with Henry on the staff of *Punch;* and Augustus was a frequent collaborator.[15]

To some of his associates Mayhew appeared as the classic type of 17 *Luftmensch,** a great schemer who never carried his schemes to completion. One remembered him as "a genius, a fascinating companion, and a man of inexhaustible resource and humor," but felt obliged to add that "indolence was his besetting sin, and his will was untutored."[16] Yet, while many of his projects were left unfinished, "indolence" hardly seems the right word for someone who produced as much as he did, and sometimes at breathtaking speed. If much of his work was incomplete and ephemeral, that was the nature of his trade; he was primarily a journalist, not, as we have come to think of him, a sociologist or historian. What is remarkable, and what distinguished him from his colleagues, was the ambitiousness of some of his projects.

*From *luft* meaning "air" and *mensch* meaning "person," thus, "air-head," or someone with his head in the clouds." [Our note.]

Mayhew's first important job, in the 1830s, was as editor of the satirical 18 journal *Figaro in London.* That experience brought him into the small group that founded *Punch* in July 1841.[17] After serving as co-editor for a few months, he became an occasional contributor when Mark Lemon assumed the sole editorship late that year. (Another *Punch* writer, Douglas Jerrold, was his father-in-law.) In the early forties when Mayhew wrote for it, *Punch* was at its most radical, satirizing and commenting on political and social issues as well as featuring the comic trivia that later became its stock-in-trade. It has been suggested that Mayhew was largely responsible for the radical tone of the magazine during these years, a supposition that derives largely from Mayhew's subsequent career.[18] But it could as easily be argued that he was influenced by *Punch* rather than the reverse. One of *Punch's* early coups was the publication of Thomas Hood's "Song of the Shirt," the famous poem of social protest which is said to have trebled the circulation of the magazine. According to one account, Lemon published it over the protests of the other contributors, including Mayhew.[19] The lesson of that episode could not have been lost on someone like Mayhew, who was so responsive to popular culture and whose livelihood was so dependent on it. This is not to say that he and others on the magazine were not genuinely interested in social issues and moved by social distress. It only suggests that they were primarily professional writers rather than publicists for a cause, and that the condition-of-England question was the liveliest journalistic subject at the time. The most serious political thinker on the staff (Mayhew himself was not a staff member, and had little to do with policy decisions) was Jerrold; it was he who had written the article in *Punch* on the meager earnings of a seamstress which had inspired Hood's "Song of the Shirt." Thus apart from the familial relationship, it was fitting that Mayhew should have dedicated to Jerrold the first volume of *London Labour and the London Poor.*

. . .

Mayhew's series in the *Chronicle* was inspired by an earlier article by him 19 on the cholera epidemic. The disease, which had appeared sporadically throughout England (and more seriously on the Continent) in 1848, returned with a vengeance the following year, taking 20,000 lives in the rest of the country and another 15,000 in London (almost 4,000 in the City alone). It reached the metropolis in the summer of 1849, peaking in mid-September. Readers of the daily death count were beginning to take comfort in the declining figures when the *Chronicle* on September 24 published an unsigned article, "A Visit to the Cholera Districts of Bermondsey." Most of the article (3,500 words, two and a half long columns in small type) was devoted to the infamous slum known as Jacob's Island. It was there, in the "Capital of Cholera" as Mayhew called it, that the epidemic had first struck in 1832, and there that Dickens had located the grisly scene of Bill Sikes's death in *Oliver Twist.* If Dickens had been inspired by newspaper accounts of that earlier epidemic, it is probable that Mayhew was now inspired by Dickens to visit that notorious site. The result was an account that almost rivaled Dickens's in its grotesqueness.

Jacob's Island was dominated by the ditch that ran through it, an open 20
sewer covered with scum and grease, filled with the refuse from the privies
lining its bank, with an occasional swollen, putrefied carcass of an animal
floating on the surface, all of which emitted the noxious vapors and "mephitic
gases" that were presumed to be the cause of the epidemic. In grisly detail
Mayhew described the inhabitants of the area (some of whose houses actually spanned the ditch), who breathed those deadly fumes, drank and washed
in that foul water, and died in their hovels, their bodies left unattended for
days. The editor of *Fraser's Magazine* was not being unduly squeamish when
he said that he could not quote the article because it was "too loathsome to
trust to the chance of its being read aloud."[20] Other journals and newspapers
were less fastidious and did reprint some of the more shocking passages.

The article attracted a good deal of attention and gave rise to the ambi- 21
tious idea of a series on "Labour and the Poor." The idea may have been
prompted by Mayhew's suggestion that there was a correlation between the
incidence of disease and the geography of poverty.

> Indeed, so well known are the localities of fever and disease, that .
> London would almost admit of being mapped out pathologically, and
> divided into its morbid districts and deadly cantons. We might lay our
> fingers on the Ordnance map, and say here is the typhoid parish, and there
> the ward of cholera; for truly as the West-end rejoices in the title of
> Belgravia, might the southern shores of the Thames be christened Pesti-
> lentia. As season follows season, so does disease follow disease in the
> quarters that may be more literally than metaphorically styled the plague-
> spots of London.[21]
>
>   . . .

"Labour and the Poor" was inaugurated in the *Chronicle* on October 18, 22
1849, prefaced by an editorial note explaining that the series would give "a
full and detailed description of the moral, intellectual, material, and physical
condition of the industrial poor throughout England." There were to be three
sets of "letters" running on successive days: one on the rural communities,
another on the manufacturing and mining areas, and a third on London.
Together, the editor hoped, they would equal or even surpass the parliamen-
tary reports in "impartiality, authenticity, and comprehensiveness," and
would provide the facts with which an "energetic Government and an enlightened Legislature" could improve the condition of the poor.

                              . . .

Mayhew's article on London . . . undertook to give an analytic account 23
of "the poor of London" in terms of the different classes of poor and the
different causes of poverty.

> Under the term poor I shall include all those persons whose incomings
> are insufficient for the satisfaction of their wants—a want being, accord-
> ing to my idea, contra-distinguished from a mere desire by a positive
> physical pain, instead of a mental uneasiness, accompanying it. The large
> and comparatively unknown body of people included in this definition I

shall contemplate in two distinct classes, viz., the *honest* and *dishonest* poor; and the first of these I purpose subdividing into the striving and the disabled—or, in other words, I shall consider the whole of the metropolitan poor under three separate phases, according as they *will* work, they *can't* work, and they *won't* work.[22]

Those who *"will* work" were further subdivided into those who received relief and those who did not, and the latter into the "improvident" and the "poorly-paid." As Mayhew warmed to his subject, especially the case of the poorly-paid, he became more impassioned, promising to inquire into the causes of their inadequate income and miserable conditions, the exorbitant rent they paid for their "waterless, drainless, floorless, and almost roofless tenements," and the usurious interest exacted by the "petty capitalist" (the pawnbroker). At this point, however, he hastened to reassert his objectivity. However sensitive he was to the wrongs done to the poor, he would not be misled by a "morbid sympathy" into seeing them only as the victims of other people's selfishness. "Their want of prudence, want of temperance, want of energy, want of cleanliness, want of knowledge, and want of morality, will each be honestly set forth."

Having laid out the plan of the series, Mayhew went on to the subject of the introductory article: the extremes of wealth and poverty, power and weakness, knowledge and ignorance, which existed side by side in London, and, more startling still, the extremes of charity and poverty. The main distinction of the present age, he found, was not the steam-engine, the railroad, or the telegraph, but the "fuller and more general development of the human sympathies," especially toward the poor. Anyone nostalgic for the "good old times" should contemplate the reign of "bluff King Hal," when 72,000 thieves and rogues were hanged, twice as many as had been felled by the recent plague; or the act in the reign of Henry VIII which stipulated the penalties for the "sturdy beggar": whipping for the first offense, cropping of the right ear for the second, and jail for subsequent offenses; or more recent times when people found their pleasure in bull-baiting and badger-baiting, dog fights and cock fights. Instead of those sports, there were now laws and societies for the prevention of cruelty to animals, and in place of bear-gardens and cock-pits there were a "thousand palaces" to cater to every variety of want, ill, or benevolent impulse: societies for the visitation of the sick, the cure of the maimed, the alleviation of the pains of childbirth, the reformation of juvenile offenders and prostitutes, the suppression of vice, and so on and on.[23] As the list unrolled, the tone became unmistakably sarcastic, almost as if Mayhew were writing a squib for *Figaro* or *Punch.* Yet his original point about the growth of the spirit of benevolence had been serious enough. Perhaps it was the vision of all those "palatial institutions," of nobles and lords giving up their sponsorship of prizefights to assume the presidency of philanthropic societies, that brought to the surface his ingrained suspicion of reformers and philanthropists. The £15,000,000 expended each year on charity suggested to him not only the "liberal extent of our sympathy" but the

enormous want and suffering requiring such large expenditures of charity and
the still more enormous wealth that could afford them.

Much of the article had the character of a "set piece," the discourse on   25
the contrasts of wealth and want being the staple of this genre. But an
occasional vignette was pure Mayhew.

> At night it is that the strange anomalies of London are best seen. Then,
> as the hum of life ceases and the shops darken and the gaudy gin palaces
> thrust out their ragged and squalid crowds, to pace the streets, London
> puts on its most solemn look of all. On the benches of the parks, in the
> niches of the bridges, and in the litter of the markets, are huddled together
> the homeless and the destitute. The only living thing that haunts the
> streets are the poor wretches who stand shivering in their finery, waiting
> to catch the drunkard as he goes shouting homewards. Here on a doorstep
> crouches some shoeless child, whose day's begging has not brought it
> enough to purchase it even the twopenny bed that its young companions
> in beggary have gone to. There, where the stones are taken up and piled
> high in the centre of the street in a flag of flame—there, round the red
> glowing coke fire, are grouped a ragged crowd smoking or dozing through
> the night beside it. Then, as the streets grow blue with the coming light,
> and the church spires and chimney tops stand out against the sky with
> a sharpness of outline that is seen only in London before its million fires
> cover the town with their pall of smoke—then come sauntering forth the
> unwashed poor, some with greasy wallets on their back, to haunt over
> each dirt heap, and eke out life by seeking refuse bones or stray rags and
> pieces of old iron. Others, on their way to their work, gathered at the
> corner of the street round the breakfast stall, and blowing saucers of
> steaming coffee drawn from tall tin cans, with the fire shining crimson
> through the holes beneath; whilst already the little slattern girl, with her
> basket slung before her, screams watercresses through the sleeping
> streets.[24]

The theme of incongruity and contrast was well served by the style,   26
passages such as this alternating with a barrage of statistics intended to point
up the "anomalies." The nighttime scene of poor wretches huddled in doorways gave way to a daytime scene of twenty-nine bankers clearing an annual
total of nine hundred and fifty-four million pounds, an average of over three
million pounds a day. In a city where a poor man might lack a roof over his
head, property was insured to the value of five hundred million pounds.
Where some poor soul was in want of dinner, two hundred and seventy
million eight hundred and eighty thousand pounds of meat was consumed
annually. (These and a series of similar figures were spelled out and sometimes italicized, as if to give them added weight.) A final set of statistics on
crime established London's preeminence in yet another respect: the number
of people taken into custody annually by the metropolitan police was equal
to the population of some of England's largest towns.

This introductory article set the agenda for the rest of the series in ways   27
Mayhew may not have intended. Instead of a systematic analysis of the types

and causes of poverty, there was more often a melange of facts, figures, images, and impressions jostling each other in bewildering confusion, with the author's voice alternately that of the dispassionate inquirer and the passionate partisan, the satiric commentator and the social accountant. The scientific impulse, the urge to define, categorize, quantify, and analyze, was always there. But so was the impulse of the dramatist, satirist, novelist, and activist. It was this combination of qualities that gave the *Morning Chronicle* articles, and, later, the four volumes of *London Labour and the London Poor,* their distinctive tone and dramatic force.

NOTES

All notes are Himmelfarb's.

1. Percy Bysshe Shelley, "Peter Bell the Third," part 3, verse 1.

2. On the etymology of "rookery" see Thomas Beames, *The Rookeries of London: Past, Present, and Prospective* (London, 1852), pp. 1–2. On the etymology of "slum" see H. J. Dyos, "The Slums of Victorian London," *Victorian Studies,* 1967, pp. 7–10; Anthony S. Wohl, *The Eternal Slum: Housing and Social Policy in Victorian London* (Montreal, 1977), p. 5. On the slums themselves, see Dyos, "Urban Transformation: A Note on the Objects of Street Improvement in Regency and Early Victorian London," *International Review of Local History,* 1957; Dyos and D. A. Reeder, "Slums and Suburbs," in *The Victorian City: Images and Realities,* ed. Dyos and Michael Wolff (London, 1973), I, 359 ff. Donald J. Olsen, *The Growth of Victorian London* (London, 1976), without focusing on the slum as such, helps put it in the perspective of the city as a whole.

3. This is the view of Francis Shepard, *London, 1808–1870: The Infernal Wen* (Berkeley, 1971), pp. 158 ff. Sheppard quotes P. G. Hall, *The Industries of London since 1861* (London, 1962) in support of his position. This is in contrast to the more familiar view expressed in the census report of 1831: "In the appropriate application of the word manufacture, none of importance can be attributed to Middlesex . . . other than that of silk." (J. H. Clapham, *An Economic History of Modern Britain: The Early Railway Age, 1820–1850* [Cambridge, 1967 (1st ed., 1926)], pp. 67–68.)

4. Emile Durkheim, *The Division of Labor in Society,* trans. George Simpson (Glencoe, Ill., 1947 [1st ed., 1893]), pp. 257 ff. This concept is used (although not with particular reference to London) by J. A. Banks, "The Contagion of Numbers," in *The Victorian City,* I, 109.

5. Asa Briggs, *Victorian Cities* (New York, 1965), p. 321, quoting Benjamin Haydon's *Autobiography* (1841). When Henry Mayhew took a balloon trip in 1856 to observe from aloft "The Great World of London," he used the same metaphor, "dense canopy of smoke," to describe the scene. (Mayhew and John Binny, *The Criminal Prisons of London and Scenes of Prison Life* [London, 1968 (1st ed., 1862)], p. 9.)

6. B. I. Coleman (ed.), *The Idea of the City in Nineteenth-Century Britain* (London, 1973), p. 101 (extract from a sermon delivered in 1844).

7. Sheppard, p. 348.

8. Jean Jacques Rousseau, *Emile, or On Education,* trans. Allan Bloom (New York, 1979 [1st ed., 1762]), p. 59.

9. Robert Vaughan, *The Age of Great Cities, or Modern Society Viewed in Its Relation to Intelligence, Morals and Religion* (Shannon, 1971 [1st ed., 1843]), pp. 227–29.

10. Robert Southey, *Sir Thomas More: or, Colloquies on the Progress and Prospects of Society* (London, 1829), I, 108.

11. The quotation is from Rousseau, *La Nouvelle Héloïse,* part II, letter 27, in *Oeuvres complètes* (Pléiade ed., Dijon, 1964), II, 303.

12. Frederick Morton Eden, *The State of the Poor: or, an History of the Labouring Classes in England* (London, 1797), I, 58–59.

13. John L. and Barbara Hammond, *The Bleak Age* (London, 1934); E. Royston Pike, *"Golden Times": Human Documents of the Victorian Age* (New York, 1972). W. L. Burns, *The Age of Equipoise: A Study of*

the Mid-Victorian Generation (London, 1964), proposes a more sober label for a period that was undeniably more stable and composed than the preceding decade.

14. The publication history is complicated and not entirely clear; see below, pp. 322, 568 n. 36. Unless otherwise noted, citations below are to the facsimile reprint, *London Labour and the London Poor,* ed. John D. Rosenberg (4 vols., New York, 1968). (For the full title and subtitles, see below, p. 322.)

15. The only full-length biography is Anne Humpherys, *Travels into the Poor Man's Country: The Work of Henry Mayhew* (Athens, Ga., 1977). Earlier biographical accounts are in the introductions to selections from his works edited by John L. Bradley, Stanley Rubinstein, and E. P. Thompson and Eileen Yeo. (See notes 18, 32, 37, 38, and 40.)

16. M. H. Spielmann, *The History of "Punch"* (London, 1895), p. 268.

17. An earlier *Punch in London* appeared in 1832, edited by Douglas Jerrold. *Punch* itself was frankly modeled on the French magazine *Charivari,* hence the *London Charivari* in its subtitle.

18. John L. Bradley, introduction to *Selections from "London Labour and the London Poor"* (London, 1965), p. xx.

19. The song inspired drawings and paintings as well as the obvious literary imitations. See T. J. Edelstein, "They Sang 'The Song of the Shirt': The Visual Iconology of the Seamstress," *Victorian Studies,* 1980.

20. *Fraser's Magazine,* Dec. 1849, p. 707.

21. *Chronicle,* Sept. 24, 1849.

22. *Ibid.,* Oct. 19, 1849.

23. "Pauper palaces" was a common expression for the workhouses. See above, pp. 187–88.

24. *Chronicle,* Oct. 19, 1849.

Questions for Discussion

1. What similarities and differences do you see between London of the 1840s and any major urban area in American in the 1990s? Do the similarities and contrasts help you better understand these two times and places? If so, how? If not, why not?

2. In paragraph 8 Himmelfarb quotes Robert Southey's description of London. Compare Southey's abundant use of metaphors and images with the kinds of metaphors people use nowadays to talk about cities, particularly the "inner city," and discuss whether his metaphors and images would be understood or accepted by a contemporary audience of newspaper readers today. If readers today would expect to see different metaphors, what are they? Are they more accurate, less accurate, or simply different than Southey's?

3. In Himmelfarb's story, the "discovery" of London's poor by the middle and upper classes was largely the work of one man, Henry Mayhew. Does it surprise you that one person can make such a difference in a society's "social imagination and conscience"?(¶13)? Are you used to supposing that one person could never affect a whole society? Can you find any modern instances that parallel Mayhew's influence in Victorian London and any other single person's influence in our society? (Would Bob Woodward and

Paul Bernstein's exposure of the Watergate scandal in the *Washington Post* during Richard Nixon's administration in 1972, which eventually led to the president's resignation, qualify as an example? Are there others?)

Suggested Essay Topics

1. Write a history of some significant period in your family's past. Even if the source you employ is mainly memory rather than documents, your purpose is to do what a good historian like Himmelfarb does: to retrieve the details of a period such that the life, motion, and feel of that period are recoverable by those who may have forgotten about it or who may never had lived it in the company of the main actors. Insofar as you can, do try to use historical documents—letters, diaries, canceled checks, budgets, appointment books, family calendars with appointments and "places to go" written on them, newspapers, interviews with family members, and so on. Picture yourself writing this history 100 years in the future and directing it to an audience composed of your family's descendants who might wish to know the details of some slice of their forebears' lives.

2. Using Himmelfarb's treatment of facts and dates as a model, write an essay directed to your classmates in which you criticize or praise some history teacher from your high school experience for either making or failing to make facts and dates important and vivid as details in the study of some historical period. Make clear how you think facts and dates should be used in the study of history by young people, and describe how they were either well used or misused by your high school history teacher.

Edith Hamilton

Edith Hamilton (1867–1963) was one of the world's leading authorities on Greco-Roman civilization. In a life that spanned nearly a century, she did not publish her first book, The Greek Way, *until she was 63. When she was 90, in a ceremony conducted in the amphitheater of Herodes Atticus at the foot of the Athenian Acropolis, she was made an honorary citizen of Greece, in recognition of her contribution and devotion to classical studies.*

In this essay Hamilton defends the position that even in the modern world, which seems on the surface to be so far removed from the world of classical antiquity, we need not only to be educated about the Greeks but also to be educated by them. Like us, they valued freedom, and their freedom, like ours, was threatened by forces pressing from within and without.

We can be educated by the Greeks if we study the spirit, the values, and the attitudes that motivated them to create and preserve a free society in the first place. By educating ourselves about the Greeks, about their failures and eventual fall from greatness, we can gain some insight into the causes that may cause us also to lose strength and purpose.

In Hamilton's view, one of the most important things the Greeks can teach us is what kind of education fosters and preserves a free society. Our education differs markedly from the Greeks's, and the contrast gives us much to think about. The Greeks understood, Hamilton argues, that a free society depends on a free spirit among its people, among individuals. Thus they directed education toward the cultivation of certain qualities and powers in individuals, on the assumption that individuals are of intrinsic worth in and of themselves. Greek education did not merely attempt to provide job skills, for the Greeks knew that no amount of professional skill could compensate for a lack of independent spirit and flexible intelligence. Every citizen was educated, says Pericles (the ruler who led Athens at the height of her glory), not to become a cog in the social machine and not to increase the gross national product but "to meet life's chances and changes with the utmost versatility and grace" (¶23).

Almost all historians believe that a knowledge of the past can enable us to face the problems of the present with deeper understanding, heightened sensitivity, and clearer heads. As you consider the contrasts and similarities that Hamilton lays out between our society and that of the Greeks, between their education and your own, consider also whether the knowledge you thus acquire about the past suggests to you any concrete recommendations for curing the ills of the present, whether in education or in society generally.

THE EVER-PRESENT PAST

First appeared in *The Saturday Evening Post* in 1958 as "The Lessons of the Past"; reprinted under the present title in *The Ever-Present Past* (1964).

Is there an ever-present past? Are there permanent truths which are   1
forever important for the present? Today we are facing a future more strange
and untried than any other generation has faced. The new world Columbus
opened seems small indeed beside the illimitable distances of space before us,
and the possibilities of destruction are immeasurably greater than ever. In
such a position can we afford to spend time on the past? That is the question
I am often asked. Am I urging the study of the Greeks and Romans and their
civilizations for the atomic age?

Yes; that is just what I am doing. I urge it without qualifications. We   2
have a great civilization to save—or to lose. The greatest civilization before
ours was the Greek. They challenge us and we need the challenge. They, too,
lived in a dangerous world. They were a little, highly civilized people, the
only civilized people in the west, surrounded by barbarous tribes and with
the greatest Asiatic power, Persia, always threatening them. In the end they
succumbed, but the reason they did was not that the enemies outside were
so strong, but that their own strength, their spiritual strength, had given way.
While they had it they kept Greece unconquered and they left behind a

record in art and thought which in all the centuries of human effort since has not been surpassed.

The point which I want to make is not that their taste was superior to ours, not that the Parthenon was their idea of church architecture nor that Sophocles was the great drawing card in the theaters, nor any of the familiar comparisons between fifth-century Athens and twentieth-century America, but that Socrates found on every street corner and in every Athenian equivalent of the baseball field people who were caught up by his questions into the world of thought. To be able to be caught up into the world of thought— that is to be educated.

How is that great aim to be reached? For years we have eagerly discussed ways and means of education, and the discussion still goes on. William James once said that there were two subjects which if mentioned made other conversation stop and directed all eyes to the speaker. Religion was one and education the other. Today Russia seems to come first, but education is still emphatically the second. In spite of all the articles we read and all the speeches we listen to about it, we want to know more; we feel deeply its importance.

There is today a clearly visible trend toward making it the aim of education to defeat the Russians. That would be a sure way to defeat education. Genuine education is possible only when people realize that it has to do with persons, not with movements.

When I read educational articles it often seems to me that this important side of the matter, the purely personal side, is not emphasized enough; the fact that it is so much more agreeable and interesting to be an educated person than not. The sheer pleasure of being educated does not seem to be stressed. Once long ago I was talking with Prof. Basil L. Gildersleeve of Johns Hopkins University, the greatest Greek scholar our country has produced. He was an old man and he had been honored everywhere, in Europe as well as in America. He was just back from a celebration held for him in Oxford. I asked him what compliment received in his long life had pleased him most. The question amused him and he laughed over it, but he thought too. Finally he said, "I believe it was when one of my students said, 'Professor, you have so much fun with your own mind.'" Robert Louis Stevenson said that a man ought to be able to spend two or three hours waiting for a train at a little country station when he was all alone and had nothing to read, and not be bored for a moment.

What is the education which can do this? What is the furniture which makes the only place belonging absolutely to each one of us, the world within, a place where we like to go? I wish I could answer that question. I wish I could produce a perfect decorator's design warranted to make any interior lovely and interesting and stimulating; but, even if I could, sooner or later we would certainly try different designs. My point is only that while we must and should change the furniture, we ought to throw away old furniture very cautiously. It may turn out to be irreplaceable. A great deal was thrown away in the last generation or so, long enough ago to show some of the results. Furniture which had for centuries been foremost, we lightly, in a few years, discarded. The classics almost vanished from our field of education. That was a great change. Along with it came another. There is a marked difference between the writers of the past and the writers of today who have been educated without benefit of Greek and Latin. Is this a matter of cause and effect? People will decide for themselves, but I do not think anyone will question the statement that clear thinking is not the characteristic which distinguishes our literature today. We are more and more caught up by the unintelligible. People like it. This argues an inability to think, or, almost as bad, a disinclination to think.

Neither disposition marked the Greeks. They had a passion for thinking   8 things out, and they loved unclouded clarity of statement as well as of thought. The Romans did, too, in their degree. They were able to put an idea into an astonishingly small number of words without losing a particle of intelligibility. It is only of late, with a generation which has never had to deal with a Latin sentence, that we are being submerged in a flood of words, words, words. It has been said that Lincoln at Gettysburg today would have begun in some such fashion as this: "Eight and seven-tenths decades ago the pioneer workers in this continental area implemented a new group based on an ideology of free boundaries and initial equality," and might easily have ended, "That political supervision of the integrated units, for the integrated units, by the integrated units, shall not become null and void on the superficial area of this planet." Along with the banishment of the classics, gobbledegook has come upon us—and the appalling size of the Congressional Record, and the overburdened mail service.

Just what the teaching in the schools was which laid the foundation of   9 the Greek civilization we do not know in detail; the result we do know. Greek children were taught, Plato said, to "love what is beautiful and hate what is ugly." When they grew up their very pots and pans had to be pleasant to look at. It was part of their training to hate clumsiness and awkwardness; they loved grace and practiced it. "Our children," Plato said, "will be influenced for good by every sight and sound of beauty, breathing in, as it were, a pure breeze blowing to them from a good land."

All the same, the Athenians were not, as they showed Socrates when   10 he talked to them, preoccupied with enjoying lovely things. The children were taught to think. Plato demanded a stiff examination, especially in mathematics, for entrance to his Academy. The Athenians were a thinking people. Today the scientists are bearing away the prize for thought. Well, a Greek said that the earth went around the sun, sixteen centuries before Copernicus thought of it. A Greek said if you sailed out of Spain and kept to one latitude, you would come at last to land, seventeen hundred years before Columbus did it. Darwin said, "We are mere schoolboys in scientific thinking compared to old Aristotle." And the Greeks did not have a great legacy from the past as our scientists have; they thought science out from the beginning.

The same is true of politics. They thought that out, too, from the   11 beginning, and they gave all the boys a training to fit them to be thinking citizens of a free state that had come into being through thought.

Basic to all the Greek achievement was freedom. The Athenians were the only free people in the world. In the great empires of antiquity—Egypt, Babylon, Assyria, Persia—splendid though they were, with riches beyond reckoning and immense power, freedom was unknown. The idea of it never dawned in any of them. It was born in Greece, a poor little country, but with it able to remain unconquered no matter what manpower and what wealth were arrayed against her. At Marathon and at Salamis overwhelming numbers of Persians had been defeated by small Greek forces. It had been proved that one free man was superior to many submissively obedient subjects of a tyrant. Athens was the leader in that amazing victory, and to the Athenians freedom was their dearest possession. Demosthenes said that they would not think it worth their while to live if they could not do so as free men, and years later a great teacher said, "Athenians, if you deprive them of their liberty, will die."

Athens was not only the first democracy in the world, it was also at its height an almost perfect democracy—that is, for men. There was no part in it for women or foreigners or slaves, but as far as the men were concerned it was more democratic than we are. The governing body was the Assembly, of which all citizens over eighteen were members. The Council of Five Hundred which prepared business for the Assembly and, if requested, carried out what had been decided there, was made up of citizens who were chosen by lot. The same was true of the juries. Minor officials also were chosen by lot. The chief magistrates and the highest officers in the army were elected by the Assembly. Pericles was a general, very popular, who acted for a long time as if he were head of the state, but he had to be elected every year. Freedom of speech was the right the Athenians prized most and there has never been another state as free in that respect. When toward the end of the terrible Peloponnesian War the victorious Spartans were advancing upon Athens, Aristophanes caricatured in the theater the leading Athenian generals and showed them up as cowards, and even then as the Assembly opened, the herald asked, "Does anyone wish to speak?"

There was complete political equality. It was a government of the people, by the people, for the people. An unregenerate old aristocrat in the early fourth century, B.C., writes: "If you *must* have a democracy, Athens is the perfect example. I object to it because it is based on the welfare of the lower, not the better, classes. In Athens the people who row the vessels and do the work have the advantage. It is their prosperity that is important." All the same, making the city beautiful was important too, as were also the great performances in the theater. If, as Plato says, the Assembly was chiefly made up of cobblers and carpenters and smiths and farmers and retail-business men, they approved the construction of the Parthenon and the other buildings on the Acropolis, and they crowded the theater when the great tragedies were played. Not only did all free men share in the government; the love of the beautiful and the desire to have a part in creating it were shared by the

many, not by a mere chosen few. That has happened in no state except
Athens.

But those free Greeks owned slaves. What kind of freedom was that?　15
The question would have been incomprehensible to the ancient world. There
had always been slaves; they were a first necessity. The way of life everywhere was based upon them. They were taken for granted; no one ever gave
them a thought. The very best Greek minds, the thinkers who discovered
freedom and the solar system, had never an idea that slavery was evil. It is
true that the greatest thinker of them all, Plato, was made uncomfortable by
it. He said that slaves were often good, trustworthy, doing more for a man
than his own family would, but he did not follow his thought through. The
glory of being the first one to condemn it belongs to a man of the generation
before Plato, the poet Euripides. He called it, "That thing of evil," and in
several of his tragedies showed its evil for all to see. A few centuries later the
great Greek school of the Stoics denounced it. Greece first saw it for what it
is. But the world went on in the same way. The Bible accepts it without
comment. Two thousand years after the Stoics, less than a hundred years ago,
the American Republic accepted it.

Athens treated her slaves well. A visitor to the city in the early fourth　16
century, B.C., wrote: "It is illegal here to deal a slave a blow. In the street he
won't step aside to let you pass. Indeed you can't tell a slave by his dress; he
looks like all the rest. They can go to the theater too. Really, the Athenians
have established a kind of equality between slaves and free men." They were
never a possible source of danger to the state as they were in Rome. There
were no terrible slave wars and uprisings in Athens. In Rome, crucifixion was
called "the slave's punishment." The Athenians did not practice crucifixion,
and had no so-called slave's punishment. They were not afraid of their slaves.

In Athens' great prime Athenians were free. No one told them what　17
they must do or what they should think—no church or political party or
powerful private interests or labor unions. Greek schools had no donors of
endowments they must pay attention to, no government financial backing
which must be made secure by acting as the government wanted. To be sure,
the result was that they had to take full responsibility, but that is always the
price for full freedom. The Athenians were a strong people, they could pay
the price. They were a thinking people; they knew what freedom means.
They knew—not that they were free because their country was free, but that
their country was free because they were free.

A reflective Roman traveling in Greece in the second century, A.D., said,　18
"None ever throve under democracy save the Athenians; *they* had sane self-
control and were law-abiding." He spoke truly. That is what Athenian education aimed at, to produce men who would be able to maintain a self-governed
state because they were themselves self-governed, self-controlled, self-reliant. Plato speaks of "the education in excellence which makes men long to
be perfect citizens, knowing both how to rule and be ruled." "We are a free
democracy," Pericles said. "We do not allow absorption in our own affairs to
interfere with participation in the city's; we yield to none in independence

of spirit and complete self-reliance, but we regard him who holds aloof from public affairs as useless." They called the useless man a "private" citizen, *idiotes,* from which our word "idiot" comes.

They had risen to freedom and to ennoblement from what Gilbert 19 Murray calls "effortless barbarism"; they saw it all around them; they hated its filth and fierceness; nothing effortless was among the good things they wanted. Plato said, "Hard is the good," and a poet hundreds of years before Plato said,

> Before the gates of Excellence the high gods have placed sweat.
> Long is the road thereto and steep and rough at the first,
> But when the height is won, then is there ease.

When or why the Greeks set themselves to travel on that road we do 20 not know, but it led them away from habits and customs accepted everywhere that kept men down to barbaric filth and fierceness. It led them far. One example is enough to show the way they took. It was the custom— during how many millenniums, who can say?—for a victor to erect a trophy, a monument of his victory. In Egypt, where stone was plentiful, it would be a slab engraved with his glories. Farther east, where the sand took over, it might be a great heap of severed heads, quite permanent objects; bones last a long time. But in Greece, though a man could erect a trophy, it must be made of wood and it could never be repaired. Even as the victor set it up he would see in his mind how soon it would decay and sink into ruin, and there it must be left. The Greeks in their onward pressing along the steep and rough road had learned a great deal. They knew the victor might be the vanquished next time. There should be no permanent records of the manifestly impermanent. They had learned a great deal.

An old Greek inscription states that the aim of mankind should be "to 21 tame the savageness of man and make gentle the life of the world." Aristotle said that the city was built first for safety, but then that men might discover the good life and lead it. So the Athenians did according to Pericles. Pericles said that Athens stood for freedom and for thought and for beauty, but in the Greek way, within limits, without exaggeration. The Athenians loved beauty, he said, but with simplicity; they did not like the extravagances of luxury. They loved the things of the mind, but they did not shrink from hardship. Thought did not cause them to hesitate, it clarified the road to action. If they had riches they did not make a show of them, and no one was ashamed of being poor if he was useful. They were free because of willing obedience to law, not only the written, but still more the unwritten, kindness and compassion and unselfishness and the many qualities which cannot be enforced, which depend on a man's free choice, but without which men cannot live together.

If ever there is to be a truly good and great and enduring republic it must 22 be along these lines. We need the challenge of the city that thought them out, wherein for centuries one genius after another grew up. Geniuses are not produced by spending money. We need the challenge of the way the Greeks were educated. They fixed their eyes on the individual. We contemplate millions. What we have undertaken in this matter of education has dawned upon us only lately. We are trying to do what has never been attempted before, never in the history of the world—educate all the young in a nation of 170 million; a magnificent idea, but we are beginning to realize what are the problems and what may be the results of mass production of education. So far, we do not seem appalled at the prospect of exactly the same kind of education being applied to all the school children from the Atlantic to the Pacific, but there is an uneasiness in the air, a realization that the individual is growing less easy to find; an idea, perhaps, of what standardization might become when the units are not machines, but human beings.

Here is where we can go back to the Greeks with profit. The Athenians   23 in their dangerous world needed to be a nation of independent men who could take responsibility, and they taught their children accordingly. They thought about every boy. Someday he would be a citizen of Athens, responsible for her safety and her glory, "each one," Pericles said, "fitted to meet life's chances and changes with the utmost versatility and grace." To them education was by its very nature an individual matter. To be properly educated a boy had to be taught music; he learned to play a musical instrument. He had to learn poetry, a great deal of it, and recite it—and there were a number of musical instruments and many poets; though, to be sure, Homer was the great textbook.

That kind of education is not geared to mass production. It does not   24 produce people who instinctively go the same way. That is how Athenian children lived and learned while our millions learn the same lessons and spend hours before television sets looking at exactly the same thing at exactly the same time. For one reason and another we are more and more ignoring differences, if not trying to obliterate them. We seem headed toward a standardization of the mind, what Goethe called "the deadly commonplace that fetters us all." That was not the Greek way.

The picture of the Age of Pericles drawn by the historian Thucydides,   25 one of the greatest historians the world has known, is of a state made up of people who are self-reliant individuals, not echoes or copies, who want to be let alone to do their own work, but who are also closely bound together by a great aim, the commonweal, each one so in love with his country—Pericles' own words—that he wants most of all to use himself in her service. Only an ideal? Ideals have enormous power. They stamp an age. They lift life up when they are lofty; they drag down and make decadent when they are low—and then, by that strange fact, the survival of the fittest, those that are low fade away and are forgotten. The Greek ideals have had a power of persistent life for twenty-five hundred years.

Is it rational that now when the young people may have to face problems harder than we face, is it reasonable that with the atomic age before them, at this time we are giving up the study of how the Greeks and Romans prevailed magnificently in a barbaric world; the study, too, of how that   26 triumph ended, how a slackness and softness finally came over them to their ruin? In the end, more than they wanted freedom, they wanted security, a comfortable life, and they lost all—security and comfort and freedom.

Is not that a challenge to us? Is it not true that into our education have come a slackness and softness? Is hard effort prominent? The world of thought can be entered in no other way. Are we not growing slack and soft in our political life? When the Athenians finally wanted not to give to the state, but the state to give to them, when the freedom they wished most for was freedom from responsibility, then Athens ceased to be free and was never free again. Is not that a challenge? 27

Cicero said, "To be ignorant of the past is to remain a child." Santayana said, "A nation that does not know history is fated to repeat it." The Greeks can help us, help us as no other people can, to see how freedom is won and how it is lost. Above all, to see in clearest light what freedom is. The first nation in the world to be free sends a ringing call down through the centuries to all who would be free. Greece rose to the very height, not because she was big, she was very small; not because she was rich, she was very poor; not even because she was wonderfully gifted. So doubtless were others in the great empires of the ancient world who have gone their way leaving little for us. She rose because there was in the Greeks the greatest spirit that moves in humanity, the spirit that sets men free. 28

Plato put into words what that spirit is. "Freedom" he says, "is no matter of laws and constitutions; only he is free who realizes the divine order within himself, the true standard by which a man can steer and measure himself." True standards, ideals that lift life up, marked the way of the Greeks. Therefore their light has never been extinguished. 29

"The time for extracting a lesson from history is ever at hand for them who are wise." Demosthenes. 30

Questions for Discussion

1. Hamilton defines being educated as being "able to be caught up into the world of thought" (¶3). What do you think she means by being "caught up"? How does her meaning compare with Whitehead's definition in "The Aims of Education" that "education is the acquisition of the art of the utilization of knowledge" (Chapter 1)?

2. According to Hamilton, the use of one's mind should be a pleasure in itself; she alludes to Robert Louis Stevenson's remark that "a man ought to be able to spend two or three hours waiting for a train at a little country station when he was all alone and had nothing to read, and not be bored for a moment" (¶6). How often do you sit down to think about something, not to daydream or lapse into random thoughts but to concentrate on an

issue, topic, or idea? Do you know people who do this? Do you know anyone who seems afraid of the silence that invites thought, who requires the sound of records, television, radio, or friends to fill up the space that might otherwise be threatened by thinking?

3. Is your education enlarging your capacity for sustained thought? Are you being given both things to think *about* and methods to think *by*? Do you find yourself mulling over the ideas from your classes—or, better yet, discussing them with friends—as if they had applications and importance outside of the requirements for the course? If not, do you think this is what you *should be* getting? What are the obstacles preventing it?

4. When Athenian democracy was strong, Hamilton argues, it was strong because citizens generally—both rich and poor, noble and common—*took responsibility* for preserving it (¶17–18). Can you find examples in American society that suggest what happens to democracy when freedom *without* responsibility becomes the aim? Is it your impression that Americans generally are willing to be responsible for making democracy work? If you think they are not willing, what do you think might account for their unwillingness?

Suggested Essay Topics

1. "In the end, more than they [the Greeks] wanted freedom, they wanted security, a comfortable life, and they lost all—security and comfort and freedom" (¶26). When college students are asked today why they go to college, they frequently cite comfort and security—a good job and a comfortable life—as their reasons for attending college. They seldom say that they want an education in order to make their contribution to freedom and democracy. In an essay or letter directed to Edith Hamilton, defend the goals of today's college students. Counter her claim that an education should be directed toward the cultivation of general powers rather than specific skills, and, since you are rejecting her claim that education helps preserve freedom, make clear what you think does help preserve it and what kind of responsibility that preservation places on individual citizens.

2. Take the opposite position from that of topic 1: In an essay directed to students you know who are bent on education for security and comfort, extend Hamilton's argument that today's education is slack and soft (¶27) and makes no real contribution to freedom in our society. Illustrate her argument with examples from trends in education generally, but especially with examples from your own education (both now and in the past). Contrast the aims of the education you have been given with the aims that Hamilton says guided Greek education—the cultivation of a sense of beauty, proportion, personal grace, excellence, and independent thought—and point out in detail where you think your education has been slack and soft. Make any recommendations you think appropriate.

Kai Erikson

It is comforting when important decisions are being made in the public sphere to think that "the authorities are in control," an assertion that offers peace to the mind. It allows us to construct a mental picture of tempered, seasoned, mature, reflective, good, and wise persons taking their time to think through a complicated issue and arrive at a solution that could not be bettered by outside critics or casual observers.

Kai Erikson (b. 1931), tracing the history of the decision to drop atomic bombs on the heavily populated cities of Hiroshima and Nagasaki at the end of World War II, throws considerable doubt on the mental picture created by "the authorities are in control." His research reveals that their "control" is highly questionable, not because they were duplicitous or because they were being manipulated against their wills by outside agents, but because they were in the grip of subtle forces difficult to identify: confusion among bureaucrats about who was really in charge of certain decisions, the forward-driving psychological inertia of a war effort that had been building with ferocious intensity for more than four years, the attitudes of those experts in charge of creating the atomic bomb, but whose ignorance in other fields (such as Japanese psychology and culture) left them incapable of predicting the effects of various alternatives, and so on. To read Erikson gives the impression that while none of the persons responsible for creating the bomb really wanted to unleash it, they seemed not to know how to devise alternatives or they assumed that "others" higher up in the chain of command had already considered those alternatives and had their good reasons for rejecting them.

In fact, it turns out that no one seems to have been seriously considering alternatives at all. No one person or committee of persons took it as his or their responsibility to think through *what else might have been done with the bomb besides dropping it on large and populous cities. The frightening point in this is not the moral or political laxity of the persons involved—for they were all doing the best they could in the circumstances—but the way in which responsibility and initiative inside a bureaucracy become so diffused that good people fail to see the points at which their own vigorous action is not only a moral responsibility, but the points at which such responsibility, once exerted, might help avoid "accidental judgments and casual slaughters."*

By tracing not only the story of these events as a historian—getting his facts, dates, and persons straight—but by drawing out the implications of the story, looking for the possible lessons that can be drawn from past events and applied to presently unfolding circumstances, Erikson illustrates not only the methods of good historiography *but its* uses, *the contributions that history may make to an enriched understanding of present conditions. The stringing out of dates and names that sometimes masquerades as the study of history should really be called something like the* memorization of chronology. *The study of history is both different and more important than the memorization of chronology. It is the attempt to tell a story constructed in part out of names and dates from the past in order to arrive at the kind of understanding of events, causes, motives, and consequences that will enlighten the understanding of our present conditions and help us avoid past errors as we create solutions to present problems.*

OF ACCIDENTAL JUDGMENTS
AND CASUAL SLAUGHTERS

From *The Nation* (August 1985).

THE BOMBINGS of Hiroshima and Nagasaki, which took place forty years   1
ago this month, are among the most thoroughly studied moments on human
record. Together they constitute the only occasion in history when atomic
weapons were dropped on living populations, and together they constitute
the only occasion in history when a decision was made to employ them in
that way.

I want to reflect here on the second of those points. The "decision to   2
drop"—I will explain in a minute why quotation marks are useful here—is
a fascinating historical episode. But it is also an exhibit of the most profound
importance as we consider our prospects for the future. It is a case history well
worth attending to. A compelling parable.

If one were to tell the story of that decision as historians normally do,   3
the details arranged in an ordered narrative, one might begin in 1938 with the
discovery of nuclear fission, or perhaps a year later with the delivery of
Einstein's famous letter to President Roosevelt.* No matter what its opening
scene, though, the tale would then proceed along a string of events—a sequence of appointees named, committees formed, reports issued, orders
signed, arguments won and lost, minds made up and changed—all of it
coming to an end with a pair of tremendous blasts in the soft morning air over
Japan.

The difficulty with that way of relating the story, as historians of the   4
period all testify, is that the more closely one examines the record, the
harder it is to make out where in the flow of events something that could
reasonably be called a decision was reached at all. To be sure, a kind of
consensus emerged from the sprawl of ideas and happenings that made up
the climate of wartime Washington, but looking back, it is hard to distinguish those pivotal moments in the story when the crucial issues were identified, debated, reasoned through, resolved. The decision, to the extent that
one can even speak of such a thing, was shaped and seasoned by a force
very like inertia.

Let's say, then, that a wind began to blow, ever so gently at first, down   5
the corridors along which power flows. And as it gradually gathered momen-

---

*In 1939, Einstein wrote a letter to President Roosevelt warning him that the Germans were
working on the development of an atomic bomb, after which funding for research to develop
the bomb first in America dramatically increased.

tum during the course of the war, the people caught up in it began to assume, without ever checking up on it, that it had a logic and a motive, that it had been set in motion by sure hands acting on the basis of wise counsel.

Harry Truman, in particular, remembered it as a time of tough and 6 lonely choices, and titled his memoir of that period *Year of Decisions.* But the bulk of those choices can in all fairness be said to have involved confirmation of projects already under way or implementation of decisions made at other levels of command. Brig. Gen. Leslie R. Groves, military head of the Manhattan Project,* was close to the mark when he described Truman's decision as "one of noninterference—basically, a decision not to upset the existing plans." And J. Robert Oppenheimer† spoke equally to the point when he observed some twenty years later: "The decision was implicit in the project. I don't know whether it could have been stopped."

In September of 1944, when it became more and more evident that a 7 bomb would be produced in time for combat use, Franklin Roosevelt and Winston Churchill met at Hyde Park and initialed a brief *aide-mémoire,* noting, among other things, that the new weapon "might, perhaps, after mature consideration, be used against the Japanese." This document does not appear to have had any effect on the conduct of the war, and Truman knew nothing at all about it. But it would not have made a real difference in any case, for neither chief of state did much to initiate the "mature consideration" they spoke of so glancingly, and Truman, in turn, could only suppose that such matters had been considered already. "Truman did not inherit the question," writes Martin J. Sherwin, "he inherited the answer."

What would "mature consideration" have meant in such a setting as 8 that anyway?

First of all, presumably, it would have meant seriously asking whether 9 the weapon should be employed at all. But we have it on the authority of virtually all the principal players that no one in a position to do anything about it ever really considered alternatives to combat use. Henry L. Stimson, Secretary of War:

> At no time, from 1941 to 1945, did I ever hear it suggested by the President, or by any other responsible member of the government, that atomic energy should not be used in the war.

Harry Truman:

> I regarded the bomb as a military weapon and never had any doubt that it should be used.

*A project established at Los Alamos, NM, in 1942 for the purpose of producing an atomic bomb before the Germans.
†Julius Robert Oppenheimer (1904–1967), American physicist and director of the Manhattan Project, 1942–1945.

General Groves:

> Certainly, there was no question in my mind, or, as far as I was ever
> aware, in the mind of either President Roosevelt or President Truman or
> any other responsible person, but that we were developing a weapon to
> be employed against the enemies of the United States.

Winston Churchill:

> There never was a moment's discussion as to whether the atomic bomb
> should be used or not.

And why should anyone be surprised? We were at war, after all, and with
the most resolute of enemies, so the unanimity of that feeling is wholly
understandable. But it was not, by any stretch of the imagination, a product
of mature consideration.

"Combat use" meant a number of different things, however, and a   10
second question began to be raised with some frequency in the final months
of the war, all the more insistently after the defeat of Germany. Might a way
be devised to demonstrate the awesome power of the bomb in a convincing
enough fashion to induce the surrender of the Japanese without having to
destroy huge numbers of civilians? Roosevelt may have been pondering
something of the sort. In September of 1944, for example, three days after
initialing the Hyde Park *aide-mémoire,* he asked Vannevar Bush, a trusted
science adviser, whether the bomb "should actually be used against the
Japanese or whether it should be used only as a threat." While that may have
been little more than idle musing, a number of different schemes were explored within both the government and the scientific community in the
months following.

One option involved a kind of *benign strike:* the dropping of a bomb on   11
some built-up area, but only after advance notice had been issued so that
residents could evacuate the area and leave an empty slate on which the bomb
could write its terrifying signature. This plan was full of difficulties. A dud
under those dramatic circumstances might do enormous damage to American
credibility, and, moreover, to broadcast any warning was to risk the endeavor
in other ways. Weak as the Japanese were by this time in the war, it was easy
to imagine their finding a way to intercept an incoming airplane if they knew
where and when it was expected, and officials in Washington were afraid that
it would occur to the Japanese, as it had to them, that the venture would come
to an abrupt end if American prisoners of war were brought into the target
area.

The second option was a *tactical strike* against a purely military target—an   12
arsenal, railroad yard, depot, factory, harbor—without advance notice. Early
in the game, for example, someone had nominated the Japanese fleet concentration at Truk. The problem with this notion, however—and there is more
than a passing irony here—was that no known military target had a wide

enough compass to contain the whole of the destructive capacity of the weapon and so display its full range and power. The committee inquiring into likely targets wanted one "more than three miles in diameter," because anything smaller would be too inadequate a canvas for the picture it was supposed to hold.

The third option was to stage a kind of *dress rehearsal* by detonating a 13 bomb in some remote corner of the world—a desert or empty island, say—to exhibit to international observers brought in for the purpose what the device could do. The idea had been proposed by a group of scientists in what has since been called the Franck Report, but it commanded no more than a moment's attention. It had the same problems as the benign strike: the risk of being embarrassed by a dud was more than most officials in a position to decide were willing to take, and there was a widespread feeling that any demonstration involving advance notice would give the enemy too much useful information.

The fourth option involved a kind of *warning shot.* The thought here was 14 to drop a bomb without notice over a relatively uninhabited stretch of enemy land so that the Japanese high command might see at first hand what was in store for them if they failed to surrender soon. Edward Teller thought that an explosion at night high over Tokyo Bay would serve as a brilliant visual argument, and Adm. Lewis Strauss, soon to become a member (and later chair) of the Atomic Energy Commission, recommended a strike on a local forest, reasoning that the blast would "lay the trees out in windrows from the center of the explosion in all directions as though they were matchsticks," meanwhile igniting a fearsome firestorm at the epicenter. "It seemed to me," he added, "that a demonstration of this sort would prove to the Japanese that we could destroy any of their cities at will." The physicist Ernest O. Lawrence may have been speaking half in jest when he suggested that a bomb might be used to "blow the top off" Mount Fujiyama, but he was quite serious when he assured a friend early in the war: "The bomb will never be dropped on people. As soon as we get it, we'll use it only to dictate peace."

Now, hindsight is too easy a talent. But it seems evident on the face of 15 it that the fourth of those options, the warning shot, was much to be preferred over the other three, and even more to be preferred over use on living targets. I do not want to argue the case here. I do want to ask, however, why that possibility was so easily dismissed.

The fact of the matter seems to have been that the notion of a demonstra- 16 tion was discussed on only a few occasions once the Manhattan Project neared completion, and most of those discussions were off the record. So a historian trying to reconstruct the drift of those conversations can only flatten an ear against the wall, as it were, and see if any sense can be made of the muffled voices next door. It seems very clear, for example, that the options involving advance notice were brought up so often and so early in official conversations that they came to *mean* demonstration in the minds of several important players. If a James Byrnes, say, soon to be named Secretary of State, were asked why one could not detonate a device in unoccupied territory, he might raise the problem posed by prisoners of war, and if the same question were asked of a James Bryant Conant, another science adviser, he might speak of the embarrassment that would follow a dud—thus, in both cases, joining ideas that had no logical relation to each other. Neither prisoners of war nor fear of failure, of course, posed any argument against a surprise demonstration.

There were two occasions, however, on which persons in a position to [17] affect policy discussed the idea of a nonlethal demonstration. Those two conversations together consumed no more than a matter of minutes, so far as one can tell at this remove, and they, too, were off the record. But they seem to represent virtually the entire investment of the government of the United States in "mature consideration" of the subject.

The first discussion took place at a meeting of what was then called the [18] Interim Committee, a striking gathering of military, scientific and government brass under the chairmanship of Secretary Stimson.* This group, which included James Byrnes and Chief of Staff Gen. George C. Marshall,† met on a number of occasions in May of 1945 to discuss policy issues raised by the new bomb, and Stimson recalled later that at one of their final meetings the members "carefully considered such alternatives as a detailed advance warning or a demonstration in some uninhabited area." But the minutes of the meeting, as well as the accounts of those present, suggest otherwise. The only exchange on the subject, in fact, took place during a luncheon break, and while we have no way of knowing what was actually said in that conversation, we do know what conclusion emerged from it. One participant, Arthur H. Compton, recalled later:

> Though the possibility of a demonstration that would not destroy human lives was attractive, no one could suggest a way in which it could be made so convincing that it would be likely to stop the war.

And the recording secretary of the meeting later recalled:

> Dr. Oppenheimer . . . said he doubted whether there could be devised any sufficiently startling demonstration that would convince the Japanese they ought to throw in the sponge.

Two weeks later, four physicists who served as advisers to the Interim Committee met in Los Alamos to consider once again the question of demonstration. They were Arthur Compton,‡ Enrico Fermi,§ Ernest Lawrence‖ and Robert Oppenheimer #—as distinguished an assembly of scientific talent as

*Stimson, see paragraph 9.

†George C. Marshall (1880–1959) was an American army officer and statesman. He originated the plan for economic recovery in Europe following World War II and received the Nobel Peace Prize in 1953.

‡Arthur Compton (1892–1962), American physicist; Nobel Prize in physics, 1927.

§Enrico Fermi (1901–1954), American physicist, Nobel Prize in physics, 1938.

‖Ernest Lawrence (1901–1958), American physicist, Nobel Prize in physics, 1939.

#Oppenheimer, see paragraph 6.

could be imagined—and they concluded, after a discussion of which we have no record: "We can propose no technical demonstration likely to bring an end to the war; we see no acceptable alternative to direct military use." That, so far as anyone can tell, was the end of it.

We cannot be sure that a milder report would have made a difference, 19 for the Manhattan Project was gathering momentum as it moved toward the more steeply pitched inclines of May and June, but we can be sure that the idea of a demonstration was at that point spent. The Los Alamos report ended with something of a disclaimer ("We have, however, no claim to special competence. . . ."), but its message was clear enough. When asked about that report nine years later in his security hearings, Oppenheimer said, with what might have been a somewhat defensive edge in his voice, "We did not think exploding one of those things as a firecracker over the desert was likely to be very impressive."

Perhaps not. But those fragments are telling for another reason. If you 20 listen to them carefully for a moment or two, you realize that these are the voices of nuclear physicists trying to imagine how a strange and distant people will react to an atomic blast. These are the voices of nuclear physicists dealing with psychological and anthropological questions about Japanese culture, Japanese temperament, Japanese will to resist—topics, we must assume, about which they knew almost nothing. They did not know yet what the bomb could actually do, since its first test was not to take place for another month. But in principle, at least, Oppenheimer and Fermi reflecting on matters relating to the Japanese national character should have had about the same force as Ruth Benedict and Margaret Mead* reflecting on matters relating to high-energy physics, the first difference being that Benedict and Mead would not have presumed to do so, and the second being that no one in authority would have listened to them if they had.

The first of the two morals I want to draw from the foregoing—this 21 being a parable, after all—is that in moments of critical contemplation, it is often hard to know where the competencies of soldiers and scientists and all the rest of us begin and end. Many an accidental judgment can emerge from such confusions.

But what if the conclusions of the scientists had been correct? What if 22 some kind of demonstration had been staged in a lightly occupied part of Japan and it *had* been greeted as a firecracker in the desert? What then?

Let me shift gears for a moment and discuss the subject in another way. 23 It is standard wisdom for everyone in the United States old enough to remember the war, and for most of those to whom it is ancient history, that the bombings of Hiroshima and Nagasaki were the only alternative to an all-out invasion of the Japanese mainland involving hundreds of thousands and perhaps millions of casualties on both sides. Unless the Japanese came to understand the need to surrender quickly, we would have been drawn by an

*Ruth Benedict (1887–1948) and Margaret Mead (1901–1978), well-known American anthropologists.

almost magnetic force toward those dreaded beaches. This has become an almost automatic pairing of ideas, an article of common lore. If you lament that so many civilians were incinerated or blown to bits in Hiroshima and Nagasaki, then somebody will remind you of the American lives thus saved. Truman was the person most frequently asked to account for the bombings, and his views were emphatic on the subject:

> It was a question of saving hundreds of thousands of American lives. I don't mind telling you that you don't feel normal when you have to plan hundreds of thousands of complete, final deaths of American boys who are alive and joking and having fun while you are doing your planning. You break your heart and your head trying to figure out a way to save one life. The name given to our invasion plan was "Olympic," but I saw nothing godly about the killing of all the people that would be necessary to make that invasion. I could not worry about what history would say about my personal morality. I made the only decision I ever knew how to make. I did what I thought was right.[1]

Veterans of the war, and particularly those who had reason to suppose 24 that they would have been involved in an invasion, have drawn that same connection repeatedly, most recently Paul Fussell in the pages of *The New Republic.* Thank God for the bomb, the argument goes, it saved the lives of countless numbers of us. And so, in a sense, it may have.

But the destruction of Hiroshima and Nagasaki had nothing to do with 25 it. It only makes sense to assume, even if few people were well enough positioned in early August to see the situation whole, that there simply was not going to be an invasion. Not ever.

For what sane power, with the atomic weapon securely in its arsenal, 26 would hurl a million or more of its sturdiest young men on a heavily fortified mainland? To imagine anyone ordering an invasion when the means were at hand to blast Japan into a sea of gravel at virtually no cost in American lives is to imagine a madness beyond anything even the worst of war can induce. The invasion had not yet been called off, granted. But it surely would have been, and long before the November 1 deadline set for it.

[1] Merle Miller notes, in *Plain Speaking: An Oral Biography of Harry S. Truman,* that Truman may have had moments of misgiving: "My only insight into Mr. Truman's feeling about the Bomb and its dropping, and it isn't much, came one day in his private library at the Truman Memorial Library. In one corner was every book ever published on the bomb, and at the end of one was Horatio's speech in the last scene of *Hamlet.*" Truman had underlined these words:

> And let me speak to the yet unknowing world
> How these things came about. So shall you hear
> Of carnal, bloody, and unnatural acts,
> Of accidental judgments, casual slaughters
> Of deaths put on by cunning and forced cause,
> And, in this upshot, purposes mistook
> Fall'n on the inventors' heads. [Erikson's note.]

The United States did not become a nuclear power on August 6, with 27
the destruction of Hiroshima. It became a nuclear power on July 16, when the
first test device was exploded in Alamogordo, New Mexico. Uncertainties
remained, of course, many of them. But from that moment on, the United
States knew how to produce a bomb, knew how to deliver it and knew it
would work. Stimson said shortly after the war that the bombings of Hiroshima and Nagasaki "ended the ghastly specter of a clash of great land
armies," but he could have said, with greater justice, that the ghastly specter
ended at Alamogordo. Churchill came close to making exactly that point
when he first learned of the New Mexico test:

> To quell the Japanese resistance man by man and conquer the country
> yard by yard might well require the loss of a million American lives and
> half that number of British. . . . Now all that nightmare picture had
> vanished.

It *had* vanished. The age of inch-by-inch crawling over enemy territory, 28
the age of Guadalcanal and Iwo Jima and Okinawa, was just plain over.

The point is that once we had the bomb and were committed to its use, 29
the terrible weight of invasion no longer hung over our heads. The Japanese
were incapable of mounting any kind of offensive, as every observer has
agreed, and it was our option when to close with the enemy and thus risk
casualties. So we could have easily afforded to hold for a moment, to think
it over, to introduce what Dwight Eisenhower called "that awful thing" to
the world on the basis of something closer to mature consideration. We could
have afforded to detonate a bomb over some less lethal target and then pause
to see what happened. And do it a second time, maybe a third. And if none
of those demonstrations had made a difference, presumably we would have
had to strike harder: Hiroshima and Nagasaki would still have been there a
few weeks later for that purpose, silent and untouched—"unspoiled" was the
term Gen. H. H. Arnold used—for whatever came next. Common lore also
has it that there were not bombs enough for such niceties, but that seems not
to have been the case. The United States was ready to deliver a third bomb
toward the end of August, and Groves had already informed Marshall and
Stimson that three or four more bombs would be available in September, a
like number in October, at least five in November, and seven in December,
with substantial increases to follow in early 1946. Even if we assume that
Groves was being too hopeful about the productive machinery he had set in
motion, as one expert close to the matter has suggested, a formidable number
of bombs would have been available by the date originally set for invasion.

Which brings us back to the matter of momentum. The best way to tell 30
the story of those days is to say that the "decision to drop" had become a
force like gravity. It had taken life. The fact that it existed supplied its
meaning, its reason for being. Elting E. Morison, Stimson's biographer, put
it well:

Any process started by men toward a special end tends, for reasons logical, biological, aesthetic or whatever they may be, to carry forward, if other things remain equal, to its climax. [This is] the inertia developed in a human system. . . . In a process where such a general tendency has been set to work it is difficult to separate the moment when men were still free to choose from the moment, if such there was, when they were no longer free to choose.

I have said very little about Nagasaki so far because it was not the   31
subject of any thought at all. The orders of the bomber command were to attack Japan as soon as the bombs were ready. One was ready on August 9. Boom. When Groves was later asked why the attack on Nagasaki had come so soon after the attack on Hiroshima, leaving so little time for the Japanese to consider what had happened to them, he simply said: "Once you get your opponent reeling, you keep him reeling and never let him recover." And that is the point, really. There is no law of nature that compels a winning side to press its superiority, but it is hard to slow down, hard to relinquish an advantage, hard to rein the fury. The impulse to charge ahead, to strike at the throat, is so strong a habit of war that it almost ranks as a reflex, and if that thought does not frighten us when we consider our present nuclear predicament, nothing will. Many a casual slaughter can emerge from such moods.

If it is true, as I have suggested, that there were few military or logistic   32
reasons for striking as sharply as we did and that the decision to drop moved in on the crest of an almost irreversible current, then it might be sensible to ask, on the fortieth anniversary of the event, what some of the drifts were that became a part of that larger current. An adequate accounting would have to consider a number of military, political and other matters far beyond the reach of this brief essay, the most important of them by far being the degree to which the huge shadow of the Soviet Union loomed over both official meetings and private thoughts. It is nearly impossible to read the remaining record without assuming that the wish to make a loud announcement to the Russians was a persuasive factor in the minds of many of the principal participants. There were other drifts as well, of course, and I would like to note a few of the sort that sometimes occur to social scientists.

For one thing, an extraordinary amount of money and material had been   33
invested in the Manhattan Project—both of them in short supply in a wartime economy—and many observers thought that so large a public expense would be all the more willingly borne if it were followed by a striking display of what the money had been spent for.

And, too, extraordinary investments had been made in men and talent,   34
both of them in short supply in a wartime economy. The oldest of the people involved in the Manhattan Project—soldiers, engineers and scientists—made sacrifices in the form of separated families, interrupted careers and a variety of other discomforts, and it makes a certain psychological sense that a decisive

strike would serve as a kind of vindication for all the trouble. The youngest of them, though, had been held out of combat, thus avoiding the fate of so many men of their generation, by accidents of professional training, personal skill and sheer timing. The project was their theater of war, and it makes even more psychological sense that some of them would want the only shot they fired to be a truly resonant one.

The dropping of such a bomb, moreover, could serve as an ending, 35 something sharp and distinct in a world that had become ever more blurred. The Grand Alliance was breaking up, and with it all hope for a secure postwar world. Roosevelt was dead. The future was full of ambiguity. And, most important, everybody was profoundly tired. In circumstances like that, a resounding strike would serve to clarify things, to give them form, to tidy them up a bit.

There are other matters one might point to, some of them minor, some 36 of them major, all of them strands in the larger weave. There was a feeling, expressed by scientists and government officials alike, that the world needed a rude and decisive shock to awaken it to the realities of the atomic age. There was a feeling, hard to convey in words but easy to sense once one has become immersed in some of the available material, that the bomb had so much power and majesty, was so compelling a force, that one was almost required to give it birth and a chance to mature. There was a feeling, born of war, that for all its ferocity the atomic bomb was nevertheless no more than a minor increment on a scale of horror that already included the firebombings of Tokyo and other Japanese cities. And there was a feeling, also born of war, that living creatures on the other side, even the children, had somehow lost title to the mercies that normally accompany the fact of being human.

The kinds of points I have been making need to be stated either very 37 precisely or in some detail. I have not yet learned to do the former; I do not have space enough here for the latter. So let me just end with the observation that human decisions do not always emerge from reflective counsels where facts are arrayed in order and logic is the prevailing currency of thought. They emerge from complex fields of force, in which the vanities of leaders and the moods of constituencies and the inertias of bureaucracies play a critical part. That is as important a lesson as one can learn from the events of 1945—and as unnerving a one.

The bombings of Hiroshima and Nagasaki supply a rich case study for 38 people who must live in times like ours. It is not important for us to apportion shares of responsibility to persons who played their parts so long ago, and I have not meant to do so here: these were unusually decent and compassionate people for the most part, operating with reflexes that had been tempered by war. We need to attend to such histories as this, however, because they provide the clearest illustrations we have of what human beings can do—this being the final moral to be drawn from our parable—when they find themselves in moments of crisis and literally have more destructive power at their disposal than they know what to do with. That is as good an argument for disarming as any that can be imagined.

Questions for Discussion

1. What has been your own understanding of the reasons why America dropped the atomic bomb on Hiroshima and Nagasaki? Has the "standard wisdom" that Erikson refers to in paragraph 23 been the main explanation you accepted? Do you still accept it after reading Erikson? Why or why not?

2. Does it seem right to you to call the last sentence of the essay Erikson's thesis sentence? If so, it is in a most unusual spot. If this is his "real" thesis, the point he has been building up to all along, how does he get away with reserving it as the final statement he makes? Does he have anything that might be called a *provisional thesis* that governs his essay up to the end when he makes his "real" thesis? If so, what is the provisional thesis? Where does he express it?

3. In what sense is this historical essay a "parable," a term Erikson uses in paragraphs 2 and 21? What is a parable? Why does Erikson's essay either qualify or not qualify as one?

4. How convincing do you find Erikson's argument in paragraphs 26–29, where he bases a good deal of his interpretation of the decision-making process about the use of the bomb on assertions about what would have happened if it had not been used. This argument is based on logic rather than on historical records or evidence. Do you find Erikson's scenario here plausible? Why or why not?

Suggested Essay Topics

1. Because you cannot be expected to do all the research that would allow you to dispute with Erikson in a detailed way about the historical record and its meaning, try to engage him on a matter of principle. Direct an essay to Erikson in which you argue that, *in principle,* the winning side in a war should never slack off in pressing any advantages it may hold, even at the cost of much civilian life, because modern wars are win-all or lose-all, and it is irresponsible for the winning side to take the chance of losing its momentum. Or, if you feel differently, argue to Erikson that, *in principle,* both sides in a war should do everything possible to avoid the unnecessary loss of civilian life, even if it means prolonging the termination of the war, and that America, on the basis of that principle, should have delayed longer in using the bomb and should have seriously considered different ways of demonstrating the power of the bomb rather than simply dropping it on Japanese cities.

2. Address an essay to the least favorite history teacher you ever had in school explaining why he or she made history such an unattractive kind of study and making recommendations about how he or she could improve its teaching. Also include an argument about your view of the *uses* of history, or what you think they should be, and make that view the basis of both your criticisms and your recommendations.

IDEAS IN DEBATE

Pieter Geyl and Arnold J. Toynbee
Edward Hallett Carr

Pieter Geyl and Arnold J. Toynbee

Few scholarly works have produced as much debate as Arnold J. Toynbee's Study of History. *Toynbee's massive comparative study of the world's civilizations continues to engage scholars in lively discussions like the one we reprint here, between historian Pieter Geyl and Toynbee himself. And in its time the* Study *provoked unusual debate among general readers. Despite its bulk—the first volume was published in 1934 and the twelfth volume completed the work in 1961—the* Study *was a steady best-seller in the years following World War II.*

Two theses in particular provoked debate among Toynbee's readers. First, Toynbee claimed that all 21 of what he considered the world's major past civilizations (each of which he studied in great detail) exhibited a common pattern in their rise and fall. Each of them began, he said, when some great threat or challenge produced a grand unified response. Working together to overcome apparently insuperable problems, men and women managed, at least 21 times in world history, to create great civilizations. But then, in every case, the spiritual center decayed, social forms fell apart, and the civilization collapsed. Though many readers were exhilarated by the offer of such a unified view of human history, many others (like Pieter Geyl in the exchange that follows) were skeptical about any effort to discern a pattern shared by all civilizations in all periods.

Even more controversial was Toynbee's second claim that Western civilization has for a long time been on the "falling" side of the curve. Some readers saw Toynbee as saying that we have lost our spiritual center and that individuals can therefore do nothing to prevent the final collapse of our civilization. As you will see in the discussion reprinted here, Toynbee explicitly denied that his view was finally pessimistic; through a spiritual rebirth we might still have a chance to reverse the downward spiral.

The debate we print here is part of a report on a conference, held about midway through Toynbee's prolonged labors, to discuss his first six volumes. In his prepared paper for the conference, Pieter Geyl said,

> I can . . . have little confidence . . . that Professor Toynbee, when later on he undertakes a set examination of our civilization and its prospects, will prove able to enlighten our perplexities; or should I not rather say that we need not let ourselves be frightened by his darkness? We need not accept his view that the whole of modern history from the sixteenth

*century on has been nothing but a downward course, following the path of rout and rally.
We need not let ourselves be shaken in our confidence that the future lies open before us,
that in the midst of misery and confusion such as have so frequently occurred in history,
we still dispose of forces no less valuable than those by which earlier generations have
managed to struggle through their troubles.*

*What we print here is a record of the more informal debate that followed the
formal papers. We have no way of knowing how much revision Professors Toynbee
and Geyl gave to their spoken words, but they have clearly kept a tone of spoken
interchange. You may have noticed that most people who debate in public "talk past"
each other most of the time, changing their opponents' points, deliberately or unconsciously, to points that are more easily crushed or dismissed. As you read this debate,
try to determine whether Toynbee and Geyl commit this kind of distortion or manage
really to understand each other. Are Geyl's points the ones that Toynbee answers?
If you had the words of only one of the speakers, would you be able to give a fair account
of the other speaker's views? To answer that question you will of course need to attend
not only to both speakers' conclusions but to the supporting reasons they offer as well.*

CAN WE KNOW THE
PATTERN OF THE PAST?

*A Discussion Between Pieter Geyl
and Arnold J. Toynbee*

From Pieter Geyl, Arnold J. Toynbee, and Pitirim Sorokin, *The Pattern of the Past: Can We Determine
It?* (1949).

PROFESSOR GEYL

The six volumes of Toynbee's *Study of History* appeared before the war,   1
but it is since the war that the book and the author have become famous. A
generation only just recovering from the terrible experiences of the war and
already anxious about the future, is reading the work in the hope of finding
in its pages the answer to its perplexities. It is indeed the author's claim to
discover for us, in the at first sight chaotic and confusing spectacle of human
history, a pattern, a rhythm.

. . .

I must come straight to the main features of the system. Has Toynbee   2
proved that the histories of civilizations fall into these sharply marked stages
of growth and disintegration, separated by breakdown? Has he proved that
the work of the creative minds, or of the creative minorities, can be successful
only in the first stage and that in the second it is doomed to remain so much
fruitless effort?

In my opinion he has not. How do I know that the difference is caused   3
by the triumphant creator acting in a growing society, and the hopelessly
struggling one in a society in disintegration? I have not been convinced of the
essential difference between the phases of civilization. There are evil tenden-

cies and there are good tendencies simultaneously present at every stage of human history, and the human intellect is not sufficiently comprehensive to weigh them off against each other and to tell, before the event, which is to have the upper hand. As for the theory that the individual leader, or the leading minority, is capable of creative achievement in a growing society only and doomed to disappointment in one that is in disintegration—that theory lapses automatically when the distinction is not admitted in the absolute form in which our author propounds it.

I am glad that you are present here, Toynbee, and going to reply. For 4 this is surely a point of great practical importance. *A Study of History* does not definitely announce ruin as did Spengler's book* by its very title. But in more than one passage you give us to understand that Western civilization broke down as long ago as the sixteenth century, as a result of the wars of religion. The last four centuries of our history would thus, according to your system, be one long process of disintegration, with collapse as the inevitable end— except for the miracle of a reconversion to the faith of our fathers.

There is no doubt, when we look around us, a great deal to induce 5 gloom. But I do not see any reason why history should be read so as to deepen our sense of uneasiness into a mood of hopelessness. Earlier generations have also had their troubles and have managed to struggle through. There is nothing in history to shake our confidence that the future lies open before us.

PROFESSOR TOYNBEE

The fate of the world—the destiny of mankind—*is* involved in the issue 6 between us about the nature of history.

In replying to Professor Geyl now, I am going to concentrate on what, 7 to my mind, are his two main lines of attack. One of his general criticisms is: "Toynbee's view of history induces gloom." The other is: "Toynbee has set himself to do something impossible. He is trying to make sense of human history, and that is beyond the capacity of the human mind." I will pay most attention to this second point, because it is, I am sure, by far the more important of the two.

Let me try to dispose of the "gloom" point first. Suppose my view of 8 history did point to a gloomy conclusion, what of it? "Gloomy" and "cheerful" are one thing, "true" and "false" quite another.

Professor Geyl has interpreted me rightly in telling you that I have 9 pretty serious misgivings about the state of the world today. Don't you feel the same misgivings? Doesn't Professor Geyl feel them? That surely goes without saying. But what doesn't go without saying is what we are going to do about it; and here Professor Geyl has been handsome to me in telling you

---

*Der Untergang des Abendlandes, 2 vols. (1918–1922); translated as The Decline of the West (1926–1928). Oswald Spengler (1880–1936) made himself internationally famous with a thesis in some ways similar to Toynbee's, but by the time Toynbee was writing, most professional historians were inclined to dismiss Spengler's claim about the *inevitable* decline of the Western world as what Toynbee calls "dogmatic determinism" (¶28).

where I stand. He has told you that I disbelieve in predestination and am at the opposite pole, on that supremely important question, from the famous German philosopher Spengler. He has told you that my outlook is the reverse of historical materialism; that, in my view, the process of civilization is one of vanquishing the material problems to grapple with the spiritual ones; that I am a believer in free will; in man's freedom to respond with all his heart and soul and mind when life presents him with a challenge. Well, that is what I do believe. But how, I ask you, can one lift up one's heart and apply one's mind unless one does one's best to find out the relevant facts and to look them in the face?—the formidable facts as well as the encouraging ones.

In the state of the world today, the two really formidable facts, as I see them, are that the other civilizations that we know of have all broken down, and that in our recent history one sees some of those tendencies which, in the histories of the broken-down civilizations, have been the obvious symptoms of breakdown. But what's the moral? Surely not to shy at the facts. Professor Geyl himself admits them. And also, surely, not to be daunted by the "sense of uneasiness" which these formidable facts are bound to give us. "I don't see any reason," said Professor Geyl just now, "why history should be read so as to deepen our sense of uneasiness into a mood of hopelessness." That is a telling criticism of Spengler, who does diagnose that our civilization is doomed, and who has nothing better to suggest than that we should fold our hands and await the inevitable blow of the axe. But that ball doesn't take my wicket, for in my view, as Geyl has told you, uneasiness is a challenging call to action, and not a death sentence to paralyze our wills. Thank goodness we do know the fates of the other civilizations; such knowledge is a chart that warns us of the reefs ahead. Knowledge can be power and salvation if we have the spirit to use it. There is a famous Greek epigram which runs: "I am the tomb of a shipwrecked sailor, but don't let that frighten off you, brother mariner, from setting sail; because, when we went down, the other ships kept afloat."

"There is nothing in history," said Professor Geyl in his closing sentence, "to shake our confidence that the future lies open before us." Those might have been my own words, but I don't quite see what warrant Professor Geyl has for using them. The best comfort Professor Geyl can give us is: "If we take care not to unnerve ourselves by trying to chart the seas, we may be lucky enough to get by without hitting the rocks." No, I haven't painted him quite black enough, for his view is still gloomier than that. "To make a chart of history," he says, "is a sheer impossibility." Professor Geyl's own chart, you see, is the "perfect and absolute blank" of Lewis Carroll's bellman who hunted the snark. Geyl, too, has a chart, like Spengler and me. We all of us have one, whether we own up to it or not, and no chart is more than one man's shot at the truth. But surely, of those three, the blank is the most useless and the most dangerous.

Professor Geyl thinks I am a pessimist because I see a way of escape in a reconversion to the faith of our fathers. "This," says Professor Geyl, "is an unnecessarily gloomy view of our situation"—like the old lady who was advised to leave it to Providence and exclaimed: "Oh dear, has it come to that?"

What was our fathers' chart of history? As they saw it, it was a tale told 13 by God, unfolding itself from the Creation through the Fall and the Redemption to the Last Judgment. As Professor Geyl says he sees it, it seems like a tale told by an idiot, signifying nothing. You may not agree with our fathers' view that history is a revelation of God's providence; but it is a poor exchange, isn't it, to swap their faith for the view that history makes no sense.

Of course, Professor Geyl is no more singular in his view than I am in 14 mine. What one may call the nonsense view of history has been fashionable among Western historians for the last few generations. The odd thing is that some of the holders of this view—I don't know whether I could count Professor Geyl among the number—defend it principally on the ground that it is scientific. Of course, it is only human that historians should have wanted to be scientific in an age when science has been enjoying such prestige. I am, myself, a historian who believes that science has an awful lot to teach us. But how strange to suppose that one is being scientific by despairing of making sense! For what is science? It is only another name for the careful and scrupulous use of the human mind. And, if men despair of reason, they are lost. Nature hasn't given us wings, fur, claws, antennae or elephant's trunks; but she has given us the human intellect—the most effective of all implements, if we are not too timid to use it. And what does this scientific intellect do? It looks at the facts, but it doesn't stop there. It looks at the facts and it tries to make sense of them. It does, you see, the very thing that Professor Geyl takes me to task for trying to do with the facts of history.

Is history really too hard a nut for science to crack? When the human 15 intellect has wrested her secret from physical nature, are we going to sit down under an *ex cathedra* dictum that the ambition to discover the secret of human history will always be bound to end in disappointment? We don't need to be told that Man is a harder—a very much harder—nut than the atom. We have discovered how to split the atom and are in danger of splitting it to our own destruction. By comparison with the science of physics, the science of man is so difficult that our discoveries in the two fields have gone forward at an uneven pace till they have got quite out of step with each other. It is partly this that has got us into our present fix. Is science to shirk trying to do anything about it? "The proper study of mankind is man," says Pope. "The human intellect," sighs Geyl, "is not sufficiently comprehensive."

I say: We can't afford such defeatism; it is unworthy of the greatness 16 of man's mind; and it is refuted by the human mind's past achievements. The mind has won all its great victories by well-judged boldness. And today, before our eyes, science is launching a characteristically bold offensive in what is now the key area of the mental battlefield. Why, she has got her nutcrackers round this nut, this human nut, already. One arm of the pincers is the exciting young science of psychology, which is opening out entirely new mental horizons for us, in the very direction in which we are most in need of longer vistas. The other is the forbidding yet rewarding discipline of statistics. Science has set herself now in good earnest to comprehend human nature, and, through understanding, to show it how to master itself and thereby to set itself free. Science, so long preoccupied with the riddles of non-human nature, has now joined in the quests of philosophy and religion, and this diversion of her energies has been timely. There is, indeed, no time to be lost. We are in for a life-and-death struggle. And, at this critical hour, is science to get no support from our professedly scientific historians?

Well, in this "mental fight," I have deliberately risked my neck by 17 putting my own reading of the facts of history on the table. I should never dream of claiming that my particular interpretation is the only one possible. There are, I am sure, many different alternative ways of analyzing history, each of which is true in itself and illuminating as far as it goes, just as, in dissecting an organism, you can throw light on its nature by laying bare either the skeleton or the muscles or the nerves or the circulation of the blood. No single one of these dissections tells the whole truth, but each of them reveals a genuine facet of it. I should be well content if it turned out that I had laid bare one genuine facet of history, and even then, I should measure my success by the speed with which my own work in my own line was put out of date by further work by other people in the same field. In the short span of one lifetime, the personal contribution of the individual scholar to the great and growing stream of knowledge can't be more than a tiny pailful. But if he could inspire—or provoke—other scholars to pour in their pailfuls too, well, then he could feel that he had really done his job. And this job of making sense of history is one of the crying needs of our day—I beg of you, believe me.

PROFESSOR GEYL

Well I must say, Toynbee, that I felt some anxiety while you were 18 pouring out over me this torrent of eloquence, wit and burning conviction, but that was of course what I had to expect from you. And now that is over I'm relieved to feel that I'm still there, and my position untouched.

Professor Toynbee pictures me as one of those men who mistake the 19 courage to see evils for gloom, and who when others sound the call for action take refuge from the dangers of our time in an illusionist optimism. But have I been saying that we are not in danger? And that no action is required? What I have said is that Toynbee's system induces the wrong kind of gloom because it tends to make action seem useless. "But I am a believer in man's free will," Toynbee replies. I know. But nevertheless, his system lays it down that the civilization which has been overtaken by a breakdown is doomed. Now Toynbee has repeatedly suggested that our Western civilization did suffer a breakdown as long ago as the sixteenth century, and that consequently, try as we may, we cannot avoid disaster. Except in one way, except in case we allow ourselves to be reconverted to the faith of our fathers. And here Toynbee exclaims: "You see, I'm not so gloomy after all." Perhaps not. But if one happens to hold a different opinion both of the efficacy and of the likelihood of application of his particular remedy, one cannot help thinking that Toynbee is but offering us cold comfort. He talks as if we cannot advance matters by "so hotly canvassing and loudly advertising," as he contemptuously puts it, "our political and economic maladies." It is the loss of religious faith that is the deadly danger. To most of us this is indeed condemning all our efforts to futility.

Of course, Toynbee, it is only your picturesque way of putting things 20 when you describe me as one of those historians who cling to the nonsense view of history. Because I cannot accept either your methods or your system it does not follow that to my mind history has no meaning. I do not believe that at any time it will be possible to reduce the past to so rigid a pattern as to enable us to forecast the future—granted. Yet to me, as to you, the greatest function of the historian is to interpret the past—to find sense in it, although at the same time it is the least scientific, the most inevitably subjective of his functions.

I am surprised that you class me with those historians who believe that 21 their view of history rests securely on scientific foundations. In fact it is you who claim to be proceeding on the lines of empiricism towards laws of universal validity, while I have been suggesting that these and other scientific terms which you are fond of using have no real meaning in a historical argument. Even just now, didn't you deduce from the conquest of the mystery of the atom the certainty that man's mind will be able to conquer the mystery of the historical process as well? In my opinion these are fundamentally different propositions.

Let me remind you especially of what I have been saying about the 22 uncertain nature of historical events, and the difficulty of detaching them from their contexts. And also of my contention that the cases and instances strewn over your pages have been arbitrarily selected from an infinite number and haven't therefore that value as evidence which you attach to them.

PROFESSOR TOYNBEE

There can be no doubt that you look upon this last point as an important 23 one. . . . I see what you're getting at. I set out to deal with history in terms of civilizations, of which there are, of course, very few specimens, but in the illustrations I give, and the points I make, I don't confine myself to these rare big fellows, I hop about all over the place, bringing up as illustrations of my points events on a much smaller scale, which to you seem to be chosen arbitrarily, because they're just a few taken out of a large number. They also, as you point out, lend themselves to more interpretations than one. Yes, I think that's fair criticism, and quite telling. In answer I'd say two things. I think, as I said a minute or two ago, the same historical event often can be analyzed legitimately in a number of different ways, each of which brings out some aspect of historical truth which is true as far as it goes, though not the whole truth. I have myself sometimes made the same historical event do double or treble duty in this way, and I don't think this is a misleading way of using facts. As I've said before, several different dissections can all be correct, each in its own line.

My second point is that I bring in these illustrations taken from the 24 small change of history, not for their own sake but to throw indirect light on the big units, which I call civilizations, which are my main concern. I helped myself out in this way because, in the very early stage in human history in which our generation happens to be living, the number of civilizations that have come into existence up to date, is still so small—not more than about twenty, as I make it out.

To take up the case of your own country, Holland, now, which I have 25 used to throw light on the rise of the Egyptian and Sumerian civilizations: you challenged my account of Holland's rise to greatness. I found my explanation of it in the stimulus of a hard country. The people of Holland had to wrest the country from the sea and they rose to the occasion. Your criticism is that I've arbitrarily isolated one fact out of several. The Dutch, you say, didn't do it by themselves, they were helped at the start by efficient outsiders, and then the country, when it had been reclaimed, turned out to have a rich soil, as well as a good situation for commerce.

Yes, of course, those are also facts of Dutch history, but my answer is 26 that they're not the key facts. If the outsiders that you have in mind are the Romans, well, the benefits of Roman efficiency were not enjoyed by Holland alone; Belgium, France and England enjoyed them as well. So Holland's Roman apprenticeship won't account for achievements that are special to Holland and that distinguish her from her neighbors. Then the fertile soil and good location: these aren't causes of Holland's great feat of fighting and beating the North Sea, they're effects and rewards of it. It is a case of "to him that hath, shall be given." What the Dutch had, before these other things were given them, was the strength of will to raise their country out of the waters. The terrific challenge of the sea to a country below sea level is surely the unique and distinguishing feature of Dutch history. With all deference to you, Geyl, as a Netherlander and a historian, I still think I'm right in picking out the response of the people of Holland to this challenge as being the key to the greatness of your country. I do also think that the case of Holland throws valuable light on the cases of Egypt and Babylonia, two other places where people have had to fight swamp and sea in order to reclaim land, and where this struggle between man and nature has brought to life two out of the twenty or so civilizations known to us.

Of course if one could lay hands on some more civilizations, one might 27 be able to study history on that scale without having to bother about little bits and pieces like Holland and England. I wish I were in that happy position, and if you now, Geyl, would help me by taking up your archeological spade and unearthing a few more forgotten civilizations for me, I should be vastly obliged to you. But even if you proved yourself a Layard, Schliemann and Arthur Evans rolled into one, you could only raise my present figure of twenty-one known civilizations to twenty-four, and that of course wouldn't help me to reduce my margin of error appreciably.

To turn for a moment to a different point, I want to correct an impres- 28
sion that I think our listeners may have got, of something else that you were
saying just now. Anyway, I got the impression myself that you still thought
I claimed to be able to foretell the future from the past, that I'd laid it down
that our own civilization was doomed. This is a very important point and I
want to make my position on it clear beyond all possibility of mistake. So let
me repeat: I don't set up to be a prophet, I don't believe history can be used
for telling the world's fortune, I think history can perhaps sometimes show
one possibilities or even probabilities, but never certainties. With the awful
warning of Spengler's dogmatic determinism before my eyes, I always have
been and shall be mighty careful, for my part, to treat the future of our own
civilization as an open question—not at all because I'm afraid of committing
myself, but because I believe as strongly as you do, Geyl, that it *is* an open
question.

PROFESSOR GEYL

Well I'm glad, Toynbee, that you've taken so seriously the objections 29
I've made to the profusion of illustrations from national histories. As to the
case of Holland, let me just say that I was not thinking of the Romans only
and not even of foreigners primarily. What I meant was that Netherlands
civilization did not have its origin or earliest development in the region which
was exposed to the struggle with the water, but, on the contrary, this region
could be described as a backward part of the Netherlands area as a whole.
And as regards the future, in one place of your book you are very near to
drawing—as you put it—"the horoscope of our civilization" from the fates
of other civilizations, and you suggest repeatedly that we have got into the
disintegration stage, which you picture to us so elaborately in your book as
leading inevitably to catastrophe. I'm glad to hear now that you did not in
fact mean to pass an absolute sentence of death over us.

PROFESSOR TOYNBEE

No, I think we simply don't know. I suppose I must be the last judge 30
of what my own beliefs are.

But now, Geyl, here is a ball I'd like for a change to bowl at you. You've 31
given me an opening by the fair-mindedness and frankness you've shown all
through our debate. You've done justice to my contention that while historical facts are in some respects unique, there are other respects in which they
belong to a class and are therefore comparable. There is truth, you say, in this,
otherwise no general ideas about history could ever be formed, but isolating
the comparable elements is ticklish work. It certainly is ticklish work. I speak
with feeling from long experience in trying to do precisely that job. But may
there not be a moral in this for you and every other historian as well as for
me? May not it mean that we ought all of us to give far more time and far
more serious and strenuous thought than many of us have ever given to this

job of forming one's general ideas? And there is a previous and, to my mind, more important job to be done before that.

We've first to bring into consciousness our existing ideas and to put these trump cards of ours face upwards on the table. All historians are bound, you see, to have general ideas about history. On this point, every stitch of work they do is so much evidence against them. Without ideas, they couldn't think a thought, speak a sentence or write a line on their subjects. Ideas are the machine tools of the mind, and, wherever you see a thought being thrown out, you may be certain that there is an idea at the back of it. This is so obvious that I find it hard to have patience with historians who boast, as some modern Western historians do, that they keep entirely to the facts of history and don't go in for theories. Why, every so-called fact that they present to you had some pattern of theory behind it. Historians who genuinely believe they have no general ideas about history are, I would suggest to them, simply ignorant of the workings of their own minds, and such wilful ignorance is, isn't it, really unpardonable. The intellectual worker who refuses to let himself become aware of the working ideas with which he is operating seems to me to be about as great a criminal as the motorist who first closes his eyes and then steps on the gas. To leave oneself and one's public at the mercy of any fool ideas, if they happen to have taken possession of one's unconscious, is surely the height of intellectual irresponsibility. 32

I believe our listeners would be very much interested to hear what you say about that. 33

PROFESSOR GEYL

This is very simple. I agree with you entirely about the impossibility of allowing, as it used to be put, the facts to speak for themselves, and the historian who imagines that he can rule out theory or, let us say, his own individual mind, his personal view of things in general, seems to me a very uninteresting being, or in the majority of cases, when he is obviously only deluding himself and covering his particular partiality with the great word of objectivity and historical science, a very naïve person, and perhaps a very dangerous one. 34

As a matter of fact this is the spirit in which I have tackled you. When you said that I was an adherent of the nonsense view of history, you were mistaking my position altogether. In my own fashion, when I reject your methods and your conclusions, I am also trying to establish general views about history. Without such views, I know that the records of the past would become utterly chaotic and senseless, and I think I should rather be an astronomer than devote my life to so hopeless and futile a study. 35

But, to me, one of the great things to realize about history is its infinite complexity, and, when I say infinite, I do mean that not only the number of the phenomena and incidents but their often shadowy and changing nature is such that the attempt to reduce them to a fixed relationship and to a scheme of absolute validity can never lead to anything but disappointment. It is when 36 you present your system in so hard and fast a manner as to seem, at any rate to me, to dictate to the future, that I feel bound to protest, on behalf both of history and of the civilization whose crisis we are both witnessing.

You have twitted me for inviting the world to sail on an uncharted 37 course. Yet I believe that the sense of history is absolutely indispensable for the life of mankind. I believe with Burckhardt that there is wisdom to be gained from the study of the past, but no definite lessons for the actual problems of the present.

PROFESSOR TOYNBEE

Well there! It looks as if, on this question anyway, our two different 38 approaches have brought us on to something like common ground. If I am right in this, I think it is rather encouraging, for this last issue we were discussing is, I am sure, a fundamental one.

PROFESSOR GEYL

Well I see, Toynbee, that our time is up. There are just a few seconds 39 left for me to pay tribute to the courage with which you, as you expressed it yourself, have risked your neck; not by facing me here at the microphone, but by composing that gigantic and impressive scheme of civilizations, which was bound to rouse the skeptics and to be subjected to their criticism. Now I am not such a skeptic as to doubt the rightness of my own position in our debate, but I am one compared with you. Perhaps you will value the assurance from such a one that he himself has found your great work immensely stimulating and that, generally speaking, in the vast enterprise in which we historians are engaged together, daring and imaginative spirits like yourself have an essential function to fulfill.

Questions for Discussion

1. Why does Geyl think that his differences with Toynbee have not just theoretical but great *practical* importance (¶4)?

2. Some historical questions are fairly easy to answer: for example, in what year did you enter high school? Others are more difficult, but not beyond meaningful speculation and argument: For example, what were your *real* reasons for going to college or for choosing this college? And some questions seem clearly beyond human capacity to answer: For example, what were Brutus' feelings as he stabbed Caesar? Does it seem to you that the question "Why do civilizations rise and fall?" is by its nature merely difficult to debate or is finally impossible to debate?

3. Clearly Toynbee and Geyl are convinced that question 2 could be addressed rationally, but few of us will ever know enough about the 21 civilizations to judge or even to debate in any detail about Geyl's and Toynbee's positions. It is not beyond us, however, to ask which of the two opponents is more convincing, given their arguments as presented. After reading the debate two or three times, choose a paragraph that seems highly persuasive, and list all the reasons you can find to explain why it carries weight for you.

4. The debate contains a good deal of comment by each speaker about the character of the other (for example, ¶18, the beginning of ¶19, and most of ¶39). Each speaker praises the other, and neither one says anything openly nasty about the other. Make two lists of characteristics, favorable and unfavorable, that Geyl attributes to Toynbee and two lists of Geyl's favorable and unfavorable qualities as stated or implied by Toynbee. (Don't list only the openly stated qualities, like the "courage" that Geyl talks about in sentence 2 of ¶39, but also the qualities that are merely implied, like Geyl's suggestion that Toynbee's work is careless and arrogant.) Does Geyl's characterization of Toynbee seem to fit what you can infer about Toynbee from his own words? Does Toynbee's Geyl fit the Geyl who speaks?

5. Study paragraph 18 carefully. What do you think Geyl is trying to accomplish with it? Would you advise Geyl to cut it, if he were preparing another printing? Why or why not?

6. In paragraph 19 Geyl suggests (especially in sentences 2–4) that Toynbee has misreported his claims. Is he justified in the claim?

7. Both men seem to agree that "facts do not speak for themselves but must be interpreted" (see, for example, ¶34). Can you state clearly the difference between them about how we should work in interpreting historical facts and making use of them in the present? Does either man take the view of facts explained by Edward Hallett Carr (pp. 785–794)? Support your answer by citing passages.

Suggested Essay Topics

1. Your life has a "history" just as each civilization does, and though that history may seem less complex, it still has consisted of so many details, from the time of your birth until now, that no one could ever list them all (see Geyl's talk about "infinite complexity" in ¶36). Your picture of your past is thus not a report of raw facts but an interpretation that in *some* ways resembles Toynbee's interpretation of civilizations. Choose some important turning point or event from your life, one that depended on your making a conscious choice. Write a history of the choice, your reasons for it, and the consequences, good or bad. You may find it helpful to address your account as a letter to your parents, correcting what you take to be their false view of the event's "history." You may also get some

hints about procedure by reading the stories of Helen Keller (Chapter 3) and Zora Neale Hurston (Chapter 4).

2. Write a two-page "history" of what happened to you yesterday. Include an appraisal of whether the day showed signs of moving you upward or downward in your life's "curve."

Edward Hallett Carr

One mark of an excellent teacher, in any scholarly discipline, is the ability to formulate and wrestle with the fundamental questions of the discipline—questions so fundamental that they are often overlooked, yet usually so elusive that no one ever finally settles them. In this essay, Edward Hallett Carr (1892–1982) takes up one such question in his own discipline, history: What is a "historical fact," and how does such a fact differ from a "mere fact about the past"? Carr addresses the question to students of history, but the issues he raises about the relative status of facts clearly apply to other disciplines and even to everyday life.

His main objective is to show that historical facts do not exist, as is sometimes assumed, in a realm separated from interpretation. He argues that it is naive and uncritical to think that facts have an objective status that remains unchanged regardless of how they are used or how they are looked at. In the common view, the facts about the Battle of Waterloo, for example, are taken as having a permanent, objective, unchanging status; they will remain the same for anyone in any time or place. In answering the question "What really happened at Waterloo?" one establishes a body of "objective" facts about the battle and then "bases" an interpretation on the facts. The possible interpretations might vary widely and new interpretations appear indefinitely, but the facts, it is held, always remain the same. And this would appear, after all, to be only common sense. Most people believe that any proposition, opinion, or datum that claims the status of a fact is unarguably true. In politics, business, medicine, mass communication, and everyday conversation, such claims as "It is a scientifically proven fact that . . . ," "It is a fact of history that . . . ," or "It is an indisputable fact that . . ." are clear claims to absolute authority, designed to preclude disagreement. A fact is a fact and that's that.

Carr holds a more complicated view. According to him, taking up any given subject requires, right from the start, that one look at it from one angle rather than another; making this choice means that not only the data that one takes as facts but also their relative importance are generated primarily by one's angle of vision, not by any intrinsic quality that facts possess in themselves.

We can illustrate his view with a non-historical example. A cone may have an objective shape, which one may choose to call a brute fact of its existence. But one still has no choice but to look at it from a given point of view at any given time, and each of these various views will always yield a different "fact." From above, the cone will look like a circle; from the side, it will look like a triangle; from the bottom, it will look like a circle with a dot in the middle; and so on. Since there is no place one can stand to obtain a 360-degree, totally encompassing view of the cone, the "facts" of its shape are going to alter whenever one alters one's point of view.

This does not mean that there is no such thing as a fact of "coneness." Nor does it mean that there are no distinctions or preferences to be made among different views of a given topic: Not all knowledge is equally good or useful. However, it does mean that facts have a dynamic, not a static, relationship to the angles of vision from which topics are viewed. Human history is full of examples. During the many centuries when demonology formed an important part of medical theory, demented behavior was explained by the "facts" of demonic possession. When everyone thought that the earth was at the center of the universe, the sun's movement around the earth was an accepted "fact." During the centuries when Euclid's theorems were unchallenged, the "fact" was that parallel lines never met, but today's non-Euclidean geometry teaches a different "fact." And so the story goes, through all the changing views and theories that human beings have held.

These earlier views cannot be dismissed as mere mistakes or falsehoods. Discredited views have not become discredited simply because thinkers "had their facts wrong." Ptolemy's epicycles could once again be used to explain the movements of the stars, if only we once again believed that the earth is at the center of the universe. Ptolemy's view and the facts it generated are not likely to be taken up again, but succeeding "facts" about astronomy and a host of other issues will be equally subject to change. Twenty years ago, for example, parents with feverish children were told to give them aspirin; today they are told to "let the fever do its job." The facts about fever depend on one's interpretation of fever, not on any intrinsic or objective "facts of the case."

The same holds true in history, science, religion, and all other fields of inquiry. What a sick person takes to be the "facts of the case" when recovery of health follows a prayer will depend on whatever beliefs he or she already holds about the power of prayer. Faced with this realization, and the need to solve real problems, one can neither abandon facts nor kowtow to them. They must be viewed with critical respect, not slavish devotion or cynical skepticism. Their limitations need to be recognized; their powers need to be respected. We cannot do without them, but we cannot live by them either—unless we know enough not to view them with uncritical naïveté.

THE HISTORIAN
AND HIS FACTS

From chapter 1 of *What Is History?* (1961).

The nineteenth century was a great age for facts. "What I want," said   1
Mr. Gradgrind in [Charles Dickens's] *Hard Times*, "is Facts. . . . Facts alone are wanted in life." Nineteenth-century historians on the whole agreed with him. When Ranke in the 1830s, in legitimate protest against moralizing history, remarked that the task of the historian was "simply to show how it really was

(*wie es eigentlich gewesen*)" this not very profound aphorism had an astonishing success. Three generations of German, British, and even French historians marched into battle intoning the magic words, "*Wie es eigentlich gewesen*" like an incantation—designed, like most incantations, to save them from the tiresome obligation to think for themselves. The positivists, anxious to stake out their claim for history as a science, contributed the weight of their influence to this cult of facts.* First ascertain the facts, said the positivists, then draw your conclusions from them. In Great Britain, this view of history fitted in perfectly with the empiricist tradition which was the dominant strain in British philosophy from Locke to Bertrand Russell. The empirical theory of knowledge presupposes a complete separation between subject and object.† Facts, like sense-impressions, impinge on the observer from outside, and are independent of his consciousness. The process of reception is passive: having received the data, he then acts on them. *The Shorter Oxford English Dictionary*, a useful but tendentious work of the empirical school, clearly marks the separateness of the two processes by defining a fact as "a datum of experience as distinct from conclusions." This is what may be called the common-sense view of history. History consists of a corpus of ascertained facts. The facts are available to the historian in documents, inscriptions, and so on, like fish on the fishmonger's slab. The historian collects them, takes them home, and cooks and serves them in whatever style appeals to him. Acton,‡ whose culinary tastes were austere, wanted them served plain. In his letter of instructions to contributors to the first *Cambridge Modern History* [1902–1910] he announced the requirement "that our Waterloo must be one that satisfies French and English, German and Dutch alike; that nobody can tell, without examining the list of authors where the Bishop of Oxford laid down the pen, and whether Fairbairn or Gasquet, Liebermann or Harrison took it up."[1] Even Sir George Clark [general editor of the *New Cambridge Modern History* (1957–1979)], critical as he was of Acton's attitude, himself contrasted the "hard core of facts" in history with the "surrounding pulp of disputable interpretation"[2]—forgetting perhaps that the pulpy part of the fruit is more rewarding than the hard core. First get your facts straight, then plunge at your peril into the shifting sands of interpretation—that is the ultimate wisdom of the empirical, common-sense school of history. It recalls the favourite dictum of the great liberal journalist C. P. Scott: "Facts are sacred, opinion is free."

Now this clearly will not do. I shall not embark on a philosophical   2

---

*"Positivists" were philosophers who claimed that positive knowledge could be based *only* on verifiable facts. Impressed by the rapid advance of science and technology they witnessed during the second half of the nineteenth century and the opening decades of this century, the positivists optimistically proposed that all disciplines—including history, and even ethics and religion—could and should be based on scientific method.

†That is, the perceiver ("subject") is separate from—has no influence on—the thing perceived ("object").

‡John Dalberg, Lord Acton (1834–1902) was a famous English historian, author of the often-repeated aphorism "Power tends to corrupt; absolute power corrupts absolutely."

discussion of the nature of our knowledge of the past. Let us assume for present purposes that the fact that Caesar crossed the Rubicon and the fact that there is a table in the middle of the room are facts of the same or of a comparable order, that both these facts enter our consciousness in the same or in a comparable manner, and that both have the same objective character in relation to the person who knows them. But, even on this bold and not very plausible assumption, our argument at once runs into the difficulty that not all facts about the past are historical facts, or are treated as such by the historian. What is the criterion which distinguishes the facts of history from other facts about the past?

What is a historical fact? This is a crucial question into which we must look a little more closely. According to the common-sense view, there are certain basic facts which are the same for all historians and which form, so to speak, the backbone of history—the fact, for example, that the Battle of Hastings was fought in 1066. But this view calls for two observations. In the first place, it is not with facts like these that the historian is primarily concerned. It is no doubt important to know that the great battle was fought in 1066 and not in 1065 or 1067, and that it was fought at Hastings and not at Eastbourne or Brighton. The historian must not get these things wrong. But when points of this kind are raised, I am reminded of Housman's remark that "accuracy is a duty, not a virtue."[3] To praise a historian for his accuracy is like praising an architect for using well-seasoned timber or properly mixed concrete in his building. It is a necessary condition of his work, but not his essential function. It is precisely for matters of this kind that the historian is entitled to rely on what have been called the "auxiliary sciences" of history—archaeology, epigraphy, numismatics, chronology, and so forth. The historian is not required to have the special skills which enable the expert to determine the origin and period of a fragment of pottery or marble, to decipher an obscure inscription, or to make the elaborate astronomical calculations necessary to establish a precise date. These so-called basic facts which are the same for all historians commonly belong to the category of the raw materials of the historian rather than of history itself. The second observation is that the necessity to establish these basic facts rests not on any quality in the facts themselves, but on an *a priori* decision of the historian.* In spite of C. P. Scott's motto, every journalist knows today that the most effective way to influence opinion is by the selection and arrangement of the appropriate facts. It used to be said that facts speak for themselves. This is, of course, untrue. The facts speak only when the historian calls on them: it is he who decides to which facts to give the floor, and in what order or context. It was, I think, one of Pirandello's characters who said that a fact is like a sack—it won't stand up till you've put something in it. The only reason why we are interested to know that

---

*"*A priori*"—literally, "from what is prior"; in other words, some facts become "basic" only because historians decide, before establishing them, that they need to be established.

the battle was fought at Hastings in 1066 is that historians regard it as a major historical event. It is the historian who has decided for his own reasons that Caesar's crossing of that petty stream, the Rubicon, is a fact of history, whereas the crossing of the Rubicon by millions of other people before or since interests nobody at all. The fact that you arrived in this building [where Carr delivered this lecture] half an hour ago on foot, or on a bicycle, or in a car, is just as much a fact about the past as the fact that Caesar crossed the Rubicon. But it will probably be ignored by historians. Professor Talcott Parsons once called science "a selective system of cognitive orientations to reality."[4] It might perhaps have been put more simply. But history is, among other things, that. The historian is necessarily selective. The belief in a hard core of historical facts existing objectively and independently of the interpretation of the historian is a preposterous fallacy, but one which it is very hard to eradicate.

Let us take a look at the process by which a mere fact about the past is transformed into a fact of history. At Stalybridge Wakes in 1850, a vendor of gingerbread, as the result of some petty dispute, was deliberately kicked to death by an angry mob. Is this a fact of history? A year ago I should unhesitatingly have said "no." It was recorded by an eyewitness in some little-known memoirs;[5] but I had never seen it judged worthy of mention by any historian. A year ago Dr. Kitson Clark cited it in his Ford lectures in Oxford.[6] Does this make it into a historical fact? Not, I think, yet. Its present status, I suggest, is that it has been proposed for membership of the select club of historical facts. It now awaits a seconder and sponsors. It may be that in the course of the next few years we shall see this fact appearing first in footnotes, then in the text, of articles and books about nineteenth-century England, and that in twenty or thirty years' time it may be a well established historical fact. Alternatively, nobody may take it up, in which case it will relapse into the limbo of unhistorical facts about the past from which Dr. Kitson Clark has gallantly attempted to rescue it. What will decide which of these two things will happen? It will depend, I think, on whether the thesis or interpretation in support of which Dr. Kitson Clark cited this incident is accepted by other historians as valid and significant. Its status as a historical fact will turn on a question of interpretation. This element of interpretation enters into every fact of history.

. . .

In the first place, the facts of history never come to us "pure," since they do not and cannot exist in a pure form: they are always refracted through the mind of the recorder. It follows that when we take up a work of history, our first concern should be not with the facts which it contains but with the historian who wrote it. Let me take as an example the great historian in whose honour and in whose name these lectures were founded. Trevelyan, as he tells us in his autobiography, was "brought up at home on a somewhat exuberantly Whig tradition";[7] and he would not, I hope, disclaim the title if I described him as the last and not the least of the great English liberal historians of the Whig tradition.* It is not for nothing that he traces back his family tree, through the great Whig historian George Otto Trevelyan, to Macaulay, incomparably the greatest of the Whig historians. Dr. Trevelyan's finest and maturest work *England under Queen Anne* was written against that background, and will yield its full meaning and significance to the reader only when read against that background. The author, indeed, leaves the reader with no excuse for failing to do so. For if, following the technique of connoisseurs of detective novels, you read the end first, you will find on the last few pages of the third volume the best summary known to me of what is nowadays called the Whig interpretation of history; and you will see that what Trevelyan is trying to do is to investigate the origin and development of the Whig tradition, and to root it fairly and squarely in the years after the death of its founder, William III. Though this is not, perhaps, the only conceivable interpretation of the events of Queen Anne's reign, it is a valid and, in Trevelyan's hands, a fruitful interpretation. But, in order to appreciate it at its full value, you have to understand what the historian is doing. For if . . . the historian must re-enact in thought what has gone on in the mind of his *dramatis personae,* so the reader in his turn must re-enact what goes on in the mind of the historian. Study the historian before you begin to study the facts. This is, after all, not very abstruse. It is what is already done by the intelligent undergraduate who, when recommended to read a work by that great scholar Jones of St. Jude's, goes round to a friend at St. Jude's [a hypothetical college at Cambridge or Oxford University] to ask what sort of chap Jones is, and what bees he has in his bonnet. When you read a work of history, always listen out for the buzzing. If you can detect none, either you are tone deaf or your historian is a dull dog. The facts are really not at all like fish on the fishmonger's slab. They are like fish swimming about in a vast and sometimes inaccessible ocean; and what the historian catches will depend partly on chance, but mainly on what part of the ocean he chooses to fish in and what tackle he chooses to use—these two factors being, of course, determined by the kind of fish he wants to catch. By and large, the historian will get the kind of facts he wants. History means interpretation. Indeed, if, standing Sir George Clark on his head, I were to call history "a hard core of interpretation surrounded by a pulp of disputable facts," my statement would, no doubt, be one-sided and misleading, but no more so, I venture to think, than the original dictum.

The second point is the more familiar one of the historian's need of imaginative understanding for the minds of the people with whom he is dealing, for the thought behind their acts: I say "imaginative understanding," not "sympathy," lest sympathy should be supposed to imply agreement. The

*The tradition of moderately liberal reform in English politics during the eighteenth and nineteenth centuries. The monument of "liberal history in the Whig tradition" is *History of England from the Accession of James II* by Thomas Babington Macauley (1800–1859). In it, Macauley unreservedly praises the Whig party as the party of progress; and progress, for Macauley, was the glorious feature of modern English history—progress of English liberty, wealth, morals, and intellect.

nineteenth century was weak in mediaeval history, because it was too much repelled by the superstitious beliefs of the Middle Ages and by the barbarities which they inspired, to have any imaginative understanding of mediaeval people. Or take Burckhardt's censorious remark about the Thirty Years' War: "It is scandalous for a creed, no matter whether it is Catholic or Protestant, to place its salvation above the integrity of the nation."[8] It was extremely difficult for a nineteenth-century liberal historian, brought up to believe that it is right and praiseworthy to kill in defence of one's country, but wicked and wrong-headed to kill in defence of one's religion, to enter into the state of mind of those who fought the Thirty Years' War. This difficulty is particularly acute in the field in which I am now working. Much of what has been written in English-speaking countries in the last ten years about the Soviet Union, and in the Soviet Union about the English-speaking countries, has been vitiated by this inability to achieve even the most elementary measure of imaginative understanding of what goes on in the mind of the other party, so that the words and actions of the other are always made to appear malign, senseless, or hypocritical. History cannot be written unless the historian can achieve some kind of contact with the mind of those about whom he is writing.

The third point is that we can view the past, and achieve our understanding of the past, only through the eyes of the present. The historian is of his own age, and is bound to it by the conditions of human existence. The very words which he uses—words like democracy, empire, war, revolution— have current connotations from which he cannot divorce them. Ancient historians have taken to using words like *polis* and *plebs* in the original, just in order to show that they have not fallen into this trap. This does not help them. They, too, live in the present, and cannot cheat themselves into the past by using unfamiliar or obsolete words, any more than they would become better Greek or Roman historians if they delivered their lectures in a *chlamys* or a *toga*. The names by which successive French historians have described the Parisian crowds which played so prominent a role in the French revolution— *les sans-culottes, le peuple, la canaille, les bras-nus*—are all, for those who know the rules of the game, manifestos of a political affiliation and of a particular interpretation. Yet the historian is obliged to choose: the use of language forbids him to be neutral. Nor is it a matter of words alone. Over the past hundred years the changed balance of power in Europe has reversed the attitude of British historians to Frederick the Great. The changed balance of power within the Christian churches between Catholicism and Protestantism has profoundly altered their attitude to such figures as Loyola, Luther, and Cromwell. It requires only a superficial knowledge of the work of French historians of the last forty years on the French revolution to recognize how deeply it has been affected by the Russian revolution of 1917. The historian belongs not to the past but to the present. Professor Trevor-Roper tells us that the historian "ought to love the past."[9] This is a dubious injunction. To love the past may easily be an expression of the nostalgic romanticism of old men and old societies, a symptom of loss of faith and interest in the present or future.[10] *Cliché* for *cliché,* I should prefer the one about freeing oneself from "the dead hand of the past." The function of the historian is neither to love the past nor to emancipate himself from the past, but to master and understand it as the key to the understanding of the present.

If, however, these [last three points] are some of the insights of what I may call the Collingwood view of history,* it is time to consider some of the dangers. The emphasis on the role of the historian in the making of history tends, if pressed to its logical conclusion, to rule out any objective history at all: history is what the historian makes. Collingwood seems indeed, at one moment, in an unpublished note quoted by his editor, to have reached this conclusion:

> St. Augustine looked at history from the point of view of the early Christian; Tillemont, from that of a seventeenth-century Frenchman; Gibbon, from that of an eighteenth-century Englishman; Mommsen, from that of a nineteenth-century German. There is no point in asking which was the right point of view. Each was the only one possible for the man who adopted it.[11]

This amounts to total scepticism, like Froude's remark that history is "a child's box of letters with which we can spell any word we please."[12] Collingwood, in his reaction against "scissors-and-paste history," against the view of history as a mere compilation of facts, comes perilously near to treating history as something spun out of the human brain, and leads . . . to the conclusion [by Sir George Clark] . . . that "there is no 'objective' historical truth." In place of the theory that history has no meaning, we are offered here the theory of an infinity of meanings, none any more right than any other— which comes to much the same thing. The second theory is surely as untenable as the first. It does not follow that, because a mountain appears to take on different shapes from different angles of vision, it has objectively either no shape at all or an infinity of shapes. It does not follow that, because interpretation plays a necessary part in establishing the facts of history, and because no existing interpretation is wholly objective, one interpretation is as good as another, and the facts of history are in principle not amenable to objective interpretation. I shall have to consider at a later stage what exactly is meant by objectivity in history.

But a still greater danger lurks in the Collingwood hypothesis. If the historian necessarily looks at his period of history through the eyes of his own time, and studies the problems of the past as a key to those of the present, will he not fall into a purely pragmatic view of the facts, and maintain that

*The view that history is neither "the past by itself" nor only "the historian's thought about" the past but "the two things in their mutual relations." Earlier in the essay, in a passage omitted in this reprinting, Carr quotes this dictum from *The Idea of History* by the British philosopher and historian R. G. Collingwood (1889–1943). Collingwood was among the philosophers of history who first rejected the "cult of facts" and stressed the interpretive role of the historian.

the criterion of a right interpretation is its suitability to some present purpose? On this hypothesis, the facts of history are nothing, interpretation is
everything. Nietzsche had already enunciated the principle: "The falseness of
an opinion is not for us any objection to it. . . . The question is how far it
is life-furthering, life-preserving, species-preserving, perhaps species-creat-
ing."[13] The American pragmatists moved, less explicitly and less wholeheart-
edly, along the same line. Knowledge is knowledge for some purpose. The
validity of the knowledge depends on the validity of the purpose.* But, even
where no such theory has been professed, the practice has often been no less
disquieting. In my own field of study I have seen too many examples of
extravagant interpretation riding roughshod over facts, not to be impressed
with the reality of this danger. It is not surprising that perusal of some of the
more extreme products of Soviet and anti-Soviet schools of historiography
should sometimes breed a certain nostalgia for that illusory nineteenth-
century haven of purely factual history.

How then, in the middle of the twentieth century, are we to define the   10
obligation of the historian to his facts? I trust that I have spent a sufficient
number of hours in recent years chasing and perusing documents, and stuffing
my historical narrative with properly footnoted facts, to escape the imputa-
tion of treating facts and documents too cavalierly. The duty of the historian
to respect his facts is not exhausted by the obligation to see that his facts are
accurate. He must seek to bring into the picture all known or knowable facts
relevant, in one sense or another, to the theme on which he is engaged and
to the interpretation proposed. If he seeks to depict the Victorian Englishman
as a moral and rational being, he must not forget what happened at Stalybridge Wakes in 1850. But this, in turn, does not mean that he can eliminate
interpretation, which is the life-blood of history. Laymen—that is to say,
non-academic friends or friends from other academic disciplines—sometimes
ask me how the historian goes to work when he writes history. The commonest assumption appears to be that the historian divides his work into two
sharply distinguishable phases or periods. First, he spends a long preliminary
period reading his sources and filling his notebooks with facts: then, when
this is over, he puts away his sources, takes out his notebooks, and writes his
book from beginning to end. This is to me an unconvincing and unplausible
picture. For myself, as soon as I have got going on a few of what I take to
be the capital sources, the itch becomes too strong and I begin to write—not
necessarily at the beginning, but somewhere, anywhere. Thereafter, reading
and writing go on simultaneously. The writing is added to, subtracted from,
re-shaped, cancelled, as I go on reading. The reading is guided and directed

*The chief "American pragmatists" were Charles Peirce (1839–1914), William James (1842–
1910), and John Dewey (1859–1952), the fathers of the American philosophical movement called
pragmatism. While pragmatism is far too eclectic and complicated to summarize in a single creed,
Carr is probably thinking of William James's view that a belief is justified if it satisfies a
"compelling need" in the believer. Dewey, dissatisfied with James's ascribing so much precedence to the will, later worked out a program for reasoning in which he tried to set the conditions
of doubt; inquiry terminates when doubt is no longer required or felt in order to act.

and made fruitful by the writing: the more I write, the more I know what I am looking for, the better I understand the significance and relevance of what I find. Some historians probably do all this preliminary writing in their head without using pen, paper, or typewriter, just as some people play chess in their heads without recourse to board and chess-men: this is a talent which I envy, but cannot emulate. But I am convinced that, for any historian worth the name, the two processes of what economists call "input" and "output" go on simultaneously and are, in practice, parts of a single process. If you try to separate them, or to give one priority over the other, you fall into one of two heresies. Either you write scissors-and-paste history without meaning or significance; or you write propaganda or historical fiction, and merely use facts of the past to embroider a kind of writing which has nothing to do with history.

Our examination of the relation of the historian to the facts of his- 11 tory finds us, therefore, in an apparently precarious situation, navigating delicately between the Scylla of an untenable theory of history as an objective compilation of facts, of the unqualified primacy of fact over interpretation, and the Charybdis of an equally untenable theory of history as the subjective product of the mind of the historian who establishes the facts of history and masters them through the process of interpretation, between a view of history having the centre of gravity in the past and the view having the centre of gravity in the present. But our situation is less precarious than it seems. We shall encounter the same dichotomy of fact and interpretation again in these lectures in other guises—the particular and the general, the empirical and the theoretical, the objective and the subjective. The predicament of the historian is a reflexion of the nature of man. Man, except perhaps in earliest infancy and in extreme old age, is not totally involved in his environment and unconditionally subject to it. On the other hand, he is never totally independent of it and its unconditional master. The relation of man to his environment is the relation of the historian to his theme. The historian is neither the humble slave, nor the tyrannical master, of his facts. The relation between the historian and his facts is one of equality, of give-and-take. As any working historian knows, if he stops to reflect what he is doing as he thinks and writes, the historian is engaged on a continuous process of moulding his facts to his interpretation and his interpretation to his facts. It is impossible to assign primacy to one over the other.

The historian starts with a provisional selection of facts and a provi- 12 sional interpretation in the light of which that selection has been made—by others as well as by himself. As he works, both the interpretation and the selection and ordering of facts undergo subtle and perhaps partly unconscious changes through the reciprocal action of one or the other. And this reciprocal action also involves reciprocity between present and past, since the historian is part of the present and the facts belong to the past. The historian and the facts of history are necessary to one another. The historian without his facts is rootless and futile; the facts without their historian are dead and meaningless. My first answer therefore to the question, What is history?,* is that it is a continuous process of interaction between the historian and his facts, an unending dialogue between the present and the past.

NOTES

All notes are Carr's.

1. [Lord] Acton: *Lectures on Modern History* (London: Macmillan & Co.; 1906), p. 318.

2. Quoted in *The Listener* (June 19, 1952), p. 992.

3. M. Manilius: *Astronomicon: Liber Primus,* 2nd ed. (Cambridge University Press; 1937), p. 87.

4. Talcott Parsons and Edward A. Shils: *Toward a General Theory of Action,* 3rd ed. (Cambridge, Mass.: Harvard University Press; 1954), p. 167.

5. Lord George Sanger: *Seventy Years a Showman* (London: J. M. Dent & Sons; 1926); pp. 188–9.

6. These will shortly be published under the title *The Making of Victorian England.*

7. G. M. Trevelyan: *An Autobiography* (London: Longmans, Green & Company; 1949), p. 11.

8. Jacob Burckhardt: *Judgments on History and Historians* (London: S. J. Reginald Saunders & Company; 1958), p. 179.

9. Introduction to Burckhardt: *Judgments on History and Historians,* p. 17.

10. Compare Nietzsche's view of history: "To old age belongs the old man's business of looking back and casting up his accounts, of seeking consolation in the memories of the past, in historical culture" (*Thoughts Out of Season* [London: Macmillan & Co.; 1909], II, pp. 65–6).

11. Robin G. Collingwood: *The Idea of History* (London: Oxford University Press; 1946), p. xii.

12. James Anthony Froude: *Short Studies on Great Subjects* (1894), I, p. 21.

13. Friedrich Nietzsche: *Beyond Good and Evil,* ch. i.

Questions for Discussion

1. In your own words re-state and develop the distinction that Carr makes in paragraph 4 between "a mere fact about the past" and "a fact of history." Do you think this is a legitimate distinction? By what criterion or process does a "mere" fact become a historical fact?

2. Paragraphs 5, 6, and 7 each begin with references to a first, second, and third point. What are the points he develops in each of these paragraphs? What argument do all three points serve?

3. In paragraph 5, when Carr asserts that "by and large, the historian will get the kind of facts he wants," is he being cynical about historians? Is he saying that they just make up facts to support their favorite views or prejudices? If so, where does he justify this view? If not, what *is* his point?

4. Is his image of fish on a slab versus fish swimming in the ocean (¶5) an effective one? What do the fish represent? In paragraph 11 he uses the metaphor of Scylla and Charybdis (if you don't know this classical allu-

*"What is history?" is the central topic of Carr's series of lectures.

sion, look it up in Book 12 of Homer's *Odyssey* or in a handbook of mythology), and in the same paragraph he makes an analogy comparing men and their environments to historians and their themes. What does each one mean? Does Carr use these devices appropriately and effectively? Do these metaphors and analogies represent the "facts" about historical research?

Suggested Essay Topics

1. Get together with an acquaintance who takes a radically different view from yours about an event or an issue. Discuss your differences long enough, taking notes, so that you can make a list of what he or she takes to be the crucial facts that support the position. In an essay directed to your fellow students, compare your version of the facts with the version you have obtained from your opponent. Make use of Carr's ideas and examples to support the point that one's list of crucial "facts" is never self-evident but in truth alters in response to many different forces. Try to identify those forces.

2. Read one of the following pairs of essays that take opposing positions, and, in an essay directed to readers who have read the pair, analyze each opponent's appeal to facts. Note the *kinds* of facts appealed to, the extent of the *authority* they are assumed to possess, the *criteria* for selecting them, and your assessment of the *appropriateness* with which they are used. (It might be helpful to re-read "How to Read an Argument" in Part One, especially section 4, "Evidence: Facts, Examples, Statistics, Analogies."
   a. John Fowles, "Why I Reject Christianity" (pp. 933–939), versus C. S. Lewis, "What Christians Believe" (pp. 940–949).
   b. C. P. Snow, "The Two Cultures" (pp. 853–863), versus Loren Eiseley, "The Illusion of the Two Cultures" (pp. 868–877).
   c. Paul Johnson, "Has Capitalism a Future?" (pp. 989–998), versus James Cone, "Capitalism Means Property over Persons" (pp. 1006–1009).

·10·

SCIENTIFIC PERSPECTIVES

Science, Knowledge, and Morality

If science would discover rather than apply—if, in other words,
men were more interested in knowledge than
in power—mankind would be in a far safer position.
E. M. Forster

[Science] is the distinctive achievement of our history, and . . . nothing less
momentous than the preservation of our culture
hangs on understanding its growth and bearing. But the
influence of science is not simply comfortable. For neither
in public nor in private life can science establish an ethic. It tells
what we can do, never what we should. Its absolute incompetence
in the realm of values is a necessary consequence of the objective posture.
Charles Coulston Gillispie

Science is much closer to myth than a scientific philosophy
is prepared to admit. It is one of the many forms of thought that have been
developed by man, and not necessarily the best.
Paul Feyerabend

I believe that the scientific method, although slow
and never claiming to lead to complete truth, is the only method
which in the long run will give satisfactory foundation for beliefs.
Julian Huxley

The separation of science and non-science is not only artificial
but also detrimental to the advancement of knowledge.
If we want to understand nature, if we want to master our physical
surroundings, then we must use *all* ideas, *all* methods,
and not just a small selection of them. The assertion, however, that there
is no knowledge outside science—*extra scientiam nulla salus*—is
nothing but another and most convenient fairy-tale.
Paul Feyerabend

Lewis Thomas

Lewis Thomas characteristically writes of science not as a repellent realm of formulas and figures but as an activity at once important, accessible, and interesting. He does this by refusing to flaunt his expertise, striving instead to communicate his own enthusiasm for ideas.

In this essay, Thomas takes a critical look at science education. He argues that it consistently errs by presenting scientific knowledge to students the way supermarkets present food to their customers—as canned goods already processed by experts and intended to be swallowed whole by the consumer. He thinks that science students should do less indiscriminate swallowing and more critical thinking and that they should learn about areas where science has more questions than answers.

Thomas states his thesis boldly: Science education should expose students to the big controversies as well as the canned goods. He then supports it with a simple plan of organization: In support of his thesis he presents the best examples of interesting controversies he knows about, with some commentary on why they are important. This pattern of organization—thesis followed by illustrative examples—is perhaps the simplest and most often used pattern in all expository writing. It is simple, direct, and clear, and Thomas employs it with a skill that any of us might emulate. His tone also presents a laudable model for this kind of essay: articulate but not pretentious, deeply involved in his subject but not self-absorbed, expert but not pedantic, and friendly but not pushy or chummy.

DEBATING THE
UNKNOWABLE

First published in *The Atlantic Monthly,* July 1981, and reprinted in *Late Night Thoughts on Listening to Mahler's Ninth Symphony* (1985).

The greatest of all the accomplishments of twentieth-century science   1
has been the discovery of human ignorance. We live, as never before, in
puzzlement about nature, the universe, and ourselves most of all. It is a new
experience for the species. A century ago, after the turbulence caused by
Darwin and Wallace had subsided and the central idea of natural selection
had been grasped and accepted, we thought we knew everything essential
about evolution. In the eighteenth century there were no huge puzzles;
human reason was all you needed in order to figure out the universe. And for
most of the earlier centuries, the Church provided both the questions and the
answers, neatly packaged. Now, for the first time in human history, we are
catching glimpses of our incomprehension. We can still make up stories to
explain the world, as we always have, but now the stories have to be confirmed and reconfirmed by experiment. This is the scientific method, and once
started on this line we cannot turn back. We are obliged to grow up in
skepticism, requiring proofs for every assertion about nature, and there is no
way out except to move ahead and plug away, hoping for comprehension in
the future but living in a condition of intellectual instability for the long time.

It is the admission of ignorance that leads to progress, not so much   2
because the solving of a particular puzzle leads directly to a new piece of
understanding but because the puzzle—if it interests enough scientists—leads
to *work.* There is a similar phenomenon in entomology known as stigmergy,
a term invented by Grassé, which means "to incite to work." When three or
four termites are collected together in a chamber they wander about aimlessly, but when more termites are added, they begin to build. It is the
presence of other termites, in sufficient numbers at close quarters, that produces the work: they pick up each other's fecal pellets and stack them in neat
columns, and when the columns are precisely the right height, the termites
reach across and turn the perfect arches that form the foundation of the
termitarium. No single termite knows how to do any of this, but as soon as
there are enough termites gathered together they become flawless architects,
sensing their distances from each other although blind, building an immensely complicated structure with its own air-conditioning and humidity
control. They work their lives away in this ecosystem built by themselves.
The nearest thing to a termitarium that I can think of in human behavior is
the making of language, which we do by keeping *at* each other all our lives,
generation after generation, changing the structure by some sort of instinct.

Very little is understood about this kind of collective behavior. It is out   3
of fashion these days to talk of "superorganisms," but there simply aren't
enough reductionist details in hand to explain away the phenomenon of
termites and other social insects: some very good guesses can be made about

their chemical signaling systems, but the plain fact that they exhibit something like a collective intelligence is a mystery, or anyway an unsolved problem, that might contain important implications for social life in general. This mystery is the best introduction I can think of to biological science in college. It should be taught for its strangeness, and for the ambiguity of its meaning. It should be taught to premedical students, who need lessons early in their careers about the uncertainties in science.

College students, and for that matter high school students, should be 4 exposed very early, perhaps at the outset, to the big arguments currently going on among scientists. Big arguments stimulate their interest, and with luck engage their absorbed attention. Few things in life are as engrossing as a good fight between highly trained and skilled adversaries. But the young students are told very little about the major disagreements of the day; they may be taught something about the arguments between Darwinians and their opponents a century ago, but they do not realize that similar disputes about other matters, many of them touching profound issues for our understanding of nature, are still going on and, indeed, are an essential feature of the scientific process. There is, I fear, a reluctance on the part of science teachers to talk about such things, based on the belief that before students can appreciate what the arguments are about they must learn and master the "fundamentals." I would be willing to see some experiments along this line, and I have in mind several examples of contemporary doctrinal dispute in which the drift of the argument can be readily perceived without deep or elaborate knowledge of the subject.

There is, for one, the problem of animal awareness. One school of 5 ethologists devoted to the study of animal behavior has it that human beings are unique in the possession of consciousness, differing from all other creatures in being able to think things over, capitalize on past experience, and hazard informed guesses at the future. Other, "lower," animals (with possible exceptions made for chimpanzees, whales, and dolphins) cannot do such things with their minds; they live from moment to moment with brains that are programmed to respond, automatically or by conditioning, to contingencies in the environment. Behavioral psychologists believe that this automatic or conditioned response accounts for human mental activity as well, although they dislike that word "mental." On the other side are some ethologists who seem to be more generous-minded, who see no compelling reasons to doubt that animals in general are quite capable of real thinking and do quite a lot of it—thinking that isn't as dense as human thinking, that is sparser because of the lack of language and the resultant lack of metaphors to help the thought along, but thinking nonetheless.

The point about this argument is not that one side or the other is in 6 possession of a more powerful array of convincing facts; quite the opposite. There are not enough facts to sustain a genuine debate of any length; the question of animal awareness is an unsettled one. In the circumstance, I put forward the following notion about a small beetle, the mimosa girdler, which undertakes three pieces of linked, sequential behavior: finding a mimosa tree and climbing up the trunk and out to the end of a branch; cutting a longitudinal slit and laying within it five or six eggs; and crawling back on the limb and girdling it neatly down into the cambium. The third step is an eight-to-ten-hour task of hard labor, from which the beetle gains no food for itself—only the certainty that the branch will promptly die and fall to the ground in the next brisk wind, thus enabling the larvae to hatch and grow in an abundance of dead wood. I propose, in total confidence that even though I am probably wrong nobody today can prove that I am wrong, that the beetle is not doing these three things out of blind instinct, like a little machine, but is thinking its way along, just as we would think. The difference is that we possess enormous brains, crowded all the time with an infinite number of long thoughts, while the beetle's brain is only a few strings of neurons connected in a modest network, capable therefore of only three *tiny* thoughts, coming into consciousness one after the other: find the right tree; get up there and lay eggs in a slit; back up and spend the day killing the branch so the eggs can hatch. End of message. I would not go so far as to anthropomorphize the mimosa tree, for I really do not believe plants have minds, but something has to be said about the tree's role in this arrangement as a beneficiary: mimosas grow for twenty-five to thirty years and then die, unless they are vigorously pruned annually, in which case they can live to be a hundred. The beetle is a piece of good luck for the tree, but nothing more: one example of pure chance working at its best in nature—what you might even wish to call good nature.

This brings me to the second example of unsettlement in biology, currently being rather delicately discussed but not yet argued over, for there is still only one orthodoxy and almost no opposition, yet. This is the matter of chance itself, and the role played by blind chance in the arrangement of living things on the planet. It is, in the orthodox view, pure luck that evolution brought us to our present condition, and things might just as well have turned out any number of other, different ways, and might go in any unpredictable way for the future. There is, of course, nothing chancy about natural selection itself: it is an accepted fact that selection will always favor the advantaged individuals whose genes succeed best in propagating themselves within a changing environment. But the creatures acted upon by natural selection are themselves there as the result of chance: mutations (probably of much more importance during the long period of exclusively microbial life starting nearly 4 billion years ago and continuing until about one billion years ago); the endless sorting and re-sorting of genes within chromosomes during replication; perhaps recombination of genes across species lines at one time or another; and almost certainly the carrying of genes by viruses from one creature to another. 7

The argument comes when one contemplates the whole biosphere, the conjoined life of the earth. How could it have turned out to possess such stability and coherence, resembling as it does a sort of enormous developing embryo, with nothing but chance events to determine its emergence? Lovelock and Margulis, facing this problem, have proposed the Gaia Hypothesis, 8 which is, in brief, that the earth is itself a form of life, "a complex entity involving the Earth's biosphere, atmosphere, oceans and soil; the totality constituting a feedback or cybernetic system which seeks an optimal physical and chemical environment for life on this planet." Lovelock postulates, in addition, that "the physical and chemical condition of the surface of the Earth, of the atmosphere, and of the oceans has been and is actively made fit and comfortable by the presence of life itself."

This notion is beginning to stir up a few signs of storm, and if it catches 9 on, as I think it will, we will soon find the biological community split into fuming factions, one side saying that the evolved biosphere displays evidences of design and purpose, the other decrying such heresy. I believe that students should learn as much as they can about the argument. In an essay in *Coevolution* (Spring 1981), W. F. Doolittle has recently attacked the Gaia Hypothesis, asking, among other things, ". . . how does Gaia know if she is too cold or too hot, and how does she instruct the biosphere to behave accordingly?" This is not a deadly criticism in a world where we do not actually understand, in anything like real detail, how even Dr. Doolittle manages the stability and control of his own internal environment, including his body temperature. One thing is certain: none of us can instruct our body's systems to make the needed corrections beyond a very limited number of rather trivial tricks made possible through biofeedback techniques. If something goes wrong with my liver or my kidneys, I have no advice to offer out of my cortex. I rely on the system to fix itself, which it usually does with no help from me beyond crossing my fingers.

Another current battle involving the unknown is between sociobiolo- 10 gists and antisociobiologists, and it is a marvel for students to behold. To observe, in open-mouthed astonishment, one group of highly intelligent, beautifully trained, knowledgeable, and imaginative scientists maintaining that all behavior, animal and human, is governed exclusively by genes, and another group of equally talented scientists asserting that all behavior is set and determined by the environment or by culture, is an educational experience that no college student should be allowed to miss. The essential lesson to be learned has nothing to do with the relative validity of the facts underlying the argument. It is the argument itself that is the education: we do not yet know enough to settle such questions.

One last example. There is an uncomfortable secret in biology, not 11 much talked about yet, but beginning to surface. It is, in a way, linked to the observations that underlie the Gaia Hypothesis. Nature abounds in instances of cooperation and collaboration, partnerships between species. There is a tendency of living things to join up whenever joining is possible: accommodation and compromise are more common results of close contact than combat and destruction. Given the opportunity and the proper circumstances, two cells from totally different species—a mouse cell and a human cell, for example—will fuse to become a single cell, and then the two nuclei will fuse into a single nucleus, and then the hybrid cell will divide to produce generations of new cells containing the combined genomes of both species. Bacteria are indispensable partners in the fixation of atmospheric nitrogen by plants. The oxygen in our atmosphere is put there, almost in its entirety, by the photosynthetic chloroplasts in the cells of green plants, and these organelles are almost certainly the descendants of blue-green algae that joined up when the nucleated cells of higher plants came into existence. The mitochondria in all our own cells, and in all other nucleated cells, which enable us to use oxygen for energy, are the direct descendants of symbiotic bacteria. These are becoming accepted facts, and there is no longer an agitated argument over their probable validity; but there are no satisfactory explanations for how such amiable and useful arrangements came into being in the first place. Axelrod and Hamilton (*Science,* March 27, 1981) have recently reopened the question of cooperation in evolution with a mathematical approach based on game theory (the Prisoner's Dilemma game), which permits the hypothesis that one creature's best strategy for dealing repeatedly with another is to concede and cooperate rather than to defect and go it alone.

This idea can be made to fit with the mathematical justification based 12 on kinship already accepted for explaining altruism in nature—that in a colony of social insects the sacrifice of one individual for another depends on how many of the sacrificed member's genes are matched by others and thus preserved, and that the extent of the colony's altruistic behavior can be mathematically calculated. It is, by the way, an interesting aspect of contemporary biology that true altruism—the giving away of something without return—is incompatible with dogma, even though it goes on all over the place. Nature, in this respect, keeps breaking the rules, and needs correcting by new ways of doing arithmetic.

The social scientists are in the hardest business of all—trying to under- 13 stand how humanity works. They are caught up in debates all over town; everything they touch turns out to be one of society's nerve endings, eliciting outrage and cries of pain. Wait until they begin coming close to the bone. They surely will someday, provided they can continue to attract enough bright people—fascinated by humanity, unafraid of big numbers, and skeptical of questionnaires—and provided the government does not starve them out of business, as is now being tried in Washington. Politicians do not like pain, not even wincing, and they have some fear of what the social scientists may be thinking about thinking for the future.

The social scientists are themselves too modest about the history of 14 their endeavor, tending to display only the matters under scrutiny today in economics, sociology, and psychology, for example—never boasting, as they might, about one of the greatest of all scientific advances in our comprehension of humanity, for which they could be claiming credit. I refer to the marvelous accomplishments of the nineteenth-century comparative linguists. When the scientific method is working at its best, it succeeds in revealing the connection between things in nature that seem at first totally unrelated to each other. Long before the time when the biologists, led by Darwin and Wallace, were constructing the tree of evolution and the origin of species, the linguists were hard at work on the evolution of language. After beginning in

1786 with Sir William Jones and his inspired hunch that the remarkable similarities among Sanskrit, Greek, and Latin meant, in his words, that these three languages must "have sprung from some common source, which, perhaps, no longer exists," the new science of comparative grammar took off in 1816 with Franz Bopp's classic work "On the conjugational system of the Sanskrit language in comparison with that of the Greek, Latin, Persian and Germanic languages"—a piece of work equivalent, in its scope and in its power to explain, to the best of nineteenth-century biology. The common Indo-European ancestry of English, Germanic, Slavic, Greek, Latin, Baltic, Indic, Iranian, Hittite, and Anatolian tongues, and the meticulous scholarship connecting them was a tour de force for research—science at its best, and social science at that.

It is nice to know that a common language, perhaps 20,000 years ago, had a root word for the earth which turned, much later, into the technical term for the complex polymers that make up the connective tissues of the soil: humus and what are called the humic acids. There is a strangeness, though, in the emergence from the same root of words such as "human" and "humane," and "humble." It comes as something of a shock to realize that the root for words such as "miracle" and "marvel" meant, originally, "to smile," and that from the single root *sa* were constructed, in the descendant tongues, three cognate words, "satisfied," "satiated," and "sadness." How is it possible for a species to show so much wisdom in its most collective of all behaviors— the making and constant changing of language—and at the same time be so habitually folly-prone in the building of nation-states? Modern linguistics has moved into new areas of inquiry as specialized and inaccessible for most laymen (including me) as particle physics; I cannot guess where linguistics will come out, but it is surely aimed at scientific comprehension, and its problem—human language—is as crucial to the species as any other field I can think of, including molecular genetics.

But there are some risks involved in trying to do science in the humanities before its time, and useful lessons can be learned from some of the not-so-distant history of medicine. A century ago it was the common practice to deal with disease by analyzing what seemed to be the underlying mechanism and applying whatever treatment popped into the doctor's head. Getting sick was a hazardous enterprise in those days. The driving force in medicine was the need to *do* something, never mind what. It occurs to me now, reading in incomprehension some of the current reductionist writings in literary criticism, especially poetry criticism, that the new schools are at risk under a similar pressure. A poem is a healthy organism, really in need of no help from science, no treatment except fresh air and exercise. I thought I'd just sneak that in.

Questions for Discussion

1. In reflecting on the strangeness of termite social behavior in paragraph 3 and on how science is far from being able to explain it, Thomas observes that "this mystery is the best introduction I can think of to biological science in college . . . [for it teaches students] early in their careers about the uncertainties in science." Do the science courses you have had teach "the uncertainties in science" and encourage discussion of them? Do you agree that they should?

2. Thomas believes that science is full of mysteries. Does it seem to you that most people think of science as full of facts—cut, dried, and proved— rather than full of mysteries? Which of these views have been held by most of the science teachers you have known? Have you found that one view is more characteristic of good science teachers than the other view?

3. Do you agree with Thomas's opening sentence that "the greatest of all the accomplishments of twentieth-century science has been the discovery of human ignorance"? State your reasons.

4. Does the Gaia Hypothesis (¶8) sound like fact or fairy tale? Most great hypotheses in the history of science sounded like fairy tales (or sheer nuttiness) when they were first advanced. This does not necessarily argue in favor of the Gaia Hypothesis, but it does argue against the cliché that science progresses because scientists stick to what can be seen, measured, and proved. For example, when Copernicus suggested that the earth goes around the sun instead of the sun going around the earth, he was contradicting what everyone could "prove" simply by watching the sky every day. As Galileo later said, Copernicus performed "a rape upon the senses"; he asked people to believe in a theory that contradicted the "facts" of everyone's experience. Likewise, Newton asked people to rely more on their imaginations than on their own eyes. Since he could perform no laboratory tests to prove his theory of gravity, he asked everyone to picture gravity operating in a frictionless universe—a kind of universe no one on earth ever experiences. (Gravity still has not been defined or measured in any conclusive way.) And in our own century, Einstein had not performed one single laboratory experiment and could offer not a single fact to back up his claims when he proposed that mass and energy are equivalent at light speeds and that the speed of light is absolute. It took decades before *any* of his claims could be verified by observation, and most of them remain untested today.

   In light of the history of great scientific discoveries, what can you conclude about the nature of scientific inquiry? If Copernicus and Newton and Einstein were dreamers, surely they were informed dreamers; though they contradicted some of the "facts" of their day, they preserved what facts they could and thought out their reasons carefully, even when they had no laboratory experiments to support their hypotheses. What, then, is the role of facts in scientific inquiry, and what is the role of imagination? When Thomas opens his essay by praising modern science for accomplishing "the discovery of human ignorance," is he trying to spur us on to find more facts, or is he appealing to our imagination? Or both? (For further reading on the role of facts in inquiry, see Edward Hallett Carr, "The Historian and His Facts," pp. 785–794. For the role of the imagination in inquiry, see Jacob Bronowski, "The Reach of Imagination," pp. 262–269.)

5. In paragraph 10 Thomas says that college students need to be exposed to the big controversies in science because "it is the argument itself that is the education." This assertion implies that *all* of education should be education-as-argument. Can you say what such an education would be? Are you getting such an education? Would you like to? How would you define its opposite? (See "What Is an Argument?" in Part One.)

Suggested Essay Topics

1. According to Thomas, "It is the admission of ignorance that leads to progress" (¶2). No doubt you have known teachers whose teaching did not reflect this view—teachers who never admitted ignorance or exposed their students to the "big arguments currently going on." Write a letter to one such teacher, arguing in support of Thomas's view of scientific education and imitating as well as you can Thomas's casual-seeming tone of geniality combined with hardheaded critical aggressiveness.

2. This is a tougher topic than the previous one and requires some library research. Picture yourself as a scientist in Copernicus' time, outraged at both the "unscientific method" and the content of Copernicus' new theory that the earth goes around the sun. Address a letter to Copernicus in which you try to persuade him of the scientific illegitimacy of contradicting so many proved facts. Point out just how well supported the accepted view of things is, and try to make him see that he is going to set science back 100 years if he gets people to believe in his nutty notions. Base your letter on library research. There *was* an enormous response to Copernicus' ideas; not only is reading some of this controversy firsthand a good introduction to the history of science, but writing about it is good practice at analysis. (See "What Is Analysis?" in Part One.)

Joseph Wood Krutch

Joseph Wood Krutch (1893–1970) was in his time one of the most widely read commentators on literature and life. Unlike many scholars, he early developed a style that proved appealing to general readers, and in a long series of popular books he goaded Americans into thought about an astonishing range of subjects: the nature of genius in the lives of authors like Edgar Allan

Poe, Samuel Johnson, Henry David Thoreau, and the great novelists, European and American; the strengths and weaknesses of modern culture; the decline of serious discussion of moral issues; and, in the latter part of his life, the wonders of the natural world.

"The Meaning of Awareness" is one of his aggressive, thoughtful efforts to understand and preserve the traditional values of humankind and the natural world. Although Krutch was by no means an opponent of science, he feared that popular misapplications of scientific, technological, and economic theories would reduce our world to what can be "covered" with formulas and statistics. While some scientists and philosophers accused him of superficiality and partiality, other readers thought of him as something like a prophet. Can you see evidence in the following piece that might lead readers to both responses?

THE MEANING OF AWARENESS

The You and the Me

Chapter 7 of *The Great Chain of Life* (1956).

For nine long years a large salamander lived her sluggish life in a damp terrarium on my window sill. Before I assumed responsibility for her health and welfare she had lived through a different life—not as different as the life of a butterfly is from that of a caterpillar, but different enough. Once she had lived in water and breathed it. Like her parents before her she still had to keep her skin damp, but now she seldom actually went into the water.

Before she was even an egg her father and her mother, prompted by some no doubt unconscious memory, had left the damp moss or leaves they had normally preferred since achieving maturity and had climbed down into some pond or pool to mate. The prompt result was a cluster of eggs embedded in a mass of jelly much like that which surrounds the eggs of common American frogs. These eggs had hatched into tadpoles easily distinguishable from those destined to become frogs or toads by the two plumes waving from their shoulders—gills for breathing the water which frogs manage to get along without even though they too are temporarily water-breathers.

Most of my specimen's subsequent history was much like that of the young frogs themselves. Legs had budded, and though the tail had not disappeared the plumes had withered away while lungs fit for air-breathing had developed. Sally, as I called her, had then left the water and become a land animal. All this took place quite gradually without any radical dissolution of the organism as a whole, as in the case of the caterpillar, and without the intervention of that dead sleep from which the caterpillar woke to find himself somebody else. Far back in time, Sally's direct ancestors had been the first vertebrates to risk coming to land, and she recapitulated their history.

The rest of my salamander's life was very uneventful but not much more so than it would have been had I left her to her own devices. In fact, returning to the water is almost the only interesting thing the amphibia ever *do*. By comparison with even the butterflies—who lead very uneventful lives as insects go—the amphibia are dull creatures indeed, seemingly without enterprise, aspiration, or any conspicuous resourcefulness.

If you or I had been permitted a brief moment of consciousness some- 5 time about the middle of the Mesozoic era, when the amphibia and the insects were both flourishing, we well might have concluded that the latter were the more promising experiment. I doubt that we would have been very likely to pick out a salamander as our ancestor. Yet the evidence seems pretty definite that nature knew better and that it is from him we come. In Old Testament terms, Amphibia begat Reptile, Reptile begat Mammal, Mammal begat Man.

Even before the Mesozoic was over the beetles were far ahead of the 6 salamanders so far as the techniques of living are concerned. "What," we might well have asked, "do the amphibia have that the insects do not?" What potentiality in them was responsible for the fact that, given the whole Ceno- zoic still to develop in, the one got no farther than the bee and the ant, while the other has ended—if this is indeed the end—in man?

Perhaps if that anticipatory visit had lasted long enough we could 7 finally have guessed the answer as easily as it can be guessed today by anyone who has kept both insects and salamanders in captivity and has observed one great difference between them. The insect goes very expertly about his busi- ness. But not even those insects who go very expertly about their very complicated business give any sign of awareness of anything not directly connected with that immediate business.

It is not merely that they are absolutely, or almost absolutely, incapable 8 of learning anything. A salamander cannot learn very much either. But the salamander has some awareness of the world outside himself and he has, therefore, the true beginnings of a self—as we understand the term. A butter- fly or a beetle does not. Hence you can make a pet out of a salamander—at least to the extent necessary to fulfill the minimum definition of that word. He will come to depend upon you, to profit from your ministrations, and to expect them at appropriate times. An insect is never more than a captive. If you help him he does not know it and he will never come to depend upon your ministrations. He does not even know that you exist. And because of what that implies, a whole great world of experience was opened up to the hierarchy of vertebrates from the salamander on up and has remained closed to the insect.

Seen from the outside, the ants who keep cows, practice agriculture, 9 make war, and capture slaves suggest human beings more strongly than any vertebrate lower than the apes. But if we could see from the inside, the psyche of even the sluggish salamander in my window terrarium would be different. In some dim way she has connected me with herself and I am part of her life.

My old housekeeper used to assure me pridefully from time to time: 10 "She knows me." That, I am afraid, was a bit of overinterpretation. I doubt very seriously that Sally could tell me and my housekeeper apart. But if either one of us approached the terrarium she would rise heavily on her short legs and amble slowly in the direction of the familiar object. We were associated in what little mind she had with the prospect of food.

Was this, many will ask, more than a mere reflex action? Did any such 11 consciousness as I have been assuming really exist? I will not answer that question in the affirmative as positively as many would answer it in the negative. But the consciousness which is so acute in us must have begun dimly somewhere and to me it seems probable that it had already begun at least as far back as the salamanders who lie, though remotely, on our own direct line of descent.

Yet if Sally just barely achieved the status of a pet she fell considerably 12 short of being what we call a domesticated animal. Considerably more awareness of the world around her and considerably more capacity to make an individual adaptation to it would be necessary for that. But because dogs and cats and horses—all of whom have, like us, a salamander in their ancestry— have that considerably greater awareness, they can live a considerable part of our lives and come to seem actual members of our family. Even they are not nearly as ingenious as bees or ants. But we recognize their nearer kinship to us.

Those ants have a culture not only analogous to ours in certain respects 13 but one also far older than ours, since the social insects have been civilized for a much longer time—perhaps thirty times longer—than we have. This was possible because they had settled down biologically—i.e., had ceased to evolve organically—long before we did. And since they were not changing rapidly, they had time to mature and to settle irrevocably into habits and customs, while we are even now still experimenting wildly—discarding habits and techniques every decade or two.

By ant standards we have never had any traditions loyally adhered to. 14 Their so-called virtues—industry, selfless devotion to the good of the community, etc.—are so strikingly superior to ours that certain fanatical critics of human nature and its ways have implied that these creatures whom the biologist calls "lower" are morally "better" than we, and have hoped that in a few million years we might become more like them. Even without going that far and leaving ourselves resolutely out of it as obviously *hors concours* [without rival], we may still find ourselves raising again the outrageous question already alluded to. By what right do we call the ants "lower" than, say, a member of a wolf pack? On what basis is the hierarchy established?

Ask that question of a biologist and he will give you ready reasons 15 satisfactory to himself. Anatomically, the insects are simpler. They show very little adaptability. They cannot learn as readily as a wolf can. They can't change their habits very much. They have come to a dead end. They have been precisely what they are for a very long time and will remain that for a very long time to come. "Progress" is something they no longer know anything about. And they are not "intelligent."

All these statements are true enough, but like so many biological dis- 16 tinctions and standards they seem just a little remote. To say that an animal is a compulsory protein feeder is, as we remarked once before, perfectly accurate but has little to do with the rich complex of meanings the word "animal" suggests to the human being who hears it. In certain contexts it is fine. In other contexts—the context of a poem, for instance—it isn't.

Indisputable accuracy does not make it much more satisfactory than Plato's definition of man—a two-legged animal without feathers. Man is certainly that and no other animal is. His definition establishes a criterion that is infallible, but also entirely irrelevant. Apply the test and you will never mistake a wolf or a bird for a man or even mistake a primate—always more or less four-footed—for one of your fellow citizens. This really is a sure way of telling your friends from the apes. But then, you would not be very likely to make a mistake anyway. The definition is perfect but also meaningless. 17

The explanation a biologist would give why a wolf is "higher" than an ant is almost equally unsatisfactory, because it does not seem to involve the thing on the basis of which we make our judgment. Should they reverse themselves tomorrow and give new reasons in similar terms for deciding that the ant is "higher" we would go right on feeling that he is not. On what, then, is this feeling based if not upon any good scientific criteria? What kind of distinctions appeal to us as genuinely meaningful? 18

Suppose you play the childish game. Suppose you ask yourself which you would rather be—a farmer ant or a robin. Only the perverse would hesitate. "A robin, of course." But why? What it would come to would certainly be something like this: "Because being a robin would be more fun. Because the robin exhibits the joy of life. Because he seems to be glad to be a robin and because it is hard to believe that an ant is glad to be what he is." Of course we can't say positively that he isn't. We cannot understand his language and he may be proclaiming to the world of other ants with what ecstasy he contemplates the fact that he is one of them. But he cannot communicate with us, and, justifiably or not, we find it hard to believe that he is glad. 19

Privately, biologists often share our prejudice. But few, I am afraid, would agree to classify animals as "higher" or "lower" on any such basis. They would reply, and rightly so far as biology is concerned, that to say a robin is higher than an ant because he has more joy in living is to cease to be scientific. Also, some might think that it smacks of immoral hedonism. Nevertheless a hierarchy ordered on that basis is meaningful in human terms as the scientific one is not. 20

If the joy of living is the most enviable good any of the lower animals can attain to and at least the second-best available to man himself, that implies in both a more general capacity which can only be called "awareness"—something that is different from intelligence as usually defined and not perfectly equatable with logic, or insight, or adaptability; also something the salamander has more of than the ant has. There is no way of measuring it, and even the psychologist would be for that reason rather loth to take it much into consideration or even to admit that it exists as distinguished from 21 reason, insight, and the rest. That it does exist in human beings, any contemplative man knows from his own experience.

The best solver of puzzles is not necessarily the man most aware of 22
living. The animal who most skillfully adapts himself to the conditions for
survival is not necessarily the one who has the greatest joy in living. And
from the standpoint of one kind of interest in living creatures it is perfectly
legitimate to think of them as "high" or "low" in proportion to the degree
of awareness they exhibit.

We can freely admit that the ant's technique of making a living is far 23
more advanced than that of the bird or, indeed, of any vertebrate animal
except man. We can see that some species of ants have reached what in terms
of human history corresponds to an agricultural society, whereas there is no
vertebrate who is not still a mere nomad hunter. But living—as some men
have got around to telling themselves—can be more important than making
a living. And making a living seems to be all the ant does, while the robin
and many another vertebrate live abundantly.

Yes, I say to myself, the "higher" animals really are higher. Even the 24
sluggish, dim-witted salamander, cold-blooded but vertebrate and with the
beginnings of a vertebrate brain, is "higher" than the industrious ant. But it
is not for any of the objective reasons either the biologist or the social
anthropologist will consent to give that I call him so.

It is because even the salamander has some sort of awareness the insects 25
have not; because, unlike them, he is on his way to intelligence, on his way
to pain and pleasure, on his way to courage, and even to a sense of honor as
the bighorn is beginning to feel it; on his way to Love, which the birds,
bungling parents though they are, can feel and the wise wasp cannot. On the
way to the joy of life, which only one or more of these things can make
possible.

Once you admit this fact there is something obviously wrong with the 26
orthodox view of the aims and methods of that evolutionary process through
which both the blindly efficient ant and the blunderingly emotional bird
arrived at their present state. According to that orthodox view "survival
value" is the key to everything. But though intelligence does have an obvious
survival value, it is by no means obvious that it works any better than the
instinct of the insect. As for the emotions, their survival value is not always
obvious at all. And if you want to include man in the scheme of evolution,
it is so far from obvious that the complexities of civilized emotional and
intellectual life have any survival value at all that many recent philosophers
have suspected them of being fatal handicaps instead.

This is a fact that raises a question for the evolutionist. If the survival 27
value of intelligence is real enough though no greater than that of instinct,
if many of our emotions and the kind of awareness upon which they depend
have no obvious survival value at all, then why have certain animals developed both to such a high degree? Why, for that matter, have either they or
we developed them at all? Doubtless an intelligent *individual* has a better
chance of individual survival than a merely instinctive one. But if nature is

careful of the type, careless of the individual, then why should that weigh anything in the scales?

Darwin himself formulated a "law." No organism, he said, ever develops a characteristic beyond the point where it is useful for survival. But, as we have been asking, how useful in that sense is intelligence or even consciousness? Doesn't instinct have an even higher survival value? 28

It is pretty generally recognized that the insects are the most successful organisms on earth. It is also generally recognized that they get along either with the dimmest consciousness and intelligence, or perhaps without any at all. It is even believed by many that they lost a good deal of what they once had because instinct proved to have a higher survival value. If all this is true does it not suggest that orthodox evolutionism may be in one respect wrong? Does it not suggest that nature (or whatever you want to call it) puts a value on things which do not have any simple survival value? Is it not possible that mammals look after their young with bumbling consciousness rather than with the expertness of instinct because nature has, in some way, been interested not merely in the survival of the fittest, but in "the fittest" for something more than mere survival? 29

This last question, in a somewhat different form, was actually asked and then left unanswered in the earliest days of Darwinism. Alfred Russel Wallace, generously acknowledged by Darwin as the co-propounder of the theory of natural selection, steadily and from the beginning maintained one difference with his more famous co-worker. It was not and could not be demonstrated, he said, that natural selection could account for "the higher qualities of man." Most notable among these "higher qualities" was, he maintained, the moral sense. 30

No doubt some manifestations of it had a survival value in society. But not all of them. Man's willingness, sometimes at least, not only to sacrifice himself but to sacrifice himself and others for an ideal, his human conviction that "survival value" is not the only value, did not in themselves have any "survival value." How then could they have arisen if it was, as Darwin said, the inviolable rule of nature that no organism can develop what is not biologically useful to it? An all-inclusive explanation of the phenomenon of life in terms of natural selection would have to account somehow for the very conception of "values which have no survival value." And no such inclusive explanation is forthcoming. 31

For the most part this question has been simply brushed aside by orthodox evolutionists. Along with other related questions it has been kept alive chiefly by "mere men of letters"—by Samuel Butler, Bergson, Bernard Shaw, and the rest. But it will not down. And there are even signs that some scientists, perhaps especially the neurologists, are less sure than they once were that the mechanistic explanation of all the phenomena of living matter is complete. But if nature has been working toward something besides survival, what is it? 32

Julian Huxley, one of the most enlightened of present-day evolutionists, has tangled with the question. Evolution, he says, implies progress. But 33

in what does "progress" consist? Certainly, as he admits, it includes something more than a mere progressive increase in the amount of living matter
on the earth. That could be achieved by the simplest forms. Nature "wants"
not merely more organisms but more complex organisms. But how can it want
them if they do not survive more abundantly? Greater complexity implies,
he says, "improvement." But what constitutes an "improved" organism? Not,
he says, mere complexity itself but a complexity which opens the way to
further "improvement." That, it seems, simply closes the circle. The question
of what constitutes "improvement" and what sort of values other than mere
survival value nature does recognize is still unanswered.

Perhaps the only way to escape from the dilemma that a Huxley recog- 34
nizes is to make an assumption bolder than he would probably be willing to
accept. But the difficulties do vanish if we are willing to accept the possibility
that what Nature has been working toward is not merely survival; that,
ultimately, it is not survival itself but Consciousness and Intelligence *themselves*—partly at least for their own sake.

If Nature has advanced from the inanimate to the animate; if she "pre- 35
fers" the living to the lifeless and the forms of life which survive rather to
those that perish; then there is nothing which forbids the assumption that she
also "prefers" conscious intelligence to blind instinct; that just as complex
organization was developed even though it had no obvious survival value for
the species, so also the awareness of itself which complex organization made
possible is also one of her goals.

Whenever man's thinking starts with himself rather than with his 36
possible origins in lower forms of life he usually comes to the conclusion
that consciousness is the primary fact. "I think therefore I am"* seems to be
the most inescapably self-evident of propositions. Only when he starts as
far away from himself as possible can he get into the contrary habit of
assuming what the nineteenth century did assume: namely, that his own
mind is so far from being the most significant thing in the universe that it
has no substantial significance at all, being a mere illusion, some sort of
insubstantial by-product of those ultimate realities which are unconscious,
automatic, and mechanical.

Ever since the seventeenth century, science actually has tended to begin 37
as far away from man himself as possible, while metaphysics has continued
to start with man's own mind. Hence the undoubted fact that for a long
time, at least, science and metaphysics either grew farther and farther apart,
or, as with the positivists, metaphysics simply surrendered to science and
tended to become no more than an abstractly stated theory of the validity of

*The quotation, one of the most famous in the history of thought, is from René Descartes'
proof for his own existence. By applying the methods of a strict skepticism to all other
"things" in the universe, Descartes could in some sense doubt their existence, but he could not
doubt that he was doubting—that is, thinking. Therefore, he concluded, *something* exists,
namely his doubting self. Do you think that Krutch is justified in employing this famous
moment as evidence for "awareness"?

science.* Yet, as we have just seen, science and positivism leave certain stubborn questions unanswered. Perhaps these questions will ultimately have to be attacked again and from the older point of view.

Aristotle is the acknowledged father of natural history. But because 38 Aristotle lived in an age when it still seemed natural to start with the human mind itself, he reached the conclusion that at least so far as man himself is concerned Contemplation is what he is "for." And if Aristotle had had any clear idea of evolution he would certainly have supposed that a more and more complete awareness, not mere survival, was what nature was aiming at.

Most present-day biologists, following the lead of the nineteenth cen- 39 tury, have no patience with any such metaphysical notions. When you come right down to it man is, they say, an animal; and there is only one thing that any animal is "for"—namely, survival and reproduction. Some animals accomplish this purpose in one way and some in another. Man's way happens to involve some consciousness of what he is doing and of why he does it. But that is a mere accident. If what we call intelligence had not had a high survival value it would never have developed. And one of the consequences of this fact is that man is most successful when he uses his intelligence to facilitate his survival. Thinking, or even awareness, for its own sake is a biological mistake. What he is "for" is *doing,* certainly not mooning over what he has done—unless of course that mooning has survival value, as under certain circumstances it may.

What we have been asking is, then, simply this: How good is the 40 evidence—even their own kind of evidence—which those who take this position can offer in its support? If they are right, then man ought biologically to be the most successful of all animals. No other ought to flourish so exuberantly or have a future which, biologically, looks so bright. But what grounds do we really have for believing anything like that to be the real state of affairs? Does conscious intelligence really work any better than instinct?

No doubt you and I are the most successful of the mammals. When we 41 take possession of any part of this earth the others go into a decline. No bear or wolf, no whale or buffalo, can successfully compete with us. But that doesn't really mean much, because all the mammals are creatures who have already started down the road we have followed so much farther than they. To some considerable extent they too are conscious, intelligent, capable of learning much from experience. Like us they are born with mental slates which, if not entirely blank, have much less written on them than is indelibly inscribed before birth on the nervous systems of many a "lower" animal.

Obviously if you are going to have to depend upon conscious intelli- 42

*Krutch uses the term *metaphysics* to refer to the branch of philosophy dealing with the nature of existence, insofar as such speculation does not depend on scientific observation. As for the "positivists," see the note on p. 786. If you are not clear about these terms—and no brief definitions can do them justice—look them up in an encyclopedia. But do not be surprised if even after you research the terms, Krutch's passage remains difficult. Krutch has telescoped large claims into a small paragraph, and since the three terms *science, metaphysics,* and *positivism* are ambiguous and controversial, any such passage will leave even the best-informed reader with some unanswered questions.

gence, then it is an advantage to have that conscious intelligence highly developed. The other mammals over whom we triumph so easily have to fight us chiefly with inferior versions of our own weapons and it is no wonder that they lose. But what of the creatures who learn little or nothing, who can hardly be said to be capable of thought, who are conscious only dimly if at all? Are they really, from the biological standpoint, any less "successful" than we or the other mammals? Can they be said to "succeed" any less well? Are they deprived of anything except consciousness itself?

It is certainly not evident that they are. As a matter of fact the insects 43 are the only conspicuous creatures indubitably holding their own against man. When he matches wits with any of the lower mammals they always lose. But when he matches his wit against the instinct and vitality of the insects he merely holds his own, at best. An individual insect is no match for an individual man. But most species of insects have done very well at holding their own as a species against him. And if you believe the biologists it is only with the prosperity of the species that Nature, or evolution, has ever, or could ever, concern herself.

Who is the more likely to be here on what evolution calls tomorrow— 44 i.e., ten million years hence? Certainly the chance that man will have destroyed himself before then seems greater than the chance that the insects will have done so. Their instincts seem not to have created for them the difficulties and the dangers man's intelligence and emotion have created for him. They have been here much longer than he and it certainly seems not improbable that they will remain here much longer also. As a matter of fact the bacteria are even more "successful" than the insects. There are far more of them alive at this moment than there are of even insects, and it is even more difficult to imagine them ever extinct. If survival is the only thing that counts in nature then why or how did any life higher than that of a bacterium ever come into being?

No answer to that question seems possible unless we are willing to 45 assume that for Nature herself, as well as for us, the instinct of the insect is "better" than the vegetative life of the bacterium, and the conscious concern of the bird for its offspring better than the unconscious efficiency of the wasp. Yet vegetation is not better than instinct and consciousness is not better than instinct if the only criterion is survival value. And if man's mind does not help him to survive more successfully than creatures having no mind at all, then what on earth can it be for? Can it be for anything except itself? Can its value be other than absolute rather than instrumental?

The bird and the man are more successful than the wasp only if you 46 count their consciousness as, itself, some kind of success. The "purpose" of parental concern cannot be merely the successful rearing of offspring, because that can be accomplished quite as successfully without any consciousness at all.

Is it not possible, then, that Aristotle was right, that contemplation is 47 not only the true end of man but the end that has been pursued ever since vertebrates took the road leading to a keener and keener consciousness? Have we been trying to understand the meaning of evolution by beginning at the wrong end? Is it possible that, for instance, the real, the only true "purpose" served by conscious concern over the young is the fact that out of it comes parental love itself? Has what evolution worked toward been not "survival" but "awareness"? Is the ultimate answer to the question "Why is a bungling mammal higher than an efficient wasp" simply that it is higher because it can experience parental love? Was it this, rather than mere survival, that nature was after all along?

Questions for Discussion

1. Krutch deals with two large and complex contrasting views of life. Can you re-formulate them, clarifying Krutch's views of the reasons underlying each?

2. At crucial points in this essay, Krutch resorts to a series of questions rather than direct assertions (especially in ¶29 and ¶47). Yet at many other points he talks as if he is not really doubtful about the answers but is rather asserting his own strong, settled beliefs. For example, he calls some of his inferences *facts* (¶26, first line; ¶27, first line), and there are other signs that he considers his opponents flatly mistaken. What does he gain, if anything, from putting his conclusions in the form of questions and his inferences in the form of facts?

3. *Awareness* is a term that, like *love* and *charity* (see the introduction to I Corinthians 13 in Chapter 5), cannot be pinned down with rigorous definition. What steps does Krutch take to ensure that his readers have a clear notion of what *he* means by this elusive concept?

4. Other authors in this book argue against narrow notions of "practicality" (for example, Wendell Berry, Chapter 1, Ursula Le Guin, Chapter 4, and Alfred Whitehead, Chapter 1.). If you have read any of these essays, compare their authors' ideas of practicality with Krutch's idea of "survival value." Does Krutch seem to be saying that nature is *im*practical or, rather, that it serves a higher practicality?

Suggested Essay Topics

1. Go through the essay once again carefully, looking for all the *assumptions* you can find for which Krutch provides no supporting evidence. For example, in paragraph 19 he assumes, without conducting an actual survey, that anyone who would not rather be a robin than an ant is "perverse" (see "Assumptions" in "How to Read an Argument, Chapter 2. After writing out these assumptions carefully, write a brief critique of each one, asking yourself whether Krutch is justified in assuming that his *readers* will see no

need for further evidence. (Note that this assignment does not ask for an organized paper. Just number your short paragraphs.)

2. Krutch assumes that animals other than human beings show "awareness." If you have ever observed any animal closely, write a short paper discussing whether all of its behavior could be explained in terms of what Krutch calls "mere survival." (It would be useful here to review Elaine Morgan, "The Man-Made Myth" (Chapter 2). Try to be as clear as possible about what kinds of behavior would satisfy Krutch's criteria for "awareness."

B. F. Skinner

The first Walden *(published in 1854) is Henry David Thoreau's (1817–1862) famous account of two years that he spent living by himself in the woods near Walden Pond (outside Concord, Massachusetts). B. F. Skinner's (b. 1904) appropriation of Thoreau's title is potentially misleading. The only way in which Thoreau's and Skinner's* Waldens *are alike is in the very general desire, as Thoreau put it, "to front only the essential facts of life." But it would be hard to imagine any two works defining the "essential facts of life" more differently than these two; their views about life could not be farther apart.*

Walden Two, in Skinner's own words, is "a novel about a utopian community . . . [that presents] an account of how I thought a group of, say, a thousand people might have solved the problems of their daily lives with the help of behavioral engineering" (from the preface of the 1976 reissue of Walden Two*). "Behavioral engineering" has been an extremely controversial concept ever since Skinner first introduced it in the 1930s. While believers think it the best tool, perhaps the only effective one, for saving the modern world from its own disasters, its critics range from people who think it foolish to those who think it simply bad science to those who think it frightening and pernicious. To this last group, "behavioral engineering" calls up science fiction images of human beings turned into unthinking robots without dignity or freedom. (In a later book Skinner argues that freedom and dignity are in fact obsolete and socially retrogressive goals, but he rejects the notion that he wants to turn people into unthinking robots [*Beyond Freedom and Dignity, *1971]).*

In Skinner's view, human nature is infinitely malleable. He believes that human infants who are subjected from birth to certain kinds of conditioning— "contingencies of reinforcement," he calls them—can be made to act and think in almost any way the conditioners desire. He sees such conditioning as a wonderfully efficient and effective way of curing the world's ills. Wisdom and common sense, he believes, are ineffective means of making the world better. They are too erratic and too little heeded. But behavioral engineering, he insists, puts individual and social improvement "within reach of a behavioral science which can take the place of wisdom and common sense and with happier results" (preface to Walden Two, *1976).*

As you read, try to determine the extent to which you think Skinner's optimistic belief in applying scientific principles directly to everyday living matches the view held by some that scientific thinking is typically divorced from ethical considerations. If behavorial engineering really works as he describes, it is clear that human beings could create any kind of social world they desire. But to whom would you want to grant the power of making the final decisions about the shape and quality of that world? And if you disagreed with the conditioners, what kind of voice do you think minority views might be given in the brave new world created by the social engineers? And who educates the social engineers anyway?

Whether you wind up being attracted to or repelled by Skinner's vision of an infinitely malleable world, he invites you to think hard about the kind of world you are willing to work for and, if you reject behavorial engineering, what other means you would recommend for making the world better.

BEHAVIORAL ENGINEERING: PROGRAMMING THE CHILDREN

Our title for chapters 13 and 14 of *Walden Two* (1948).

The quarters for children from one to three consisted of several small   1
playrooms with Lilliputian* furniture, a child's lavatory, and a dressing and locker room. Several small sleeping rooms were operated on the same principle as the baby-cubicles. The temperature and the humidity were controlled so that clothes or bedclothing were not needed. The cots were double-decker arrangements of the plastic mattresses we had seen in the cubicles. The children slept unclothed, except for diapers. There were more beds than necessary, so that the children could be grouped according to developmental age or exposure to contagious diseases or need for supervision, or for educational purposes.

We followed Mrs. Nash to a large screened porch on the south side of   2
the building, where several children were playing in sandboxes and on swings and climbing apparatuses. A few wore "training pants"; the rest were naked. Beyond the porch was a grassy play yard enclosed by closely trimmed hedges, where other children, similarly undressed, were at play. Some kind of marching game was in progress.

As we returned, we met two women carrying food hampers. They spoke   3
to Mrs. Nash and followed her to the porch. In a moment five or six children came running into the playrooms and were soon using the lavatory and dressing themselves. Mrs. Nash explained that they were being taken on a picnic.

*Lilliput is the land of extraordinarily small human beings created by Jonathan Swift in his great satire *Gulliver's Travels* (1726).

"What about the children who don't go?" said Castle.* "What do you   4
do about the green-eyed monster?"

Mrs. Nash was puzzled.   5

"Jealousy. Envy," Castle elaborated. "Don't the children who stay home 6
ever feel unhappy about it?"

"I don't understand," said Mrs. Nash.   7

"And I hope you won't try," said Frazier,† with a smile. "I'm afraid we 8
must be moving along."

We said good-bye, and I made an effort to thank Mrs. Nash, but she 9
seemed to be puzzled by that too, and Frazier frowned as if I had committed
some breach of good taste.

"I think Mrs. Nash's puzzlement," said Frazier, as we left the building, 10
"is proof enough that our children are seldom envious or jealous. Mrs. Nash
was twelve years old when Walden Two was founded. It was a little late to
undo her early training, but I think we were successful. She's a good example
of the Walden Two product. She could probably recall the experience of
jealousy, but it's not part of her present life."

"Surely that's going too far!" said Castle. "You can't be so godlike as 11
all that! You must be assailed by emotions just as much as the rest of us!"

"We can discuss the question of godlikeness later, if you wish," replied 12
Frazier. "As to emotions—we aren't free of them all, nor should we like to
be. But the meaner and more annoying—the emotions which breed unhappiness—are almost unknown here, like unhappiness itself. We don't need them
any longer in our struggle for existence, and it's easier on our circulatory
system, and certainly pleasanter, to dispense with them."

"If you've discovered how to do that, you are indeed a genius," said 13
Castle. He seemed almost stunned as Frazier nodded assent. "We all know
that emotions are useless and bad for our peace of mind and our blood
pressure," he went on. "But how arrange things otherwise?"

"We arrange them otherwise here," said Frazier. He was showing a 14
mildness of manner which I was coming to recognize as a sign of confidence.

"But emotions are—fun!" said Barbara.‡ "Life wouldn't be worth living 15
without them."

"Some of them, yes," said Frazier. "The productive and strengthening 16
emotions—joy and love. But sorrow and hate—and the high-voltage excite-
ments of anger, fear, and rage—are out of proportion with the needs of
modern life, and they're wasteful and dangerous. Mr. Castle has mentioned
jealousy—a minor form of anger, I think we may call it. Naturally we avoid
it. It has served its purpose in the evolution of man; we've no further use for
it. If we allowed it to persist, it would only sap the life out of us. In a
cooperative society there's no jealousy because there's no need for jealousy."

---

*Augustine Castle is a philosopher who, reflecting Skinner's dislike of philosophy, is portrayed
as smug, narrow-minded, and a bit dense.

†T. E. Frazier is the "behavioral engineer" who has founded the community called Walden Two.
He is Skinner's spokesperson in the novel.

‡Barbara Macklin is characteristically made to speak from an "emotional" point of view.

"That implies that you all get everything you want," said Castle. "But 17 what about social possessions? Last night you mentioned the young man who chose a particular girl or profession. There's still a chance for jealousy there, isn't there?"

"It doesn't imply that we get everything we want," said Frazier. 18 "Of course we don't. But jealousy wouldn't help. In a competitive world there's some point to it. It energizes one to attack a frustrating condition. The impulse and the added energy are an advantage. Indeed, in a competitive world emotions work all too well. Look at the singular lack of success of the complacent man. He enjoys a more serene life, but it's less likely to be a fruitful one. The world isn't ready for simple pacifism or Christian humility, to cite two cases in point. Before you can safely train out the destructive and wasteful emotions, you must make sure they're no longer needed."

"How do you make sure that jealousy isn't needed in Walden Two?" 19 I said.

"In Walden Two problems can't be solved by attacking others," said 20 Frazier with marked finality.

"That's not the same as eliminating jealousy, though," I said. 21

"Of course it's not. But when a particular emotion is no longer a useful 22 part of a behavioral repertoire, we proceed to eliminate it."

"Yes, but how?" 23

"It's simply a matter of behavioral engineering," said Frazier. 24

"Behavioral engineering?" 25

"You're baiting me, Burris.* You know perfectly well what I mean. The 26 techniques have been available for centuries. We use them in education and in the psychological management of the community. But you're forcing my hand," he added. "I was saving that for this evening. But let's strike while the iron is hot."

We had stopped at the door of the large children's building. Frazier 27 shrugged his shoulders, walked to the shade of a large tree, and threw himself on the ground. We arranged ourselves about him and waited.

"Each of us," Frazier began, "is engaged in a pitched battle with the rest 28 of mankind."

"A curious premise for a Utopia," said Castle. "Even a pessimist like 29 myself takes a more hopeful view than that."

"You do, you do," said Frazier. "But let's be realistic. Each of us has 30 interests which conflict with the interests of everybody else. That's our original sin, and it can't be helped. Now, 'everybody else' we call 'society.' It's a powerful opponent, and it always wins. Oh, here and there an individual prevails for a while and gets what he wants. Sometimes he storms the culture of a society and changes it slightly to his own advantage. But society wins

*Professor Burris, the narrator of *Walden Two,* is a former graduate school friend of T. E. Frazier.

in the long run, for it has the advantage of numbers and of age. Many prevail against one, and men against a baby. Society attacks early, when the individual is helpless. It enslaves him almost before he has tasted freedom. The 'ologies' will tell you how it's done. Theology calls it building a conscience or developing a spirit of selflessness. Psychology calls it the growth of the superego.*

"Considering how long society has been at it, you'd expect a better job. 31 But the campaigns have been badly planned and the victory has never been secure. The behavior of the individual has been shaped according to revelations of 'good conduct,' never as the result of experimental study. But why not experiment? The questions are simple enough. What's the best behavior for the individual so far as the group is concerned? And how can the individual be induced to behave in that way? Why not explore these questions in a scientific spirit?

"We could do just that in Walden Two. We had already worked out a 32 code of conduct—subject, of course, to experimental modification. The code would keep things running smoothly if everybody lived up to it. Our job was to see that everybody did. Now, you can't get people to follow a useful code by making them into so many jacks-in-the-box. You can't foresee all future circumstances, and you can't specify adequate future conduct. You don't know what will be required. Instead you have to set up certain behavioral processes which will lead the individual to design his own 'good' conduct when the time comes. We call that sort of thing 'self-control.' But don't be misled, the control always rests in the last analysis in the hands of society.

"One of our Planners, a young man named Simmons, worked with me. 33 It was the first time in history that the matter was approached in an experimental way. Do you question that statement, Mr. Castle?"

"I'm not sure I know what you are talking about," said Castle. 34

"Then let me go on. Simmons and I began by studying the great works 35 on morals and ethics—Plato, Aristotle, Confucius, the New Testament, the Puritan divines, Machiavelli, Chesterfield, Freud—there were scores of them. We were looking for any and every method of shaping human behavior by imparting techniques of self-control. Some techniques were obvious enough, for they had marked turning points in human history. 'Love your enemies' is an example—a psychological invention for easing the lot of an oppressed people. The severest trial of oppression is the constant rage which one suffers at the thought of the oppressor. What Jesus discovered was how to avoid these inner devastations. His technique was to *practice the opposite emotion.* If a man can succeed in 'loving his enemies' and 'taking no thought for the morrow,' he will no longer be assailed by hatred of the oppressor or rage at the loss of his freedom or possessions. He may not get his freedom or possessions back, but he's less miserable. It's a difficult lesson. It comes late in our program."

"I thought you were opposed to modifying emotions and instincts until 36

*According to Skinner, none of the "ologies" refers to anything real or yields real knowledge.

the world was ready for it," said Castle. "According to you, the principle of 'love your enemies' should have been suicidal."

"It would have been suicidal, except for an entirely unforeseen conse- 37 quence. Jesus must have been quite astonished at the effect of his discovery. We are only just beginning to understand the power of love because we are just beginning to understand the weakness of force and aggression. But the science of behavior is clear about all that now. Recent discoveries in the analysis of punishment—but I am falling into one digression after another. Let me save my explanation of why the Christian virtues—and I mean merely the Christian techniques of self-control—have not disappeared from the face of the earth, with due recognition of the fact that they suffered a narrow squeak within recent memory.*

"When Simmons and I had collected our techniques of control, we had 38 to discover how to teach them. That was more difficult. Current educational practices were of little value, and religious practices scarcely any better. Promising paradise or threatening hell-fire is, we assumed, generally admitted to be unproductive. It is based upon a fundamental fraud which, when discovered, turns the individual against society and nourishes the very thing it tries to stamp out. What Jesus offered in return for loving one's enemies was heaven *on earth,* better known as peace of mind.

"We found a few suggestions worth following in the practices of the 39 clinical psychologist. We undertook to build a tolerance for annoying experi- ences. The sunshine of midday is extremely painful if you come from a dark room, but take it in easy stages and you can avoid pain altogether. The analogy can be misleading, but in much the same way it's possible to build a tolerance to painful or distasteful stimuli, or to frustration, or to situations which arouse fear, anger or rage. Society and nature throw these annoyances at the individual with no regard for the development of tolerances. Some achieve tolerances, most fail. Where would the science of immunization be if it followed a schedule of accidental dosages?

"Take the principle of 'Get thee behind me, Satan,' for example," Frazier 40 continued. "It's a special case of self-control by altering the environment. Subclass A_3, I believe. We give each child a lollipop which has been dipped in powdered sugar so that a single touch of the tongue can be detected. We tell him he may eat the lollipop later in the day, provided it hasn't already been licked. Since the child is only three or four, it is a fairly diff—"

"Three or four!" Castle exclaimed. 41

"All our ethical training is completed by the age of six," said Frazier 42 quietly. "A simple principle like putting temptation out of sight would be acquired before four. But at such an early age the problem of not licking the lollipop isn't easy. Now, what would you do, Mr. Castle, in a similar situa- tion?"

"Put the lollipop out of sight as quickly as possible." 43

*He is referring to World War II. Skinner wrote *Walden Two* in the early summer of 1945 (recounted in the preface of the 1976 reprint).

"Exactly. I can see you've been well trained. Or perhaps you discovered 44
the principle for yourself. We're in favor of original inquiry wherever possible, but in this case we have a more important goal and we don't hesitate to
give verbal help. First of all, the children are urged to examine their own
behavior while looking at the lollipops. This helps them to recognize the need
for self-control. Then the lollipops are concealed, and the children are asked
to notice any gain in happiness or any reduction in tension. Then a strong
distraction is arranged—say, an interesting game. Later the children are reminded of the candy and encouraged to examine their reaction. The value of
the distraction is generally obvious. Well, need I go on? When the experiment
is repeated a day or so later, the children all run with the lollipops to their
lockers and do exactly what Mr. Castle would do—a sufficient indication of
the success of our training."

"I wish to report an objective observation of my reaction to your story," 45
said Castle, controlling his voice with great precision. "I find myself revolted
by this display of sadistic tyranny."

"I don't wish to deny you the exercise of an emotion which you seem 46
to find enjoyable," said Frazier. "So let me go on. Concealing a tempting but
forbidden object is a crude solution. For one thing, it's not always feasible.
We want a sort of psychological concealment—covering up the candy by
paying no attention. In a later experiment the children wear their lollipops
like crucifixes for a few hours."

" 'Instead of the cross, the lollipop,   47
About my neck was hung,' "

said Castle.

"I wish somebody had taught me that, though," said Rodge, with a 48
glance at Barbara.*

"Don't we all?" said Frazier. "Some of us learn control, more or less by 49
accident. The rest of us go all our lives not even understanding how it is
possible, and blaming our failure on being born the wrong way."

"How do you build up a tolerance to an annoying situation?" I said. 50

"Oh, for example, by having the children 'take' a more and more painful 51
shock, or drink cocoa with less and less sugar in it until a bitter concoction
can be savored without a bitter face."

"But jealousy or envy—you can't administer them in graded doses," I 52
said.

"And why not? Remember, we control the social environment, too, at 53
this age. That's why we get our ethical training in early. Take this case. A
group of children arrive home after a long walk tired and hungry. They're
expecting supper; they find, instead, that it's time for a lesson in self-control:
they must stand for five minutes in front of steaming bowls of soup.

---

*Rogers, a former student of Professor Burris's and Barbara's fiancé. The obscure "glance at
Barbara" may be Rogers's way of alluding to control of sexual passion.

"The assignment is accepted like a problem in arithmetic. Any groaning 54 or complaining is a wrong answer. Instead, the children begin at once to work upon themselves to avoid any unhappiness during the delay. One of them may make a joke of it. We encourage a sense of humor as a good way of not taking an annoyance seriously. The joke won't be much, according to adult standards—perhaps the child will simply pretend to empty the bowl of soup into his upturned mouth. Another may start a song with many verses. The rest join in at once, for they've learned that it's a good way to make time pass."

Frazier glanced uneasily at Castle, who was not to be appeased.   55

"That also strikes you as a form of torture, Mr. Castle?" he asked.   56

"I'd rather be put on the rack,"* said Castle.   57

"Then you have by no means had the thorough training I supposed. You 58 can't imagine how lightly the children take such an experience. It's a rather severe biological frustration, for the children are tired and hungry and they must stand and look at food; but it's passed off as lightly as a five-minute delay at curtain time. We regard it as a fairly elementary test. Much more difficult problems follow."

"I suspected as much," muttered Castle.   59

"In a later stage we forbid all social devices. No songs, no jokes—merely 60 silence. Each child is forced back upon his own resources—a very important step."

"I should think so," I said. "And how do you know it's successful? You 61 might produce a lot of silently resentful children. It's certainly a dangerous stage."

"It is, and we follow each child carefully. If he hasn't picked up the 62 necessary techniques, we start back a little. A still more advanced stage"— Frazier glanced again at Castle, who stirred uneasily—"brings me to my point. When it's time to sit down to the soup, the children count off—heads and tails. Then a coin is tossed and if it comes up heads, the 'heads' sit down and eat. The 'tails' remain standing for another five minutes."

Castle groaned.   63

"And you call that envy?" I asked.   64

"Perhaps not exactly," said Frazier. "At least there's seldom any aggres- 65 sion against the lucky ones. The emotion, if any, is directed against Lady Luck herself, against the toss of the coin. That, in itself, is a lesson worth learning, for it's the only direction in which emotion has a surviving chance to be useful. And resentment toward things in general, while perhaps just as silly as personal aggression, is more easily controlled. Its expression is not socially objectionable."

Frazier looked nervously from one of us to the other. He seemed to be 66 trying to discover whether we shared Castle's prejudice. I began to realize, also, that he had not really wanted to tell this story. He was vulnerable. He was treading on sanctified ground, and I was pretty sure he had not estab-

---

*The rack was an instrument of torture used in the Middle Ages.

lished the value of most of these practices in an experimental fashion. He could scarcely have done so in the short space of ten years. He was working on faith, and it bothered him.

I tried to bolster his confidence by reminding him that he had a professional colleague among his listeners. "May you not inadvertently teach your children some of the very emotions you're trying to eliminate?" I said. "What's the effect, for example, of finding the anticipation of a warm supper suddenly thwarted? Doesn't that eventually lead to feelings of uncertainty, or even anxiety?" 67

"It might. We had to discover how often our lessons could be safely administered. But all our schedules are worked out experimentally. We watch for undesired consequences just as any scientist watches for disrupting factors in his experiments. 68

"After all, it's a simple and sensible program," he went on in a tone of appeasement. "We set up a system of gradually increasing annoyances and frustrations against a background of complete serenity. An easy environment is made more and more difficult as the children acquire the capacity to adjust." 69

"But why?" said Castle. "Why these deliberate unpleasantnesses—to put it mildly? I must say I think you and your friend Simmons are really very subtle sadists." 70

"You've reversed your position, Mr. Castle," said Frazier in a sudden flash of anger with which I rather sympathized. Castle was calling names, and he was also being unaccountably and perhaps intentionally obtuse. "A while ago you accused me of breeding a race of softies," Frazier continued. "Now you object to toughening them up. But what you don't understand is that these potentially unhappy situations are never very annoying. Our schedules make sure of that. You wouldn't understand, however, because you're not so far advanced as our children." 71

Castle grew black. 72

"But what do your children get out of it?" he insisted, apparently trying to press some vague advantage in Frazier's anger. 73

"What do they get out of it!" exclaimed Frazier, his eyes flashing with a sort of helpless contempt. His lips curled and he dropped his head to look at his fingers, which were crushing a few blades of grass. 74

"They must get happiness and freedom and strength," I said, putting myself in a ridiculous position in attempting to make peace. 75

"They don't sound happy or free to me, standing in front of bowls of Forbidden Soup," said Castle, answering me parenthetically while continuing to stare at Frazier. 76

"If I must spell it out," Frazier began with a deep sigh, "what they get is escape from the petty emotions which eat the heart out of the unprepared. They get the satisfaction of pleasant and profitable social relations on a scale almost undreamed of in the world at large. They get immeasurably increased efficiency, because they can stick to a job without suffering the aches and pains which soon beset most of us. They get new horizons, for they are spared 77 the emotions characteristic of frustration and failure. They get—" His eyes searched the branches of the trees. "Is that enough?" he said at last.

"And the community must gain their loyalty," I said, "when they dis- 78 cover the fears and jealousies and diffidences in the world at large."

"I'm glad you put it that way," said Frazier. "You might have said that 79 they must feel superior to the miserable products of our public schools. But we're at pains to keep any feeling of superiority or contempt under control, too. Having suffered most acutely from it myself, I put the subject first on our agenda. We carefully avoid any joy in a personal triumph which means the personal failure of somebody else. We take no pleasure in the sophistical, the disputative, the dialectical." He threw a vicious glance at Castle. "We don't use the motive of domination, because we are always thinking of the whole group. We could motivate a few geniuses that way—it was certainly my own motivation—but we'd sacrifice some of the happiness of everyone else. Triumph over nature and over oneself, yes. But over others, never."

"You've taken the mainspring out of the watch," said Castle flatly. 80

"That's an experimental question, Mr. Castle, and you have the wrong 81 answer."

Frazier was making no effort to conceal his feeling. If he had been riding 82 Castle, he was now using his spurs. Perhaps he sensed that the rest of us had come round and that he could change his tactics with a single holdout. But it was more than strategy, it was genuine feeling. Castle's undeviating skepticism was a growing frustration.

"Are your techniques really so very new?" I said hurriedly. "What 83 about the primitive practice of submitting a boy to various tortures before granting him a place among adults? What about the disciplinary techniques of Puritanism? Or of the modern school, for that matter?"

"In one sense you're right," said Frazier. "And I think you've nicely 84 answered Mr. Castle's tender concern for our little ones. The unhappinesses we deliberately impose are far milder than the normal unhappinesses from which we offer protection. Even at the height of our ethical training, the unhappiness is ridiculously trivial—to the well-trained child.

"But there's a world of difference in the way we use these annoyances," 85 he continued. "For one thing, we don't punish. We never administer an unpleasantness in the hope of repressing or eliminating undesirable behavior. But there's another difference. In most cultures the child meets up with annoyances and reverses of uncontrolled magnitude. Some are imposed in the name of discipline by persons in authority. Some, like hazings, are condoned though not authorized. Others are merely accidental. No one cares to, or is able to, prevent them.

"We all know what happens. A few hardy children emerge, particularly 86 those who have got their unhappiness in doses that could be swallowed. They become brave men. Others become sadists or masochists of varying degrees of pathology. Not having conquered a painful environment, they become preoccupied with pain and make a devious art of it. Others submit—and hope to inherit the earth. The rest—the cravens, the cowards—live in fear for the rest of their lives. And that's only a single field—the reaction to pain. I could cite a dozen parallel cases. The optimist and the pessimist, the contented and the disgruntled, the loved and the unloved, the ambitious and the discouraged—these are only the extreme products of a miserable system.

"Traditional practices are admittedly better than nothing," Frazier went   87 on. "Spartan or Puritan—no one can question the occasional happy result. But the whole system rests upon the wasteful principle of selection. The English public school of the nineteenth century produced brave men—by setting up almost insurmountable barriers and making the most of the few who came over. But selection isn't education. Its crops of brave men will always be small, and the waste enormous. Like all primitive principles, selection serves in place of education only through a profligate use of material. Multiply extravagantly and select with rigor. It's the philosophy of the 'big litter' as an alternative to good child hygiene.

"In Walden Two we have a different objective. We make every man a   88 brave man. They all come over the barriers. Some require more preparation than others, but they all come over. The traditional use of adversity is to select the strong. We control adversity to build strength. And we do it deliberately, no matter how sadistic Mr. Castle may think us, in order to prepare for adversities which are beyond control. Our children eventually experience the 'heartache and the thousand natural shocks that flesh is heir to.'* It would be the cruelest possible practice to protect them as long as possible, especially when we *could* protect them so well."

Frazier held out his hands in an exaggerated gesture of appeal.   89

"What alternative *had* we?" he said, as if he were in pain. "What else   90 could we do? For four or five years we could provide a life in which no important need would go unsatisfied, a life practically free of anxiety or frustration or annoyance. What would *you* do? Would you let the child enjoy this paradise with no thought for the future—like an idolatrous and pampering mother? Or would you relax control of the environment and let the child meet accidental frustrations? *But what is the virtue of accident?* No, there was only one course open to us. We had to design a series of adversities, so that the child would develop the greatest possible self-control. Call it deliberate, if you like, and accuse us of sadism; there was no other course." Frazier turned to Castle, but he was scarcely challenging him. He seemed to be waiting, anxiously, for his capitulation. But Castle merely shifted his ground.

"I find it difficult to classify these practices," he said. Frazier emitted a   91 disgruntled "Ha!" and sat back. "Your system seems to have usurped the place as well as the techniques of religion."

"Of religion and family culture," said Frazier wearily. "But I don't call   92 it usurpation. Ethical training belongs to the community. As for techniques, we took every suggestion we could find without prejudice as to the source. But not on faith. We disregarded all claims of revealed truth and put every principle to an experimental test. And by the way, I've very much misrepre-

*From *Hamlet,* by William Shakespeare.

sented the whole system if you suppose that any of the practices I've described are fixed. We try out many different techniques. Gradually we work
toward the best possible set. And we don't pay much attention to the apparent success of a principle in the course of history. History is honored in
Walden Two only as entertainment. It isn't taken seriously as food for
thought. Which reminds me, very rudely, of our original plan for the morning. Have you had enough of emotion? Shall we turn to intellect?"

Frazier addressed these questions to Castle in a very friendly way and   93
I was glad to see that Castle responded in kind. It was perfectly clear, however, that neither of them had ever worn a lollipop about the neck or faced
a bowl of Forbidden Soup.

Questions for Discussion

1. In the preface to the 1976 reprint of *Walden Two,* Skinner details the kinds
   of improvements he pictures as a result of behavorial engineering.
   "Psychotic and retarded persons would lead better lives, time and energy
   of teachers and students would be saved, homes would be pleasanter social
   environments, people would work more effectively while enjoying what
   they were doing, and so on." Then in the next sentence he identifies these
   goals as "the kinds of achievements traditionally expected from wisdom
   and common sense." Are these goals in fact the ones that you would
   identify as the primary ones for wisdom and common sense to achieve?
   If not, which goals would you want to include? Regardless of where you
   would place different kinds of goals, which other ones do you think need
   to be included? While Skinner's goals are clearly important, do you find
   it curious that these goals are the only ones mentioned? Which other
   important goals are silently subordinated in his "and so on"?

2. Comment on the awareness or lack of awareness of ethical issues in Skinner's account of the advantages of behavorial engineering. Does Skinner
   seem adequately or inadequately sensitive to issues of individual right to
   self-determination? Why or Why not?

3. Presumably in Skinner's ideal society, behavorial engineering will be able
   to avoid turning into social oppression (although he never really makes
   this clear) by operating on consensus: People will agree to what they want
   before the conditioning procedures are implemented. But what do you
   picture happening to minority views and dissenting opinions in such a
   world? Who gets the final say about the qualities the conditioners instill
   in their citizen-subjects?

4. Where do Skinner's criteria come from for defining the kind of feelings and
   opinions society desires most? From science? If so, how does science establish criteria? From religion? Skinner thinks religion superfluous and illu-

sory. From history? Perhaps, but whose version of it? From objective
reasoning? Perhaps, but would you accept Skinner's reasoning, which lists
psychotics and retarded persons leading better lives *first* in his catalog of
the advantages of behavorial engineering?

5. Do you think Skinner's recommended technique of making children wait
to begin eating is a good way to teach self-control? How much distance
is there between learning this kind of self-control and learning to control
one's impulses to envy, greed, lust, or aggression? Do these all exist on the
same psychic and emotional plane as hunger? If they do not, what critique
of Skinner's reasoning does this seem to suggest?

Suggested Essay Topics

1. Write an essay, scenario, or short story in which you depict the kinds of
educational principles *you* would recommend for achieving the same goals
that Skinner desires: the teaching of self-control and the stifling of envy,
aggression, and competitiveness.

2. Write a dialogue in which you picture Frazier (or Skinner) debating the
best means of educating children with any other appropriate author in this
book: Rich, Plato, Whitehead, Arnold, or some other thinker whose views
will make an instructive contrast.

Mary Midgley

*In this probing and insightful essay, Mary
Midgley (b. 1919) undertakes the arduous task of simultaneously defending and
criticizing science, especially certain tendencies in evolutionary theorizing. While she
defends both the content and the methods of evolutionary science as important, at the
same time she criticizes the tendency of some evolutionary scientists to draw exaggerated
conclusions about the character and destiny of the universe based on evolutionary
postulates.*

*On the basis of facts as uncovered by evolutionary research, some scientists
conclude that the world is a terrifying battleground dominated by each person's or
society's inevitable drive to ensure survival and dominance. Other scientists, however,
looking at the same data, draw no such pessimistic conclusions, but see the world
instead as the site of inevitable progressions that include the gradual improvement
(sometimes, it is claimed, the perfection) of human nature itself and of society. The
extreme forms of these pessimistic and optimistic pictures of the world are not, says
Midgley, scientific in any sense and threaten both the prestige and the progress of
science by claiming scientific legitimacy for views that can best be explained not as
scientific theories but as moralistic, atheistic, or religious melodramas.*

Midgley is not attacking the scientific impulse to draw big pictures of the world.

She sees such pictures as the beginning point of all inquiries, whether scientific, religious, economic, or of some other kind. What she attacks is the tendency on the part of some scientists to claim that certain versions of the evolutionary picture are scientific conclusions, which they are not, or that they possess a scientific character in themselves.

In the end Midgley argues that the reliance on certain antitheses prevalent in modern discourse about both religion and science is dysfunctional to both. For the past century, for example, is has been common to divide the world up into a set of opposing characteristics that place science, rationality, and hard knowledge on one side of a dividing line and religion, spirituality, and intuition on the other. Midgley makes it clear that such antitheses as these are inadequate and in fact mask the way science works. She argues, for example, that scientific pictures of the world, including the evolutionary picture of human development, are attempts to stitch together a meaning for human existence; they are not simply the results of empirical research. No good scientist, she says, merely collects and stores facts. Any good scientist collects facts to fit some big picture to which belief has already been committed. Instead of such beliefs being unscientific, they are in fact essential to scientific research and the maintenance of scientific energy.

Much of what Midgley says is, of course, controversial. Some scientists may feel that their objectivity is being impugned and that their scienticic research is being either trivialized or coopted by a religious or at least unscientific point of view. But Midgley argues her case pointedly and cogently. Whether you agree or disagree, try to form your responses as cogently and concretely as she forms her arguments.

EVOLUTION AS A RELIGION

From chapters 1, 8, and 12 of *Evolution as a Religion* (1985).

SCIENCE AND SYMBOLISM

The theory of evolution is not just an inert piece of theoretical science. 1 It is, and cannot help being, also a powerful folk-tale about human origins. Any such narrative must have symbolic force. We are probably the first culture not to make that its main function. Most stories about human origins must have been devised purely with a view to symbolic and poetic fittingness. Suggestions about how we were made and where we come from are bound to engage our imagination, to shape our views of what we now are, and so to affect our lives. Scientists, when they find themselves caught up in these webs of symbolism, sometimes complain, calling for a sanitary cordon to keep them away from science. But this seems to be both psychologically and logically impossible.

Our theoretical curiosity simply is not detached in this way from the rest of our life. Nor do scientists themselves always want it to be so. Some of the symbolic webs are ones which they approve of, and promote as part of the ideal of science itself. For instance, Jacques Monod, as an atheistical biochemist, does not just rejoice at getting rid of the theistic drama. He at once replaces it by another drama, just as vivid, emotive and relevant to life, in which Sartrian man* appears as the lonely hero challenging an alien and meaningless universe:

> It is perfectly true that science attacks values. Not directly, since science is no judge of them and *must* ignore them; but it subverts every one of the mythical or philosophical ontogenies upon which the animist tradition, from the Australian aborigines to the dialectical materialists, has based morality, values, duties, rights, prohibitions.
>
> If he accepts this message in its full significance, man must at last wake out of his millenary dream and discover his total solitude, his fundamental isolation. He must realize that, like a gypsy, he lives on the boundary of an alien world; a world that is deaf to his music, and as indifferent to his hopes as it is to his sufferings or his crimes.[1]

But "discovering his total solitude" is just adopting one imaginative stance among many possible ones. Other good scientists, very differently, have used the continuity of our species with the rest of the physical world to reprove human arrogance and to call for practical recognition of kinship with other creatures. Many, like Darwin and the great geneticist Theodosius Dobzhansky,† have held that an attitude of awe and veneration for the wonders of the physical world is an essential condition for studying them properly. Others have talked in a more predatory way about the joys of the chase and the triumph of catching facts. Both motives, and many others, are evidently so habitual in science that they are only not mentioned because they are taken for granted.

It seems often to be assumed that they are therefore irrelevant, that Science itself is something so pure and impersonal that it ought to be thought of in complete abstraction from all the motives that might lead people to practise it. This, unfortunately, cannot work because of the importance of world-pictures. Facts are not gathered in a vacuum, but to fill gaps in a world-picture which already exists. And the shape of this world-picture—determining the matters allowed for it, the principles of selection, the possible range of emphases—depends deeply on the motives for forming it in the first place.

Imagination, which guides thought, is directed by our attitudes. For instance, predatory and competitive motives tend to produce a picture dominated by competition and predation—one in which these elements do not only play their part, as they did for Darwin, but are arbitrarily and dogmati-

---

*A reference to the French existential philosopher and novelist Jean-Paul Sartre (1905–1980), who portrayed individuals as pitted in lonely and isolated (but potentially heroic) opposition to a neutral universe, their job being to *assert* meaning in a world that possesses none intrinsically.
†Russian-born American geneticist (1900–1975), known especially for work on the philosophical implications of evolution.

cally isolated as sole rulers. Thus, in a familiar distortion which will concern us repeatedly, the sociobiologist M. T. Ghiselin flatly declares:

> The evolution of society fits the Darwinian paradigm in its most individualistic form. The economy of nature is competitive from beginning to end. Understand that economy, and how it works, and the underlying reasons for social phenomena are manifest. They are the means by which one organism gains some advantage to the detriment of another. No hint of genuine charity ameliorates our vision of society, once sentimentalism has been laid aside. What passes for co-operation turns out to be a mixture of opportunism and exploitation. The impulses that lead one animal to sacrifice himself for another turn out to have their ultimate rationale in gaining advantage over a third, and acts for the good of one "society" turn out to be performed for the detriment of the rest. Where it is in his own interest, every organism my reasonably be expected to aid his fellows. Where he has no alternative, he submits to the yoke of servitude. Yet, given a full chance to act in his own interest, nothing but expediency will restrain him from brutalizing, from maiming, from murdering—his brother, his mate, his parent, or his child. Scratch an "altruist" and watch a "hypocrite" bleed.[2]

As we shall see, this claim is essentially pure fantasy, not only unsupported by the empirical facts which are supposed to be its grounds, but actually contrary to them, such as they are. Is this a quite exceptional aberration? Some will suspect that it must be, not only because the world-picture involved is a bad one, but because scientists ought to be so impartial that they either do not have anything so unprofessional as a world-picture at all, or, if they have one, do not let it affect their work.

But this is a mistaken ideal. An enquirer with no such general map would only be an obsessive—someone who had a special motive for collecting facts indiscriminately. He would not be a person without an attitude, or without special motives, but one with motives so odd as to inhibit the kind of organizing activity which normally shapes people's ideas into some sort of coherent whole. Merely to pile up information indiscriminately is an idiot's task. Good scientists do not approximate to that ideal at all. They tend to have a very strong guiding imaginative system. Their world-picture is usually a positive and distinctive one, with its own special drama. They do not scrupulously avoid conveying any sense of dark and light, of what matters and what does not, of what is to be aimed at and what avoided at all costs. They use the lights and shadows to reveal the landscape. Like those who argue usefully on any other subject, they do their best work not by being neutral but by having strong preferences, being aware of them, criticizing them carefully, expressing them plainly and then leaving their readers to decide how far to share them.

Symbolism, then, is not just a nuisance to be got rid of. It is essential. Facts will never appear to us as brute and meaningless; they will always organize themselves into some sort of story, some drama. These dramas can indeed be dangerous. They can distort our theories, and they have distorted the theory of evolution perhaps more than any other. The only way in which we can control this kind of distortion is, I believe, to bring the dramas themselves out into the open, to give them our full attention, understand them better and see what part, if any, each of them ought to play both in theory and in life. It is no use merely to swipe at them from time to time, like troublesome insects, while officially attending only to the theoretical questions. This will not make them go away, because they are a serious feature of life.

DARWIN'S BALANCE

The drama that attends a theory need not, then, be mere melodrama. 7 When sensationalism is present it is either irrelevant or—if it really belongs to a theory—shows that that theory is bad. The drama that goes with a good theory is simply the expressive aspect of the theory itself. In order of time, it is often conceived in advance of much of the supporting evidence. But when further facts accumulate, it ought to respond to them by refining and subtilizing its cruder outlines. This process usually makes it less extreme and one-sided, and so moves it away from the gratuitous sensationalism which marks melodrama. That does not make it less stirring or less important for life; it can make it more so. This imaginative and emotional deepening is part of the growth of a theory, not just a chance ornament. When the young Darwin immersed himself in the arguments about cosmic purpose in Paley's* theological textbook *The Evidences of Christianity,* and repeatedly read *Paradise Lost* on exploring trips from the *Beagle,* †³ he was neither wasting his time nor distorting his scientific project. He was seriously working his way through a range of life-positions which lay on the route to the one he could finally use.

The result of this long preliminary pilgrimage was to make his own 8 picture unusually balanced and inclusive. To keep it so is, however, terribly hard. He himself made clear that he felt this difficulty deeply, and was constantly dissatisfied with his efforts, constantly changing his books to do justice to some neglected angle. The vastness of the truth and the one-sidedness of formulae always haunted him.

· · ·

The destructive message of this book is a somewhat dismal one. It concerns the sort of trouble which arises when, with writers less careful than Darwin, the dramas take over. About evolution, theory itself has again and again been distorted by biases flowing from over-simple, unbalanced world-pictures. The trouble does not, of course, lie in mere wish-fulfilment of the obvious kind which paints the world as we should like it to be. It involves

*William Paley (1743–1805), English theologian and utilitarian philosopher.
†The ship on which Darwin first visited the Galápagos Islands, where he observed many of the natural phenomena that supported his theory.

being obsessed by a picture so colourful and striking that it numbs thought about the evidence required to support it. Standards of proof then fall headlong.

. . .

FALSE LIGHTS

There are two distortions in particular which will mainly concern us in   9
this book, and they had better be indicated, however crudely, right away. Neither is new; both have often been denounced. But both persist, not just in the minds of outsiders ignorant of evolutionary theory, but also in those of many scientists who develop and expound it. The first is the better known and the more obviously pernicious. It is the "Social Darwinist" idea, expressed by Ghiselin, that life has been scientifically proved to be essentially competitive, in some sense which exposes all social feeling as somehow mere humbug and illusion. The phrase "survival of the fittest" has been used, ever since Herbert Spencer* first coined it, to describe an individualistic law showing such things as co-operation, love and altruism to be unreal, a law which (somewhat mysteriously) both demands and predicts that they should always give way to self-interest. This has often been exposed as nonsense. Since many very successful species of social animals, including our own, have evolved these traits, have survived by them and continue to live by them, their unreality cannot be the message of evolutionary theory. But because of its strong dramatic force, as well as various political uses, this notion persists through repeated attempts to correct it, and often twists up the ideas even of those who think they are helping to get rid of it. It is especially troublesome in the American sociobiology debate, a topic to which I shall have to give a rather disproportionate amount of attention, simply because its wide publicity makes it, just now, the most prominent hotbed of noisy errors about evolution.

The second main distortion may be called Panglossism,† or the Escalator   10
Fallacy. It is the idea that evolution is a steady, linear upward movement, a single inexorable process of improvement, leading (as a disciple of Herbert Spencer's put it) "from gas to genius"⁴ and beyond into some superhuman spiritual stratosphere. This idea, first put forward by Jean-Baptiste Lamarck‡ at the beginning of the century,⁵ convinced Spencer instantly and completely. It did not convince Darwin at all. He thought it vacuous, pointed out the obscurity of the metaphor "higher," and relied on no such paid-up cosmic insurance policy to bail out the human race. He developed his own view of

---

*English philosopher (1820–1903) who, in a series of books beginning with *Principles of Psychology* (1855), applied Darwin's theory of evolution to social phenomena.

†Pangloss was the philosopher—(ridiculed by Voltaire in his great satire *Candide* (1759)—who claimed that everything that happened was for the best and that the world was getting better and better.

‡French naturalist (1744–1829) and forerunner of Darwin, who proposed that changes in environment cause changes in animals and plants, resulting in adaptive modification, and that such acquired characteristics are then transmitted genetically to offspring.

selection on the humbler model of a bush—a rich radiation of varying forms, in which human qualities cannot, any more than any others, determine a general direction for the whole. Here too, however, what he rejected has been kept by many people as a central feature of the idea of evolution and seen as a key part of "Darwinism." Still unsupported by argument, it too continues to produce some extremely strange theorizing, and in its less obvious way also to do a great deal of damage. These two kinds of drama are, in fact, the shapes into which the two main strands of feeling about evolution naturally develop, if they are not held in balance and forced to correct each other. They are the hypertrophied forms of cosmic optimism and cosmic pessimism respectively. Since both these moods are common, theory-builders often oscillate between them rather casually, and produce views which owe something to both. Unluckily, this is not the same thing as the synthesis which Darwin attempted. It can merely give us the worst of both worlds.

. . .

CLAIMS FOR THE FUTURE OF SCIENCE

Let us turn now to . . . [the] kind of prophecy, concerned mainly with   11
the rosy future of science itself, but also indicating the route by which it is to bring about a general reform of life. It is from the sociobiologist Edward O. Wilson:

> When mankind has achieved an ecological steady state, probably by the end of the twenty-first century, the internalization of social evolution will be nearly complete. About this time biology should be at its peak, with the social sciences maturing rapidly . . . cognition will be translated into circuitry. Learning and creativeness will be defined as the alteration of specific portions of the cognitive machinery regulated by input from the emotive centers. Having cannibalized psychology, the new neurobiology will yield an enduring set of first principles for sociology. . . . Skinner's dream of a culture predesigned for happiness will surely have to wait for the new neurobiology. A genetically accurate and hence completely fair code of ethics must also wait.[6]

This means, however, that we shall get it in the end, once the neurobiologists have done their stuff. Wilson admits indeed that some of us may not like this future world when we get it, partly, it seems, because of worries about genetic engineering. But this will be due to our unscientific attitude. It affects neither the dogmatic confidence of the prediction, nor the desirability of the outcome from the impersonal, scientific point of view.

The point about dogmatic confidence is interesting. Scrupulous modera-   12
tion in making factual claims is commonly seen as a central part of the scientific attitude. Julian Huxley, listing the bad habits which infest religion, naturally mentions "dogmatism" and "aspiring to a false certitude" among them and explains that science corrects these vices.[7] Remarks like those just quoted do not on the face of it seem to meet this standard.

When I have complained of this sort of thing to scientists, I have   13 sometimes met a surprising defence, namely, that these remarks appear in the opening or closing chapters of books, and that everybody knows that what is found there is not to be taken literally; it is just flannel for the general public. The idea seems to be that supplying such flannel constitutes a kind of a ritual. If so, it must surely strengthen our present unease, since addiction to ritual is another fault supposed to be the mark of religion. The point might of course just be the more practical one of selling books. But if grossly inflated claims to knowledge of the future are made for that reason, then there is either common dishonesty for personal profit, or an attempt to advance the cause of science by methods which disgrace it, and which (again) have always been considered a disgrace to religion. Putting these prophecies in a special part of the book does not disinfect them. It cannot be more excusable to peddle groundless predictions to the defenceless general public, who will take them to have the full authority of science, than to one's professional colleagues, who know much better what bees infest one's bonnet. These bold prophecies of an escalating future are often combined, as they are here, with the vision of one's own Science in a gold helmet finally crushing its academic rivals: again, scarcely a monument to scientific balance and caution.

DRAWBACKS OF THE ESCALATOR MODEL

Is all this euphoria, however, actually dangerous? If the escalator myth 14 really has got out of hand, what harm does it do?

In one way, certainly, it does much less harm than the egoistic myth of 15 universal cut-throat competition. Optimism in general, even when it is muddled, tends to do less harm than pessimism. Faith in life, and in the human race, is certainly a better thing to have around than a supposedly science-based conviction of universal bloody-mindedness and hypocrisy. But once we are clear about that, we need to notice some objections, and as they have had much less attention than those which arise to the competitive myth, they may need more emphasis.

In the first place, faith in life and in the human race becomes much less 16 evident when we turn from those who rely on continued natural growth, like Teilhard* and Dobzhansky, to the champions of genetic engineering. Calling for surgical methods always shows less faith in the patient's constitution and more in the skills of the surgeon. The question, *in what do you put your faith?* is central to the whole enquiry. Those who put it in genetic engineering seem to give us what we now get so often here, an answer which misses the point of the question. They want us to put faith in certain techniques, or at most in the intellectual skills and capacities which make those techniques possible. But all these are means. What we need is to hear about aims, and about the faculties in all of us which reach out to those aims. What we get is a recom-

*Teilhard de Chardin (1881–1955), French paleontologist and philosopher, who theorized that humans are presently evolving, mentally and socially, toward a final spiritual unity.

mendation to entrust change to a certain set of experts, whose training has not called on them to pay any attention to conflicting aims at all.

The genetic engineering proposal, however, is not a necessary part of the escalator myth. Is there anything harmful about that myth itself, if we consider it in its more natural and consistent form as a simple prediction of steady, indefinite future human genetic progress to heights hitherto undreamed of? 17

I have already touched on the objection that this prediction, if it is taken as certain and infallible, gives a quite unwarranted sense of security, and can easily distract us from the need for other changes. If it is not taken as certain, but still as providing the only guideline towards safety, it admits the dangers but tells us, without argument, to rely on one particular way of escaping them rather than others, namely genetic engineering. And I think that those who do rely on it are in fact led by this way of thinking, not by any real evidence that this is a better prospect than other possible means of salvation. What, however, if no special question is raised about inevitability, but this progress is simply presented as the destiny offered to the human race? This somewhat vaguer picture is inspiring but a trifle dazzling. It may help us in assessing it to let the objector open the argument. 18

The central difficulty is that this story is arbitrarily human-centered, and that its view of humanity is at present arbitrarily intellect-centred. Its human-centredness distorts both evolutionary theory and our attitude to the natural world. By what right, and in what sense, can we consider ourselves as the directional pointer and aim-bearer of the whole evolutionary process? Does this mean what is often taken for granted today in controversy about the treatment of plants and animals, that all other organisms exist only as means to our ends? Kant and other philosophers have said this, many people believe it, yet it remains extremely obscure.[8] The idea that things are *there* for some external purpose seems to need a theological context, and this view did of course grow out of one. But that context will not subjugate everything to man. Certainly Judaeo-Christian thinking made the human race much more central than many other religions do, but it still considered man to be God's steward. Divine aims were always paramount, and God had created all his creatures for his own purposes, not for man's. Non-human beings count in this picture as having their own special value. Redwoods and pythons, frogs, moles and albatrosses are not failed humans or early try-outs for humans or tools put there to advance human development. 19

When this is spelled out, people today usually accept it, yet the escalator picture tends quietly and constantly to obscure it. Lamarck, who invented the escalator concept, did consider all non-human animals to be standing behind man, engaged on the same journey, and this still persisting idea does inevitably suggest that they are inferior and expendable. It obscures our enormous ignorance about their lives, about what it is like to be (say) a whale, a gorilla, an elephant, a mouse or a battery chicken, and supports our natural conviction that anything we don't do or experience can't have any value. The more we put aside this obviously hasty and inadequate myth, and notice the 20 endless variety of existing creatures, the more we shall be driven to forget the linear metaphor of height, and return to the more Darwinian image of the radiating bush.

WHICH WAY IS UP?

Is there, however, still a fixed upward dimension? Does the bush have 21 a human tip? Are we in some sense the point of the whole? I have never myself felt the need to say this, but very many people do, and the point must be taken seriously. It may well be that any intelligent species, able to meditate on such things, must in some way think of itself as central in the whole world, because in its own world it is so. It may be morally necessary to treat our own destiny as the most important thing conceivable, if only because we cannot easily conceive anything greater. But this by no means licenses us to separate it from all others and pursue it at their expense, nor does it mean, as escalator-fanciers sometimes kindly suggest, that our duty to those behind us is to help them to become like ourselves as quickly as possible. The moral consequences of a serious attitude to our own destiny are excellent, but those of a contemptuous attitude to other destinies are quite another matter. The two should not be linked at all.

Turning from morals to theory, could this way of thinking license us to 22 predict that the next thing the bush will do is to grow taller? Change in human societies is now almost entirely a cultural, not a genetic matter, and it can as easily be for the worse as for the better. It is commonly recognized today that we badly need to be clear about this, since the belief in inevitable progress can be, and has been, used to justify bad changes which were preventable. Even, therefore, if we had reason to expect genetic change, this would not show that such change was good, nor that it was outside our control. And even if we had sound theoretical grounds for expecting the genetic development of our own species into something still greater and more distinctively human, this could scarcely show that we were the single supremely valuable object which gave point to the whole evolutionary process. There does not have to be any such one object. And since there are no such theoretical grounds either—since this expectation has no place in Darwinian theory, and came to Lamarck and Spencer simply as a welcome, self-justifying hunch—it is very remarkable that scientifically educated people still continue to ask the question which stands as title to the last chapter of William Day's book, from which I have already quoted, the question "Where is evolution headed?"[9]

THE FUTURE AS MAGNIFYING
MIRROR

How does this question arise? If we look at the literature which asks it 23 and attempts to give it answers, a very simple answer becomes almost unavoidable. It is a way of dramatizing morals. One can give a peculiar force to the praise and exaltation of particular ideals by presenting them as a piece of foresight, a glance at a real, attainable though perhaps distant future. This is an ancient, natural and legitimate device, which lies at the root of prophecy. Both bad and good futures can be used, but if the moral leverage is to work, both must be presented as only possible. There must still be time to work for this "future" or avert it. Both author and reader must therefore be clear that the vision is an imaginary one, and this literature must be kept separate from the relatively humdrum business of prediction. Sober predictions about the likely future development of terrestrial life would not carry any such moral message. They would not necessarily make human affairs central at all, but would refer to them only in so far as they seem likely to affect the development of ecosystems. But the prophecies which now concern us are not in the least like this. They are quite simply exaltations of particular ideals within human life at their own epoch, projected on to the screen of a vague and vast "future"—a term which, since Nietzsche* and Wells, is not a name for what is particularly likely to happen, but for a fantasy realm devoted to the staging of visionary dramas.

In their content, these dramas plainly depend on the moral convictions   24 of their author and of his age, not on scientific theories of any kind. Nietzsche, who laid down the ground-rules of this game, used Darwinian ideas and language as a pedestal for his own preferred ideal type, the unsocial, anarchic, creative individual, his enlarged and exalted self:

> Ye lonely ones of to-day; ye that stand apart, ye shall one day be a people; from you, that have chosen yourselves, a chosen people shall arise—and from it, the Superman. . . .
> And the Great Noon shall be when man standeth in the midst of his course between beast and Superman. . . . Dead are all gods; now will we that the Superman live.[10]

And, more prosaically:

> The problem I raise here is not what ought to succeed mankind (the human being is an *end*) but what type of human being one ought to *breed*, ought to *will*, as more valuable, more worthy of life, more certain of the future.[11]

The mark of this favoured and expected type is not just that he is free from the trammels of existing religion and morality, but that he is a fully unified human being, free from the many bad habits which at present divide our nature. He is to reunite spirit and intellect, which now wither in pretentious isolation, with their strong roots in the body, the imagination and the passions. Although externally he is isolated, contemptuous of social links with

*Friedrich Wilhelm Nietzsche (1844–1900), German philosopher, poet, and philologist known for espousing the doctrine of the perfectibility of humans through forcible self-assertion and for glorification of the superman or overman (übermensch).

his fellows, internally he balances this isolation by the strongest possible integration of his nature. Indeed Nietzsche's hostility to outward social bonds is largely a protest against their tendency to fragment the individual's being. And, among contemporary influences which promote this fatal division, he thinks the exaltation of the bare intellect, especially in its scientific form, every bit as pernicious as the Christian religion:

> The harsh helot condition to which the tremendous extent of science has condemned every single person to-day is one of the main reasons why education and *educators* appropriate to fuller, richer, *deeper* natures are no longer forthcoming. Our culture suffers from nothing *more* than it suffers from the superabundance of presumptuous journeymen and fragments of humanity.[12]

And again:

> *From a doctorate exam.*—"What is the task of all higher education?"—To turn a man into a machine—"By what means?" He has to learn how to feel bored. "How is this achieved?"—Through the concept of duty. . . . "Who is the perfect man?" The civil servant.[13]

Thus Nietzsche; do we like his future? If not, the Jesuit biologist Teil- 25 hard de Chardin offers us quite a different one, in which Nietzsche's twin abominations, physical science and Christianity, are both to be exalted and to find their final synthesis. It was Teilhard who invented the phrase "Omega man," using it to describe a future being, raised above us both spiritually and intellectually, whose destiny it is to complete the divine plan for this earth by perfecting it at the mental level—to add a nöosphere, or intellectual realm, to the living realm, or biosphere, which is already present. (Teilhard seems also to have invented the term *biosphere,* and should be given the credit for that useful move.) In this ideal future, the idea of brotherly love and of the mystical union of individuals in the whole—an ideal which would have been pure ratsbane to Nietzsche—plays a central part, and traditional Christianity, however difficult it may be to fit in with this ambitious scheme, is certainly still conceived as the main guiding thread.

SCIENTISTS AS SUPERMEN

Do both these suggestions strike some readers today as a trifle crazy? 26 It cannot be too strongly emphasized how much this impression of craziness depends on current moral and intellectual habits. What will our own look like, to those who have ceased to share them? And what is actually in the minds of those who make parallel suggestions today?

I shall go on using William Day's book *Genesis on Planet Earth,* because 27 it seems to me to put exceptionally clearly ideas which are very widely accepted, and seldom as well expressed. Day writes throughout as if only one

sort of improvement could possibly be in question, namely a rise in intelligence, and he treats *intelligence* as a term which could not possibly be ambiguous or need analysis. To increase this intelligence is, he says, the purpose of
all life: an idea which he presents as needing no defence or explanation. His
language about this is flagrantly teleological,* indeed vitalist:

> Life has endured, generation after generation, producing more than can
> live, sacrificing many that the most fit may survive. Species have followed
> species, rung after rung, in a continuous climb of the ladder called evolu-
> tion. And in that long ascent, life has retained rapport with its surround-
> ings by evolving its window on the universe—intelligence.[14]

What is meant by speaking of intelligence as a window, and why should such
a window furnish the point of the whole? If windows matter so much, must
it not be because what we see through them is important, and if it is, must
there not be other valuable things besides intelligence? Windows are a means.
Is the function we are talking about just the acquiring and ordering of information? or does it include certain deep ways of responding to it? Those who
originally put this great stress on intelligence into European thought meant
by it something enormously wider than mere ordered storage. Both Plato and
Aristotle, who differed so much on countless other points, agreed in making
the point of the whole intellectual enterprise consist in the contemplation to
which it led: the awareness of a vast outer whole, within which human
thought operates, and of which it can form only the faintest image. Day sees
no such difficulty. Reality for him is what we make it through science:

> It is into all reality that life, led by man, is expanding. Reality is no longer
> restricted to the horizons of the senses, but extends to the far reaches
> conceived by the mind. Physical reality may or may not be finite, for what
> exists is what we perceive, or identify as reality, and how far we can
> extend reality is uncertain.[15]

Resisting the temptation to go into all the implications of this—does it
actually mean that reality is what physicists say it is, and if so how do they
know what to say?—I stick to the point which now concerns us, namely that
the central business of the mind, the work for which "life" has evolved it,
is here physical science. Omega man emerges as quite simply a superscientist.
Only at one point does it look as if he might have any other interests: where
Day says that man's "intelligence has evolved where, unlike any other form
of life, he is touching on a new dimension. It is man's spirituality, psyche and
superego, and that part of man [*sic*] that makes him the forerunner of Omega
man."[16] But these mysterious dimensions have already been mentioned and
been explained as being simply physical: "real dimensions of time and space,
beyond our reach in size and perception."[17] Materialism is not being compromised. To settle that point finally, Day goes on [italics added]:

*Purposeful, having a goal established by plan; not happening merely at random.

A type of intelligence more evolved than man's could conceive of a reality *and exercise control over it* in a manner beyond our ability to comprehend. What comprehension *and powers over nature* Omega man will be able to command can only be suggested by man's image of the supernatural.[18]

The mention of spirituality proves to have been only a ritual one. The real point of all this intelligence, and therefore of evolution itself, was, it turns out, simply to put more physical power in the hands of the quasi-deified human species, even though that species seems already to have a great deal more physical power than it knows what to do with.

· · ·

BALANCING THE WORLD

I have been arguing that the contrast between science and religion is unluckily not as plain, nor the relation between them as simple, as is often supposed, and have been discussing some elements which can equally form part of either. Thoughtful scientists have often mentioned this problem, but a great many of their colleagues, and of the public generally, cling to the reassuringly simple opposition. What often seems to happen is that a great number of different antitheses are mixed up here, and used rather indiscriminately, as each happens to be convenient, to give colour to the idea of a general crusade of light against darkness. We could group them roughly like this:

1	science	v.	superstition partiality error magic wish-fulfilment dogmatism blind conformism childishness
2	common sense science rationalism logic	v.	intuition mysticism faith
	materialism	v.	idealism animism vitalism mind-body dualism commonsense agnosticism
3	hard	v.	soft
	progress	v.	tradition
	determinism	v.	free will
	mechanism	v.	teleology
	empiricism	v.	rationalism metaphysics

scepticism	v.	credulity
reason	v.	feeling or emotion
objective	v.	subjective
quantity	v.	quality
physical science	v.	the humanities
realism	v.	reverence
specialism	v.	holism
prose	v.	poetry
male	v.	female
clarity	v.	mystery

SHIFTING PARADIGMS

A mental map based on this strange group of antitheses, a map which 30 showed them all as roughly equivalent and was marked only with the general direction "keep to the left," has for the last century usually been issued to English-speaking scientists with their first test-tube and has often gone with them to the grave. In spite of its wild incoherence, it still has great influence, though at least two recent developments within science itself have lately shaken it, and more are to be expected. The first shock is the series of changes whereby modern physics now shows indeterminacy as lying near the centre of causation, and solid matter as dissolving, on inspection, into non-solid energy. This is a severe upset to the crucial notions of mechanism and determinism. What perhaps cuts deepest, however, is something symbolic which looks more superficial and which would not matter at all if people were really only interested in facts and not in drama. It is the disturbance to the notion of "hardness," a metaphor whose application is entirely mysterious, but which has somehow served to keep the whole left-hand column together.

At present, this change results in a flow of popular books such as *The Tao of Physics* by Fritdjof Capra and *The Dancing Wu Li Masters* by Gary Zukav,[19] which suggest that energy is spirit, and that what modern physics teaches is, give or take a mantra or two, very much what Zen masters and Hindu sages have been saying for centuries, or possibly millennia. Whatever else may be thought about this, it does at least point to the need to look again at our list of antitheses. On the face of things, these books do draw attention to the arbitrary narrow-mindedness which has been imposed on scientists, and call for science to look outward, though at times they also seem to convey the opposite message: science, especially physics, is already far more spiritual, and therefore more all-sufficient, than we have so far supposed. At least, however, the traditional set of antitheses is broken up. Serious physicists seem at present more aware than many biologists of its confusions and inadequacies. David Bohm's comment, extracts from which we saw earlier, deserves now to be quoted more fully:

> At the end of the nineteenth century, physicists widely believed that classical physics gave the general outlines of a complete mechanical explanation of the universe. Since then, relativity and quantum theory have overturned such notions altogether. It is now clear that no mechanical

explanation is available, not for the fundamental particles which constitute all matter, inanimate and animate, nor for the cosmos as a whole (e.g.
it is now widely accepted among cosmologists that in "black holes" there
is a singularity, near which all customary notions of causally ordered law
break down). So we are now in the strange position that whereas physicists are implying that, fundamentally and in its totality, inanimate matter
is not mechanical, molecular biologists are saying that whenever matter
is organized so as to be alive, it is completely mechanical.

Of course, molecular biologists generally ignore the implications of
physics, except when these implications support their own position. In
this connection, it might be appropriate for them to consider that the
nineteenth-century view of physics was enormously more comprehensively and accurately tested than is now possible for the current views of
molecular biology. Despite this, classical physics was swept aside and
overturned, being retained only as a simplification and an approximation
valid in a certain limited domain. It is not likely that modern molecular
biology will sooner or later undergo a similar fate?

What is needed for unrestricted objectivity is a certain tentative and
exploratory quality of mind that is free of final conclusions. [Without this,
there is an] ever-present danger that knowledge in broad and deep fields
may give rise to the sort of 'hubris' described above, in which there is an
unquestioned belief in the complete validity of current forms of thinking.
. . . If [this] is allowed to continue in science, this latter will in all probability eventually suffer the sort of decline of influence which has already
befallen the religious view of the world. Indeed, there are already signs
of such a trend.[20]

The second shock was delivered by recent discoveries about the functions of brain hemispheres. In its early days, this was often read, in a way
which is itself a notable indicator of the underlying dramas expected, as a
story about the "dominance" of one hemisphere, namely of course the calculating, articulate, scientific one, over the other, which was intuitive, humble
and not really very distinctively human. Further research, however, has
steadily shown more and more serious functions for the right-hand hemisphere, and has led increasingly to the acceptance of Kipling's picture expressed at the beginning of this chapter,* where it is utterly vital to have, and
to keep in balance, the two separate sides of one's head. The idea of the ruling
hemisphere had been just one more version of a simple but very powerful
hierarchical view of mental function which long dominated neurology, and
which Peter Reynolds, the comparative ethologist, has lately christened "the
Victorian brain."[21] This showed brain evolution dramatically as a series of
successive conquests, in which at each level of life a new brain area and its
faculties came in to rule the rest, culminating in man and the final victory of
the cerebral cortex, or some specially splendid part of it. To keep this dominance order clear, functions were neatly confined to particular structures, and
the belief that *Homo sapiens* possessed not just a better cortex but entirely

---

*Midgley earlier quotes a Kipling poem, omitted here, in which the speaker says he would rather
suffer anything than "lose / Either side of my head."

distinct organs to carry his higher faculties was at first hotly defended by Owen* against Huxley.† Detailed neurological work has, however, worn away almost every aspect of this seductive picture. As Stephen Walker, a neurological psychologist, says,

> One still has a sense of regret that this charming and convincing tale must be discarded. The weight of evidence is now if anything more in favour of the unhelpful suggestion . . . that all the fundamental parts of the vertebrate brain were present very early on, and can be observed in lampreys.[22]

Moreover, new developments do not at all follow the simple pattern of conquest and takeover. Functions are neither handed over wholesale to grander organs nor fully determined by them; they seem to involve very complex interactions between wide ranges of brain areas, in which it is seldom safe to say either that any one area takes no part, or that any one dominates or "rules" any others. No doubt each makes its own distinctive contribution, to which adjectives like "higher" might sometimes usefully be applied, but the only social metaphor which seems appropriate for these transactions is co-operation. The brain, in short, works as a whole, and our understanding of it has been very much held back by the fact that, as Walker remarks, "there is a tendency to want to appoint some brain division as 'in charge' of all the others, and this sets the stage for phylogenetic takeovers of the executive position."

Brain evolution, in short, is not a simple success story establishing the right of all left-hand members in our antitheses to subdue their partners. Since the members of the two sets are in any case such a mixed lot as to make this wholesale arrangement impossible, we had better look at them separately on their merits.

FINDING THE RIGHT ENEMY

Which among these antitheses are really the ones we need, which of them give clear ground for a crusade? The ones in the first group seem the most promising for crusaders. In them science stands opposed to something undoubtedly bad. But in these cases it is certainly not the only opponent of the evils in question. Superstition and the rest find their opposites in clear thinking generally, and a particular superstition is as likely to be corrected by history or logic or common sense as by one of the physical sciences. The second group deals in ideas which are more ambitious, more interesting, but also much more puzzling, because we at once need definitions of the terms involved, and cannot easily give them without falling into confusion. The odd

*Sir Richard Owen (1804–1892), English anatomist and paleontologist, early opponent of Darwin's theory of evolution.

†Thomas Henry Huxley (1825–1895), English biologist, who defended Darwin's theories so persistently that he earned the nickname "Darwin's Bulldog."

tendency of both rationalism and common sense to jump the central barrier is only one indication of the difficulties. In the third group, we have contrasts which are a good deal clearer. But they do not seem to provide material at all suitable for a crusade. They describe pairs of complementary elements in life and thought, both members of which are equally necessary, and indeed could scarcely be identified except in relation to each other as parts of a whole. We no longer want that truculent little "v." to divide them. They go very well together, and crusaders must avoid trying to set them at logger-heads. Thus it does not matter here that "reason" appears on both sides; we no longer want to reduce all these contrasts to a single underlying shape. The lines of division cross each other. Different distinctions are needed for differ-ent purposes.

How hard it is to relate these various antitheses clearly can be seen in 35 Bertrand Russell's very interesting and influential paper "Mysticism and Logic." Russell's main enterprise here is an admirable attempt to move the whole debate into our group 3, to show apparently warring elements as both necessary and complementary:

> Metaphysics,* or the attempt to conceive the world as a whole by means of thought, has been developed, from the first, by the union and conflict of two very different human impulses, the one urging men towards mysti-cism, the other urging them towards science. . . . In Hume,† for instance, the scientific impulse reigns quite unchecked, while in Blake‡ a strong hostility to science co-exists with profound mystic insight. But the great-est men who have been philosophers have felt the need both of science and of mysticism; the attempt to harmonize the two was what made their life, and what always must, for all its arduous uncertainty, make philoso-phy, to some minds, a greater thing than either science or religion. . . . Mysticism, is, in essence, little more than a certain intensity and depth of feeling in regard to what is believed about the universe. . . . Mysticism is to be commended as an attitude towards life, not as a creed about the world. The metaphysical creed, I shall maintain, is a mistaken outcome of the emotion, although this emotion, as colouring all other thoughts and feelings, is the inspirer of whatever is best in Man. Even the cautious and patient investigation of truth by science, which seems the very antithesis of the mystic's swift certainty, may be fostered and nourished by that very spirit of reverence in which mysticism lives and moves.[23]

Russell has got a lot of things right here. He has "got in," as they say, 36 many items from the right-hand column of our antitheses in legitimate rela-tion to science. He has got in emotion and poetry, indeed he has got in Blake,

---

*The study of things transcending physical nature, thus frequently associated with inquiries into the spiritual and the religious dimensions of reality.

†David Hume (1711–1776), Scottish philosopher whose skepticism restricted knowledge to what we learn from direct experience; strong opponent of all forms of metaphysics.

‡William Blake (1757–1827), English artist, poet, and mystic, violently opposed to science's "despiritualizing" effects.

with his criticisms of Newton.* He sees that emotion is so far from being an opponent of science, or a menace to it, that emotion of a suitable kind is necessary for science, and that part of that emotion can quite properly be called "reverence." He sees that something of the sort is necessary for metaphysics too.

The word *metaphysics* here is not of course used in the abusive sense to   37
mean mere empty vapouring. It is used in its proper sense of very general conceptual enquiry, covering such central topics as the relation of mind and matter, free will and necessity, meaning, truth and the possibility of knowledge, all in an attempt (as Russell rightly says) to make sense of the world as a whole. In this sense, naturally, views like materialism and empiricism, and also sceptical enquiries like those of Hume, Ayer and Popper are themselves part of metaphysics just as much as what they oppose or enquire into. When A. J. Ayer began his book *Language, Truth and Logic*[24] with a chapter called "The Elimination of Metaphysics," and went on to explain that the word was for him virtually equivalent to "nonsense," he was, in any ordinary sense of that word, simply doing metaphysics himself—expounding one theory of meaning among many others. Empty vapouring is *bad* metaphysics. There is a lot of it about, but it cannot make the study unnecessary.

Russell, who had the advantage of having started his philosophical life   38
as a disciple of Hegel, was not tempted, as Hume and his disciples were, to suppose that good metaphysics merely meant cutting down one's thoughts on such topics to a minimum. He knew that, far from that, even highly constructive metaphysicians like Plato and Heraclitus, Leibnitz and Hegel often had something very important to say, especially about mathematics. Yet he was now a convert to empiricism, and he wanted to set limits on the thought-architecture of these bold rationalists. His solution was, on the whole, to concentrate on the emotional function of this large-scale, constructive metaphysics, and on the intellectual function of science and of more sceptical philosophy. Thus mystical, constructive metaphysics was to supply the heart of the world-grasping enterprise, while science supplied the head.

THE MANY-SIDEDNESS OF SCIENCE

This is a bold and ingenious idea, but something has gone wrong with   39
it. He has fitted the head of one kind of enquiry on to the heart of another. Constructive metaphysics has its own thoughts, and science its own motives. If the word *science* means what it seems to mean here—primarily the search for particular facts—then it is powered emotionally by the familiar motive of detailed curiosity. If it means the building of those facts into a harmonious, satisfying system, then it draws upon a different motive, the desire for intellectual order; which is also the motive for metaphysical endeavour. Without this unifying urge, science would be nothing but mindless, meaningless col-

*Isaac Newton (1642–1727), English physicist and mathematician, who conceived the idea of universal gravitation.

lecting. At the quite ordinary scientific level, before any question of mystically contemplating the whole comes in, the system-building tendency, with its aesthetic criteria of elegance and order, is an essential part of every science, continually shaping the scrappy data into usable patterns. Scientific hypotheses are not generated by randomizers, nor do they grow on trees, but on the branches of these ever-expanding thought systems.

This is why the sciences continually go beyond everybody's direct experience, and do so in directions that quickly diverge from that of common sense, which has more modest systems of its own. And because isolated systems are always incomplete and can conflict with each other, inevitably in the end they require metaphysics, "the attempt to conceive the world as a whole," to harmonize them.

To what are interestingly called *lay* people, however, these intellectual constructions present problems of belief which are often quite as difficult as those of religion, and which can call for equally strenuous efforts of faith. This happens at present over relativity, over the size and expansion of the universe, over quantum mechanics, over evolution and many other matters. Believers are—perhaps quite properly—expected to bow to the mystery, admit the inadequacy of their faculties, and accept paradoxes. If a mystical sense of reverence is, as Russell suggested, the right response to the vast and incomprehensible universe, then science itself requires it, since it leads us on directly to this situation. It cannot therefore be right to call mysticism and science, as Russell does, two distinct, co-ordinate "human impulses." Mysticism is a range of human faculties; physical science, a range of enquiries which can, at times, call these faculties into action. But long before it does so, it has passed the limits of common sense, transcended experience and begun to ask for faith.

At this stage, there is often a real problem about what kind of thinking [42] is going on, and whether it ought to be stopped. If, for instance, we ask whether the universe is finite, are we still talking about anything at all? If so, do we know what it is? The most general concepts used by any science—concepts like life, time, space, law, energy—raise serious headaches, affecting their use in actual problems. To resolve these, however, we often need not more facts but a better way of fitting these concepts into their neighbours, of stating the wider problems which surround them, of "conceiving the world as a whole." Science quite properly calls on the whole range of our cognitive faculties, but it is not alone in doing so, nor can it define their whole aim. It is a part of our attempt to understand the universe, not the whole of it. It opens into metaphysics.

NOTES

All notes are Midgley's.

1. Jacques Monod, *Chance and Necessity,* trans. Austryn Wainhouse (London, Fontana, 1974), p. 160.

2. M. T. Ghiselin, *The Economy of Nature and the Evolution of Sex* (Berkeley, Cal., University of California Press, 1974), p. 247.

3. For both these influences see Gillian Beer's excellent discussions in *Darwin's Plots; Evolutionary Narrative in Darwin, George Eliot and Nineteenth Century Fiction* (London, Routledge & Kegan Paul, 1984), especially pp. 30–40 and 83–8.

4. Quoted by James Moore, *The Post-Darwinian Controversies; A Study of the Protestant Struggle to Come to Terms with Darwin in Great Britain and America 1870–1900* (Cambridge, Cambridge University Press, 1979), p. 167, from Edward Clodd.

5. In his *Philosophie Zoologique* (1809) and *Histoire Naturelle des Animaux sans Vertèbres* (1815–22).

6. Edward O. Wilson, *Sociobiology; The New Synthesis* (Cambridge, Mass., Harvard University Press, 1975), pp. 574–5.

7. Julian Huxley, *Religion without Revelation* (London, Benn, 1927), p. 372.

8. See for instance the essay on 'Duties towards animals and spirits' in Kant's *Lectures on Ethics,* trans. Louis Infield (London, Methuen, 1930). I have discussed these difficulties in *Beast and Man* (Brighton, Harvester Press, 1979), pts. 4 and 5, and in *Animals and Why They Matter* (Harmondsworth, Penguin, 1983) throughout.

9. William Day, *Genesis on Planet Earth; The Search for Life's Beginning* (2nd edn, New Haven, Conn., Yale University Press, 1984).

10. *Thus Spake Zarathustra,* pt. I, 'Of virtue that giveth', trans. A. Tille and M. Bozman (London, Dent, Everyman edn., 1930), pp. 68–9.

11. *The Antichrist,* sec. 3, trans. R. J. Hollingdale (published with *Twilight of the Idols*) (Harmondsworth, Penguin, 1968), p. 116.

12. *Twilight of the Idols,* sec. 3, 'What the Germans lack', trans. R. J. Hollingdale (Harmondsworth, Penguin, 1968), p. 61.

13. Ibid., sec. 29, 'Expeditions of an untimely man', p. 83.

14. Day, op. cit., p. 381.

15. Ibid., p. 389.

16. Ibid., p. 391.

17. Ibid., p. 390.

18. Ibid., p. 391.

19. Fritdjof Capra, *The Tao of Physics* (London, Wildwood House, 1975) and Gary Zukav, *The Dancing Wu Li Masters* (London, Fontana, 1982).

20. In John Lewis (ed.), *Beyond Chance and Necessity* (London, Garnstone Press, 1974), pp. 128–35.

21. See Peter Reynolds, *On the Evolution of Human Behaviour* (Berkeley, Cal., University of California Press, 1981) pp. 35–6, 68 and 222–4.

22. Stephen Walker, *Animal Thought* (London, Routledge & Kegan Paul, 1983), p. 145.

23. Bertrand Russell, 'Mysticism and logic', reprinted in *Mysticism and Logic* (London, Allen & Unwin, 1917), pp. 9, 10 and 16.

24. London, Gollancz, 1936.

Questions for Discussion

1. Some people, says Midgley, hold to the "mistaken ideal" that "scientists ought to be so impartial that they either do not have anything so unprofessional as a world-picture at all, or, if they have one, do not let it affect their work" (¶ 4–5). Try to determine by class discussion how prevalent this view of scientific objectivity is among your classmates. How convincing or unconvincing do you and others find Midgley's description of scientific

objectivity? What reasons would you use in arguing either for or against her views?

2. Summarize in your own words the positions of Herbert Spencer and Jean-Baptiste Lamarck (¶ 9–10) and Darwin's objections to their views. Can you and your classmates come up with references to evolutionary theory that you have heard that treat evolutionary theory as if it explains social relationships as well as biological development? Can you specifically recall hearing the phrase "survival of the fittest" applied to society, as if competition among corporations or countries could be explained by the model of biological competition? What does such an application mean? Did anyone in class know that this phrase was introduced by the sociologist, Herbert Spencer, and not by Darwin?

3. Sift through Midgley's essay and copy in your notebook the metaphors used both by and about science and scientists, and note any repetitions. Discuss the possibility of substituting "literal" language for the metaphors? Can it be done, or do metaphors seem an essential part of scientific discourse? If so, what does this do to the conventional notion of scientific discourse as based solely on hard facts? If metaphors are not essential, should scientists make every attempt not to use them? Support your opinions with specific reasons.

4. Which sets of antitheses in paragraph 29 seem to you and your classmates a natural way of categorizing things? Why? Which, if any, do not seem natural? Why not? What diversity of opinions exist among members of the class? Are there any discernible preferences for the right-hand list over the left-hand list (or vice versa)? If there are, on what grounds are the preferences explained or defended? Can you determine if religious believers tend to prefer one list and agnostics or atheists the other? If so, what does this suggest about the nature of the lists? If not, what does this suggest about deeply shared cultural values?

5. What does Bohm (¶ 31) mean by the term *hubris,* which appears near the end of the quoted passage? Does Midgley provide other examples of the kind of hubris he is referring to in other quotations?

6. In paragraph 30 Midgley says that two developments in the twentieth century have shaken people's faith in the validity of the antitheses that she outlines in paragraph 29. Explain in your own words the nature of these two developments. Which of the two was more widely known among your classmates?

7. Paraphrase Russell's point in the passage quoted in paragraph 35. Why does Midgley think Russell provides help in escaping the sterility of overdrawn antitheses? What is Midgley's criticism of Russell's point (¶ 39)?

Suggested Essay Topics

1. Write a précis: a summary of an argument that preserves the main points and structure of the original while condensing it greatly. Midgley's essay has 12 sections, each with its own heading. Using these headings and

placing them in the same order as in Midgley's essay, write a three- or four-sentence summary of each subsection so that you wind up with a condensed but accurate paraphrase of her whole argument. This kind of exercise is not the same as doing original analysis, but when you are dealing with complex arguments such as Midgley's, it can be a useful way of making sure you understand what you are reading.

2. In an essay directed to your classmates, your instructor, a scientist, or a religious believer (whichever seems most appropriate to you), explain either the accuracy or the inaccuracy of the list of antitheses that Midgley lays out in paragraph 29. Whether the list seems to you helpful or unhelpful, right or wrong, explain (if you support the list) what it tells us about different kinds of knowledge, experience, or reality. If you do not support the list, explain why knowledge, experience, and reality cannot really be divided this way. If you choose this latter tack, you will have to show in addition that some other division would be better or that no divisions should be made at all.

IDEAS IN DEBATE

C. P. Snow
Loren Eiseley

C. P. Snow

*The British writer C. P. Snow (1905–
1980) could write about the distinctive character of the literary and scientific cultures
because he not only knew them both intimately but spanned them in a distinguished
and unusual way. He is thus an exception to the generalizations he makes about both
the literary culture (or, as we in America would tend to say, the humanistic outlook
or humanistic tradition) and the scientific culture (or scientific outlook). That he was
himself an exception does not, of course, invalidate his generalizations; it simply
underscores what a remarkable man he was. He spanned the two cultures by working
professionally as both a trained scientist and a publishing novelist. He was a physicist
at Cambridge from 1930 to 1950, and at the same time he wrote an 11-volume
sequence of novels, collectively titled* Strangers and Brothers *(1940–1970), that
focuses on contemporary English society and documents the corrupting influence of
power.*

*The split between humanists and scientists that Snow described in 1956 has
in the intervening decades both grown and shrunk. At the theoretical level the split
has shrunk, but at the institutional level and in the eyes of the general public the split
has grown. At the theoretical level the work of such theorists and philosophers of science
as Jacob Bronowski, Loren Eiseley, Stephen Toulmin, Norwood Russell Hanson,
Thomas Kuhn, Paul Feyerabend, Harold Brown, and Michael Polanyi has taught
contemporary scientists to see that their modes of operation and those of the humanists
are not as different as they were thought to be in 1956 when Snow published his
original review, "The Two Cultures," in the* New Statesman. *In the past 35 years
scientists have become much less naïve about such issues as the status of a fact, the
nature of objectivity, and the limits of empiricism. And humanists are probably much
more knowledgeable now than Snow's literary colleagues were in 1956 about the
general trends and controversies in scientific theory—though probably not much more
knowledgeable about the details of scientific research. Generally, then, the two cultures
have more of a speaking, or at least nodding, relationship today, at the theoretical level,
than they had in the 1950s.*

*At the institutional level, however, at the places where scientists actually
conduct their research and humanists write their books, the specialization that Snow
deplores has driven the two cultures even farther apart. In both the humanities and
the sciences the topics of inquiry over the past three decades have become even more*

specialized and thus more subdivided. The result is that a historian who has a general knowledge of trends in scientific theory these days will nevertheless be as ignorant as ever about the actual research that fuels theoretical controversy. What is more—and this is something new—humanists now find themselves in the same position of ignorance about research and theories, even those of other humanists. And in science today an organic chemist has a nearly impossible task trying to understand the work of a mathematical chemist. In other words, the split nowadays is not just between the humanists and the scientists but among the subdivisions within these two broad camps.

The split between scientists and humanists has also grown larger in the eyes of the general public since the 1950s. We have no statistical proof of this assertion, but it seems a logical consequence of the increasing specialization we just referred to. In the 1950s, as Snow reports, science was brash and optimistic. Since then science has had to endure a degree of suspicion and hostility that it once seemed immune to—primarily on occasions when technology has proved threatening, as in the near meltdown at the Three Mile Island nuclear facility, as in the injurious consequences of the Agent Orange defoliation of forests in Vietnam, or as in the deterioration of the ozone layer caused by atmospheric pollution. These problems, however, do not lead most people to reject science. Indeed, the remedies people look to are almost always scientific. Science is supposed to tell us how to make safer defoliants, more reliable nuclear power plants, more efficient, pollution-scrubbing smokestacks, and so on. And beyond that, most people still think of science as the source of the only true—or at least the most true—understanding of both the natural world and human nature.

While science has retained its prestige as a source of both true and useful knowledge, the humanities have lost prestige on this scale of measurement. Fewer people now seem to turn to the study of languages, history, literature, or philosophy for solving either social or personal problems. Thus in the more than 35 years since Snow's essay, science has maintained its position in society or even enhanced it, but the humanities have lost ground. B.A. degrees in the humanities and student enrollments in humanities courses have been steadily declining. In this and other ways, the split between the two cultures has become an even more formidable problem now than it was when Snow first called our attention to it.

As you read, try to extend and amplify Snow's reasons for thinking that the split between the sciences and the humanities is unfortunate and potentially disastrous. Also consider your own attitudes toward either culture in light of what you want out of your education or the qualities of mind you think a well-educated person should possess. If Snow is right, we should all share a common literacy in both science and the humanities. But as you know, science and humanities majors all too often not only avoid courses in the "other" culture (to whatever extent possible) but are downright hostile to them. Consider how far your own literacy (and that of your friends) extends in the sciences and humanities. Does it extend far enough? Far enough for what?

THE TWO CULTURES

From *The Two Cultures: And a Second Look* (1965).

It is about three years since I made a sketch in print of a problem which 1
had been on my mind for some time.[1] It was a problem I could not avoid just
because of the circumstances of my life. The only credentials I had to rumi-
nate on the subject at all came through those circumstances, through nothing
more than a set of chances. Anyone with similar experience would have seen
much the same things and I think made very much the same comments about
them. It just happened to be an unusual experience. By training I was a
scientist: by vocation I was a writer. That was all. It was a piece of luck, if
you like, that arose through coming from a poor home.

But my personal history isn't the point now. All that I need say is that 2
I came to Cambridge and did a bit of research here at a time of major scientific
activity. I was privileged to have a ringside view of one of the most wonderful
creative periods in all physics. And it happened through the flukes of war—
including meeting W. L. Bragg* in the buffet on Kettering station on a very
cold morning in 1939, which had a determining influence on my practical
life—that I was able, and indeed morally forced, to keep that ringside view
ever since. So for thirty years I have had to be in touch with scientists not
only out of curiosity, but as part of a working existence. During the same
thirty years I was trying to shape the books I wanted to write, which in due
course took me among writers.

There have been plenty of days when I have spent the working hours 3
with scientists and then gone off at night with some literary colleagues. I
mean that literally. I have had, of course, intimate friends among both scientists and writers. It was through living among these groups and much
more, I think, through moving regularly from one to the other and back
again that I got occupied with the problem of what, long before I put it on
paper, I christened to myself as the "two cultures." For constantly I felt I
was moving among two groups—comparable in intelligence, identical in
race, not grossly different in social origin, earning about the same incomes,
who had almost ceased to communicate at all, who in intellectual, moral
and psychological climate had so little in common that instead of going
from Burlington House or South Kensington to Chelsea,† one might have
crossed an ocean.

In fact, one had travelled much further than across an ocean—because 4
after a few thousand Atlantic miles, one found Greenwich Village‡ talking
precisely the same language as Chelsea, and both having about as much

*Sir William Lawrence Bragg (1890–1971), Cavendish professor of experimental physics at
Cambridge (1938–1954) and co-winner with his father of the 1915 Nobel Prize in physics.
†Chelsea has a long history as a literary and artistic section of London. In the eighteenth
century Swift, Steele, and Smollett lived there. Later, Turner, Rossetti, Whistler, Leigh Hunt,
and Carlyle lived there.
‡A famous literary and artistic section of New York City.

communication with M.I.T.* as though the scientists spoke nothing but Tibe-
tan. For this is not just our problem; owing to some of our educational and
social idiosyncrasies, it is slightly exaggerated here, owing to another English
social peculiarity it is slightly minimised; by and large this is a problem of
the entire West.

By this I intend something serious. I am not thinking of the pleasant   5
story of how one of the more convivial Oxford greats dons†—I have heard
the story attributed to A. L. Smith—came over to Cambridge to dine. The date
is perhaps the 1890's. I think it must have been at St John's, or possibly
Trinity.‡ Anyway, Smith was sitting at the right hand of the President—or
Vice-Master—and he was a man who liked to include all round him in the
conversation, although he was not immediately encouraged by the expressions of his neighbours. He addressed some cheerful Oxonian chit-chat at the
one opposite to him, and got a grunt. He then tried the man on his own right
hand and got another grunt. Then, rather to his surprise, one looked at the
other and said, "Do you know what he's talking about?" "I haven't the least
idea." At this, even Smith was getting out of his depth. But the President,
acting as a social emollient, put him at his ease by saying, "Oh, those are
mathematicians! We never talk to *them.*"

No, I intend something serious. I believe the intellectual life of the   6
whole of western society is increasingly being split into two polar groups.
When I say the intellectual life, I mean to include also a large part of our
practical life, because I should be the last person to suggest the two can
at the deepest level be distinguished. I shall come back to the practical
life a little later. Two polar groups: at one pole we have the literary intellectuals, who incidentally while no one was looking took to referring to
themselves as "intellectuals" as though there were no others. I remember
G. H. Hardy once remarking to me in mild puzzlement, some time in the
1930's: "Have you noticed how the word 'intellectual' is used nowadays?
There seems to be a new definition which certainly doesn't include Rutherford or Eddington or Dirac or Adrian or me.§ It does seem rather odd,
don't y' know."[2]

Literary intellectuals at one pole—at the other scientists, and as the most 7
representative, the physical scientists. Between the two a gulf of mutual
incomprehension—sometimes (particularly among the young) hostility and
dislike, but most of all lack of understanding. They have a curious distorted
image of each other. Their attitudes are so different that, even on the level
of emotion, they can't find much common ground. Non-scientists tend to

---

*Massachusetts Institute of Technology in Boston, a famous school of science and engineering.
†A don is a tutor in an English university.
‡St. John's and Trinity are colleges at Cambridge University.
§All great scientists: Ernest Rutherford (1871–1937) was awarded the 1908 Nobel Prize for
chemistry, Arthur Stanley Eddington (1882–1944) was an English astronomer and Cambridge
professor, P. A. M. Dirac (1902–1984) was instrumental in the development of quantum the-
ory, and Edgar Douglas Adrian (1889–1977) was an English physiologist who won (with Sir
Charles Sherrington) the Nobel Prize for medicine in 1932.

think of scientists as brash and boastful. They hear Mr. T. S. Eliot,* who just for these illustrations we can take as an archetypal figure, saying about his attempts to revive verse-drama that we can hope for very little, but that he would feel content if he and his co-workers could prepare the ground for a new Kyd or a new Greene.† That is the tone, restricted and constrained, with which literary intellectuals are at home: it is the subdued voice of their culture. Then they hear a much louder voice, that of another archetypal figure, Rutherford, trumpeting: "This is the heroic age of science! This is the Elizabethan age!" Many of us heard that, and a good many other statements beside which that was mild; and we weren't left in any doubt whom Rutherford was casting for the role of Shakespeare. What is hard for the literary intellectuals to understand, imaginatively or intellectually, is that he was absolutely right.

And compare "this is the way the world ends, not with a bang but a 8 whimper"‡—incidentally, one of the least likely scientific prophecies ever made—compare that with Rutherford's famous repartee, "Lucky fellow, Rutherford, always on the crest of the wave." "Well, I made the wave, didn't I?"

The non-scientists have a rooted impression that the scientists are shal- 9 lowly optimistic, unaware of man's condition. On the other hand, the scientists believe that the literary intellectuals are totally lacking in foresight, peculiarly unconcerned with their brother men, in a deep sense anti-intellectual, anxious to restrict both art and thought to the existential moment. And so on. Anyone with a mild talent for invective could produce plenty of this kind of subterranean back-chat. On each side there is some of it which is not entirely baseless. It is all destructive. Much of it rests on misinterpretations which are dangerous. I should like to deal with two of the most profound of these now, one on each side.

First, about the scientists' optimism. This is an accusation which has 10 been made so often that it has become a platitude. It has been made by some of the acutest non-scientific minds of the day. But it depends upon a confusion between the individual experience and the social experience, between the individual condition of man and his social condition. Most of the scientists I have known well have felt—just as deeply as the non-scientists I have known well—that the individual condition of each of us is tragic. Each of us is alone: sometimes we escape from solitariness, through love or affection or perhaps creative moments, but those triumphs of life are pools of light we make for ourselves while the edge of the road is black: each of us dies alone. Some scientists I have known have had faith in revealed religion. Perhaps

*Thomas Stearns Eliot (1888–1965) was a leading poet and critic for most of his career. He won the Nobel Prize for literature in 1948.
†Robert Greene (ca. 1558–1592) and Thomas Kyd (1558–1594) were relatively minor literary figures of the sixteenth century. Snow's point is that if Eliot and other literary people are content merely to prepare the way for minor writers, they are indeed motivated by a conservative impulse quite different from the high ambitions of the scientists.
‡The last two lines of Eliot's poem "The Hollow Men."

with them the sense of the tragic condition is not so strong. I don't know. With most people of deep feeling, however high-spirited and happy they are, sometimes most with those who are happiest and most high-spirited, it seems to be right in the fibres, part of the weight of life. That is as true of the scientists I have known best as of anyone at all.

But nearly all of them—and this is where the colour of hope genuinely   11
comes in—would see no reason why, just because the individual condition is tragic, so must the social condition be. Each of us is solitary: each of us dies alone: all right, that's a fate against which we can't struggle—but there is plenty in our condition which is not fate, and against which we are less than human unless we do struggle.

Most of our fellow human beings, for instance, are underfed and die   12
before their time. In the crudest terms, *that* is the social condition. There is a moral trap which comes through the insight into man's loneliness: it tempts one to sit back, complacent in one's unique tragedy, and let the others go without a meal.

As a group, the scientists fall into that trap less than others. They are   13
inclined to be impatient to see if something can be done: and inclined to think that it can be done, until it's proved otherwise. That is their real optimism, and it's an optimism that the rest of us badly need.

In reverse, the same spirit, tough and good and determined to fight it   14
out at the side of their brother men, has made scientists regard the other culture's social attitudes as contemptible. That is too facile: some of them are, but they are a temporary phase and not to be taken as representative.

I remember being cross-examined by a scientist of distinction. "Why do   15
most writers take on social opinions which would have been thought distinctly uncivilised and démodé at the time of the Plantagenets? Wasn't that true of most of the famous twentieth-century writers? Yeats, Pound, Wyndham Lewis, nine out of ten of those who have dominated literary sensibility in our time—weren't they not only politically silly, but politically wicked? Didn't the influence of all they represent bring Auschwitz* that much nearer?"

I thought at the time, and I still think, that the correct answer was   16
not to defend the indefensible. It was no use saying that Yeats, according to friends whose judgment I trust, was a man of singular magnanimity of character, as well as a great poet. It was no use denying the facts, which are broadly true. The honest answer was that there is, in fact, a connection, which literary persons were culpably slow to see, between some kinds of early twentieth-century art and the most imbecile expressions of anti-social feeling.[3] That was one reason, among many, why some of us turned our backs on the art and tried to hack out a new or different way for ourselves.[4]

---

*One of Hitler's death camps in which millions of Jews were killed during World War II. The scientist Snow quotes is suggesting that the political attitudes of the literary culture helped make Auschwitz possible.

But though many of those writers dominated literary sensibility for a 17
generation, that is no longer so, or at least to nothing like the same extent.
Literature changes more slowly than science. It hasn't the same automatic
corrective, and so its misguided periods are longer. But it is ill-considered of
scientists to judge writers on the evidence of the period 1914–50.

Those are two of the misunderstandings between the two cultures. I 18
should say, since I began to talk about them—the two cultures, that is—I have
had some criticism. Most of my scientific acquaintances think that there is
something in it, and so do most of the practising artists I know. But I have
been argued with by non-scientists of strong down-to-earth interests. Their
view is that it is an over-simplification, and that if one is going to talk in these
terms there ought to be at least three cultures. They argue that, though they
are not scientists themselves, they would share a good deal of the scientific
feeling. They would have as little use—perhaps, since they knew more about
it, even less use—for the recent literary culture as the scientists themselves.
J. H. Plumb, Alan Bullock and some of my American sociological friends have
said that they vigorously refuse to be corralled in a cultural box with people
they wouldn't be seen dead with, or to be regarded as helping to produce a
climate which would not permit of social hope.

I respect those arguments. The number 2 is a very dangerous number: 19
that is why the dialectic is a dangerous process. Attempts to divide anything
into two ought to be regarded with much suspicion. I have thought a long
time about going in for further refinements: but in the end I have decided
against. I was searching for something a little more than a dashing metaphor,
a good deal less than a cultural map: and for those purposes the two cultures
is about right, and subtilising any more would bring more disadvantages than
it's worth.

At one pole, the scientific culture really is a culture, not only in an 20
intellectual but also in an anthropological sense. That is, its members need
not, and of course often do not, always completely understand each other;
biologists more often than not will have a pretty hazy idea of contemporary
physics; but there are common attitudes, common standards and patterns of
behaviour, common approaches and assumptions. This goes surprisingly
wide and deep. It cuts across other mental patterns, such as those of religion
or politics or class.

Statistically, I suppose slightly more scientists are in religious terms 21
unbelievers, compared with the rest of the intellectual world—though there
are plenty who are religious, and that seems to be increasingly so among the
young. Statistically also, slightly more scientists are on the Left in open
politics—though again, plenty always have called themselves conservatives,
and that also seems to be more common among the young. Compared with
the rest of the intellectual world, considerably more scientists in this country
and probably in the U.S. come from poor families.[5] Yet over a whole range
of thought and behaviour, none of that matters very much. In their working,
and in much of their emotional life, their attitudes are closer to other scientists
than to non-scientists who in religion or politics or class have the same labels

as themselves. If I were to risk a piece of shorthand, I should say that naturally they had the future in their bones.

They may or may not like it, but they have it. That was as true of the 22 conservatives J. J. Thomson and Lindemann as of the radicals Einstein or Blackett: as true of the Christian A. H. Compton as of the materialist Bernal: of the aristocrats de Broglie or Russell as of the proletarian Faraday: of those born rich, like Thomas Merton or Victor Rothschild, as of Rutherford, who was the son of an odd-job handyman. Without thinking about it, they respond alike. That is what a culture means.*

At the other pole, the spread of attitudes is wider. It is obvious that 23 between the two, as one moves through intellectual society from the physicists to the literary intellectuals, there are all kinds of tones of feeling on the way. But I believe the pole of total incomprehension of science radiates its influence on all the rest. That total incomprehension gives, much more pervasively than we realise, living in it, an unscientific flavour to the whole "traditional" culture, and that unscientific flavour is often, much more than we admit, on the point of turning anti-scientific. The feelings of one pole become the anti-feelings of the other. If the scientists have the future in their bones, then the traditional culture responds by wishing the future did not exist.[6] It is the traditional culture, to an extent remarkably little diminished by the emergence of the scientific one, which manages the western world.

This polarisation is sheer loss to us all. To us as people, and to our 24 society. It is at the same time a practical and intellectual and creative loss, and I repeat that it is false to imagine that those three considerations are clearly separable. But for a moment I want to concentrate on the intellectual loss.

The degree of incomprehension on both sides is the kind of joke which 25 has gone sour. There are about fifty thousand working scientists in the country and about eighty thousand professional engineers or applied scientists. During the war and in the years since, my colleagues and I have had to interview somewhere between thirty to forty thousand of these—that is, about 25 per cent. The number is large enough to give us a fair sample, though of the men we talked to most would still be under forty. We were able to find out a certain amount of what they read and thought about. I confess that even I, who am fond of them and respect them, was a bit shaken. We hadn't quite expected that the links with the traditional culture should be so tenuous, nothing more than a formal touch of the cap.

As one would expect, some of the very best scientists had and have 26 plenty of energy and interest to spare, and we came across several who had read everything that literary people talk about. But that's very rare. Most of the rest, when one tried to probe for what books they had read, would modestly confess, "Well, I've *tried* a bit of Dickens," rather as though Dickens were an extraordinarily esoteric, tangled and dubiously rewarding writer, something like Rainer Maria Rilke. In fact that is exactly how they do regard

---

*In other words, differences of social class, political leaning, and wealth among the scientists are all outweighed by common attitudes about the future based on scientific aspirations and outlook.

him: we thought that discovery, that Dickens had been transformed into the type-specimen of literary incomprehensibility, was one of the oddest results of the whole exercise.*

But of course, in reading him, in reading almost any writer whom we 27 should value, they are just touching their caps to the traditional culture. They have their own culture, intensive, rigorous, and constantly in action. This culture contains a great deal of argument, usually much more rigorous, and almost always at a higher conceptual level, than literary persons' arguments— even though the scientists do cheerfully use words in senses which literary persons don't recognise, the senses are exact ones, and when they talk about "subjective," "objective," "philosophy" or "progressive,"[7] they know what they mean, even though it isn't what one is accustomed to expect.

Remember, these are very intelligent men. Their culture is in many ways 28 an exacting and admirable one. It doesn't contain much art, with the exception, an important exception, of music. Verbal exchange, insistent argument. Long-playing records. Colour-photography. The ear, to some extent the eye. Books, very little, though perhaps not many would go so far as one hero, who perhaps I should admit was further down the scientific ladder than the people I've been talking about—who, when asked what books he read, replied firmly and confidently: "Books? I prefer to use my books as tools." It was very hard not to let the mind wander—what sort of tool would a book make? Perhaps a hammer? A primitive digging instrument?

Of books, though, very little. And of the books which to most literary 29 persons are bread and butter, novels, history, poetry, plays, almost nothing at all. It isn't that they're not interested in the psychological or moral or social life. In the social life, they certainly are, more than most of us. In the moral, they are by and large the soundest group of intellectuals we have; there is a moral component right in the grain of science itself, and almost all scientists form their own judgments of the moral life. In the psychological they have as much interest as most of us, though occasionally I fancy they come to it rather late. It isn't that they lack the interests. It is much more that the whole literature of the traditional culture doesn't seem to them relevant to those interests. They are, of course, dead wrong. As a result, their imaginative understanding is less than it could be. They are self-impoverished.

But what about the other side? They are impoverished too—perhaps 30 more seriously, because they are vainer about it. They still like to pretend that the traditional culture is the whole of "culture," as though the natural order didn't exist.† As though the exploration of the natural order was of no interest either in its own value or its consequences. As though the scientific edifice of the physical world was not, in its intellectual depth, complexity and articulation, the most beautiful and wonderful collective work of the mind

---

*This was "the oddest result" because Dickens is the last writer who could be justifiably accused or accurately described as being artistically incomprehensible. He was the most popularly admired and widely read author of the nineteenth century. Calling Dickens esoteric is like calling elevator music experimental.

†By "the natural order" he simply means "nature."

of man. Yet most non-scientists have no conception of that edifice at all. Even if they want to have it, they can't. It is rather as though, over an immense range of intellectual experience, a whole group was tone-deaf. Except that this tone-deafness doesn't come by nature, but by training, or rather the absence of training.

As with the tone-deaf, they don't know what they miss. They give a 31 pitying chuckle at the news of scientists who have never read a major work of English literature. They dismiss them as ignorant specialists. Yet their own ignorance and their own specialisation is just as startling. A good many times I have been present at gatherings of people who, by the standards of the traditional culture, are thought highly educated and who have with considerable gusto been expressing their incredulity at the illiteracy of scientists. Once or twice I have been provoked and have asked the company how many of them could describe the Second Law of Thermodynamics. The response was cold: it was also negative. Yet I was asking something which is about the scientific equivalent of: *Have you read a work of Shakespeare's?*

I now believe that if I had asked an even simpler question—such as, 32 What do you mean by mass, or acceleration, which is the scientific equivalent of saying, *Can you read?*—not more than one in ten of the highly educated would have felt that I was speaking the same language. So the great edifice of modern physics goes up, and the majority of the cleverest people in the western world have about as much insight into it as their neolithic ancestors would have had.

Just one more of those questions, that my non-scientific friends regard 33 as being in the worst of taste. Cambridge is a university where scientists and non-scientists meet every night at dinner.[8] About two years ago, one of the most astonishing discoveries in the whole history of science was brought off. I don't mean the Sputnik*—that was admirable for quite different reasons, as a feat of organisation and a triumphant use of existing knowledge. No, I mean the discovery at Columbia by Yang and Lee. It is a piece of work of the greatest beauty and originality, but the result is so startling that one forgets how beautiful the thinking is. It makes us think again about some of the fundamentals of the physical world. Intuition, common sense—they are neatly stood on their heads. The result is usually known as the non-conservation of parity.† If there were any serious communication between the two cultures, this experiment would have been talked about at every High Table in Cambridge. Was it? I wasn't here: but I should like to ask the question.

There seems then to be no place where the cultures meet. I am not going 34 to waste time saying that this is a pity. It is much worse than that. Soon I shall come to some practical consequences. But at the heart of thought and creation

---

*In 1958 the Russians put the first man-made satellite, *Sputnik,* into orbit around the earth.

†Tsung-Dao Lee (b. 1926) and Chen Ning Yang (b. 1922) devised a set of experiments in 1956 that led to extensive revisions of basic theory in atomic and sub-atomic physics. For their accomplishments, generally known as the non-conservation of parity, they were awarded the Nobel Prize for physics in 1957.

we are letting some of our best chances go by default. The clashing point of two subjects, two disciplines, two cultures—of two galaxies, so far as that goes—ought to produce creative chances. In the history of mental activity that has been where some of the break-throughs came. The chances are there now. But they are there, as it were, in a vacuum, because those in the two cultures can't talk to each other. It is bizarre how very little of twentieth-century science has been assimilated into twentieth-century art. Now and then one used to find poets conscientiously using scientific expressions, and getting them wrong—there was a time when "refraction" kept cropping up in verse in a mystifying fashion, and when "polarised light" was used as though writers were under the illusion that it was a specially admirable kind of light.

Of course, that isn't the way that science could be any good to art. It 35 has got to be assimilated along with, and as part and parcel of, the whole of our mental experience, and used as naturally as the rest.

I said earlier that this cultural divide is not just an English phenomenon: 36 it exists all over the western world. But it probably seems at its sharpest in England, for two reasons. One is our fanatical belief in educational specialisation, which is much more deeply ingrained in us than in any country in the world, west or east. The other is our tendency to let our social forms crystallise. This tendency appears to get stronger, not weaker, the more we iron out economic inequalities: and this is specially true in education. It means that once anything like a cultural divide gets established, all the social forces operate to make it not less rigid, but more so.

The two cultures were already dangerously separate sixty years ago; but 37 a prime minister like Lord Salisbury could have his own laboratory at Hatfield, and Arthur Balfour had a somewhat more than amateur interest in natural science. John Anderson* did some research in inorganic chemistry in Leipzig before passing first into the Civil Service, and incidentally took a spread of subjects which is now impossible.[9] None of that degree of interchange at the top of the Establishment is likely, or indeed thinkable, now.[10]

In fact, the separation between the scientists and non-scientists is much 38 less bridgeable among the young than it was even thirty years ago. Thirty years ago the cultures had long ceased to speak to each other: but at least they managed a kind of frozen smile across the gulf. Now the politeness has gone, and they just make faces. It is not only that the young scientists now feel that they are part of a culture on the rise while the other is in retreat. It is also, to be brutal, that the young scientists know that with an indifferent degree they'll get a comfortable job, while their contemporaries and counterparts in English or History will be lucky to earn 60 per cent as much. No young scientist of any talent would feel that he isn't wanted or that his work is ridiculous, as did the hero of *Lucky Jim,* and in fact, some of the disgruntlement

*John Anderson (1882–1958) was chancellor of the exchequer, 1943–1945.

of Amis* and his associates is the disgruntlement of the under-employed arts graduate.

There is only one way out of all this: it is, of course, by rethinking our education. In this country, for the two reasons I have given, that is more difficult than in any other. Nearly everyone will agree that our school education is too specialised. But nearly everyone feels that it is outside the will of man to alter it. Other countries are as dissatisfied with their education as we are, but are not so resigned.

The U.S. teach out of proportion more children up to eighteen than we do: they teach them far more widely, but nothing like so rigorously. They know that: they are hoping to take the problem in hand within ten years, though they may not have all that time to spare. The U.S.S.R. also teach out of proportion more children than we do: they also teach far more widely than we do (it is an absurd western myth that their school education is specialised) but much too rigorously.[11] They know that—and they are beating about to get it right. The Scandinavians, in particular the Swedes, who would make a more sensible job of it than any of us, are handicapped by their practical need to devote an inordinate amount of time to foreign languages. But they too are seized of the problem.

Are we? Have we crystallised so far that we are no longer flexible at all?

Talk to schoolmasters, and they say that our intense specialisation, like nothing else on earth, is dictated by the Oxford and Cambridge scholarship examinations. If that is so, one would have thought it not utterly impracticable to change the Oxford and Cambridge scholarship examinations. Yet one would underestimate the national capacity for the intricate defensive to believe that that was easy. All the lessons of our educational history suggest we are only capable of increasing specialisation, not decreasing it.

Somehow we have set ourselves the task of producing a tiny *élite*—far smaller proportionately than in any comparable country—educated in one academic skill. For a hundred and fifty years in Cambridge it was mathematics: then it was mathematics or classics: then natural science was allowed in. But still the choice had to be a single one.

It may well be that this process has gone too far to be reversible. I have given reasons why I think it is a disastrous process, for the purpose of a living culture. I am going on to give reasons why I think it is fatal, if we're to perform our practical tasks in the world. But I can think of only one example, in the whole of English educational history, where our pursuit of specialised mental exercises was resisted with success.

It was done here in Cambridge, fifty years ago, when the old order-of-merit in the Mathematical Tripos† was abolished. For over a hundred years, the nature of the Tripos had been crystallising. The competition for the top

*Kingsley Amis's novel *Lucky Jim* (1953) satirizes the stuffiness and provinciality of the English educational system. The hero is a historian, not a scientist, and part of his problem is that he can't get a job.

†The Mathematical Tripos was the final examination instituted in the first half of the eighteenth century for honors in mathematics.

places had got fiercer, and careers hung on them. In most colleges, certainly in my own, if one managed to come out as Senior or Second Wrangler, one was elected a Fellow out of hand. A whole apparatus of coaching had grown up. Men of the quality of Hardy, Littlewood, Russell, Eddington, Jeans, Keynes, went in for two or three years' training for an examination which was intensely competitive and intensely difficult. Most people in Cambridge were very proud of it, with a similar pride to that which almost anyone in England always has for our existing educational institutions, whatever they happen to be. If you study the flysheets of the time,* you will find the passionate arguments for keeping the examination precisely as it was to all eternity: it was the only way to keep up standards, it was the only fair test of merit, indeed, the only seriously objective test in the world. The arguments, in fact, were almost exactly those which are used today with precisely the same passionate sincerity if anyone suggests that the scholarship examinations might conceivably not be immune from change.

In every respect but one, in fact, the old Mathematical Tripos seemed 46 perfect. The one exception, however, appeared to some to be rather important. It was simply—so the young creative mathematicians, such as Hardy and Littlewood, kept saying—that the [Tripos] had no intellectual merit at all. They went a little further, and said that the Tripos had killed serious mathematics in England stone dead for a hundred years. Well, even in academic controversy, that took some skirting round, and they got their way. But I have an impression that Cambridge was a good deal more flexible between 1850 and 1914 than it has been in our time. If we had had the old Mathematical Tripos firmly planted among us, should we have ever managed to abolish it?

NOTES

All notes are Snow's.

1. "The Two Cultures," *New Statesman,* 6 October 1956.

2. This lecture was delivered to a Cambridge audience, and so I used some points of reference which I did not need to explain. G. H. Hardy, 1877–1947, was one of the most distinguished pure mathematicians of his time, and a picturesque figure in Cambridge both as a young don and on his return in 1931 to the Sadleirian Chair of Mathematics.

3. I said a little more about this connection in *The Times Literary Supplement,* "Challenge to the Intellect," 15 August 1958. I hope some day to carry the analysis further.

4. It would be more accurate to say that, for literary reasons, we felt the prevailing literary modes were useless to us. We were, however, reinforced in that feeling when it occurred to us that those prevailing modes went hand in hand with social attitudes either wicked, or absurd, or both.

5. An analysis of the schools from which Fellows of the Royal Society come tells its own story. The distribution is markedly different from that of, for example, members of the Foreign Service or Queen's Counsel.

6. Compare George Orwell's *1984,* which is the strongest possible wish that the future should not exist, with J. D. Bernal's *World Without War.*

*A flysheet is a small, loose advertising sheet, like a handbill; in this case it refers to campus leaflets espousing particular points of view.

7. *Subjective*, in contemporary technological jargon, means "divided according to subjects." *Objective* means "directed towards an object." *Philosophy* means "general intellectual approach or attitude" (for example, a scientist's "philosophy of guided weapons" might lead him to propose certain kinds of "objective research"). A "progressive" job means one with possibilities of promotion.

8. Almost all college High Tables contain Fellows in both scientific and non-scientific subjects.

9. He took the examination in 1905.

10. It is, however, true to say that the compact nature of the managerial layers of English society—the fact that "everyone knows everyone else"—means that scientists and non-scientists do in fact know each other as people more easily than in most countries. It is also true that a good many leading politicians and administrators keep up lively intellectual and artistic interests to a much greater extent, so far as I can judge, than is the case in the U.S. These are both among our assets.

11. I tried to compare American, Soviet and English education in "New Minds for the New World," *New Statesman*, 6 September 1956.

Questions for Discussion

1. Poll your class to see if the "two cultures" split is visible within it. Are the people who prefer humanities courses also fond of or excited by science courses? And vice versa? How many people enjoy switching back and forth equally?

2. In 1802 William Wordsworth (1770–1850), Romantic poet, wrote in his preface to *Lyrical Ballads:*

   > The knowledge both of the poet and the man of science is pleasure; but the knowledge of the one cleaves to us as a necessary part of our existence, our natural and unalienable inheritance; the other is a personal and individual acquisition, slow to come to us, and by no habitual and direct sympathy connecting us with our fellow-beings. The man of science seeks truth as a remote and unknown benefactor; he cherishes and loves it in his solitude: the poet, singing a song in which all human beings join with him, rejoices in the presence of truth as our visible friend and hourly companion. Poetry is the breath and finer spirit of all knowledge; it is the impassioned expression which is in the countenance of all science.

   Discuss with your classmates what you think this passage means and whether you think it is true. Is Wordsworth privileging literary culture over scientific culture? Or does he simply see each kind of culture as covering a different domain of human knowledge and experience? Support your views with the best reasons you can create.

3. In 1821, a few years after Wordsworth wrote his preface, another Romantic poet, Percy Shelley (1792–1822), also undertook to compare literary culture with scientific culture in *A Defence of Poetry*. Looking about him at a world in which industrialization and economic expansion seemed to be impoverishing at least as many people as it was enriching, he observed:

   > We have more moral, political and historical wisdom, than we know how to reduce into practice; we have more scientific and economical knowl-

edge than can be accommodated to the just distribution of the produce which it multiplies. The poetry in these systems of thought, is concealed by the accumulation of facts and calculating processes. . . . We want [i.e., lack] the creative faculty to imagine that which we know; we want the generous impulse to act that which we imagine; we want the poetry of life: our calculations have outrun conception; we have eaten more than we can digest. The cultivation of those sciences which have enlarged the limits of the empire of man over the external world, has, for want of the poetical faculty, proportionally circumscribed those of the internal world; and man, having enslaved the elements, remains himself a slave.

Is Shelley being fair to science by implying that the means by which men are making themselves rich are also impoverishing their social sympathies? Can you think of examples in which science has been used both ways—that is, to alleviate human suffering and to create it at the same time? And if both kinds of examples are plentiful, is science's failings the fault of science or of something else? If something else, what?

4. Twelve years after Shelley's *Defence,* in 1833, John Stuart Mill (1806–1873)—philosopher, logician, and economist—wrote an essay called "What Is Poetry?" in which he asserts that the opposite of poetry is

not prose, but matter of fact, or science. The one addresses itself to the belief; the other, to the feelings. The one does its work by convincing or persuading; the other, by moving. The one acts by presenting a proposition to the understanding; the other, by offering interesting objects of contemplation to the sensibilities.

How readily do you think this view of literary culture contributes to the popular notion that artists are impractical and irrational, guided by emotions and impulse rather than facts? Is this cliché true? Can you think of examples that contest it? Examples that support it? What do you think is the truth of the matter? Give reasons.

5. Fifty years after Mill's essay, in 1882, Matthew Arnold (1822–1888), poet and essayist, maintained in an essay titled "Literature and Science" (see Chapter 2) that science yields important and true knowledge but cannot tell us what to do with such knowledge, cannot tell us how to relate it to the arenas of conduct and behavior. The humanities, he claims, are necessary for making these connections and therefore cannot be allowed to decline as science advances.

Interesting, indeed, these results of science are, important they are, and we should all of us be acquainted with them. But what I now wish you to mark is, that we are still, when they are propounded and we receive them, we are still in the sphere of intellect and knowledge. And for the generality of men there will be found, I say, to arise, when they have duly taken in the proposition that their ancestor was "a hairy quadruped furnished with a tail and pointed ears, probably arboreal in his habits," there will be found to arise an invincible desire to relate this proposition to the sense in us for conduct, and to the sense in us for beauty. But this the men of science will not do for us, and will hardly even profess to do. They will give us other pieces of knowledge, other facts, about other animals and their ancestors, or about plants, or about stones, or about stars; and they may finally bring us to those great "general conceptions of the universe, which are forced upon us all," says Professor Huxley, "by the progress of physical science." But still it will be *knowledge* only which they give us; knowledge not put for us into relation with our sense for conduct, our sense for beauty, and touched with emotion by being so put; not thus put for us, and therefore, to the majority of mankind, after a certain while, unsatisfying, wearying.

As you sit day after day in your college courses, do you ever experience the feeling that Arnold here attributes to "the generality of men," the feeling that you are learning more than you know how to use, more than you know the worth of, more than you can relate to the other pieces of knowledge you are learning in other classes? If so, has Arnold put the case accurately for you, or would you put the emphasis in different places? And what about the sense of beauty Arnold alludes to? What do you take him to mean by this? Do you need the sense that knowledge has to be somehow turned to the beautification of life before it has earned its way in the world? Can you provide examples one way or the other? How would you define *beauty* in this context?

6. After reading these selections by nineteenth-century figures on humanistic versus scientific culture, what changes, if any, in your view of Snow's version of the two cultures have been created? Is it possible that the two cultures he sees were at least a century in the making? How could you corroborate this statement by referring to the quotations? What counterexamples could you provide?

7. Some critics have noted that Snow's analysis simply ignores many areas of modern thought, particularly the social sciences. He has little to say about history, sociology, anthropology, and political science. Where do you think he would place these subjects, if he did include them in his twofold scheme? Do you think his analysis would have to be greatly modified if he wrote an essay on "the *three* cultures"?

Suggested Essay Topics

1. At the time of Snow's essay in the 1950s, he was right to see the humanists and scientists as constituting the two dominant constituencies in the university, but today there is another constituency separate from these two traditional groups: the people in the professional or pre-professional schools. People getting degrees in business, pharmacy, dance, theater, communications, and many other fields are in neither the humanities nor the sciences. The question is, should they be, or at least should they be made to learn enough about the humanities and sciences as to achieve a minimal kind of literacy in both?

   In an essay directed to your classmates, answer these questions with the best reasons you can find for either forcing people in professional programs to take humanities and science courses or exempting them from such requirements. State what you think the minimal requirements should be, and make clear what your criteria for "minimal" are. If, for example, you would only require them to take, say, three hours of literature, say why that is enough. Enough in relation to what?

2. Write an essay to your instructor in which you attack or support Arnold's claim that the knowledge of science cannot be related to the questions we most want answers to—questions about how to live, how to make life meaningful or beautiful—and that scientific knowledge will therefore always remain incomplete unless complemented by knowledge from the humanities (and possibly other sources as well).

Loren Eiseley

Loren Eiseley (1907–1977) both admits and contests C. P. Snow's assertion that the humanities and sciences form two antagonistic, mutually unintelligible cultures in today's world. He admits that as an institution, as a profession, science has separated itself from the methods and insights of religion, art, and speculation—the areas of human creativity studied by the humanities. He even provides examples of this split, as when he tells of the young science colleague who, when he finds Eiseley reading J. R. R. Tolkien, sneers, "I wouldn't waste my time with a man who writes fairy stories." (¶7) Eiseley is clear that science has become "a professional body, and with professionalism there tends to emerge a greater emphasis upon a coherent system of regulations" (¶20) that produce a "deliberate blunting of wonder" (¶19).

But Eiseley is also clear that this division is a product of misunderstanding, that it occurs only at superficial levels within both humanistic and scientific activity. It is an illusion—a dangerous illusion with potentially disastrous consequences, to be sure—but an illusion nevertheless. The molds that the humanists and scientists cast each other in, Eiseley says, "are always useful to the mediocre conformist" (¶22)— useful, that is, to the thinker who has no sense of wonder, no personal vision, and therefore nothing original to say. But "happily," he continues later, "the very great in science . . . have been singularly free of this folly" (¶38), and he goes on to cite Leonardo da Vinci, Newton, Darwin, and Einstein as great scientific thinkers who all "retained a simple sense of wonder . . . [and who] all show a deep humility and an emotional hunger which is the prerogative of the artist" (¶38). "Creation in science," says Eiseley, "demands a high level of imaginative insight and intuitive perception" (¶25), which leaves us free to conclude, as indeed Eiseley implies, that the fence building, sloganeering, and sneering that go on between the mediocre professionals in both cultures are the opposite of creative. Such hostility is stultifying and deadening, and it leads to that curious feature of the modern mind noted by Santayana, the mind that has "seemed to lose courage and to become ashamed of its own fertility" (¶3).

As you read, ask yourself how much the conformist molds seem to characterize the thinking about scientists and humanists at your college or university. How much, and how uncritically, have you accepted such polarized, cliché-ridden thinking yourself? It would be odd if you had not accepted it, for, as both Snow and Eiseley agree, it pervades much of the thinking today not only about scientists and humanists but by scientists and humanists. Finally, ask yourself whether Snow and Eiseley have given you good reasons for re-thinking any prejudices you may have held and in what ways your education and society at large would both benefit if the rift between the two cultures were closed.

THE ILLUSION OF
THE TWO CULTURES

From *The American Scholar* (1964) and *The Star Thrower* (1978).

Not long ago an English scientist, Sir Eric Ashby, remarked that "to train young people in the dialectic between orthodoxy and dissent is the unique contribution which universities make to society." I am sure that Sir Eric meant by this remark that nowhere but in universities are the young given the opportunity to absorb past tradition and at the same time to experience the impact of new ideas—in the sense of a constant dialogue between past and present—lived in every hour of the student's existence. This dialogue, ideally, should lead to a great winnowing and sifting of experience and to a heightened consciousness of self which, in turn, should lead on to greater sensitivity and perception on the part of the individual.

Our lives are the creation of memory and the accompanying power to extend ourselves outward into ideas and relive them. The finest intellect is that which employs an invisible web of gossamer running into the past as well as across the minds of living men and which constantly responds to the vibrations transmitted through these tenuous lines of sympathy. It would be contrary to fact, however, to assume that our universities always perform this unique function of which Sir Eric speaks, with either grace or perfection; in fact our investment in man, it has been justly remarked, is deteriorating even as the financial investment in science grows.

More than thirty years ago, George Santayana* had already sensed this trend. He commented, in a now-forgotten essay, that one of the strangest consequences of modern science was that as the visible wealth of nature was more and more transferred and abstracted, the mind seemed to lose courage and to become ashamed of its own fertility. "The hard-pressed natural man will not indulge his imagination," continued Santayana, "unless it poses for truth; and being half-aware of this imposition, he is more troubled at the thought of being deceived than at the fact of being mechanized or being bored; and he would wish to escape imagination altogether."

*George Santayana (1863–1952), Spanish-American poet and philosopher and Harvard professor.

"Man would wish to escape imagination altogether." I repeat that last   4
phrase, for it defines a peculiar aberration of the human mind found on both
sides of that bipolar division between the humanities and the sciences, which
C. P. Snow has popularized under the title of *The Two Cultures.* The idea is not
solely a product of this age. It was already emerging with the science of the
seventeenth century; one finds it in Bacon.* One finds the fear of it faintly
foreshadowed in Thoreau. Thomas Huxley† lent it weight when he referred
contemptuously to the "caterwauling of poets."

Ironically, professional scientists berated the early evolutionists such as   5
Lamarck and Chambers for overindulgence in the imagination. Almost eighty
years ago John Burroughs observed that some of the animus once directed by
science toward dogmatic theology seemed in his day increasingly to be vented
upon the literary naturalist. In the early 1900s a quarrel over "nature faking"
raised a confused din in America and aroused W. H. Hudson to some dry and
pungent comment upon the failure to distinguish the purposes of science
from those of literature. I know of at least one scholar who, venturing to
develop some personal ideas in an essay for the layman, was characterized by
a reviewer in a leading professional journal as a worthless writer, although,
as it chanced, the work under discussion had received several awards in
literature, one of them international in scope. More recently, some scholars
not indifferent to humanistic values have exhorted poets to leave their personal songs in order to portray the beauty and symmetry of molecular structures.

Now some very fine verse has been written on scientific subjects, but,   6
I fear, very little under the dictate of scientists as such. Rather there is evident
here precisely that restriction of imagination against which Santayana in-
veighed; namely, an attempt to constrain literature itself to the delineation
of objective or empiric truth, and to dismiss the whole domain of value,
which after all constitutes the very nature of man, as without significance and
beneath contempt.

Unconsciously, the human realm is denied in favor of the world of pure   7
technics. Man, the tool user, grows convinced that he is himself only useful
as a tool, that fertility except in the use of the scientific imagination is
wasteful and without purpose, even, in some indefinable way, sinful. I was
reading J. R. R. Tolkien's great symbolic trilogy, *The Fellowship of the Ring,* a few
months ago, when a young scientist of my acquaintance paused and looked
over my shoulder. After a little casual interchange the man departed leaving
an accusing remark hovering in the air between us. "I wouldn't waste my time
with a man who writes fairy stories." He might as well have added, "or with
a man who reads them."

As I went back to my book I wondered vaguely in what leafless land-   8

*Francis Bacon (1561–1626), philosopher and author whose works were instrumental in further-
ing the development of modern science.
†Thomas Henry Huxley (1825–1895), English biologist, best known in his own day as "Darwin's
bulldog" for his spirited defense and popularization of evolutionary theory.

scape one grew up without Hans Christian Andersen, or Dunsany, or even
Jules Verne.* There lingered about the young man's words a puritanism
which seemed the more remarkable because, as nearly as I could discover, it
was unmotivated by any sectarian religiosity unless a total dedication to
science brings to some minds a similar authoritarian desire to shackle the
human imagination. After all, it is this impossible, fertile world of our imagination which gave birth to liberty in the midst of oppression, and which
persists in seeking until what is sought is seen. Against such invisible and
fearful powers, there can be found in all ages and in all institutions—even the
institutions of professional learning—the humorless man with the sneer, or
if the sneer does not suffice, then the torch, for the bright unperishing letters
of the human dream.

One can contrast this recalcitrant attitude with an 1890 reminiscence 9
from that great Egyptologist Sir Flinders Petrie, which steals over into the
realm of pure literature. It was written, in unconscious symbolism, from a
tomb:

"I here live, and do not scramble to fit myself to the requirements of 10
others. In a narrow tomb, with the figure of Néfermaat standing on each side
of me—as he has stood through all that we know as human history—I have
just room for my bed, and a row of good reading in which I can take pleasure
after dinner. Behind me is that Great Peace, the Desert. It is an entity—a
power—just as much as the sea is. No wonder men fled to it from the turmoil
of the ancient world."

It may now reasonably be asked why one who has similarly, if less 11
dramatically, spent his life among the stones and broken shards of the remote
past should be writing here about matters involving literature and science.
While I was considering this with humility and trepidation, my eye fell upon
a stone in my office. I am sure that professional journalists must recall times
when an approaching deadline has keyed all their senses and led them to
glance wildly around in the hope that something might leap out at them from
the most prosaic surroundings. At all events my eyes fell upon this stone.

Now the stone antedated anything that the historians would call art; it 12
had been shaped many hundreds of thousands of years ago by men whose
faces would frighten us if they sat among us today. Out of old habit, since
I like the feel of worked flint, I picked it up and hefted it as I groped for words
over this difficult matter of the growing rift between science and art. Certainly the stone was of no help to me; it was a utilitarian thing which had
cracked marrow bones, if not heads, in the remote dim morning of the human
species. It was nothing if not practical. It was, in fact, an extremely early
example of the empirical tradition which has led on to modern science.

The mind which had shaped this artifact knew its precise purpose. It 13
had found out by experimental observation that the stone was tougher,
sharper, more enduring than the hand which wielded it. The creature's mind

*Andersen (1805–1875), Edward Plunkett (1878–1957), eighteenth baron of Dunsany, and Verne
(1828–1905) were all writers of fairy tales or adventure stories popular with children.

had solved the question of the best form of the implement and how it could be manipulated most effectively. In its day and time this hand ax was as grand an intellectual achievement as a rocket.

As a scientist my admiration went out to that unidentified workman. How he must have labored to understand the forces involved in the fracturing of flint, and all that involved practical survival in his world. My uncalloused twentieth-century hand caressed the yellow stone lovingly. It was then that I made a remarkable discovery.

In the mind of this gross-featured early exponent of the practical approach to nature—the technician, the no-nonsense practitioner of survival— two forces had met and merged. There had not been room in his short and desperate life for the delicate and supercilious separation of the arts from the sciences. There did not exist then the refined distinctions set up between the scholarly percipience of reality and what has sometimes been called the vaporings of the artistic imagination.

As I clasped and unclasped the stone, running my fingers down its edges, I began to perceive the ghostly emanations from a long-vanished mind, the kind of mind which, once having shaped an object of any sort, leaves an individual trace behind it which speaks to others across the barriers of time and language. It was not the practical experimental aspect of this mind that startled me, but rather that the fellow had wasted time.

In an incalculably brutish and dangerous world he had both shaped an instrument of practical application and then, with a virtuoso's elegance, proceeded to embellish his product. He had not been content to produce a plain, utilitarian implement. In some wistful, inarticulate way, in the grip of the dim aesthetic feelings which are one of the marks of man—or perhaps I should say, some men—this archaic creature had lingered over his handiwork.

One could still feel him crouching among the stones on a long-vanished river bar, turning the thing over in his hands, feeling its polished surface, striking, here and there, just one more blow that no longer had usefulness as its criterion. He had, like myself, enjoyed the texture of the stone. With skills lost to me, he had gone on flaking the implement with an eye to beauty until it had become a kind of rough jewel, equivalent in its day to the carved and gold-inlaid pommel of the iron dagger placed in Tutankhamen's tomb.

All the later history of man contains these impractical exertions expended upon a great diversity of objects, and, with literacy, breaking even into printed dreams. Today's secular disruption between the creative aspect of art and that of science is a barbarism that would have brought lifted eyebrows in a Cro-Magnon cave. It is a product of high technical specialization, the deliberate blunting of wonder, and the equally deliberate suppression of a phase of our humanity in the name of an authoritarian institution, science, which has taken on, in our time, curious puritanical overtones. Many scientists seem unaware of the historical reasons for this development or the fact that the creative aspect of art is not so remote from that of science as may seem, at first glance, to be the case.

I am not so foolish as to categorize individual scholars or scientists. I am, however, about to remark on the nature of science as an institution. Like all such structures it is apt to reveal certain behavioral rigidities and conformities which increase with age. It is no longer the domain of the amateur, though some of its greatest discoverers could be so defined. It is now a professional body, and with professionalism there tends to emerge a greater emphasis upon a coherent system of regulations. The deviant is more sharply treated, and the young tend to imitate their successful elders. In short, an "Establishment"—a trade union—has appeared.

Similar tendencies can be observed among those of the humanities   21
concerned with the professional analysis and interpretation of the works of the creative artist. Here too, a similar rigidity and exclusiveness make their appearance. It is not that in the case of both the sciences and the humanities standards are out of place. What I am briefly cautioning against is that too frequently they afford an excuse for stifling original thought or constricting much latent creativity within traditional molds.

Such molds are always useful to the mediocre conformist who instinc-   22
tively castigates and rejects what he cannot imitate. Tradition, the continuity of learning, are, it is true, enormously important to the learned disciplines. What we must realize as scientists is that the particular institution we inhabit has its own irrational accretions and authoritarian dogmas which can be as unpleasant as some of those encountered in sectarian circles—particularly so since they are frequently unconsciously held and surrounded by an impenetrable wall of self-righteousness brought about because science is regarded as totally empiric and open-minded by tradition.

This type of professionalism, as I shall label it in order to distinguish   23
it from what is best in both the sciences and humanities, is characterized by two assumptions: that the accretions of fact are cumulative and lead to progress, whereas the insights of art are, at best, singular, and lead nowhere, or, when introduced into the realm of science, produce obscurity and confusion. The convenient label "mystic" is, in our day, readily applied to men who pause for simple wonder, or who encounter along the borders of the known that "awful power" which Wordsworth characterized as the human imagination. It can, he says, rise suddenly from the mind's abyss and enwrap the solitary traveler like a mist.

We do not like mists in this era, and the word imagination is less and   24
less used. We like, instead, a clear road, and we abhor solitary traveling. Indeed one of our great scientific historians remarked not long ago that the literary naturalist was obsolescent if not completely outmoded. I suppose he meant that with our penetration into the biophysical realm, life, like matter, would become increasingly represented by abstract symbols. To many it must appear that the more we can dissect life into its elements, the closer we are getting to its ultimate resolution. While I have some reservations on this score, they are not important. Rather, I should like to look at the symbols which in the one case denote science and in the other constitute those vaporings and cloud wraiths that are the abomination, so it is said, of the true scientist but are the delight of the poet and literary artist.

Creation in science demands a high level of imaginative insight and 25
intuitive perception. I believe no one would deny this, even though it exists
in varying degrees, just as it does, similarly, among writers, musicians, or
artists. The scientist's achievement, however, is quantitatively transmissible.
From a single point his discovery is verifiable by other men who may then,
on the basis of corresponding data, accept the innovation and elaborate upon
it in the cumulative fashion which is one of the great triumphs of science.

Artistic creation, on the other hand, is unique. It cannot be twice dis- 26
covered, as, say, natural selection was discovered. It may be imitated stylistically, in a genre, a school, but, save for a few items of technique, it is not
cumulative. A successful work of art may set up reverberations and is, in
this, just as transmissible as science, but there is a qualitative character
about it. Each reverberation in another mind is unique. As the French novelist François Mauriac has remarked, each great novel is a separate and distinct world operating under its own laws with a flora and fauna totally its
own. There is communication, or the work is a failure, but the communication releases our own visions, touches some highly personal chord in our
own experience.

The symbols used by the great artist are a key releasing our humanity 27
from the solitary tower of the self. "Man," says Lewis Mumford, "is first and
foremost the self-fabricating animal." I shall merely add that the artist plays
an enormous role in this act of self-creation. It is he who touches the hidden
strings of pity, who searches our hearts, who makes us sensitive to beauty,
who asks questions about fate and destiny. Such questions, though they lurk
always around the corners of the external universe which is the peculiar
province of science, the rigors of the scientific method do not enable us to
pursue directly.

And yet I wonder. 28

It is surely possible to observe that it is the successful analogy or symbol 29
which frequently allows the scientist to leap from a generalization in one field
of thought to a triumphant achievement in another. For example, Progres-
sionism in a spiritual sense later became the model contributing to the discovery of organic evolution. Such analogies genuinely resemble the figures and
enchantments of great literature, whose meanings similarly can never be
totally grasped because of their endless power to ramify in the individual
mind.

John Donne gave powerful expression to a feeling applicable as much 30
to science as to literature when he said devoutly of certain Biblical passages:
"The literall sense is always to be preserved; but the literall sense is not
always to be discerned; for the literall sense is not alwayes that which the
very letter and grammar of the place presents." A figurative sense, he argues
cogently, can sometimes be the most "literall intention of the Holy Ghost."

It is here that the scientist and artist sometimes meet in uneasy opposi- 31
tion, or at least along lines of tension. The scientist's attitude is sometimes,
I suspect, that embodied in Samuel Johnson's remark that, wherever there is
mystery, roguery is not far off.

Yet surely it was not roguery when Sir Charles Lyell* glimpsed in a few   32
fossil prints of raindrops the persistence of the world's natural forces through
the incredible, mysterious aeons of geologic time. The fossils were a symbol
of a vast hitherto unglimpsed order. They are, in Donne's sense, both literal
and symbolic. As fossils they merely denote evidence of rain in a past era.
Figuratively they are more. To the perceptive intelligence they afford the hint
of lengthened natural order, just as the eyes of ancient trilobites† tell us
similarly of the unchanging laws of light. Equally, the educated mind may
discern in a scratched pebble the retreating shadow of vast ages of ice and
gloom. In Donne's archaic phraseology these objects would bespeak the principal intention of the Divine Being—that is, of order beyond our power to
grasp.

Such images drawn from the world of science are every bit as powerful   33
as great literary symbolism and equally demanding upon the individual imagination of the scientist who would fully grasp the extension of meaning
which is involved. It is, in fact, one and the same creative act in both domains.

Indeed evolution itself has become such a figurative symbol, as has also   34
the hypothesis of the expanding universe. The laboratory worker may think
of these concepts in a totally empirical fashion as subject to proof or disproof
by the experimental method. Like Freud's doctrine of the subconscious, however, such ideas frequently escape from the professional scientist into the
public domain. There they may undergo further individual transformation
and embellishment. Whether the scholar approves or not, such hypotheses
are now as free to evolve in the mind of the individual as are the creations
of art. All the resulting enrichment and confusion will bear about it something suggestive of the world of artistic endeavor.

As figurative insights into the nature of things, such embracing concep-   35
tions may become grotesquely distorted or glow with added philosophical
wisdom. As in the case of the trilobite eye or the fossil raindrop, there lurks
behind the visible evidence vast shadows no longer quite of that world which
we term natural. Like the words in Donne's Bible, enormous implications
have transcended the literal expression of the thought. Reality itself has been
superseded by a greater reality. As Donne himself asserted, "The substance
of the truth is in the great images which lie behind."

It is because these two types of creation—the artistic and the scien-   36
tific—have sprung from the same being and have their points of contact even
in division that I have the temerity to assert that, in a sense, the "two
cultures" are an illusion, that they are a product of unreasoning fear, professionalism, and misunderstanding. Because of the emphasis upon science in
our society, much has been said about the necessity of educating the layman
and even the professional student of the humanities upon the ways and the
achievements of science. I admit that a barrier exists, but I am also concerned

*Lyell's (1795–1875) *Principles of Geology* (1830–1833) earned him the popular title of "father of
geology."
†Fossils of Paleozoic marine arthropods.

to express the view that there persists in the domain of science itself an occasional marked intolerance of those of its own membership who venture to pursue the way of letters. As I have remarked, this intolerance can the more successfully clothe itself in seeming objectivity because of the supposed open nature of the scientific society. It is not remarkable that this trait is sometimes more manifest in the younger and less secure disciplines.

There was a time, not too many centuries ago, when to be active in 37 scientific investigation was to invite suspicion. Thus it may be that there now lingers among us, even in the triumph of the experimental method, a kind of vague fear of that other artistic world of deep emotion, of strange symbols, lest it seize upon us or distort the hard-won objectivity of our thinking—lest it corrupt, in other words, that crystalline and icy objectivity which, in our scientific guise, we erect as a model of conduct. This model, incidentally, if pursued to its absurd conclusion, would lead to a world in which the computer would determine all aspects of our existence; one in which the bomb would be as welcome as the discoveries of the physician.

Happily, the very great in science, or even those unique scientist-artists 38 such as Leonardo, who foreran the emergence of science as an institution, have been singularly free from this folly. Darwin decried it even as he recognized that he had paid a certain price in concentrated specialization for his achievement. Einstein, it is well known, retained a simple sense of wonder; Newton felt like a child playing with pretty shells on a beach. All show a deep humility and an emotional hunger which is the prerogative of the artist. It is with the lesser men, with the institutionalization of method, with the appearance of dogma and mapped-out territories, that an unpleasant suggestion of fenced preserves begins to dominate the university atmosphere.

As a scientist, I can say that I have observed it in my own and others' 39 specialties. I have had occasion, also, to observe its effects in the humanities. It is not science *per se;* it is, instead, in both regions of thought, the narrow professionalism which is also plainly evident in the trade union. There can be small men in science just as there are small men in government or business. In fact it is one of the disadvantages of big science, just as it is of big government, that the availability of huge sums attracts a swarm of elbowing and contentious men to whom great dreams are less than protected hunting preserves.

The sociology of science deserves at least equal consideration with the 40 biographies of the great scientists, for powerful and changing forces are at work upon science, the institution, as contrasted with science as a dream and an ideal of the individual. Like other aspects of society, it is a construct of men and is subject, like other social structures, to human pressures and inescapable distortions.

Let me give an illustration. Even in learned journals, clashes occasionally 41 occur between those who would regard biology as a separate and distinct domain of inquiry and the reductionists who, by contrast, perceive in the living organism only a vaster and more random chemistry. Understandably, the concern of the reductionists is with the immediate. Thomas Hobbes was expressing a similar point of view when he castigated poets as "working on mean minds with words and distinctions that of themselves signifie nothing, but betray (by their obscurity) that there walketh . . . another kingdome, as it were a kingdome of fayries in the dark." I myself have been similarly criticized for speaking of a nature "beyond the nature that we know."

Yet consider for a moment this dark, impossible realm of "fayrie." Man 42 is not totally compounded of the nature we profess to understand. He contains, instead, a lurking unknown future, just as the man-apes of the Pliocene contained in embryo the future that surrounds us now. The world of human culture itself was an unpredictable fairy world until, in some pre-ice-age meadow, the first meaningful sounds in all the world broke through the jungle babble of the past, the nature, until that moment, "known."

It is fascinating to observe that, in the very dawn of science, Francis 43 Bacon, the spokesman for the empirical approach to nature, shared with Shakespeare, the poet, a recognition of the creativeness which adds to nature, and which emerges from nature as "an art which nature makes." Neither the great scholar nor the great poet had renounced this "kingdome of fayries." Both had realized what Henri Bergson was later to express so effectively, that life inserts a vast "indetermination into matter." It is, in a sense, an intrusion from a realm which can never be completely subject to prophetic analysis by science. The novelties of evolution emerge; they cannot be predicted. They haunt, until their arrival, a world of unimaginable possibilities behind the living screen of events, as these last exist to the observer confined to a single point on the time scale.

Oddly enough, much of the confusion that surrounded my phrase, "a 44 nature beyond the nature that we know," resolves itself into pure semantics. I might have pointed out what must be obvious even to the most dedicated scientific mind—that the nature which we know has been many times reinterpreted in human thinking, and that the hard, substantial matter of the nineteenth century has already vanished into a dark, bodiless void, a web of "events" in space-time.* This is a realm, I venture to assert, as weird as any we have tried, in the past, to exorcise by the brave use of seeming solid words. Yet some minds exhibit an almost instinctive hostility toward the mere attempt to wonder or to ask what lies below that microcosmic world out of which emerge the particles which compose our bodies and which now take on this wraithlike quality.

Is there something here we fear to face, except when clothed in safely 45 sterilized professional speech? Have we grown reluctant in this age of power to admit mystery and beauty into our thoughts, or to learn where power

---

*In nineteenth-century physics, matter was viewed as determinate and predictable. It was thought that when physics finally succeeded in isolating the smallest particle of matter, the ultimate building block of reality would be revealed. Today, however, physics has given up the idea that there *is* an ultimate particle. Reality seems much more mysterious to physics today than it did 100 years ago. The smallest particles seem to be neither solid matter nor electromagnetic waves, yet they sometimes act like both. And the ultimate "facts" in particle physics seem not to be the predictable motion of solid particles but statistically "guessed at" *events*.

ceases? I referred earlier to one of our own forebears on a gravel bar, thumbing a pebble. If, after the ages of building and destroying, if after the measuring of light-years and the powers probed at the atom's heart, if after the last iron is rust-eaten and the last glass lies shattered in the streets, a man, some savage, some remnant of what once we were, pauses on his way to the tribal drinking place and feels rising from within his soul the inexplicable mist of terror and beauty that is evoked from old ruins—even the ruins of the greatest city in the world—then, I say, all will still be well with man.

And if that savage can pluck a stone from the gravel because it shone 46 like crystal when the water rushed over it, and hold it against the sunset, he will be as we were in the beginning, whole—as we were when we were children, before we began to split the knowledge from the dream. All talk of the two cultures is an illusion; it is the pebble which tells man's story. Upon it is written man's two faces, the artistic and the practical. They are expressed upon one stone over which a hand once closed, no less firm because the mind behind it was submerged in light and shadow and deep wonder.

Today we hold a stone, the heavy stone of power. We must perceive 47 beyond it, however, by the aid of the artistic imagination, those humane insights and understandings which alone can lighten our burden and enable us to shape ourselves, rather than the stone, into the forms which great art has anticipated.

Questions for Discussion

1. What logic or principle of development connects the first three paragraphs of Eiseley's essay with paragraph 4, in which he seems to focus on his thesis? What would be gained or lost if the first three paragraphs were dropped?

2. Once you are sure of the meanings of *dialectic, orthodoxy,* and *dissent,* do you agree that "to train young people in the dialectic between orthodoxy and dissent is the unique contribution which universities make to society" (¶1)? Do you feel that this *should* be the aim of university teaching? Why or why not? Do you feel that this aim governs the teaching at your institution? If not, and if you think it should, what obstacles can you identify as blocking that aim? And finally, can you offer any remedies for the removal or at least the mitigation of these obstacles?

3. If you were the editor of this book and wanted to write a footnote explaining Eiseley's meaning in the first two sentences of paragraph 2, how could you make use of Jacob Bronowski's essay "The Reach of Imagination" (Chapter 4) in writing a commentary? Is there a quotation in Bronowski's essay that amplifies and thus helps clarify Eiseley's point? Offer it to the rest of your class for discussion.

4. Do you agree with Santayana that people are so imprisoned by their notions of practicality that "the hard-pressed natural man will not indulge his imagination unless it poses for truth; and being half-aware of this imposition, he is more troubled at the thought of being deceived than at the fact of being mechanized or being bored" (¶3)? Can you provide examples of people who think of imaginative works as, if not downright deceiving, at least not leading to useful truth? How would you use material from the essays by Ursula Le Guin and E. M. Forster (Chapter 4) to help clarify the issues raised in this question?

5. Eiseley's prose offers a flood of allusions to other writers and thinkers, including fairy-tale writers, philosophers, poets, anthropologists, literary critics, and, of course, natural scientists. The richness of his thinking seems directly related to the richness of this wide-ranging reading. How much of your own education is dominated by the desire to acquire something like this richness for yourself, to build it into the quality of your own mind? If this is not a personal goal for you, on what grounds do you reject or neglect it? Do most of your friends and peers hold to this goal? Do your teachers hold to it, either for themselves or for you? Should they? If those who do not hold to this goal were to adopt it, what differences would it make in their teaching and testing?

6. What fundamental traits in human nature does Eiseley see expressed in the decorative (or at least non-utilitarian) markings on the flint ax (¶16)? How does he use these markings as evidence in this argument that the division between the two cultures is merely an illusion?

Suggested Essay Topics

1. If you have ever had any teachers whose prejudiced views about either the sciences or the humanities have helped to reinforce the split between the two cultures, pick one such teacher now, either a scientist or a humanist, and address an essay in the form of a letter to that person, arguing that such prejudices are unreasonable and in the end deny to both the sciences and the humanities what is most creative in them. You will of course want to use Snow and Eiseley as sources for some of your ideas, but add any thinking of your own that will support the argument.

2. If you are majoring in neither the sciences nor the humanities but instead in some social science or pre-professional program such as business, nursing, accounting, or radio and television, and if you know that some of your peers or teachers in your field think that *both* the sciences and humanities are boring, irrelevant, or impractical, write an essay in the form of a letter to one of them arguing that people in the technical fields need the insights of the sciences and the humanities as much as anyone else; give the best reasons you can to support your claims.

·11·

RELIGIOUS PERSPECTIVES

Belief Versus Unbelief

We have just enough religion to make us hate, but not
enough to make us love one another.
Jonathan Swift

The fairest thing we can experience is the mysterious.
It is the fundamental emotion which stands at the cradle of true art
and true science. He who knows it not, who can no longer
wonder, can no longer feel amazement, is as good as dead,
a snuffed-out candle.
Albert Einstein

For my own part, the sense of spiritual relief which comes from
rejecting the idea of God as supernatural being is enormous. I see no
other way of bridging the gap between the religious
and the scientific approach to reality.
Julian Huxley

Incomprehensible? But because you cannot understand a
thing, it does not cease to exist.
Blaise Pascal

Religion is a passion for righteousness, and for the spread of
righteousness, conceived as a cosmic demand.
William Ernest Hocking

Many people . . . have been extremely religious and extremely wicked.
R. H. Thouless

Truth is the supreme God for me. Truth is God.
Gandhi

Religion . . . is the opium of the people.
Karl Marx

My country is the world, and my religion is to do good.
Thomas Paine

James Baldwin

If you are middle class, whether black or white, you may be personally unfamiliar with the emotionally charged kind of religious experience, sometimes intense to the point of hysteria, that James Baldwin (1924– 1987) tells about in this excerpt from his autobiography. If you are middle class, whether black or white, you almost certainly know little of the role that religion plays in the lives of people whose everyday problem of existence is coping with, adjusting to, and surviving life in the ghetto. Baldwin, African-American novelist, essayist, and short-story writer, was born and raised in the ghetto of Harlem, coming into young manhood right before the onslaught of World War II. In his account of involvement with the church, which included local fame as a child preacher and evangelist, he illustrates one of the church's most important roles in the ghetto: its use as a kind of protection against hopelessness, despair, and danger.

Ghettos are dangerous places. Black Americans are forced to live in them against their will. Born innocent but guilty—innocent as moral agents, guilty for being black—ghetto residents are forced into second- or third-class citizenship; forced to know that their children have no hope of living better lives than their parents; and forced to endure the humiliations of poverty, filth, disease, and violence that other people living in the same society are never forced even to acknowledge, must less endure. It is no wonder that such places become dangerous. The frustration, resentment, and rage that builds up in such environments turns ghettos into social pressure cookers always simmering with explosive anger.

The major dangers of the ghetto are faced and endured by ghetto residents themselves. Living in a socially sealed environment, the outbursts of cynicism, hopelessness, and violence turn inward and wreck the lives of people in the ghetto, not the lives of those who live outside it. According to Baldwin and other black writers of the twentieth century, ghetto residents feel the danger. It is like a palpable presence. Parents fear to let their children out of the house or apartment: There are the dangers of street gangs, police harassment, pimps, whores, racketeers, hoodlums, hobos, winos, and 100 other threats. There is fear of the present and fear that the future will never be different.

From what sources do people living in such conditions find comfort and nonviolent release? Too often what is sought is neither comfort nor release, but simple escape: through the needle, through crime, or through alcohol. More dangers. In the midst of such dangers, ghetto churches, as Baldwin reveals, serve as an escape vent for feeling, a comfort against hopelessness, and a barrier behind which people attempt to protect themselves from outside dangers. Perhaps it is true that the role of most churches is more social than theological, but in that case it is also true that the nature of that social role will vary immensely from one social setting to another. The social role of the suburban church with its Little League teams; its winter skiing trips for youth groups; its lovely buildings of colonial red brick and white steeples or Gothic battlements and stained glass; and its boxes of food, old clothes, and abandoned toys gathered for the "underprivileged" at Thanksgiving and Christmas is not the social role of the ghetto church with its desperate emotionalism, its sense of the frailty against the outside rage and violence, and its difficulty in making religion seem real in a setting that is like a hallucination of hatred or a nightmare of despair.

Baldwin knows the ghetto. He knows the role of religion and churches in the ghetto. He has "been there," as people say—lived there—in both body and mind. The clarity of his insight and the lucidity of his prose invite us all to think hard about the intersections of religion, reality, rage, and fear in certain American settings.

DOWN AT THE CROSS: LETTER FROM A REGION IN MY MIND

From *The Fire Next Time* (1964).

I underwent, during the summer that I became fourteen, a prolonged religious crisis. I use the word "religious" in the common, and arbitrary, sense, meaning that I then discovered God, His saints and angels, and His blazing Hell. And since I had been born in a Christian nation, I accepted this Deity as the only one. I supposed Him to exist only within the walls of a church—in fact, of *our* church—and I also supposed that God and safety were synonymous. The word "safety" brings us to the real meaning of the word "religious" as we use it. Therefore, to state it in another, more accurate way, I became, during my fourteenth year, for the first time in my life, afraid—afraid of the evil within me and afraid of the evil without. What I saw around me that summer in Harlem was what I had always seen; nothing had changed. But now, without any warning, the whores and pimps and racketeers on the Avenue had become a personal menace. It had not before occurred to me that I could become one of them, but now I realized that we had been produced by the same circumstances. Many of my comrades were clearly headed for the Avenue, and my father said that I was headed that way, too. My friends began to drink and smoke, and embarked—at first avid, then groaning—on their sexual careers. Girls, only slightly older than I was, who sang in the choir or taught Sunday school, the children of holy parents, underwent, before my eyes, their incredible metamorphosis, of which the most bewildering aspect was not their budding breasts or their rounding behinds but something deeper and more subtle, in their eyes, their heat, their odor, and the inflection of their voices. Like the strangers on the Avenue, they became, in the twinkling of an eye, unutterably different and fantastically *present*. Owing to the way I had been raised, the abrupt discomfort that all this aroused in me and the fact that I had no idea what my voice or my mind or my body was likely to do next caused me to consider myself one of the most depraved people on earth. Matters were not helped by the fact that these holy girls seemed rather to enjoy my terrified lapses, our grim, guilty, tormented experiments, which were at once as chill and joyless as the Russian steppes and hotter, by far, than all the fires of Hell.

Yet there was something deeper than these changes, and less definable, that frightened me. It was real in both the boys and the girls, but it was, somehow, more vivid in the boys. In the case of the girls, one watched them turning into matrons before they had become women. They began to manifest a curious and really rather terrifying single-mindedness. It is hard to say exactly how this was conveyed: something implacable in the set of the lips, something farseeing (seeing what?) in the eyes, some new and crushing determination in the walk, something peremptory in the voice. They did not tease us, the boys, any more; they reprimanded us sharply, saying, "You better be thinking about your soul!" For the girls also saw the evidence on the Avenue, knew what the price would be, for them, of one misstep, knew that they had to be protected and that we were the only protection there was. They understood that they must act as God's decoys, saving the souls of the boys for Jesus and binding the bodies of the boys in marriage. For this was the beginning of our burning time, and "It is better," said St. Paul—who elsewhere, with a most unusual and stunning exactness, described himself as a "wretched man"—"to marry than to burn." And I began to feel in the boys a curious, wary, bewildered despair, as though they were now settling in for the long, hard winter of life. I did not know then what it was that I was reacting to; I put it to myself that they were letting themselves go. In the same way that the girls were destined to gain as much weight as their mothers, the boys, it was clear, would rise no higher than their fathers. School began to reveal itself, therefore, as a child's game that one could not win, and boys dropped out of school and went to work. My father wanted me to do the same. I refused, even though I no longer had any illusions about what an education could do for me; I had already encountered too many college-graduate handymen. My friends were now "downtown," busy, as they put it, "fighting the man." They began to care less about the way they looked, the way they dressed, the things they did; presently, one found them in twos and threes and fours, in a hallway, sharing a jug of wine or a bottle of whiskey, talking, cursing, fighting, sometimes weeping: lost, and unable to say what it was that oppressed them, except that they knew it was "the man"—the white man. And there seemed to be no way whatever to remove this cloud that stood between them and the sun, between them and love and life and power, between them and whatever it was that they wanted. One did not have to be very bright to realize how little one could do to change one's situation; one did not have to be abnormally sensitive to be worn down to a cutting edge by the incessant and gratuitous humiliation and danger one encountered every working day, all day long. The humiliation did not apply merely to working days, or workers; I was thirteen and was crossing Fifth Avenue on my way to the Forty-second Street library, and the cop in the middle of the street muttered as I passed him, "Why don't you niggers stay uptown where you belong?" When I was ten, and didn't look, certainly, any older, two policemen amused themselves with me by frisking me, making comic (and terrifying) speculations concerning my ancestry and probable sexual prowess, and for good measure, leaving me flat on my back in one of Harlem's empty lots. Just before and then during the Second World War, many of my friends fled into the service, all to be changed there, and rarely for the better, many to be ruined, and many to die. Others fled to other states and cities—that is, to other ghettos. Some went on wine or whiskey or the needle, and are still on it. And others, like me, fled into the church.

For the wages of sin were visible everywhere, in every wine-stained and urine-splashed hallway, in every clanging ambulance bell, in every scar on the faces of the pimps and their whores, in every helpless, newborn baby being brought into this danger, in every knife and pistol fight on the Avenue, and in every disastrous bulletin: a cousin, mother of six, suddenly gone mad, the children parcelled out here and there; an indestructible aunt rewarded for years of hard labor by a slow, agonizing death in a terrible small room; someone's bright son blown into eternity by his own hand; another turned robber and carried off to jail. It was a summer of dreadful speculations and discoveries, of which these were not the worst. Crime became real, for example—for the first time—not as *a* possibility but as *the* possibility. One would never defeat one's circumstances by working and saving one's pennies; one would never, by working, acquire that many pennies, and, besides, the social treatment accorded even the most successful Negroes proved that one needed, in order to be free, something more than a bank account. One needed a handle, a lever, a means of inspiring fear. It was absolutely clear that the police would whip you and take you in as long as they could get away with it, and that everyone else—housewives, taxi-drivers, elevator boys, dish-washers, bartenders, lawyers, judges, doctors, and grocers—would never, by the operation of any generous human feeling, cease to use you as an outlet for his frustrations and hostilities. Neither civilized reason nor Christian love would cause any of those people to treat you as they presumably wanted to be treated; only the fear of your power to retaliate would cause them to do that, or to seem to do it, which was (and is) good enough. There appears to be a vast amount of confusion on this point, but I do not know many Negroes who are eager to be "accepted" by white people, still less to be loved by them; they, the blacks, simply don't wish to be beaten over the head by the whites every instant of our brief passage on this planet. White people in this country will have quite enough to do in learning how to accept and love themselves and each other, and when they have achieved this—which will not be tomorrow and may very well be never—the Negro problem will no longer exist, for it will no longer be needed.

People more advantageously placed than we in Harlem were, and are, 4 will no doubt find the psychology and the view of human nature sketched above dismal and shocking in the extreme. But the Negro's experience of the white world cannot possibly create in him any respect for the standards by which the white world claims to live. His own condition is overwhelming proof that white people do not live by these standards. Negro servants have been smuggling odds and ends out of white homes for generations, and white people have been delighted to have them do it, because it has assuaged a dim guilt and testified to the intrinsic superiority of white people. Even the most doltish and servile Negro could scarcely fail to be impressed by the disparity between his situation and that of the people for whom he worked; Negroes who were neither doltish nor servile did not feel that they were doing anything wrong when they robbed white people. In spite of the Puritan-Yankee equation of virtue with well-being, Negroes had excellent reasons for doubting that money was made or kept by any very striking adherence to the Christian virtues; it certainly did not work that way for black Christians. In any case, white people, who had robbed black people of their liberty and who profited by this theft every hour that they lived, had no moral ground on which to stand. They had the judges, the juries, the shotguns, the law—in a word, power. But it was a criminal power, to be feared but not respected, and to be outwitted in any way whatever. And those virtues preached but not practiced by the white world were merely another means of holding Negroes in subjection.

It turned out, then, that summer, that the moral barriers that I had 5 supposed to exist between me and the dangers of a criminal career were so tenuous as to be nearly nonexistent. I certainly could not discover any principled reason for not becoming a criminal, and it is not my poor, God-fearing parents who are to be indicated for the lack but this society. I was icily determined—more determined, really, than I then knew—never to make my peace with the ghetto but to die and go to Hell before I would let any white man spit on me, before I would accept my "place" in this republic. I did not intend to allow the white people of this country to tell me who I was, and limit me that way, and polish me off that way. And yet, of course, at the same time, I *was* being spat on and defined and described and limited, and could have been polished off with no effort whatever. Every Negro boy—in my situation during those years, at least—who reaches this point realizes, at once, profoundly, because he wants to live, that he stands in great peril and must find, with speed, a "thing," a gimmick, to lift him out, to start him on his way. *And it does not matter what the gimmick is.* It was this last realization that terrified me and—since it revealed that the door opened on so many dangers—helped to hurl me into the church. And, by an unforeseeable paradox, it was my career in the church that turned out, precisely, to be my gimmick.

For when I tried to assess my capabilities, I realized that I had almost 6 none. In order to achieve the life I wanted, I had been dealt, it seemed to me, the worst possible hand. I could not become a prize-fighter—many of us tried but very few succeeded. I could not sing. I could not dance. I had been well conditioned by the world in which I grew up, so I did not yet dare take the idea of becoming a writer seriously. The only other possibility seemed to involve my becoming one of the sordid people on the Avenue, who were not really as sordid as I then imagined but who frightened me terribly, both because I did not want to live that life and because of what they made me feel. Everything inflamed me, and that was bad enough, but I myself had also become a source of fire and temptation. I had been far too well raised, alas, to suppose that any of the extremely explicit overtures made to me that summer, sometimes by boys and girls but also, more alarmingly, by older men and women, had anything to do with my attractiveness. On the contrary, since the Harlem idea of seduction is, to put it mildly, blunt, whatever these people saw in me merely confirmed my sense of my depravity.

It is certainly sad that the awakening of one's senses should lead to such a merciless judgment of oneself—to say nothing of the time and anguish one spends in the effort to arrive at any other—but it is also inevitable that a literal attempt to mortify the flesh should be made among black people like those with whom I grew up. Negroes in this country—and Negroes do not, strictly or legally speaking, exist in any other—are taught really to despise themselves from the moment their eyes open on the world. This world is white and they are black. White people hold the power, which means that they are superior to blacks (intrinsically, that is: God decreed it so), and the world has innumerable ways of making this difference known and felt and feared. Long before the Negro child perceives this difference, and even longer before he understands it, he has begun to react to it, he has begun to be controlled by it. Every effort made by the child's elders to prepare him for a fate from which they cannot protect him causes him secretly, in terror, to begin to await, without knowing that he is doing so, his mysterious and inexorable punishment. He must be "good" not only in order to please his parents and not only to avoid being punished by them; behind their authority stands another, nameless and impersonal, infinitely harder to please, and bottomlessly cruel. And this filters into the child's consciousness through his parents' tone of voice as he is being exhorted, punished, or loved; in the sudden, uncontrollable note of fear heard in his mother's or his father's voice when he has strayed beyond some particular boundary. He does not know what the boundary is, and he can get no explanation of it, which is frightening enough, but the fear he hears in the voices of his elders is more frightening still. The fear that I heard in my father's voice, for example, when he realized that I really *believed* I could do anything a white boy could do, and had every intention of proving it, was not at all like the fear I heard when one of us was ill or had fallen down the stairs or strayed too far from the house. It was another fear, a fear that the child, in challenging the white world's assumptions, was putting himself in the path of destruction. A child cannot, thank Heaven, know how vast and how merciless is the nature of power, with what unbelievable cruelty people treat each other. He reacts to the fear in his parents' voices because his parents hold up the world for him and he has no protection without them. I defended myself, as I imagined, against the fear my father made me feel by remembering that he was very old-fashioned. Also, I prided myself on the fact that I already knew how to outwit him. To defend oneself against a fear is simply to insure that one will, one day, be conquered by it; fears must be faced. As for one's wits, it is just not true that one can live by them—not, that is, if one wishes really to live. That summer, in any case, all the fears with which I had grown up, and which were now a part of me and controlled my vision of the world, rose up like a wall between the world and me, and drove me into the church.

As I look back, everything I did seems curiously deliberate, though it certainly did not seem deliberate them. For example, I did not join the church of which my father was a member and in which he preached. My best friend in school, who attended a different church, had already "surrendered his life to the Lord," and he was very anxious about my soul's salvation. (I wasn't, but any human attention was better than none.) One Saturday afternoon, he took me to his church. There were no services that day, and the church was empty, except for some women cleaning and some other women praying. My friend took me into the back room to meet his pastor—a woman. There she sat, in her robes, smiling, an extremely proud and handsome woman, with Africa, Europe, and the America of the American Indian blended in her face. She was perhaps forty-five or fifty at this time, and in our world she was a very celebrated woman. My friend was about to introduce me when she looked at me and smiled and said, "Whose little boy are you?" Now this, unbelievably, was precisely the phrase used by pimps and racketeers on the Avenue when they suggested, both humorously and intensely, that I "hang out" with them. Perhaps part of the terror they had caused me to feel came from the fact that I unquestionably wanted to be *somebody's* little boy. I was so frightened, and at the mercy of so many conundrums, that inevitably, that summer, *someone* would have taken me over; one doesn't, in Harlem, long remain standing on any auction block. It was my good luck—perhaps—that I found myself in the church racket instead of some other, and surrendered to a spiritual seduction long before I came to any carnal knowledge. For when the pastor asked me, with that marvelous smile, "Whose little boy are you?" my heart replied at once, "Why, yours." 8

The summer wore on, and things got worse. I became more guilty and more frightened, and kept all this bottled up inside me, and naturally, inescapably, one night, when this woman had finished preaching, everything came roaring, screaming, crying out, and I fell to the ground before the altar. It was the strangest sensation I have ever had in my life—up to that time, or since. I had not known that it was going to happen, or that it could happen. One moment I was on my feet, singing and clapping and, at the same time, working out in my head the plot of a play I was working on then; the next moment, with no transition, no sensation of falling, I was on my back, with the lights beating down into my face and all the vertical saints above me. I 9 did not know what I was doing down so low, or how I had got there. And the anguish that filled me cannot be described. It moved in me like one of those floods that devastate counties, tearing everything down, tearing children from their parents and lovers from each other, and making everything an unrecognizable waste. All I really remember is the pain, the unspeakable pain; it was as though I were yelling up to Heaven and Heaven would not hear me. And if Heaven would not hear me, if love could not descend from Heaven—to wash me, to make me clean—then utter disaster was my portion. Yes, it does indeed mean something—something unspeakable—to be born, in a white country, an Anglo-Teutonic, antisexual country, black. You very soon, without knowing it, give up all hope of communion. Black people, mainly, look down or look up but do not look at each other, not at you, and white people, mainly, look away. And the universe is simply a sounding drum; there is no way, no way whatever, so it seemed then and has sometimes seemed since, to get through a life, to love your wife and children, or your friends, or your mother and father, or to be loved. The universe, which is not merely the stars and the moon and the planets, flowers, grass, and trees, but *other people,* has evolved no terms for your existence, has made no room for you, and if love will not swing wide the gates, no other power will or can. And if one despairs—as who has not?—of human love, God's love alone is left. But God—and I felt this even then, so long ago, on that tremendous floor, unwillingly—is white. And if His love was so great, and if He loved all His children, why were we, the blacks, cast down so far? Why? In spite of all I said thereafter, I found no answer on the floor—not *that* answer, anyway— and I was on the floor all night. Over me, to bring me "through," the saints sang and rejoiced and prayed. And in the morning, when they raised me, they told me that I was "saved."

Well, indeed I was, in a way, for I was utterly drained and exhausted, and released, for the first time, from all my guilty torment. I was aware then only of my relief. For many years, I could not ask myself why human relief had to be achieved in a fashion at once so pagan and so desperate—in a fashion at once so unspeakably old and so unutterably new. And by the time I was able to ask myself this question, I was also able to see that the principles governing the rites and customs of the churches in which I grew up did not differ from the principles governing the rites and customs of other churches, white. The principles were Blindness, Loneliness, and Terror, the first principle necessarily and actively cultivated in order to deny the two others. I would love to believe that the principles were Faith, Hope, and Charity, but this is clearly not so for most Christians, or for what we call the Christian world.

I was saved. But at the same time, out of a deep, adolescent cunning I do not pretend to understand, I realized immediately that I could not remain in the church merely as another worshipper. I would have to give myself something to do, in order not to be too bored and find myself among all the wretched unsaved of the Avenue. And I don't doubt that I also intended to best my father on his own ground. Anyway, very shortly after I joined the church, I became a preacher—a Young Minister—and I remained in the pulpit for more than three years. My youth quickly made me a much bigger drawing card than my father. I pushed this advantage ruthlessly, for it was the most effective means I had found of breaking his hold over me. That was the most frightening time of my life, and quite the most dishonest, and the resulting hysteria lent great passion to my sermons—for a while. I relished the attention and the relative immunity from punishment that my new status gave me, and I relished, above all, the sudden right to privacy. It had to be recognized, after all, that I was still a schoolboy, with my schoolwork to do, and I was also expected to prepare at least one sermon a week. During what we may call my heyday, I preached much more often than that. This meant that there were hours and even whole days when I could not be interrupted—not even by my father. I had immobilized him. It took rather more time for me to realize that I had also immobilized myself, and had escaped from nothing whatever.

The church was very exciting. It took a long time for me to disengage   12 myself from this excitement, and on the blindest, most visceral level, I never really have, and never will. There is no music like that music, no drama like the drama of the saints rejoicing, the sinners moaning, the tambourines racing, and all those voices coming together and crying holy unto the Lord. There is still, for me, no pathos quite like the pathos of those multicolored, worn, somehow triumphant and transfigured faces, speaking from the depths of a visible, tangible, continuing despair of the goodness of the Lord. I have never seen anything to equal the fire and excitement that sometimes, without warning, fill a church, causing the church, as Leadbelly* and so many others have testified, to "rock." Nothing that has happened to me since equals the power and the glory that I sometimes felt when, in the middle of a sermon, I knew that I was somehow, by some miracle, really carrying, as they said, "the Word"—when the church and I were one. Their pain and their joy were mine, and mine were theirs—they surrendered their pain and joy to me, I surrendered mine to them—and their cries of "Amen!" and "Hallelujah!" and "Yes, Lord!" and "Praise His name!" and "Preach it, brother!" sustained and whipped on my solos until we all became equal, wringing wet, singing and dancing, in anguish and rejoicing, at the foot of the altar. It was, for a long time, in spite of—or, not inconceivably, because of—the shabbiness of my motives, my only sustenance, my meat and drink. I rushed home from school, to the church, to the altar, to be alone there, to commune with Jesus, my dearest Friend, who would never fail me, who knew all the secrets of my heart. Perhaps He did, but I didn't, and the bargain we struck, actually, down there at the foot of the cross, was that He would never let me find out.

He failed His bargain. He was a much better Man than I took Him for.   13 It happened, as things do, imperceptibly, in many ways at once. I date it—the slow crumbling of my faith, the pulverization of my fortress—from the time,

*Leadbelly, or Huddie Ledbetter (1885–1949), was an American blues singer of black and Cherokee descent. His compositions include "Rock Island Line" (1942) and "Good Night, Irene" (1943).

about a year after I had begun to preach, when I began to read again. I justified this desire by the fact that I was still in school, and I began, fatally, with Dostoevski.* By this time, I was in a high school that was predominantly Jewish. This meant that I was surrounded by people who were, by definition, beyond any hope of salvation, who laughed at the tracts and leaflets I brought to school, and who pointed out that the Gospels had been written long after the death of Christ. This might not have been so distressing if it had not forced me to read the tracts and leaflets myself, for they were indeed, unless one believed their message already, impossible to believe. I remember feeling dimly that there was a kind of blackmail in it. People, I felt, ought to love the Lord *because* they loved Him, and not because they were afraid of going to Hell. I was forced, reluctantly, to realize that the Bible itself had been written by men, and translated by men out of languages I could not read, and I was already, without quite admitting it to myself, terribly involved with the effort of putting words on paper. Of course, I had the rebuttal ready: These men had all been operating under divine inspiration. *Had* they? *All* of them? And I also knew by now, alas, far more about divine inspiration than I dared admit, for I knew how I worked myself up into my own visions, and how frequently—indeed, incessantly—the visions God granted to me differed from the visions He granted to my father. I did not understand the dreams I had at night, but I knew that they were not holy. For that matter, I knew that my waking hours were far from holy. I spent most of my time in a state of repentance for things I had vividly desired to do but had not done. The fact that I was dealing with Jews brought the whole question of color, which I had been desperately avoiding, into the terrified center of my mind. I realized that the Bible had been written by white men. I knew that, according to many Christians, I was a descendant of Ham,† who had been cursed, and that I was therefore predestined to be a slave. This had nothing to do with anything I was, or contained, or could become; my fate had been sealed forever, from the beginning of time. And it seemed, indeed, when one looked out over Christendom, that this was what Christendom effectively believed. It was certainly the way it behaved. I remembered the Italian priests and bishops blessing Italian boys who were on their way to Ethiopia.

Again, the Jewish boys in high school were troubling because I could find no point of connection between them and the Jewish pawnbrokers and landlords and grocery-store owners in Harlem. I knew that these people were Jews—God knows I was told it often enough—but I thought of them only as white. Jews, as such, until I got to high school, were all incarcerated in the Old Testament, and their names were Abraham, Moses, Daniel, Ezekiel, and Job, and Shadrach, Meshach, and Abednego. It was bewildering to find them so many miles and centuries out of Egypt, and so far from the fiery furnace.

14

*Fyodor Dostoevski (1821–1880), Russian novelist whose novels are powerful explorations of people's search for faith, meaning, and truth. His novels include *Crime and Punishment* (1866) and *Brothers Karamazov* (1879–1880). His subtle and penetrating analyses of faith would have been no comfort to the shallow emotionalism of the young Baldwin.

†See Genesis 9:20–27.

My best friend in high school was a Jew. He came to our house once, and afterward my father asked, as he asked about everyone, "Is he a Christian?"—by which he meant "Is he saved?" I really do not know whether my answer came out of innocence or venom, but I said coldly, "No. He's Jewish." My father slammed me across the face with his great palm, and in that moment everything flooded back—all the hatred and all the fear, and the depth of a merciless resolve to kill my father rather than allow my father to kill me—and I knew that all those sermons and tears and all that repentance and rejoicing had changed nothing. I wondered if I was expected to be glad that a friend of mine, or anyone, was to be tormented forever in Hell, and I also thought, suddenly, of the Jews in another Christian nation, Germany. They were not so far from the fiery furnace after all, and my best friend might have been one of them. I told my father, "He's a better Christian than you are," and walked out of the house. The battle between us was in the open, but that was all right; it was almost a relief. A more deadly struggle had begun.

Being in the pulpit was like being in the theatre; I was behind the scenes 15 and knew how the illusion was worked. I knew the other ministers and knew the quality of their lives. And I don't mean to suggest by this the "Elmer Gantry" sort of hypocrisy concerning sensuality; it was a deeper, deadlier, and more subtle hypocrisy than that, and a little honest sensuality, or a lot, would have been like water in an extremely bitter desert. I knew how to work on a congregation until the last dime was surrendered—it was not very hard to do—and I knew where the money for "the Lord's work" went. I knew, though I did not wish to know it, that I had no respect for the people with whom I worked. I could not have said it then, but I also knew that if I continued I would soon have no respect for myself. And the fact that I was "the young Brother Baldwin" increased my value with those same pimps and racketeers who had helped to stampede me into the church in the first place. They still saw the little boy they intended to take over. They were waiting for me to come to my senses and realize that I was in a very lucrative business. They knew that I did not yet realize this, and also that I had not yet begun to suspect where my own needs, *coming up* (they were very patient), could drive me. They themselves did know the score, and they knew that the odds were in their favor, And, really, I knew it, too. I was even lonelier and more vulnerable than I had been before. And the blood of the Lamb had not cleansed me in any way whatever. I was just as black as I had been the day that I was born. Therefore, when I faced a congregation, it began to take all the strength I had not to stammer, not to curse, not to tell them to throw away their Bibles and get off their knees and go home and organize, for example, a rent strike. When I watched all the children, their copper, brown, and beige faces staring up at me as I taught Sunday school, I felt that I was committing a crime in talking about the gentle Jesus, in telling them to reconcile themselves to their misery on earth in order to gain the crown of eternal life. Were only Negroes to gain this crown? Was Heaven, then, to be merely another ghetto? Perhaps I might have been able to reconcile myself even to this if I had been able to believe that there was any loving-kindness to be found in the haven I represented. But I had been in the pulpit too long and I had seen too many monstrous things. I don't refer merely to the glaring fact that the minister eventually acquires houses and Cadillacs while the faithful continue to scrub floors and drop their dimes and quarters and dollars into the plate. I really mean that there was no love in the church. It was a mask for hatred and self-hatred and despair. The transfiguring power of the Holy Ghost ended when the service ended, and salvation stopped at the church door. When we were told to love everybody, I had thought that that meant *everybody*. But no. It applied only to those who believed as we did, and it did not apply to white people at all. I was told by a minister, for example, that I should never, on any public conveyance, under any circumstances, rise and give my seat to a white woman. White men never rose for Negro women. Well, that was true enough, in the main—I saw his point. But what was the point, the purpose, of *my* salvation if it did not permit me to behave with love toward others, no matter how they behaved toward me? What others did was their responsibility, for which they would answer when the judgment trumpet sounded. But what *I* did was *my* responsibility, and I would have to answer, too—unless, of course, there was also in Heaven a special dispensation for the benighted black, who was not to be judged in the same way as other human beings, or angels. It probably occurred to me around this time that the vision people hold of the world to come is but a reflection, with predictable wishful distortions, of the world in which they live. And this did not apply only to Negroes, who were no more "simple" or "spontaneous" or "Christian" than anybody else—who were merely more oppressed. In the same way that we, for white people, were the descendants of Ham, and were cursed forever, white people were, for us, the descendants of Cain. And the passion with which we loved the Lord was a measure of how deeply we feared and distrusted and, in the end, hated almost all strangers, always, and avoided and despised ourselves.

But I cannot leave it at that; there is more to it than that. In spite of everything, there was in the life I fled a zest and a joy and a capacity for facing and surviving disaster that are very moving and very rare. Perhaps we were, all of us—pimps, whores, racketeers, church members, and children—bound together by the nature of our oppression, the specific and peculiar complex of risks we had to run; if so, within these limits we sometimes achieved with each other a freedom that was close to love. I remember, anyway, church suppers and outings, and, later, after I left the church, rent and waistline parties where rage and sorrow sat in the darkness and did not stir, and we ate and drank and talked and laughed and danced and forgot all about "the man." We had the liquor, the chicken, the music, and each other, and had no need to pretend to be what we were not. This is the freedom that one hears in some gospel songs, for example, and in jazz. In all jazz, and especially in the blues, there is something tart and ironic, authoritative and double-edged. White Americans seem to feel that happy songs are *happy* and sad songs are *sad*, and that, God help us, is exactly the way most white Americans sing them—sounding, in both cases, so helplessly, defenselessly fatuous that one dare not speculate on the temperature of the deep freeze from which issue their brave and sexless little voices. Only people who have been "down the line," as the song puts it, know what this music is about. I think it was Big Bill Broonzy who used to sing "I Feel So Good," a really joyful song about a man who is on his way to the railroad station to meet his girl. She's coming home. It is the singer's incredibly moving exuberance that makes one realize how leaden the time must have been while she was gone. There is no guarantee that she will stay this time, either, as the singer clearly knows, and, in fact, she has not yet actually arrived. Tonight, or tomorrow, or within the next five minutes, he may very well be singing "Lonesome in My Bedroom," or insisting, "Aint' we, ain't we, going to make it all right? Well, if we don't today, we will tomorrow night." White Americans do not understand the depths out of which such an ironic tenacity comes, but they suspect that the force is sensual, and they are terrified of sensuality and do not any longer understand it. The word "sensual" is not intended to bring to mind quivering dusky maidens or priapic black studs. I am referring to something much simpler and much less fanciful. To be sensual, I think, is to respect and rejoice in the force of life, of life itself, and to be *present* in all that one does, from the effort of loving to the breaking of bread. It will be a great day for America, incidentally, when we begin to eat bread again, instead of the blasphemous and tasteless foam rubber that we have substituted for it. And I am not being frivolous now, either. Something very sinister happens to the people of a country when they begin to distrust their own reactions as deeply as they do here, and become as joyless as they have become. It is this individual uncertainty on the part of white American men and women, this inability to renew themselves at the fountain of their own lives, that makes the discussion, let alone elucidation, of any conundrum—that is, any reality—so supremely difficult. The person who distrusts himself has no touchstone for reality—for this touchstone can be only oneself. Such a person interposes between himself and reality nothing less than a labyrinth of attitudes. And these attitudes, furthermore, though the person is usually unaware of it (is unaware of so much!), are historical and public attitudes. They do not relate to the present any more than they relate to the person. Therefore, whatever white people do not know about Negroes reveals, precisely and inexorably, what they do not know about themselves.

White Christians have also forgotten several elementary historical details. They have forgotten that the religion that is now identified with their virtue and their power—"God is on our side," says Dr. Verwoerd*—came out of a rocky piece of ground in what is now known as the Middle East before color was invented, and that in order for the Christian church to be established, Christ had to be put to death, by Rome, and that the real architect of the Christian church was not the disreputable, sunbaked Hebrew who gave it his name but the mercilessly fanatical and self-righteous St. Paul. The

17

*Hendrik Frensch Verwoerd (1901–1966), South African prime minister (1958–1966) who established resettlement of blacks and rigorously enforced the policy of apartheid.

energy that was buried with the rise of the Christian nations must come back into the world; nothing can prevent it. Many of us, I think, both long to see this happen and are terrified of it, for though this transformation contains the hope of liberation, it also imposes a necessity for great change. But in order to deal with the untapped and dormant force of the previously subjugated, in order to survive as a human, moving, moral weight in the world, America and all the Western nations will be forced to reëxamine themselves and release themselves from many things that are now taken to be sacred, and to discard nearly all the assumptions that have been used to justify their lives and their anguish and their crimes so long.

"The white man's Heaven," sings a Black Muslim minister, "is the black man's Hell." One may object—possibly—that this puts the matter somewhat too simply, but the song is true, and it has been true for as long as white men have ruled the world. The Africans put it another way: When the white man came to Africa, the white man had the Bible and the African had the land, but now it is the white man who is being, reluctantly and bloodily, separated from the land, and the African who is still attempting to digest or to vomit up the Bible. The struggle, therefore, that now begins in the world is extremely complex, involving the historical role of Christianity in the realm of power—that is, politics—and in the realm of morals. In the realm of power, Christianity has operated with an unmitigated arrogance and cruelty—necessarily, since a religion ordinarily imposes on those who have discovered the true faith the spiritual duty of liberating the infidels. This particular true faith, moreover, is more deeply concerned about the soul than it is about the body, to which fact the flesh (and the corpses) of countless infidels bears witness. It goes without saying, then, that whoever questions the authority of the true faith also contests the right of the nations that hold this faith to rule over him—contests, in short, their title to his land. The spreading of the Gospel, regardless of the motives or the integrity or the heroism of some of the missionaries, was an absolutely indispensable justification for the planting of the flag. Priests and nuns and school-teachers helped to protect and sanctify the power that was so ruthlessly being used by people who were indeed seeking a city, but not one in the heavens, and one to be made, very definitely, by captive hands. The Christian church itself—again, as distinguished from some of its ministers—sanctified and rejoiced in the conquests of the flag, and encouraged, if it did not formulate, the belief that conquest, with the resulting relative well-being of the Western populations, was proof of the favor of God. God had come a long way from the desert—but then so had Allah, though in a very different direction. God, going north, and rising on the wings of power, had become white, and Allah, out of power, and on the dark side of Heaven, had become—for all practical purposes, anyway—black. Thus, in the realm of morals the role of Christianity has been, at best, ambivalent. Even leaving out of account the remarkable arrogance that assumed that the ways and morals of others were inferior to those of Christians, and that they therefore had every right, and could use any means, to change them, the collision between cultures—and the schizophrenia in the mind of

Christendom—had rendered the domain of morals as chartless as the sea once was, and as treacherous as the sea still is. It is not too much to say that whoever wishes to become a truly moral human being (and let us not ask whether or not this is possible; I think we must *believe* that it is possible) must first divorce himself from all the prohibitions, crimes, and hypocrisies of the Christian church. If the concept of God has any validity or any use, it can only be to make us larger, freer, and more loving. If God cannot do this, then it is time we got rid of Him.

Questions for Discussion

1. If you are a church goer—or if you have ever been—what would you describe as the social role of the church you know best? In addition, that is, to the religious functions that members find served by the church, what social needs get met? What values, attitudes, and expectations about life are collectively affirmed when the church people you know get together for programs, dinners, and other social functions?

2. Do you find the social functions of your church useful? In what ways? Do you think most members view the social functions as central or peripheral to the church's mission? How do you think it should be viewed? Why?

3. What does Baldwin mean in paragraph 5 when he describes the church as a "gimmick" (or, at the end of ¶8, the "church racket") that he used "to lift him out, to start him on his way"?

4. Baldwin reports that as a child he took it for granted that God was white (¶9). If you believe in God, how do you picture the divine existence? Your thought-out definition may not involve personifying God, but it is very likely that, underneath your thought-out definition, you have, like most people, a mental picture of God as something like a human being. Is your image of the divine based on pictures you saw in books as a child? Do you view God as a person of your own sex and color? Of your own color, but not your sex? Why or why not? What would be the psychological effect of imagining God as black if you were white, especially if being white were a despised thing in a black society?

Suggested Essay Topics

1. In an essay directed to your classmates, undertake to describe, first, the main *features* and, second, the main *effects* of your religious beliefs. In this first part you are not being asked to defend your beliefs, only to present an orderly and accurate description of them. (This may be harder than it sounds.) In the second part of the essay try to say what effects your religious beliefs have, what role they play in your everyday life. One way to get at this issue is to imagine specific instances of how you might live

your life differently—recent decisions you might have made differently or recent actions that you might or might not have performed—if you did not hold the beliefs that you claim.

2. If you are not a religious believer, write an essay directed to your class-mates explaining why you feel no necessity to have a religious life. Whether you are completely indifferent toward religion, whether you are actively hostile, whether you feel nostalgic about religion, wishing you could believe in it, but simply unable to, or whether you hold some other attitude about it, look closely enough within yourself to discover just what that attitude is, what components make it up, and then undertake, first, to describe accurately what those components are and, second, to explain why you hold to them.

Elie Wiesel

Elie Wiesel (b. 1928), novelist and biblical commentator, winner of the Nobel Prize for literature, has written book after book since World War II, seeking a way to talk about religious questions while living with memories of the Nazi holocaust. How can a Jew—how can anyone—believe in and talk about God's loving care for his "chosen people" knowing that 6 million Jews and countless others were massacred? How can any sensitive person speak joyfully of "the sacred" after such an event? How can anyone have the courage or effrontery to affirm God's creation in the light of such horrors?

Wiesel has pursued such questions mainly in his novels, among them The Gates of the Forest, The Town Beyond the Wall, *and* A Beggar in Jerusalem. *Here we meet him in a different role, traditional in Jewish culture: that of the spiritual inquirer who wrestles with moral and spiritual problems by writing commentary on the mysterious stories in the Torah about the patriarchs, Israel's "founding fathers." In this essay, Wiesel comments on Genesis 22, in which God commands Abraham to sacrifice his son, Isaac. This powerful story has always raised difficult questions, and Wiesel says the questions troubled him even as a child. Why do the innocent suffer? How can God ask of anyone such a terrible sacrifice as that of a son? How could Abraham have enough faith to accept such an awful command? And why is the story told just* this *way?*

Wiesel finds the story of Abraham and Isaac raising the same questions that are raised by the Nazi holocaust, and, as you might expect, he arrives at no simple, unambiguous reassurance about the meaning of evil and suffering in the world. But he does offer a path to the kind of spiritual insight, often humorous but always profound, that Jewish commentators have traditionally exhibited in the Midrash—a *term that refers both to a way of interpreting scripture and to the content of the accumulated stories and interpretations that the method has produced over millennia.*

It is important when reading commentary of this kind not to worry about the literal historical status of the stories themselves. Their value lies not in their factuality but in their meaning, and such meaning is always oblique and allusive, usually tentative, and sometimes downright puzzling—like the experience of evil and suffering in life itself.

THE SACRIFICE OF ISAAC

A Strange Tale About Fear, Faith, and Laughter

From "The Sacrifice of Isaac: A Survivor's Story," in *Messengers of God: Biblical Portraits and Legends* (1976).

This strange tale is about fear and faith, fear and defiance, fear and laughter.   1

Terrifying in content, it has become a source of consolation to those   2
who, in retelling it, make it part of their own experience. Here is a story that contains Jewish destiny in its totality, just as the flame is contained in the single spark by which it comes to life. Every major theme, every passion and obsession that make Judaism the adventure that it is, can be traced back to it: man's anguish when he finds himself face to face with God, his quest for purity and purpose, the conflict of having to choose between dreams of the past and dreams of the future, between absolute faith and absolute justice, between the need to obey God's will and to rebel against it; between his yearnings for freedom and for sacrifice, his desire to justify hope and despair with words and silence—the same words and the same silence. It is all there.

As a literary composition, this tale—known as the *Akeda*—is unmatched   3
in Scripture. Austere and powerful, its every word reverberates into infinity, evoking suspense and drama, uncovering a whole mood based on a before and continuing into an after, culminating in a climax which endows its characters with another dimension. They are human—and more: forceful and real de-spite the metaphysical implications. At every step, their condition remains relevant and of burning gravity.

This very ancient story is still our own and we shall continue to be   4
bound to it in the most intimate way. We may not know it, but every one of us, at one time or another, is called upon to play a part in it. What part? Are we Abraham or Isaac? We are Jacob, that is to say, Israel. And Israel began with Abraham.*

Let us reread the text.   5

Once upon a time there lived a man for all seasons, blessed with all   6
talents and virtues, deserving of every grace. His name was Abraham and his

---

*Isaac's son, Jacob, received the name "Israel" when he strove with the angel and prevailed (Genesis 32). The name later designated the 12 tribes, represented in Genesis by Jacob's 12 sons.

mission was to serve as God's messenger among men too vain and blind to recognize His glory. Tradition rates him higher than Moses—whose Law he observed; higher even than Adam—whose errors he was asked to correct.

Abraham: the first enemy of idolatry. The first angry young man. The first rebel to rise up against the "establishment," society and authority. The first to demystify official taboos and suspend ritual prohibitions. The first to reject civilization in order to form a minority of one. The first believer, the first one to suffer for his belief. Alone against the world, he declared himself free. Alone against the world, he braved the fire and the mob, affirming that God is one and present wherever His name is invoked; that one is the secret and the beginning of all that exists in heaven and on earth and that God's secret coincides with that of man.

And yet. Notwithstanding his total faith in God and His justice, His kindness as well, he did not for a moment hesitate to take God to task as he tried to save two condemned cities from destruction:* How can You—who embody justice—be unjust? He was the first who dared query God. And God listened and answered. For unlike Job, Abraham was protesting on behalf of others, not of himself. God forgave Abraham everything, including his questions. God is God and Abraham was His faithful servant; one was sure of the other. To test his will and vision, God had made him leave the security of his father's home, challenge rulers and engage their armies in battle, endure hunger and exile, disgrace and fire. His trust in God was never shaken. So loyal was he to God that he was rewarded with a son who became symbol and bearer of grace and benediction for generations to come.

Then one day God decided once more to test him—for the tenth and last time: Take your son and bring him to Me as an offering. The term used is *ola,* which means an offering that has been totally consumed, a holocaust. And Abraham complied. Without an argument. Without questioning or even trying to understand, without trying to stall. Without a word to anyone, not even his wife Sarah, without a tear; he simply waited for the next morning and left the house before she awakened. He saddled his donkey, and accompanied by his son and two servants, started on the road to Mount Moriah. After a three-day journey—which according to Kierkegaard† lasted longer than the four thousand years separating us from the event—father and son left the servants and donkey behind and began their ascent of the mountain. When they reached the top they erected an altar and prepared for the ritual. Everything was ready: the wood, the knife, the fire. Slaughterer and victim looked into each other's eyes and for one moment all of creation held its breath. The same fear penetrated the father and the son. A Midrash describes Isaac's fear. Stretched out on the altar, his wrists and ankles bound, Isaac saw the Temple in Jerusalem first destroyed and then rebuilt, and at the moment of the supreme test, Isaac understood that what was happening to him would happen to others, that this was to be a tale without an end, an experience to

*Sodom and Gomorrah (see Genesis 18).
†Søren Kierkegaard (1813–1855), Danish philosopher and religious thinker.

be endured by his children and theirs.* Never would they be spared the
torture. The father's anguish, on the other hand, was not linked to the future;
by sacrificing his son to obey God's will, Abraham knew that he was, in fact,
sacrificing his knowledge *of* God and his faith *in* Him. If Isaac were to die,
to whom would the father transmit this faith, this knowledge? The end of
Isaac would connote the end of a prodigious adventure: the first would
become the last. One cannot conceive of a more crushing or more devastating
anguish: I shall thus have lived, suffered and caused others to suffer for
nothing.

And the miracle took place. Death was defeated, the tragedy averted.   10
The blade that could have cut the line—and prevented Israel from being
born—was halted, suspended.

Was thus the mystery resolved? Hardly. As one plunges into Midrashic   11
literature, one feels its poignancy. It leaves one troubled. The question is no
longer whether Isaac was saved but whether the miracle could happen again.
And how often. And for what reasons. And at what cost.

As a child, I read and reread this tale, my heart beating wildly; I felt dark   12
apprehension come over me and carry me far away.

There was no understanding the three characters. Why would God, the   13
merciful Father, demand that Abraham become inhuman, and why would
Abraham accept? And Isaac, why did he submit so meekly? Not having
received a direct order to let himself be sacrificed, why did he consent?

I could not understand. If God needs human suffering to be God, how   14
can man foresee an end to that suffering? And if faith in God must result in
self-denial, how can faith claim to elevate and improve man?

These were painful questions, especially for an adolescent, because they   15
did not fit into the framework of the sin-punishment concept, to which all
religious thought had accustomed us.

. . .

To me the *Akeda* was an unfathomable mystery given to every genera-   16
tion, to be relived, if not solved—one of the great mysteries of our history,
a mystery so opaque that it obscures not only the facts but also the names
of the protagonists.

Why did Abraham, the would-be slaughterer, become, in our prayers,   17
the symbol of *hesed:* grace, compassion and love? A symbol of love, he who
was ready to throttle his son?

And Isaac, why was he called Isaac? *Yitzhak?* He who will laugh? Laugh   18
at whom? At what? Or, as Sarah thought, he who will make others laugh?
Why was the most tragic figure in Biblical history given such a bizarre name?

. . .

*The "Temple in Jerusalem" is Solomon's Temple, first built on the summit of Mt. Moriah where
Abraham and Isaac's story takes place. Its history of repeated construction and destruction here
symbolizes the history of the sufferings of the Jews.

What do we know about his [Abraham's] life and his person? Many   19
things told to us by the Bible and expounded upon by the Midrash. We are
treated to an abundance of precise and picturesque details on both his private
and public activities. We are informed about his habits, his moods, his business relationships, his difficulties with his neighbors, his servants and his
concubines. He was rich, hospitable, friendly and giving; he invited strangers
into his home without asking who they were or what the purpose of their
visit might be. He welcomed the hungry and helped the poor, angels and
beggars alike, offering them both shelter and food.

. . .

He evidently was a restless man who could not stay idle long. He was   20
forever seeking new stimulation, new certainties; he abhorred all routine. He
would go from Haran to Canaan, sometimes pushing as far as Damascus, in
his search for worthy adversaries. He was an explorer of some stature who
affronted kings and robbers, and enjoyed defeating them, exulting when he
broke their pride.

Yet his greatest adventure was his encounter with God—an encounter   21
which was a result of deliberate choice on both sides. They addressed one
another as equals. According to the Midrash, God said to Abraham: *Ani yekhidi
veata yekhidi*—I am alone and you are alone, alone to know and proclaim it.
From that moment on, their dialogue took place under the implacable sign of
the absolute: they were to be both partners and accomplices. Before, says
legend, God reigned only in heaven; it was Abraham who extended his rule
unto the earth.

. . .

And one begins to wonder, since God and he loved one another so much   22
and collaborated so closely, why these tests? Why these ordeals and torture?
Because God tests only the strong. The weak do not resist or resist poorly;
they are of no consequence. But then, what good is it to resist, since God
knows the outcome in advance? Answer: God knows, man does not.

Most commentators assume that Abraham was tested for his own good.   23
To serve as an example to the peoples of the world and to earn him their
leaders' reverence. And also to harden him; to awaken in him an awareness
of his own strength and potential.

Of course, this does not satisfy everyone: the idea that suffering is good   24
for Jews is one that owes its popularity to our enemies.

And indeed there is another explanation, though not a very original one,   25
that brings into the picture an old acquaintance, always present in moments
of crisis and doubt: Satan. Source of all evil, supreme temptor. The easy, glib
answer, the scapegoat. The crafty gambler, the unabashed liar. The servant
who conveniently carries out the Master's dirty work, accepting all blame and
anathema in His place. The sacrifice of Isaac? God had nothing to do with it;
it was all Satan's doing. God did not want this test; Satan demanded it. The
inhuman game was Satan's scheme and he bears full responsibility. Satan: the
ideal alibi.

Just as he did with Job—who is frequently compared to Abraham for   26 more than one reason—Satan used gossip to distort and embellish history. On his return from an inspection tour on earth, he handed his report to the Almighty while telling Him his impressions. Thus he came to his surprise visit with Abraham, who was celebrating the birth of his beloved son Isaac. Rejoicing, sumptuous meals, public festivities, Satan did not spare the superlatives, as usual. And do You know, said he perfidiously, do You know that Your faithful servant Abraham has forgotten You—You? Yes indeed, his good fortune has gone to his head; he forgot to set aside an offering for You. He thought only of his joy, as though it did not come from You; he fed all his guests, yet he neglected to offer You the youngest of his sheep, if only as a modest token of his gratitude. God was not convinced. He answered: No, no, you're wrong to suspect My faithful Abraham; he is devoted to Me, he loves Me, he would give Me all that he possesses—he would give me his son were I to ask him. Really? said Satan. Are You sure? I'm not. And God was provoked and felt compelled to accept the challenge. The rest can be found in Scripture.

The Biblical narrative is of exemplary purity of line, sobriety and terseness. Not one superfluous word, not one useless gesture. The imagery is striking, the language austere, the dialogue so incisive, it leaves one with a knot in one's throat. 27

. . . And, some time afterward, God put Abraham to the test. He said to him: Abraham. And he answered: Here I am. And He said: Take your son, your favored one, Isaac, whom you love, and go to the land of Moriah and offer him there as a burnt offering on one of the heights which I will point out to you. 28

This time Abraham did not answer: *Here I am;* he did not answer at all. He went home, lay down and fell asleep. The next morning he rose, awakened his son and two of his servants, and started out on his journey. At the end of three days—at the end of a silence that lasted three days—he saw the appointed place in the distance. He halted, and instructed the servants: *You stay here with the ass. The boy and I will go up there; we will worship and we will return to you.* 29

Abraham took the wood for the burnt offering and gave it to his son, Isaac. He himself took the firestone and the knife; and the two walked away together. 30

The last sentence gives us the key: one went to face death, the other to give it, but they went together; still close to one another though everything already separated them. God was waiting for them and they were going toward Him together. But then Isaac, who until that moment had not opened his mouth, turned to his father and uttered a single word: *Father.* And for the second time Abraham answered: *Here I am.* Was it because of the silence that followed this painfully hushed affirmation? Isaac began to feel uneasy; he wanted to be reassured or at least understand. 31

And Isaac said: Here is the firestone and the wood; but where is the sheep for the burnt offering? 32

Embarrassed, suddenly shy, Abraham tried to equivocate: *God will see to the sheep for His burnt offering, my son. And the two of them walked on together.* 33

The march continued. The two of them alone in the world, encircled by 34

God's unfathomable design. But they were *together.* Now the repetition renders a new sound while adding to the dramatic intensity of the narrative.

And Isaac began to guess, to understand. And then he knew. And the 35 father and the son remained united. Together they reached the top of the mountain; together they erected the altar; together they prepared the wood and the fire. Everything was ready, nothing was missing. And Isaac lay on the altar, silently gazing at his father.

And Abraham picked up the knife to slay his son. Then an angel of the Lord called 36 *to him from heaven: Abraham, Abraham! And he answered: Here I am.*

For the third time he answered: *Here I am.* I am the same, the same person 37 who answered Your first call; I answer Your call, whatever its nature; and even were *it* to change, *I* would not.

And the angel said: Do not raise your hand against the boy or do anything to him. 38 *For now I know that you fear God, since you have not withheld your son, your favored one, from Me.*

All is well that ends well. The sacrifice took place, yet Isaac remained 39 alive: a ram was slaughtered and burned in his stead. Abraham reconciled himself with his conscience. And the angel, exulting, renewed before him shining promises for the future: his children, as numerous as the stars reflected in the sea, would inherit the earth. Abraham once more plunged into the magnificent dream which would always remind him of his covenant with God. No, the future was not dead. No, truth would not be stifled. No, exile would not go on indefinitely. Abraham should have returned home a happy and serene man. Except that the tale ends with a strange sentence which opens rather than heals the wounds: *Vayashav avraham el nearav*—And Abraham returned to his servants. Note the singular: *Vayashav,* he returned. He, Abraham. Alone. And Isaac? Where was Isaac? Why was he not with his father? What had happened to him? Are we to understand that father and son were no longer together? That the experience they just shared had separated them—albeit only *after* the event? That Isaac, unlike Abraham, was no longer the same person, that the real Isaac remained there, on the altar?

These profoundly disquieting questions provoked passionate responses 40 in the Midrash, where the theme of the *Akeda* occupies as important a place as the creation of the world or the revelation at Sinai.

The Midrash, in this case, does not limit itself to stating the facts and 41 commenting upon them. It delves into the very heart and silence of the cast of characters. It examines them from every angle; it follows them into their innermost selves; it goes so far as to imagine the unimaginable.

. . .

On the morning of the third day, says the Midrash, Abraham could 42 distinguish the appointed place from afar—just as the people did later before Sinai. He turned to his son and asked: Do you see what I see? Yes, replied Isaac, I see a splendid mountain under a cloud of fire. Then Abraham turned to his two servants and asked: And you, what do you see? The servants, passive onlookers, saw nothing but the desert. And Abraham understood that the event did not concern them and that they were to stay behind. And that the place was indeed the place.

And so the father and the son walked away together—*ze laakod veze léaked,* 43 the one to bind and the other to be bound, *ze lishkhot veze lishakhet,* the one to slaughter and the other to be slaughtered—sharing the same allegiance to the same God, responding to the same call. The sacrifice was to be their joint offering; father and son had never before been so close. The Midrashic text emphasizes this, as if to show another tragic aspect of the *Akeda,* namely, the equation between Abraham and Isaac. Abraham and Isaac were equals, in spite of their opposing roles as victim and executioner. But Abraham himself, whose victim was he? God's? Once more the key word is *yakhdav,* together: victims together. Together they gathered the wood, together they arranged it on the altar, together they set the stage for the drama to unfold. Abraham, says the text, behaved like a happy father preparing to celebrate his son's wedding, and Isaac like a groom about to meet his bride-to-be. Both were serene, at peace with themselves and each other.

But then, suddenly, for a brief moment, Isaac reentered reality and 44 grasped the magnitude and horror of what was to come: Father, what will you do, Mother and you, afterward? — He who has consoled us until now, answered Abraham, will continue to console us. — Father, Isaac went on after a silence, I am afraid, afraid of being afraid. You must bind me securely. And a little later: Father, when you shall speak to my mother, when you shall tell her, make sure she is not standing near the well or on the roof, lest she fall and hurt herself.

Our attention thereafter is centered on Isaac stretched out on the altar. 45 We watch him as Abraham gazes straight into his eyes. Abraham was weeping, his tears streaming into the eyes of his son, leaving a scar never to be erased. So bitterly did he weep that his knife slipped from his hands and fell to the ground. Only then, not before, did he shout in despair, and only then did God part the heavens and allow Isaac to see the higher sanctuaries of the *merkava,* of creation, with entire rows of angels lamenting: *Yakhid shokhet veyakhid nishkat*—Look at the slaughterer, he is alone and so is the one he is about to slaughter. All the worlds in all the spheres were in tumult: Isaac had become the center of the universe. He could not be allowed to die, not now, not like this. And die he would not. The voice of an angel was heard: Do not raise your hand against the boy, Abraham. Isaac must live.

Why did an angel intervene rather than God Himself? The Midrash 46 answers: God alone may order death, but to save a human life, an angel is enough.

A profoundly generous and beautiful explanation, but I have another 47 which I prefer. Mine allows me to do what until now I could not; namely, to identify not only with Isaac but also with Abraham.

The time has come for the storyteller to confess that he has always felt 48 much closer to Isaac than to his father, Abraham.

I have never really been able to accept the idea that inhumanity could 49

be one more way for man to move closer to God. Kierkegaard's too convenient theory of occasional "ethical suspension" never appealed to me. Kierkegaard maintains that Abraham concealed Isaac's fate from him in order to
protect his faith in God; let Isaac lose faith in man rather than in man's
Creator. These are concepts rejected by Jewish tradition. God's Law—we
said it earlier—commits God as well; but while God cannot suspend His
law, it is given to man—to man and not to God—to interpret it. However,
faith in God is linked to faith in man, and one cannot be separated from the
other.

Let us once again examine the question: Why didn't Abraham tell Isaac   50
the truth? Because he thought the *Akeda* was a matter strictly between himself
and God; it concerned nobody else, not even Isaac.

Thus I place my trust in man's strength. God does not like man to come   51
to him through resignation. Man must strive to reach God through knowledge and love. God loves man to be clear-sighted and outspoken, not blindly
obsequious. He respected Job because he dared to stand up to Him. Abraham
had interceded on behalf of the two sinful cities long before the test with
Isaac.

A double-edged test. God subjected Abraham to it, yet at the same time   52
Abraham forced it on God. As though Abraham had said: I defy You, Lord.
I shall submit to Your will, but let us see whether You shall go to the end,
whether You shall remain passive and remain silent when the life of my
son—who is also Your son—is at stake!

And God changed his mind and relented. Abraham won. That was why   53
God sent an angel to revoke the order and congratulate him; He Himself was
too embarrassed.

And suddenly we have another *coup de théâtre* [sudden dramatic turn of   54
events]. Abraham never ceases to astonish us: having won the round, he
became demanding. Since God had given in, Abraham was not going to be
satisfied with one victory and continue their relationship as though nothing
had changed. His turn had come to dictate conditions, or else . . . he would
pick up the knife—and come what may!*

Let us listen to the Midrash: 55

When Abraham heard the angel's voice, he did not cry out with joy or
express his gratitude. On the contrary, he began to argue. He, who until now
had obeyed with sealed lips, suddenly showed inordinate skepticism. He
questioned the counterorder he had been hoping and waiting for. First he
asked that the angel identify himself in due form. Then he demanded proof
that he was God's messenger, not Satan's. And finally he simply refused to
accept the message, saying: God Himself ordered me to sacrifice my son, it
is up to Him to rescind that order without an intermediary. And, says the
Midrash, God had to give in again: He Himself finally had to tell Abraham
not to harm his son.

This was Abraham's second victory; yet he was still not satisfied.   56

*The ellipses in paragraphs 54 and 57 are Wiesel's.

Listen . . .   57

When Abraham heard the celestial voice ordering him to spare his son   58
Isaac, he declared: I swear I shall not leave the altar, Lord, before I speak my
mind. — Speak, said God. — Did You not promise me that my descendants
would be as numerous as the stars in the sky? — Yes, I did promise you that.
— And whose descendants will they be? Mine? Mine alone? — No, said God,
they will be Isaac's as well. — And didn't You also promise me that they
would inherit the earth? — Yes, I promised you that too. — And whose
descendants will they be? Mine alone? — No, said God's voice, they will be
Isaac's as well. — Well then, my Lord, said Abraham unabashedly, I could
have pointed out to You before that Your order contradicted Your promise.
I could have spoken up, I didn't. I contained my grief and held my tongue.
In return, I want You to make me the following promise: that when, in the
future, my children and my children's children throughout the generations
will act against Your law and against Your will, You will also say nothing and
forgive them. — So be it, God agreed. Let them but retell this tale and they
will be forgiven.

We now begin to understand why Abraham's name has become synon-   59
ymous with *hesed*. For indeed he was charitable, not so much with Isaac as
with God. He could have accused Him and proved Him wrong; he didn't. By
saying yes—almost to the end—he established his faith in God and His
mercy, thus bringing Him closer to His creation. He won and—so says the
Midrash—God loves to be defeated by His children.

But unlike God, Satan hates to lose. Unlike God, he takes revenge,   60
however and against whomever he can. Defeated by Abraham and Isaac, he
turned against Sarah, appearing before her disguised as Isaac. And he told her
the *true* story that was taking place on Mount Moriah. He told her of the
march, the ritual ceremony, the heavenly intervention. Barely had Satan
finished talking, when Sarah fell to the ground. Dead.

Why this legend? It has a meaning. Abraham thought that the *Akeda*   61
was a matter between himself and God, or perhaps between himself and his
son. He was wrong. There is an element of the unknown in every injustice,
in every adventure involving total commitment. One imposes suffering on a
friend, a son, in order to win who knows what battles, to prove who knows
what theories, and in the end someone else pays the price—and that someone
is almost always innocent. Once the injustice has been committed, it eludes
our control. All things considered, Abraham was perhaps wrong in obeying,
or even in making believe that he was obeying. By including Isaac in an
equation he could not comprehend, by playing with Isaac's suffering, he
became unwittingly an accomplice in his wife's death.

Another text, even more cruel, goes further yet. It hints that the tragic   62
outcome could, after all, not be averted. Hence the use of the singular verb:
Vayashav avraham el nearav. Yes, Abraham did return alone. One does not play
such games with impunity.

Of course, this hypothesis has been rejected by tradition. The ancient 63 commentators preferred to imagine Isaac shaken but alive, spending the unaccounted-for years at a yeshiva or perhaps even in paradise, but eventually returning home.*

Yet popular imagination—collective memory—adheres rather to the 64 tragic interpretation of the text. Isaac did not accompany his father on the way back because the divine intervention came too late. The act had been consummated. Neither God nor Abraham emerged victorious from the contest. They were both losers. Hence God's pangs of guilt on Rosh Hashana, when He judges man and his deeds. Because of the drama that took place at Mount Moriah, He understands man better. Because of Abraham and Isaac, He knows that it is possible to push some endeavors too far.

That is why the theme and term of the *Akeda* have been used, through- 65 out the centuries, to describe the destruction and disappearance of countless Jewish communities everywhere. All the pogroms, the crusades, the persecutions, the slaughters, the catastrophes, the massacres by sword and the liquidations by fire—each time it was Abraham leading his son to the altar, to the holocaust all over again.

Of all the Biblical tales, the one about Isaac is perhaps the most timeless 66 and most relevant to our generation. We have known Jews who, like Abraham, witnessed the death of their children; who, like Isaac, lived the *Akeda* in their flesh; and some who went mad when they saw their father disappear on the altar, with the altar, in a blazing fire whose flames reached into the highest of heavens.

We have known Jews—ageless Jews—who wished to become blind for 67 having seen God and man opposing one another in the invisible sanctuary of the celestial spheres, a sanctuary illuminated by the gigantic flames of the holocaust.

. . .

But the story does not end there. Isaac survived; he had no choice. He 68 had to make something of his memories, his experience, in order to force us to hope.

For our survival is linked to his. Satan could kill Sarah, he could even 69 hurt Abraham, but Isaac was beyond his reach. Isaac too represents defiance. Abraham defied God, Isaac defied death.

What did happen to Isaac after he left Mount Moriah? He became a 70 poet—author of the *Minha* service†—and did not break with society. Nor did he rebel against life. Logically, he should have aspired to wandering, to the pursuit of oblivion. Instead he settled on his land, never to leave it again, retaining his name. He married, had children, refusing to let fate turn him into a bitter man. He felt neither hatred nor anger toward his contemporaries who did not share his experience. On the contrary, he liked them and showed

*A yeshiva is an academy for studying the Talmud, the body of Jewish law and tradition. The notion of Isaac at a yeshiva is, of course, whimsical.

†A daily afternoon liturgy.

concern for their well-being. After Moriah, he devoted his life and his right to immortality to the defense of his people.

At the end of time, say our sages, God will tell Abraham: Your children 71 have sinned. And Abraham will reply: Let them die to sanctify Your name. Then God will turn to Jacob and say: Your children have sinned. And Jacob will reply: Let them die to sanctify Your name. Then God will speak to Isaac: Your children have sinned. And Isaac will answer: *My* children? Are they not also Yours? Yours as well?

It will be Isaac's privilege to remain Israel's *Melitz-Yosher,* the defender 72 of his people, pleading its cause with great ability. He will be entitled to say anything he likes to God, ask anything of Him. Because he suffered? No. Suffering, in Jewish tradition, confers no privileges. It all depends on what one makes of that suffering. Isaac knew how to transform it into prayer and love rather than into rancor and malediction. This is what gives him rights and powers no other man possesses. His reward? The Temple was built on Moriah. Not on Sinai.

Let us return to the question we asked at the beginning: Why was the 73 most tragic of our ancestors named Isaac, a name which evokes and signifies laughter? Here is why. As the first survivor, he had to teach us, the future survivors of Jewish history, that it is possible to suffer and despair an entire lifetime and still not give up the art of laughter.

Isaac, of course, never freed himself from the traumatizing scenes that 74 violated his youth; the holocaust had marked him and continued to haunt him forever. Yet he remained capable of laughter. And in spite of everything, he did laugh.

Questions for Discussion

1. Can you summarize Wiesel's point in one topic sentence (for example, "God is good, after all," or "The meaning of suffering is such-and-such or so-and-so")? If so, can you get your classmates to agree with your summary? If your summaries seem even less satisfactory than usual, why is that so?

2. Do you or any other members of your class know of interpretations of the story of Abraham and Isaac that Wiesel does not offer? If so, discuss how they differ from his.

3. For some religious thinkers, religion is best explained in full-fledged systematic *theologies,* organized accounts of the nature of God and His creation (perhaps the most famous example is the *Summa Theologica* of St. Thomas Aquinas, a monumental intellectual inquiry running to thousands of pages). Neither the Torah nor the Christian Bible is like that. Like Wiesel,

they seem to say that the truth about religion is expressed better in stories than in propositions or arguments. Do you think that there are some truths that are somehow "beyond" direct statement? That some genuine knowledge cannot be proved with argument? Or do you think that whatever cannot be stated in straightforward propositions must be something other than "truth" or "knowledge"—poetry, perhaps, or myth?

Suggested Essay Topics

1. Most of our suggested topics in this book have asked you to present an argument, a systematic defense of some belief, with your reasons worked out as fully as possible. Here is your chance to try a freer kind of exploration. Choose any story from the Torah or Bible (or any other scripture you may know) and tell it again, but more fully, adding your own hunches about the characters' motives or the probable outcomes. For example, you might dramatize the scene between Cain and Abel in Genesis 4, trying to understand the point of view of both characters. Or you might try the story of Mary and Martha in the New Testament (Luke 10:38–42). Try to tell your story in a tone that suggests, like Wiesel's, that you are engaged in a genuine search for meaning.

2. For Wiesel the holocaust was a supreme test of his religious faith, and he sees God's command to Abraham presenting a similar kind of supreme test. Can you think of experiences of evil or suffering in your own life that, though less grand in scale, presented to you the same *kind* of challenge? If so, write an essay in the form of a letter to someone you trust, recounting the argument with yourself (or perhaps the quarrel with God) that your experience produced. You may not want—or you may not be able—to settle the issues you raise, or you may feel ready to affirm or reject the religious views that were challenged by your experience. If you do take a settled position, however, try to give reasons for it. Merely asserting how you "feel" about God or religion will not make an interesting statement.

Rosemary Radford Ruether

This essay was written in 1972 at the height of various anti-establishment, quasi-revolutionary movements that had begun in the late 1950s with civil rights agitation and ended in the early seventies with the conclusion of the Vietnam War and the beginning of Watergate. In the midst of this 15-year ferment, feminists began making powerful arguments against the restrictiveness and injustice of traditional roles for women. Feminist arguments, not all of them made by women, began to surface in literary criticism; in politics; in business; in sports; in historical analysis; in legal analysis; in reformulations of sex, marital, and parenting roles; in criticism of advertising and mass media; in the arts; and in theology—to mention only a few areas. (See our Chapter 8.) Regardless of the arena of discussion, the general feminist theme is (1) that women have been the victims of suppression and exploitation that are sometimes explicitly hostile but often disguised as preferential treatment (the "woman on a pedestal" treatment), (2) that they have been disallowed from participating fully in the prestige and power traditionally reserved for men, and (3) that this enforced diminishment of their development as persons, not to mention the social loss of their contributions as thinkers and problem solvers, is bad not only for women but also for men and ultimately for the whole society.

In theology the feminist discussion continues on many fronts: the role of women in church history, the role of women in contemporary church leadership, the criticism of male-centered concepts ("God the father"), the reinterpretation of biblical doctrines, and so on. In this essay, Rosemary Radford Ruether (b. 1936) presents a critique of one of the main ideas in the Christian view of the world: the idea that body and matter are inferior to and hostile to mind and spirit and that the most perfect form of existence is one in which mind and spirit finally separate themselves forever from entanglements with their inferior components, body and matter. One traditional Christian view is that this blessed separation comes after death, in heaven, where the disembodied soul is seen as enjoying a perfect and eternal existence.

For Ruether, this dualistic view of the world's structure and man's nature (see the introduction to Plato's "Allegory of the Cave," in Chapter 6, for further discussion of dualism) has its roots in two sources: Neo-Platonism and apocalyptic Judaism (see the notes at bottom of p. 910). "Christianity," she says, "brought together both of these myths: the myth of world cataclysm [based on apocalyptic Judaism] and the myth of the flight of the soul to heaven [based on Platonic notions]" (¶23). But she is not primarily interested in a historical analysis. Of more importance to her is showing that the influence of this dualism has been in many ways pernicious. It has helped justify, for example, the systematic subjugation of women in Christian thinking, which has traditionally aligned women with the inferior elements of body, sensuality, earth, and matter, and aligned men with the superior elements of intellect, spirit, and high-mindedness. The arrangements and duties of domestic living have been given to women, while men have given themselves the tasks of pursuing "higher" goals (power, prestige, victory, competition, civilization, and so on) and portrayed themselves as driven by "higher" motives (theoretical, intellectual, patriotic, spiritual).

Ruether undertakes to expose and challenge this pernicious body- and soul-splitting dualism reinforced and sustained by Christian doctrines. She also proposes an alternative view. As you read, try to establish where her historical analysis turns into evaluation, whether or not you agree with her criticism of Christian doctrines, and to determine the content of her alternative. Keep in mind that as a professor of theology (at Garrett Theological Seminary in Evanston, Illinois), Ruether is offering her criticisms not as an unbeliever, as an atheist, or as a church-hater, but as a Christian theologian and scholar. Whether or not you think this gives her criticism more force, it is clear that as a Christian, a theologian, a scholar, and a woman, the issues have an inevitable importance for her. If they were just Ruether's issues or just women's issues, they would be more suitable for discussion by special-interest groups than by college freshmen. The truth is, however, that regardless of our religion and our sex, the notions that Christianity has offered about the relationship between body and mind, man and nature, and men and women are so deeply ingrained in our society that they are an important influence on us all. Do you find that Ruether's basic claims about the sexist bias in Christian thought are well supported? Even if you disagree, do you find her challenge to traditional Christian thinking vital and useful? Or does it seem dangerous and subversive? Will it serve to weaken or strengthen the beliefs of Christians? Regardless of how we each answer these questions, Ruether invites us to examine afresh our notions about truth and about the kind of world we want to live in.

MOTHEREARTH
AND THE MEGAMACHINE

A Theology of Liberation in a Feminine, Somatic, and Ecological Perspective

From *Womanspirit Rising: A Feminist Reader in Religion* (1979).

Christianity, as the heir of both classical Neo-Platonism and apocalyptic Judaism,* combines the image of a male, warrior God with the exaltation of the intellect over the body. . . . These world-negating religions carried a set of dualities that still profoundly condition the modern world view. 1

All the basic dualities—the alienation of the mind from the body; the alienation of the subjective self from the objective world; the subjective retreat of the individual, alienated from the social community; the domination or rejection of nature by spirit—these all have roots in the apocalyptic-Platonic religious heritage of classical Christianity.† But the alienation of the masculine from the feminine is the primary sexual symbolism that sums up all these alienations. The psychic traits of intellectuality, transcendent spirit, and autonomous will that were identified with the male left the woman with the contrary traits of bodiliness, sensuality, and subjugation. Society, through the centuries, has in every way profoundly conditioned men and women to play out their lives and find their capacities within this basic antithesis. 2

This antithesis has also shaped the modern technological environment. The plan of our cities is made in this image: The sphere of domesticity, rest, and childrearing where women are segregated is clearly separated from those corridors down which men advance in assault upon the world of "work." The 3

Classical Neo-Platonism refers to the view, based on doctrines in Plato, that the world is divided into a duality between spirit and mind on the one hand and matter and body on the other. *Apocalyptic Judaism* refers to the Jewish belief that when the Messiah appears, the Jews will be freed from subjection to their enemies and restored to national greatness and religious purity. At the time of the rise of Christianity and the Jews' subjection to the Romans, this version of Judaism was held with special fervor by some.

†In other words, because part of Christianity's heritage goes back to Neo-Platonism and apocalyptic Judaism, Christianity is implicated in the destructive dualism of these religious views.

woman who tries to break out of the female sphere into the masculine finds not only psychic conditioning and social attitudes but the structure of social reality itself ranged against her.

The physical environment—access to basic institutions in terms of space   4
and time—has been shaped for the fundamental purpose of freeing one half of the race for the work society calls "productive," while the other half of the race remains in a sphere that services this freedom for work. The woman who would try to occupy both spheres at once literally finds *reality itself* stacked against her, making the combination of maternal and masculine occupations all but impossible without extraordinary energy or enough wealth to hire domestic help.

Thus, in order to play out the roles shaped by this definition of the male   5
life-style, the woman finds that she must either be childless or have someone else act as her "wife" (i.e., play the service role for her freedom to work). Women's liberation is therefore *impossible* within the present social system except for an elite few. Women simply cannot be persons within the present system of work and family, and they can only rise to liberated personhood by the most radical and fundamental reshaping of the entire human environment in a way that redefines the very nature of work, family, and the institutional expressions of social relations.

Although widespread hopes for liberty and equality among all humans   6
rose with the *philosophes* * of the Enlightenment, hardly any of these ideologies of the French Revolution and the liberal revolutions of the nineteenth century envisioned the liberation of women. The bourgeoisie, the workers, the peasants, even the Negro slaves were more obvious candidates for liberation, while the subjugation of women continued to be viewed as an unalterable necessity of nature. When the most radical of the French liberals, the Marquis de Condorcet, included women in the vision of equality, his colleagues thought he had lost his senses and breached the foundations of the new rationalism. The ascendency of Reason meant the ascendency of the intellect over the passions, and this must ever imply the subjugation of women.

An embarrassed silence or cries of ridicule likewise greeted this topic   7
when it was raised half a century later by another consistent libertarian, John Stuart Mill. Only after a long struggle from the nineteenth to the early twentieth century did women finally break down the barriers that separated them from the most basic rights to work, education, financial autonomy, and full citizenship—and even these freedoms are not universally secured today.

The reaction against and suppression of the Woman's Liberation Move-   8
ment has been closely tied to reactionary cultural and political movements, and the emancipated woman has been the chief target of elitism, fascism, and neoconservatism of all kinds. The Romantic Movement traumatized Europe's reaction to the French Revolution, reinstated the traditional view of women in idealized form, while the more virulent blood-and-soil reactionaries of the

---

*The *philosophes* were radical political theorists and philosophers whose criticism of the old order of things in the eighteenth century prepared the way for the French Revolution.

nineteenth century expressed a more naked misogynism. Literary figures such as Strindberg and Nietzsche couldn't stress strongly enough their abhorrence of women. At the turn of the century, Freud codified all the traditional negative views of the female psychology, giving them scientific respectability for the new psychological and social sciences. These negative stereotypes have been a key element in the repression of the women's movement through the popular mass media.*

In Nazism, the reactionary drive against the libertarian tradition cul- 9 minated in a virulent revival of racism, misogynism, elitism, and military and national chauvinism. Its victims were Jews, Communists, Social Democrats, and libertarians of all kinds—and, finally, the nascent women's movement.

In America, the period from World War I to the 1960s was characterized 10 by a successive revival of anti-Negro racism, anti-Semitism, the destruction of the American Left, and finally the cold war militarization of society based on a fanatic anti-Communism. In this same period, a continuous reactionary pacification of the women's movement deprived women of many of their earlier gains in educational and professional fields.

This modern backlash against the libertarian tradition seeks to reinstate 11 attitudes and social relations whose psychic roots run back through the Judeo-Christian and classical cultures into the very foundations of civilization building. The cry for liberty, equality, and fraternity challenged the roots of the psychology whereby the dominant class measured its status in terms of the conquest of classes, nations, races, and nature itself.

Lewis Mumford, in his monumental work on the foundations of ancient 12 civilization, *The Myth of the Machine,* and its supplementary volume on modern technological society, *The Myth of the Machine: The Pentagon of Power,* has shown how civilization has been founded on a subjugation of man to machinery. A chauvinist, paranoid psychology has directed men's productive energies into destruction rather than the alleviation of the necessities of all, thus aborting the promise of civilization. The subjugation of the female by the male is the primary psychic model for this chauvinism and its parallel expressions in oppressor-oppressed relationships between social classes, races and nations. It is this most basic symbolism of power that has misdirected men's psychic energy into the building of the Pentagon of Power, from the pyramids of ancient Egypt to the North American puzzle-palace on the Potomac.

The psychosocial history of the domination of women has not been 13 explored with any consistency, so the effort to trace its genesis and develop-

---

*In paragraphs 7–10 Ruether is giving a quick historical overview of attitudes toward the liberation of women since the French Revolution, which erupted in 1789: In paragraph 7 she shows John Stuart Mill's case in the middle of the nineteenth century for the liberation of women being met with silence or ridicule; in paragraph 8 she argues for the negative effects of Romanticism and the reactionary attitudes of Nietzsche, Strindberg, and Freud at the end of the nineteenth century and the beginning of the twentieth; in paragraph 9 she alludes to the undermining of the women's movement by Nazism in the mid-twentieth century; and in paragraph 10 she argues that racial and ethnic prejudice and the paranoia caused by the cold war, which lasted until the 1960s, have also undermined the liberation of women. That brings her up to the time of the writing of this article, 1972.

ment here can only be very general. However, it appears that in agricultural societies sexist and class polarization did not immediately reshape the religious world view. For the first two millennia of recorded history, religious culture continued to reflect the more holistic* view of society of the neolithic village, where the individual and the community, nature and society, male and female, earth Goddess and sky God were seen in a total perspective of world renewal. The salvation of the individual was not split off from that of the community; the salvation of society was one with the renewal of the earth; male and female played their complementary roles in the salvation of the world. This primitive democracy of the neolithic village persisted in the divine pantheons of Babylonia, despite the social class stratification that now appeared.

In these early civilizations, this holistic world view was expressed in the public celebration of the new year's festival, wherein the whole society of humanity and nature experienced the annual death of the cosmos and its resurrection from primordial chaos. In this cult, the king, as the personification of the community, played the role of the God who dies and is reborn from the netherworld. His counterpart was a powerful feminine figure who was at once virgin and mother, wife and sister, and who rescued the dying God from the power of the underworld. The king united with her at the end of the drama to create the divine child of the new year's vegetation. The crisis and rebirth encompassed both society and nature: The hymns of rejoicing celebrated the release of the captives, justice for the poor, and security against invasion, as well as the new rain, the new grain, the new lamb and the new child.

Somewhere in the first millennium B.C., however, this communal world view of humanity and nature, male and female, carried over from tribal society started to break down, and the alienations of civilization began to reshape the religious world picture. This change was partly aggravated by the history of imperial conquest that swept the people of the Mediterranean into larger and larger social conglomerates where they no longer felt the same unity with the king, the soil or the society.

The old religions of the earth became private cults for the individual, no longer anticipating the renewal of the earth and society but rather expecting an otherworldly salvation of the individual soul after death. Nature itself came to be seen as an alien reality, and men now visualized their own bodies as foreign to their true selves, longing for a heavenly home to release them from their enslavement within the physical cosmos. Finally, earth ceased to be seen as man's true home.

Hebrew religion is significant in this history as the faith of a people who clung with particular tenacity to their tribal identity over against the imperial powers of civilization. Hebrew society inherited kingship and the new year's festival of the temple from their Canaanite neighbors. But Yahwism repressed

*Holistic refers to the wholeness and interconnectedness of things—the opposite of their division into dualistic and antagonistic categories.

the feminine divine role integral to this cult and began to cut loose the festival itself from its natural base in the renewal of the earth.

This desert people claimed the land as a divine legacy, but they imag- 18 ined a manner of acquiring it that set them against the traditional cult of the earth. They took over the old earth festivals but reinterpreted them to refer to historical events in the Sinai journey. The messianic hopes of the prophets still looked for a paradisal renewal of earth and society, but this renewal broke the bonds of natural possibility and was projected into history as a future event.

So the pattern of death and resurrection was cut loose from organic 19 harmonies and became instead an historical pattern of wrath and redemption. The feminine imagery of the cult was repressed entirely, although it survived in a new form in the symbol of the community as the bride of Yahweh in the Covenant. But the bride was subordinate and dependent to the male Lord of Hosts, who reigned without consort in the heavens, confronting his sometimes rebellious, sometimes repentant people with punishment or promises of national victory.

The hopes for a renewal of nature and society, projected into a once and 20 for all historical future, now came to be seen as less and less realizable within history itself. And so the prophetic drive to free man from nature ended in the apocalyptic negation of history itself: a cataclysmic world destruction and angelic new creation.

In this same period of the first millennium B.C., we find in classical 21 philosophy a parallel development of the alienation of the individual from the world. Like the prophets, the philosophers repudiated the old nature Gods in their sexual forms of male and female divinities, and maleness was seen as bodiless and intellectual.

For Plato, the authentic soul is incarnated as a male, and only when it 22 succumbs to the body is it reincarnated in the body of a female and then into the body of some beast resembling the evil character into which it has fallen. The salvation of the liberated consciousness repudiates heterosexual for masculine love and mounts to heaven in flight from the body and the visible world. The intellect is seen as an alien, lonely species that originates in a purely spiritual realm beyond time, space, and matter, and has been dropped, either as into a testing place or, through some fault, into this lower material world. But space and time, body and mutability are totally alien to its nature. The body drags the soul down, obscuring the clarity of its knowledge, debasing its moral integrity. Liberation is a flight from the earth to a changeless, infinite world beyond. Again we see the emergence of the liberated consciousness in a way that alienates it from nature in a body-fleeing, world-negating spirituality.

Christianity brought together both of these myths—the myth of world 23 cataclysm and the myth of the flight of the soul to heaven. It also struggled to correct the more extreme implications of this body-negating spirituality with a more positive doctrine of creation and incarnation. It even reinstated, in covert form, the old myths of the year cult and the virgin-mother Goddess.

But the dominant spirituality of the Fathers of the Church finally ac- 24
cepted the antibody, antifeminine view of late antique religious culture.
Recent proponents of ecology have, therefore, pointed the finger at Christianity as the originator of this debased view of nature, as the religious sanction
for modern technological exploitation of the earth.

But Christianity did not originate this view. Rather, it appears to corre- 25
spond to a stage of development of human consciousness that coincided with
ripening classical civilization. Christianity took over this alienated world
view of late classical civilization, but its oppressive dualities express the basic
alienations at work in the psychosocial channelization of human energy since
the breakup of the communal life of earlier tribal society.

What we see in this development is a one-sided expression of the ego, 26
claiming its transcendental autonomy by negating the finite matrix of existence. This antithesis is projected socially by identifying woman as the incarnation of this debasing threat of bodily existence, while the same polarized
model of the psyche is projected politically upon suppressed or conquered
social groups.

The emphasis upon the transcendent consciousness has literally created 27
the urban earth, and both abstract science and revolution are ultimate products of this will to transcend and dominate the natural and social world that
gave birth to the rebellious spirit. The exclusively male God who creates out
of nothing, transcending nature and dominating history, and upon whose
all-powerful wrath and grace man hangs as a miserable, crestfallen sinner, is
the theological self-image and guilty conscience of this self-infinitizing spirit.

Today we recognize that this theology of rebellion into infinity has its 28
counterpart in a world-destroying spirituality that projects upon the female
of the race all its abhorrence, hostility and fear of the bodily powers from
which it has arisen and from which it wishes to be independent. One can feel
this fear in the threatened, repressively hostile energy that is activated in the
dominant male society at the mere suggestion of the emergence of the female
on an equal plane—as though equality itself must inevitably mean *his* resub-
jugation to preconscious submersion in the womb.

This most basic duality characterizes much recent theology. Karl Barth, 29
despite his model of cohumanity as the essence of the creational covenant,
insists on the relation of super- and subordination between men and women
as an ordained necessity of creation. "Crisis" and "secular" theologians such
as Bultmann and Gogarten continually stress the transcendence of history
over nature, defining the Gospel as the freedom of the liberated consciousness
to depart endlessly from natural and historical foundations into the content-
less desert of pure possibility. Such theologians are happy to baptize modern
technology as the expression of the freedom mediated by the Gospel to
transcend and dominate nature.

Today, both in the West and among insurgent Third World peoples, we 30
are seeing a new intensification of this Western mode of abstractionism and
revolution. Many are convinced that the problems created by man's ravaging
of nature can be solved only by a great deal more technological manipulation.

The oppressed peoples who have been the victims of the domination of the elite classes now seek to follow much the same path of pride, transcending wrath, separatism and power in order to share in the benefits of independence and technological power already won by the dominant classes.

Yet, at the same time, nature and society are giving clear warning signals 31 that the usefulness of this spirituality is about to end. Two revolutions are running in contrapuntal directions. The alienated members of the dominant society are seeking new communal, egalitarian life-styles, ecological living patterns, and the redirection of psychic energy toward reconciliation with the body. But these human potential movements remain elitist, privatistic, esthetic and devoid of a profound covenant with the poor and oppressed of the earth.

On the other hand, the aspirations of insurgent peoples rise along the 32 lines of the traditional rise of civilization through group pride, technological domination of nature and antagonistic, competitive relationships between peoples. Such tendencies might be deplored by those who have so far monopolized technology and now believe they have seen the end of its fruitfulness, but they must be recognized as still relevant to the liberation of the poor and oppressed from material necessity and psychological dependency.

We are now approaching the denouement of this dialectic. The ethic of 33 competitiveness and technological mastery has created a world divided by penis-missiles and countermissiles that could destroy all humanity a hundred times over. Yet the ethic of reconciliation with the earth has yet to break out of its snug corners of affluence and find meaningful cohesion with the revolutions of insurgent peoples.

The significance of the women's revolution, then, may well be its 34 unique location in the center of this clash between the contrapuntal directions of current liberation movements. Women are the first and oldest oppressed, subjugated people. They too must claim for themselves the human capacities of intellect, will, and autonomous creative consciousness that have been denied them through this psychosocial polarization in its most original form.

Yet women have also been identified with nature, the earth, and the 35 body in its despised and rejected form. To simply reject this identification would be to neglect that part of ourselves we have been left to cultivate and to buy into that very polarization of which we have been the primary victims. The significance of our movement will be lost if we merely seek valued masculine traits at the expense of devalued feminine ones.

Women must be the spokesmen for a new humanity arising out of the 36 reconciliation of spirit and body. This does not mean selling short our rights to the powers of independent personhood. Autonomy, world-transcending spirit, separatism as the power of consciousness raising, and liberation from an untamed nature and from subjugation to the rocket-ship male—all these revolutions are still vital to women's achievement of integral personhood. But we have to look beyond our own liberation from oppression to the liberation of the oppressor as well. Women should not buy into the masculine ethic of competitiveness that sees the triumph of the self as predicated upon the subjugation of the other. Unlike men, women have traditionally cultivated a communal personhood that could participate in the successes of others rather than seeing these as merely a threat to one's own success.

To seek the liberation of women without losing this sense of commu- 37
nal personhood is the great challenge and secret power of the women's revolution. Its only proper end must be the total abolition of the social pattern of domination and subjugation and the erection of a new communal social ethic. We need to build a new cooperative social order out beyond the principles of hierarchy, rule, and competitiveness. Starting in the grass roots local units of human society where psychosocial polarization first began, we must create a living pattern of mutuality between men and women, between parents and children, among people in their social, economic, and political relationships and, finally, between mankind and the organic harmonies of nature.

Such a revolution entails nothing less than a transformation of all the 38
social structures of civilization, particularly the relationship between work and play. It entails literally a global struggle to overthrow and transform the character of power structures and points forward to a new messianic epiphany that will as far transcend the world-rejecting salvation myths of apocalypticism and Platonism as these myths transcended the old nature myths of the neolithic village. Combining the values of the world-transcending Yahweh with those of the world-renewing Ba'al in a post-technological religion of reconciliation with the body, the woman and the world, its salvation myth will not be one of divinization and flight from the body but of humanization and reconciliation with the earth.

Our model is neither the romanticized primitive jungle nor the modern 39
technological wasteland. Rather it expresses itself in a new command to learn to cultivate the garden, for the cultivation of the garden is where the powers of rational consciousness come together with the harmonies of nature in partnership.

The new earth must be one where people are reconciled with their labor, 40
abolishing the alienation of the megamachine while inheriting its productive power to free men for unalienated creativity. It will be a world where people are reconciled to their own finitude, where the last enemy, death, is conquered, not by a flight into eternity, but in that spirit of St. Francis that greets "Brother Death" as a friend that completes the proper cycle of the human soul.

The new humanity is not the will to power of a monolithic empire, 41
obliterating all other identities before the one identity of the master race, but a polylinguistic appreciativeness that can redeem local space, time, and identity. We seek to overcome the deadly Leviathan of the Pentagon of Power, transforming its power into manna to feed the hungry of the earth. The revolution of the feminine revolts against the denatured Babel of concrete and steel that stifles the living soil. It does not merely reject the spirit child born

from the earth but seeks to reclaim spirit for body and body for spirit in a messianic appearing of the body of God.

Questions for Discussion

1. After discussing the world view of neolithic tribal societies, Ruether says, "Somewhere in the first millennium B.C., however, this communal world view of humanity and nature, male and female, carried over from tribal society started to break down . . . and men now visualized their own bodies as foreign to their true selves, longing for a heavenly home to release them from their enslavement within the physical cosmos" (¶15–16). To what extent do you see this dualistic antagonism between soul and body, earth and heaven still residing in Christianity (or other religions) today? How do Christians in your experience feel about the demands, impulses, and constraints of physical life?

2. How would you paraphrase paragraph 26 in your own words?

3. How difficult would it be for you to visualize God as a female? If you pray, can you imagine praying to a female God? What feelings would be aroused by the attempt? Can you account for them?

4. Today women are going into the pastoral ministry more than ever before. To those of you for whom attending a church pastored by a woman would be a new experience, can you say whether it would make you uncomfortable? Why or why not? To those of you who may have been in a church when a female pastor followed a male, can you give an account of the range of parishioners' reactions? If some responses were sexist, did they fade with time? How has the situation worked out?

5. To those of you who are Catholic, how would you feel about attending a mass conducted by a female priest? Would it undermine for you the authenticity or efficacy of the ritual? Why or why not?

6. In paragraphs 36–37 Ruether makes it clear that she does not want changes that will merely place women in the same roles and give them the same attitudes that men have traditionally held. How would you state her goals more fully in your own words? If she does not want merely to turn the present system upside down, what does she want?

Suggested Essay Topics

1. This topic is based on discussion question 6. In an essay addressed to someone to whom you think feminist arguments are either novel or repugnant, write an essay in which you, first, try to give, as completely as possible, an explanation in your own words of Ruether's position (you may quote Ruether if you wish) and, second, attempt to provide examples

of your own to support her case, concluding with an evaluation of her final alternative.

2. In paragraph 5 Ruether states, "Women simply cannot be persons within the present system of work and family, and they can only rise to liberated personhood by the most radical and fundamental reshaping of the entire human environment in a way that redefines the very nature of work, family, and the institutional expressions of social relations." In an essay written as a letter addressed to Ruether, give the best reasons you can muster for either agreeing or disagreeing with the position advanced in the quotation. If you agree, detail some of the "radical and fundamental" reshapings of the "entire human environment" that you think should come first, and cite the advantages you think will follow. If you disagree, provide concrete illustration of the disadvantages that will follow by adopting her views.

Walter T. Stace

Walter T. Stace (1886–1967), for many years a professor of philosophy at Princeton, undertakes here to define religion in the most basic terms possible. From his point of view, being religious has little to do with going to church, professing creeds, or believing conventionally in the existence of a personal God. Religion lies not in outward beliefs or activities but in an inner disposition of the soul that all human beings share. The "impulse [that] lies deep down in every human heart"—the religious impulse in its most basic form—is "the hunger of the soul for the impossible, the unattainable, the inconceivable" (¶ 6).

The most unattainable achievement for a human being—a creature—would be to enter a state beyond creatureliness: not by dying, for dying is in the nature of creatures, but by going beyond creaturely existence altogether. To exist but to have none of the transitory properties of existence—that is the impossible. Yet that condition is exactly what human beings most want—so argues Stace—even as they are aware that they will never achieve it.

Other aspects of conventional religion, such as moral codes and belief in a personal God, are not necessarily irrelevant to the religious impulse, but they are not synonymous with it. And religion is not to be debased by finding, or fabricating, "explanations" for it. Religion can be neither accounted for nor explained away by theories of social behavior, human psychology, logic, or reason. The fundamental characteristic of religion is an inescapable paradox: To be religious means knowing that I cannot have what I want, that I can never fully understand the mystery of what I want (cannot, at least, fully name it or explain it), and that I persist in longing for it against any hope of ever achieving it.

WHAT RELIGION IS

Chapter 1 of *Time and Eternity: An Essay in the Philosophy of Religion* (1952).

"Religion," says Whitehead, "is the vision of something which stands   1
beyond, behind, and within, the passing flux of immediate things; something
which is real, and yet waiting to be realized; something which is a remote
possibility, and yet the greatest of present facts; something which gives
meaning to all that passes, and yet eludes apprehension; something whose
possession is the final good, and yet is beyond all reach; something which is
the ultimate ideal, and the hopeless quest."[1]

These words evidently express a direct intuition of the writer. They well   2
up from his own personal religious experience and therefore stir the depths
in us who read. What he says is not a faded copy of what someone else has
felt or thought or seen, as the majority of pious utterances are—hackneyed
and wornout clichés, debased by parrot-like repetition, although they too,
poor dead things, once issued fresh-minted from a living human soul. Here
and there amid the arid hills of human experience are well-springs and
fountain-heads of religious intuition. They are the original sources of all
religion. They need not always be of great grandeur. They may be humble
rivulets of feeling. Or they may give rise to great rivers of refreshment
flowing through the centuries. But always, great or small, they bear upon
themselves the stamp of their own authenticity. They need no external proof
or justification. Indeed they are incapable of any. We know them because the
God in us cries out, hearing the voice of the God in the other, answering back.
The deep calls to the deep.

Whitehead's words are of this kind.   3

Note first their paradoxical character. To the "something" of which they   4
speak are attributed opposite characters which barely avoid, if they do avoid,
the clash of flat contradiction. Each clause is a balance of such contradicting
predicates. The meaning cannot be less than that paradox and contradiction
are of the very essence of that "something" itself.

Note, too, the final words. That something which man seeks as his   5
ultimate ideal is the "hopeless quest." This is not a careless expression, an
exaggeration, a loose use of words. It is not rhetoric. If this phrase had come
at the beginning of the passage, it might have been toned down in the
succeeding sentences. But it strikes the final note. It is the last word.

And one can see why. For religion is the hunger of the soul for the   6
impossible, the unattainable, the inconceivable. This is not something which
it merely happens to be, an unfortunate accident or disaster which befalls it
in the world. This is its essence, and this is its glory. This is what religion
means. The religious impulse in men *is* the hunger for the impossible, the
unattainable, the inconceivable—or at least for that which is these things in
the world of time. And anything which is less than this is not religion—
though it may be some very admirable thing such as morality. Let it not be
said that this makes religion a foolish thing, fit only for madmen—although

indeed from the world's point of view the religious man *is* a madman. For, mad or not, this impulse lies deep down in every human heart. It is of the essence of man, quite as much as is his reason.

Religion seeks the infinite. And the infinite by definition is impossible,   7 unattainable. It is by definition that which can never be reached.

Religion seeks the light. But it is not a light which can be found at any   8 place or time. It is not somewhere. It is the light which is nowhere. It is "the light which never was on sea or land." Never was. Never will be, even in the infinite stretches of future time. The light is non-existent, as the poet himself says. Yet it is the great light which lightens the world. And this, too, the poet implies.

Religion is the desire to break away from being and existence altogether,   9 to get beyond existence into that nothingness where the great light is. It is the desire to be utterly free from the fetters of being. For every being is a fetter. Existence is a fetter. To be is to be tied to what you are. Religion is the hunger for the non-being which yet is.

In music sometimes a man will feel that he comes to the edge of break-   10 ing out from the prison bars of existence, breaking out from the universe altogether. There is a sense that the goal is at hand, that the boundary wall of the universe is crumbling and will be breached at the next moment, when the soul will pass out free into the infinite. But the goal is not reached. For it is the unspeakable, the impossible, the inconceivable, the unattainable. There is only the sense of falling backward into time. The goal is only glimpsed, sensed, and then lost.

One thing is better than another thing. Gold is perhaps better than   11 clay, poetry than push-pin. One place is pleasanter than another place. One time is happier than another time. In all being there is a scale of better and worse. But just because of this relativity, no being, no time, no place, satisfies the ultimate hunger. For all beings are infected by the same disease, the disease of existence. If owning a marble leaves your metaphysical and religious thirst unquenched, so will owning all the planets. If living on the earth for three-score years and ten leaves it unsatisfied, neither will living in a fabled Heaven for endless ages satisfy it. For how do you attain your end by making things bigger, or longer, or wider, or thicker, or more this or more that? For they will still be *this* or *that*. And it is being this or that which is the disease of things.

So long as there is light in your life, the light has not yet dawned. There   12 is in your life much darkness—that much you will admit. But you think that though this thing, this place, this time, this experience is dark, yet that thing, that place, that time, that experience is, or will be, bright. But this is the great illusion. You must see that all things, all places, all times, all experiences are equally dark. You must see that all stars are black. Only out of the *total* darkness will the light dawn.

Religion is that hunger which no existence, past, present, or future, no   13 actual existence and no possible existence, in this world or in any other world, on the earth or above the clouds and stars, material or mental or spiritual, can ever satisfy. For whatever is or could be will have the curse on it of thisness or thatness.

This is no new thought. It is only what religious men have always said. To the saint Narada the Supreme Being offered whatsoever boon his heart could imagine—abundance of life, riches, health, pleasure, heroic sons. "That," said Narada "and precisely that is what I desire to be rid of and pass beyond." It is true that the things here spoken of—health, riches, even heroic sons—are what we call worldly, even material, things. But they are symbolic only. They stand for all things of any kind, whether material or non-material—for all things, at least, which could have an existence in the order of time, whether in the time before death or in the time after. 14

It is true that simple-minded religious men have conceived their goal as a state of continued existence beyond the grave filled with all happy things and experiences. But plainly such happy things and experiences were no more than symbolic, and the happy heavens containing such things have the character of myth. To the human mind, fast fettered by the limits of its poor imagination, they stand for and represent the goal. One cannot conceive the inconceivable. So in place of it one puts whatever one can imagine of delight; wine and houris if one's imagination is limited to these; love, kindness, sweetness of spiritual living if one is of a less materialistic temper. But were these existences and delights, material or spiritual, to be actually found and enjoyed as present, they would be condemned by the saint along with all earthly joys. For they would have upon them the curse, the darkness, the disease, of all existent things, of all that is this or that. This is why we cannot conceive of any particular pleasure, happiness, joy, which would not *cloy*, which—to be quite frank—would not in the end be boring. 15

"In the Infinite only is bliss. In the finite there is no bliss," says the ancient Upanishad.[2] And we are apt to imagine that this is a piece of rhetoric, or at least an exaggeration. For surely it is not strictly speaking true that in the finite there is no happiness at all. No doubt the saint or the moralist is right to speak disparagingly of the mere pleasures of sense. But is there, then, no joy of living? What of the love of man and woman, of parent and child? What of the sweetness of flowers, the blue of the sky, the sunlight? Is it not quite false that there is no bliss in these? And yet they are finite. So we say. But we fail to see that the author of the verse is speaking of something quite different from what we have in mind, namely of that ultimate bliss in God which is the final satisfaction of the religious hunger. And we think that this ultimate blessedness differs only *in degree* from the happy and joyful experiences of our lives. Whereas the truth is that it differs *in kind.* The joys, not only of the earth, but of any conceivable heaven—which we can conceive only as some fortunate and happy prolongation of our lives in time—are not of the same order as that ultimate blessedness. We imagine any joyful, even ecstatic, experience we please. We suppose that the blessedness of salvation is something like this, only more joyful. Perhaps if it were multiplied a million times. . . . But all this is of no avail. Though we pile mountain of earthly joy upon mountain of earthly joy, we reach no nearer to the bliss which is the 16 end. For these things belong to different orders; the one, however great, to the order of time; the other to the order of eternity. Therefore all the temporal joys which we pile upon one another to help our imaginations, are no more than symbolic, and the accounts of possible heavens mere myths.

Hence the religious soul must leave behind all things and beings, including itself. From being it must pass into Nothing. But in this nothing it must still be. Therefore also what it seeks is the being which is non-being. And God, who is the only food which will appease its hunger, is this Being which is Non-Being. Is this a contradiction? Yes. But men have always found that, in their search for the Ultimate, contradiction and paradox lie all around them. Did we not see that the words of Whitehead, with which we opened this chapter, must mean at least that contradiction and paradox lie at the heart of things? And is there any more contradiction here than we find—to give the most obvious example from traditional theology—in the doctrine of the Trinity? That, too, proclaims in unmistakable terms that there is contradiction in the Ultimate. The rationalizing intellect, of course, will not have it so. It will attempt to explain away the final Mystery, to logicize it, to reduce it to the categories of "this" and "that." At least it will attempt to water it down till it looks something like "common sense," and can be swallowed without too much discomfort! But the great theologians knew better. In the self-contradictory doctrine of the Trinity they threw the Mystery of God uncompromisingly in men's faces. And we shall see that all attempts to make religion a purely rational, logical, thing are not only shallow but would, if they could succeed, destroy religion. Either God is a Mystery or He is nothing at all.

NOTES

Both notes are Stace's.

[1] A. N. Whitehead, *Science and the Modern World,* chapter 12.
[2] Chandogya Upanishad.

Questions for Discussion

1. Do you agree with Stace's final assertion that "either God is a Mystery or He is nothing at all"? Do you think Stace argues this point convincingly? What parts of the supporting argument do you find particularly strong or weak?

2. According to Stace, the religious impulse "lies deep down in every human heart" (¶ 6). Granting Stace his definition of *religious impulse* as a paradoxical yearning for the unattainable, do you agree with the assertion that this

impulse is universal? What forms of behavior in human beings do you think either confirm or contradict the assertion?

3. Can you confirm from your own experience or observation the assertion that people indeed "hunger for the impossible"? Is it your impression that people consistently yearn for some glimpse of or contact with something beyond and above creatureliness? Or does it seem to you that people generally accept the terms of human existence without much regret or complaint?

4. Keeping in mind the extreme claims for science that Midgley (pp. 829–848) cites, does it seem fair to suggest that some devotees of science have, as Midgley's title suggests, turned science itself into a religion? Can you think of ways in which modern science fits Stace's definition of religion as a yearning for the unattainable or for the absolute?

5. Do the devoutly religious people you know seem fairly or adequately described by Stace's analysis? If not, do you think, after reading Stace, that they are less religious than you formerly thought? Or do you think he has left important considerations out of his discussion? If the latter, what has he omitted?

Suggested Essay Topics

1. Describe an experience—preferably one that recurs often enough to form a pattern, but a unique one will do—in which you are aware of having "hungered for the impossible." (Make sure that you are talking about hungering for the impossible in the same sense that Stace means. Wanting new clothes for the weekend dance when you have only $10 does not qualify.) Then either use Stace's argument to explain this hunger as a religious impulse and the pursuit of its fulfillment as a religious experience or refute Stace's argument by explaining your hunger in non-religious terms. (You might want to say, for example, that your feelings were merely a product of psychological or social conditioning—a product of the way you've been raised. But you will not want to admit that your desire for the impossible has anything to do with seeking an escape from the limitations of creatureliness.)

2. Spend a Sunday morning listening to as many television evangelists and preachers as you can. Choose one who interests you and evaluate, as you think Stace would, the degree of genuine religiousness you find either in the messages delivered or in the personality you can infer behind the messages.

   It is important here not to slide from possible objections you may have to the surface opinions of the preachers into the automatic judgment that they are not genuinely religious. It is inherent in Stace's view that true religion can be expressed in many different—and no doubt often surprising—forms.

Desmond Mpilo Tutu

Should churches take stands on political and social issues? Should churches agitate against injustice; bring political pressure to bear on oppressive governments; and use their resources to support the poor, the homeless, and the downtrodden even though they may not be members of any church at all?

Desmond Tutu (b. 1931), a bishop of the Catholic church and a black South African, answers these questions with a resounding and unambiguous "yes!" In the following excerpts from three sermons all focusing on the relationship between politics and religion, Bishop Tutu asserts repeatedly that the Church cannot focus on the vertical relationship that human beings have with God, but must also focus on the horizontal relationships that human beings have with each other. While obedience to God is the central task of humankind, this does not preclude, in fact it clearly includes, tending to the suffering that goes on among our fellow creatures.

In Bishop Tutu's view, the very fact that God came to earth as a human being to save human beings bestows an honor and status on human existence that demands an indignant response when human character is degraded, when possibilities are artificially limited, and when oppression creates unnecessary suffering and despair.

Bishop Tutu's courage in speaking out so strongly in criticism of both the government and the Dutch Reformed Church, which has always supported the South African government, is eloquent testimony to the depth of his own dedication to the principles he espouses. It is dangerous to criticize oppressive governments while living within their jurisdiction, especially if one is a critic of black skin in white-dominated South Africa. Yet the bishop continues to speak with both passion and clarity, challenging all who want a merely comfortable religion, inspiring those who are downtrodden with hope, and illustrating what it means to turn the Kingdom of God into a real force within an earthly context of oppression and suffering.

POLITICS AND RELIGION— THE SEAMLESS GARMENT

From *Hope and Suffering: Sermons and Speeches* (1983).

A familiar remark which has become almost a parrot cry is "Don't mix religion with politics!" It is a remark which is made not because a politician in his election campaign introduces a moral or religious element. No, we almost always hear it when a particular political, social or economic fact of life is criticized as being inconsistent with the Gospel of Jesus Christ as most Christians understand it. Politicians and others will utter that cry if, for instance, someone were to say that it is unchristian to neglect the development of rural areas because the inhabitants of those rural areas will be unable to resist the temptation to emigrate to the urban areas, where they will invariably help to cause slums to emerge. They will often not be able to compete on equal terms for jobs with their city counterparts, and so they will swell the ranks of the unemployed. They won't be able to find cheap accommodation because there is no longer such a commodity in the city, and so they will be reduced to putting up some kind of shelter on any available space, and a slum will have begun. If the Church demonstrates a concern for the victims of some such neglect or exploitation or denounces the widening gap in the country between the very few who are rich and the vast majority who are poor (a gap that seems almost always to widen rather than narrow), then the Church will be accused of meddling in affairs it knows very little about. This kind of criticism will reach crescendo proportions if the Church not merely provides an ameliorative ambulance service, but aims to expose the root causes; if it becomes radical (which refers to the roots of the matter) then it will arouse the wrath of those who benefit from the particular inequitable status quo. It could expose itself then to harassment and worse in its concern for justice, for an equitable distribution of wealth, in its call for the eradication of corruption, for an end to the abuse of power, the need to empower the powerless. And so when you work for a more just, participatory and sustainable society whose members share in crucial decision-making about the issues that are important for their lives, that is when you hear the cry, "Don't mix religion with politics!"

It is strange that this happens only when a particular socio-political and   2
economic policy is denounced as being unchristian or unjust. If that same policy is described by religious leaders as being in accordance with Christianity, then there is no question in this instance of religious persons being accused of mixing religion with politics. The White Dutch Reformed Church (DRC) in South Africa for a long time sought to provide scriptural justification for the Nationalist Party policy of apartheid. Nowhere was the cry uttered that this was mixing politics with religion; whereas when other South African Christians declared apartheid to be abhorrent to the Christian conscience, then people were told that religion and politics belonged in separate categories and that it was wrong to mix them. We need to add in fairness to the DRC that one hears less and less today that apartheid can be justified scripturally.

The same point about not mixing politics with religion or vice versa is   3
made by those who think that religion does have a bearing on what happens in politics. These persons tend to have an attenuated doctrine of reconciliation and want to avoid confrontation at all costs—to speak about a neutral God in situations of conflict, of injustice and oppression. They say God does not take sides and so the Church should not take sides, but must be somewhere in the middle. In an attempt to exercise a ministry of reconciliation such people present reconciliation as an easy option for Christians, and they speak about the need to be forgiving, especially to the victims of injustice, without making a call for repentance by the perpetrators of the injustice and for a redress of the unjust system—they will do this to such an extent that profound Christian words such as "reconciliation and forgiveness" are rejected with contempt by the poor and exploited because they appear to want

them to acquiesce in their condition of oppression and exploitation and powerlessness. It appears then as if Christianity is interpreted by those advocates as an anaemic reconciliation aimed at their domestication. It is forgotten that reconciliation is no easy option, nor does it rule out confrontation. After all, it did cost God the death of His Son to effect reconciliation; the cross of Jesus was to expose the sinfulness of sin when He took on the powers of evil and routed them comprehensively. No, just as there can be no cheap grace so there can be no cheap reconciliation, because we cannot cry, "peace, peace" where there is no peace.

We must, therefore, examine the biblical evidence to see what the   4 scriptures say about liberation. Do they say God is concerned only about individual salvation and has no interest in the redemption of the socio-political and economic matrix in which individuals live? Does it say the world is religiously and ethically neutral and of no consequence to salvation and the final consummation of all things, that what happens in the market place, in the courtroom, or in Parliament is of no particular religious significance, and that all that matters to God is what is confined to the sacred sphere of the ecclesiastical? Does it say God is in fact not really interested too much in what happens from Monday to Friday but only in that which happens on Sunday, and that He does not much care about the plight of the hungry, the dispossessed, the voiceless, powerless ones—that He does not take sides? When two persons are engaged in a conflict and one of them is considerably stronger than the other, to be neutral is not just and fair and impartisan because to be neutral is in fact to side with the powerful.

. . .

African and Black Theology must be concerned—and vitally con-   5 cerned—with liberation because, as we have shown, liberation is a serious preoccupation at the present time and it is not seen as being an alternative to personal salvation in Jesus Christ. No, it is seen in Africa as the inescapable consequence of taking the Gospel of Jesus Christ seriously. Only a spiritually, politically, socially and economically free Africa, where Christianity today is expanding faster than anywhere else in the world, can make a distinctive contribution to the life of the body of Jesus Christ and to the world community as a whole. Of course, there are differences between these two kinds of theology and there must be differences because in a sense these two kinds of theology develop from different contexts. African theology on the whole can afford to be a little more leisurely though I am not convinced of this, because Africa by and large is politically independent but there is not the same kind of oppression which is the result of White racism in South Africa.

Black Theology arises in a context of Black suffering at the hands of   6 rampant White racism. And consequently Black Theology is much concerned to make sense theologically of the Black Experience whose main ingredient is Black suffering, in the light of God's revelation of Himself in the Man, Jesus Christ. It is concerned with the significance of Black Existence, with liberation, with the meaning of reconciliation, with humanization, with forgiveness. It is much more aggressive and abrasive in its assertions, because of a burning and evangelistic zeal, as it must convert the Black man out of the stupor of his subservience and obsequiousness, to the acceptance of the thrilling and demanding responsibility of full human personhood, to make him reach out to the glorious liberty of the sons of God. It burns to awaken the White man to the degradation into which he has fallen by dehumanizing the Black man, and so it is concerned with the liberation of the oppressor equally as with that of the oppressed. It is not so naïve as to think that only economic or political oppression are what matter. But liberation must thus be understood in a total sense as removal of all that which keeps us in bondage, all that which makes us less than what God intended us to be.

. . .

The Church exists primarily to worship and adore God. It must praise   7
His most Holy Name. But it can never use this as a form of escapism. Precisely because it worships such a God it must take seriously the world He has created and which He loved so much that He gave His only begotten Son for it. Christians remember the strictures of the Old Testament prophets against an empty and formalistic worship. At the beginning of this paper we quoted examples of these prophetic denunciations. Jesus Himself reminded His followers that they could not offer an acceptable sacrifice on the altar if they had not been reconciled to their brother (Matthew 5:24), and the evangelist declares that anyone who claims to love God but hates his brother is a liar, because how can he love God whom he has not seen when he hates the brother whom he has? Our so-called vertical relationship with God is authenticated and expressed through our so-called horizontal relationship with our neighbour. Christianity knows nothing about pie in the sky when you die, or a concern for man's soul only. That would be a travesty of the religion of Jesus of Nazareth, who healed the sick, fed the hungry, etc. Christianity has been described as the most materialistic of the great religions. Jesus showed that for the spiritual God, His kingdom must have absolute centrality; but precisely because this was so, because He turned Godwards, He of necessity had to be turned manwards. He was the Man for others precisely because He was first and foremost the Man of God. If it must needs be so for the Son of God, it could not be otherwise for His Church.

The Church is constantly tempted to be conformed to the world, to   8
want influence that comes from power, prestige and privilege, and it forgets all the while that its Lord and Master was born in a stable, that the message of the angels about His birth was announced first not to the high and mighty but to the simple rustic shepherds. The Church forgets that His solidarity was with the poor, the downtrodden, the sinners, the despised ones, the outcasts, the prostitutes, the very scum of society. These were His friends whom He said would go to heaven before the self-righteous ones, the Pharisees, the scribes, the religious leaders of His day. The Church thinks to its peril that it must sanctify any particular status quo, that it must identify with the powerful and uphold the system which will invariably be exploitative and oppressive to some extent. When it succumbs to the temptations of power and identifies with a powerful establishment, then woe betide that Church

when that system is overthrown, when the powerless, the poor come into their own! It will go down with that system as happened especially to the Roman Catholics in Mozambique, and the Anglican Church in Zimbabwe and now the Roman Catholics in Zimbabwe.

The Church is always in the world but never of the world, and so must always maintain a critical distance from the political set-up so that it can exercise its prophetic ministry, "Thus saith the Lord", to denounce all that is contrary to the divine will whatever the cost. The Church has only one ultimate loyalty and that is to its Lord and Master Jesus Christ. The Church knows therefore that it will always have to say to worldly rulers whose laws are at variance with the laws of God that "We had much rather obey God than man" (Acts 4:19).

The Church must be ever ready to wash the disciples' feet, a serving Church, not a triumphalistic Church, biased in favour of the powerless to be their voice, to be in solidarity with the poor and oppressed, the marginalized ones—yes, preaching the Gospel of reconciliation but working for justice first, since there can never be real reconciliation without justice. It will demonstrate in its very life that Jesus has broken down the wall of partition, and so in its common life there will be no artificial barriers to any Christian being able to participate fully.

A Church that is in solidarity with the poor can never be a wealthy Church. It must sell all in a sense to follow its Master. It must sit loosely to the things of this world, using its wealth and resources for the sake of the least of Christ's brethren.

Such a Church will have to be a suffering Church, one which takes up its cross to follow Jesus. A Church that does not suffer is a contradiction in terms if it is not marked by the cross and inspired by the Holy Spirit. It must be ready to die, for only so can it share in Christ's passion so as to share His resurrection.

> A grain of wheat remains a solitary grain unless it falls into the ground and dies; but if it dies, it bears a rich harvest. The man who loves himself is lost, but he who hates himself in this world will be kept safe for eternal life. If anyone serves me, he must follow me; where I am, my servant will be. Whoever serves me will be honoured by my Father. (John 12:24–26)

I pray that for the sake of our children, for the sake of our land and for God's sake, the Dutch Reformed Church will be converted to its true vocation as the Church of God, because if that were to happen, if it were to stop giving spurious biblical support to the most vicious system—apartheid—since Nazism, if it were to become truly prophetic, if it were to be identified with the poor, the disadvantaged, the oppressed, if it were to work for the liberation of all God's children in this land, then, why, we would have the most wonderful country in the world. If it does not do these things and do them soon, then when liberation comes it will be consigned to the outer darkness for having retarded the liberation struggle and for misleading the Afrikaner. That is my fervent prayer for my fellow Christians in the Dutch Reformed Church. Woe betide all of us if the grace of God fails to move this great Church, and all churches, to be agents of the great God of the Exodus, the liberator God.

Questions for Discussion

1. A common cliché in American society is, "Never discuss politics or religion." Is there a truth that lies buried in this cliché? If so, what is it? If not, what truth is the cliché trying to express, even if it fails? How would Bishop Tutu most likely respond to this cliché?

2. Do you think Bishop Tutu is right to insist that the Church take a political stand with regard to political and social oppression? Or do you think he is illegitimately making his theology serve his politics? What reasons can you articulate to support whichever of these views you take?

3. Compare Bishop Tutu's comments about the white Dutch Reformed Church with Martin Luther King, Jr.'s, comments about the white, church-going moderates in "Letter From Birmingham Jail" (Chapter 6), a document that King wrote in response to a published criticism of his civil-rights activities in Birmingham written by several white clergymen. Are Tutu and King in basic agreement about the role the Church should play with regard to political activism? What similarities and differences between their two situations do you see? How do these similarities and differences help illuminate the whole issue?

4. How would you feel or react if you read in the papers that your minister, priest, or rabbi had been arrested and jailed for participating in a protest demonstration designed to protest rent gouging in slum apartments? Would you feel the same if he or she had been arrested for protesting some other issue, such as environmental pollution? How would you feel if your female minister, rabbi, or priest (there are still no female priests in the Catholic church, although women have recently been admitted to the priesthood in the Episcopal church) were arrested and jailed for participating in a protest against sexual harassment in downtown offices and businesses? How do you think most people in your church or temple would react? With whose reactions would you be most in agreement, most in disagreement?

Suggested Essay Topics

1. Imagine that Bishop Tutu, as a guest speaker in your church or temple, has just given the essay reprinted here as a sermon and that there has been a lot of disagreement among the congregation about the rightness of his claim that politics and religion are a "seamless garment." The religious leader of your church has invited any interested member of the congrega-

tion to make a written contribution to the controversy for publication in a special, enlarged edition of the church newsletter. You decide to write. Your audience is not Bishop Tutu so much as the members of your own church. You must decide whether to try to address (1) everyone or mainly (2) those who support Bishop Tutu's position or (3) those who do not support his position. Your job is to find reasons that will be effective in convincing people that the position you take on this issue is thoughtful and coherent.

2. Try to accomplish the following three tasks in an essay directed to your classmates. First, characterize the attitude that most church people or temple goers you know would take, or do take, toward the issue of whether the Church should or should not "get involved" in speaking out against social and political injustices. Second, in response to whatever you have described as your church's typical attitude on this issue, offer what you take to be constructive criticisms, pointing out that the attitude should be more this, or less that, or something else altogether. Third, discuss the reasons you offer for changing attitudes and describe the possible effects both in the Church and society if attitudes are changed in the way you would like to see them changed.

Ideas in Debate

John Fowles
C. S. Lewis

John Fowles

Do you believe in God? Do you believe in the divinity of Jesus? Do you believe in the goodness of Jesus, but not his divinity? Do you believe in the Church as the arm of God on earth? Do you believe in Jesus, but not in the Christian church that claims to be founded on his life and principles? Do you revere Christianity as the one true religion? Do you respect Christianity as one plausible and valid religion among many other plausible and valid religions? Do you respect Christianity, but think that it is outmoded, that it has served its purpose? Do you despise Christianity and all that it stands for?

From the time of the Roman emperor Constantine's conversion to Christianity in the fourth century and, in the sixth century, the conversion to Christianity of some of the tribes living on the British Isles, Christianity gradually became the dominant power both politically and spiritually on the European continent. It achieved its height of power, influence, and wealth during the Middle Ages and the Renaissance. During this time the Catholic church was a storehouse of knowledge and an instrument of learning; a patron of the arts; an arbiter of political conflicts; an immense landowner; a sprawling bureaucracy providing employment to scores of thousands of church clerics; an establisher of hospitals; an outfitter and a justifier of armies; and, through its parish priests, monks, nuns, and friars, it reached into and, indeed, did much to govern the everyday lives of aristocrats, peasants, and monarchs alike.

The Church met its first significant conflict early in the seventeenth century from the men of science who were getting modern science underway: Copernicus, Kepler, Galileo, and others. Not that these early scientists were atheists or even agnostics—far from it; they almost always described their purposes as dedicated to the glory of God. However, although they were religious, they were not as obedient to the Church as the Church often desired. Not all of them were punished by the Church as was Galileo, but some of them were. All of them did something—some more, some less—to offer an interpretation of natural phenomena that gradually threw the literal interpretation of the Bible into question. In addition, attitudes that prevailed among intellectuals during the period known as the Enlightenment (roughly 1660–1800), particularly the antagonism of Enlightenment philosophers to what they called the "superstitions" of the Church, put the church on the defensive as it had not been since the days of the Roman persecutions. Where the Church emphasized the necessity of faith, the Enlightenment emphasized reliance on reason. The writings of such thinkers as

Voltaire, Thomas Paine, Benjamin Franklin, James Mill, Jeremy Bentham, and John Stuart Mill proved corrosive to the faith that many people had automatically invested in religion.

*In the popular mind science has been considered as the main opponent of religion and the Church from the seventeenth century until now. As modern science really began to build up steam in the nineteenth century with its discoveries in geology (Lyell, 1830s), improvements in the telescope (Herschel, 1840s), historical criticism of the Bible (Straus and others in Germany, 1830s and 1840s), and especially, with the publication of Charles Darwin's two books on evolution—*On the Origin of Species by Means of Natural Selection *(1859) and* The Descent of Man and Selection in Relation to Sex *(1871)—the Church was not only put on the defensive but put to rout. Matthew Arnold, speaking of Christianity in his poem "Dover Beach" (1867), says*

> The Sea of Faith
> Was once, too, at the full, and 'round earth's shore
> Lay like the folds of a bright girdle furled.
> But now I only hear
> Its melancholy, long, withdrawing roar,
> Retreating to the breath
> Of the night wind, down the vast edges drear
> And naked shingles* of the world.

The past 20 years have seen scientists—especially those on the cutting edges of certain disciplines, such as particle physics and astronomy—admitting to religious beliefs and feelings. During this same period, religion has come to seem less hostile to science. Nowadays, both religion and science seem to see crass materialism as a common enemy more important than their traditional conflict over such matters as the authenticity of Jesus's miracles or the Virgin Birth. Still, in the eyes of most people, science is the winner of the tug-of-war for influence that began in the seventeenth century. Most people would probably say science that science dominates modern society the way the Church did in the Middle Ages. If it is science that has created many of our problems, it is to science that we turn for the solution of those problems, not religion.

*In the selection you are about to read, John Fowles (b. 1926), modern British novelist (*The Collector, The Magus, The French Lieutenant's Woman, Daniel Martin, *and others), lays out a set of beliefs about religion that touches on all of these issues. He speaks of evolution, scientific evidence, skepticism, religious mystery, faith, and moral conduct. As you read, try to determine just where Fowles draws the line between his admiration and support for religion and the Church on the one hand and his disapproval of both on the other.*

---

*Gravel beaches.

WHY I REJECT CHRISTIANITY

Our title. From *The Aristos* (1970).

> *I conjecture; you refute. This is not the dialogue; only my side of the dialogue. All precepts are ultimately descriptions of the preceptor; not of a truth or a humanity, but of his truth and his humanity.*

> *I believe in the essential sanity of man, and this is a memorial to that belief.*

1* Other philosophies of life.

2 I reject some of these as I might reject certain houses to live in; I do not reject them as houses for anyone else to live in, I do not deny them utility in part, beauty in part, meaningfulness in part; and therefore I do not deny them truth as defined below in part.

3 Ernst Mach:† A piece of knowledge is never false or true—but only more or less biologically and evolutionarily useful.

4 All dogmatic creeds are approximations: these approximations form a humus from which better approximations grow.

CHRISTIANITY

5 In a hundred years ecclesiastical Christianity will be dead. It is already a badly flawed utility.

6 The current ecumenical mania, the "glorious new brotherhood" of churches—futile scrabbling behind the wainscots of reality.

7 The best Christianity is that which accepts the War and the task of alleviating the suffering caused in the War; in short, that which maintains that compassion, charity and good acts are the principal human duties.

8 The best Christianity is based on the third of the three attributes of the It: total sympathy. This Christianity was instituted by a man of such active philosophical and evolutionary genius that it is little wonder that he was immediately called (as it was a necessary part of his historical efficacy that he should be) divine.

9 Christianity has protected the most precarious, because most evolved, section of the human race from itself. But in order to sell its often sound evolutionary principles it has been obliged to "lie"; and these "lies" have made it temporarily more, but now finally less, effective.

10 In no foreseeable future will many of the general social laws and attitudes stated or implied in Christianity be archaic; this is because they are based on compassion and common sense; but the metaphysical galimatias to which they are still linked increasingly alienates minds that see no neces-

*The paragraph numbers are Fowles's own. Because our right-margin paragraph numbers would be redundant, we will avoid them here.

†Ernst Mach (1838–1916), Austrian physicist and philosopher who investigated the physics of physiology and psychology of the senses.

sity for anything but compassion and common sense—that is, for humane rationality.

11　There is in every great religion a process akin to the launching of space vehicles; an element that gives the initial boost, the getting off the ground, and an element that stays aloft. Those who cling to Christian metaphysical dogma are trying to keep launcher and launched together.

12　First the buttress of dogmatic faith strengthens, then it petrifies; just as the heavy armor of some prehistoric reptiles first enabled them to survive and then caused them to disappear. A dogma is a form of reaction to a special situation; it is never an adequate reaction to all situations.

13　The Bet Situation: however much evidence of historical probability the theologians produce for the incredible (in terms of modern scientific credibility) events of the life of Jesus, they can never show that these events took place verifiably in the way they claim they took place. The same is finally true, of course, of any remote historical event. We are always reduced, in the bitter logical end, to the taking of some such decision as the Kierkegaardian step in the dark or the Pascalian* *pari;* and if I refuse to believe these incredible events took place, then it can be said that I am doing no more than take my own blind step in the opposite direction. It is, absolutely, as rational, or irrational, to disbelieve as to believe. A certain kind of blind believer, not confined to Christianity but common in it since the days of Tertullian,† uses the apparent absurdity, and the consequent despair, of our never being able to establish any certainty of belief as both a source of energy for the step in the dark and an indication of the direction in which it should be taken. Because, by any empirical human definition of what constitutes knowing finally, I cannot know anything finally, I must leap to some state that does permit me to know finally—a state of certainty "above" or "beyond" attainment by empirical or rational means. This to me is as if, finding myself in doubt and in darkness, I should decide, instead of cautiously feeling my way forward, to leap; not only to leap, to leap desperately; and not only to leap desperately, but into the darkest part of the surrounding darkness. There is an obvious emotional heroic-defiant appeal about this violent plunge from the battlements of reason; and an equally obvious lack of spiritual glamour in the cautious inching forward by the dim light of probability and the intermittent flicker (in this remote region) of scientific method. But I believe, and my reason tells me I am right to believe, that the step in the dark constitutes an existential betrayal and blasphemy, which is the maintaining that scientific probability should play no part in matters of faith. On the contrary I believe that probability must play a major part.

---

*Søren Kierkegaard (1813–1855), Danish philosopher who spoke of the "leap of faith" necessary to religious belief, and Blaise Pascal (1623–1662), French mathematician and philosopher, who argued that the most reasonable gamble (the *pari,* as in parimutuel betting) is to "bet" on God's existence.

†Tertullian (A.D. ca. 155–after 220), one of the early church fathers.

I believe in the situation and cosmos described in the first group of notes because it seems to me the most probable. And I find the less sublime analogy of the horse race a better one than that of the step in the dark. From a race card, that is, in bare terms of strict logic, it may seem that all the horses in a race have the same chance; but we know that in reality there is such a thing as "form," or a science of probability. No one but Jesus has been born of a virgin or has risen on the third day, and these, like the other incredible facts about him, are running at very long odds indeed. It is countless thousands of millions to one that I am right in refusing to believe in certain aspects of the Biblical accounts of his life, and countless thousands of millions to one that you, if you do believe them, are wrong.

14 To take these incredible aspects from his life does not diminish Jesus; it enhances him. If Christians were to say that these incredible events and the doctrines and rituals evolved from them are to be understood metaphorically, I could become a Christian. I could believe in the Virgin Birth (that the whole of evolution, of whatever is the case, fathers each child); in the Resurrection (for Jesus has risen again in men's minds); in the Miracles (because we should all like to perform such generous acts); in the Divinity of Christ and in Transubstantiation (we are all complementary one to another, and all to the It); I could believe in all these things that at present excommunicate my reason. But Christians would call this lack of faith.

15 Intelligent Athenians of the fifth century knew their gods were metaphors, personifications of forces and principles. There are many signs that the athenianization of Christianity has begun. The second coming of Christ will be the realization that Jesus of Nazareth was supremely human, not supremely divine.

16 Between Jesus and his church I choose Jesus: between Jesus and humanity, I choose humanity.

17 It is not what Jesus made of mankind, but what mankind made of him.

18 The Christian churches, contrary to the philosophy of Jesus himself, have frequently made their own self-continuance their chief preoccupation. They have fostered poverty, or indifference to it; they have forced people to look "beyond" life; they have abused the childish concept of hell and hell-fire; they have supported reactionary temporal powers; they have condemned countless innocent pleasures and bred centuries of bigotry; they have set themselves up as refuges and too often taken good care that outside their doors refuge shall be needed. Things are better now; but we have not forgotten that things were not better till history presented the churches with a clear choice: reform or die.

19 Worst of all, the churches have jealously caged Jesus. What right have they to say that he cannot be approached except through them? Must I believe in the Olympians and practice ancient Greek religious rituals before I can approach Socrates?

20 Peter's worst and last treachery was to found the church: but it is a treachery we are only just beginning to understand. The church has become not the body and spirit of Jesus; but a screen and barrier round him.

21 Jesus was human. He believed he was what he claimed to be. That he was not what he claimed to be is trivial, not vital, because he was human.

22 The man on the crucifix. He cries "Unnail me" and yet they make him stay there. They like to see his blood. It is salable.

23 There is no redemption, no remission; a sin has no price. It cannot be bought back till time itself is bought back.

24 Children learn very early the double vision a dogmatic church induces. They pray to God and nothing happens. They learn that there are two modes of behavior, an absolute one in church, and a relative one outside. They are taught science and then ordered to believe what is palpably unscientific. They are told to revere the Bible, and yet even children can see that it is in one way a rag bag of myths, tribal gibberish, wild vindictiveness, insane puritanism, garbled history, absurdly one-sided propaganda—and in another way a monument of splendid poetry, profound wisdom, with the universal human story of Jesus.

25 It is not the child who adopts double standards that is to blame; it is the churches that perpetuate them.

26 To claim of something that it belongs to a special category of absolute truth or reality is to pronounce its death sentence: there is no absolute truth or reality.

27 If Jesus came to Rome tomorrow, he would catch the next plane to Peking.

28 After Platonism some such development as Christianity was inevitable; there would always have been a Jesus, and a Christianity.

29 The Greeks were fatalists and pragmatists, and could tolerate insoluble mysteries. But the pompous Romans and the romantic Celts, faced with the darkness, had to solve and dissolve it, at whatever cost to reason. Like nature, history creates, then abhors the vacuum.

30 It was certain that Plato's hypothesis of the Idea would be misapplied. Fear of death did this. An enemy would say Christianity obscures reality; a friend, that it softens it. If the necessity of the situation is that it should be softened, misted, muffled, then Christianity is good. There are many such situations. If to a man dying of cancer Christianity makes dying of cancer an easier death, not all the arguments of all the anti-Christians could make me believe Christianity, in this situation, is not true. But this truth is a kind of utility, and in general I think it probable that clear glass is of greater utility than frosted.

31 Arian* was concerned that Christianity should be intellectually and eternally right; Athanasius,† that it should be psychologically and histori-

---

*Arius (A.D. ca. 250–336), Greek ecclesiastic who placed a Platonic construction on Christian theology; founded Arianism, which was declared heretical by the Council of Nicea in 325.

†Athanasius (A.D. ca. 293–373), Greek theologian and lifelong opponent of Arianism.

cally right. Arian saw what was; Athanasius, what would sell. Arian was a Greek, and Athanasius a Copt.*

32   The mousetrap mechanism of Christianity: Lord, show me myself! Desolation. Lord, show me thyself. Consolation. It abases and consoles; it strips and clothes.

33   Evolution is like a tall building. It needs stage after stage of scaffolding. Religion after religion, philosophy after philosophy. One cannot build the twentieth floor from the scaffolding of the first.

34   These last two millennia—much knowledge and little self-control. Christianity, like Buddhism and Mohammedanism, has disciplined and consoled the Many. But the great religions prevent the Many from looking and thinking. The world would not at once be a happier place if they looked and they thought; but this is no defense of dogmatic religions.

35   Does one snatch a cripple's crutch away because it is not the latest sort? Is it even enough to put the latest sort in his hands? He may not know how to use it. But this is not an argument against the latest sort of crutch.

36   Religious faith: mystery. Rational faith: law. The fundamental nature of reality is mysterious—this is a scientific fact. In basing themselves on mystery, religions are more scientific than rational philosophies. But there are mysteries and mysteries.

37   Any philosophy that tries to dispense with the mystery that lies at each core, in each moment of existence, is doomed to stresses and conflicts no less serious than those forecast by Marx, on economic grounds, of capitalist society.

38   Official Stalinist art: the futility of trying to remove mystery from any field of human activity.

39   Any great religion will have a practical moral appeal to men of other races; but the essential appeal will be racial, and more accessible to the originating race or racial group than to any other race.

40   Any religion that appeals more to one racial group than to another is in some sense inadequate.

41   Christianity has foolishly tried to particularize the fundamental mystery. The essential and only mystery is the nature of what the Christians call "God" or "Providence." But the church has introduced a fairground of pseudo-mysteries, which have no relation to truth, but only to the truth that mystery has power.

42   A religion finally endures according to its refusal to define the central mystery; or at least according to its willingness to jettison inadequate or constricting past symbolizations of that mystery. In this, the great oriental religions could have taught Christianity much.

43   What was impetus in a superstitious age has become dead weight in a scientific one.

44   But man is starved of mystery: so starved that even the most futile

---

*A member of Egyptian early Church, for example, because Athanasius was not Greek, he was not inclined to theoretical absolutism.

enigmas have their power still. If no one will write new detective stories, then people will still read the old ones.

45 Parthenogenesis* makes Jesus unique; the mystery of this impudent uniqueness is so pleasurable that we cannot resist it.

46 Christianity is a horse and cart.

47 In most parts of the world the horse and cart has been superseded by the automobile. But we do not say of the horse and cart that it is untrue, or that simply because the automobile is generally more useful and faster all horses and carts should be abolished.

48 There are still places where the horse and cart is indispensable. Where it is used and useful it is evolutionarily true.

49 Militant antireligious movements are based on this mechanization fallacy: that the most efficient machine must be the best. But it is the most effective machine in the circumstances that is the best.

50 Christians will say that to regard their religion as no more than a convenient mechanism, and convenient only for a certain stage of history, for certain situations, is to destroy its soul. But it is their intransigent refusal seriously to reform and reinterpret their religion that parks it in desuetude.

51 For every Christian who believes in all the dogma of his church, there are a thousand who half believe because they feel a man should believe in something. If the old religions survive, it is because they are convenient receptacles of the desire to believe; and because they are, though poor ones, ports; and because they at least try to satisfy the hunger for mystery.

52 All the old religions represent a barbarous waste of moral energy; ramshackle water mills on a river that could serve hydroelectric dynamos.

53 All gods alleged to be capable of intervention in our existence are idols; all images of gods are idols; all prayer to them, all adoration of them, is idolatry.

54 Gratitude for having been born and for existing is an archetypal human feeling; so is gratitude for good health, good fortune and happiness. But such gratitude should be ploughed back into the life around one, into one's *manner* of being; not thrown vaguely into the sky or poured into that most odious of concealed narcissisms, prayer. Religion stands between people's gratitude and the practical uses they might put its energy to. One good work is worth more than a million good words; and this would be true even if there were an observing and good-mark-awarding god "above" us.

55 I reject Christianity, along with the other great religions. Most of its mysteries are remote from the true mystery. Though I love and admire the founder, though I admire many priests and many Christians, I despise the church. It is because men want to be good and do good that it has survived so long; like Communism, it is inherently parasitical on a deeper

*The Virgin Birth.

and more mysterious nobility in man than any existing religion or political creed can satisfy.

Questions for Discussion

1. Would most church people you know agree with Fowles's assertion in paragraph 7, or would they maintain that charity, compassion, and good deeds are an insufficient definition of the moral duties of human beings? Would they insist, in addition, that one "be saved," "confess Christ," "be baptised," or "have taken the sacraments"? What is your own view on this matter? Why do you believe as you do?

2. Do you agree or disagree with Fowles's assertion in paragraph 14 that denying Jesus's miracles enhances his status, not diminishes it? Why or why not?

3. What is the view of the Church that Fowles advances in paragraphs 18–20, 24, 34, 41, and 50? Do you agree or disagree with this view? Why or why not?

4. How would you state Fowles's meaning in paragraph 52 in your own words? Is the metaphor particularly appropriate here or not? Can you create an alternative metaphor of your own that captures the same meaning?

5. Although Fowles's piece starts out as an apparently disconnected series of assertions, it turns out that the whole piece makes a more coherent argument than one expects. Can you identify the points at which he begins to develop themes and ideas that are connected to each other? Do you agree that the whole piece makes an argument—a loose one, but nevertheless an argument? Why or why not?

Suggested Essay Topics

1. Taking paragraphs 54 and 55 as a freestanding mini-essay, write an essay directed to Fowles in which you support his view here by extending it, giving examples to support it, and developing it into a convincing position instead of a bare statement. Or, if you disagree with his point, write an essay direct to Fowles in which you show him why he is wrong by laying out the best reasons that you can.

2. In imitation of Fowles's style and organization here, create a string of assertions about your own religious and antireligious beliefs. Like Fowles, try to make your assertions epigrammatic, yet try to make them gradually reveal the development of a related set of ideas, such that an overall view is built up despite the seemingly fragmentary nature of the building units. Direct the essay to your classmates.

C. S. Lewis

*A widely recognized literary critic and his-
torian, C. S. Lewis (1898–1963) is now perhaps best known as an author of
children's stories (the "Narnia" tales) and as a witty, intelligent defender of Christianity.*

*The task faced by all authors who set out to defend a given set of beliefs varies
greatly, depending on how sympathetic their readers are when they begin. For many
centuries, Christian authors writing in Europe or America could assume that most of
their readers were to some degree ready to take their arguments seriously. But from
the seventeenth century onward, the number of unbelievers increased rapidly. In our
century, Christian "apologists" (as defenders of the faith have traditionally been
called) have had to assume that most of their readers begin reading in either a skeptical
or a hostile frame of mind. As Lewis reports of himself in his autobiographical work*
Surprised by Joy *(1955), proclaiming oneself an atheist in one's early youth became
an almost automatic, normal step required of anyone with serious intellectual interests.*

*Lewis's reconversion was by no means automatic, and the struggle between
doubt and belief that he fought with himself made him one of the best-informed and
most effective Christian writers of modern times. Because he had himself felt the force
of every conceivable argument against belief, he was able to meet doubting readers as
no "automatic" Christian could. In a series of satirical works (the best known is* The
Screwtape Letters*), in science fiction (for example,* Perelandra*), and in direct
argument of the kind we print here, he attempted to remind unbelievers that the issues
of belief and doubt are, as he says in paragraph 8, extremely complex and difficult—at
least as difficult as his proof for the existence of God (in ¶6). His chief target often
seems to be those who "put up a version of Christianity suitable for a child of six and
make that the object of their attack" (¶9).*

*Be sure to read the preceding essay by John Fowles for comparison with this
one. Like Fowles, Lewis is master of a style that seems to make complex issues crystal
clear. In reading Lewis, as in reading Fowles, it is a good idea, at least the second
time round, to have pencil in hand, tracing the connections between conclusions and
reasons.*

WHAT CHRISTIANS BELIEVE

From book 2 of *Mere Christianity* (1943, 1945, 1952).

THE RIVAL CONCEPTIONS OF GOD

I have been asked to tell you what Christians believe, and I am going   1
to begin by telling you one thing that Christians do not need to believe. If
you are a Christian you do not have to believe that all the other religions are
simply wrong all through. If you are an atheist you do have to believe that
the main point in all the religions of the whole world is simply one huge

mistake. If you are a Christian, you are free to think that all these religions, even the queerest ones, contain at least some hint of the truth. When I was an atheist I had to try to persuade myself that most of the human race have always been wrong about the question that mattered to them most; when I became a Christian I was able to take a more liberal view. But, of course, being a Christian does mean thinking that where Christianity differs from other religions, Christianity is right and they are wrong. As in arithmetic—there is only one right answer to a sum, and all other answers are wrong: but some of the wrong answers are much nearer being right than others.

The first big division of humanity is into the majority, who believe in 2 some kind of God or gods, and the minority who do not. On this point, Christianity lines up with the majority—lines up with ancient Greeks and Romans, modern savages, Stoics, Platonists, Hindus, Mohammedans [Muslims], etc., against the modern Western European materialist.*

Now I go on to the next big division. People who all believe in God can 3 be divided according to the sort of God they believe in. There are two very different ideas on this subject. One of them is the idea that He is beyond good and evil. We humans call one thing good and another thing bad. But according to some people that is merely our human point of view. These people would say that the wiser you become the less you would want to call anything good or bad, and the more clearly you would see that everything is good in one way and bad in another, and that nothing could have been different. Consequently, these people think that long before you got anywhere near the divine point of view the distinction would have disappeared altogether. We call a cancer bad, they would say, because it kills a man; but you might just as well call a successful surgeon bad because he kills a cancer. It all depends on the point of view. The other and opposite idea is that God is quite definitely "good" or "righteous," a God who takes sides, who loves love and hates hatred, who wants us to behave in one way and not in another. The first of these views—the one that thinks God beyond good and evil—is called Pantheism. It was held by the great Prussian philosopher Hegel and, as far as I can understand them, by the Hindus. The other view is held by Jews, Mohammedans and Christians.

And with this big difference between Pantheism and the Christian idea 4 of God, there usually goes another. Pantheists usually believe that God, so to speak, animates the universe as you animate your body: that the universe almost *is* God, so that if it did not exist He would not exist either, and anything you find in the universe is a part of God. The Christian[s'] idea is quite different. They think God invented and made the universe—like a man making a picture or composing a tune. A painter is not a picture, and he does not die if his picture is destroyed. You may say, "He's put a lot of himself into it," but you only mean that all its beauty and interest has come out of

---

*A materialist believes in the existence of only matter. Thus the materialist considers spirit, including the divine, an illusion. [Our note.]

his head. His skill is not in the picture in the same way that it is in his head, or even in his hands. I expect you see how this difference between Pantheists and Christians hangs together with the other one. If you do not take the distinction between good and bad very seriously, then it is easy to say that anything you find in this world is a part of God. But, of course, if you think some things really bad, and God really good, then you cannot talk like that. You must believe that God is separate from the world and that some of the things we see in it are contrary to His will. Confronted with a cancer or a slum the Pantheist can say, "If you could only see it from the divine point of view, you would realise that this also is God." The Christian replies, "Don't talk damned nonsense."* For Christianity is a fighting religion. It thinks God made the world—that space and time, heat and cold, and all the colours and tastes, and all the animals and vegetables, are things that God "made up out of His head" as a man makes up a story. But it also thinks that a great many things have gone wrong with the world that God made and that God insists, and insists very loudly, on our putting them right again.

And, of course, that raises a very big question. If a good God made the world why has it gone wrong? And for many years I simply refused to listen to the Christian answers to this question, because I kept on feeling "whatever you say, and however clever your arguments are, isn't it much simpler and easier to say that the world was not made by any intelligent power? Aren't all your arguments simply a complicated attempt to avoid the obvious?" But then that threw me back into another difficulty.

My argument against God was that the universe seemed so cruel and unjust. But how had I got this idea of *just* and *unjust?* A man does not call a line crooked unless he has some idea of a straight line. What was I comparing this universe with when I called it unjust? If the whole show was bad and senseless from A to Z, so to speak, why did I, who was supposed to be part of the show, find myself in such violent reaction against it? A man feels wet when he falls into water, because man is not a water animal: a fish would not feel wet. Of course I could have given up my idea of justice by saying it was nothing but a private idea of my own. But if I did that, then my argument against God collapsed too—for the argument depended on saying that the world was really unjust, not simply that it did not happen to please my private fancies. Thus in the very act of trying to prove that God did not exist—in other words, that the whole of reality was senseless—I found I was forced to assume that one part of reality—namely my idea of justice—was full of sense. Consequently atheism turns out to be too simple. If the whole universe has no meaning, we should never have found out that it has no meaning: just as, if there were no light in the universe and therefore no creatures with eyes, we should never know it was dark. *Dark* would be without meaning.

---

*One listener complained of the word *damned* as frivolous swearing. But I mean exactly what I say—nonsense that is *damned* is under God's curse, and will (apart from God's grace) lead those who believe it to eternal death. [Lewis's note.]

THE INVASION

Very well then, atheism is too simple. And I will tell you another view   7
that is also too simple. It is the view I call Christianity-and-water, the view
which simply says there is a good God in Heaven and everything is all
right—leaving out all the difficult and terrible doctrines about sin and hell and
the devil, and the redemption. Both these are boys' philosophies.

It is no good asking for a simple religion. After all, real things are not   8
simple. They look simple, but they are not. The table I am sitting at looks
simple: but ask a scientist to tell you what it is really made of—all about the
atoms and how the light waves rebound from them and hit my eye and what
they do to the optic nerve and what it does to my brain—and, of course, you
find that what we call "seeing a table" lands you in mysteries and complica-
tions which you can hardly get to the end of. A child saying a child's prayer
looks simple. And if you are content to stop there, well and good. But if you
are not—and the modern world usually is not—if you want to go on and ask
what is really happening—then you must be prepared for something difficult.
If we ask for something more than simplicity, it is silly then to complain that
the something more is not simple.

Very often, however, this silly procedure is adopted by people who are   9
not silly, but who, consciously or unconsciously, want to destroy Christianity. Such people put up a version of Christianity suitable for a child of six
and make that the object of their attack. When you try to explain the Christian doctrine as it is really held by an instructed adult, they then complain
that you are making their heads turn round and that it is all too complicated
and that if there really were a God they are sure He would have made
"religion" simple, because simplicity is so beautiful, etc. You must be on your
guard against these people for they will change their ground every minute
and only waste your time. Notice, too, their idea of God "making religion
simple": as if "religion" were something God invented, and not His statement
to us of certain quite unalterable facts about His own nature.

Besides being complicated, reality, in my experience, is usually odd. It   10
is not neat, not obvious, not what you expect. For instance, when you have
grasped that the earth and the other planets all go round the sun, you would
naturally expect that all the planets were made to match—all at equal distances from each other, say, or distances that regularly increased, or all the
same size, or else getting bigger or smaller as you go farther from the sun. In
fact, you find no rhyme or reason (that we can see) about either the sizes or
the distances; and some of them have one moon, one has four, one has two,
some have none, and one has a ring.

Reality, in fact, is usually something you could not have guessed. That   11
is one of the reasons I believe Christianity. It is a religion you could not have
guessed. If it offered us just the kind of universe we had always expected, I
should feel we were making it up. But, in fact, it is not the sort of thing
anyone would have made up. It has just that queer twist about it that real
things have. So let us leave behind all these boys' philosophies—these over-

simple answers. The problem is not simple and the answer is not going to be simple either.

What is the problem? A universe that contains much that is obviously bad and apparently meaningless, but containing creatures like ourselves who know that it is bad and meaningless. There are only two views that face all the facts. One is the Christian view that this is a good world that has gone wrong, but still retains the memory of what it ought to have been. The other is the view called Dualism. Dualism means the belief that there are two equal and independent powers at the back of everything, one of them good and the other bad, and that this universe is the battlefield in which they fight out an endless war. I personally think that next to Christianity Dualism is the manliest and most sensible creed on the market. But it has a catch in it. 12

The two powers, or spirits, or gods—the good one and the bad one—are supposed to be quite independent. They both existed from all eternity. Neither of them made the other, neither of them has any more right than the other to call itself God. Each presumably thinks it is good and thinks the other bad. One of them likes hatred and cruelty, the other likes love and mercy, and each backs its own view. Now what do we mean when we call one of them the Good Power and the other the Bad Power? Either we are merely saying that we happen to prefer the one to the other—like preferring beer to cider—or else we are saying that, whatever the two powers think about it, and whichever we humans, at the moment, happen to like, one of them is actually wrong, actually mistaken, in regarding itself as good. Now if we mean merely that we happen to prefer the first, then we must give up talking about good and evil at all. For good means what you ought to prefer quite regardless of what you happen to like at any given moment. If "being good" meant simply joining the side you happened to fancy, for no real reason, then good would not deserve to be called good. So we must mean that one of the two•powers is actually wrong and the other actually right. 13

But the moment you say that, you are putting into the universe a third thing in addition to the two Powers: some law or standard or rule of good which one of the powers conforms to and the other fails to conform to. But since the two powers are judged by this standard, then this standard, or the Being who made this standard, is farther back and higher up than either of them, and He will be the real God. In fact, what we meant by calling them good and bad turns out to be that one of them is in a right relation to the real ultimate God and the other in a wrong relation to Him. 14

The same point can be made in a different way. If Dualism is true, then the bad Power must be a being who likes badness for its own sake. But in reality we have no experience of anyone liking badness just because it is bad. The nearest we can get to it is in cruelty. But in real life people are cruel for one of two reasons—either because they are sadists, that is, because they have a sexual perversion which makes cruelty a cause of sensual pleasure to them, or else for the sake of something they are going to get out of it—money, or power, or safety. But pleasure, money, power, and safety are all, as far as they go, good things. The badness consists in pursuing them by the wrong method, 15 or in the wrong way, or too much. I do not mean, of course, that the people who do this are not desperately wicked. I do mean that wickedness, when you examine it, turns out to be the pursuit of some good in the wrong way. You can be good for the mere sake of goodness: you cannot be bad for the mere sake of badness. You can do a kind action when you are not feeling kind and when it gives you no pleasure, simply because kindness is right; but no one ever did a cruel action simply because cruelty is wrong—only because cruelty was pleasant or useful to him. In other words badness cannot succeed even in being bad in the same way in which goodness is good. Goodness is, so to speak, itself: badness is only spoiled goodness. And there must be something good first before it can be spoiled. We called sadism a sexual perversion; but you must first have the idea of a normal sexuality before you can talk of its being perverted; and you can see which is the perversion, because you can explain the perverted from the normal, and cannot explain the normal from the perverted. It follows that this Bad Power, who is supposed to be on an equal footing with the Good Power, and to love badness in the same way as the Good Power loves goodness, is a mere bogy. In order to be bad he must have good things to want and then to pursue in the wrong way: he must have impulses which were originally good in order to be able to pervert them. But if he is bad he cannot supply himself either with good things to desire or with good impulses to pervert. He must be getting both from the Good Power. And if so, then he is not independent. He is part of the Good Power's world: he was made either by the Good Power or by some power above them both.

Put it more simply still. To be bad, he must exist and have intelligence 16 and will. But existence, intelligence and will are in themselves good. Therefore he must be getting them from the Good Power: even to be bad he must borrow or steal from his opponent. And do you now begin to see why Christianity has always said that the devil is a fallen angel? That is not a mere story for the children. It is a real recognition of the fact that evil is a parasite, not an original thing. The powers which enable evil to carry on are powers given it by goodness. All the things which enable a bad man to be effectively bad are in themselves good things—resolution, cleverness, good looks, existence itself. That is why Dualism, in a strict sense, will not work.

But I freely admit that real Christianity (as distinct from Christianity- 17 and-water) goes much nearer to Dualism than people think. One of the things that surprised me when I first read the New Testament seriously was that it talked so much about a Dark Power in the universe—a mighty evil spirit who was held to be the Power behind death and disease, and sin. The difference is that Christianity thinks this Dark Power was created by God, and was good when he was created, and went wrong. Christianity agrees with Dualism that this universe is at war. But it does not think this is a war between independent powers. It thinks it is a civil war, a rebellion, and that we are living in a part of the universe occupied by the rebel.

Enemy-occupied territory—that is what this world is. Christianity is the 18 story of how the rightful king has landed, you might say landed in disguise, and is calling us all to take part in a great campaign of sabotage. When you go to church you are really listening-in to the secret wireless from our friends: that is why the enemy is so anxious to prevent us from going. He does it by playing on our conceit and laziness and intellectual snobbery. I know some-one will ask me, "Do you really mean, at this time of day, to re-introduce our old friend the devil—hoofs and horns and all?" Well, what the time of day has to do with it I do not know. And I am not particular about the hoofs and horns. But in other respects my answer is "Yes, I do." I do not claim to know anything about his personal appearance. If anybody really wants to know him better I would say to that person, "Don't worry. If you really want to, you will. Whether you'll like it when you do is another question."

THE SHOCKING ALTERNATIVE

Christians, then, believe that an evil power has made himself for the present the Prince of this World. And, of course, that raises problems. Is this state of affairs in accordance with God's will or not? If it is, He is a strange God, you will say: and if it is not, how can anything happen contrary to the will of a being with absolute power? [19]

But anyone who has been in authority knows how a thing can be in accordance with your will in one way and not in another. It may be quite sensible for a mother to say to the children, "I'm not going to go and make you tidy the schoolroom every night. You've got to learn to keep it tidy on your own." Then she goes up one night and finds the Teddy bear and the ink and the French Grammar all lying in the grate. That is against her will. She would prefer the children to be tidy. But on the other hand, it is her will which has left the children free to be untidy. The same thing arises in any regiment, or trade union, or school. You make a thing voluntary and then half the people do not do it. That is not what you willed, but your will has made it possible. [20]

It is probably the same in the universe. God created things which had free will. That means creatures which can go either wrong or right. Some people think they can imagine a creature which was free but had no possibil-ity of going wrong; I cannot. If a thing is free to be good it is also free to be bad. And free will is what has made evil possible. Why, then, did God give them free will? Because free will, though it makes evil possible, is also the only thing that makes possible any love or goodness or joy worth having. A world of automata—of creatures that worked like machines—would hardly be worth creating. The happiness which God designs for His higher creatures is the happiness of being freely, voluntarily united to Him and to each other in an ecstasy of love and delight compared with which the most rapturous love between a man and a woman on this earth is mere milk and water. And for that they must be free. [21]

Of course God knew what would happen if they used their freedom the wrong way: apparently He thought it worth the risk. Perhaps we feel inclined to disagree with Him. But there is a difficulty about disagreeing with God. He is the source from which all your reasoning power comes: you could not [22] be right and He wrong any more than a stream can rise higher than its own source. When you are arguing against Him you are arguing against the very power that makes you able to argue at all: it is like cutting off the branch you are sitting on. If God thinks this state of war in the universe a price worth paying for free will—that is, for making a live world in which creatures can do real good or harm and something of real importance can happen, instead of a toy world which only moves when He pulls the strings—then we may take it it is worth paying.

When we have understood about free will, we shall see how silly it is 23 to ask, as somebody once asked me: "Why did God make a creature of such rotten stuff that it went wrong?" The better stuff a creature is made of—the cleverer and stronger and freer it is—then the better it will be if it goes right, but also the worse it will be if it goes wrong. A cow cannot be very good or very bad; a dog can be both better and worse; a child better and worse still; an ordinary man, still more so; a man of genius, still more so; a superhuman spirit best—or worst—of all.

How did the Dark Power go wrong? Here, no doubt, we ask a question 24 to which human beings cannot give an answer with any certainty. A reasonable (and traditional) guess, based on our own experiences of going wrong, can, however, be offered. The moment you have a self at all, there is a possibility of putting yourself first—wanting to be the centre—wanting to be God, in fact. That was the sin of Satan: and that was the sin he taught the human race. Some people think the fall of man had something to do with sex, but that is a mistake. (The story in the Book of Genesis rather suggests that some corruption in our sexual nature followed the fall and was its result, not its cause.) What Satan put into the heads of our remote ancestors was the idea that they could "be like gods"—could set up on their own as if they had created themselves—be their own masters—invent some sort of happiness for themselves outside God, apart from God. And out of that hopeless attempt has come nearly all that we call human history—money, poverty, ambition, war, prostitution, classes, empires, slavery—the long terrible story of man trying to find something other than God which will make him happy.

The reason why it can never succeed is this. God made us: invented us 25 as a man invents an engine. A car is made to run on gasoline, and it would not run properly on anything else. Now God designed the human machine to run on Himself. He Himself is the fuel our spirits were designed to burn, or the food our spirits were designed to feed on. There is no other. That is why it is just no good asking God to make us happy in our own way without bothering about religion. God cannot give us a happiness and peace apart from Himself, because it is not there. There is no such thing.

That is the key to history. Terrific energy is expended—civilisations are 26 built up—excellent institutions devised; but each time something goes wrong. Some fatal flaw always brings the selfish and cruel people to the top and it all slides back into misery and ruin. In fact, the machine conks. It seems to start up all right and runs a few yards, and then it breaks down. They are trying to run it on the wrong juice. That is what Satan has done to us humans.

And what did God do? First of all He left us conscience, the sense of right and wrong: and all through history there have been people trying (some of them very hard) to obey it. None of them ever quite succeeded. Secondly, He sent the human race what I call good dreams: I mean those queer stories scattered all through the heathen religions about a god who dies and comes to life again and, by his death, has somehow given new life to men. Thirdly, He selected one particular people and spent several centuries hammering into their heads the sort of God He was—that there was only one of Him and that He cared about right conduct. Those people were the Jews, and the Old Testament gives an account of the hammering process. {27}

Then comes the real shock. Among these Jews there suddenly turns up a man who goes about talking as if He was God. He claims to forgive sins. He says He has always existed. He says He is coming to judge the world at the end of time. Now let us get this clear. Among Pantheists, like the Indians, anyone might say that he was a part of God, or one with God: there would be nothing very odd about it. But this man, since He was a Jew, could not mean that kind of God. God, in their language, meant the Being outside the world Who had made it and was infinitely different from anything else. And when you have grasped that, you will see that what this man said was, quite simply, the most shocking thing that has ever been uttered by human lips. {28}

One part of the claim tends to slip past us unnoticed because we have heard it so often that we no longer see what it amounts to. I mean the claim to forgive sins: any sins. Now unless the speaker is God, this is really so preposterous as to be comic. We can all understand how a man forgives offences against himself. You tread on my toe and I forgive you, you steal my money and I forgive you. But what should we make of a man, himself unrobbed and untrodden on, who announced that he forgave you for treading on other men's toes and stealing other men's money? Asinine fatuity is the kindest description we should give of his conduct. Yet this is what Jesus did. He told people that their sins were forgiven, and never waited to consult all the other people whom their sins had undoubtedly injured. He unhesitatingly behaved as if He was the party chiefly concerned, the person chiefly offended in all offences. This makes sense only if He really was the God whose laws are broken and whose love is wounded in every sin. In the mouth of any speaker who is not God, these words would imply what I can only regard as a silliness and conceit unrivalled by any other character in history. {29}

Yet (and this is the strange, significant thing) even His enemies, when they read the Gospels, do not usually get the impression of silliness and conceit. Still less do unprejudiced readers. Christ says that He is "humble and meek" and we believe Him; not noticing that, if He were merely a man, humility and meekness are the very last characteristics we could attribute to some of His sayings. {30}

I am trying here to prevent anyone saying the really foolish thing that people often say about Him: "I'm ready to accept Jesus as a great moral teacher, but I don't accept His claim to be God." That is the one thing we must not say. A man who was merely a man and said the sort of things Jesus said {31} would not be a great moral teacher. He would either be a lunatic—on a level with the man who says he is a poached egg—or else he would be the Devil of Hell. You must make your choice. Either this man was, and is, the Son of God: or else a madman or something worse. You can shut Him up for a fool, you can spit at Him and kill Him as a demon; or you can fall at His feet and call Him Lord and God. But let us not come with any patronising nonsense about His being a great human teacher. He has not left that open to us. He did not intend to.

Questions for Discussion

1. Lewis clearly sees that many of his readers will find some of his views shocking, perhaps most obviously his claim that Satan is literally real. Does he take any steps to lead his readers gently into the more controversial territory? Do the steps work? To put it another way, did you feel, by the end of the first few paragraphs, that the author could on the whole be trusted, even if you could not fully accept his arguments?

2. Fowles implies that he was once a believer who learned better. Lewis tells us that he was once an unbeliever who learned better (¶1). Do they increase their persuasiveness by making this kind of claim? Why or why not?

3. Lewis's tone remains serious throughout, and he does not pause to relate illustrative anecdotes. (He does of course engage in frequent witty thrusts, but his tone is on the whole serious.) Do you find his style heavy or pompous? How would you describe the "person" behind the writing here? Be as detailed as you can, giving both intellectual and moral qualities.

4. Work out in discussion with your classmates the exact line of argument in the section called "The Invasion." Give special attention to the logic in paragraph 12. When writers give us "only two possibilities," we should always be on our guard. Only if there *really* are no other possibilities must we accept their choice, and it is worth remembering that in most human issues the possibilities are not limited to two. Has Lewis played fair with his sharp choice between Christianity and Dualism? If you think of other possibilities, be sure that they are not merely other versions of one of his.

5. Later in the essay Lewis gives us a sharp choice among three possibilities: either Christ was who he said he was, or he was mad, or he was the Devil of hell (¶31). Is this a logical division of the possibilities? Why or why not? Again it is useful to ask yourself whether there are any other possibilities.

6. Whether we agree with them or not, both Fowles and Lewis can teach us a good deal about how to present a case effectively. Lewis is especially skillful in this essay in organizing a body of difficult material into a clear sequence of steps. Trace those steps and ask about each of them: Why does he take it at *this* point? Once you have done that kind of reading of a

variety of complicated essays, your own powers of organization will inevitably increase. (See "Why Use a 'Reader' in a Writing Course?" in Part One.)

Suggested Essay Topics

1. If you consider yourself a Christian, write a letter to Lewis, explaining to him how his version of Christianity is similar to or different from yours. Your purpose, in the latter case, is not to convert him but to persuade him to see your view as something that he should take into account.

2. If you are an unbeliever in Christianity or a believer in some other religion, write a letter to either Lewis or Fowles, disagreeing with any points in their arguments that seem faulty. Be sure that you have understood the point before trying to refute it.

·12·

ECONOMIC PERSPECTIVES

Capitalism Attacked and Defended

Money is indeed the most important thing in the world;
and all sound and successful personal and national morality should
have this fact for its basis.
George Bernard Shaw

But man has almost constant occasion for the help of his brethren,
and it is in vain for him to expect it from their
benevolence only. He will be more likely to prevail if he can
interest their self-love in his favour, and show them that it is for
their own advantage to do for him what he requires of
them. . . . It is not from the benevolence of the butcher, the brewer,
or the baker, that we can expect our dinner, but from
their regard to their own interest.
Adam Smith

A fool and his money are soon parted.
Old proverb

Money is like muck, not good except it be spread.
Sir Francis Bacon

You pays your money and you takes your chances.
Popular saying

The love of money is the root of all evil.
I Timothy 6:10

He that wants [i.e., lacks] money, means, and content
is without three good friends.
Shakespeare

Wine maketh merry: but money answereth all things.
Ecclesiastes 10:19

Celeste MacLeod

Celeste MacLeod (b. 1931) has spent a lifetime thinking and writing about contemporary American society. She travels abroad to get new perspectives and then comes home to fling herself into work for such organizations as the Sierra Club, the National Women's Political Caucus, the Women's National Book Association, and the American Civil Liberties Union. In this essay she questions both the legitimacy and the usefulness of the traditional American Dream, the Horatio Alger myth that in America, the land of not just opportunity but endless opportunity, anyone, literally anyone, can "make it big" with just a little luck and a lot of hard work.

What if it simply isn't true? What if conditions in American society and in the American economy have changed such that the opportunities for "making it big" are simply not there anymore—or at least are there for only a few? What if the homeless and the poor aren't just lazy, incompetent, or the victims of outlandish accidents? What would you be, if your parents' plant or business closed down, an event not outlandish at all, but one that happens somewhere every day? How close to the financial edge does your own family run? If your family's income suddenly disappeared, how long could you maintain middle-class amenities, style, and comfort?

In the meantime, the gap between the poor and the wealthy grows larger, and yet we persist in believing that America is the land of opportunity for all. It's the "for all" part that MacLeod questions in this essay, and she grounds her discussion in the view that the American myth of "endless" opportunity was a function of psychology rather than economics. The apparently endless frontier gave Americans throughout the eighteenth and nineteenth centuries a corresponding feeling of "endless" opportunity: If things didn't work out in one place, you could always pull up stakes and move on to the next set of opportunities—the next land rush, the next gold rush, the next boomtown, the next oil field—and there would lie your chance to "make it big." However, in the twentieth century, since the truth about that frontier has finally asserted itself namely, that it is not endless at all, MacLeod suggests that perhaps we now need to recognize that opportunity is not endless either.

If opportunity is not endless, if limits have been reached, then it is also possible that Americans may need to scale back their expectations about the good life. It is possible that too many people wanting too many things both in and out of their lives dangerously strains the economy. It may be that in order for all of us to live well, some of us who live superlatively well may have to scale back and those of us who are only doing "well" may need to quit aspiring to "superlatively well" status.

These are issues raised by MacLeod, whose voice is not that of the detached academic or theoretical economist, but that of the concerned and dedicated American, the layperson with a view. She is engaged, passionate, and committed. If you take her concerns seriously, she will force you, whether you agree with her or not, to clarify your own views about important issues in American society.

HORATIO ALGER, FAREWELL

From *Horatio Alger, Farewell* (1980).

THE DREAM AND THE REALITY

Upward mobility was the essence of the American dream. In the new land of democracy and freedom, everyone who tried hard enough could rise and become rich—according to the dream. Individual initiative and persistence were automatic stairsteps to financial success. Horatio Alger, a nineteenth-century American minister, wrote more than 100 novels for boys that illustrated the dream in action; Alger's heroes invariably went from rags to riches through hard work and virtue. 1

Two interlocking premises supported the American dream—unlimited opportunity and an endless frontier to provide that opportunity. Without the frontier, the dream could not have survived. 2

The dream of riches for everybody originated in the United States, but it has become one of our most popular exports. The idea that everyone who works hard enough can become wealthy, regardless of social class or advantages (and irrespective of the economic and political situation in one's country), has universal appeal. It is a modern-day fairy tale wherein effort is the magic wand and every person turns into his or her own fairy godmother. The inherent justice of such a tale, its suitability as an inspirational piece for children, makes the story an unbeatable favorite. The American dream has helped raise expectations across the globe. 3

Belief in the dream has a special advantage for those who embrace its tenets: It serves as a screen that shuts out the real world, at least temporarily. The reality is that opportunity is shrinking, in the United States and elsewhere. When the frontiers ended, so did the basis of the dream. 4

Although a highly visible minority of individuals in the United States and other Western countries are better off financially than ever before, the common experience is that jobs are increasingly difficult to find. How to earn a living is becoming a dilemma instead of a choice for more and more people 5 entering adulthood. Vast numbers of young people—ranging from unskilled laborers who quit school at sixteen through holders of doctoral degrees from prestigious universities—cannot find jobs. Their problem is not a lack of effort or individual initiative; it is a lack of jobs. More people are looking for work than there are jobs available for them to fill. Automation has been a primary factor in eroding the dream's promise of jobs for everybody; techno- logical innovations have caused great numbers of unskilled and semiskilled workers to be replaced by machines.

In the past, migration was the trump card of the poor. If all else failed,   6 you could leave home and seek opportunity in some other place. You could emigrate (leave your native land and enter another nation as an immigrant), or you could migrate (move within your own country, often from farm to city after the coming of the Industrial Revolution).

Today emigration is closing as an option for the poor. The countries that   7 used to absorb large numbers of immigrants regularly (i.e., United States, Canada, Australia) are experiencing high rates of unemployment themselves, so they no longer want or need the poor and unskilled as immigrants. To the contrary, it is the rich and the highly skilled technicians who are welcome as immigrants these days.

Migration within one's own country is still open, and it remains a   8 popular option. Whenever unemployment increases, so does migration, even though the areas people move to in search of work often have higher rates of unemployment than the communities they left behind. But the dream says that opportunity awaits them someplace, and so people keep moving, hoping to find it in the next town.

This book is about the end of the American dream. The focus is on   9 young people and migration, because the young are hit the hardest by job scarcity, and they are also the most likely to leave home in search of the dream.

Part One introduces "the new migrants"—young adults eighteen to   10 thirty years old, who have left their communities in hopes of finding a better life in a different part of the country. The new migrants come pre- dominantly from poor or working-class homes and, like the majority of the American population, most of them are white. They are not new in the sense of being the first of their kind, because migration—especially west- ward migration toward the frontier—has long been a traditional way for young Americans to seek the dream; today's young migrants are new in that they reflect a resurgence: A combination of historical and economic events during the 1960s and 1970s caused the new migrants to leave home in renewed numbers.

The new migrants have been confused with "hippies," the middle-class   11 youths (also predominantly white) whose rebellion against the dream in the mid-1960s brought them worldwide notoriety. A few critics of the American scene applauded the revolt, but the general public developed a deep revulsion toward the rebels, who were also closely associated with psychedelic drugs.

These young people were too lazy to work, the popular argument went; they had been ruined by permissiveness and their immoral way of life.

When the new migrants went on the road in search of opportunity, they were thought to be running from affluence instead of looking for it, thought to be avoiding work instead of trying to find it. 12

Dr. Henry Miller, professor of social welfare at the University of California, takes a different view of the new migrants. Miller, whose specialty is "youth on the move," has studied youth migration patterns of the past as well as those in recent times, and he finds the new migrants closer in kind to the hobos at the turn of the century, or the migrants of the Great Depression, than to the beats or hippies. As Miller explained when interviewed at Berkeley: 13

> There's a popular myth floating around that the poverty of youth is self-imposed, but the fact is, we've produced a generation of young people for whom there are no jobs. The labor market cannot absorb them, so they seek other routes. Periodically in history there have been cataclysmic events that coughed up great numbers of people and made them wander about looking for ways to survive. The Plague of 1386 is a classic example, but our own Depression is closer. In 1933 alone, the Southern Pacific Railroad apprehended six hundred thousand people riding the rails illegally. A quarter of them were under twenty-five. We're in the midst of another upheaval now, although we haven't acknowledged it.

Acknowledging this upheaval and its effects on young people from the bottom layers of American society would shake the dream at its foundations. The belief that a job exists *a priori* for anyone who really wants to work is a central tenet of the American dream.

Even the revelation in the 1960s that black Americans and other nonwhite citizens were being excluded from the dream was resolved in a manner that left the core of the dream's mythology untouched. Racial prejudice was isolated as the demon that was blocking their chances to climb the ladder of success. The remedy was simple: Remove the demon from the foot of the ladder, add some programs to compensate for past blockage, and then every American would enjoy unlimited opportunity for upward mobility. 14

The antipoverty programs of the Great Society did help some black people, but failed to eliminate poverty (and, in fact, made scant inroads on improving the lives of the poorest people). The programs, or the people they served, were blamed: The wrong incantation had been used to drive out the demon; the government bureaucracy was at fault; or the poor were not trying hard enough. To suggest that some people remained poor and jobless despite earnest efforts to succeed would have been blasphemous, for unlimited opportunity to get rich was considered a sacred natural resource that we could never run out of in the United States. 15

It is still so regarded by many an affluent American. Not only does the American dream include a job for everybody who wants to work, it also 16 promises big money to those who try hard enough. A million dollars is just around the corner if you go after it. Horatio Alger will turn over in his grave if you say otherwise. Books and television specials about the few who do make millions reinforce this belief, but little is heard about those who tried and failed.

The grandiose expectations that the American dream instills in its 17 young people make the reality all the more painful when the new migrants arrive in yet another city and cannot make it. They are not only poor and unemployed, they are also failures—in their own eyes and in the eyes of society.

Americans still have the highest expectations in the world, but other 18 nations are catching up. In western Europe, young people from the working class are also leaving their hometowns in increasing numbers in search of brighter futures. In England they flock into London by the hundreds each month, coming mainly from areas of high unemployment such as the Midlands, Glasgow, or Ireland. In France they go to Paris, in Belgium to Brussels; or, because of the Common Market, Belgians may move to London, while British youths settle in Brussels. They expect good jobs to await them in their new locations, but, like their American counterparts, they are usually disappointed.

In every country the poor and the unskilled are the most adversely 19 affected by the dwindling of economic opportunity. Well-educated people from middle-class homes are also experiencing serious job problems, because far more people aspire to professional or executive positions than any country can use in those capacities; but the highly trained can go down the job ladder, if necessary, while those who start out at the bottom can go no lower. They may find themselves pushed out of the job market altogether—and then castigated by society for not working.

The situation is bleak, but not hopeless. The final chapters of this book 20 will discuss some possible directions for change and make a few suggestions, but no four-point plan for reshaping the world economy will be presented. The emphasis will be on readjusting our thinking to fit reality—changing the nature of the dream, as individuals and as nations. We cannot work out viable solutions to the world's growing unemployment problems as long as we cling to obsolete beliefs; it is like trying to win a sports-car race with a horse and buggy.

. . .

INCREASED PRODUCTION: THE
CONVENTIONAL ECONOMIC
SOLUTION

In conventional economic theory, increased production is considered 21 the answer to every nation's problems. The conventional economists, who advise businesses and governments alike, evaluate a country's economy in terms of how much goods it produces; to them nothing is more important than a country's Gross National Product (GNP).

Even John Maynard Keynes, the British economist who recommended 22 government spending as the way out of the Great Depression, based his theory on increased production. When savings are depleted during a severe recession, he said, the government should put money into circulation through public projects, to "prime the pump"; then available capital will build up, businesses can increase their production, and the system, now repaired, will run smoothly again.

John Kenneth Galbraith is the economist who attacked the theory that 23 increasing production always improves a nation's well-being. In his book *The Affluent Society* (1958) Galbraith argued that when a country could not produce enough goods to satisfy the basic needs of its citizens for food, clothing, and shelter (as in the days of Smith, Ricardo, and Malthus), it made sense to concentrate on the increased production of goods above all else; but when a country was more than able to meet the needs of its people (in terms of its capacity to produce goods), as in the case of the United States, when it was in fact an affluent society, it no longer made sense to keep pushing increased production as the nation's number-one goal.

Galbraith introduced the theory of social balance, which he defined as 24 "a satisfactory relationship between the supply of privately produced goods and services and those of the state."[21] Production of more goods increases the need for more services; for example, if we produce more automobiles, we will need more highways, traffic control, and parking spaces. But in the United States this social balance is out of whack, said Galbraith. The country keeps producing more goods—often goods of marginal utility, for which citizens feel no need until an advertising campaign creates a desire for them—while the money for needed services in cities and states is hard to come by. The result is a devastation of our cities and countryside that affects everyone, he said.

Galbraith argued for a better balance between the production of goods 25 and the social services provided by the state. By implication he urged economists to take cognizance of this changed situation and adjust their systems to include social as well as monetary values.

Although Galbraith's book was primarily about the United States, his 26 argument that the capacity now exists to produce enough goods to satisfy everyone's basic need for food, shelter, and clothing appears to have some validity for other nations as well in terms of the world's ability to produce enough goods to supply everyone. Millions of people still die of starvation and malnutrition every year, but the problem is more one of economic distribution than of an inability to produce enough food for them. People die because they lack the money to buy food. Relief agencies may distribute free food to starving people during severe famines or other emergencies, but usually you need money to get food, or the seeds, equipment, and land to grow it; and to have money, you need to be able to make a living. Which brings us back to the question of whether increased industrial production of goods is the only way to improve the lives of people in a given country.

An African Textile Mill

The late British economist E. F. Schumacher said no—increasing pro- 27
duction, by itself, wasn't the answer. Schumacher was one of that small group
of maverick economists like Galbraith who challenged the conventional economic wisdom. The way to help the developing nations become self-sufficient, said Schumacher, was to encourage the use of "intermediate technology"—that is, small-scale projects that made a virtue of employing the local
people. In his essay "2 Million Villages," Schumacher made his point by
describing a visit to a textile mill in Africa:

> The manager showed me with considerable pride that his factory was
> at the highest technological level to be found anywhere in the world. Why
> was it so automated? "Because," he said, "African labor, unused to indus-
> trial work, would make mistakes, whereas automated machinery does not
> make mistakes. The quality standards demanded today," he explained,
> "are such that my product must be perfect to be able to find a market."
> He summed up his policy by saying, "Surely my task is to eliminate the
> human factor."[22]

The mill's equipment and raw materials all had to be imported, and the 28
sophisticated equipment demanded that all higher management and maintenance personnel be imported. By the standards of the conventional wisdom,
this mill was a sound project: It increased production and the country's GNP
as well as helping its balance of payments on the iternational market. The fact
that the mill created virtually no jobs for African workers and that the foreign
goods shipped into the country in exchange would be consumed by a tiny
elite (of which the manager was one), because most people were too poor to
buy them, would be irrelevant to the calculations of trained economists. But
politically this textile mill, which helped the rich become richer while the
poor remained poor from lack of a way to make a living, was like one more
piece of dynamite stored up for a future explosion, an explosion of the
have-nots that could ultimately affect both the nation's GNP and the mill
itself.

Selling Shirts on the World Market

Increased production remains the standard solution to unemployment, 29
although, as we have just seen, this solution may be illusory. The example
of what happened to Sri Lanka illustrates another problem that may arise
when increased production alone is viewed as the answer to a nation's economic woes.[23]

Sri Lanka (formerly Ceylon), the island at the tip of India, has a high 30
rate of unemployment and considerable poverty. After wide-scale riots there
in 1971, the Western nations decided they had better help Sri Lanka make
more jobs for its people or the country might be wooed successfully by the
Soviet bloc. Economists analyzed the country's situation and recommended

establishing a garment industry there. The World Bank lent the country $20 million to establish the industry, and Western shirtmakers came in to teach the managers and workers how to cut the fabric and use the newly purchased sewing machines to make quality shirts that could compete on the world market. Labor is cheap in Sri Lanka, so the shirts would sell for less than those made in Europe or the United States.

All went according to plan until the Sri Lankans tried to sell their shirts. 31 Then they discovered that the same Western nations that had encouraged them to make shirts for the international market did not want to buy them. The sale of Sri Lankan shirts might adversely affect the garment industries of those nations, where labor costs are higher.

Sri Lanka ran into the free-trade-versus-protection controversy: Should 32 countries restrict imports or charge tariffs on foreign goods to protect their own manufacturers, or is it better to allow goods to enter freely and let those who can compete most effectively win out? Should quotas be worked out to give every country the chance to sell some shirts, or does economic reality dictate that whichever country can capture the market for a given commodity should do so? In the context of the free-trade-versus-protection controversy, if one country wins, another has to lose.

Part of the problem is overproduction. More shirts are being manufac- 33 tured in the world than there are customers to buy them. Millions of other people may be in dire need of more shirts, but, unless they have the money to pay for them, they will not function as consumers of shirts, because no company increases its profits by giving away its shirts, nor does a country help its balance of payments that way.

As long as countries view their economic development primarily in 34 terms of increasing production, there will be controversy over who sells what to whom, and the likelihood of international dissension will remain high. This is an old story. But other effects of spiraling production, made possible by our massive technological breakthroughs, are causing a new problem that earlier generations never heard of—environmental overload.

The Destruction of the Environment

Another reason for deemphasizing the production of goods as the pri- 35 mary way of making a living is the havoc it is wreaking on our planet. Polluted waters and smoggy air have become commonplace in and around industrial areas throughout the world. As economist Robert Heilbroner puts it, "We are running out of the sheer absorptive capacity for the dangerous by-products of an ever-growing industrial output. . . .* There was a time when every act of production, by adding a needed bit to the skimpy pile of social wealth, justified itself without question. But as our air darkens and our lakes putrefy, as our population continues to swell and our reserve of resources shrink, that easy equation of *more* with *better* is no longer possible to make."[24]

*MacLeod's ellipsis.

Heilbroner,* Galbraith,† and Toffler‡ all recommend a further conver- 36
sion to a service-oriented society. This does not mean that production should
stop altogether or that industrial nations should return to rural village economies, as a handful of environmental purists suggest; it means trying to achieve
a better social balance between goods and services. Toffler sees two benefits
from the shift: "First, a service society can help us solve many accumulated
social, community, and environmental problems bequeathed to us by the
unrestrained economic growth policies of the past two decades. Second, a
service-oriented society is less dependent on high inputs of energy and resources than is a traditional industrial society."[25]

When a garment factory in Manhattan closes down or moves to Korea 37
because shirts made at home are too expensive to compete on the world
market, it means that more young people who might have become garment
workers are likely to end up as new migrants. The same is true of garment
factories that close in Manchester, England—or steel mills or automobile
factories that shut down in any nation. We cannot escape the international
connection of jobs and commerce in the modern world.

Nor in the long run can we escape the need to put the production of 38
goods in perspective and stop worshipping growth per se.

NOTES

All notes are MacLeod's.

21. Galbraith, *The Affluent Society*, p. 201.

22. Schumacher, E.F. *Small is Beautiful: Economics as if People Mattered*, Intro. by Theodore Roszak. New
York: Harper & Row, 1973, p. 194.

24. Heilbroner, pp. 303 and 305. *B.

25. Toffler, p. 84, *B.

HORATIO ALGER, FAREWELL

A nation that no longer needs the full-time labor of all its people does 39
not have to be in trouble; instead, the nation could consider this cause for
rejoicing. This was the belief in the 1950s when machines began replacing
workers at an astonishing rate. Now people would have more time for leisure
pursuits, the theorists said, time to develop their spiritual and intellectual
sides, time to become fuller human beings who could help build an even
better world.

But it didn't turn out that way. We never reconciled the moral impera- 40
tive "If you don't work, you don't eat" with the reality of not enough jobs
to go around. The Protestant work ethic, combined with the dream of unlim-

*Heilbroner, Robert L. *The Worldly Philosophers: The Lives, Times, and Ideas of the Great Economic Thinkers*,
4th ed., New York: Simon & Schuster, 1972.

†Galbraith, John Kenneth. *The Affluent Society*. New York: New American Library, 1958.

‡Toffler, Alvin. *The Eco-Spasm Report*. New York: Bantam, 1975.

ited opportunity for all, kept us from reassessing the job situation in the light of technological changes and making the necessary adjustments.

People without jobs were accused of not wanting to work, of preferring 41 welfare to jobs. In fact, the work imperative is as strong among the jobless as among those who receive regular paychecks, if not stronger. Most adults want to work; they do not want to be dependent on welfare or charity. When tomato-picking machines began putting farm workers out of jobs in California, the pickers did not rejoice at the prospect of relaxing on the dole; they mounted a campaign to try to stop the development of machines that were taking away their jobs, jobs that many an optionaire would consider boring, menial labor.[1]

Plenty of people from all walks of life would enjoy a moratorium from 42 work in youth or middle age, a period when they could relax, travel, and do as they pleased. And we all need vacations. But there are few adults who do not want some kind of work to structure their life around. This goes beyond the need for money and a moral imperative to work; it is a matter of needing something to do, some activity that gives direction and purpose to life. Even boring work may be better than doing nothing at all full time.

Ultimately, we will need to develop different kinds of jobs, and a greater 43 variety of job arrangements: for example, shorter hours; job sharing; longer vacations; more adult education to help people develop new interests they can pursue if they retire early; programs open to teen-agers that will give them satisfying experiences while keeping them off the regular job market a year or so longer. Numerous other innovative arrangements could be devised and tried if people put their minds to it.

We already have the technological capability to create jobs for all, but 44 two stumbling blocks keep us from making the necessary transition: the myth of the American dream and inflation. In this final chapter we will consider both impediments to change, starting with inflation and working back to the need to relinquish the dream—the central thesis of this book.

THE INFLATION MENACE

When inflation is rampant, few people will want to share jobs or work 45 shorter hours if it means less pay; conversely, government and business will not agree to full-time pay for less work during a period of inflation. Other arrangements would involve government spending for programs or pensions, again unacceptable during inflation, a time when people are pushing to decrease existing government spending, not add to it. Therefore, before we can make significant changes, we must solve the problem of inflation.

What is causing inflation? The nation's top economists disagree. Just as 46 Supreme Court justices naturally interpret the law according to their individual social and political beliefs, so economists fit the causes of inflation into their own economic theories: Conservative economists blame government spending and call for a balanced federal budget, while liberal economists blame high profits and massive spending and call for controls on prices and wages. I would not attempt to fathom inflation's complex web of causality, except to suggest that some of the points stressed in this book—our expectation of continuous upward mobility and our worship of riches—are intimately tied up with the causes of our current inflation. Changing the dream may thus have the secondary benefit of helping to lessen inflation.

In 1958 John Kenneth Galbraith wrote, "Discrimination against the public services is an organic feature of inflation."[2] That observation has been borne out with a vengeance in the current crisis, and not only in the United States. Canada and Britain both dumped labor governments in 1979 and elected Conservatives who pledged to cut domestic government spending. 47

The situation is curious. Scores of nations are facing a similar crippling inflation at the same time, so even an untrained observer might suspect a link between the various inflations; yet in most countries domestic spending is getting the blame. 48

In the United States, social services—especially to the poor—are being cut back, and the government is viewed by many as a robber who is stealing part of everybody's paycheck. This antigovernment feeling reached its climax in 1978 in California, with the passage of Proposition 13. 49

Inflation and Proposition 13

For more than a decade a real-estate executive named Howard Jarvis had been leading a movement to cut property taxes in California; although his initiative got on the ballot regularly,* it failed, because Californians did not want to give up the local services that property taxes support. But in 1978, with inflation rampant, Proposition 13 (the Jarvis-Gann initiative) won a sweeping victory. 50

Jarvis, who assured Californians that his measure would only cut the fat from government, emerged as a folk hero. He was photographed with James Ware, who had won the Republican primary for state controller by endorsing Proposition 13. Ware said jubilantly, "Like Howard Jarvis, I've been on the ballot for 15 years. Now, we're both part of a new revolution to save the American dream." 51

But victory was not as sweet as expected. Instead of trimming the fat off government, it was the lean that went, because the people with the knives were not about to trim themselves away. Public libraries were closed a few days a week, city-run day camps and summer schools were canceled, day-care centers for children of working mothers were closed, as were some neighborhood medical clinics. These closures did not bother people who had enough money to pay for private services in these areas, but even the most ardent supporters of Proposition 13, it turned out, did not want to close down the police and fire departments in their cities in order to cut the cost of government. 52

Cities and counties had to apply to the state for relief, which lessened 53

*Under California law, if enough citizens sign petitions, a proposed law change can appear on the next ballot as an initiative measure.

local control. And although property owners did have a little more money to spend, with escalating inflation this money did not change their financial picture much, unless they owned vast amounts of property.

What people were really rebelling against when they voted for Proposi- 54 tion 13 was the rising price of ground beef, the fact that, no matter how much money they earned, they never got rich the way one was supposed to in America. What had happened to the promises of the dream?

It was appropriate that Proposition 13 occurred in California, the land 55 at the end of the frontier where people had once rushed in from all corners of the globe expecting to pull gold nuggets out of the earth and became millionaires overnight. The state where the American dream—a dream of money, money, and more money—had appeared to be a sure thing. Now they wondered—could the dream still happen?

Robert J. Ringer says "Yes!" in his 1979 best-seller *The Restoration of the* 56 *American Dream.* Ringer's message has much in common with the theme of his earlier book, *Looking Out for Number One,* but his style is distinctly different; the earlier, snappy, anecdotal style is replaced with a dignified tone that befits the high priest of libertarianism. Preaching that government is the evil that keeps Americans from achieving their dream of riches, Ringer recommends phasing out all taxes and gradually eliminating government services and government employees. Essential workers, such as postmen and firemen, "would be legitimate private employees performing the same functions as before, only better, less expensively and more efficiently than in the old government-employment days." Ringer urges Americans to "Make an unwavering commitment to become fiercely independent and individualistic."[3]

The Restoration of the American Dream may be inspirational to people who 57 share Ringer's beliefs and ideals, but the book offers no effective plan for establishing his anarchic utopia. Ringer is such a staunch individualist that he opposes all group action—even joint action by conservatives to restrain the government.

Prices continued to rise in 1979, and although many big businesses and 58 some speculators made enormous profits, most people were worse off, because wage increases were not as great as price increases. At the end of 1978 President Carter had asked business and labor to restrict their increases voluntarily in order to help fight inflation; but in the first quarter of 1979, profits earned by businesses increased 26.4 percent over the same period a year earlier, while labor raises, for the most part, kept within the suggested 7-percent guideline.[4]

With the people in an antigovernment mood, the president did not 59 invoke price and wage controls, as some economists urged. The people got less government—and more inflation.

The Role of Government

How much should the government govern? Americans still yearn for 60 small government, for the town meetings of old New England where every citizen could participate directly and Washington was a distant image that people thought about every four years. They love tales of the old West where, according to legend, one "good guy" sheriff was personnel enough to restore law and order in a town and keep it that way. Small government sufficed when there were few people, and land and resources were plentiful. But today the United States is a complex nation with a large population, and it requires a complex government in order to function.

But what about waste, inefficiency, and corruption in government? 61 Aren't there legitimate complaints against the government, and shouldn't we try to correct them? Certainly. The machinery of government—any government—does have a tendency to become large and unwieldy; at times it is inefficient; sometimes it is corrupt. Government needs to be watched constantly. It also needs to be checked and evaluated periodically, so programs that aren't working can be removed, red tape can be spliced, and services can be streamlined. Old services may need to go in order to make room for new ones of greater urgency.

In one sense the government is like a large house that becomes cluttered 62 through long and active use. Sensible people do not burn down their house because it is cluttered and move into a small tent in hopes of avoiding future clutter. Instead, they clean out their house periodically.

What we need to strive for is not less government but better govern- 63 ment. A return to the laissez-faire economy recommended by Ringer would not bring most citizens an increased chance to earn a better living; to the contrary, it would decrease their opportunities by enabling those with the greatest financial resources and political clout (the big corporations and banks) to grow even larger and more powerful. The Constitution gives us the machinery with which to impeach a president who tries to grab too much power; but where is the machinery to oust the head of a conglomerate who assumes the role of dictator in formulating national policies that will enrich himself and his associates while impoverishing others?

Who Pays the Bill?

It costs money to run social programs. Earlier chapters have stressed the 64 need for a variety of programs to help the new migrants and other people in the nonaffluent society find jobs and decent places to live. These programs will not make a profit, so the business sector will not be interested in running them. Nonprofit organizations lack the financial resources to operate large-scale programs. Only one institution is capable of running long-range social programs—the government, which was set up in part to help promote the general welfare of its citizens. But where will the government get the money to pay for these programs?

The answer should be obvious by now, in the context of this argument. 65 People pay to support their government through taxes, and the tax rate is geared to one's ability to contribute. In theory, our graduated-income-tax laws laready provide for this; in practice, the system does not always operate that way.

Wage earners are forced to pay their fair share of taxes, because taxes 66 are deducted from their paychecks; if all their income goes for living expenses, as is the case with virtually everyone in the nonaffluent society, there is none left over for tax-shelter investments. At the same time, middle-income citizens—those around the base of the affluence pyramid, and some with incomes considerably larger—may pay higher taxes than many of the rich and super-rich if they do not search avidly for loopholes. But those in the middle resent the unfairness of the situation.

It is this type of inequality that taxpayers should revolt against. If the 67
top rates are too high now to be realistic, as some argue, they should be lowered somewhat—and collected without fail. (The obscene housing prices in California and many other states would surely be lower if our tax structure did not encourage people to invest and speculate in real estate as a method of escaping taxes.)

But as long as the dream of riches remains the dominant goal, and the 68
wealthy are held up as role models of success—with their tax evasions considered smart instead of immoral—there is little chance of significant tax reform. Nor can other important changes occur while we cling to the myth of unlimited opportunity and venerate the super-rich.

A TIME FOR CHANGE

Personal expectations keep rising throughout the world. At the same 69
time, technological innovations keep increasing the world's ability to produce enough basic goods for all and eradicate poverty. Everyone should be better off. Instead, poverty perversely remains, and the divisions between rich and poor grow wider.

We are pursuing outmoded economic goals. The philosophy that championed rugged individuals in competition for the land and resources of the frontier, with the winner taking all, belongs in the archives of history.

It is time to say, "Horatio Alger, farewell." The hallowed dream of 70
millions for everyone who works hard enough is obsolete. There is, quite simply, not enough wealth or natural resources on earth for every person to be rich, or even affluent, no matter how hard we all work; nor is a higher standard of living for all likely to spread across the United States or any other country in the future through improved technology and increased production of goods. In order to give everyone the chance to make a living and escape poverty, we will have to scale down our conception of how rich is rich enough.

The United States did attempt to eradicate poverty and lessen the in- 71
come gap during the 1960s, but there was no corresponding drive to lessen the concentration of wealth. We assumed that there was plenty for all. Today, only those who bury their heads in the sand (or remain in executive suites far from the masses of population) can still believe that fairy tale.

Lowering Our Expectations
People at every income level, except the very bottom, need to lower 72
their expectations. Now when a leader exhorts the people to lower their

expectations for the common good, he speaks to those in the middle and lower income ranges, because they constitute the majority; he does not exhort those in the highest income brackets to buy one less luxury car or beachfront retreat. The wealthy are exempted from retrenchment. This has got to change.

People in the middle and lower income ranges will not be convinced that   73
they should tighten their own belts as long as others live in opulence. If we are to lower our expectations, then those in the top income brackets must also reduce their standard of living (and the number of their investments) and learn to find satisfactions in life that do not depend on having more money and power than other people. We can no longer afford to allow enormous holdings of personal and corporate wealth to accumulate and multiply.

Changing Our Perceptions of Success

Another significant change must occur before people in the nonaffluent   74
society will relinquish the dream of riches—a change that strikes at the core of the dream. We must stop ranking people as failures if they do not make enough money to become affluent.

Labor specialist B. J. Widick summed up workers' grievances about this   75
attitude of the affluent society in *Auto Work and Its Discontents:* "They [workers] do have a grievance against society, with its middle-class values, and that is the general contempt in which factory workers, in particular assembly-line workers, are held, making it doubly difficult for blue-collar workers to maintain a sense of personal pride and dignity."

Workers are placed in a double bind: They are regarded as inferior if   76
they remain in the nonaffluent society; but when they try to climb up, as the dream encourages them to do, they find that the affluent society has no place for them.

As earlier chapters have stressed, far more people want professional jobs   77
than the country can use in that capacity. Higher pay and greater intellectual stimulation motivate this aspiration in part, but the desire for status—the determination to be ranked as somebody in the community—is an equally strong goad.

It is time to stop preaching upward mobility as the only way to go, time   78
to give recognition to people who are satisfied (or at least willing) to stay where they are—and who perform much of the labor that keeps our society going. By pretending to be a classless society, we rob the working classes of status and dignity.

A Different Dream

Now that there are no more frontiers or undiscovered continents for   79
rugged individuals to conquer, we need a different dream. The challenge facing the United States and other Western nations in the coming century is whether they can end dire poverty, put limits on individual and corporate wealth, and usher in full employment without also inaugurating the totalitarian excesses that have so often accompanied attempts to effect such changes in communist nations. An equitable balance between the rights of the indi-

vidual and the needs of the community and nation has yet to be worked out in most countries in either power bloc, but it is essential that we work toward this goal.

On the international level, cooperation and compromise are the key 80 words of the future, if we are to prevent the holocaust of a nuclear war.

The multiple changes that occurred in our age have rendered both 81 capitalism and communism in their traditional forms obsolete as adequate economic solutions for the centuries ahead. We are sorely in need of new comprehensive economic theories, carefully formulated plans of the magnitude of those put forth by Adam Smith and Karl Marx in the past, but based on the world in which we now live.

Meanwhile, the new migrants wend their way from city to city in search 82 of opportunities that do not exist for them. Without help from their governments, and encouragement to lower their expectations, the new migrants will remain wanderers, part of a growing army of unemployed youths in Europe and the United States who have become surplus commodities in their own countries. Their presence mocks the Alger myth, and undermines their nations' priorities.

When countries with the capability of putting men on the moon and 83 developing hydrogen bombs declare that it is impossible for them to devise methods of employing all their people who want to work, then something is clearly amiss with their systems and values. It is time for changes.

The end of the American dream may seem sad, even tragic, to some 84 people. But it need not be a time for mourning. In the United States we have come through our childhood as a nation and lived through a stormy adolescence in the past two decades. Perhaps we are ready for a new dream, a mature dream that does not center on individual desires for grandiose wealth and the power to play God. It could be that in the century ahead, a different dream can serve us just as well or better.

NOTES

All notes are MacLeod's.

1. Chavez.
2. Galbraith, *The Affluent Society,* p. 209.
3. Ringer, Robert J. *The Restoration of the American Dream,* San Francisco: QED, 1979, p. 280.
4. "Huge Profits Anger the White House," *San Francisco Chronicle,* January 3, 1977, 3. (Reprinted from the Washington Post.), pp. 1 and 16.

Questions for Discussion

1. Are there members of your class who have examples of the Horatio Alger myth in their family histories: immigrants who came to this country pen-

niless and are now well off; forebears who lit out for the West with nothing but portable possessions and made it big; relatives who lost everything from fire, flood, or accident and then recovered all they had and more; or other relatives who started life as nobodies and then rose to political or social prominence? Discuss among yourselves the possible influences that such stories have had on the expectations you hold for your own lives, and how you are likely to feel if those expectations do not come true.

2. If there are no, or few, examples of such rags-to-riches success, does the scarcity of examples raise doubts about the reality of the Horatio Alger version of the American Dream? Your class, obviously, does not constitute much of a sample, but it probably is a sufficiently representative group to allow you to speculate about the social and economic realities for people of your like social and income group.

3. For the last 25 years in America, young adults starting life seem to do less well economically than their parents did at their children's time of life. Young people starting out today often cannot afford to buy a home, must delay starting a family because of finances, and both partners in a marriage must often work whether they want to or not just to make ends meet. How vividly do people in your class feel that the American economy offers them less advantageous or less plentiful opportunities for economic success and security than it offered their parents?

4. How many people in your class expect to continue receiving financial help from their parents after they graduate from college? How many expect to go back home and live until they have gotten themselves established? How many of these people's parents relied on *their* parents in the same way when *they* started out? Are there any suggestive differences in the degree or amount or kind of help youth today expect compared to that expected by their own parents in their youth? If so, what causes these differences? How can they be explained? What do they suggest, if anything, about the condition of the Horatio Alger dream in American society today?

Suggested Essay Topics

1. In an essay directed to your parents, speculate on your future life in comparison to the life they have had up to this point. Your title could be something like, "What does the future hold for me?" or "Times are different now," or "1950s expectations vs 1990s expectations"—something that suggests an attempt to look back simultaneously on your parents' life and to look forward on your own life and to learn something from whatever contrasts or similarities you see.

2. At the end of MacLeod's essay, she refers to "a different dream" (¶79), suggesting that, once we have said farewell to the Horatio Alger myth, we need to replace it with some other, new, and better American Dream of what constitutes the good life. In an essay directed to your classmates, either rebut MacLeod's position about the American Dream, showing good

reasons why her views are weak or unfounded, or try your hand at describing or inventing a "new" American Dream, suggesting in concrete terms how the expectations of your generation should differ from the expectations of most of your parents.

E. M. Forster

The English novelist and essayist E. M. Forster (1879–1970) published his most famous novel, A Passage to India, *in 1924. It was the money from American sales of this novel (alluded to in ¶1) that enabled him to buy the woods that gave him the title of this essay.*

"My Wood" is a good example of indirect argument. On the surface the essay is all about Forster himself—the effect on his character of owning property. But under the surface is another topic, related to the first but larger and more general. It is an indirect argument about the evils of an economic system that encourages us to think that owning things is a worthy objective in life—even the highest objective, a sufficient substitute for all other experiences. Our economic system implies that if we own enough things, we don't have to be intelligent, clever, creative, or compassionate. We don't even need to know how to enjoy ourselves.

Forster's larger argument is strongly hinted but not developed outright. Because Forster talks only about his own feelings and experience, he must make it clear that his references to himself are really observations about human beings in general, as they live under our economic system. Forster quietly but insistently places his own story within larger contexts ranging from biblical stories to the example of a man who ruins his woods by walling them off. In each case it is impossible to apply Forster's judgments only to him (although he asks you, tongue in cheek, to do so). In reality his judgments extend to the whole social system that holds up ownership of things as the main objective of life.

As you read, try to determine what kind of response to his indictment of our economic and social system Forster is asking for. Is he calling for political revolution? For moral reform? For a reaffirmation of religious principles? Or does he have some other aim in mind altogether?

MY WOOD

From *Abinger Harvest* (1936). "My Wood" was written in 1926.

A few years ago I wrote a book which dealt in part with the difficulties of the English in India. Feeling that they would have had no difficulties in India themselves, the Americans read the book freely. The more they read it the better it made them feel, and a cheque to the author was the result. I bought a wood with the cheque. It is not a large wood—it contains scarcely any trees, and it is intersected, blast it, by a public footpath. Still, it is the first property that I have owned, so it is right that other people should participate in my shame, and should ask themselves, in accents that will vary in horror, this very important question: What is the effect of property upon the character? Don't let's touch economics; the effect of private ownership upon the community as a whole is another question—a more important question, perhaps, but another one. Let's keep to psychology. If you own things, what's their effect on you? What's the effect on me of my wood?

In the first place, it makes me feel heavy. Property does have this effect. 2
Property produces men of weight, and it was a man of weight who failed to get into the Kingdom of Heaven. He was not wicked, that unfortunate millionaire in the parable, he was only stout; he stuck out in front, not to mention behind, and as he wedged himself this way and that in the crystalline entrance and bruised his well-fed flanks, he saw beneath him a comparatively slim camel passing through the eye of a needle [Mark 10:25] and being woven into the robe of God. The Gospels all through couple stoutness and slowness. They point out what is perfectly obvious, yet seldom realized: that if you have a lot of things you cannot move about a lot, that furniture requires dusting, dusters require servants, servants require insurance stamps, and the whole tangle of them makes you think twice before you accept an invitation to dinner or go for a bathe in the Jordan [II Kings 5:1–14]. Sometimes the Gospels proceed further and say with Tolstoy that property is sinful; they approach the difficult ground of asceticism here, where I cannot follow them. But as to the immediate effects of property on people, they just show straightforward logic. It produces men of weight. Men of weight cannot, by definition, move like the lightning from the East unto the West [Matthew 24:27], and the ascent of a fourteen-stone* bishop into a pulpit is thus the exact antithesis of the coming of the Son of Man. My wood makes me feel heavy.

In the second place, it makes me feel it ought to be larger. 3

The other day I heard a twig snap in it. I was annoyed at first, for I 4 thought that someone was blackberrying, and depreciating the value of the undergrowth. On coming nearer, I saw it was not a man who had trodden on the twig and snapped it, but a bird, and I felt pleased. My bird. The bird was not equally pleased. Ignoring the relation between us, it took fright as soon as it saw the shape of my face, and flew straight over the boundary hedge into a field, the property of Mrs. Henessy, where it sat down with a loud squawk. It had become Mrs. Henessy's bird. Something seemed grossly amiss here, something that would not have occurred had the wood been larger. I could not afford to buy Mrs. Henessy out, I dared not murder her, and limitations of this sort beset me on every side. Ahab did not want that vineyard [I Kings 21]—he only needed it to round off his property, preparatory to plotting a new curve—and all the land around my wood has become necessary to me in order to round off the wood. A boundary protects. But—

*A stone is a British weight equal to 14 pounds.

poor little thing—the boundary ought in its turn to be protected. Noises on the edge of it. Children throw stones. A rettle more, and then a little more, until we reach the sea. Happy Canute!* Happier Alexander!† And after all, why should even the world be the limit of possession? A rocket containing a Union Jack,‡ will, it is hoped, be shortly fired at the moon. Mars. Sirius. Beyond which . . . But these immensities ended by saddening me. I could not suppose that my wood was the destined nucleus of universal dominion—it is so very small and contains no mineral wealth beyond the blackberries. Nor was I comforted when Mrs. Henessy's bird took alarm for the second time and flew clean away from us all, under the belief that it belonged to itself.

In the third place, property makes its owner feel that he ought to do 5 something to it. Yet he isn't sure what. A restlessness comes over him, a vague sense that he has a personality to express—the same sense which, without any vagueness, leads the artist to an act of creation. Sometimes I think I will cut down such trees as remain in the wood, at other times I want to fill up the gaps between them with new trees. Both impulses are pretentious and empty. They are not honest movements towards money-making or beauty. They spring from a foolish desire to express myself and from an inability to enjoy what I have got. Creation, property, enjoyment form a sinister trinity in the human mind. Creation and enjoyment are both very, very good, yet they are often unattainable without a material basis, and at such moments property pushes itself in as a substitute, saying, "Accept me instead—I'm good enough for all three." It is not enough. It is, as Shakespeare said of lust, "The expense of spirit in a waste of shame": it is "Before, a joy proposed; behind, a dream." Yet we don't know how to shun it. It is forced on us by our economic system as the alternative to starvation. It is also forced on us by an internal defect in the soul, by the feeling that in property may lie the germs of self-development and of exquisite or heroic deeds. Our life on earth is, and ought to be, material and carnal. But we have not yet learned to manage our materialism and carnality properly; they are still entangled with the desire for ownership, where (in the words of Dante) "Possession is one with loss."

And this brings us to our fourth and final point: the blackberries. 6

Blackberries are not plentiful in this meagre grove, but they are easily 7 seen from the public footpath which traverses it, and all too easily gathered. Foxgloves, too—people will pull up the foxgloves, and ladies of an educational tendency even grub for toadstools to show them on the Monday in class. Other ladies, less educated, roll down the bracken in the arms of their gentlemen friends. There is paper, there are tins. Pray, does my wood belong to me or doesn't it? And, if it does, should I not own it best by allowing no one else to walk there? There is a wood near Lyme Regis, also cursed by a

*Danish king who ruled all of England for about 20 years in the eleventh century.
†Alexander the Great (356–323 b.c.), who conquered all of the civilized world from Macedonia into Egypt.
‡The British flag.

public footpath, where the owner has not hesitated on this point. He had built high stone walls each side of the path, and has spanned it by bridges, so that the public circulate like termites while he gorges on the blackberries unseen. He really does own his wood, this able chap. Dives in Hell did pretty well, but the gulf dividing him from Lazarus could be traversed by vision, and nothing traverses it here [Luke 16:19–26].* And perhaps I shall come to this in time. I shall wall in and fence out until I really taste the sweets of property. Enormously stout, endlessly avaricious, pseudo-creative, intensely selfish, I shall weave upon my forehead the quadruple crown of possession until those nasty Bolshies† come and take it off again and thrust me aside into the outer darkness.

Questions for Discussion

1. State in your own words the four effects that owning the wood had on Forster. Begin your statement something like this: "Property has four main effects on the moral character of the owner. . . ."

2. What "shame" is Forster talking about in paragraph 1? Does he mean this literally or tongue-in-cheek? Can you decide without reading farther into the essay? How far must you go before you know?

3. "Don't let's touch economics," he says in paragraph 1. Does he mean this literally or tongue-in-cheek? How do you know?

4. In paragraph 4 what mixture of reactions is elicited by the two words "My bird"? How do the words work? What happens to the effect of the paragraph if you omit these two words?

5. At the end of his essay (¶7) and at the end of his experience of ownership, Forster pictures himself sitting within his walled-up woods, "enormously stout, endlessly avaricious, pseudo-creative, [and] intensely selfish." Is he merely trying to get a laugh, or is he saying what he really thinks about persons who fall prey to the temptations of an acquisitive economic system? Does the description "go too far," or does it express a fair moral judgment?

6. The last two sentences of paragraph 2 exhibit a typical stylistic device of this essay: a fairly complex sentence in formal English followed by a simple sentence in colloquial English. Does this mixing of styles work for or against Forster's effectiveness? What happens to the effectiveness of any given paragraph if you make all of the sentences in it either consistently formal or consistently colloquial?

*The "rich man" in the story is actually unnamed but is traditionally called Dives, the Latin word for "rich man."

†Bolsheviks, that is, Communists, who are ideologically opposed to the private ownership of property.

Suggested Essay Topics

1. Most of us know people who are out-and-out moneygrubbers—grade-A materialists whose only way of valuing anything is to look at the price tag. Imagine yourself sending these people a copy of Forster's essay, setting yourself the task of writing an introduction to it that will (without pointing the finger at them directly) force them to read it as a judgment on their materialism. You will have to make your introduction more than a summary; it must clarify the underlying value judgments that make this essay a reproof to your audience's intense acquisitiveness.

2. At the end of paragraph 5 Forster distinguishes "materialism and carnality" on the one hand from "the desire for ownership" on the other, and he quotes Dante to the effect that to own things is to lose them. Write an essay to your instructor in which you explain what this distinction means. This may seem difficult at first, but think of Forster's blackberries as a clue about how to start. Enjoying the blackberries is a carnal and material pleasure, surely an innocent one, but wanting to *own* the blackberries turns out to be something quite different. Consider whether this truth about the blackberries also applies to other things, such as possessiveness between men and women or domination of children by parents. Find enough examples to illuminate the meaning, and perhaps even show the validity, of the distinction.

Joyce Carol Oates

In a chapter dealing with defenses of and attacks on capitalism, is it fair, does it make sense, to include a story? Many people would say that works of art have no definite political, moral, or economic messages to deliver. They would say that art and aesthetics are one kind of human activity and that politics and economics are another kind of activity and that the second kind is incompatible with the first kind. Admittedly, this story makes no explicit point about either politics or economics. Oates (b. 1938) indulges in no long sermons on economic doctrine such as we find in the novels of Ayn Rand, nor does she undertake any obvious kind of exposé such as Frank Norris's early twentieth-century novels about the meatpacking industry, nor does she focus with hostility on a certain group of persons as did Sinclair Lewis, whose novels openly attacked the lives and values of "main street" American businesspeople.

Nonetheless, Oates's story carries a strong economic message. It is not about economic doctrine but about the way lives are lived, damaged, or destroyed among people whose economic level places them so far above other citizens that they have no view of how the poor, the desperate, and the deviants live or die. In addition, the "haves" in Oates's story have become so owned by their possessions and their positions that they can no longer see each other's emotional or spiritual needs, even when those needs belong to members of their own families. Affluence has swallowed them up, and they can see life only in monetary terms. The parents in the story think they are solving the problems of a shoplifting daughter, for example, by buying her the gloves she had stolen, completely failing to see—not really wanting *to see—that owning new gloves was never the issue.*

Thus the political and economic realities of the different characters in Oates's story are not present only as background, as they must always be for all of us, but also subtly emerge as determinative of the story's action, of the characters' understanding of themselves, and of their eventual destinies. In addition, the author implies a strong judgment about these political and economic realities, especially the economic ones, a judgment that challenges many of the most revered dicta that Americans hold about the worthiness of making money, getting ahead in the world professionally, and having enough consumer goods, physical comfort, and social prestige to give one's neighbors envious heartburn.

HOW I CONTEMPLATED THE WORLD FROM THE DETROIT HOUSE OF CORRECTION AND BEGAN MY LIFE OVER AGAIN

From *The Wheel of Love* (1965).

Notes for an essay for an English class at Baldwin Country Day School; poking around in debris; disgust and curiosity; a revelation of the meaning of life; a happy ending. . . .*

1

I. EVENTS

1. The girl (myself) is walking through Branden's, that excellent store. Suburb of a large famous city that is a symbol for large famous American cities. The event sneaks up on the girl, who believes she is herding it along with a small fixed smile, a girl of fifteen, innocently experienced. She dawdles in a certain style by a counter of costume jewelry. Rings, earrings, necklaces. Prices from $5 to $50, all within reach. All ugly. She eases over to the glove counter, where everything is ugly too. In her close-fitted coat with its black fur collar she contemplates the luxury of Branden's, which she has known for many years: its many mild pale lights, easy on the eye and the soul, its elaborate tinkly decorations, its women shoppers with their excellent shoes and coats and hairdos, all dawdling gracefully, in no hurry.
Who was ever in a hurry here?

2

3

2. The girl seated at home. A small library, paneled walls of oak. Someone is talking to me. An earnest husky female voice drives itself against my ears,

4

*Oates's story is printed here complete and uncut. All ellipses throughout are Oates's.

nervous, frightened, groping around my heart, saying, "If you wanted gloves why didn't you say so? Why didn't you ask for them?" That store, Branden's, is owned by Raymond Forrest who lives on DuMaurier Drive. We live on Sioux Drive. Raymond Forrest. A handsome man? An ugly man? A man of fifty or sixty, with gray hair, or a man of forty with earnest courteous eyes, a good golf game, who is Raymond Forrest, this man who is my salvation? Father has been talking to him. Father is not his physician; Dr. Berg is his physician. Father and Dr. Berg refer patients to each other. There is a connection. Mother plays bridge with. . . . On Mondays and Wednesdays our maid Billie works at. . . . The strings draw together in a cat's cradle, making a net to save you when you fall. . . .

3. *Harriet Arnold's.* A small shop, better than Branden's. Mother in her black coat, I in my close-fitted blue coat. Shopping. Now look at this, isn't this cute, do you want this, why don't you want this, try this on, take this with you to the fitting room, take this also, what's wrong with you, what can I do for you, why are you so strange . . . ? "I wanted to steal but not to buy," I don't tell her. The girl droops along in her coat and gloves and leather boots, her eyes scan the horizon which is pastel pink and decorated like Branden's, tasteful walls and modern ceilings with graceful glimmering lights.

4. Weeks later, the girl at a bus-stop. Two o'clock in the afternoon, a Tuesday, obviously she has walked out of school.

5. The girl stepping down from a bus. Afternoon, weather changing to colder. Detroit. Pavement and closed-up stores; grill work over the windows of a pawnshop. What is a pawnshop, exactly?

II. CHARACTERS

1. The girl stands five feet five inches tall. An ordinary height. Baldwin Country Day School draws them up to that height. She dreams along the corridors and presses her face against the Thermoplex Glass. No frost or steam can ever form on that glass. A smudge of grease from her forehead . . . could she be boiled down to grease? She wears her hair loose and long and straight in suburban teenage style, 1968. Eyes smudged with pencil, dark brown. Brown hair. Vague green eyes. A pretty girl? An ugly girl? She sings to herself under her breath, idling in the corridor, thinking of her many secrets (the thirty dollars she once took from the purse of a friend's mother, just for fun, the basement window she smashed in her own house just for fun) and thinking of her brother who is at Susquehanna Boys' Academy, an excellent preparatory school in Maine, remembering him unclearly . . . he has long manic hair and a squeaking voice and he looks like one of the popular teenage singers of 1968, one of those in a group, *The Certain Forces, The Way Out, The Maniacs Responsible.* The girl in her turn looks like one of those fieldsful of girls who listen to the boys' singing, dreaming and mooning restlessly, breaking into high sullen laughter, innocently experienced.

2. The mother. A midwestern woman of Detroit and suburbs. Belongs to the 9
Detroit Athletic Club. Also the Detroit Golf Club. Also the Bloomfield Hills
Country Club. The Village Women's Club at which lectures are given each
winter on Genet and Sartre and James Baldwin, by the Director of the Adult
Education Program at Wayne State University. . . . The Bloomfield Art Association. Also the Founders Society of the Detroit Institute of Arts.
Also. . . . Oh, she is in perpetual motion, this lady, hair like blown-up gold
and finer than gold, hair and fingers and body of inestimable grace. Heavy
weighs the gold on the back of her hairbrush and hand mirror. Heavy heavy
the candlesticks in the dining room. Very heavy is the big car, a Lincoln, long,
and black, that on one cool autumn day split a squirrel's body in two unequal
parts.

3. The father, Dr. ———. He belongs to the same clubs as # 2. A player of 10
squash and golf; he has a golfer's umbrella of stripes. Candy stripes. In his
mouth nothing turns to sugar, however, saliva works no miracles here. His
doctoring is of the slightly sick. The sick are sent elsewhere (to Dr. Berg?),
the deathly sick are sent back for more tests and their bills are sent to their
homes, the unsick are sent to Dr. Coronet (Isabel, a lady), an excellent psychiatrist for unsick people who angrily believe they are sick and want to do
something about it. If they demand a male psychiatrist, the unsick are sent
by Dr. ——— (my father) to Dr. Lowenstein, a male psychiatrist, excellent
and expensive, with a limited practice.

4. Clarita. She is twenty, twenty-five, she is thirty or more? Pretty, ugly, 11
what? She is a woman lounging by the side of a road, in jeans and a sweater,
hitchhiking, or she is slouched on a stool at a counter in some roadside diner.
A hard line of jaw. Curious eyes. Amused eyes. Behind her eyes processions
move, funeral pageants, cartoons. She says, "I never can figure out why girls
like you bum around down here. What are you looking for anyway?" An
odor of tobacco about her. Unwashed underclothes, or no underclothes, unwashed skin, gritty toes, hair long and falling into strands, not recently
washed.

5. Simon. In this city the weather changes abruptly, so Simon's weather 12
changes abruptly. He sleeps through the afternoon. He sleeps through the
morning. Rising he gropes around for something to get him going, for a
cigarette or a pill to drive him out to the street, where the temperature is
hovering around 35°. Why doesn't it drop? Why, why doesn't the cold clean
air come down from Canada, will he have to go up into Canada to get it, will
he have to leave the Country of his Birth and sink into Canada's frosty
fields . . . ? Will the F.B.I. (which he dreams about constantly) chase him over
the Canadian border on foot, hounded out in a blizzard of broken glass and
horns . . . ?

"Once I was Huckleberry Finn," Simon says, "but now I am Roderick 13
Usher." Beset by frenzies and fears, this man who makes my spine go cold,
he takes green pills, yellow pills, pills of white and capsules of dark blue and

green . . . he takes other things I may not mention, for what if Simon seeks me out and climbs into my girl's bedroom here in Bloomfield Hills and strangles me, what then . . . ? (As I write this I begin to shiver: Why do I shiver? I am now sixteen and sixteen is not an age for shivering.) It comes from Simon, who is always cold.

III. WORLD EVENTS

Nothing.   14

IV. PEOPLE AND CIRCUMSTANCES CONTRIBUTING TO THIS DELINQUENCY

Nothing.   15

V. SIOUX DRIVE

George, Clyde G. 240 Sioux. A manufacturer's representative; children, a dog; 16
a wife. Georgian with the usual columns. You think of the White House, then of Thomas Jefferson, then your mind goes blank on the white pillars and you think of nothing. Norris, Ralph W. 246 Sioux. Public relations. Colonial. Bay window, brick, stone, concrete, wood, green shutters, sidewalk, lantern, grass, trees, black-top drive, two children, one of them my classmate Esther (Esther Norris) at Baldwin. Wife, cars. Ramsey, Michael D. 250 Sioux. Colonial. Big living room, thirty by twenty-five, fireplaces in living room library recreation room, paneled walls wet bar five bathrooms five bedrooms two lavatories central air conditioning automatic sprinkler automatic garage door three children one wife two cars a breakfast room a patio a large fenced lot fourteen trees a front door with a brass knocker never knocked. Next is our house. Classic contemporary. Traditional modern. Attached garage, attached Florida room, attached patio, attached pool and cabana, attached roof. A front door mailslot through which pour *Time Magazine, Fortune, Life, Business Week, The Wall Street Journal, The New York Times, The New Yorker, The Saturday Review, M.D., Modern Medicine, Disease of the Month* . . . and also. . . . And in addition to all this a quiet sealed letter from Baldwin saying: *Your daughter is not doing work compatible with her performance on the Stanford-Binet.* . . . And your son is not doing well, not well at all, very sad. Where is your son anyway? Once he stole trick-and-treat candy from some six-year-old kids, he himself being a robust ten. The beginning. Now your daughter steals. In the Village Pharmacy she made off with, yes she did, don't deny it, she made off with a copy of *Pageant Magazine* for no reason, she swiped a roll of lifesavers in a green wrapper and was in no need of saving her life or even in need of sucking candy, when she was no more than eight years old she stole, don't blush, she stole a package of *Tums* only because it was out on the counter and available, and the nice lady behind the counter (now dead) said nothing. . . . Sioux Drive. Maples,

oaks, elms. Diseased elms cut down. Sioux Drive runs into Roosevelt Drive. Slow turning lanes, not streets, all drives and lanes and ways and passes. A private police force. Quiet private police, in unmarked cars. Cruising on Saturday evenings with paternal smiles for the residents who are streaming in and out of houses, going to and from parties, a thousand parties, slightly staggering, the women in their furs alighting from automobiles bought of Ford and General Motors and Chrysler, very heavy automobiles. No foreign cars. Detroit. In 275 Sioux, down the block, in that magnificent French Normandy mansion, lives ——— ——— himself, who has the C—— account itself, imagine that! Look at where he lives and look at the enormous trees and chimneys, imagine his many fireplaces, imagine his wife and children, imagine his wife's hair, imagine her fingernails, imagine her bathtub of smooth clean glowing pink, imagine their embraces, his trouser pockets filled with odd coins and keys and dust and peanuts, imagine their ecstasy on Sioux Drive, imagine their income tax returns, imagine their little boy's pride in his experimental car, a scaled-down C——, as he roars around the neighborhood on the sidewalks frightening dogs and Negro maids, oh imagine all these things, imagine everything, let your mind roar out all over Sioux Drive and DuMaurier Drive and Roosevelt Drive and Ticonderoga Pass and Burning Bush Way and Lincolnshire Pass and Lois Lane.

When spring comes its winds blow nothing to Sioux Drive, no odors of 17 hollyhocks or forsythia, nothing Sioux Drive doesn't already possess, everything is planted and performing. The weather vanes, had they weather vanes, don't have to turn with the wind, don't have to contend with the weather. There is no weather.

VI. DETROIT

There is always weather in Detroit. Detroit's temperature is always 32°. Fast 18 falling temperatures. Slow rising temperatures. Wind from the north northeast four to forty miles an hour, small craft warnings, partly cloudy today and Wednesday changing to partly sunny through Thursday . . . small warnings of frost, soot warnings, traffic warnings, hazardous lake conditions for small craft and swimmers, restless Negro gangs, restless cloud formations, restless temperatures aching to fall out the very bottom of the thermometer or shoot up over the top and boil everything over in red mercury.

Detroit's temperature is 32°. Fast falling temperatures. Slow rising tem- 19 peratures. Wind from the north northeast four to forty miles an hour. . . .

VII. EVENTS

1. The girl's heart is pounding. In her pocket is a pair of gloves! In a plastic 20 bag! Airproof breathproof plastic bag, gloves selling for twenty-five dollars on Branden's counter! In her pocket! Shoplifted! . . . In her purse is a blue comb, not very clean. In her purse is a leather billfold (a birthday present from her grandmother in Philadelphia) with snapshots of the family in clean plastic

windows, in the billfold are bills, she doesn't know how many bills. . . . In her purse is an ominous note from her friend Tykie *What's this about Joe H. and the kids hanging around at Louise's Sat. night? You heard anything?* . . . passed in French class. In her purse is a lot of dirty yellow Kleenex, her mother's heart would break to see such very dirty Kleenex, and at the bottom of her purse are brown hairpins and safety pins and a broken pencil and a ballpoint pen (blue) stolen from somewhere forgotten and a purse-size compact of Cover Girl Make-Up, Ivory Rose. . . . Her lipstick is Broken Heart, a corrupt pink; her fingers are trembling like crazy; her teeth are beginning to chatter; her insides are alive; her eyes glow in her head; she is saying to her mother's astonished face *I want to steal but not to buy.*

2. At Clarita's. Day or night? What room is this? A bed, a regular bed, and 21 a mattress on the floor nearby. Wallpaper hanging in strips. Clarita says she tore it like that with her teeth. She was fighting a barbaric tribe that night, high from some pills she was battling for her life with men wearing helmets of heavy iron and their faces no more than Christian crosses to breathe through, every one of those bastards looking like her lover Simon, who seems to breathe with great difficulty through the slits of mouth and nostrils in his face. Clarita has never heard of Sioux Drive. Raymond Forrest cuts no ice with her, nor does the C—— account and its millions; Harvard Business School could be at the corner of Vernor and 12th Street for all she cares, and Vietnam might have sunk by now into the Dead Sea under its tons of debris, for all the amazement she could show . . . her face is overworked, over-wrought, at the age of twenty (thirty?) it is already exhausted but fanciful and ready for a laugh. Clarita says mournfully to me *Honey somebody is going to turn you out let me give you warning.* In a movie shown on late television Clarita is not a mess like this but a nurse, with short neat hair and a dedicated look, in love with her doctor and her doctor's patients and their diseases, enamored of needles and sponges and rubbing alcohol. . . . Or no: she is a private secretary. Robert Cummings is her boss. She helps him with fantastic plots, the canned audience laughs, no, the audience doesn't laugh because nothing is funny, instead her boss is Robert Taylor and they are not boss and secretary but husband and wife, she is threatened by a young starlet, she is grim, handsome, wifely, a good companion for a good man. . . . She is Claudette Colbert. Her sister too is Claudette Colbert. They are twins, identical. Her husband Charles Boyer is a very rich handsome man and her sister, Claudette Colbert, is plotting her death in order to take her place as the rich man's wife, no one will know because they are *twins.* . . . All these marvelous lives Clarita might have lived, but she fell out the bottom at the age of thirteen. At the age when I was packing my overnight case for a slumber party at Toni Deshield's she was tearing filthy sheets off a bed and scratching up a rash on her arms. . . . Thirteen is uncommonly young for a white girl in Detroit, Miss Brook of the Detroit House of Correction said in a sad newspaper interview for the *Detroit News;* fifteen and sixteen are more likely. Eleven, twelve, thir-teen are not surprising in colored . . . they are more precocious. What can we

do? Taxes are rising and the tax base is falling. The temperature rises slowly but falls rapidly. Everything is falling out the bottom, Woodward Avenue is filthy, Livernois Avenue filthy! Scraps of paper flutter in the air like pigeons, dirt flies up and hits you right in the eye, oh Detroit is breaking up into dangerous bits of newspaper and dirt, watch out. . . .

Clarita's apartment is over a restaurant. Simon her lover emerges from   22
the cracks at dark. Mrs. Olesko, a neighbor of Clarita's, an aged white whisp of a woman, doesn't complain but sniffs with contentment at Clarita's noisy life and doesn't tell the cops, hating cops, when the cops arrive. I should give more fake names, more blanks, instead of telling all these secrets. I myself am a secret; I am a minor.

3. My father reads a paper at a medical convention in Los Angeles. There he   23
is, on the edge of the North American continent, when the unmarked detective put his hand so gently on my arm in the aisle of Branden's and said, "Miss, would you like to step over here for a minute?"

And where was he when Clarita put her hand on my arm, that wintry   24
dark sulphurous aching day in Detroit, in the company of closed-down barber shops, closed-down diners, closed-down movie houses, homes, windows, basements, faces . . . she put her hand on my arm and said, "Honey, are you looking for somebody down here?"

And was he home worrying about me, gone for two weeks solid, when   25
they carried me off . . . ? It took three of them to get me in the police cruiser, so they said, and they put more than their hands on my arm.

4. I worked on this lesson. My English teacher is Mr. Forest, who is from   26
Michigan State. Not handsome, Mr. Forest, and his name is plain unlike Raymond Forrest's, but he is sweet and rodent-like, he has conferred with the principal and my parents, and everything is fixed . . . treat her as if nothing has happened, a new start, begin again, only sixteen years old, what a shame, how did it happen?—nothing happened, nothing could have happened, a slight physiological modification known only to a gynecologist or to Dr. Coronet. I work on my lesson. I sit in my pink room. I look around the room with my sad pink eyes. I sigh, I dawdle, I pause, I eat up time, I am limp and happy to be home, I am sixteen years old suddenly, my head hangs heavy as a pumpkin on my shoulders, and my hair has just been cut by Mr. Faye at the Crystal Salon and is said to be very becoming.

(Simon too put his hand on my arm and said, "Honey, you have got to   27
come with me," and in his six-by-six room we got to know each other. Would I go back to Simon again? Would I lie down with him in all that filth and craziness? Over and over again.

a Clarita is being betrayed as in front of a Cunningham Drug Store she is nervously eyeing a colored man who may or may not have money, or a nervous white boy of twenty with sideburns and an Appalachian look, who may or may not have a knife hidden in his jacket pocket, or a husky red-faced man of friendly countenance who may or may not be a member of the Vice Squad out for an early twilight walk.)

I work on my lesson for Mr. Forest. I have filled up eleven pages. Words   28
pour out of me and won't stop. I want to tell everything . . . what was the
song Simon was always humming, and who was Simon's friend in a very new
trench coat with an old high school graduation ring on his finger . . . ? Simon's
bearded friend? When I was down too low for him Simon kicked me out and
gave me to him for three days, I think, on Fourteenth Street in Detroit, an
airy room of cold cruel drafts with newspapers on the floor. . . . Do I really
remember that or am I piecing it together from what they told me? Did they
tell the truth? Did they know much of the truth?

VIII. CHARACTERS

1. Wednesdays after school, at four; Saturday mornings at ten. Mother drives   29
me to Dr. Coronet. Ferns in the office, plastic or real, they look the same. Dr.
Coronet is queenly, an elegant nicotine-stained lady, who would have studied with Freud had circumstances not prevented it, a bit of a Catholic, ready
to offer you some mystery if your teeth will ache too much without it. Highly
recommended by Father! Forty dollars an hour, Father's forty dollars! Progress! Looking up! Looking better! That new haircut is so becoming, says Dr.
Coronet herself, showing how normal she is for a woman with an I.Q. of 180
and many advanced degrees.

2. Mother. A lady in a brown suede coat. Boots of shiny black material, black   30
gloves, a black fur hat. She would be humiliated could she know that of
all the people in the world it is my ex-lover Simon who walks most like
her . . . self-conscious and unreal, listening to distant music, a little bowlegged
with craftiness . . .

3. Father. Tying a necktie. In a hurry. On my first evening home he put his   31
hand on my arm and said, "Honey, we're going to forget all about this."

4. Simon. Outside a plane is crossing the sky, in here we're in a hurry.   32
Morning. It must be morning. The girl is half out of her mind, whimpering
and vague, Simon her dear friend is wretched this morning . . . he is wretched
with morning itself . . . he forces her to give him an injection, with that needle
she knows is filthy, she has a dread of needles and surgical instruments and
the odor of things that are to be sent into the blood, thinking somehow of
her father. . . . This is a bad morning, Simon says that his mind is being
twisted out of shape, and so he submits to the needle which he usually scorns
and bites his lip with his yellowish teeth, his face going very pale. *Ah baby!*
he says in his soft mocking voice, which with all women is a mockery of love,
*do it like this—Slowly—*And the girl, terrified, almost drops the precious needle
but manages to turn it up to the light from the window . . . it is an extension
of herself, then? She can give him this gift, then? *I wish you wouldn't do this to
me,* she says, wise in her terror, because it seems to her that Simon's danger—
in a few minutes he might be dead—is a way of pressing her against him that
is more powerful than any other embrace. She has to work over his arm, the

knotted corded veins of his arm, her forehead wet with perspiration as she pushes and releases the needle, staring at that mixture of liquid now stained with Simon's bright blood. . . . When the drug hits him she can feel it herself, she feels that magic that is more than any woman can give him, striking the back of his head and making his face stretch as if with the impact of a terrible sun. . . . She tries to embrace him but he pushes her aside and stumbles to his feet, *Jesus Christ,* he says. . . .

5. Princess, a Negro girl of eighteen. What is her charge? She is closemouthed   33 about it, shrewd and silent, you know that no one had to wrestle her to the sidewalk to get her in here; she came with dignity. In the recreation room she sits reading *Nancy Drew and the Jewel Box Mystery,* which inspires in her face tiny wrinkles of alarm and interest: what a face! Light brown skin, heavy shaded eyes, heavy eyelashes, a serious sinister dark brow, graceful fingers, graceful wrist-bones, graceful legs, lips, tongue, a sugarsweet voice, a leggy stride more masculine than Simon's and my mother's, decked out in a dirty white blouse and dirty white slacks; vaguely nautical is Princess's style. . . . At breakfast she is in charge of clearing the table and leans over me, saying, *Honey you sure you ate enough?*

6. The girl lies sleepless, wondering. Why here, why not there? Why Bloom-   34 field Hills and not jail? Why jail and not her pink room? Why downtown Detroit and not Sioux Drive? What is the difference? Is Simon all the difference? The girl's head is a parade of wonders. She is nearly sixteen, her breath is marvelous with wonders, not long ago she was coloring with crayons and now she is smearing the landscape with paints that won't come off and won't come off her fingers either. She says to the matron *I am not talking about anything,* not because everyone has warned her not to talk but because, because she will not talk, because she won't say anything about Simon who is her secret. And she says to the matron *I won't go home* up until that night in the lavatory when everything was changed. . . . "No, I won't go home I want to stay here," she says, listening to her own words with amazement, thinking that weeds might climb everywhere over that marvelous $86,000 house and dinosaurs might return to muddy the beige carpeting, but never will she reconcile four o'clock in the morning in Detroit with eight o'clock breakfasts in Bloomfield Hills . . . oh, she aches still for Simon's hands and his caressing breath, though he gave her little pleasure, he took everything from her (five-dollar bills, ten-dollar bills, passed into her numb hands by men and taken out of her hands by Simon) until she herself was passed into the hands of other men, police, when Simon evidently got tired of her and her hysteria. . . . *No, I won't go home, I don't want to be bailed out,* the girl thinks as a *Stubborn and Wayward Child* (one of several charges lodged against her) and the matron understands her crazy white-rimmed eyes that are seeking out some new violence that will keep her in jail, should someone threaten to let her out. Such children try to strangle the matrons, the attendants, or one another . . . they want the locks locked forever, the doors nailed shut . . . and this girl is no different up until that night her mind is changed for her. . . .

IX. THAT NIGHT

Princess and Dolly, a little white girl of maybe fifteen, hardy however as a   35
sergeant and in the House of Correction for armed robbery, corner her in the
lavatory at the farthest sink and the other girls look away and file out to bed,
leaving her. God how she is beaten up! Why is she beaten up? Why do they
pound her, why such hatred? Princess vents all the hatred of a thousand silent
Detroit winters on her body, this girl whose body belongs to me, fiercely she
rides across the midwestern plains on this girl's tender bruised body . . .
revenge on the oppressed minorities of America! revenge on the slaughtered
Indians! revenge on the female sex, on the male sex, revenge on Bloomfield
Hills, revenge revenge. . . .

X. DETROIT

In Detroit weather weighs heavily upon everyone. The sky looms large. The   36
horizon shimmers in smoke. Downtown the buildings are imprecise in the
haze. Perpetual haze. Perpetual motion inside the haze. Across the choppy
river is the city of Windsor, in Canada. Part of the continent has bunched up
here and is bulging outward, at the tip of Detroit, a cold hard rain is forever
falling on the expressway . . . shoppers shop grimly, their cars are not parked
in safe places, their windshields may be smashed and graceful ebony hands
may drag them out through their shatterproof smashed windshields crying
Revenge for the Indians! Ah, they all fear leaving Hudson's and being dragged to
the very tip of the city and thrown off the parking roof of Cobo Hall, that
expensive tomb, into the river. . . .

XI. CHARACTERS WE ARE FOREVER
ENTWINED WITH

1. Simon drew me into his tender rotting arms and breathed gravity into me.   37
Then I came to earth, weighted down. He said *You are such a little girl,* and he
weighed me down with his delight. In the palms of his hands were teeth
marks from his previous life experiences. He was thirty-five, they said. Imagine Simon in this room, in my pink room: he is about six feet tall and stoops
slightly, in a feline cautious way, always thinking, always on guard, with his
scuffed light suede shoes and his clothes which are anyone's clothes, slightly
rumpled ordinary clothes that ordinary men might wear to not-bad jobs.
Simon has fair, long hair, curly hair, spent languid curls that are like . . .
exactly like the curls of wood shavings to the touch, I am trying to be
exact . . . and he smells of unheated mornings and coffee and too many pills
coating his tongue with a faint green-white scum. . . . Dear Simon, who would
be panicked in this room and in this house (right now Billie is vacuuming next
door in my parents' room: a vacuum cleaner's roar is a sign of all good things),
Simon who is said to have come from a home not much different from this,
years ago, fleeing all the carpeting and the polished banisters . . . Simon has

a deathly face, only desperate people fall in love with it. His face is bony and cautious, the bones of his cheeks prominent as if with the rigidity of his ceaseless thinking, plotting, for he has to make money out of girls to whom money means nothing, they're so far gone they can hardly count it, and in a sense money means nothing to him either except as a way of keeping on with his life. *Each Day's Proud Struggle,* the title of a novel we could read at jail. . . . Each day he needs a certain amount of money. He devours it. It wasn't love he uncoiled in me with his hollowed-out eyes and his courteous smile, that remnant of a prosperous past, but a dark terror that needed to press itself flat against him, or against another man . . . but he was the first, he came over to me and took my arm, a claim. We struggled on the stairs and I said, "Let me loose, you're hurting my neck, my face," it was such a surprise that my skin hurt where he rubbed it, and afterward we lay face to face and he breathed everything into me. In the end I think he turned me in.

2. Raymond Forrest. I just read this morning that Raymond Forrest's father, 38 the chairman of the board at ———, died of a heart attack on a plane bound for London. I would like to write Raymond Forrest a note of sympathy. I would like to thank him for not pressing charges against me one hundred years ago, saving me, being so generous . . . well, men like Raymond Forrest are generous men, not like Simon. I would like to write him a letter telling of my love, or of some other emotion that is positive and healthy. Not like Simon and his poetry, which he scrawled down when he was high and never changed a word . . . but when I try to think of something to say it is Simon's language that comes back to me, caught in my head like a bad song, it is always Simon's language:

> *There is no reality only dreams*
> *Your neck may get snapped when you wake*
> *My love is drawn to some violent end*
> *She keeps wanting to get away*
> *My love is heading downward*   5
> *And I am heading upward*
> *She is going to crash on the sidewalk*
> *And I am going to dissolve into the clouds*

XII. EVENTS

1. Out of the hospital, bruised and saddened and converted, with Princess's 39 grunts still tangled in my hair . . . and Father in his overcoat looking like a Prince himself, come to carry me off. Up the expressway and out north to home. Jesus Christ but the air is thinner and cleaner here. Monumental houses. Heartbreaking sidewalks, so clean.

2. Weeping in the living room. The ceiling is two storeys high and two 40 chandeliers hang from it. Weeping, weeping, though Billie the maid is *probably*

listening. I will never leave home again. Never. Never leave home. Never leave this home again, never.

3. Sugar doughnuts for breakfast. The toaster is very shiny and my face is 41
distorted in it. Is that my face?

4. The car is turning in the driveway. Father brings me home. Mother em- 42
braces me. Sunlight breaks in movieland patches on the roof of our traditional
contemporary home, which was designed for the famous automotive stylist
whose identity, if I told you the name of the famous car he designed, you
would all know, so I can't tell you because my teeth chatter at the thought
of being sued . . . or having someone climb into my bedroom window with
a rope to strangle me. . . . The car turns up the black-top drive. The house
opens to me like a doll's house, so lovely in the sunlight, the big living room
beckons to me with its walls falling away in a delirium of joy at my return,
Billie the maid is *no doubt* listening from the kitchen as I burst into tears and
the hysteria Simon got so sick of. Convulsed in Father's arms I say I will never
leave again, never, why did I leave, where did I go, what happened, my
mind is gone wrong, my body is one big bruise, my backbone was sucked
dry, it wasn't the men who hurt me and Simon never hurt me but only
those girls . . . my God how they hurt me . . . I will never leave home
again. . . . The car is perpetually turning up the drive and I am perpetually
breaking down in the living room and we are perpetually taking the right exit
from the expressway (Lahser Road) and the wall of the restroom is perpetually banging against my head and perpetually are Simon's hands moving
across my body and adding everything up and so too are Father's hands on
my shaking bruised back, far from the surface of my skin on the surface of
my good blue cashmere coat (drycleaned for my release). . . . I weep for all
the money here, for God in gold and beige carpeting, for the beauty of
chandeliers and the miracle of a clean polished gleaming toaster and faucets
that run both hot and cold water, and I tell them *I will never leave home, this is
my home, I love everything here, I am in love with everything here.* . . .

   I am home.   43

Questions for Discussion

1. Why does the girl in the story steal the gloves from Branden's store? Is her
   parents' pulling of social strings—"fixing" things for her—the wrong or
   right response to her act? Why?
2. What judgments about the mother and father are you led to make by
   paragraphs 9 and 10?
3. The Detroit weather seems to be used symbolically in this story—as a
   symbol of what? Is the symbolic treatment effective? Why or why not?

4. What do you learn about the central character when she lists "Nothing" under "III. World Events" (¶ 14)? You know from the story that the year is 1968—the year Robert Kennedy and Martin Luther King were assassinated, the year of the police riots at the Democratic national convention in Chicago, the year when anti-war protests against the Vietnam conflict were more vociferous than they had ever been, the year that an incumbent president was forced out of running for re-election because of his failure to end either the war or the protests against it, and the year in which it became clear that America was actually going to send a crew of astronauts to the moon (which happened the next year). In other words, 1968 was one of the most turbulent, dramatic, and vivid years the nation had experienced since the Second World War. Most people felt, at the very least, that it was impossible not to have opinions about public affairs, if not impossible to be acually involved firsthand. Yet to the central character of Oates's story, world events are "nothing." What does this blankness toward the outside world reveal about the girl, her upbringing, her problems, and possible solutions? Does it suggest any reasons that help explain her inability to understand why Princess and Dolly beat her up?

5. Why is the girl in the story so loyal to Simon? To what lengths does her loyalty carry her in helping to support his drug habit? Does paragraph 31 help you answer this question?

6. When the girl weeps (in the last sentence) "for all the money here, for God in gold and beige carpeting," what does she mean? In what sense is God in these things? For whom? And why does it make her weep?

7. Is the girl's homecoming happy or sad? Why? Will she be OK from now on? Why or why not?

Suggested Essay Topics

1. American society is full of double messages about money. On the one hand, we talk as if we were all convinced of money's limited importance as embodied in a whole cluster of clichés such as "Money can't buy love," "Money can't buy happiness," "You can't take it with you," "I'd rather be happy than rich," "Love of money is the root of all evil," "Easy come, easy go," and "Take time to smell the flowers." On the other hand, we also talk as if we were convinced that nothing is more important than money as embodied in a cluster of contrasting clichés that, revealingly, are not as explicit as the clichés against money. The clichés that laud money are more like code words or phrases. "Getting ahead," for example, makes no explicit reference to money, but everyone knows that money and the things money can buy are referred to. "Let's stick to the 'bottom line,' " a metaphor from accounting that is consistently applied to almost every area of life, is more explicit but still refers to money only metaphorically. "Stick to practicalities" is even less direct but in many contexts translates into "Look at things from a economic point of view first." And most Americans are either proud or envious rather than shocked or outraged that some

corporate executives are paid millions of dollars a year while other people in the same society are starving.

In light of all these double messages and contradictory attitudes about money (you can probably come up with other examples on your own), write an essay (using your classmates as an audience) in which you analyze the relationships among the family members and attempt to explain (a) why the girl acts as she does, (b) how the parents are to blame (or are blameless) for the girl's troubles, (c) how her difficulties might have been avoided, and (d) how money has played a role in the development of character and events.

2. Write about the events of the story from three different points of view, employing three different voices. The first voice is that of Simon, who was reared in a family much like the girl's own. He is speaking to the girl and evaluating people such as his own family and hers. The second voice is that of the girl's father, explaining to her, after her return home, why people such as Clarity and Simon are not fit companions and expressing his opinions about how they got where they are, why they live as they do, and what they should do with themselves. The third voice is your own as you attempt to reconcile the other voices, take sides with one or the other, or construct a view of the situation different from either. In your own voice, directed not to the girl but to a general reader (who you may assume has read the other two accounts), you are trying to sort out the rights and wrongs of this situation, determine who merits sympathy and who merits blame, and suggest changes that should be made.

IDEAS IN DEBATE

Paul Johnson
Herbert Schmertz
J. Robert Nelson
Eugene McCarthy
James Cone

Paul Johnson

*P*aul Johnson (b. 1928), British historian, author, and former editor of the New Statesman, first delivered "Has Capitalism a Future?" as a speech at a conference of bankers. Johnson's objective is to go on the "ideological offensive" (¶37) and "to teach the world a little history" (¶38) in order to defend capitalism against those he considers its five main enemies: academic leftists, ecological doomsayers, intrusive governments, union activists, and Soviet totalitarianists. He measures the value of capitalism as an economic system exclusively by the amount of national wealth it has generated. By comparing the rate of national economic growth in later historical times (after capitalism's emergence as the dominant economic system of the West) with the rate of economic growth in earlier times, Johnson claims to have clearly assessed its value: "Industrial capitalism, judged simply by its capacity to create wealth and to distribute it, is a phenomenon unique in world history. One could argue that it is the greatest single blessing ever bestowed on humanity" (¶11).

Following Johnson's essay are four responses (by Herbert Schmertz, J. Robert Nelson, Eugene J. McCarthy, and James Cone) to his question, "Has capitalism a future?" Each respondent disagrees with parts of his position. It is clear that Johnson has an ax to grind and that he is speaking as an advocate, but it is not so clear, at least at first glance, whether his critics are simply looking for weaknesses in his arguments or whether they are grinding their own axes in a biased way. It may be helpful to know that Herbert Schmertz is a corporation executive; J. Robert Nelson is a professor of theology; Eugene McCarthy is a former presidential candidate, former senator, and author; and James Cone is a black theologian.

As you read, try to assess the validity of arguments raised on both sides of the issues. Note that Johnson's facts are not disputed by any of his respondents, regardless of whether they like or dislike his position. Once again we see that facts seldom determine the positions that people take on issues. Everyone accepts Johnson's facts, yet everyone has a different picture of their significance. (For more on this topic, read

HAS CAPITALISM A FUTURE?

This essay and the four responses to it are from *Will Capitalism Survive?* (1979), edited by Ernest W. Lefever.

1   Seen against the grand perspective of history, capitalism is a newcomer. I would date it, in its earliest phase in England, only from the 1780s. We now possess some knowledge of economic systems going back to the early centuries of the third millennium B.C. I could outline, for instance, the economic structure of Egypt under the Old Kingdom, about 2700 B.C. Our knowledge of how civilized societies have organized their economic activities thus covers a stretch of more than 4,600 years. And in only about two hundred of those years has industrial capitalism existed. As a widely spread phenomenon, it is barely one hundred years old.

2   (Before I go any further, let me define my term: by "capitalism" I mean large-scale industrial capitalism, in which privately financed, publicly quoted corporations, operating in a free-market environment, with the back-up of the private-enterprise money market, constitute the core of the national economy. This is a rather broad definition, but I think it will do.)

3   The next point to note is the remarkable correlation between the emergence of industrial capitalism and the beginnings of really rapid economic growth. Throughout most of history, growth rates, when we have the statistical evidence to measure them, have been low, nil, or minus. A century of slow growth might be followed by a century of decline. Societies tended to get caught in the Malthusian Trap: that is, a period of slow growth led to an increase in population, the outstripping of food supplies, then a demographic catastrophe, and the beginning of a new cycle.

4   There were at least three economic "Dark Ages" in history, in which a sudden collapse of the wealth-making process led to the extinction, or virtual extinction, of civilized living, and the process of recovery was very slow and painful. The last of these three Dark Ages extinguished Roman civilization in Western Europe in the fifth century A.D. Not until the thirteenth century were equivalent living standards achieved; the recovery thus took eight hundred years.

5   Society again fell into a Malthusian trap in the fourteenth century. Again recovery was slow, though more sure this time, as intermediate technology spread more widely and methods of handling and employing money became more sophisticated. As late as the first half of the eighteenth century, however, it was rare for even the most advanced economies, those of England and Holland, to achieve 1 per cent growth in any year. And there is a possibility that mankind would again have fallen into a Malthusian trap toward the

end of the eighteenth century if industrial capitalism had not made its dramatic appearance.

And it *was* dramatic. By the beginning of the 1780s, in England, an unprecedented annual growth rate of 2 per cent had been achieved. During that decade, the 2 per cent was raised to 4 per cent. This was the great historic "liftoff," and a 4 per cent annual compound growth rate was sustained for the next fifty years. Since this English, and also Scottish, performance was accompanied by the export of capital, patents, machine tools, and skilled manpower to several other advanced nations, the phenomenon soon became international.

A few more figures are necessary to show the magnitude of the change that industrial capitalism brought to human society. In Britain, for instance, in the nineteenth century, the size of the working population multiplied fourfold. Real wages doubled in the half-century 1800–1850, and doubled again, 1850–1900. This meant there was a 1600 per cent increase in the production and consumption of wage-goods during the century. Nothing like this had happened anywhere before, in the whole of history. From the 1850s onward, in Belgium, France, Austria-Hungary, and above all in Germany and the United States, even higher growth rates were obtained; and feudal empires like Japan and Russia were able to telescope into a mere generation or two a development process that in Britain had stretched over centuries.

The growth rates of twelve leading capitalist countries averaged 2.7 per cent a year over the whole fifty-year period up to World War I. There was, it is true, a much more mixed performance between the wars. The United States, which in the forty-four years up to 1914 had averaged a phenomenal 4.3 per cent growth rate, and which in the seven years up to 1929 had increased its national income by a staggering 40 per cent, then saw its national income fall 38 per cent in a mere four years, 1929–32.

But after World War II, growth was resumed on an even more impressive scale. In the 1950s, for instance, the twelve leading capitalist economies cited before had an average annual growth of 4.2 per cent. In Germany it was as high as an average of 7.6 per cent. In all the West European economies, the rate of investment in the 1950s was half again as high as it had ever been on a sustained basis. In several such countries it was over 20 per cent of the GNP; in Germany and the Netherlands it was 25 per cent, in Norway even higher. Moreover, this high capital formation took place not at the cost of private consumption but during a rapid and sustained rise in living standards, particularly of industrial workers. These tendencies were prolonged throughout the 1960s and into the 1970s. For the mature economies, the second industrial revolution—1945–1970—was entirely painless. This was also largely true in Japan, which achieved even higher investment and growth rates in an effort to catch up with the United States and Europe.

In short, after nearly five recorded millennia of floundering about in poverty, humanity suddenly in the 1780s began to hit on the right formula: industrial capitalism. Consider the magnitude of the change over the last two centuries or less. We all know the wealth of present-day West Germany. In the year 1800, in the whole of Germany fewer than 1,000 people had annual incomes as high as $1,000. Or again, take France. France now has more automobiles per capita even than Germany, and more second homes per family than any other country in Europe. In the 1780s, four-fifths of the French families spent 90 per cent of their incomes simply on buying bread— only bread—to stay alive.

In short, industrial capitalism, judged simply by its capacity to create 11 wealth and to distribute it, is a phenomenon unique in world history. One could argue that it is the greatest single blessing ever bestowed on humanity. Why, then, are we asking, "Has capitalism a future?" The answer is clear enough: because capitalism is threatened.

The idea has got around that industrial capitalism is unpopular and 12 always has been, that it is the work of a tiny minority who have thrust it upon the reluctant mass of mankind. Nothing could be further from the truth. The storage economies of remote antiquity were often hideously unpopular. So was the slave-based economy, combined with corporatism, of the classical world. Agricultural feudalism was certainly unpopular, and mercantilism had to be enforced, in practice, by authoritarian states.

But from the very start industrial capitalism won the approval of the 13 masses. They could not vote in the ballot box, but they voted in a far more impressive manner: with their feet. The poorest member of society values political freedom as much as the richest. But the freedom he values most of all is the freedom to sell his labor and skills in the open market, and it was precisely *this* that industrial capitalism gave to men for the first time in history. Hence it is a profound error of fact, in my view, to see what Blake called the "dark, satanic mills" of the industrial revolution as the enslavement of man. The factory system, however harsh it may have been, was the road to freedom for millions of agricultural workers. Not only did it offer them an escape from rural poverty, which was deeper and more degrading than anything experienced in the cities, but it allowed them to move from status to contract, from a stationary place in a static society, with tied cottages and semi-conscript labor, to a mobile place in a dynamic society.

That was why the common man voted for industrial capitalism with his 14 feet, by tramping from the countryside to the towns in enormous numbers, first in Britain, then throughout Europe. And tens of millions of European peasants, decade after decade, moved relentlessly across the Atlantic in pursuit of that same freedom, from semi-feudal estates and small holdings in Russia, Poland, Germany, Austria-Hungary, Italy, Ireland, Scandinavia, to the mines and factories and workshops of New York, Chicago, Pittsburgh, Cleveland, Detroit. It was the first time in history that really large numbers of ordinary people were given the chance to exercise a choice about their livelihood and destiny, and to move, not as members of a tribe or conscript soldiers, but as free individuals, selling their labor in the open market.

They voted for industrial capitalism with their feet not only because 15 they felt in their bones that it meant a modest prosperity for their children and grandchildren—and on the whole they have been proved abundantly right—but because they knew it meant a new degree of freedom for themselves. Indeed, the success of industrialization, despite all its evils, continues to persuade countless ordinary men and women, all over the world, to escape the poverty and restraints of the rural status society and to enter the free labor markets of the towns. Hence the growth of megalopolises all over the world—Calcutta and Bombay, Teheran and Caracas, Mexico City and Djakarta, Shanghai and Lagos, Cairo and Johannesburg. There are now literally scores of million-plus cities all over the Third World. This never-ending one-way flow from countryside to city is plainly a voluntary mass choice, for most governments fear and resent it, and many are attempting, sometimes savagely but always ineffectively, to halt or reverse it. It is more marked in the free-market economies, but it is noticeable everywhere.

Short of evacuating the cities by force and terror, as is now apparently 16
being practiced in parts of southeast Asia, there is no way to stop this human flood. There seems to be an almost irresistible urge in human beings to move away from the status society to contractual individualism, the central feature of industrial capitalism. This operates even in totalitarian societies, as witness the efforts, for instance, of the Chinese and Polish governments to limit the urban explosions they are experiencing.

If industrial capitalism is unique in its wealth-producing capacity and 17
also has the endorsement of the people, then why is it under threat? And who is threatening it?

THE INTELLECTUAL
AND MORAL BATTLE

Let me look at five principal elements. The *first,* and in some ways the 18
most important, is that *the free-enterprise idea is losing, if it has not already lost, the intellectual and moral battle.* Not long ago I went into Blackwell's, the great book shop at Oxford University. I wandered over the huge room that houses the books on politics and economics, and having been disagreeably surprised by what I saw there, I made a rough calculation. New books extolling the economic, social, and moral virtues of Communism and collectivism—and there were literally hundreds and hundreds from all over the world—outnumbered books defending free enterprise, or merely seeking to take an objective view of the argument, by between five and six to one. This overwhelming predominance of collectivism was not due to any sinister policy on the part of Blackwell's, which is a highly efficient capitalist enterprise. It was a marketing response to demand on the part of students and teachers. And this was not one of the new slum universities of recent years, some of which have been virtually shanghaied by Marxist factions, but Oxford University, one of the free world's greatest centers of learning, where the battle of ideas is fought under the best possible conditions.

There can be no doubt that the intellectual and moral assault on free 19
enterprise, and the exaltation of Marxist collectivism, that is such a striking feature of the 1970s is directly related to the huge expansion of higher

education, put through at such cost to the capitalist economies in the 1960s. Now there is in this a huge and tragic irony. For in the 1950s, the decade when the university expansion was planned, it was the prevailing wisdom among the leading thinkers of the West that the growth of higher education was directly productive of industrial growth—that the more university graduates we turned out, the faster the GNPs of the West would rise. This was the thesis outlined by President Clark Kerr of Berkeley in his 1963 Godkin lectures at Harvard, and it was a thesis put forward in Britain with immense effect by Sir Charles, now Lord Snow. Kerr said: "What the railroads did for the second half of the last century, and the automobile for the first half of this century, may be done for the second half of the twentieth century by the knowledge industry: that is, to serve as the focal point for national growth." He added that more graduates would not only mean a bigger GNP but act as a reinforcement for middle-class democracy, with all its freedoms.

To speak of the "knowledge industry" was to ask for trouble. Knowl- 20 edge is not a manufactured commodity. There is knowledge for good and knowledge for evil, as the Book of Genesis says. The 1960s, during which most Western nations doubled and some even trebled their university places, did not reinforce democratic freedoms or enlarge the GNP or strengthen the free-enterprise system. They produced the students' revolts, beginning in Paris in 1968. They detonated the Northern Ireland conflict, which is still harassing Britain. They produced the Baader-Meinhoff Gang in West Germany, the Red Brigade in Italy, the Left Fascist terrorism of Japan. They produced an enormous explosion of Marxist studies, centered on the social sciences and especially sociology and on a new generation of school and university teachers who are dedicated, by a sort of perverted religious piety, to the spread of Marxist ideas.

There are ironies within the general irony. The new university of the 21 air, created in Britain at enormous expense to bring higher education to adults and therefore christened the Open University, has become virtually closed to any teacher not of proven Marxist opinions. Nuffield College, Oxford, founded by the great capitalist pioneer Lord Nuffield, who created the British automobile industry, has become a center of trade-union ideology, of the very ideas that slowly but surely are putting the British automobile industry out of world markets and out of business. Warwick University, created in the 1960s as a powerhouse of ideas and clever graduate executives for the West Midlands industrial complex, Britain's biggest, has become a seminary of Marxist and pseudo-Marxist agitators dedicated to the destruction of the wealth-producing machine that brought their university into existence.

I could go on. It is true, of course, that student unrest, as such, has 22 quieted down. But the steady diffusion of ideas hostile to our free system continues remorselessly. Industrial capitalism and the free-market system are presented as destructive of human happiness, corrupt, immoral, wasteful, inefficient, and above all, doomed. Collectivism is presented as the only way out compatible with the dignity of the human spirit and the future of our

race. The expanded university threatens to become not the powerhouse of
Western individualism and enterprise but its graveyard.

THE ECOLOGICAL PANIC

There is a *second* threat, what I have called *the "ecological panic."* This   23
movement, again, began with the best intentions. I well remember when
Rachel Carson's book *The Silent Spring* first appeared in the *New Yorker.* The
wave of concern that followed was justified. We were tending to ignore some
of the destructive side effects of very rapid industrial expansion. The steps
then taken, notably the clean-air policies and the policies for cleansing lakes
and waterways, have been spectacularly successful. Thanks to smokeless
fuel, London fogs, which were real killers, have been virtually eliminated; the
last really serious one was in 1952. The Thames is now cleaner and has greater
quantities of fish, and more varieties, than at any time since before the days
of Spenser or Shakespeare. Similar successes are now being registered in the
United States, which adopted such legally enforceable remedies somewhat
later than Britain did. These are examples of what can be done by the
thoughtful, unemotional, systematic, and scientifically justified application of
conservation and anti-pollution policies.

But most of these were put in motion before the ecological panic started.   24
Once ecology became a fashionable good cause, as it did in the late 1960s,
reason, logic, and proportion flew out the window. It became a campaign not
against pollution but against growth itself, and especially against free-enterprise growth—totalitarian Communist growth was somehow less morally
offensive. I highly recommend Professor Wilfred Beckerman's *In Defence of
Economic Growth.* Beckerman is one of the best of our economists and was a
member of the Royal Commission on Environmental Pollution; he knows the
subject better perhaps than any other working economist, and his book is a
wonderfully sane and lucid summary of it.

I have never yet been able to persuade any committed ecology cam-   25
paigner even to look at this book. Of course not. Such persons have a faith,
and they do not want to risk it. One of the most important developments of
our time is the growth, as a consequence of the rapid decline of Christianity,
of irrational substitutes for it. These are not necessarily religious or even
quasi-religious. Often they are pseudo-scientific in form, as for instance the
weird philosophy of the late Teilhard de Chardin. The ecology panic is
another example. It is akin to the salvation panic of sixteenth-century Calvinism. When you expel the priest, you do not inaugurate the age of reason—you
get the witch doctor. But whereas Calvinist salvation panic may have contributed to the rise of capitalism, the ecology panic could be the death of it.

If the restrictions now imposed on industrial development had operated   26
in eighteenth-century England, the industrial revolution could not have taken
place. It would in effect have been inhibited by law—as of course many
landowners of the day wished it to be—and legal requirements would have
eliminated the very modest profits by which it originally financed itself. We

would still be existing at eighteenth-century living standards, and wallowing in eighteenth-century levels of pollution, which were infinitely worse than anything we experience today. (If you want to see what they were like, visit the slums of Calcutta or Djakarta.)

As it is, the ecology panic has been a potent destructive force. The 27 panic-mongers played a crucial role in persuading the Middle Eastern oil producers, especially Iran, to quadruple the price of oil in the autumn of 1973, the biggest single blow industrial capitalism has suffered since the Wall Street crash of 1929. That was the beginning of the profound recession from which we have not yet emerged. In the end, as was foreseeable at the time, the huge rise in oil prices did not do anyone any good, least of all the oil producers. But it ended the great post-war boom and robbed Western capitalism of its tremendous élan, perhaps for good. As Browning put it, "Never glad confident morning again." And it is significant that the ecological lobby is now striving with fanatic vigor and persistence to prevent the development of nuclear energy, allegedly on the grounds of safety. Now it is a fact, a very remarkable fact in my view, that throughout the West (we have no figures for Russia or China) the nuclear power industry is the only industry, the *only* industry, which over a period of thirty years has not had a single fatal industrial accident. This unique record has been achieved by the efforts of the industry itself and the responsible governments, without any assistance from the ecolobby. But of course they would *like* a few fatal accidents. That would suit their purposes very well.

In Britain we had a long public enquiry, what we call a statutory en- 28 quiry, into whether or not it was right to go ahead with the enriched-uranium plant at Windscale. The enquiry was a model of its kind. The ecolobby marshalled all the scientific experts and evidence they could lay their hands on. At the end the verdict was that there was no reason whatever why the program should not proceed. Did the ecolobby accept the verdict? On the contrary. They immediately organized a mass demonstration and planned various legal and illegal activities to halt the program by force. It is notable that a leading figure in this campaign is the man who is perhaps Britain's leading Communist trade unionist, Mr. Arthur Scargill of the Mine-workers. He has never, so far as we know, campaigned against Soviet nuclear programs, peaceful or otherwise. It is true that most people in the movement in the United States, Britain, France, Germany, and Italy, so far as I have been able to observe, are not politically motivated; they are simply irrational. But irrationality is an enemy of civilized society, and it is being exploited by the politically interested.

BIG GOVERNMENT VS. THE MARKET

A *third* factor in the future of capitalism is *the growth of government.* Indus- 29 trial capitalism—or rather, the free-enterprise economy—and big government are natural and probably irreconcilable enemies. It is no accident that the industrial revolution took place in late eighteenth-century England, a time of minimum government. Of all the periods of English history, indeed of European history, it was the time when government was least conspicuous and active. It was the age, very short alas, of the Night Watchman state. As a matter of fact, the industrial revolution—perhaps the most important single event in human history—seems to have occurred without the English government's even noticing. By the time the government did notice, it was, happily, too late.

It is almost inevitable that government, particularly an active, interventionist government, should view free enterprise with a degree of hostility, since it constitutes a countervailing power in the state. The tendency, then, is to cut free enterprise down to size, in a number of ways. In the United States the characteristic technique is government regulation and legal harassment, and this of course has been far more pervasive and strident since the ecolobby swung into action. In Britain the technique is both direct assault—nationalization—and slow starvation. In a way, nationalization is ineffective, since it allows the public to make comparisons between the performance of the nationalized sector and that of the free sector, nearly always to the latter's advantage.

Starvation is more insidious. By this I mean the progressive transfer of resources, by taxation and other government policies, from the private to the public sector. In 1955, for instance, public expenditure in Britain as a proportion of the GNP was just over 40 per cent. By 1975, twenty years later, it had risen to nearly 60 per cent. This was accompanied by a record budget deficit of about $22 billion, itself a further 11½ per cent of the GNP. Of course, the tax money had to be provided, and the deficit serviced, by the private sector. We have, then, an Old Man of the Sea relationship in which the parasitical Old Man is growing bigger, and poor Sinbad smaller, all the time. The shrinking productive sector has to carry the burden of an ever-expanding loss-making public sector. Thus Britain's authorized steel industry will lose $1 billion this year, and it has been authorized by statute to borrow up to $7 billion, guaranteed by government and taxpayer. Now the interesting thing is that in Britain the public sector and the civil service generally are now paying higher wages, providing better conditions, and giving larger pensions—which in a growing number of cases are index-linked and thus inflation-proof—than the private sector can possibly afford. And of course they are financing these goodies out of tax-guaranteed deficits—that is, from the dwindling profits of the private sector. This is what I call the starvation technique. When a private firm goes bust, provided it is big enough, the state takes over, the losses are added to the taxpayer's bill, and the private sector has one more expensive passenger to carry.

In this technique, the *fourth* factor, *the trade unions,* play an important part. In Britain it is demonstrably true that the legal privileges of the trade unions, which virtually exempt them from any kind of action for damages (including, now, libel), led directly to restrictive practices, over-manning, low productivity, low investment, low wages, and low profits. Thus trade-union action tends, in itself, to undermine the performance of industrial capitalism as a wealth-creating system. In Britain, the trade unions can rightly claim that capitalism is inefficient, because they make sure it is inefficient. Ford workers in Britain, using exactly the same assembly-line machinery as in West Germany, produce between 20 per cent and 50 per cent fewer automobiles. ICI Chemicals, one of the best companies in Britain, nevertheless has a productivity performance 25 per cent lower than its Dutch and German competitors. A recent analysis shows this is entirely due to over-manning and restrictive practices.

The private sector in Britain is now threatened by two further union 33 devices: the legally enforced closed shop, which compels workers to join designated unions on pain of dismissal without compensation or legal redress, and new plans to force firms to have up to 50 per cent worker directors, appointed not by the work force themselves nor even necessarily from among them but by and from the trade-union bureaucracy (Bullock Report). This has to be seen against the explicit policy of some groups within the unions of driving private-sector firms to bankruptcy by strikes and harassment, so that the state will then have to take them into the public sector.

What is happening in Britain will not necessarily happen elsewhere. But 34 there are many ways in which the present U.S. administration seems determined to follow Britain's example. The West Germans, too, are now beginning to adopt some of the institutions that flourish in British trade unionism, notably the shop stewards' movement. Businessmen all over the free world may despise the performance of British industry, but trade unionists all over the world admire and envy the power of British trade unionists and are actively seeking to acquire it for themselves.

THE TOTALITARIAN THREAT

Let me end on a word of warning. I have said nothing of the *fifth* threat 35 to industrial capitalism and the free-enterprise system—*the threat from without.* But this is bound to increase as the military superiority of the Soviet Union over the United States is reinforced. I have never thought that the Communist system would triumph by a direct assault. I have always assumed that it would first establish an overwhelming military predominance and then, by pressure and threats, begin to draw the political and economic dividends of it. If the United States opts out of the competitive arms race with the Soviet Union while supposedly providing merely for its own defense, then we must expect to see this fifth threat hard at work winding up industrial capitalism and free enterprise all over the world.

Therefore, when we ask, "Has capitalism a future?," I answer: It all 36 depends on the United States. West Germany and Japan, it is true, have strong free-enterprise economies; they also have a tradition of state capitalism, and would adapt themselves with surprising speed and readiness to a new collective order. France already has a huge public sector and a long tradition of *dirigisme* [state-controlled finance] or *étatisme* [state socialism]. All three are Janus-faced. Britain, I believe, is profoundly anti-collective and will remain so if it continues to be given the choice. But its private-enterprise system is now very weak, and its business and financial elites are demoralized and defeatist.

I myself think that capitalism will survive, because of its enormous 37 intrinsic virtues as a system for generating wealth and promoting freedom. But those who man and control it must stop apologizing and go on the ideological offensive. They must show ordinary people that both the Communist world and the Third World are parasitical upon industrial capitalism for their growth technology, and that without capitalism, the 200 years of unprecedented growth that have created the modern world would gradually come to an end. We would have slow growth, then nil growth, then minus growth, and then the Malthusian catastrophe.

Those who wish to maintain the capitalist system must endeavor to 38 teach the world a little history. They must remind it, and especially the young, that though man's achievements are great, they are never as solid as they look. If man makes the wrong choice, there is always another Dark Age waiting for him round the corner of time.

Herbert Schmertz

DEMOCRACY, TYRANNY, AND CAPITALISM

While I am all for capitalism and see many valid points in Paul John- 1 son's argument, I get uneasy when I see it posed—as I think Johnson does— as the antithesis to Marxism or "Marxist collectivism." Marxism is at best a theory about history and at worst what the economist P. T. Bauer has called "an all-embracing secular messianic faith." Capitalism is neither. It is a historical phenomenon, as Johnson points out, but even by his own definition it is an economic system: a device, a means, a way to go about certain economic business. It is hardly a theory about history, and much less is it the force that must be set in the lists to combat the messianic faith of Marxist collectivism. I would guess that the faith of capitalists is invested in far more profound and transcendent realities than capitalism. What they see and fear in Marxist collectivism is not so much its menace to capitalism as its menace to freedom.

This distinction is important. There is some danger that readers of 2 Johnson's essay may come away believing that the struggle is between capitalism and Marxism. That is to wage the battle on Marxism's ground and in Marxism's terms, and it renders the contest deceptively simple. Marxism's argument is only superficially with capitalism: witness the cordiality of Marxist states when they are in need of high technology. At its essence,

Marxism's argument is about who shall make choices; it is a quarrel with freedom and democracy.

Given this perspective, I am somewhat hesitant about the broad scope 3 of Johnson's thesis. That the industrial revolution was an epochal event must be admitted, but Europe was by no means sick and poor when the industrial revolution began. Revolutionary economic changes had been initiated in the sixteenth century with the voyages of discovery and the considerable stimulation of trade, industry, and finance provoked by these discoveries. And—at least on this side of the ocean—we tend to assign even more importance to the revolution of ideas that might be said to have begun with the Magna Carta, developed in the Enlightenment, and culminated in the American Revolution: the idea that governments must answer to the people.

From such a perspective, the threats to capitalism outlined by Johnson 4 seem less formidable. We have seen that the university student's infatuation with collectivism tends to fade rather quickly once he begins to work within the capitalistic system and learns to recognize its virtues. We have seen, in the United States at least, a growing public realization that balance is necessary in questions that pit environmentalism against the need for energy, economic growth, and jobs; people are becoming more enlightened about the tradeoffs required in a progressive society. Americans have already begun a more careful definition of the role to be played by government in relation to enterprise and the market economy, as evidenced by the deregulation of airline fares and the movement toward decontrol of prices for natural gas and crude oil.

These are arguments that capitalism has begun to win on the basis of 5 facts and experience—on pragmatic, economic grounds. I would say that it is all very well to go on the "ideological offensive" but that one must be careful not to confuse ideology and economics, lest—as in Marxism—the one poison the other.

Many writers and scholars present capitalism as a scheme of social 6 organization, a remarkable fortress of ideology and philosophy concerning the right to private property, strict limitation of government power, and dedication to free markets or the market economy. Yet capitalism itself has displayed, in the main, a positive aversion to ideology, to declaring itself the one true way that men should live and work. Its claims—and demonstrated virtues—have mainly to do with the economic sphere. This is why multinational corporations are able to operate successfully and usefully in so many countries, with so many ideological shadings in their governments. For they enable economics to stand apart from politics.

Still, I suppose we are observing the phenomenon Bertolt Brecht de- 7 scribed when he said that to avoid ideology in our day is not to escape it. Presenting capitalism as a scheme of social organization gives the scholar a convenient rhetorical device to oppose to socialism or "Marxist collectivism." He can then argue private property vs. public ownership, market economy vs. centrally controlled economy, or limited government vs. all-pervasive government.

But the scheme of social organization in, say, the United States is not   8
capitalism but democracy. Americans, if asked, do not describe themselves as
capitalists. Capitalism, to the man in the street, is not the ideological fortress
underlying his liberties but an economic system that has worked rather well
(as Johnson points out) for almost every group or individual who got involved
with it. As long as we talk about capitalism in terms of what it is—an
economic device of proven value—it can generally hold its own in the public
dialogue. But we shall send people scurrying off in droves if we attempt to
load the nature and fate of Western civilization onto the back of capitalism.
I think Americans know very well that what Marxism can imperil is their
liberty, not their capitalism.

It is worth remembering that to offer a convincing catalogue of the   9
dangers or abject failures of socialism does not, in itself, convert one's listeners to capitalism. This seems to have mystified a fair number of capitalist
intellectuals; it is perhaps further evidence of the perils encountered when
ideology and economics are confused.

Can we look at capitalism without its ideological freight? Perhaps by   10
thinking of it as simply a "competitive market economy" we can consider it
as an economic system. As Johnson describes most forcefully, capitalism has
worked phenomenally well in achieving material abundance, the wide distribution of goods, and a steady increase in personal opportunity. I think we can
discern in the system of capitalism some sort of inner affinity with the human
desire to work, to make or build or accomplish something of one's own, and
an even deeper affinity with the human desire to change, to improve not only
one's self but also one's environment. Capitalism has not created these needs;
it has merely provided a marvelous means for fulfilling them. When critics
complain that capitalism has aggravated spiritual unease or restlessness in
Western civilization, they overlook the possibility that this very restlessness
has perhaps created and formed the civilization. Capitalism has been not a
primary cause but an efficient vehicle.

Johnson's warning that capitalism can be smothered, dismantled, and   11
destroyed is valid. I think there is some danger that this will happen in the
United States, but I am, on the whole, optimistic that it will not. Even in the
worst of times, many of us have persisted in believing that the American
public—given more information—would come to see that the market pros-
pers in liberty and atrophies under command.

That lesson of history is so clear that it cannot forever be ignored. It is   12
an idea that is currently in disfavor among many American intellectuals. But
the public is of a different mind. The public current is now running strongly
against big government and excessive, costly regulation—witness California's
Proposition 13* and similar tax revolts. The public demand is for change, for
a thorough pruning of the huge, remote bureaucracies that have been inter-

---

*The first of several state laws passed by referendum limiting the size of state budgets and
establishing limits on taxes.

fering so relentlessly not only with the free market but with almost everyone's life and work.

And even the intellectual community is beginning to resist the unneces- 13 sary interference of government in what had been an effective and highly successful market economy. In 1978 the new president of Yale University, A. Bartlett Giamatti, went to some length in his inaugural address to remind the Yale community of the dangers to Yale of "governmental intrusion" and to stress that private educational institutions "are an integral part of the private sector." He called for an end to the "ancient ballet of mutual antagonism" between private enterprise and private education, and said further: "There is a metaphor that informs the private business sector as it informs the private educational sector, and that is the metaphor of the free marketplace."

And of course there are other striking signs of the change in public 14 opinion. Legislators themselves are becoming disenchanted with the unpredictable distortions and misallocations of resources that result from large-scale government interference in the operations of the market economy. They are coming to see the truth in Friedrich Hayek's observation that the competitive free market does not mean a national abdication from planning; rather, "competition means decentralized planning by many separate persons."

Inherent in the competitive market economy, in capitalism, there *is* a 15 plan—a sort of unorchestrated harmony that represents not only the decisions of "many separate persons" but also the larger frame of public decisions and reasonable regulations that channel enterprise toward goals aligned with the democratic ideal. This is not true *laissez-faire* capitalism—if indeed there has ever been such a creature outside books—but rather a system in which the public sector takes pains to foster responsive, adaptable, innovative, and democratic markets. That system worked in an extraordinary, unprecedented way to advance the material well-being and range for personal autonomy of all those who took part in it. Today the public, much of the intellectual community, and many of the nation's political leaders show a growing appreciation of that system's worth—heartening evidence that capitalism does indeed have a future.

J. Robert Nelson

CAPITALISM: BLESSING AND CURSE

Paul Johnson's description of the astounding effects of industrial capi- 1 talism within two hundred years reminds us of other remarkable developments in this relatively brief period. Except for some realms of philosophy, religion, literature, and the arts—visual, auditory, and culinary—our present civilization is wholly different from that of the eighteenth century. He is probably correct in comparing the slums and peasants' hovels of Europe in that century to those in the poorest lands of the Southern Hemisphere today. In hundreds of respects our present world, whether brave or not, is certainly new. And for millions of people it is manifestly better in three broad categories—health, education, and welfare.

Johnson does not choose to argue that the capitalist economy had a great   2
deal to do with the generally improved lot of countless human beings who, thanks to science and technology, will now live to maturity and old age. Before the advent of capitalism, utter poverty, malnutrition, and mortal diseases were common conditions; the primary question was not how to *enhance* life but how to *survive.* Industrial capitalism is sustaining growing numbers of human beings at a higher level of health and material well-being. No one can deny that this is largely the result of a sense of individual worth, initiative, aspiration, and competition. These human qualities had for centuries been denied and suppressed in the common people. They were like white roots and stems found under flat rocks. The plants are alive, but barely so; only when they are uncovered and exposed to sunlight can they grow and develop color. The use of technology to make a profit on invested capital, encouraged by increasingly democratic political societies, was like the lifting of a heavy stone from Western Europe and America.

Johnson does not overstate the case for crediting capitalism—both the   3
ideology and the economic system—for much of what the developed countries enjoy and take for granted. He could have extended the catalogue of its good influences. But he could also have noted the conditions and strictures that have been imposed upon the exuberant free enterprise of the nineteenth century. Government regulation, brought about by democratically elected legislatures, shows that citizens recognized dangers and evils inherent in that economic system. They have seen capitalism for what it is: both a blessing and a curse.

Perhaps this perception of paradox derives from the religious force   4
usually associated with the rise of capitalism—Calvinism. To those most conscious of being God's elect and most obedient to his will is attributed the famous work ethic. But whether or not they were Calvinists, many of the early capitalists were indeed tirelessly industrious, thrifty, and imbued with a sense of rightness and destiny. How could they avoid believing that divine and benign Providence had given to the British the nearly inexhaustible natural resources of a world empire and to Americans the unexplored and as yet unexploited North American continent (though the new Jerusalem they felt called to build in the green lands of England and New England turned out to be more commercial than heavenly).

The same Providence that gave them resources and inspired resource-   5
fulness also required justice and mercy. While the early capitalists, who could be described as "God-fearing," had a limited concept of what justice required, they did give expression to mercy through acts of philanthropy that partially

expiated their sin of acquisitiveness. Many colleges, universities, libraries, museums, charitable institutions, and foundations owe their existence in large measure to the "plagued conscience" of Christian and Jewish capitalists.

But this was not enough to offset the ill effects on the population of economic control by large corporations. As the era of robber barons gave way to the era of big business, the necessity of government regulation was apparent. Implicit in the motivation for regulation was a biblical teaching: the same heart of man that rejoices in the blessings of prosperity remains wicked and exceedingly self-centered. If there is any truth in the saying that there was more Methodism than Marxism in the rise of British socialism, a similar observation about religious influence is appropriate to America's willingness to accept the Rooseveltian reforms that rendered fully obsolete the concept of *laissez-faire*.   6

Paul Johnson's discussion of the relation between government and business is inadequate. It is merely contentious to say that industrial capitalism and big government are irreconcilable enemies. He has a legitimate complaint against *excessive* controls by government, but he goes much further and appears to preclude *proper* controls. He implies that the only alternative to big government's power over the economy is no control at all.   7

His discussion of labor unions leads to a similarly erroneous conclusion: better none at all than what we have in Britain and America today. This is unfortunate, since many who are sympathetic with Johnson's opposition to Marxism and Communism cannot believe that our national government and labor unions are equally perilous to a good society.   8

His polemic against the false gods and false hopes of Communism certainly is justified; but it would be more compelling if he had shown that the outrages of which industrial capitalism stands accused are easily matched, or exceeded, by those in socialist countries. These have to do with three kinds of exploitation: human, international, and ecological. Critics and dedicated opponents of capitalism have convincing reasons for faulting the corporate powers of free (or nearly free) enterprise. Countless workers and their dependents have suffered abuses and deprivations; natural resources of less developed countries have been pillaged for the profit of the rich ones; our air, water, and soil have been polluted. Johnson is not disposed to mention these vulnerable aspects of capitalist societies, which are the prime targets of both the academic Marxists and the pamphleteers. Neither does he admit the extent to which industrial capitalism is linked with, and dependent upon, the European and American production of military hardware and all the ancillary materials and services useful only to defense and warfare. Remembering that it was a representative of capitalist interests, President Eisenhower, whose last testament was a grave warning against the "military-industrial complex," we may find all the less convincing Johnson's generalization that industry and government are natural enemies.   9

These arguments can readily be turned back against Marxist apologists for socialist and Communist states and economies. When one thinks only of the Soviet Union's control over Eastern Europe, its expropriation of raw   10 materials and manufactured products for itself, its spoliation of the natural environment, and its abysmal record of human degradation and oppression, it is obvious that the Communist pot has no basis for calling the capitalist kettle black. To make these points would strengthen the case for capitalism as an imperfect yet preferable mode of production and distribution.

Johnson's animosity toward what he calls the "ecolobby" is excessive and perplexing. He gives the impression that he believes in industry's willingness and capability to care for the plundered planet by itself. Evidence abounds to show that this is an ill-founded belief—a point dramatized in March 1979 when the world turned horrified eyes on the Three Mile Island nuclear power reactor near Harrisburg, Pennsylvania. Although its malfunction and threatened explosion of radioactive materials were brought under control with no human death or injury, the catastrophic possibility was enough to negate such blithe cases for developing nuclear power as Johnson's. 11

Though his style is engaging and articulate, Johnson falls short of making a satisfying apologia for industrial capitalism in our time. This is disappointing. There is merit in his trenchant observations about Marxists. He is right to point to the erosion of both the ideologically informed will and the political conditions that can make capitalism work as it should—i.e., for the common good. Not socialism but social mutuality and human solidarity must now determine our evaluation of any economic or political system. 12

Eugene J. McCarthy

CORPORATIONS HAVE CORRUPTED CAPITALISM

Little can be said against Paul Johnson's case for the productive power of capitalism, whether a particular capitalist's motivation was to amass wealth (as the economist Carl Snyder observed years ago, "Deep as are our prejudices against avarice and greed, it cannot be denied that they have been great forces for the building of the modern economic world"), to demonstrate personal power and achievement (as in the case of empire-builders like Andrew Carnegie and James Hill), or to contribute to human welfare. Today the theoretical challenge, if it can properly be called that, is not to traditional capitalism but to capitalism as it is manifested in the corporation. 1

When economists began to write about the economics of "imperfect competition," they signaled the end of the pure economics of Adam Smith and of capitalism. Today nearly 80 per cent of the productive activity in the United States is controlled by corporate organizations operating under charters granted by the states. These corporations are not free, competing entities 2 but institutions given special privileges and advantages over individuals by legal social decision.

James Kent, in his *Commentaries on American Law,* published early in the nineteenth century, observed that "the number of charters of incorporation" was increasing in the United States with a disturbing rapidity. "We are multiplying in this country to an unparalleled extent the institution of corporations," he said, "and giving them a flexibility and variety of purpose unknown to the Roman or to the English law."

Competition does not rule the economy of the United States today. More and more, differences between the largest corporations and the government are settled not within a framework of law but by negotiation. For example, when Du Pont was ordered to divest itself of General Motors stock some seventeen years ago, the existing antitrust laws and penalties were not applied. Congress passed special legislation to work out the transition. In much the same way, the taxation of insurance companies and of oil companies has been settled by negotiation rather than by the application of public judgment and law.

The government's dealings with the steel industry in recent years demonstrate the same relationship. During the Korean War, when President Truman tried to prevent a slowdown in steel production by issuing an executive order to take over the industry, the independence of the industry was sustained by the Supreme Court.

Subsequent challenges to the industry were handled differently. The Kennedy administration responded to a major increase in the price of steel not by attempting to apply the existing law or by executive order but by public denunciation and, according to some reports, by midnight calls from the FBI to steel-company officials.

In the Johnson administration, the presidents of steel companies were called to the White House for "jawboning" sessions, generally approved by the press and politicians. The message was not that competition, the free economy, and the law of supply and demand should be allowed to prevail but that prices should be kept down. The steel-company officers, champions of free enterprise and of capitalism, surrendered, seeming to accept the idea that if prices were fixed in Pittsburgh, that would be an "action in restraint of trade." It was rather as if an English king had called in the nobles and said: "If you agree to these things in my presence, you will be able to do them. But if you agree to them among yourselves in Wales, you will be in deep trouble."

It has been suggested that the U.S. government seek the equivalent of diplomatic representation on the boards of major corporations, especially those that are deeply involved in foreign business and finance.

What we have in America is not a free, competitive, capitalistic system but a kind of corporate feudalism. In the feudal system, according to a schoolboy's definition, everyone belonged to someone and everyone else belonged to the king. In the modern order, nearly every worker belongs to some corporation, and everyone else belongs to the government, federal, state, or local.

A corporately controlled economy has left us with a situation in which   10
there is widespread poverty, serious unemployment, the wasting of resources,
shortages, and inflation. The corporation is not wholly responsible for these
conditions. Undoubtedly outside policy or forces, such as war and government fiscal policies and regulations, have an adverse affect on the general
economy and specifically on some institutions and businesses.

The concept of the corporation as an instrument for the conduct of   11
business and financial affairs is a valid one. But it is a concept that must prove
its vitality in practice. If the corporation is to be privileged by law, as it is now,
and if it is to control most of the powers on which the material well-being
of the nation depends, then it must become more effective and more responsible, both socially and economically.

James Cone

CAPITALISM MEANS PROPERTY OVER PERSONS

Some perspectives differ so radically from my own that I hardly know   1
where to begin in responding to them. Having read Paul Johnson's address
several times, I still find it hard to believe that he can so uncritically support
capitalism in the face of the vast human suffering arising from it. How should
I respond to a point of view that seems completely insensitive to many human
factors that I regard as important?

I will focus my comments on the *selective* character of Paul Johnson's   2
argument for industrial capitalism. Because I am a black American whose
value system has been shaped in the historical context of an oppressed people's struggle for justice, I cannot avoid evaluating a given sociopolitical
perspective in terms of how it helps or hinders that struggle. If one takes the
general principle of "justice for the poor" as the criterion, Johnson's apology
for capitalism is completely unconvincing. He shows little or no concern for
oppressed humanity in Europe, the United States, and the Third World. It is
as if they do not exist.

When a people's existence is not recognized, it means that their suffer-   3
ing is considered to have no bearing on the value of a given political system
if that system continues to serve the interests of those for whom it was
created. That was why white North Americans could speak of the United
States as the "land of the free" while they held Africans as slaves. Similarly,
Paul Johnson can speak of capitalism as "the greatest single blessing ever
bestowed on humanity" even though the vast majority of people have been
victimized by it. He seems to be saying that as long as the white European
and American ruling classes benefit from the profits of capitalism, its short-

comings in contributing toward the liberation of the poor from their poverty cannot count significantly against its value for humanity. Value is defined in terms of material profit for the rich, not economic and political structures for the benefit of all. It is this implication that makes his viewpoint reprehensible from my ethical perspective.

For whom does Johnson speak and for what purpose? I think the answer 4 is obvious. He speaks for the haves and not the have-nots, for the rich and not the poor, for whites and not blacks, for the United States and Europe and not for Asia, Africa, and Latin America. His purpose is to show that recent threats to industrial capitalism arise not from the masses of people but rather from university intellectuals, trade unions, big government, ecology campaigners, and the Soviet Union. This selective focus and his caricature of the opponents of capitalism define the character of his address; he thereby limits the possibility of genuine dialogue with anyone whose perspective has been shaped by solidarity with the victims of industrial capitalism.

Johnson's defense of industrial capitalism centers on its ability to pro- 5 duce an "unprecedented annual growth rate" in Europe and North America. Aside from Japan, there is no mention in this connection of any country in the Third World. Nor does he say anything about the relation between the wealth of Europe and the United States and the poverty in Asia, Africa, and Latin America. Is he suggesting that this wealth is in no way connected with and dependent upon slavery and colonization in the Third World? Because the examples he gives of the value of industrial capitalism are almost exclusively limited to Europe and the United States, I am particularly interested in how he would explain the huge gap between the rich and the poor on both continents, but especially in Asia, Africa, and Latin America. And why does he not mention that though the United States has only 6 per cent of the world's population, it consumes over 30 per cent of the world's natural resources?

I contend that capitalism is under threat not because it has received a 6 bad press from university intellectuals, ecology campaigners, and trade-union people, nor because of big government or even the outside danger of the Soviet Union, but because the so-called free-enterprise system is not free at all; it is actually controlled by multinational corporations.

I agree with Johnson that the capitalist economies of the United States 7 and Europe have produced a lot of wealth. But I also know that the masses of people on both continents do not receive their just share of that wealth. While legislators in the United States enact laws almost yearly that appear to guarantee a fairer distribution, statistics show that the very rich still control a hugely disproportionate amount of the nation's wealth. This rich ruling class makes up only 0.5 per cent of the population but controls over one-fourth of the nation's privately held wealth and yearly income, including 50–86 per cent of all corporate stock (see Jonathan Turner and Charles Staines, *Inequality: Privilege and Poverty in America,* Goodyear, 1976).

When these economic factors are set in a racial context, the injustice is 8 even more striking. Blacks and other U.S. minorities are especially victimized, because their color is an additional factor contributing to the economic injustice inflicted upon them. Aside from the small minority of black professionals who are needed to create the appearance of equality in the United States, blacks and other ethnic minorities are the last hired and often the first fired. Their unemployment rate is always four to ten times higher than that of whites. They are forced to live in urban ghettoes with no real opportunity to participate in shaping the laws that affect their community.

People who share Paul Johnson's perspective like to delude themselves 9 into thinking that the poor enjoy living in poverty. They nourish this delusion by spending most of their time talking to rich capitalists and their supporters rather than to the poor. Yet they like to claim that they know what the poor think. What they label as the "poor" perspective is nothing but the reinforcement of the ruling-class point of view. In the United States I have met many white people who share Johnson's viewpoint. They were plentiful during the civil-rights struggle in the 1950s and '60s, and today they are even more vocal in advocating the essential justice of the American capitalist system. When poor black people, during the 1960s, reacted in violent rebellion against intolerable economic conditions, white oppressors simply attributed such behavior to the influence of outside agitators and gave a military response that left many blacks dead in the streets.

Economic conditions in U.S. cities are no better today for the masses of 10 blacks than they were in the 1960s. But I am sure that urban police departments are better prepared for any disturbance that black people's poverty may motivate them to create. People who share Paul Johnson's perspective seem to be more concerned about eliminating social unrest through the power of the police than about eliminating the economic conditions that create the unrest.

Paul Johnson either is unaware of the gross injustices created by capital- 11 ism or has simply chosen to ignore them. If he thinks that the growth of megalopolises all over the world is evidence of a popular endorsement of capitalism, he is grossly mistaken. Poor people migrate to urban centers because they are trying to survive in a situation of maldistributed wealth. Whatever else may be said about the wealth that capitalism generates in the United States, poor blacks and other minorities do not benefit from it.

When capitalism's wealth is viewed in an international context, the 12 injustice it creates appears even greater. The wealth of Europe and the United States is directly determined by the poverty of the people of Asia, Africa, and Latin America. This is the historical significance of slavery and colonization, which today are continued in the economic domination of the Third World by the United States and Europe. Despite the Western world's verbal defense of human rights and freedom, its continued economic and military support of the dictator governments of South Africa, South Korea, Chile, and many other states completely invalidates what it says.

Although I am a Christian whose ethical perspective is derived primarily 13 from that tradition, I do not need to appeal to Christianity to demonstrate the gross immorality of economic arrangements defined by capitalism. One needs only to be sensitive to human beings and their right to life, liberty, and the pursuit of happiness to question seriously what Paul Johnson advocates. Capitalism is a system that clearly values property more than persons. That is why it is losing the moral and intellectual battle. And perhaps it is why Paul Johnson appeals to material statistics as evidence for the inherent value of capitalism rather than to the quality of life it makes possible for all people.

Questions for Discussion

1. In paragraph 15 of "Has Capitalism a Future?" Johnson pictures peasants and poor people all over the world going to the cities in a "never-ending one-way flow from [the] countryside." He calls this movement "plainly a voluntary mass choice." From what you know of poor people in cities either in the past or present, does this seem an accurate description of the urban poor?

2. Johnson calls the environmentalists' objections to industrial growth "ecological panic." What effect is the word *panic* designed to have on the reader?

3. Schmertz accuses Johnson of confusing capitalism as an economic system with democracy as a social system. Does this seem a well-placed criticism? Does Schmertz seem less or more eager than Johnson for capitalism to survive? Are Johnson and Schmertz appealing to the same *interests* in their readers? If so, what are they? If not, how do they differ?

4. Is McCarthy an opponent of capitalism? If not, what *does* he oppose? When he says that "competition does not rule the economy of the United States today" (¶4), is he saying that it should or should not? *Why* has competition disappeared from the American economy, and what should be done either to keep it out or to bring it back in?

5. What use does Nelson make of his observation that "the same heart of man that rejoices in the blessings of prosperity remains wicked and exceedingly self-centered" (¶6)? Does this remark provide support for Johnson's position? If so, how? If not, why not?

6. Nelson says that Johnson's attack on ecological advocates is "perplexing" (¶11). Does he really seem perplexed in the rest of the paragraph? If not, why do you think he uses this term? If you think his perplexity is genuine, what is he perplexed about?

7. Cone claims that Johnson "speaks for the haves and not the have-nots" (¶4). Do you think this is a fair accusation? Can you find evidence in Johnson's essay either to support or to refute it?

8. By putting Johnson's facts into the contexts of race and social class, Cone makes them look much less laudatory than Johnson does. Which writer do

you think is being more careful with his facts? Are they speaking *at* each other or *past* each other?

Suggested Essay Topics

1. Select *one* of Johnson's respondents and make a list of three or four of his specific criticisms. Then write a letter to the critic in Johnson's name, addressing the criticisms in detail and answering them with information from "your" (Johnson's) essay, showing the critic that he has somehow failed to read you correctly.

2. Write a letter to Johnson, using evidence from all four of Johnson's respondents, to support a series of claims showing that Johnson has unfairly presented his argument for industrial capitalism.

Acknowledgments

St. Thomas Aquinas, "The Production of Woman." From *The Summa Theologica.* From *Basic Writings of Saint Thomas Aquinas,* edited by Anton C. Pegis. Copyright © 1945 by Random House, Inc. Reprinted by permission of the Estate of Anton C. Pegis.

Matthew Arnold, "Literature and Science." From *Discourses in America,* 1885.

Margaret Atwood, "A Disneyland of the Soul." From *The Writer and Human Rights,* edited by the Toronto Arts Group for Human Rights. Copyright © 1983 by Margaret Atwood. Reprinted by permission of Margaret Atwood.

James Baldwin. From *The Fire Next Time.* Copyright © 1962 by James Baldwin, renewed 1990. Used by arrangement with the James Baldwin Estate.

Wendell Berry, "The Loss of the University." From *Home Economics.* Copyright © 1987 by Wendell Berry. Published by North Point Press and reprinted by permission.

Bruno Bettelheim and Karen Zelan, "Why Children Don't Like to Read." From *On Learning to Read: The Child's Fascination with Meaning* by Bruno Bettelheim and Karen Zelan. Copyright © 1981 by Bruno Bettelheim and Karen Zelan. Reprinted by permission of Alfred A. Knopf, Inc.

Sissela Bok. From *Lying: Moral Choice in Public and Private Life* by Sissela Bok. Copyright © 1978 by Sissela Bok. Reprinted by permission of Pantheon Books, a Division of Random House, Inc.

André Brink. Excerpts from *Writing in a State of Siege: Essays on Politics and Literature* by André Brink. Copyright © 1983 by Andre Brink. Reprinted by permission of Summit Books, a division of Simon & Schuster, Inc.

Jacob Bronowski, "The Reach of Imagination." From *Proceedings of the American Academy of Arts and Letters and the National Institute of Arts and Letters,* 2nd series, 17 (1967). Copyright © 1967 by the American Academy of Arts and Letters. Reprinted by permission of the American Academy and Institute of Arts and Letters.

Edward Hallett Carr. From *What Is History?* by Edward Hallett Carr. Copyright © 1961 by Edward Hallett Carr. Reprinted by permission of Alfred A. Knopf, Inc.

Robert Coles, "On the Nature of Character: Some Preliminary Field Notes." From *Daedalus* 110 no. 4 (Fall 1981). Reprinted by permission of *Daedalus, Journal of American Academy of Arts and Sciences.*

James Cone, "Capitalism Means Property Over Persons." From *Will Capitalism Survive?* edited by Ernest W. Lefever (Washington, D.C.: Ethics and Public Policy Center, 1979). Copyright © 1979 by the Ethics and Public Policy Center. Reprinted by permission of the publisher.

Richard Dawkins. Reprinted from *The Selfish Gene* (1976; 1989) by permission of Oxford University Press.

Frederick Douglass, "The Meaning of July Fourth for the Negro." From *The Life and Writings of Frederick Douglass,* Vol II, edited by Phillip S. Foner.

Andrea Dworkin. From *Pornography* by Andrea Dworkin. Copyright © 1979, 1980, 1981 by Andrea Dworkin. Used by permission of the publisher, Dutton, an imprint of New American Library, a division of Penguin Books USA Inc.

Loren Eiseley. From *The Star Thrower* by Loren Eiseley. Copyright © 1978 by the Estate of Loren C. Eiseley, Mabel L. Eiseley, Executrix. Reprinted by permission of Times Books, a Division of Random House, Inc.

Ralph Ellison, "Battle Royal." From *Invisible Man* by Ralph Ellison. Copyright © 1947, 1948, 1952 by Ralph Ellison. Reprinted by permission of Random House, Inc.

Kai Erikson, "Reflections on the Bomb: Of Accidental Judgments and Casual Slaughters." From *The Nation* (August 1985). Copyright © 1985 by The Nation Company, Inc. Reprinted by permission of The Nation Company, Inc.

E. M. Forster, "My Wood." From *Abinger Harvest* by E. M. Forster. Copyright © 1936, 1964 by Edward Morgan Forster. Reprinted by permission of Harcourt Brace Jovanovich, Inc., and Edward Arnold, Ltd.

John Fowles, "Christianity" (pp. 102–110; numbers 3–32). From *The Aristos: A Self-Portrait in Ideas,* Chapter 7. Copyright © 1964, 1968, 1970 by John Fowles. Reprinted by permission of Little, Brown and Company.

Francine Frank and Frank Ashen, "Of Girls and Chicks." From *Language and the Sexes* by Francine Frank and Frank Ashen. Copyright © 1983 by Francine Frank and Frank Ashen. Reprinted by permission of State University of New York Press.

Sigmund Freud, "Femininity." From *New Introductory Lectures On Psycho-Analysis* by Sigmund Freud, translated and edited by James Strachey. Reprinted by permission of W. W. Norton & Company, Inc. Copyright 1933 by Sigmund Freud. Copyright renewed 1961 by W. J. H. Sprott.

Genesis 1–2:3, from *The Torah,* 2nd ed. Copyright © 1962 by the Jewish Publication Society. Reprinted by permission of the publisher.

Pieter Geyl and Arnold J. Toynbee, "Can We Know the Pattern of the Past?" Reprinted from *The Pattern of The Past: Can We Determine It?* by Pieter Geyl, Arnold J. Toynbee, and Pitirim A. Sorokin. Copyright © 1949 by Beacon Press. Reprinted by permission of Beacon Press.

William Golding, "Thinking as a Hobby." Copyright © 1961, 1989 by William Golding. Reprinted by permission of Curtis Brown, Ltd. First printed in *Holiday* magazine.

Mary Ellen Goodman. From *Awareness in Young Children,* Chapter 2. Published by Addison-Wesley Press, Inc. Copyright by Addison-Wesley Press, Inc.

Stephen Jay Gould, "The Median Isn't the Message." From *Discover* magazine (June 1985). Reprinted by permission of Stephen Jay Gould.

Edith Hamilton, "The Ever-Present Past" from *The Ever-Present Past* by Edith Hamilton.

1945, 1952 by William Collins Sons & Co., Ltd. Reprinted by permission of William Collins Sons & Co., Ltd.

Eugene J. McCarthy, "Corporations Have Corrupted Capitalism." From *Will Capitalism Survive?* edited by Ernest W. Lefever (Washington, D.C.: Ethics and Public Policy Center, 1979). Copyright © 1979 by the Ethics and Public Policy Center. Reprinted by permission of the publisher.

Mary McCarthy, "Artists in Uniform." From *On the Contrary* by Mary McCarthy. Copyright © 1953 by Mary McCarthy. Reprinted by permission of the author.

Celeste MacLeod. Excerpts from "The Dream and the Reality," "The International Connection," and "Horatio Alger, Farewell." From *Horatio Alger, Farewell: The End of the American Dream* by Celeste MacLeod. Copyright © 1980 by Celeste MacLeod. Reprinted by permission.

Malcolm X. From *The Autobiography of Malcolm X,* with the assistance of Alex Haley. Copyright © 1964 by Alex Haley and Malcolm X. Copyright © 1965 by Alex Haley and Betty Shabazz. Reprinted by permission of Random House, Inc.

Margaret Mead, "The Mind Is Not Sex-Typed." From *Blackberry Winter: My Earlier Years* by Margaret Mead. Copyright © 1972 by Margaret Mead. Reprinted by permission of William Morrow & Co.

Mary Midgley, "Evolution as a Religion." From *Evolution as Religion: Strange Hopes and Stranger Fears* by Mary Midgley. Copyright © 1985 by Mary Midgley. Reprinted by permission of Methuen & Co.

Elaine Morgan, "The Man-Made Myth." From *The Descent of Woman* by Elaine Morgan. Copyright © 1972 by Elaine Morgan. Reprinted by permission of Stein and Day Publishers and Souvenir Press Ltd.

J. Robert Nelson, "Capitalism: Blessing and Curse." From *Will Capitalism Survive?* edited by Ernest Lefever (Washington D.C.: Ethics and Public Policy Center, 1979). Copyright © 1979 by the Ethics and Public Policy Center. Reprinted by permission of the publisher.

Susan Neville, "Cousins." From *The Invention of Flight* by Susan Neville. Copyright © 1984 by Susan Neville. Reprinted by permission of the University of Georgia Press.

Friedrich Nietzsche, "The Ugliness of Woman." From *Beyond Good and Evil* by Friedrich Nietzsche, translated by Walter Kaufmann. Copyright © 1966 by Random House, Inc. Reprinted by permission of the publisher.

Joyce Carol Oates, "How I Contemplated the World from the Detroit House of Correction and Began My Life Over Again." From *The Wheel of Love.* Copyright © 1965 by Joyce Carol Oates. Reprinted by permission of Vanguard Press.

C. K. Ogden and I. A. Richards. Excerpts from *The Meaning of Meaning* by C. K. Ogden and I. A. Richards. Copyright © 1946 by Harcourt, Brace and Company. Reprinted by permission of Harcourt Brace Jovanovich, Inc.

George Orwell, "Politics and the English Language." From *Shooting an Elephant and Other Essays* by George Orwell. Copyright © 1946, 1974 by Sonia Brownwell Orwell. Reprinted by permission of Harcourt Brace Jovanovich, Inc., the estate of the late Sonia Brownwell Orwell, and Martin Secker & Warburg, Ltd.

Cynthia Ozick, "The Moral Necessity of Metaphor." From *Metaphor and Memory*. Copyright © 1989 by Cynthia Ozick. Reprinted by permission of Alfred A. Knopf, Inc.

Plato, "Censorship." From *The Republic* in *The Dialogues of Plato* translated by Benjamin Jowett, 4th ed. Copyright © 1953 by the Jowett Copyright Trustees. Reprinted by permission of Oxford: Claredon Press.

Karl R. Popper, "Utopia and Violence." From *Conjectures and Refutations: The Growth of Scientific Knowledge* (2nd ed., 1965.) Copyright © 1963, 1965 by Karl L. Popper. Reprinted by permission of the author.

Ayn Rand, "I Owe Nothing to My Brothers." From *Anthem* by Ayn Rand. Copyright © 1946 by Pamphleteers, Inc. Reprinted by permission of Dr. Leonard Peikoff, Executor, Estate of Ayn Rand.

Chief Red Jacket and the Missionary, "Native American Episode." Speeches by Chief Red Jacket and the Reverend Mr. Cram. From *Indian Speeches: Delivered by Farmer's Brother and Red Jacket, Two Seneca Chiefs* (1809).

Adrienne Rich, "Claiming an Education." Reprinted from *Lies, Secrets, and Silence, Selected Prose, 1966–1978,* by Adrienne Rich, by permission of W. W. Norton and Company, Inc. Copyright © 1979 by W. W. Norton and Company, Inc.

Phyllis Rose, "Heroic Fantasies, Nervous Doubts." From the *New York Times* "Hers" column of March 22, 1984. Copyright © 1984 by Phyllis Rose. Reprinted by permission of Georges Borchardt, Inc., and the author.

Peggy Rosenthal, "Words and Values." From *Words and Values: Some Leading Words and Where They Lead Us* by Peggy Rosenthal. Copyright © 1984 by Peggy Rosenthal. Reprinted by permission of Oxford University Press, Inc.

Betty Roszak and Theodore Roszak, "The Human Continuum." From *Masculine/Feminine: Readings in Sexual Mythology and the Liberation of Women* by Betty Roszak and Theodore Roszak. Reprinted by permission of HarperCollins Publishers.

Rosemary Radford Ruether, "Mortherearth and the Megamachine: A Theology of Liberation in a Feminine, Somatic, and Ecological Perspective" by Rosemary Radford Ruether. From *Christianity and Crisis* (April 12, 1972). Copyright © 1972 by Rosemary Radford Ruether. Reprinted by permission of *Christianity and Crisis.*

St. Paul, "I Corinthians 13." From *The New English Bible.* Copyright © by the Delegates of the Oxford University Press and the Syndics of the Cambridge University Press 1961, 1970. Reprinted by permission.

Scott Russell Sanders, "The Inheritance of Tools." From *The Paradise of Bombs* by Scott Russell Sanders. Copyright © 1986 by Scott Russell Sanders; first appeared in *The North American Review.* Reprinted by permission of the author and the author's agent, Virginia Kidd.

Margaret Sanger, "The Turbid Ebb and Flow of Misery." From *An Autobiography by Margaret Sanger.* Copyright © 1938 by W. W. Norton & Co., Inc. Reprinted by permission of Dr. Grant Sanger.

Herbert Schmertz, "Democracy, Tyranny, and Capitalism." From *Will Capitalism Survive?* edited by Ernest W. Lefever (Washington, D.C.: Ethics and Public Policy Center). Copyright © 1979 by the Ethics and Public Policy Center. Reprinted by permission of the publisher.

Essays by Alfred North Whitehead. Copyright © 1929 by Macmillan Publishing Co., Inc., renewed © 1957 by Evelyn Whitehead. Reprinted by permission of Macmillan Publishing Co.

Elie Wiesel, "The Sacrifice of Isaac: A Strange Tale About Fear, Faith and Laughter." From *Messengers of God: Biblical Portraits and Legends* by Elie Wiesel, translated by Marion Wiesel. Copyright © 1976 by Elie Wiesel. Reprinted by permission of Random House, Inc.

Richard Wright. Excerpt from *Black Boy* by Richard Wright. Copyright © 1937, 1942, 1945 by Richard Wright. Reprinted by permission of HarperCollins Publishers.

Author Index

Rhetorical Index